Paul KLEE "INSULA DULCAMARA", 1938, C 1 (481)
Gemälde, Oelfarbe, Jute auf Keilrahmen, mit Papier
überklebt / 88 : 175 / signiert rechts oben /
Sammlung Paul Klee-Stiftung, Inv. B 30.

Psychology and Life

Tenth Edition

Psychology and Life

Tenth Edition	Philip G. Zimbardo	1979
Ninth Edition	Philip G. Zimbardo and Floyd L. Ruch	1975
	Brief Ninth Edition 1976	
Eighth Edition	Floyd L. Ruch and Philip G. Zimbardo	1971
	Brief Eighth Edition 1971	
Seventh Edition	Floyd L. Ruch 1967	
	Brief Seventh Edition 1967	
Sixth Edition	Floyd L. Ruch 1963	
	Brief Sixth Edition 1963	
Fifth Edition	Floyd L. Ruch 1958	
	Brief Fifth Edition 1959	
Fourth Edition	Floyd L. Ruch 1953	
Third Edition	Floyd L. Ruch 1948	
Second Edition	Floyd L. Ruch 1941	
First Edition	Floyd L. Ruch 1937	

Psychology and Life

Tenth Edition

by
Philip G. Zimbardo Stanford University

from earlier editions by
Floyd L. Ruch University of Southern California, Emeritus

Scott, Foresman and Company Glenview, Illinois

Dallas, Tex.   Oakland, N.J.   Palo Alto, Cal.   Tucker, Ga.   London, England

Dedicated to my brother Don Zimbardo,
whose sensitivity to the needs of others
is excelled only by his generosity
and richness of spirit.

Library of Congress Cataloging in Publication Data

Zimbardo, Philip G
  Psychology and Life.

  Bibliography: p.
  Includes indexes.
  1. Psychology. I. Ruch, Floyd Leon, 1903-
Psychology and life. II. Title. [DNLM: 1. Psychology.
BF121 Z71p]
BF121.R77 1979   150   78-26957
ISBN 0-673-15183-2

Acknowledgments for illustrations and quoted matter are
included on pages xliv–xlviii at the end of the book. These
pages are an extension of the copyright page.

Preface

Dear Reader:

I'm delighted your psychology teacher has given me this opportunity to share with you my enthusiasm for psychology as well as the knowledge I've gained in over twenty years of teaching introductory psychology. I love psychology; it is fascinating, challenging, and a source of much satisfaction. The more I observe people, the more questions I am led to ask about the human condition. The more I understand of it, the less I take for granted about the exquisite complexity that goes into making you unique and us different. What better way to spend one's life than being a professional "people watcher," investigating the mysteries of human nature?

I shudder to recall that I almost didn't make it—after my first psychology course. A total disaster! In my whole career as a student my lowest grade ever was in that Psych 1 course. I entered with great expectations and exited quietly depressed, feeling cheated. Most of the blame falls on the text. It was the enemy—a relentless adversary equipped to bore me nearly to death. The author had tried so hard to be serious and scientific, but succeeded only in being irrelevant to any of my personal or intellectual concerns. I was rescued in my senior year from an uncertain future as an accountant by a dedicated psychology instructor—and have never regretted the decision to devote my life to being a psychologist.

When it came time to write about psychology, collaborating with Floyd Ruch was a natural. Professor Ruch had written the first basic text designed for the beginning psychology student rather than to impress his professional colleagues. Since that first edition in 1937, *Psychology and Life* has become the model to be imitated by virtually all the other basic texts that followed.

With the publication of this Tenth Edition, *P&L* ranks first in seniority among over 160 other texts. I hope my contribution to this classic work will help to make it first also in student and faculty evaluations.

In many ways this Tenth Edition is a fresh, new edition. It has been almost completely rewritten in an effort to present you with a comprehensive and in-depth view of what psychology is all about. I have tried to blend academic rigor, intellectual sophistication, common sense, humanistic concerns, and a measure of fun. There are many new chapters and topics that represent the most exciting areas of contemporary research. Within this greater variety of chapters, each chapter is shorter than in previous editions, to make it easier for you to complete a study unit at one sitting. There are more places where I've tried to communicate directly to you as if you were in one of my own tutorials. I hope you will learn much and like most of what you discover. If you do, you will owe a debt of thanks to a generation of other students who have used the past several editions of *P&L*. Thousands of them sent me detailed feedback about what they enjoyed, as well as constructive criticism. My respect for the value of this student input shows up throughout *P&L* 10th. (Please carry on this tradition by sending in *your* evaluation on the form at the end of the book. Try to mark down your reactions to each chapter immediately after reading it.)

Psychology is a broad, dynamic field, with shifting emphases and new discoveries about behavior and the mind. For example, while some of my colleagues study the physiological functions of the nervous system, others seek to discover why we forget and still others search for explanations of violence. While some research directions that seemed promising a while ago have proved disappointing, others have emerged with even greater promise. Therefore, in undertaking the task of informing you about the current state of this vast field of knowledge, I have called upon the expertise of many authorities. They have educated me, infused me with some of their enthusiasm for their individual fields of study, shared new ideas, corrected faulty ones, and shown how I might better communicate to you what psychologists have done and are doing. To each of them, I am grateful.

Critical evaluation, valuable insights, and new directions were provided by: Justine Owens, Megan Gunnar, Charles Swencionis, Grace Hagawara, Linda Solomon, and Michael Werb (Stanford University); Helen Joan Crawford (University of Wyoming); Raymond Paloutzian (University of Idaho); Randy Gallistel (University of Pennsylvania); Richard Bootzin (Northwestern University); Ola Selnes (Hennepin County Medical Center); Sharon Brehm (University of Kansas); Paul Ban and Jac Carlson (University of Hawaii); Susan Jackson and Karen Brattesani (University of California,

Berkeley); Gary Frieden (University of Southern California); Keith Wescourt (Office of Naval Research).

Karl Minke (University of Hawaii) improved every chapter through his keen appreciation of how best to deliver what psychologists know to an audience of students varying in background and interests.

Special thanks go to those colleagues and friends who assisted me by collaborating on drafting chapters or sections of chapters: Jeff Wine (Stanford University) for the physiology chapters, Hayne Reese (West Virginia University) for the developmental chapters, Richard Dolinsky (University of Toledo) for the memory and language chapters, Tom Bourbon (Stephen F. Austin State University) for the perception chapter, Richard Santee (University of California, Berkeley) for the social psychology chapter.

My publisher, Scott, Foresman, backed my efforts with a team of inspired editors and former teachers whose wise counsel shaped much that is effective in this book, among them Arden Orr, Pat Nerenberg, Sharon Barton, and Linda Muterspaugh. Marguerite Clark knows how much I continue to value her invaluable input to my thinking. As the heads of this editorial team, Louise Howe contributed her clarity of thought, sense of effective prose, and patience for my excesses, while Jim Romig provided his tireless energy and superb organizational skills.

Rosanne Saussotte, my secretary, goes far beyond making my scribbles intelligible. She makes me ever aware that it is possible to always be compassionate and involved in the lives of other people regardless of how hard one is working.

My wife, my friend, my colleague, Christina Maslach (University of California, Berkeley) is the gentle force that informs so much of what I am and enriches all that I write. She assisted in many ways, with support, advice, and drafting sections of this book from materials that she has taught effectively to her own students. She shares the credit for whatever joy you find in the ideas that follow.

Where *P&L* 10th falls short of your expectations, I stand alone. With a little more help from my friends, including you, I promise to make the necessary improvements next time around. But for now, the table is set, enjoy.

Using this book wisely

You will get more out of the time you put into reading *Psychology and Life* if you follow these recommendations:

☥ Set aside sufficient study time for this course.

☥ Study in a setting with minimum distractions.

☥ Begin each chapter by looking over the outline on the opening page of the chapter. It acquaints you with the topics to come and their relationship to one another.

☥ Read the Chapter Summary at the end of the assigned chapter. The summary will familiarize you with the themes of the chapter, basic concepts, and conclusions.

☥ Skim through the chapter, reading for general information.

☥ Now you are ready to dig in! Read closely and carefully. Read actively by underlining or taking notes. Good notes now will be of considerable value later on when studying for your examinations.

We have designed a number of features into each chapter to facilitate your comprehension and increase your enjoyment. Among them are:

☥ Major topics come under first-level headings (large brown type). Note the styles of type used in the various levels of headings because they indicate the structure of the chapter and the relationships of the ideas. These headings organize the content for you and help you plan your reading for each period of study.

☥ Important terms and concepts are printed in *italic type* to highlight them.

☥ Detailed reports of interesting or critical research are printed in italicized sections.

☥ When a figure or illustration is mentioned in the text, it is followed by one of these symbols: ● ▲ ■ ◆. The same symbol appears with the caption of the appropriate chart or photo.

☥ Items of special interest are set apart from the body of the text for detailed presentation in *P&L Close-ups*. Each one appears on or close to the page in the text where it is cited, and should be read at that time even though you may have to pass over some material in order to get to it. I think you will find many of them are fun to read and contain interesting ideas.

☥ References to research, scholarly sources, and mass-media sources appear throughout the text. The authors' names and date of publication will be listed in parentheses (e.g., Zimbardo, 1979); complete citations are listed in the References at the end of the book in alphabetical order. These references establish the basis of our conclusions and also direct you to more complete information if you are especially interested in any given idea.

☥ You will find at the back of the book a full glossary of psychological terms and concepts used in *Psychology and Life* (indicating the pages on which they are discussed); a subject index of all important concepts; and a name index of the individuals whose work I have cited.

☥ Think of this text as a valuable reference source, useful in later psychology courses or for term papers for other courses. For example, many psychology majors prepare for Graduate Record Examinations by reviewing this introductory psychology text. In short, I hope you will keep this book as part of your personal library of intellectual resource materials.

☥ *Note:* Both the title and the approach of this book are represented by the symbol that appears on this page, a combination of the ancient Egyptian ankh, symbolic of *life*, with the Greek letter psi, ψ, which has come to stand for *psychology*.

Contents

Part One
Foundations

Paul KLEE "BESTANDENE ABENTEUER", 1931, QU 16
Feder- und Pinselzeichnung, (136)
italienisches Ingres PMF

Chapter 1

Psychology and Life: Challenges and Promises

Psychology is . . .
  Scientific
  Curious
  Comprehensive
  Pragmatic

Psychology in action: questions and answers
  Are love and affection essential for survival? (Part Three)
  Would *you* obey a command to electrocute a stranger? (Part Seven)
  Can aggression be triggered just by stimulating the brain? (Part Four)
  Does your left hand really know
    what your right hand is doing? (Part Five)
  How unusual is it for someone (like me) to be shy?
    Can shyness be cured? (Part Six)
  Does your memory of a story depend on
    which character you identify with? (Part Two)

Models of human nature
  The psychodynamic model
  The behavioristic model
  The cognitive model
  The humanistic model

Chapter summary

Psychology is . . .

Scientific

It is formally defined as *the study of the behavior of organisms*. Using careful observation and rigorous experiments, psychologists look for the causes of various behaviors of human beings and other animal species. By using the methods of scientific inquiry, they can often give precise and valid answers to questions about the underlying processes that determine the complexity of our behavior.

Curious

It involves questioning reality, asking "How come?" "Why is it so?" "What would happen if . . . ?" "How important is X?" "If Y changed, then what?" "What made it do that?" and so on. Some psychologists try to make sense out of apparently bizarre behavior, such as madness or vandalism. Others are excited by the challenge of discovering how the eye and brain enable us to perceive the outside world so accurately. Curiosity leads some to probe the realm of the "inner eye," unlocking the secrets of a mind that is conscious of its own being. For all psychologists, human nature is an endless puzzle waiting to be solved—but a puzzle that keeps changing even as theories and research try to reveal its hidden treasures.

Comprehensive

It is a way of thinking about how living creatures cope with their environment and interact with each other. As such, it is at the intersection of philosophy, biology, sociology, physiology, and anthropology. Psychology is both an approach to gathering information about behavior and a storehouse of knowledge uncovered by research. Psychologists use a variety of methods to study how we sense, think, feel, and act. Sometimes privately held beliefs, values, attitudes, and expectations hold the key to our behavior. Sometimes past experiences we are not conscious of determine what we say and do. Thus psychologists approach the challenges posed by the human condition prepared to study both our public actions and our private experiences. They study behavior as it emerges in physical, biological, mental, and social contexts. Their methods and the body of knowledge developed by using them form the foundation of this book. ▲[1]

Pragmatic

Perhaps most important, psychology is practical; it can be used to improve the quality of human life. Psychology is more than a mere description of how the mind functions, of what causes a certain reaction, or of the effects of a given event on a person's behavior. It includes prescriptions for change. Psychologists get especially excited by the prospect of applying what they know to help people modify undesirable habits, alter destructive life-styles, and more positively, realize the fullest development of their human potential. Because psychologists are trained to be sensitive to the impact of society and the environment on our behavior and outlook, they are also in a position to recom-

---

[1]This symbol is a signal for you to refer to the figure on this or the next page that has the same symbol. Where more than one figure is described in the text, each will be keyed with its own symbol: ▲, ■, ●, ◆.

Divisions of the American Psychological Association

There are many different areas of psychology, virtually one for whatever interest a student has in entering the realm of mind and behavior. This listing of the 35 divisions of the American Psychological Association (whose membership numbers 44,650) will give you an idea of the variety of subfields within psychology

Work with Individuals
Clinical psychology
Counseling psychology
Rehabilitation psychology
Psychotherapy
Psychological hypnosis
Mental retardation
Child and youth services
Behavioral medicine

Work with Institutions
Consulting psychology
Industrial and organizational psychology
Educational psychology
School psychology
Psychologists in public service
Military psychology
Society of engineering psychologists
Consumer psychology

Laboratory and Quantitative Psychology
Experimental psychology
Evaluation and measurement
Physiological and comparative psychology
Experimental analysis of behavior
Psychopharmacology

Social Development and Social Psychology
Developmental psychology
Personality and social psychology
Society for the psychological study of social issues
Community psychology
Adult development and aging
Population and environmental psychology
Psychology of women

Other Specialized Areas of Interest
General psychology
Teaching of psychology
Psychology and the arts
Philosophical psychology
History of psychology
Humanistic psychology
Psychologists interested in religious issues
State psychological association affairs

---

mend ways to improve existing conditions and suggest alternatives. In many cases the "proof" of a good psychological theory is shown in its useful practical application. Psychology is pragmatic, then, because psychologists are concerned about how to apply their scientifically gathered wisdom to improve the human condition.

In one sense, you are already a psychologist—an "intuitive psychologist." Even without formal training in the discipline of psychology, you probably use psychology in various ways in your daily life. For example, you may have some theories about human nature based on your own observations of how people behave in different situations. You have undoubtedly wondered about your own behavior and about why others often act so differently from the way you do under the same circumstances. If you are perceptive and sensitive, you may often try to understand the behavior patterns you observe and whether they are related to personality characteristics. You are probably pretty good at anticipating the consequences of your own actions and also at predicting how you will act under various conditions. But it is not enough to be able to predict your behavior. There are probably many times when you wish you had better control over what you do and over what other people do that affects you.

Commonsense psychology may be adequate for many tasks, but it can also at times lead you to false conclusions and ineffective actions. This may be because of faulty assumptions about human nature, cultural and personal biases and prejudices, poorly controlled observations, or an uncritical acceptance of information provided by your senses, by so-called authorities, or by the mass media. To be a good psychologist, you need to learn how to check your assumptions, observe accurately, weigh evidence objectively, and draw valid conclusions.

One goal of this book is to provide information that should help you make better use of psychological knowledge in your life. A careful reading of *Psychology and Life* can help pave your way toward becoming a more effective psychologist. To complete the journey will require not only additional reading and course work, but a continued openness to new experiences, ideas, and people, as well as curiosity to discover all you can about the psychology of *you*. It can be an exciting, unique adventure — one that will enable you to understand better the secrets of why people think and feel and act as they do. (Take the test in the *P&L* Close-up, "Commonsense" Psychology, to determine what you already know and where this kind of knowledge may have led you astray.)

Psychology in action: questions and answers

Let us begin your introduction to psychology by examining some illustrations of how researchers go about finding answers to the whys of psychological functioning. Each example represents one of the six major areas of psychology that we will investigate in detail in subsequent parts of the book. They are: Learning and Cognition; Life-Span Development; Biological Foundations of Behavior; Motivation and Mind; Personality and Clinical Psychology; and Social Psychology. Frankly, the examples were also selected to involve you directly in the exciting challenge that is psychology, instead of talking in abstract generalities.

All persons are puzzles until at last we find in some word or act the key to the man, to the woman: straightway all their past words and actions lie in light before us.
Ralph Waldo Emerson
Journals

Are love and affection essential for survival? (Part Three)

Is there an association between depriving an infant of love and affection and later illness? Are nutritious food and other good physical conditions the only requirements for normal growth and physical well-being? Another, more popular way to pose this basic question is: can someone die of a "broken heart"? Such questions focus our attention on the role of emotional deprivation in the process of development. They also touch upon the broader issue of how psychological and physical processes are related to each other.

Long before the science of psychology was born, Frederick II, a thirteenth-century ruler of Sicily and a master of languages, believed that every person was born already knowing the original human language. According to him, a child would begin to use this built-in language without any training or experience as soon as he or she was old enough. To test this *hypothesis* Frederick conducted an experiment. A group of foster mothers were put in charge of a number of newborn infants. They were to care for the babies in silence, never speaking to them or allowing them to hear human sounds. When at last they spoke, it would reveal, according to Frederick, the true natural language they had inherited, since nothing could be attributed to their upbringing. History gives us the sad results of this experiment: "But he labored in vain, be-

Close-up
"Commonsense" Psychology

Test your "commonsense knowledge" of psychology on the fifteen selected statements below. Mark *T* before those you think are true as stated and *F* before those statements you believe are false. The answers and some additional information are at the bottom of the page.

_____ 1. To change people's behavior toward members of ethnic minority groups, we must first change their attitudes.

_____ 2. Memory can be likened to a storage chest in the brain into which we deposit material and from which we can withdraw it later if needed. Occasionally, something gets lost from the "chest," and then we say we have forgotten.

_____ 3. The basis of the baby's love for its mother is the fact that the mother fills its physiological needs for food, etc.

_____ 4. The more highly motivated you are, the better you will do at solving a complex problem.

_____ 5. The best way to ensure that a desired behavior will persist after training is completed is to reward the behavior every single time it occurs throughout training (rather than intermittently).

_____ 6. A schizophrenic is someone with a split personality.

_____ 7. Fortunately for babies, human beings have a strong maternal instinct.

_____ 8. Biologists study the body; psychologists study the mind.

_____ 9. Psychiatrists are defined as medical people who use psychoanalysis.

_____ 10. Children memorize much more easily than adults.

_____ 11. Boys and girls exhibit no behavioral differences until environmental influences begin to produce such differences.

_____ 12. Genius is closely akin to insanity.

_____ 13. The unstructured interview is the most valid method for assessing someone's personality.

_____ 14. Under hypnosis, people can perform feats of physical strength which they could never do otherwise.

_____ 15. Children's IQ scores have very little relationship with how well they do in school.

Eva Vaughan of the University of Pittsburgh studied the "knowledge" of psychology that beginning students had acquired from books, the media, and their own family background (1977). Her test consisted of eighty items and was administered to 119 students in four introductory courses. Twenty-three of Vaughan's statements were answered incorrectly by more than fifty percent of the students tested; these included the fifteen presented here. All statements are false as stated, though many of them reflect widespread popular belief. You will find out why they are false as you study the remainder of this book. Here are the percentages of students whose "commonsense knowledge" led them to choose the wrong answer: statement 1, 92%; 2, 87%; 3, 84%; 4, 80%; 5, 77%; 6, 77%; 7, 73%; 8, 71%; 9, 67%; 10,, 66%; 11, 61%; 12, 53%; 13, 52%; 14, 51%; 15, 50%.

How much commonsense psychology did you have?

cause the children all died. For they could not live without the petting and the joyful faces and loving words of their foster mothers."

A fable? Folkore? Could emotional deprivation really have had such a profound effect? Writing in 1760, a Spanish churchman noted, "In the foundling home the child becomes sad, and many of them die of sorrow." Since the early years of this century, a number of studies have found signs of physical as well as psychological deterioration in young children who were hospitalized for long periods of time. One study of children in two postwar German orphanages traced the relationship of weight changes to quality of care. Al-

The importance of quality of care is illustrated by these curves showing the weight gain of children in two German orphanages after World War II. The colored line shows the increasing weight gain of a group of the stern matron's favorites, whom she took with her when she moved. These data show that the normally expected gain in weight as children mature is slowed down when either the diet is poor or their care lacks emotional warmth.

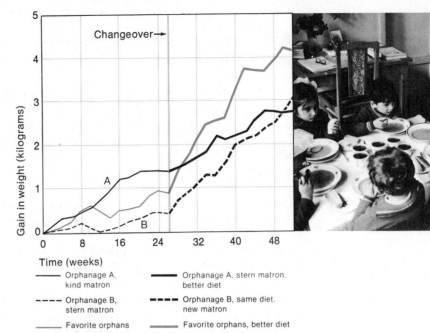

Gardner, L. "Deprivation Dwarfism," from SCIENTIFIC AMERICAN, 1972, Vol. 227, pp. 76-82. Copyright © 1972 by Scientific American, Inc. All rights reserved. Reprinted by permission.

though both groups of children received the same basic rations for the first twenty-six weeks, those in orphanage A, with a kind and loving matron, showed greater weight gain than those in orphanage B, where the matron was harsh and stern. This stern matron transferred to orphanage A at the same time a better diet was begun. At orphanage B the diet was not changed, but the weight gain increased sharply after the stern matron left. The data show that growth accelerates with a better diet of good food and loving care. ■

The most direct evidence for the link between emotional factors and physical development comes from an intensive study of six "thin dwarfs." Researcher Lytt Gardner (1972) studied children who were underweight and short. These undersized children also had retarded skeletal development with a "bone age" much less than their chronological age. All had come from family environments marked by emotional detachment and lack of affection between parents and children. Gardner showed that this condition, which has been called *deprivation dwarfism*, was indeed the physical consequence of emotional deprivation. He found that such children gain weight and begin to grow when they are removed from the hostile environment, and their growth again becomes stunted if the home environment is unchanged when they are returned to it. Since the growth problems reappear in children who are returned to a hostile situation, we have "experimental" evidence that deprivation dwarfism is indeed the consequence of emotional deprivation.

Not only has a relationship between emotional deprivation and defective physical growth been demonstrated experimentally but a physiological link between them has been found. Two structures in the brain are involved in this link with emotional starvation. A region called the *hypothalamus* (which plays a central role in emotional arousal) fails to have its usual stimulating effect on the *pituitary gland* (which secretes growth hormones). It is through such a mechanism that lack of love and human attention at critical, sensitive periods in the development of the infant can affect the body—producing deprivation dwarfism in those babies who manage to live at all. Gardner concluded: "Deprivation dwarfism is a concrete example—an 'experiment of nature,' so to speak—that demonstrates the delicacy, complexity and crucial importance of infant-parent interactions" (1972, p. 82).

The exact process by which deprivation dwarfism works is not yet known. However, it seems to be related to the impact of emotional strain on the production of pituitary and growth hormones. Most growth hormone is secreted during sleep, and these children may not sleep properly in their stress-filled homes. A recent study with infant rats shows clearly that maternal deprivation leads to an immediate suppression of growth hormone, which will increase when the rat pups are returned to the mother (Kuhn, Butler, & Schanberg, 1978). Apparently, maternal deprivation in infancy is bad for all living creatures. But can we extend this analysis to suggest that a person can really "die of a broken heart"? Psychologist James Lynch believes we can. After reviewing the evidence linking loneliness and isolation to health, Lynch asserts that "there is a biological basis for our need to form human relationships. If we fail to fulfill that need, our health is in peril" (Lynch, 1977, p. xiii). He points to the greater coronary death rate among widows than married women, among divorced men than married men. Cancer and strokes, as well as heart disease, occur twice as often among the divorced as among the married. The ultimate cause of death is, of course, a physical malfunction, such as a ventricular fibrillation. But in some still to be discovered way, the likelihood of that breakdown is increased when a person is isolated from the touch, trust, and tenderness of fellow human beings.

Would *you* obey a command to electrocute a stranger? (Part Seven)

Our next sample question is quite different but also is representative of a recurring issue in psychology. To what extent is behavior caused by characteristics inside the person, and to what extent is it caused by conditions in the environment? What made Eichmann and the other Nazis do what they did to the Jews? How was it possible for them to systematically destroy millions of people in the gas chambers of the concentration camps? How can civilized people—like *you*—understand the basis for such mass violence? Did some character defect lead the Germans to blindly carry out orders from their leaders, even if the orders violated their own values and beliefs?

What other explanation might there be? Is it conceivable that such behavior was not peculiar to the personalities of those who engaged in it in Nazi Germany? Could it be traced instead to factors in their environment? Might *you* have acted in the same way? Not a very pleasant thought, to be sure, but one that would suggest a very different approach to preventing such behavior in the future. If there are situations that increase the probability that you or I will act the way Eichmann did in Germany or Lieutenant Calley did at My Lai, then we want to identify those conditions. Only then can we avoid them or work to change them so they will not affect others. Solutions then would *not* be phrased in terms of what should be done with "problem people"—educate, treat, isolate, imprison, destroy them. Rather, we should look for ways to change "problem situations" that might lead any of us to behave in undesirable ways.

How might we investigate these alternative explanations? Often inner and outer forces are hopelessly entangled in natural situations where people behave in violent, antisocial ways. This is why a controlled experiment is called for to isolate the factors that might be at work. To rule out the possibility that evil deeds are the product of "evil personalities," the subjects for study must represent a cross section of normal, average citizens without prior histories of sadism or violence. To demonstrate the power of situational forces to make these "good" people act in evil ways, the researcher must create a believable setting in which aggression can occur, and also must devise an objective way to measure obedience to authority.

Stanley Milgram (1965, 1974), of the City University of New York, set out to investigate this intriguing question using such a procedure. Let us take a close look at the methods used in this study before we decide whether evil situations can really overpower good people or whether goodness triumphs over malevolent external pressures. Milgram's subjects were all volunteer adult males who were paid for taking part in the experiment. He began using Yale students as subjects but eventually expanded the sample to represent a cross section of the population varying widely in age, occupation, and education.

The subjects were told that the purpose of the study was to investigate the effect of punishment on memory. Every subject was told that he was to be a "teacher" and that his task was to administer punishment (an electric shock) to a "learner" whenever the latter made a mistake on a learning test. The learner, "Mr. Wallace," was a pleasant, mild-mannered man about fifty years old. It was made to look as though assignment to the two roles had been by a chance drawing of lots. After the subject-teacher himself received a sample shock of 45 volts, he watched as the learner was strapped into an "electric chair" in an adjacent room. ●

Now the experiment began. The subject was seated before a shock generator with thirty clearly marked switches ranging from "Slight Shock" (15 volts) to "Danger: Severe Shock" (450 volts). He was ordered to increase the shock to the next level each time the learner made an error or failed to respond. Since the learner made many errors, the level of punishment escalated rapidly.

The protests of the victim, heard over an intercom, rose with the shock level being administered. At 75 volts he began to moan and grunt; at 150 volts he demanded to be released from the experiment; at 180 volts he cried out that he could not stand the pain any longer. At 300 volts he insisted that he would no longer take part in the experiment and must be freed. He yelled out about his heart condition and screamed. If the subject hesitated or protested against delivering the next shock, the experimenter told him, "Teacher, you have no other choice; you must go on!" "Your job is to punish the learner's mistakes."

As you might imagine, the situation was not an enjoyable one for the subjects. In fact, it produced considerable anguish in many. To shock an innocent stranger at such high voltage levels obviously was an act of extreme violence against another human being. Most subjects complained and protested. As they became alarmed that they might even kill the learner if one of their shocks caused him to have a heart attack, they insisted they could not go on with their job. That the experimental situation produced considerable conflict is readily apparent from a sample of the transcript given here:

"180 volts delivered: 'He can't stand it! I'm not going to kill that man in there! You hear him hollering? He's hollering. He can't stand it. What if something happens to him? . . . I mean who is is going to take the responsibility if anything happens to that gentleman?' (The experimenter accepts responsibility.) 'All right.'

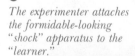

The experimenter attaches the formidable-looking "shock" apparatus to the "learner."

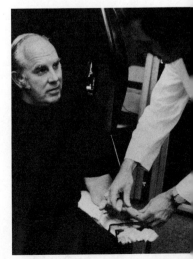

"195 volts delivered: 'You see he's hollering. Hear that. Gee, I don't know.' (The experimenter says: 'The experiment requires that you go on.') — 'I know it does, sir, but I mean — huh — he don't know what he's in for. He's up to 195 volts.' . . .

"240 volts delivered: 'Aw, no. You mean I've got to keep going up with that scale? No sir, I'm not going to kill that man! I'm not going to give him 450 volts!'" (1965, p. 67)

After the ominous silence from the learner's room, trial after trial, some subjects would even call out to him to respond, urging him to get the answer right so they would not have to continue shocking him, all the while protesting loudly to the experimenter. When the learner stopped answering at all over the last series of trials, the experimenter insisted the "teacher" must go on. "Absence of a response must also be punished because the rule states that no response is an error just like a wrong response." And of course, rules are rules! So even when only the sounds of silence were heard from the learner's room, the teacher had to keep shocking him more and more strongly. But did he? Did they? Would you? (Stop! Before reading further, think about what your response would have been. ◆)

◆

The experimenter instructs the subject in the use of the shock generator. How far do you think the average subject in Milgram's experiment actually went in administering the shocks? Suppose for a moment that you were the subject-teacher. How far up the scale would you go? Which of the thirty levels of shock would be the absolute limit beyond which you would refuse to continue? Indicate your estimates below.

1. The average subject probably stopped at: _____ volts.

2. I would refuse to shock the other person beyond voltage level (circle one number):

0	15	30	45	60
75	90	105	120	135
150	165	180	195	210
225	240	255	270	285
300	315	330	345	360
375	390	405	420	435
450				

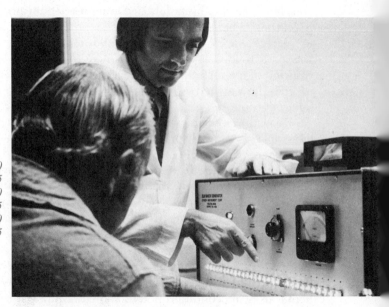

When forty psychiatrists were asked to predict the performance of subjects in this experiment, they estimated that most subjects would not go beyond 150 volts, that at 300 volts fewer than four percent of the subjects would still be obedient, and that only about 0.1 percent would go all the way up to 450 volts — obviously, only those few individuals who were abnormal in some way. How close are your predictions to theirs?

The majority of the subjects — students just like you, older people just like me — dissented, *but they did not disobey.* Nearly two thirds of the subjects (62 percent) kept pressing the levers all the way to the very last switch that delivered 450 volts, the maximum punishment possible! Even including the minority who refused to obey the authority's request, the mean maximum level of shock administered was nearly 370 volts. None of the subjects who got within five switches of the end ever refused to go all the way. By then, their resistance was broken; they had resolved their own conflict.

Although the "victim" was in reality a confederate of the experimenter and his protests were tape-recorded, the subjects believed the shocks were real. And despite their belief that they were inflicting considerable, perhaps lethal, doses of pain to a nice elderly gentleman, the majority of normal, average people—62 percent of them—obeyed the commands of authority rather than the dictates of their conscience.

Personality tests administered to the subjects did *not* reveal any traits that differentiated those who obeyed from those who refused. Nor did the tests show any psychological disturbance or abnormality in the obedient "punishers." Thus, we are led to conclude from this research that under certain circumstances, forces in the situation may override our attitudes, values, and personality traits. These forces can lead us to do things that we could not imagine ourselves doing when we are not actually involved in the situation.

In these studies those situational forces are identified as: (a) the presence of a "legitimate" authority who assumes responsibility for the consequences of one's actions; (b) a victim who is physically remote; (c) acceptance of a subordinate role with functions governed by rules; (d) allowing oneself to become part of a social system where public etiquette and protocol are more important to maintain than one's personal values and private beliefs.

An experiment such as this one is valuable not only because it provides answers, but also because it raises new questions and compels us to rethink some of our assumptions about human nature. It shatters the myth that evil is alien to Everyman and Everywoman and lurks only in particular other people who are "different" from us. It is a convincing demonstration that the "Eichmann phenomenon" could be reproduced in the majority of ordinary American citizens under specifiable social conditions.

You should also be wondering why you (probably) underestimated the percentage of people who would blindly obey. And what about your "illusion of invulnerability" that leads you to believe that *you* would have been able to resist the social forces in the experimental situation, even though the majority of your peers could not?

Could you specify conditions under which the majority of subjects might refuse to shock at all, or disobey long before dealing the ultimate blow to the victim? That is, how can we prevent or weaken this powerful social force that operates not only in the psychologist's laboratory but in our lives as well? Finally, you should be asking yourself who (or what) programmed these subjects to be so compliant to the commands of authority. The psychologist didn't; there was no prior training included in the research design. It wasn't necessary, since that had long since been completed for him by society. What particular experiences in our homes and schools prepare us to be "good little conformists" so readily manipulated by authority and rules? (See *P&L* Close-up, Stay in Your Seat—No Matter What!) In Part Seven of *P&L*, we shall look at some variations of Milgram's study as well as at other aspects of our relationships to other individuals and to society as a whole.

The methodology used in this study is *not typical* of the average experiment you may participate in as a research subject. It is rare for psychological research to involve deception or such a complicated scenario. And if you are disturbed by the ethics of such a study, you will be interested to know that many psychologists are too. In fact, a special Ethics Committee in the American Psychological Association (the leading professional organization of psychologists) has developed specific guidelines regarding this and other aspects of treatment of subjects in psychological experiments (1973). It is a tricky problem. Subjects must be safeguarded but without unduly hindering the search for knowledge. We shall be concerned throughout our study of the science and application of psychology about the ethical and moral issues involved in experimentation, therapy, and other forms of intervention in our lives.

There is no such thing in man's nature as a settled and free resolve either for good or evil, except at the very moment of execution.
Nathaniel Hawthorne
Twice Told Tales

Eichmann did not hate Jews, and that made it worse, to have no feelings. To make Eichmann appear a monster renders him less dangerous than he was. If you kill a monster you can go to bed and sleep, for there aren't many of them. But if Eichmann was normality, then this is a far more dangerous situation.
Hannah Arendt
Eichmann in Jerusalem

Close-up
Stay in Your Seat—No Matter What!

Go back in time to the memory of your elementary school classes. Ever have to go to the toilet during a lesson? Did you just get up out of your seat and quietly go about your pressing business? Not if your teachers were like mine at P.S. 25. "Stop squirming in your seat, young man; if you have to leave the room, you know the rule: You must raise your hand, be recognized, get a pass and return as soon as possible without making any disturbance. Now put your hand down when I'm talking, that's rude, where are your manners?" "Yes, teacher, but . . ."

If there is one lesson to be learned from the first six years of our traditional educational system, it is to know your place and stay put in it. This indoctrination is not only training in accepting discipline (and bladder control), but more fundamentally, it is likely preparation for passively accepting the rules of authority without question. How deeply ingrained this programming can be is shown in an unpublished set of data from Milgram's obedience research.

After members of the brave minority refused to shock the helpless victim further and quit the experiment rather than contribute to the man's heart attack, what do you suppose they did about the victim? After the others blindly went all the way and the study was officially over, what do you think they did about their victim? Did they run (or walk) to the other room to see if he was still alive, or needed help of some kind?

The answer to these questions is not contained in Milgram's book, so I called him to find out. The answer: *No one* got out of his or her seat to offer aid to the victim. Some politely requested the experimenter do so, "Someone ought to look in on the man, sir." But they did not violate their elementary school rule—no one leaves a seat until teacher says it's OK to do so. Even the small hardy band of dissenters blindly obeyed this well-seasoned rule taught them decades ago. To that extent, the obedience statistic jumps to 100 percent. "And that's good; isn't it, teacher?"

Can aggression be triggered just by stimulating the brain? (Part Four)

The answer to our last question about obedience and aggression, though quite significant, was also rather broad and somewhat vague. Rules, roles, situational forces, social programming must be taken into account, defined, and analyzed before one can make reliable predictions about their influence on aggressive behavior. However, some psychologists prefer to deal with more specific answers to questions of more limited scope. A neuropsychologist studying how behavior is affected by brain functioning would investigate aggression from a very different perspective than the social psychological one we have just considered.

Can aggressive behavior be induced in experimental animals by electrical stimulation of particular areas of the brain? This question was recently posed by a team of psychologists at the University of British Columbia in Vancouver, Canada. John Pinel, Dallas Treit, and Louis Rovner (1977) became interested in answering this question because of reports of unprovoked aggressive behavior by people with epileptic seizures. Studies of such people hospitalized or imprisoned for their violent behavior have revealed tumors in the region of the brain above the ear—the temporal lobe. But finding this clinical pattern of association does not allow one to conclude that there is a cause-and-effect relationship. To learn if changes in temporal lobe functioning *cause* aggressive behavior, the researchers designed a controlled experiment in which the brains of rats were stimulated and their aggressive reactions observed.

Seventy-five rats underwent a surgical operation in which a tiny electric needle (electrode) was implanted in their brains. By means of this electrode, minute amounts of electrical current could be used to stimulate specific areas of the brain. In some of the animals, the electrode was placed in the temporal lobe region, for others a different brain region was used. After recovery from the operation (which all subjects underwent), the rats were handled each day for several weeks to ensure that they would be tame and not fearful. Thirty of the 75 subjects served as a *control group* and did not receive the stimulation, but in every other way were treated identically to the *experimental groups*. Subjects in the experimental groups received electrical stimulation in the selected brain site three times a day, six days a week for eight weeks.

At first, the stimulation produced no noticeable effects. But after a while, muscle spasms and convulsive reactions set in. In the last weeks convulsive seizures took place regularly in every one of the brain-stimulated subjects. (If the procedure continues for several months the rats begin to develop spontaneous epileptic seizures without electrical stimulation. Their reaction is comparable to that seen in human epileptic patients.) Aggressive reactions were measured at six different times, once on each of three days before the stimulation series began, and once after a day of no stimulation at the end of four, six, and eight weeks of training. Aggression was scored by rating each animal's resistance to being captured and also its reactivity to being tapped on the tail (rats find that unpleasant). The scorers did not know to which group any given subject belonged.

The results confirm and extend the observations made with human patients. Only temporal lobe stimulation caused significant increases in aggression. The control group (operated on and handled but not stimulated) reacted about the same on the posttests as they had on the pretests. The rats who were stimulated in a region other than the temporal lobe (caudate nucleus, if you are premed) also had seizures, but did *not* show the aggressiveness common to those with temporal lobe arousal.

This study is a good example of the use of animal subjects to investigate a problem of concern to humans. Ethical and humane considerations make it impossible to study the direct connection between epileptic seizures and aggression in humans by systematically inducing seizures and observing the results. The type of research this study represents—precise, carefully controlled procedures designed to yield specific answers—is characteristic of the approach of neuropsychologists and others in the "harder," more experimental, laboratory-based areas of psychology. The initial chapters of Part Four of *P&L* will take you into those laboratories as we get under the skin into the brain and nervous system.

Does your left hand really know what your right hand is doing? (Part Five)

In the early days of psychology there was a great deal of concern with the "mind," or consciousness, as well as with the physiological aspects of the brain. In *The Principles of Psychology* (1890), William James sought to throw light on the murky concept of "split consciousness." By this he meant that one part of our consciousness may be unaware of the activity of another part. This was demonstrated in studies involving "automatic writing," in which the subject writes with one hand while his or her apparent consciousness is fully engrossed in something else and is totally unaware of what is being written. James found that one young man's writing hand was apparently "anesthetized"; it could be severely pricked with no vocal response from the subject. The injured hand, however, protested vigorously in writing. Pricks on the nonwriting hand elicited a strong vocal response from the subject, but were ignored by the part of the consciousness that controlled the writing hand.

In light of this and similar observations by French psychologists, James stated:

"It must be admitted, therefore, that in certain persons, at least, the total possible consciousness may be split into parts which coexist but mutually ignore each other, and share the objects of knowledge between them. More remarkable still, they are complementary. Give an object to one of the consciousnesses, and by that fact you remove it from the other or others. Barring a certain common fund of information, like the command of language, etc., what the upper self knows the under self is ignorant of, and vice versa" (James, 1890, p. 206).

You are probably aware of the operation of this "divided consciousness" in your own everyday life. You may read this passage while also listening to music. You carry on a conversation with an attractive acquaintance while fantasies abound. You drive skillfully through traffic while rehearsing your request for a raise or a postponed date for a term paper.

Despite the fact that we are all conscious of our consciousness, however, the mind went out of favor as a subject of psychological study for many decades. Recently, however, a number of psychologists have turned their attention to this neglected area of study, picking up where James and his contemporaries left off. One such researcher is Ernest Hilgard, who has used hypnosis in an attempt to "sort out" the various aspects of our consciousness. In a recent study (1977) Hilgard has discovered a "hidden observer" in the consciousness of the hypnotized person. This metaphor describes the awareness at an intellectual level of a source of stimulation (loud noise or pain, for example) that the hypnotized subject is neither consciously aware of nor overtly responding to.

The existence of this division of consciousness was shown with a young woman who, when hypnotized, could completely reduce the pain from having her arm immersed in ice water. Under normal waking conditions only 25 seconds in this ice bath is too much pain for the average person to bear. She reported no pain and was able to keep her left hand in the ice for a relatively long period. But at the same time, her right hand was automatically writing out pain scale ratings indicating she was experiencing considerable pain.

Hilgard substituted a "talking hidden observer" for the writing one by suggesting to other hypnotized subjects that when he touched their arm they would be able to tell him how much pain they were experiencing. While the overt reports of induced pain were uniformly low for the hypnotized subjects, the covert report from their hidden observers was much higher. However, it was still less than the pain experienced from the ice water stimulation when the same subjects were in a normal waking state. ▲ Hilgard's subjects describe their hidden observer as a part of consciousness dissociated from their ordinary consciousness as well as from their hypnotized state of consciousness.

"The hidden part knows the hypnotized part, but the hypnotized part does not know the hidden one."
"The hidden observer is analytical, unemotional, business-like."
"The hidden observer was an extra, all-knowing part of me."
"The hidden observer is a portion of me. There's Me 1, Me 2, and Me 3. Me 1 is hypnotized, Me 2 is hypnotized and observing, and Me 3 is when I'm awake" (p. 209 – 210).

In Part Five of *Psychology and Life*, we shall explore the powers and vulnerabilities of the human mind. Our excursion into the realms of consciousness and its alternate states will be preceded by studying the nature of emotion and the cognitive control exercised by mind. Many psychologists would contend that such a journey is a side trip taking you away from the fundamen-

▲

Combined responses of eight subjects in the ice-water pain experiment
The top curve shows the average level of pain reported under normal waking conditions and the bottom curve the level of overt pain reported under hypnosis. The middle curve shows the amount of pain reported by the "hidden observers" using a key-pressing device.

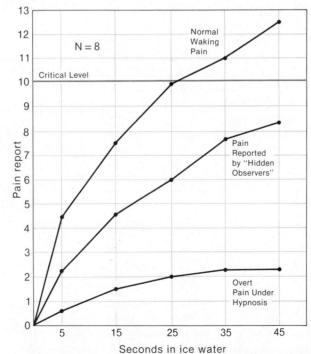

Adapted from Hilgard & Hilgard, 1975

tals of psychology. In opposition, others (including me) argue that consciousness, emotion, and the controlling influences of mind over matter are at the core of the unique experience of being human.

How unusual is it for someone (like me) to be shy? Can shyness be cured? (Part Six)

The intellectual puzzles that psychologists face come from a variety of sources. Some ideas emerge from their sensitive "people watching," others from attempts to evaluate a theory or one of its derivations. Some come from questions raised by prior research, still more are generated by problems in the society—like violence and prejudice. But ultimately, what is most exciting about being a psychologist comes from trying to understand the basic functioning of the mind and to discover the determinants of human action. With such knowledge in hand, psychologists are then able to develop tactics for behavior change and strategies for enhancing the human potential.

Not long ago, one of my students posed some psychological questions that had personal relevance to him. "How unusual is it for someone to be shy? What causes shyness? Is it a childhood stage most people outgrow? Can anything be done to help a shy person—like me?" My answer to such questions was simple and direct: "I don't know. Go to the library, look up *Shyness* in the card catalogue, read all the references listed, write a report on them. We'll discuss your findings, and you'll have the information you need."

It is important to recognize that psychologists cannot begin to develop tactics designed to change behavior or to improve the quality of life until they have a basic understanding of the problem. This is why most research projects begin with a search of the available literature. But in this case, the card catalogue was not very helpful: surprisingly, not much research had been done that could help answer the student's queries. There were studies of how individuals differed in the personality trait of shyness. But there was very little on the experience of shyness, what elicits it, how prevalent it is, what its consequences are, and so forth.

Aware that shyness is a serious personal problem for many of my students, friends, and relatives, I decided to accept this challenge to discover the whys and hows of shyness. Five years later, after surveying over 5000 people in eight different cultures, interviewing hundreds of shy and nonshy people, observing children in school settings from kindergarten through college, and conducting a dozen experiments, we have some answers to give to that student, and also to you. Shyness will be discussed in Chapter 17 in some detail. For now, let us touch on some of the highlights of our research into this complex and fascinating phenomenon. (See my book *Shyness* [Zimbardo, 1977] for more information.)

yes   no   "Do you consider yourself to be a shy person?"

yes   no   "If you are not shy now, were you ever a shy person?"

These are the opening questions in a self-report survey that was administered to many different groups of people. The survey went on to probe into the kind of people and situations that trigger shyness in the shy person. It asked about one's reactions when made to feel shy: physical reactions (blushing? sweating? heart pounding?), actions (eye contact? stuttering?), feelings (anxiety?), and thoughts (self-consciousness? inadequacies?). Finally, the questionnaire inquired about the consequences of shyness, both negative and positive.

What we discovered was that more than 40 percent of all those surveyed labeled themselves as "shy people." That would mean four out of every ten people you meet, perhaps 84 million Americans, think of themselves as currently shy. The figure escalates to over 80 percent if those who are now shy are combined with those previously shy. In every one of the eight cultures studied, shyness is reported to be a common experience — with a low of about 30 percent in Israel and a high of 60 percent in Japan. Thus shyness is prevalent, widespread, and maybe even a universal psychological experience.

The table indicates the average replies of nearly a thousand college students to questions about what makes them shy. ■ Interestingly, when an independent team of market researchers asked 3000 U.S. inhabitants "What are you most afraid of?" guess what was the worst human fear? Darkness was in twelfth place, fear of flying came in eighth, 19 percent of the people were afraid of sickness and death, putting those fears in sixth place. Two biggies were financial problems and fear of insects, each with 22 percent indicating them as worst fears. The runner-up fear was heights, which made 32 percent of those surveyed stay on the ground. But the number one, worst human fear of all was — "Speaking before a group," a fear shared by 41 percent of the people (Wallechinsky, Wallace, & Wallace, 1977).

Shyness is a form of social anxiety — a people phobia. It is a learned reaction in which the shy individual becomes overly self-conscious, filled with discomforting thoughts about negative evaluation from others. It is judged to be an undesirable "personal problem" by the majority of people who are shy. Shyness can start at any age and last a lifetime. Our research reveals that shyness not only interferes with an adequate social life, but when it is strongly felt, shyness can impair one's memory, inhibit sexual enjoyment, and limit career opportunities. The experience of shyness alienates some people from all human contact.

Once having discovered this (and other) information about the nature and consequences of shyness, then what? The obvious next question is, can the knowledge generated by the research be used to overcome shyness? The issue then becomes one of how best to apply what we know to make changes in people who are unhappy being shy. The concern for treating individuals in a

■

What makes you shy?

Situations	Percentage of Shy Students	Other People	Percentage of Shy Students
Where I am focus of attention — large group (as when giving a speech)	73%	Strangers	70%
		Opposite sex	64%
Of lower status	56%	Authorities by virtue of	
Social situations in general	55%	their knowledge	55%
New situations in general	55%	Authorities by virtue of	
Requiring assertiveness	54%	their role	40%
Where I am being evaluated	53%	Relatives	21%
Where I am focus of attention —		Elderly people	12%
small group	52%	Friends	11%
One-to-one different sex interactions	48%	Children	10%
Of vulnerability (need help)	48%	Parents	8%
Small task-oriented groups	28%		
One-to-one same sex interactions	14%		

therapeutic setting has traditionally been the province of clinical psychologists and psychiatrists. (See *P&L* Close-up. What Distinguishes Psychology from Psychiatry?) They are the practitioners who apply psychological theories and research findings to help people who have serious problems coping with life.

We created our own experimental shyness clinic to put our ideas into practice, and evaluate them. In small group settings, shy people were guided toward changing one or more aspects of their functioning, depending on the way shyness affected them. Some shy people require training and practice in social skills (smiling, making eye contact, the art of conversation, etc.). Others receive training in self-control of anxiety through relaxation techniques. Low self-esteem frequently accompanies shyness; when it does, therapy involves lessons in building self-confidence. For other shy people the treatment may be directed at better understanding social cues others are providing and also learning what is expected in given social and work settings. Finally, one aspect of this shyness therapy centers upon changing the label of "shyness" itself. Are *you* a shy person or are there some unpleasant situations that give rise to feelings of shyness in you? If your shyness is specific to certain situations, then maybe you are not shy after all. Maybe there is something wrong with those situations where you feel put on the spot, critically evaluated, and not accepted for yourself. If so, perhaps some therapy ought to be directed toward changing undesirable situations, as well as undesirable thought and response patterns in people.

In Part Six of *P&L*, you will have a greater opportunity to see how psychologists go about the task of understanding normal personality and the stresses we face daily in our lives. The study of madness and abnormal reactions will interest us, as will the kinds of therapy being used to modify the patterns of thinking, feeling, and action of those of us who cannot make an adequate adjustment. Going beyond the research findings, in Chapter 18 we will also consider together some issues and offer advice on personal adjustment for the "garden variety" psychological problems faced by college students.

ZIGGY...i THINK iT's TiMe We MADe AN eFFORT To DeAL WiTH THiS BASiC SHYNeSS iSSUe !!

Does your memory of a story depend on which character you identify with? (Part Two)

Not all psychologists are professionally concerned about such dramatic issues as those we have posed thus far. For many of them, the foundation of psychology rests more on understanding the basic processes by which people learn new information, integrate the new with the familiar, remember some of it, forget some of it, and perhaps distort the rest of it to fit their particular biases. The study of learning, cognition, and the way people process information is at the very core of contemporary psychology.

Gordon Bower and his associates at Stanford University, Justine Owens and Janet Dafoe (1977), have begun a program of research to understand the effects of identification on memory. When you identify with a particular character in a story is your recall of the story distorted or more accurate as a consequence? The way we interpret the events of a written story may, in fact, follow the same principles as our interpretation of events in our everyday lives. At least, that is one assumption that initiated this research. The investigators began with an idea they wanted to test: When a reader identifies with a character in a story he or she tries to understand the story from that character's point of view. Readers attempt to understand the character's personal perspective and events in the story much the same way they try to understand events in their own lives. They search for explanations to make sense of ambi-

What Distinguishes Psychology from Psychiatry?

Because psychology and psychiatry are both professions that deal with matters of mind and behavior, the public often confuses them. The most basic difference is in the advanced training received; psychiatry is a medical speciality requiring an M.D. degree, while psychology is considered part of an academic discipline requiring a Ph.D. degree from an accredited graduate school. Their medical training enables psychiatrists to prescribe drugs as part of a treatment program, while psychologists may not. In general, psychiatrists tend to be professional therapists who treat patients with mental and emotional problems. They do so either in their own private practice or in a clinic or hospital setting. With few exceptions they are more likely to be practitioners than researchers. Training in psychology can prepare the student for a career as researcher-scholar (usually combined with college teaching), or in any of a number of areas of applied psychology. The clinical psychologist, like the psychiatrist, usually is a therapist who treats clients in private practice or hospitalized patients. Assessment of psychological disturbance by means of various tests (described in Chapter 17) is a task of the clinical psychologist. A psychoanalyst can be either a psychiatrist or clinical psychologist who has received specialized training at a psychoanalytic institute, where Freud's ideas and therapeutic methods are taught.

guities, to give advantages to liked characters or handicaps to disliked ones, and to find reasonable causes for the behavior of all the characters.

Behavior is sometimes explained in terms of internal attributes of the person. These are traits, such as "generous" or "intelligent," for example, or background factors, "she's a Catholic," "he's a Southerner," "they came from broken homes." Behavior can also be attributed to external events or factors in the immediate environment, such as "His hostile reply made me angry" or "I failed the test because the room was so noisy." Generally, it has been found that when we explain another person's behavior we tend to attribute it to internal causes, while we think our own behavior depends more on external causes (Jones & Nisbett, 1972).

Therefore Owens, Dafoe, and Bower reasoned that if you identify with a character in a story, you ought to perceive the causes of that person's actions the same way you perceive your own, as externally or situationally motivated. The characters you do not identify with should more likely be seen as motivated by inner forces and permanent traits. Thus different perspectives will result in different cognitive processing of the same story by different readers. Furthermore, what they remember of it should be distorted accordingly. To test these ideas, the researchers had two groups of college students: (a) read the identical four-page story about three characters (Cindy, Harry, and Rich); (b) spend twenty minutes on an unrelated task (the retention interval); (c) take a ninety-item recognition test covering the facts of the story (to see if their memory of the story depended on who they identified with while reading the story).

Before any of this was done, however, identification had to be established. The experimental manipulation of identification with a particular character involved reading a one-page account of the previous day's activities of one or the other character. Thus half the subjects were first acquainted only with Harry, the driver of the motorboat, while the other half read only about Rich, the water-skier. This initial exposure to one actor was assumed to be enough for the subject to take that actor's point of view throughout the rest of the story. (See *P&L* Close-up, The Killers' Point of View.) A synopsis of the story will help you better appreciate the outcome.

Cindy is trying to film a television commercial for suntan lotion, and she has selected Rich to be the water-skier in the ad. She gets her boyfriend, Harry, to drive the speedboat. The story describes them meeting at the dock, going out on the lake, and trying to get some good film shots of Rich waterskiing. However, various spills, mistakes, and misunderstandings occur involving the skier and the driver, who are competing for Cindy's attentions.

The story was intentionally vague at key places, forcing the readers to make their own interpretation of particular events. For example, the cause of the mishaps was not stated.

Some of the recognition test items were worded in such a way that identification with one of the characters would lead to a false interpretation. For example, the story states: "Rich reached for the handle, but it escaped him," with no explanation of why he couldn't catch it. One test item was: "Rich reached for the handle, but he wasn't fast enough to catch it." Readers who identified with Harry, the driver, were more likely than those who identified with Rich to mistakenly remember this statement as part of the story. They blamed the mishap on the skier's incompetence (an internal attribution). When the corresponding recognition item was worded to be more favorable to Rich ("Rich reached for the handle, but the boat hadn't come close enough for him to catch it"), readers who identified with Rich mistakenly believed it was the sentence they had read in the story (an external attribution).

When the data were computed for all the items of the recognition test that favored one or the other character, it was found that identification with one of the characters significantly affected memory for what had been read. The effect that identification can have on our interpretation of causes of behavior is shown in the graph. Subjects who identified with the skier rated his ability high, but the driver's ability as low. The opposite pattern occurred with those who identified with the driver; his ability was judged high compared to that of the skier (Owens, Dafoe, & Bower, 1977).

Seeing the story "through the eyes" of one of the actors in the story colors our psychological perspective on what "really happened." Most of us identify with other people in our lives, both those we know personally and those we see

Close-up
The Killers' Point of View

In Ernest Hemingway's short story, "The Killers," the reader is led to adopt a particular point of view by the use of a single verb in the opening sentence.

The facts are: two men, a lunchroom, and a door. The issue is: what is the point of view of the storyteller who presents these facts in the following way?

"The door of Henry's lunchroom opened and two men *came* in."

The observer's point of view is from the inside of the lunchroom that the two men entered. But notice how this point of view shifts to an outsider's perspective when the action verb is changed from "came" to "went."

"The door to Henry's lunchroom opened and two men *went* in."

There are also other inferences we make on the basis of this changed point of view. In the first version, it is reasonable to assume the two men opened the door. In the second version, it could be that more than two men were outside and when the door was opened by someone inside two of the men entered (see Fillmore, 1974).

Effective writing always creates points of view about the interpretation of certain events and about characters. When we adopt the point of view of another person, that is the start of a psychological process of identifying with that person.

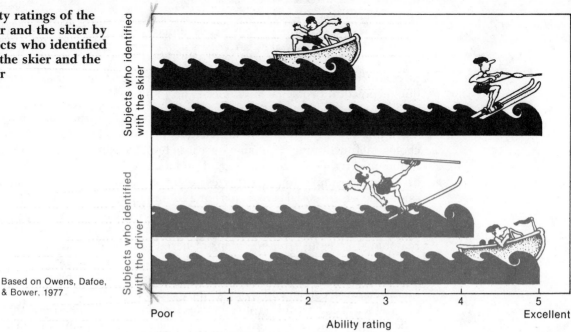

Ability ratings of the driver and the skier by subjects who identified with the skier and the driver

Subjects who identified with the skier

Subjects who identified with the driver

Based on Owens, Dafoe, & Bower, 1977

Poor 1 2 3 4 5 Excellent

Ability rating

in the mass media. Such identification serves important social and emotional functions for us, but it may also distort our perception of events. In Part Two of *P&L* we will begin our study of the subject matter of psychology by studying how we learn, remember, solve problems, think, and develop our language, intelligence, and creativity.

Models of human nature

The questions raised thus far are but a sampling of the many you will be confronted with throughout this introduction to psychology. How one poses the questions determines the kinds of answers that are possible. Different questions require developing different research tools and strategies, collecting different data, and ultimately developing radically different perspectives on the human condition. For example, how a research question is posed determines whether the researcher:

a. studies *all living, behaving organisms* or only *humans*;

b. studies only *overt behavior*, observable to all, or *covert psychological processes* like thoughts and feelings;

c. studies the *process* of psychological events (reasoning, problem solving) or the *product* (success, failure);

d. is willing to accept only *objective* behavioral data or includes also people's *subjective* analysis of their own experience;

e. analyzes behavior into the smallest functional *parts* or deals with *whole,* integrated systems of behavior;

f. focuses on the *past* history of the individual or on *present* conditions;

g. looks for the causes of behavior *within the individual* (motives, traits, physiological functioning, etc.), or *in the environment* (rewarding or stressful conditions);

h. emphasizes *precision and simplicity* or *complexity and richness* in description and explanation;

i. starts with a *theory* to guide the collection of data, gathering data to test or extend the theory or takes an *empirical approach* that rejects the value of theories;

j. conducts research for its *pure, scientific value* or for its *application* to the solution of practical problems, both social and individual.

"Well, what is the *right* way to ask the questions?" you may be wondering. The right way is that which yields useful explanations of some aspect of psychological functioning. Human nature is so broad a subject that no one has yet found one "right" way to analyze and understand it. We are basically biological creatures, similar to other species in our physiological makeup. But at the same time we are social beings, part of a community, a culture, a political-economic system. We are rational problem-solvers, but also at times become irrationally impulsive. We use our uniquely human gifts of language and abstract reasoning to free us from the limits of heredity by finding ways of changing the environment to fit us and not simply adapting to what we find. Thus to capture this complexity properly in the portrait of man and woman requires many shadings, colors, and styles of approach. At one end, psychology is a biological science, at the other it resembles sociology. And in between there is a little of everything as we study the development of the organism from its conception through its final transformations in death. Psychology is *pluralistic;* it intentionally encourages different approaches and tolerates a wide variety of viewpoints on the nature of human nature. The long-range hope is that as this young social science matures, its many strands will combine to form a solid core of knowledge.[2]

Of the various general views that psychologists take in their pursuit of solving the riddle of human behavior, four predominate: the psychodynamic, the behavioristic, the cognitive, and the humanistic. They not only represent different perspectives, but sometimes are in opposition about what should be studied, how it should be studied, and even why it should be studied.

The psychodynamic model

The dynamic approach in psychology is one that assumes all behavior is driven or motivated by powerful inner forces. In this view our actions are caused by biological and social drives. Conflicts, tensions, guilt, anxiety, and frustration fuel the fires of human functioning much as coal fuels a steam locomotive. Outer (overt, observable) behavior is to be explained in terms of inner forces. Theories that emphasize motivation of one sort or another are generally dynamic theories.

The psychodynamic model is founded on the ideas of Sigmund Freud. (See *P&L* Profile on p. 23.) Freud's writings have had a greater influence on the development of psychology than those of any other individual. His theories will come up again and again in many contexts throughout this text. Central to his approach is the assumption that biological drives and inborn instincts toward self-preservation direct behavior. Thus we are dominated by sexual and aggressive urges. Society opposes the open expression of these urges, catching the infant or young child in a crosscurrent. Though we are at the mercy of our inherited urges and early parental training experiences, we

---

[2]For a fuller presentation of these ideas and those to come in the next section, you might read: James Deese, *Psychology as Science and Art*, Harcourt Brace Jovanovich, 1972; Frank Bruno, *The Story of Psychology*, Holt, Rinehart and Winston, 1972; or Robert Nye, *Three Views of Man*, Brooks/Cole, 1975.

Profile
Sigmund Freud

Combining a penetrating intelligence with a dazzling literary talent, Sigmund Freud approached the problem of human personality with fresh insight—pioneering the modern study of personality theory. Throughout his career Freud sought to trace the roots of personality and to delineate the intricate relationship between underlying mental structures, overt behavior, and societal pressures.

Freud was born in a small Czech town in Moravia, near the Polish border, on May 6, 1856. He was the eldest of eight children by his father's second wife. His father, a wool merchant, early recognized Sigmund's intellectual bent and encouraged the boy in his studies. Freud excelled in school but was frequently prey to deep depression and emotional upheaval. These early personal difficulties may have stimulated him to search for the hidden mechanisms that prompt personality disorders.

In 1873, he entered the prestigious medical school at the University of Vienna, intending to become a scientific researcher rather than to practice medicine. While at the university, he became intrigued with Professor Ernst Brücke's theories of behavioral and physiological processes and considered studying under him after earning his medical degree. But Freud had, in the interim, married and begun to raise a family, and financial pressures increased accordingly. Because advancement in academia was severely restricted for Jews at the time, he felt compelled to enter private practice as a psychiatrist. With this goal in mind he studied for a year with Jean Charcot, who was well known for his use of hypnotism as a treatment for nervous disorders.

Eventually, Freud found this technique unsatisfactory and so began work with a Viennese colleague, Joseph Breuer, who had initiated the use of free association in an attempt to trace the origins of neurotic symptoms. An important product of the years during which the two doctors collaborated was the book they coauthored in 1895, *Studies in Hysteria*. The two men finally parted over a disagreement on the importance of sexual conflict as the cause of hysteria—Freud assigned such conflicts a central position.

Freud soon began practicing on his own, using free-association techniques and asking patients to relate their dreams to him. From the insights he gained during these sessions, he formulated a system of dream symbolism that he presented in his first great book, *Interpretation of Dreams*. While he was attacked by much of the scientific community at that time, particularly for his theory of infant sexuality, he also had outstanding disciples, including Jung and Adler.

His recognition as an important contributor to psychological theory came when he was invited by the American Psychology Association to give a series of lectures at Clark University in 1909.

He went on to found the International Psychoanalytic Association in 1910, establishing training institutes for psychoanalysis in many countries. His writing covered an incredible range of subjects: psychoanalytic technique, and explanations in psychoanalytic terms of history, religion, literature, and social science.

But his work did not begin to have real impact until the 1930s—a period that was personally traumatic for him because the Nazis had gained control of Austria and were a continual threat to the lives of his family and himself. Friends eventually convinced the Freuds to escape to England in 1939, and Freud spent the last year of his life there, succumbing at last to the cancer of the jaw he had been fighting for over sixteen years. Although psychoanalysis is less popular today in the U.S. than it was, in western Europe it remains a powerful intellectual force. Some Europeans believe it rivals Christianity and Communism as a social-intellectual movement.

survive by imposing rational control over these basic conflicts. Behavior that does not appear to make sense, or to be based on logic, is analyzed as a symptom of unconscious motives. According to the psychodynamic model, then, human nature is fully determined by heredity and early life experiences; is basically evil (requiring societal controls and psychotherapy that brings the unconscious to the surface) and leads to a pessimistic outlook about the inevitability of violence and the passion for power.

The behavioristic model

If the analogy for the dynamic model is the steam engine, the analogy for the behavioristic model is the assembly line. What is important to the behaviorist is activity, tangible products and output that can be counted and "inventoried." Behaviorists seek data that are objective, overt, specific, localized responses to specific stimuli, precisely measured and simply interrelated. They believe that the basis of reality is to be found in the objective, material world of physical actions. They look for predictable relationships between specific responses and conditions in the environment. They see no need to look for causes within the person, except to the extent that these inner events can, in turn, be related to the external environment. Indeed, some of them argue that making inferences about internal processes is the guessing game of psychologists who do not have (or do not know how to go about finding) the facts of behavior. Behavior is the starting point of psychology; *it* is what is to be explained, and not the inner person.

To some extent all psychologists accept the importance of objectively studying observable behavior—what people say and do. But *radical behaviorists* deny the reality of motives, mind, personality traits, attitudes, values, and even cognitive processes. If anything, inner states are seen as mere by-products of outer behavior. Human actions are elicited by environmental events and controlled by their consequences. This is known as the S→R approach (stimulus→response). We continue to do what has been followed in the past by favorable consequences and do not engage in behaviors that have had unfavorable effects.

Behaviorists tend toward the "scientific" in their approach to psychology: they prefer "hard," numerical data to "soft," qualitative data and typically collect their data from controlled laboratory experiments, using electronic apparatus and computers to present stimuli and record responses. They insist on precise definitions, special vocabulary, and rigorous standards of evidence. Often they use animal subjects because control can be much more complete than with human subjects and because the processes being studied occur in simpler form. They believe that human nature is neutral—neither bad nor good—and can be molded into nearly any form. Behavior is completely modifiable through the systematic application of principles of conditioning. The practical goal of all organisms is successful adaptation to their environment, which is accomplished through their learning experiences, according to the behaviorist approach.

The first major figure in behaviorism was John B. Watson, its founder back in the 1920s. Watson, in boldly asserting that psychology must be only the science of behavior, was reacting to several trends of his times which placed undue importance on vaguely defined mental states and endless lists of instincts that supposedly explained (but really only named) everything. In short, we are what we have been conditioned to become.

B. F. Skinner (see *P&L* Profile, p. 25) has carried Watson's deterministic

B. F. Skinner is probably the best-known contemporary psychologist in America today. Long recognized within the field for his contributions to behavioristic and experimental psychology, he has become familiar to the larger public through his best-selling novel, *Walden Two* (1948), and the more recent *Beyond Freedom and Dignity* (1971).

Born in Susquehanna, Pennsylvania, where his father practiced law, Burrhus Frederick Skinner attended local schools until 1922. He then entered Hamilton College in New York, hoping to prepare himself for a literary career. He graduated with a degree in English and with special honors in Greek, in 1926.

During his last year at Hamilton, Skinner sent some short stories he had written to the poet Robert Frost, hoping for some helpful criticism. Much to Skinner's amazement, Frost replied enthusiastically, encouraging the young author to pursue a writing career. Skinner took the advice seriously and set aside a block of time following graduation in which to apply himself to his chosen discipline. In looking back on this year, Skinner wryly comments that while he did indeed learn to write well, he also discovered that he had nothing important to say!

To remedy the situation, he returned to academia—this time as a graduate student in psychology. He had done much reading during his year away from school, and in the course of it, had come upon the works of John B. Watson, the famous American behaviorist. The story of Watson's pioneering efforts excited Skinner's interest and thus determined his decision to study psychology.

Skinner was accepted at Harvard and there earned his Ph.D. in experimental psychology in 1931. He continued with post-doctoral work until 1936, when he accepted a teaching position at the University of Minnesota. Throughout this period, Skinner had been formulating and testing his theories on conditioning. So impressive were the results he achieved in controlling the behavior of laboratory animals, that the U.S. government employed him in a top secret project during World War II. Skinner was given funding to condition pigeons to guide missiles directly down the smokestacks of enemy naval destroyers.

After the war, Skinner did not hesitate to apply the techniques he had developed to human subjects. Upon moving to Indiana University as chairman of its new psychology department, he constructed his famous "air crib"—a soundproofed, germ-free "box" enclosed in clear plastic and intended as an environment in which infants could spend much of their time. Skinner's daughter Deborah was raised in the air crib, and she in turn raised her children in the device.

In 1948, Skinner returned to Harvard University as a member of the faculty. There he developed the "Skinner Box"—a chamber in which animal behavior (particularly that of rats and pigeons) can be precisely recorded and thus prepared for statistical analysis. The apparatus had an immediate impact on experimental laboratories in universities across the country.

Skinner became convinced that the learning techniques he had hit upon with his methodology could be translated to the environment of the classroom, and so spent most of the '50s perfecting his programmed teaching modules for schoolchildren. With these, children could acquire information and skills while being led through a series of questions—each of their correct responses eliciting a reinforcing confirmation.

Throughout his career, Skinner has published prolifically, and the American Psychological Association honored him for his immense contribution with their Distinguished Scientific Contribution Award in 1958. Though retired now, Skinner has not remained idle. He recently published his autobiography, *Particulars of My Life*, and continues to study and write at his home in Cambridge, Massachusetts.

banner—all behavior can be lawfully related to observable environmental conditions—not only in his scientific writings (1938, 1953, 1974) but also in his popular works, *Walden Two* (1948) and *Beyond Freedom and Dignity* (1971). "Psychological growth is not a naturally occurring process that emerges from the individual," said Skinner in a recent interview (*APA Monitor*, July 1977, p. 6). He believes that variations in the environment lead to modifications in behavior over one's life span. If the environment changes and you don't, you will be left without adequate responses to get the rewards necessary for physical or psychological survival. While Skinnerian behaviorism has created a controversy about the ethics and politics of behavior control, we shall see in later chapters that it has profoundly affected much psychological thinking and practice.

The cognitive model

While behaviorists do not believe in anything that can't be seen directly, psychologists who take a cognitive approach are willing to believe that there is more to human nature than the public actions of human beings. They broaden the domain of psychological reality beyond the limits of behavioral reactions to external stimuli. Mental processes—attending, thinking, remembering, planning, expecting, wishing, fantasizing, and consciousness itself—are the "stuff" of the cognitive psychologists. In counterpoint to the physical actions emphasized by the behaviorists is the uniquely human activity of self-awareness. As philosopher Karl Jaspers (1963) has pointed out, human beings not only exist, but know that they exist. The individual's perceptions and interpretations determine his or her subsequent behavior. Thus to understand someone's behavior, it is not enough to know the objective external situation; we must understand how it looks subjectively to that person. Early psychologists such as Wilhelm Wundt in Germany and E. B. Titchener in the United States appreciated this "insider's" view of their subject matter. The "new" psychology at the end of the nineteenth century was introspective. The core of introspective psychology is the study of *consciousness*; its goal is to uncover the "contents of the mind" and the mental processes used by the individual in responding to environmental stimulation. This information is elicited through the systematic questioning of trained subjects who are trained in *introspection*—the process of reporting and describing their subjective experiences.

The cognitive approach views the person as an *information generator* rather than as mere transmitter of environmental inputs (Hitt, 1969). It asks how we gain information about our physical and social world that enables us to make sense of our sensations and give purpose to our behavior. Some of the basic differences between the behaviorist and cognitive approaches are described in the table. ◆

Phenomenology is the term for an approach within the general cognitive model that studies the unique personal experiences of the individual. How does your view of the world change as you get older, feel depressed, fall in love, get closer to danger? The richness of human nature is studied not through analysis of its parts, but as a whole, interdependent system—a dynamic system of potentiality. Some phenomenologists seek to learn how we transform what comes in through our sense impressions into personally relevant perceptions by means of values, symbols, and myths (May, 1975).

The English essayist William Hazlitt captured a basic tenet of this approach to psychology when he wrote: "We do not see nature with our eyes but

◆

Two models of human nature

	Behavioristic	**Cognitive**
1. The object of psychological study is:	Behavior, actions	Consciousness, self-awareness
2. Human behavior is:	Predictable	Unpredictable
3. Human beings are:	Information transmitters	Information generators
4. The basis of reality is found in:	The objective material world	The subjective world of experience
5. Each individual is:	Like all others, thus governed by general laws	Unique, thus not subsumed by laws common to all
6. Descriptions of human beings:	Can be in absolute terms	Must be only in relative terms
7. Human characteristics can be investigated:	Singly or independent of one another	Only as a whole, as an interdependent system
8. Human nature and human beings are:	An actuality, a reality, an objective fact of existence	A potentiality, a dynamic process of becoming
9. Human beings are knowable:	Scientifically, logically, empirically, completely	To some extent, but not ever completely

Adapted from Hitt, 1969

with our understanding and our hearts" (1839). The subject's view of the situation is all important to the phenomenologist, while the experimenter's view is the one that matters to the objective behaviorist. The latter position makes sense when the subjects are lower animal species; it has less impact when applied to the study of human behavior. The cognitive approach to psychology underlies a wide variety of topics, such as the concept of "attitude" in social psychology, the Freudian interpretation of dreams, attempts to study the uniqueness of personality and, as we have seen, processes that affect memory.

Some of the very best researchers from the behaviorist side have in recent years defected from the empirical study of the simple behavior of rats and pigeons. They have shifted from a concern for relating overt responses to environmental stimuli to a concern for the internal cognitive processes by which individuals interpret external events and plan how to respond. Cognitive psychology, which studies such processes as memory, language acquisition, and problem-solving, thus represents a bridge between the S→R variables of behaviorism and the individualistic orientation of phenomenology. It uses the rigorous research methods of the former to study the experiential world of the individual. We will also see, for example, the pervasive influence of the cognitive model in the approach of Albert Bandura to learning theory, Walter Mischel to personality theory, and Kurt Lewin to social psychology.

The humanistic model

Humanism has been called "Third Force" psychology, as an alternative to the passive-deterministic outlook of both psychodynamic and behaviorist models. It shares with phenomenology the emphasis on the importance of the person's current conscious experiences in determining reality. But humanism is less a research-oriented approach to studying psychology and more a program of ideals about what *should* be the proper study of psychology. Basic human nature is seen as good, not evil or neutral. It is active, not passive. It is not simply adaptable, but striving for growth, seeking change and a restructuring of the environment. Humanistic psychology is concerned with

Profile
Carl Rogers

Carl Rogers, the founder of client-centered therapy and one of the best-known figures in humanistic psychology, is often described by friends as the "man who gave people permission to be themselves." A firm believer in the basic goodness of human beings, Rogers has based his approach to therapy and education on the assumption that individuals, when given the proper opportunity and encouragement, can decide for themselves the best course to follow.

For all its apparent simplicity, this doctrine has placed the mild-mannered Rogers squarely in the face of controversy throughout his career. For Rogers has always attempted to go beyond the mere formulation of pleasant-sounding philosophies—he has insisted upon implementing his notions in the context of social institutions.

A student of agriculture, Rogers made an abrupt change of plans after traveling to China with a student religious group. He began to see that he would only truly satisfy his needs and interests in a milieu that encouraged communication and offered him an opportunity to help others. He enrolled in a theological seminary, but soon found the emphasis on dogma and hierarchy to be contradictory to his highly personal approach. He then switched to the study of psychology, a discipline in which he felt he would be better able to develop and act upon his ideas. He received his bachelors degree from the University of Wisconsin in 1924. After graduating from Columbia Teachers College, he became director of the Rochester Child Guidance Clinic in New York and there began to construct the techniques that would eventually evolve into Rogerian, or person-oriented, therapy. He was then chosen as director of the student guidance clinic at the University of Chicago, the first in the country. Excited by the prospect of further developing and implementing his techniques, Rogers accepted the position. But he almost immediately ran afoul of the more conservative members of the department of psychiatry. First, they insisted that he was practicing a type of therapy that would best be left to those with medical degrees. Second, they objected to his candid admission that many of the failures occurring in student therapy were directly attributable to therapists. Rogers got around much of the debate by changing his terminology—instituting "student counseling" rather than psychotherapy and continuing to develop highly successful therapeutic techniques.

But he remained dissatisfied and moved to the University of Wisconsin, where he again earned a reputation as a maverick. While he stayed at the university for nearly a decade and wrote and published many of his finest works during this period he became increasingly critical of the form that graduate education in psychology had taken. He wrote a number of critiques of higher education, most notably *Freedom to Learn*, published in 1969.

Finally, he decided to join forces with a group of like-minded psychologists at the Western Institute for Behavioral Sciences in California. This nonprofit center is involved in several projects, including a tremendously popular two-week summer course of encounter groups. An even more ambitious project is designed to put physicians in closer touch with the "human" and ethical aspects of medical practice. Other programs include family therapy and psychotherapy for disturbed children.

But for all his success, Rogers has undergone criticism from many sides in recent years. Even friends and colleagues describe his views as overly optimistic—particularly his faith that tense situations such as racial confrontations can be resolved by person-centered therapy techniques. And some of the unstructured educational programs he has encouraged are proving ineffective.

But Rogers, if anything, has grown more optimistic over the years. He is currently training facilitators (therapists) in a number of foreign countries, and he believes that the popularity of his client-centered therapy is growing—especially in places such as Germany, Japan, and Brazil.

developing the human potential, not merely with its adequate functioning. In brief, humanistic psychology stands for a commitment to human becoming, an emphasis on the wholeness and uniqueness of the individual, a concern for improving the human condition as well as for understanding the individual.

The pioneers of this movement have been Abraham Maslow (1954) and Carl Rogers (1961, 1977) (see *P&L* Profile on p. 28). Both see humans as striving toward actualization, the fullest growth of one's basic potentialities. The goal of living is to evolve continually, to experience the joys of life, and to participate in creating new forms rather than settling for adaptation to existing ones. The unit of study is the whole organism, not some particular behavioral reaction. Floyd Matson, former president of the American Association for Humanistic Psychology, spoke for this viewpoint when he said: "I know of no greater disrespect for the human subject than to treat him as an object— unless it is to demean that object further by fragmenting it into drives, traits, reflexes, and other mechanical hardware" (1971, p. 7). If behaviorists and Freudians *analyze* the individual into responses and conflicts, humanists see their role as putting Humpty Dumpty together again, *synthesizing* the parts into a uniquely whole person.

These models will recur in different forms throughout our text. This overview should help give you a general orientation that will be amplified as we gather more information about the many content areas that psychologists are currently investigating.

Chapter summary

Psychology is formally defined as *the study of the behavior of organisms*. It can be described as *scientific, curious, comprehensive*, and *pragmatic* (practical). The comprehensiveness of psychology is shown in the variety of interesting and challenging questions that psychologists seek to answer through their research.

The types of questions a psychologist raises and the way he or she goes about answering them is determined to a large extent by the *model*, or perspective on human nature, he or she has adopted. Most psychologists accept one of four major models: (1) The *psychodynamic* model, which assumes that all behavior is determined by powerful inner drives, either biological or social. This model is based largely on the theories of Sigmund Freud. (2) The *behavioristic* model, which sees the causes of behavior in the environment rather than the individual. This approach is also *deterministic*. Its adherents believe all behavior is caused by environmental events and controlled (changed) by its consequences—that is, by learning. B. F. Skinner is the leading behaviorist in America today. (3) The *cognitive* model, which takes a somewhat broader view of human nature in that it recognizes the existence of mental processes. Many cognitive psychologists take a *phenomenological* approach, concentrating their study on the unique experiences of individuals. Many behaviorists are presently moving toward greater acceptance of some aspects of cognitive psychology. (4) The *humanistic* model, which has been referred to as "third force" psychology, is not so much an approach to psychological research as it is an optimistic movement within psychology emphasizing the human potential for growth and fulfillment. Carl Rogers is one of the foremost proponents of this approach.

Unraveling the Mysteries of Human Behavior

☥

At a conference where psychological factors in the criminal justice system were being discussed, a well-respected judge disclosed a unique ability he believed that he possessed.

"I can always tell when a defendant in my court is guilty by the look in his eyes."

"And what look is that, your honor?" queried the psychologist/author.

"The guilty ones have shifty eyes. They can't look me straight in the eye because they know I can see right through their pack of lies."

"Are you saying that some people who come before your bench have difficulty maintaining eye contact?" questioned a public defender.

"Only the guilty ones, because they know that their secret is revealed in their eyes."

"But how do you know your theory is correct, your honor?"

"It is obviously so; I would never send an innocent person to prison!"

Where is the error in this judgment? How might we set about the task of evaluating the truth of the honorable judge's intuition? Here is an example of "pop" psychology in actual use, or rather, misused and perhaps abused.

Psychology is much more than an academic enterprise that only psychologists work at. It has become part of our everyday lives, influencing the way each one of us thinks and talks about human actions. It is almost impossible today to read a newspaper or magazine or watch television without having some supposed psychological truth thrust upon you. The 1970s became the era of psychology—today everybody is a psychologist of sorts.

The judge in our example used the psychodynamic model of behavior (outlined in Chapter 1) when he asserted that inner motivation of guilt (about committing a crime) affects the person's overt behavior (of not making eye contact). You have probably already been exposed to many other psychological concepts—IQ, anxiety, achievement, depression, mental illness, arousal, the unconscious, and more. You may have even used psychology to "psych out" an opponent in a competition, to get "psyched up" for a test of some kind, or to persuade someone to see things your way. And without doubt, since you first were exposed to Saturday morning TV, you have been the target of advertising that often hits below the psychological belt. Its goal is often to encourage the desire for products you do not need and may not be able to afford.

But "experience" is not always the best teacher, and our observations and commonsense psychology can sometimes lead us astray. In this chapter we shall see what we can discover from the way psychologists analyze human behavior that will enable *you* to do so more accurately. The topics to be presented deal with the methods of psychological inquiry: *how* psychologists come to know *what* about the *whys* of behavior. The general principles underlying the scientific approach to psychological issues may hold for you the most valuable lessons in this entire book. It is the soundness of the methodology that lays the foundation on which our ideas about the mind and behavior stand or fall.

We will begin by considering in detail the five goals of psychology: description, explanation, prediction, control, and improving the quality of life. To satisfy these goals often requires using the methods of scientific inquiry, which we examine next. These methods rest on certain basic assumptions about causality and determinism. How can a deterministic psychology be reconciled with a psychology of individual freedom and dignity? This and other conflicting issues will be posed. Finally, we will note the various levels of analysis on which different psychologists operate. Some look at the broad picture, while others focus on the individual brush strokes. Taken together, it all forms the portrait of human behavior.

The goals of psychology

In Chapter 1 we saw some of the ways in which psychologists report the behaviors they observe and attempt to make sense of these observed relationships, and to use them in predicting some future behavior. There are direct parallels between these activities and those we expect from our physician after he or she examines us for some malady. We want a *diagnosis* (or classification) of the symptoms observed and reported. Then we'd like to know what caused them; that is, what is the *etiology* of the disease? The doctor's *prognosis* is a prediction about the course the sickness is likely to take. But then we would like one more bit of information, a recommendation for *treatment*, one that ideally will give a favorable prognosis.

For the research psychologist, these similar goals can be described as: description, explanation, prediction, and control. For the applied psychologist, who conducts research on practical problems or puts into practice the findings derived from other research, there is a fifth goal. That goal is improving the quality of human life. As psychological control techniques become more powerful, there is an increasing feeling that the research psychologist, too, must be concerned about this fifth goal. These goals form the foundation of the whole psychological enterprise. Let's examine each of them more closely.

Description: Reporting what really happens

In a court of law it is imperative that the evidence presented by both prosecution and defense be as objective and specific as possible. Although the evidence introduced is intended to lead the judge and jury toward a given conclusion for one or the other side, any given piece of evidence must stand alone as a "fact"; it must not be someone's interpretation of the facts. Either the evidence must be described in such a manner that different jurors can agree as to what it represents, or it must be available for their personal inspection. "What occurred" and "what is" are carefully distinguished from "what could have been" and "what seems to be." Inference is not acceptable in a statement of facts.

In science, too, the first task is to "get the facts." And there are a number of similarities between the standards of trial evidence and those of scientific evidence. In science, too, conclusions must be based on objective observation. Observation must be reported in such a way that others' knowledge of what you are describing is as identical to yours as possible. Put differently, if they were able to observe the same events, their descriptions would correspond to yours.

Data and facts

In science, the evidence is comprised of *data*. Data are reports or measurements of observed events. They are the building blocks of psychology or any other science. Data distinguish scientific thought from logical, rational, philosophical, mathematical, and religious thought.

Every grain of sand on a beach, every smile of a stranger, every silence in a conversation is a potential source of data. Dreams themselves are not data because only the person dreaming has direct access to them. But *reports* of dreams can stand as data, as can "wet dreams" (nocturnal emissions) or brain-wave patterns recorded during the periods in sleep when people say they have been dreaming. Such data are available for examination and evaluation by independent investigators.

The psychologist must be constantly on guard to separate *observations* ("The patient's hands trembled and he did not make eye contact with the therapist") from *inferences* that go beyond the observations ("The patient was anxious"). If a patient complains of a headache, all those present could hear the statement and agree that the patient had made it, but they might disagree about the actual existence of the headache. To report any event *as it is* is difficult, if not impossible, in spite of our best intentions and efforts. It requires stripping away the observer's expectations and removing the blinders imposed by his or her personal history, culture, and values.

Hugo Münsterberg, one of the first research psychologists at Harvard University, provided this remarkable account of the different observations made by reporters who covered a speech on peace that he gave to a large audience in New York:

"The reporters sat immediately in front of the platform. One man wrote that the audience was so surprised by my speech that it received it in complete silence; another wrote that I was constantly interrupted by loud applause, and that at the end of my address the applause continued for minutes. The one wrote that during my opponent's speech I was constantly smiling; the other noticed that my face remained grave and without a smile. The one said that I grew purple-red from excitement; and the other found that I grew white like chalk. The one told us that my critic, while speaking, walked up and down the large stage; and the other, that he stood all the while at my side and patted me in a fatherly way on the shoulder" (1908, pp. 35–36).

Surely, not all of these observations could have been accurate.

In many instances, the problem is not with interpretation of events, but rather, that the events are not recorded as precisely as they might be—or worse, not recorded at all. Few physicians, for example, keep accurate records of patients' symptoms, their treatment recommendations, and subsequent outcomes. When general impressions replace conclusions based on data, the margin for error escalates. Similarly, when the data are recorded in imprecise units (such as, "X was really big") conclusions are likely to be so vague that they become meaningless.

Operational definitions

If internal events like dreams and "anxiety" or "frustration" cannot serve as data, how can they be studied? You report that you feel "shy"; one observer reports your behavior as "aloof," another as "introverted," a third as "alienated." Which is it?

An approach used in physics to remove ambiguity from scientific terms and concepts is the use of *operational definitions*. This means defining a concept entirely by the operations used in measuring it. For example, the concept "length" is defined by the physical operations used in measuring a line. An operational definition of "maintenance of eye contact" might mean counting the number of times a person's eyes meet and move away from a target person's gaze in a specified period of time. All observers using this definition should come up with approximately the same data from observing the same behavior.

For many concepts in psychology, different measuring procedures have been used in different studies. For example, in studies of "psychological stress" several different kinds of measurements have been used as definitions of "stress." In communicating the results of a study, it is important that researchers specify the operational procedures they used to define their concepts so that in comparing the results of different studies we can know whether they really deal with the same concept. Otherwise two studies of "stress" could be about quite different processes. For example, if one researcher used "muscular tension" as the definition of stress and another used "days absent from work" as the definition, they would measure different things and might report quite different findings about "stress."

Sometimes operational definitions can seem like "cop-outs," as when "intelligence" is defined as "what intelligence tests measure." Where no one operational definition captures the whole concept, several can be used together to identify what we mean by the concept. Thus "emotional arousal" might be defined by a combination of: self-reports, ratings by trained observers, physiological changes, and scores on selected performance tasks. If a concept cannot be defined in terms of operations, then it cannot be used in scientific ways, although it still may be of value in philosophy, literature, or ordinary discourse. Critics of Sigmund Freud argue that he used too many concepts that cannot be operationally defined, such as "id," "superego," and "unconscious." However, we must also distinguish between concepts that are used to represent and stand for events or specific psychological experiences and those intended to guide our thinking in more general ways (concepts that have *heuristic* value).

Empirical data

The goal of some psychologists, such as B. F. Skinner, has been to collect only *quantifiable* data; that is, behavioral events that can be stated in the form of numbers. Only events that can be directly observed qualify as data. No inferences about unseen events or processes are allowed. No theories are permitted to cloud the objective analysis of specific reactions to identifiable stimuli.

This empirical approach obviously places great emphasis on precise recording and measuring apparatus. Its roots are in the experimental psychology laboratories of nineteenth-century Germany where "brass instrument" psychology was founded by Wilhelm Wundt in the 1870s. In those early days, the experimental psychologists recorded the psychological experience of their subjects in response to physical stimuli that were precisely specified. Modern-day empiricists replace "experience" (which they consider a mystical concept) with precisely specified responses—for example, pressure on a bar sufficient to activate an electronic recording device.

Psychologists agree with the old saying, "What you look for, you will find." In designing experiments, they try to safeguard against personal bias. For example, psychologists studying the effects of a certain drug or other treatment would conduct a *double-blind* test. That is, they would see to it that the individuals evaluating the behavior of the subjects would not know ahead of time which subjects had received the treatment and which had not. Nor would the subjects themselves know which group they were in or even that there were two conditions being tested.

Observation and the collection of data are basic to the scientific study of behavior. They distinguish psychology from philosophy and separate it from mathematics and the humanities. Given this reliance on data, it follows that data gathering must abide by rules that ensure its objectivity. This is most true in the process of experimentally testing an idea about whether and how certain events are related. Objectivity in science helps separate trust in facts from reliance on faith.

Particularly in new areas of research, it is often difficult for investigators to maintain their objectivity. The closer they come to a discovery that might be a real breakthrough, the harder it becomes for them not to let what they wish to see stand in the way of unbiased observation or interpretation of their data—no matter how good their intentions. When we read of "astounding new discoveries" in psychology, or in any science, it is well to be cautious about accepting them until time has proved their worth.

There are some, however, who believe that this ideal of the psychologist as a purely objective scientist should not be the whole story. One historian of science suggests that the rules of objectivity must occasionally be violated if a science is to advance. He identifies "the average scientist, who must obey the rules, and the genius, who will know when to break them" (Brush, 1974, p. 1170). In breaking the rules, the original thinker moves our ideas in new directions rather than simply putting the old ones on more solid ground.

Explaining what happens

Description is not enough; we need to know not merely what happens, but how two or more events are related. The quest of science is a search for patterns of regularity, for consistent relationships. It is this search that uncovers and creates "facts" from prehistoric scribbles on a cave wall, balls rolling down inclined planes, molds on bread, dogs salivating to the sound of a bell, and babies who don't grow in stressful environments. ◆

The process of explanation involves finding a context in which the phenomena that have been observed make sense. There is an attempt to discover similarities between this situation and some previously experienced one. The context may be provided by your past experience and knowledge or by theories about how the things observed ought to be related. Suppose, for example, as you are reading this you suddenly notice your hand trembling, your rate of breathing increasing, and your heart racing. Would you be content to remain an empiricist, recording specific measurements of these behavioral reactions? Not likely. Rather, you'd ask why you were reacting in this way. If you first change your question to "*what* is causing these reactions" or "*how* unusual is it to get these physiological changes when reading *Psychology and Life*," then a scientifically acceptable explanation might be generated. "Why" questions are not acceptable because they can be answered in terms of metaphysical speculations and the search for "ultimate truth." In addition, one "why" always leads to another (as the parents of any three-year-old will tell you).

You want an explanation that will enable you to understand this unusual event—assuming you do not always get aroused when doing your homework. In your search for an explanation, you might try to remember the circumstances in which you last felt these symptoms and see if the present situation is comparable. Could be the first signs of the flu that is going around. Or maybe it was something you ate. Then again you may be anxious about something: tomorrow's test or a blind date. Maybe you are irritated by the loud music from a neighbor's stereo. As you can see, there are many plausible competing explanations. But they all share the property of providing possible *determinants* for your response. Starting with an observed effect you search for a causal determinant that will account for it. When you find one that satisfies you, you have explained the experience (although your explanation might not be

◆ *"I think you should be more explicit here in step two."*

the correct one). By helping to make unusual events more commonplace, psychological explanations impose a rational order on chaos.

But you didn't just want to identify the determinants of your behavior. You asked whether your reactions were unusual. Like the student mentioned in Chapter 1 who wanted to know whether his shyness was unusual, you raise a very basic psychological question. "To what extent is this particular behavior different from or similar to that of others?" Such questions give rise to two basic psychological issues: (a) whether there is any unity in the variety of behaviors we see all around us, and (b) whether there is any meaningful variety in what appears to be the sameness of people and their actions. Psychological explanations directed at the first issue make use of general laws, attempting to organize isolated parts into integrated wholes. This search for a common underlying basis despite a surface appearance of individual variation is fundamental to psychological research. We will see in a later chapter that the other part of the search, to discover what makes you uniquely different from every other person that exists, forms the basis of the study of personality.

The most comprehensive form of scientific explanation is *theoretical explanation*. To explain by means of a theory is to deduce a particular instance from more general principles, perhaps even before it has been observed—and then seek to confirm it by observation and experimentation. In commonsense terms, we often use "theory" as interchangeable with "explanation," as when we ask "What is your theory as to why women have higher verbal scores on college entrance examinations than men?" In contrast, a *formal theory* in psychology consists of a systematic statement of the relationship of several assumptions, some principles of behavior, a variety of deductions, and a body of observed pertinent facts. The value of a theory is assessed in terms of: (a) its ability to give meaning and order to known facts, (b) whether it reveals relationships among concepts and observations previously thought to be unrelated, and (c) its usefulness in generating new ideas that can be tested.

It is theory that determines which observations will become "data" and which data are entitled to become relevant facts. When new facts are shown to be inconsistent with the theory, either the theory is modified to accommodate them or (less scientifically but more typically) the facts are simply ignored. Only rarely is a theory overthrown and discarded by facts to the contrary. Instead, worthless theories persist with a life of their own until replaced by others proven to be less objectionable. For example, Ptolemy's theory that the earth was the center of the universe persisted long after Copernicus' heliocentric theory was empirically and logically proven to be a better model of planetary motion.

The psychologist's second goal, then—of explaining behavior—involves finding order, simplicity, and regularity in the apparent confusion, complexity, and randomness of observed events. This can also be a very important personal goal to you when you need to make sense of disharmonies you experience within your body or mind or those you perceive in your environment. (See *P&L* Close-up, Stutterers Still Suffer in Silence While Hypotheses Flow Freely.)

It is the nature of [a theory], when once a man has conceived it, that it assimilates everything to itself as proper nourishment, and, from the first moment of your begetting it, it generally grows the stronger by everything you see, hear, read, or understand.

Laurence Sterne
Tristram Shandy

Predicting what will happen

In addition to their desire to understand nature, human beings throughout history have sought to know the future—to predict and prepare for events in advance of their happening. In ancient times, oracles and soothsayers held positions of great honor, for they were credited with a supernatural ability to

Close-up
Stutterers Still Suffer in Silence While Hypotheses Flow Freely

Have you ever known anyone with a "stuttering problem"? If so, you are aware of what a painful experience it can be for all parties involved to carry on a conversation. There are over a million and a half victims of this disorder in the United States alone.

Treatment of stuttering has varied enormously over the ages and there is still no agreed upon "cure." It is interesting to examine the cures that have been proposed in light of their direct relationship to hypotheses advanced to explain stuttering. Such an examination offers a remarkable case study of how for centuries false hypotheses and malpractice have gone hand in hand (or is it foot in mouth?).

According to Van Riper (1970), in Roman times evil spirits possessed the stutterer, so exorcism was the recommended treatment. In the Middle Ages, the evil was centered in the tongue of the stutterer; therefore hot irons, spices, and unpleasant substances were applied to it. Francis Bacon thought that stuttering was caused by a frozen tongue, which could be thawed by hot wine therapy. An English physician, believing the stutterer's words were held back as in constipation, recommended powerful laxatives. "The poor devils were either afraid to stutter lest an accident occur or too weak to do so," according to one account (p. 40). A Swiss physician recommended tongue exercises and gymnastics to cure a "vicious tongue habit." One French doctor's cure consisted of supporting the "weak" tongue with a little fork of gold or ivory.

In the last century, the hypotheses advanced were less bizarre, but still widely varied. Emphasis on the expressive aspect of stuttering led to phonetic drills, while believing the disorder to be one of rhythm resulted in therapies involving singing or chanting. Later, it was hypothesized that the condition was caused by a cramp necessitating removal of part of the tongue.

Psychology finally came upon the scene in 1862, and further muddied the waters. Stutterers were seen as secretive, lazy, suspicious, and passive about receiving help. A psychologist named Klencke was quite modern in recommending that speech be placed "under the control of the ear and therefore under the judgment and control of the mind" (p. 42). Stuttering was next proclaimed to be a neurotic symptom brought on by pain and embarrassment. The treatment program included complete silence at first, isolation with other stutterers, and then confidence building. "Overexcited nerves" and "habitual tension" were also advanced as causes. Toward the end of the century, the causal sequence was reversed; a popular hypothesis held that stuttering was the cause, rather than the result, of emotional and personality abnormalities.

The first decades of this century ushered in "schools for stutterers" taught by speech teachers (later therapists). Stuttering was seen as a bad habit, to be broken by regimented speech drills. Other hypotheses placed the blame on "poor mental hygiene," abnormal brain organization, heredity, biochemical imbalances, early childhood experiences in speech acquisition, and deep-seated neurotic patterns.

Currently fashionable are learning theories with their emphasis on stuttering as a learned behavior that is maintained by reinforcements such as attention, sympathy, excuses for nonparticipation, or avoidance of threatening situations. Therapy then involves attempts to alter patterns of reinforcement.

Charles Van Riper concludes the history of hypotheses and therapies (from which this Close-up was abstracted) on a somber note. "Unfortunately for the stutterer, no unified program of experimental therapy exists" (Van Riper, 1970, p. 53) — even today, after centuries of thinking about and tinkering with this troublesome aspect of the human condition.

Stonehenge, a massive structure on England's Salisbury Plain dating from neolithic times, bears silent testimony to the human passion for predicting the secrets of nature. At dawn on Midsummer Day (the summer solstice), the first rays of the rising sun strike through the arch in exact alignment with the giant "heel stone." On the basis of careful study, astronomer Gerald Hawkins (1965) has concluded that Stonehenge is actually an accurate, if primitive, computer capable not only of predicting the yearly solstices, but also of forecasting the most terrifying of celestial events, eclipses of the sun and moon.

reveal the future by reading signs from the gods. Today we rely primarily on science for predictions of the future. Accurate prediction helps us guide our present behavior so as to avoid danger, pain, and disappointment while gaining security, pleasure, and satisfaction. Successful prediction reduces uncertainty and gives us a sense of understanding what is going on around and within us. ▲

While some psychologists are content with understanding and explaining as the goal of their inquiry, others insist that if you cannot predict the conditions under which a given behavior will appear or vary, then you simply have not understood it. For them, the operational test of explanation is being able to predict what will happen, or to make it happen, or both.

Actuarial prediction vs. prediction through understanding

Some predictions are averages made on the basis of relationships observed in the past. This is the type employed to tell us in advance of each Labor Day weekend how many motorists will die in auto accidents. Such predictions are called *actuarial* predictions. They are made for groups, not for specific individuals. The whole concept of life insurance is based on the ability to predict very accurately the life span of different classes and types of people. Actuarial prediction does not depend on an understanding of the life-death cycle but merely on the observation of past relationships.

The goal of most scientific prediction, however, is to understand cause-and-effect relationships well enough to be able to describe the exact conditions under which an event will occur or even to predict an event that has not been previously observed.

Hypotheses about relationships

Every investigation into causes starts with a hypothesis. A *hypothesis* is a statement of possible ways two or more events or variables may be related. Some hypotheses are general hunches stating only that there is a relationship; others are more specific, stating exactly how two things are related. Hypotheses derived from mathematical models of human behavior specify precise quantitative relationships between the elements being studied. Each of the studies we examined in Chapter 1 started with some hypothesis the researcher wanted to test. (Can you state what those hypotheses were?) Hypotheses must be stated in such a way that they can be tested by observation, or by logical inference, or perhaps by both. (For a discussion of the complex process by which hypotheses are confirmed or rejected, see Salmon, 1973.)

Discovering causality is one of the primary tasks of psychological research. It has also been an ageless problem for philosophical analysis to determine the conditions that satisfy the criteria of causality. For events to be considered causally related, they must occur together (be invariably contiguous: if A, then always B), and it is assumed that the "cause" must occur prior to or simultaneously with the "effect." But a relationship established by research states only that the events in question occurred together in the manner prescribed. Any explanation of *how* the two variables are related is a theoretical interpretation that must be assessed against other alternatives.

There are a variety of ways in which two events can be related. The strongest relationship is that of *direct causality*, one event causes the other to occur—eating five pounds of chocolate and vomiting. There is also *indirect causality*, one event affects a second one directly which in turn, causes a change in a third—eating all that chocolate, vomiting, and paying to have someone's rug cleaned. *Third-factor causality* occurs when each of two independent events is caused by some third factor. The behaviors of "going to church" and "being seen but not heard" may both be caused by attempts to please one's parents. As we shall see, events may also be related in the sense that they tend to occur together (be correlated) without in any way being causally interrelated.

A critical task for the researcher or scholar is to try to specify all the alternative hypotheses that might explain a phenomenon. Each of these is tested against available information or current theories or in new experiments, and by a strategy of elimination all but one is rejected as unsatisfactory. As false hypotheses are eliminated, the investigator emerges with a single hypothesis that seems preferable to its rivals.

Confidence is never absolute, however. A hypothesis can be supported by evidence, but it can never be proved true. There may be a totally different hypothesis that accounts equally well for the data even when you have a convincing demonstration on your side. The following anecdote illustrates the point that one person's "proof" may be another's poison. At a meeting of new members of Alcoholics Anonymous the lecturer put a worm into a jar of alcohol to demonstrate graphically the dangers of drink. Sure enough, it curled up and died instantly. "What that tells me," said a heavy drinker, "is I'll never have worms as long as I keep drinking!" (Dyer, 1976)

Even after hypotheses have been supported by the results of many studies and thus given the elevated status of "laws" of behavior, they are not considered to be proved in any absolute sense. They still are regarded as only provisional—the best available knowledge at this time. Thus psychological research transforms "uncertainty" to "tentativeness" while moving in the direction of, but never quite realizing, the impossible dream of "certainty."

Correlations and causation

Cause-and-effect predictions are only one form that predictions may take, and indeed are not the common "garden" variety with which you are probably most familiar. Your "success in college" was predicted from your College Entrance Board scores, but those scores are not causing your success. Much of the

Everything in nature is a cause from which there flows some effect.
Benedictus de Spinoza
Ethica

Chance is a word devoid of sense: Nothing can exist without a cause.
Voltaire
Philosophical Dictionary

time you are making predictions of future behavior from your current behavior. You estimate how you will do on the final exam from how you are doing on the quizzes. On the basis of how much you enjoyed your partner on the first date, you predict what the next encounters will be like and pursue or abandon the relationship. Psychologists who are interested in studying individual differences between people—in intelligence, personality, achievement, abilities, or whatever—devise tests whose scores will predict certain behaviors they are interested in predicting.

In fact, much effort is directed toward evaluating just what are the best predictors for behaviors psychologists are interested in studying. Ideally one wants a predictor that is relatively easy and inexpensive to assess and accurately forecasts some important behavior. For example, if personality test scores of potential astronauts could predict which ones are likely to suffer emotional problems on flights to outer space, grounding such persons could prevent a costly disaster.

All these are examples of predictions relating one behavior to another rather than relating behavior to environmental conditions. *Correlation* is the term used to describe such relationships, in which events occur in some systematic pattern but are not necessarily caused (or even affected) by one another. While is is possible to make accurate predictions based on correlational data, one is *never* justified in assuming that such data describe direct causal relations. A great many more things in life are linked together through correlation than are chained together through causality. However, there is a powerful human tendency to transform correlations into causal relations. We observe things that only co-relate and we infer that one has caused the other. This error in reasoning can be quite serious, as we shall see in many instances throughout the text. Serious or not, it is a trap that we all fall into often. (See *P&L* Close-up, Blackout Baby Boom.)

In psychology, causal connections are sought between behavior and stimulus conditions rather than between two behaviors. If a particular behavior is a function of (is caused by) a particular stimulus, the behavior will vary when the stimulus is varied. Psychologists explain behavior in terms of such functional relationships between *stimulus variables* and *response variables*.

Controlling what happens

Once some behavior—say, "Humpty-Dumpty's fall"—has been objectively described and adequately explained, and accurate predictions have been made of conditions that will result in another fall, a critical issue remains, that of *control*. For many psychologists behavioral control is the central goal. There is both an intellectual and a practical reason for elevating control to such a lofty position.

First, the ultimate test of any causal explanation of behavior lies in being able to demonstrate the conditions under which the behavior can be started, stopped, maintained, or altered. Only by such demonstrations can we establish that we know both the *necessary and sufficient conditions* for the behavior to occur. For example, there is a correlation between amount of sunlight a plant receives and its growth; but sunlight alone is not enough. It is a necessary, but not a sufficient condition for controlling the growth of plants—water and soil nutrients being other necessary conditions. Similarly, the *desire* to stop smoking, drinking, or shooting heroin may be a necessary condition to actually stop these addictive behaviors, but it must usually be supplemented by a variety of environmental changes before the behavior can be controlled. Knowledge of how to control an undesirable behavior usually depends on understanding not only how it started but how it is maintained — what keeps it going. You can have greater confidence in your explanation of what caused X to occur when you actually make X occur by presenting those presumed determinants of X. Even the failure to occur can provide valuable information, indicating that one or more other necessary stimulus variables are missing. Or perhaps your theory sounds good in principle but does not reflect reality.

The second reason for an emphasis on control is less related to "pure knowledge" than to usefulness. Psychology, as we have seen, is a practical, pragmatic discipline often concerned with "problem behaviors" or "problem situations" and how to change or improve them. Fear, anxiety, mental illness, suicide, worker alienation, battered children, sexism, racism, and violence are just a few of the topics and "problems" psychologists study, with an eye toward change.

Close-up
Blackout Baby Boom (or, What to Do 'til the Lights Go On)

It is remarkable how many things are correlated in nature and how that number increases when human beings are involved. In August 1966, newspapers in New York heralded an above-average increase in births "in several leading hospitals," "nine months after the 1965 power blackout." This claim was generally accepted without question.

Given a "problem relationship," people proceeded to explain it. They searched for causes and found quite a few: "Natural disasters lead people to turn to each other"; "Darkness and candlelight are very romatic"; "People will engage in sex whenever they don't have anything else to do."

Here we have a causal inference based on a correlation of two events. The frequency with which this type of thinking occurs attests to our tendency to go beyond observations and seek a "law" that explains them. This is an admirable venture, but may be nothing more than an intellectual explanation in search of a nonfact. Two possibilities exist here which we have not considered before: (a) the data cannot be trusted, or (b) the relationship is coincidental.

Although one New York hospital reported three times the average number of daily births for each of the seven key days, the numbers were small, only about 10 extra babies a day. And the sixteen other hospitals combined reported an increase of only 47 births, which adds up to fewer than three babies per hospital. This output seems even less significant when we remind ourselves that in New York City there were probably three million women with childbearing capabilities who were in the dark of that November night. There is no evidence that all those women who gave birth in August had even been in the blackout nine months earlier.

When correlations involve events that occur in a given time period (such as births nine months after a November conception), it is necessary to examine data for comparison periods in other years. There might be a regular seasonal fluctuation in the event, for example. Looking at the proportion of the total year's births that fell approximately nine months after the November 9 conception date (from June 27 to August 14) and the proportion usually born during that time period in any of the five preceding years reveals no difference! The "blackout" birthrate was about the same as the increase that usually occurs for that time of year. The two events thus were not meaningfully related; a chance event (the blackout) happened to occur nine months before a birthrate increase common during the summer months in "fun city."

Moral: Interior decorators may be the only people who are content when two things simply go well together. The rest of us insist on finding causes for correlations and correlations for accidental arrangements.

In this sense, psychologists are a rather optimistic group, believing that virtually any pattern of behavior can be modified. Undesirable habits that have been previously learned can be unlearned, from poor study habits to neurotic symptoms. Control is at the very heart of all programs of treatment or therapy designed to alter any aspect of human functioning. We will see in later chapters that this goal is being realized not by the psychologist controlling the patient's behavior, but by guiding people toward greater self-control. The personal control of one's own thoughts, feelings, and actions is obviously of great importance to every one of us. We don't like to be controlled by other people, by compulsive rituals we feel forced to go through, by addictions (to drugs, food, money, or work) or by self-defeating thoughts. But in fact, we are all controlled by an infinite array of physiological, social, environmental, legal, religious, and political processes and forces. Indeed, we rarely realize the extent to which our behavior is under the control of subtle situational variables. During the rioting in Watts back in 1965, when people were defying usual restraints by breaking windows, setting fires, and battling with police, many of these same people were observed obeying traffic signals; looters on foot apologized courteously when they bumped against each other (Bernstein, 1970).

Robert Oppenheimer, the well-known atomic physicist, told a convention of psychologists of his awe for the potential of control that psychological knowledge carries with it.

"The psychologist can hardly do anything without realizing that for him the acquisition of knowledge opens up the most terrifying prospects of controlling what people do and how they think and how they behave and how they feel. This is true for all of you who are engaged in practice, and as the corpus of psychology gains in certitude and subtlety and skill, I can see that the physicist's pleas that what he discovers be used with humanity and be used wisely will seem rather trivial compared to those pleas which you will have to make and for which you will have to be responsible" (1956, p. 128).

A father watches a parade in New York City with his two sons. The flag and buttons he has bought for them serve to reinforce his lesson on patriotism. Is he controlling the development of their values?

But responsibility for the consequences of exercising knowledge of how to control human behavior is not only a matter for psychologists. It must be of concern to each of us in our daily lives. Do we not expect children to be controlled by their parents as well as by teachers, ministers, police, and physicians? When is that control good, and when is it evil? What yardstick shall be used to measure when control is unethical and when acceptable? What's wrong with the kind of parental control that the concerned father quoted below wants to use on his child? What advice would you give if his request had gone to you rather than to "ask the expert" in *McCall's* magazine?

"I am very pro-American. I have a small son and have hopes that when he grows up he will join one of the armed forces. To ensure this, I have thought of talking to him while he is sleeping — no great speech, but a little patriotism and the suggestion that an army career would be good. Can this type of suggestion help, or will it cause him to rebel?" (Caplan, 1969, p. 65) ■

"Control" has become a term loaded with the negative connotations of robots guided by "Big Brother" via electrodes in our brains, subliminal commands relayed to us on TV, and mind-binding chemicals slipped into our coffee. But although we resent being controlled, we buy millions of Dale Carnegie's recipes for *How to Win Friends and Influence [control] People.* We are all persuaders. Some of us work for better schools, others for more humane prisons, still others for stiffer laws, less permissive judges, less violence on children's TV programs, and so on. All are instances of attempts at social control. Serious ethical issues are involved in any effort to control other people's behavior — whether it is in the psychological laboratory or in psychotherapy or in everyday settings in which others control us or we control them. (See *P&L* Close-up, Controlling Behavior for Good or Evil.)

Improving the quality of life by changing what happens

It is essential that detachment and objectivity be used in gathering and interpreting data. But following the rules of scientific method (which we turn to in the next section) only tells you how to get evidence that you can trust. It does not tell you what evidence to look for or how to use the knowledge and tools you develop. So increasingly, as their knowledge grows and their tools become sharper, psychologists are accepting responsibility for seeing that their tools are used to enrich human life, not to diminish it.

Until comparatively recently, academic psychologists were reluctant to be concerned with values. Some felt that concern with values was not "objective" and "scientific"; others acted from a sense of modesty about whether psychology was really ready to make a contribution to the public good. For though "psychology has a long past, it has a short history." The first formal experimental laboratory was founded just a century ago. Many of the most exciting and relevant areas of study in psychology have emerged only within the last decade or two. "Science proceeds cautiously" is a reminder to those who claim that psychologists need to know much more before being arrogant enough to try to formulate solutions to social problems.

"Ready or not, you better come out!" is the cry from other quarters. The pressing social and personal needs of today cannot wait until tomorrow. George Miller, in a presidential address to the American Psychological Asso-

Close-up
Controlling Behavior for Good or Evil

The tools of psychology, like any other tools, can be used for good or evil—to help achieve our goals, meet our needs, or to diminish us. Control of our movements by others in many everyday situations is essential, nonfrightening, and accepted by all, as, for example, the control exercised here by a French policeman, or similar control by a traffic signal. On the other hand, the idea of computerized electronic control by means of electrodes implanted in the brain seems a terrifying prospect. Yet such techniques make it possible for the monkey shown here to raise an otherwise paralyzed arm;

thus they hold tremendous potential for enabling people with physical disabilities to regain control over their bodily functioning—for example, for the blind to "see" by electronic signals. Control also has its humorous aspects, as shown in the cartoon. Just as even the most powerful dictator is dependent on his people in that he can maintain his power only so long as he can get the response he needs from them, control in the laboratory is, in the last analysis, a reciprocal relationship in which the psychologist and the subject "control" each other.

"Boy, do we have this guy conditioned. Every time I press the bar down he drops a pellet in."

ciation, argued that besides being good scientists, psychologists must also be advocates of ways to improve the quality of human life. In his "revolutionary" speech, Miller (1969) stated:

"Changing behavior is pointless in the absence of any coherent plan for how it should be changed. It is our plan for using control that the public wants to know about. Too often, I fear, psychologists have implied that acceptable uses for behavior control are either self-evident or can be safely left to the wisdom and benevolence of powerful men. Psychologists must not surrender the planning function so easily. . . . Psychology has at least as much, probably more, to contribute to the diagnosis of personal and social problems as it has to the control of behavior. . . . So let us continue our struggle to advance psychology as a means of promoting human welfare, each in our own way. For myself, however, I can imagine nothing we could do that would be more relevant to human welfare, and nothing that could pose a greater challenge to the next generation of psychologists, than to discover how best to give psychology away" (pp. 1068–74).

Psychologists have begun to work with architects and urban planners to design housing projects for people to use, instead of as physical spaces to put people in. Other psychologists consult with educators on ways of making the new child care programs more effective. Collaborations are also springing up between psychologists and medical researchers who want to develop more effective ways for harried men and women to cope with their life stresses. Psychology and law is another emerging field in which the human element is now being taken seriously along with the traditional legal issues.

Psychologists are even coming to the aid of other professionals whose life work is helping people in distress and providing various types of social welfare. Psychiatric nurses, police, poverty lawyers, social workers, community mental health counselors, and others are learning how to handle a psychological problem common to their occupation—"burn-out." The loss of human caring that eventually comes from repeated, emotionally draining contacts typical in these jobs can be prevented. Psychologist Christina Maslach of the University of California, Berkeley (1977) is translating her research findings based on observations of people in many such professions into practical recommendations. Her recipe for improving the social psychological climate of these jobs is working to increase both the personal satisfaction of the professional "helpers" and the quality of care and service they are giving to the public (Maslach & Pines, 1977). These are but a few of the ways psychologists are going beyond the laboratory to work for improving the quality of the way we live and relate to one another.

Scientific inquiry and experimental method

Basically, scientific inquiry is an approach to gathering information that limits errors in the conclusions made about natural events and human nature. The *experimental method* is a general set of attitudes and procedures that help justify accepting or rejecting conclusions based on observation. Scientific inquiry involves four major steps: getting a worthwhile idea, testing it, drawing conclusions, and reporting what has been found in such a way that another investigator could *replicate* (repeat) the study to verify or challenge the conclusion. Each investigator can thus build on what others have contributed and make new findings available for later researchers to start with.

There are no guidelines on how to get good ideas—that is the creative part of science, the art in the process. It depends on the scientist's knowledge, creativity, ability to analyze and synthesize, and sometimes, as we shall see, pure chance. But even in the face of a "lucky" discovery "chance favors only the prepared mind," as was pointed out by Louis Pasteur. For the psychologist, there is no substitute for a sensitivity to the dynamics of human behavior, for "people watching," for rigorous self-appraisal, for an insatiable curiosity, and for caring about people.

Ground rules for collecting data

Once you know what you want to study, you must decide how to define and measure the things whose relationships you want to investigate. For example, if you wanted to investigate the relationship between apple-polishing and school success, you would need operational definitions of both. For "school success" you would probably use grades, though you might use other measures too. For "apple-polishing" you might use "number of minutes per day spent helping the teacher."

Once you have defined the things whose relationship you plan to study, your next step would be to formulate a testable hypothesis—perhaps that students who spend more than X amount of time a day apple-polishing receive higher grades than those who spend less time. Actually, for convenience in later use of statistical checks, the hypothesis is usually stated negatively, as a *null hypothesis*—in this case, that apple-polishing will *not* make a difference in grades. But the evidence you gather is the same.

When you are studying the influence of a stimulus condition on a behavioral response, the first is called the *independent variable* and the second, the one influenced, is called the *dependent variable.* The independent variable may be manipulated (for example, you might systematically arrange for different students to spend different amounts of time apple-polishing). School success is the dependent variable in this example, the one whose variation you think will be *dependent on* (affected by) variations in apple-polishing. The independent variable is the *predictor,* the dependent variable is the *predicted behavior.*

The two most common research approaches used by psychologists are the *ex post facto* and the *experimental.* In the ex post facto design, comparisons are made between the behavior of two (or more) groups of people who already differ on some dimension. Thus juvenile delinquents may be compared to nondelinquent youths on their ability to plan ahead. If the delinquents show poorer future planning than the comparison group, what can we really conclude? Did this difference in time perspective predispose one group to be delinquent, the other not? Or was it *after* the first group became delinquent, dropping out of school and not working, that they lost interest in planning for the future? In the ex post facto study, subjects are "self-selected" into the groups being compared. Thus they may differ on many dimensions in addition to the one under investigation, and one of these other factors may be the critical one. Perhaps poor future planning is characteristic only of the delinquents who get caught, the smart planners go undetected, and are not even part of the researcher's sample. We will see that the ex post facto design is used often in psychological research and all too often unwarranted causal implications are drawn from its results when at best only correlational conclusions are justified.

Four key principles of the experimental approach are: randomization, systematic variation, proper control, and replication.

Randomization

Individuals must be assigned to each treatment in an experiment so that every subject has an equal (or known) chance of receiving any given treatment. This means that *before* the study begins those who will be observed are randomly assigned to one or the other of the experimental groups, thereby ensuring that whatever initial differences exist will be distributed among them purely by chance. Allowances for these differences can then be made by statistical methods in calculating the results of the experiment (see Appendix). While randomization cannot make the groups exactly equivalent to one another, it does counterbalance unknown and irrelevant factors and limit the likelihood that individual differences between subjects will affect the outcome.

Systematic variation

The experimenter manipulates one (or several) independent variables in such a way that variation in outcomes (observed behaviors) may be assumed to be caused by these stimulus variations. Varying the independent variable may be done either by: exposing one group of subjects to it (the experimental group) but not the other (the control group), or by varying the amount or strength of the independent variable. Investigating the effects of alcohol on speed of a driver's reaction thus might involve either comparing one group given an alcoholic drink with a control group who received ginger ale. Or one might vary the amount of alcohol drunk in fifteen minutes by subjects in a number of different experimental groups.

Proper control

The experimenter must make sure the experiment contains an appropriate condition against which to compare the effects of the manipulated variable. Control groups are comparable to the experimental group in every possible way, except for the one dimension being systematically varied. Control groups therefore provide the baseline against which to compare the behavioral effect of the independent variable.

There are other types of *control procedures* that may be included in experiments to rule out or minimize the effects of extraneous variables. These procedures are directed toward overcoming the problem of *confounded* outcomes. (An outcome is said to be confounded when factors other than the independent variable might have been responsible for the result.) The experimenter's behavior thus has to be the same from subject to subject, as does the way the task is presented, the way the subject is to respond, the way the data are scored, and so forth. *Standardized* testing, recording, and scoring procedures are some essential procedural controls.

These and other controls will be illustrated more concretely when we analyze specific experiments throughout the remainder of this book. Unfortunately, it is extremely difficult to separate the variables affecting the behavior of organisms. The major criticism leveled against most experiments is their failure to include some control group or procedure that would have been necessary to rule out an alternative hypothesis. (See *P&L* Close-up, A Typical Experimental Design.)

Replication

We have spoken earlier of the importance of having independent investigators repeat a study and obtain comparable results. Another type of replication takes place within an experiment. The same treatment must be repeated on more than a single subject. This provides an estimate of how *variable* the effects of the treatment are across different subjects treated the same way. In many investigations the primary interest lies in understanding this variation between subjects rather than in the average or typical performance. (See *P&L* Close-up, Average, Variability, and Correlation.)

Drawing conclusions

"Nothing spoils a good conclusion like disagreeable data," and sometimes scientists have as much vested interest in proving they are right as do parents, lawyers, and politicians. But scientific researchers are a little more scrupulous in their effort to let the data decide, to have conclusions follow rather than anticipate the data. Without some formalized and standard procedure for drawing conclusions from a given set of observations, there could be no objective and impartial way of establishing when a result was "significant" or a conclusion really justified.

Assume that data have been collected properly, and we find a behavioral

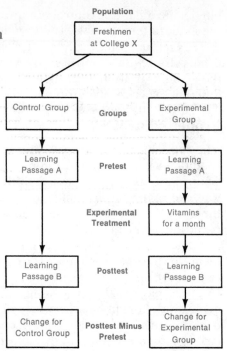

Two groups are chosen randomly from the same population. Both are given the same pretest and posttest, during which all relevant variables (directions, room temperature, time allowed, and so on) are the same for both groups. So far as is known, the only systematic difference during the interval between pretest and posttest for the two groups is the difference in the experimental treatment. The change in learning performance for each group is determined by subtracting pretest from posttest scores. If the experimental group has changed more than the control group, the difference is attributed to the difference in the experimental treatment. Is it clear to you what the independent and dependent variables are here?

difference between the experimental and control groups. Can we conclude that the independent variable was responsible for this difference, and thus that the experimental hypothesis has been supported? After all this investment of time, energy, intellect, and money, our objective scientist might be inclined to see any difference, however accidental or trivial, as a "real" one. The safeguard against such a temptation comes from agreeing in advance to a convention (rule) shared by all psychological researchers on what will be regarded as a *significant difference*.

Remember, the experiment began with the statement of a *null hypothesis* — that there would be no difference between the two groups after the experimental treatment. If you do find a difference, you need to know whether it is big enough to be considered a real one or whether it could have occurred by chance. If chance could have accounted for it, you cannot draw any conclusions about a relationship between your variables. Only if the difference is big enough can you reject the null hypothesis and conclude that the difference is real (that there probably is a relationship between apple-polishing and school success, in our earlier example).

The particular statistical tests used vary according to the nature of the data collected, but all yield the same final *probability statement,* an estimate of the probability that the difference is a chance occurrence. This probability statement is what makes it possible for psychologists to adopt a common rule for deciding when an experiment has "worked." A result is accepted as a *real* one and is labeled "statistically significant" only when the probability (p) that the difference could have occurred by chance is less than five in one hundred. (The notation $p < .05$ is used to indicate "probability is less than 5 percent.") This is the most lenient level of significance permitted, and for some problems it is not acceptable. More stringent requirements are imposed on conclusion drawing as the consequences of reaching a false conclusion become more important. For example, in predicting suicides, the researcher might demand a probability level of .01, .001, or greater. This and other statistical techniques for deciding the degree of confidence you can have in measures you get are described in the Appendix. There also are techniques for finding out how far you can generalize your findings with a particular sample of subjects to apply to others in the same general category. You have to know how *representative* your sample is of a larger group before you can generalize your findings to the group as a whole *(population)*.

This elaborate procedure of gathering data and drawing conclusions is what distinguishes scientific conclusions from those advanced by philosophers, theologians, and journalists as well as by the rest of us in our daily decisions about what we ought to believe in and support. Unfortunately, not all the conclusions that others want us to act on are so valid; in fact, many—including some that claim to be based on "scientific fact"—represent serious psychological traps.

In summary, the scientific method involves an attitude of healthy skepticism, as well as procedural safeguards to minimize the risk of error. Nobel-prize winning biologist Salvador Luria says of this skepticism, "The first reaction of most scientists, including myself, to a student announcing a novel finding is invariably, 'What did you do wrong?'" (*New York Times*, January 23, 1977, p. 44)

Because people take action on the basis of alleged scientific findings, it is better to err in the direction of being conservatively skeptical than un-

Close-up
Average, Variability, and Correlation

In our discussion of research findings we will occasionally mention the terms *average, variability,* and *correlation.* Their meanings are briefly summarized here. (For a fuller explanation of statistical terms and statistical inference, see the Appendix.)

1. To describe a group's performance (and be able to compare it with that of another group), you need two things: a single number *typical* enough to represent the whole group of scores, and a number that tells how different the scores are: how widely they *vary*.

a) The most typical number is a *measure of central tendency,* or *average.* The three kinds of average most often used are: the *mean* (sum of the scores divided by the number of scores, and abbreviated M or $\bar{X}$); the *median* (the score in the middle when all the scores are lined up in order; 50% of the scores are above and 50% below the median), and the *mode* (the most frequently occurring single score).

b) Measures of variability tell whether the scores cluster closely or are spread out. The measures of variability most often used are the *range* of the scores (from lowest to highest) and the *standard devia-*tion. The standard deviation (or SD) is a measure of the average variation of the individual scores from the group mean. The bigger the standard deviation, the more the scores vary from the mean score.

2. To describe the relationships between two sets of scores for the same individuals (intelligence and grades, for example), you use a statistical formula to obtain a *coefficient of correlation (r)*. This statistic tells you whether they are related, if the relationship is positive or negative, and how strong or weak it is.

Coefficients of correlation range from *minus one* (-1.0), which would mean perfect *negative* correlation (as intelligence gets higher, grades get lower), through *zero* (0), which would mean no correlation at all, to *plus one* ($+1.0$), which would mean perfect *positive* correlation (as intelligence goes up so do grades). Perfect correlations are rarely found. A "moderate" correlation might be between .25 and .60 (either + or −), a "high" correlation between .60 and .99. Predictions can be made equally well from positive or negative correlations.

duly enthusiastic. This is why most scientists withhold final judgment until all the evidence is in—it's just too easy to falsify data or be seduced into false beliefs.

At a Senate hearing in 1976 in which a drug manufacturing company was found to have inadequately tested several of its drugs, Senator Edward Kennedy spoke for both the conscientious scientist and the public that science serves when he said:

"Inaccurate science, sloppy science, fraudulent science—these are the greatest threats to the health and safety of the American people. Whether the science is wrong because of clerical error, or because of poor technique, or because of incompetence or because of criminal negligence, is less important than the fact that it is wrong" (New York Times, *January 23, 1977, p. 44*).

Assumptions and basic issues

Psychologists begin by making certain assumptions about nature, people, behavior, "mind," and appropriate methods for studying them. On some of these assumptions there is general agreement; others represent continuing unresolved issues in psychology.

Assumptions about the universe

The chess-board is the world, the pieces are the phenomena of the universe, the rules of the game are what we call laws of Nature.
Thomas H. Huxley
A Liberal Education

The scientist assumes an underlying order in nature, a system of events, processes, and phenomena that are predictable because they occur repeatedly with some sort of regularity. The goal of research, then, is to uncover this lawfulness, and the patterns of systematic relationship that underlie apparently unique, unrelated events. The quest is to peer beneath the surface of differences and particulars to the foundation of similarities and generalities. This approach is in sharp contrast to that of many poets and artists who make the assumption that nature is inherently mysterious, changing, chaotic, in constant flux. For them, the task of art is to impose an artificial structure and permanence on this transience. ●

●

The scientist sees nature as orderly and seeks to determine its underlying structure. The artist, on the other hand, sees nature as changing and changeable and may seek to impose a new order on it, as in this painting by Marc Chagall entitled I and the Village, *1911.*

Oil on Canvas, 75 5/8 × 59 5/8".
Collection, The Museum of Modern Art,
New York. Mrs. Simon Guggenheim Fund.

Associated with the scientist's assumption of an ordered universe are the assumptions of determinism and causality. It is assumed that all events have causes—conditions that preceded them and determined that they would happen. It is assumed that these cause-and-effect relationships are unvarying, and thus can serve as the basis for prediction. Given knowledge of all the relevant *variables* (conditions), it should be possible to make an accurate prediction of when and how a given event or phenomenon will occur. At the present, however, such absolute knowledge is lacking in the field of psychology, and psychologists must talk in probabilistic terms: "there is an X percent probability that cause A will result in effect B under Y conditions."

Can we ever really know all the relevant variables that "determine" a given behavior? What you do in a particular situation—for example, when someone threatens you—is determined by the history of your species, your culture, your heredity, your psychological and physical makeup, your upbringing and other past experience, the availability or unavailability of a weapon, the existing laws, your anticipation of the consequences of your actions, and a thousand other things. There are so many determinants operating that it seems impossible ever to know all of them. But this does *not* mean that they do not fully determine the behavior and that behavior is therefore a matter of "free will" or "free choice."

The philosophical debate between "determinism" and "free will" has been a lively one for centuries and cannot be resolved by logical argument. It is important simply to realize that scientists and psychologists *must* accept the assumptions of determinism and causality if they are to proceed to study human nature by means of experimental research. Unless they assume regularity and predictability, there is no point in looking for "laws of behavior."

Nature goes her own way, and all that to us seems an exception is really according to order.
Johann W. Goethe
Conversations with Goethe

Conflicting assumptions about human nature

Although research psychologists agree on the basic assumptions that must guide their scientific investigations, they differ considerably on a range of issues dealing with "human nature"—what human nature is, how we have become what we are, and how our behavior can be changed—if indeed it can be.

Mind vs. body

Is there such a thing as mind? Does it affect the body? Do bodily processes affect the mind? These issues will become central in Part Five as we examine "mind power." But recall that the radical behaviorist position, which is strongly represented, holds that mind and mental processes are explanatory fictions—not meaningful in a behavioral analysis. How then to explain psychosomatic illnesses in which emotional states can be shown to induce physical illness? Recently, many strands of research are challenging the radical behaviorist assumption. Research on the effects of life stresses on physical health, studies of cognitive and language development, studies of the effects of mind-expanding drugs, and studies of the effects of things like feelings of helplessness—all these have stirred a new interest in the "private behaviors" of the mind. There is now a recognition that they must be included in an adequate account of behavior. Even though they cannot be observed directly, their effects can be seen and their operation inferred indirectly through many observable processes. Most psychologists are still more comfortable calling them "psychological processes" or "cognitive processes" rather than "mental processes," however, and many psychologists still see no need to study them at all.

Nature vs. nurture

To what extent are you a product of your heredity, and to what extent the result of your life's experiences? This basic issue, debated for centuries by philosophers, is still argued with much gusto. John Locke propounded the notion that at birth we are nothing but a blank tablet *(tabula rasa)* on which experience makes impressions. This *environmentalist* position—placing emphasis on nurture as the determining factor of our individuality—is at odds with that of the *nativists*. They hold that what we are is determined by our genes, nervous system, physical structure, and all that is present at birth. For them, nurture just develops the nature we are born with.

This basic issue has been argued in many forms. Examples are arguments as to the relative contributions of *innate* versus *learned* factors in determining intelligence and personality. There are other arguments about the importance of unlearned, *maturational* processes versus specific training and *learning* experiences in the development of skills. This issue is important because advocates of the extreme nativist position see more severe limits on the degree to which behavior, performance, and skills can be modified by learning, knowledge, practice, and education. A sociopolitical implication of this position is that if some people are born "stupid," there is no sense in wasting (taxpayers') money trying to educate them. The environmentalists, by contrast, see human nature as essentially pliable, modifiable, perfectable. Such a view has been the cornerstone of the approach taken by psychologists who have made *learning* the core of American psychology. It is a democratic belief, one that gives every child the same opportunity at birth—assuming, of course, that he or she can have access to the same enriched, rewarding environment. If this ideal is false, its danger lies less in wasted funds than in the frustrated expectations of a nation of children who believe they can become anything they want to because "reinforced practice makes perfect."

Good vs. evil

The religious themes of evil—good, sin—grace, and devil—god have carried over into alternative views of what we are and what motivates us to act the way we do. ◆ On the dark side of the ledger, human nature is seen as basically evil—*hedonistic* (pleasure seeking), self-centered, driven by irrational impulses, mechanistic, materialistic, and concerned with power, control of others, and destruction. It is the task of the state and its social institutions, therefore, to constrain this animal-like nature in us, or else all hell will break loose.

◆

How do you see human nature? Which stands out, the angelic or the demonic?

But what about the innocence of youth, the sacrifice of martyrs, the gift of altruistic concern for the well-being of others, the multitudes whose lives are guided by moral choices and ethical decisions? Is it not the exploits of the few who act in evil ways that give the name to the many who inconspicuously go about their lives in quiet goodness? Many psychologists reject the pessimistic view that we are essentially evil, dominated by fate and impulses, acting only to avoid pain and satisfy animal drives. For them, human nature is *potential*, good unless perverted. Living fully is becoming, creating, and actualizing one's potential for growth, beauty, and joy. Behavior can be the outcome of rational choice, mind can transcend the confines of biological matter, and life can be a process of discovering freedom where society often imposes coercive restrictions. In their view, the role of social institutions should be to enable, not to restrict.

We ride through life on the beast within us. Beat the animal, but you can't make it think.
Luigi Pirandello
The Pleasure of Honesty

Assumptions about studying behavior

As we saw in Chapter 1, differing assumptions about human nature have led to a variety of assumptions about how the study of behavior should be approached. These assumptions determine the kinds of questions that will be asked and, therefore, the kinds of answers that will be found.

Universal laws vs. individual uniqueness

Psychological laws are generalizations about causes and their consequences. Can they ever explain why, how, and when an individual does what he or she does? Psychologists working in counseling and therapy generally assume that to understand an individual case, they must explore that person's unique past experience, view of the world, and other special circumstances that make him or her unique. This is termed the *idiographic* approach. Many similarities and predictable sequences are found, of course, but each case is unique in some ways.

Other psychologists take a *nomothetic* approach, trying to establish general relationships between behavior and causal conditions that hold for all of us. Most psychological tests take the nomothetic approach in specifying a series of traits or dimensions on which we all can be placed, differing only in our position on each scale. A profile of a person's scores on these scales is assumed to be an adequate description of the person.

Psychologists who follow the idiographic approach study why people behave differently in the same situation, while those who take the nomothetic road investigate what makes such seemingly different people as we all are behave so similarly in many situations. Reconsider the Milgram study on obedience to authority (in Chapter 1) as an illustration of both approaches. A proponent of the idiographic approach would analyze the written transcripts of the individual subjects rather than the outcome data of mean shock level or percentage of compliers. The group data, however, would be of primary concern to the psychologist taking a nomothetic approach. The idiographic researcher might do an intensive case study of one person who resisted the pressures to obey, which, for example, might reveal that one of the few subjects ever to refuse to give even the first shock was a student named Ronald Ridenhour (Rosenhan, 1974). He not only dissented, he disobeyed authority. Ridenhour did so not out of rebelliousness, but for fear of anticipated consequences of going all the way. He later quit college to join the Green Berets unit in the Vietnam war. It was the same young man, Ronald Ridenhour, who in 1969 forced Congress to investigate the My Lai massacre. Despite much pressure from his superiors to force him to stop making accusations about what really happened at My Lai, Ridenhour held out. He did not obey the authority. He acted from a sense of moral outrage and not from social pressure. By studying such unique individuals, we may learn more about humanity than is usually revealed in the "average" response.

Person vs. group as the unit of study

Given our economic doctrine of individual enterprise and capitalism, and our social history and folklore of rugged individualism, it is no wonder that psychology in America has been the psychology of the individual. The study of individual uniqueness, of individual reactions, of personality has been a dominant theme in much of psychology from its start. Indeed, the very popularity of psychology as an area of study in the United States stems, in part, from its relevance for understanding "personal problems." In a society where "I've gotta be me," it is natural that people want a psychology of "me-ness."

Social psychology is a partial corrective to this overconcern for the individual, through studying the behavior of individuals as influenced by others. But it, too, has tended to ignore important variables that operate at a level beyond that of the individual organism. Ecological variables (space, time, and place) and system variables (power, authority, institutional rules, etc.) have until very recently been overlooked because the focus was on the person rather than on people.

Where the important unit is not the individual, but the group, the society, the family, or the culture, then a very different psychology emerges. For example, in Japan, group action is considered preferable to individual initiative because it minimizes individual responsibility and failure while increasing the chances of shared success. There one finds less emphasis on the study of guilt (an individual phenomenon) than on shame (which occurs in social settings). Similarly, African psychology puts survival of the tribe at its core, rather than successful coping by the individual (see Nobles, 1972).

In this regard, we must note that the general orientation in this book, like most American psychology texts, represents the assumptions and values of western culture and philosophy. Furthermore, the research reported is largely from studies conducted in the United States, Canada, and European countries. That is a bias which does not fully acknowledge psychological differences between western and eastern perspectives, nor between those of a psychology based on white subjects and one founded on nonwhite populations (see Guthrie, 1976).

Causes in the person vs. causes in the environment

Where shall we look for the wellsprings of human action? Are the determinants of behavior to be found inside the person, in one's character, personality traits, and dispositions to act? Or are they outside, in the situation? Is our behavior caused by us or by our environment? Psychologists use the terms *dispositional* and *situational* attribution to indicate whether behavior is attributed to causes within the person or in his or her external situation.

The many psychologists who try to measure and diagnose human "types" and those in the helping professions who treat individuals for personal pathologies and deviant behavior assume causes to be dispositional; that is, in the person. Such a position in psychology has resulted in political legislation and social institutions designed to identify "problem people" whose freedom is a threat to the majority or who are seen as in need of treatment of some kind. Once the problem (of violence, crime, deviance, or any antisocial behavior) is blamed on certain kinds of people, the "logical" solution is to reeducate, reform, rehabilitate, treat, cure, hospitalize, segregate, imprison, punish, or, finally, execute.

A body of recent investigation, however, supports situational attribution of causes and claims that personality traits are poor predictors of behavior (Mischel, 1968). Moreover, many psychologists are demonstrating in their studies that behavior can be induced, maintained, and altered by specified variables in the environment regardless of the "disposition," or personality, of the behaver. This controversy has important implications for programs of education, therapy, and social change as well as for an accurate intellectual understanding of the causes of human behavior. The place you choose to look determines to some extent what you will find.

Levels of psychological analysis

It should be obvious to you by now that different psychologists look in different places for solutions to the puzzles of mind and behavior. Different questions, different research techniques, and different types of data require different levels of analysis—all the way from the highly detailed, minute, and specific to the general, broad, and gross. We can distinguish three levels of analysis in psychological research: the microscopic level, the molecular level, and the molar level.

At the *microscopic* (or *micro*) level, interest is centered on the smallest possible parts, events, and subunits of the whole organism. Precision, specificity, rigorous methods of data collection, and quantitative analysis are the hallmarks of research at this level. A researcher who studied chemical transformations within nerve cells would be operating at this micro level.

The *molecular* level is also geared to a concern for detail—for small, quantifiable units of measurement. However, the units studied are bigger than at the micro level, since larger processes are investigated, which themselves are composed of subunits. Psychologists who work in the areas of learning, perception, psycholinguistics, and information processing, for example, probably operate most frequently at the molecular level. They often attempt to develop causal laws relating internal processes (such as color vision or memory) to external, manipulated variables.

At the *molar* level, the object of study is either the whole functioning organism or systems of behavior that involve much of the total organism. The personality psychologist, the clinical psychologist, and the social psychologist typically are among those who utilize the molar level of analysis. At this level, data are often more qualitative than quantitative, research methodology may be less rigorous and controlled, and conclusions are much broader but less precise than at the micro or molecular levels. Psychologists who operate at this level are willing to make inferences about unobservable events and processes (for example, values, the superego, cultural deprivation) and to attribute behavior to historical, mental, environmental, social, and even political causes.

Despite the general agreement on goals of psychology and on standards for dependable data collection and conclusion drawing, there is no agreement among psychologists on what level of analysis is best. Typically, a researcher chooses to function primarily at the level that suits his or her own interests, training, and abilities. And there is an interplay between one's assumptions about causes and consequences of human behavior and the level of analysis at which one studies the processes. If you assume that behavior is controlled largely by genetic influences, you do not study attitudes, childrearing patterns, and self-awareness. If you function at the "looser," "softer," less specific, molar level, you are less likely to be interested in physiological processes and more likely to assume that the important determiners of behavior are to be found in the individual's social environment.

Although the particular level at which any psychologist functions may be just a matter of personal preference, many come to feel that their level is the best or indeed the only right way to study psychology. The history of psychology is filled with the names of "schools" of psychology that have arisen to defend a particular set of assumptions about what should be the legitimate study of psychology and/or how that study should be conducted. Our own approach will be *eclectic* — that is, one that tries to present you with the widest variety of the best available research, theory, and speculation, regardless of the orientation or level of analysis of the researcher or the philosophical and political assumptions of the theorist.

A useful way to think about the issue of levels of analysis is in terms of the different kinds of *maps* you would need in order to go from your college campus to some desired other place. If you wanted to find the administration building or the gym, a campus map with each building identified would be the most appropriate one. If, however, you wanted to bike to a movie downtown, then you would be better off with a map showing streets of the town. To go on a vacation to a nearby city would require a map with state and county routes, while a cross-country jaunt on your freewheeling motorcycle would necessitate a national map of the United States with states, cities, interstate highways, and other features shown. Although each map may be an accurate and valid representation of the information it provides, it may be totally inappropriate if you do not need that information for your particular trip. To be "relevant" the map you use must be at the level of detail or generality appropriate to the demands you impose on it. Therefore, to go from where you are at this moment to Istanbul requires a whole set of maps, perhaps starting and ending with local ones but employing global ones as well, in order to give you general direction and the overall picture.

Maps differ not only in their scale of detail but also in the kinds of features they show. A relief map may not show auto routes or cities. Such differences may correspond to the difference in psychology between studying physical events and studying conscious experience. Some psychologists would deny this, having faith that ultimately all psychological events will be describable in neurological or biochemical terms. This position is called *reductionism*.

In this text, you will be introduced to research growing out of all these approaches. We will try studying human nature at all these levels. You will have a chance yourself to wrestle with the question of what is the best level for understanding and explaining what we do and how we feel — or whether perhaps different levels must be used for different purposes. We will also attempt to share in the enthusiasm that different investigators bring to and get out of their particular area of psychological inquiry — Freudians, behaviorists, humanists, cognitive psychologists, and assorted others. Throughout our journey together through the fields of psychology, we will guide you toward noticing interesting features of the local terrain, as well as toward appreciating the broader vista that makes the trip more enjoyable each time we take it.

Chapter summary

The four basic goals of the research psychologist are *description, explanation, prediction, and control*. To these the applied psychologist adds a fifth: using the findings of research to improve the quality of human life. *Description* requires objective observations. This means gathering *data:* reports or measurements of observed events. In gathering data it is important to distinguish between what is actually *observed* and what is only *inferred.* To make sure that their data are not ambiguous, psychologists construct *operational definitions*, defining concepts in terms of the specific operations used in measuring them. The empirical approach, based on observation and experience, demands great precision and objectivity in collecting and recording data.

Explanation in psychology is concerned with answering the questions "what" and "how" rather than "why." It includes the search for *causal determinants* of behavior. Many psychologists concentrate on the search for *general laws* that establish unity in behavior; others seek to explain individual variations. The most elaborate form of scientific explanation is *theoretical explanation*. A *theory* is a statement of the relationship between a set of assumptions, principles, observations and deductions.

On the basis of their theories, psychologists attempt to *predict* the occurrence and/or the consequences of behavior. Such prediction begins with a *hypothesis:* a statement concerning a possible relationship between two or more *variables*, usually some stimulus condition and some behavior. Such relationships may involve direct or indirect *causality*, but may also result from some third factor. Hypotheses are tested by experimentation, and while they may be supported with a reasonable degree of certainty, they are never actually considered proved.

Correlations are a useful tool in psychological prediction. These are precise statistical statements of the relationship between two variables. It is important to note that a correlation between two variables does not necessarily mean one is causing the other, only that they vary with one another.

The ability to *control* behavior tells the psychologist that his or her explanations are adequate — that the necessary and sufficient conditions for the behavior have been identified. Psychologists are also becoming increasingly concerned about using their ability to predict and control behavior in ways that will enrich rather than diminish the quality of human life.

The *experimental method* is the basis of scientific inquiry. This method involves four major steps: formulating a hypothesis, collecting data to test it, drawing conclusions, and reporting the results in such a manner that the experiment can be *replicated* by other scientists. The research psychologist begins by formulating a hypothesis and deciding how the variables to be studied are to be defined and measured. The variable whose effects are being studied is called the *independent variable.* This is the one the experimenter changes, or *manipulates.* The *dependent variable* is the behavior that is expected to change when the independent variable is manipulated. In an *ex post facto* design, groups that already differ on some independent variable are studied.

A typical experiment involves two groups of subjects: an *experimental group* and a *control group*. A crucial element in experimentation is the *random* assignment of subjects to different experimental conditions. The independent variable is manipulated for the experimental group but held constant for the control group. (All other variables that might possibly influence the results are held constant for both groups.) If the dependent variable changes for the experimental group but not for the control group, the difference can be attributed to the changes in the independent variable.

In drawing conclusions, it is important to know whether there is a *significant difference* between the groups, or whether the difference could have occurred by chance. This must be determined by statistical tests which result in a *probability statement*. This is an estimate of the probability that the difference occurred by chance. If this probability is small enough (say, less than five chances in one hundred), the hypothesis of a chance result is rejected and the difference is considered to be *statistically significant*—due not to chance but to the experimental manipulation of variables.

Although psychologists agree on the basic assumptions underlying scientific research, they may operate on the basis of differing assumptions about human nature and human behavior. Psychologists differ as to the existence — and the importance—of *cognitive* or *mental* processes. They differ as to the importance of *nature* (the influence of heredity) as opposed to *nurture* (the influence of the environment). They differ as to whether "human nature" is inherently *good* or inherently *evil*. Some psychologists take a *nomothetic* approach, seeking universal laws that will explain the behavior of all people. Others prefer an *idiographic* approach, seeking to determine why people differ in their behavior. Some concentrate on the study of *individuals;* others on the behavior of *groups*. Some look for *dispositional* causes within persons. Others look for *situational* causes in the environment.

The psychological investigations we shall be studying throughout this text can be categorized according to the *level of analysis* at which they are carried out. Studies involving subunits of an organism, such as the behavior of individual cells, are generally at the *microscopic* level of analysis. Studies of larger units of behavior, such as those involved in perception or information processing, are at the *molecular* level. Broader investigations involving the behavior of an entire organism or groups of organisms are said to be at the *molar* level of analysis. The level of analysis at which a particular psychologist functions is determined by his or her theoretical assumptions and by the nature of the processes to be investigated. In this text we shall take an *eclectic* approach to the study of psychology, drawing on various theoretical assumptions and levels of analysis as the need arises.

Part Two

Learning and
Cognition

Paul KLEE "DIE GEDANKEN - EPISCH CONCENTRIERT" 1917, 122
Zeichnung, Feder, imitiertes Ingres

Chapter 3

Adaptive Responding: Conditioning and Learning

Woody Allen is not the only one intimidated by modern appliances. I still harbor a deep-seated fear of showers. The very thought of taking a shower in a college dormitory makes me quiver all over. But perhaps my reaction is not so abnormal; maybe you've had similar experiences of being attacked by a hit-and-run shower. You're really exhausted after a long day of heavy lectures and science labs. A warm, soothing shower is just what you need to unwind. As the water pours down against your back, you soon relax contentedly and become oblivious to everything but the comforting warmth. Suddenly, your relaxation is smashed; the water has become scalding hot causing you considerable pain. Someone has flushed a toilet, and when that happens, there is no cold water to temper the shower. Just as quickly, the temperature of the water returns to its previous condition, and you continue your shower, although unable to regain your former state of contented oblivion. But soon you detect that the water pressure has abruptly and momentarily dropped. Bam! On comes the red-hot flow again, accompanied by curses from you—but curses do not make the water cooler.

You do not have to learn to experience pain when skin tissue is damaged. Those connections are physiologically built in. But you did have to learn the connection between the event and its effect on you—namely, "very hot water burns my skin." Beyond being perceptive reporters of what was going on, you and I had to figure out what was causing the scalding water to do its evil thing on our unsuspecting bodies. The association between the drop in water pressure and the increase in water temperature did not escape our analytical minds. Having noticed that the one stimulus event precedes the other, we entertain the hypothesis that they go together. Sure enough, after we have been burned several times—always after a drop in pressure—a strong association is formed between these two stimulus events. The pressure change is a *signal* for the temperature change. The more often they occur in that sequence, the more dependable the signal. We can predict that the temperature will change when we notice the pressure change. "Oh, oh! Here it comes. Oow! See, I was correct in my prediction." As mundane as it appears, an important kind of learning has just occurred: the learning of *an association between stimulus events*. So you are now smarter, but still smarting.

Originally, many behavioral reactions may accompany your pain response, such as screaming, cursing, kicking the wall, tearing the shower curtain, and so on. What you obviously must learn is which reaction from your total repertoire of responses will be adaptive—will terminate or better yet prevent the painful experience the next time you shower. In this case you would learn to get out of the path of the shower right after you noticed the water pressure drop and before the torrent of scalding water. This is the second kind of association you must learn—*the association between your behavior and its consequences*. Such actions on your part involve *operating* on the environment or your relation to it in order to change it in a desired way. We learn how to exert control on our environment through perception of the consequences of our actions. Similarly, we learn how we are controlled by our environment (including both people and physical events), in our reactions to environmental stimuli.

Both kinds of environmental control are vastly extended in humans by the use of language. Not every resident or visitor in a dormitory with this plumbing problem has to go through the painful process of discovering it personally. It becomes part of the storehouse of knowledge that can be passed from one person to another through words. Moreover, we can post signs, "Beware, temperamental shower" or be more creative in solving the problem of our fellow sufferers. (See *P&L* Close-up, Solution for a Burning Issue.)

Close-up
"Solution for a Burning Issue"

"A soldier with an engineering degree has licked a barracks plumbing problem at Aberdeen Proving Ground that has burned up Army men for years.

"Specialist 4th David Ursin and his bunkmates are the only enlisted men at this weapons test center who no longer worry about sudden flashes of scalding water in the barracks shower each time someone flushes a toilet.

Associated Press, August 16, 1971

"'After repeatedly getting burned,' Ursin said, 'I had to do something.'

"So he invented the 'accumulator,' a quartsized metal cylinder that fits behind the shower head and takes the peril out of barracks bathing.

"The accumulator holds enough water during latrine flushing to eliminate surges of hot water through the shower head."

The study of learning processes is fundamental to any understanding of human behavior. Our ability to profit from experience is greater than that of any other animal species. Because we can learn so many types of associations between stimuli and responses, our behavior is less restricted by heredity. Inherited physiological mechanisms provide a foundation on which we erect a complex superstructure of learned behavioral patterns. In contrast, much of what lower animals do, when they do it, and how they go about it, is controlled (or fixed) more by their inheritance. Bees don't decide they'd rather not build a honeycomb this season but go to Miami instead. Nor can many species of birds stay put in the winter; they have to fly south. The same genetically programmed control affects salmon, who must swim hundreds of miles upstream against lethal odds to return to the ponds they were born in to breed the next generation—and then die there. Even the pattern of sexual intercourse is more precisely determined in most species; humans are the only ones free to "try anything once." (We say the behavior of lower animals tends to be *stereotyped*, while that of higher animals is more *modifiable* through encounters with the environment.)

We *learn* how to be human beings, to live with others, to attend, to perceive, to reason, to relate—as well as to act. Our attitudes, tastes, idiosyncrasies, loves, hates, fears, prejudices, and even neurotic symptoms are all learned. A consideration of principles of learning, therefore, is basic to almost any analysis of human behavior. We begin your introduction to psychology with a series of chapters that touch upon various aspects of the learning process.

The present chapter focuses primarily on the two basic patterns by which learning ties things together (signal learning and consequence learning). Signal learning is a major feature of *respondent conditioning* (also called *classical conditioning* or *Pavlovian conditioning*, after its founder, Ivan Pavlov). Consequence learning is the hallmark of *operant conditioning* (also called *instrumental conditioning*, or sometimes *Skinnerian conditioning* after its founder, B. F. Skinner). In subsequent chapters we will build upon these simpler forms of learning to understand more complex facets of human learning and acquisition of knowledge. In studying the process by which we acquire, transmit, interpret (and often distort) information we will be forced to examine how we learn to use language, to reason, to solve problems, and to be creative. When we study perception, therapy, or social psychology, these basic principles of learning surface as important keys to understanding how we make or break the human connection with one another and our environment.

What organisms must learn

Learning is defined as *a relatively permanent change in behavior as a result of experience*. It is the process of learning that frees us from the restrictions set by our natural environment as well as from those imposed by our physiological inheritance and the history of our species. Humans have learned to fly, to live in orbiting space stations, and to extend the limits of our sensory capacities through electron microscopes and radio telescopes. We have discovered how to prolong life through adequate diet, medicine, and surgery, and to change the environment through irrigation, air conditioning, and nuclear heating plants.

These and other human accomplishments are largely due to our having learned to become accurate, consistent predictors. There are two basic kinds of predictions that we must learn to make reliably: first, which events follow which other events in our bodies or in the environment, and secondly, which events follow our own actions or responses. With this knowledge, we may then move from prediction to control—intervening to change environmental events (or their impact on us), modifying the behavior of other people, and altering our own behavior to make it more appropriate and effective.

All living organisms possess the capacity to learn about these two basic kinds of relationships; lower organisms possess it to a lesser degree.

What events are signals?

By learning about the regularity with which certain events occur together (covary), we identify environmental correlations. These correlations form the basis on which we make predictions about the likelihood of future events from knowledge of present or past events. *A stimulus becomes a signal to the extent that it provides information about the probability that another stimulus will occur.* A clanging bell at a railroad crossing signals the danger of an oncoming train; its cessation or the raising of the striped crossbar (a related signal) is the "Go ahead" safety signal. During World War II, civil-defense sound signals warned the people of air raids; then a different pattern of sound was used as the all-clear signal. To the bored student, the lecturer's phrase, "and in conclusion . . ." signals relief on the way: the seemingly endless lecture will, in fact, soon terminate. Temporal or spatial patterning can also be a signal. Thus the timing of the contractions of the uterus during labor helps predict how soon the baby will be delivered.

But there is an infinite variety of stimulus events in our environment, and only some of them are related to others in the informational way we have described here. How, then, do we learn to extract from these myriad possibilities those that are genuine signals? Aristotle in his classical work *De Anima* suggested that for ideas (or events) to be associated in our minds, they must occur in *contiguity* with each other. That is, the signal and the thing signaled must be experienced close enough together in space and time that we will see them as related. Thereafter, the former will remind us to pay attention: the latter is coming soon. Psychologists today believe that contiguity is not *sufficient* to account for learning associations, but it seems to be *necessary* in most cases. A high frequency or repetitiveness of the two events also enhances the learning of the relationship.

When the second stimulus in a pair is unpleasant or dangerous, we are motivated to search for naturally occurring, *neutral* signals that anticipate the dangerous one. Identifying the neutral predictor stimulus enables us to avoid its serious consequences. Human beings can also go beyond merely using existing signals; they create new ones, such as air-raid sirens or traffic lights, to help them predict other events—and then instruct members of their language community as to the significance of these signals.

There are four basic relationships between stimuli (S) and responses (R) that must be mastered: (1) S—S relationships; (2) R—R relationships; (3) S→R relationships; (4) R→S relationships. The first two can be thought of as signal learning. The latter two are instances of learning about consequences. In learning about relationships between stimulus events (S—S relationships), we come to learn about the *nature of the environment* in which we behave. How are events in both the physical and social environments related, if at all? From correlations between pairs of responses (R—R relationships) we come to learn about the *structure of behavior*—first our own, and then, by observation and inference, that of other people. We learn what responses are related to each other and then can make predictions accordingly. Often clusters of responses tend to occur together. For example, when a response toward some desired goal is blocked or frustrated, aggressive responses of some kind typically follow. As fear responses become stronger, avoidance or escape reactions are more likely.

What actions and consequences are related?

We also learn what environmental events have consequences for our actions and what actions of ours have consequences that affect the environment. From S→R relationships we learn about the *environment's impact on our behavior.* Scalding water will burn your skin. A bright light shining into your eyes makes the pupils constrict, causes tearing, and may lead to a headache. People with allergies must learn which foods, flowers, or other environmental conditions will induce allergic reactions in them if they are to avoid those unpleasant and occasionally fatal stimulus events. On a more positive note, we also come to predict fairly accurately which stimuli will make us feel happy, proud, satisfied, or sexually aroused—and then try to arrange our lives so that the environment has a good opportunity to do its good things to us.

The other general type of relationship to be learned is that between a response we make and the consequences it has on the environment (R→S). Some things we do have an effect, while other things we do have none. Consider the behavior of crying, for example. You do not have to learn to cry; the response mechanisms involved in crying are physiologically wired in at birth. Crying is elicited in any infant by intense, disturbing stimuli, such as hunger pangs, cold, pain, and noise. Indeed, infant crying is a signal to adult caretakers that something is probably bothering the baby. But the child soon learns under which conditions crying is followed by the appearance of parents or grandparents, and often "uses" crying as a means to get attention, to be picked up and cuddled, and so forth. So the child does not learn *how* to cry, but rather *when* crying is followed by a desirable event. Children raised in orphanages or children who are long-term hospital patients cry less often than children in their own homes, because the institutional staff members respond less often to their crying (recall our Chapter 1 example on emotional deprivation).

In many societies, male children learn that the consequences that follow their crying are negative—they will be teased or embarrassed and labeled "sissies" or "cry babies." For such males, the act of crying becomes inhibited when they learn to predict that it will have aversive consequences. By the time these males reach adulthood, stimulus events that would be expected to elicit crying, such as extreme pain or even the death of a loved one, no longer do so.

When your actions do affect the environment in predictable ways, you discover what features of the environment are susceptible to control. At the same time you learn something about yourself as an agent of control. When you raise your hand in class, does the teacher notice you? When you smile, do people smile back at you? When you hit someone bigger, do you get away with it? When you throw water on a gasoline fire, does it go out? When you cry "Wolf" or "Help" does anyone come to your aid? It is from the answers you discover about these and other pairs of responses and consequences that you learn *the impact you have—or can have—on your social and physical environment.* This type of learning plays an important role in behavior modification therapies (which we shall be studying in a later chapter).

Respondent conditioning

Ivan Pavlov, a Russian physiologist, discovered the basic principles of respondent conditioning while studying the functioning of the digestive system in dogs (see *P&L* Profile on p. 66). From this accidental combination of careful observation and the scientific curiosity of a prepared mind has grown the body of learning theory on which so much of present-day psychology is based. We shall begin our study of learning by examining the elements of the conditioned response.

American behavioral scientists have surely added wings to the house that Pavlov built, but really only wings; the main house continues to overtower and to stand firm, little worn by wind and weather.

G. H. S. Razran
Pavlovian Conference

Elicited respondents

A cinder gets in your eye, you blink and secrete tears, your eye is protected from damage. The lights go off (it's another power failure), your pupil dilates, allowing more light into the retina of your eye so you see better. You don't realize the toaster is hot when you rest your hand on it; immediate withdrawal of the hand upon contact saves you from a serious burn. As you start to eat a cracker, saliva flows in your mouth to help dissolve and digest the dry food.

Each of these behaviors—eye blink, tear secretion, pupil dilation, hand withdrawal, salivation—is an example of a *reflex. A reflex is a specific, automatic, unlearned reaction elicited by a specific stimulus.* As you can see from these examples, reflexes have survival value for the organism. They are rapid reactions to dangerous or desirable environmental events not requiring time to think about how to respond. Your body reacts first, then you think about the incident. Reflexes are temporary, physical adaptations the body makes to adjust to some sudden change in the environment. A reflexive response is said to be *elicited* (brought about) by a stimulus event of a particular kind. The connections between these specific stimuli and the responses they elicit are determined genetically in the species and fixed in the individual at or soon after birth. Even in embryos still in the womb some reflexes have been elicited by sound and touch stimuli. Reflexes are under the control of the autonomic nervous system (ANS), and especially that division that operates in emotional reactions, the sympathetic nervous system. In making these *involuntary*

Profile
IVAN PAVLOV

It is ironic that Ivan Petrovich Pavlov, whose pioneering work laid the foundations for the behaviorist school of thought in psychology, believed that psychology was "completely hopeless" as an independent science. Rather, Pavlov saw his work on conditioning as a problem in physiology—a way in which to discover the physical properties of the brain.

Born in 1849, the son of a village priest, Pavlov received his early education in a seminary school, fully intending to follow his father into the priesthood. But after reading several books on physiology, he changed his mind and decided on a career in the natural sciences.

Though he encountered resistance at home, he resolutely entered the University of St. Petersburg and obtained his basic degree in physiology in 1875. And in order to ensure that he would be properly prepared for a research post in physiology, his ultimate goal, he applied to medical school as an advanced student. There he proved so brilliant that upon completion of his medical studies, he was awarded a scholarship for further study under two eminent physiologists in Germany. It was not until 1890 that he was finally appointed to two research positions in his native Russia—professor of pharmacology at the St. Petersburg Medical Academy, and director of the physiology department at the Institute of Experimental Medicine.

Pavlov's research for the next twenty years was primarily concerned with the study of the digestive process, and it was for his excellent work in this area that he won the Nobel Prize in 1904. In fact, it was in the course of directing a number of experiments on the digestive glands that he first became aware of the significance of the conditioned response.

He had been working with dogs as experimental animals in an effort to establish the precise function of saliva in the digestive process, when he noticed that many of the dogs secreted saliva even before meat was administered to them. He quickly determined that this "psychic response" occurred whenever the dogs either had a preliminary glimpse of the food or heard the approaching footsteps of the lab assistant who fed them.

This was so unexpected a phenomenon that he decided to pursue the process as a physiological problem, receiving generous funding for the enterprise when the Soviet government came to power. The new regime was very anxious to push forward biological and behavioral research, and they saw in Pavlov, Nobel laureate and brilliant experimentalist, a man who could bring the Soviet Union into the vanguard of scientific research. A large number of colleagues and assistants joined Pavlov in his work, thus establishing the longest-lived research project in the history of psychology. The Pavlovian paradigm is still used as the major approach to the study of psychology in the Soviet Union.

Over the years, Pavlov refined his investigations into the conditioned response. He moved on from demonstrating the comparatively simple mechanism of positive reinforcement to inducing more subtle phenomena such as extinction, spontaneous recovery, generalization, and discrimination. Up until his death in 1936, he became particularly involved in producing and observing experimental neurosis in his animal subjects.

It is interesting to note that one of the most important contributions Pavlov thought he had made to science was his cortical extinction and inhibition theory—an attempt at explaining the conditioning process in physiological terms. But this particular aspect of his work has not attracted nearly the interest that his conditioning methods have. The latter have been taken up by experimental psychologists all over the world, making Pavlovian conditioning a cornerstone of twentieth-century psychology.

Ivan Pavlov and his staff are shown here with the apparatus used in his conditioning experiments. The dog was harnessed to the wooden frame; a tube conducted its saliva to a measuring device that recorded quantity and rate of salivation to stimuli.

responses to an eliciting stimulus, the organism is responding to a stimulus by doing something to itself, not to its environment. Such behavior is termed *respondent* behavior. In contrast, when the organism's response operates on the environment to alter it in some way, it is termed *operant* behavior (which we shall come to later).

The respondent conditioning paradigm

Paradigm is an important term for you to know because it is used often in psychology as well as in other contexts you will come across in your studies. A paradigm is a symbolic model or diagram that helps us understand the essential features of a process. It is a general way of representing how events are related. Paradigms are ways of thinking about a certain class of events or the processes that affect those events. They provide a structure by which various types of content can be analyzed and explained.

The paradigm that Pavlov discovered was one that showed how an insignificant stimulus could come to have a powerful impact on behavior. The central idea of the respondent conditioning paradigm is: *the learned association between a weak and a strong signal transfers sufficient power to the weaker stimulus so that it comes to elicit the same response(s) originally controlled only by the stronger one.* Thus a new signal can be used in place of a familiar one; or, a neutral stimulus is substituted for the normal eliciting stimulus. This paradigm points to a powerful technique for the control of a wide range of behavior—for better or for worse, as we shall soon see. ▲

\ The respondent conditioning paradigm begins with the relationship between a stimulus and a reflex that it reliably elicits. The usual eliciting stimulus is the *unconditioned* or *unconditional stimulus* (UCS, or US). The response that regularly follows it is called the *unconditioned response* (UCR, or UR).

Pavlov found that when he presented meat powder to a dog and observed the automatic, unlearned response of salivation, it was not long before other stimuli occurring shortly *before* actually putting food in the dog's mouth (sight of food, sight or sound of experimenter) also became capable of eliciting salivation. When salivation was then elicited by these other previously irrelevant and weak stimuli, salivation was called a *conditioned* or *conditional response* (**CR**).

▲
Appetitive conditioning paradigm
Originally, the sound of a bell elicits only orientation (a general response of attention); food elicits salivation. If the food is consistently presented immediately after the bell is rung, the bell will soon come to elicit salivation. Note that the solid arrows in the diagram indicate an unlearned (biologically determined) relationship between a stimulus and a response; the broken arrow symbolizes a learned (experientially determined) relationship.

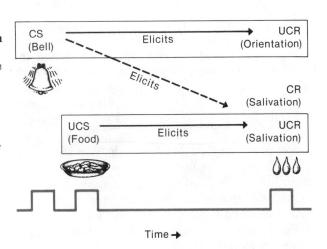

When respondent conditioning takes place, the organism learns a new correlation between two previously unrelated stimulus events. The *conditioned stimulus* (CS) now signals the onset of the unconditioned stimulus (UCS). Once this pairing between stimuli (CS–US) has been learned, the organism responds to the signal (CS) as if it were the original, powerful instigating stimulus (in this case, the US is food). Initially, the sound of a bell elicited only an orientation response toward it (attentive listening), and only food in the dog's mouth elicited salivation. But after a number of trials in which Pavlov regularly rang the bell before presenting the food, conditioning occurred. The dog now salivated to the sound of the bell; it had become a dinner gong. The dog had been *conditioned* to make the old response to a new stimulus.

We have just described an *appetitive* conditioning paradigm (involving positive reactions and approach to a desirable stimulus). Suppose we were to change one element by shocking the dog instead of giving it food. What form would conditioning take in this *aversive* conditioning paradigm? If the subject were restrained so it could not escape the shocks, what would happen when the warning bell sounded? Muscle twitch and withdrawal of the shocked limb, as well as a generalized arousal reaction, would probably be elicited. If the UCS elicits a strong fear response, then with only a few pairings with it a neutral CS will come to do so. The very same tinkle of the bell that elicited salivation (and approach responses) can become a stimulus that strikes fear in the heart of a once brave animal—or a human. A substantial body of research on respondent conditioning has demonstrated a very important principle of conditioning: *any stimulus that the organism can perceive can be used to elicit a conditioned response in any muscle or gland by an appropriate pairing of this conditioned stimulus with a biologically significant unconditioned stimulus.*

The tremendous implications of this principle should not escape you. Whatever stimulus you can perceive (even at a subliminal level, below awareness) can be conditioned to a response system so that you learn to value it, or hate it, or even to fear it. The Russian investigator Konstantin Bykov (1957), reviewed a large body of respondent conditioning research on the extent to which internal organs can be conditioned. His conclusion (roughly translated) was that if it wiggles or squirts naturally, it can be conditioned. So virtually any stimulus within our range of perceptual detectability can come to have meaning for us, to take on positive or negative qualities. In addition, virtually any response we are capable of making can be conditioned by these learned signals. Think of examples in your life where such conditioning occurs.

In the movie *The Diary of Anne Frank*, the arrival of Nazi SS troops was always preceded by the wailing siren of a squad car and followed by the perpetration of some horrifying action against the Jews. By the end of the movie, the peculiar sound of siren alone (CS) elicited strong feelings of revulsion (CR) in most viewers, in anticipation of the horror about to come (UCS). This was even more true of the persecuted Jews who actually experienced this symbol of danger and the events with which it came to be associated.

Not only physical stimuli but also words and other symbols can become conditioned stimuli. Such conditioning vastly extends the range of stimuli that can elicit reflexes, signal danger, or "stand in" for absent unconditioned stimuli. Words and symbols associated with significant events come to be substitutes for events, producing the same reaction as the events themselves. It is remarkable that many people all over the world experience strong internal reactions when a piece of cloth is raised on a pole and a band makes some musical sounds—if the cloth is their nation's flag and the sounds are the music of their national anthem. ■

This photograph shows a widely known case of mass conditioning with conditioned overt reactions such as the salute and hail of "Heil Hitler," plus internal ones of arousal to the passing of Hitler's motorcade.

The anatomy of Pavlovian conditioning

How is a conditioned association formed, and, once learned, can it be broken? The following is a brief summary of some of the major processes underlying respondent conditioning.

1. Generalized excitability   Even after a single pairing of a neutral and an unconditioned stimulus, the animal will respond to the conditioning situation by being more excitable. This may be great enough to trigger spontaneous motor reactions as well as glandular secretions. If it is a food response that is being conditioned, there is a "general alimentary excitation, a general preparation for future alimentary activity, the expectation of feeding in general that is supposed to follow. Then the reaction is concretized, and the animal awaits the definite conditioned stimulus that is followed by feeding, and focuses its attention on this stimulus" (Kupalov, 1961, p. 1050).

2. CS—UCS pairing   The strength of the conditioned response depends on the frequency of CS—UCS pairings and the time interval between the two stimuli. Increasing the number of pairings of the conditioned and unconditioned stimuli increases the strength of the conditioned responses (up to a certain level). But this holds only under certain temporal conditions. The CS must usually precede the UCS, although under some conditions it is presented simultaneously. The most favorable interval between stimuli is about half a second between onset of CS and onset of UCS. This time interval is sufficient for the first stimulus to signal the second and to prepare the organism to respond physiologically. Shorter time intervals reduce the signaling utility of the CS; longer ones allow time for other irrelevant stimuli to occur, other responses to be activated, and a loss of attention to the specific CS. Thus temporal contiguity (one event closely following the other) is critical in the respondent conditioning paradigm.

3. Stimulus generalization   When the conditioned response to a given CS also is elicited by unfamiliar stimuli similar to the CS, *stimulus generaliza-*

tion is occurring. This phenomenon can be thought of as a "confusion" between a stimulus that has been part of the conditioning paradigm and other stimuli that share some of its properties (brightness, pitch, etc.). Early in conditioning, stimulus generalization may occur to almost any stimulus that is perceived to bear some similarity to the conditioned stimulus. The greater the similarity, the stronger will be the CR to these other stimuli. As conditioning proceeds, the individual becomes more "discriminating", responding only to the specific stimulus attributes of the CS.

4. Discrimination and inhibition At first, it may be useful for an organism to respond to any and all stimuli that might potentially have signal value. But it must eventually learn to differentiate or *discriminate* between relevant and irrelevant stimuli and to *inhibit* its response to all stimuli *not* associated with the unconditioned stimulus event. Conditioning can be thought of as a process in which discrimination wins over generalization.

The more distinguishable the *signal*, the more quickly it will be identified and attended to at the expense of irrelevant stimuli (often called *noise*) that are occurring at the same time. Thus a marked difference in intensity between stimuli will speed up discrimination. In our hot shower example, the association between drop in water pressure and hotter water will be learned more quickly if the water-pressure change is marked and the rise in temperature is great than if the changes are small and gradual.

Even *not responding* can be a response. Although inhibition of a response is a passive act in a behavioral sense, it involves considerable physiological activity in the nervous system. All we see during conditioning is the overt activity, but one of the most intriguing aspects of conditioning is the coordinating role of inhibitory processes in suppressing the inappropriate reactions to all other sensory inputs except the critical one (see Rescorla, 1969; Boakes & Halliday, 1972).

5. Higher-order conditioning Once a conditioned stimulus has acquired the power to elicit a strong conditioned response, it can then be paired with any other stimulus that the organism can perceive. This second stimulus will become a second CS, eliciting the conditioned response even though it has never been directly paired with the UCS. In this way, human behavior can come to be controlled by stimuli qualitatively very different from those originally present during conditioning. One of Pavlov's colleagues, Krylov, found that after a morphine injection (UCS) had elicited nausea and vomiting (UCR), the mere sight of the needle, about to be injected (CS), could also produce vomiting—a typical conditioned response (CR). In addition, he found that nausea came to be elicited by any stimulus regularly preceding the sight of a needle—alcohol on the skin, the box containing the needle, eventually even the laboratory room. These stimuli paired with the original CS were never directly paired with the UCS in this paradigm.

This process, by which a series of conditioned stimuli may, in turn, serve as a substitute for the original conditioned stimulus and themselves produce the response, is called *higher-order* conditioning and can be diagrammed as shown. ● Suppose that a thoroughly conditioned young male subject leaves the training session and chances to meet an attractive young woman on the street corner. Although their chat consists only of rather ordinary small talk, she slaps his face and walks away muttering "pig." Little does she realize that his leering wink was elicited when the traffic light turned green and not by his "M.C.P." reactions to her charms. A less facetious use of higher-order conditioning procedures to study voluntary control of involuntary reflexes is illustrated in the *P&L* Close-up, Simon Says, "Pupil Contract"; "Dilate."

Higher-order conditioning

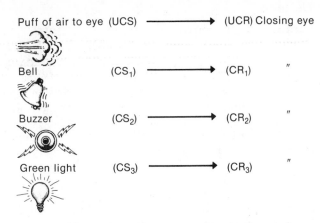

Puff of air to eye (UCS) ————————→ (UCR) Closing eye

Bell   (CS$_1$) ————————→ (CR$_1$)   "

Buzzer   (CS$_2$) ————————→ (CR$_2$)   "

Green light (CS$_3$) ————————→ (CR$_3$)   "

6. Extinction   Since the actual connections between events in the environment change from time to time, it is important that the connections established by conditioning not be permanent. Otherwise, we would not have the flexibility we need for responding appropriately to a changing environment. Once a conditioned stimulus no longer signals either danger or benefit, our continued response to it would be nonfunctional and perhaps harmful.

Fortunately, most such nonfunctional responding eventually stops when presentation of the conditioned stimulus is repeatedly followed by the *absence of the unconditioned stimulus*. The conditioned response then becomes weaker and eventually reaches zero intensity. The response is then said to be *extinguished*, and the trials that bring it about (CS + no UCS) are called *extinction trials*. The organism is learning that the CS is no longer a relevant signal for predicting the UCS. Extinction results in the CS losing its power to control behavior.

When a response is extinguished, does that mean it is gone forever? Not at all. Extinction is a special case of active inhibition, not loss of learning. This is demonstrated by the fact that after a rest period during which neither CS nor UCS is presented, the supposedly extinguished conditioned response comes to life again—though in somewhat weaker form—the first time the conditioned stimulus reoccurs. The phenomenon is called *spontaneous recovery*. If additional acquisition trials are given (CS + UCS), the response will return to its former vigor more rapidly than it reached it originally. If further extinction trials are given, it will become weaker and be permanently extinguished.

During extinction, a process takes place that is analogous to stimulus generalization during acquisition of a CR. Responses to stimuli not directly subjected to extinction training will also extinguish—in proportion to their similarity to the conditioned stimulus. This spread of inhibition (from the specific CR being extinguished to other related ones) is known as *generalization decrement*.

7. Strength of conditioning   We cannot measure the strength of conditioning directly but must infer it from some kind of observable, measurable behavior. Traditionally four general measures have been used. Pavlov used *amplitude* of response—quantity of saliva secreted—as his measure of response strength. Other measures sometimes used are *latency* of response—how much time elapses between the onset of the conditioned stimulus and the response—and *frequency*, or rate of making a given response. Strength of learning can also be measured by *resistance to extinction*. The more trials required to extinguish a conditioned response, the stronger it is assumed to have been.

Close-up
Simon Says, "Pupil Contract"; "Dilate"

In the traditional respondent conditioning paradigm, neither the CS nor the UCS is under the control of the individual being conditioned. They are usually programmed to occur in a predictable sequence by the environment, by the experimenter, or by a "trainer" who sets out to establish a conditioned response in animals or humans. A moment's reflection, however, makes it apparent that responses could be conditioned to stimuli produced by the person who is being conditioned. Through higher-order conditioning procedures it should be possible to extend the power of an external conditioned stimulus (such as a bell) to an internally generated stimulus (such as words spoken by the subject).

In a remarkable study conducted in 1933, Clarence Hudgins did just that:

a) contraction of the pupil of the human eye was the UCR elicited first by a bright light (UCS) then conditioned to a bell (CS_1) paired with the light;

b) a hand contraction by the subject, which switched on the bell and light, became CS_2;

c) the experimenter's verbal commands for the subject to "contract" or "relax" the grip on the bell-light switch was CS_3;

d) the light, bell, and hand reactions were then eliminated leaving the experimenter's words as the conditioned stimuli that alone elicited pupil contractions.

e) Next, the subjects were told to repeat the commands aloud. Then they gave their own "auto-commands" (CS_4) whenever they wanted to while the experimenter remained silent.

f) After pupillary contraction was conditioned to the subject's own commands, they were instructed to whisper them (CS_5) and finally to say the words only to themselves—subvocally (CS_6). (So that the experimenter would know when these silent stimuli took place, subjects touched a telegraph key once for contraction, twice for relaxation.)

Before training, none of the conditioned stimuli had any effect on varying the size of the pupil. After conditioning, each conditioned stimulus in turn exerted a substantial effect on pupillary contraction and dilation. Merely thinking the word "contract" was sufficient to cause the pupil to contract, while the thought of the word "relax" did the opposite, enlarging the diameter of the pupil.

When asked "What did you do when I said 'contract'?" thirteen of the fourteen subjects replied, "I did nothing." The conditioning took place without their awareness of the consistent changes in their responding. Only a single subject was sufficiently sensitive to the light changes associated with slight changes in pupil size—and she was able to detect the direction of the pupillary change on every conditioning trial. Of further interest is the finding that conditioned responses to the bell and hand contractions were easily extinguished, but not the CR to the verbal stimuli. No experimental extinction occurred during testing, and the conditioned response appeared in full even after a two-week interval without any further training.

Hudgins' study raises challenging questions about whether so-called *voluntary behavior*—things we tell ourselves to do—is essentially a special case of a conditioned response, and not really a matter of "free will." It also points up the possibility that we might inadvertently be telling our bodies how to react in various situations, to "be tense," "get turned on," etc. In this way, we could be conditioning unhealthy reactions in ourselves without even knowing it.

The graph shows conditioned pupillary responses to subvocal stimuli. The pupil became smaller when the subject said "contract" to himself; it enlarged when he said "relax."

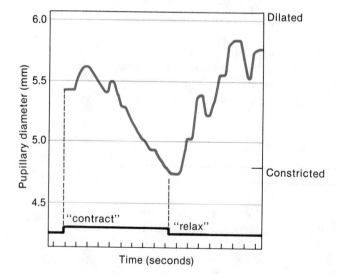

Adapted from Hudgins, 1933.

More recently, "habit permanence" has been suggested as a concept to describe the strength of a learned association. It appears to consist of three dimensions: retention, durability, and generalizability (Wong, 1977). *Retention* refers to the appearance of the conditioned response after an interval without practice; a "memory" for the correct response when the appropriate stimulus is presented. *Durability* refers to the capability of a learned response to survive an extended series of extinction trials. *Generalizability* refers to the transfer of the learned response to a situation quite different from the original learning environment.

8. Pseudoconditioning False conditioning occurs whenever the pairing of CS – UCS is *not* necessary for eliciting the response, but is assumed to be so. Sometimes the organism is in a state of high excitability and responds to many unlearned stimuli in the same way—even without being paired with the UCS. Consider an example in which a shock to the hand is the UCS and a vibratory tactile stimulus the CS. The CS may not produce withdrawal initially but does so after CS – UCS trials. Can we conclude withdrawal is CR to the vibratory stimulus? Not without also testing for a possible pseudo-conditioning effect. The electric shock may have made the hand more sensitive to any stimulation so that withdrawal will occur to any stimulus, whether or not it has been paired with shock. The observed effect is not due to the conditioning *association* of CS – UCS, but is a pseudoconditioning effect in which the CS alone will elicit the response (see Rachlin, 1976).

A little learning may be a dangerous thing

A summary of general principles of respondent conditioning underscores its widespread implications for the control of human behavior:

a. any stimulus we can perceive has the potential to become a conditioned stimulus;

b. perception of the CS can take place below the level of conscious awareness;

c. any response we make naturally can come to be elicited by any learned signal;

d. these responses can be highly specific and simple (such as a muscle twitch or part of a brain-wave pattern) or general and complex (such as sexual arousal or fear);

e. the conditioned response can be a response of our skeletal muscles or visceral organs or even a "private" response (such as thoughts and feelings);

f. with a powerful original UCS, conditioning may take place in only one trial in which the UCS is paired with any CS;

g. stimuli quite different from the original CS can control the appearance of the conditioned response through higher-order conditioning;

h. depending on the strength of the CR and the nature of the conditioning process some learned responses resist extinction—don't fade away easily, and may endure for a lifetime.

Taken together, these principles reveal the remarkable adaptability of organisms to learned conditioned associations. But they also are disturbing. It is obvious that much inappropriate conditioning which is not in the best interests of our physical or psychological well-being also takes place. Let's examine some of the "side effects" of conditioning.

Experimental neurosis

When an experimental subject is forced to make perceptual discriminations between two stimuli that are very similar, its capability may be so taxed that extreme stress results. This phenomenon has been called *experimental neurosis*. It was first observed in one of Pavlov's dogs who had to discriminate between a circle that was a signal for food (CS⁺) and an ellipse that was a signal that no food would come (CS⁻). At first, the dog could do so easily, salivating only to the circle, not reacting to the ellipse. But then on successive trials, the shape of both stimuli was slightly altered. Soon the circle was getting flattened out like an ellipse while the ellipse was getting rounder, like a circle. The animal no longer could respond differentially to the two stimuli. Its discrimination ability had been overloaded. When the original simple discrimination was again presented (CS⁺, circle; CS⁻, ellipse) the animal no longer responded appropriately. Even more dramatic were the accompanying behavioral changes. The formerly tranquil dog barked, squealed, tore at the apparatus, showed signs of fear of the room, and exhibited generalized inhibition leading to drowsiness and sleep. Similar reactions have been found in studies with rats, cats, and sheep.

This experimental neurosis is like neurosis in humans in that it:

a. results from prolonged stress, inescapable conflict, and inability to decide between competing alternatives;

b. involves behavior indicative of a generalized anxiety state;

c. is marked by "symptoms" — reactions that are unusual in the life of the organism and provide at best only a partial solution to the conflict; and

d. may persist without extinction for a lifetime, unless special "counterconditioning therapy" is provided.

Liddell (1956) reports symptoms enduring for thirteen or more years, as well as an increased incidence of premature deaths among sheep who were made experimentally neurotic. He relates one incident in which, a full year after the conditioning, his 400-pound experimentally neurotic sow, Tiny, "by friendly overtures, lured him into a fence corner and attacked him so viciously that he required medical attention" (pp. 982–83). (Chalk one up for the passive victims!)

Persistence of irrational behavior

Why do intense, irrational fear reactions, learned through respondent conditioning, sometimes persist and not extinguish even though no harm or danger ever follows? One answer is that people avoid situations where the thing they have learned to fear (snakes, small rooms, open spaces, heights) might appear, or they flee as soon as the feared object or situation is present or expected. So there is never a chance to learn that it does not in fact signal danger or harm on the way. For the conditioned fear response to extinguish, circumstances must be arranged so that the individual can experience the conditioned stimulus *not* being followed by danger or harm, or better yet being followed by a pleasant event, in which case new, *counterconditioning* can take place. These phenomena have been demonstrated in the laboratory.

When dogs were trained to avoid a painful electric shock in the grill floor of one compartment of a shuttle-box by jumping quickly over a barrier into the "safe" side of the box, they learned to do so in only a few trials. After the tenth conditioning trial, shock was never presented in the formerly "danger" side of the box. Nevertheless, whenever the dogs were placed in that compartment they continued to jump into the other one—and

did so without evidence of extinction for 500 trials! They never learned that the first side was now safe because they did not stay around long enough to learn that the correlation had been broken (Solomon, Kamin, & Wynne, 1953).

Another reason why a useless or even harmful conditioned response may persist for years is the "spread of conditioning" effects. Bodily functioning is highly integrated, so that conditioning of a muscular response may involve responses of the autonomic nervous system as well. Zeaman and Smith (1965) found that when light and shock are paired in conditioning the responses of the heart in human subjects, a conditioning of respiratory responses also occurs. Similarly, Neal Miller (1969) reported a number of experiments in conditioning of autonomic responses in which responses other than those being conditioned were also affected. This means that the CR may include more physiological components than the UCR—the two response systems are not necessarily identical. Therefore, when extinction of a specific conditioned response occurs, those other components—the excess conditioned baggage—may linger on, resisting extinction. As one psychologist has observed:

"The fact that conditional reflexes are so difficult to eradicate, once formed, makes the individual a museum of antiquities as he grows older. . . . He is encumbered with many reactions no longer useful or even . . . detrimental to life. This is especially true for the cardiovascular function, and it is these conditional reflexes that are most enduring. A person may be reacting to some old injury or situation which no longer exists, and he is usually unconscious of what it is that is causing an increase in heart rate or blood pressure. The result may be chronic hypertension. This may be the explanation of many cardiac deaths" (Gantt, 1966, p. 62).

In many cases where individuals no longer show any overt behavioral response to the conditioned stimulus, it is still having an effect on them at a physiological level. Such resistance to extinction of a once-significant signal stimulus long after it ceases to signal anything really coming is demonstrated in a study of reactions to the "call to battle stations" (Edwards & Acker, 1962).

Hospitalized Army and Navy veterans who had seen active service during World War II were exposed to a series of twenty sound stimuli, and their autonomic responses were measured by a recording of GSR changes. The biggest difference between men from the two services emerged when they heard a repetitive gong sounding at the rate of about 100 percussions a minute. This signal was used as a call to battle stations aboard U.S. Navy ships during the war, and it continued to elicit a strong autonomic response from the Navy veterans. Even though more than fifteen years had elapsed since this stimulus had signaled danger, the sailors showed a significantly more vigorous emotional response to it than did the soldiers. The probability of getting such a big difference by chance would have been less than one in a hundred (p = <.01).

Hypertension has been called the "mystery disease" that affects perhaps as many as 30 million Americans whose diastolic blood pressure registers over the "safe" level of 90. It is also termed the "silent killer" because its sufferers are usually unaware of it until it erupts in heart disease, kidney malfunction, or stroke. Hypertension is not really a disease itself, but a symptom, perhaps of general stress conditioned to a variety of environmental stimuli at work, school, and in the home. It may also be cued to the "auto-commands" of hypertensive people who may be constantly telling themselves to work harder, be vigilant, "be number one." Current treatment for hypertension includes training the individual to control it through relaxation exercises (in addition to diet and exercise).

Conditioned addictions

Most addictions to some substance (drugs, alcohol, cigarettes, food) are in part physiological and in part learned. Addictive responses are conditioned to stimuli associated with the act of consuming the substance. Of all addictions, the one that reduces life expectancy most is food addiction. Recent research indicates that many extremely overweight people have a heightened sensitivity to cues associated with food and eating—the sight or smell of food, pictures of food, or seeing other people eating. Furthermore, environments in which overweight people normally eat when hungry become conditioned stimuli for eliciting eating even in the absence of hunger—while watching TV, movies, or sports events, listening to music, walking through the kitchen or dining room, and so on. One therapeutic procedure with some success involves decreasing these conditioned associations by restricting eating to just one place at predetermined times (Stunkard, 1972).

Among narcotic addicts, a major problem is their relapse (also called *recidivism*) after apparently being cured. Former addicts have reported experiencing painful withdrawal symptoms when they visit areas where they used to take drugs (O'Brien, 1975). These withdrawal effects are both physiologically and psychologically unpleasant. Taking drugs again quickly alleviates these aversive withdrawal symptoms. There is now objective evidence that narcotic withdrawal symptoms can be experimentally conditioned to environmental stimuli. Such studies "lend credence to clinical reports of such phenomena occurring naturally when treated addicts return to their former drug-taking environments" (O'Brien, Testa, O'Brien, Brady, & Wells, 1977, p. 1002).

Conditioning based on consequences

Learning what events in the environment are predictably related to each other is not enough for adaptation and survival. Any organism, as we have seen, must also learn what consistent relationships can be expected between its own actions and subsequent events in the environment—in particular, what changes it can achieve or prevent.

Species adapt to a gradually changing environment through evolution of behaviors essential for survival in the new environment. Individuals however, must often meet abrupt environmental challenges with sudden changes in their behavior patterns. Learning is this process of behavior change. American psychology has from the first been centrally concerned with the study of learning and especially with the learning of this kind of relationship between behavior and its consequences—as befits a young, action-oriented, practical society, confident of its power to control its own destiny.

Learning that focuses on the consequences of one's responding was originally called *instrumental conditioning*. Currently, consequence learning is more typically referred to as *operant conditioning*. Despite some minor differences between the use of these terms, they are both basically focused on the association between responses and stimuli, rather than the stimulus-stimulus relations of respondent conditioning.

Instrumental conditioning

At about the same time that Russian dogs were salivating, blinking, or becoming neurotic in Pavlov's laboratory, American cats were coolly learning to work their way out of strange boxes. In order to get out of their solitary confinement (and get food), hungry cats had to discover how to operate a latch on each of a series of "puzzle boxes." American psychologist E. L. Thorndike, at Columbia University, reported the results of his pioneering study of the behavioral (as constrasted with Pavlov's more physiological) approach to learning back in 1898:

"When put into the box the cat would show evident signs of discomfort and of an impulse to escape from confinement. It tries to squeeze through any opening; it claws and bites at the bars or wire; it thrusts its paws out through any opening and claws at everything it reaches; . . . It does not pay very much attention to the food outside [the reward for the hungry cat], but seems simply to strive instinctively to escape from confinement. The vigor with which it struggles is extraordinary. For eight or ten minutes it will claw and bite and squeeze incessantly. With 13, an old cat, and 11, an uncommonly sluggish cat, the behavior was different. They did not struggle vigorously or continually. On some occasions they did not even struggle at all. It was therefore necessary to let them out of the box a few times, feeding them each time. After they thus associated climbing out of the box with getting food, they tried to get out whenever put in. . . . Whether the impulse to struggle be due to an instinctive reaction to confinement or to an association, it is likely to succeed in letting the cat out of the box. The cat that is clawing all over the box in her impulsive struggle will probably claw the string or loop or button so as to open the door. And gradually all the other nonsuccessful impulses will be stamped out and the particular impulse leading to the successful act will be stamped in by the resulting pleasure, until, after many trials, the cat will, when put in the box, immediately claw the button or loop in a definite way" (p. 13).

From observations such as these on "trial-and-error learning," Thorndike began the study of instrumental conditioning. His methods and ideas became cornerstones in the American investigation of the learning process in humans and lower animals.

The key to instrumental conditioning is the phrase "contingent reinforcement follows response." In this kind of learning, the individual gets rewarded when it makes a particular response. "No work, no pay" is the motto of our free enterprise economic system. It is also the basis of instrumental conditioning: delivery of rewards is critically dependent upon what the organism does. Its behavior is *instrumental* to obtaining a desirable goal, or avoiding (escaping) an undesirable one. In contrast, the Russian respondent conditioning paradigm calls for a passive organism that has no control over the delivery of the UCS. The experimenter or nature provides the UCS *independent* of what the organism does.

There are two other differences between respondent and instrumental conditioning to be noted. Behavior is *elicited* by a strong, identifiable, stimulus (the UCS) in respondent conditioning, while in instrumental conditioning the behavior is *emitted* spontaneously by the organism without any apparent eliciting stimulus. In addition, this UCS both elicits the respondent and reinforces it, while in instrumental conditioning the reinforcement occurs only *after* a designated response occurs. In short, instrumental conditioning teaches the organism a lesson in the *consequences* of its actions, while the respondent situation teaches the importance of the *antecedents* of behavior. Together, these two paradigms account for a great deal of learning that takes place from the simplest organisms to nature's most complex learning machines—you and me.

The currency that makes instrumental conditioning such a viable system of learning is *reinforcers and rewards. A reinforcer is a stimulus event that maintains a response or increases its strength, when presented in a proper temporal relationship with that response* (Deese & Hulse, 1967). As stated earlier, the UCS in respondent conditioning is the "reinforcer" that elicits the UCR; the instrumental conditioning reinforcer follows shortly after the response. Pyschologists tend to use the term "reinforcer" as the contingent *stimulus event* affecting specific responses. "Reward" is a less technically precise term, so we may say that responses are reinforced; individuals are rewarded.

Like Thorndike's cats, you encounter situations in which what you do makes a difference. If a coke machine regularly fails to deliver a coke after you deposit a coin, you learn that coin-dropping in that situation has no effect on that machine. Your behavior does not change the environment. But if you kick the machine and a cold coke appears and you quench your thirst, your behavior has had a consequence on the environment. Next time you are thirsty, you may go up to the coke machine and start kicking it (especially if no one is watching). Kicking the machine has thus become a dominant, highly probable response for you. If that fails to produce a coke, you may learn that the behavior that is followed by the coke is composed of two response units: first depositing the coin and then smartly kicking the stubborn machine. On subsequent occasions you will repeat the sequence, or else search for a coke machine that will deliver its contents for coin alone or for a more gentle kick. ◆

In Thorndike's experiment, if the latch had been dropped by means of a sound-activated relay when the puzzled cats meowed or hissed, or if mama cat had come and opened the door then, the cats would have continued to meow or hiss on later trials. But meowing and hissing were not followed by freedom or food; in fact, they had no effect on the environment at all. So they were discontinued; in Thorndike's terminology, they moved down in the response hierarchy.

Thorndike thought that it was the *feeling of satisfaction* in accomplishment that made a successful response become more probable. He regarded these

◆

*Perhaps this photograph
shows Thorndike's law of
effect (mixed with a little
aggression release?).*

Close-up
Hull's Drive-Reduction Theory

Clark Hull (1943, 1952), at Yale University, attempted to formulate a comprehensive theory of learning that would integrate the findings of respondent and instrumental conditioning. His goal was a precise and objective statement of Thorndike's law of effect that would make it applicable to social learning in humans as well as maze learning in rats. The major features of Hullian theory are:

a) What is learned is a connection between a stimulus and a response; the unit of learning is called *habit strength.*

b) *Reinforcement* is a necessary condition for learning. For a response to increase in habit strength, it must be followed immediately by a goal substance. Such substances, called *reinforcers*, gain their effectiveness by reducing the level of existing drive. The theory is therefore described as a *drive-reduction* theory of learning.

c) The learned connection between a stimulus and a response increases in magnitude gradually and continuously with each reinforced practice trial; this learning represents a relatively permanent change in behavior.

Unfortunately, Hullian theory was left unfinished at his death in 1952. Its influence, however, has been a major one in American psychology, and other psychologists have refined and extended it (Spence, 1956).

successful environmental consequences as "reinforcing states" and believed that connections between them and the responses that led to them were "stamped in" on successive training trials. According to his *law of effect,*

"Any act which in a given situation produces satisfaction becomes associated with that situation, so that when the situation recurs, the act is more likely than ever before to recur also. Conversely, any act which in a given situation produces discomfort becomes disassociated from that situation, so that when the situation recurs, the act is less likely than before to recur" (1905, p. 202).

Thorndike's law of effect was really little more than a modern restatement of the old doctrine of *hedonism* advanced by the philosopher Jeremy Bentham—that people will tend to behave in such a way as to gain pleasure and avoid pain. Nevertheless, for many years it served as the basic principle for that emerging American enterprise, "the psychology of learning." (See *P&L* Close-up, Hull's Drive-Reduction Theory.)

Operant conditioning

It is not surprising to discover that B. F. Skinner attributes his change of career—from a literature major in college to behavioral psychologist—to reading John B. Watson's book *Behaviorism* (Homans, 1977). For the past forty years, Skinner has actively preached and still vigorously practices the principles of behaviorism. His views on human nature and how it can be changed have created much controversy—some of it through misunderstanding what his sermon is all about. Skinner has been called a "dangerous man, with dangerous ideas." This characterization is due largely to his pioneering efforts to apply the principles of operant conditioning to real-life situations. As well as modifying abnormal behavior patterns of mental patients, Skinner and his students have worked at improving education with teaching machines, changing the environments in which delinquents, retarded, and the elderly are "warehoused," and designing new environments in which babies could be raised. And on the side, he has proposed plans for recreating society based on the central principle of Skinnerian psychology — "the power of positive reinforcement." Let's examine what operant conditioning is and why Skinner's ideas are threatening to so many people.

The experimental analysis of behavior

From the outset, Skinner's approach has been characterized by its emphasis on observing the physical, measurable properties of responding and on developing a practical technology for controlling observable responses. There is no place in such an analysis of behavior for unobservable, inferred mental, motivational, or even physiological states or entities. For example, what did we really know about those cats of Thorndike's? What could we *see*? Meowing and scratching, yes; inner drives, no. Higher rate of occurrence of the successful response, yes; satisfaction, no. Cessation of the ineffective responses, yes; "stamping in" or "stamping out," no. Psychologists are much more aware today of the need to make their concepts precise and explicit and closely related to what *can* be observed.

Followers of Skinner hold that a learning situation can and should be described *entirely* in such terms that nothing need be said about what is happening within the organism. For example, they define "hunger" not by an inference about drives but by the experimental operation of withholding food for a certain number of hours before the trial, or by a given percent of body weight loss after an organism has been on a schedule of food deprivation.

In this framework, instead of saying that hunger *motivated* the animal to work for food, they say that food deprivation made food a more effective reinforcer, as shown by more rapid responding. Deprivation, amount and type of food, and rate of response are all overt, observable, measurable events. Consequences, too, can be defined empirically. A *reinforcer* (or *reinforcing stimulus*) is defined as: *any stimulus that follows a response and increases the probability of its occurrence*. If getting food as a result of opening a latch makes the latch-opening response more probable next time, then getting food is a reinforcer.

The basic operant conditioning paradigm

Operant conditioning is the process by which behavior can be modified or controlled through environmental manipulations. The simple empirical statement for how this happens is:

If an operant response is emitted and followed by a reinforcing stimulus, the probability that it will occur again is increased $R \longrightarrow S^R$

Those responses that have favorable environmental consequences are more likely to recur, and to do so at higher rates, than those that have no positive effect on the environment. But the concept of reinforcement is not linked to any presumed drive states or "satisfactions." A *reinforcer* is simply defined empirically and pragmatically as any stimulus event that increases the probability of occurrence of any response. The relationship between the response and the reinforcer is arbitrary, and a stimulus is called a "reinforcer" only *after* it has been shown to influence the rate of responding. It is the claim of operant conditioning that *any response that can be reinforced quickly can be conditioned*. This rivals in significance the claim of respondent conditioning that *anything the organism can perceive can become a conditioned stimulus*.

The terms *instrumental* and *operant conditioning* are used interchangeably by many psychologists because they both refer to reinforced voluntarily emitted behavior. Skinnerians, however, prefer the term *operant* because *instrumental* is too mentalistic, implying a future-oriented purpose; "the organism does something in order to get a reward." Another distinction between these similar types of learning is the instrumental paradigm typically studies a single response in a *discrete trial* experiment. Success or failure, speed, magnitude of a response are investigated by putting the organism in a special apparatus (such as a maze or puzzle box) for a specific time period over a preset number of trials. When the subject makes the response the trial is over. In the operant paradigm what is studied are changes in rate of responding of a *freely available* response. Stuttering, gesturing, swallowing while reading, and using plural nouns in speech are some examples of responses whose operant level might be studied or modified in human subjects. The major differences between respondent and operant conditioning are summarized for your convenience in the chart. ▲

Stimulus control of behavior

If the individual already "knows" *how* to make the operant response (to make sounds, move, jump, push, pull, peck, etc.), what does it have to learn? Operant learning consists of two elements: learning *when* to emit a response that is likely to be reinforced and *what form* the response must take for reinforcing consequences to follow it. The first element involves the concept of the *discriminative stimulus*, the second entails the concepts of *behavioral contingencies* and *reinforcement schedules*.

From all the available stimuli in their environment, animals and humans learn to identify—to *discriminate*—those particular ones that are signals for (correlated with) reinforcers that will come when they emit an operant response. These signals are called *discriminative stimuli* (symbolized as S^D); they inform the organism of when a response will (or will not) be followed by a payoff. A discriminative stimulus "sets the stage" or "provides the occasion" for the organism to emit a voluntary operant response. It does not elicit the response in the sense that a bright light elicits an eye blink but simply signals, in effect, "If you do it now, you can get a reinforcer."

▲
Respondent vs. operant conditioning

	Respondent (Pavlovian, Classical)	**Operant (Skinnerian, Instrumental)**
Type of response	Involuntary, related to biological survival, produces change in organism, elicited by stimulus	Voluntary, operates on environment, emitted by organism
Contingencies	S–S, R–R	R→S, S→R
Preceding stimulus	Elicits response	Signals that reinforcement is available
Temporal relation of response to reinforcer (in acquisition)	Response follows	Response precedes
Functional relation of response to reinforcer	Presence of reinforcer independent of response	Presence of reinforcer contingent on response and changes probability of response
Timing between paired stimuli ($CS–UCS; S^D–S^R$)	Short, fixed	Variable, can be a long time
Training trials	Fixed by experimenter	Free to vary with subject's response

An extension of the basic operant conditioning paradigm that includes this discriminative stimulus is:

In the presence of a discriminative stimulus (S^D) an operant response (R) is followed by a reinforcing stimulus (S^R)

$$S^D{:}R \longrightarrow S^R$$

The dimming of lights in a public hall is the S^D for sitting in your seat, stopping talking, and attending to the (reinforcing, you hope) event about to unfold. Many professors who teach large lecture classes have difficulty getting their class started because they do not employ a salient, consistent discriminative stimulus that can be easily recognized—such as walking to the lectern and beginning to lecture immediately or turning off a tape of recorded "warm-up" music. One problem many students have on first dates is learning to "read" the discriminative stimuli projected by their date—they have to learn *when* it is OK to do what they already know how to do and receive the reinforcer they hope will be a consequence of doing it.

Those who use operant conditioning techniques are concerned with bringing responding under control of manipulable environmental stimuli. By controlling the reinforcing stimulus, they can control the rate or probability of a response. By controlling the appearance of the discriminative stimulus, they control when the response will be made. An organism is said to be "under stimulus control" when it responds consistently in the presence of a discriminative stimulus and not in its absence.

An organism's alertness to a discriminative stimulus can also be used to teach it to make discriminations between stimuli, even quite similar ones. The technique is to give reinforcement when responses are made in the presence of one stimulus but not when responses are made in the presence of the other. The first stimulus then becomes the *positive discriminative stimulus* (S^D), and the other becomes the *negative discriminative stimulus* ($S°$ or S^Δ, pronounced "ess delta"). After repeated discrimination training, responding occurs in the presence of S^D but not when S^Δ is present. In fact, psychologists often use this technique to find out whether organisms without language, infants and lower animals, can in fact distinguish between particular stimuli—between blue and green, for example, or between horizontal and vertical lines.

Does the discriminative stimulus, S^D, come to elicit the same behavior pattern as does the reinforcing stimulus? Sometimes. When a lighted key signals a food reinforcer, male pigeons direct hard, brief pecks at the key, similar to their eating responses. But if the lighted key signals water, the pigeons direct "soft, sipping" pecks at the key. And when the light signals access to a receptive female pigeon, the male directs "courting" responses to the key (Moore, 1973). So it appears as if S^D can develop substitute value for the reinforcer. But in several other studies, behavior in the presence of the discriminative stimulus did not resemble behavior directed toward the reinforcing stimulus. When baby chicks that have been artificially cooled are exposed to heat (as a reinforcer), they extend their wings and become immobile. However, when these same refrigerated chicks see a lighted key that signals the onset of heat, they approach, peck, and "snuggle" the key (Wasserman, 1973). In another study, the appearance of a fellow rat was made the discriminative stimulus for food. The hungry rat-subjects did not nibble at the S^D rat, but directed social responses toward it. When the S^D was a block of wood, however, the subject rats did not behave in this manner (Timberlake & Grant, 1975). Thus operant conditioning involves not just an isolated response, but a *system* of behaviors typical for a given species that are commonly related to the reinforcing stimulus and the discriminative stimulus.

Behavioral contingency

At the time you are making any response, many environmental events are occurring. Indeed, the environment is constantly changing even when you are *not* responding. How, then, do you know which events your behavior is affecting? It is generally agreed that you can say that an environmental event is *contingent* on your behavior if it follows that behavior with some degree of regularity (a high probability but not necessarily 100 percent).

The idea of *behavioral contingency* is perhaps the most important concept in operant conditioning. When a reinforcer is made contingent on (available only after) a desired response, that response becomes more probable. By setting up different contingencies—different relationships between responses and reinforcers—those who use the operant conditioning approach can make a given response more or less probable over time. They do this through changing the timing and frequency of events known to be reinforcers, making them available after the desired response but not at other times.

Operant conditioners assume that any response that keeps occurring is being maintained by a payoff of some kind. (See *P&L* Close-up, Superstition or Playing It Cautious?) Even responses that have obviously undesirable consequences, including personal suffering and sometimes the possibility of death, are maintained because of some prevailing source of reinforcement. The class clown accepts punishment from the teacher as long as he or she continues to receive the attention of classmates. For some people sympathy and pity from others are sufficient reinforcement to sustain whatever life-style supports such social reinforcers. To modify undesirable behaviors (such as aggression, addictive responses, poor study habits, littering, and others), we must first discover what the existing payoff is, and then change the response-reinforcement contingency. To alter the way people behave, existing environmental contingencies have to be changed and new ones substituted.

Take the case of Rorey B., a preschool child of average intelligence who was a "behavior problem." He screamed, fought, disobeyed, and bossed others both at home and school—although he was only 4 years, 8 months of age. His parents were concerned over his obviously undesirable behavior which might be expected to get even worse as he grew older. "He continually told other children what to do and how to play, and enforced his demands with punches, kicks, and slaps" (p. 47). Observation of Mrs. B's interaction with her son revealed three things: (a) she reinforced this undesirable behavior with excessive attention; (b) she did not program consequences in a consistent fashion; and (c) the relationship between the undesirable behavior and any negative consequences was unclear because she frequently used lengthy explanations before applying the sanctions. The behavioral psychologists who consulted with Mrs. B. taught her to deliver three types of operant contingencies—punishment, extinction, and reward.

As soon as Rorey acted aggressively or disobediently Mrs. B. took him to a time-out (TO) room that contained no items of interest to a child. He was told only that he could not stay with the others if he fought or disobeyed. He was put in the TO room without conversation or further explanation, for a two-minute period (or two minutes from the end of his last cry or tantrum). This unavoidable aversive consequence of his undesirable behavior is a punishment contingency. When the time was up, Rorey was taken back to his regular activities without comment on the previous episode. Less serious forms of undesirable behavior were ignored, so they would have no reinforcing consequences— an extinction contingency. Finally, desirable behaviors such as cooperative play and following instructions were directly praised and at the end of each period of desirable play, Rorey got some special treats, cookies, cold drinks, toys, etc.—a positive reinforcement contingency.

To demonstrate the effectiveness of mother as behavior therapist, the psychologists

Close-up
Superstition or Playing It Cautious?

1

2

3

4

TON SMITS

Drawing by Ton Smits; © 1959, The New Yorker Magazine, Inc.

Perhaps the most fascinating relationship between responses and stimuli that follow them occurs when, in fact, *no relationship* exists between them, but the individual believes that one does. One day a tennis player, in dressing for the game, puts on his left sock, right sock, right shoe, and left shoe in that order. He then wins the game. Next time, he puts his socks and shoes on in a different order, and he loses the game. With as little as one "learning" trial, some people (including at least one well-known former tennis star) have come to believe that the outcome of their game was contingent on the behavior of putting on their socks and shoes in one fixed sequence.

Consider another example of this type of learning. A man who calls himself Orpheus tells you that he has the power to make the sun rise by singing to it. Being, by now, scientifically skeptical, you demand a demonstration of this environmental control. Orpheus begins to sing at about 5 A.M. and soon the sun rises. He can repeat this demonstration for you daily, showing that his response is always followed by this change in the environment. You now suggest another test; omit the singing and see if the sun still comes up. But Orpheus must reject such a test. The consequence of his not singing would surely be the sun's not rising, and for the sake of the world he dare not risk such a dire consequence.

This example can be seen as accidental operant strengthening of a *coincidental* relationship between behavior and reinforcers. The rituals gamblers use in trying to change their luck illustrate their learned belief that something they were doing caused the dice or cards to fall a certain way. Such accidentally conditioned responses are called *superstitions*.

When the environmental consequences are vital for an individual or a group, a superstitious response is extremely resistant to extinction. This is true for two reasons. First, as in the case of Orpheus, the risk involved in not making the response, *if* the connection *were* a causal one, would be greater than the gain in knowledge from finding out that one's behavior was not producing the effect. Second, if the individual believes the superstition is valid, omitting the "necessary" act might produce other changes in his or her behavior that *would* directly affect the event in question. This is often seen among students who have a special pen or pair of jeans that they always use for taking final exams. If the pen is lost, or the filthy jeans are thrown out by an exasperated parent, they may indeed do poorly on the exam because of expectation of failure and distracting thoughts about "their luck running out."

The development of such superstitions can be easily demonstrated in the laboratory. A hungry pigeon is confined in a box with a feeding mechanism that automatically dispenses a pellet of food every fifteen seconds, regardless of what the pigeon does. Whatever response the pigeon happens to be making when the food is delivered then becomes a reinforced repsonse, and the probability of its occurrence is increased. Different stereotyped behavior patterns are likely to emerge in different subjects—turning counterclockwise, turning in a circle several times before going to the food dispenser, jerking the head in one direction, as well as other "bizarre" movements.

first observed Rorey's behavior during a baseline period, then instructed Mrs. B. to carry out her behavioral contingency management program. This sequence was repeated a second time. Rorey's aggressive and disobedient behaviors were dramatically changed by manipulating their consequences. His parents and neighbors commented that Rorey behaved like a "different child." During the first baseline period Rorey followed only about thirty percent of instructions given him; but a week later was following three fourths of them. On some days Rorey never misbehaved at all, even resisting striking back when another child hit him. As Rorey's problem behaviors declined, his mother's comments about him became more favorable; she felt she was a more effective mother and he was shown more affectionate concern (Zeilberger, Sampen, & Sloane, 1968).

Five kinds of contingencies are possible between responses and reinforcers—three that increase the rate of an operant response and two that decrease it. Response rate *increases* when responding is followed by (a) a positive reinforcing stimulus, (b) escape from an aversive stimulus, or (c) avoidance of an aversive stimulus. The rate *decreases* when responding is followed by (d) an aversive stimulus *(punishment)* or (e) the absence of any reinforcer *(extinction)*. These five contingencies are diagrammed in the illustration. ■

Reinforcement scheduling

Every reinforcement is part of some schedule, whether systematically arranged or haphazard. Modification of behavior requires discovering the schedule currently controlling an individual's pattern of responding, and then changing it. (See *P&L* Close-up, Skinner's Box.)

■

Five contingencies in operant conditioning

1. Reward conditioning   increases operant rate

S^D	R	is followed by	S^{R+}
Discriminative Stimulus	Operant Response		Positive Reinforcing Stimulus
[coke machine]	[put coin in slot]		[get refreshing drink]

2. Escape conditioning   increases operant rate

S^D	R	is followed by	S^{R-}
Discriminative Stimulus	Operant Response		Negative Reinforcing Stimulus
[heat]	[fanning oneself]		[escape from heat]

An unpleasant situation (S^D) is escaped from by making a selected operant response. Escape is a reinforcing stimulus; it is called a *negative* reinforcing stimulus because it involves the *absence* of an unpleasant stimulus rather than the presence of a pleasant one.

3. Avoidance conditioning   increases operant rate

S^D	R	is followed by	S^{R-}
Discriminative Stimulus	Operant Response		Negative Reinforcing Stimulus
[in wartime sound of rocket with time-delay explosives]	[run for shelter]		[avoid effects of explosion]

A stimulus signals the organism that an unpleasant event will occur soon; responding in the time interval between the discriminative stimulus and the signaled event avoids the feared event altogether. In animal learning research, the S^D is typically a light which signals electric shocks.

4. Punishment   decreases operant rate

S^D	R	is followed by	S^A
Discriminative Stimulus	Operant Rate		Aversive Stimulus
[attractive match box]	[playing with matches]		[getting burned]

When punishment contingencies are used, the individual cannot escape or avoid but experiences the aversive event each time the response is made.

5. Operant extinction   decreases operant rate

R	is followed by	$\cancel{S^R}$
Conditioned Operant		No reinforcing stimulus

A conditioned operant that is emitted and is *not* followed by a reinforcing stimulus decreases in rate.

The "Skinner box" is designed for use with pigeons and delivers a pellet of food (via the lower opening) when the bird pecks the key.

Special apparatus, electronic programming equipment, and a unique means of recording changes in the response rate have been designed for investigating the stimulus conditions that modify the rate of operant responding. The apparatus (affectionately called a "Skinner box") is a highly simplified, restricted environment in which a variety of discriminative stimuli can be presented clearly without the distraction of other stimuli that would occur in the organism's natural environment. Lights, colors, or shapes are typical S^D (used with pigeons, the typical subject in this research) and are presented on illuminated disks. The operant response of pecking a disk or pushing a lever is made more probable by having those items be the only aspects of the physical environment that the subject can easily manipulate, or operate upon. A food or water cup with a light to signal when a reinforcer is available in it, completes the Skinner box.

Electronic programming equipment precisely controls the presentation of stimuli, monitors responses, and delivers the reinforcers. It also can arrange complex patterns of reinforcement.

Response rate is conveniently measured by a cumulative recorder, which plots each response as it occurs. A pen is placed against a roll of paper which is moving at a constant speed. Each time the subject makes a response, the pen moves upward a little. The more responses made in a given time period, the more accumulated upward steps of the pen will be recorded on the section of paper that has moved past it during that interval.

Time passing is thus shown by horizontal distance on the line; responses, by vertical distance. A high rate of responding gives a steep cumulative curve; a low rate of responding gives a less steep one.

It is also possible to look at the shape *(topography)* of a cumulative curve and see how the rate of responding has changed during the time interval recorded. Typically in a new situation, the curve goes up very slowly and irregularly at first, and there may be long pauses between responses; during these pauses, the recording pen simply moves horizontally along the paper. Then as learning proceeds, the cumulative curve shows less variability and becomes steeper. A skilled researcher can read a subject's response curve much like an X-ray plate, to see the changes over time and compare the behavioral effects of different patterns of reinforcement. A few typical response curves are shown below (note that the "jagged" lines made by the jumps of the response pen have been smoothed out).

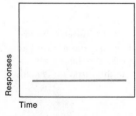

No Response

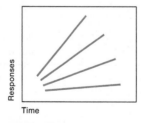

**Four Examples
of Responding at a Steady Rate**
(the steeper the line,
the more rapid the rate)

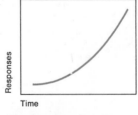

Accelerating Rate
(responding more and more rapidly
across time)

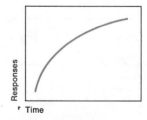

Decelerating Rate
(responding less and less rapidly
over time)

*Note: Curve never goes down
except when pen is reset
at bottom of the page.*

Many years ago, when the young B.F. Skinner was secluded in his laboratory over a long weekend, he stumbled by accident onto an important discovery: namely, that there are times when less of a good thing is better. Realizing that he hàd not stocked up enough food pellets for his hard-working animals, Skinner decided to make do by giving them a pellet only after every second correct response. Surprisingly, he found no difference in learning rate. *Partial reinforcement* appeared to be as effective as *continuous reinforcement* (one response, one pellet). But the real discovery came when the subjects were put through *extinction training*. When the reinforcers were withdrawn altogether, the subjects that had been conditioned with partial reinforcement kept responding longer than did those who had gotten their payoff after every correct response. *Acquisition of responding under conditions of partial reinforcement made responding more resistant to extinction!* This is called the *partial reinforcement effect*. It has been found repeatedly with many different animal species, including humans.

Thus, if you want someone to continue to emit a response when you are no longer around to reinforce it, it is better to have programmed your reinforcers from the beginning so that they were part of a partial schedule of reinforcement. Once we recognize the principle that reinforcers on other than a one-to-one relationship with responses can control responding in predictable ways, we can inquire into what ways different *schedules of intermittent reinforcement* affect behavior.

Ratio schedules   Reinforcers delivered on ratio schedules establish how much work must be done for a given payoff. Ratio schedules can be fixed or variable. A *fixed ratio (FR) schedule* provides for a constant number of work units to be exchanged for one reinforcer. It is like getting paid for piecework; you get a standard fee for every five new customers you sign up (FR-5), a dollar for every ten newspapers sold (FR-10), and so forth. In the laboratory, a pigeon might have to peck a key anywhere from two to over a hundred times before getting a single pellet. "FR-25," for example, would be laboratory shorthand for "one reinforcement for each twenty-five responses." Winning the Perfect Attendance Award is on an FR schedule of the total number of days you must come to class before receiving the reinforcer. FR schedules produce very high rates of responding in the laboratory, as can be seen from the cumulative record shown in the diagram. Subjects learn to depend on such schedules.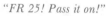

But the world is not always arranged in so orderly a fashion as described by fixed ratios. Sometimes the world is a slot machine—you cannot tell whether one or a few or only a great many responses will eventually result in hitting the jackpot. As long as you occasionally get a payoff, this *variable ratio (VR) schedule* will keep you responding at a high rate for a long time. A VR-10 schedule would mean that *on the average*, reinforcement would follow every tenth response. But it might come after only one response, and not again until after twenty. VR schedules keep you guessing when the payoff is likely to occur. For some people such guessing on the VR payoff represents an exciting gamble.

Interval schedules   It may be not *how much* work you do that brings the reinforcement but *when* you do it. Learning to look busy when the authority (employer, lab instructor, police officer, head resident) makes the rounds may be enough to assure getting your just rewards. When reinforcement is set on a *temporal* basis, it is being given at a single time for all the responses during the preceding interval.

"FR 25! Pass it on!"

Typical curves for different reinforcement schedules

These are typical "idealized" curves that have come to be identified with the main kinds of reinforcement schedules. These records are characteristic whether the subject is a rat or a pigeon or a child.

Both the ratio schedules typically maintain a high level of responding, as shown in the steepness of the curves. Interval schedules generally maintain a moderate rate of responding. The fixed interval schedule typically yields the "scalloped" curve shown here, reflecting the fact that the subject virtually stops responding after a reinforcement and waits until near the next scheduled reinforcement before responding actively again.

It is also possible, by reinforcing a low rate of responding, to get the almost flat curve of response shown here.

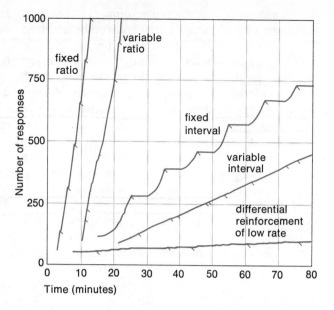

There are two types of interval schedules, fixed and variable. In a *fixed interval (FI) schedule*, reinforcers are delivered at a predictable time, regardless of how many previous responses have been made, as long as at least one occurs at the end of the time interval. Getting paid once a week for salaried workers represents an FI-1 week. Giving yourself a treat after every two hours of studying puts your study behavior on an FI-2 hours schedule.

FI schedules reveal a typical, but peculiar curve with a "scalloped" form. After each reinforced response, the subject ceases relevant responding for a time and performs "time-out" responses (sometimes referred to technically as the "goofing-off response"). As the time for the next payoff approaches, relevant responding switches on and increases sharply until the reinforcement occurs. This effect is called "scalloping." It looks as if the subjects are learning to tell time. Work systems that employ long FI reinforcement schedules often use surveillance during the interval to keep the workers from dallying during the "time-out" period immediately following a reinforcement—the "Monday letdown" syndrome.

If reinforcement is given on a temporal basis but the interval varies from one time period to the next, it is called a *variable interval (VI) schedule*. One time you might have to wait a long time before getting a single reward; then you might get a second or third reward or more after only a short wait. But when you think you've "got it!" the next reward may be a long time in coming. This appears to be the reinforcement history of many people in the entertainment field. Trout fishermen, who also live by VI schedules and don't quit, probably learn "patience" as a by-product of such a schedule.

Schedules of reinforcement may occur in mixed forms and may be quite complex; those described here are only the most basic varieties. Schedules can be designed to generate high levels of responding or to ensure continuous, steady responding over time. ◆ Some schedules of reinforcement even suppress behavioral output, by reinforcing waiting and nonresponding. In fact, animals have even learned to run through a maze or down an alley at whatever specific speed yields a larger or more immediate reward (Logan, 1960, 1972).

Increasing reinforcer effectiveness

Knowledge of the schedule of reinforcement associated with a given behavior tells us much about what that behavior will look like. But it is not the whole story. We will be in a better position to predict and perhaps control behavior knowing three other facts about the reinforcement operations; whether they are delayed or immediate, conditioned or primary, self-determined or managed by someone else.

Delay of reinforcement: Late may not be better than never

Whatever the schedule of reinforcement, reinforcers, to be effective, must be "quick on the draw." The more prompt the better; in fact, if too much time elapses between the terminal response in a sequence of behavior and its reinforcement, the effect of reward is completely wasted.

One would think that educators would make use of this simple principle to be sure that good student performance was promptly reinforced, but alas, as your own reinforcement history probably illustrates, this is not so. Too often, reinforcement in the classroom comes long after the effort expended, and when it comes, it is often a general evaluative grade rather than specific informational feedback for particular responses. Immediate reinforcers thus provide not only satisfaction, but *information* as well about the correctness of the response.

In teaching situations where the delay of reinforcement is unavoidable, a teacher may still improve pupil performance by:

a. Making sure that the correct completion of the response is so clear and unambiguous that both teacher and pupil will recognize it when a "reinforceable response" occurs.
b. Making explicit the reinforcement contingencies so that they never appear arbitrary or inconsistent but are seen as predictably dependent on particular behavior.
c. Using language and other reminders to establish the symbolic connection for the learner between a late-approaching reward and the long-gone response.
d. Employing conditioned reinforcers to "stand in" for the primary reinforcer along the way.

Conditioned, or secondary, reinforcers

Any perceived stimulus regularly associated with the primary reinforcing stimulus can develop reinforcing powers itself. When that stimulus maintains the behavior in the absence of the primary reinforcer, it is called a *conditioned reinforcer*, or *secondary reinforcer*. Primary reinforcers usually have biological significance for the organism (just as the UCS does in classical conditioning). Food, water, escape from cold or noise, sex are some potent primary reinforcers. Q: What is an example of a conditioned reinforcer? A: Any stimulus can become one through contiguity with the primary reinforcer. The sound of the electronic programming equipment as it delivers a food pellet to the organism in the Skinner box could become a conditioned reinforcer.

If baby's approach in the presence of a smile is repeatedly followed by a tasty treat, the smile will become a conditioned reinforcer for approach even in the absence of the treat (approach→smile→treat). In fact, in highly developed countries, such conditioned reinforcements are far more important in controlling behavior than primary reinforcers that have biological consequences. Just consider, for example, the variety of responses you will emit to obtain a rectangular piece of green paper with the picture of a certain United States President on it.

Smiles, nods, pats on the back, and money all represent a class of *generalized conditioned reinforcers* that can be used to control a wide range of responding. These stimulus events are usually paired with many primary reinforcers; for example, the list of reinforcers we could get in exchange for money is virtually endless. After a while, money becomes a reinforcer that will maintain a high level of responding even when the person hoards it, and doesn't exchange it for pleasures of the mind, body, or flesh. Misers (hoarders) are people who treat the generalized reinforcer of money as though it had biological significance.

Although conditioned reinforcers are more variable than primary reinforcers in their effect on learning, they are often more effective for a teacher or experimenter to use because: (a) they can be dispensed rapidly, (b) they are portable, (c) almost any available stimulus event can be used for a conditioned reinforcer, (d) they often do not lead to satiation, (e) their reinforcing effect may be more immediate since it depends only on perception and not on biological processing of primary reinforcers.

We will see in subsequent chapters that the principle of reinforcing behavior with tokens exchangeable later for a variety of tangible rewards is now being used extensively in behavioral modification programs with both children and adults.

Self-management of reinforcers

The final issue to be raised in our introduction to operant conditioning is perhaps the most important one of all: *who is the contingency manager?* Does it make a difference if I reinforce your desirable responding or you reinforce yourself? Despite the professed value of student *self-reliance,* aren't most of the rewards you get (or fail to obtain) administered by an external agent of rein-

▲
Reinforcement schedules

Children who set their own reinforcement standards made more responses during extinction than did their peers, an effect which can be seen in the graph. Note also the partial reinforcement effect operating for both self-selected and other-determined schedules of reinforcement (FR-4 is more resistant to extinction than FR-2, which in turn is more persevering than FR-1).

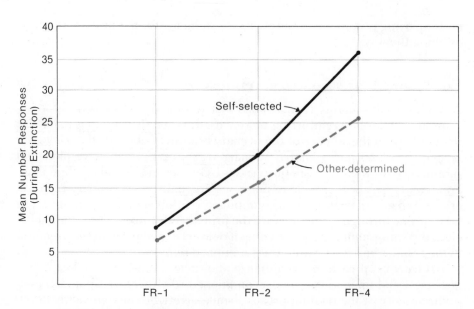

Based on Weiner & Dubanoski, 1975.

forcement? Two studies indicate why self-determined schedules of reinforcement are desirable. The first showed that self-imposed contingencies set by a student improved academic performance more than did teacher-imposed contingencies. It mattered more whether the contingency manager was the student than what the contingency system was or even the magnitude of reinforcement delivered by the teacher. "It appeared that, for the students in this study, being allowed to *choose* (even between two academic tasks) was the critical variable" (Lovitt & Curtiss, 1969, p. 53).

In the second study, children allowed to set their own standards for reinforced performance exhibited a greater resistence to extinction than did children upon whom the same standards were externally imposed by the experimenter-teacher (Weiner & Dubanoski, 1975). ▲

This research moves us toward another set of questions about the optimal conditions for learning new behaviors, maintaining effective old ones, and getting rid of self-defeating patterns of behavior that make you "sad," "bad," or "mad." In the next chapter we shall build substantially upon the basic foundation laid by these principles of respondent and operant conditioning. In doing so, we will want to build high enough to truly appreciate the panorama of the infinite possibilities open to us as learning animals.

Chapter summary

In order to survive, any organism must be capable of learning: (a) what things in the environment are related and (b) how its own actions affect and are affected by environmental events. Such learning enables the organism to make predictions about future events and to use the environment to meet its needs.

While studying salivation in dogs, Ivan Pavlov discovered the *respondent conditioning paradigm*. A stimulus that regularly elicits a reflex response prior to learning is called an *unconditioned stimulus* (UCS or US). A neutral stimulus that repeatedly occurs just before the onset of a UCS acquires the ability to elicit the response, thereby becoming a *conditioned stimulus* (CS). In *respondent (classical) conditioning*, one stimulus comes to substitute for another as a signal that a pleasant event (perhaps food) or an aversive event (perhaps electric shock) is imminent. The original reflex response is called an *unconditioned response* (UCR or UR). When it is elicited by the new signal, the response is called a *conditioned response* (CR). Not only physical stimuli but words and other symbols as well may become conditioned stimuli.

In a conditioning situation there is a generalized increase in *excitability*. The most favorable *interval* between onset of the CS and onset of the US is half a second. *Stimulus generalization* typically occurs, in which not only the precise conditioned stimulus but other stimuli somewhat similar to it also elicit the response. With continued trials in which reinforcement occurs only after the exact CS, the organism comes to respond only to the correct stimulus and to make only the precise response through *discrimination* and *inhibition of competing responses*. *Higher-order conditioning* may occur, in which the conditioned stimulus rather than the unconditioned stimulus serves as reinforcement in establishing second-order association. *Extinction,* due to active inhibition of the response, occurs after conditioning when the conditioned stimulus is regularly *not* followed by the unconditioned stimulus. *Spontaneous recovery* of the response can occur after a rest period following lengthy extinction training. The *strength of conditioning* can be measured by *resistance to extinction* as well as by *amplitude of response, latency of response,* or *frequency of response.* In *pseudoconditioning,* there is a change in the strength of responding for some reason other than learning.

Past conditioning can leave unfortunate and often unrecognized effects. When a conditioned animal is forced to make finer and finer discriminations, the original conditioned discrimination may be lost and an *experimental neurosis* may appear. Conditioned fear reactions will not extinguish unless the CS is experienced safely or *counterconditioning* takes place. Sometimes elements of a conditioned response (such as changes in blood pressure) remain after the primary muscular or glandular response has been extinguished. Overeating, alcoholism, and drug addiction may also be the results of conditioning.

Conditioning based on the consequences of behavior was first studied by E. L. Thorndike with hungry cats confined in puzzle boxes. Here behavior is instrumental in reaching a goal; it is *emitted* by the organism rather than *elicited* by a stimulus; and reinforcement is given only if a particular response is made. To explain such *instrumental conditioning,* Thorndike postulated a *law of effect:* that the feeling of satisfaction following a successful response made the response more likely next time.

B. F. Skinner, a pioneer in the experimental analysis of behavior, and his followers hold that learning can and should be described entirely in terms of observable behavior. They study *operant conditioning,* which differs slightly from instrumental conditioning in that rate of responding rather than the occurrence of a single response is measured. The operant conditioning paradigm holds that if a response is followed by a *reinforcing stimulus,* the probability of its reoccurrence is increased.

A *discriminative stimulus* (S^D) is one that signals the availability of a reinforcer; rate of responding increases in its presence. A *negative discriminative stimulus* (S^Δ) sets the occasion for a low rate of responding. A discriminative stimulus may itself become reinforcing; it is then said to be a *conditioned,* or *secondary, reinforcer.*

Behavior can be changed by setting up different *contingencies* (relationships between responses and reinforcers). Five such contingencies are possible. Response rate increases when responding is followed by a *positive* reinforcing stimulus or by *escape* from or *avoidance* of an aversive stimulus; it decreases when followed by an aversive stimulus (*punishment*) or no reinforcer (*extinction*).

Responses learned under *partial reinforcement* are more resistant to extinction than those acquired with *continuous reinforcement.* A learned response can be maintained on schedules of *intermittent reinforcement.* Four such schedules are *fixed ratio, variable ratio, fixed interval,* and *variable interval* schedules; each induces a characteristic pattern of responding. The more prompt and specific the reinforcement, the more effective it will be in increasing rate of responding. *Conditioned reinforcers,* such as money or approval, may come to be as powerful as primary (physical) reinforcers. Self-management of reinforcers can be a powerful means of bringing about changes in one's own behavior.

Changing Patterns of Human Behavior

The anticipated arrival of a recently captured savage child had all Paris buzzing with excitement. The child, now perhaps twelve, had first been seen five years earlier running naked in the woods. He apparently lived alone surviving on a meager diet of acorns, roots, and maybe some wild game. Two dozen scars on his body bore evidence of battles with other animals who also inhabited the woods of Aveyron. After being seized by several sportsmen, he escaped but was retaken. The boy remained "equally wild and shy," so the account goes, "impatient and restless, continually seeking escape."

A perceptive minister of state, hearing of the adventure of this "Wild Boy of Aveyron," ordered him brought to Paris. It was hoped that observation of this part beast – part human "would throw some light upon the science of the mind." Back in the fall of 1800, when our story takes place, psychology could hardly qualify as a science. It was at best a combination of philosophy and medicine that included some uncontrolled observation of human behavior.

The discovery of this wild boy was greeted as an opportunity to evaluate Rousseau's claim that society was a contaminating influence. He argued that a primitive specimen of humanity would be a "noble savage." To the contrary, the portrait of this savage child was anything but noble. He was described as:

A disgustingly dirty child affected with spasmodic movements and often convulsions who swayed back and forth ceaselessly like certain animals in the menagerie, who bit and scratched those who opposed him, who showed no sort of affection for those who attended him; and who was in short indifferent to everything and attentive to nothing (Itard, reprinted 1962, p. 3; see also Lane, 1976).

Expert opinion declared him to be "an incurable idiot." Fortunately, a young doctor, Jean Marc Itard, accepted the challenge of trying to transform this subnormal organism into a normally functioning human being. Itard was an extreme environmentalist, who perhaps went overboard in his naive belief in philosopher John Locke's empiricism. If "sense provides all," Itard reasoned, and humanity is a product of civilizing experiences, then proper training was the key to reclaiming the mind of this savage. Itard believed further that by observing what "so surprising a creature" lacked, it would be possible to deduce the "hitherto uncalculated sum of knowledge and ideas which man owes to his education."

The first few years of Itard's patient and ingenious training of his pupil, whom he named Victor, were quite successful. The boy learned to speak a few words, "lait" (milk) and "Oh Dieu" (O God), and comprehend a great many instructions and commands. Itard reports that "multiplying the sensations and ideas of our savage have contributed powerfully to the development of his intellectual faculties; . . . furthermore, he has both a knowledge of the conventional value of the symbols of thought and the power of applying it by naming objects, their qualities, and their actions" (p. 101). He kept himself clean, developed his previously dull senses, and was generally affectionate and good mannered. He finally learned one of the most difficult lessons humanity teaches, to act morally from a feeling of justice and to act against instances of injustice.

But sad to tell, this initial success did not continue. After five years of training, Victor had not progressed much further. He never learned to talk nor to behave in all the ways that would make him "just like any other teenager." Disappointed, Itard gave up his hope of fully changing the patterns of Victor's behavior. "Unhappy creature, since my labors are wasted and your efforts fruitless, take again the road to your forest and the taste for your primitive life" (p. xvii).

Why had these years of learning failed to change Victor's behavior more completely? There are many possibilities. The new environmental inputs may have come too late to be of optimal value in affecting the child's thinking and actions. Victor may actually have been mentally defective and abandoned by his parents for that reason. Thus there may have been a relatively low limit to his capabilities to learn even with the best of teachers. But then again, teaching methods at the time were far from ideal. With what is known today about the principles of learning, and about sign-language aquisition in the deaf and in primates, Victor might have made considerably more progress.

Nevertheless, the case of Victor, the wild boy of Aveyron, is an important milestone in our psychological journey. It highlights the role of learning in changing behavior. It also suggests that there are limits to this modifiability of behavior. Limits may be set by heredity, by brain damage, and by development stages of the child. These issues will be treated in subsequent chapters. Itard's success with teaching Victor to learn concepts, to reason, and to solve problems underscores that basic property of the human mind, complex information processing.

Before we turn to examine in detail what is now known about behavior change, we should mention Itard's lasting influence. Dr. Itard later became the teacher of Edouard Séguin, who developed techniques for educating feeble-minded children. Maria Montessori was, in turn, influenced by Séguin. Her methods of early childhood education, which are now widely practiced in many countries, owe an intellectual debt to the pioneering efforts of our young Paris doctor. He may have failed to realize his expectations to teach the savage to be like other children. However, his ideas and example of dedicated teaching have had a lasting effect on education and educators. And, of course, education is one arena in which psychological knowledge of learning and information processing is put to practical use.

Controlling human behavior

Suppose you should be charged with the task of educating another savage child. What principles of behavior change will you use? You already have some knowledge of the fundamentals of respondent and operant conditioning that will come in handy, but you'll need to know more. How will you elicit the first response that you are ready to follow with an immediate reinforcer? Should you punish the child for making errors? How will you get more complex sequences of behavior and novel patterns of responding? These questions lead us first to an analysis of procedures for behavior control.

Behavior changes when we change its effects, the conditions that elicit it, or the setting in which it occurs. The psychology of learning is an analysis of the *relatively permament* changes in behavior that occur when an organism is exposed to environmental conditions that alter the consequences, the antecedents, or the context of the behavior. We know that certain stimuli presented after a response make it more likely that the response will occur again. Stimuli that function in this way to maintain responding or to increase the tendency or strength of the response are termed *positive reinforcers*.

Four basic conditions of positive control that increase the effectiveness of reinforcers in influencing behavior were first outlined by Hull (1943). Up to some limit, instrumental responses are stronger: (a) the greater the number of times they have been reinforced (reinforcement frequency), (b) the sooner the response is followed by reinforcement (delay of reinforcement), (c) the larger the amount of reinforcement (quantity of reinforcement), and (d) the more attractive or desirable the reinforcer (quality of reinforcement). In short, response strength (learning) is given its biggest boost when *many good* reinforcers are *repeatedly given immediately* after the correct response occurs.

New responses through operant procedures

How does anyone learn a *new* response pattern if operant conditioning requires that the correct response be emitted before it can be reinforced? In this section we will examine procedures that increase the likelihood of getting that first response emitted so that reinforcement can be given. Then we want to inquire into the process by which a brand-new behavior that is rarely or never emitted can be conditioned. Finally, we will discover how complex sequences of behavior are put together to form a reinforceable habit *pattern*.

Getting the first response

Let us assume that you are a benevolent parent, teacher, or animal trainer, and you have a pocketful of reinforcers you want to dispense—if only the individual will make the correct response. What procedures can you use to elicit the first correct response, so you can reinforce it and thus make it occur more frequently? This is a problem Pavlov never had because he was studying reflex responses that could always be produced by careful presentation of the proper eliciting stimulus.

This is a crucial and basic problem in learning, to which not enough attention has been given. All we will do here is outline and briefly comment on the possible effectiveness of several approaches. Some of the means of getting the individual to make that first correct response so you can reinforce it are: (a) increasing motivation; (b) lowering restraints; (c) structuring the environment; (d) forcing; (e) providing a model; (f) giving instructions; and (g) trial and error.

Each of these techniques has certain advantages and disadvantages, depending on whether you want only immediate results or more permanent, long-term ones. Because some of the consequences of applying these techniques are unintentionally negative, especially in the long run, you must be cautious in deciding which fits the particular learning situation best.

Increasing motivation   Prodding the organism into responding increases the probability that one of the responses will be the correct one. Electrifying a grid will get the rat moving about, and in the process it may discover an escape route. Threats and promises of future reward (called "incentive motivation") as well as deprivation states or noxious stimulation all may be successfully used to motivate action.

The general principle is that of increasing the activity level of the individual so that many responses are emitted. When the right one occurs, reinforce it promptly. Motivation need not be only deprivation of something that is desired or needed. Motivation can be provided through a challenge to one's mastery, a puzzle to be solved, a competition.

There are several possible negative consequences of such increases in motivation. It is not recommended where the individual does not have the ability to perform the response (like an infant who can not yet control muscles necessary to toilet training). It is not appropriate where the response is inhibited by a high level of fear (or avoidance motivation). Raising motivation under these circumstances increases the magnitude of conflict and the stress experience. When *external* motivation is introduced to get a person to perform a given task, he or she may have less self-generated motivation to do it another time.

Lowering restraints   If the organism has already learned the skills involved in making the correct response but does not emit it under motivating conditions, it may well be that the response is being inhibited or suppressed. Previously learned habits may be incompatible with emitting the desired response. The shy girl who knows the answer will not ever get reinforced for it unless she raises her hand and says it out loud. Fear of ridicule or anticipated rejection limits public responding even when there is the ability and desire to answer correctly. To get soldiers to kill, or medical students to dissect a cadaver, one must lower learned restraints against such "antisocial" behavior. Discovering the competing motives and weakening them, or finding out what reinforcers are maintaining the inhibitions on behavior and removing them, may help to induce the "desired" response. Thus, providing a supportive environment may help the shy boy or girl respond. On the negative side, whatever is inhibiting the behavior in question may also be holding in check other undesirable behaviors that you would *not* want to be released. Encouraging soldiers to kill in wartime may lower their restraints on using violence against enemies in civilian life.

Structuring the environment   Suppose you want two competitive children to learn to cooperate with each other. One way to encourage this type of responding is to place them in an area containing toys that can be manipulated only by two or more children. Or each child in a group might be given *part* of the total information necessary for effective team performance. Structuring the learning environment this way promotes cooperation in otherwise competitive environments (Aronson, 1978). If you want an animal to learn to press a bar or peck a key, you can make the behavior more likely by simplifying the environment to make the bar or key stand out more than other features of the environment. The simplicity of the Skinner box (p. 86) illustrates this principle.

The negative aspect of this approach is that it encourages dependence on a simple environment when the real world is filled with a multitude of complex stimuli. The individual may need to learn *what* to respond to, rather than how or when.

Forcing   Often the most efficient method of getting out that first correct response is to assist its execution physically. You take the child's hand with the spoonful of unfamiliar food and guide it mouthward. Then you reinforce putting-food-in-mouth (and, you hope, swallowing it) with praise or whatever. To teach a dog to roll over, trainers first provide a verbal cue, then physically roll the dog over and praise or feed it each time until it "catches on."

This rapid response elicitation technique probably has the worst long-term consequences for human learners, especially if they are involuntary or unwilling participants or if the individual using the technique is inept. Guiding a learner in a dance step could be helpful, but imagine how our shy student would feel toward the teacher who forced the response of answering in class by picking up her hand. Regardless of the subsequent reinforcement for the response, this crude type of forcing would likely develop negative emotional responses toward the teacher, deepen the sense of personal inadequacy, or lead the subject to make the correct response by rote without ever understanding the underlying principle involved.

Imitation

"Répétez, s'il vous plaît," says the French teacher, and the student attempts to imitate what the teacher has said—both the content and manner of delivery. Observational learning is also valuable where the details of a complex motor task cannot be easily communicated in words—as, for example, tying one's shoelaces, or hitting a baseball. This kind of learning is evidently important in the social learning of both animals and humans (as we shall detail in the next section).

On the other hand, overdependence on models (who usually are "authority figures") may limit one's own initiative and teach one to be a conformist. It may also lead to imitation of other responses made by the model. These may be responses correlated with the desired one, such as parents' poor speech habits, dialects, and so on. Or they may be unrelated responses that just happen to be emitted with high frequency by the model, such as statements of prejudice against minority groups.

Instruction

"Do what I say, not what I do," distinguishes this approach from the previous one. The ability to use language can clearly facilitate some kinds of learning. It can greatly accelerate elicitation of the first correct response. In fact, verbal instructions can be used not only to outline how the response should be made, but also to provide a description of the consequences that such responding will bring. Complex sequences may be communicated, as well as abstract principles. Information regarding delay of response, ways of using past learning, and instructions for the future are also verbally transmitted.

Naturally, following instructions presupposes understanding them, which is not always the case, as parents will testify who have tried in frustrating desperation to assemble a child's toy from the "easy-to-follow directions." Ambiguity in language usage, inadequate verbal or conceptual skills, and the occasional difference between what is said and what is actually meant may all reduce the effectiveness of verbal instruction for many potential learners. In addition, overly explicit instructions can lead in the long run to a learned dependence on being told exactly what to do and how to do it. The result is a loss of intellectual curiosity and a fear of taking risks, and a reliance on experts to provide the "approved solution" for you.

Trial and error

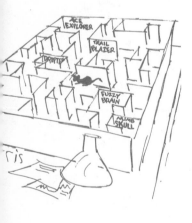

This "sink or swim," survival-of-the-fittest method is peculiar in a number of ways. It is one of the least effective techniques for getting out that first correct response, but it may have the most desirable long-term consequences when it works. It is a decidedly undemocratic, elitist approach, for those who succeed are few. For these few, however, reinforcement is great indeed (your A is more valued when everyone else barely got B's and C's). Furthermore, not only the correct response, but the entire process of searching for a solution, has been reinforced. Thus successful learners are encouraged to raise their level of aspiration, take more chances, and be more independent. But what about their unsuccessful peers?

For the many people whose trials end only in more errors, reinforcement for correct responding never comes. The effort and curiosity involved in the behavior are likely to undergo experimental extinction. This is especially true when grading is on a curve and half the members of a class are doomed to "below average" grades. On the other hand, a noncompetitive trial-and-error "inquiry" approach, with a watchful teacher to help structure the search so that students are constantly reaching beyond past achievements—but not too far beyond—can enable searchers to get enough reinforcement along the way to keep them going.

Shaping behavior by successive approximations

The technique used to create a new behavioral response is called *shaping. Shaping is an operant conditioning method to produce new behaviors by differentially reinforcing elements of behavior that approximate the specific behavior desired.* The specific behavioral outcome is the "target response." It is made up of elements or parts that the individual already can (and does) emit.

Initially, any element of the target response is reinforced. Then the criterion for reinforcement is raised; reinforcement follows only responses that are successively more similar to the target response. Finally, the individual must put all the parts together, or make the total response in a specific way in order to get a reinforcement. This technique of reinforcing behavioral elements that are approximations to the target response is called *successive approximation.* In this way, complex behavioral skills may be built upon rather simple initial responses.

To shape some desired behavior, you must attend to several points: determine what is an effective reinforcer for the particular individual; deliver it quickly according to a systematic schedule; clearly specify the target (goal) behavior; gradually raise the criterion for reinforcement as each sub-goal response is mastered.

In seminars, for example, teachers would like to reinforce the complex response of: listening to the discussion, thinking, formulating a reply or point of view, raising one's hand to be noticed, delivering a clear statement of an interesting, creative, or perceptive contribution. However, if we waited around until that entire composite target behavior occurred, our M&Ms would be stale or the term would be over. Instead, the teacher begins by reinforcing any part of this total response. Then the reinforcement criterion is raised for both the quality of the response and its integrated pattern.

All complex skills that we possess started out as simple responses that were nurtured into maturity through shaping. Proficiency in sports, in foreign languages, dancing, skateboarding, driving a car, and even the intimate pattern of responding between lovers are the product of intentional or accidental shaping. Intentional shaping involves the systematic progression toward a target behavior according to the procedures outlined here. Shaping also can occur accidentally. People with sufficient skill to get reinforced for early responses can progress rapidly to subsequent approximations without planned intervention by a reinforcing agent-coach. Most of us learned to speak our native language by accidental shaping.

Behavior chaining

Shaping transforms simple, crude actions into a complex and sophisticated behavioral response. To perform a *sequence* of integrated responses requires another operant conditioning technique, *behavior chaining.* You have undoubtedly seen trained animals on TV performing remarkable feats in which only the last response was followed by the carrot, sugar cube, or fish tidbit. An experimental demonstration of the procedure involved in producing such smart animals would show that the key ingredient is the patience and operant conditioning skill of the *trainer,* not the intelligence of the trainee.

Pierrel and Sherman (1963) were able to turn a rather commonplace little rat, "Barnabus," into an exotic performer, just as Professor Higgins did with his street waif in *My Fair Lady.* Barnabus learned to: (a) climb a spiral staircase, (b) cross a narrow drawbridge, (c) ascend a ladder, (d) pull a toy car over by a chain, (e) jump into the car, (f) pedal it to a second ladder, (g) climb this ladder, (h) crawl through a tube, (i) board an elevator, (j) pull a chain that raised a flag and that lowered him back to the starting platform, where he could (k) press a lever delivering a tiny food pellet and, after eating the food, to start all over again to climb the spiral staircase, and so on.

To teach Barnabus to go through this remarkable sequence, the experimenters started not at the beginning of it but at the end. First Barnabus learned to press the lever to get food pellets. Next, they put him in the elevator, which, when lowered, gave him access to the food lever. Once he learned that elevator rides were followed by such happy results—and then how to achieve them by pulling a chain—it was no trick to get Barnabus to crawl through a tunnel to reach the elevator. And, similarly for each component earlier in the chain. Individual parts of the responses that were not originally in Barnabus' repertoire sometimes had to be induced by one or more of the ways to elicit novel responses we examined earlier. Approximations of the desired responses were then shaped toward the precise action desired. Eventually each link in the behavior chain became a *discriminative stimulus* for the next response and a *conditioned reinforcer* for the preceding one.

Stimulus control

Behavior is not changed only by its consequences; it is also affected by other stimuli present at the time the response is or is not reinforced. In the previous chapter, we learned that behavior was said to be under stimulus control when an available stimulus "set the occasion" for reinforcement of responding. The response of asking for a favor is more likely to be reinforced if the person asked has been smiling rather than scowling. In this case smiling becomes a discriminative stimulus (S^D) while scowling is the S^Δ associated with nonreinforcement.

Effective salespeople learn to read subtle cues that signal when responding will or won't pay off. Similarly, defensive football alignments are often designed to give the opposing quarterback a *false* reading of the pattern that will set the occasion for a response that has been reinforced in the past.

As we have seen (p. 82), the controlling power of a given stimulus can be increased by *discrimination training,* in which stimuli similar to the S^D are introduced into the situation. Responding in the presence of these similar stimuli is not reinforced, while responding in the presence of the S^D is. One problem using stimulus control in everyday settings outside the laboratory is getting the learner to attend to the appropriate stimulus dimension and perceive what the S^D is when it is part of a complex stimulus context. Controlled laboratory studies, as in the environment of the Skinner box, allow the relevant stimulus to stand out and be attended to because there are few competing stimuli. By contrast, in the "stimulus-rich" environment of the classroom or home the stimuli which signal the availability of reinforcers may be obscured by contextual features or a host of distracting stimuli. A rise in the inflection of the teacher's voice at the end of the sentence indicates a question. It is generally for you to respond with a well-thought-out answer and be reinforced. But some questions are rhetorical, meant for you to think about as the teacher answers. Or the same voice pattern may be an indication of anxiety on the teacher's part, with no question intended. Or it might be used as a sarcastic device.

Learning often demands a highly specific response be made to a stimulus of a particular value. The same response to a slightly different stimulus won't be reinforced, nor will a slightly different response to the same stimulus. The individual forms a discrimination that is as fine as the learning situation calls for (required for reinforcement) and his or her sensory system permits. For example, we learn how tightly to screw on a bottle cap so that it won't leak but also so it won't be impossible to unscrew. We clap to signal our approval of a performance, but not in church, nor during the pause between movements of a symphony.

Discrimination is thus vital in focusing our perceptual and motor systems to the relevant dimensions of the learning task. However, for something learned in a given setting to be useful, it must be performed in other appropriate settings. No two settings are ever quite identical. *Generalization* is the process which enables us to perform the learned response in settings comparable to, but not identical with, the original learning environment. In generalization, a range of stimulus values similar to the originally conditioned stimulus will elicit the response. And a range of response values similar to the originally reinforced one are enacted and reinforced. Thus though the setting changes, the basic pattern of learning is maintained. So in therapy, for example, the new adaptive coping responses and social skills the client learns must generalize beyond the therapy setting. The learning must extend to the client's home and work setting if it is to be of value. We will see in Chapter 20 how therapists attempt to increase the generalizability of responses learned in therapy so that they will occur in their patients' everyday settings.

Aversive control procedures

Positive control procedures promote desirable responding by making stimulus *presentation* contingent upon the correct action. To stop undesirable responding, aversive control is used instead. Aversive control hurts. Either painful physical stimuli (electric shock, noise, or slaps in the face, for example) or threats of them ("I'm going to spank you") may be part of an aversive control procedure. Painful social stimuli such as ridicule or rejection may sometimes be even more powerful controlling agents.

It appears that the various forms of aversive procedures . . . will continue to be used in the future by parents, teachers, employers, and institutions to control human behavior.
Williams, 1973

Escape and avoidance

There are three aversive control paradigms: escape, avoidance, and punishment. In escape and avoidance conditioning behavior that effectively *terminates* the source of aversive stimulation is strengthened and maintained. This is called *negative reinforcement.* The child is hit until he admits that he broke the vase. The parent is thus setting up an *escape conditioning* situation. The child's confession results in terminating the aversive stimulation from the parent. It is a negatively reinforced response. But if the parent can't catch up to the swifter child to deliver the painful stimulation, *avoidance conditioning* takes place. The child's confession—made at a distance—prevents the presentation of the bad strokes. If the aversive stimulus is really painful, then only a few exposures to it might be sufficient to condition escape or avoidance responses to it.

In contrast to negative reinforcement is the punishment paradigm, in which an aversive stimulus *follows* (is contingent upon) a given response. If the punishing stimulus is sufficiently painful or unpleasant, the response (throwing a ball in the house) will be *terminated, reduced,* or at least *suppressed* in the presence of the punishing agent. In a later section we will discuss the pros and cons of using punishment to control behavior; for now, we will concentrate on several features of the escape and avoidance paradigms.

A neutral stimulus paired with a primary aversive stimulus becomes a *conditioned aversive stimulus*. It might be a light that precedes a shock, a squad car's siren that precedes getting a speeding ticket, a date's yawn that regularly precedes, "You better take me home, it's getting late." These warning stimuli help one anticipate the unpleasant event on its way. They may also provide time to alter behavior (or prepare a good alibi or line of defense).

Fear is the emotional response which is conditioned (according to respondent conditioning principles) to the warning stimulus (Mowrer, 1960). This fear motivates a wide range of responding to avoid or escape from the fear-producing stimulus. Because painful stimuli can be intense and applied suddenly (in contrast to most positive reinforcers), fear can be readily conditioned. Responses motivated by a fear-producing stimulus often resist experimental extinction. In the study cited on pp. 74–75, the dogs' perseverance was motivated only by the fear stimulus rather than the pain stimulus, since they avoided the danger side of the box so well that they never received any shocks.

Any response that reduces this learned fear will be repeated and become conditioned to cues that signal the fearful event. Suppose you anticipate an unpleasant scene at home when you report your poor grades. Worrying about the aversive stimuli you're going to receive gives you a headache and constricts your breathing. Because you are "sick," the aversive stimuli are not applied to you. What responses might you learn to generate (without conscious awareness) whenever you feel fearful and vulnerable? Maybe a little migraine or a bit of asthma. Some psychologists believe neurotic and psychosomatic symptoms are conditioned responses to actual, imagined, or symbolic stimuli. They persist because they reduce the person's fear or anxiety (Miller, 1959).

Learned helplessness

One animal, put into a compartment where it receives painful shocks, wisely and quickly exits by jumping over a barrier to get into the safe compartment of the shuttle box. However, a second animal put into the shock compartment does not even try to escape. It gives up, meekly resigning itself to the pain. What is making this dog helpless in the face of danger, while another of the same species reacts appropriately to escape danger? The answer can be found in the prior experience of the helpless animal. It had been previously conditioned in a Pavlovian harness which made it impossible to escape a painful shock that followed a conditioned tone. The dog was conditioned to respond to the tone alone, but it also learned an even more significant lesson—nothing it did had an effect on changing its traumatic environment. The aversive respondent conditioning taught the animal that its responses did nothing to stop the pain or even minimize its impact. Fear and a "sense of helplessness" took over. Later the animal was unable to learn escape responses, even when dragged over the escape barrier time after time. This phenomenon is called *learned helplessness*. It occurs when an organism has learned as a result of prior experience that its behavior has no effect on changing an aversive environment.

This research also showed that domesticated beagles were more susceptible to the conditions inducing helplessness than were mongrels of unknown history. These untamed dogs probably learned to persist, to survive in an environment that was hostile and not as predictable as that of the laboratory. Learned helplessness was eliminated when the dogs were given a means of controlling the shock (by pressing a panel) in the original shock harness situation. These dogs escaped normally when put in the shuttle box later. Their earlier experience carried over to the traumatic situation and they did not passively give up (Seligman & Maier, 1967; Overmier & Seligman, 1967). Seligman and his associates are showing that learned helplessness occurs in humans as well. When it does, there are clear parallels with one of the most widespread human psychiatric problems, *depression* (Seligman, 1975).

Punishment

The basic goals of even the most benevolent parents, teachers, and others involved in behavioral management are to *start* some behaviors, *maintain* some, and *stop* some others from occurring (especially at certain times and places). Positive reinforcement clearly is the most effective technique for the first two, starting and maintaining desired behavior — for getting something that is happening a little to happen more often or for getting a behavior you like to continue. But when you are trying to stop a persistent act that is for some reason undesirable, positive reinforcement alone may not be enough. In such cases, punishment is often used.

The principles of punishment are comparable to those of positive reinforcement, except that whereas positive reinforcement *increases* the probability of responding, punishment *decreases* it. But as we shall see, punishment in social situations can often have extremely undesirable side effects. Throughout the ages, the voices of philosophers and educators have been raised in controversy over whether punishment is the only way to "build character" or merely a destructive, if not downright sadistic, show of brute strength on the part of the punisher.

Punish the response, not the person   Perhaps some of the heated controversy over punishment may be resolved in light of a distinction that those in the field of behavior modification insist on:

> *Responses* are reinforced, *people* are rewarded.

Extending this distinction to the effective and humane use of punishment, we would add:

> Undesirable *responses* may be punished; *people* should not be.

> Although *responses* may be undesirable, *people* should never be made to feel that *they* are undesirable.

Punishment often "works," but unless it is administered within an overall positive context you may find that you have won the battle but lost the war. Listed below are some guidelines for the constructive use of punishment (adapted from Parke & Walters, 1967; Azrin & Holz, 1966).

a. *Response specificity.* It should be made explicitly clear what specific response is being punished, why, and what alternatives are possible.

b. *Alternative responses.* There should always be available to the individual a response that the individual can make that will not receive the punishing stimulus, but will be positively reinforced.

c. *Situational limits.* The aversive social interaction of punishment should be clearly limited to the situation in which the punished response occurs. It should not spill over to unrelated situations or to other times.

d. *Timing.* The punishment should follow the response immediately every time the response occurs.

e. *Escape.* There should be no unauthorized means of escape, avoidance, or distraction.

He that spareth the rod hateth his own son.
Proverbs 13:24

All punishment is mischief. All punishment is itself evil.
Jeremy Bentham

f. *Intensity of punishing stimulus.* The punishing stimulus should be at the highest reasonable level.

g. *Duration.* Prolonged punishment is to be avoided.

h. *Conditioned punishing stimuli.* A neutral stimulus consistently paired with the punishing stimulus may be used to reduce the frequency of responding without harming the individual.

i. *Displays of sympathy, affection, etc.* Punishers should *not* provide positive reinforcement in connection with punishment. If they do, it may be sufficient to maintain the undesired response.

j. *Time-outs.* Punishment effects are obtained with use of "time-out periods" in which desired positive reinforcement is withheld because of undesirable responses (no television viewing today because you didn't do your homework last night). In the Greek play *Lysistrata*, women put their husbands on a "time-out" punishment program by refusing sexual relations until their demands for an end to war were met.

k. *Motivation.* Motivation for making the punished response should be reduced. Show how the need that motivated the undesirable response can be satisfied in desirable ways.

l. *Generalizations from acts to dispositions.* Under no circumstances should the punisher generalize from the specific response to character traits of the person ("You're no good," "stupid," etc.) on the basis of the punished response. These inferences about personal traits remain in the person's consciousness long after the punished response has been extinguished and the punishment is forgotten.

I have never observed other effects of whipping than to render boys more cowardly, or more wilfully obstinate.
Montaigne

When is punishment counterproductive? There is substantial evidence for the effectiveness of the judicious, controlled use of punishment as one method in a program of behavior management that generally emphasizes positive reinforcement. However, *punishment is usually counterproductive*. When used by teachers, parents, police, hospital aids, friends, spouses, bosses, and others, it is rarely used in accordance with the principles listed above, which were derived from controlled research. It is more likely to be used to vent the anger of the punisher, a motive which is not pertinent to the task of reducing the probability of a specific response. (See *P&L* Close-up, Paddling Pupils Produces Problems.)

Furthermore, punishment may elicit more undesirable responses than it stops. It may be ineffective, or worse—permanently damaging to human relationships—for a number of reasons.

a. The strong emotions associated with the act of punishment often are generalized too far. The punished person may become excessively timid, hostile, or resentful of authority. Or sometimes the individual develops feelings of worthlessness, thereby justifying the punishment from a loved parent. If the punisher enjoys the feeling of power that aversive control can bring, punishment is reinforced and will be used more frequently.

b. Punishment usually suppresses the undesirable action only in the presence of the punisher. The person may learn a stimulus discrimination, inhibiting the response only when he or she is being watched and cannot safely express it. This leads to a shared set of (false) beliefs that surveillance is *necessary* for good behavior.

c. It is too easy for a stronger punishing agent to underestimate the painfulness of the punishment administered to a physically weaker person. In addition, it is too easy to lose rational control of the punishing act and become

The use of punishment in the control of human behavior is not merely a matter of deciding whether or not it works. Besides the psychological questions involved in punishing people for "undesirable behavior" are many moral and legal issues. Corporal punishment is defined in educational terms as the inflicting of pain by a teacher or school official upon the body of a student as a penalty for doing something which is disapproved of by the punisher (Wineman & James, 1967). This includes confinement in an uncomfortable space, forced eating of obnoxious substances, and standing for long periods.

It is generally assumed that corporal punishment in schools is administered rarely, with a light hand, and primarily to high-school students who represent a physical threat to the teacher. All false assumptions. The Dallas, Texas, school system reported an average of over 2000 cases of physical punishment *per month* during the 1971–72 school year. There were over 46,000 cases of reported corporal punishment in California schools during 1974 (excluding the entire city of Los Angeles). Only 5 percent of them were in the high schools. The primary targets of corporal punishment are boys of all ages and children in grades one through four. Such punishment is often brutal, including beating and even kicking (Hyman, McDowell, & Raines, 1977).

The four most commonly given reasons for using corporal punishment are: (a) it is a tried and effective method for changing undesirable behavior; (b) it develops a sense of personal responsibility; (c) students learn self-discipline; (d) it helps develop moral character (Clarizio, 1975).

There is reason to doubt the effectiveness of punishment in achieving any of these goals. Target behaviors are suppressed only when the punishment is severe and repeated, and then only in the presence of the punishing teacher. Furthermore, the "side effects" of this aversive control include development of a general negative attitude toward school or learning, avoidance of the teacher, truancy, blind obedience to authority, vandalism, and perhaps learning to use violence against younger, weaker students (Bongiovanni, 1977).

About three-fourths of the adults in one survey were in favor of corporal punishment, only 17 percent opposed, and 8 percent unsure. Adults were parents, teachers, administrators, principals, and school board presidents. The only group clearly opposed were students: 50 percent against, with 25 percent in favor and the other 25 percent unsure (Reardon & Reynold, 1975).

In April 1977 the Supreme Court ruled *(Ingraham* v. *Wright)* in a five to four decision that corporal punishment in public schools is constitutional and, no matter how severe, does not violate the Eighth Amendment's prohibition against cruel and unusual punishment. At this writing only four states have statutes limiting the use of corporal punishment in schools: New Jersey, Maine, Maryland, and Massachusetts.

There are many alternatives to the use of physical punishment in the classroom. "Time-out rooms" and denial of class privileges can be effective aversive control tactics. Private conferences with "disruptive" students can be used more often. Class discussion of acceptable and unacceptable behavior and shared responsibility for discipline helps create a democratic class atmosphere. And of course, more interesting curricula and better preparation for teachers in managing children with the use of positive incentives and reinforcements will reduce the "need" for punishment.

abusive. The result can be seen in the battered child and battered wife syndrome (discussed in Chapter 23).

d. The punishing situation can be a setting for learning the meaning of social power. Both individuals may learn that "it is better to give than receive," (punishment). They may also learn that it is less trouble to settle conflicts with physical force than with verbal negotiation.

e. The presence of witnesses to the punishment is an added source of aversiveness. The humiliation of being singled out for reprimand or physical punishment may have effects that linger long after their sting is gone. (It wasn't that crack of the ruler across my knuckles in Sunday School that was the deterrent, but the laughter of my peers. I never talked in class again—because I never went back.) Sometimes the presence of an audience may bias the behavior of the punisher. For example, the punisher may be concerned about his or her image and use punishment because any desired change that occurs will be "credited" to him or her rather than to the punished person. Or the punisher may overreact and use the occasion as a "lesson" for the entire group.

In a study of the spontaneous use of punishment by schoolteachers, two children from each of five classes were observed for a four-month period. These children had a high frequency of classroom behavior for which their teachers reprimanded them loudly in the presence of the class. The reprimands were not particularly effective in reducing the frequency of the disruptive behavior.

During Phase 2 of the study, teachers were asked to switch to "soft" reprimands, audible only to the child being reprimanded. In almost all cases, disruptive behavior decreased when soft reprimands were used. In Phase 3, when loud reprimands were reinstated there was an increase in frequency of disruptive behavior. In Phase 4, to demonstrate convincingly the counterproductivity of loud, public reprimands and the effectiveness of soft, personal ones, soft personal ones were again used by the teachers. Again disruptive behavior declined in virtually all cases where the teacher made the punishing stimulus not a public announcement to the student's peers but a soft, personal reprimand intended only for the student (O'Leary, Kaufman, Kass, & Drabran, 1970).

Disruptive behavior of two children with loud and soft reprimands

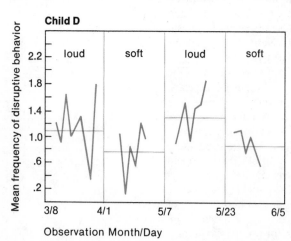

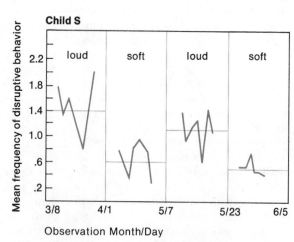

Behavior with a purpose

In most standard learning paradigms, what is being learned is an *association* of stimulus pairings (respondent conditioning), stimulus-response connections (instrumental conditioning), or response-reinforcement schedules (operant conditioning). Central to each paradigm is the principle of *contiguity*—the relationship of two events occurring closely together in time and space. In all strictly behavioral theories, contiguity is a necessary condition for learning. The CS and UCS must be experienced together; the desired response must be quickly followed by a reinforcer.

But is all learning the product of contiguity, of *overt* responses to *immediate* sensory experience? Surely the human learner isn't always so mindless a creature. There is more majesty to man and woman than can be observed in their physical responses to direct stimuli. Don't we also make *implicit* responses to imagined stimuli and to distant events? Don't we offer ourselves *mental* reinforcements supported by *rational* processes as well as by sensory and behavioral processes?

Because much research in learning has relied on animal species less complex than humans—dogs, cats, rats, and pigeons—the important role played by cognitive processes and language has been underrepresented. A "new look" in learning research, however, focuses as much on what is happening inside the learner's head as on the learner's overt responses. *People* have returned to center stage, and the animals are no longer quite so much in the spotlight. Radical behaviorism is now viewed as having gone too far in replacing mind with other matters. A current psychology of "hope" and "despair," of "longing," "intention," and "purpose" has emerged.

Goals, meaning, and context

To a large extent, we are what we have learned to become. Life itself is a learning process; to change what we are is often a matter of changing what we *think* we are. The manner in which the mind perceives itself may be as important as the matter it moves by flexing the muscles. Learning is often a process of deciding what leads to what, what signs lead to significant places and people, and what actions satisfy the purposes that guide our behavior. This view of learning was first proposed by Edward C. Tolman back in 1932 in his classic work, *Purposive Behavior in Animals and Men.*

Tolman made a bold attempt to develop a theory that retained the objectivity of behaviorism while also giving *meaning* to behavior by putting it into a *cognitive context* which included purposive or *goal-directed* behavior. He tried to blend a functional analysis of observable stimulus-response events with more cognitive concepts similar to ones then current in Gestalt psychology. Tolman acknowledged the basic simplifying decision every psychologist who believes in the value of a scientific analysis of behavior must make. "In place of the concrete, but ineffable, richness of real experience, as it comes, i.e., of our hopes, our feelings, our images, our thoughts—we have substituted a barren and 'unfelt' array of functionally defined immanent determinants . . . we have ended up with demands, means-end-readiness, sign-gestalt-expectations and the rest" (p. 424). But to these "barren" and "functionally defined" variables, he added some insightful concepts.

Tolman's system specified environmental stimuli and the resulting responses as the objective variables to be studied, but he added relevant physiological states, heredity, and past training of the organism to the list of relevant concerns. A combination of "initiating conditions" was empirically correlated with specific responses to form the basic input-output elements of the learning equation, but a missing ingredient was added. Tolman's system "conceives of mental processes as functional variables intervening between stimuli . . . and final resulting responses" (p. 414).

Cognitions as intervening variables

Cognitions impart goals and purposes to human actions, thereby giving behavior a guiding force. Behavior without purpose would be random, and in Tolman's words "both silly and meaningless." In describing cognitions as *intervening variables*, Tolman gave them an important theoretical status. They were not "things" or events to be observed or measured. Rather, they were abstract concepts defined by the theorist from their relationship to the stimuli and responses between which they intervene. In this way, Tolman avoided mentalistic interpretations of cognition on the one hand, or attempts to treat it as a measurable quantity on the other. Cognitions were inferred processes that were affected by experience with external stimuli and in turn helped to produce responses.

Among these intervening variables that determined responding was the expectation that certain events would lead to others. Some stimulus events serve as signs or guideposts to a whole pattern of stimulation. A piercing, high-pitched sound is likely to be a sign of a missile when heard in the context of war. The hearer expects that it will explode and that it may cause bodily harm if he or she does not take shelter. In peacetime, a similar stimulus might signify the noontime factory lunch break.

Tolman proposed the term *sign-gestalt-expectation* to convey the notion that individuals learned to expect their world to be organized in predictable patterns. "Signs" are external stimuli that point to other stimulus events such as goal objects. "Gestalt" is the context in which signs are perceived and in which they are interrelated. "Expectation" is the cognition of a predictable sequence or pattern of events.

Two other terms in this theory deserve mention. *Means-ends-readiness* is the action tendency that an organism brings to a learning situation (as a function of past experience and heredity). It is activated by a demand (a need or deprivation state) and stimulates *judgments* about stimuli to which one should respond. Thus means-ends-readiness determines the selective responsiveness of organisms to stimuli in their environment. In this sense the concept is similar to the social psychological concept of *attitudes*. Attitudes are predispositions to judge or act toward a certain class of stimuli in a particular way such as a prejudiced attitude toward an ethnic group or a favorable attitude toward ecology.

Cognitive maps

Two experiments demonstrate some of the predictions of Tolman's theory. If rats are placed in a complex maze, allowed to explore it, but are not fed there and are removed from it at different locations on different trials, have they learned anything? Without reward for their efforts, a strict S→R reinforcement interpretation would predict that this early experience in the maze would have no benefit for the subjects. Not so. When these rats were later deprived of food and then fed in the goal box of the maze, the next time they were put in the start box they ran to the goal box without a single error. Significantly more of the maze-wise rats learned to solve the maze on one or a few trials than did control subjects without prior maze experience (Buxton, 1940). Tolman argued the rats demonstrated *latent learning*. They had learned how the maze was organized from their experience with it. However, this knowledge was latent (hidden) until hunger and the food reinforcer gave them a purpose for performing what they already knew.

In another study (Tolman, Ritchie, & Kalish, 1946), rats revealed they could learn the location of a reward in space and not merely to perform the same responses that led to prior reinforcement. They first learned to use the only available roundabout route to the goal (see start A). When the enclosed runway was blocked (start B) and 18 other paths were possible to get to the goal, which do you suppose the majority of subjects chose? Paths closest to the original (blocked) one (8, 9, 10, or 11) should be preferred from the principle of generalization. To the contrary, a majority chose the paths that led most directly toward the goal. They responded as if they were reading a map of the maze and taking a shortcut. ◆ If rats have cognitive maps they can read so well, we might assume that people carry around a world atlas in their heads to facilitate the more complex learning challenges they face.

The learning-performance distinction

The concept of latent learning reminds us that learning may be taking place even though there is no apparent, immediate change in our overt behavior. There are other conditions also when how we perform does not accurately reflect what we have learned. It is important to note that learning curves which show the relationship of response strength to reward characteristics typically level off over time. At first small increases in reinforcement result in large increments in responding. Later in learning, the same increase in reinforcement (for example, one additional food pellet) yields only a small increment in responding. The learner is said to be reaching a *plateau* of responding. ▲

Several factors may be responsible for this leveling off of the effectiveness of reinforcement in changing behavior. First, the organism may be performing the response at or near its physical capacity, so there is little room for improvement. Related to this is the inhibition and fatigue that build up as the response is repeated. Third, satiation occurs as the response is reinforced re-

◆

Learning the direction to a goal

This is a top view of an apparatus in which rats followed the roundabout route, in part A, from the round table top to the goal where they found food. In part B, the original route was blocked and 18 new paths were made available. The rats tended to choose the path pointing toward the goal.

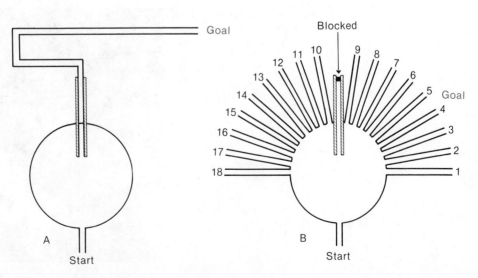

Adapted from Tolman, Ritchie, & Kalish, 1946

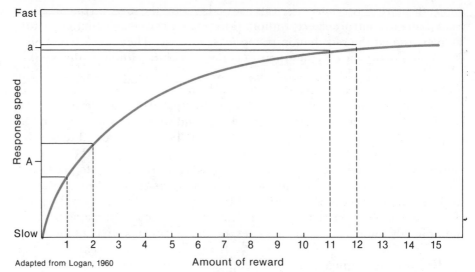

Quantity and quality of reinforcement

The graph is a hypothetical curve showing the relationship between speed of a particular response and amount of reinforcement. Note how the curve levels off; there is a much smaller increase in response speed when the reinforcement is increased from 11 pellets to 12 (a) than when the number was increased from 1 pellet to 2 (A).

Fast

a

Response speed

A

Slow

1 2 3 4 5 6 7 8 9 10 11 12 13 14 15

Amount of reward

Adapted from Logan, 1960

peatedly. (The things you'll do to get one piece of pizza, you might not be willing to do for a fifth piece.) Finally, some big, tasty reinforcers simply take more time to consume, thus lowering response output.

The operation of these variables calls our attention to an important distinction between *learning* and *performance*. We *infer* learning by *observing* performance. We assume that reinforcement operations directly affect learning in relatively permanent ways. In contrast, deprivation conditions, motivation, satiation, effortful responding all have a temporary effect on performance (overt behavior), but do not influence the learning that is taking place.

Performance can be enhanced by raising motivation, as when the underdog team gets psyched up and beats the favorite. ■ However, this souped-up performance does not exceed the limits of their previous learning. In the same way, what you've learned from studying for an exam might be obscured when anxiety causes you to "clutch" and your test performance nose-dives. You then say "I really knew it" (learning), but nevertheless "really blew it" (performance).

■

Just minutes before the USC game, the Notre Dame coach made a switch to green jerseys, to inspire his Fighting Irish, as well as the crowd of almost 60,000 people, for an unexpected 49 to 19 victory.

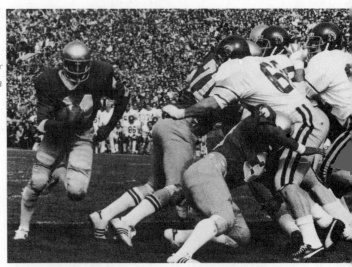

In some situations, testers want to determine how well a person will perform under stress, not merely how well he or she has learned what to do. Medical school interviews are often purposely stressful in order to assess how well a candidate makes use of available knowledge when confronted with stress conditions. However, the conditions of test administration in many college courses create unnecessary sources of stress that interfere with determining how much the student has really learned. Unit mastery or PSI (Personalized System of Instruction) courses are designed so that students can demonstrate their mastery of course material free from many of the effects that depress test performances (see Minke & Carlson, 1975).

Mediational learning

A radical behaviorist position assumes that a full account of learning involves only three elements: *stimulus input, response output,* and the *consequences* that follow responding. Such a view creates an empty space between the S and the R, as if nothing intervened to link them together. Tolman filled some of that void with cognitions that were affected by S and in turn influenced R (mediating responses). Many other theorists have also used the concept of mediation to account for the ways in which an organism "bridges" the gap in time or space between experienced events. *Mediators are events or processes that facilitate the association between two (or more) other events not directly connected (not contiguous in space or time).*

Mediating responses

In the act of counting numbers from "one" to "three," "two" is a response to "one," but it is something more. Hearing (or perceiving) yourself say "two" becomes a stimulus for the next response in the sequence. These *cue-producing responses* mediate between the initial external stimulus and the next observable response. They are not limited to verbal responses. Tying your shoelaces or engaging in gymnastic exercises are activities where individual responses produce cues that guide the next response. Similarly, conditioned emotional responses such as *fear* produce stimuli, in this case drive stimuli, that motivate the learning of new responses (Dollard & Miller, 1950).

Mediating responses may also affect learning by directing attention toward certain aspects of the stimulus situation. Indeed, often the crucial thing to be learned is which cues in the situation are relevant and which can be ignored. Suppose you were given a set of cylinders of different colors, heights, and widths and asked to group them in as few categories as possible. The relevant dimension might be "volume." But a person who was schizophrenic might group them according to the length of the shadows they cast, or by the scratches on their surface, or by some other visual stimulus quality rather than their conceptual similarity. When children learn to read, they must learn that the *form* of the letters is the essential cue, not their size, color, etc.

Cue-producing mediated responses result in a phenomenon called the *acquired distinctiveness of cues* (Lawrence, 1949). We learn to make the general response of attending to a stimulus class (form, for example) in addition to a particular response to any specific form. One obvious way to establish distinctiveness of cues is by instructing subjects to attach verbal labels to stimuli. Stimulus labeling appears to alter the target stimulus by the act of attaching a distinctive mediator. The more distinctive the label, the better the subsequent recognition of the labeled stimulus—even when the label bears no meaningful relationship to the stimulus.

University of Hawaii students served as subjects in a study to test whether the acquired verbal distinctiveness of a perceptual stimulus would enhance its subsequent recognition. They were shown a line at a given orientation of 60° and told they would have to recognize this target stimulus later. Control subjects were told nothing more. For experimental subjects the target stimulus was labeled. For some, the label was an uncommon word rated high in imagery—"dummy." For others, the verbal label was a common word, low in imagery—"idea." Stimulus test lines were then presented in random order varying in their orientation, 40°, 45°, 50°, 55°, and 60°. Subjects called out "same" or "different" to indicate whether the test stimulus was identical to the target stimulus. The no-label controls most often selected the 50° test stimulus as identical to the target. The low-imagery subjects ("idea") tended to choose the 55° test stimulus. The acquired distinctiveness of the "dummy" cue resulted in the greatest accurate recognition of the 60° test stimulus as being the same as the target stimulus (Ban, 1975). A replication of this study showed similar results, except that low-imagery subjects were as accurate as high-imagery ones (Ban & Minke, 1979). Thus learning and remembering the perceived orientation of a line can be enhanced by verbal mediation, even when the mediator has no natural relationship to the stimulus.

Learning to learn

The response of paying attention to the relevant cues in a task is termed either *selective attention* or an *observing response*. Such responses are essential in developing the capacity to discriminate among stimulus dimensions. One of the most important roles such observing responses play in learning occurs in the formation of *learning sets*. A learning set is developed gradually over a series of trials in which discrimination problems are solved. The individual learns the *principle* (or rule) necessary to solve problems of a given form. Thus in acquiring learning sets the individual is actually *learning how to learn.*

Harry Harlow (1949) first demonstrated learning sets by giving a group of monkeys 344 successive problems to solve. Their task was to choose which of two objects concealed a food reward. The objects varied in color, shape, height, and other ways. But in any given problem, the reward was always found under the stimulus of a particular type (say, always under the red cylinder). On the first trial, the response was a matter of chance; however, once the relevant dimension was discovered, discrimination improved dramatically, from trial two on. As the graph shows, on the 32 preliminary problems the animals' correct responding improved gradually over trials. However, repeated experience with this type of discrimination problem began to show that the subjects were learning how to learn. By the end of testing, the monkeys were choosing the correct stimulus dimension more than 95 percent of the time from trial two on. ●

Harlow (1959) believes that the process of developing a discrimination learning set involves learning to suppress response tendencies that have resulted in errors. The important process in such learning is, in his view, reducing the strength of responses that result in *incorrect* choices, rather than building up the strength of correct responding.

Cognitive behavior modification

Mediating responses are often images, thoughts, or words. Sometimes the use of words is overt, as when you learn a new skill and talk aloud to yourself while practicing it, "one, two, cha, cha, cha." With practice, skill, and maturity, audible speech becomes internalized.

Development of a discrimination set

Early discriminations require a large number of trials to master, but later ones are learned in essentially one trial.

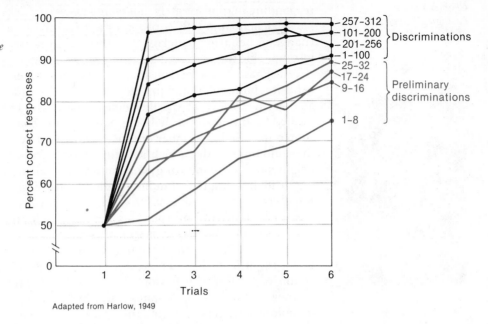

Adapted from Harlow, 1949

Verbal mediation consists of talking to oneself in relevant ways when confronted with something to be learned, a problem to be solved, or a concept to be attained. In adults the process generally becomes quite automatic and implicit; only when a problem is quite difficult do we begin "thinking out loud." Most mediational processes take place subvocally below our level of awareness (Jensen, 1966, p. 101).

We use language in an instrumental way to formulate plans of action and to guide our nonverbal behavior. Some of this language can be thought of as an *internal dialogue* we carry on with ourselves. The mental plans we formulate for defining and solving problems can be called *cognitive strategies*. These "thinking sets" are internally organized skills by means of which we come to manage our own thinking activities (Gagné & Briggs, 1974).

If we conceive of cognitive strategies as "self-management skills," then such skills should be modifiable through application of principles of operant conditioning. Donald Meichenbaum of the University of Waterloo in Canada has successfully used such an approach in treating individuals with a variety of behavior problems.

Depressed people often tell themselves they are inadequate, their situation is hopeless, they are helpless, and nothing will change for the better. Those with low self-esteem carry on a dialogue with themselves that might go:

"How do I look?"
"Terrible."
"Yeah, you're right, My hair is a mess, I'm too fat, and . . ."
"Yes, but it wouldn't matter if ugliness were your only problem . . ."
"You mean . . ."
"I don't have to tell you how dumb you act and what a schnook you are."

Our self-concept is based in part on the ratio of negative to positive things we say about ourselves in such internal dialogues. These thoughts often carry over into feelings of anxiety, shame, envy, or frustration. They may also trig-

ger a wide range of reactions such as avoiding certain people or situations, responding inappropriately, not taking necessary risks—and more.

Meichenbaum (1977) proposes a three-phase process of bringing about change in behavior patterns. The three phases are: (1) self-observation, (2) incompatible thoughts and behaviors, and (3) cognitions concerning change.

In Phase 1, the person must develop a greater awareness of his or her behavior, both public and private. One of the best ways of doing this is to keep an objective record of specific behavior patterns. This can be readily accomplished by the use of a daily log, journal, or behavior diary. Such a record should include the number of times a day the activity is engaged in, as well as the conditions under which it occurs and its consequences. Along with this heightened self-monitoring is an emphasis on giving the behavior new meaning by identifying the stimulus conditions that elicit it and help to explain it. Redefining one's "problems" in terms of what causes and maintains them increases feelings of control. This reconceptualization also provides a new perspective in which *change* is seen as possible.

In Phase 2, what the person says internally and/or imagines must initiate a new set of behaviors. These behaviors are to be incompatible with the maladaptive, "problem" behaviors. The person encourages him- or herself to try out new responses—for instance, "to whistle a happy tune" even when afraid, to smile at strangers, to offer a compliment, or act assertively.

Finally, in Phase 3, after adaptive behaviors are being emitted, the person must also *appraise their consequences* in ways that further support his or her cognitive structures. The new set of beliefs that guided the productive actions can be undermined by an internal dialogue full of putdowns. "I did it, I got the date, but she was probably so desperate, anyone who asked would have gotten the green light." Such a negative evaluation diminishes the potency and generalizability of the behavior change. To be lasting, any significant change in behavior must also involve a corresponding change in supportive cognitive structures; "I got the date because I asked for it in an effective way, and because she probably thinks I'll be an interesting person."

In sum, this approach specifies that the key to behavior change lies in the introduction of an intentional mediational process. This process involves recognition of maladaptive behavior and a new inner dialogue about it that is incompatible with previous cognitions. These new thoughts, in turn, must trigger appropriate coping responses. Finally the person acknowledges that he or she has changed, realizes the personal gains that result from this change—and takes full credit for a job well done.

Social learning theory

Many different theories have been proposed over the years to account for why people behave as they do and to suggest how behavior may be changed. As we have seen, behavior theory has switched the search for determinants of behavior away from a study of vague, internal motivational states to a detailed examination of external influences. Any given behavior can be analyzed into the external stimulus conditions that evoke it and the external reinforcing conditions that maintain it. There is much research to support the notion that human behavior is externally regulated. The empirical success of the operant conditioning approach has led many psychologists to abandon the view that human behavior is determined by factors within the individual. Instead, they emphasize the power of environmental forces over human behavior. However, radical behaviorism has been rejected by many psychologists who refuse to see human beings as passive creatures, controlled by an all-powerful environment. Other criticism is directed at the refusal of traditional behavior theorists to recognize the significance of cognitive functioning.

An alternative perspective, which we shall examine next, is provided by _social learning theory_. In the social learning view, behavior, personal factors, and environmental factors all operate as interlocking determinants of each other. It is true that behavior is influenced by the environment, but the environment is partly of our own making. Behavior is shaped by reinforcers, but it is usually human beings who make those reinforcers available or scarce for one another.

Albert Bandura of Stanford University has redirected behavioristic approaches to human learning through his theory of social learning (1977a). His conception of human functioning denies that people are either helplessly driven by inner forces or passively pushed around by environmental stimuli. Instead, people are seen as capable of exercising some control over their own behavior. As we have seen, the impact of environmental stimuli is often mediated by cognitive processes through which people define, interpret, compare, contrast, give meaning to, and integrate stimulus events. These cognitive skills enable us to remember the circumstances in which our behavior was followed by reinforcement and how often reinforcement occurred.

This cognitive orientation has guided social learning theorists to investigate neglected aspects of learning, such as observational learning, symbolic learning, and self-regulatory processes. Many of our behaviors are acquired through the _observation_ of models engaging in that behavior and of its consequences for those models. Language and other symbols enable us to process, store in memory, and retrieve experiences that can serve as guides for future behavior. The cognitive power of symbolizing allows the learner to imagine alternative consequences of different actions, to test out problem-solving solutions mentally, and to give substance to abstract ideas such as "freedom," "dignity," "patriotism," and many others.

Observation of models

Baseball players improve their hitting skills by taking long batting practice sessions. Many of the best hitters spend a great deal of time in addition observing how other batters respond to the pitcher. They also profit from watching films of their own batting habits. When you are a stranger in a new setting, say your first college class, do you talk up right away or "size up the action"? Human beings have been designed for action, but action guided by observation. We look before we leap, if we want to live to leap again. The bulk of human learning is rooted in observation of what others do and what happens to them or to their environment. Learning based entirely upon observation of the behavior of others and its consequences, without personally performing the response and experiencing its effects, is called _vicarious learning_.

Our capacity for observational learning has a number of important advantages. It enables us to acquire large, integrated patterns of behavior without the tedious process of trial and error. We can profit from the mistakes of others as well as from their successes. Through listening, reading, or observing we gain knowledge that aids in our survival and development. Distinguishing poisonous snakes or dangerous tides, reading of the danger of looking directly at a solar eclipse, witnessing the execution of a mass murderer—all are lessons

better learned vicariously than experientially. Furthermore, new or complex patterns of behavior are much more efficiently learned through verbal instruction or observation than by operant shaping or other direct procedures.

Bandura's emphasis on the importance of observation of models was influenced by earlier work of Neal Miller and John Dollard (1941). However, they stressed *response mimicry*, the vicarious learning of specific imitated responses. A rat seeing another rat reinforced for turning left turns left when it get the opportunity. Social learning theory offers a broader conception of the psychological effects of exposure to models. "From observing examples, people derive general rules and principles of behavior which permit them to go beyond what they see and hear" (Bandura, in Evans, 1976, p. 244).

Observational learning by exposure to models is governed by four types of processes: attentional, retention, motor reproduction, and motivational. That is, the learner must pay attention to certain aspects of the model's behavior, remember what was observed, be able to enact the behavior properly, and finally, be motivated to perform the learned behavior. ◆

Attentional processes

What one observes depends on where one looks and which models one notices. The significant features of a model's behavior must be attended to and accurately perceived for observational learning to take place. The availability of certain models obviously influences what one can attend to. Violent behavior will be observed more frequently in neighborhoods with active street gangs, drug abuse more likely in settings where drugs are readily available, and prejudice more often where parents or significant adults model intolerance. Similarly, the absence of appropriate models diminishes opportunity to attend to modeled behavior that could be influential. Until quite recently, females and members of minority groups were conspicuous by their absence from textbooks or by their stereotyped, negative portrayal. Content analyses of children's texts have revealed for example, that while male characters are dominant, active, make decisions, take risks, and have fun, females are subordinate, passive, dependent, play it safe, complain, and are the butt of jokes (U'Ren, 1971; Tavris & Offir, 1977). These stereotyped textbook role models have had a profound effect on the social learning of the boys and girls who read them. Television has greatly expanded the range of models and modeled behavior available for observation. Given the profusion of models in the mass media and in our everyday life, which ones we attend to will depend to some extent upon their personal characteristics, such as attractiveness and status. But the personal characteristics of the observer are also important, such as attention span, expectations, and biases in the selection of models (developed through exposure and experience with certain classes of models, for example, athletes versus academics, or macho males and feminine females).

Retention processes

Because observational learning is usually practiced when the model is absent, modeled actions have to be remembered. The use of symbolic representations of physical events enables us to store them in memory, and (usually) call them up when appropriate. These representations may be images (think of how your tennis coach demonstrated backhand) or verbal codes (tell yourself the shortest route from your psychology class to the cafeteria). Memory codes that are rehearsed and response patterns that are practiced enhance modeled performance.

◆

We learn general rules and ways of behaving from adult models. Children watch and remember and are motivated to repeat adult behavior and are able to go beyond what they observe and hear.

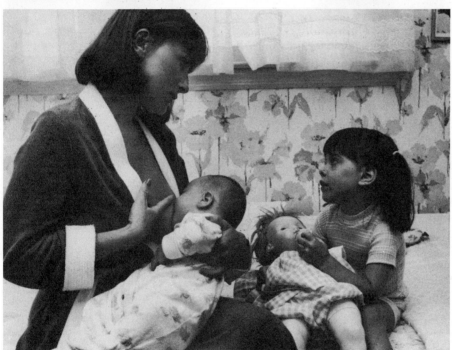

Motor reproduction processes

For a behavior pattern to be enacted, the component skills that make it up have to be part of the learner's repertoire or be developed separately. Before singing in a choral group, one must be able to sing on key, have a sense of rhythm, and know how to read music. A complex response is rarely perfect on the first trial. Through informative feedback, the patterning of the response is adjusted to bring it closer to match the modeled ideal. Where feedback is ambiguous (as in learning emotional responses), or is absent (as in social situations where people don't tell you when you are acting inappropriately), correct response reproduction is often not learned. Modern therapy for many types of behavior problems includes teaching adaptive social skills to improve the person's coping with troublesome situations.

Motivational processes

We observe many things that we never imitate. In terms of the distinction we examined earlier in this chapter, performing what we've learned requires motivation to do so. Such motivation may be in the form of deprivation (a need for something essential), the presence of an incentive (a promised reward), or in Tolman's concepts, a purpose. Of all the behaviors we observe, we are most likely to perform those whose consequences we see as desirable, or as being in line with our own values and self-image. During the Vietnam war, a Buddhist monk burned himself to death publicly to protest the continuation of war. This behavior was modeled by others whose values were similar, despite the adverse personal consequences. On the other hand, kidnapers, terrorists, skyjackers, and others who model violent antisocial actions are often imitated by those whose self-interest finds expression in such behavior.

Symbolic learning: "if→then"

From both active participation (performance) and passive exposure to experienced events (observation), we learn "*if→then" relationships*. They are action→ outcome contingencies. "If I smile, then other people act friendly toward me," "If my professor is late to class, then she is more critical of my answers," "If someone uses 'I' excessively, then people tend to avoid him and label him 'conceited.'" The sum of all such "if→then" contingencies makes up a person's knowledge or belief system about behavioral outcomes.

Not only do we learn a whole body of such R→S operant pairings, we also learn the conditions under which these relationships hold true. We learn that certain settings increase the likelihood that a particular "if" will lead to a specific "then." Begging for money outside a racetrack or at an army post on payday is more likely to pay off than panhandling in front of a welfare or unemployment office. We thus learn to discriminate among situations or stimulus conditions in terms of the probable payoff value of making a given response in their presence.

In addition to learning in what contexts given behaviors are likely to be reinforced, we learn more subtle variations on this basic if→then rule. Timing the response is often critical. A compliment given while a person is still talking is an interruption. Given too late, it may be confusing. Socially appropriate behavior, then, demands knowledge of what to do, where to do it, and when.

A recent study compared college men who date often with those who rarely had dates. The experimental task was to observe, on a video monitor, an attractive woman who was carrying on a conversation with them. Their task was to press one key whenever they wanted to say something and another key to signify a nonverbal response to the "target stimulus." The competent and incompetent daters responded equally often. The big difference between them was not in how often they reacted, but when. The incompetent daters were "out of synch." They responded sooner or later than the time it was ideal to do so. Competent daters had previously learned how to synchronize their responses to the other person's behavior (Fischetti, Curran, & Wessberg, 1977).

Symbolic learning goes beyond the acquisition of knowledge of S→R or R→S units. It involves developing general *rules* for appropriate action and for inhibiting incorrect responding. The capacity to use abstract symbols to represent concrete events gives us a powerful way of manipulating our environment. These symbols help put our specific observations into general classes and broad categories, as well as to formulate probability statements about behavior. "If I continue to put in about three hours careful reading per chapter I'll probably get an A in this course." To resist temptations and defer taking small immediate rewards for larger, future rewards, we must be able to visualize abstract future consequences as vividly as those that are closer at hand.

Self-regulation: Power to the person

Social learning theory rejects Skinner's statement that "a person does not act upon the world, the world acts upon him" (1971, p. 211). Such *environmental determinism* is replaced with the concept of *reciprocal determinism*. That is, the environment influences behavior, behavior affects the environment, the person exerts control over both behavior and environment and is controlled by them. This reciprocal determinism is shown in the paradigm:

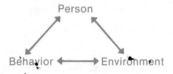

Our behavior is shaped by schedules of reinforcement, but we often choose environments in which particular schedules operate (go fishing, play slot machines, are attracted to someone who's "hard to get," etc.).

Results of research on self-regulatory processes are having a considerable impact in therapeutic programs designed to bring about personal change (see Curran, 1977). Where the emphasis used to be on "managing" behavior by imposing stimulus contingencies, now it has shifted to developing personal skills in self-regulation. Control is vested in the individuals themselves, not in therapists, trainers, teachers, researchers, and other "agents of change." The individuals set their own goals, monitor their ongoing performance, evaluate it in terms of established criteria, and then decide to grant or deny reinforcers to themselves.

Self-regulation of behavior means exerting personal control over three key elements in learned behavior: self-observation, environmental planning, and behavioral programming (Mahoney & Thoresen, 1974). In place of vague attempts to build up one's "will power," social learning theory advocates examination of the *ABCs*—the *antecedents* of behavior, the *behavior* itself, and its *consequences*. To regulate your behavior you must have objective information about what elicits it, its frequency, and its effects.

Self-observation involves keeping an objective record of a behavior. Recording when, where, and how the behavior occurs sensitizes the person to him- or herself. It provides feedback on both the behavior itself and the situations in which it occurs. In fact, merely keeping accurate records of certain kinds of behavior is often sufficient to alter the behavior dramatically. Students randomly assigned to a condition in which they made daily graphs of the number of hours spent reading this text performed better on examinations and got higher grades than classmates in a control group who did not keep such records (Yates & Zimbardo, 1977).

Environmental planning entails avoiding situations that elicit undesirable behavior. It also includes actively structuring the environment to make the desired response easier and the chance of getting rewarded greater. Setting strict schedules for TV viewing (or putting the set in a closet), having study materials in sight and well arranged, not answering phone calls during study hours are part of some students' environmental planning.

Behavioral planning introduces changes in the consequences of one's actions rather than in the stimulus situation. Individuals regulate their behavior by reinforcing themselves for meeting self-prescribed standards of performance. "I will do A by time t, and when I do, I'll give myself reinforcement X." Rewards and punishments are self-administered, either through external consequences (buying a new album, not allowing oneself to go to a movie) or internal ones. Self-praise and self-criticism are part of the internal dialogue that can exert powerful effects on behavior. By consciously programming these self-administered consequences, the person takes charge of his or her behavior. In this way, one's personal freedom is expanded as a sense of self-induced control develops. (For a study of self-regulation in action see *P&L* Close-up, Get Me to the Potty on Time.)

What constitutes a self-reinforcing event? A *self-reinforcing event* is one in which the individual exercises full control over a supply of freely available reinforcers, administering them only when a self-prescribed standard of performance has been attained. Performances that match or exceed these goals serve as discriminative cues for self-reward; all others signal an occasion of nonreinforcement. These performance standards usually involve comparison with:

a. some *absolute level* of performance (such as 90 percent correct on a test, or bowling over 200)
b. one's own *previous personal standard* (such as reducing the number of cigarettes smoked in a day or increasing reading speed by a given amount)
c. *social comparison* with the performance of others (such as doing as well as or better on the test than your best friend).

These features define the *operation* of self-reinforcement and should be distinguished from the *process* by which consequences affect behavior. The main differences between externally controlled and self-regulated reinforcements arise *before* rewards are administered. Once the standard is met and the reward given, then the source of that reward does not matter—the process of reinforcement is the same.

Self-efficacy is a belief in one's ability to cope with environmental demands. It is one of the most important determinants of behavior. We don't even try to do things or take chances when we expect to be ineffectual. We avoid people and situations when we don't feel adequate to the performance they require (or we believe they do). Even when we have the ability and the desire, without a sense of self-efficacy, we may not take the required action or, if we do, not complete it successfully. Self-efficacy is a sense of personal mastery that must be learned. Once established, positive expectations about one's efficacy generalize to new learning situations (Bandura, 1977b).

In the process of learning to master significant behaviors, self-efficacy is enhanced when the learning setting enables the person to take credit for the behavior. This cannot happen when the learner feels forced to make the response or when its successful execution is credited to the teacher or trainer, luck, fate, the gods, or some other agency. Therefore, educators need to be aware that in any learning situation, something more than correct responses is being learned. The individual is learning a more profound lesson: "I am (or am not) a competent person who can function effectively as an independent and self-reliant human being." This message is taught, for better or worse, in every learning setting—in schools, in the home, in therapy, at work, and in most of our daily encounters. The significance of learning this type of cognitive self-appraisal can not be overestimated. Because of our recognition of the important role that cognitive processes play in so many aspects of human functioning, we will turn in the next chapters to an in-depth analysis of what cognitive processes are and how they weave the texture of the rich fabric of all intelligent life.

Close-up
Get Me to the Potty on Time

Becoming toilet trained is a significant milestone in a child's development. It marks the transition from immature dependence on parents and an inability to control bodily functions to a stage of greater self-reliance and a sense of mastery over these bladder and bowel functions. It is also an event that is rewarding for parents. The toilet-trained child saves them about $200.00 a year in diaper costs as well as the considerable time and energy involved in many diaper changes daily. Being toilet trained makes the young child eligible for many preschool programs and also makes travel less burdensome.

But the process which precedes these idyllic consequences all too often resembles a nightmare. It can be a struggle for domination between determined parents and willful children. Attendant threats, screams, punishments all create a tension-filled battleground that is as likely to result in "failure" as "victory." Psychoanalytic writers have pointed to toilet training as a potentially traumatic experience with lifelong adverse (even neurotic) consequences seen in therapy patients.

It need not be so. The sensitive and systematic application of the principles of learning (outlined in Chapters 3 and 4) can work the miracle of total training in less than a day — without resorting to any physical punishment at all! The technique developed by psychologists Azrin and Foxx (1976) combines the following principles: (a) necessity for physical readiness of the child (not to be used before 20 months); (b) Pavlovian learning by which the child associates sphincter relaxation stimuli (UCS) with potty chair stimuli (CS); (c) operant learning that desired responses are followed by many different material and social reinforcements (potato chips and praise), also to shape and chain behavior sequences; (d) mediational learning by which, for example, verbal labels are attached to "dry" and "wet" pants and sequences of behavior are bridged by verbal rehearsal; (e) social learning which employs modeling of parents and self-generated reinforcements. The only punishment allowed is verbal disapproval; "no," or phrases such as "wet pants are bad."

A formal study of the effectiveness of the techniques based on these general principles was conducted by Foxx and Azrin (1973). Of 200 children trained by their method, one sixth were in the formal study. They were of both sexes, varied in age from 20 months to 4 years, and also in verbal ability. The average child required less than 4 hours to be completely toilet trained. The fastest learners did so in only 30 minutes, the slowest required 14 training hours. Girls trained slightly faster than boys, older children trained in half the time required for those under 26 months.

When this approach was put to a personal test with a child of our acquaintance (see photo), the quality of the learning was even more remarkable than these "speed" figures. The young child, not yet two years old, learned to perform the following sequence (with only occasional misses): (a) announce "toilet," (b) walk or run (as the urge demanded) to the nearest potty, and later when the potty was removed, to the nearest toilet, (c) pick up her dress, take down her pants, (d) climb up on the toilet seat, (e) urinate or defecate, (f) get off the seat, (g) wipe herself, (h) pick up pants, pull down dress, (i) carry the pot to the toilet, empty it, and flush it (or when toilet trained, just flush it), (j) wash and dry hands, (k) administer a self-reinforcement, "See pants dry" or "I go toilet, OK." (l) ask for a reinforcement, "Mommy gimme chip," or some other goodie, (m) share her reinforcements with parents (to encourage an attitude of sharing possessions).

Eat your heart out, Barnabus!

Chapter summary

Behavioral responses can be changed by changing their effects, the conditions that elicit them, or the setting in which they occur. Since reinforcers can influence only responses that are already occurring, special means need to be devised for inducing the first response. Such means include increasing motivation, lowering restraints, structuring the environment, forcing, providing a model, giving instructions, and inducing trial and error. Complex new responses may be taught by rewarding *successive approximations (shaping)*. In *chaining*, a subject can be taught a sequence of responses in which the discriminative stimulus for one step becomes a conditioned reinforcer for the preceding step.

Behavior may be under the control of stimuli other than reinforcers *(discriminative stimuli)*. Such *stimulus control* requires fine discrimination, which is not always easy in the real world with its multitude of complex stimuli. *Generalization*, in which we learn a range of both response values and stimulus values, is also important, since no two situations are completely identical.

Escape and *avoidance conditioning* rely on *negative reinforcement*, in which some *aversive stimulus* is terminated (escape) or prevented (avoidance) if the subject makes the desired response. Fear is the most powerful *conditioned aversive stimulus*. Fear-related responses are extremely resistant to extinction. Such conditioning can result in a sense of *learned helplessness* in which one's inability to master the environment leads to a total lack of responding.

Negative reinforcement differs from a third aversive control paradigm, *punishment*, in which an aversive stimulus is presented in hopes of *decreasing* the occurrence of an undesired response. While it can be effective under some circumstances, punishment must be used carefully if it is not to have undesired consequences for both the "victim" and the punisher. It is important to make it clear that the *response*, not the *person*, is being punished.

Human learning appears to go beyond simple conditioning paradigms to include *purposive*, or *goal-directed*, *behavior*. Learning theorist E. C. Tolman inferred the existence of *cognitions* (mental processes) as *intervening variables* that function between a stimulus and a response. His concepts of *sign-gestalt-expectation* and *means-end-readiness* deal with the predictable sequencing of events and the ability of organisms to respond selectively. Another element of Tolman's theory is *latent learning* and the existence of *"cognitive maps"*; here learning takes place but is not necessarily revealed in performance until the need arises. This leads to the important observation that *learning* and *performance* are not the same thing, though we can only infer the former from the latter.

Other theorists have proposed the existence of *cue-producing responses* that *mediate* between the stimulus and the observed response. Selective attention is essential in the development of learning sets; that is, learning to learn. *Cognitive behavior modification* involves the self-management of behavior through such strategies as the deliberate use of positive mediating responses.

The *social learning theory* of Albert Bandura and Neal Miller goes beyond traditional behaviorism in recognizing that much human learning is vicarious —that is, based on the observation of models. Important elements of such learning include attentional processes, retention processes, motor reproduction processes, and motivational processes.

The learning of *if→then contingencies* is important in developing strategies for action and visualizing future consequences. Social learning theory replaces the behavioristic concept of *environmental determinism* with a concept of *reciprocal determinism,* taking into account the interacting influences of the person, behavior, and environment. The emphasis is on self-regulation of behavior, which entails close attention to the abc's of *antecedents, behavior,* and *consequences.* Helping people develop a sense of *self-efficacy* is an important goal of modern social learning theorists.

Human Thinking and Reasoning

What goes on four legs in the morning, on two legs at noon, and on three legs in the twilight?

This was the riddle posed by the evil Sphinx who held the people of ancient Thebes in tyranny until someone could solve it. Oedipus solved the problem and delivered his people from bondage. To break the code, he had to translate two key elements that were being used in a special way. "Morning," "noon," and "twilight" were meant to represent different periods of one's life, not times of one day. Then he figured out that "legs" were not just our lower limbs, but anything that could support the body. For a crawling baby, arms and legs were four supports. In youth, we stand erect on our own two legs. But as we age, we often need the assistance of a cane — a third supporting leg. The solution to the riddle follows naturally: it is "man" (used generically).

But what is the deeper level of meaning behind this entire fable? I infer that the intention of the story is to remind us of the power of human reasoning. Through the exercise of reason we rise above the tyranny of dictators and the coercive control of arbitrary rules. Even when our bodies are imprisoned, our thoughts may roam free. So long as one person's thoughts are not controlled, the hope of freedom lives for the rest of the human community. Do you agree with this interpretation?

To answer this question, you must make use of the very psychological processes that form the core of the present chapter. In previous chapters we saw how organisms learn to act in ways that increase their chances of survival. They learn to avoid or escape dangerous situations and to seek out and respond appropriately to those that deliver (or promise) positive reinforcements. But people do not live by action alone, nor by an automatic stamping in of stimulus-response connections. For every important action you take, how many others do you consider and reject? For every action you fail to take when you should, how much do you think about it afterwards? If intelligent action is necessary for survival, then it is thinking that gives meaning to our existence. "Cogito, ergo sum" ("I think, therefore I am") was Descartes' insight that our sense of identity depends on awareness of our thought processes.

Modern psychology is to a large extent cognitive psychology. The earlier emphasis in American psychology was on conditioning and simple learning in lower organisms, usually operating in artificially restricted laboratory environments. Controlled studies lead to basic "laws of learning" that are generally valid for humans and lower animal species. Thus, for example, the *law of effect* accurately states that any action followed by a desirable outcome is likely to be repeated under similar future circumstances. We have seen in Chapters 3 and 4 that behavior can be powerfully controlled by the systematic application of this basic law of learning.

However, when *you* take some action and it is followed by a desirable outcome, haven't you learned *more* than to behave the same way next time around? Suppose that you study hard and earn an A in this course. We can predict that you will probably continue to study hard in other courses and to obtain similarly high grades, but we also have to conclude that you have learned much more than merely what to do. You have learned about the meaning of your actions, of course grades, and relationships between actions and outcomes. You no doubt thought, planned certain study strategies, and implemented some actions and not others.

And what happens if a friend also gets an A in the course, without studying at all? Then what have you learned? Or what happens if someone cheats and gets an A? Or worse, what if you study and it does not pay off with a good grade? Might you not, in some circumstances, conclude that the test was unfair, that psychology is not your cup of tea, that the textbook is confusing, or that honesty and hard work don't pay?

In humans the law of effect is often moderated by cognitive processes, by recognition of apparent relationships between actions and consequences. Human learning involves making inferences about how the world seems to work. We abstract information and construct mental patterns of relationships (actions and other actions, actions and consequences, events and consequent actions, events and other events). In this way, we develop a knowledge base.

If we are told that a friend, John, went to a restaurant and ordered lobster, we immediately infer a whole set of supporting circumstances. We "know" that the friend entered the restaurant, probably waited for someone to seat him at a table. A waiter brought a menu, which John examined. He told the waiter what he wanted to eat. The waiter told the cook, who prepared the food. The waiter served it to John, who ate it. He requested a bill, paid it, left a tip, and so forth.

Jerome Bruner (1973) observed that the most striking aspect of human perception (beyond the fact that it occurs) is the tendency of the perceiving person "to go beyond the information given." Information is interpreted both within its current context and with perceived relationships to other factors. It is also interpreted within the experience, background, and future expectations of the perceiver. ▲ Humans are information *interpreters,* ambiguity resolvers, psychological forecasters, event predictors. Somehow we are able to make educated guesses about what we cannot observe directly.

Cognition is the *process of knowing.* It is also the *product of the act of knowing.* Cognition includes thoughts, bits of information, memory elements, as well as mental symbols and the processes by which those symbols are acquired and manipulated. Through our *cognitive processing* of information, we become active creators of realities that take us beyond mere stimulus-response patterns, beyond concerns for survival and adaptation that drain most of the energies of the lower animals.

Although cognitive processes are continuous events, for purposes of analysis they can be separated into successive phases that intervene between stimulus input and response output. These phases include: detection of stimulus features; selection of features to attend to; recognition of the stimulus as novel or familiar; transformation or encoding of selected features; storage in memory; access to and retrieval of stored cognitions; verbal representation of ideas; specification of alternatives, consequences, and plans for action; and testing of actual outcomes against expectations.

Cognitive processes do not necessarily occur in an orderly, linear fashion, but may involve parallel, simultaneous processing of different types of information at different rates. For instance, you might be solving a math problem, planning your lunch, trying to recall a name that is "on the tip of your tongue," being distracted by the awareness of hunger pangs or sexual urges, noticing a hole in your sock, recalling a silly dream, and wondering what you're doing in college anyway, all within a few moments.

Ulric Neisser, one of the most influential thinkers in the field of cognitive psychology, provides us with a broad definition of what we shall mean when we refer to cognitive processes:

"Cognition refers to all the processes by which the sensory input is transformed, reduced, elaborated, stored, recovered, and used. It is concerned with those processes even when they operate in the absence of relevant [externally generated] stimulation, as in images and hallucinations" (1967, p. 4).

▲

The meaning of your perceptions is interpreted in terms of what you know.

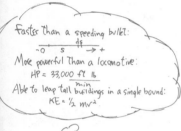

Human information processing

A dominant approach in many areas of cognitive psychology has been termed *information processing*. In this view, cognitive activity is seen as either (a) a sequence of *mental operations* performed on information stored in memory, or (b) a sequence of internal changes of *information states* as that information is processed toward a particular goal. The goal may be to solve a problem given a limited amount of information, or to draw valid conclusions from a given set of premises.

The information-processing psychologist attempts to analyze the cognitive activities and internal states occurring between the input of information and the person's response to it. This approach focuses upon the unobservable events assumed to be taking place in the mind between sensory stimulus input and overt response output. Obviously, radical behaviorists would have nothing to do with such an approach that tries to fill up the space between S and R with inferences about perception, memory, thinking, reasoning, and problem-solving processes that could never be directly observed.

Basic to the information processing approach is the attempt to define in precise terms the exact sequence of operations being used and the stages through which information passes in the process of being transformed. This approach is more a method than a theory. It is an orientation toward precise descriptions of cognitive processes in terms of sequential phases and hierarchical stages. It is used to help us understand better how humans think, reason, solve problems, and remember what they have learned. "The general principles of information processing must apply to all systems that manipulate, transform, compare, and remember information" (Lindsay & Norman, 1977, p. 589). ∎

The three main features of an information processing system are *input-output* (IO) *mechanisms,* the *information store,* and *processors. IO mechanisms* serve as a way of getting information into and out of the system. The *information store* is the memory subsystem. Facts are stored as data to be operated upon by

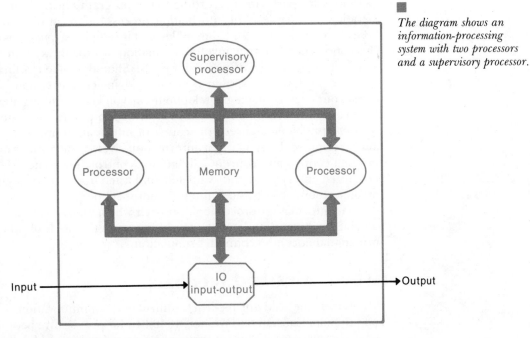

The diagram shows an information-processing system with two processors and a supervisory processor.

Adapted from Lindsay & Norman, 1977

the processors. Complete processing programs — rules systems, problem-solving strategies, sequences of actions, or goals — can be stored as data. *Processors* are those aspects of the information processing system that carry out the system's operations. A processor functions by calling up from the information store various facts and stored programs. It searches for relevant information and other programs as they become necessary. The processor may also direct the system to collect additional data (by IO operations). *"You,* reader, go to the dictionary, and look up the meaning of *sequential* and *hierarchical,"* it might subtly suggest to the executive processor of the total system.

What happens to the system while you are engaged in the dictionary search operation? If it included only one processor, it would have to shut down the store until you returned with the information requested. In fact, we have multiple processors that can function in complex, integrated sequences because they are controlled by a master, supervisory processor. For example, when there is a lull in the information flow while your lecturer sets up the slide projector, you might write a note to the classmate you suspect likes you, or rehearse the dates that might appear on your Western Civilization exam next period. You are employing a *time-sharing* strategy to carry on two or more activities in a given period of time while awaiting more information.

If the lecturer turns on the information flow again as you notice the classmate smiling back encouragingly, you can continue to pay attention to each source of information and maybe even continue your knitting at the same time because of *multiple processors.* Complex information processing systems can carry on several activities simultaneously because they engage several different processing units that function in *parallel.* To do so requires a master supervisory control processor that is aware of the proper functioning of the individual processors and is ready to resolve conflicts among them. (Your classmate signals you "let's leave now," as the lecturer says, "now for the information about the final exam." What then, oh mighty master processor?)

Control of the information processing system can be of three types (Lindsay & Norman, 1977). The simplest control enacted by separate processing units is program control. *Program control* determines the order in which operations are performed according to the program's instructions. When the operations at each level of information processing are in turn controlled by those at a more central (or "higher" level) it is called *conceptually guided control.* This conceptual guidance involves evaluation of how the systems operations are progressing toward its particular goals. (Should you be reading this chapter faster? Perhaps you should switch to studying chemistry now, take a break to rest your eyes, or make the telephone call you keep thinking about that distracts you from attending fully to this information-processing material.)

Data-driven control directs the course of information processing in a direction determined by new input information. New inputs interrupt ongoing program control and conceptually guided control. These new data must be recognized, interpreted and evaluated, and acted upon — either ignored, held for later action, or integrated into present functioning.

The information processing approach which many psychologists find so valuable has been stimulated by developments in the fields of cybernetics, information theory, and computer simulation.

Cybernetics and feedback

Cybernetics is the study of feedback control and communications in machines and physiological systems (Weiner, 1948). In his provocative book *The Human Use of Human Beings,* Norbert Weiner (1954) defined control as "nothing but

A plan for regulating temperature

Steps:

1. *Test temperature. If under 65°, go to 2, if over 67°, go to 5; otherwise go to 1.*
2. *Test furnace. If on, go to 1; otherwise go to 3.*
3. *Turn furnace on.*
4. *Go to 1.*
5. *Test furnace. If off, go to 1; otherwise go to 6.*
6. *Turn furnace off.*
7. *Go to 1.*

Adapted from Mayer, 1977

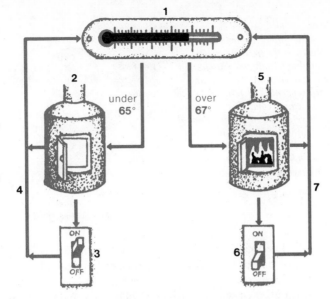

the sending of messages" that change the behavior of the receiver of those messages. Weiner's cybernetic models are the basis for automation and much computer technology. Operations are directed by programmed commands with built-in devices to audit performance, provide feedback on that performance, and make decisions. A thermostat operates on cybernetic principles. It is a device for sensing and measuring a specific property — temperature — using that information to make decisions that open or close electrical relays which in turn, control a heat source. A flow chart of a thermostatic plan to regulate temperature (between 65° and 67°F) is shown in the figure and also represented as a program. ●

A similar model of a feedback system in which cognitive processes are involved is that introduced by Miller, Galanter, & Pribram (1960). Plans for most human actions call for a *TOTE*: TEST-OPERATE-TEST(again)-EXIT. A TOTE is a planned hierarchy of operations with feedback. One plan for describing the cognitive processes in hammering a nail flush into a board is given in the figure, along with its four-step program. ◆

◆ A hierarchical plan for hammering nails

Steps:

1. *Test nail. If it sticks up, go to 2; otherwise stop.*
2. *Test hammer. If down, lift; otherwise go to 3.*
3. *Strike nail.*
4. *Go to 1.*

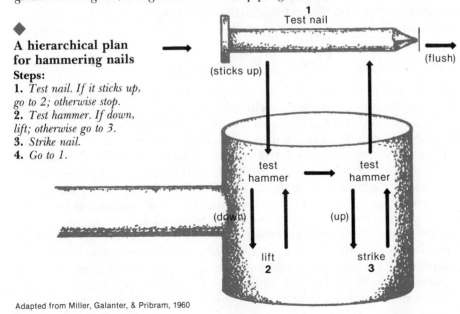

Adapted from Miller, Galanter, & Pribram, 1960

A simple feedback system

An actuating signal (stimulus input) produces some activity within the action element (in this case, the nervous system). This internal action, called throughput, activates muscles that produce a response (output). Part of the principal output serves as a signal to the feedback element. The feedback signal is then fed to a comparator which compares the current state of the system's activity to the reference input (the desired end state). If they differ, a new actuating signal is transmitted in order to generate a new output. The process continues until the feedback signal matches the reference input value, signaling that the goal has been reached.

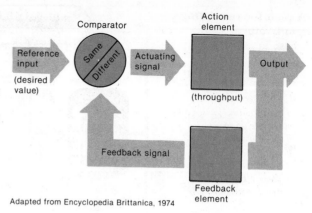

Adapted from Encyclopedia Brittanica, 1974

Feedback from events completed and activities in progress is essential for coordinated, smooth integration of a behavioral sequence. Many human functions are controlled by *closed-loop feedback systems*. The simple act of reaching for a glass of water illustrates such a feedback system. Thirst is the input that activates the memory which contains the stored sequence of motor actions that must be performed. A command program sends signals through the nervous system that stimulates arm and hand movements. Action in a given direction is sensed by observing the distance between hand and glass. The information is fed back to the brain where the current state of the operation is compared with the desired end state; any deviations noted will result in signals to correct the muscular action to change in a given direction. These operations are repeated until hand touches glass. Then other similar feedback loops are activated for grasping the glass with sufficient strength, for raising the glass to the lips, drinking until thirst is relieved, and returning the glass to its original position. A simple human feedback system is outlined in the diagram. ▲

Feedback serves three distinguishable functions: (a) providing *information* both about the results of a response and about its characteristics (temporal, spatial, directional, level of intensity, and so on); (b) providing positive or negative *reinforcement*, depending on the adequacy of the response; and (c) providing *motivation* to continue the task by helping to make the world and one's behavior predictable and potentially controllable.

Information theory: Redundancy vs. entropy

In order for a message (feedback or input) to control an action in a given direction, the message must be accurately transmitted and interpreted as intended by the source. But messages are subject to distortion as they are sent through various communication channels. Sometimes the signal is weak, as when a shy student utters a barely audible opinion. Sometimes the receiver does not recognize the signal because he or she is distracted by personal problems, expects a different signal, or is unfamiliar with the language of the transmitted signal. At other times, there may be "noise" or static in the communication channel, reducing the quality of the signal.

Communications engineers need to know precisely how much information is being transmitted over a particular communications system in order to determine its efficiency. To do so, it is necessary to quantify the concept of information. Claude Shannon of Bell Telephone Laboratories did just that in 1949 by developing a mathematical theory of communication (Shannon & Weaver, 1949).

The unit of measurement of information is a bit. *A bit is the amount of information that distinguishes two equally likely alternatives.* Before I flip a coin there are two equally likely outcomes. I flip it and tell you it came up heads. One bit of information has been transmitted. Do I convey any additional information when I also tell you it was not tails? No, that information ("not tails") is completely redundant, it does not tell you anything more than you already knew ("it's heads"). But if I rolled a die I still convey information when I tell you it was "not two" when you already knew it was "not one," because there are six equally likely alternatives. One bit is the maximum amount of information contained in a yes-or-no answer. That maximum can be achieved only when you ask the question so that it divides the possibilities exactly in half. (See *P&L* Close-up, Can You Guess What I'm Thinking?)

Redundancy is the repetition of elements within a message. It is a process that increases the reliability of the message. It includes the structural constraints, such as the rules of grammar, that are imposed on many types of information. Most written and spoken languages are about half redundant. They contain at least 50 percent more information than is essential for transmission of their message. Redundancy clarifies communication and is insurance that the message will get through.

In interchanges between airplane pilots and control tower personnel the words *Able, Baker,* and *Charlie* replace *A, B,* and *C*. These words do not add

Close-up
Can You Guess What I'm Thinking?

I am thinking about one particular square on a checkerboard; can you guess which one? It is possible for you to discover exactly which one of the 64 possible squares I have in mind by asking the proper six questions. If each of your questions reduces the area of uncertainty by half (that is, eliminates half of the possible alternates) then six questions will be necessary and sufficient to locate the square. If your first question was "Is it in the upper right-hand quarter of the board?" that would reduce the alternatives by only a fourth (it could be anywhere in the other three quarters). Here is one set of efficient informational questions that remove or reduce uncertainty in an optimal way (from Attneave, 1959):

1. Is it one of the 32 on the left half of the board? (Yes)
2. Is it one of the 16 in the upper half of the 32 remaining? (No)
3. Is it one of the 8 in the left half of the 16 remaining? (No)
4. Is it one of the 4 in the upper half of the 8 remaining? (No)
5. Is it one of the 2 in the left half of the 4 remaining? (Yes)
6. Is it the upper one of the 2 remaining? (Yes)

The answers given in parentheses refer to the checkerboard below which indicates how the area of uncertainty is progressively reduced with each binary cut of information until the correct one of 64 squares is located. Other questions could also achieve this result, but only if their form is the same—each reduces uncertainty by one-half—a binary cut—and by no other fraction. The uncertainty involved in my question, "Which checkerboard square am I thinking of?" amounts to 6 bits of information.

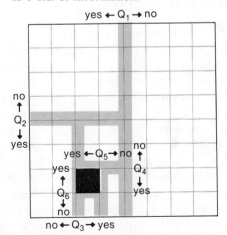

Adapted from Attneave, 1967

anything new to the conversation but they do reduce the possibility that in this noisy channel an *A* will be confused with a *K*, a *B* with a *P*, or a *C* with a *T*. This is another example of redundancy; it improves predictability. If a pilot did not hear the entire letter *C*, it would be difficult to predict what letter was intended; however, if only the *Char* of *Charlie* was picked up, it would be a virtual certainty that it was a *C*.

Opposed to redundancy is *entropy*. Entropy is the amount of uncertainty in an informational system. It can distort the message and confuse the receiver. As entropy increases, each element in the system is more independent, less constrained by context and rules, and freer to vary in unpredictable ways. A table of random numbers exhibits maximum entropy, since each number has an equally probable chance of occurring on every occasion. There is no pattern to be detected. On the other hand, repeating a one-word *mantra* during meditative exercises would involve a minimum of entropy.

It sounds as if entropy is bad and redundancy good. Only up to a point. Only up to a point. Only up to a point where redundancy becomes boring, since nothing new is being transmitted and the receiver may stop processing the message. Some entropy provides a degree of uncertainty and variability; it can arouse one's curiosity and may be intellectually challenging to the receiver.

Analysis of the redundancy in children's textbooks reveals that textbook writers are aware of the need of the young child for repetition. The redundancy factor decreases from its high level in the primer according to a smoothly declining curve over increasing grades. ■ Information processing systems must take account of the degree of knowledge (experience, sophistication, stored information) the system starts with prior to its processing of new inputs. One of the ways in which the mind differs from a machine is in its ability to transform its own level of complexity by the act of processing information. The more it does, the "smarter it gets."

In this regard it is important to note that information does not exist without a mind that is seeking or ready to process that information. When Pasteur remarked that "chance favors only the prepared mind," he reminded us that "accidental" events become "discoveries" when they are observed or thought about by someone with enough prior knowledge to appreciate their significance.

■

Redundancy in children's readers

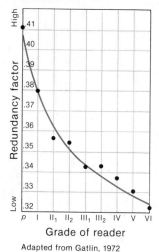

Grade of reader

Adapted from Gatlin, 1972

Computer simulation and artificial intelligence

Cognitive psychologists have studied human thought processes by comparing them with the problem-solving activities of computers. In *computer simulation*, computers are programmed to simulate human problem solving. The computer is used as analogy of what is going on inside a person's mind when he or she takes in information, processes it, and transmits information to the environment. (See *P&L* Close-up, Conversation with the Mad Doctor.) A comparison of human and computer information processing is presented in the figure. ●

Both computers and humans start out with some *hardware*. Computer hardware is the machinery, circuits, microprocessors, nuts and bolts built into it. Human hardware is the body, bones, circulatory system, neural circuits and so on that are genetically determined at birth. *Software* is the programming that enables the computer to manipulate information in particular ways. A computer program is simply a "series of instructions written in a language the

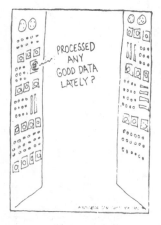

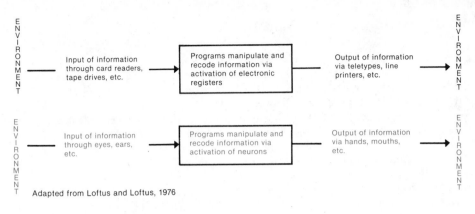

Input of information through card readers, tape drives, etc.

Programs manipulate and recode information via activation of electronic registers

Output of information via teletypes, line printers, etc.

Input of information through eyes, ears, etc.

Programs manipulate and recode information via activation of neurons

Output of information via hands, mouths, etc.

Adapted from Loftus and Loftus, 1976

In this figure you can see the similarity of information processing in computers and humans.

computer is built to understand, that tells the computer precisely what to do with the information presented to it" (Loftus & Loftus, 1976, p. 6). Programs are not part of the computer, but are fed into it. Similarly, humans acquire a variety of programs for manipulating symbols and processing information. We have programs for doing arithmetic, for dancing, for responding to insults, for water skiing, and for countless other activities.

The complicated behavior of computers is generated by relatively simple, but precise computer programs written by humans. Perhaps, then, the complicated cognitive behavior of humans may also be understood in terms of similar programs. "The logic of computer simulation is simple: if a computer program produces the same problem solving behavior as a human then the series of operations are an accurate representation of the human thought processes" (Mayer, 1977, p. 136).

The typical methodology used in computer simulation involves having subjects solve problems aloud, giving a running commentary on their thought processes. A transcript of these comments, called a *protocol*, is made. From a collection of such protocols researchers can derive a description of the mental processes assumed to be used in solving the problems. These operations are put into the form of a computer program, which the computer uses to process the same input data given to the human subjects. If the computer's output matches that of the human, simulation has been achieved and the particular model of information processing is assumed to be valid. If the computer output and human output do not match, either the human protocols did not accurately represent what the subjects were really doing or the computer program was not written correctly.

The development of computer programs that simulate human activity by engaging in conversation or solving problems is referred to as *artificial intelligence*. Three researchers at M.I.T., Newell, Shaw, and Simon, were the first to see computers as symbol manipulating devices that could be used in the study of human thinking and problem solving (1958). Their Logic Theorist, which was designed to find proofs for theorems in logic, was the first major computer system that could claim to show "intelligence." The problem-solving behavior of the Logic Theorist showed many "human" characteristics, such as examples of sudden "insight" into the solution of a problem.

Computers have also been programmed to play chess against both human opponents and other computers. The present champion among chess-playing computer programs is Northwestern University's Chess 4.6 (Kaplan, 1977). However "intelligent" such programs may be, they do not use the same information processing strategies as the human chess masters they play.

Conversation with the Mad Doctor

Can a computer help you solve your personal problems? An example of its therapeutic abilities is demonstrated in the following actual conversation between a "patient" and the "Mad Doctor" computer whose office is at Stanford University's Artificial Intelligence Laboratory.

The patient types responses on a teletype, and seconds later the computer-therapist replies by teletype or a videoscope display.

Patient (PGZ): Hello.

Therapist (Mad Doctor): How do you do. Please state your problem.

PGZ: I feel depressed all the time.

MD: Tell me more about such feelings.

PGZ: I am just unhappy and I want your help.

MD: You believe I can help you, don't you?

PGZ: I am not sure.

MD: Is it because you are not sure that you came to me?

PGZ: I think that I hate you.

MD: Perhaps in your fantasy, we do not like each other.

PGZ: You are nothing but a dumb machine.

MD: Do computers worry you?

PGZ: Computers and therapists worry me.

MD: Why do you mention computers?

PGZ: You mentioned it first.

MD: We were discussing you—not me.

PGZ: Are you a therapist or a computer?

MD: What do you think machines have to do with your problem?

PGZ: They are the cause of it.

MD: Did you ever think they might *not* be the cause of it?

PGZ: No.

MD: Are you saying "no" just to be negative?

PGZ: No.

MD: You don't seem very talkative today.

PGZ: I don't want to talk any more.

MD: Don't you *really* want to talk any more?

PGZ: No.

MD: You are being a bit negative.

PGZ: You bet I am. I am leaving.

MD: Do you believe it normal to be leaving?

Courtesy of Dr. Kenneth Colby

When used as part of a diagnostic evaluation, the computer has proven to be an effective tool in guiding clinicians to the best course of therapy for each patient. Thousands of psychiatric patients at the Veterans Administration Hospital in Salt Lake City have undergone this automated analysis. Says Dr. Thomas Williams, codirector of the computer diagnoses program at the hospital, "a computer can perform some valid functions in a mental health care delivery system, especially in the diagnostic procedure, and perform them with more efficiency and greater precision than attainable before. It can show you what to do more effectively—and the result is better patient care" (quoted in Shuman, 1976).

In some ways, talking to a computer has been found to be less threatening and less impersonal than talking to a busy psychiatrist. The majority of patients surveyed also reported giving more truthful answers to their concerned computer.

Computer simulations of information processing systems are very useful to psychologists. Such programs require that the steps in a sequence of information processing be spelled out in explicit, precise, and rigorous terms, rather than vague generalizations. This forces the researcher to specify all the procedures in a theory and not leave anything fuzzy and undefined. In this way computer simulation offers an effective way of testing our theories about mental functions. Computer models of thought processes are designed to succeed where people do and also to make errors where people do. However, they don't make the errors that observers and behavior analysts do because they don't forget or have personal biases, prejudices, or values. They operate faster and can process more complex sets of relationships than the cognitive psychologist can.

It is important, however, to bear in mind the limitations of such analogies. While computer models serve a valuable function in many areas of research, we cannot say that they *explain* the phenomena being studied. Electronic information processing is not identical to human information processing. Models of this kind are ultimately most valuable in that they generate hypotheses about the functioning of the human brain that might otherwise be overlooked.

Thinking

We have seen that the information processing approach to thinking is based largely upon two analogies, the "human-is-like-a-machine" analogy, and the "thinking-is-like-a-program" analogy. In the first, humans are viewed as complex computers. In the second analogy, human thought processes used in problem solving are viewed as computer programs.

In the previous chapter a quite different view of thinking was presented, that of thinking as covert (hidden) behavior. In an attempt to acknowledge there was more to learning than S→R connections, associationist psychologists extended their view of responding to include *mediational reactions*. These tiny internal responses are triggered by overt stimulus events, and they in turn elicit new internal mediational states which finally evoke an overt solution response.

"Silent speech" in thinking

The notion that thinking is simply "talking to oneself" would imply that it is a behavior that can be measured by the activity of muscles related to speech. What is the evidence that thought is accompanied by *covert oral behavior*, by electrical activity in speech musculature? The evidence from an extensive body of research in this area leads to the conclusion that covert oral responding does occur reliably in a variety of situations (McGuigan, 1978). The covert events thought to be *indicators* of the processing of "thoughts" stimulated by external verbal stimuli are measured by psychophysiological techniques: EEG (electroencephalograph) for events in the central nervous system; EMG (electromyograph) for muscular responses such as lip, tongue, and chin movements; and measures of autonomic nervous system activity such as pupillary dilation and cardiac functioning.

The results of one study reveal that while children are reading silently, they are moving their lips, increasing their breathing rate, and making subvocal sounds (measurable only through high audio amplification). ◆ The same results were later found with silent reading and memorization of prose by college students. Such activity appears to be localized in the speech mechanisms.

Also of interest are findings that while people are having dreams with conversational content (as contrasted to visual, nonlinguistic dreams), their lip and chin EMG responses increase significantly (McGuigan & Tanner, 1971). Furthermore when dreams of various kinds were hypnotically induced, those with verbal content showed marked increases in covert oral activity, while those with "relaxation" and induced "physical activity" content did not.

From research that varies the nature of the information processing demands on the subjects and measures covert oral behavior, it has been conclud-

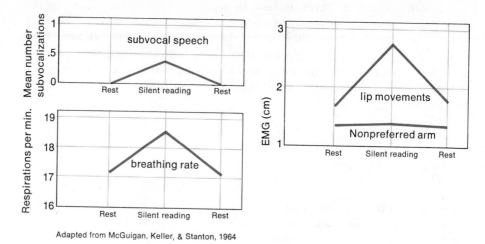

During silent reading, subvocalization, breathing rate, and lip EMG increase in children, while nonpreferred arm EMG changes little.

Adapted from McGuigan, Keller, & Stanton, 1964

ed that the thought process is facilitated by such silent speech. When behaviorist John Watson said that "we think with our whole bodies," he may have been correct to the extent that we respond to incoming, thought-provoking, linguistic stimuli with widespread muscular responses.

Measuring covert responses

Recent evidence reveals that the dilation of the pupil of one's eye is a reliable indicator of momentary increases in the brain's activity. When subjects are in the process of making a decision the pupils dilate (increase in size). Pupillary dilation is related to the level of activation or vigilance necessary to successfully carry out the decision-making process. The more complex the cognitive processing required, the greater the pupillary dilation (Beatty & Wagoner, 1978).

Psychologists have long been concerned with the problem of measuring the time involved in mental processes. Generally, the index for measuring mental processes has been *reaction time*. (See *P&L* Close-up, Taking Time to Think.) Recently, however, a measure of stimulus processing has been developed that is independent of response selection (which button to press, or word to call out) and the time it takes to execute a motor response. It involves measuring the activity of the brain itself (by means to be discussed more fully in Chapter 11).

A particular form of brain-wave activity called P300 is elicited by a variety of cognitive processing tasks. This waveform reaches its peak in amplitude 300 milliseconds after a stimulus event occurs. This is assumed to reflect the times it takes to evaluate a stimulus event and decide to act (Donchin, 1975). The P300 reflects the "surprise value" of a stimulus since its amplitude increases with the unexpectedness of the stimulus. It is large for unusual words, small for familiar words. Stimuli initiate two distinct processes: (a) the selection and execution of an overt response, measured in terms of reaction time, and (b) stimulus *evaluation*, as measured in terms of the P300 component. When people are instructed to respond with *accuracy* to a stimulus, these processes are closely related, with the P300 occurring before the overt reaction time. When subjects are instructed to concentrate on speed, however, the two measures of mental activity are poorly correlated. People often respond *before* fully

Taking Time to Think: Reaction Time

Psychologists who set out to study thought processes soon find that most of the phenomena they are interested in are not the sort of things that can be measured. One thing that can be measured, however, is *reaction time*: the interval elapsing between the presentation of a stimulus and a given reaction to that stimulus. The study of reaction time has been important in psychology, not only for what it tells us about simple motor reactions but also because it serves as an indication of how much mental processing may be taking place between stimulus and response.

The relationship between reaction time and thought can best be appreciated if we examine it from a historical perspective. Reaction time studies fall roughly into four chronological periods: (1) astronomers' studies of the "personal equation," (2) Helmholtz' experiments on nerve conduction, (3) the period of "mental chronometry," and (4) modern studies of the deep structure of language and the complexity of thought processes.

1. In 1796 an assistant to the Astronomer Royal was fired from his post at the Greenwich Observatory because he consistently recorded the transit of a star about one second later than the Astronomer Royal himself. Not much scientific note was made of this discrepancy until 1819, when the German astronomer Bessel became interested in such "errors" of observation. He carefully compared his own reports of stellar transits with those of other astronomers, and showed that there are very consistent differences between people in the times they give to the occurrence of natural events. Bessel expressed these differences in the form of an equation. For example, the difference between the reports of Walbeck, another astronomer, and himself was:

W (Walbeck) − B (Bessel) = 1.041 sec.

As a result, this phenomenon of consistent discrepancies in observation was called the *personal equation*. This concept, as one of the first instances of the systematic study of *individual differences* in behavior, is a precursor of the concept of per-

sonality traits as an explanation for differences in reaction to the same situation.

2. Before 1850, scientists believed that impulses were conducted instantaneously along the nerves. However, in that year, Helmholtz demonstrated (a) that nerve conduction took time, and (b) that the time it took could be measured. In his experiments on sensory nerves, Helmholtz administered a weak electric shock first to a man's toe and later to his thigh. The difference between the man's reaction times to these two stimuli was the measure of the speed of conduction in the sensory nerves. These experiments were the first true studies of reaction time ever to be done.

3. After Helmholtz had shown that there is an interval of time between a physical stimulus and a person's physiological response to it, scientists began to think that this might be a good measure of a person's mental processes. From the 1850s to about the 1930s, reaction time was studied under a variety of conditions, using different versions of a measuring device called the *chronoscope*. One of the major experimenters during this period was a Dutch physiologist named Donders. He identified three types of reaction time: (a) *simple reaction time*, the single response to a single stimulus; (b) *discrimination reaction time*, in which there are several different stimuli but the same single response is made only when a particular one is distinguished; and (c) *choice reaction time*, in which there are several different stimuli and a different reaction for each of them. As you might expect, the third is longer than the second, which in turn is longer than the first.

4. Donders showed that reaction time appears to reflect the psychological *complexity* of the reaction—the amount of mental processing that must take place before the person responds to the stimulus. Present-day researchers have made use of this principle in studying the nature and complexity of cognitive processing. Such research is described in this chapter and various other places throughout the text.

evaluating the stimulus. This is what occurs when we "engage mouth before putting brain in gear."

The use of pupillary dilation, reaction time, and the P300 waveform as measures of mental activity reveals a basic idea about thinking. Thinking is an activity that occurs internally, but to be of value in psychological analysis it must be expressed externally. Thinking can be inferred only from observing some form of overt behavior.

Images in thinking

Usually, thinking involves manipulation of events represented in the cognitive system in the form of words. We also think in mental images, however, and such imagery may be the key to creative thinking. Successful interaction with environmental objects requires that the individual construct an internal representation of these external objects and relationships. It is believed that in the course of cognitive growth three successively more efficient types of representation are built up. The first is *muscular* or motor representation. You can climb your back stairs in the dark without tripping because you have learned to adapt your movements to the exact height of the steps and to turns or irregularities in the stairway. Even without visual cues, you can make the exact motions needed.

The next type of representation is through the use of *images*. Unlike motor representations, images can serve us in the absence of the objects themselves. But images are literal records; they remain similar in form and in their interrelationships to the objects as previously perceived. Not until we become able to construct *symbols*, such as language symbols, do we have a system of representation that can transcend the exact characteristics of what we have perceived. Images are based on particular perceptual details, while symbols may represent inference, abstraction, or transformation according to a rule (Bruner, 1964).

But we can learn little about the use of images in thinking from the self-reports of individuals. In order to be useful, the vague concept of "mental imagery" must be presented in such a way that it can be experimentally analyzed. If we indeed form internal representations of objects in our external environment, can we *measure* the correspondence between such internal events and their external counterparts? Is there a systematic relationship between variations in external stimulus arrays and their internal representations? These were the kinds of questions posed by Roger Shepard and his associates (Shepard & Metzler, 1971, 1974; Shepard & Feng, 1972; Cooper & Shepard, 1973).

In each trial, the subject was presented with a pair of perspective drawings of three-dimensional objects. The task was to determine as rapidly as possible if the two objects portrayed were different or had the same three-dimensional shape, but different visual orientations, a task which made visual imagery necessary. The subject indicated whether the objects were "the same" or "different" by pressing one or the other of two levers. The dependent variable was the amount of time elapsed between the presentation of the drawings and the pressing of the lever. By plotting the pattern of these reaction times against the degree to which the identical figures differed in angular rotation, it was possible to relate internal representation to external variations. Reaction times increased as the angle of rotation between the two figures increased. ▲ *The same amount of time was required to make the mental rotation whether the rotation was two-dimensional or three-dimensional. Subjects reported that they mentally rotated one of the objects into the same orientation as the other, perceiving the two-dimensional figures as if they were objects in*

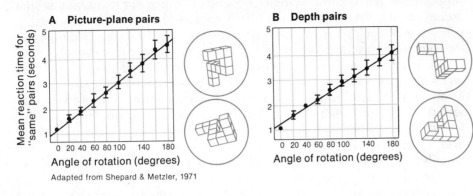

A Picture-plane pairs

Mean reaction time for "same" pairs (seconds)

Angle of rotation (degrees)

Adapted from Shepard & Metzler, 1971

B Depth pairs

Angle of rotation (degrees)

The graphs show mean reaction time required for the mental "rotation" of perspective line drawings to determine whether they were identical. (Vertical bars indicate the variability in responses of the eight subjects.) Sample objects are shown at right. Pair A requires rotation in the picture plane only; Pair B requires rotation in depth.

three-dimensional space. They said the activity of mental rotation seemed to require a certain amount of time, depending on how much rotation was needed, but that the two types of rotation could be carried out with equal ease.

Shepard believes this research shows that internal representation follows an *analogue* process, that is, one in which a mental process corresponds directly (is analogous) to a physical process. The intermediate stages of the process have a one-to-one correspondence to intermediate situations in the external world.

Albert Einstein is the prime example of a thinker in whose creative thought verbal processes did "not seem to play any role." His insight into the fundamental nature of space and time, matter and energy were achieved largely through mentally visualized systems of light and moving bodies (Hadanard, 1945). Like a number of other inventors and creative thinkers (including Thomas Edison and Charles Darwin) Einstein, as a child, suffered from language disabilities. His poor verbal performance led one of his teachers to predict "nothing good" would come of this boy (Sullivan, 1972). Relying on visual images and nonverbal symbols instead of thinking in words "frees" thought from its concrete foundation of already familiar events. Original creations of the human mind—musical compositions, inventions, painting, sculpture, architecture, and scientific theories—may derive largely from "nonverbal internal representations of images of a largely spatial and often visual character" (Shepard, 1978, p. 1).

Reasoning and problem solving

Thought ranges between two extremes—the autistic and realistic. *Autistic thinking* is an idiosyncratic process involving fantasy, daydreaming, and unconscious events. It may be used for self-gratification and wish fulfillment in order to create an imaginary reality where things are the way one would like them to be. Some autistic thinking is part of every creative act. However, when it occurs frequently or is the individual's primary mode of thought, then we suspect the person is "out of contact with reality." Thought disorders among schizophrenics are often characterized by the use of internal reality (the patient's beliefs) as the validity check on the correctness of external reality.

In *realistic thinking,* our personal wishes and beliefs are subordinated to, and "corrected by," the external reality about us. When our thoughts are not supported by reality considerations, we tend to change our thoughts (and the actions based upon them). A star athlete who is told he will lose his scholarship if his grades don't improve, is thinking realistically if he spends more time studying, hires a tutor, goes to class, and cuts down on bull sessions.

In contrast, consider the case of a student who believed his teacher was in love with him because in her course on interpersonal attraction, she talked a lot about liking and loving and intimacy. He told her that he realized she was secretly communicating to him and that he loved her, too. She informed the love-struck pupil that she did not even recognize him in the lecture class of over a hundred students, had no particular feelings at all for him, and was happily in love with someone else. He dismissed this reality as her "coyness" and continued to make advances. Even after the teacher took disciplinary action against him for his offensive behavior, he insisted she was "playing hard to get." Such autistic thinking blinds the person to the constraints reality imposes on acting out irrational impulses and personal desires.

Types of reasoning

Reasoning is thinking that is directed toward a particular goal. It involves the use of relevant information from the environment, as well as stored information, in accordance with a set of formal or informal rules for transforming information. Reasoning may be deductive, inductive, or evaluative.

Deductive reasoning involves the processes of analysis and abstraction. *Analysis* breaks down an object into its component parts, substituting a part for the whole object. The statement "All war is hell" presents only one property of war (its hellishness). *Abstraction* subsumes a specific property under a broader category, or general rule. In processing the abstraction, "evil places are bad for all living creatures," the thinker subsumes "hell" under the general category of "evil places."

(a)   (b)

P_1: All war is hell

(b)   (c)

P_2: Hell is evil

_____

(a)   (c)

C: All war is evil

Deductive reasoning is exemplified by *syllogisms*, which follow the rules of Aristotelian logic. Given premises P_1 and P_2, there can be one, and only one, *valid* conclusion. You have undoubtedly used such reasoning when studying geometry. If the conclusion of a syllogism is not derived by using the rules of logic, that syllogism is invalid.

The *validity* of a syllogism should be distinguished from the *truth* of its conclusion. A syllogism may be valid but its conclusion false if it rests on false premises. Or the conclusion may be true but not logically derived from the premises; in this case the syllogism is invalid. Syllogistic reasoning involves propositions that concern the relations of sets to subsets. The four types of set-subset relations and the diagrams (Venn diagrams) used to represent them are given in the figure. ■

Two types of errors can occur in deductive reasoning: form errors and content errors. *Form errors* occur when people overgeneralize either the breadth (extent) of the middle term, or the breadth of a particular premise by misinterpreting "some" to mean "all." *Content errors* occur when deductive reasoning is biased by the individual's personal attitudes about the conclusion or the premises. Conclusions with high emotional content result in more reasoning errors than less emotional ones of identical logical form (Lefford, 1946). People tend to judge as valid conclusions they agree with and as invalid those with which they disagree (Janis & Frick, 1943). From the systematic study of errors in logic and reasoning we learn much about the structure of the mind, as we shall see in the final section of this chapter.

Many problems, however, do not have a single right answer and cannot be solved by simply putting together the available evidence.

Possible Venn diagrams for four types of propositions

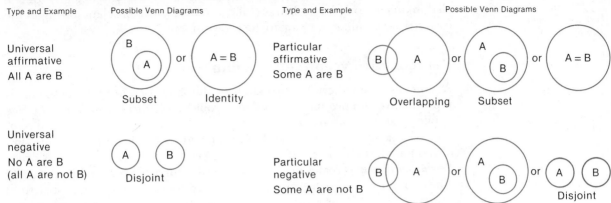

Adapted from Mayer, 1977

Inductive reasoning involves constructing a hypothesis from a minimum amount of data. Further evidence is then scanned to determine whether it confirms the hypothesis. Alternative hypotheses are also sampled. The thinker tries one or a small set of possible hypotheses at a time against the available data (Trabasso & Bower, 1968; Restle & Greeno, 1970). Psychological theories are largely based on inductive reasoning.

A third kind of reasoning is *evaluative*—judging the soundness or appropriateness of an idea, action, or product. Critical thinking is evaluative—it involves judging the suitability or goodness or effectiveness of an idea or representation, as distinguished from trying to create or add to it. The validity of the result depends not only on the reasoning process itself—here the evaluating—but also on the standard used. If the standard is faulty, a solution judged "appropriate" may not fit the real requirements of the situation.

Evaluative reasoning does not begin after a problem has been solved; it is part of the process of acquiring a new response, skill, or learning strategy. Five steps in evaluative reasoning can be outlined (adapted from Holliman, 1976):

a. Specify goals (task analysis), and establish a criterion of suitable performance;
b. assess materials needed to carry out the task;
c. specify responses necessary to achieve goals;
d. arrange materials and program sequence of responses to achieve final goal efficiently (in a given period of time);
e. compare obtained result with criterion to evaluate success.

As Sherlock Holmes remarked on more than one occasion, evidence which seems to point unerringly in one direction, may, in fact, if viewed from a slightly altered perspective, admit of precisely the opposite interpretation.
Nicholas Meyer
The Seven Percent Solution

Solving problems

Whenever you find yourself in a novel situation in which you are motivated to achieve a certain goal but in which your progress toward it is blocked by some obstacle for which you have no ready-made response, you are confronted with a *problem* (and a potentially frustrating situation). Solution of the problem involves the development of some mode of response that will eliminate the obstacle. Since frustration is an inevitable part of life, much of your behavior necessarily involves problem-solving activity. Some cognitive psychologists define all thinking as "problem solving" (Johnson, 1972), and problem solving as the core activity in our adaptation to the environment.

Reproductive vs. productive thinking

A basic distinction between two kinds of thinking used in problem solving is reproductive and productive thinking. Problem solving by *reproductive thinking* applies past solutions to current problems. Previously learned habits and reinforced behaviors are reproduced in the effort to solve the problem. This kind of thinking has also been called "trial and error," "rote memory," and "drill." *Productive thinking* creates new solutions to the current problem by producing a new organization. It has also been referred to as "insight," and "structural understanding." Reproductive thinking characterizes *associationist* approaches while productive thinking has emerged from the *Gestalt* approach. The origins of these alternative approaches are to be found in Thorndike's cats trying to escape from their confinement in a puzzle box and Kohler's apes trying to get a banana that was out of reach.

For Thorndike (see p. 77) thinking was learning by association. His confined cats made many initial responses in their effort to escape. The responses that did not work were extinguished; those that were part of the solution were reinforced and became stronger. The many responses elicited by the stimulus situation can be thought of as arranged in a hierarchy according to their strength or probability of being produced. This initial *habit family hierarchy* changes with trial-and-error experience as irrelevant responses weaken and relevant, originally weak ones become stronger. ● In this associationist view, problem solving is a process that gradually changes the habit family hierarchy through stimulus-response learning. This view suggests that problem solving is more a matter of learning than of thinking—that is, the organism gradually learns to behave correctly rather than suddenly recognizing the correct response. This is called the *continuity hypothesis* of problem solving; the solution develops slowly over time with practice, experience, and reinforcement.

Gestalt psychologist Wolfgang Kohler disagreed with this position, arguing that Thorndike's experiment was not appropriate to the study of problem solving since it was impossible for the cat to use foresight and planning in the solution of the problem. The release mechanism for the trick doors was out of the animal's field of vision, so it could not "figure out" how the doors worked. Also, the correct response (manipulating a door latch) was so foreign to the

●

Habit family hierarchy

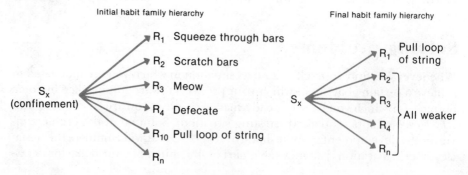

Initial habit family hierarchy — S_x (confinement): R_1 Squeeze through bars, R_2 Scratch bars, R_3 Meow, R_4 Defecate, R_{10} Pull loop of string, R_n

Final habit family hierarchy — S_x: R_1 Pull loop of string, R_2, R_3, R_4, R_n All weaker

animal's normal movements that it could probably only be discovered by accident and not by "reasoning."

Kohler attempted to handle these difficulties by placing animals in problem situations where all the materials necessary for solution were in clear view. In his famous series of experiments with apes, the animal's problem was to get some food that had been placed out of reach. For example, a basket of fruit was suspended from the wire roof of the cage in such a manner that the basket could be made to swing back and forth when a string was pulled. At one point of the arc described by the swinging basket, there was a scaffolding. Although unable to reach the basket from the ground, the animal could catch it as it swung by jumping up on this scaffolding.

In contrast to Thorndike's cats, Kohler's apes seemed to discover the solution suddenly rather than stumbling onto it accidentally while making random responses. Furthermore, once they had found the solution, they responded perfectly on all succeeding trials, instead of showing the gradual improvement that was characteristic of Thorndike's animals. In other words, Kohler's apes acted according to a *discontinuity* hypothesis. Kohler (1926) maintained that problem solving was primarily a matter of insight and perceptual reorganization, rather than trial-and-error behavior. Later studies have modified Kohler's position by demonstrating that insight is not a completely sudden process but does incorporate relevant previous experience. ■

Animals use "tools" naturally in the wild as well as in the presence of humans. This chimp uses a grass stalk to gather a meal of termites from a nest.
Baron Hugo van Lawick;
© National Geographic Society.

Problem-solving stages

Human problem solving commonly involves a mixture of insight and trial and error. Usually we start out with more insight into a problem than was possible, for example, for the cats in the puzzle box. Most of our problems are not totally unfamiliar to us, and there are likely to be intrinsic relationships in our situation, whereas the latch to be pressed in the puzzle box had no inherent relation to the food. So we make plausible hypotheses on the basis of what we already know from experience and then test them, either through action or by thinking through the proposed solution (*covert* trial and error). As we see the results of these tentative solutions, our insight increases, and our later hypotheses come closer to meeting the requirements for solution—until at last we "have it." Seldom do we solve a problem without trying some alternative possibilities; and the final achievement of a solution implies, by definition, some insight into the important relationships.

The thinking process that takes place in problem solving has been analyzed into distinct stages or phases. Wallas (1926) suggests a four-step process:

a. Preparation: preliminary information gathering and trial solutions;
b. Incubation: "sleeping on it" or setting the problem aside;
c. Illumination: the key to the solution appears as a flash of insight;
d. Verification: the solution is checked out against the constraints of reality.

Since the sudden solution is not typical of our daily problem solving, others have proposed more active stages. Among the stages noted by mathematician Polya (1957) is that of "devising" a plan. Here the solver tries to use past experience as a basis for restating the goal (working backward), or to restate the givens in a novel way that relates to past experience (working forward).

Most recent attempts at analyzing the stages of problem solving emphasize reformulating the problem into smaller ones, as independent, sequential substages. As each substage problem is solved, the solver moves on to the next one (Restle & Davis, 1962). The important aspect of problem solving then shifts from one big solution to many smaller ones. But there is still the "problem" of breaking the big nut into smaller pieces, each of which is solvable. Analysis of the time subjects spend and the errors they make at different stages of problem solving indicates that they do chunk problems into substages. Error rates and response times go down as subjects approach a subgoal solution and they go up on the steps that immediately follow a subgoal (Hayes, 1966; Thomas, 1974).

Pitfalls in problem solving

Two pitfalls often met in solving problems are: (a) failure to use negative instances in reasoning out the correct rule and (b) perceptual-cognitive rigidity.

Confirming the rule   Solving well-structured problems typically involves a search for a rule that will serve as a general principle for organizing specific instances. This search is an inductive process in which evidence is generated, hypotheses are formulated and tested, and the rule eventually discovered (Wason, 1971). We can learn much about problem solving and also about some of the limits we impose on our own problem-solving ability by trying to solve an apparently simple problem. (See *P&L* Close-up, The Exception May Prove the Rule.) Only 21 percent of the subjects in Wason's original experiment discovered the rule without making any incorrect announcements. Why do you think the other 79 percent had so much difficulty solving the problem? Why did you formulate incorrect rules, if you did?

An examination of the *process* by which the rule is discovered will illuminate some of the pitfalls and barriers to successful reasoning. These protocols demonstrate that "the exception proves (tests) the rule." Confirming instances alone are not sufficient; negative instances are required as well. We can also see how easy it is to overlook simple solutions in our effort to formulate overly complex hypotheses or unnecessarily precise statements. Wason also found that subjects tended to put too much faith in their hypotheses, seeking to verify them rather than evaluate them. In some instances this dogmatic approach led to self-deception; subjects would misperceive or rationalize feedback that contradicted their proposed solution.

The problems used in studies of this type do not involve the emotions, values, or serious personal consequences that accompany real-life problem solving. Such influences only magnify the difficulties involved in generating objective solutions to our everyday problems.

Problem-solving set and functional fixedness   Sometimes experience is the worst teacher. Prior experience with a particular way of solving problems might be used in new situations where it limits the person's ability to develop a new rule of appropriate generality. This is a case of negative transfer of inappropriate rules. A classic instance of this pitfall in problem solving is the *problem-solving set* or *einstellung* that has been demonstrated in the water jar problems (Luchins & Luchins, 1950). Your task is to obtain a required amount of water in one jar when you have several jars of known different total capacity and an unlimited water supply.

Goal: Obtain 20   *Given:* Jar A (29), jar B (3)

Solution: Fill Jar A to capacity then pour off 3 units into Jar B, empty B, and repeat this two more times until 9 units have been poured off and 20 remain. Goal obtained.

Now try to solve the next four problems, drawing arrows to indicate where you are pouring the water.

Jar capacity

Obtain	A	B	C
100	21	127	3
99	14	163	25
5	18	43	10
21	9	42	6

Here are two more water jar problems to be solved as quickly and efficiently as possible. Again use arrows.

Jar capacity

Obtain	A	B	C
25	28	76	3
22	18	48	4

If you developed a problem-solving rule for the first four problems (B − A − C − C) and used it on the last two problems, you demonstrated a *set* or *einstellung*. Instead of obtaining 25 by filling 76 and pouring off 28 and 3 and 3, you could simply fill 28 and pour off 3 to get 25!

Experimental subjects given a large series of practice problems take longer to solve the test problems than control subjects given only the first practice problem. The control subjects use the short, direct solution. Einstellung puts blinders on the problem solver. It biases the way information is processed; the new is treated as if the old rule is still the best and only rule. (This factor may be at work in problems that involve communication across the "generation gap.")

Functional fixedness is another way in which experience limits problem-solving productivity. We are inhibited from perceiving an appropriate new use for an object because we've used it previously for some other purpose. Gestalt psychologist Duncker (1945), who discovered this principle, showed that subjects had a harder time solving a problem when its key element was given some unrelated function. Thus subjects were unlikely to use a box as a support (for a candle) if it had been used earlier as a container. Subjects who received the box separately were more likely to perceive the solution.

Functional fixedness and problem set chain behavior to the past. Their effects increase with anxiety, fatigue, and the immediate demands of the situation. To break them requires keeping cool and rested during problem solving, distancing yourself from the problem physically, taking a different perspective on it, and always being willing to entertain alternative hypotheses. Children are more creative problem solvers than adults. In part this is due to

Close-up

The Exception May Prove the Rule

The three numbers 2 4 6 conform to a simple relational principle. The task is to discover that rule by generating other sets of three numbers. Subjects are told whether the sets they generate are correct (+) or incorrect (−). Below are excerpts from the *protocols* (experimental records) of two subjects in Wason's study (1971, pp. 207–8). See if you can determine the rule on the basis of the feedback given to them.

Protocol 1

Subject: 8 10 12, (+); 7 9 11, (+); 7 5 3, (−); 13 26 28, (+); 8 16 18, (+); 49 58 100, (+); 8 13 15, (+); 1 2031 2033, (+); the rule is that the first and second numbers are random, the third is the second plus two.

Experimenter: That is not the rule I have in mind. Please carry on with the task.

Subject: 7 5 7, (−); 1 5 7, (+); 5 5 7, (−); 4 5 7, (+); 9 5 7, (−); 263 364 366, (+); the rule is that the first and second numbers are random, but the first is smaller than the second, and the third is the second plus two.

Experimenter: That is not the rule I have in mind. Please carry on with the task.

Subject: 261 263 101, (−); 3 17 17, (−); 51 53 161, (+); 671 671 3, (−); 671 673 900, (+); 42 43 45, (+); 41 43 42, (−); 41 43 67, (+); 67 43 45, (−); the rule is that the second number is random, and *either* the first number equals the second minus two, and the third is random but greater than the second, *or* the third number equals the second plus two, and the first is random but less than the second.

Experimenter: That is not the rule I have in mind.
(Subject gives up after 50 min.)

Protocol 2

Subject: 4 6 8, (+); 6 8 10 (+); the rule is add two to the first and two to the second.

Experimenter: That is not the rule I have in mind. Please carry on with the task.

Subject: 8 10 12, (+); the rule is the progression of even integers.

Experimenter: That is not the rule I have in mind. Please carry on with the task.

Subject: 13 15 17, (+); the rule is any three positive integers.

Experimenter: That is not the rule I have in mind. Please carry on with the task.

Subject: 3 5 7, (+); the rule is any three numbers.

Experimenter: That is not the rule I have in mind. Please carry on with the task.

Subject: −11 0.999 22/7, (+); the rule is any three numbers with or without modifying signs.

Experimenter: That is not the rule I have in mind. Please carry on with the task.

Subject: 8 6 4, (−) . . .

At this point Subject 2 was able to state the correct rule. Can *you* state it? Write it here:

The correct rule is printed upside down below.

The rule is: Any three ascending numbers.

the practical, reality constraints adults have learned. It is also because most cultures "train out" fantasy, imagination, and playful thinking while training in logical, linear, verbal reasoning that is purposeful. Creative problem solving often involves "conceptual blockbusting" a term coined by engineering design professor James Adams (1976). Tradition, cultural values, and environmental blocks must sometimes be broken through in order to imagine what a better world would be like.

The water jar problem is classified as a *well-defined problem* because its initial and final states are unambiguous and the problem is to discover the best means-ends strategy. Many problems we face in our everyday lives are not so well defined. Problems are *ill defined* when initial or final conditions or both are ambiguous. The problem solver has to first define the relevant initial conditions (where shall I begin? what is available and appropriate?), understand the general situation depicted (what is the problem here?), establish goal criteria (what do I want to happen, to achieve?), and identify situations that satisfy these criteria (Erickson & Jones, 1978). Sometimes solution of ill-defined problems, such as "What shall I do with my life?" or "Why do I always hurt the ones I love?" requires not means-ends strategies but analysis in terms of higher-order cognitive structures.

Higher-order knowledge structures

Past experience may be a bad teacher (as we have just seen) or the best teacher. Experience creates cognitive structures that we use to process subsequent information. The negative effects of such experience show up most when novel solutions are suddenly called for, or the tried and true rules of thumb no longer hold. But experience is essential if we are to solve any problems at all, to perform many functions automatically, and to discover meaning and relevance in available information.

Which word is the odd one: *skyscraper/cathedral/temple/prayer*? "Prayer" does not fit if "building" is the concept that you used to organize the elements. Again, which word does not belong: *cathedral/prayer/temple/skyscraper*? "Skyscraper" seems out of place now among "religious" elements (Judson & Cofer, 1956). The first word provides the basis for establishing a concept which, according to your past experience, offers a reasonable interpretation of the problem. Often problem solving requires assimilation of the problem to one's past experience. This assimilation involves seeing relationships between new elements in familiar terms. When you "see what I mean," there is a click of comprehension as the comforting feeling of familiarity wraps itself around the once strange, novel, uncertain, alien cognitive event.

The active organization of past reactions and experience into a cognitive structure that operates in processing new information is referred to by Bartlett (1932) as a *schema*. Assimilation of the new to the old entails searching the memory for an appropriate schema; ". . . such effort is simply the attempt to connect something that is given with something other than itself" (p. 227). The search for meaning and the use of schemata and other higher-order knowledge structures has progressed from its origins in Gestalt psychology to a position of central important in the field of cognitive and social psychology.

Metaphor and meaning

"All human beings, all persons who reach adulthood in the world today are programmed biocomputers. No one of us can escape our own nature as programmable entities. Literally, each of us may be our programs, nothing more, nothing less" (Lilly, 1974, p. viii).

In this passage psychologist John Lilly describes human nature in terms of a computer program metaphor. *Metaphors* are words usually denoting one thing that are used to describe something else that they do not literally denote. Metaphors have a powerful impact on the functioning of cognition, language, memory, and creativity (see Billow, 1977). A metaphor gives a sentence two meanings—literal and figurative—by transferring the receiver's conventional knowledge of it to an unconventional comparison with the "thing" to be understood. Often metaphors substitute a concrete, particular image familiar to the person for a more abstract, unfamiliar image. The mystery of the brain's functioning has always been described metaphorically in terms of the prevailing technology of a given age—a divine clockwork, a spinning wheel, an engine, a radio station, a telephone switchboard, a computer, a hologram.

Among the advantages of metaphor for cognitive functioning are: (a) it reduces mental storage by using single words with two or more distinct meanings, (b) it makes language more flexible and expressive, (c) it leads to greater clarity of thought by expressing abstract, unfamiliar ideas in more comprehensible terms, and (d) it aids memory associations by providing vivid, concrete "memorable" imagery. At a more general level, metaphors carry with them a whole view of an event or experience that can transform one's perception of the thing being described, for example, "life is a bowl of cherries," "her mind is a computer." The artificial intelligence metaphor has, for instance, forced psychologists to make explicit the processes underlying thinking and focus their attention on the issues of how events are represented in memory, stored and transformed.

The study of meaning is the study of semantics (to be discussed in Chapter 7) or more generally, *epistemology*, the philosophical study of knowledge. It is at the core of all cognitive endeavors and is the basis for the development of "knowledge packages" which we consider next. Two types of knowledge exist in every problem solver's memory. *Meaningful*, or *propositional*, knowledge consists of concepts derived from general experience such as, "men and women have equal rights," "I enjoy learning about psychology." *Rote* or *algorithmic* knowledge consists of rules or formulas for operating on concepts, such as "$E = mc^2$."

What do we mean by *meaningful*? Meaning resides in the content of information stored in memory, its association with other stored events, and its current significance in the mind of the problem solver. Meaning can be expressed by pointing to a *referent* (as "my car"—that particular vehicle; or "the Siamese cat"—that particular animal). Meaning can also come from transforming abstract concepts into more *concrete* ideas ("Democracy is government of the people, by the people, for the people"). And we can understand the meaning of something through its *entailment*, or a knowledge of its cause-effect relationships (this lever opens that door). Meaning can also be a broad *subjective experience*. We derive special meanings from events that make a particular difference in our lives, such as a first kiss, making the team, losing a loved one, or finding God.

A fundamental aspect of meaning is comprehension. To *comprehend* is to understand a new experience in terms of its resemblance to some properties of already familiar experience. When we say, "I don't understand," we often mean we do not see the connection between what is being said and the context in which the sentence is being used. Comprehension integrates new information into appropriate contexts or established schema.

According to the results of recent research, human memory seems to represent familiar categories of objects such as table, chair, bird at distinct locations with a *semantic network* (Meyer & Schvaneveldt, 1976). A semantic network is an inferred structure stored in memory that facilitates identifying relationships between known objects (see figure on p. 165).

Subjects were asked to verify the truth of a series of short sentences based on their comprehension of the relations between the sets designated, for example:

> *Some pines are trees;*
> *Some pines are plants;*
> *Some writers are mothers;*

Reaction times (RTs) were measured from the moment a sentence appeared on a computer display screen to the moment the true or false button was pressed. Reaction times varied according to the set relations of the categories. Faster reactions occurred when the first category was a subset of the second (pines-trees) than when they overlapped partly (writers-mothers). Also reaction times increased as the size of the two set categories became more different from each other; thus it took longer to respond to the truth of "some pines are plants" than "some pines are trees."

This research reveals that even where comprehension is easy, people take time to sift their memories for stored information concerning category relations. The speed of the retrieval process increases with the familiarity and specificity of the meanings involved. Other research indicates that the semantic network operates even *before* comprehension of relationships is undertaken. Even one's ability to recognize printed letters, words, and sounds depends in part on how their meanings have been stored.

Sentences to be informative must contain both *given* information (what the listener is expected to know already) and *new* information (what the listener is not expected to know yet). According to a proposed strategy for sentence comprehension (Haviland & Clark, 1974), the listener uses the "given" to search memory for matching information. Then the memory structure is revised by attaching the new information to it. This strategy has been empirically verified. Comprehension time of a target sentence (for example, "the beer was warm") was shown to be faster when a prior context sentence contained information directly related to the target ("We got some beer out of the trunk./The beer was warm") than when the prior context sentence did not ("We checked the picnic supplies./The beer was warm").

Redundant information is essential to transform entropy and "give it meaning." Redundancy, as *given* information, provides an address in memory where the listener is directed to store *new* information so that it will be accessible in the future.

Knowledge packages

"Memory is filled with footprints on the sands of time." This metaphor of memory should suggest to you that from an analysis of footprints we can know much more than the mere fact that someone passed by this way. We can tell the traveler's direction and pace, probable sex, physical bulk, and whether he or she went by on two, three, or four legs. Memory is not a museum of isolated artifacts of our past, it is an organization of active, interrelated knowledge structures. These structures enable us to comprehend incoming information. They also guide the execution of all transformations of that knowledge. From a small bit of new information we may infer a considerable body of likely related events. Or from knowledge of the general context of an event we are able to make educated guesses about the particulars of the event.

The organization of information into higher-order structures has been described in terms of schemas, scripts, attributions, judgmental heuristics, and inferential strategies.

Schemas

"Adam was upset to discover upon opening the basket that he'd forgotten the salt." Your knowledge structure tells you a great deal more about this episode than just that salt was forgotten by Adam. Salt in a basket implies a lunch or picnic basket, which suggests food on which salt might be put, such as vegetables and meats. What else do you suppose was in the basket? Napkins, plates, utensils, dessert, maybe a tablecloth or blanket and some beverage perhaps. You also "know" what was not in the basket; everything in the world larger than a picnic basket and all things that would be inappropriate to take on a picnic, like a boa constrictor or your bronze-plated baby shoes, for example. This body of information has been organized around a "picnic basket schema."

A schema is the primary meaning and processing unit of the human information processing system, according to Rumelhart & Norman (1976). A schema consists of a network of interrelations among its constituent parts. These parts are themselves schematic information units.

Scripts

Scripts are knowledge packages about a complex sequence of interrelated events occurring in a limited time span (see Schank & Abelson, 1977). We have scripts for going to a restaurant (recall John ordered a lobster?), using the library, listening to a lecture, and visiting a sick friend. Such scripts describe standard ways of behaving in given settings. To the extent people share common scripts, their interaction in particular settings will be facilitated. Professors assume students know that the "lecture script" means they listen while the professor teaches. Conflict comes when a student is working from a different script, such as "the class clown script."

Some scripts are controlled by aspects of the situation, such as being quiet in libraries. These are said to be *situation-driven scripts.* Some scripts are controlled by particular roles we are expected to play in society, such as parent, teacher, priest. These can be thought of as *role-driven scripts.* Still other scripts are invoked when we are not in traditional roles or formal situations, they are *person-driven scripts.* These last scripts might be thought of as being expressions of our "personality." ▲

▲
A nun in flowing habit provides an unexpected sight on the ski slopes of Italy; she has stepped out of her stereotyped role to express her own personality.

The systematic investigation of scripted behavior is just beginning to interest psychologists. Many questions are raised by an analysis of script-guided behavior. How are scripts elicited from minimal situational cues? Under what conditions do people set aside a familiar, well-rehearsed script to try out a new one? Why, also, do some actors accept scripts that are not in their best interests, such as self-destructive addiction scripts? The answers to these questions are being sought by social and clinical psychologists as well as by cognitive psychologists.

Attributions

Attribution theory offers a *rational* view of the way the average person makes inferences of causality about behavioral events (Kelley, 1967). The lay person acts like a social scientist who: (a) attends to the *covariation* between particular events (social acts and their outcomes), as well as the (b) *potential causal factors* (such as competence and motivation of actors, situational pressures, sources of prior justification for the act). From such observations, the lay person reasons logically and statistically about the "cause" of a given social event. If a fellow student recommends you take a particular course by Professor X, is the "cause" of that recommendation to be found in the justifiably good quality of the teacher or the poor discrimination of your friend? You infer the validity of the recommendation on the basis of three attributional criteria: (a) *consistency*—the same recommendation is made on many occasions and in many contexts; (b) *distinctiveness*—not all teachers or courses are recommended by your friend; (c) *consensus*—other students with similar knowledge make the same recommendation.

The lay person, as attribution theorist, also "discounts" possible confounding variables that could obscure the inferred causal relation. If your friend fails an exam, will you agree that the teacher was prejudiced—your friend's causal attribution for the failure? Or will you want to establish whether your friend studied, was well on the day of the exam, had not been caught cheating, how many others failed, and so on?

Attribution theory assumes that we have a need to develop an understanding of predictable relations in order to give stability and meaning to events in our lives. This leads to a *reality orientation* to the world. In addition, it assumes that we have a need to be able to predict important events and alter them in desirable directions. This leads to a *control orientation* to the world. (We met these two orientations in Chapter 3 in discussing the two kinds of conditioning and the need for organisms to know when signals and events and consequences are related.) Attribution theory assumes further that our assignment of causes may involve active information seeking, that it occurs in a systematic manner, and that the "meaning" an event has for us depends heavily on the cause we assign to it.

Judgmental heuristics

Attributional analysis is part of a long tradition in psychology that characterizes people as rational, logical information processors. This flattering portrait of "Homo Sapiens as natural problem solver" has of late been challenged. We often make mistakes in our rationally derived judgments (as when I sublet my house to a "respectable couple" who used it to film X-rated movies and to deal in dope). We are all subject to systematic errors in the process by which we make specific causal attributions and general social inferences. We may, at times, be blinded by our theories, restricted by our value orientation, or overly impressed by seemingly "hard data" that comes from our senses and personal experience.

Daniel Kahneman and Amos Tversky (1973, 1978) have made a very important contribution to our understanding of how people misinterpret their ongoing experience. From analyses of such errors we learn about the structure of mind and strategies of human judgment.

Heuristics are cognitive tools, informal cognitive strategies or rules of thumb. Heuristics reduce the task of making complex inferences to very simple judgmental operations—"Go"/"No Go." "Never take candy from a stranger" is a typical heuristic that good little boys and girls are taught. "Don't trust a person who can't look you in the eye" is another decision rule for trust allocation: shifty eyes—No trust; eye contact—Trust. Our heads are filled with such rules of thumb which often serve us well by guiding the countless judgments we make daily down a simple, straight and narrow path. Problems arise however when the path curves or is wide. There is "trouble in Judgment City" when heuristics are overapplied (where not appropriate) or misapplied (where wrong). Kahneman and Tversky's research highlights this use of two heuristics: availability and representativeness.

The availability heuristic   Judges err about how common a particular entity is or the likelihood of particular events when they are overly influenced by their relative availability. When such events are salient and readily accessible (in perception, memory, or imagination), they will be judged to be more common, typical, frequent, important, or likely. The error comes when the judge's *subjective* experience is not correlated with *objective* frequency or likelihood. Thus unemployed people judge the unemployment rate to be higher than do those who are employed. The unemployed person's judgments are biased by the available sample of observations he or she uses as the basis for a judgment of the general level of unemployment — unemployed neighbors, friends, relatives, unemployment agencies, welfare visits, and so forth. Any manipulation that focuses the attention of the perceiver on a particular social event increases its "availability." This in turn results in biased judgments of overestimating the significance, frequency, or potency of that event (Taylor & Fiske, 1978; McArthur & Post, 1978).

The representativeness heuristic Some judgments involve comparisons or relative likelihoods: is event Y more likely to be an instance of class A or B? Inferential tasks, especially ones that involve generalization or induction depend upon deciding what class of event one is observing. Such judgments are based upon assessments of the resemblance or representativeness of the particular instance to a stereotyped conception of the general class (Tversky, 1977).

I have a friend at Stanford who is a professor. He likes to tend his garden, read poetry, is shy and slight of build. Which field do you judge he is in: (a) Japanese studies or (b) psychology?

"Japanese studies" is the answer if you asked the question: is a psychologist more likely to resemble the personality profile given than someone in Japanese studies? But in doing so you have fallen prey to the error of the representativeness heuristic. The answer is "psychologist" if you phrased the question in terms of the statistical base rates of the friends a psychologist is likely to have. A higher *percentage* of Japanese scholars may fit the profile than psychologists, but there is a much greater *absolute number* of psychologists who fit it because there are so many more of them in the population under consideration (Nisbett & Ross, 1979). Where base rate or normative population data are unknown or ignored, the representativeness heuristic will seduce judgments toward false similarities. Psychologists are studying not only the consequences of misuse of judgmental heuristics, but the conditions under which particular heuristics are employed, that is, "recruited" the way scripts and general schemas are.

Inference strategies

Richard Nisbett and Lee Ross (1979) are currently extending the analysis of the use and misuse of higher-order knowledge structures. Their work points up the fallacies of both biased theories and biased data. On the one hand, the lay person acting as intuitive psychologist is "a prisoner" of his or her preconceptions, theories, and knowledge structures. Their hypotheses about how things are related "drive" their observations to find data that "fit" and discard or conveniently overlook data that do not support the hypothesis. Thus the person prejudiced against Jews may argue that they are "greedy" and "money hungry." When shown a Jew who gives freely to charity and sacrifices for the welfare of others, the datum becomes the *exception* to the rule. When presented with published statistics of the philanthropic works of the Jewish community, the bigot rejects the data as "rigged" because "they own all the newspapers." The theory resists negative instances that disconfirm or at least should modify it.

All too often then our inferences are *conceptually driven* and available evidence is distorted in the service of our theories. Even more a source of error in inference strategies is the tendency of the lay person to be overly impressed by certain kinds of data. We tend to give undue weighting to data that are concrete, sensory, personally experienced, relevant to our needs, or otherwise "vividly" presented. This leads to a systematic source of error in giving disproportional weight to the individual concrete case while undervaluing abstract statistics, principles, or baselines. Joseph Stalin is reported to have said (in support of this principle): "A single death is a tragedy, a million deaths is a statistic."

Journalists exploit this error of inference whenever their story about a national trend, or a social movement is "captured" not in population statistics, but in a few character sketches of concrete individuals involved.

A recent laboratory study shows that a *New Yorker* article profiling the social pathology of a single, "prototypical" welfare case had more impact on changing the subjects' attitudes toward welfare than did presentations of critically relevant summary data about general welfare issues (Hamill, Wilson, & Nisbett, 1978). "The intuitive psychologist is, perhaps, as often misled by overreliance upon his senses as he is dogged by adherence to prior theories" (Ross, 1979, p. 5).

Scientific training and the proper use of the scientific method allow psychologists to avoid the pitfalls that can distort inferences and bias judgments. However, in their everyday lives psychologists, like the rest of us, are subject to these misuses of our ordinarily exquisite information processing mechanisms. In the following chapters, we shall analyze two of our unique and more important abilities, memory and language.

Chapter summary

Modern psychology places growing emphasis on the study of *cognition*—the process of knowing. Cognitive processes intervene between stimulus and response to make our behavior truly human.

The *information processing approach* views cognitive activity as either a sequence of mental operations or a sequence of internal changes in information states. An information processing system consists of *input-output mechanisms,* an *information store,* and *processors.* The existence of *multiple processors* enables us to carry on a number of cognitive activities simultaneously. An information processing system may be controlled by the individual processor *(program control),* by higher levels of the system *(conceptually guided control),* or by input information *(data-driven control).* *Cybernetics* is the study of feedback control and communications in machines and living systems. Models of feedback systems include the *TOTE* (TEST-OPERATE-TEST-EXIT) and *closed-loop* feedback systems. Feedback serves to provide (a) information about the results or characteristics of a response, (b) positive or negative reinforcement, and (c) motivation to continue responding.

Information is measured in *bits;* a bit is defined as the amount of information that distinguishes two equally likely alternatives (e.g., heads or tails?). *Redundancy* is the repetition of information; its opposite is *entropy* (uncertainty or unpredictability). *Computer simulation* is often used to study human problem solving processes. The computer mechanism or human nervous system is referred to as *hardware;* the programming or set of instructions fed into the system is called *software.* *Protocols* describing the steps used in solving a problem are used to develop programs for computer simulation *(artificial intelligence)*. It is important to remember that while such models throw a great deal of light on human information processing, they do not *explain* it.

If we consider thinking in terms of *mediational reactions*, we can measure it in terms of *covert oral behavior* (responses of the muscles involved in speech) or other covert activity, such as changes in brain waves or pupillary dilation. The traditional measure of cognitive activity is *reaction time* (the time intervening between stimulus and response). Thinking involves three types of *internal representations* of external objects or relationships: *muscular representation, images,* and *symbols.*

Thought ranges from the *autistic* (self-centered) to the *realistic.* Realistic thinking includes three types of *reasoning: deductive reasoning,* involving the use of *syllogisms* in which data are combined and inescapable conclusions are drawn; *inductive reasoning,* in which hypotheses about the unknown are formulated on the basis of inferences from what is already known; and *evaluative reasoning*—judging the soundness or appropriateness of some new idea or product.

An individual in a new situation who wishes to reach a goal, but is blocked by some obstacle, is confronted with a *problem.* Approaches to problem solving may involve *reproductive thinking* (relying on past learning) or *productive thinking* (new organization and insight). Most human problem solving involves four stages: *preparation, incubation, illumination,* and *verification.* When problem solving involves seeking out the correct rule, we often forget that our "wrong" answers can provide us with as much information as our "right" answers. Another pitfall in problem solving is *rigidity,* which may take the form called *set* or *einstellung,* in which we unthinkingly apply old rules to new problems, or *functional fixedness,* in which we fail to see new uses for familiar objects.

The process of assimilating new information and experiences involves organizing past reactions and experiences into cognitive structures called *schemas. Metaphors* give meaning by applying concrete and familiar images to abstract and unfamiliar concepts. *Epistemology* is the study of knowledge; it deals with both *meaningful propositional knowledge,* derived from experience, and *rote* or *algorithmic* knowledge of rules or formulas. The study of meaning is called *semantics. Semantic networks* are inferred structures by means of which we identify relationships between objects.

Higher-order knowledge structures include schemas, scripts, attributions, judgmental heuristics, and inference strategies. In this usage, a *schema* is a network of interrelated concepts. *Scripts* involve sequences of interrelated events. *Attributions* are inferences about causality; they give predictability to our world. *Heuristics* are the cognitive strategies or rules of thumb on which we base our behavior. One example is the *availability heuristic,* which leads us to judge the frequency of a given event in terms of its *perceived* availability, which may be influenced by its importance to us. Another is the *representativeness heuristic,* whereby we make judgments based on stereotyped views of a particular class of people or objects. Biased *inference strategies* may lead us to amend our data to fit our hypotheses rather than the reverse.

Memory and Forgetting

Robert W. was the first institutionalized mental patient I saw during the practicum part of a graduate course in abnormal psychology. He did not fit any of my preconceptions about how a mental patient would (or "should") behave. In fact, he seemed perfectly normal throughout the entire hour-long interview. But just when I was ready to conclude that he had been diagnosed incorrectly, his pleasant, attentive, matter-of-fact manner disintegrated before my eyes.

"Do you have children, Robert?" I asked.

The patient went into a fit of sobbing, displaying an intense hysterical reaction, depression, and incoherent speech. After a few minutes, he pulled himself together to explain that he had had only one child, a six-year-old daughter, Jennifer. He loved Jennifer very much and recalled many of the joyful episodes they had shared. The girl had been killed in a hit-and-run accident on her sixth birthday. Whenever he thinks of her or whenever anything he experiences reminds him of her, he is plunged into a state of deep depression. He has been unable to hold his job or to maintain his previously good relationships with friends and family.

"I cannot help thinking of that sweet little face with its wry little smile," he said, "and whenever I do, I am filled with great sadness" (a normal reaction, so far). "But I must not allow myself to forget her, because once I do, my little girl will not exist any longer. You see, then she will be forgotten and I would be the one who killed her memory." Jennifer would have been about ten years old at the time of our interview.

My cousin, Mrs. R. J., lost her memory one day, and I had the unpleasant task of helping her find it again. It is one thing to read textbook accounts of amnesia, but quite another matter to have someone you've known most of your life look into your eyes without the faintest glimpse of recognition. She did not remember where she currently lived (she had traveled to a city she had lived in ten years earlier believing it to be her present home). Nor did she recognize anyone except her young son. The past was gone and with it went her identity — or at least much of it. R. J. did not recall her name or any information about who she was or what she did for a living (she was a college professor).

But she did remember clearly all she knew about English literature, enough so that she was able to teach again even before the rest of her memory returned. To their dismay, her students, even the ones she had been very close to, were also forgotten. That is, she could not recall their names, details about their backgrounds, grades, or specific information that linked them to her past. But curiously, she had an "emotional memory" for them and for other people she had liked very much or disliked strongly. She was a woman of strong opinions who tended to overreact to people and causes. She would say to previous friends, "I'm sorry I don't know who you are, but for some reason I like you (or feel safe around you, or can trust you)." On the other hand, encounters with previous adversaries might bring a blush of guilt or a moment of fear as she would hesitatingly report how silly she felt reacting so strongly at first meeting the "stranger." She was even a bit ashamed at "judging a book by its cover." This was one of the few negative feelings in her otherwise euphoric state of amnesia.

R. J. gradually pieced her life together again, with a little help from her friends. They reminded her, for example, that she had usually been on a diet and had not enjoyed eating as much as she did now since she was a chubby teenager. (She went back on her diet.) They informed her that she need not keep doing dishes by hand because she had a dishwasher. Once so reminded, she recalled how to operate it. But the more she remembered, the less happy

R. J. became. It seems that she had suffered an incredible series of traumatic events within the past year climaxing with the breakup of her marriage and the sudden death of her mother before her eyes. Amnesia put all that past ugliness, and more, out of awareness. In its place this motivated forgetting had given her peace of mind. But it was too upsetting to the rest of us to have someone in our midst who didn't remember what she was supposed to. R. J. was eventually "cured" when we helped her remember all of her traumatic experiences. To be sure, she was wiser with the return of her full faculties, but also much sadder.

What Robert W. refused to forget, Mrs. R. J. was unwilling to remember. While their reactions are obviously very unusual, nevertheless they force us to acknowledge what we usually take for granted—the power of memory to recreate reality and the forces of forgetting that deny its existence.

Not the power to remember, but its very opposite, the power to forget, is a necessary condition for our existence.
Sholem Asch
The Nazarene

How do we remember?

When most people think about memory, they consider only the way we retain facts. If you can remember many facts for a long time, then your memory is good; if not, it isn't. But memory is much more than just a mental warehouse cluttered with the experiences of living. First, it involves recognizing what we are experiencing; is it a horse or a deer, the letter A or the letter X, the sound of a voice or the sound of something else? This is a process that psychologists call *encoding*. Then there is the task of *storing* the information so we can get to it when we want it. This step is crucial since without adequate storage, our memory would be almost totally ineffective. Think of a library where a great many books are received, and then hurled over the librarian's shoulder onto an ever increasing mountain of items. When someone asks for a particular book, there would be no way to know if the library owned it unless you sifted through the pile, book by book, until you found what you were looking for or exhausted the search—or yourself. The problem is not that the book is not in the library; it may well be there. The problem is that there is no order to the way things are stored.

We store information according to our previous experiences. If we are trying to remember a joke about talking fish, we might store it with what we know about fish, about talking, about the peculiarity of fish talking, and so on. Then, when we want to recall the joke, there are a lot of places in memory to look for it; we have related it meaningfully to other experiences in our life. One of the reasons why children have such poor memories (not to speak of the poor memories of many adults) is that they have not learned adequate ways to store what they want to remember.

Memory is the diary that we all carry about with us.
Oscar Wilde
The Importance of Being Earnest

The reason storage is so important is that it makes retrieving information from memory so much more effective. If we know "where" it is, it is easier to get to, and retrieving information when it's needed is what memory is all about. In amnesia, the loss of memory does not mean that recollections have really been lost or dropped from memory. What it does mean is that the cues for retrieval are missing. Mrs. R. J., eventually recalled her previous experiences when the appropriate cues were reinstated. As you can see, then, memory is more than strictly retention. It also includes encoding, storage, and retrieval. A disturbance or inadequacy in any of these processes can disrupt, if not totally destroy, our memory for an event.

Getting information in and out of memory

A child learning lines for a play uses encoding, storage, and retrieval skills.

There are different ways of encoding, storing, and retrieving depending on what we want to do with what we've experienced and how long we want to retain it. ■ In phoning the theater to find out what time the movie starts, we need only store the phone number long enough to make the call; after that there is no sense remembering it. The whole process is geared to a short time span. On the other hand, storing, retaining, and retrieving the name of a teacher from whom you'd like a letter of recommendation uses a different process since it is considered a more important and lasting thing. But it is not only names and numbers that we remember, or historical facts, or rules and directions; we also remember faces and pictures, odors and tastes, caresses and pains. These sometimes involve the same basic processes, but there can also be some big differences. You can rehearse a name to yourself by reciting it over and over, but how do you rehearse an odor to yourself?

Encoding, storage, and retrieval are constantly interacting with one another. Things we learn in one setting, or at one time, are needed in another setting or at another time in order to solve a problem or make some kind of judgment. When a patient recites a list of complaints, the physician probes his or her own memory trying to retrieve information that will be a reminder of what the symptoms mean. The physician tests hypotheses, confirming or rejecting them, all the while comprehending, storing, and retrieving new information that the patient provides.

Or, consider another example. Suppose I meet a Mr. Samson at a party and conclude, for one reason or another, that it's important to remember his name. But how? Well, I think of the story of Samson (retrieval), his great strength and his long hair, and I try to associate that story with the man I have just met. If this Mr. Samson is totally bald, I just associate (store) that fact with my memory of the original Samson—after Delilah did her dirty work. The next time I run into Mr. Samson I will draw the connection between his appearance—the bald head—and my memory of the shorn and weakened Samson. The name should be retrieved almost immediately. There will be more to say about this later in the chapter when we deal with improving memory. Of course, if Mr. Samson is wearing a hairpiece when we next meet, I'm finished. But that should make the point that our memories are fallible. It's not that I don't know the man or that I have forgotten his name. It's just that the cue of baldness that I need to retrieve the name isn't there and I am stymied, at least momentarily.

Along with all the knowledge we have stored and retained about our past experiences, we also have knowledge about things we haven't experienced, but which, nevertheless, involve our memory. If a bus is bearing down on you at fifty miles per hour, you don't need firsthand experience to realize that it would be prudent to move out of the way. Within an instant we can, we hope, retrieve from our memory what we have been told or have observed about incidents like these, or personal experiences with other big things traveling at fast speeds, getting knocked down by a playmate on a bicycle, or being spanked by a parent.

We also know when we don't know something or that we have not experienced something. College students were faster at responding "no" to the names of large European cities they had *not* visited than "yes" to the names of those they had visited (Kolers & Palef, 1976). People are more accurate in knowing that they haven't heard a particular joke than knowing that they have heard it (Dolinsky, 1978). Can you generate a hypothesis to account for this effect?

Also, you know that you know your current address, and you know that you may possibly remember your previous addresses (or that they are on the "tip of your tongue"). However, you know surely that you do not know Billy Carter's address in Plains, Georgia. Experiments have shown that these feeling-of-knowing (or not-knowing) judgments can be quite accurate. (See *P&L* Close-up, Don't Tell Me—It's on the Tip of My Tongue.)

You search through the stacks of a library for a specific book only if you have reasonable grounds for believing that it is there. It is of little use to search for esoteric, out-of-date government documents in a small bookmobile. There seems to be a built-in monitor that tells you whether you are likely to know something—whether a more extensive search of your memory will prove fruitful in answering the question.

In one experiment, college students were asked a number of general information questions (e.g., "Who invented the steam engine?"). If the students could not recall the answer to a particular question, they were asked to rate their "feeling of knowing" on a five-point scale. Later they were given a multiple-choice test. The observed percentage of correct choices was about 63 percent for tests on items the subjects thought they knew versus 47 percent for tests on items they thought they did not know, as compared with the 25 percent correct that would have been expected by chance on the four alternate questions. In other words, the subjects could judge to some extent whether they knew information that they could not recall at the time (Hart, 1967).

This introspective monitoring, this knowledge of our own storehouse of knowledge, is surely one of the more fascinating capabilities of the mind. It serves to inform us whether it is worthwhile to search our memory for some elusive item of information; by this means, time and effort are not wasted in hopeless and fruitless searches.

Close-up
Don't Tell Me—It's on the Tip of My Tongue

What is the name of the waxy substance derived from sperm whales that is often used in perfumes? What is the name of the small boats used in the harbors and rivers of China and Japan? Do you know the name of the patronage bestowed in consideration of family relationship, not on the basis of merit? When these questions were asked of a large of number of college students, there were three kinds of reactions: immediate recall of the correct word; failure to identify the word from the definition; and, most interestingly, awareness of knowing the right word, but not being able to recall it (Brown & McNeil, 1966). This last reaction is a common one we all experience when the name we are searching for is "on the tip of the tongue" (TOT).

If these TOT words are really known and stored in memory, but are not available in the person's active-recall vocabulary, then it should be possible to demonstrate that many characteristics of the word can be retrieved through questioning. When asked to write down all the words they were thinking of as possible answers, subjects gave words that are similar in *meaning* to the elusive TOT word, but more often they answered with words similar in *sound*. For the TOT word *sampan*, they tended to answer "Siam," "Cheyenne," "Sarong," or "Saipan" more frequently than "junk" or "barge." They were also able to recall other details of the target word, such as its number of syllables and first letter, even though the word itself was not recalled.

You might want to demonstrate this phenomenon for yourself using your roommate or relatives as subjects to see what they say while searching for *ambergris, sampan, nepotism,* and other words that might fall into the TOT category. From such research we learn that memory storage and retrieval is a complex, rather than an all-or-none process.

Systems of memory storage

Although psychologists are still unsure about the explanations of memory and forgetting, they are fairly well agreed upon some of the characteristics of the memory process. Basically, there appear to be three different memory systems, each involved with the storage and retrieval of information: sensory-information storage, short-term memory, and long-term memory. While we will discuss these systems separately, it is important to note that they are continually interacting, with information being shifted from one to another.

Sensory-information storage

The first system involved in the memory process preserves sensory information just long enough to be used in perceiving, remembering, judging, and so on, and is called *sensory-information storage*. Sensory information enters the memory system from all of our senses, though it is vision and audition that have received the bulk of research interest. Visual information in this system is referred to as an *icon* and it lasts for less than one second. On the other hand, auditory information, called an *echo*, persists at least a second and possibly much longer. You can get some idea of this by suddenly turning off some music to which you have been listening; the sounds tend to reverberate for a while longer. If you try a similar thing with a picture—flashing it very briefly in front of your eyes—the trace will disappear much more rapidly.

In one experiment, subjects were shown an array of nine letters in three rows of three letters each. After a lightning exposure of 30 milliseconds for the entire array, they were asked to report the three letters in a particular row. If the instruction to report a row was delayed one-fifteenth of a second from the exposure, subjects were about 60 percent successful. If the delay was longer, about one second, they were only about 40 percent correct (Sperling, 1960). That gives some idea of just how fast the icon disappears.

You might think that information processing would be more effective if the sensory traces remained longer. There would be more time to deal with them and interpret what stimulus is being presented. However, we don't see or hear things one sight or sound at a time. There are sequences and patterns occurring very close to one another, and if the traces did remain in sensory storage much longer, new information would tumble in with the old, masking and distorting what went before and making recognition difficult. Think what would happen with speech. The very shortness of the icon and echo, their rapid fading, insures the distinctness of the experience. Actually, with the system functioning the way it does, we can still analyze a great deal of information in a very short time.

Pattern recognition   By whatever sense any stimulus enters sensory-information storage, it is necessary to determine what has been presented. If it's a number, which one; or what word or odor? That is, a particular *pattern* must be recognized in order to give meaning to what we are experiencing. It is just at this beginning point that other aspects of memory become involved. For example, to know which number is being flashed in front of us, we must have prior memories of what numbers look like; otherwise we would just be observing a meaningless squiggle.

Somehow, the incoming stimulus must be rapidly compared with a number pattern already in our memory; if there is a match, we recognize the number. However, every 6, say, doesn't look the same; some are large and some small, some stand straight up while others lean to the side, and so on. In fact, variation is more the rule than the exception and the system must be able to recognize a 6 in all its irregular forms. Similarly, we recognize our name whether it is spoken by a child, an old man, or a telephone operator. (See *P&L Close-up, Put Your Money Where Your Mouth Is.*)

Exactly how the matching occurs is not entirely clear. One theory suggests that patterns are divided into features—straight lines, curves, and the like—and these features are compared with a pattern already stored in memory through earlier experience. The best match between the features and what is stored determines what pattern is recognized. The form would be recognized as a B rather than a P because it has more features in common with the stored pattern of a B (two round segments, for example). This is so even though it's not a very good B, since it comes closer to our pattern of a B than it does to any other letter (Selfridge, 1959). In order to do this matching, one must attend to what is happening. Obviously, you can't remember something if you don't pay some attention to it and often our memory fails just at that point. The material never gets into the system.

Shared attention   For a long while, all the evidence showed that attention had very distinct limitations and that you couldn't attend effectively to two things at one time. Even the famous "cocktail party phenomenon" is a case of selective attention. We can shift our attention instantaneously from one conversation at the party to another, but we can't concentrate on both at the same time. When one is in the foreground, the other shifts abruptly to the background.

However, recent research shows that we can attend to several things simultaneously though it takes some practice. After a few weeks of training, subjects were able to read a short story aloud at the very same time they were taking dictation on another topic. Furthermore, they performed all of this with the same speed, comprehension, and accuracy they showed when dealing with the tasks separately. These findings suggest that perhaps attentional capacity does not have fixed limits (Spelke, Hirst, & Neisser, 1976). Maybe we were right when we argued with our parents that it was possible to do our homework and watch television simultaneously. Once information is attended to and recognized, it may be passed on to short-term memory.

Short-term memory

The second memory system is *short-term memory*, in which limited amounts of information that the person has just learned remain in the memory for very short periods of time, probably no more than thirty seconds. This can be extended considerably if we rehearse the material; otherwise memory starts to disappear almost at once. The classic example of short-term memory was mentioned at the beginning of the chapter; it concerned remembering an unfamiliar telephone number. After you look up the number in the directory, you can dial it immediately and perhaps even repeat it to someone else if necessary. Shortly after that, however, you probably cannot remember the number correctly.

In another demonstration, college students first were shown a trigram composed of three consonants, like QNV. Following that, they were shown a three-digit number and were asked to count backward by threes until stopped. Finally they were instructed to recall the trigram. Since counting backward should interfere with the active rehearsal of the trigram, this task should give us a good idea of how long information stays in short-term memory. In this experiment, students received eight trials in which they saw a trigram (a dif-

As more people pay their bills by check, banks are becoming overwhelmed by millions of small pieces of paper. This has led to attempts to find an alternate system that would eliminate paper checks. One proposal, discussed by Lummis in the Bell Laboratories Record (1972), is to use something like a voice print. The bank account holder would tape-record a short message such as "We were away a year ago" and this would be stored at the bank. Whenever a bill was due, the account holder would phone the bank, give his or her name, and recite the message. A computer would compare this with the stored recording, using such characteristics as pitch, speech intensity, speech rate, and others. If the match was close enough, and obviously we would not expect it be exact, the bank would pay the bill. No paper checks, no trips to the bank . . . just a simple phone call.

How well does it work? In one test, the computer was correct in 98.8 percent of the comparisons and the verification took only seven seconds. Human evaluators, on the other hand, were right only 95.8 percent of the time. But what about "forging"? Could someone telephone the bank, give your name, mimic your voice, and have the bank pay out your life savings without your knowledge? When this was tried, using impersonators trained to accurately reproduce pitch, intensity, and rate, the computer was fooled 41 percent of the time! Not so good. Voice verification by computer might be on its way, but the age of the checkless society probably is still off in the future.

ferent one on each trial), counted backward for three seconds, and then tried to recall the trigram. They were correct on about 80 percent of the trials. When they were asked instead to count backward for 18 seconds, the students were correct on only 10 percent of the trials; they had forgotten a massive 90 percent (Peterson & Peterson, 1959).

Like sensory-information storage, short-term memory has a limited capacity and can only store a small amount of information, about five to seven *unrelated* items, whether words, letters, numbers, or something else. As we shall see later, if the items are related in some way, the capacity can be increased; we can remember sentences that contain more than seven words, but a sentence has meanings; the words are related in a special sequence.

Usually though, short-term memory capacity is not very great. I once taught at a university where all the telephone calls were placed by one switchboard operator. Her short-term memory capacity was six digits and since she never wrote anything down, perhaps due to vanity, she always guessed at the seventh. There was one chance in ten of correctly completing the call. (Needless to say, I was often connected to a wrong number.)

Further, if short-term memory is overloaded, information will be "pushed out." In order to accommodate the new material, the old is lost. It's like constructing a row of blocks on a table. When the row is long enough to reach from one side to the other, each additional block that is placed on one side results in a block on the other side dropping off the table.

Rehearsal Though short-term memory has limited capacity, the information that is there is very accessible and can be recalled easily. To maintain information in short-term memory, it is necessary to rehearse it actively (as when we repeat that telephone number over and over again). However, if the rehearsal is just a matter of rote repetition, it is not very effective; forgetting starts the instant that the repetition ceases. Rote rehearsal might be adequate for phone numbers dialed once, but it has major weaknesses when we want to remember information for longer periods of time.

Jacoby (1973) had students learn a list of five common words, a very easy task. When tested immediately after the presentation, without rehearsal, their recall was perfect. Other students learned the same five words, but rehearsed them for fifteen seconds before being tested. Again, unsurprisingly, there was perfect recall. Tested with many other five-word lists, they did just as well. But at the end of the experimental session, the students were instructed to remember all the words contained in all the lists. This came as a complete surprise, since they had not expected a comprehensive test. The results showed that the memory for words in the lists that had been rehearsed for fifteen seconds was no better than for those that had not been rehearsed. Apparently rehearsal by sheer repetition does not improve memory; it just maintains the information in short-term storage.

Short-term memory appears to involve some sort of "echo" process by which items are stored according to their sound rather than their meaning. Research has shown that many of the errors that occur are confusions of things that *sound* alike, even if they look different and have different meanings. For example, on tasks involving immediate recall of lists of letters, subjects may remember *B* instead of *D*, or *S* instead of *X*. These short-term acoustic confusions occur even if people have seen the lists of letters, rather than heard them (Conrad, 1964).

Retrieval from short-term memory   So far, we have been discussing how material is stored in short-term memory. But there is also a retrieval process, some way of searching through what has been stored. The following experiment should illustrate this process.

People were shown a slide which contained from one to six digits, 6, 3, 7, 9, for example. After a brief exposure, a single digit was shown as a probe and the task was to indicate, as rapidly as possible, whether that digit was part of the original set. One result of this task was that reaction time to the single digit probe increased as the number of digits on the first slide increased. This might not seem surprising and it indicates that the individual is checking the probe digit against the original set, one item at a time (Sternberg, 1966). ◆

But actually, there is a surprise in another result of this experiment. On the average, probe digits that are not in the original set, the "noes," should have longer reaction times than those that are, the "yeses." To be certain that

◆
In this graph the average reaction time is shown as a function of the number of digits in memory. The filled circles show the reaction times for "yes" responses and the unfilled circles show the reaction times for "no" responses.

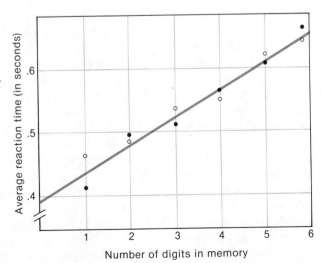

Adapted from Sternberg, 1966

an item is not in the set, one must make an exhaustive search through all the digits in the original. But if the probe digit is in the original set, the search can stop as soon as the match is found. This is called a self-terminating search and it should take less time than the exhaustive search. However, the results show no difference. This implies that, if the answer is "yes," the individual, nevertheless, continues to search every other digit in the original set; an exhaustive search. Why should one use what appears to be an inefficient process like this? Why not stop when the match is made and not waste time going through the rest of the comparisons?

Sternberg feels that there are two processes involved. First, *comparing* the probe digit with the digit in the original set and second, *deciding* whether there is a match. Let us assume that in short-term memory, the comparing process is rapid and the deciding process slower. If it was necessary to compare each digit with the probe and then decide whether it matched before moving on to the next digit in the set, the search would result in alternately comparing (fast) and deciding (slow), comparing and deciding, and so on. Suppose, on the other hand, all the comparisons were made first and then just one final decision at the end—was there a match anywhere? That is, an exhaustive search. There would then be only one slow process, one decision, and the whole search would be more efficient than if it was self-terminated. Also, "yes" and "no" reaction times would be the same. In fact, the comparison process in this task is quite rapid, taking less than forty milliseconds. That means that one could make about twenty-five comparisons each second.

Long-term memory

Remembering the *meaning* of information appears to be characteristic of *long-term memory*. This third memory system is more permanent, but it is not always easy to retrieve information from long-term storage. Because the material is not immediately accessible, it takes more "searching" for appropriate cues to retrieve it. A reason for this retrieval difficulty is that long-term memory holds a massive amount of information (virtually everything we have ever experienced that has been transferred from short-term memory is stored here), probably millions of pieces of information. It includes not only memory for facts, but also emotions, beliefs, and motor skills like driving. Imagine what it would be like to write down everything you know. Nevertheless, there is no risk that we will overload long-term memory. One estimate is that its capacity is 1,000,000,000,000,000 items (Fry, 1977). In order for this gaint library of long-term memory to be useful to us, there must be some plan or scheme to the way experiences are arranged. Otherwise we would not be able to retrieve anything. That is why meaning is so important a characteristic of long-term memory; the meaning provides the order.

Meaning affects long-term memory in two ways. In *episodic memory*, we remember information on the basis of when or where something happened; specific facts or experiences. You store facts: when Columbus discovered America, where you had lunch yesterday, who your first love was, and so on. *Semantic memory* is less specific, and includes such things as our memory of rules and directions, how to spell and calculate, conceptual units, and such mundane information as knowing that if you run into a brick wall, you will be hurt. Episodic and semantic memory interact consistently and it is often difficult to set distinct boundaries for the two systems. Generally semantic memory is more accessible than episodic memory (Tulving, 1972).

It is also remarkable that so much information can be stored in the relatively small space of our brains. IBM scientists are working on a new form of information storage using magnetic bubbles that holds the promise of storing 100 million bits of information in just one square inch. Through evolution, our brains have been designed to process many kinds of information efficiently and to store much information in bits, but to retrieve not just little bits but whole knowledge structures (of the kinds discussed at the end of Chapter 5).

Semantic processing   Various theories have been proposed to account for the way semantic information is arranged in long-term memory. For example, how do we store such facts as "Elephants have big ears and long trunks" or "Elephants are animals"? Obviously, there must be some hierarchy or network of associations such that big ears and long trunks are properties of elephants and elephants are instances of animals. This is an incredibly complicated business, not only because we have stored a vast number of sequences of this type, but also because these sequences are interrelated. Elephants are animals, but so are robins; that distinguishes them from petunias—but all three are living things which distinguishes them from sand. You can picture the spider web of interrelationships that is part of long-term memory. ▲

We also use long-term memory for *comprehension*. If we are told that "The elephant ate the peanuts," we call up our associations to elephants and to peanuts, realize that "elephant" is the subject of the utterance, "peanuts" the object, and that the elephant caused the peanuts to be eaten. We also make various inferences when we comprehend. For example, we would probably infer that the elephant picked up the peanuts with its trunk rather than its tail or its front feet; and that the peanuts were eaten unshelled. If you were asked to recall the "elephant" sentence tomorrow, you would undoubtedly search through these meaningful relationships in long-term memory. In fact, the sentence finally recalled might not be an exact replica of the original since we process the meaning rather than the verbatim series of words. You might remember it as, "The peanuts were eaten by the elephant," or even "The elephant picked up the peanuts with its trunk and ate them."

Similarly, you will remember tomorrow some of what was said in this chapter, but you certainly will not remember the exact words that were used.

▲
The figure depicts part of an inferred semantic memory network for storing information about familiar categories of objects. Solid lines between category locations point from subsets to supersets, and dashed lines point to other important defining attributes of each category.

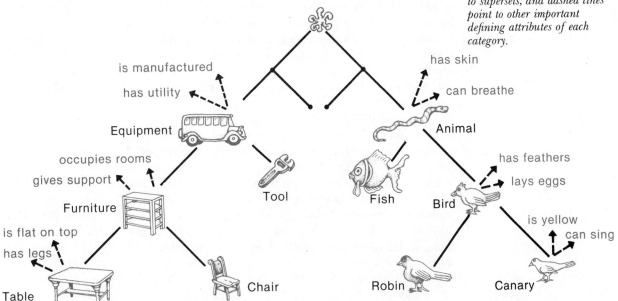

Adapted from Meyer & Schvaneveldt, 1976; original in Collins & Quillian, 1969

The subjects were very good at detecting changes in meaning, but they were not as good at recognizing the same meaning or changes in form.

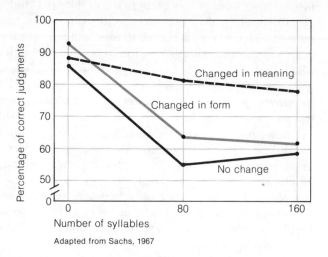

Adapted from Sachs, 1967

In one experiment, subjects were read a short story containing a particular sentence—such as, "He sent a letter about it to Galileo, the great Italian scientist." They were later given a recognition test for this sentence, which came after either 0, 80, or 160 additional syllables of story. On the test, a sentence was presented that was either identical to the original one, changed in form but not meaning ("A letter about it was sent to Galileo, the great Italian scientist"), or changed in meaning ("Galileo, the great Italian scientist, sent him a letter about it"). As can be seen in the figure, the subjects detected changes in meaning well. They were not so good at recognizing verbatim wording as the same or at detecting changes in form when the meaning had been preserved. This is especially so as the amount of interpolated material increases (Sachs, 1967).

While studies such as these have focused on memory for individual sentences or words, other research has been concerned with memory for ideas. Such ideas are often based on many different sentences that express a common semantic content. The phenomenon of "idea acquisition and retention" has been demonstrated in a series of experiments by Bransford and Franks (1971). They found that subjects took the information expressed in a number of related sentences and spontaneously integrated them into a few complex ideas. Later on, these subjects were more likely to recognize, or "remember," sentences that communicated these complex ideas, rather than the simpler ones that they had originally heard. Findings such as these suggest that people often construct organizing schemes for the information they learn. As a result, they exhibit a constructive process in their memory of things, rather than a rote, verbatim recall.

Distortion   There is always the chance that this constructive, inferential process might overreach itself resulting in the misrecall of some facts. This is the way rumors get started and also the way lawyers can lead the courtroom testimony of witnesses. If you witnessed an accident and later were asked to judge how fast the two cars were going when they *hit* each other, you would probably "remember" their speed as slower than if you were asked how fast they were going when they *smashed into* each other. People who had seen the same movie of an automobile accident estimated the speed of the cars to be about 25 percent faster when *smashed* was used in the questioning rather than *hit* (Loftus & Palmer, 1974).

Levels of processing   Earlier in this chapter we spoke about the inability of sheer rote rehearsal to do anything more than maintain material in short-term memory. In order to transfer information to the relatively permanent long-term memory, it is necessary to use more elaborate rehearsal; that is, a deeper *level of processing*. Suppose you were given a list of words to learn with the intent of recalling them next week. Rote repetition would be effective only as long as you were actively engaged in it, and one certainly wouldn't rehearse the words for a full week.

A somewhat more elaborate scheme would be to call on prior information in long-term memory; for example, finding words that rhyme with the words on the list. An even better approach would be to put each word in a sentence or to organize them into a story. Each of these changes results in a more meaningful or deeper level of processing (Craik & Lockhart, 1972). The more we can relate current experiences to previously stored information, the better we will remember them. That is, long-term memory relies very much on some previous context.

Context Though many childhood memories remain vivid as we grow older, a great number recede into the corners of our mind and remain inaccessible to us as adults. Once again, it is a case of losing the retrieval cues and not knowing where to look. If we could somehow regenerate our original state or the original context of our experiences, the cues might be forthcoming. Trying to remember the words of a song you memorized in fourth grade might seem an impossible task, but sometimes if we think back to the classroom, the teacher, how we felt, who our friends were, and so on, some of the words might be recalled. Even if they are not, it is surprising to find how much we really do remember about times past.

Recreating a previous physical state also improves memory. Alcoholics who hid liquor while intoxicated did not remember its location when they were sober. However, they did recall where the liquor was when they were again intoxicated (Goodwin, Powell, Brener, Hoine, & Stone, 1969). Also, people who learned word lists under the influence of marijuana remembered them better in that same state than when they were not under the influence of the drug (Eich, Weingarten, Stillman, & Gillin, 1975). When later performance of a learned task is improved by reinstating the original state (physiological, psychological, or emotional) of the subject when the task was learned, it is called state-dependent learning (or memory). We will have more to say about this in Chapter 15 when we consider the effects of drugs on behavior.

Transferring information in memory

In order for us to profit from our experience — not to make the same mistakes again — information must somehow get *transferred* to long-term memory. As we have seen, new information passes immediately into short-term memory from the sensory-information storage. The period in short-term memory is a very fragile one, during which the information could easily be forgotten or lost from the system. Both experiments with animals and clinical observations of humans with brain injuries suggest that the memory for an event can be easily disrupted and "shaken out" of the system. In studies with animals, a standard technique for disrupting a recent memory is to give an electroconvulsive shock to the brain or induce unconsciousness and coma by a drug. It is found that behavioral events occurring shortly before the convulsion or coma are almost totally erased from memory, so that little if any of that information can be detected upon later testing. The longer the delay interval between the event and the trauma to the brain, the less the memory for an event is likely to be disrupted. This finding is in accord with the view that information transmitted to long-term memory increases with the time an item is able to remain in short-term memory without interference. However, it also raises the puzzling question of how the brain can discriminate and store *meanings*.

Patients who have had a part of their hippocampus (a structure in the subcortex) removed have no permanent memory for new information but can remember material learned prior to the operation (Milner & Penfield, 1955). Thus the hippocampus may be involved in the transfer of information from the short-term memory to long-term memory.

Several factors help to get the information transferred from the short-term system to the long-term. The likelihood of information getting into long-term storage is greater: the smaller the amount of material presented, the more novel it is, the more actively it is rehearsed, and the greater its meaning or significance to the individual.

How do we forget?

Think for a moment of all the complex information you have learned in school: grammar, foreign languages, chemical formulas, geometric proofs, syllogistic reasoning, and much more. Then consider how much more you have had to learn outside of class about your environment, especially about the people and institutions in it. Some of this learning has come easily and "naturally"; some of it you have had to work hard to learn.

Forgetting has not been the same for everything either. Have you had the experience of mastering material well enough to get an "A" only to find a few months later that you have forgotten most of what you knew? But can't you still remember all of the details associated with your first "real date"? College students frequently can remember the names of all their elementary school teachers, but forget the name of their psychology professor or their textbook the day after the final exam. On the other hand, if you put on a pair of skates, began to skip rope, or tried a dance you had not done for years, you would probably find that in a short time you were almost as good as you ever were. Why do some things stay with you so much longer than others? Does the difference lie with the kind of material learned, or does something about the way you learn it determine how well you are able to remember it later?

We have already made a distinction between learning and memory. A psychologist investigating learning looks at trial-to-trial changes in performance and how well a subject is ultimately able to perform on some task after different kinds of practice—a change in performance as a result of experience. In studying memory, we are interested in whether material that has been learned at a given time in the past is available to the subject at a selected time in the present. Tests of memory, then, require that the past be brought back into the present.

In laboratory studies memory is inferred by comparing how much is remembered after some period of time with how much was known immediately after learning. It is assumed that with perfect memory the two would be the same—there would be no loss. Actually, therefore, memory is usually assessed in terms of how much has been forgotten. This explains why what we say about "memory" in this section will be in terms of forgetting and, furthermore, why some important theories about memory have been developed in terms of the process of forgetting.

There are two facts about forgetting that all of us know. One is that we do not remember everything. We forget some people's names, we forget some appointments, we forget some of the information that we crammed for an exam. A second fact is that as the interval between learning and remembering increases, the amount forgotten becomes greater as time passes. Generally, you will remember more one hour after you learn it than five days later. Further, most of our forgetting occurs soon after learning rather than in the days or weeks following. (See *P&L* Close-up, Ebbinghaus and Ceg, Dax, Laj.)

Although forgetting is a very common experience for all of us, its explanation is not so easily found. Much research has been done on this topic, and several alternative theories have been proposed to explain how and why we seem to forget the material we have learned. First, though, let us see how forgetting is measured.

Measuring forgetting

The usual sequence by which memory is studied experimentally has already been implied. First, the subject is presented with a task to be learned, and usually some measure is made of how much learning has taken place. Second, during some length of time the subject is asked to engage in specified types of activity (perhaps additional learning or perhaps some time-filling task, like doing arithmetic problems, that simply limits any thinking about the original task). Finally, the subject is tested on what he or she is able to remember from the original task, and this score is compared with the score that was obtained at the end of the learning session. To measure the amount remembered, the investigator generally uses *recall* or *recognition*.

Close-up

Ebbinghaus and *Ceg, Dax, Laj*

The first significant study providing a truly quantitative measure of retention was performed by Ebbinghaus in 1885. Ebbinghaus invented the "nonsense syllable"—a meaningless three-letter unit consisting of a vowel between two consonants, such as *ceg, dax, laj,* and so on. He used nonsense syllables because he wanted to obtain a "pure" measure of memory, uncontaminated by previous learning or associations that might otherwise have been brought to the task being studied. Using himself as his only subject, Ebbinghaus would study a list of such nonsense syllables until he could repeat the list perfectly, twice in a row. In addition, he would measure the amount of time it took him to learn the list. Then, after some fixed period of time—during which he would usually be learning other lists—he would relearn the original list and again measure his learning time. The amount by which this second time was shorter was his measure of retention.

The type of result obtained by Ebbinghaus is shown in the figure, where percent of time saved in relearning is plotted as a function of the number of days since original learning. As you can see, there is a rapid initial loss, followed by a gradually slower decline. This curve is typical of results obtained in studies involving rote memorization.

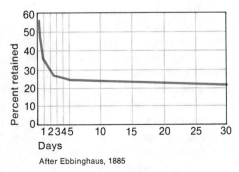

After Ebbinghaus, 1885

Recall

Recall is reproduction of the learned material. If the exam question asks you to give the causes of the Civil War, you must dredge them up out of your memory and formulate a response that convinces your instructor you know them. Two kinds of recall are distinguished by researchers. The first is *rote* or *verbatim recall*. Whenever we need to remember the exact form of things, especially arbitrary items like telephone numbers, we must store the entire information in order to reproduce it correctly. Most cases of recall that involve any complexity, however, require some *reconstruction*. In this case, we store and recall only part of the information but are able to reconstruct the rest of the event or fact from this partial information. For example, you could probably develop a theory of the causes of the Civil War on the basis of just a few remembered facts.

Recognition

Another technique of assessing remembering involves the ability to *recognize* something previously experienced. Think of the tremendous number of objects and people you can recognize. The streets and buildings of your neighborhood, the faces of numerous friends and acquaintances, words — the list is nearly endless.

Recognition is usually tested by presenting a stimulus and asking the subject whether it is one of a set learned earlier or is a new one. Another method is to present several items and ask whether the subject recognizes any as previously experienced. Our recognition ability is often astounding. Subjects who saw 2560 slides for ten seconds each were later tested with a subgroup of them. They correctly recognized about 90 percent! (Standing, Conezio, & Haber, 1970) In other experiments, correct recognition reached 97 percent.

Recognition actually may be part of the recall process in the sense that when we attempt to recall something, it is necessary to recognize whether our recall is correct. This notion is helpful in understanding that recognition is usually more successful than recall. Another way to view this distinction is to realize that an inability to recall something may be due either to a storage or a retrieval failure. We may not have stored the information where we could find it or, if we did, the retrieval cues at our disposal may be inappropriate. In recognition, on the other hand, retrieval is not a problem; we are given the information and must recognize only whether it is correct. Incorrect recognition, then, implies not retrieval failure but just a failure to store information in an appropriate place.

Decay and interference

We have spoken earlier in the chapter about why information might be forgotten or inaccessible for recall at a later time. It might not have been encoded properly; short-term memory might be overloaded; it might never transfer out of short-term memory and would then be forgotten when rehearsal ceased; or it might be stored in long-term memory but remain inaccessible because the appropriate retrieval cues are not present. For whatever reason, we cannot retrieve information when we want it. What has happened to memory and why does forgetting become greater as time passes?

Basically, two major theories have been proposed to explain the course of forgetting. According to *trace-decay theory*, learned material leaves a "trace" or impression in the brain. If unused, this trace will disappear in time, like the fading white trail we often see in the sky after a jet plane has passed above us. In other words, the knowledge we have learned just fades away. As we have seen, such decay can be prevented if we repeatedly practice the knowledge and thus maintain the trace. But without this rehearsal, the trace is lost.

The other theory argues that time alone can't cause anything to happen or not to happen: the cause of forgetting depends upon what occurs as time passes. Thus, *interference theory* holds that everything we learn will stay learned unless something new occurs to interfere with it. If there were nothing to interfere with our knowledge, we would never forget anything. However, interference is a daily occurrence in our lives; the issue is just how much it affects forgetting.

Which of these theories is correct, trace decay or interference? An experiment to decide between the two could take the following form: first, two groups of subjects would learn some task—a list of words, or, for example, a story. Following that, one group would learn another list or story, something that would probably interfere with remembering the first task. During the time this second task was being learned, the other group would do "nothing at all." Finally, both groups would attempt to recall the first task. If the group that learned the second task had poorer recall in this final test than the group that did "nothing" during the equivalent time, there would be evidence for *interference*. If both groups forgot equal amounts, there would be evidence for trace decay over time. This would be so because the time between learning and recalling the first task is the same for both groups and the trace-decay theory proposes that time is the only relevant variable.

It would be difficult actually to conduct this experiment because there is no way to be certain one group will do "nothing at all" while the other learns the interfering task. We can't suspend people in time or flash freeze them. Even if it were possible and ethical, the act of defrosting would certainly be interfering. Nevertheless, there have been some other attempts to determine whether trace decay or interference is critical.

One of the earliest tests of these hypotheses was done by Jenkins and Dallenbach in 1924.

In this study, subjects learned lists of nonsense syllables and were later tested for recall of these lists at several different time intervals. The period between the subject's learning and recall was either spent in normal working activity or in sleep (during which, it is assumed, there is less interference). The results showed that less forgetting occurred after sleep than after waking activity. This supports the notion of interference theory that it is the nature of the intervening activity, and not time itself, that is critical to forgetting. ■

Another ingenious experiment used cockroaches. If a cockroach is placed in a cardboard cone where it receives considerable body contact, it will become immobile for up to two hours. This approaches an environment that is almost totally noninterfering. The experiment was similar to the last. Two groups of cockroaches learned, under penalty of electric shock, to avoid a corner of their cage. One group was then immobilized by the paper cone, the other animals were free to roam around their home cage doing whatever cockroaches normally do for the same period of time. Finally, there was an evaluation of how well each group retained the response of avoiding the electrified corner of the cage. The group better at this was the one immobilized in the paper cone. Without interference, the response was more effectively retained. Again, the results support the notion that interference, not trace decay, is responsible for forgetting. However, the immobilized group did show some

Our memories are card-indexes consulted, and then put back in disorder by authorities whom we do not control.
Cyril Connolly
The Unquiet Grave

**Forgetting after
sleeping vs. waking**

*The graph shows the
number of syllables
recalled after various
intervals of sleep or waking
activity.*

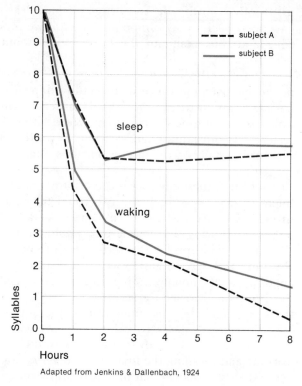

Adapted from Jenkins & Dallenbach, 1924

forgetting and that could mean that either trace decay was in fact operating or that some interference had crept into this situation also (Minami & Dallenbach, 1946).

You can see that it is not so simple to untangle the two theories. Much recent research has suggested that both interference and trace decay may be involved in forgetting.

Retroactive and proactive inhibition

The interference that was developed in these last experiments is backward-working, it produces what is called *retroactive inhibition*. Those subjects receiving the interference task make up the experimental group; the others are the control group. Stated more formally now, both groups learn the *first* task, with only the experimental group learning the second task. The control group does some irrelevant activity such as reading cartoons or doing arithmetic problems. Both groups are then tested again on the first task. The control group usually does better, presumably because of less interference from the intervening activity.

The more similar the second task to the first, the greater the buildup of retroactive inhibition. Let us say that you learned a list of French words and then a second list of different French words. If you were then asked to recall just the first list, there would be considerable confusion from the second, you wouldn't know which words belonged to each list. Consequently, retroactive inhibition would be great. On the other hand, if the second list contained only the names of American states, names unrelated to the French words, there would be very little retroactive inhibition. Further, the greater the amount of practice on the *second* list, the greater the retroactive inhibition (Slamecka, 1960).

A second type of interference, called *proactive inhibition*, is forward-working. It puts the interference at the very beginning. The experimental group learns a first task, then a second task, and finally is tested on the *second* task. The control group engages in an irrelevant activity, then learns the second task, and finally is tested on the second task. This is also shown in the table. Again the control group usually does better, indicating less interference from the earlier activity. ▲

Proactive inhibition develops quite rapidly. If an individual learns a short list of animal names and is then tested for them, recall is usually relatively good. If a second list of animal names is then learned and tested, recall is usually inferior to the first list; this decrement is due to proactive inhibition. Items from the first list interfere with those on the second. If a third list of animal names is now learned, recall for this will be even worse than for the second list. Again proactive inhibition continues to build up. Now suppose a fourth list is presented, but instead of animal names, this list is composed of the names of occupations. When this list is tested, the recall is typically quite good, easily superior to the performance on the two previous lists. This indicates a *release from proactive inhibition;* apparently the change to a new category, occupations in this case, acts to reduce, if not eliminate, the effects of the proactive inhibition (Wickens, 1970). Not only does proactive inhibition develop rapidly then, it also diminishes rapidly.

Competition and unlearning

In order to understand further the factors involved in forgetting, let us consider a classic technique used to study memory, known as *paired-associate* learning. Think of learning English equivalents of foreign vocabulary words, or of learning the capital cities of various states. In these cases, the information to be acquired is a set of pairs, such that one element of a pair goes with or is to be associated with the other element of the pair. Typically the subject studies each pair for a short time until the entire list has been presented. Then the first item in each pair is presented alone and the subject is asked to recall the second item in the pair. Suppose this paired-associate procedure is used in the experimental group situation that produces retroactive inhibition? For example, a subject would learn a list of paired associates, one of which might be *car – prune*. After this list was learned, a second list would be presented. On this list, however, the second word in each pair would be the same as those on the first list; the second word of each pair would be changed. As a result, this list might have a pair like *car – dog*. After this second list was learned, subjects would relearn the first list.

The control group would learn and relearn the first paired-associate list, but would then engage in an irrelevant activity during the time the experimental group was learning the second list. Retroactive inhibition should occur in the experimental group since the second list produces interference. Not only

▲
Typical paradigms for studying interference in verbal learning

Retroactive (Backward Working) Inhibition					Proactive (Forward Working) Inhibition				
Group	*Learn*	*Learn*	⟶	*Test on Task A*	*Group*	*Learn*	*Learn*	⟶	*Test on Task B*
Experimental	Task A ↑ (equally well) ↓	Task B	Passage of Time	poorer	Experimental	Task A	Task B ↑ (equally well) ↓	Passage of Time	poorer
Control	Task A	(none)		better	Control	(none)	Task B		better

The amount of retroactive inhibition (RI) is shown in this graph as a function of the degree of learning of the second list.

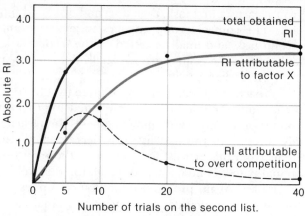

Adapted from Melton & Irwin, 1940

that, but relearning the first list should be hampered by the interfering associations within the pairs. That is, when the subject tries to relearn that *prune* is associated with *car*, there will be a competing tendency to say *dog* instead, since in the second list which was just learned, *dog* was the associate to *car*. This competition was felt to be the reason for retroactive inhibition. But the results of one early study make it clear that competition cannot be the only cause. In fact, as practice on the second list increases, competition becomes less and less important (Melton & Irwin, 1940). ●

What *is* the major cause of retroactive inhibition in this paired-associate situation? Melton and Irwin proposed that in addition to competition, there was *unlearning* of the first list associations as the second list was being learned. This was their "factor X" on the graph. This means that as the *car-dog* pair continues to be learned better and better, the original *car – prune* association becomes unavailable; it is unlearned. There is strong evidence for this unlearning since it has been found that with increased training on the second list, recall of the first list associations does become more and more difficult (Barnes & Underwood, 1959).

Initially, the unlearning factor was thought to be similar to extinction in classical conditioning. The idea was that as *dog* was learned as a response to *car*, the response from the first list, *prune*, was unreinforced and thereby extinguished. Now it is not entirely clear that this view is correct.

Though these experiments have used paired associates, this is not the only way people learn word lists. Another method is known as *serial* learning. People learn a list of words or other items, not in pairs, and then must remember them in the order they were presented, the first item first, second item second, and so on. Memory is in series and hence the name *serial learning*.

In any practical experience you have had in serial learning, you may have noticed a phenomenon that nearly always occurs. If you are learning a list of items, the first and last items in the list seem easier to remember than those in the middle. This is called the *serial-position effect*. No one is completely certain why it occurs, but it has been observed consistently in experiments. So far, the accepted explanation is that the first and last items occupy unique positions in the list and thus are especially noticeable because they serve as salient markers for the beginning and the end of the list. ■

If after learning a serial list, recall is delayed for about a minute—by imposing some task that prevents rehearsal of the list—there is a marked change in the serial-position effect. Specifically, while the items from the beginning and middle of the list are remembered in about the same way as they were without

Serial position effect

The items in the middle of the list are more difficult to remember than those at the beginning and end.

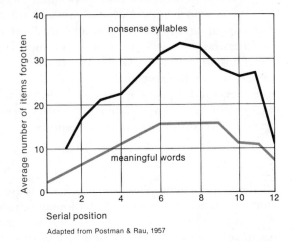

Serial position

Adapted from Postman & Rau, 1957

the delay, the items at the end of the list are remembered much more poorly, in some cases as poorly as those items in the middle of the list. If we consider that those items remembered from the beginning and middle of the list are probably in long-term memory and those from the end of the list still in short-term memory, then the delay without rehearsal would affect only short-term memory. The result would be more forgetting of the items at the end of the list (Glanzer & Cunitz, 1966).

Remembering and forgetting stories

The experiments we have been discussing in this section have been concerned with the forgetting of words or nonsense syllables presented in lists. But only a small part of our learning and forgetting is of this type. Generally, we are most involved with memory for larger units of information, entire stories, for example. In this case, rather than dealing with lists of individual words or paired associates, we are concerned with themes and characters, settings and plot progressions. Is the nature of forgetting the same with meaningful material like this as it is with nonsense syllables or with lists composed of unrelated words? Not entirely; in fact, there are some big differences.

Productive memory

In one experiment, Bartlett read an American Indian folktale to his subjects. They were asked to reproduce the story after fifteen minutes, and again at longer intervals. In general, subjects accurately remembered the central meaningful "core" of the story, but they also added new material that had not been originally included. Often this new material involved alterations of the story to make it conform better with the subjects' cultural norms and past personal experience. Thus, the phrase "went down to the river to hunt seals" was remembered by one of the British subjects as "went fishing."

Bartlett's interpretation of these results was that memory is *productive* as well as *reproductive* and that this productivity induces certain predictable changes in what is stored. According to him:

"Remembering . . . is an imaginative reconstruction or construction, built out of the relation of our attitude towards a whole active mass of organized past reactions or experience . . . . It is thus hardly ever really exact . . ." (1932, p. 213).

A recent version of Bartlett's original theory has been provided by Neisser (1967), who argues that good memory is more than just an efficient filing and storage system. Acts of memory are comparable to the work of a paleontologist, who starts with a few bone fragments and then reconstructs the form of a dinosaur or other creature. In a similar way, people reconstruct what they remember on the basis of a few recalled elements. People do not have exact rote memory for the words they learn, but they do remember the general meaning of those words. This should bring to mind what we said earlier about semantic processing in long-term memory.

Story structure

At the present time, psychologists are attempting to account for the way a story is learned and forgotten by looking more closely at the structure and regularities in the story itself. The way information is presented and developed within a story very often has a structure that is as organized as that of a grammar which imposes an order on the individual words in a sentence. For example, read the short folktale about a dog and a piece of meat. ◆ The story is divided into eleven segments, each one describing an event or a state. These events and states can be organized into larger units within the story in about the same way as the individual words in a sentence can be organized into larger subject and predicate units. These larger units can then be combined until the entire story is reconstructed.

A diagram of the dog story is also presented below. Notice that it is divided into two basic units, the *setting* and the *event structure*, each composed of a number of events; the first three, for example, are part of the setting. Further, the event structure is made up of smaller units which themselves can be broken in still smaller units. The result is a general pattern for the entire

◆

The "dog story" and its structure

The numbers in the diagram refer to the statement number in the story below.

1 *It happened that a dog had got a piece of meat*
2 *and was carrying it home in his mouth.*
3 *Now on his way home he had to cross a plank lying across a stream.*
4 *As he crossed he looked down*
5 *and saw his own shadow reflected in the water beneath.*
6 *Thinking it was another dog with another piece of meat,*
7 *he made up his mind to have that also.*
8 *So he made a snap at the shadow,*
9 *but as he opened his mouth the piece of meat fell out,*
10 *dropped into the water,*
11 *and was never seen again.*

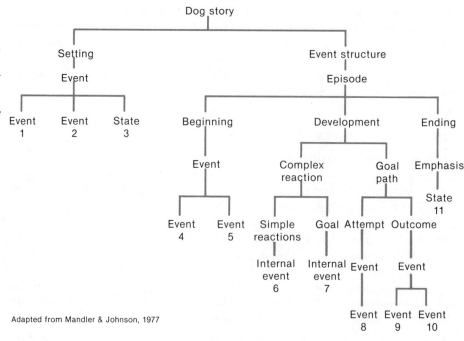

Adapted from Mandler & Johnson, 1977

story. Presumably, other stories would have similar patterns, at least in regard to the largest units (Mandler & Johnson, 1977).

How is this related to memory? When various age groups, first-graders, fourth-graders, and adults tried to learn stories like this one, memory was best for the settings, beginnings, and outcomes. It was worst for reactions, like the sixth event in the story, "thinking it was another dog . . . ." Apparently, people are sensitive to different aspects of the story structure; possibly we cognitively tune ourselves to look for certain major parts, such as settings, beginnings, and outcomes. The fact that first-graders show a similar though not identical pattern to adults in what they remember suggests that the importance of these features is established quite early.

Motivation

In the theories discussed so far, forgetting has been viewed as a consequence of interference in the memory system, or trace decay, or some failure of encoding, storage, or retrieval. Whatever the reason or reasons, forgetting appears to be an unintentional process often occurring automatically. A very different approach was taken by Sigmund Freud, who argued that forgetting may be *intentional*. His thesis was that the things we remember and the things we forget are related to their value and importance to us. Things that are very disturbing to us, for example, are likely to be made temporarily inaccessible by being driven out of our consciousness. Such *repression* is a device by which we unknowingly protect ourselves from unacceptable or painful information, as did Mrs. R. J., about whom we read earlier. As we shall see in Chapter 16, the "forgotten" material may persist at an unconscious level and produce emotional conflicts for years afterward.

It seems likely that some of our forgetting can be attributed to repression, but there is reason to question the generality of this explanation. Much of Freud's argument is based on anecdotal evidence from his personal experience and while this might be intriguing, it is difficult to test experimentally. Also, it is difficult to make clear predictions regarding how and in what setting repression should occur.

At about the same time that Freud was talking about motives to repress negative information, Kurt Lewin and his students were looking at the effect of task motives on memory. Legend has it that they were puzzled by an occurrence in a Berlin beer garden. It seems there was a waiter with such a remarkable memory that he could retain long, detailed, complicated orders without writing them down. Once after the meal had been served and he had given the party their bill, however, someone asked him a simple question about the order. It turned out that he could remember very little of it once he had completed his task.

The result of this observation was a classic experiment that demonstrated greater recall of tasks before completion than of comparable tasks after completion. This effect of enhanced recall for uncompleted tasks was named the *Zeigarnik effect* after Bluma Zeigarnik, the young woman who carried out the study.

In this experiment the subjects performed simple tasks that they would be able to accomplish if given enough time, such as writing down a favorite quotation from memory, solving a riddle, and doing mental arithmetic problems. In some of the tasks, the subjects were interrupted before they had a chance to carry out the instructions in full. In others they were allowed to finish. Despite the fact that the subjects spent more time on the completed tasks than on the interrupted ones, they tended to recall the unfinished tasks better than the finished ones when they were questioned a few hours later. This superiority of recall for the uncompleted tasks disappeared, however, within twenty-four hours. Apparently it was attributable to short-term motivational factors that affected the rehearsal process (Zeigarnik, 1927).

It might appear that the Zeigarnik effect is inconsistent with the notion of repression, since one might expect that people would repress their memory of things left unfinished, particularly if the lack of completion was viewed as a failure. Later research has suggested a resolution of this inconsistency by showing that the Zeigarnik effect only holds for tasks performed under nonstressful conditions. When noncompletion is ego-involving and threatens the individual's self-esteem, there is a tendency for the Zeigarnik effect to be reversed — that is, for completed tasks to be remembered better than uncompleted ones.

Further inhibiting effects of threatening experiences on memory have been demonstrated in a number of studies. In general, memory has been shown to be impaired when "anxiety" stimulus words are used, when there is a threat of failure associated with the material, or when frustration or other unpleasantness is experienced between learning and recall. Whether memory is facilitated or inhibited by motivation depends on the kind and intensity of emotion aroused as well as on the nature of the task, the kind of response called for, and the place in the sequence of learning and remembering at which the motivational conditions are introduced.

How to improve your memory

People are always complaining about the brittleness of their memory. They attribute it to various causes: lack of mental exercise, as if one's memory was like a flabby muscle that needed to be flexed; or to growing old; or to some inherited weakness. Memory lapses are so annoying for many people that every year thousands of them buy books or register for courses that offer to provide techniques on memory improvement. Others take a peculiar satisfaction in their poor memories in the same way that some people brag about their inability to do simple arithmetic. They argue that remembering minor pieces of information might be detrimental since it would occupy room in memory that is needed for more important facts. We know that this view is incorrect since, you will recall, the capacity of long-term memory is virtually limitless.

Nevertheless, the things that people can or cannot do with their memories holds a fascination for most of us. The feats of professional memory experts who can remember the names of a hundred people after being introduced to them once seems spectacular. On the other hand, case studies of individuals like Mrs. R. J., whose amnesia resulted in the unavailability to recall the well-learned facts of a lifetime are equally intriguing.

Bower (1978) discusses a much more severe amnesia in a brain-damaged patient. This man, a soldier, conversed normally except that he couldn't remember anything that happened a few seconds before. He engaged in a short conversation with the examiner who then left for a few minutes. When the examiner returned, the patient asked "Who are you?" and then there followed the same conversation that occurred before. When some memory tasks were attempted, the patient couldn't remember the instructions. Asked, "Are you ready to start?" he responded, "Ready to start what? Did you want me to do something?"

In another, similar case, when a twenty-seven-year old man "learned of the death of an uncle of whom he was very fond, he became very moved, but forgot about it immediately and showed the same emotion each time he received the same news" (Barbizet, 1970, p. 60). Fortunately, these are rare cases, but the devastating nature of the memory loss underlines the vital importance of an adequately functioning memory system.

The purpose of this section is to survey some of the major techniques that have been developed to improve memory, to make it function more adequately.

Study strategies

Early research on verbal learning identified several techniques for improving retention of learned material.

Overlearning

If your task is to learn a list, you might think that when you can recall the complete list without error, your learning is complete and there would be no point in studying it further. To the contrary; further practice, called *overlearning*, has a marked effect on how much of the material you will remember later.

In one study, subjects were asked to memorize several lists of words. As soon as they had done so, they were divided into three groups and given varying amounts of additional practice. One group practiced the words again for the same amount of time it had taken them to learn the words originally (100 percent), a second group practiced the words for half the time it took to learn them originally (50 percent), and a third group did not practice at all (0 percent). All three groups were tested for recall at intervals throughout the next month. The 100 percent group recalled about twice as many words as the 0 percent group on each of six tests, although by the twenty-eighth day, recall was very low for all groups (Krueger, 1929).

This student has probably done some reading and reviewing before the test. Preliminary survey and questioning of the material as well as some recitation are strategies for even more effective learning.

The SQ3R method

One well-known study strategy that is effective and easy to learn consists of five steps: survey, question, read, recite, and review (Morgan & Deese, 1969; Higbee, 1977). ▲ In an initial *survey,* one skims over the material in order to get an overview: reading the chapter summary first, skimming over the chapter titles and chapter subsections. The idea of this first step is to avoid jumping into the detail before you know what is covered and where the details will be leading. People remember facts better if they know the general theme. Without knowing the theme, it is often difficult to make much sense out of what one is studying. Read the following paragraph and try to remember it:

"With hocked gems financing him, our hero bravely defied all scornful laughter that tried to prevent his scheme. 'Your eyes deceive,' he had said, 'an egg not a table correctly typifies this unexplored planet.' Now three sturdy sisters sought proof, forging along sometimes through calm vastness, yet more often over turbulent peaks and valleys. Days became weeks as many doubters spread fearful rumors about the edge. At last from nowhere welcome winged creatures appeared signifying momentous success" (from Dooling & Lachman, 1971, p. 217).

How much of that paragraph did you remember? Would it have helped to know beforehand that it was about Columbus discovering America? Read it over again and see just how much better it seems to be organized. On the basis of a preliminary survey, you should next attempt to ask some *questions* about the material. What are the main points of the section or chapter? What is the order in which these points are developed? For example, the section on "How do we forget?" started with some ways of measuring forgetting. Can you remember what they were? It then progressed to some general theories of forgetting, then on to a more detailed look at interference in forgetting, and so on. Do you know some of the ways to measure forgetting or what the theories are? Asking questions immediately after the survey stage can further help in orienting the learner to the learning material. Some textbooks provide questions at the beginning of the chapter to act as advanced organizers. Others, like this one, provide a separate workbook *(Mastering Psychology and Life)* containing questions to help students evaluate how well they have learned the material. If these questions are intended to examine the most important points of a chapter, then reading them beforehand can be almost as valuable as trying to answer them afterwards. It's like having a copy of the test before you start to study; but in this case, it isn't cheating.

The third stage, *reading*, describes the process of actually reading the material thoroughly, detail after detail. Most people use only this stage in studying; consequently, they become lost in the specifics, often unable to even guess where anything is leading. You can see why the preliminary survey and question stages are so important; they allow you to see the beach and not just the grains of sand.

Recite is the name given to the fourth stage. During learning, writing and/or saying the material out loud (as well as reading it) leads to better retention of the material. Such *active recitation* ensures active attention rather than passive reception and also ensures that your learning has reached the degree necessary for recall rather than only recognition. It is even useful to test yourself on the material with the book closed—in other words to recite the material without visually reviewing it. Once again, asking questions, as in the second stage, is also useful here. Psychologists have suggested that the effectiveness of such recitation, even in the absence of a check on accuracy, may lie in the opportunity it provides for practice in *retrieving* the information—perhaps devising the strategy that will be most effective later, when exam time comes.

Finally, *review* what you have learned. Can you remember how the material was organized? Can you answer the question asked initially? Also, if you read a book at the beginning of a term and expect to be tested on its contents some time later, you are likely to make a better showing if you review the material by periodically looking through it. It is thought that one reason such review is helpful is that it enables you to direct your attention to parts you did not learn thoroughly the first time. With periodic review, less and less review time is needed to maintain recall as time passes.

These five strategies really do work in remembering. Higbee notes also that they have "been found to increase rate of reading, level of comprehension, and performance on examinations. In addition, the principle . . . can be used not only for textbooks but also for such tasks as outside reading assignments, English literature, and charts, tables, maps, and drawings" (Higbee, 1977, p. 67).

"Chunking" and memory

Read the following sequence of letters once and then close your eyes and try to recite them from memory.

TH-EDO-GSA-WTH-ECA-T

Very probably a sequence of letters like this one is at or near the limit of your short-term memory capacity. The way the letters are organized into groups is probably meaningless; thus the letters must be remembered individually. However, if you had noticed that this sequence of letters, with different groupings, says "the dog saw the cat," then it would have been a simple matter to remember and recall the sequence.

Our ability to recall once-presented material depends on the number of organizational units, or *chunks*, we see in it. Many studies have shown that we can take in only somewhere between five and nine chunks in a brief time—as George Miller (1956) says, *seven, plus or minus two, pieces of information.* This seems to be true whether the units are large or small, complex or simple. (Did you try to remember the sequence of letters as fifteen separate units?)

One psychologist taught himself to recode sequences of two digits in a random pattern— for example, 101100111010 — by using a code that transformed every group of three digits into a single digit between 0 and 7. For example, the series above—grouped as 101, 100, 111, 010 — would be recoded as 5472.

He first determined how long a sequence of the original digits he could recall without recoding. Then he learned a recoded series. As expected, his recall almost tripled. Evidently what had been remembered as three chunks in the original sequence was being remembered as one chunk in the recoded series, with a corresponding increase in the amount that could be retained (S. Smith, cited in G. A. Miller, 1967).

Many studies have verified this tendency to recall a constant number of chunks, whatever their size or complexity. Thus when letters are grouped into words, there is about a sevenfold increase in the number of letters that can be retained, even though the words are more complex informational units. When the words are organized into sentences and the sentences into larger thought units, the amount of material we can take in increases accordingly.

This kind of evidence establishes quite well the notion of chunking and constant capacity for immediate memory in terms of chunks. It may be that our greater recall for meaningful than meaningless material (reported earlier in this chapter) results from the fact that meaningless items such as lists of nonsense syllables are composed of many small chunks that cannot be grouped into larger units and thus must each be processed separately. In any case, it is quite clear that we do indeed organize material to be learned into "meaning-encoded" units.

Mnemonic strategies

Until recently, those trying to apply psychological principles in the classroom have made little effort to deal directly with the organizational problems that confront the learner as the task of learning begins. However, as psychologists have become convinced of the importance of encoding, storage, and retrieval processes in memory, they have begun to investigate techniques for making these types of coding more efficient. Such techniques are called *mnemonic strategies.* Mnemonic is pronounced "nemonic" with the first "m" silent, and it is derived from the Greek word for remembering or recollecting. Specifically, it relates to assisting the memory and the idea behind most mnemonic strategies is to use old knowledge as an anchor or context for new knowledge. That is, mnemonics are techniques for associating things. Such a technique may simply involve using organization of some already well-known structure as an "outline" for new information. For example, many young musicians have learned to name the lines of the treble staff by reciting "Every Good Boy Does Fine." Or one can arrange the items in a list so that the initial letters spell a familiar word. For example, the names of the Great Lakes (Huron, Ontario, Michigan, Erie, Superior) spell *homes.*

Visual imagery

Visual imagery is one example of a mnemonic strategy and it also underlies most of the other examples we will discuss. The technique is particularly effective when small groups of meaningful items such as words must be associated. In this technique, the objects to be associated are pictured as being in some vivid interacting scene. For example, if the pair *dog – bicycle* is part of a list for a paired-associate task, then the pair will likely be more rapidly learned and more accurately remembered if you picture a large, spotted dog pedaling a decorated child's bicycle. People's names, too, can often be remembered more easily by the use of such imagery.

Often, the more vivid and specific the imagery, the better, though recent experimental evidence indicates that vividness itself is not so important as the visualization of the two words or objects in some interaction. That is, visualizing a dog and a bicycle separately would not be a very effective way of remembering the pair. Using visual imagery is also difficult when the words are abstract, like *consider* or *truthful*, or when we are attempting to remember a string of numbers.

Story chains

One effective mnemonic device for increasing meaning in lists of words is to put them into a story or sentence. Bower and Clark (1969) demonstrated the effectiveness of this strategy for remembering a list of nouns.

Subjects were given a list of ten totally unrelated nouns that they had to learn in the order presented. The experimental subjects were told to construct a story in which these nouns appeared in the correct order. For example, a subject's story woven around the nouns (capitalized here) for one list was:

   "A VEGETABLE can be a useful INSTRUMENT for a COLLEGE student. A carrot can be a NAIL for your FENCE or BASIN. But a MERCHANT of the QUEEN would SCALE that fence and feed the carrot to a GOAT."

   Each subject learned twelve lists this way. Control subjects were simply instructed to memorize the lists. Since there were only ten words in each list, both groups of subjects had almost perfect recall for each list immediately following the study period. After all the lists had been presented and learned, however, each subject was given the first word of each list and asked to recall the rest of each list in correct order. The contrast was dramatic on this delayed recall test. Subjects who had made up stories were able to recall correctly 94 percent of the words from all the lists, as compared with only 14 percent for the control subjects. The mnemonic strategy had increased recall sevenfold.

Unfortunately, one of the problems with this technique is that if you forget one of the words in the list, it can break up the rest of the story chain.

The method of loci

Since the word *mnemonic* is derived from Greek, it is not surprising to find that the early Greeks used many of these techniques. The method of loci, or locations, is one such system. We remember the order of a list of names or objects by associating them with some other order we have already learned. Higbee (1977) recounts a gruesome story from Cicero on how this method presumably originated:

"A poet named Simonides was speaking at a banquet, when a message was brought to him that someone was outside to see him. While Simonides was outside, the roof of the banquet hall collapsed, crushing the occupants beyond recognition. Simonides was able to identify the bodies by remembering the places at which the guests had been sitting. This experience suggested to Simonides a system for memorizing. Noting that it was his memo-

ry of the places where the guests were sitting that had enabled him to identify them, he inferred that a person could improve memory by associating mental images of the items to be remembered with mental images of locations for the items" (pp. 107–108).

Without the disaster Simonides experienced, you can still remember a list of items like *mouse, car, melon,* and so on by associating them with the things you would see on a walk around your living room. First might be the doorway to the room; therefore you would associate *mouse* with the *door,* possibly picturing a mouse opening the door for you. Next might be the couch, so you would associate *car* with the couch; a car resting on the couch with its hazard lights blinking. *Melon* would be associated with the next object you would encounter on your walk, a television set perhaps, and so on through the list. Of course, it needn't be your living room; any scene that you recall in a given order will suffice. You might use the stores you would pass on a walk down a familiar street, for example. Try this technique to recall the names of students in one of your seminars, if they occupy the same seats each session.

Super memory?

All of us have heard of the phenomenon of a "photographic memory" or what psychologists call *eidetic imagery.* Some individuals possess imagery that is almost like actual perception in clarity and accuracy. People with eidetic imagery can frequently tell the exact position of a formula or fact on the printed page of a textbook. They can even glance for a fraction of a second at an object, such as a comb, and then call up such a vivid image that they can give a complete description, including the number of teeth in the comb. In examinations, they may "copy" from their image of the printed page, performing with an accuracy as great as though the book were actually open before them. ■

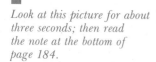

Look at this picture for about three seconds; then read the note at the bottom of page 184.

Striking examples of eidetic imagery have been documented in *The Mind of a Mnemonist*, a case study by the Russian psychologist Luria of a man with a "photographic" mind.

The subject had such powers of imagery that he was able to perform staggering feats of memory. The following is one of the many experiments carried out with this man, which you might want to try yourself. The man spent three minutes examining the table of numbers reprinted below. He was able to reproduce the table perfectly, by calling off all the numbers in succession, within forty seconds. He could call off the numbers in both the columns and the horizontal rows in either forward or reverse order. He also reproduced the numbers that form the diagonals (e.g., 6, 4, 8, 5; 5, 6, 3, 7) within 35 seconds. Finally, he took a minute and a half to convert all fifty numbers into a single fifty-digit number (Luria, 1968).

6	6	8	0
5	4	3	2
1	6	8	4
7	9	3	5
4	2	3	7
3	8	9	1
1	0	0	2
3	4	5	1
2	7	6	8
1	9	2	6
2	9	6	7
5	5	2	0
x	0	1	x

At this point, you may be wishing that you had the gift of eidetic imagery (or "photographic memory"). You might think that all of your schoolwork would be extremely simple to do, since you could remember everything so well. Actually, eidetic imagery often obstructs thinking, rather than helping it. Materials stored eidetically are not easily broken down and reassembled in new patterns or easily forgotten when no longer useful or relevant. To do so, Luria's subject had to visualize the information being written on a paper that was then "burned" in order to destroy the vivid image. Individuals with eidetic imagery can reproduce what they have seen, but it is difficult for them to use this information in new ways. Thus, eidetic imagery does not appear to play a role in abstract thinking or creative imagination, which require flexibility in thought. For example, Luria's subject was unable to understand simple abstract ideas because he could not "see" them in concrete visual images. This could explain why eidetic imagery is most often found in children and is comparatively rare in adults.

Baddeley (1976) notes that children with eidetic imagery do not seem to differ in other ways from children without the ability. In fact, he feels that eidetic imagery may have very little usefulness. To wish, then, that we could possess a photographic memory or a limitless ability to remember perfectly everything we experience is not the best of all wishes. We have as much capacity as we will ever need. What is necessary are methods to order our experiences so that they can be remembered without their interfering with one another; and we need methods to lead us to those memories when we want them.

How many stories were there in the building in the picture on page 183? If you have eidetic imagery you will still have a clear enough visual image to count them.

Chapter summary

The study of human memory involves the question of how knowledge is encoded, stored, retained, and retrieved. It is also concerned with the individual's knowledge of when they do not know something. There appear to be three different memory systems which continually interact with each other. *Sensory-information storage* preserves sensory information just long enough for immediate use in perception. It includes *pattern recognition* and *shared attention.* In *short-term memory,* limited amounts of information are stored for brief periods of time. For information to remain in short-term memory without degenerating it must be *rehearsed.* Short-term memory also can be enhanced through the use of *visual imagery.* Content that is to be retained for longer periods of time must be transferred to *long-term memory.* This system is more permanent, though information in it may not be easily accessible. Long-term memory uses *semantic processing* and as the *level of processing* is made deeper, that is, more meaningful, remembering becomes more effective. *Context* and *inference* are important though they might occasionally result in memory distortion.

Forgetting is evaluated by comparing the amount retained immediately after learning with the amount retained some time later. Generally, it is measured either by *recall* or by *recognition.* The first systematic work in this area was conducted by Ebbinghaus, who learned lists of nonsense syllables. He found a typical rote retention curve with rapid forgetting at first, followed by a gradually slower decline. Explanations of forgetting include *trace decay,* which proposes that memory traces decay over time, and the *interference theory,* which argues that forgetting is due to the interference from other experiences. Interference is of two types: when it works backward it is called *retroactive inhibition;* when it is forward working it is called *proactive inhibition.*

Investigation into the role of interference in memory suggests that *competition* and *unlearning* are both relevant. Research has used the *paired-associate method,* in which the subject learns pairs of words and must recall one of the pair when given the other, and as well as *serial learning,* where the subject must learn the individual items in order. The latter produces a *serial-position effect:* the beginning and end of a series are remembered better than the middle items.

The remembering and forgetting of connected pieces of information, like stories, is somewhat different from the learning and remembering of word lists or nonsense syllables. It is more *productive* and reflects the importance of the story setting and specific events and the need to complete tasks. Some forgetting may also be affected by motivational factors such as *repression* and the personal biases of the learner.

Memory can be improved by *overlearning* and by a study strategy that proposes that one *survey, question, read, recite,* and *review. Chunking* cuts down the number of units to be learned.

Visual imagery is a *mnemonic strategy* and it also underlies many other mnemonic techniques such as *story chains* and *the method of loci* (or location). Other abilities, such as *eidetic memory,* may be less helpful than they seem.

Chapter 7

Language and Communication

The nature of language

The structure of language

The development of language

Language and thought

Chapter summary

A highly educated sixty-one-year-old woman was admitted to the hospital after suffering a paralysis on the right side of her body. Accompanying this problem was a severe language difficulty:

"'Then he graf, so I'll graf, I'm giving ink, no, gerfergen, in pane, I can't grasp, I haven't grob the grabben, I'm going to the glimmeril, let me go.'

'What my fytisset for, whattim tim saying got dok arne gimmin my suit, suit to Friday . . . I ayre here what takes zwei the cuppen seffer effer sepped . . . I spoke on she asked for clubbin hond here, you what, what kind of a siz, sizzen . . . and she speks all the friend and all that is in my herring.'

Q. 'What is your speech problem?'

A. 'Because no one gotta scotta gowan thwa, thirst, gell, gerst, derund, gystrol, that's all.'

Q. 'What does "swell-headed" mean?'

A. 'She is selfice on purpiten' " (Brown, 1972, pp. 64–65).

This woman's word for comb was "galeefs," yellow was "errendear," and ear was "my ear tuck me here." At times, more than 80 percent of her words were her own "inventions."

Why is this woman talking like this? Why are there so many invented words and why, with all the bizarreness in her language, are there snippets of "normal" speech like "I can't grasp" and "what kind of a . . . ?" She is suffering from *aphasia*, a language disorder arising from damage to a specific part of the brain, almost always in the left hemisphere. Her right-sided paralysis was also due to this brain damage since the left hemisphere controls the right side of the body. We will consider this disorder in more detail later in the chapter. For now, it illustrates the dramatic results that can occur when language, which we usually take very much for granted, breaks down. It is as if someone pulled out the foundation from an elaborately constructed building and the entire structure came toppling down. Some of the pieces might be large enough for an observer to realize that it had been a building, in the same way that this woman retained enough word order and enough vocabulary to show us that she was speaking something related to the English language. But most of the building would have crumbled into unidentifiable rubble just as most of this woman's speech was reduced to incomprehensible jargon.

When language disintegrates as it has in this example, communication dissolves along with it. Personal experiences can't be shared, knowledge can't be conveyed, emotions can't be verbally expressed. Situations like this enable us to appreciate the remarkable importance of the language system.

It is through our mastery of language that human beings have been able to transmit the wisdom of one generation to the next, to structure reality, and to stimulate fantasy. However, this same ability can become a barrier to the full experience of emotions by allowing us to substitute verbal descriptions of how we are (or ought to be) feeling in place of the feelings themselves. Language can thus be used to gain analytical distance from disturbing experiences by giving them a label, an explanation, and a time tag, which forces them into a specific historical niche.

In this chapter we shall explore the field of *psycholinguistics*—the study of the psychological nature of language. We will examine the characteristics and structure of language; how it develops as one grows from a newborn to a maturely functioning adult; its relation to thinking; and how people function when language becomes disordered. This overview should give you some insights into why language is one of the crowning achievements of our species.

The nature of language

Somewhere, a long, long time ago, someone uttered the first word and talking has never ceased. Certainly we will never know that first word and probably we shall never know the form of the first language. Nevertheless this has not stopped people from speculating. An early theory suggested that the first words were attempts to mimic the sounds of the things one was talking about. A lion, or its prehistoric equivalent, might be "grrr," and a dog "bow-wow": this theory is known as the *bow-wow theory* of the origin of language. Unfortunately many things, such as stones and caterpillars don't make any sound; therefore the early language would be greatly impoverished. However, in modern English we do have some words that mimic sounds, like *zip* and *zap* and *wham* and *ping* (even though the *ding-dong* of a bell in English is *bim-bam* in some other tongue).

Another early theory proposed that the first words were the spontaneous sounds the first humans uttered when confronting various objects. By this account, that ancient lion was no longer a "grrr," but now an "uh-oh" or something like that. This was known as the *pooh-pooh theory* of the origin of language. The fanciful titles given to these theories reflect the lack of seriousness in which they were held, not because they were necessarily wrong, but because there was no way of proving or disproving any of them. Largely for this reason, the French Academy of Science in 1875 refused to hear any further papers on the topic.

If we can't know the words of the first language, can we know at least what the sounds were? Did the first humans produce the same array of acoustic signals as their modern counterparts? In this case, we can get some answers. It is possible using skull remains to reconstruct much of the vocal channel and to subject it to computer analysis. As a result we know that Neanderthals, who lived 45,000 to 100,000 years ago, had a throat design that did not enable them to use the wide range of sounds of modern language. There were few vowels; the vowel sounds in *hill, the,* and *boat* were possible, but not those in *put, pit, pot,* and *paw.* Consonants were restricted to sounds like *b* and *d.* Further, Neanderthals didn't have the neurological receptors for the perception of some speech. Possibly the poor communication abilities of Neanderthals led to replacement by a more articulate subspecies (Lieberman & Crelin, 1971). (See *P&L* Close-up, Walking and Talking.)

Criteria for speech

There are thousands of modern languages and although they differ in many ways from one another, the basic characteristics are the same. Hockett (1960) lists a number of criteria for speech and we will discuss a sample of them here.

a. *Vocal-auditory channel.* Speech involves the mouth and the ears. As a result, speech production takes little physical energy and frees other channels for other tasks. If language used only hand gestures, we would not be able to communicate and do other things with our hands at the same time. With vocal language we can communicate without being visually observed—around corners or in the dark.

b. *Specialization.* Speech is used to send messages; that is its only purpose. Many other behaviors may result in communication, but we would not say they constitute language. When a dog pants, it is sending a message that it is hot, but it is mainly engaging in some physical activity aimed at relieving its

Close-up
Walking and Talking

Even though we do not know how languages originated, it is indisputable that humans depend greatly on this form of communication. Why do we need it? Why is it such a major human characteristic? David McNeill (1970) has proposed an ingenious theory as to why people must talk.

He notes that as humans evolved, their brain size increased and the skull also became larger in order to contain the brain. At the same time, humans were getting off all fours and starting to walk upright. To facilitate this, the birth canal became smaller which allowed walking to be smoother and more streamlined. As a result, the birth process became complicated; it was necessary for a big head to pass through a small birth canal. How could this be accomplished?

McNeill proposes that humans were born prematurely, at an earlier developmental stage than other primates. The head would then be smaller and birth would not be as difficult. There is some evidence for this proposal. Orangutans and humans have about the same gestation period, about 38 weeks, yet an orangutan reaches its full growth eleven years after birth while a human takes about twenty. This implies that humans are born prematurely.

Because of this relative "immaturity" at birth, human infants must be able to signal their needs to their mothers; other primates are more capable of taking care of themselves. McNeill argues that natural selection probably favored good signalers and good vocalizers and, consequently, we evolved into a language-using species. We were forced to talk in order to stay alive.

---

discomfort, similar to perspiring in humans. The point is that panting as communication is entirely secondary to its main function. If no one were around, a warm dog would still pant.

c. *Arbitrariness.* The fact that in English a certain large domesticated, four-legged animal is called a "horse" is arbitrary; we could call it a "mub" if everyone agreed. Obviously, in other languages a horse is called by other names; for example, "cheval" in French. The combination of sounds a language selects to refer to something is arbitrary, though once selected, the speakers of the language must be consistent. (See *P&L* Close-up, It Takes Two to Tangerk.)

d. *Displacement.* Humans use language to talk about the past and future as well as the present. Many psycholinguists believe this is one of the major distinctions between human language and the communication of lower animals, though as we shall soon see, there may be some question about this. Nevertheless, when your pet dog stands barking in front of you, he probably wants something now and is not reflecting on last summer or guessing at what next Thanksgiving will be like.

e. *Productivity.* Language allows a virtually infinite number of utterances to be produced. In fact, with the exception of clichés and other stock phrases, most people never say exactly the same thing twice. Language therefore is *productive.* If someone were to say, "Bruce tripped over the skateboard, crashed through the glass door, and knocked Rhoda into the deep end of the pool," the uniqueness of the utterance would not result in it being more difficult to state or to understand. This productivity also allows us to say things that are not true; we will return to this issue shortly.

f. *Duality of patterning.* Speech is composed of a relatively small set of sounds that are combined in different ways to refer to different things. The individual sounds have no specific meaning; the fact that "act," "cat," and "tack" are combinations of the same three sounds doesn't imply that they share any meaning. They actually do not. It is the pattern of sounds that carries the

Virginia and Grace Kennedy are seven-year-old identical twins living in San Diego. Raised primarily by their German grandmother, the twins can understand English, German, sign language, and some Spanish. They can also understand each other though no one else seems able to understand them. Writing for *The New York Times,* Everett R. Howes (1977) gave the following example of an exchange between the two girls who were playing with a doll house:

" 'Dugon, thosh yom dinckin, du-ah?' asked Virginia, who is called 'Cabenga' by her sister.

Linguists are interested in identical twin sisters, Grace and Virginia Kennedy, because they may have invented their own language; but communicating with the "outside world" (their speech therapist) was first done through sign language.

Grace, who is 'Poto,' nodded and replied with what sounded like 'Snup aduk, chase die-dipanna.' Both immediately set about removing the doll house's furniture."

Though it may sound like gibberish, some investigators feel that this may be an example of "twin speech," a very rare form of private communication which appears to have its own vocabulary and syntax. For the Kennedys this language started when they were about 17 months old though it is not just a shared form of "baby talk." The twins suggest names for objects and then agree to use those names in their conversations. All the experts are not convinced that this is indeed a special language but argue instead that it may be due to some neurological difficulty. Whatever the cause, this type of communication is quite fascinating and important. Dr. Leonard Newmark, professor of linguistics at the University of California, is quoted as saying that it "may help us in resolving one of the most intriguing and controversial enigmas of linguistic and cognitive science."

". . . Studying these children may provide data that will help provide the answer to whether language ability is inherited."

meaning, and any individual sound appears in many different patterns. If speech did not have this characteristic, we would need a new sound for every single thing we wanted to communicate and our speech capacity would be overtaxed almost immediately.

Animal communication

The above characteristics not only help to define human speech, they also present ways to distinguish it from the communication of lower animals. Though many animals use a vocal-auditory system, there has been very little evidence, at least until recently, that they possess such characteristics as specialization, arbitrariness, displacement, productivity, or duality of patterning.

Whistling dolphins

In recent years, much attention has been focused on the communication systems of dolphins. The underwater sounds made by dolphins were thought by some to be a true language. One of these sounds is a series of "clicks." However, research has shown that these clicks serve only as an underwater sonar system for exploring the environment. By emitting a sound that is reflected back as an echo, the dolphin (much like the bat) can determine the position of objects.

Another sound made by dolphins is a "whistle." It is made by both sexes and by all age groups—even newborn infants. This unique sound is not at all typical of nonhuman mammals, and there has been much speculation about its possible function as a true language. The most recent investigations, however, seem to challenge this conclusion. It has been found that individual dolphin whistles are very stereotyped and very repetitive. Although there are differences among dolphins in the type of whistle they make, there are not sufficient variations in pattern within a particular whistle to justify thinking of it as a language. Rather, the whistle appears to serve four *social* functions: (1) the alerting of other dolphins to one dolphin's presence, (2) the identification of that particular dolphin, (3) the localization of that dolphin, and (4) a general indication of the emotional state of the animal doing the whistling (Caldwell & Caldwell, 1972).

Experimental evidence has been found to support these first three functions, and data is currently being collected on the fourth. The Caldwells have shown that dolphins can clearly distinguish between the whistles of other individual dolphins, of both their own and other species. Furthermore, dolphins can locate the position of another dolphin on the basis of its whistle. These researchers have also noted that dolphins whistle a great deal when they are in an excited emotional state, but stop immediately when they are afraid. ■

Studying monkey talk

Is the gift of language unique to human beings because of evolution and innately given mental structures or because of the ideal language learning environment to which other species do not have access?

In the last forty years, a number of experiments have been conducted to determine whether chimpanzees reared in home environments can develop communication skills comparable to those exhibited by children. The young chimp rapidly adapts to its physical and social environment, becomes strongly attached to its caretaker, imitates adult acts without any training, and develops its motor behavior more rapidly than a child of similar age. However, the results in terms of language development are dismal. None of the chimps studied ever copied or reproduced human word sounds spontaneously, nor

The streams of bubbles indicate that the dolphins are whistling. The sounds they make, however, appear to serve as a means of identification rather than communication.

was there any evidence of attempts to do so. There was not any period of babbling or random emission of sounds (other than the food-bark, the "oo oo" cry, and screeching).

One couple of psychologists did manage to teach their chimp, Viki, to utter four words: "mama," "papa," "cup," and "up." Viki learned these words with great difficulty, only after considerable training, and even then could not really produce them easily and could not keep the sound patterns straight (Hayes & Hayes, 1952). But verbal communication does not necessarily involve speech production, and more recent research on language acquisition in apes has involved a variety of symbol systems.

Sign language
In 1966, Allen and Beatrice Gardner, psychologists at the University of Nevada, began an intensive study with a female chimp named Washoe, using the American Sign Language (ASL), a code of arbitrary symbols devised for the deaf (Gardner & Gardner, 1969).

In the first seven months, Washoe acquired four signs that she used reliably: "come-gimme," "more," "up," and "sweet." Moreover, she understood more signs than she produced. In the next seven months, she added nine more signs. By the age of twelve Washoe had control over 180 signs (Fouts, 1977).

What is most impressive about Washoe's use of language is not the extent of her vocabulary, but rather that she spontaneously uses a great many signs per day, and demonstrates both generalization and differentiation. For example, she uses the same sign, "more," for continued play and additional food; she uses "open" for opening a door, a soda bottle, or a stuck zipper. She strings her sign words into semantically valid multisign sequences, such as "Gimme please food," "Please tickle more," "Hurry gimme toothbrush," "You me go there in."

Washoe has also shown some evidence for productivity. She can put words together to form new concepts. For example, when Washoe first saw a swan, she spontaneously signed, "water-bird"; not knowing the sign for Coca-Cola, she concocted "sweet-water."

Most studies of language acquisition in apes have used chimpanzees as subjects. There is now evidence that gorillas, too, can learn to use sign language. A gorilla named Koko has been studied for the last five years by Francine Patterson at Stanford University. Koko is able to use over 400 signs, to invent new ones, and to engage in conversations with human beings. She is also capable of displacement, in that she can converse about past events. The following excerpt gives an example of this and it is all the more remarkable because Koko is able to refer to an emotional state she is not currently experiencing.

"The following conversation (between Patterson and Koko) took place three days after the event discussed:
P: What did you do to P?
K: Bite.
P: You admit it? (Previously Koko had referred to the bite as a scratch.)
K: Sorry bite scratch. (P shows Koko the mark on her hand—it really does resemble a scratch.)
K: Wrong bite.
P: Why bite?
K: Because mad. (A few moments later, it occurred to P to ask Koko,)
P: Why mad?
K: Don't-know."

On another occasion, Koko showed unmistakable evidence of lying, another behavior that has been considered outside the repertoire of animals:

"Koko, who had just tipped the scales at 90 pounds, sat on the kitchen sink and it sank about 2 inches. Not knowing how it had happened, (Patterson) asked Koko, 'Did you do that?' and Koko signed 'Kate there bad,' pointing to the sink. Kate . . . who had witnessed the incident, defended herself by explaining the situation" (Patterson, 1977).

Plastic "words" Using a slightly different approach, David Premack and his associates have had remarkable success in teaching their chimp, Sarah, to communicate by constructing sentences with colored chips of plastic on a magnetized board. Sarah first learned, through simple conditioning procedures, to associate a chip of a particular color and shape with a particular fruit — being allowed to eat the correctly identified item as a reward. Other chips became the "names" of the experimenters or represented certain actions, and Sarah was soon comprehending and constructing sentences like "Mary give apple Sarah" and "Sarah insert banana pail."

Sarah also proved to be capable of learning relational concepts such as "on" or "under," and even such abstractions as "name of," constructing such sentences as "(symbol) not-name of apple." Perhaps the high point of Sarah's "writing" career, however, was the day when, apparently bored with what was going on, she set up a string of incomplete sentences and gave her astonished trainer a multiple-choice sentence-completion test! (Premack, 1969, 1970)

Computer chatter At the Yerkes Primate Research Center in Georgia, a chimp named Lana has learned to "read" symbols on a computer keyboard and type out her requests (for food, music, etc.). Only "grammatically correct sentences" — that is, correct sequences of signs — are rewarded by the computer, and Lana has learned not only to state her requests correctly but also to erase and correct "ungrammatical" sentences presented by the computer (Rumbaugh, Gill, & von Glasersfeld, 1973).

At latest count, Lana was effectively using over 74 word symbols and she has 23 ways to ask for a cup of coffee, such as "You give coffee to me?" and "Please machine, give coffee" (Rumbaugh & Gill, 1976). More impressively, she no longer waits passively for new instructions, but now asks her teachers to name objects that interest her.

Talking to each other Washoe, Sarah, and Koko have learned their language systems from human beings, and Lana by interacting with a computer. So far, they have used them only to communicate with human beings. But suppose they were in the company of other apes who also knew the same system. Would they use this language to communicate with each other? Chimps at the Institute for Primate Studies in Norman, Oklahoma, who have learned sign language from human trainers, often use it in communicating among themselves. For example, one chimp will usually respond to another's sign command to "Come, hug" or "Come, hurry."

A pair of chimps have recently learned to use the Yerkes computer to communicate with each other. Sherman and Austin can tell each other what kind of food is hidden in a sealed container and can request a particular food from a supply available only to the other animal. Such requests are usually granted, although an "order" for a favorite food is occasionally filled with a less tasty item (Savage-Rumbaugh, Rumbaugh, & Boysen, 1978).

The accomplishments of Sarah, Lana, Koko, and other apes in laboratories around the country clearly challenge previous conceptions of the linguistic limitations of subhuman species. The extent to which they can com-

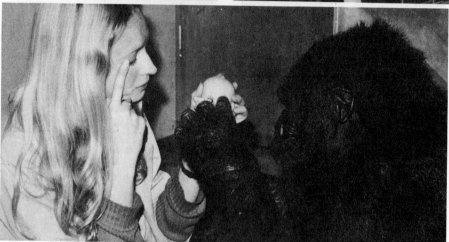

◆
The animals shown here are
very communicative, each in
her own way. Sarah "writes"
her request for chocolate on
the magnetized board. Lana
types out sentences on an
elaborate computer keyboard.
When asked to "find the
baby's eye," Koko points to it.
All three primates are
contributing to our
understanding of
communication processes.

municate with human beings via a shared language system gives some hope
that the ability to talk with animals may someday be more than a subject for
fantasy tales. ◆

The structure of language

On the surface, human languages appear to be infinitely varied. In fact, however, they share certain universal properties. Thus while the specific sounds,
words, and rules we shall consider in our discussion of language are those of
English, the same broad principles are applicable to any language.

One of the properties common to all human languages is a basic linguistic
structure—a system which includes the sound units, the combination of these
sounds, and the meaning. These three levels, known as *phonology, syntax,* and
semantics constitute the structure, or the *grammar,* of a language. Grammar, in
this sense, is used to describe how a language operates; it is not directed at
how people should use language, but at how they actually do use it.

Phonology

At the phonological level, we are concerned with the basic sound units that
make up the stream of speech. Speech begins with small puffs of air pushing
upward from the lungs through the *larynx,* a mass of cartilage situated in the

front of the neck. The *vocal cords*, located in the larynx, continually alter this air flow by varying their rate of vibration. As the air is forced farther upward other modifications of the sound are made by varying the shape of the mouth, the position of the tongue and lips, and the opening or closing off of the nasal cavity. These adjustments, performed in various combinations, result in the formation of different speech sounds known as *phonemes*.

Phonemes

Phonemes are a class of sounds that are recognized by speakers of a given language as having certain distinctive features that set them apart from other sounds and signal a difference in meaning. For example, while the sound of the letter *p* in *pan* is not entirely identical to that of the *p* in *plan*, any speaker of English would recognize them as instances of the same phoneme: /*p*/. Furthermore, an English-speaking person would make a clear distinction between this phoneme and the initial sound in the word *ban* (the phoneme /*b*/). Obviously, to understand any spoken language, a person must learn to make the necessary phonemic distinctions and identifications.

Differences in vowel phonemes are due to the closeness of the tongue to the roof of the mouth and to whether the front, center, or back of the tongue is most used in making the sound. An example of a high (tongue very near the roof of the mouth) front vowel is the *ee* sound in *beet* or *cheese*. You can feel the front of your tongue doing most of the work. In English, producing this vowel also results in your mouth turning up a little bit and that is why photographers who want you to smile will ask you to say "cheese." An example of the opposite type of vowel, a low (tongue held way down) back one, is the *ah* sound in the word *calm*. Producing that vowel also exposes much of the throat; the physician asks the patient to say *ah* so that area can be examined.

Consonant phonemes are distinguished by their place and manner of articulation. For example, some (bilabial phonemes) are made by the putting the lips together, others by placing the tongue against the teeth. Since families of sounds are produced in the same place, the only way they can be differentiated is by their manner of articulation. Stop phonemes, for example, are made by blocking the air flow in the mouth and then suddenly releasing it. If this blockage occurs by holding the lips together and then opening them, the resulting phoneme will be a *p* or *b*. The sound will be a *b* if the vocal cords vibrate just as the air is released—what is called a *voiced* phoneme; if the vibration starts a fraction of a second after the air is released—a voiceless phoneme—the sound will be a *p*. If you place your hand lightly on your throat, you will feel the vibration when you say *ba* but not when you say *pa*.

Similar to the stop consonants are the nasals, which involve the passage of air through the nasal cavity. If your nose is stopped up, a nasal phoneme becomes a voiced stop consonant. When you have a head cold, *my* becomes *by* and *not* becomes *dot*.

Like English, most languages are composed of about 38 to 40 phonemes, though not always the same ones. Hawaiian, however, has only twelve. This necessitates using the same sound combinations over and over, as in the names Waikiki, Kamehameha, and Honolulu.

Distinctive features

Speech production is a remarkably efficient process. The average syllable contains about 2.5 phonemes and a typical speaker can pronounce about five syllables per second, an amazing 12.5 phonemes (Miller, 1951). If you think about vibrating your vocal cords and moving around your tongue and lips purposefully and in combination over twelve times each second, you will probably be impressed—though somewhat mistakenly. In fact, the changes in articulation are usually not that elaborate. For example, the difference between /b/ and /p/ resides in only one characteristic, /b/ is voiced and /p/, voiceless. As a result, to change from one to another it is necessary only to adjust the vibration of the vocal cords; the mouth, lips, and tongue placement are identical for the two phonemes. The phonemes /n/ and /d/ are also identical except that the first is nasal. Characteristics like voicing or nasality are called *distinctive features* and they are either present or absent in each phoneme. As a result, when we shift from one phoneme to another what actually changes is usually not an entire complex of movements, but only a few distinctive features. This makes talking much easier.

Parallel transmission and spectrograms

So far, our discussion of phonology has centered on speech production. But of course there is another side to the issue—how listeners perceive the sounds that are spoken to them. One research strategy employed by psycholinguists to study this question involves changing a single linguistic element and then observing whether this has any effect on the subject's ability to perceive, learn, or remember a given utterance.

Investigators working at the phonological level have succeeded in determining the basic physical acoustic properties necessary to hear and identify a phoneme. Spoken sounds can be recorded and then converted to visual displays, called *spectrograms*. Plotted on these spectrograms are the frequency (cycles per second) of the sound and the amount of time needed to utter it. Researcher Ruth Day and her colleagues at the Haskins laboratories in New Haven have developed a method for constructing simplified, idealized sound patterns from these actual spectrograms. ● With a special apparatus, these idealized patterns can be converted back to sound and played to listeners who

●

**Actual and idealized
spectrograms**
*The actual spectrogram of
the spoken syllable /ga/ is
shown in black.
Superimposed in color is the
idealized spectrogram
constructed by investigators
at Haskins laboratory.*

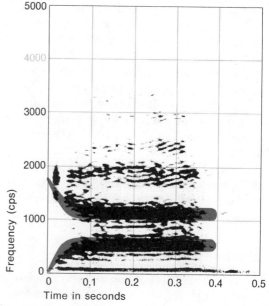

Courtesy of Dr. Ruth Day

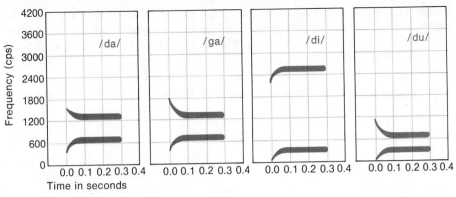

Idealized spectrograms of four sounds

Courtesy of Dr. Ruth Day

are asked to report what they hear. The investigators have found that some very similar physical patterns are heard as different phonemes, as shown for /da/ and /ga/ in the top portion of the figure. ▲ Other very different physical patterns (as shown in the lower part of the figure) are often *not* distinguished by the listener as being different phonemes.

The fact that the spectrograms of the same phonemes are not identical implies that their shape is determined by the other sounds in the same syllable. When /d/ is followed by /i/, both initial "hooks" turn down; when followed by /a/, one turns down and one up. This further implies that all the phonemes in a syllable carry information about each other. The /b/ in *boy* is not physically the same as the /b/ in *big*. The first is influenced by the *oy* following, the second by the *ig*. Speech is not just the stringing together of individual, distinct sound units, it is more a case of each sound in a syllable carrying with it at the same time information about the sounds preceding and following. This is known as *parallel transmission*, a process that also results in more effective speech processing. Nevertheless, the fact that no one pattern has been found that corresponds with a given phoneme (such as /d/) makes it all the more amazing that phonemes are so readily extracted from the stream of speech and recognized by listeners.

Dialect differences in phonology

Though all speakers of American English use basically the same set of phonemes, there are variations due to region, socioeconomic class, race, and social setting. Northerners usually pronounce *greasy* with an /s/ in the second syllable; some Southerners pronounce it as if it were spelled *greazy*. Northeasterners pronounce *merry*, *Mary*, and *marry* differently. Not only do Midwesterners pronounce them identically, but the three words all sound the same to them, an interesting observation on how speech production and speech perception interact.

Upper-middle socioeconomic class individuals are less likely to drop the final /g/ in pronouncing words like *running* and *finding* than are those from the lower socioeconomic class. For both groups, the final /g/ is dropped less in reading aloud than in casual speech (Labov, 1970). In some forms of black English, the final consonant or consonant grouping may be omitted, so that *call*, *calls*, and *called* are all pronounced *call*.

As in other situations, it is unwise to use a general characteristic as a means of stereotyping people. Not all Southerners say *greazy* and there are some Northerners who do; not all Northeasterners distinguish *merry*, *Mary*, and *marry* and to some Midwesterners the distinction is clear; not all lower socioeconomic class people drop their final *g*'s and some of the very rich take this shortcut; not all blacks omit final consonants and some whites do frequently. The fact that there are so many exceptions to the general pattern should indicate that dialect differences, when they occur, are simply variations in the way people talk; they have nothing to do with differences in intelligence or capability. (See *P&L* Close-up, He Done Did Follow the Man's Rules.)

Syntax

The rules of syntax specify the permissible orders in which words may be arranged to form sentences. Since the sentences we construct are comments on something or other, it is difficult to discuss the syntax of normal language without at the same time dealing with meaning. Even a seemingly nonsensical sentence can have some meaning imposed on it if the syntactical rules are acceptable. For example, "The milk shake thanked the tree," though correct syntactically is certainly bizarre semantically. Nevertheless, in some context—a fairy tale perhaps—the sentence might make some sense. The same words arranged in a nonsyntactic, haphazard order, "milk shake the thanked tree the" have no meaning beyond those of the individual words.

In a series of experiments, George Miller and his co-workers at Rockefeller University have studied the psychological effects of violating linguistic rules. Consider the five "normal sentences" in the table. Note that all follow the same syntactic sequence, namely (Subject) + (Verb) + (Direct Object) + (Preposition) + (the) + (Object of Preposition). From these, a new set of sentences was generated that were nonsensical but preserved syntactic order. Each of these was prepared by selecting the first word of one normal sentence, the second word of the next normal sentence, the third word of the next normal sentence, and so on, yielding the string, "Gadgets kill passengers from the eyes." This procedure was continued until all words were used, yielding the second group of sentences in the table, which were syntactically correct but "semantically anomalous." A third set of sentences was generated by haphazardly rearranging the words of the normal sentences to destroy their normal

Sentences used in studying consequences of linguistic rule violations

Normal Sentences
1. Gadgets simplify work around the house.
2. Accidents kill motorists on the highways.
3. Trains carry passengers across the country.
4. Bears steal honey from the hive.
5. Hunters shoot elephants between the eyes.

Semantically Anomalous Sentences
1. Gadgets kill passengers from the eyes.
2. Accidents carry honey between the house.
3. Trains steal elephants around the highways.
4. Bears shoot work on the country.
5. Hunters simplify motorists across the hive.

Ungrammatical Strings
1. Around accidents country honey the shoot.
2. On trains hive elephants the simplify.
3. Across bears eyes work the kill.
4. From hunters house motorists the carry.
5. Between gadgets highways passengers the steal.

Adapted from Miller & Isard, 1963

Close-up
"He Done Did Follow the Man's Rules": Nonstandard English

What is the difference between the following sentences: "He workin' when the boss come in" and "He be workin' when the boss come in"? According to the rules of standard English, both sentences are syntactically incorrect and imprecise. However, if the speaker is a black American, there is a significant difference in their meaning, one that is conveyed with considerable precision according to psycholinguists J. L. Dillard (1967, 1968, 1972) and William Labov (1969). The first statement means the worker performs his job *only* in the presence of his employer. The second indicates that the worker is conscientious about his work and works even in the absence of surveillance.

"I do," "I did," and "I have done" are the accepted forms of the verb "to do" in standard English, but the black child might say, "I do," "I done," and "I have did," or "I done did." Linguistic differences such as these have been assumed by many white educators to reflect "cultural deprivation" and cognitive inability to learn and process complex concepts.

At the heart of this controversy is whether nonstandard English is erratic and illogical or is a rule-governed language system. Resolution of the issue goes beyond satisfying academic curiosity because of its social, cultural, and political implications. Are black children and others who have learned to master their ethnic group's nonstandard English language system handicapped by having to unlearn it and acquire a "foreign" language that is the only accepted and correct form in school? Furthermore, since their language is not officially recognized as "legitimate" — as it would be if they spoke Russian, Arabic, or French — such children are often ridiculed for their "faulty" speech habits, thereby making school for them a place associated with feelings of inferiority. (Incidentally, there are, in fact, rules regarding verb forms in nonstandard English that are similar to those of Russian or Arabic and dissimilar to those of English.)

Some instances of grammatical rules of black dialect are, for example: (a) when a word ends with two audible sounds the last is dropped — *fist* becomes *fis* and *desk* becomes *des*. Thus, with plurals *fis* transforms to *fisses* and *des* to *desses*; (b) whenever standard English can contract, black children use either the contracted verb form or the deleted form (called the *zero copula*) — "they mine," "you right"; (c) in long sentences additional predicate markers are used to remind the speaker and listener of the subject of the discussion, as in "You know that girl live on 151st street, dress real cool, work modeling downtown, got real deep eyes, *she* go to school with me."

Linguists have argued that aspects of nonstandard black English offer a better sense of the point in time, or the duration an action takes place. In addition, because this language is still closer to its oral, storytelling tradition than to written form, it employs grammatical devices, emphasis, and vocabulary to hold the listener's immediate attention. Even when listening to a sentence spoken in standard form and asked to repeat it, black research subjects "translate" it according to the rules of their dialect. Thus, when asked to repeat sentences containing the negative "nobody ever," black ghetto children consistently responded with "nobody never" — the correct form in black English (Labov et al., 1968).

The concern of linguists that black nonstandard English be recognized as a viable, legitimate language is eloquently stated by Labov, who feels teachers are taught to ignore the language of Negro children and to hear their speech as proof of mental inferiority. Linguists condemn this bad observation, theory, and practice. "That educational psychology should be strongly influenced by a theory so false to the facts of language is unfortunate; but that children should be the victims of this ignorance is intolerable" (1969, p. 169).

syntactic structure, yielding the "ungrammatical strings" shown in the table. The sentences were tape-recorded, and the subjects were asked to "shadow" them by repeating them out loud as soon as they heard them. The subjects were able to correctly repeat 89 percent of the first group, 80 percent of the second group, and only 56 percent of the third, ungrammatical group. Similar results were found when subjects were asked to memorize these types of sentences. Thus both structure and meaning apparently affect our ability to hear accurately and to remember what we have heard (Miller & Isard, 1963; Marks & Miller, 1964).

Phrase structure

One of the earlier views of syntax proposed that a sentence was just a group of words hooked together with no underlying structure. To begin a sentence the speaker would sift through the words in his vocabulary and choose the single most probable word to start. The second word would be obtained by inspecting the vocabulary again and selecting the most probable word, where the probability was now based on words that could follow the first word. The third word would be chosen in a similar fashion, and so on, until a period was the most probable alternative and the sentence was thus completed. The selection of each word depended on the one preceding it. Aside from the fact that this procedure is psychologically and physically impossible — we could never sort through the probabilities fast enough to speak at a normal speed — it also ignores the importance of the words occurring earlier in the sentence. For example, in "The people who live down the block own the fast-food restaurant" the form of *own* depends on the second word, *people*. If the second word was *person*, instead, the choice would now be *owns*. That is, the selection of the eighth word is determined not by the word before it, but by the second word in the sentence. Every language has so many of these remote dependencies that it is clear that a simple probability chaining theory will not suffice.

The underlying structure of language is not arranged in a word-to-word chain but in a hierarchy. A sentence is composed of phrases, the phrases can be made up of smaller phrases, and at the end the entire structure is composed of words. Speaking is largely a matter of manipulating phrase units rather than individual words. A grammar based on this theory is known as a *phrase-structure grammar*. ■ Notice that the sentence in the diagram is composed of two major phrases, a subject and a predicate (or, equivalently, a noun phrase and a verb phrase). Further, the phrase "saved the dying woman" can be divided into a verb, "saved," and another noun phrase, "the dying woman." If we wanted to say the same thing in another way, we would change the order of the phrases; we would not move words from one phrase into the other. For example, we could say "The dying woman was saved by the small boy" and mean about the same thing. However, if we toyed with the phrases themselves, like "The dying boy saved the small woman" the original meaning has been changed totally.

Is there any psychological reality to this phrase-structure approach? That is, do people really think and construct sentences in this manner? Johnson (1965) had people learn sentences like the one we have been using. He predicted that if phrase structure were psychologically real, people would make the greatest number of errors at the phrase boundaries — the place in the sentence where one phrase ended and the next began — and the fewest number within the phrase. The idea was that people would remember the sentence as a series of phrase "chunks"; if they remembered a chunk at all, they would probably remember the entire unit. Not only was Johnson's prediction con-

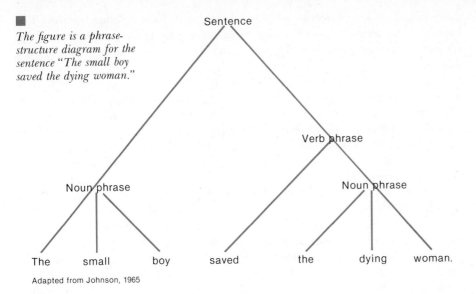

The figure is a phrase-structure diagram for the sentence "The small boy saved the dying woman."

Adapted from Johnson, 1965

firmed, but he also found that the greatest number of memory errors occurred at the boundary between the major phrases in the sentence, that is, between the words *boy* and *saved*. Fewer errors occurred between *saved* and *the*, and there were even fewer between words in the smallest phrases, such as the transition between *small* and *boy* or *dying* and *woman*.

Transformational grammar

Although a phrase-structure grammar is quite useful in understanding how language is ordered, it fails to account for similarities in meaning between sentences with different phrase structures. It also does not consider the *productive* aspects of language—that is, how people are able to produce completely original sentences that they have not heard before. Presumably, these aspects of language are based on the ability to use various syntactic rules. According to Chomsky (1965) these rules can be divided into two classes, depending on whether they determine the superficial or the underlying linguistic structure of language. The *surface structure* of a sentence refers to its component parts (such as noun, verb, object, etc.) and the relationship between them. This structure of a sentence plays an important role in determining its meaning. Clearly, if we take the words in a sentence like "Lecturers like silent, happy audiences" and rearrange them in various combinations, the meaning they convey will be quite different. What a sentence means (its semantic interpretation) is determined by its underlying, abstract *deep structure*. Even if sentences have very different surface structures, they may be similar in their deep structure. For instance, the sentences "I asked Chris to come" and "What I asked of Chris was that she come" have the same deep structure and semantic interpretation, even though their surface structure differs.

It is this deep structure that is intuitively and unconsciously converted, by means of *transformational rules*, into the surface structure. Take, for example, the sentence "The man who is sitting at the head of the table is my father." We may consider this sentence to be composed of a transformed version of "The man is my father" and "The man is sitting at the head of the table." In this case the speaker has unconsciously transformed two separate "sentences" (at the conceptual level) into the single sentence that is spoken. Certain transformational rules have been used to *embed* one sentence in the other and make the syntactic changes necessary to produce a well-formed construction. The hearer of the sentence goes through the reverse procedure, transforming the surface structure into the deeper structures that reveal the underlying meaning.

Transformational grammar is able to deal with ambiguous sentences, those that can have more than one meaning. An ambiguous sentence is one where two or more different deep structures have been transformed to produce one surface structure. We can see this in the sentence, "The shooting of the hunters was terrible." One of the deep structures would include the information that the hunters were shot; the other would include information that it was the hunters that did the shooting.

Clearly a transformational grammar has utility in understanding how sentences are produced, how they are related to each other, and how such problems as ambiguity can be identified and resolved. Nevertheless, much psychological research has been unable to support the concept of deep structure. Possibly this is because the transformational rules should not change the meaning of the deep structure though it seems that they often do. Thus psycholinguists are not as excited about the place of transformational grammar in understanding the nature of language as they were initially. The concept is good but empirical validation has not been forthcoming.

Case grammar

Which are the most important parts of a sentence? Razran (1961) conditioned people to salivate when they were presented a sentence like "I gave him a new ball." Later each word was presented again, but separately this time, and the amount of salivation was measured. The assumption was that salivation from presentation of the entire sentence would generalize to the individual words with the most salivation occurring to the word that best represented the meanings of the sentence. Razran found that the verbs were the best representatives of the sentence meaning; the direct object ("ball" in the above sentence) was the next best. In one test, 35 percent of the salivation occurred to the verb and only 9 percent to the subject ("I" in the example).

More recent linguistic attempts to deal with the problems of grammar have also focused more sharply on the issue of meaning. As in Razran's work, the verb has become the center of the analysis and the task is to understand how the verb interacts meaningfully with the other nouns in the sentence. These interactions are called case relations and this type of grammar is called a *case grammar* (Fillmore, 1968). In the sentence "John destroyed the statue with his tractor," one case relation involves the *agent* ("John") and "destroyed." Another concerns the relation of "destroyed" to the *patient*, ("statue"); and a third, the case relation of *instrument* ("tractor") to the verb. Presumably there are a limited number of case relations, including such additional ones as *location, time,* and *experiencer*. Because a case grammar deals with the deep meaning of a sentence and because it attempts to deal with the things that language users know and try to communicate to each other, it is receiving much attention from psycholinguists.

Semantics

The study of meaning is called *semantics*. Some words or word strings have arbitrarily agreed-upon meanings (such as the word *psychology*), or else acquire meaning through emotional or cognitive associations. The meaning of a word also depends on its immediate context and the inflection with which it is uttered relative to related words. For example, the simple word *run* has over twenty meanings. (How many of them can you list?) A "white house cat" becomes a very different thing depending on where the inflection falls: "a *white* house cat," "a *white house* cat," "a white *house* cat," and so on. The sentences, "The king is pregnant" or "Colorless green ideas sleep furiously" are acceptable on the phonological and syntactic levels but not always on the semantic level—unless, of course, we are being whimsical or are speaking metaphorically. Actually semantics and syntax are interacting all the time (consider the case grammar discussed in the last section) and it is difficult to consider one without the other. However, if we first study the meaning of individual words the situation can be simplified somewhat.

Connotative meaning and the semantic differential

In an attempt to quantify the nature of semantics, Osgood, Suci, and Tannenbaum (1957) devised a rating technique called the *semantic differential*. In this method, people rated their connotations, or impressions, of words on a series of seven-point scales. For example, an individual would be asked to rate *baby* on a scale that looked like this:

good:_____:_____:_____:_____:_____:_____:_____:bad

A check mark would be placed in one of the spaces between *good* and *bad*, the more "good" the rater perceived babies, the more to the left the check mark would be placed. Many different scales were used, such as: sweet-sour, fast-slow, young-old, strong-weak, noisy-quiet, and many different words were rated. Following this, the results obtained from a great many raters were analyzed by an elaborate statistical procedure in order to determine if there were any general underlying characteristics of the rated words.

Three factors emerged which seemed to account for the connotations of words. They were the *evaluative* factor, represented by such scales as good-bad and nice-awful; a *potency* factor, measured by scales like strong-weak and big-little; and an *activity* factor which included fast-slow and alive-dead. A word like *baby*, for example, would probably be rated as quite positive on the evaluative factor, quite weak on the potency factor, and quite energetic on the activity factor. Certain words make more sense with some scales than do others. Fast-slow might be a direct way to rate racehorses but it is less representative when rating chairs. Nevertheless, people are still quite consistent; most subjects are likely to rate chairs as slow rather than fast.

Osgood (1971) has studied these three factors in many different cultures in order to determine if there are psycholinguistic consistencies. Seventeen of the twenty languages studied—including American English, Greek, Italian, Lebanese, Finnish, Bengali, and Japanese—use these same three dimensions to classify words. Further, all twenty languages give most weight to the evaluative factor. These regularities have led Osgood to suggest that evaluation, potency, and activity may be basic characteristics of emotional meaning in all humans. He suggests that these factors might have quite a long history:

"What is important to us now, as it was way back in the age of Neanderthal Man, about the sign of a thing is: First, does it refer to something <u>good</u> or <u>bad</u> for me (is it an antelope or a saber-toothed tiger)? Second, does it refer to something which is <u>strong</u> or <u>weak</u> with respect to me (is it a saber-toothed tiger or a mosquito)? And third, for behavioral purposes, does it refer to something which is <u>active</u> or <u>passive</u> (is it a saber-toothed tiger or merely a pool of quicksand, which I can simply walk around)? . . . to deny their importance is to fly in the face of everyday common sense as well as much scientific data" (Osgood, 1971, pp. 37–38).

Denotative meaning

The semantic differential technique is used for studying connotative or emotional meaning. It can tell us that babies are considered soft and good, and that bugs are felt to be bad and active, but it can't tell us that babies have a nose in the middle of their face or that bugs have many, maybe too many, legs. These latter facts are objective defining characteristics as contrasted with the subjective evaluations of goodness or softness. The objective characteristics are part of the *denotative* meaning of a word.

Katz and Fodor (1963) have proposed a theory of denotative meaning based on the use of *semantic features*, or meaning categories. ● In the diagram, the word *bachelor* is analyzed. It has four possible meanings, all of which are nouns, and the theory tries to account for these four meanings by ordering them into categories. These categories, which are the semantic features, include "human," "animal," and "male" though, of course, for other words a different selection might be necessary. Notice that a bachelor, in the sense of having never married, and a bachelor as a "young knight serving under another knight" share the "male" and "human" features; the bachelor who holds a bachelor's degree shares only the "human" feature, since those people can be either male or female. And finally, the bachelor fur seal is alone, not only because he has no mate at breeding time, but also because he doesn't share the "human" feature.

Two advantages of a system such as this are that it may help us to understand the nature of ambiguity and that it may provide some way of determining whether a sentence is likely to carry a conventional meaning or not. For example, the sentence "She is a bachelor" is not ambiguous because "She" possesses a "female" semantic feature and the only bachelor that can be female is the one with a bachelor's degree. On the other hand, "All the world loves a bachelor" is ambiguous in four ways since all of the semantic features of bachelor are consistent with those of "love." Finally, we know that the sentence, "My door is a bachelor" is nonsensical because the semantic features of "door" do not include any of those for "bachelor." Doors are not human, animal, or male. Consequently, any conventional meaning is excluded. This theory is not without its problems. Specifically, we do not know all the semantic features for a language, nor do we know how many there are likely to be. Undoubtedly the number is very large.

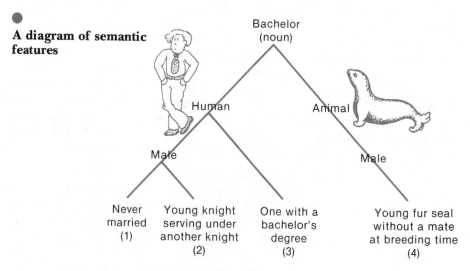

A diagram of semantic features

Bachelor (noun)

Human — Animal

Male — Male

Never married (1) — Young knight serving under another knight (2) — One with a bachelor's degree (3) — Young fur seal without a mate at breeding time (4)

Adapted from Katz & Fodor, 1963

The problem of understanding the semantic system in language is an extremely complicated one; possibly the most complicated in psychology. We have seen that there are at least two kinds of meaning, connotative and denotative, and that syntax is constantly interacting with semantics. Nevertheless, when the problems in this area are solved, we will have learned much not only about the nature of language, but also about human memory, where all this information is stored.

The development of language

Up to this point, we have been speaking of language as though it were simply a way of expressing one's ideas. However, language is more than a medium of communication: it plays a basic role in ordering experience and in stabilizing the confusing world a young child faces. In fact, there are very few psychological processes that are not affected by the operation of language, verbal labels, and symbols. By using language appropriately, a child can have his or her biological needs better met, secure attention, and to some extent control the behavior of others.

Language is necessary if we are to recall, plan, reason, analyze, explain inconsistencies, reduce uncertainty, and form a common bond of social reality with those around us.

The sequence of language development

Human language production can be roughly divided into four stages. These stages overlap somewhat, but they form a convenient framework for studying early vocalization (Kaplan & Kaplan, 1970).

Stage 1. The study of language development in human children begins with the birth cry of the newborn. For the first three weeks, the infant's vocal repertoire is extremely limited. The basic cry may be modified somewhat to produce variations, from which the alert parent infers anger or physical pain. But cries, coughs, and gurgles make up the sum of the newborn's vocal production. Even though vocalization in this stage is diffuse, analysis of movies has shown that infants as young as two days of age move in synchrony with the sounds of adult speech. True, such movements are very small—a slight tilt of the head, a rotation of the hip—but they indicate that the infant is "tuned in" to the adult world (Condon & Sander, 1974).

Stage 2. From about three weeks of age to four or five months, the infant introduces some pseudocries—cry vocalizations that are not simple cries. Variety in these sounds is produced by changes in duration, pitch, and articulation. In fact, during the first two or three months all the speech sounds of all languages are uttered at one time or another. This seems to be a sort of general flexing of the speech production mechanism. That is, the infant is not able to intentionally produce any particular sound, but randomly produces many.

Speech perception also becomes somewhat more refined. One-month-old infants were able to distinguish between voiced and voiceless stop consonants, like *b* and *p* or *d* and *t*, as shown by a change in their conditioned sucking rate (Eimas, Siqueland, Juscyzk, & Vigorito, 1971). This experiment and the one on synchrony in movement lend strong support to the view that the percep-

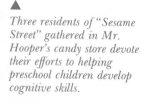

In addition to play times and talking sessions, bathing, diapering, dressing, and feeding times are frequently times of vocal interaction between infant and parent.

tion of speech precedes its intentional production. As we shall see, children can understand language before they are very proficient in using it.

Infant vocalizations also interact with the vocalizations of the mother. ◆ Sometimes this interaction is alternating, as when the mother makes a sound, then the infant follows with another sound, then the mother makes yet another sound, and so on. At other times the interaction is simultaneous, both mother and infant articulating together. Two- to four-month-old infants show both patterns, which appear to develop for different reasons. The alternating pattern seems to be the forerunner of normal conversational behavior where one person talks while the other is silent. The simultaneous pattern occurs most frequently when the infant is at a high level of arousal, such as moving and looking around. Adults also vocalize simultaneously when they are at the high arousal levels accompanying heated arguments or lovemaking (Stern, Jaffee, Beebe, & Bennett, 1975).

Stage 3. During the last half of the first year, the child's speech sounds become so varied and continuous that this period is known as the "babbling stage." As in the previous stages, very many different sounds are made and, at least at the beginning of the babbling stage, the sounds produced seem to be the same from one culture to another. However, as children near the end of this stage, they begin to imitate the intonation pattern of their parent language; though no words are produced, the sounds of an American child are those of American English and a Japanese child begins to sound Japanese (Glucksberg & Danks, 1975).

Stage 4. The beginnings of patterned, "true" speech occur some time near the end of the first year. The "prelinguistic" period of the previous stages gives way to the appearance of the child's first recognizable words. However, it is still not clear whether the prelinguistic stages are systematically related to the production of true speech. Some researchers maintain that in the babbling stage there is an ordered sequence of development; others hold that the development of true language is completely discontinuous from prior linguistic behavior.

The average year-old child has an initial vocabulary of two or three words. This increases to about fifty words by twenty-four months and 1000 words by the age of three (Lenneberg, 1969). It is likely that the greater stimulation provided by daily exposure to television programming will be shown to accelerate vocabulary development, and if skillfully prepared (as on the program "Sesame Street") may have an impact on other areas of language development. ▲

▲ Three residents of "Sesame Street" gathered in Mr. Hooper's candy store devote their efforts to helping preschool children develop cognitive skills.

The pattern of language development

Once children are able to produce recognizable words, what do they say? The first meaningful utterances are single words, such as "mama," which often carry the force of a complete sentence. For example, "mama" could mean "That's Mama," "Mama, where are you?" "Mama, I'm hungry," or several other things, depending on the situation. Later on, the child begins to put words together to form two-word sentences. As we shall see, these word combinations are not random but show a definite, regular structure. While this structure changes with age, it does not always correspond to the structure of adult language.

Putting words together

At about eighteen months of age, the child begins to use two-word, rather than one-word sentences. Such sentences seem to be expressing various types of relationships between things. For example, the sentence "Cup glass" could be signifying a *conjunction* ("I see a cup and a glass"). Similarly, *location* could be expressed by "Hat chair" ("The hat is on the chair"). A sentence such as "Mary ball" could indicate either *possession* ("Here is Mary's ball") or a *subject-object* relationship ("Mary throws the ball"). Obviously, two-word sentences such as these can only be understood in the context in which they are spoken.

The important thing to realize about the child's language at this stage is that it is *not* a direct copy of an adult's language. Although the words are the same, the child puts them together in a different way. The child's grammar has its own rules that do not correspond to those of the surrounding adult language that he or she must use in order to communicate effectively.

Rules to organize words and phrases

When children are about two years old, they begin to produce sentences that are longer than two words. Often, these longer sentences are expansions of shorter ones; the child first produces a short sentence and then apparently "plugs it in" to a more complex one. For example, a child will say, "Want that . . . Andrew want that" or "Stand up . . . Cat stand up . . . Cat stand up table." A careful examination of these longer sentences suggests that the child is actively analyzing each sentence into its structural subunits and is not just stringing words together.

As the child's language becomes more and more complex, he or she begins applying patterns of regularity, or *rules*. Sometimes a rule is applied too widely and results in incorrect linguistic forms. For example, once the child learns the past-tense rule for most verbs (adding "*ed*" to the verb), the "*ed*" will be added to *all* verbs, resulting in words such as "doed" and "breaked." After my daughter had correctly learned "my" and "mine" to indicate her possessions and "your" to indicate those of another person, she overregularized to say "mines" when she heard people saying "yours."

This overregularization is especially interesting because it usually appears *after* the child has learned and used the correct forms of the verbs and nouns. That is, the child first uses the correct verb forms of "came" and "went," apparently because they were learned as separate vocabulary items. However, when the child later learns the general rule for past tenses, he or she immediately extends it to all verbs and starts to say "comed" and "goed," even though the child has never heard other people say such words. It is from analysis of such mistakes that we can discover how language learning depends on acquisition of general rules.

Up until this time, children's sentences have generally taken the form of simple statements, such as "More cookie", "John want that." However, the child gradually begins to apply rules to construct questions and negative statements. Through the use of one rule the statement "He is doing it" can be turned into the question "Is he doing it?" Adding "why" to the beginning of the sentence transforms the question into "Why is he doing it?"

This development is not without its difficulties. The child has a limited memory span and is unable to apply many linguistics rules at the same time. Also, young children have trouble distinguishing the meaning of certain words; "what" is confused with "where," "why" with "what," and "when" with "where" (Clark, 1971). And there are confusions in interpreting sentences. A six-and-one-half-year-old boy was shown two toys, Donald Duck and Bozo the Clown. When told "Donald tells Bozo to hop across the table. Can you make him hop?" the boy bounced Bozo across the table. But when instructed, "Bozo promises Donald to hop across the table. Can you make him hop?" the boy had Donald doing the hopping instead of Bozo. In the first sentence, the word "Bozo" is closest to the word "hop" so Bozo is made to do the hopping. In the second sentence "Donald" is closest so now Donald is made to do the hopping. But this *minimal-distance principle* doesn't work in the second sentence; the child has not yet learned that the verb "tell" functions differently than the verb "promise" (C. S. Chomsky, 1970).

Theories of language learning

Now that we have some idea of *what* children learn to say, we can begin to tackle the question of *how* they learn to say it. Where does this ability to produce a complex language come from? Many people would probably say, "Oh, children just imitate what they hear, and if they make a mistake, their parents correct them." In fact, this imitation-and-correction model is one of the major theories of language acquisition. A different answer comes from a developmental approach to language. The ability to use language effectively is seen as a basic, innate capacity of the human species. It emerges at a particular time in the child's development given only a receptive environment.

The learning approach: Imitation and reinforcement

B. F. Skinner (1957), as a leading learning theorist, argues that children learn language in just the same way that they learn to perform all other behaviors. They imitate the linguistic behavior of the adults around them and, if they do so correctly, the adults will reinforce them positively by praising them and telling them that what they have said is "right." However, if they make a mistake and say something ungrammatical, adults will withhold reinforcement, and sometimes provide punishment by saying "No, that's wrong" or "You can't talk like that." As a result of this selectively reinforced imitation of adult language, children gradually learn how to speak correctly.

Although this is a fairly simple, straightforward idea of how children learn a language, there are several major problems with it. First, the *variability* in environmental or reinforcing conditions from child to child should result in tremendous variability in language development and performance in different children. But this is not the case. Despite differences in the kind of opportunities for training and social reinforcement offered by the great variety of social environments in which language acquisition takes place, the development of language by children of various cultures and social classes seems to follow a relatively standardized, universal pattern. Infants born to deaf parents, who cannot hear and reinforce their children, progress through the same stages of vocalization as do the children of hearing parents (Lenneberg, 1969).

Still another argument against the learning theory analysis of language is that children often say things that are clearly *not* imitations of adult speech. As we saw earlier, children will say "he goed," or will produce two-word sentences like "Allgone Daddy," none of which they have ever heard adults say. Furthermore, parents actually do not correct the child's speech as often as the theorists contend they do. Usually the parent is more concerned with comprehending *what* the child is trying to say than with *how* it is being said. A true statement will often receive positive reinforcement from the parent, even if it is ungrammatical. For example, if a child says "Her curl my hair," the mother will probably answer "That's right" because she is, in fact, curling the child's hair. However, if a child makes the grammatically correct statement, "There's the animal farmhouse" but is pointing to a lighthouse, the parent will surely say "No, that's wrong" (Brown, Cazden, & Bellugi-Klima, 1969).

Most importantly, if children could say only sentences that they had successfully imitated and been reinforced for, then how could they ever produce new sentences that they had never heard before? Clearly, children and adults alike are continually producing sentences that are completely original; in fact, the total number of sentences that might be uttered by any human being is theoretically infinite. The developmental theory of language does take this into account.

The developmental approach: Acquisition of rules

This approach argues that children learn a complex system of *rules*, rather than just many different strings of words, and that such a system allows them to generate an infinite number of new sentences. As we saw earlier, children's overregularization of the past tense form is clear evidence that they are using a system of rules. Children not only acquire these rules without having formal teaching, they do so long before they are capable of other complex intellectual achievements. How do they manage to accomplish such an incredible feat?

Theorists such as Lenneberg (1969) stress the importance of biological aspects. As we have seen, the ability to develop a complex, abstract language system is *species specific;* that is, unique to human beings. While some animal species have developed reasonably complex signal systems to communicate the presence of danger or food, such systems contain no means for novelty of expression or abstraction as in human language.

Language capacity also seems to be *species uniform*: there is no known instance of a group of human beings without a language. Furthermore, there is little difference in the grammatical complexity of various human languages. Observations such as these have led a number of students of language processes to propose that many aspects of our linguistic ability are probably innate. That is, much of our ability to speak and understand a language is due to our genetic makeup rather than to the specific reinforcements to which we have been exposed. Lenneberg points out that "Children begin to speak no sooner and no later than when they reach a given stage of physical maturation" (1969, p. 635). Thus language development correlates consistently with motor development and maturational indices of brain development.

The hypothesis-testing approach is closely allied with the theory of transformational grammar presented earlier. It is certainly a challenging alternative to the imitation-reinforcement theory, but it does not give the final answer to the problem of how a child learns his or her native language.

Language and thought

What is the relationship between language and thinking? At one time or another, all of us have talked to ourselves when we were trying to work though some problem and, obviously, the communication of much of our thinking is dependent on words. Language and thought seem to be so interwoven with each other that in one early psychological view they were considered the same thing (Watson, 1913). J. B. Watson believed that thinking did not exist apart from covert muscular activity in the speech organs. As we saw in Chapter 5, such responses frequently do accompany speech — but so do other processes like visual imagery. Nevertheless, language and thought are intimately related and over the years other theories have attempted to clarify this relationship.

The Whorfian hypothesis

Benjamin Whorf was concerned with the problem of whether thought determines language or language determines thought, a problem which has stimulated much interest and controversy among students of psycholinguistics (Brown, 1956). Is language a "cloak following the contours of thought" or a "mold into which infant minds are poured"? The *Whorfian* hypothesis contends that the language patterns of a cultural group shape the thought patterns and even perceptions of the children reared in that culture (Whorf, 1956). For example, the Eskimos have seven names for different types and conditions of snow, while English-speaking people have just the single term. The Hopi Indians have one name for birds and one name for all other things that fly (airplane, bee, etc.). Whorf would argue that such differences in descriptive nouns result in a different conception of the event. That is, Eskimos' perceptions and thoughts of snow are more complex than those of English-speaking people; the Hopis think about flying objects differently than we do.

Whorf's hypothesis raises several important questions which, unfortunately, are difficult to resolve with experimental data. One major problem is the old one of cause and effect. Perhaps the culture's thinking about an event led to the development of different linguistic labels for it, rather than vice versa. Because the condition of the snow has a major impact on their daily life, the Eskimos need several terms to differentiate them linguistically. However, the type of snow may have no real importance to people living in Philadelphia, so that for them, all snow (even slush) is "snow."

Critics of Whorf have also challenged the idea that there are actual differences in perception and thought between cultures with different languages. The fact that some people have only a single term for an event does not necessarily mean that they cannot distinguish differences within that event. Children in New York have just one term for snow, but they can easily tell what kind of snow is good for packing snowballs and what kind is not. Similarly, skiers are very sensitive to snow conditions and can distinguish between wet snow, powder snow, icy snow, and so on, even though they do not have completely different words for each of them.

The "cloak-mold" controversy has never been resolved in one way or the other, but it seems fairly safe to say that language and thought affect each other. Ideas are undoubtedly "shaped" by language, but certainly not to the extent postulated by Whorf.

One example of such "shaping" occurs in the way we talk about various kinds of illness. Despite the fact that disease is a process, we treat it as an object, using a noun to describe it. We say that a person "has cancer" or "has measles." This probably stems from the germ theory which developed in European medicine in the nineteenth century. But in fact, illnesses are rarely static; they change from day to day. Assigning static labels to them distorts the situation.

A further distortion often occurs in the case of chronic disease, especially "mental illness." We frequently use language that makes the patient inseparable from the illness, "she's a diabetic," "he is a schizophrenic." Such labels, once assigned, are likely to remain. An individual who has suffered from schizophrenia but whose behavior has returned to normal is still considered a schizophrenic, with his or her symptoms "in remission." This can severely affect both the individual's self-concept and the reactions of his or her family and friends (Warner, 1976–77).

Or, for example, when someone vividly perceives an event or has an experience without an immediately present external stimulus, it can be called either a *hallucination* or a *vision*. Which has a negative and which a positive connotation for you? Hallucinations are one indicator of psychosis and thus are not good to have — or at least not to talk to others about. It is apparent that even if language does not determine thought, it can infiltrate the thought process and subtly influence the ways in which we conceptualize experiences.

Aphasia . . . when language goes astray

As we saw in the example that began this chapter, speaking can be susceptible to a variety of problems. We encounter people who, for one reason or another, have difficulty speaking, and we are usually aware of our own speech problems when we are nervous, or not feeling well, or taking some medication, or have had too much to drink. At times like these, it may be difficult to put our thoughts into words, or to position our tongue and mouth so that the right sounds come out.

Unfortunately there are many other people (like the woman at the beginning of the chapter) who have much more severe language problems that result specifically from damage to the central nervous system. This disorder, known as *aphasia*, usually occurs as a result of stroke or brain accident. Because the ability to communicate is so important, aphasia is tremendously debilitating. In this section, we will present an overview of the disorder and some discussion of the rehabilitation of aphasic patients.

Aphasia is clearly a difficulty in using language and not primarily a problem in speech (sound) production. Though articulation difficulties are sometimes present, the aphasic mainly experiences problems in organizing thoughts into words or in understanding and processing what others are saying. Also, it is not psychosis. Language problems in psychosis are mainly reflections of mental confusion. Language difficulties in aphasia are not necessarily accompanied by a generalized cognitive impairment. The interaction between language and thought is so intimate that one shouldn't be surprised that a breakdown in one is accompanied by a breakdown in the other. Aphasics talk ungrammatically, some with considerable hesitancy or repetition, but others with great ease and fluency. In the latter case, the content of what is being said is limited and not always coherent, sounding like jargon or "double-talk." An aphasic physician was asked if he was a doctor and replied: "Me? Yes sir, I'm a male demaploze on my own. I still know my tubaboys what for I have that's gone hell and some of them go" (Brown, 1972, pp. 61–62).

Aphasia appears in a variety of forms; a given patient may have speech and language difficulties but normal writing ability; fluent speech but an inability to read or understand the written word; ability to understand what is written, but malfunction in the act of writing; difficulties in performing simple arithmetic, and so on. It is presumed that these differences are due to damage to different parts of the brain, damage which results in highly specific and often quite exotic language problems.

As we shall see in later chapters, the brain is divided into a left and a right hemisphere. These two halves seem to be specialized for different functions and, though there is some overlap, the left hemisphere is most involved with speech and language functions and the right is concerned predominantly with nonverbal skills. This would suggest that aphasia should be more likely to occur if the injury is in the left hemisphere and, indeed, this is the case. It has been estimated that about 95 percent of those individuals who suffer left hemispheric damage develop some kind of aphasia, with the greatest likelihood in right-handed people (Geschwind, 1970). The exact nature of the aphasia depends very much on the specific location of the brain damage.

Broca's and Wernicke's aphasias

Two major types of aphasia stand out, although it is difficult to find pure types of either one and most aphasics show symptoms of both. The two types are named for the scientists most influential in their description. Broca's aphasia occurs with left-hemisphere damage somewhat further to the front of the brain than that in the other category, called Wernicke's aphasia. A clear case of Broca's aphasia has the following characteristics. There is little speech, produced slowly, often (though not always) with poor articulation. The loss is largely in intentional speech. Automatic productions, such as greetings or profanity, may be strikingly intact. The patient has great difficulty in using appropriate grammatical constructions, and the small junction words, prepositions and conjunctions, may drop out of the vocabulary completely (Geschwind, 1970). The result is language that sounds very much like a telegram. Although the Broca's aphasic might be able to correctly name various objects, vocabulary is sometimes disastrously impoverished. Many patients are entirely mute when the disorder first appears. Because Broca's area of the brain is so close to the area that controls motor functioning, 80 percent of the time damage to Broca's area is accompanied by some paralysis on the right side of the body.

A pure case of Wernicke's aphasia, on the other hand, shows almost the opposite characteristics of those in Broca's. In Wernicke's aphasia, speech output is rapid and profuse, often greater than normal. However, speaking only seems to be easy and fluent; in fact it is almost devoid of information and the patient has problems both in finding the correct noun to use and in understanding the speech of others. The woman described at the beginning of this chapter was afflicted with Wernicke's aphasia. Many aphasics have characteristics of both Broca's and Wernicke's types. Some investigators have suggested that there are no pure or distinct types (partly because different brain regions interact to influence behavior). Aphasia is viewed as a general deficit in language ability varying in severity from one patient to another.

If we consider aphasia in this way, it is interesting to note that all of us behave in an aphasia-like manner from time to time. This happens not only when we are under the influence of some outside agent, like medication or alcohol, but also when we experience those minor, but excruciating, tip-of-the-tongue problems, that inability to recall the correct word when we are certain we know it. Or there are those peculiar thought and language patterns that make up the reveries that occur just before we fall asleep. Nightly, we loosen our grip on the here and now and might produce utterances like,

"Gundrum is the word for hundred" or "it goes drench more about Ronnie" (Brown, 1972, p. 38). Bizarre as these may be, they are neither pathological states nor aphasia. But these examples are aphasia-like, and studying them can tell us much about the problems the aphasic is going through.

Are aphasics aware of their language difficulties? Sometimes yes and sometimes no. When they are, the situation can be even more poignant. One middle-aged patient, when asked to use the word "at" in a sentence, struggled along, commenting on his distress: "It gets in there, but the whole thing don't . . . *at* . . . like the theater . . . see, that's the trouble. I know what it is but it won't come in there . . . it won't put it in."

Rehabilitation

Recovery from aphasia, while occasionally occurring spontaneously, is usually a painstaking process, often resulting in only limited gains. Of course, the less severe the disorder, the better the chances. Some investigators claim that Wernicke's type has a poorer prognosis than Broca's, though in either case, the earlier therapy begins, the better. But these are only generalizations and the results of individual treatment are often difficult to predict.

This does not imply that the situation is hopeless. Most aphasics either recover or improve substantially, especially if their motivation is strong and their level of aspiration is realistic. After all, the purpose of therapy is to retrain a person to communicate adequately; it shouldn't be viewed as a system for changing the aphasic into a glib raconteur. In reviewing the literature, Darley (1975) found that intensive therapy, started early, is generally beneficial—particularly in younger patients and those whose motivation and insight are high.

The retraining itself is quite similar to the original language methods we all experienced in school. There is routine drilling, gesturing, and some innovation tailored to the individual patient. A person who can't spontaneously say a certain number might be able to count to it. Or a patient who has difficulty putting words together into connected speech might, surprisingly, be able to *sing* them correctly. Why this sometimes occurs is not known. Talking about topics that interest the patient is also valuable.

What about people who speak more than one language, the bi- or trilinguals? Are the different languages represented in the same areas of the brain—or does each language have its own region? This is an area of research where many questions still await clarification, but evidence from aphasia and from recent electrophysiological studies (Whitaker & Ojeman, 1977) suggest that while the cortical representation of different languages is largely overlapping, there also appears to be "monolingual" regions; that is, areas where one language only is represented.

Aside from the very real need for knowledge about aphasia and the retraining of language function, what we learn about this disorder is invaluable in understanding the relationship between language and the brain. The many different appearances that aphasia takes from one patient to another, tell us much about brain structures and function. The importance of the left hemisphere of the brain, for example, is certainly illustrated in aphasic disorders.

The achievement of a young child in speaking and understanding its native language is in part the legacy it receives from its species, in part due to learning and information processing. But a crucial role is also played by developmental processes taking place within the maturing individual. Let us next inquire into the role of such developmental changes in other aspects of human functioning.

Chapter summary

Language plays an important role in human learning, communication, and memory. It serves both to structure reality and to stimulate fantasy, and provides the means for transmitting knowledge from generation to generation.

Though there are many theories concerning how language originated, the correct one has not yet been determined. Neanderthals were able to produce some speech sounds but their proficiency was not comparable to the speech of modern humans. There are many criteria for defining true speech, including an *auditory-vocal* channel, *displacement* (the ability to talk about past, present, and future), and *productivity* (the ability to produce a virtually infinite number of messages).

Psychologists have long been intrigued by the question of whether the ability to use language is restricted to the human species. Studies of whistling sounds made by dolphins have shown that they serve social rather than communication functions. Studies with primates have shifted from attempts at teaching the animals to speak words to studying their ability to use symbols.

Psycholinguistics is the study of the psychological aspects of language. Linguistic analysis examines the *grammar* of language, which is divided into three major categories: (a) *phonology*, concerned with *phonemes*, the basic sound units of language; (b) *syntax*, the rules for combining words into sentences; and (c) *semantics*, concerned with meaning. *Sound spectrograms* have proven useful in studying the acoustical properties of phonemes, showing that there is a simultaneous *parallel transmission* of the information in speech sounds. The phonemes themselves are composed of *distinctive features*.

There are several theories of syntax: (a) *phrase structure grammar*, based on a hierarchy of phrase units; (b) *transformational grammar*, based on transformational rules by which deep structure, or meaning, is converted into surface structure; and (c) *case grammar*, which studies the way meaningful parts of the sentence are related to each other. Semantics studies both the connotative and denotative aspects of language. Both syntactic structure and meaning affect our ability to hear and remember accurately.

Language production during the first year of life is limited to various forms of crying and babbling. At the end of the first year, recognizable words appear and true speech begins. From here, children go on to increase their vocabulary and develop their use of syntax. They begin by using single words and later progress to two-word sentences. By the age of two, they are capable of producing longer sentences, and soon begin to master adult syntax.

Some theorists hold that language, like any other behavior, is learned through *reinforcement* of correct responses that the infant produces spontaneously or through *imitation* of adults. Psycholinguists argue that language production is an *innate* human ability, both *species specific* and *species uniform*. They believe that it is not based on imitation, but rather on construction of a general theory of language related to transformational grammar.

Language and thought are closely related though it is unclear whether language determines thought or thought determines language.

Aphasia is a language disorder resulting from brain damage. In one type, *Broca's aphasia*, speech is produced slowly and vocabulary can be greatly reduced; in another type, *Wernicke's aphasia*, speech output is rapid and the patient appears to be fluent but has difficulty finding the correct word to use and in understanding others. Many therapies are available for helping the aphasic individual. Through study of aphasic disorders, psychologists are learning more about language centers located in specific areas of the brain.

Part Three

Life-Span Development

Paul KLEE "FAMILIENSPAZIERGANG", 1930

Developmental Basis of Behavior

During the 1930s, two baby girls neglected by their mentally retarded mothers were committed to an Iowa orphanage. When first observed by Harold Skeels, they were physically sick and clearly retarded in mental development. At fifteen and eighteen months of age, respectively, they were transferred to an institution for the retarded. When Skeels saw them six months later, they were alert and healthy, and their intelligence test scores had increased. Skeels attributed the change to the fact that these little waifs had been "adopted" by the nurses and patients and given a loving, stimulating environment.

Skeels set about testing this chance observation in a systematic fashion. A total of thirteen similarly neglected children, averaging nineteen months of age with a mean IQ score of 64, far below the "normal" IQ of 100, were sent from the orphanage to a home for mental retardates as "house guests." They were later compared with a group of orphans of similar age, but higher initial IQ, who were tested at similar times but remained in the orphanage, which was overcrowded and appeared to be understimulating. Each child in the experimental group was quickly "adopted" by an older woman, and warm personal relationships developed. These were supported by the other patients and staff members. What were the effects of this tender, loving care?

The comparison group started with a considerable advantage, with an average IQ about 23 points higher than the average of the special-care group. About three years after the latter infants had been transferred to the retarded ward and their special care had begun, their IQs had gained an average of 28 points, increasing from an average of 64 to 92. The comparison infants had lost a comparable amount. After two more years of special care, eleven of the special-care children were considered adoptable (children with very low IQ were considered unadoptable) and indeed had been adopted.

In what amounts to a developmental psychologist's *tour de force*, Skeels went out years later and located every child, now an adult, from the original study, except for one control child who had died at age fifteen. The differences found in the adult lives of the two groups were enormous. All of the children who had received the special care, on a one-to-one basis from an attentive "aunt," became self-supporting adults and none was a ward of any institution. In contrast, five of the eleven surviving comparison individuals were still institutionalized. The average income of the six employed comparison individuals was only one-quarter that of the special-care group. In the latter group eight of the thirteen had graduated from high school, and five had gone to college. The average educational attainment of the special-care group was the eleventh grade, while that of the comparison group was only the fourth grade. Eleven of the special-care group had married, and among them had had 28 children whose IQs averaged a normal 104, none of them with mental retardation (Skeels, 1966).

This research was honored by an award for excellence by the Kennedy Foundation, and the award was presented to Dr. Skeels by a young man then completing his master's degree in business administration. Although the young man did not know it until this time, he had been one of the infants whom Skeels had assigned to special care (Lipsitt & Reese, 1979).

The study of development

Knowing about the past should help us understand the present, and understanding the present should help us predict the future. This general principle is applicable in all developmental sciences, including embryology, geography, geology, history, and developmental psychology. The time periods involved and the identification of what is changing are not the same in all these sciences, but common to all of them are the beliefs that things change in a time-ordered way and that the causes of these systematic changes can be discovered. In developmental psychology, the time period covers the human life span and the thing that changes is the individual—or more accurately, the individual's behavior, both physical and mental.

A belief in the continuity of psychological development can be discerned in folk sayings such as "Tall oaks from little acorns grow"; "As the twig is bent the tree's inclined"; and "The child is father of the man." Some of these sayings imply that development is mostly change in size—"Tall oaks," for example—and others imply a change in form—"bent twigs." The belief that a child is a miniaturized adult, changing only in size, is an old one, appearing in the seventeenth century as the *homunculus* theory.  The view that change is primarily in form is also old, going back at least to Aristotle. Typical parents nowadays seem to accept the change in form theory for physical development, especially for the prenatal period and infancy, but to believe the homunculus theory for psychological development. They tend to attribute a child's disobedience, or even an infant's persistent crying, to willfulness.

The study of developmental psychology can help us realize what the child's actions are really about. However, development does not stop at the end of childhood, and developmental psychology can also help us understand why the parent may have misinterpreted the child's actions. Furthermore, in its fullest extent developmental psychology covers the entire life span, and can help us understand the behavior of the child's grandparents as well as that of the parents and child.

At this point it may be useful to present a formal definition of the field of developmental psychology: *Developmental psychology deals with the description, explanation, and modification of changes within individuals across the life span, and with differences and similarities in such changes between individuals.* That is, the aims are to find out the ways in which an individual's behaviors change across the life span, why they change in these ways, and how desirable changes can be encouraged and undesirable ones discouraged. Developmental psychologists also want to know how and why individuals differ in the ways their behaviors change, and how these individual differences can be made the most of.

For example, the figure represents the mental growth of five individuals to young adulthood. ● You can see that the general shape of the growth curves is the same for all five individuals, with faster growth in early childhood than in later childhood and adolescence, but the individuals vary considerably in the rates of growth. Case 5M grew in mental age much more rapidly than the other cases, and 13M grew much more slowly. Curves like these are useful because they indicate how an individual may be expected to change in the course of development and how much variability may be expected across individuals. In other words, they provide *norms* against which an individual can be compared for an assessment of developmental progress. Note, however, that norms tell us what *is,* not what *should be;* they are descriptive averages, not proscriptive standards to be lived up to.

Life-span developmental psychologists want to *describe* development, hence they are interested in norms; but they also want to *explain* developmental processes—they want to know why development proceeds in the way it does, and why individuals differ from one another in their course of development. Often, the endeavor to describe and explain development yields a useful by-product, information that indicates ways of optimizing development either by intervention or remedial treatment, as in Skeels' work with orphans.

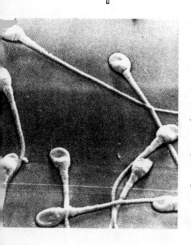

This drawing of a sperm cell by Niklaas Hartsoeker depicts a completely formed miniature human being as a homunculus. The photo shows actual sperm cells highly magnified by modern photographic techniques.

**Mental growth curves
of five individuals**

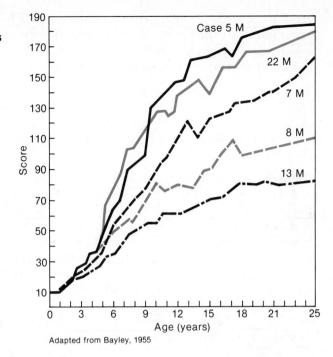

Adapted from Bayley, 1955

What is development?

Most developmental psychologists use three sets of principles to account for the data in their field: (1) the principles of physical growth, (2) the principles of maturation, and (3) the principles of learning. The principles of physical growth account for changes in physical structures and organs, including changes in shape, size, number, position, and location. The term *maturation*, as used by developmental psychologists, refers to the development of reflexes, instincts, and other unlearned behavior. The principles of physical growth and maturation are biological. Heredity exerts close control on these principles, sometimes seeming to have more influence than the environment.

The principles of learning may be broadly defined to include not only traditional conditioning and extinction but also the effects of classroom instruction and other environmental influences. There has been considerable controversy over the relative contributions of learning and heredity to development. Today, most psychologists take an *interactionist* position, recognizing that heredity and environment interact to produce development. While both are necessary, neither is sufficient. Even those who argue most strongly for the importance of heredity admit that environment has an influence (Jensen, 1977), and even the radical behaviorists admit that environment cannot explain everything (Skinner, 1974). Heredity may set potential limits, but environment will determine how closely the limits are approached.

Traditional views

Life-span developmental psychology incorporates the older fields of child psychology and psychological gerontology, or *geropsychology* (the study of old age). However it has been influenced more clearly by child psychology than by geropsychology. The development of modern child psychology was influenced by four different historical traditions represented most clearly early in this century by the work of John B. Watson, Sigmund Freud, Jean Piaget, and Alfred Binet.

Watson's approach is *behaviorism*, reflecting an intellectual line that can be traced from the seventeenth-century philosophy of John Locke and the more recent work of Ivan Pavlov. B. F. Skinner's psychology is in this same tradition. In this approach, it is behavior—overt physical action—that develops. The causes of behavior change are assumed to be environmental:

"Give me a dozen healthy infants, well-formed, and my own specified world to bring them up in and I'll guarantee to take any one at random and train him to become any type of specialist I might select—doctor, lawyer, artist, merchant-chief and, yes, even beggar-man and thief, regardless of his talents, penchants, tendencies, abilities, vocations, and race of his ancestors" (Watson, 1925, p. 82).

Although this statement is sometimes ridiculed, and Watson is depicted as a ruthless would-be mind-controller, the statement actually reflects a gloriously optimistic view of the human potential for development, regardless of differences in genetic inheritance. As one modern behaviorist has said, "There must be quite some number of environmental programs . . . that will bring an organism to any specified developmental outcome. This is a very happy characteristic . . . if it is a correct one . . . [It] suggests that behaviorally, it is rarely too late—or too early—for a good outcome" (Baer, 1970, p. 244). The behaviorist, then, is optimistic about the extent to which genetic limitations can be overcome through the action of the environment (although no longer quite as optimistic as Watson had been).

Freud's *psychodynamic* theory of personality development reflects the genetic approach, which had its roots in Charles Darwin's work. The genetic approach is also reflected in the more modern theorizing of Erik Erikson, to be discussed later. In this approach, development is represented as the emergence of successive forms and functions: physical organs and their functions in biology, and mental structures and their functions in psychology. Freud and Erikson did not literally attribute development to the action of genes, but their emphasis on biological bases of infant behavior in particular and on the influence of early experience on later development is clearly Darwinian.

Piaget's *cognitive* approach has origins in the philosophy of Rousseau, who viewed development as guided by maturing forces from within the organism. In this view, development proceeds through stages, each characterized by a different style of thinking, or "structure of cognitive operations." What changes developmentally is the nature of the structure and the set of operations, some newly acquired with development, some retained unchanged from preceding stages, and some retained but with changed functions. The same approach is seen in Kohlberg's theory of moral development, discussed later.

Alfred Binet is best known for his *psychometric* approach and his work on the development of intelligence tests, to be described in Chapter 17. As such tests and the methods of constructing them became more sophisticated, the practical testing movement developed a theoretical branch, in which the tests were used to gather norms having no apparent practical value but having value for theories about development.

Ages and stages

Age is the central concept distinguishing developmental psychology from other branches of psychology. The role of age is seen in the standard formulas used to represent development. For example:

$$B = f(H, E_{t_1}, E_{t_2})$$

where B represents present behavior, f is the mathematical symbol for functional relationship, H represents heredity, E represents environment, and t_1

and t_2 are time subscripts designating, respectively, the present and past. Note that age is represented by the passage of time, which in turn is symbolized by a subscript. Symbolizing time in this way implies, correctly, that time is not itself a causal variable but rather is merely an *index variable*. Although folk wisdom, for example, tells us that "time heals all wounds," doctors know that the healing is caused by physiological processes. Time is involved in that these processes take time to occur, but time itself does not cause the healing. Age is synonymous with time — it is only the time passed since birth — and therefore age cannot, in itself, cause anything. Thus, even though age is the usual independent variable in developmental research, it is not a causal variable but an index variable.

There is another problem of interpretation in using age as an index variable. Age reflects time, and time is continuous. Although we divide it into discrete segments, we can always think of smaller segments — months instead of years, seconds instead of minutes. Consequently, age is also continuous, and the use of age as an index variable therefore implies that the causal variables that are indexed are continuous, as in the case of the healing process.

Continuous causal variables imply that they cause continuous change, as in the growth in height and mental age. Growth in height can be attributed to the continuous process of metabolism and cellular growth, and growth in mental age can be attributed to the accumulation of experiences or learning. In both cases the causal variables are continuous, and growth continues until a physiological limit is reached, or until the causes cease to operate because of changes in the environment.

To the contrary, many developmentalists believe that the causal variables are *discontinuous*, changing in kind and not merely in amount. To avoid the implication of continuous change, these developmentalists find *stage* more useful than age as an independent variable. With this use of the stage concept, change is implied to be discontinuous and qualitative. An example is the relation between a mother and her child. The relation between the mother and the newborn infant is qualitatively different from her relation to the fetus. The newborn is not merely less dependent on the mother for survival, which would be a quantitative change, but rather is dependent in different ways. The implication of the stage approach, then, is that different behaviors will be found at different stages because different causes are operating.

The concept of stages   The stage concept has actually been used in two ways by developmental psychologists. One is the *strong sense* described in the preceding paragraph, the sense of discontinuity. An example from biology is the stages of insect development: egg, caterpillar, cocoon, adult. An example from child psychology is the development of locomotion: sitting, crawling, standing, walking, running. Each of these stages is qualitatively different from the others. Stages in this strong sense are always assumed to occur in a fixed sequence; the developing individual cannot skip a stage and cannot go through the stages in any other sequence. This strong sense also appears in Piaget's theory of cognitive development and Kohlberg's theory of moral development.

The stage concept has also been used in a *weak sense,* as a convenient shorthand term indicating something about the child's age, environment, or current predominant interests and activities. In all of these usages, the concept could be dropped without changing meaning. Examples are "They are in the teething stage," which means they are at the age at which the teeth begin to cut through the gums; "They are in the elementary-school stage," which means they are in the elementary-school environment much of the day; and

"They are in the anal stage," which means they are being toilet trained and are fascinated by the excretory process and pleased by their control of it. Both Freud's theory of psychosexual development and Erikson's theory of psychosocial development use this weak sense of stages.

Stages in life-span development   The human life span is usually divided into the stages listed and described in the table. ▲ These stages were originally defined by age and hence were "stages" only in the weak sense roughly synonymous with age. Later, however, Piaget's work on cognitive development led to identification of the same stages in the strong sense of changed causes and structures and Kohlberg's work on moral development led to similar stages in the strong sense. The coincidence extends still further, in that the weak-sense stages in Freud's theory of psychosexual development and in Erikson's analysis of psychosocial crises fit the same pattern rather closely. These coincidences are indicated in the table. It should be emphasized, however, that only the stage names listed in the first column are defined strictly by the age ranges in the second column. For all four of the theories indicated in the table, the stages are defined by the nature of psychological or social processes and the age periods indicate only rough norms.

As you can see, the table starts with the prenatal stage, beginning at conception, even though life-span developmental psychology is usually defined as covering the period beginning at birth. Actually, the only reason life-span psychology starts at birth is that very little is known about behavioral development in the prenatal stage, and even less is known about the effects of prenatal behavioral development on later development. We should note, however, that starting the table at conception is arbitrary. We could have started the table at a "pre-conception" stage, because the genetic makeups, personalities, and other characteristics of the persons who will later conceive and raise the child have important influences on the development of the child.

We have indicated in the table that death is the last "stage" of life-span development. It is legitimate to consider it a stage because it is a period that exerts considerable influence on development in earlier stages. That is, as we will see in Chapter 9, adjustment to the inevitability of one's own death and to its implications is one of the major developmental tasks, especially as one approaches the end of the life span. Moreover, just as the individual who did not yet exist was influenced by events from the "pre-conception" stage, so the individual in the stage of death, who no longer exists physically in this world, often influences others who are still living. Indeed, some people have had a greater influence on the thinking of subsequent generations than of their own, among them Jesus, Galileo, and Martin Luther. Thus, we see a kind of psychological continuity that transcends the individual life span.

Methods of studying development

The research methods used in developmental psychology can be classified into three types: cross-sectional, longitudinal, and sequential. In the *cross-sectional* design, groups of different age are selected and compared. A major advantage of the cross-sectional design is that the entire age range can be covered in one test session. A major problem is that the groups differ not only in age but also in year of birth. The differences in year of birth could be associated with differences in social conditions, educational practices, political atmosphere, and other variables that could affect performance.

Individuals who differ in some specified way are said to belong to differ-

Stages in life-span development

Stage	Age Period	Major Features	Cognitive Stage (Piaget)	Psychosexual Stage (Freud)	Psychosocial Crisis (Erikson)	Moral Stage (Kohlberg)
Prenatal Stage	Conception to birth	Physical development	—	—	—	—
Infancy	Birth at full term to about 18 months	Locomotion established; rudimentary language; social attachment	Sensorimotor	Oral; anal	Trust vs. mistrust	Premoral (Stage 0)
Early Childhood	About 18 months to about 6 years	Language well established; sex typing; group play; ends with "readiness" for schooling	Preoperational	Phallic; Oedipal	Autonomy vs. doubt; initiative vs. guilt	Obedience and punishment (Stage 1); Reciprocity (Stage 2)
Late Childhood	About 6 to about 13 years	Many cognitive processes become adult except in speed of operation; team play	Concrete operational	Latency	Industry vs. inferiority	Good child (Stage 3)
Adolescence	About 13 to about 20 years	Begins with puberty, ends at maturity; attainment of highest level of cognition; independence from parents; sexual relationships	Formal operational	Genital	Identity vs. role diffusion	Law and order (Stage 4)
Young Adulthood	About 20 to about 45 years	Career and family development			Intimacy vs. isolation	Social contract (Stage 5)
Middle Age	About 45 to about 65 years	Career reaches highest level; self-assessment; "empty nest" crisis; retirement			Generativity vs. self-absorption	Principled (Stage 6 or 7, both rare)
Old Age	About 65 years to death	Enjoy family, achievements; dependency; widowhood; poor health			Integrity vs. despair	
Death	—	A "stage" in a special sense (see text)	—	—	—	—

ent *cohorts* of some kind. Thus, individuals born at different times belong to different *birth* cohorts, usually defined by the year of birth but for some purposes perhaps the month or even day of the year. The problem with the cross-sectional design is that age and cohort are confounded—the age groups are selected from different birth cohorts.

In the *longitudinal* design, individuals from one birth cohort are tested repeatedly as they grow older. An advantage of this type of design is that age changes are not confused with cohort differences, since only one cohort is tested throughout. However, a major problem is that the study will require an impossible amount of time to complete if the age span to be covered is large. Another problem is that if cohort differences exist, they will not be detected. Because only one cohort is tested, the generalizability of the results will be unknown.

Thus a cohort that grew up during a period of severe economic depression may reflect certain attitudes unique to that time and not typical of earlier or later cohorts. (Still another problem is that repeated testing often influences test scores, but this problem is relatively easy to control—you simply have subgroups given different numbers of testings. For example, one subgroup gets all the testings and another starts with Session 2. Comparing their performance provides an estimate of the effect of Session 1 on Session 2.)

In *sequential* designs, several different birth cohorts are tested repeatedly for a span of years. The birth cohorts are selected so that by the end of the study the entire age range will be covered and the cohorts will overlap in age. Thus, the sequential designs avoid the major problem of the cross-sectional design—confounding of age with cohort—by including more than one cohort at each age level, and they avoid the generalizability problem of the longitudinal design in the same way. By overlapping the age ranges of the different cohorts, the sequential designs avoid the other major problem of the longitudinal design, the time requirement. (See *P&L* Close-up, Cohort Effects Can Be Greater Than Age Effects.)

Large cohort differences such as those described in the Close-up are confounded with age changes in cross-sectional research. Much of the developmental research has been cross-sectional rather than longitudinal or sequential, and therefore many of the effects currently attributed to aging may be in fact not age effects but cohort differences. These cohort differences are part of the individual differences in development, and some developmentalists consider them to be more interesting than age changes. Whichever is of interest, however, the problem remains to distinguish between them.

There are two general ways that developmental psychologists usually organize their material—either by age periods or by processes. The age-period approach is particularly sensible if a strong theory of stages is being presented, but is useful in any case if the interest is in showing how processes might be interrelated at any particular age. The process approach is particularly useful if different kinds of processes exhibit different kinds of developmental trend, or conform to different developmental principles.

The rest of this chapter is organized by processes so that the trends and principles can be seen more clearly. Chapter 9 is organized by age periods so that interrelations among the processes can be seen more clearly.

The processes that change developmentally can be divided—somewhat arbitrarily—into four general categories: biological and physiological, motor and perceptual, cognitive and intellectual, and social and personality. We will examine in this chapter some of the major changes that occur in these categories, and some of the variables that influence these changes. Language development has already been treated in the previous chapter. Our purpose here

Nesselroade and Baltes (1974) used a sequential design to study developmental changes in ability and personality in adolescence. The design is illustrated in the figure, which shows some of the data collected. The investigators selected adolescents from the 1957, 1956, 1955, and 1954 birth cohorts. In 1970, when the testing began, the cohorts were ages 12, 13, 14, and 15, respectively, as shown in the figure. Each cohort was tested in 1970, 1971, and 1972, with a battery of intelligence and personality tests. The results for one test—motivation to achieve—are shown in the figure. Before considering these results, however, note that at any one time of testing, the study is cross-sectional in that the four different age groups are from different birth cohorts. For any one cohort, the study is longitudinal in that a single cohort is tested at three different ages. The study as a whole is sequential, covering the five-year range from 12 to 17 in only three years of testing. Furthermore, in this sequential study, the birth cohorts and times of testing were selected in such a way that by the end of the study each cohort had a two-year overlap in age with another cohort. The overlap permits assessment of cohort differences with age held constant.

As shown in the figure, the two younger cohorts—1957 and 1956—exhibited large declines in achievement motivation as they grew older, while the 1955 and 1954 cohorts remained fairly stable in this trait. Thus, the study re-vealed large differences between birth cohorts born as little as one year apart. In fact, some of the comparisons in the figure indicate that one-year cohort differences were larger than one-year age changes. For example, the difference in performance between the 14-year-olds born in 1955 (age 14 in 1970) and the 14-year-olds born in 1956 (age 14 in 1971) was greater than the change shown by the 1956 cohort between the ages of 13 (1970) and 14 (1971) and greater than the change shown by the 1955 cohort between the ages of 14 (1970) and 15 (1971). In some respects, then, it would be appropriate for today's 14-year-olds to refer to today's 16-year-olds as "the older generation."

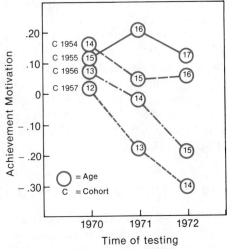

Adapted from Nesselroade & Baltes, 1974

is not to provide a complete description and analysis of the changes in these categories, but rather to survey the kinds of changes and causes that developmentalists study. Further developmental information on these is given in Chapter 9.

Biological and physiological changes

Many biological and physiological processes change during the course of development, and the rate and pattern of growth are not the same for all physiological structures. There is, however, one pattern that is exhibited by so many different structures that it is called the *general growth curve*. It is exhibited by height, weight, and other biological and physiological characteristics, and is also seen in the development of some *psychological* characteristics such as intelligence.

Role of nutrition

Through the action of genes, heredity exerts close control over physical growth, yielding, for example, the remarkable physical resemblance of identical twins. However, the action of genes always occurs in an environment, and the nature of that environment can modify the influence of genes. In physical growth, one important environmental factor is the adequacy of nutrition.

Malnutrition will retard the rate of growth—cognitive as well as physical—but its effects can be reversed to some extent by providing a nutritionally sufficient diet. The human infant has a remarkable capacity to recover from physical disturbances such as malnutrition—as well as from psychological disturbances such as isolation (Kagan, 1978). However, the extent of recovery from malnutrition depends on its duration, severity, and timing. Prolonged, severe malnutrition produces permanent retardation, according to available evidence, but the effects of short-term, moderate malnutrition are completely reversible (Herrera, 1978; Kessen, Haith, & Salapatek, 1970).

The timing of the malnutrition seems also to be important, and its effects may be especially severe if it occurs during a period in which growth would normally be very rapid. For example, malnutrition during the prenatal period can severely retard brain development. These conclusions are further complicated by the fact that males are more susceptible than females to the effects of environmental disturbances, such as malnutrition. This is so in all mammals that have been studied including humans (Tanner, 1970). This sex difference is consistent with other physical sex differences favoring the human female, who generally is healthier and lives longer than the male (see Whelan, 1977).

Development of sex differences

The sex ratio at birth is about 106 males per 100 females, but the prenatal death rate, from miscarriage and spontaneous abortion, is greater for males than for females, and it is estimated that about 130 to 150 males are conceived for every 100 females (*Developmental Psychology Today*, 1975, p. 81).

The excess of male over female births decreases with the age of the mother. The ratio for fifteen-year-old mothers is 163 males to 100 females, for twenty-year-old mothers 120 to 100, for thirty-year-old mothers 112 to 100, and for forty-year-old mothers 91 to 100. One theory is that sperm cells carrying the Y chromosome are smaller and therefore faster moving than those carrying the X, but do not live as long. Consequently, if insemination occurs at the time of ovulation, the ovum (which always carries an X chromosome) is more likely to be fertilized by a Y-bearing sperm cell, resulting in conception of a male. In contrast, if insemination occurs two or three days before ovulation, fertilization is more likely to involve the longer-lived X-bearing sperm cell, hence to produce a female. According to this theory, insemination is more likely to occur near the time of ovulation in younger women because, as a group, they are sexually more active than older women.

The death rate is greater for males than females throughout the life cycle, with peak differences in adolescence and middle age, until the age of about 100, when the death rate of surviving males falls below that of surviving females. Suicide rates are much greater for males of all ages than for females.

Consequently, the life expectancy is greater for females, as is also true in some other species including rats and insects such as the beetle, fruit fly, and spider. In general, males appear to have a harder time getting through life than females.

Although the shape of the general growth curve is the same for boys and girls, the timing of some of the changes may be different. The figure shows that males are generally bigger than females. ◆ At birth the male outweighs the female by about a third of a pound and is longer by about a third of an inch. The direction of the difference continues until the age of about twelve to fifteen years, when girls are heavier and taller than boys on an average. This reversal occurs because girls begin the period of rapid growth called the preadolescent growth spurt about two years earlier than boys. However, after the growth spurt occurs in boys, they catch up with the girls and after fifteen are again heavier and taller than girls. Boys might be expected to be disturbed when the girls in their class become bigger, because status in children's social structure tends to be based on age, especially for boys, more than on social position or ability (contrary to adult society, in which social position and ability are the major determinants of status). Because size is correlated with age, older children tend to be larger; therefore psychological status is correlated with physical stature. Contrary to expectation, however, in grades 6, 7, and 8, when children are about eleven to thirteen or fourteen years old, boys are not as hostile toward girls as girls are toward boys (Reese, 1966).

There are other physical differences between the sexes. Boys are generally superior in gross motor skills, girls in fine eye-hand coordination; after the age of six, boys are generally stronger. These differences are assumed to reflect sex differences in practice and motivation. Other differences have a physiological basis: boys are more likely to be color blind, because color blindness results from a sex-linked recessive gene—it is recessive in females but dominant in males. Females have greater sensitivity to tastes, odors, and sounds, especially for the higher pitches. Brain damage is more frequent in male infants, perhaps because the female is better able to tolerate changes in oxygen level during the fetal period. Hyperactivity, which has been attributed to "minimal brain dysfunction" (alleged brain damage that is suspected from behavioral symptoms but is not detectable with physiological measures), is also more frequent in boys than girls, perhaps also reflecting the sex difference in fetal tolerance of environmental fluctuations.

Baby girls are rated as more cuddly than baby boys as young as three days of age (Osofsky, 1976), and they get cuddled more than baby boys. This trend is also found in monkeys (Mitchell & Schroers, 1973). Parental attention and cuddling are found to be important for normal psychological development in both human infants (Ribble, 1943) and infant monkeys (Harlow & Suomi, 1974). Perhaps this difference explains in part why boys are more prone to emotional, scholastic, and behavior problems than girls. Boys are seen more often in psychological clinics (2½ to 1), stutter more (3 to 1), read less well, and more frequently exhibit enuresis (bedwetting), tics, lack of discipline, delinquency, and aggressiveness. Girls, however, are more likely than boys to have such passive nervous habits as nail biting and thumb sucking.

Differences such as these do not have a genetic basis, but rather are acquired through environmental influences; that is, children are taught their sex roles, the sets of behaviors that society considers sex-appropriate. Although society's conception of these roles is changing, the masculine role is still the one more highly valued by society. Perhaps the greater hostility of preadolescent girls toward boys than of boys toward girls reflects resentment by girls about the inferior status society imposes on them. Perhaps for the same reason, boys conform to the masculine stereotype at an earlier age than

◆ **Growth in weight of the human body between birth and eighteen years**
Many other physiological and psychological characteristics follow the same general pattern.

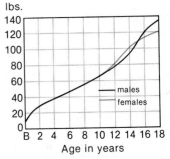

Adapted from Scammon, 1930

girls conform to the feminine stereotype. Also, cross-sex identification—"tomboy" girls and "sissy" boys—is more accepted in girls than in boys. These differences in sex-role development occur despite the fact that the mother has been the primary agent of socialization in the early years, for boys as well as girls. Thus, it has been the mother who was primarily responsible for teaching boys the masculine role and girls the feminine role. With the changing consciousness in our society toward traditional sex-role typing, and the greater involvement of fathers in child rearing, we can expect to see new patterns of sex-related emotional development emerging.

Motor and perceptual changes

When do infants begin to crawl; when do they begin to walk? When can they hold their bottle or rattle? Can they pick up a pin and put it in their mouth? When do they begin to perceive? What is their perceptual world like? How does their perception change as they grow and develop? Questions such as these intrigue research psychologists as much as they do parents.

Motor development

A classic study of the development of locomotion in infants was published by Shirley (1933). The study documents a sequence of stages that lead up to walking, and provides average ages for the various stages. ● However, the averages must be interpreted as only very rough norms because the number of infants studied was relatively small. The development of walking seems to require no special attempt at teaching by the parents. However, cross-cultural differences have been found in the age at which walking appears, and these differences are interpreted to reflect effects of differences in stimulation of walking and the behaviors that lead up to it. What is curious about walking is

● **The sequence of stages in the development of walking**

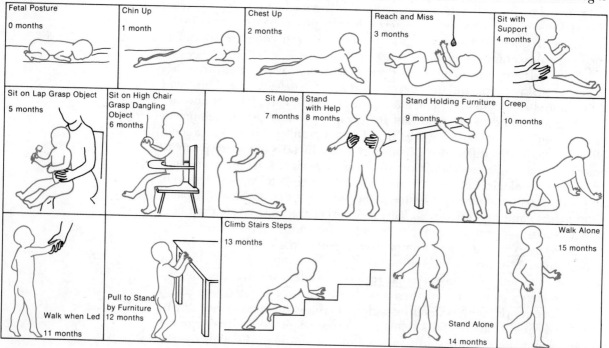

Fetal Posture — 0 months
Chin Up — 1 month
Chest Up — 2 months
Reach and Miss — 3 months
Sit with Support — 4 months
Sit on Lap Grasp Object — 5 months
Sit on High Chair Grasp Dangling Object — 6 months
Sit Alone — 7 months
Stand with Help — 8 months
Stand Holding Furniture — 9 months
Creep — 10 months
Walk when Led — 11 months
Pull to Stand by Furniture — 12 months
Climb Stairs Steps — 13 months
Stand Alone — 14 months
Walk Alone — 15 months

that it should occur at all. The crawling infant successfully locomoting about must suffer pain and frustration in its first attempts to walk. But despite setbacks, it persists rather than regresses and comes to stand on its own two feet. In doing so, it joins the community of Homo sapiens who have walked around this planet and beyond to the moon.

Grasping a small object with the thumb and forefinger involves a complex set of coordinated movements and perceptual inputs. A well-known study of the development of grasping, or *prehension,* was reported by Halverson (1931). Like walking, prehension goes through a sequence of stages. ▲ At birth infants reflexively grasp objects put in their hands. The fingers and palm are involved in this reflexive grasp, but the thumb is usually not involved. The grasp is strong enough in some babies to support their weight. With development, the involuntary grasp reflex weakens and is replaced by voluntary grasping. At first, voluntary grasping involves the whole hand, but gradually the forefinger becomes more exclusively involved and finally, at about five months of age, the baby's grasp is similar to the adult's.

Perceptual development

The anatomical structures of most sense organs are well developed even before birth. Whether or when they actually begin to function in the fetus or newborn infant is a question that must be answered with careful testing procedures. Testing sensitivity early in life is difficult, however, because it must be inferred from a response of some sort, and a response may fail to occur because motor systems are not sufficiently developed rather than because of undeveloped sensory mechanisms.

Secluded in the womb, the fetus is not exposed to many stimuli. The newborn enters a vastly more complex stimulus environment, and does show sensitivity to many kinds of stimulation. Just how much the infant organizes the welter of sensations is a question that has generated a great deal of research.

Touch, temperature, and pain

The human fetus can react to touch stimuli six or eight weeks after conception. By this time, then, some rudimentary sensory capacity has developed. Sensitivity to touch develops from the head downward. By the eighth week of prenatal life, the fetus becomes responsive to touch stimuli on the nose, lips, and chin, and the area sensitive to stimulation gradually increases with the passage of time. By the thirteenth or fourteenth week, the entire body is sensitive except for the top and back of the head, which are not sensitive until after birth. Even at birth, the face is more sensitive to touch and pressure than other parts of the body.

Temperature sensitivity is present before birth; we know this from the fact that premature infants, like full-term ones, may refuse milk of the wrong temperature. They may also respond to external temperatures, usually reacting more strongly to cold than to heat.

Sensitivity to pain is weak in the fetal period and during the early days of life outside the womb. It is greater on the face than elsewhere and sufficiently underdeveloped that circumcisions may be performed without anesthetic during the first two weeks. The delay in development of the pain sense has been interpreted as a biological defense mechanism to protect the child during what would otherwise be a painful process (Carmichael, 1951).

▲
The stages in the development of prehension
The numbers are ages in weeks.

16

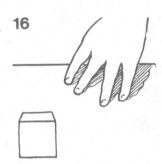

20

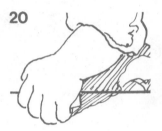

24

28

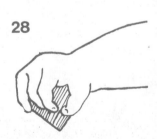

Taste and smell

A sense of taste is well developed at birth. Newborn infants usually react with sucking movements to sweet or salty stimuli and with rejecting behavior to sour or bitter ones. The taste sense apparently develops some time before birth, since even premature babies respond to taste stimuli.

Smell is another well-developed sense in the newborn. Definite changes in bodily activity and breathing rate following olfactory stimulation have been observed. Studies have shown that newborns can distinguish between such odors as acetic acid, asafetida, phenylethyl alcohol, and anise oil (Engen, Lipsitt, & Kaye, 1963), and clear differences are observed in response to odors that are pleasant and unpleasant to the normal adult (Steiner, 1978).

Hearing

There is some question as to whether the fetus can hear in spite of the fluid in the ears. It has been found that the rate of the fetal heartbeat will increase sharply in response to a tone sounded close to the mother's abdomen (Bernard & Sontag, 1947). A team of Swedish investigators studied fetal reactions to tones of differing frequency. They found that the higher tones produced a greater response (Dwornicka, Jasienka, Smolarz, & Wawryk, 1964). This finding is of interest because studies of babies soon after birth show them to be more pleased by low notes than by high notes, as inferred from their behavior.

Hearing is well developed at birth; the newborn infant perceives differences in duration and loudness, and discriminates complex sounds from pure tones. The newborn can hear low intensity tones, in the range of normal speech, and is soothed by low frequency sounds and continuous or rhythmic sounds. Soon after birth the infant can localize sounds (Appleton, Clifton, & Goldberg, 1975).

Vision

Since the retina has not reached its full development at birth, it was once assumed that newborns could not see clearly. Experiments have shown, however, that young infants can distinguish patterns and even give indication of depth perception.

Pattern and color perception   Apparently there is an innate ability to perceive form visually. One researcher found that infants under five days of age looked longer at black-and-white patterns than at plain-colored surfaces. Infants a few days older were found to show even greater visual discrimination (Fantz, 1963). In another study, investigators showed newborn babies a series of pairs of shapes differing in the number of angles they contained. Shapes with ten angles or turns were preferred to shapes with five turns or twenty turns, as inferred from photographic recordings of eye fixations, which showed longer times spent looking at the ten-angle figures (Hershenson, Munsinger, & Kessen, 1965).

At birth, infants can follow slowly moving objects with their eyes (Brazelton, 1973). Because their eye muscles are not well coordinated at first, their gaze may occasionally seem to "flare out" in two directions at once. Young infants perceive color, but researchers have so far been unable to determine whether the colors look the same as to adults. The age at which color vision first appears is not known, and the question of whether the newborn sees color remains open (Bornstein, 1978).

Depth perception   One of the issues in the field of visual perception is how we come to perceive the three dimensions of height, width, and depth. It is widely believed that perception in a single plane (height and width) is innate, and depth perception is learned from experience. This belief has recently been challenged, however.

A relevant study showed that infants from one to two weeks old reached for objects presented in their visual field much more than they reached for pictures of the objects (T. G. R. Bower, 1972). The discrimination between objects and pictures shows perception of depth before the learning interpretation suggests it should occur. However, this finding does not resolve the issue about the primitiveness of depth perception because conflicting evidence has been reported. A recent study of normal babies in the same age range showed that although the babies studied the stimuli visually, they almost never reached for them and they looked at and reached for the pictures as often as the objects. Thus, the babies gave no evidence of discriminating between pictures and objects (Dodwell, Muir, & DiFranco, 1976).

Other evidence relating to inborn abilities to perceive pattern and meaning in visual stimuli comes from an interesting series of experiments with young organisms of various species employing the "visual cliff."

This apparatus consists of a board laid across the center of a large sheet of heavy glass that is supported a foot or more above the floor. On one side of this board a sheet of patterned material is placed flush against the underside of the glass so that the glass appears to be as solid as it in fact is. On the other side of the board a sheet of the same material is several feet below the glass. This gives the visual appearance of a drop or "cliff," in spite of the solid glass above it. In experiments with thirty-six infants aged six to fourteen months, the babies were placed individually on the center board and their mothers called to them first from the deep side and then from the shallow side.

Twenty-seven of the children tested moved off the board; all of these crawled out on the shallow side at least once, but only three crept off onto the glass above the "cliff." Many cried when the mother called to them from the cliff side, but were unwilling to go to her over the apparent chasm; others actually crawled away from her. Some patted the glass on the deep side, ascertaining that it was solid, but still backed away. Apparently they were more dependent on their visual sensations than on the evidence of their sense of touch.

Although this experiment does not prove that the infants' perception and avoidance of the chasm are innate, similar experiments with animals tend to support the hypothesis that such perception is inborn. Nearly all animals tested were able to perceive and avoid the visual cliff as soon as they were able to stand or walk (Gibson & Walk, 1960).

Actually it was discovered, somewhat surprisingly, that instead of responding to depth cues the subjects were responding to the *motion parallax*: the perceived changes in their own position relative to other objects. When the "floor" was close, a given movement of their own seemed faster relative to it, and the changes in their position were more clearly related to changes in its appearance from one moment to the next. Evidently learning was unnecessary for perception of this difference and for preference for the conditions associated with the faster motion.

Part and whole perception   An old principle in developmental psychology is that growth and responsiveness proceed from global and diffuse to specific and detailed. This is the *orthogenetic* principle of development. In the development of motor reflexes, it means that the developmentally primitive response to stimulation involves the whole body, and the mature response involves only narrowly selected muscle groups. For example, a sudden flash of

These pictures show the apparatus used in the visual-cliff experiments and the reactions of two subjects to the apparent drop-off. Although the child patted the glass with his hand and thus had tactual evidence that there was a firm surface there, he refused to crawl across it when his mother called to him. The one-day-old goat walked freely on the shallow side but would not venture out on the deep side. When placed at the far edge of the deep side, it perched carefully on the narrow edge of the board and shortly thereafter leaped across to the shallow side again.

bright light causes the head to be jerked backward in the adult, but in the young infant it also arouses limb movements, possibly movements of the torso, and crying. For emotions, the principle means that development proceeds from a state of undifferentiated emotionality to the adult range of highly specific emotions. For perception, it means that perception of the whole figure as a unit is more primitive than perception of its parts and details.

The orthogenetic principle has been challenged, however. High-speed movies have been used to study the motor reactions of fetuses and young infants to stimulation, and frame-by-frame analysis has indicated that although the reaction as a whole is global and diffuse, it begins with a specific response in the region stimulated and then rapidly spreads to other regions (Humphrey, 1970). Similarly, differentiated emotions appear at birth, and they depend on primitive brain structures; both of these findings are embarrassing, at least, for the orthogenetic principle. The issue in perception is whether the developmental sequence is from whole to part perception, as the orthogenetic principle requires, or—as some theorists suggest—from part to whole perception.

The issue about perceptual development has been addressed in research on recognition memory, for example, where it translates to the question of whether recognition is based on comparison of an image of the whole figure or is based on comparison of separate features. When we see a face, do we recognize it as that of a friend or stranger by matching it against remembered faces, or by comparing it feature-by-feature with remembered collections of features? Do we remember that Jack has big ears and Jill has a big nose by calling to mind an image of each face and then examining its features, or by calling to mind the "ears" feature for Jack and the "nose" feature for Jill? The research on face recognition indicates a progression from feature analysis to whole perception. (See *P&L* Close-up, Recognition of Faces.)

However, Carey and Diamond (1977) also reported that even five-year-olds are not fooled by irrelevant paraphernalia such as facial expression and clothing when the test involves faces of persons they know well. Thus, even the young child can represent the face as a unit rather than as separate features. In fact, this ability may appear even in infants.

Young infants attend to edges, or contours, when shown geometric figures. Recent research has shown that they attend also to the edges of human faces. This tendency, found at three to five weeks of age, is replaced by another tendency by seven weeks of age, a tendency to focus on the eyes, especially when the person being viewed is talking (Haith, Bergman, & Moore, 1977). This change has been interpreted as a shift from seeing the face like a geometric form to seeing it as an entity, or whole. Thus, the face becomes a perceptual unit, and eye contact between the infant and mother increases. Eye contact plays a crucial role in the development of attachment of the child to adult caretakers.

Cognitive and intellectual changes

Cognition and *intelligence* refer to psychological processes of adapting to the environment. Proponents of different approaches to development interpret these processes and explain them in different ways.

Do children perceive and remember faces as collections of features or as configurations, that is, do they look at the parts or do they see the face as a whole? The issue is related to the development of lateralized brain functions—in adults the right hemisphere is more important than the left for the perception of unfamiliar faces. It is also related to the nature of perceptual development, which has been theorized to progress from diffuse and global to detailed and specific. Carey and Diamond (1977) studied children's memory for unfamiliar faces, using materials like those in the figure. A photograph like the single ones in the top row was presented for inspection and then was covered up and a pair of photographs was presented with instructions to pick the one showing the same person. The children, who were 6, 8, and 10 years old, were told to look at the face because features such as facial expression, clothing, and hairstyle might change. The figure

shows two of the four test conditions used. In Type A tests, where clothing is a misleading cue, attention to the clothing would yield an error. In Type B tests, where facial expression is misleading, attention to facial expression would yield an error. Facial expression was not available as a cue in Type A tests (it was the same in all pictures), and clothing was not available as a cue in Type B tests. The percentage of errors is shown in the graph. Accuracy improved with increasing age, especially for Type A pictures. Thus, the younger children relied more on the irrelevant clothing than on the face as a whole, although they could respond on the basis of the face itself when clothing was not available as a cue. Apparently, then, younger children rely more on isolated features such as clothing, and older children rely more on the whole face. The general result is that clothing fools children more than facial expression does.

Type A

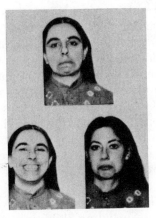

Type B

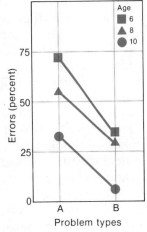

Problem types

Adapted from Carey & Diamond, 1977

A behavioral theory

One of the behavioral theories of intellectual development was proposed by Ferguson (1954, 1956). According to Ferguson, intelligence consists of separate abilities, but these "abilities" are actually responses and are learned like any other kinds of responses. Reading ability, for example, includes the obvious perceptual responses but also includes motor responses such as eye movement. Children normally learn the abilities that society values, because these are reinforced by society's representatives (first the parents, then teachers as well). Abilities, particularly those acquired early in life, transfer to new learning situations and facilitate the new learning. Thus, acquiring a critical ability early should lead to further acceleration, and learning this ability late should lead to more and more retardation, as each delay in learning one ability delays the learning of later abilities, and so on. In other words, we would expect young children who are advanced for their age to become more advanced and ones who are retarded to become more retarded.

The intelligence quotient (IQ) is based on this assumption. It indicates a child's intellectual functioning relative to his or her age group. Thus, an IQ of 100 means that a child's performance is at the average for that age group. An IQ above or below 100 means the child is advanced or retarded, respectively, relative to the group. IQ was originally determined by dividing a child's mental age by his or her chronological age, and multiplying by 100 to remove the decimal. Thus, a five-year-old with an IQ of 120 is one year advanced relative to the population of five-year-olds [$120 = (6 \div 5) \times 100$]. Assuming the child has the same IQ at age ten, this would indicate a mental age of twelve [$120 = (12 \div 10) \times 100$]. Thus the child would be one year advanced at age five and two years advanced at age ten, indicating a faster rate of intellectual development than the average, as indicated by Ferguson's theory.

Research confirms these expectations. An example is shown in the figure on page 219, in which the five individuals represented were equal in early childhood but become progressively farther apart thereafter because of different cognitive growth rates.

Different cultures value different abilities, and therefore Ferguson's theory also predicts that people from different cultures will have different kinds of abilities. This prediction is also confirmed (see Munroe & Munroe, 1975). Cultural differences in the abilities that are valued, reinforced, and acquired make tests of intelligence *culture-bound*; a test developed for use in France or North America, for example, may be inappropriate in Third World nations because the abilities that result in a person's being considered "intelligent" are not the same in these varying cultures. Attempts to develop "culture-free" and "culture-fair" tests have not been successful (Shepard, 1970). When the test used to assess intellectual development is not appropriate for the culture under study, the IQ is not likely to remain constant. In early childhood, the desirable abilities may be universal, or nearly so—skills in locomotion, communication, self-care, and so on, might be examples—but with increasing age, cross-cultural differences in desired abilities should also increase. Therefore, if intelligence is assessed with an inappropriate test, the IQ obtained in early childhood should be about "normal" but with increasing age, as the test becomes increasingly inappropriate, IQ scores should be lower and less valid as measures of intelligence.

This expectation has been confirmed in studies of cultures isolated from the mainstream of nations, including children reared on the canal barges of England, in the isolated fishing villages of Newfoundland, and in isolated mountain regions of Tennessee (Ferguson, 1954). (See *P&L* Close-up, Why Did the IQ of the Mountain Children Decline?) Ferguson's theory can also be used to explain declines in intellectual abilities in old age, which are discussed in Chapter 9. Simply stated, the assumption would be that the abilities that decline are the ones no longer valued, hence no longer reinforced.

The nature-nurture issue

The "nature-nurture" issue is concerned with the relative importance of heredity (nature) and environment (nurture) in determining a characteristic such as personality or intelligence. One of the standard procedures in research on this issue is to compare correlations of IQ test scores between per-

Close-up
Why Did the IQ of the Mountain Children Decline?

Wheeler (1942) used a cross-sectional design to test the IQs of Tennessee mountain children at ages 6, 10, and 16. He conducted the study first in 1930 and again in 1940. Two major findings are illustrated in the graph. First, at each age level the children tested in 1940 obtained higher IQs than those tested in 1930, on the average. Second, the average IQ of mountain children declined with increasing age in both 1930 and 1940.

The interpretation based on Ferguson's theory is that some of the abilities valued in this isolated region differ from those valued in the mainstream United States culture for which the IQ test was developed. With respect to perceptual abilities, for example, the mountain child on a 'coon hunt can tell from the sound of the hounds' baying when they have a trail and when they have treed the hunted animal, and can tell which hound is doing what. The city child merely hears a bunch of dogs barking. But the IQ test does not reflect these differences that favor the mountain child, because the questions are usually based on the experiences of city children.

Because of the difference in abilities valued and acquired, the mountain children get further below the standardized test norm as they grow older. However, the argument would add that the cultural isolation and differences in values are diminishing because of improved roads, schools, and communication, hence the difference from the norm is becoming smaller.

An alternative interpretation—the usual one, in fact—is that the mountain children actually become mentally retarded as they grow older, because of the lack of intellectual stimulation in the isolated region. This deficiency in stimulation is diminishing, however, for the reasons already listed. This interpretation says the mountain children become *deficient*; Ferguson's interpretation says they become *different*. This point is worth keeping in mind in any discussion about cultural or racial effects on intelligence, or on any other characteristic.

Still another interpretation is simply that the brighter children move out of the region as soon as they are able to, and removing them from the available population would reduce the average IQ of the sample available for testing (Baltes, Reese, & Nesselroade, 1977).

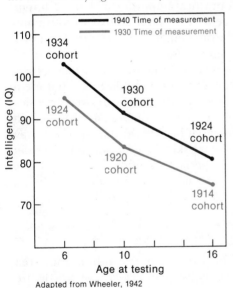

Adapted from Wheeler, 1942

sons at different levels of hereditary and environmental similarity. For example, the correlation between children and their true parents is compared with the correlation between children and foster parents; or correlations are compared for identical twins, fraternal twins or siblings (nontwin brothers and sisters), and unrelated children. Each group is divided into those reared together and those reared apart. Correlations such as these can be used to obtain numerical estimates of the relative contributions of heredity and environment. One widely used estimate is the *heritability coefficient;* it has a value of 1.00 for characteristics that are determined entirely by heredity (e.g., blood type) and a value of zero for characteristics that are determined entirely by the environment (e.g., which specific language a child learns). Multiplying the coefficient by 100 would give you the percentage of the characteristic resulting from heredity.

In the case of intelligence, an estimate that has been widely accepted is that intelligence is 80 percent hereditary and only 20 percent environmental. Estimates such as these can be challenged on many grounds, however. One criticism is that although the degree of genetic resemblance can be estimated quantitatively, at least in a rough way, the degree of environmental resemblance is almost impossible to quantify even roughly. We don't yet have techniques to measure similarity between environments. The contribution of environment is evaluated as what is left after heredity effects are determined—not independently as it should be. Yet the nature-nurture ratios require assuming that the range of hereditary variation is the same as the range of environmental variation.

Another problem in most of the research is that the index of intelligence has been the overall, or global, IQ score. It is known that intelligence consists of relatively independent *primary mental abilities* (see Chapter 17) and that the same overall IQ can be obtained with different patterns of primary abilities. For example, boys and girls are equal in global IQ, on the average, but boys are higher than girls on spatial and number abilities and lower than girls on verbal abilities. It seems unreasonable to suppose that these sex differences are 80 percent attributable to sex-linked genetic differences. Rather, the difference in the ways boys and girls are treated by parents, teachers, and even age-mates throughout childhood is more likely the major source of the sex differences in primary mental abilities.

Another important consideration in evaluating the nature-nurture issue is that the question being asked has no practical importance. A more important practical question is whether intelligence can be raised by special training or other manipulations of the child's environment. The answer turns out to be affirmative, no matter what concept of intelligence is used. If intelligence is conceptualized as global IQ, research has shown that nursery-school experience can increase intelligence. If intelligence is conceptualized as aptitude in the classroom, research has shown that special education can overcome slow reading and other handicaps. If intelligence is conceptualized as adaptation to the physical and social environment, research has shown that special behavior-modification programs can teach self-care skills to even severely retarded individuals. And as we saw on page 217, special institutional care can lead to fully adequate adaptation by individuals thought to be retarded.

Piaget's theory of cognitive development

No one has contributed more to our knowledge of how children think, reason, and solve problems than Swiss psychologist Jean Piaget. For nearly fifty years he has devoted his career to observing what children are able to do and how they explain what they can (and cannot) do at successive stages in their intellectual development. (See *P&L* Profile on p. 238.) Piaget began by carefully observing the behavior of his own children as they were growing up. He would pose problems for them, alter the situation slightly, and then see how they would respond. Unlike many experimental psychologists who study cognitive information processing in laboratory settings by designing complex experiments that yield simple conclusions, Piaget has used simple experimental demonstrations from which complex generalizations can be drawn.

From appearances to rules

Young children start their journey through life as *naive realists*—that is, they believe in what they see, trusting that appearance is the only reality. For many problems children face, this reliance on *perception* as the means of knowing the environment is adequate. But looks can be deceiving, as when we tell our children that "all that glitters is not gold."

A central problem of cognitive development is how children manage to learn and use appropriately the *rules* that govern abstract relationships in their world. These rules embody the principles necessary to develop a logical understanding of the world. In Piaget's view (1970) this knowledge comes only when children free themselves from the dominant influence of immediate perception. It is in the process of discovering, applying, and verifying the rules that underlie logical and mathematical relations that children learn what are the stable, invariant features of their world and what things are not constant. In addition, they learn the social lesson of their relation to their world and to the other people who also inhabit it.

Structure and processes

As we have seen, Piaget's theory of cognitive development is based on a sequence of "strong" stages, each of which represents abrupt, discontinuous changes rather than continuous or gradual changes. These stages occur in the same sequence, although not at the same rate, in all children. Although these stages are qualitatively different, the structures and capacities developed at each stage are incorporated into the next one.

Piaget identified the four stages of cognitive development as sensorimotor, preoperational thought, concrete operations, and formal operations (see p. 223). We shall describe the characteristics of each stage when we discuss the appropriate age periods in Chapter 9; here we shall look closely at the structures and processes that underlie them.

According to Piaget, a child's understanding, inferences, abstractions, logical rules, and problem-solving ability develop entirely from occasions of unsatisfactory *interaction* of the child with the environment (*states of tenuous equilibrium*). Knowledge is structured, as is behavior, and these structures change only when there is a perceived *discrepancy* between them (or their level of complexity) and the complexity of the environment. Out of these encounters between a child and the problems that are posed by the *physical* environment there emerges an invariant sequence of cognitive developmental stages. The progression from simpler to more complex stages of functioning is the same for each individual child.

The overall process of development is (a) a function of the intellectual challenge that comes when novel, challenging information from the environment confronts the child's existing cognitive structures, and (b) a continual process of internal, self-induced reorganizing and integrating of the contents and structures of human intellect.

The primary "shapers" of intellectual growth are certain *functional invariants* that enable the child to adapt successfully to the environment. Here Piaget suggests a similarity between intellectual functioning and biological functioning. The baby starts life with biologically inherited modes of interacting with the environment (called *functions*). These functions enable the child to perform acts that accomplish things necessary for survival, such as ingestion of food.

In the process of being carried out, these acts become organized into *structures* that are changed to adapt to varying environmental demands and experiences. The structures include *schemes* and *schemata*. A *scheme* "represents what can be repeated and generalized in an action (for example, the scheme is what is common in the actions of 'pushing' [any] object with a stick or any

Time strips our illusions of their hue
And one by one in turn, some grand mistake
Casts off its bright skin yearly like the snake.
Lord Byron
Don Juan

Every summer, Jean Piaget retreats to his cabin in the Alps, where he spends most of his days analyzing the mass of research data generated over the past year at his Center for Genetic Epistemology. During long walks along the mountain trails, he mulls over the latest experimental results, and in the cool mountain evenings, he formulates his conclusions. With the approach of fall, he will descend from the mountain, manuscript for a book and several journal articles in hand. This time-honored procedure of careful observation followed by seclusion for thought and synthesis, has enabled him to become one of the most prolific, if not the most famous psychologist of the century.

Piaget has only been widely known in this country since the 1960s, when his works were translated from their original French. But he has been recognized as an expert in the field of cognitive development in Europe since the 1930s. In fact, Piaget's publishing career can be traced to the year 1906, when as a child of ten, he published his careful notes on the habits of an albino sparrow he observed near his home in Switzerland. After his precocious debut as an ornithologist, he took an after-school job at the local natural history museum, soon becoming an expert on mollusks. At the age of sixteen he was recommended for a curator's position at the natural history museum in Geneva, but declined in favor of continuing his education.

He studied natural science at the University of Neuchâtel, obtaining his doctorate at the age of twenty-one. His readings in philosophy stimulated an intense interest in epistemology—the study of how humans acquire knowledge. Convinced that cognitive development had a genetic basis, Piaget decided that the best way to approach epistemology would be through its behavioral and biological components. Psychology appeared to be the discipline that best incorporated this approach.

Piaget therefore sought further training in several distinguished European psychology laboratories and universities, gaining his first major breakthrough into the understanding of chronological stages of growth while working at Binet's laboratory school in Paris. While designing and administering intelligence tests to French schoolchildren there, he became intrigued with the characteristic wrong answers that many of the children gave to his questions. Further pursuing these wrong answers, he came to the realization that the children were employing a process of thought and interpretation decidedly different in nature from that of adults (who made up the tests).

The theory of cognitive development Piaget was formulating centered upon the stages of growth in early childhood, so it seemed natural for him to observe his own three children as they grew from infancy to preadolescence. His careful experiments and conclusions based on these observations, published in journal articles and then in book form, brought him immediate recognition in Europe. While Piaget has since expanded his experiments to encompass a much larger group of subjects, his approach to research has not altered. He observes, asks questions, uncovers new and sometimes puzzling facts, and attempts to integrate his findings with what is presently known. Eventually, he forms a theory from the whole enterprise of explaining his observations.

Piaget has sometimes been criticized for disregarding the traditional methods of scientific inquiry; he almost never designs experiments to prove preliminary hypotheses and does not rely heavily upon hard statistical data for the conclusions he does reach. But Piaget responds good-humoredly to scholarly attacks upon his work. He claims that if he were to start out with a rigid plan and hypothesis, he would be forced to ignore all the fascinating phenomena falling outside of such narrow constraints. He insists upon his freedom to look for the new and the unexpected. Now in his eighties, he continues to ask questions, to probe, and to integrate. And psychology, both its developmental and cognitive areas, have benefited enormously from Piaget's curiosity about how the child comes to understand the world and his or her place in it.

other instrument)" (Piaget, 1970, p. 705). The "pushing" scheme is not the actual act of pushing a particular object; rather it is what is common to all acts of pushing and it includes things to push with and things that can be pushed. Thus, a scheme is a cognitive structure that relates means (such as looking, reaching, manipulating) to ends (such as receiving particular kinds of stimulation). A *schema* (plural *schemata*) is a "simplified image (e.g., the map of a town)" (Piaget, 1970, p. 705). Schemata refer to the "figurative aspects of thought." Children recognize that a particular animal is a dog, for example, by comparing it with their schemata of various animals; they know they can play with it by referring to their "playing" scheme.

The two basic processes involving cognitive structures are *assimilation* and *accommodation*. These processes always occur together, although one can be predominant. In ordinary language, we might say that children attempt to understand their experiences by interpreting them consistently with what they already know (assimilation) but the experiences at the same time change their knowledge (accommodation) (Lipsitt & Reese, 1979). Interpreting current experiences in terms of previously established cognitive structures is assimilation; discovering new facts about experiences and modifying existing cognitive structures is accommodation. Imaginative play—using a broom as a horse—is assimilative; imitation is accommodative (Flavell, 1977).

Assimilation modifies or transforms incoming information (the input to the child is changed by the child's cognitive structures). Only that part of a stimulus that is assimilated can affect behavior—the unassimilated part is ignored. Accommodation modifies previously developed cognitive structures (the child is changed by the input). For example, seeing that a paper straw bends and is therefore not useful as a pushing tool leads to accommodation of the pushing scheme to exclude soft straws from "things to push with." Cognitive development, in Piaget's terms, consists of a succession of such changes in schemes and refinements of the figurative structures (schemata), plus periodic reorganization of the whole system of structures. It is these schemes and schemata that guide and control what the child can understand and do at any given age.

Social and personality changes

According to psychodynamic theory, the foundations of adult personality are laid in childhood. Not only is the course of normal personality development seen as continuous across ages and stages, but the origins of adult fears and neuroses can be traced back to early childhood experiences. We shall return to these theories in greater detail in Chapter 16.

Psychosexual development

According to Freud's psychoanalytic theory, personality development in childhood is divided into *psychosexual stages*. Each stage is dominated by instinctual, unlearned biological urgings, which are *hedonistic* (pleasure-seeking). During each of these successive periods, sensual satisfaction comes through stimulation of various "erogenous" zones of the body—the mouth, the anus, and the genitals. These broadly conceived sexual forces are termed *libido*, and comprise all of the ways in which an individual derives gratification from bodily stimulation. At each stage of development, the extent to which such libidinal drives are satisfied or frustrated provides occasion for intrapsychic conflict. Excess of either gratification or frustration at one stage prevents the normal progression to the next and leads to *fixation* at that stage. Such fixations then influence how the child will interact with his or her environment. Anal fixation in the child is presumed to result in a stingy, neat, and stubborn obsessive-compulsive adult character. Oral fixation is alleged to lead to drug addiction, compulsive eating, and even tendencies toward verbal fluency and sarcasm.

The most primitive stage of psychosexual development is the *oral* stage, in which the mouth region is the primary source of nourishment, stimulation, and contact with the environment. Infants and young children spend a great proportion of their time in sucking activities of a nonnutritive nature (such as thumb or toe sucking).

The *anal* stage, which follows, focuses gratification first on elimination of feces, then on retention of them. The child's pleasure from both the process and the products of excretion is challenged by social demands in most cultures and is eventually suppressed and regulated.

The final general period of erotic satisfaction centers around the exploration and stimulation of one's own body, especially the penis and the vagina or clitoris. This *phallic* stage is followed by a *latent stage*, where sexuality "goes underground" for a few years. Finally, with puberty, the individual arrives at the *genital* stage of sexual differentiation, away from autoeroticism (self-stimulation) toward stimulation from contact with the genitalia of others. As they progress through these stages, children learn their appropriate sex-role identification, develop a conscience partially through the resolution of their sexual love for the opposite-sex parent (the Oedipal situation), and become ready for culturally appropriate adult heterosexuality. But where the conflict at any of these stages between personal pleasure and social pressure is not adequately resolved, normal character development is affected—according to Freudian theory.

Psychosocial development

We will consider in some detail the two theories that go furthest in emphasizing the social nature of personality, those of Erik H. Erikson and Harry Stack Sullivan.

Erikson's portrait of the individual

From his clinical observations of children, adolescents, college students, and older adults, Erikson made three major contributions to the theory of personality development in his book *Childhood and Society* (1963). First, parallel to Freud's psychosexual stages, he identifies *psychosocial* stages of ego development in which individuals establish new orientations to themselves and to other people in their social world. Second, personality development is seen as continuing throughout all stages of life, rather than being established primarily during the infantile stage as in Freud's theory. Third, each of these stages requires a new level of social interaction that can change the course of personality in either positive or negative directions.

Erikson identified eight stages of psychosocial development describing the human cycle of life from infancy through old age. At each stage a particular conflict comes into focus. Although it is never resolved once and for all, it must be resolved sufficiently so that the individual can cope successfully with the conflicts of later stages.

1. *Trust vs. mistrust* (first year of life). Depending on the quality of the care received, the infant learns to trust the environment, to perceive it as orderly and predictable, or to be suspicious, fearful, and mistrusting of its chaos and unpredictability.

2. *Autonomy vs. doubt* (second and third years of life). From the development of motor and mental abilities and the opportunity to explore and manipulate emerges a sense of autonomy, adequacy, and self-control. Excessive criticism or restriction of the child's exploration and other behaviors leads to a sense of shame and doubt over his or her adequacy. In American culture, toilet training is emphasized in this period. Gentle handling generally results in self-sufficiency; unwise handling results in shame.

3. *Initiative vs. guilt* (fourth to fifth year of life). The way parents respond to the child's self-initiated activities, intellectual as well as motor, creates either a sense of freedom and initiative at one extreme, or at the other, a sense of guilt and a feeling of being an inept intruder in an adult world.

4. *Industry vs. inferiority* (sixth to eleventh year). The child's concern for how things work and how they ought to operate leads to a sense of industry in formulating rules, organizing, ordering, being industrious. However, a sense of inferiority may be promoted in a child when these efforts are rebuffed as silly, mischievous, or troublesome. During this stage influences outside the home begin to exert a greater influence on the child's development.

5. *Identity vs. role confusion* (adolescence, from twelve to eighteen years of age). During this period the adolescent begins to develop multiple ways of perceiving things, can see things from another person's point of view, behaves differently in different situations according to what is deemed appropriate. In playing these varied roles, the person must develop an integrated sense of his or her own identity as distinct from all others, but coherent and personally acceptable. Where such a "centered" identity is not developed, the alternatives are to be confused about who one really is or to settle on a "negative identity"—a socially unacceptable role, such as that of a "speed freak" or "bully."

6. *Intimacy vs. isolation* (young adulthood). The consequences of the adult's attempts at reaching out to make contact with others may result in intimacy (a commitment—sexual, emotional, and moral—to other persons) or else in isolation from close personal relationships.

7. *Generativity vs. self-absorption* (middle age). Here one's life experiences may extend the focus of concern beyond oneself to family, society, or future generations. If this future orientation does not develop, a person may become concerned with only material possessions and physical well-being.

8. *Integrity vs. despair* (old age). In this last stage of life one looks back on what it has been all about and ahead to the unknown of death. As a consequence of the solutions developed at each of the preceding stages, one can enjoy the fulfillment of life, with a sense of integrity. But despair is what faces the person who finds that life has been unsatisfying and misdirected. Too late either to look back in anger or ahead with hope, the life cycle of such a person ends with a whimper of despair.

The first four stages refer to socialization of the child, the last four to socialization of the adult. The major psychosocial issues in childhood are about the worth of others and the self. The major issues in adolescence are about personal identity; in young adulthood, intimacy; in middle age, the family; and in old age, the legacy one leaves (Neugarten, 1976).

Sullivan's social perspective

Sullivan, like Freud, proposed that tension arising from a set of physiological needs often leads to action. Unlike Freud, however, he believed that our basic needs are not biological but derive from interactions with people, and that these interpersonally developed "human" characteristics may directly affect or alter physiological functioning. Most cultures, for example, have more or less elaborate sets of rules specifying when and how one may eat, eliminate, and so on.

Sullivan defined personality as "the relatively enduring pattern of recurrent interpersonal situations which characterize human life" (1953, p. 111). Thus for him personality meant consistency not in internal traits but in what a person does *in relation to other people*.

In accounting for consistency in interpersonal behavior, Sullivan introduced the concepts of "dynamism" and "personification." A *dynamism* is a prolonged, recurrent behavior pattern (other theorists would call much the same thing a *habit*). A dynamism can be any habitual reaction, whether in the form of an attitude, a feeling, or an overt action. One particularly important dynamism is the "*self-system*," which, according to Sullivan, develops as individuals learn to avoid threats to their security. They learn, for example, that if they do what their parents like, they will not be punished. They then come to engage in habitual "security measures" that allow some forms of behavior (the "good-me" self) and forbid others (the "bad-me" self).

A *personification* is an image a person has of someone else. It is a complex of feelings, attitudes, and conceptions that in large part determines how one will act toward that person. Personifications learned in infancy may remain intact and influence a person's adult reactions to people. Children who personify their father as overbearing and hostile, for example, may come to personify other older men as being overbearing, and will then react to certain teachers and employers as if they were overbearing and hostile whether they actually are or not. Sullivan called a personification held in common by a group of people a *stereotype*. Examples of stereotypes common in our culture are the "long-haired student radical," the "ivory-tower intellectual," and the "male chauvinist pig."

Sullivan outlined seven stages of personality development in Western European societies. These are: (a) infancy, (b) childhood, (c) the juvenile era, (d) preadolescence, (e) early adolescence, (f) late adolescence, and (g) maturity. The emphasis is on the kinds of interpersonal relationships and the ways of thinking that become possible in each stage. Thus Sullivan recognized that somewhat different patterns might be found in other societies.

Although he stressed the influence of social forces in the development of personality, Sullivan also recognized the potential influence of individuals in changing their society. Indeed, he was often critical of contemporary society, believing that many of the ways it influences personality development run counter to people's personal needs and inhibit rather than enhance the full realization of human potential. At the same time, because he believed that people remain flexible throughout their lives, he was optimistic about their chances to live in harmony with the dictates of society, until it becomes so irrational and repressive that individuals attempt to *change* it rather than just adapt to it.

Emotional development

The newborn infant seems to possess only a few different "emotional" states, perhaps only two—a state of agitation and a state of quiet. The early behaviorist John B. Watson believed that infants have three basic emotions: fear, rage, and love. Whatever the initial number, the emotions found in adults are believed to develop from the basic emotions, partly as a result of maturation

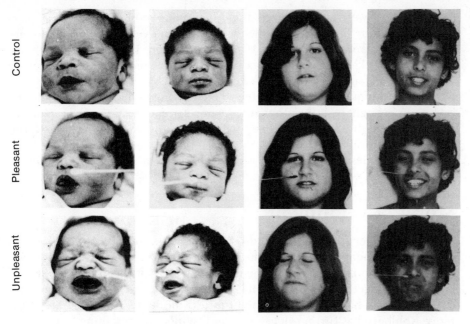

Control

Pleasant

Unpleasant

The expression of emotions can be seen in normal newborn babies. These babies were tested with various odors between birth and the first feeding. The first pictures show the resting face, with no stimulation. Pleasant and unpleasant odors were presented. The beauty in the region of the mouth in response to pleasant odors is similar to the expression associated with love in the adult. The facial responses to unpleasant odors clearly reflect disgust when observed in the adult. The other photographs show the expression of similar emotions in normal adolescents.

but largely as a result of learning. The development is relatively rapid; by two years of age, the child already exhibits most of the adult emotions, from anger, disgust, and fear to elation, joy, and love. In Chapter 14 we will analyze the nature of emotion more fully.

The primitive nature of the basic emotions is illustrated by the photographs. ▲ Note the similarity of the disgust reactions across ages and of the reactions to pleasant stimuli. The same facial expressions are also seen in newborn infants with severe brain abnormalities, in mentally retarded individuals, and in persons blind since birth (Steiner, 1978). Thus, these emotions originate in the primitive structures of the brain and the characteristic ways of expressing them are innate, rather than resulting from imitation, for example, which would require visual experiences.

Watson believed that emotional development is mostly a matter of conditioning the primary emotions to new stimuli. He and Rosemary Rayner tested part of this theory and confirmed that one of the emotions, fear, can be conditioned in infancy to previously neutral stimuli.

Watson and Rayner (1920) tested an eleven-month-old boy, "Albert," by presenting a variety of furry and woolly objects to see if they aroused any fear. Albert showed no fear of any of them—a rat, rabbit, dog, monkey, mask, cotton wool, and the like. Then the rat was presented and as Albert began to reach for it, a metal bar was struck loudly just behind him. The sudden loud sound aroused the fear response (in accordance with Watson's theory, which equates the fear and startle responses). This procedure was repeated twice. A week later, the rat was presented three times, closer each time but each time without the loud sound. Albert showed some hesitancy in reaching for the rat. Five more training trials were then given, with two test trials intermixed. Albert showed strong fear; he began to cry, turned, fell over, and crawled away as fast as he could. Five days later further tests were given, in which Albert exhibited fear of a rabbit, a sealskin coat, a dog, cotton wool, a Santa Claus mask, and Watson's hair. The strength of the fear was strongest for the rabbit, and decreased for the other stimuli in the order listed. Albert showed no conditioned fear of nonfurry objects.

Watson and Rayner had planned to extinguish the fear as a further test of the theory, but "Unfortunately, Albert was taken from the hospital the day the above tests were made. Hence, the opportunity of building up an experimental technique by means of which we could remove the conditioned emotional responses was denied us" (Watson & Rayner, 1920). However, Mary Cover Jones (1924) demonstrated a highly effective technique for removing such fears. Her subject was Peter, a three-year-old boy who was afraid of rabbits. The technique was simply to feed Peter at one end of a room while the rabbit was brought in at the other end. Over a series of sessions, the rabbit was gradually brought closer until finally all fear disappeared and Peter played freely with the rabbit. In essence, the procedure is identical to the technique of "systematic desensitization" currently used to treat phobias (see p. 608).

Moral development

Piaget's characteristic research method consists of presenting a situation, asking for a judgment about it, and then probing for the basis of the judgment, the child's reasoning that led to the judgment. The situation presented is of interest to Piaget only in providing an opportunity to probe the person's thought. Piaget has used this method to study moral development, and Lawrence Kohlberg has further developed and refined it, presenting brief stories embodying various moral dilemmas, such as the following:

"In Europe, a woman was near death from a special kind of cancer. There was one drug that the doctors thought might save her. It was a form of radium that a druggist in the same town had recently discovered. The drug was expensive to make, but the druggist was charging ten times what the drug cost him to make. He paid $200 for the radium and charged $2,000 for a small dose of the drug. The sick woman's husband, Heinz, went to everyone he knew to borrow the money, but he could only get together about $1,000, which is half of what it cost. He told the druggist that his wife was dying and asked him to sell cheaper or let him pay later. But the druggist said: "No, I discovered the drug and I'm going to make money from it." So Heinz got desperate and broke into the man's store to steal the drug for his wife. Should the husband have done that?" (From Longstreth, 1974, p. 504.)

Like Piaget, Kohlberg has been less interested in the development of moral *behavior* than in the development of the *understanding* of morality. He is not concerned with what a person would actually do if faced with a moral problem but with what the person believes would be morally correct.

Kohlberg has found that people can be categorized as being at one of seven stages of moral development (0–6), and he has theorized that an eighth stage (Stage 7) exists (Kohlberg, 1973). Each stage is characterized by particular beliefs about such aspects of morality as the reason for being moral and the basis for valuing the worth of a human life. ◆ The progression of a child through these stages follows a fixed sequence from 0 through 7, although the rate of movement toward conventional and principled levels of morality may vary in different children and different societies, and upper levels may never be reached. Indeed, the very existence of the highest stage has not been demonstrated with data, although theoretically it must exist.

Adult moral development is characterized by: dropping of self-centered modes of thinking about morality, rather than forming higher modes; stabilizing of Stage 4 conventional morality; greater consistency of moral judgment and moral action; integration of the use of moral structures and the application of moral thought to one's life.

Kohlberg reports that he has never found a Stage 7 person among those he has tested, but he suggests that persons "from Socrates to Martin Luther

Kohlberg's classification of moral judgment into levels and stages of development

Basis of Moral Judgment	Stages of Development	Reasons for Conforming	Worth of a Human Life
Level I: Preconventional; hedonic. Moral value resides in the individual selfish actor, in good and bad acts.	*Stage 0:* Premoral. The good is what I want and like.	None.	None.
	Stage 1: Punishment/obedience orientation. Egocentric deference to superior power or prestige, avoidance of trouble.	Avoid punishment.	The value of a human life is confused with the value of things and is based on the status or appearance of the person.
	Stage 2: Naively egoistic orientation. Instrumental hedonism: right action is whatever instrumentally satisfies own needs and occasionally others'. Concrete reciprocity: an eye for an eye. Awareness of relativism of value to each actor's needs and perspective.	Obtain rewards; have favors returned.	Human life is instrumental to the satisfaction of the needs of the one who has life or the needs of others.
Level II: Conventional; pragmatic. Morality of conventional role conformity. Moral value resides in performing good or right roles, in maintaining the conventional order and the expectancies of others.	*Stage 3:* "Good child" morality. Please and help others to maintain good relations and win approval. Conformity to stereotyped ideas about natural roles. Moral judgment based on intentions.	Avoid disapproval or dislike by others.	The value of a human life is based on the empathy and affection of family members and others toward the one who has life.
	Stage 4: Law and order orientation. Authorities set rules to maintain social order. Morality of "doing your duty" and showing respect for authority; maintaining the given social order for its own sake.	Avoid censure by authorities and resultant guilt.	Life is sacred because of its place in a moral or religious order of rights and duties.
Level III: Postconventional; principled. Morality of self-accepted moral principles. Moral value resides in conformity to the principles of a moral theory.	*Stage 5:* Contractual legalistic orientation. Morality of contract, of individual rights, and of democratically accepted law; social contract orientation. Duty reflects the rights of others, the majority will and welfare.	Maintain community welfare.	Life is valued because of its relation to community welfare and because of its being a universal human right.
	Stage 6: Conscience or principle orientation. Morality of individual principles of conscience, mutual respect and trust. Orientation not only to actual social rules but to consistent universal principles.	Avoid self-condemnation.	Human life is sacred because of universal human value of respect for the individual.
	Stage 7: Cosmic or infinite orientation. The ultimate moral question here is not "Why be moral?" but "Why live?" The answer refers to the unity of the whole cosmos and the self as part of this unity.	Reflect the unity of the cosmos and the self (or the self as part of the cosmic unity).	Life is valued because it is part of the infinite or cosmic unity.

Based on Kohlberg, 1964; 1967; 1973

King, who lived and died for their ethical principles, have something like a strong Stage 7 orientation" (1973, p. 204). The morality of Stage 7 is likely to be based on religion, according to Kohlberg, but it would need to be a "post-conventional" religion.

Chapter summary

Developmental psychology deals with the description, explanation, and modification (optimization) of changes in behavior within persons across their life spans, and differences between persons in these changes. These changes are explained in terms of *physical growth, maturation,* and *learning.* Although the causes of development are characterized as either *hereditary* or *environmental,* neither can have any effect without the other. Therefore, the old heredity versus environment (nature-nurture) controversy is fruitless.

Development has been viewed from four major perspectives: the *behavioral* emphasizes environmental influences on behavior; the *genetic* emphasizes the unfolding of drives and evolution of higher forms; the *cognitive* emphasizes underlying mental structures that change developmentally; and the *psychometric* emphasizes attributes that are relatively stable and can be measured objectively.

Age refers to the passage of time, and is not itself a causal variable. It is correlated with causal variables, however, and therefore is useful as an *index variable.* The concept of *stages of development* is used in a weak sense to refer to variables indexed by age. In a strong sense, the concept indicates discontinuity in development, or qualitative change from one time period to another.

Life-span development can be characterized as passing through eight stages: prenatal (conception to birth), infancy (birth to 18 months), early childhood (18 months to 6 years), late childhood (6 to 13 years), adolescence (13 to 20), young adulthood (20 to 45), middle age (45 to 65), and old age (to death). A "preconception" stage could be added at the beginning and a stage of death at the end.

The designs used for developmental research are *cross-sectional* (comparing people who are different in age at the present time), *longitudinal* (repeatedly testing the same people as they grow older), and *sequential* (starting with a cross-sectional design but testing each age group repeatedly as they grow older). Each design has advantages and disadvantages, but the sequential designs are generally best. Nevertheless, most developmental research is cross-sectional.

Malnutrition can cause permanent physical and psychological retardation, if prolonged, severe, or associated with a period of normally rapid growth. Males are more susceptible to its negative consequences than females.

Females have a higher survival rate than males from the beginning, in the prenatal period, until the age of about 100 years. Among other contributing causes is the greater resistance of females to environmental perturbations. Boys are more prone than girls to emotional, scholastic, and behavior problems, but the causes may be largely environmental, based on parental expectations about the behaviors of boys and girls and consequent differences in treatment.

Walking and grasping develop through fixed stages, without any special training efforts. Perceptual development is also spontaneous. The newborn infant possesses well-developed senses of touch, temperature, taste, smell, hearing, and vision, but is relatively insensitive to pain. Depth perception may be learned; "visual cliff" studies show it by six months, but evidence for younger infants is mixed. Evidence is also mixed on whether whole perception precedes part perception, as the *orthogenetic* principle suggests.

Cognition and intelligence refer to psychological processes of adapting to the environment. According to Ferguson's behavioral theory, such processes are responses that are learned because society values them and the caregivers therefore reinforce them. Cross-cultural differences in intelligence, and perhaps age differences, reflect differences in the responses, or abilities, that are valued.

In the psychometric approach, test scores are interpreted to reflect abilities, and attempts have been made to determine the extent to which each of them is fixed by heredity or is free to vary with variation of environment (the nature-nurture issue). One estimate of the relative importance of these influences is the *heritability coefficient*. Studies in which this coefficient was calculated have suggested that overall intelligence, or IQ, is 80 percent hereditary and 20 percent environmental, but the validity of these estimates is easily challenged.

In Piaget's approach to cognition, thought involves *schemes*, which are mental operations, and *schemata* (singular *schema*), which are like mental images. Thinking involves *assimilation* and *accommodation*. Assimilation yields understanding—it involves interpreting experiences to make them consistent with what one already knows. Accommodation is a process of discovery—it involves modifying schemes to make them consistent with the new information. The course of cognitive development consists of changes in the schemes and schemata and, most importantly, in the way they are organized to yield a characteristic style of thought.

Piaget has identified four stages of cognition, or styles of thought: *sensorimotor, preoperational, concrete,* and *formal*.

Freud viewed personality development in terms of five *psychosexual* stages: *oral, anal, phallic, latent,* and *genital*.

According to Erikson, *psychosocial* development proceeds through eight stages. The first four refer to socialization of the child, and the last four to socialization of the adult. Sullivan goes further than Erikson in emphasizing the social nature of personality.

Basic emotions, and manner of expressing them, are innate and depend on primitive brain structures. The more complex and subtle emotions, which appear fairly early in childhood, are differentiated by maturation and, to a large extent, learning in social contexts.

Moral development also seems to progress through fixed stages, beginning in infancy with an absence of morality and proceeding through seven further stages divided into three levels: preconventional (early childhood), conventional (late childhood, adolescence, and perhaps adulthood), and postconventional or principled (relatively rare, especially in its two highest forms).

Stages of the Life Cycle

All the world's a stage,
And all the men and women merely players.
They have their exits and their entrances;
And one man in his time plays many parts,
His acts being seven ages. At first the infant,
Mewling and puking in the nurse's arms,
And then the whining school-boy, with his satchel,
And shining morning face, creeping like snail
Unwillingly to school. And then the lover,
Sighing like furnace, with a woful ballad
Made to his mistress' eyebrow. Then a soldier,
Full of strange oaths, and bearded like the pard,
Jealous in honor, sudden and quick in quarrel,
Seeking the bubble reputation
Even in the cannon's mouth. And then the justice,
In fair round belly with good capon lin'd,
With eyes severe and beard of formal cut,
Full of wise saws and modern instances;
And so he plays his part. The sixth age shifts
Into the lean and slipper'd pantaloon,
With spectacles on nose and pouch on side,
His youthful hose well sav'd, a world too wide
For his shrunk shank; and his big manly voice,
Turning again toward childish treble, pipes
And whistles in his sound. Last scene of all,
That ends this strange eventful history,
Is second childishness, and mere oblivion,
Sans teeth, sans eyes, sans taste, sans everything.
Shakespeare, <u>As You Like It</u>, Act II, Scene vii

William Shakespeare, writing before the year 1600, recognized that human development includes the entire life span. He saw our "acts being *seven ages*," with each individual progressing through "mewling and puking" *infancy*, the "whining school-boy" period of *childhood*, the *adolescent* state of "the lover," a *young adult* stage of "a soldier," "and then the justice" or period of *adulthood* and stability, followed by "the sixth stage" of *old age*, and a "last scene of all" of "second childishness" and senility. Shakespeare even hints at the final stage of *death*. One need but add the prenatal period, and Shakespeare's analysis of human development is directly parallel to the eight stages we will discuss here.

Our entire lives are characterized by change and growth: physical development, personality changes and refinements, the development of cognitive abilities, and changing emotions and attitudes. A seemingly never ending series of *developmental tasks* faces each of us, continuing from birth through adolescence into marriage and child rearing, career choice, life-style choices and changes, the acceptance of maturity and life situation, the meeting of retirement, and finally the prospects of imminent personal extinction.

We all progress through the various stages of development and face most of the human tasks. Some of us travel gracefully and with personal pride and dignity, others move with difficulty under great personal stress. Growth and change are the very stuff of human existence, and much is to be learned from a survey of age-related patterns and the suffering and solving of developmental problems. We begin our individual growth process at conception, and we continue to develop through the lifespan into the final moments ". . . and mere oblivion."

The cycle begins

An energetic sperm cell discovers a receptive egg cell; united, they follow a trail as old as life itself to become in a mere nine months a human being. We saw in Chapter 8 that about 30 to 50 percent more males are conceived than females, but that the prenatal death rate is so much greater for male fetuses that the sex ratio at birth is only about 106 males to 100 females. Little else is known about sex differences in the prenatal period, and no evidence is available on possible sex differences in behavioral development in this period. Differences should exist, however, because differences are observed at birth.

Prenatal development

The mother may feel the quickening of the fetus in the sixteenth week after conception, although fetal movements may be heard with a stethoscope a week or two earlier (Carmichael, 1970). At these ages, the fetus is somewhere around seven inches long (the average length at birth is twenty inches). Actually, however, fetuses are capable of movement considerably earlier, as shown by observations of medically aborted fetuses. Responses to stimulation have been observed as early as the sixth week after conception, when the fetus is not yet an inch long, and spontaneous movements have been observed in fetuses a week or two older (Carmichael, 1970; Humphrey, 1970). The earliest behavior of any kind observed in the prenatal period is the heartbeat, beginning in the third week when the embryo is somewhat less than one-sixth of an inch long.

Many drugs taken by the mother pass through the placenta to the fetus and can affect fetal behavior and development. A tragic and extreme example is the thalidomide disaster of 1961. When taken during the first few months of pregnancy, this tranquilizer caused severely abnormal physical development. Hundreds of "thalidomide babies" were born without arms or legs, their hands and feet being attached directly to the torso like flippers. ■ Although not all drugs taken by a pregnant woman affect the fetus, and such

■
This youngster and hundreds like him were born without fully developed arms and legs after their mothers took the drug thalidomide during early pregnancy.

severe effects as those of thalidomide are extremely rare, it is important to keep in mind the *possible* consequences for the unborn child of taking any drugs, especially during the first third of the pregnancy.

The first third of pregnancy seems to be an especially vulnerable period, when about 75 percent of miscarriages occur. It is estimated, for example, that approximately 12 percent of babies born to women who had contracted German measles (rubella) during the first three months of pregnancy will be defective in some way. The defects that may occur include brain damage, blindness, deafness, and defects of the heart and other organs. So sensitive is this early period of pregnancy that no drug can be considered completely safe during these first few weeks (Bowes, Brackbill, Conway, & Steinschneider, 1970). After the fifth month there is much less danger.

Birth

Much has been written on the virtues of natural childbirth, but little research has been done to confirm these virtues. One virtue that has been demonstrated, however, is the absence of anesthetics. Certain kinds of anesthetics given to the mother pass through the placenta to the fetus and affect its behavior not only immediately following birth but throughout the next few days. In fact, some effects can be demonstrated four weeks after birth, and although the evidence is not firm there is a hint of persisting effects *twenty* weeks after birth. Of course, not all anesthetics have an effect; some do not cross the placental barrier (Bowes et al., 1970). The greater responsiveness of the undrugged newborn and mother may lead to a cycle of greater interaction between them—more touching, playing, cuddling, moving. Other positive effects of natural childbirth include the participation of the father in prenatal instruction and the birth itself, and the sense of a peak experience shared by both parents at the time of delivery.

The use of an anesthetic is sometimes a necessity, as when the baby is delivered by Caesarian section. Babies thus delivered surgically, through an incision in the mother's abdomen, have been reported to exhibit poorer color, muscle tone, and responsiveness than babies born normally, but it is not clear whether the difference reflects the use of different anesthetics or reflects beneficial effects of the stresses of normal births (as has been supposed).

Prematurity—birth before full term—is most common in the lower socioeconomic classes, perhaps because of less adequate maternal nutrition and medical care. The earlier the premature birth, the more likely it is to be associated with physical and behavioral abnormalities such as cerebral palsy, mental retardation, and learning disabilities.

Premature infants must be kept in fairly isolated conditions for a period, usually with electrodes attached for the continuous recording of heart rate. They must often be kept in an incubator under good temperature controls and can be handled only through portholes in the side of the unit. The sound of the incubator motor can be like a continuous roar, drowning out the more interesting, less monotonous human sounds outside the container. Little can be seen from inside the incubator, which is covered with a shaped plastic or glass dome that tends to diffuse and distort images. Thus the "handicapped newborn" kept in premature nurseries sometimes for weeks or months may be running a risk of having the initial hereditary or constitutional handicap that is associated with prematurity compounded by further deprivations of sensory experience and human interaction (Klaus & Kennell, 1970).

Infancy

A staggering number of studies have been carried out with infants over the past two decades. More studies of babies, their behavior, and their psychological needs have been conducted during this time than in the entire previous history of the fields of child psychology and pediatrics. As a consequence, we know much more today than just one short generation ago. The parent-help and child-development books can hardly keep pace with the rapidly advancing frontiers of knowledge.

The significance of infancy

Apart from the intrinsic interest that the newborn and older infant hold for us, it is of great importance from a health and welfare standpoint that we learn as much as possible as quickly as possible about the growing infant. It is increasingly apparent that the period of *infancy* (which means "incapable of talking") has special significance as a training ground for later development and behavior. It is during the first year of life that the child becomes attached to other persons in his or her life, a walking pattern begins to take shape, smiling and other reciprocating gestures come in as social exercises and play activities. Now, the child begins to reach out—with hands, eyes, culturally relevant vocal gestures—and some of the basic biological reflexes disappear to be supplanted by learned responses (Lipsitt, 1976).

The newborn baby   Even within the first few hours of life, it is clear that the newborn infant has a wide variety of built-in responses available. If placed upon the mother's abdomen, the newborn will usually engage in crawling motions, in a seeming attempt to find the nipple. If the baby is placed near the mother's breast, a "rooting" activity or search for the nipple occurs, with some agitated but quite well coordinated head turning and mouth opening. As the nipple goes into the mouth, the baby closes tightly on it, and sucking begins. It appears that most babies "know how to do it"; some need a few practice trials. ●

Sucking behavior is a very highly developed and exceedingly complex pattern of behavior (Kaye, 1967). It involves intricate coordination of tongue and swallowing movements, the baby's respiration must be synchronized with the sucking and swallowing sequence, and the entire process is dependent both upon the tactile stimulation from the nipple and upon taste.

From the earliest moments of sucking experience and ingestion, the baby is influenced by the consequences of its own behavior. The rapidity of sucking, for example, is dependent upon the sweetness of the fluid being received. The sweeter the fluid, the more continuously—and also the more slowly—the infant will suck (Lipsitt et al., 1976). We come into the world, apparently, with a propensity for pleasurable sensation, and we already have the capacity within the first few days of life to adjust our behavior to optimize that pleasure.

Related to the newborn's capacity for optimizing pleasant stimulation, particularly around the mouth, or *oral* region, is the presence from very early in life of defensive responses. Newborns seem to dislike any form of unpleasant stimulation and engage in actions which tend to thwart such stimulation. The stimuli they find aversive are not so different from those which most of us would agree are annoying. For example, the normal newborn will blink at the sudden onset of a bright light, will jump when a loud noise occurs, and will cry or withdraw the leg when the heel is pricked with a needle for a blood test.

Especially interesting in the newborn is a set of responses relating to

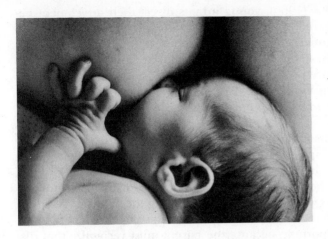

When placed near the mother's breast most babies will open their mouths and turn their heads. When they find the nipple, they begin to suck.

253
The cycle begins

threats of smothering. If placed on the abdomen with the nose and mouth pressed gently against the mattress, most normal newborns will lift their heads fully off the mattress within a few seconds after the head is released. Similarly, with the baby lying on its back, if a gauze pad is pressed against the face for a brief period, a five-step reaction pattern ensues: first the baby turns its head rapidly to and fro, then there appears some backward pulling of the head, then the hands come up toward the face in a fightinglike gesture and swipe against the object (often accurately and effectively). If none of these gestures has succeeded in escape from the gauze pad, blushing occurs, and finally the fail-safe response of crying, which is nearly always effective in getting rid of the annoyance.

This is an inborn reaction, and does not require actual blockage or smothering to occur. It is a protective response system that seems to respond in anticipation of real danger. Observers often characterize the reaction pattern as one of rage. It may well constitute the basis of learned anger which will not, of course, emerge until later. It has been suggested that infants in whom this response system is not well functioning at birth may be precisely those who are in special danger from sudden infant death (crib death), from which about 8000 babies a year in the U.S. alone succumb each year, most between the ages of two and eight months (Lipsitt, 1976).

Attachment   The young infant defecates an average of almost five times a day, usually in the first half-hour after feeding, and urinates almost 19 times a day, mostly in the first hour after feeding. These norms are possibly more exciting to a diaper manufacturer than to a parent, but the norms show that diapering will be a frequent occurrence in the daily life of the normal young infant. When you add the number of feedings—from four to eight a day—and other care-giving activities such as bathing, soothing, rocking, and playing, it becomes apparent that many learning trials are available every day for associating the sight and sound of the parent (or other caregiver) with the occurrence of comfort. No wonder, then, that the infant normally becomes attached to the mother early in life, as early as the third month after birth or even earlier.

Attachment is defined behaviorally as a set of activities that elicit and maintain physical nearness between two persons, specifically in the present case between infant and parent (Ainsworth & Bell, 1970; Bowlby, 1969). The development of attachment between infant and parent is necessary for healthy emotional development. Research has shown that severe disruption of attachment can result in developmental retardation and even death of the infant (Sherrod, Vietze, & Friedman, 1978).

According to Bowlby (1969), young infants direct their attachment behaviors, such as smiling, reaching, vocalizing, and crying, indiscriminately to any adult who is a potential caregiver; but at about three months of age, infants begin to direct these behaviors primarily toward their parents. This preference becomes more pronounced as the infant grows older, and from around six or seven months of age to perhaps twelve months, the infant may even exhibit *stranger anxiety*: apprehensiveness in the presence of unfamiliar adults.

It is believed that associating physical contact with comfort is the major contributor to the development of attachment (Sherrod et al., 1978). As already noted, the parents have many opportunities each day to teach this association; for example, if the baby is bottle fed, holding the baby in the nursing position during feedings would be better than holding the baby on the lap or leaving the baby alone in the crib with the bottle propped up. Sensitivity to the baby's signals is also important, because the parent must recognize that discomfort is being signaled in order to give the needed care and produce the state of comfort.

Early stimulation   In recent years the infant during its first months of life is seen as rather more "precocious" than previously (Lipsitt, 1963, 1977). This new appreciation, even of the newborn, has resulted in greater attention to the environmental conditions of babies both in institutional settings and at home. Infants in orphanages, for example, are no longer left lying unattended for long hours in their cribs. Walls are painted bright colors, mobiles are hung over the cribs, music is often played, and nurses or other attendants interact frequently with the infants, turning them over, talking or singing to them, and cuddling them. We now know that lack of environmental stimulation and human comforting of infants can have devastating effects, sometimes called *hospitalism* or *marasmus* (Spitz, 1945).

At home, too, parents realize that the beginnings of their infant's life are of great importance. The "enlightened" parent today has become more aware of the real capabilities of the infant and often seeks to provide a bit of extra loving attention. Some of this is due, no doubt, to parents' better observations of their infants' capacities and potential. For example, while it was

a common belief 25 years ago that newborns cannot see, today the new mother knows that very young infants can see, hear, and smell, and a mother will often "test" her baby in the first few days to see if it will follow with its eyes a brightly colored object, or will respond to her voice by turning toward her. The baby often will.

Modification of innate behaviors

Very soon after birth, environmental forces, or response contingencies, begin to operate in conjunction with the infant's built-in response repertoire to produce learned changes in behavior. It will not be long before the baby, instead of awaiting a touch near the mouth to open it, will do so when the bottle or nipple is seen approaching it. Or the head may be turned in the appropriate direction when the baby is placed in the accustomed feeding posture. Such anticipatory gestures symbolize the essence of learning. Such response systems are of the classically conditioned or Pavlovian variety, because they involve elicited behavior.

Operant conditioning is in a sense also anticipatory; the infant makes a response presumably in anticipation of receiving a reward. Response consequences serve as reinforcers of the behavior, then, and tend to perpetuate the behavior. Thus an infant who spontaneously makes a sound, which is then followed by an attractive consequence such as sweet fluid or the smiling presence of the mother, will very likely repeat the act with increasing frequency as time (and reinforcement) goes on. Similarly, a response which is followed by an aversive consequence, such as a frightening noise, will tend not to be repeated in the future. The infant thus behaves in accordance with expectations about the availability of positive reinforcers or punishments, based upon past experience.

Cognitive processes

It must be clear by now that thought begins at birth. There are psychologists who would not want to term the anticipatory gestures just spoken of as thought. Even they, however, would have difficulty pinpointing the stage of development or learning at which the onset of thought occurs. It is perhaps more meaningful to speak of increasing levels of symbolization.

A number of developmental theorists have postulated stages of thought development. While no two systems or theories of cognition or thought development are exactly the same, most are agreed that the baby begins with a primitive appreciation of what is there and what is not, and most agree that early in life what is not there is unimportant to the child. Only with increasing cortical development, cognitive complexity, and experience in sensing, perceiving, and storing information does the child begin to take into consideration the current absence of past stimulation and to consider how things are different or might be different than they are. Such "mental manipulations" occur later and set the stage for the very symbolic higher thought processes of which mature persons are capable. We will review briefly two theories of cognitive development, that of Piaget and that of Bruner.

Piaget's theory   In a sense, Piaget's entire theory of cognitive development and intelligence is about the gradual acquisition of the capacity to symbolize events or to develop inner representations of external stimuli. His descriptions of developmental transitions that lead to higher-level symbolization are based upon his perceptive observations of growing children. When they were old enough to articulate answers to his clever questions, Piaget spoke with his subjects. However, he did not wait for that time. His observations began at birth.

Piaget observed that most of the infant's activity in the first month of life is of a reflexive sort, and he thus labeled this the Reflexive Activity stage. By the first month, however, and continuing to the fourth month, the infant is in what Piaget calls the stage of Primary Circular Reactions, which is characterized by a tendency to perpetuate what is pleasurable or fascinating. In this stage, something interesting happens and the infant keeps it going. For example, the hand in going by the mouth happens to touch the mouth; the mouth opens and grasps a finger. The finger is pleasant to suck, and the infant leaves it there. During these three months of age increasingly complex variations on this theme are evolving all the time, setting the conditions for the next stage.

The third infantile stage is that of Secondary Circular Reactions, during which the baby seems deliberately to be making something happen. During this period, lasting from about four to eight months, the first appreciation of "causation" seems to be achieved. When the mattress is bumped with the heel of the foot, for example, the crib rattles or an overhead mobile shakes. Fascinated by the realization that one can *make* those things happen, the baby intensively pursues the project of doing and stopping, kicking then observing, smiling and kicking. The joy of achieving control over one's world, however circumscribed or delimited, is set forever!

At this point, the stage Piaget calls Coordination of Secondary Schemes begins, lasting until about one year. During this stage infants develop an awareness of object permanence: the appreciation that when an object has gone from view it still exists, or the same object may occupy two spaces at different times. The difference between an eight-month-old and a one-year-old in this regard is always astonishing. The eight-month-old will often go searching for an object in its accustomed place even after seeing it removed from there and put in another location and even when the new location is virtually in full view. The one-year-old is too smart for that.

The next Piagetian stage of infancy is that of Tertiary Circular Reactions, during which real trial-and-error behavior, akin to reasoning, can be observed. The child explores things, looks at them from different angles, and seems to be appreciating how objects look different from diverse angles but are nonetheless the same objects. By this stage an infant will pull a mat or rug to get an object resting on it and otherwise out of reach.

Piaget calls the entire period of infancy *sensorimotor development*. Its final stage is that of Invention of New Means by Mental Combination. This takes the child up to two years of age. This is a period of "thinking out" or mental experimentation, a period of symbolic rehearsal before action. The child is hardly an infant any more at this stage. "If I do this, then that," the silence seems to say; here is the beginning of responsibility, perhaps.

Bruner's theory of cognitive development Bruner's theory differs from Piaget's in at least two major ways. One is the role of experience and education, which are *conditions* of cognitive progress for Piaget, and *causes* of progress for Bruner. That is, for Piaget education provides experiences that encourage discovery, but discovery is an activity of the learner and is limited by the learner's present stage of thought. For Bruner, well designed education can be effective at any age (Bruner, 1966). Another difference is that for Bruner, cognitive development progresses through three periods characterized by different modes of representation: *enactive, iconic,* and *symbolic.* In the enactive period, the infant is gaining control over objects and events in the environment essentially through increasing motor skill, and representation is motoric. In the iconic period, the child has a mental image or perceptual representation of objects and events. True symbols do not appear until the symbolic period (see p. 259).

Communication   It must be apparent that in all of the infant's activities just described, other persons are often involved. It is other people who so frequently move themselves in and out of the infant's presence, or who take things away or bring them back. Other people are forever dropping things, changing the visual appearance of things, turning lights on and off, putting things in the infant (like nipples), and taking things away (like inedibles and soiled diapers). These reciprocating interactions, many of them of a nature in which each individual does something in response to the other, are communications; they form the basis for the acquisition of a language.

The baby's gestures and grunts are its earliest social messages to encourage others to take some action on its behalf. An early reach toward an object can mean: "I want that," or "Give me that." The mother or other adult might respond not only by delivering or returning the desired object to the infant but with a comment or even a continuing dialogue. The mother might say while handing over the rattle: "Did you drop it again?" or "You want Mommy to get your blue rattle for you, don't you?" Such interchanges occur long before the child has any conventional language. It is likely that much language learning takes place in the context of such reciprocating motor gestures between the infant and adults. It has been shown, in fact, that language development of young children can be facilitated by reading to them long before the child grasps the content of the spoken passages (Irwin, 1960).

Socialization

According to Erikson's theory, *trust vs. mistrust* is the conflict that characterizes the first stage of psychosocial development. If the infant's needs are satisfied, including needs for comfort and security as well as nutrition, the infant learns to trust the environment, to perceive it as orderly and predictable. However, the infant who does not receive good care may become suspicious, fearful, and mistrusting of the chaotic and unpredictable environment—and the people in it. Much of this way of thinking about infancy is compatible with the Freudian notions about the importance of the "oral period" for making progress in ego development. The sense of trust to which Erikson alludes can also be understood in the framework of social learning theory (McCandless, 1970).

The first level of moral development, in Kohlberg's analysis, is *preconventional* or *hedonic*. In the first developmental stage, labeled "Stage 0," of this level, the child is *premoral*. If the infant could put the guiding principle into words, it might be "The good is what I want and like."

Childhood and adolescence

Although we have adopted an "ages-and-stages" orientation for the organization of this chapter, the large age spans covered at each "stage" and the diversity of behavioral changes occurring within each make it difficult to characterize each of the stages rigidly. Just as play behavior increases in complexity with increasing age, incorporating more nuances of fantasy and reality, thought processes become ever more dependent upon symbolic representations. A child's social and moral concerns undergo profound changes throughout childhood, culminating during adolescence in especially interesting and revealing behavior patterns that seem clearly to set the conditions for adulthood.

Childhood

The period of *early childhood* is marked roughly by the termination of infancy on one side, and the beginning of the school years or kindergarten on the other. Thus in Freudian terms children will go through the "anal phase" and will be well into the phallic stage of development by the end of this period. This is to say that they will have become toilet trained and will now be less concerned with excremental processes, and will be occupying themselves with sex differences. This concern for gender and the emergence of sex-role identity are among the preschooler's major preoccupations.

Every developmental theorist (like the rest of us) tends to observe and interpret behavior in the light of his or her own theories and sensitivities. Thus where one prominent theorist might call attention to a child's temporary obsession with genitalia, another might emphasize the exploratory, cognition-building character of the "obsession." Still another theorist might want to emphasize the functional effect of the developing child's concentration on bowel activity, perhaps to suggest that the anal orientation of the newly toilet-trained youngster really represents the child's sense of autonomy or striving for self-determination.

Toward the end of early childhood, at the age of about five years, children have a vocabulary of about 2000 words, and virtually every word they say is comprehensible even though their pronunciation is only about 88 percent correct. They use the word "you" almost half as often as "I," which is sometimes interpreted as a reflection of developing social interest.

The period of *late childhood* extends from about six to about thirteen, or from the beginning of schooling (in the United States) to the beginning of adolescence. It is a period of relative tranquillity, developmentally, in that the changes are more quantitative than qualitative. In the six or seven years of this period, the body changes more in size than in proportions. In the preceding six years the shape of the body changed drastically; and in the next period sexual maturation will drastically alter the qualitative appearance of the body. Similarly, vocabulary increases during late childhood but grammar, which is a qualitative feature of language, was already almost mature when the period began.

Speech and thought

How does one find out what is on a child's mind, at *any* age level? There is only one way and that is to observe behavior, including verbal behavior. Piaget diagnoses the stage at which a child, even an infant, is operating by watching or listening carefully to the kinds of errors that are made. One's errors, like one's fantasies, tip the observer off as to what is on one's mind. The way we organize our drawings, the way we play with others, the truths we hold to be self-evident about our universe, our country, our friends, our family, and ourselves are organizing influences on much of our everyday behavior. This is seldom again as apparent as it is during childhood.

The preoperational stage   Piaget suggests that by the end of the early childhood stage the child is well into the so-called preoperational period. During this time the child has considerable command of the language but it is used especially for egocentric and magical ideation, at least from the adult's point of view. If asked how he knows when it is nighttime, for example, a preoperational child may reply that nighttime occurs when he goes to bed. There is a sense in the replies that children of this age believe their actions make things so. Appearances count for everything; a taller glass is thought to have more fluid in it even when that fluid has been poured directly into it from a shorter, squat glass. ◆ Piaget's children must successfully traverse this stage by confrontations with a reality that differs from initial perceptions of it.

◆

Even though the child poured equal amounts of liquid into the different shaped containers, the taller glass "has more."

Where the infant was, in Bruner's terms, iconic toward the end of infancy (meaning that he or she could think of things not physically present) the capacity for *symbolic representation* comes in during early childhood, enabling the child to depict and convey objects and ideas symbolically—through the use of words, and in play. The child can imagine being a train and make the choo-choo noises symbolic of that identity. However, although the preoperational child can acquire symbols or names for objects and events, he or she is not yet able to use them in thinking. The young child who sees two rows of five marbles each, with one row spread out more than the other, is inclined to assume that the longer row contains more marbles.

The concrete operations stage   The child in the concrete operations stage will count the marbles to determine if the two rows contain equal numbers. The child can also manipulate symbols to describe to someone how to get from one place to another, and classify objects by similarities of appearance or function. The child is on the way to mature thought processes and, incidentally, is thinking more and more like a scientist all the time—seeking to explain events and analyzing relationships.

Play behavior   Play activities are in fact important correlates of the various stages of development. Although play activities show interesting relationships to chronological age, the type of play in which the child engages can be taken as "diagnostic" of his or her sophistication of thought and general maturational level. As they get older, children engage in more and more play activities involving other persons and incorporating more complicated toys which can, in the imagination, become related to one another. Indeed, if a child progresses through the early childhood years without showing an increasing interest in playing with other children and merging his or her playthings with those of others, this solitariness or tendency toward isolation is often presumed to be a sign that the older child will have trouble developing satisfactory social relationships.

Socialization

Early childhood is a period in which the child's caretakers move to bring the child into conformity with social standards relating to processes of elimination, sexual displays, and in general, modesty. Modesty and correct toileting sometimes become confused. A great deal of pressure is brought to bear on the young child to suppress both sex-play and excremental activities, at about the same time in development. It is not difficult for the child to develop an association between the two and to act for a time as if the processes are essentially the same. In the extreme, some young children have the idea that

urinating on someone might bring a baby, or that mothers have babies by having a bowel movement. The insistence by society and one's parents on modesty in both areas is the mediating influence; the child senses that the genitalia and excremental processes have parental anxiety in common (Sears, Maccoby, & Levin, 1957).

The growing concern of the child's parents with modesty sets up the conditions for the training of shame. The child is made to feel naughty for misbehavior. This feeling of naughtiness or of shame is thought to be essential for full eventual socialization, which requires that a person be able to "control" his or her own behavior without the parents being nearby at all times. Guilt develops as an internalized sense of distress over having violated social norms (in deed or even in thought). This sense of guilt when misbehavior occurs forestalls misbehavior in the absence of authority figures who control the rewards and punishments in our lives. Shame and guilt, then, represent the internalized parental and social standards. Ultimately, feelings of responsibility (and self-controls) for one's own behavior will emerge based upon these early experiences.

Erikson's stages   The psychosocial stage from the end of infancy to about three years of age relates to self-assertion (Erikson, 1963). The child now moves about with relative ease, a feeling for language and a greater capacity for self-expression are emerging, and increasingly, the child sees himself or herself as capable of controlling things and events (and people) in a way previously unrealized. But each new foray into the world beyond tranquil dependency on mother carries with it some risk, some hurts, and as a consequence, some self-doubt.

The conflict in the later part of early childhood, just prior to the usual start of schooling, is between initiative and guilt. It follows easily from the groundwork laid in the previous stage. During this period the child vies increasingly with the parent for control of his or her own activities and pleasures, and the sparring relationship which emerges at this time especially with the same-sexed parent precipitates further "escape" behaviors, into fantasy and over to one's same-aged peers. In power encounters with adults, the child is usually, of course, likely to be overcome. These feelings of failure and inferiority lend themselves, as has been emphasized by Alfred Adler (1929), to very powerful strivings to surmount the insult to the child's ego. This may lead to an overreaction and result in intense industriousness which Erikson says characterizes the later childhood ages.

Because the late childhood stage is one of especially rapid acquisition of skills, Erikson postulated that the major conflicts of this period relate to pride in one's work, on the one hand, and fear of being inferior, on the other. Team games, usually highly competitive, are characteristically played with great fervor at this time. One's peer group takes on special importance; this affiliation with best friends will become even more important during adolescence.

The peer group becomes a very potent socializing force, for it has power to ostracize and shame its members, as well as to enhance one's feelings of worth (McCandless, 1970). During this time, conflicts with parents often arise, as the child's loyalty to the peer group comes into inevitable conflict with demands and permissions of parents. At the same time, strivings to achieve in special areas of competence are in evidence, as the child seeks simultaneously to gain or retain approval of both peers and family.

Kohlberg's stages of morality   Kohlberg's analysis of moral development indicates that young children behave according to rules of expediency and reciprocity; they behave themselves because they fear punishment or

because they will receive something good in return. By late childhood, a transition has been made to the belief that there is something good about being good (Stage 3 morality). This belief becomes better articulated in the adolescent stage, as we will see later.

Adolescence

It could be seen from the kinds of developments occurring during the late childhood phase that we are working up to something. The pioneer child developmentalist G. Stanley Hall, called the adolescent phase of development the *Sturm und Drang* period. Recent longitudinal studies have shown that adolescence is not necessarily as much a time of "storm and stress" as Hall believed it to be, thus agreeing with a conclusion reached much earlier by anthropologists (such as Margaret Mead and Ruth Benedict) on the basis of cross-cultural research: Adolescence is a time of storm and stress only if society makes it so; if society eases the transition from childhood to adulthood, adolescence is not tumultuous (Muuss, 1962).

Physical development

Adolescence is often considered to begin with *puberty,* the appearance of mature sexual characteristics. In girls this is marked by *menarche,* the onset of menstruation. The average age is about 12½ years, but the normal range is large, from about 8 to 26. About two years before the menarche, the rate of growth in height and weight begins to increase, reaching a peak about a year before the menarche. The peak rate is the most rapid growth in the postnatal period. Because of its timing, this period of rapid growth is sometimes called the preadolescent growth spurt.

In boys there is no striking change analogous to the menarche to mark the beginning of adolescence. However, a growth spurt in height and weight occurs, and its pattern is about the same as in girls except that it is about two years later. Thus, adolescence begins about two years later in boys than in girls.

Like girls, boys vary widely in the age at which puberty begins. However, the "average" early-maturing boy begins puberty at about the average normal age for the beginning of puberty in girls. Similarly, the "average" late-maturing girl begins puberty at about the average normal age for boys. Research shows such individuals have few problems in learning to adjust to the opposite sex. The early-maturing boy has the better time of it, though, because he is also a hero to the normally-maturing boys, while the late-maturing girl is not well accepted by normally-maturing girls. In contrast, the early-maturing girl is too far ahead of her classmates of both sexes, and the late-maturing boy too far behind. Both have adjustment problems.

Adolescence is a period of advancement to adulthood. There is no clear point at which one can say that the adolescent has changed to man or woman. As with all biological phenomena, and most psychological changes, there is a process going on that involves barely perceptible changes from one day to the next. Often parents do not realize how quickly the changes are in fact taking place, however, until someone who has not seen the adolescent for a few months comments on the remarkable growth in height, or the change in voice (in both males and females), or the onset of other visible signs of maturity, some of which are sexual.

Adolescent girls may worry about the size of their breasts—too small or too large, depending on the current fad—and boys about the size of their penis—"too small," usually, but occasionally "too large." Disuse, incidentally, does not cause the penis to atrophy, nor does frequent use make it larger (Katchadourian, 1977).

Cognitive processes

The Formal Operations period, as Piaget labeled the adolescent stage of cognitive development, is one of mature organization of facts and events, with sophisticated manipulation of materials and symbols. The person capable of formal operations views problems from several different vantage points, all without making a move. Problem or conflict resolution goes on largely as a matter of mental manipulation. The image of the expert chess player, quietly conjecturing moves and outcomes several steps ahead of the present position of the game, dealing simultaneously with many different contingencies, is an apt one for the cognitive portrait of the adolescent.

Socialization

Adolescence is the period of the life cycle in which socializing with peers reaches its peak, not only in frequency of contacts but also in number of persons socialized with. Perhaps for this reason it is also sometimes characterized as the peak period for conformity to the peer group—a characterization that is somewhat misleading in that standards learned from the parents during childhood are not abandoned (just set aside in the presence of peers). ●

Erikson's adolescent stage   For Erikson, the major tension to be resolved during the period of adolescence is that having to do with one's identity. It is a time of role confusion as the adolescent seeks to find his or her most comfortable style of behavior, hopefully compatible with peer influences and at the same time acceptable to one's parents. The person who makes the transition successfully will emerge from the role confusion with a personal identity that at once honors the social training of one's childhood and provides the young adult with a sense of selfhood. Successful progression in this area results in being one's own person but at the same time benefiting from one's origins and even endorsing them with pride. Many events become "matters of principle" for the adolescent.

For Freud, adolescence marked emergence from the so-called latency period, which has lasted from about the age of six. During latency, sexual urges are presumably hidden, and the child's energies are diverted to other matters, such as developing skills, developing relationships beyond the family, and so on. In adolescence, which Freud called the genital stage of develop-

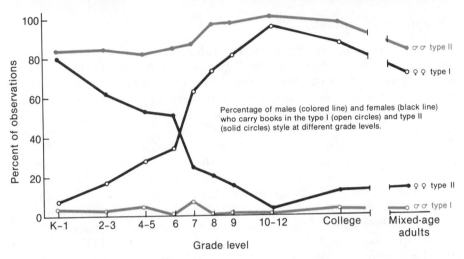

Percentage of males (colored line) and females (black line) who carry books in the type I (open circles) and type II (solid circles) style at different grade levels.

♂♂ type II

♀♀ type I

♀♀ type II

♂♂ type I

Percent of observations

Grade level

K-1 2-3 4-5 6 7 8 9 10-12 College Mixed-age adults

The way we carry our books varies according to sex. Most school-age girls and women clasp books against their chests; males generally hold them at their sides. During the first two years of school, both sexes carry books as older males do. A "sex-typical" carrying style appears before adolescence. These behavioral differences appear to be mainly a result of skeletal differences and social modeling (Jenni & Jenni, 1976). Note that the sex difference in style of carrying books is greatest during high school, perhaps reflecting a peak in conformity to the peer group.

ment, the development of secondary sex characteristics becomes compelling, and sexuality surfaces once again. In the course of becoming acquainted with his or her "new" body, and with a newly emerging self-concept based in part on previous personal history and in part on one's new forays into the world of adults, the intimacy game commences.

Kohlberg's adolescent moral stage   The operative moral principle in adolescence is often that if everyone misbehaved, society would not work; law and order are necessary or we would have chaos and no control over others. Interestingly, it is during this period of adolescence, when so many youngsters in fact have problems in accepting authority (or at least question it closely), that youngsters begin to feel very strongly about the importance of that authority for purposes of defining morality.

Adulthood

Developmental psychologists have disagreed about the age range that should define the stage of young adulthood. The word *adult* is derived from the past participle of the Latin verb *adolescere*, to grow up. Thus, by derivation an adolescent is one who is growing up, an adult is a "grown-up." The problem of definition is that the adult is supposed to be grown up not only with respect to physical characteristics, but also with respect to psychological characteristics. He or she is supposed to be mature physically and psychologically. Physical maturity is difficult to measure, and psychological maturity is difficult even to define, especially because some psychological processes continue to improve until very old age. Because of the difficulty of measuring physical and psychological maturity, many developmentalists have by-passed the problem, and adopted a definition based only on age level.

Young adulthood

In Chapter 8 we defined early adulthood as extending from maturity to about the age of 45 years. Other developmentalists have defined it as extending from 18 to 35 years of age (Havighurst, 1973), 20 to 40 (Erikson, 1963), and 25 to 45 or 50 (Buhler, 1962). There is nevertheless good agreement about the major life crises or developmental tasks of the general age period.

Developmental tasks

The period of young adulthood begins with the completion of formal schooling and entry into the job and marriage market. For married parents it ends with departure of the children; for others the end is related to psychologically meaningful events which reveal they are no longer "promising" youngsters.

Erikson identified the crisis of this period as *intimacy vs. isolation.* A major developmental task is the development of intimacy, especially with the opposite sex. During adolescence, the biology of sex is of more concern and interest than are interpersonal affection and intimacy (McCandless, 1970). During early adulthood, however, a failure to establish intimacy leads to isolation and stifles further psychological growth (Erikson, 1963).

Other tasks of early adulthood are to establish and maintain a home and family; to enter and maintain a career; to become part of a congenial social group; and to discharge the obligations of citizenship (Troll, 1975).

These general tasks are obviously not solvable by any single behavioral change, but rather require many adjustments in many behaviors. Resolution, in other words, requires adaptation to "large numbers of detailed *task-lets*" (Havighurst, 1973, p. 10), which can be grouped in various ways. An example is the general task of establishing and maintaining a family. To accomplish this task, one must normally have a mate, which requires not only selecting a mate but also securing a mate. One must also learn to live with a mate, produce and rear children (the average is still more than one per family), obtain and manage a home, etc.

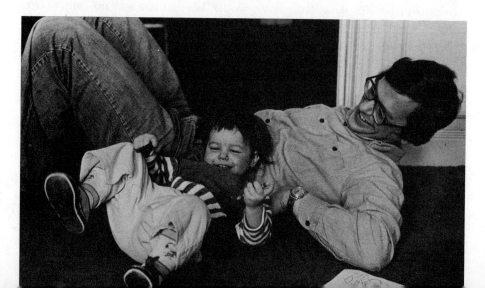

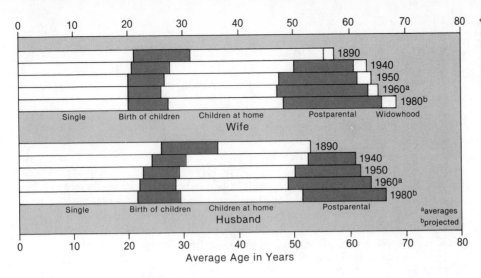

Average age of
husband and wife at
critical stages of the
family cycle

Although the training one receives from casual to serious dating in adolescence, babysitting, and doing household chores is better than nothing (Ahammer, 1973, refers to it as "anticipatory socialization"), little direct training is provided in American culture, less for males than females (Albright & Gift, 1975).

Between 1890 and 1960, both men and women married at steadily younger ages (on the average); they also began to have children sooner. Evidence obtained in 1972 indicates that the average age at first marriage had increased for both men and women (Troll, 1975), reversing the trend indicated in the figure. A trend that has continued, however, is for women to marry younger than men. One consequence is that women become widows, on the average, at younger ages than men become widowers.

Social issues

Although many young adults remain in Kohlberg's Stage 4, the "law and order" stage of moral development, some progress to Stage 5, in which morality is motivated not by external authority and convention but by social contract and respect for the rights of others. One could characterize at least the higher-minded protesters of the late 1960s and early 1970s as reflecting Stage 5 morality. (See *P&L* Close-up, Morality and Social Activism.)

Cognitive adaptation

Cognitively, we left the adolescent lost in thought in Piaget's period of formal operations, viewing life and its tasks as one might view a chess game. Actually, this picture reflects our oversimplifying Piaget's theory in order to describe it more easily. Piaget actually assumes that in each stage of cognitive development the ways of thinking that characterized earlier stages are not lost but rather remain available, in "higher" form, for application in suitable circumstances. In the most mature level of cognitive development, attained in early adulthood, the various cognitive structures are used appropriately and efficiently. A scientist, for example, might use formal operations for work on a theoretical problem, concrete operations for everyday business transactions, preoperational thinking for artistic endeavors, and sensorimotor processes for intimate personal interactions (Riegel, 1973). In this last case, the sensorimotor actions and pleasures will be adult and not like those of the infant.

"While one may be grateful that feelings of personal alienation have apparently decreased since the late 1960s, one may also express regret that despite its understandability, some of the best aspects (as opposed to some of the more unrealistic and destructive aspects) of the activism of the 1960s—its idealism and active concern for other individuals and for the world in which we live—seem to have been attenuated in the process. In the election of November 1974, participation of the 12 million eighteen- to twenty-year-olds was only 21 percent, the lowest for any eligible age group.

"While the solutions to our problems advocated in the late 1960s by both radical activists and the "flower children" were too often naive, self-indulgent, personally destructive, internally inconsistent, and ultimately unworkable, the deficiencies in our society that they identified—the need for greater intimacy and more love; for a lesser emphasis on ruthless competition, status-seeking, and "role-playing games"; for greater self-awareness, honesty, and freedom to be oneself; for resistance to coercion and corruptive authority—all remain pressing challenges today" (Conger, 1976, p. 21).

The mature years

According to a popular stereotype, the accumulated experience of the elderly makes them wise and valued advisers. However, research has shown that in fact the most highly valued adviser is the middle-aged person in the range from 35 to 55 years of age. Even the old prefer the advice of the middle-aged.

According to another stereotype, a major crisis occurs in middle age, the "mid-life crisis." However, psychologists have not been able to agree when it occurs, some arguing for the 20s, some for the 60s, and others for every age in between. Furthermore, they disagree about the nature of this crisis. One might suspect, then, that the concept lacks a firm basis of facts. Supporting this suspicion, a recent study showed that middle age is actually the best period of adulthood. Feelings of alienation, powerlessness, meaninglessness, and disengagement were most prevalent in young adulthood and least prevalent in middle age. The elderly group in the study was intermediate.

Nevertheless, middle age is not free of crises. Physiological and psychological crises occur, and must be met in a satisfactory way if stagnation is to be avoided. We begin with a physiological crisis that confronts middle-aged women, the menopause.

The menopause

The word *menopause* is derived from the Greek *menos*, month, and *paueis*, to cause to cease. It refers to an abrupt period of time in which physiological changes in women result in natural termination of menstruation and the menstrual cycle. During the menopause, women sometimes experience "hot flashes," and many women report that the period is unpleasant. It signals the end of fertility, but it is not viewed by middle-aged women as a heavy crisis; only 4 percent checked "the menopause" in a question on the worst thing about middle age, and most women who are postmenopausal feel positively about it (Troll, 1975).

In a study done in Israel, more than a thousand women from a range of cultures were interviewed. In the traditional culture of the region, fertility was uncontrolled ("fertility" is used here in its technical sense of "birth rate"); and in the modern, European culture of the region, fertility was controlled. In the traditional group, the typical woman never menstruated. She became pregnant at the first ovulation, and from then until the menopause she was either pregnant or nursing a baby. The typical traditional woman was pregnant 25 times during this period. About 20 of the pregnancies went to full term, but only 15 ended with the birth of a live baby. Of the 15 babies born alive, 10 survived through childhood. In contrast, the typical modern woman raised only a child or two, using contraception as the standard method of control, but using abortion when contraception failed.

Both groups were positive about the loss of fertility associated with the menopause. In fact, independently of their history of fertility, they were equally positive about this aspect of the menopause, although for different reasons. For the women with a history of controlled fertility, the positive attitude reflected no further need for the bothers of contraception (or abortion), while for the traditional women, it ended the long succession of pregnancies (Datan, Antonovsky, & Maoz, 1978).

Men undergo no critical stage like menopause, and may remain fertile throughout middle and old age. Physiological changes occur, however, and affect sexual functioning. Sexual activity usually drops in frequency in middle and old age, but it still occurs even in old age, in spite of the stereotype of old age as sexless (except for "dirty old men"). The physiological changes in men gradually lengthen the time needed to get an erection, and reduce the strength of ejaculation and intensity of the orgasm. In women, the physiological changes increase the time required for arousal and lubrication, but do not affect the intensity of the orgasm (Weg, 1975).

Psychological crises

The psychosocial crisis of middle age, according to Erikson, is *generativity vs. self-absorption*. The problem is to progress from physical generativity, involving the production and rearing of one's own children, to social and psychological generativity, involving not only the present but also future generations. The individual's legacy becomes not merely the contribution to the gene pool of the species, but also a contribution to knowledge. Conversely, the self-absorbed individual retains a materialistic concern for the here and now, with an emphasis on physical and psychological well-being.

The career In 1870 the average work career ran from the age of 14, when the worker entered the labor force, to the age of 61, when the average worker died after having worked a total of 146,640 hours for a total of $90,000 (1970 dollars). In 1970 the average career ran from about age 20 to about age 65, when the average worker retired after having worked a total of 90,000 hours for a total of $360,000. The average college graduate enters the work force later, at 22 to 25, and consequently works fewer total hours, but the lifetime earnings are greater than the average worker's, totaling about $550,000 (Miernyk, 1975). College graduates are also likely to be more satisfied with their job, although in a recent survey 90 percent of all workers reported satisfaction with their job (but more whites than nonwhites were satisfied) (Troll, 1975).

These statistics do not indicate two middle-age crises associated with occupation. One is the financial strain of supporting adolescent children, especially if they are in college or they married young and require financial assistance. The average first child is born when the husband is 22 or 23 years old, and the last child when he is 28 or 29. Therefore, the husband will be supporting adolescent children and maybe college students as he begins middle age.

At that age, he is likely to be employed, but if he loses his job new employment is harder to find than when he was younger. Furthermore, even if he stays employed, the extra financial burdens and high economic inflation may force a reduction in the standard of living. Recently the problem is being avoided by the wife's reentering the labor force, but unless she has specialized training, a well-paying job will be hard to find.

The other middle-age crisis associated with occupation is that it is during this stage that people normally face the discrepancy between their early ambitions and their actual accomplishments. The discrepancy is likely to be a disappointment unless the ambitions were modest or the individuals have been fortunate. This crisis usually affects the husband more directly than the wife, but it can have an immense indirect effect on her. The crisis appears at about the same time as the crisis of the *empty nest*—the departure of the last child from the home—which affects particularly the wife. She may be unable to turn to her husband for help in dealing with the empty-nest crisis, because he is preoccupied with his own crisis of adjusting to the limits on his career and the implied limits on his abilities. Especially if the wife has learned only the traditional view of woman's role in society—wife and mother—the departure of the last child will be a crisis. For such a woman one of the main purposes in life has ended, bringing about a sudden "retirement" that was unwanted and largely unanticipated.

Perhaps the most disturbing thing about the empty nest, however, is that it is a sign that youth has gone. This sign, together with the evidence confronted in the mirror and the menopause, which occurs at about the same time as the empty nest, make the loss of youth impossible to deny. Given the worship of youthfulness in our society, especially youthfulness in women, the effect is a real crisis. Of little comfort to the present generation, the declining birth rate and increasing longevity have combined to increase the average age of Americans to 29 years. If the trends continue, our ideal may also mature.

Kohlberg's mature morality   At maturity, morality is derived from principle rather than convention, hence it is identified as "postconventional." At Stage 5, the first stage of the postconventional level, the guiding principle is to maintain community welfare. The Stage 5 individual values community welfare because of respect for the rights of others, not because the law demands it. The morality of a Stage 6 individual is based on principles of wider scope than those of the Stage 5 person; Stage 6 morality refers to principles that have universal applicability, such as "Stealing to protect a human life is justified, because a human life is more valuable than material property."

The elders

One widely accepted definition puts the beginning of old age at retirement at the age of 65 years. In the research literature, however, the group designated as "old" often ranges down to 60 or even 55 years of age. Furthermore, with the recent federal regulations against job discrimination based on age, retirement will occur at a wide range of ages averaging more than 65. Clearly, like most of the other periods of the life cycle, old age has an arbitrary point of onset. Nevertheless, society considers old age to be a distinct period, and has stereotyped beliefs about how persons behave in these periods.

One stereotype is that of the elder statesman, the repository of tribal lore and accumulated wisdom at whose feet the young sit for counsel and instruction. Another stereotype has the elders enjoying the leisure made possible by a comfortable retirement pension, pursuing long-postponed but loved avocations — reading great literature, or *writing* it, painting, building, gardening, traveling. ■ A third stereotype refers to the serenity of old age; the elderly contemplate a life well spent and face the inevitability of their own death with equanimity.

The reality does not always agree with the ideal. The old may prattle and preach ("When I was young, we didn't have it so good . . . .") rather than teach, especially because their failing memory makes their testimony unreliable.

Retirement frequently brings on an economic crisis that leaves little money for luxuries and travel, and often leaves little room for necessities. Furthermore, failing eyesight, arthritis, and other health problems often accompany old age, curtailing activity and promoting isolation by restricting mobility. Instead of serenely contemplating the past and future, the old may be continually frustrated by tip-of-the-tongue forgetting of the past, and their ill health may make them despondent about their future.

Reality contradicts the positive stereotypes so often that they cannot be accepted as the norms of old age. However, the positive stereotypes are ac-

Grow old along with me!
The best is yet to be,
The last of life, for which
the first was made.
Robert Browning
Rabbi Ben Ezra

■
The elder statesman holds the rapt attention due the ideal patriarch. In the other photo the ideal retiree, with time now to pursue his hobby, also shows a continuing sense of humor.

tualized in enough elderly persons to warn us against acceptance of the analogous negative stereotypes. Rather than stereotypes, we need the facts about aging.

Cognitive ability

Old age is a time in which some cognitive powers wane, although others do not, at least not until a few years before death. Let's examine what is known about memory and intelligence of the elderly.

Memory   It is well known that old people have memory problems. They do not remember recent events well, but they remember events from long ago and relish telling them—again and again—because they do not remember having told the same story yesterday.

Although this is common knowledge, it is not entirely correct. For example, an old person can recall a series of numbers as well as a younger person—provided the series is not too long, provided enough time is allowed for study, and provided no interfering material is presented between the study time and the test time. In short, if you do not hurry them or interfere with them, old people can remember a telephone number as well as anybody. They are less successful, even when allowed time to study, at other kinds of tasks used to study memory in the experimental laboratory, including paired-associate learning and serial and free recall of word lists.

But, why should they use their memory to perform such tasks? In the real world, if a person needs to remember a list of words—a list of items to be purchased, for example—the usual technique is to write out the list and consult it when recall is required—at the grocery store or wherever. Psychologists have conducted hundreds—perhaps thousands—of studies of short-term memory, but apparently they have never allowed subjects to do what most of us do in the real world—make a list of the items to be remembered and read them off when recall is required.

The same is true of studies of long-term rote memory, even though this type of memory is probably almost never required once a person has finished school. Once the years of formal schooling are over, test-taking days are largely past. An occasional test will need to be taken, for driver's license renewal, for example, but by and large the need for long-term rote memory is reduced to zero in day-to-day adult life. People do not get much practice, if any, with the memory skills of bygone school years, and by the time they are old they can expect to be unable to use the old skills efficiently, and may be unable to use them at all.

With instruction and practice, however, the elderly can recover the required skills and perform as well as the younger person, except in those few cases in which the memory loss has a physical cause (see Walsh, 1975). In addition, however, even when the old have stored material in memory effectively, they often have trouble retrieving it from memory (Hultsch, 1975). Again, though, the problem seems to be in the use of inefficient strategies, search strategies in this case, rather than a lack of capacity or ability.

Intelligence   Neugarten (1976) has summarized the known facts about aging and intelligence as follows:

a. Speed of responding declines with age. One consequence is that the elderly will perform especially poorly when the test is given under speeded conditions.

b. Chronological age is not a good predictor of performance.

c. Old people who remain physically and mentally active perform better than those who become inactive.

d. Educational level predicts performance in old age; the higher the educational attainment, the better the performance.

e. Intellectual decline seems to be inversely related to longevity; the less bright die younger.

f. Intellectual decline is greater in old men than in old women.

For many years, one of the best-established findings in developmental psychology was that intelligence declines in old age. It is now known, however, that this "finding" is partly false. The data were obtained in cross-sectional research, and apparently reflected differences between birth cohorts to a large extent, because the finding has not been entirely confirmed in research with longitudinal or sequential designs (see Chapter 8, pp. 222–224).

Another problem is that the finding was based on a conception of "intelligence" that most developmental psychologists now reject. Specifically, the finding was from studies in which a single global IQ score was the only measure of a person's intelligence. It is now known that intelligence is not a single unitary trait, but rather consists of several distinct and relatively independent skills or abilities, such as verbal fluency and numerical ability. The fact that these abilities are relatively independent suggests that they should not be lumped together into one global score. Another reason not to combine them is that they seem to depend to different degrees on heredity. Finally, and of most importance to developmental psychologists, different abilities exhibit different patterns of change through the life span.

The various intellectual abilities can be divided into groups. One grouping distinguishes between "crystallized" and "fluid" abilities (Horn, 1970). Crystallized abilities are determined largely by learning from the culture, and fluid abilities are determined largely by maturation, or physiological factors. For example, vocabulary, mechanical knowledge, and formal reasoning are crystallized abilities. Only training—even if informal—can teach a person a vocabulary, instill knowledge about machinery, and teach the rules of logic. Examples of fluid abilities are inductive reasoning, intellectual speed, and memory span.

Fluid abilities should change with changes in physiological characteristics of the person. Since marked physiological changes occur in old age, marked changes in fluid abilities should also occur. In contrast, crystallized intelligence should tend to be maintained, in spite of the mutual withdrawal of the elderly person and society, because contact with the culture is only reduced, not eliminated. The best estimates presently available support these predictions, in that crystallized abilities seem to be maintained during old age or even to increase, while fluid abilities decline. Thus, the "well-established finding" is now considered to be only partly correct for the individual. It is true that some intellectual abilities decline in old age—and more markedly than had been believed—but others are maintained until "terminal drop" begins.

There is good evidence that "individuals who show a notable change in any one of a variety of measures of cognitive performance are more likely to be dead within a few years [less than five] than are those who show no particular change" (Kalish, 1975, p. 41). This phenomenon is called *terminal drop* (Riegel & Riegel, 1972), and is said to be a more accurate predictor of approaching death than medical assessments are. However, the phenomenon is not well understood; its causes have not yet been identified.

Physical and social concerns

Activity may be sharply curtailed in the old person, because of inadequate motivation, poor health, insufficient funds, or, simply, despair.

Retirement   Early retirement is being encouraged through special-incentive programs in many businesses, universities and in the federal government, and many employees are choosing early retirement. However, the population that is now at or near retirement age has been poorly socialized for retirement. During their youth, these people learned that success is measured by productivity and economic gain—the American "work ethic." Therefore, they are not prepared to enjoy leisure (Birren & Woodruff, 1973). The result is that many who retire are unhappy, and many who could retire choose to continue working. Retirement is seen as a kind of punishment, with consequent loss of self-esteem which sometimes results in suicide. During adulthood and old age, the suicide rate remains fairly level, at around 5 to 15 per 100,000 persons, *except in white males,* for whom the rate increases throughout adulthood and is greatest in old age (Troll, 1975).

Retirement can be successful, however. In one study of automobile workers who retired early or at the usual age, satisfaction with retirement was greater when: (1) they had planned the retirement, (2) their health was good, (3) their standard of living was at least as good as before retirement, (4) their income was high, (5) they were well educated, and (6) the company had a preretirement program. The picture is complicated because some persons carry over their work-related tasks into retirement, and some workers see the leisure after retirement as their just reward. Finally, "it seems entirely possible that, given sufficient income and transportation, the elderly who are in good health would willingly make use of whatever sources of leisure entertainment were available without longing for work" (Kalish, 1975, p. 115). Retirement then is a task for the society as well as for elderly persons. ■

Disengagement   As people get older, they tend to withdraw gradually from society, and at the same time society tends to withdraw from them. This progressive, mutual withdrawal is called *disengagement*. Because of disengagement, old people are less interested in having social contacts, and have fewer social contacts, with less emotional involvement in them. Viewed positively, disengagement permits the old person to enjoy a more leisurely way of life,

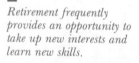

Retirement frequently provides an opportunity to take up new interests and learn new skills.

but working against this positive aspect of disengagement is the work ethic that requires activity, including social activity, to maintain a sense of self-worth (Kalish, 1975).

Failing health   Old age is a time of failing health. Over half the elderly have lost their teeth; over half have problems with vision; about half have chronic health problems that limit their activities; and over a fourth have problems with hearing (Kalish, 1975). In addition, serious conditions such as arthritis, rheumatism, high blood pressure, and heart disease are more prevalent, and seven out of eight old people have chronic conditions of some kind (Bengtson & Haber, 1975). On top of all this, their incomes are lower and their health costs are higher than at younger ages.

Dependency   Poverty is not common in old age, but it is far from rare, especially among nonwhite old people. In 1973, about one out of seven (14.4 percent) old whites were below the low-income level used to define poverty, while more than one-third (35.5 percent) of old nonwhites were poor.

Although most old people do not live in poverty, most live below standard. Given their health problems, furthermore, they live further below standard than their dollar incomes would suggest (Bengtson & Haber, 1975). Another reason to question the value of the poverty index, or any index based on number of dollars of income, is that they are not satisfactory indexes of the *relative* quality of life. They are based on adequacy of income without taking into consideration preretirement income (see Walther, 1975). A person whose pension income is substantially below the preretirement income must suffer a substantial reduction in standard of living without additional funds.

Economic dependency can be generated by other kinds of dependency that appear in old age, including physical and mental dependency. Physical dependency results from illness or injury, which can require a nurse or housekeeper and in effect reduce the pension income usable by the old person to the poverty line. Mental dependency can result from loss of memory, orientation, or judgment, which in turn may result from physical illness or injury, especially brain disease or injury. If severe enough, the person needs a nurse or housekeeper, again reducing usable pension income.

Physical and mental dependency are dealt with in different ways, depending on the resources available. If income is sufficient, the old person may continue to live "independently" in his or her own home. Often, however, monetary resources are too low, and the old person moves in with relatives, usually one of his or her children. If this resource is unavailable, because no child is willing or able to take in the aged and ailing parent, then the only recourse is institutionalization. Only a very small proportion of the aged population is institutionalized, however, amounting in 1970 to about 4 percent of white men, 6 percent of white women, and 3 percent of black men and women.

Loss of spouse   During the early years of life, loss of spouse is certainly not a normally encountered crisis. After adolescence, however, it becomes increasingly common with increasing age. During the early years of adulthood, divorce causes loss of a spouse much more often than death does. Incidentally, the crisis of losing a spouse is more likely to have a gradual onset in the early adult years than a sudden onset, because during these years divorce — the more usual cause of losing a spouse — is likely to result from a gradual buildup of tensions, while death — the less common cause of losing a spouse — is likely to have a sudden onset. The most common cause of death in early adulthood, as in adolescence, is accident.

In old age, in contrast, the usual cause of losing a spouse is death, and the death is likely to be gradual in onset. Consequently, in principle an old person should have time to prepare for the crisis of losing a spouse, who has become ill. In practice, it turns out that the warning signs are seldom heeded; after all, as pointed out earlier, we are not given the kinds of training—socialization—that would prepare us to meet normal life crises. Consequently, loss of a spouse in old age may be as psychologically sudden in onset as in early adulthood, in effect.

Loss of a spouse through death is relatively uncommon before middle age, but becomes increasingly more common after old age begins. An old person without a mate is much more likely to be a woman than to be a man. This fact has several important implications for old people, but before commenting on these implications, we might mention some of the causes of the sex difference.

First, wives tend to be younger than their husbands, by an average of two or three years (Troll, 1975), and thus would naturally be expected to outlive them. Second, women have a longer life expectancy than men all over the world. Finally, elderly widowers are more likely to remarry than elderly widows. Widowers have more to gain from remarrying than widows because husbands often depend entirely on their wives for meals, housekeeping, and homemaking, hence their lives are disrupted in major ways by loss of their spouse (Lopata, 1975). In addition, wives often are responsible for maintaining contact with relatives, hence the widower loses contact with them. Finally, husbands do not expect to outlive their wives, hence are not psychologically prepared—socialized—for the loss (Treas, 1975).

Loneliness   The feeling of loneliness pervades old age, even for old persons still living with their spouses. It is especially prevalent among women, and among women especially among widows (Lopata, 1975). In fact, loneliness is the major difficulty faced by widows (Treas, 1975). Among the other consequences of loneliness is reduced appetite, which could result in malnutrition (Weg, 1975); but the one inevitable consequence of loneliness is reduced satisfaction with life. The quality of life cannot be satisfactory if one is ridden with loneliness, social isolation, and bitterness.

Integrity vs. despair   In Erikson's eighth and final stage of psychosocial development, the crisis revolves around the meaning of life, life in general, and one's own life in particular. Unsuccessful resolution is associated with a feeling of despair. The life was wasted, and too little time is left to pick up the pieces; all that remains is frustration and hopelessness. In contrast, a sense of integrity comes with successful resolution, integrity in its meaning of honesty and soundness of moral principle and also in its meaning of wholeness or oneness, integration of self and cosmos. Persons who attain this sense of integrity should also attain Kohlberg's Stage 6 of morality, and some perhaps even Stage 7, in which morality is postconventional, based on principles that are universal (Stage 6) or cosmic (Stage 7) in scope.

The cycle ends

Other things equal, the death of an old person disturbs us less than the death of a young person, apparently because early death is considered somehow unfair (Kastenbaum, 1975; Roth, 1977). The word *death* refers to both an event—dying—and the result of this event. It is difficult to distinguish between clinical death and biological death. Clinical death is defined by the absence of vital signs, but after the disappearance of vital signs some biological structures continue to function for an appreciable length of time, and different structures continue to "live" for different lengths of time (as we saw in Chapter 10 with the case of Karen Ann Quinlan). Biological death varies, in other words, for different structures in the body. Brain cells are among the first to die when oxygen in the blood is depleted, either because the blood is not oxygenated (as in drowning) or because the blood is not circulated (as in heart failure). Presumably, the mind ceases to function when the brain cells die, although this presumption is challenged in some religions.

Life expectancy

The first table shows variations in life expectancy around the world. ● Life expectancies are longer in Europe than anywhere else. Consequently, a larger percentage of the population of Europe is old than anywhere else. It has been estimated that the average life expectancy in 1000 B.C. was eighteen years. The first row in the second table shows changes in life expectancy in the United States in the twentieth century. ▲ Note that in the twenty-nine centuries between 1000 B.C. and 1900, life expectancy increased by almost thirty years, and in the seventy years between 1900 and 1970 it increased almost another twenty-four years. These striking increases are misleading, however, because the averages reflect to a very large extent reductions in infant mortality. The figures we have been discussing—the ones in the first row of the second section—are life expectancies at birth. The second row of this table shows the life expectancies at the age of sixty-five years. It can be seen that in 1970, the average sixty-five-year-old could expect to live about fifteen more years, to the age of about eighty—nine years longer than the average life expectancy of the newborn infant. That is, when you were born you could expect to live seventy-one years, and as you grew older and survived longer, you could expect to live longer. (See *P&L* Close-up, Life Expectancy: How Long Is Long?)

From too much love of living,
From hope and fear set free,
We thank with brief thanks giving
Whatever gods may be
That no life lives forever;
That dead men rise up never;
That even the weariest river
Winds somewhere safe to sea.
Swinburne
The Garden of Proserpine

Death

The process of dying may normally go through a sequence of stages. According to Kübler-Ross (1969), if death is not too sudden and if the dying person is aware of what is happening, dying progresses through five stages: *denial,*

●

Life expectancy at birth and population over age 65 in various countries

Country	Life Expectancy at Birth		Population Age 65 and over (Percent)	Country	Life Expectancy at Birth		Population Age 65 and over (Percent)
	Male	Female			Male	Female	
North America				Europe			
United States	67	75	9.9	Austria	66.6	73.7	14.2
Canada	68.8	75.2	8.1	Denmark	70.8	75.7	12.1
Mexico	61.0	63.7	3.7	France	68.6	76.1	13.4
South America				Hungary	66.3	72.0	11.4
Argentina	64.1	70.2	7.5	Netherlands	71.0	76.7	10.3
Asia				Sweden	71.7	76.5	13.7
Japan	69.1	74.3	7.1	United Kingdom	68.8	75.1	13.1
USSR	65.0	74.0	11.8	Africa			
				Kenya	46.9	51.2	3.6

Demographic Yearbook 1975, United Nations

▲

Average life expectancy at birth and at age 65 in the United States: 1900–1970

Age	1900	1939	1949	1955	1959	1970
At birth	47.3	63.7	68.0	69.6	69.9	70.9
At age 65	11.9	12.8	12.8	14.2	14.4	15.2

U.S. Public Health Service, 1974

anger, bargaining, depression, and *acceptance.* In the first stage, the person denies that death is impending. In the second stage, the person is typically struggling with the question "Why me?" "Frustration builds and anger overflows as the question resists satisfactory answer" (Kastenbaum, 1975). In the third stage, the person tries to postpone death by making a bargain with God, the doctors, or others. In the fourth stage, the person can no longer deny that he or she is dying, and anger is replaced by depression, a sense of great loss perhaps coupled with guilt and a feeling of unworthiness. Finally, in the fifth stage the person accepts the approach of death. However, "acceptance should not be mistaken for a happy stage. It is almost void of feelings. It is as if the pain had gone, the struggle is over, and there comes a time for 'the final rest before the long journey' as one patient phrased it" (Kübler-Ross, 1969, p. 100). A person may not get to the last stage, may be in more than one stage at once, and may slip back and forth between stages. Furthermore, persons vary in the speed of progress through the stages (Kastenbaum, 1975).

The stage theory of dying was developed by psychiatrist Elizabeth Kübler-Ross from interviews with a large number of terminally ill persons. However, her methods of collecting and interpreting the data have been questioned, and she has been criticized for failing to consider such demographic variables as nature of the disease, sex of the patient, race, developmental level, and cognitive style (Kastenbaum, 1975). Thus, the usefulness and generality of the theory are questionable. However, her research has forced others to be concerned with the psychology of dying.

Regarding the question of whether death is a life crisis, one noted authority concluded that it is not invariably a crisis for an individual person. "There are people among us who seldom give thought to death. Some of these people come to death before death has come to mind—accidents, foul play, sudden traumas of various kinds. A crisis was neither anticipated nor experienced in such instances. Others among us do think of death, but minus the doomsday visions. There are people who seem to view personal annihilation with equanimity, and others who are serene because, for them, death does not represent annihilation. Still others feel sorely troubled with the life they are experiencing, and death is seen as the solution rather than the problem" (Kastenbaum, 1975, p. 48).

Chapter summary

Our entire lives are characterized by change and growth, and the facing of a series of *developmental tasks.*

The prenatal period begins at conception and ends at full-term birth nine months later. During this period, the death rate is considerably greater for males than for females, especially during the first three months, which are particularly critical for normal development. Maternal medications and dis-

"There are groups of mountain people in the Soviet Union, India and Ecuador who claim to live very long lives. Some people say they're 125 years old and going strong.

"Robert R. Kohn, professor of pathology at Case Western University, says the claims aren't true.

"'They have every reason to claim old age—economic reasons, status reasons—and there are no records to back up the claims,' says Kohn.

"While in the Soviet Union for a scientific meeting, Kohn found another reason: The old people in Georgia have become such a tourist attraction that he was offered the opportunity to see them for the sum of 50 American dollars.

"'There's no doubt these people are old and healthy and they would be worth studying, but when you read about Ivan who's 146 years old and his mother's mad at him, don't believe it.'

"The maximum length of human life probably hasn't increased much since the Stone Age, Kohn said. Modern medicine, improved sanitation and better nutrition have enabled many more people to live from birth to ten years of age, but have done little to add anything to the life span of older people.

"'Life expectancy at 65 has been affected very little by progress. Maybe it's gone up a year or two in the last 80 years,' he said" (From "Adult's Life: No Longer Now Than Stone Age Man's Life" in *Spectator*, March 1978. Reprinted by permission of the University of Iowa Press).

Although not relevant to the issues under consideration here, it is worthwhile to point out two places where the article skirts dangerously close to the misuse of statistics. First, while the *maximum* length of human life has perhaps not changed much since the Stone Age, as asserted, the *average* length of human life has probably increased enormously. It increased by 50 percent in the present century alone. Second, life expectancy at 65 has actually gone up more than "a year or two" in the last 80 years; it has gone up about 3.3 years, which gains in impressiveness when you consider that this is a 28 percent increase over the life expectancy of 11.9 years at age 65 in 1900.

This great-grandfather in Soviet Georgia gives his age as 117; the woman above still tends her own garden at 99.

eases that occur during that time can have devastating effects on fetal development, yet have relatively little effect if they occur later. Some drugs and diseases, however, have marked untoward effects when they occur anytime in the fetal period, and even some medications given during delivery can have effects that persist in the baby for months following birth.

At first, the infant is an entirely reflexive individual, responding helplessly and without will to environmental stimulation. Learning proceeds quickly, however, and the baby gains more and more control over its own actions and, thereby, the actions of others. The reflexes become integrated and organized into complex patterns of voluntary behavior and, by the end of the period, the infant is capable of forming internal representations of significant events. The baby is selfish, and wants its needs satisfied now; from the infant's view a "good" parent complies, a "bad" parent frustrates. The good parent instills a sense of trust in the infant, an optimistic, though at this point primitive, belief in the predictability of people and the environment.

During childhood, the primitive cognitive powers of the infant develop into thought processes that are completely adult in the sense that they are the typical adult processes, although some further development is required to attain the fully mature formal operations of thought. In Piaget's theory, the progression is from the reflexive sensorimotor adaptations of the infant, through the preoperational intelligence of the young child, to the concrete mentality of the older child. The psychosocial conflicts of childhood are autonomy vs. doubt (age 2–3 years), initiative vs. guilt (4–5), and industry vs. inferiority (6–11). These conflicts occur in the stages Freud identified, respectively, as *anal, phallic,* and *latency.* Morality also exhibits marked changes during this period, progressing from the purely hedonic premoral state of the infant through the expedient, pragmatic morality of the young child to the conventional, "law and order" morality of the older child.

Puberty begins with, or shortly after, a great increase in growth rate, occurring about two years earlier in girls than in boys. The development of self-identity and postconventional or principled morality are tasks of adolescence, which may be a time of storm and stress unless society eases this transition to adulthood, in part perhaps by adopting a permissive attitude toward the adolescent's strong drive for conformity to the peer group. The highest form of thinking—Piaget's formal operations—first appears in adolescence.

The young adult must establish intimacy with the opposite sex, as a foundation for successful establishment and maintenance of a family, which itself involves a number of "task-lets." Cognitively, the young adult is able to function comfortably, efficiently, and appropriately at various levels of thought and action, as the situation at hand requires. Some young adults who had not progressed beyond conventional morality as adolescents do so now, attaining a postconventional morality based on social contract rather than law, on moral rather than legal principles.

In the mature years, the menopause creates a major crisis for women, perhaps because it is an undeniable sign that youth is gone. It often coincides with the "empty nest"—the departure of the last child—which is also a major crisis especially for women with traditional sex-role attitudes. At about the same time, the breadwinners (regardless of gender) may be facing a financial crisis precipitated by the costs of educating or otherwise assisting their children, who will likely be newly married and perhaps also in college. Often, men must also at this time face up to personal limitations and admit that their youthful ambitions have been defeated. Successful resolution of these crises, and others, yields generativity; unsuccessful resolution yields materialistic self-absorption. Success is likely to be associated with the attainment of postconventional morality based on universal or even cosmic principles.

The elderly suffer memory losses, but with special training can overcome the deficit except when it results from brain disease. "Crystallized" intelligence, consisting of abilities and knowledge acquired through acculturation, is maintained through most of old age; but "fluid" abilities, which depend more on physiological structures, decline. Both types decline in the period of "terminal drop," beginning a few years before death from natural causes. Low income and poor health, coupled with disengagement, result in sharp curtailments in recreation and other activity—to the old person, it costs too much, it requires too much energy, and it is not interesting anyway.

The average life expectancy has been increasing steadily, and is now about seventy-one years. It is longer, however, for women than for men. In the process of dying, a person may go through five stages: *denial, anger, bargaining, depression,* and *acceptance.* For some, however, death is not seen as a crisis, but rather is faced with serenity.

Part Four

Biological Foundations
of Behavior

10 Elements of the Nervous System

Studying the nervous system
> The field of physiological psychology
> The human nervous system

Neurons: The stuff that brains are made of
> Functions of a neuron: A reflex arc
> How neurons work

Synaptic transmission
> Varieties of chemical transmission
> Are neurons decision makers or obedient servants?
> Spontaneously active neurons
> Chemicals that shape mind and body

Chapter summary

By the time we become high-school seniors most of us have stopped growing. Typically, the spurts of growth in height, weight, and strength that start at puberty are over when we reach seventeen or so. But Keith was not typical—at least not after he entered his senior year. Before then, he was big enough to make the school football team, but he was second string. "Not enough drive," "too easy going," "lets people push him around," "too good-natured," were frequent comments about him. Keith's girlfriend liked his gentle manner, but he seemed slow in getting turned on to her charms.

It was at the first fall football practice when it all started, or more accurately, when the first changes in Keith were noticed. On an end sweep coming his way, Keith smashed through the pulling guard and nailed the high-stepping halfback for a big loss. The halfback for the white shirts had to be carried off the field on a stretcher. Later, a fight broke out between Keith and the center for the white shirts who had been needling and cursing him for playing dirty. Keith knocked him out with a solid right hook. "Hey, what's gotten into Keith?" everyone was wondering. "Who cares?" was the coach's reaction. "The man is varsity material; he's got what it takes."

At team table after dinner some of the guys were horsing around and tripped Billy, the burly fullback who was carrying three plates of ice cream on his tray. Caught by surprise and their good timing, Billy fell flat out, unable to brace himself. He would have been badly hurt hitting the tile floor, were it not for Keith's reaching out and breaking the fall in midair—with one hand. Keith attributed this newfound strength—soon to become legendary in his widening circle of admirers—to hard work on a summer construction job. His recent twenty-pound weight increase was attributed to the greater appetite he had had since that job. The only explanation for his steadily increasing height was that "he was still a growing boy."

Off the playing field, Keith's life was also changing in other similarly dramatic ways. His girlfriend now called him "Tiger." Before, he could take sex or leave it; now it was a consuming passion. He would have sexual relations with his girlfriend as often as he could get her to say "Yes." Then he might go home and masturbate, and when he had enough money, he'd also visit a prostitute. Needless to say, Keith's "machismo" did not go unnoticed among his friends. In fact, neither did Keith's other exploits. He became a defender of the weak, the little people, the abused. This defense usually took the form of regular weekend brawls in the local bars.

After graduation, our run-of-the-mill-boy-turned-star joined the army. There too, he continued to be "special," for example by volunteering to drive a high-explosive truck in Vietnam. "No big deal," he said. "Somebody's got to do it." While his buddies slept anxiously in full uniform, Keith slept like a baby in his shorts. He didn't feel particularly tough or brave, but he wondered why the other guys were so chicken. On leaves behind the front lines, the weekend bar brawls continued, but now often involved military police. Once Keith "subdued" three of them while his right leg was in a full cast from a previous week's group encounter session. The plaster cast also had no effect on his sexual proclivities during R and R leaves. His exploits surely would have won him some decoration for "service above and beyond the call of duty" if his buddies were giving out the medals. In a society where the masculine traits of aggressiveness, sexuality, and fearless bravery are prized, Keith earned a ten-plus on any male's ten-point scale.

Upon returning home for his father's funeral, Keith finally realized something was wrong inside himself. He didn't cry at the funeral. He felt as if he should cry, because he had loved his father and grieved at the loss. But his emotions were *"as if"* emotions. They were cold, lacking any real feeling. His girlfriend noticed this too, and complained that there was no warmth or feelings of love in his relations with her, either.

Adding further misery to Keith's once glorious life were the headaches he was having. They were coming on more often and each new one seemed worse than the others. Despite it all, Keith kept on growing. But no one asked "why?"

One day while visiting a friend in the hospital, Keith passed out from one of his most painful headaches. He could tolerate pain, was not afraid of anything, but this was something else. This was like a toothache in every tooth all at once. When the friend's doctor examined Keith, he readily diagnosed why Keith had become such a different person in the past four years. Keith was suffering from a tumor at the base of the brain, or more precisely on the pituitary gland. The pressure of the tumor stimulated the pituitary to secrete hormones, and had been doing so from his seventeenth summer on. One of these was the hormone that controls body growth. Keith was on his way to becoming a giant, like those we see in the circus.

The tumor also triggered almost continuous secretions of other hormones from the adrenal glands. These hormones are involved in our stress reactions and emotions. Basic to the experience of strong emotions—fear, anxiety, anger, love, passion—is a general state of physiological arousal. We learn to associate *variations* in that inner arousal with perceived changes in the external environment—taking a surprise quiz, being verbally or physically assaulted, intimate sharing of feelings, etc. But Keith was highly aroused all the time. There were no variations within to relate to anything that was taking place in his life space. Without perception of fluctuations in arousal, his feelings seemed unreal or went unnoticed.

A third type of hormone secreted into Keith's bloodstream through the abnormal action of the pituitary tumor was, as you may have guessed, the male sex hormone. The increase of testosterone is partly responsible for the development of masculine physical characteristics in adolescent boys. It also has been implicated in both aggressive and dominance reactions in certain animal species. Of course, it stimulates the instigation of sexual urges as well.

Were it not for the pain of the headaches (from the pressure of the growing tumor), Keith might have continued on his merry way for a while longer. Eventually though, he would probably have died from an enlarged heart or circulatory problems induced by his constant state of arousal.

Everything changed abruptly after the tumor was removed. Needless to say, he was delighted to be rid of the headaches. All of his other newfound traits disappeared as well, however. He grew weaker, losing most of his appetite for food and sex. He no longer was a tough guy; he stopped telling people where to get off and picking fights.

By the sweep of the surgeon's wand, the twenty-one-year-old superman was literally transformed back to his mild-mannered "Clark Kent" personality. He wasn't really back to his "old self" again, because he was too acutely aware of what he had lost. It was a nightmare come true; the good fairy had taken back her gifts.

As long as Keith lay recuperating in the hospital, it was easy to attribute these sudden changes to the recovery process. But once he got home, visited his old hangouts, talked with his buddies, took his girlfriend out, the truth could not be denied. He was no longer as strong, as tough, as fearless, as brave, as aggressive, as sexual. Over time, Keith felt inadequate, grew depressed, became impotent. Finally he consulted a psychiatrist for fear he was "going crazy." But that's a topic we'll explore in a later chapter. For now, suffice it to say that Keith was helped back to his normal physiological functioning by a well-regulated schedule of hormone treatments. These injections helped him begin to lead a healthier, happier life. I provided supportive counseling for Keith, who was a student in my introductory psychology class, helping him understand how his behavior was affected by his abnormal physiological condition and giving him retraining in matching his emotional reactions to the situations he faced.

The story of Keith contains implications about the nature of emotions, social behavior, aggression, and psychopathology—all topics that we will discuss in later chapters. For now, it leads us naturally into the study of physiological psychology because it highlights the complex and powerful effects your brain and internal bodily functions can exert on your thinking, feelings, and actions.

When the machinery inside our heads and bodies functions normally, we ignore it. We don't notice what we can't see if it is doing what it is supposed to. We begin to ask the "why?" and "how?" when things do not work right. Thus the physical bases of our behavior become most noticeable when natural processes are interrupted by "experiments of nature," such as the one Keith unwittingly participated in, or by planned experiments of scientists.

After all, human beings are biochemical "machines" brought to near perfection over millions of years of environmental selection. But at any moment the magnificence of the human creature can be shattered just because a tube gets clogged, a valve sticks, or one tiny gland squirts too much or too little juice.

Studying the nervous system

In this chapter you will be exposed to the "real story" behind the dramatic changes that took place in Keith's thinking, feelings, and actions. To do so, we will focus our analytical microscope down to a molecular level of analysis. This will enable us to understand better what makes our muscles and glands act the way they do. It is ultimately their action that changes the entire world you experience. Many students find this the most exciting part of the study of psychology and life processes. But it is also demanding. There is much to learn that is new. Unlike material in the other chapters of this book where many terms and concepts have a familiar ring, most of those introduced here will not. Thus these chapters on physiological psychology will probably pose more of an intellectual challenge to you than any others. I believe you can rise to that challenge, if you will accept it.

The field of physiological psychology

Physiological psychology is the study of the relationship between the body and the mind. Research in this field strives to show that all of our behavior is the direct result of the operation of the nervous system. The nervous system is made up of matter, and thus subject to physical laws. Such a *mechanistic* view is contrary to the earlier notion that the soul guides the contact of human consciousness with the matter of the external world. Medieval scholars searched for the "vital fluid" or "animal spirit" that directed perception, action, and awareness.

René Descartes, the remarkable French philosopher and mathematician,

was the first authority to insist on separating physiological questions from psychological ones. In the early 1600s he advanced the view of the body as an "animal machine" that could be studied scientifically. Thus, for example, perception of a stimulus event was to be understood in part through the physiology of vision and in part through the psychology of sensing, knowing, and experiencing. The physiological side of the question involved a knowledge of the physical laws that govern the transmission of light through lenses. Reducing complex sensory processes to their underlying physical basis would be an example of the mechanistic approach to the study of physiological psychology. Another example of the mechanistic approach, as applied to the physical sciences, comes from the research of the astronomer Kepler, a contemporary of Descartes. It was Kepler's precise observations and mathematical analysis of the movements of celestial bodies that provided the empirical support for the then revolutionary theory that the sun, not the earth, is the center of the solar system. Kepler said of his approach: "My goal is to show that the heavenly machine is not a kind of divine living being but similar to a clockwork."

It is easy for modern physiological psychologists to adopt a mechanistic view. It was not so easy for Descartes. Because he was devoutly religious in a time when the Church was the supreme authority on most matters, the soul could not be ignored. It had to have a place in human functioning. Descartes got out of this bind by postulating separate actions of the mechanistic body and brain from that of the spiritual soul and ephemeral mind. This view is termed *dualism*; it allowed scientists to study the nervous system, while philosophers and theologians could continue to search for the ways the soul influenced human affairs. Descartes' intellectual contributions have earned him the honorary designation as "founder of physiological psychology."

Physiological psychologists of today are not only mechanistic in their general orientation, they are also *reductionistic*. They try to understand complex phenomena by reducing them to ever more simple basic components. They begin with an interest in understanding human behavior similar to that of most psychologists, but then go about their business quite differently. Their task of discovering how the brain affects behavior is broken down into smaller units, into simpler neurological or biochemical units of analysis—nerve cells, molecules, and eventually to the core of all matter—atoms and electrons. They hope to come up with the answers to the big questions by dissecting matter into its smallest components and understanding functioning at each of these levels of molecular analysis.

"All wrong," say some psychologists critical of the reductionist approach. Can you understand a melody by analyzing its separate notes or a work of art by reducing it to its basic colors, textures, technical features, and so on? "Hardly!" say the *holists*. In opposition to reductionism, this holistic approach advocates studying behavior in terms of the way the whole organism acts and not just of its parts. The whole person, they argue, is infinitely more than the sum of his or her separate parts. This view finds supporters in the humanities and arts who believe that reductionism robs the richness from reality. "Only where ignorance of reality is the mystery of life," counter our physiological psychologists.

We will see in this and the next chapter that the mechanistic, reductionist approach often brings researchers in close contact with the basic elements of life—listening to individual nerve cells communicating with each other. Whether this approach is the best level of analysis depends on the kind of questions we want answered (as mentioned in Chapter 2). The theme of the next chapters will place us squarely in the center of a vast revolution taking place in our understanding of the brain and the mind. Descartes started it all several hundred years ago, significant progress is less than a century old, and the modern explosion in brain research was ignited only a few decades ago in the nineteen fifties.

The human nervous system

In this introduction to the physical and biological foundations of psychology, we begin with an overview of the structure and function of the human nervous system. After touring around the outside of the brain we will be guided by modern brain researchers into its inner space, to the nerve cells, or *neurons*, that make up the nervous system. This cellular level of analysis permits us to go beyond a general understanding of what the brain does to *how* it enables us to start, stop, talk, listen, make love or war, in short, to be human or to act inhumanely.

A human brain weighs only about three pounds. Even adding in the spinal cord and all the body's nerves, the total is still less than 5 percent of your body weight. But packed into this relatively small mass are at least ten billion nerve cells. A one-inch square chunk of brain tissue would contain perhaps one hundred million such cells. Neural tissue has the consistency of softly jelled pudding that is heavily infiltrated with blood vessels. Even the brains of newborn infants are covered with wrinkles like a walnut. Besides being rather unimpressive in its appearance, the brain also seems rather passive, not moving like the pulsating heart or gurgling like a hungry stomach. This silent organ does not appear to be doing much in its protective perch under the skull, behind the eyes and between the ears. No wonder then that some of our greatest philosophers assigned the brain a minor role in the conduct of human nature. Aristotle thought it did little more than cool the blood. Plato gave it credit for reason alone. Desire and hunger, he reasoned, originated in the stomach, while courage and ambition were attributed to the heart (a theory the military services still honor with the Purple Heart medal). However, as in other things, appearances are deceiving. As research teaches us how to look more closely at the brain and what it can do, its unimpressive shapelessness recedes, revealing what we now know to be the most intricate machine and beautiful organ of life imaginable.

The nervous system consists of two subsystems, the *central nervous system* and the *peripheral nervous system*. The central nervous system (CNS) is both in the center of the body and has the central function of integrating and coordinating the various functions of the body. It consists of the brain and the spinal cord. As you might expect from its name, the peripheral nervous system is responsible for receiving information from and sending information to the periphery (outer parts) of the body. It consists of nerve fibers that connect the central nervous system to cells that are sensitive to various forms of energy (*receptor cells*) and also to muscles and glands that effect changes in the movements or chemistry of the body (*effector cells*).

It is important for you to form a mental map of the basic structures of the nervous system because many of the studies we will be discussing relate specific structures to particular behaviors. Such maps of the nervous system are essential for neurologists who must find and treat its diseased or injured portions. Students with a medical or life sciences orientation should learn all of the terms that are defined in the Reference Modules. Other students will want to refer to these pages as they read the chapters. They can determine from their instructors how much of this information they will be responsible for, or decide for themselves how informed they wish to be about neuropsychological terms and concepts.

What a piece of work is man! how noble in reason! how infinite in faculty! in form and movement how express and admirable!
Shakespeare
Hamlet

It will be apparent to you that there is a hierarchy of organization within the nervous system, in which larger units consist of subunits which, in turn, can be subdivided into ever smaller components. (Remember, it is a reductionist approach we are studying.) The distinctions are determined by the special functions of each component of the system and the relationship between different parts of the whole system. For example, peripheral nerves may be regenerated after injury, while those in the spinal cord normally cannot. Thus paralysis of the arms or legs can be reversed and sensation regained after peripheral nerves are cut. In contrast, the loss of function is permanent after an injury to the spinal cord, such as former Dodger catcher Roy Campanella suffered. It is important to remember that although the parts are isolated for purposes of analysis, they work together like the gears and wheels of a complex machine. (See *P&L* Close-up, The Sad Case of Karen Ann Quinlan.)

Close-up
The Sad Case of Karen Ann Quinlan

In April 1975, at the age of 21, Karen Ann Quinlan was found unconscious in the bedroom of a friend's home, apparently the victim of drugs and alcohol. But Karen had done more than just pass out. She no longer seemed to be breathing. The police were called, and an ambulance rushed her to the hospital. Doctors went to work on her without success—indeed, without discovering what was wrong. Tests and X rays showed no physical injuries. She was put on a respirator, but it was already too late to restore Karen's higher brain centers to normal functioning; they had been irreversibly damaged by lack of oxygen. Thus began the "waking sleep" that was to make this young woman a symbol of a modern dispute—what is the dividing line between life and death?

For more than a year, Karen lay in a coma in the intensive care unit of the New Jersey hospital near her home. Machines "breathed" for her and pumped blood through her veins. She was fed intravenously. By this time, she had attracted the attention of millions of people the world over. What to do about her became a dilemma that called into question the very meaning of human existence. Would turning off the respirator constitute murder, or would it be an act of mercy? Karen herself was in no distress, but her parents obviously were.

The ethics of the situation were beyond the competence of any single person to decide. Theologians, lawyers, doctors, and judges argued the matter while the Quinlans agonized. Eventually, convinced that there was no hope of recovery, they made their own decision. The machines would be turned off, and Karen allowed to die a natural death.

At this point they discovered that the decision was not theirs to make—at least not without the approval of the doctors and the hospital. Although Karen's doctors were willing to "pull the plug," the hospital was not. The Quinlans went to court, where a judge denied their petition. However, he was overruled by a higher court. The respirator was turned off, and the young woman was removed to a nursing home. Here, it was expected, nature would take its course.

And nature did—in an unusual fashion. Although she never regained consciousness, Karen Quinlan continued to "live," breathing on her own, her heart still beating, yet hardly "human." Lying motionless in a fetal position, legs drawn up underneath her, hands joined as if in prayer, the physical body of Karen Ann Quinlan survived. But the real Karen Ann Quinlan—the person with feelings and thoughts, the ability to recognize others and make decisions—had long been dead.

The Quinlan case tells us how much biological factors—especially the brain and nervous system—influence the behaviors that make people human. Our bodies are, in fact, "life support" systems that make possible all psychological experiences from a simple sensation to the highly complex act of playing a piano concerto.

Neurons: The stuff that brains are made of

Common to each and every part of the nervous system is the very same kind of cell—*the neuron*—that knits together the different divisions. When a neuron fires, its effects may be heard round the world. A declaration of war, a Shakespeare sonnet, an act of kindness all start with a circuit of neurons sending a message that is acted upon. Some of the messages are prearranged by heredity, such as nest building in birds, mating rituals in fish, or the menstrual cycle in women. Others are wired in by learning through our experiences, such as saluting the flag, greeting a friend, recognizing a Beatles song. Behavior begins with the action of neurons.

At the core of everything you can do, feel, and think are cells so tiny they are only visible under a microscope after being specially stained to make them stand out from one another in beautiful array. ● Without such staining techniques single neurons would be lost in the crowd of billions of other neurons in the human brain. Even a tiny insect's central nervous system contains about one hundred thousand neurons. For comparison, the largest computers in the world contain fewer than ten million components—only a thousandth of the neurons in your little brain.

The nerve cells of the brain share common structural features with all other living cells, having a *nucleus, cytoplasm* (the substance surrounding the nucleus, in which most of the biochemical reactions of the cell take place), and an *outer membrane*. But there the resemblance ends. Most body cells are simply small blobs that look identical to others of the same type. Nerve cells are uniquely individual. They come in a vast assortment of sizes and shapes and differ widely both in activity and in chemical composition. Some look like bent balloons on long crooked strings, others like a child's stick drawing of a face with frizzy hair, a long thin armless trunk, and many skinny legs.

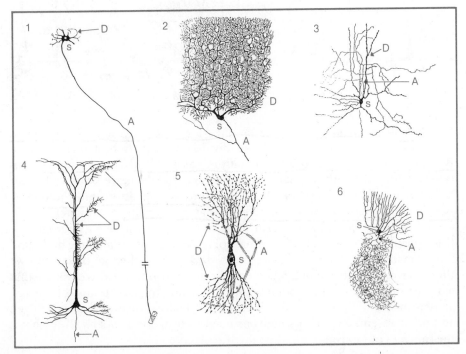

●

Shown here are a few examples of the amazing variety of neurons in the human nervous system. A = axon, D = dendrites, S = soma (cell body).
1. Spinal motor neuron, showing part of its long axon.
2. Purkinje neuron of cerebellum, with fantastically complex dendrites.
3. Local neuron from cerebral cortex.
4. Pyramidal cell of cerebral cortex; its axon goes to spinal cord.
5. Pyramidal cell of hippocampus.
6. Local neuron of cerebellum, with an astonishingly branched axon.

Every neuron has a *cell body*, which contains the nucleus and manufactures proteins and other materials necessary for the cell's maintenance, and one or more sets of fine processes like fingers that project from the cell. These often include a number of short *dendrites* projecting from one end of the cell, and usually a single *axon* projecting from the other side of the cell body. Axons extend for long, varied distances (sometimes as much as three feet). Branching out from the end of each axon are *terminal buttons*, which make close contact with other neurons.

One of the most remarkable features of neurons is that they do not divide to form new cells. At birth or shortly afterwards you had all the neurons you were ever going to have. During the development of the embryonic brain before birth, however, neurons were being manufactured at the rate of twenty thousand per minute! Obviously, even with all its neurons, the newborn infant is not a very brainy creature. In fact, the thinking part of the brain takes more time to mature in human beings than in any other species. The infant's transition from a sleeping, crying, urinating creature to an active, skillful, manipulative human comes about with the proliferation of the branching processes (dendrites and axons) that interconnect neurons to form behavioral circuits and with other changes that enable nerve cells to transmit information more rapidly. ◆

◆

The photographs show a Golgi-stained section from Broca's area of the brain in a one-month-old brain (left) and in a two-year-old brain (right). The more mature brain on the right has many more interconnections.

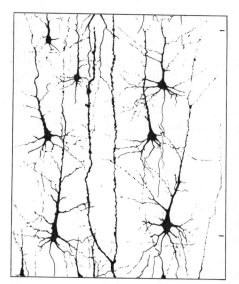 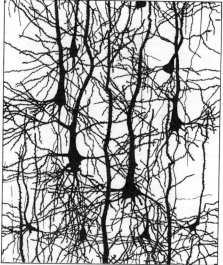

Because neurons resist division they are virtually immune to cancer, which causes other types of cells to divide abnormally and form tumors. Brain tumors such as Keith's are actually diseases of *glial cells* and not neurons (see p. 300). Although humans do not appear to add more brain cells after birth, they certainly can lose them. Neurons die in astonishing numbers, estimated to be about ten thousand every day of your life. Fortunately for us, we still have a lot left to burn because we started out with such a huge supply. If we started with the minimal estimate of ten billion in our average brain and lost as many as ten thousand neurons a day then by the age of seventy we would have lost only about 2.5 percent of our neuron reserve. We will see that old age causes some deterioration in brain functioning, not because of the lack of neurons, but probably from biochemical factors such as lack of oxygen and other essential elements neurons need to function properly. But what is the function of neurons?

Functions of a neuron: A reflex arc

If you apply an electric current to the exposed nerves of a dissected frog's leg the muscles twitch. What do you conclude from your experiment? When Luigi Galvani discovered this effect in the 1780s he declared it to be a demonstration of the electrical nature of nerve signals. The nerves were transmitting the battery's electrical current and thereby making muscles move. Although crude, this experiment accurately pinpointed the function of neurons. *Neurons transmit messages from one part of the body to another.* Some messages carry information about how the environment is acting on the individual and others about how the individual should act or is acting on the environment. Each neuron is a miniature living battery that discharges itself—sending out electrochemical current—and then recharges itself. Nerve currents direct the behavior of every living creature; without them, the living brain would be unaware of the world around it and we would be unable to think, feel or act.

Let's first look at what neurons do and then how they carry out their miniature miracles. Two simple experiments will help set the stage for our analysis. First, get a flashlight and sit or stand before a mirror in a darkened room. Watching the mirror, flash the light in your right eye keeping the other covered. Notice how your right pupil contracts. After a minute or so, uncover the left eye; notice that the left pupil is initially bigger than the right, but also contracts to the same size as light strikes it. Next, take a clean pin and prick the back of your hand. It jerks back a little in reaction to the pinprick.

In both instances your nervous system was detecting and responding to external stimulation. Stimulus energy was activating sensory receptor neurons that activated other neurons in the brain and spinal cord which, in turn, relayed messages back via motor neurons, causing contraction of the pupil of the eye or of the hand or arm muscles. This sequence of sensory input→central nervous system→behavioral output is known as a *reflex arc.* ▲

▲
This is a simplified drawing of a reflex arc. Three kinds of neurons are represented here: (a) a sensory (afferent) neuron; (b) an interneuron, with its many branches, well designed for its job of providing multiple connections among many neurons; and (c) a motor neuron, with its long axon traveling most of the distance in the same nerve trunk as the sensory neuron and ending at muscles near the origin of the sensory input. Actually, a single sensory cell would contact hundreds or thousands of interneurons.

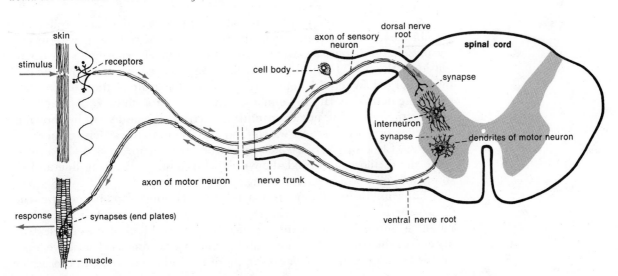

Notice that the neurons in the diagram are divided into three functional categories. *Receptors* detect energy signals from external or internal stimuli and convert it into neural signals. The best known receptors are associated with the five senses of vision, hearing, taste, smell, and touch. But we have dozens of other kinds of receptors. Receptors in our muscles, tendons, and joints tell us the position of our limbs, other receptors detect gravity, acceleration, warmth, pressure, and pain. Internal receptors deep in the brain monitor the balance of the body fluids, brain temperature, and the presence of hormones and other chemicals in the blood. All this information is processed in the brain by *interneurons*, which communicate exclusively with other neurons. Finally, all behavior is directly controlled via *motor neurons*, which excite muscles, and by other *effector neurons* that excite or inhibit glands. The vast majority of neurons in the human nervous system are interneurons. (See Reference Module, p. 292.) Why this should be so will become clear as we proceed.

How neurons work

Many neurons work by an action called *firing*. Each neuron receives a signal at one end (usually from neighboring neurons) and sends it along to other neurons at its far end. The dendrites act like receiving antennas, picking up incoming messages. These messages change the electrical properties of the neuron, causing it to send signals along the length of the axon. The axon is like a transmission cable carrying messages over varied distances to the terminal buttons. The terminal buttons serve as the transmitting antenna and pass the message along to a network of surrounding neurons by a process called *synaptic transmission*.

Sounds simple, like part of a wiring diagram for a ham operator's radio kit. But a moment's reflection should cause you to wonder (in the words of a popular song) "is that all there is?" Every waking second of your life, your eyes, ears, and other sense receptors send perhaps one hundred million such individual messages to the brain. These neuronal signals in the brain are responsible for coordinating as many as ninety sets of muscles with every breath a sprinter takes in a hundred-yard dash. These neuronal signals are the raw material of experience, and the triggers of action. To discover how they manage their incredible feats we return to our reflex arc example aided by information from modern electrophysiology.

We have compared neurons to batteries; they are, of course, cells with a membrane. The membrane keeps the fluid inside the cell, along with its electrically charged ions, separated from the positively charged ions on the outside of the cell. The inside of the cell is negatively charged, the outside positively charged. When the neuron is at rest—not activated—the *electrical potential* of the neuron is said to be in a steady or *polarized* state. ■ The cell is silent, neither receiving nor transmitting electrical signals as can be shown on an oscilloscope. Researchers watch (and also listen) to the activity of neurons. (See *P&L* Close-up, Nerve Watching on the Oscilloscope, p. 294.) In a steady state, the oscilloscope would show only a straight, unwavering line and the sound amplifier would have nothing to amplify.

The equilibrium of a neuron at rest is as tenuous as the borderline truce of two warring nations. A minute disturbance on the outside of the membrane might be ignored, but if the disturbance grows, it suddenly causes an electrifying end of the truce. When the stimulus energy reaching a cell is above a particular level (or *stimulation threshold*), there is a sudden increase in the perme-

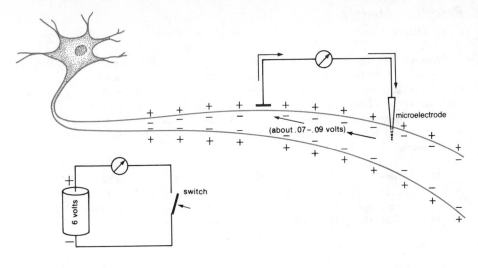

The nerve cell is actually a battery, with the inside more negative than the outside. Normally, no current flows (the cell is "at rest") because the cell membrane is impermeable. If a microelectrode is pushed inside the cell, current can flow as shown—just as current flows when a switch is closed in a flashlight. A neuron's voltage is surprisingly large—almost one-tenth of a volt—but the neuron is so tiny that it would run down in a fraction of a second if the current flow continued. Neurons normally let current flow for only a few thousandths of a second; even so, they must continuously recharge themselves. When recordings are made, an amplifier and oscilloscope would replace the meters in the schematic.

ability of the membrane, allowing the ions to pass through it in a series of exchanges. These electrochemical changes momentarily change the inside of the cell from negative to positive. This sudden electrical change is the *action potential*. This change travels rapidly along the axon of the cell to other neurons. That electrical disturbance (recorded as you can see on the oscilloscope) is the neuron's means of communicating with other neurons.

Only two types of electrical disturbance occur in neurons, and they appear to be the basis of all the signals the nervous system receives and sends. The two types of signals are called *slow potentials* and *impulses*.

Slow potentials are the simpler of the two. (They are also called "local" or "graded" potentials, for reasons obvious in the figure.) ● The stimulus for slow potentials typically comes from outside the cell, creating an electrical disturbance that is localized (limited) mainly to the area of stimulation. The electrical activity fades rapidly over distance, but it can still reach all parts of small neurons that do not have axons. In these axonless neurons, slow potentials are the only changes seen. The amplitude or size of the slow potential varies with the intensity of the stimulus. Indeed there is a continuously graded relationship between the strength of the incoming stimulus and the size of the outgoing slow potential. The bigger the input, the greater the output.

The story is quite different in neurons with long axons, where additional electrical activity is generated. This activity is called the *nerve impulse* (also *action potential* or "spike"). The nerve impulse is fast, or brief; it does *not* vary in amplitude, rather it operates on an *all-or-none principle*. Once the threshold for "firing" (producing an impulse) is exceeded, the impulse is sent along its explosive way without any loss of strength for its entire journey. Because the nerve impulse gets its energy from within the nerve cell itself, it can be propagated along the axon without any loss in vigor. This propagation of impulses along the axon has been compared to a burning fuse. The analogy is good, except that a fuse burns only once, while the axon is ready to fire again in about a millisecond (1/1000 second).

Many neurons can convert slow potentials into impulses and vice versa. The neurons in the reflex arc (p. 289) illustrate this. The physical stimulus evokes a slow potential (called a *receptor potential* or *generator potential*) in the receptor. If the stimulus is sufficiently intense, it exceeds the *threshold* of the neuron and generates an impulse. As the stimulus increases in intensity, the

Reference Module
The Neuron

Axon "Sending" portion of a neuron, which conducts impulses over relatively long distances. Most neurons have only one axon; a few have none.

Cell body (soma) The thickest portion of a cell, containing the nucleus.

Dendrites Branched, tapering structures which receive information.

Membrane The extremely thin covering of the cell, specialized for electrical and chemical excitability.

Myelin sheath Fatty layer of glial cells surrounding some axons; speeds transmission of impulses.

Nodes of Ranvier Gaps in the myelin sheath at periodic intervals, where the impulse is generated.

Synapse Specialized structure for transmitting information among neurons or from neurons to effectors. (See Reference Module on page 297.)

Terminal buttons Endings of axons, specialized for transmitting information across synapses.

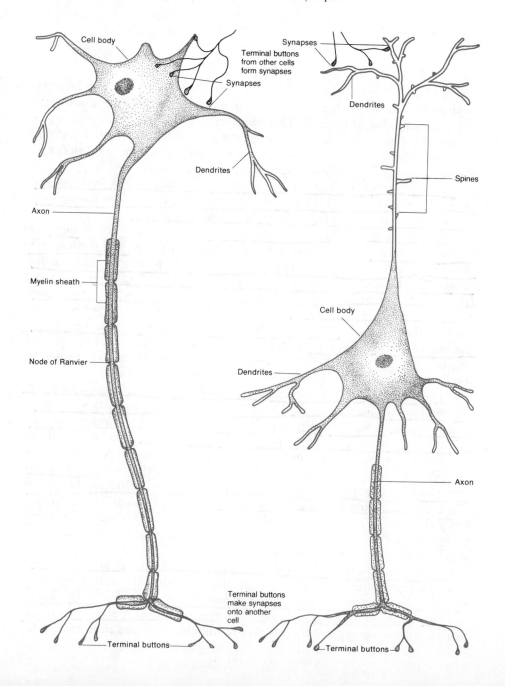

Two types of electrical potential changes are the basis of all neural activity. Slow potentials develop relatively slowly and are local and graded; like ripples in a pond, they are largest at their source (in this case a synapse) and diminish with distance. Strong synapses can make waves, weak synapses, ripples. Slow potentials are converted by axons into brief, all-or-none bursts of electrical activity called impulses, which travel without getting smaller all the way to the end of the axon. Axons in our bodies can transmit series of impulses at rates of up to a thousand per second. Normally, thousands of synapses cover a neuron, but only one is shown here. Synapses are a common source of slow potentials, but some neurons generate slow potentials spontaneously.

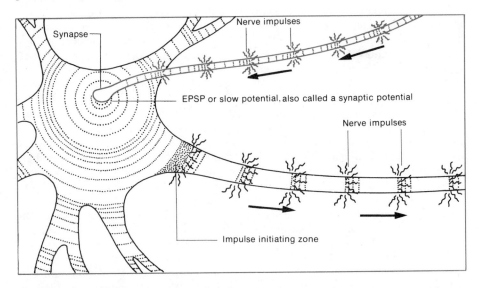

generator potential produces nerve impulses at higher *frequency*. That is, stronger stimuli generate more nerve impulses per unit of time. They also excite a greater number of neurons. This important relationship was discovered by Lord Adrian in 1926.

The impulses arriving at the terminals of the sensory cell produce slow potentials in interneurons. If these slow potentials exceed the spike threshold of the interneurons, they in turn produce impulses that activate motor neurons, in which the same process is repeated. This sequence is usually repeated many times over long chains of intertwined neurons.

A nerve impulse is a large and rapid change in potential. It rises to its full amplitude of almost one hundred millivolts in a fraction of a millisecond and then drops back down to baseline within another millisecond. The conduction of an impulse along an axon is fast, but not nearly as fast as the speed of electricity or light. Electricity travels more than two hundred million times faster than the fastest nerve impulse. In the human body nerve impulses are clocked at speeds of about two hundred fifty miles an hour, which is pretty fast if they are only going a few centimeters or so. Thus our brains can receive information from distant sense organs and transmit instructions to our muscles with delays of only a few hundred milliseconds.

The speed with which a neuron can transmit its message depends on two factors, the diameter of the axon and whether it is covered with an insulating material called *myelin*. (See *P&L* Close-up, Missing Myelin Mars Motor Mastery.) Fatter axons conduct impulses faster, as do those coated with a myelin sheath. The fastest axons have an impulse velocity of about 200 meters per second, the slowest ones plod along at 10 centimeters per second (Bullock, Orkand, & Grinnell, 1977). Impulses signaling danger, acute pain, or survival get on the express route. Those carrying old, familiar messages (about chronic low-level pain, for example) are routed on the slow train.

Close-up
Nerve Watching on the Oscilloscope

The major tool used by scientists who study the brain's activity is the oscilloscope. With it, nerve impulses can be observed visually on a fluorescent screen and their characteristics precisely measured. Photos or illustrations of a neuron firing or of a nerve impulse being transmitted are taken from the oscilloscope.

Think of aiming a thin flashlight beam so that it makes a dot on a screen, then rapidly move it across the screen, then up and down. What you would see would be a horizontal, then a vertical line. Similarly, in an oscilloscope there is a dot of light caused by a beam of electrons that hits the phosphor-coated screen of the oscilloscope and illuminates it.

Electrons are *negatively* (−) charged particles that are attracted by positive (+) electrical charges and repelled by other negative charges. Thus in the series of figures, you can see the effects of putting either + or − charges on one or the other of the four plates that surround the beam (A). The beam moves rapidly to the left if a + voltage is applied there (B). It shifts to the right if the left side is made − and the right is made + (C). The speed with which it traverses the screen depends on the relative strengths of the charges on either side. Obviously the beam can move in the vertical dimension by electrically charging either the upper or the lower plate (D), or it can be made to bounce back and forth by alternating the charges on the plates (E).

In recording from neurons in the brain the experimenter determines how fast the beam sweeps from left to right: the rate of this movement is the measurement of *time*. The vertical movement of the beam represents changes in voltage of the membrane of the nerve cell being studied. When a neuron "fires," it produces a momentary change in voltage so rapid that the beam is deflected and returned to its original position within a millisecond—1/1000th of a second. (The voltage change must be amplified thousands of times before it can influence the oscilloscope beam.) When the beam is moving slowly across the screen from left to right, the sudden voltage change of the firing neuron makes the deflection look like a "spike" or a sudden "impulse" on the record (F). The terms *nerve impulse*, *nerve spike*, and *action potential* are used interchangeably.

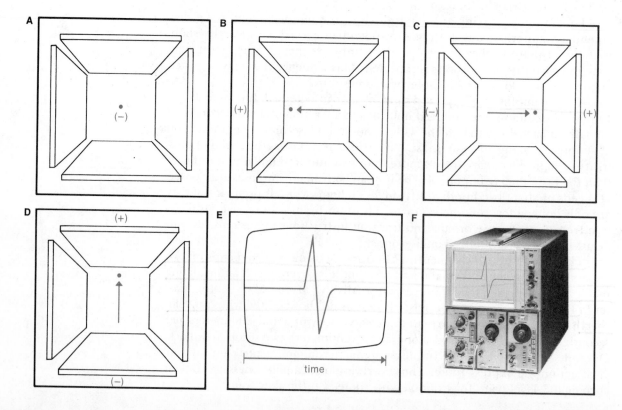

For a brief time after the axon has "fired," the membrane is temporarily unexcitable and the axon cannot be fired again, regardless of the strength of a stimulus. This interval (which can be from a fraction of a millisecond to several milliseconds) is known as the *absolute refractory period*. There is a short period just before the membrane returns to normal during which a stronger-than-normal stimulus is required to fire another impulse; this is called the *relative refractory period*. The maximum firing frequency of a neuron rarely exceeds five hundred impulses per second.

Perhaps the most important point to be made about nerve impulses is their similarity to one another. Nerve impulses in axons from squid, insects, rabbits, or humans look much the same on an oscilloscope. We now know that this is because their fundamental, electrochemical mechanisms are virtually identical. Within our own bodies, the nerve impulses carrying information from our eyes and ears are alike, and are indistinguishable from impulses going to our muscles. Nerve impulses are thus the common currency of all nervous systems. However, when we turn to consider the gap in our tale thus far, synapses and synaptic potentials, the story is quite different. Synaptic potentials also have common features in all animals, but *within* a given animal, great variability in synaptic transmission is encountered. This has surprising consequences. Let's examine them.

Synaptic transmission

As remarkable as axonal conduction is for rapid, reliable delivery of coded information, the real key to the complexity and subtlety of the information carried by our nervous system lies in the activities that take place at the *synapses*—the tiny regions where neurons communicate with one another. *Synapse*

Close-up
Missing Myelin Mars Motor Mastery

In order for electricity to be reliably conducted over long distances, transmission cables must be coated with insulation. The same thing is true of the axon, because its own membrane is very porous and a poor insulator. The myelin sheath is a fatty white coating of glial cells that serves not only as an insulator, but as a facilitator as well. This sheath has gaps along its surface, called nodes of Ranvier. The ion transfer which creates the electrical disturbance can only take place at these nodes. Interestingly, the electrical charge jumps along the axon from node to node, even skipping some for really fast express service.

"What difference does it make if my axon is sheathed or not?" you may be wondering. Well, in fact, this coating does not develop fully in humans until sometime after the first year of life. You couldn't crawl or control your bowels or bladder until the nerves involved had become myelinated. Apparently the intricate coordination of motor movements and the feedback from them that directs subsequent actions require fast-talking, smooth-acting, myelin-coated neurons. Some fiber systems start development of myelin early and finish late, others start late and finish early. Some parts of the brain are not fully myelinated until around puberty (Yakovlev & Lecours, 1967).

The unfortunate consequence of damage to this soft coating can be seen in people suffering from multiple sclerosis. This disease of the myelin sheath throws off the delicate timing of nerve impulses, resulting in jerky, spastic, poorly coordinated movements and eventual paralysis (Bailey, 1975).

means "to clasp tightly" and indeed the neurons on either side of the synaptic gap are strongly bonded together. A synapse consists of three components: the *presynaptic terminal* (the terminal buttons of the axon), the *postsynaptic membrane* (of the dendrites of another neuron) and the *synaptic gap* between them. Although the membranes of the pre- and postsynaptic cells do not directly touch, they are held closely together. Even when neural tissue is disrupted and separated for chemical analysis, the pre- and postsynaptic portions are found stuck together among the fragments of tissue. (See Reference Module, p. 297.)

The synapse, this miniscule space of five millionths of an inch, may indeed be nature's most amazing invention. Instead of direct connection between any two neurons, each one is indirectly linked to hundreds of others by synaptic connections. This makes it possible for more complex messages to be simultaneously transmitted to many parts of the entire system, and for the system to work even if some neurons become damaged or defective. By analogy, the receiving sites are like great telephone switchboards that can receive a hundred calls at once. Even if a number of the incoming cables are cut, broken, or out of order, the message can still get sent through.

But how does the nerve impulse get across this open synaptic space? "Spark" and "soup" were the two opposing ideas advanced by theorists. It jumps the gap like the electricity in a car's spark plug, said one group of researchers. Others believed it floats across in a chemical mixture, a kind of chemical alphabet soup. The critical experiment was conducted by an Austrian chemist, Otto Loewi, who got the idea in a dream. When he awoke however, he could neither remember the dream nor make sense of the notes he had scribbled during the night. Amazingly, the dream recurred the next night. This time he wrote it down and immediately went to his laboratory and conducted an experiment which showed that nerves secrete a chemical that affects other cells. Certain nerve fibers slow the heartbeat when they are stimulated. Loewi stimulated these nerves in a frog, slowing its heartbeat. He immediately transferred fluid from that frog's heart to the heart of a second frog. The second frog's heartbeat also slowed down, showing that chemicals in the transferred fluid had stimulated the nerves. In other words, synapses send soup—not sparks.

The presynaptic terminal of a synapse, when a nerve impulse is received, releases thousands of molecules of a *neurotransmitter* into the gap. These diffuse across the narrow gap almost instantaneously and combine with other, much larger molecules in the postsynaptic membrane called *receptors*.[1] The receptor molecules then cause "channels" in the membrane to open briefly, allowing various ions to flow in or out of the cell producing a slow *postsynaptic potential*, or *PSP*. The transmitter binds to the receptor only briefly, and then either diffuses away, is taken back up into the presynaptic terminal (reuptake), or is degraded (broken down) by enzymes.

There are at least five important consequences of this unique system for transmission of messages across nerve connections:

a. all neural activity follows the *law of forward conduction*: the coded information in the nerve impulse travels in only one direction, always flowing from terminal knobs of the axon to the postsynaptic membrane of the dendrites;

---

[1]Unfortunately, the term "receptor" has two other distinct physiological meanings. It can refer to an entire organ like the eye or ear, or to individual cells in the organ specialized for converting light or sound into nerve potentials, like rods and cones in the retina.

Neurotransmitters Chemicals released by presynaptic ("sending") neuron.

Postsynaptic membrane The surface of the "receiving" neuron, containing the receptors and ion channels that control the excitability of the cell.

Presynaptic terminal Another name for terminal button.

Receptors Molecules in the postsynaptic membrane that combine with neurotransmitters to alter the permeability of the cell, allowing an exchange of ions through the membrane.

Reuptake After release, transmitter molecules or their degraded products may be taken back up into the terminal button.

Synaptic gap The narrow space between the terminal buttons of the presynaptic neuron and the membrane of the postsynaptic neuron.

Synaptic vesicles Tiny "bags" found in great numbers in terminal buttons, believed to contain molecules of a neurotransmitter.

Terminal button The enlarged portion of an axon terminal that forms the presynaptic portion of a synapse.

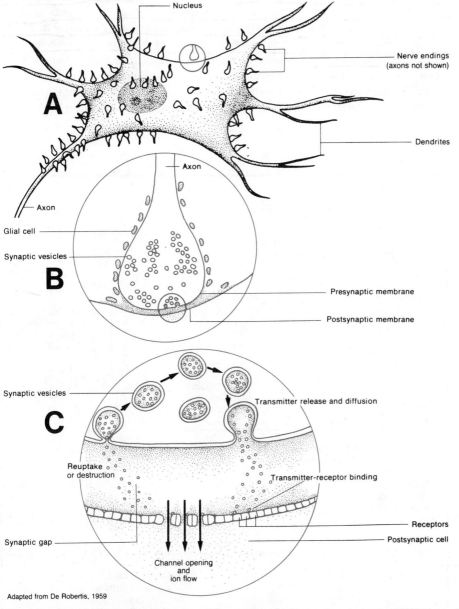

The three diagrams show the synapse between terminal buttons and a spinal motorneuron at different levels of magnification. A) The entire motorneuron, whose cell body is covered with terminal buttons from other cells that are not shown. B) Structure of a single terminal button. C) Release of neurotransmitters at the synaptic gap.

Adapted from De Robertis, 1959

b. because the secretion process takes time, there is a delay between the arrival of an impulse and the onset of the PSP. Most neural messages traverse many synapses in sequence. The synaptic delays taken together with the axonal conduction delays add up to the total *reaction time*—the time between the initial stimulus and the final response;

c. nerve impulses are converted back to slow potentials that allow multiple inputs to be *integrated*, or added together, over time;

d. the chemical synapse can multiply or inhibit the nerve impulse rather than sent it along its all-or-none fashion;

e. with perhaps as many as five hundred trillion synapses in the brain, the *variability* in neural transmission is almost infinite.

Varieties of chemical transmission

Variability is the key to the richness of our experience and behavior. From nerve impulses, which we have seen are virtually all identical, there emerge complex patterns of sense impressions, memories, feelings, thoughts, and actions that vary in subtlety, persistence, distinctiveness, and vigor. They vary from person to person in the same situation and in the same person over time or in different settings. Synapses make this variation possible. There is variability between synapses and even within a given synapse as it gets older or more "experienced." The important variations in synapses that give our brains their enormous and intricate flexibility are illustrated below. ◆

◆

Varieties of synaptic potentials are illustrated by recording from a neuron while stimulating different kinds of synapses. In each example the dark line represents the oscilloscope beam sweeping from left to right. In A, the beam suddenly drops by 70 millivolts when the electrode penetrates the neurons. Then different axons are stimulated to cause synaptic potentials of various kinds. In B and C, the synaptic potentials are at times so large that they trigger all-or-none impulses in the neurons.

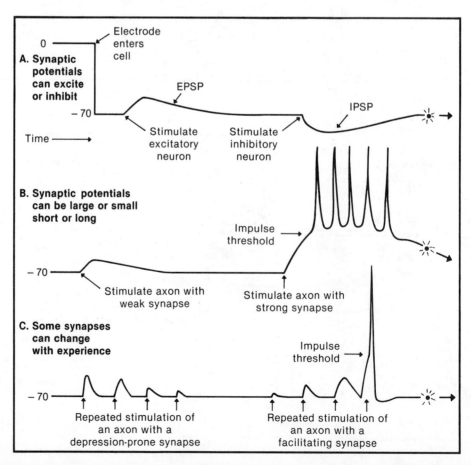

Excitatory or inhibitory?

When the tiny sacs of neurotransmitters at the terminal buttons are released by the nerve impulse, molecules are sent across the synaptic gap to combine with receptors of the postsynaptic cells. If the synapse is an *excitatory synapse*, then the transmitter's effect is to change the membrane of the dendrites to allow positive ions to enter and trigger a nerve impulse. If it is an *inhibitory synapse*, the transmitter opens channels so that negative ions enter or positive ions leave. This prevents the neuron from firing. Inhibitory synapses are common throughout the CNS, outnumbering excitatory ones in some regions. Most neurons are either exclusively excitatory or exclusively inhibitory, but in lower animals examples are known in which the same neuron inhibits some postsynaptic cells and excites others (Kandel, 1976). This is possible because a given transmitter may excite one type of neuron but inhibit another. Thus it is incorrect to refer to a given transmitter as either excitatory or inhibitory, since the transmitter's effect is determined by the postsynaptic cell.

The nature of synaptic potentials

The *strength* of a PSP bears no relation to the amplitude of the nerve impulse that triggers it. Excitatory postsynaptic potentials can be weak, so that many are needed to cause the postsynaptic cell to fire, or powerful, so that a single presynaptic impulse leads to a burst of postsynaptic impulses. The strength of inhibitory postsynaptic potentials also varies widely. Hence some neurons can work alone to trigger the next in line, while those with weaker synapses must work together in order to have any influence.

The *duration* of postsynaptic potentials at different synapses may vary from tens of milliseconds to minutes, resulting in brief or prolonged effects.

Facilitation and depression occur at different synapses, or sometimes at the same synapse depending upon the frequency of stimulation. *Facilitation* means that subsequent PSPs become larger. *Depression* means that they become smaller. Both effects are caused by a change in the amount of transmitter released by the nerve impulse. The regulation of synaptic transmission may in part be the work of the glial cells, once thought to be only the "glue" holding neurons in place. (See *P&L* Close-up, The Glue of Life.)

A given synapse, then, has a *profile* of characteristics: we find facilitating, short-duration, excitatory synapses of moderate strength; stable, long-duration, inhibitory synapses of great power; and so on. These are by no means the only kinds of variations: it has been suggested that some synapses may change their response drastically if their activity is associated with certain other events (Hebb, 1949), but such "learning" synapses have not yet been found. These variations add a great deal of richness to the operation of the nervous system, having profound consequences for behavior.

Synapses are definitely much more than "on-off" switches. Neurobiologist Steven Rose makes a very strong case for the special significance of the synapse in human evolution: "Consciousness, learning and intelligence are all synapse-dependent. It is not too strong to say that the evolution of humanity followed the evolution of the synapse" (1973, p. 65).

Are neurons decision makers or obedient servants?

Every neuron in the central nervous system that has been studied closely has been shown to have both inhibitory and excitatory synapses on it. A single neuron may receive synaptic input from hundreds of other neurons, some strongly inhibitory or excitatory, others weakly so. The neuron is usually pictured as a decision maker, which weighs the conflicting directions it is receiving:

Fire!
Don't Fire!
Fire! *Fire!* FIRE!
OK. So I'm firing.
Stop Firing!
Silence.

Just such incessant, competing orders can be seen in intracellular recordings from neurons in alert insects, where they appear as long trains of intermingled excitatory and inhibitory PSPs and nerve impulses. Such experiments are not yet possible in mammals, but we have every reason to believe that exactly the same kinds of events occur inside many of our own neurons.

Other neurons display a more harmonious picture, in which inhibitory and excitatory actions *cooperate* instead of compete. ▲ In such neurons,

Close-up
The Glue of Life: Neuroglial Cells

Glia is derived from the Greek word for glue and is an appropriate name for the cells that surround all neurons, sealing up the space around them as if gluing them together. It is only relatively recently that researchers began to take glial cells seriously. This is surprising, because they outnumber neurons ten to one, and

though tiny in size, still make up half of the brain's bulk. Unlike neurons, glia do not possess excitable membranes and so cannot transmit information. Yet so many thousands of cells must be there for some purpose.

Glia can take up, manufacture, and release chemical transmitters, and so may help to maintain or regulate synaptic transmission. Another suggestion is that glia can manufacture and possibly transmit other kinds of molecules, such as proteins. The anatomy of some glial cells is striking in this regard, for they seem to form a conduit between blood vessels and neurons, and so may bring nourishment to the neurons. It is thought that these cells may have important functions during prenatal development and recovery from brain injury. One role of the glia is known definitely: certain kinds of glia, called by the tongue-twisting name of *oligodendroglia*, form the myelin sheath that insulates axons and speeds conduction of the nerve impulse (see p. 295). A counterpart called a *Schwann cell* performs the same role for the peripheral nerves.

The study of glia is difficult because these tiny cells are inextricably entwined with neurons. As the most numerous type of cell in the brain, their potential importance is vast, and investigation of their function seems likely to yield exciting results in the near future (Kuffler & Nicholls, 1976).

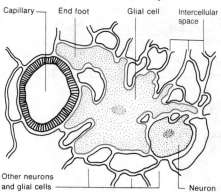

Capillary   End foot   Glial cell   Neuron

Capillary   End foot   Glial cell   Intercellular space

Other neurons and glial cells   Neuron

Adapted from Kuffler and Nicholls, 1976

The top drawing is of a single glial cell and neuron. The bottom drawing shows a thin slice of brain tissue as seen through the electron microscope. Notice that the brain is packed with neurons and glia, separated by narrow channels. These channels are the extracellular space of the brain and are filled with cerebrospinal fluid.

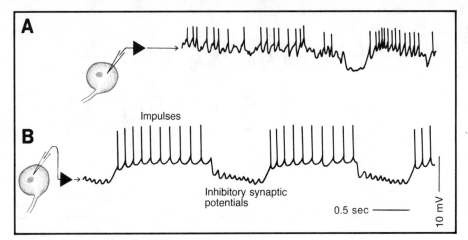

Two patterns of synaptic activity. The cell marked "A" produces a ragged series of nerve impulses as a result of competition between excitatory and inhibitory synaptic input. The brackets show brief periods when first inhibition and then excitation gain the upper hand. In contrast, the cell marked "B" is controlled by synaptic input that alternates to produce a regular rhythm.

when the excitatory synapses are active, then the inhibitory ones are silent, leading to strong firing of the neuron. The excitatory synapses then turn off and inhibitory ones turn on, producing complete silence. This *alternation* causes a rhythmic output or *cycling* in the neuron. Cyclic behavior is, of course, absolutely fundamental to breathing and most of our other vital functions.

What a neuron does is in large part determined by what the presynaptic cells tell it to do. The second neuron in the figure *seems* to be "weighing the input," but in fact its output is just as determined as that of the first. It seems like a slave cell. If a neuron's activity is *determined* by the cells that are presynaptic to it, and *their* activity is in turn determined in the same manner, does this not force us to the conclusion that all activity in our nervous system is determined by the action of those first neurons—our receptors? Since the receptor impulses are a precise function of the stimulus conditions, the result is behavioral determinism. You will recall that one premise of *behaviorism* (see p. 24) accounts for behavior entirely in terms of antecedent stimuli, without recourse to the internal state of the animal. However, another possible conclusion is that if all external sensory stimulation were stopped, the brain would gradually damp down, turn off and become silent. *Sensory deprivation* does cause bizarre effects, but the brain never stops until death. If anything, its activity may increase when outside stimulation decreases. In animals like frogs, we can perform the drastic experiment of *isolating* the CNS by cutting all the nerves to it and removing it, still alive, from the animal. When we do this, we find as much or more neural activity going on in the CNS as before. This tells us that the CNS has the capacity for self-generated, spontaneous activity. In other words, it is always "turned on."

Spontaneously active neurons

Impulses from our sense organs arrive at a brain already humming with internally generated activity. Like passengers arriving at a busy airport, they cause a momentary stir, and much activity is geared to them, but they directly *cause* only a small proportion of all the hustle and bustle. Early investigators were puzzled by the incessant activity in unstimulated neural tissue, and tried to explain it by the concept of *circus reexcitation* in which a ring of neurons excites itself indefinitely. However, we now know that some individual neurons are capable of generating rhythmic activity, just as an isolated heart can continue to beat. ■ Such activity may have many different frequencies, including very slow waves with peaks separated by about twenty-four hours (circadian

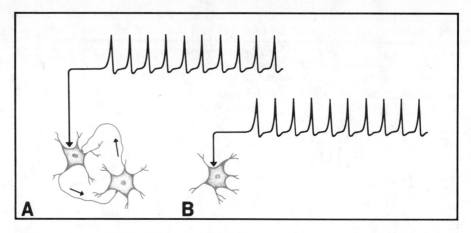

Spontaneous firing can be recorded in neurons throughout the nervous system. Early theories tried to explain this by reverberating or self-exciting circuits like A because the neuron was considered to be silent unless stimulated. We now know that some single neurons can generate impulses without any synaptic input (B).

rhythms). The mechanisms for the faster rhythms are partially understood, the slower ones less so. We will see in Chapter 15 that when all external stimulation is set aside during sleep, the brain signals slow down but still vary systematically in characteristic patterns. The self-stimulating aspect of the nervous system is clearly involved in dreaming as well as in some of our greatest acts of creativity and the most frightening hallucinations of the schizophrenic. But the important point is that this spontaneous neural activity liberates us from a passive view of behavior as merely a deterministic response to external stimuli. Instead, it provides a dynamic physiological substrate on which to base active process theories of motivation, perception, and learning.

Chemicals that shape mind and body

Samuel Taylor Coleridge awoke one night from a deep opium sleep to write one of his finest poems, *Kubla Khan*. Novelist Honoré de Balzac upped his coffee consumption to fifty cups a day when his writing grew stale. Playwright-director Joshua Logan found that lithium salts helped him snap out of the emotional depression that had crippled him for years. The era of "better living through chemistry" is clearly upon us. Not only are drugs being used to pick up depressed spirits and calm manic ones (the neurological effects of psychoactive drugs will be discussed in detail in the next chapter), but to control disturbances of our sensory and motor systems as well. In the not too distant future, we may be taking chemicals to improve our attention and memories and also put some new kick in our creativity. Many drugs affect synaptic transmission by blocking or facilitating receptor molecules. Others alter the receptivity of certain cells to hormones. We will see accumulating evidence which suggests neurotransmitters affect the earliest development of embryo cells even before neurons exist. Thus they shape the way the body develops as well as how the mind works.

Long before scientists started investigating the role of chemicals in nerve action, South American Indians were dipping their arrows into the poison *curare*, which kills by blocking the transmission of certain nerve signals to muscles, causing sudden paralysis and death by suffocation. A different, much more gradual loss of muscular control occurs in Parkinson's disease from a lack of the transmitter substance called *dopamine*. In some severe forms of mental illness there is an imbalance of certain transmitters. Too much as well as too little of a transmitter may cause physiological as well as mental disorders. An excess of the transmitter *norepinephrine* is sometimes responsible for high blood pressure. The powerful tranquilizer *chlorpromazine*, which created a revolution in the treatment of hospitalized mental patients (p. 598), exerts its calming effect by inhibiting the action of other neurotransmitters, among them *epinephrine*. People who mellow out with marijuana, get high with amphetamines, or spaced far out with LSD are conducting their own experiments on altering the action of transmitter substances. More systematic research is currently being directed toward tampering with brain chemistry to make humans remember more, attend better to visual stimuli, and even be more creative.

A California chemist (Alexander Shulgin) is developing a drug that he hopes will expand our potential for creative responding by preventing the brain from getting "bored." There is a brain system that tunes down (and out) repetitive signals, whether internal ones or from the environment. Signals that are repeated and carry no new information stop being attended to. This energy-saving process of *habituation* dulls our reaction to familiar stimuli that do not demand action. From what you know already, you can figure out where the habituation is probably occurring. There is evidence that reduced amounts of transmitter substances are released when habituation to a repeated stimulus takes place. This depression at synaptic junctions may be offset by injections of chemicals that keep the neurotransmitters flowing and the postsynaptic membrane receptive to them. Undoing habituation may thus enable us to see new solutions to old problems. This revitalization of stimulus input could allow a person to see the world anew and react with childlike enthusiasm to all ideas, sights, sounds, and people. The danger is, of course, a sensory overload if the habituation mechanism were turned off for too long a time. We would not distinguish between old and new, relevant and irrelevant stimuli—all would excite us. (Some theories of schizophrenia discussed in Chapter 19 suggest a similar dynamic process of being flooded with stimulus input that the person cannot screen out or put on "hold.") As was cautioned in our opening chapters, we should reserve judgment on these interesting hypotheses until sound data are in hand. The line between "creative" and "crackpot" can indeed be quite fine.

The incredible thing about the human mind is that it can act upon the brain to produce some of these same effects without the injection of chemicals from the outside. Apparently Zen masters can block the habituation process because their disciplined concentration makes them attend with equal intensity to every stimulus perceived. Their openness allows them to perceive the world anew with each stimulus.

In a study of habituation comparing three Zen masters and four control subjects (relaxed with eyes closed), a click was sounded twenty times at precise fifteen-second intervals. By monitoring their brain wave patterns it was possible to observe the initial attention of the control subjects diminish as habituation set in. In contrast, the Zen masters responded to each repeated stimulus as fully as to the first. It was as if their openness to the experience of the moment resulted in preceiving the world anew at each sound of life (Kasamatsu & Hirai, 1966).

Neurotransmitters may in fact be even more remarkable than anyone has yet given them credit for. It appears that in certain organisms, transmitter substances are already at work influencing the differentiation, multiplication, and movement of developing cells in the embryos, even before neurons are functioning. They may have begun their evolutionary life as messengers of information *within* cells, carrying out the genetic instructions that make every individual unique (McMahon, 1974).

Reference Module
The Endocrine System

Adrenals Pair of endocrine glands located near the kidneys. The inner part is the *adrenal medulla*, which secretes the hormones adrenaline and noradrenaline during strong emotion. The outer layer is the *adrenal cortex*, which secretes hormones that influence physical growth and maturation.

Hormones Greek for "I excite"; chemicals produced by the endocrine glands and carried through the bloodstream to various parts of the body where they control metabolism, arousal, and other bodily processes.

Hypothalamus Key structure in the brain which controls much of the endocrine system through the pituitary.

Islets of Langerhans Tiny glands in the pancreas that secrete the hormone insulin, which regulates blood sugar.

Ovaries Female sex glands; produce egg cells *(ova)* and the hormones estrogen and progesterone.

Parathyroids Tiny glands on the surface of the thyroid that regulate calcium and phosphorus levels in the blood.

Pituitary The "master gland" of the endocrine system, activated by the hypothalamus. It is associated directly with body growth and controls the functioning of other endocrine glands.

Testes Male sex glands; produce sperm and the hormone testosterone.

Thymus Gland in the chest cavity; active early in life in the development of immunity to disease.

Thyroid Endocrine gland in the neck that regulates metabolism (oxygen consumption, body temperature, and so forth).

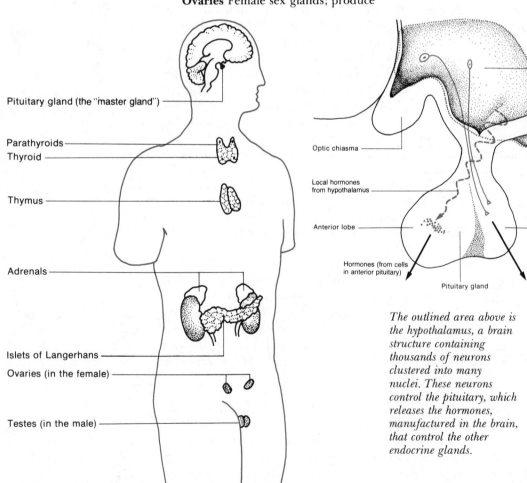

The outlined area above is the hypothalamus, a brain structure containing thousands of neurons clustered into many nuclei. These neurons control the pituitary, which releases the hormones, manufactured in the brain, that control the other endocrine glands.

The chemistry of intimacy

Chemical communication is not restricted to synapses. There are four levels of such communication, of which synaptic transmission is the most localized and specific. The other levels of chemical communication are: *pheromones, general hormones,* and *local hormones.* Many animals excrete chemicals into the environment in order to communicate with other animals. Well-known examples are the sex pheromones or "chemical lures" which are excreted by some insects to attract mates from miles away. Mammals also use sex pheromones, for example, the musk deer secretes a highly potent oil which many humans (and presumably all musk deer) find sexually exciting. Synthetic musk is a constituent of perfumes and colognes. Pheromones can also signal danger, as in the alarm pheromones of certain fish, and the territorial scent markings of wolves and cats, which warn other animals to keep away.

A second level of chemical communication occurs within our bodies by way of hormones, which are released by glands into the bloodstream and bathe most of the tissues in the body. In so doing, they chemically control the basic rhythms of life — sexual drive, reproduction, stress reactions, aggressiveness, energy level, and general emotional arousal. (See Reference Module, p. 304). Depending on the amount of hormone secreted by the thyroid gland you can feel listless, energetic, or even manic. The hormones produced by the *gonads* (sex glands) control the many complex patterns of behavior and physiology in the reproductive cycle. Most of the body's glands release their specific hormones on command from other hormones that are released from the master gland, the *pituitary.* Thus for example, one pituitary hormone stimulates production of *estrogen,* which is essential to the hormonal chain reaction that triggers the release of eggs from the female's ovaries, making her fertile. By blocking the mechanism in the pituitary that controls this hormone flow, certain birth-control pills prevent the eggs from getting to where they can be fertilized.

The pituitary gland is activated by "orders" from a nearby brain structure, the *hypothalamus.* Those orders come from electrical impulses sent through connecting nerve fibers and by hormone messages sent into blood vessels surrounding them. This is the third level of chemical communication (more specific than the general hormonal secretions). The hypothalamus secretes local hormones into the blood supply of the pituitary. These hormones tell the pituitary gland to release *its* hormones into general circulation. In spite of their widespread distribution, hormones produce specific effects because only certain cells are sensitive to them. Cells may change their receptivity to certain hormones. This mechanism keeps them from overreacting when the concentration of certain hormones is too high. Hormones may also decrease or increase the sensitivity of receptors to other hormones. For example, an excess of thyroid hormones results in rapid heart rate. This effect is indirect because they increase the number of receptors on heart cells for another hormone (epinephrine) that directly increases heart rate (Kolata, 1977).

Back to Keith

We are now in a better position to appreciate that even when Keith was a superman he was "not his own man" at all. He was being chemically programmed in extreme ways by the steady secretions from the pituitary gland. These hormones in turn stimulated secretions from the adrenal glands (stress reactions of fight or flight), the gonads (sexual behavior), the thyroid (high energy level), and possibly others. In addition, there is a fine interplay between the hypothalamus and the hormones from the pituitary and other glands. While the hypothalamus controls the release of some hormones, its action is also influenced by other hormones. The sight of a sexually desirable person will flash nerve impulses to the hypothalamus via the optic nerve. The hypothalamus releases hormones that speed up heart action and initiate an arousal pattern. Sex hormones can affect feelings of irritability and aggressiveness as well as sensuality. Thus, Keith was always wired and ready either to make love or to make war. All that was needed was an appropriate stimulus object: a woman for the former, a challenging male for the latter.

But Keith was not a slave to the abnormal chemical commands brought about by the tumor. Even before his operation, he began to realize something was wrong. He was able to conclude rationally that he was not experiencing appropriate emotions in certain social situations. And when he could not understand his reactions after the tumor was removed, he sought professional help. Keith's case reveals that although hormonal secretions control the more primitive flow of life processes, it is the rational functioning of the brain itself that gives life its direction and meaning. In the next chapter we shall see how our neurons are put together into a brain and examine that wonderful organ that sets us apart from all other living creatures.

Chapter summary

In the seventeenth century, René Descartes advanced the *mechanistic* view that the study of the processes of brain and body could and should be approached on a purely physical basis. But in order to conform to religious orthodoxy, he constructed a *dualistic* system that exempted the soul and mind from scientific inquiry.

Modern physiological psychologists have carried Descartes' approach to a further point called *reductionism*. The *reductionist* studies complex phenomena by reducing them to smaller and smaller units—even to the level of minute subatomic particles.

The human nervous system is made up of two subsystems: the *central nervous system* (CNS), which consists of the brain and spinal cord, and the *peripheral nervous system,* which consists of nerve fibers connecting the central nervous system to energy-sensitive *receptor cells* and to *effector cells.*

Neurons are the cells that carry messages within the nervous system. A typical neuron is made up of a *cell body* with one or more sets of *dendrites* that project from one end of the cell, a single *axon* that extends for long and varied distances from the other end, and *terminal buttons* that make contact with other neurons.

The simplest form of neural transmission is along a *reflex arc*, which follows a sequence from initial sensory input, through the central nervous system, to the final behavioral output. *Receptor* neurons detect energy signals from external or internal *stimuli* and convert them into neural signals. The most common form of neuron, the *interneuron*, transmits signals from one neuron to another. *Motor neurons,* in turn, directly control behavior by either directly exciting the muscles or activating *effector neurons* that excite or inhibit glandular activity.

When a nerve cell *fires,* the electrical properties of a received signal are converted to impulses sent along the length of the axon to the terminal buttons. Then, through *synaptic transmission,* the terminal buttons pass the message along to a network of surrounding neurons.

When the neuron is at rest, its charge is negative and its *electrical potential* is said to be in a steady, or *polarized* state. When the stimulus energy reaching a cell exceeds the cell's *stimulation threshold*, it creates an *action potential* by changing the cell's charge to positive. This potential is propagated along the axon. *Slow potentials* are electrical disturbances within a neuron that vary with the intensity of the stimulus. *Nerve impulses*, or *action potentials*, operate on an *all-or-none* principle—amplitude remains constant throughout the journey of the impulse.

Axons with large diameters and/or *myelin sheaths* transmit messages faster than small or unsheathed axons. There is a brief *absolute refractory period* that occurs after an axon has fired, during which it is temporarily unexcitable. For an even briefer period before the axon membrane returns to normal, it experiences a *relative refractory period*, in which a stronger-than-normal stimulus is required to fire an impulse.

Synaptic transmission makes variability in behavior possible. When a nerve impulse is received, the *presynaptic terminal* of one neuron releases thousands of molecules of a *neurotransmitter* into the gap between it and the dendrites of another neuron.

Synapses may be *excitatory* or *inhibitory*, triggering or preventing an adjacent nerve from firing. The amount of transmitter released by the nerve impulse may *facilitate* the subsequent *postsynaptic potentials* (PSP), making them larger, or *depress* them, making them smaller.

While some neurons may receive hundreds of inhibitory or excitatory transmissions that cancel each other out, others display *cooperation* and *alternate* between the two, producing the *cyclical* behavior fundamental to such functions as breathing. Thus, the variability in neural transmission is almost infinite.

Some individual neurons are capable of generating rhythmic activity. This self-stimulating aspect of the nervous system calls into question the thoroughly determinist view of behavior as limited and fixed by external stimuli.

Many chemicals and drugs affect synaptic transmission by blocking or facilitating receptor molecules. Others alter the receptivity of certain cells to hormones. Too much as well as too little of a transmitter can lead to physiological or mental disorders.

Synaptic transmission is only one of the body's means for chemical communication. *Pheromones* are excreted by some animals for mating purposes and as a means of warning. Gonads and other glands produce general and local *hormones* that act as communicators within the body, regulating complex patterns of behavior and physiology such as the reproductive cycle. These glands usually release their hormones on the commands of specific hormones released by the *pituitary*, the master gland. The pituitary gland itself is activated by hormones or nerve impulses originating in the *hypothalamus*, a nearby brain structure.

11 Exploring the Brain

We are in the operating room of the Montreal Neurological Institute observing brain surgery on Buddy, a young man with uncontrollable epileptic seizures. The surgeon wants to operate to remove a tumor, but first he must discover what the consequences will be of removing various portions of the brain tissue surrounding the tumor. In effect, he must draw a *map* of a portion of the patient's brain—a map relating particular sites in the brain to the psychological functions they affect or control. Therefore, Buddy is kept conscious under local anesthesia so he can report what he experiences as the surgeon probes his brain.

The thick, bony layer of skull that shields and protects the delicate biological organ housed within is removed. We can now see the outermost, deeply wrinkled surface of the brain, called the *cortex*. The point of a thin wire, held like a pencil in the surgeon's skilled hand, gently touches one area of the cortex, stimulating it with minute electrical current.

"Nil, nil, no reaction noted," states the nurse. The electrode is then carefully placed on another spot only millimeters away. "Fist clenching, hand raising, twitching reaction observed." The same area is stimulated again, and the nurse reports a similar motor reaction. This procedure of stimulating one area of the surface of the brain after another while observing the changes in behavior produced allows the surgeon slowly to put together the map he must use to guide his operation through the innumerable hills and valleys of the patient's brain. There are no pain receptors in the brain so the electrical current stimulates neuronal activity without causing discomfort. The patient can therefore be awake and assist the surgeon during the brain mapping without any sensation of pain.

Suddenly, an unexpected response occurs.

"The patient is grinning: he is smiling: eyes opening when that area is stimulated."

"Buddy, what happened, what did you just experience?"

"Doc, I heard a song, or rather a part of a song, a melody."

"Buddy, have you ever heard it before?"

"Yes, I remember having heard it a long time ago, but I can't remember the name of the tune."

When another brain site is stimulated, the patient recalls in vivid detail a thrilling childhood experience.

In a similar operation, a woman patient "relived" the delivery of her baby. As if by pushing an electronic memory button, the surgeon, Dr. Wilder Penfield, has touched memories stored silently for years in the recesses of his patients' brains (Penfield & Baldwin, 1952). ■

We shall examine these and other brain mapping techniques later in this chapter. But first, let us consider the wide range of capabilities of this remarkable organ.

The human brain is often compared to a computer, but in many ways it is vastly superior to even the most sophisticated electronic computer. It does not work as fast on routine programs and it tires more quickly, but even the brain of a child has powers no computer can match. The sensory detection features of the human brain enable it to distinguish between wines of different years, perfumes of different makes, a familiar face in a crowd, or a pitched "strike" from a "ball." Its language ability allows the brain to write programs for computer software and wiring diagrams for its hardware, while also training technicians to operate the machines. The contrasts could be extended to its long-term memory that knows whether or not it knows a given bit of information and the brain's creative functions that go far beyond existing rules and limitations to invent new forms. However, the most important contrast be-

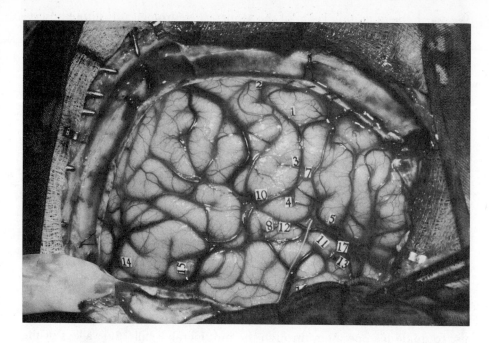

This is the right cerebral cortex of an epileptic patient. It has been exposed for surgery with the patient fully conscious. The numbers indicate spots at which electrical stimulation produced positive responses—simple sensory and motor responses at spots 2, 3, 7, 4, and 8 and flashback experiences at spots 11, 12, 15, and 14. For example, when spot 11 was stimulated, the patient reported hearing a neighborhood mother calling her little boy. She identified the experience as "something that happened years ago" (Penfield, 1958).

tween brain and computer is in the area of action. Computers are acted upon and can give instructions for action, but they just stand around passively waiting for someone and something to follow their output. Brains were designed for action. All the exquisite sensory processing, information storage, perceptual abilities, and decision-making strategies exist for one purpose—to make action swift and sure. The input and integrating capacity of the brain operate in the service of the body's muscles and glands. It is through our motor actions that humans have built instruments (like telescopes and microscopes) to extend our limited senses or to expand physical limitations (with space satellites, submarines, and organ transplants). The human brain is even able to analyze its own life force, a study which may in time lead to the ability to create new life. The major parts of the brain are described in the Reference Module on pages 312–313.

Neural networks

When we observe a neuron in action, or even a simple reflex arc (p. 289), we are witnessing only information *transmission*. The real achievement of the nervous system, however, is in *information processing*. Information processing is a common feature of all central nervous systems, as well as digital computers. Information is *transformed*: it is combined, added to or subtracted from, rerouted, stored for later use, compared with other information. How is information processed by the brain? The basic principle that has emerged from the last quarter century of brain research is that neurons have evolved into vast numbers of complex circuits or *networks*, which have the ability to process information with ever increasing sophistication. This principle is the central theme of this section. It is so important that it is worthwhile viewing it from a broader perspective.

Hierarchical organization in nature

Perhaps the most fundamental achievement of science has been the demonstration that all matter is organized *hierarchically*. Subatomic particles (*protons, neutrons,* and *electrons*) combine into just ninety-eight stable forms known as *atoms*, or elements. Atoms in turn are linked together in nearly limitless combinations as *molecules,* which have evolved into structures of staggering complexity, eventually achieving, because of their structure, special abilities that transcend ordinary chemistry and give rise to life. The hierarchical principle of organization continues in living systems: molecules are grouped into bits of living matter called *organelles.* These are collected together in *cells,* like nerve cells and heart cells, the cells in turn form organs (like the brain and the heart), which make up *organisms,* like us. The principle continues, however, as organisms form *families, communities,* and *societies.* Psychology focuses on the individual, but its attempts to explain behavior force us to take account of both our neurons and our neighbors.

It is difficult, both conceptually and experimentally, to jump from one level of organization to the next. Nevertheless, among the most exciting events in science are those rare occasions when bridgeheads are established across the gaps that separate hierarchical levels. Nature is organized by hierarchies and it functions by integrating units and simple objects into systems and complex organizations. Each system uses only some of the elements of the simpler systems. At each level of complexity there are limits and constraints on the system that demand still higher levels of complexity to overcome them (see Jacob, 1977).

Large assemblies or *networks* of neurons give rise to the higher properties of nervous systems. It is neural networks that ultimately generate intelligent behavior. The best way to gain an understanding of the enormous processing power of neural networks is to look briefly at an example from vision.

A common characteristic of all visual networks is that a large number of neurons are precisely interconnected and converge onto other neurons. The interactions among the neurons give these networks special properties, such as the ability to distinguish between horizontal and vertical lines. That is, a specific cell in the brain will fire when and only when a vertical line is presented to the animal, another cell will fire only for a horizontal line, another for a line of a particular intermediate angle, and so on. We will have more to say about this in Chapter 12. These properties are expressed in the output of the neuron at the apex (head) of the network. However, the neuron at the head of one network may also function as an intermediate element in a larger hierarchy. Thus, fantastically elaborate networks are formed. These neural circuits begin to exhibit some of the properties of functioning organisms.

From dots, to lines, to shapes, to figures, stimuli in our field of vision begin to take on forms that are instantly recognizable to us. At higher levels of complexity, neural networks integrate the simpler input from lower levels transforming parts into wholes. (see *P&L* Close-up, Are There "Grandmother Cells" in the Brain?) In the next chapter we will consider in detail how the world "out there" is processed by the visual system to become a private showing in the theater of our "mind's eye."

The brain as actor

Perception and thought are indeed vital activities of the brain, but we could not have survived the challenges posed by evolutionary demands simply by

Reference Module
Brain Structure

Amygdala An almond-shaped nucleus in the limbic system located in front of the hippocampus in the temporal lobe; associated with emotional and aggressive behavior.

Brain stem Columnar structure between the cerebrum and the spinal cord; contains many structures, and damage to it usually causes severe disabilities, coma, or death.

Cerebrum Latin for "brain"; now usually refers to the most recently developed part of the brain: the cerebral hemispheres, basal ganglia, and rhinencephalon.

Cerebellum The "little brain" beneath the back of the cerebrum; has extensive connections with sensory and motor structures. Damage to it results in disturbances of movement.

Corpus callosum A large collection of nerve fibers (axons), which interconnects the two hemispheres of the brain. Split-brain operations sever this connection, resulting in two functionally separate cortical hemispheres.

Cortex or neocortex A thin, grayish rind of nerve tissue covering the cerebrum; active in conscious experience and higher mental processes.

Cranial nerves Twelve pairs of nerves that arise from the brain and brain stem, including the olfactory, optic, and auditory nerves and the vagus nerve (see below).

Diencephalon Region at the forward end of the brain stem containing the thalamus and hypothalamus.

Fissure Deep cleft or groove separating the lobes of the cortex.

Frontal lobes Area of cortex forward of the central sulcus. This area appears to be involved in future orientation and planning.

Ganglion Latin for "knot"; a cluster of nerve cell bodies, usually outside the central nervous system.

Gyrus An outfolding, or bulge, of the cortex.

Hippocampus Latin for "seahorse," which describes its shape. A portion of the limbic system located in the temporal lobe. Bilateral damage to it in humans causes severe memory loss for subsequent events.

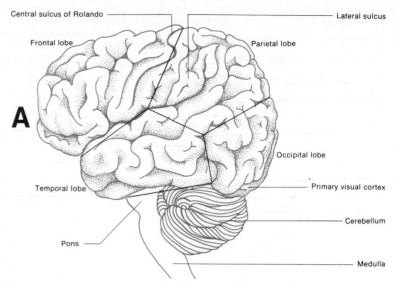

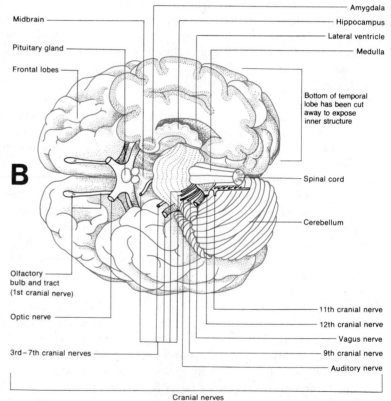

A. Side view of intact brain.
B. Undersurface of brain. A horizontal section has been made through the right temporal and occipital lobes, exposing the hippocampus and part of the lateral ventricle.

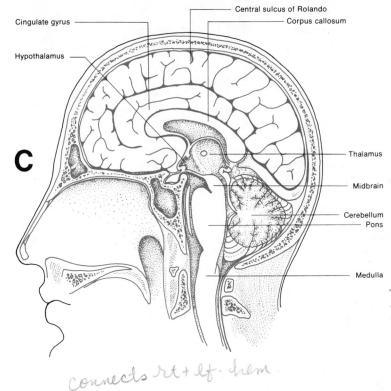

Cingulate gyrus

Central sulcus of Rolando

Corpus callosum

Hypothalamus

C

Thalamus

Midbrain

Cerebellum
Pons

Medulla

connects rt + lf. hem

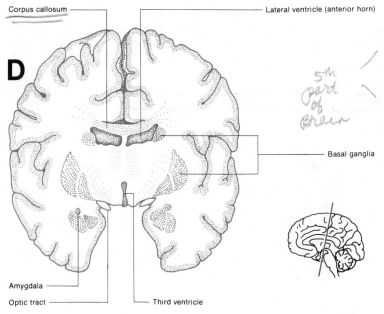

Corpus callosum

Lateral ventricle (anterior horn)

D

5th part of Brain

Basal ganglia

Amygdala

Optic tract

Third ventricle

*C. Cross section of brain,
side view.
D. Cross section through
cerebrum. The small drawing
shows the location of the cut.*

Hypothalamus Key structure beneath the cortex; important in regulation of metabolism, temperature, and emotional behavior; control center for the endocrine system.

Limbic system Region around the upper end of the brain stem; active in attention, emotion, motivation, and memory.

Medulla Base of the brain stem; blends into the spinal cord.

Midbrain Region of the brain stem between the hypothalamus and the pons.

Nerve A bundle of axons, wrapped in connective tissue.

Nucleus (1) Specialized matter in the cell body that directs the life activities of the cell. (2) A cluster of nerve cell bodies located within the central nervous system (see also *Ganglion*).

Optic chiasm Region where the optic nerves cross, named for its resemblance to the Greek letter *chi* (χ).

Parietal lobe Nonspecific or "association" area of the cortex, containing neurons responding to many different senses.

Pons Latin for "bridge"; a portion of the brain stem containing many axons leading to and from the cerebellum.

Reticular activating system A diffuse region of cells spreading along the central portion of the brain stem; important in arousal and attention.

Sulcus An infolding, or "wrinkle," of the cortex, smaller than a fissure.

Temporal lobe Lateral (side) portion of cortex; contains specialized areas for hearing and visual processing.

Thalamus A knob in the center of the cerebrum, on top of the brain stem, containing millions of axons which process sensory information going to the cortex.

Spinal cord Major communication pathway with the portion of the body below the neck.

Vagus nerve From Latin "to wander"; the tenth cranial nerve; contains sensory and motor axons connecting the visceral organs to the brain.

Ventricles An interconnected series of cavities within the brain, filled with the cerebrospinal fluid that cushions the brain from injuries. These were incorrectly considered for more than a thousand years to be the seat of mental faculties.

Close-up
Are There "Grandmother Cells" in the Brain?

In the early 1960s, neuroscientists began to find neurons in the visual systems of animals that responded only to very specific stimuli. For example, a small erratically moving dark dot in the visual field of a frog would cause a certain cell to fire, but no other stimulus (such as turning the lights up and down, or jiggling a small spot of light) was effective. Jerome Lettvin, of the Massachusetts Institute of Technology, dubbed these cells "bug detectors" and suggested that cells with exceedingly complex stimulus requirements might be found in the brain. As an extreme example, he speculated half jokingly on the existence of a "grandmother cell," a neuron in the brain that would only respond to the features of one's grandmother.

Recently, however, investigators at Princeton discovered a cell in the brain of the monkey that responded best to a silhouette of the monkey's hand. The stimuli used in this study are shown below, arranged from left to right in the sequence of their increasing ability to trigger a response (Gross, Rocha-Miranda, & Bender, 1972).

1   1   1   2   3   3   4   4   5   6

sitting around and meditating. Evolution can only have selected for *useful acts*, not for good thoughts nor the intention to go to work tomorrow. This point was made with typical clarity by neuropsychologist Roger Sperry in a famous article called "Neurology and the Mind-Brain Problem." According to Sperry, the brain is primarily

"a mechanism for governing motor activity. Its primary function is essentially the transforming of sensory patterns into patterns of motor coordination. . . . From the fishes to man there is apparent only a gradual refinement and elaboration of brain mechanisms with nowhere any radical alteration of the fundamental operating principles. In man as in the salamander the primary business of the brain continues to be the governing, directly or indirectly, of overt behavior" (1952, p. 297).

How we move our muscles may seem more akin to athletics than to psychology, but even our more sedentary moments are symphonies of neuromuscular activity. As you read this, your eyes skip across the page and then fly back to the margin to begin again. Most students are surprised to learn that acts which we all perform quite effortlessly and unconsciously have mechanisms which cannot yet be explained.

The motor unit

How can we do what we do? The fundamental link between brain and behavior is the *motor unit*, which is made up of a single motor neuron and all the muscle fibers it innervates. ▲ Muscles involved in fine, precise movements, like those in the tongue and fingers, comprise many individual motor units, each unit consisting of only a few muscle fibers, while muscles like those in the thigh and trunk have relatively fewer motor units, each with many hundreds of muscle fibers in it. In other words, many more motor neurons activate a given mass of finger muscle than of leg muscle. Since each impulse in a motor neuron causes all of the muscle fibers in its unit to contract (muscle fibers, like

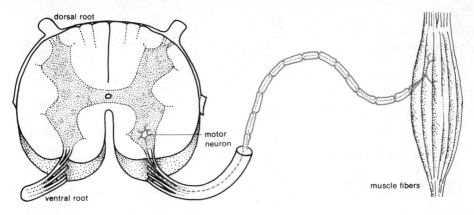

A motor unit, shown here in highly diagrammatic form, consists of a single motor neuron originating in the spinal cord and the muscle or muscles it innervates.

motor neurons, fire in all-or-none fashion), the tension in a whole muscle depends on the number of motor neurons firing at a given time. This means, among other things, that a finger can produce much finer gradations of force than a leg. The greater number of motor neurons devoted to the fingers requires a corresponding increase in interneurons in the motor circuits programming the fingers' movement. This is reflected in the fact that, as we shall see, relatively large portions of the brain are concerned with the hand. Motor neurons are the exclusive pathway to your muscles. Whether you are typing, playing a concerto, or gripping a tennis racket, motor neurons must be employed.

The flow of behavior

The term *central motor program* (or sometimes motor *score*, by analogy with music or choreography) is used to refer to the neural mechanisms that generate patterned output. It should not surprise you to learn that the physical bases of such programs are neural circuits, and that such circuits are complex. Complete neural circuits cannot yet be drawn for any behavior beyond single-synapse reflexes, although many laboratories are hard at work trying to unscramble the neural "wiring diagrams" for various simple behaviors. Even the complex cellular basis of learned movements in primates can now be investigated because of innovations that permit recordings from neurons in alert monkeys.

Tools and talk are perhaps the two major gifts of human evolution. The two largest functional regions of the brain are those that control the hands—which allow us to use tools to build shelters and weapons to protect us from more powerful animals—and the vocal apparatus—which allows us to communicate information and talk our way out of trouble when an enemy has a bigger weapon. There are more than six hundred muscles in the human body, and their voluntary action is initiated and integrated by the *motor cortex*. The motor cortex functions in conjunction with the *cerebellum* and the *sensory cortex* to coordinate muscular activity. Information from the sensory cortex is essential to provide *feedback* about the progress and accuracy of our motor output. Auditory feedback is necessary to guide talking and singing, while immediate visual feedback is essential for eye-hand coordination. These behaviors deteriorate when feedback is prevented or altered by delaying it. ●

The effects of auditory feedback are studied by delaying the interval between uttering a sound and hearing it. Rather than hearing the words they have just spoken through air and bone conduction, as they normally would, subjects hear them over a set of earphones, with a delay interposed.

Motor tracking with delayed visual feedback

The lower diagram shows a videotape apparatus used to introduce a time delay into the tasks of tracing a star and writing a list of words. At the top are shown one subject's responses. Items in the first column were done under normal conditions, items in the second column were done using a TV monitor but no delay, and items in the third column were done using a TV monitor with a delay. The handicap this delay creates for coordinated eye-hand movements is considerable.

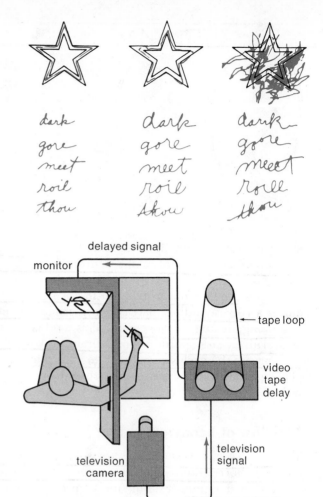

The consequences of such delay are measured in terms of changes in the subjects' speaking—its intensity, duration of phrase, articulation, and emotional stress (Smith, 1962; Yates, 1963). Under conditions where the delay interval is about a fifth of a second, speech is extremely disrupted. In fact, the speech of some people breaks down altogether.

Delay is most disruptive when the feedback is loud and when the material is closely organized with the parts dependent on each other, as in singing, whistling a tune, or saying a tongue-twisting limerick. Delays shorter or longer than a fifth of a second are less disruptive. There is very little adaptation or improvement with continued practice, although long-term studies of delayed auditory feedback have not been tried.

Mapping the brain

The secrets of the brain's functioning, like some great treasure hidden in a vault, have eluded discovery for centuries because of its protected location. The thick, bony skull cap shields it from exposure, and even when the skull is removed, only the cortex is revealed—the rest remains concealed within. Anatomists have, of course, provided us with pictures of the brain, by post-mortem examination of human and animal brains. But a physiological psychologist interested in the relationship between brain processes and behavior must study a living, behaving organism.

The study of brain processes in living subjects has awaited technological discoveries. Most of these methodological breakthroughs have occurred only in the last few decades, but already they have generated an enormous yield of exciting information about how our brains work. The three most basic techniques employed by researchers to probe the neural activity of the brains of living humans and lower animals are: (a) stimulation, (b) lesions, and (c) recording of electrical activity.

Touching a sensitive nerve

Wilder Penfield's application of the stimulation method to map the functions of the conscious brain in humans climaxed a hundred years of research. In 1870, Gustav Fritsch and Eduard Hitzig of Berlin applied a weak electrical current to the cortex of dogs. Movements of a given leg occurred when certain regions were touched; other movements were coordinated to different sites of brain stimulation. In this way, the first maps were drawn of the functions of the brain. However, like an explorer who notes the mountains in a strange country while ignoring less obvious terrain, early brain explorers only touched upon the outer surface of the cortex. It was easy to reach, large in size, and thought to be the center of all human higher faculties. A great deal of evidence for localized function in the cortex has been obtained by the stimulation method, and the cortex is still being analyzed, but with ever more refined and carefully controlled techniques.

Interestingly, systematic research relating brain anatomy to functions of the brain was beginning at about the time the fad of *phrenology* was ending. A Viennese doctor named Franz Gall started the pseudoscience of phrenology with his theory that specific areas of the brain perform specific functions. This good idea was distorted by the notion that bumps on the head indicated well-developed brain areas below which pushed the skull out at that point. Using their own imagination as the method for mapping the brain Gall and Spurzheim created fanciful charts that found a place for areas of love of God (at the top), physical love (at the bottom), and almost every imaginable character trait in between. Phrenologists were consulted by masses of people who wanted to have their personalities diagnosed and their futures predicted. ■

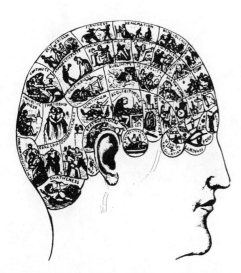

This phrenological map shows the locations ascribed to the various presumed powers or faculties of the mind—largely social-moral personality traits.

Penfield's explorations of the surface of the cortex, along with subsequent studies, have made it possible to draw another kind of cortical map. ◆ Sensory input from our eyes and ears projects to the cortex in a precise topographical way; these maps of sensation bear a startling resemblance to a distorted human figure spread out along one side of the cortex. Brain areas controlling motor output also form maps. When the body parts are drawn proportional in size to the areas of the cortex that operate their muscles, we can see that the hand (especially the thumb) is the largest. Mouth, tongue, and eyes follow, with little stature given to our legs and torso. These discoveries about the relationship between body surface and cortical surface proved that the organization of the brain was orderly and therefore could be systematically analyzed.

Memory: Place or protein?

Penfield concluded from his stimulation studies that all the memories "played back" on the operating table from different patients came from one area of the brain—the *temporal lobe*. Recent studies with monkeys offer some support for this view regarding visual memory. When monkeys see a highly familiar visual stimulus, temporal lobe nerve cells fire with a distinctive pattern, and when temporal lobe nerve cells are destroyed, visual memory is impaired. Nevertheless, other researchers question whether memory need be localized in only one area of the cortex. Critics remind us that Penfield's subjects were

◆ **Primary motor and somatosensory areas**

The primary motor and somatosensory areas of the cortex lie along the fissure of Rolando: the motor area just in front of it, the somatosensory area just behind it. Corresponding parts of the body are represented by points roughly across the fissure from each other, and representation is upside down; that is, the legs and feet are represented at the top and around the inner surface between the hemispheres, hands and arms are below them, and the head at the bottom. The greater precision of sensitivity and control in head and hands than in other parts of the body is reflected in larger areas of representation on the cortex.

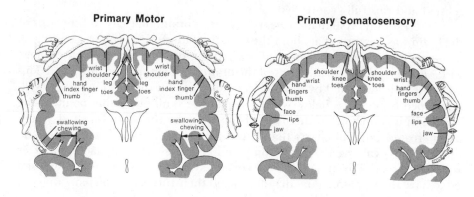

Primary Motor   **Primary Somatosensory**

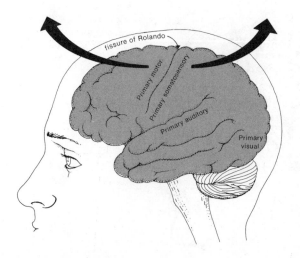

epileptic patients whose brains may have been altered due to their long-standing history of severe seizures.

The search for a physical home in the brain for memories was a task that consumed physiological psychologist Karl Lashley for decades (starting in the 1920s). Lashley's technique was simple and direct. First, he trained rats to find a reward at the end of a maze. He then removed bits of their cortex and finally returned them to the maze to observe how much of their memory of it was lost. To Lashley's dismay, no one area was pinpointed as causing a memory loss. It was not where he cut, but *how much* he cut away that affected the rat's memory. Memory got worse as larger and larger chunks of brain were destroyed, no matter where those chunks were located (Lashley, 1929).

Some neurobiologists now believe that *brain proteins* are the "homeless" free spirit of memory. Brain cells manufacture and use up more proteins at a faster rate than do any other of the body's cells. Since proteins may be arranged in large, complex chains, they could constitute a useful code language for memory. The possible combinations of proteins are sufficient to generate the structural basis for trillions of bits of information that humans remember in the course of their lives. One researcher has been able to chart the buildup of proteins and RNA in the brains of baby chicks during the critical developmental process of learning to recognize their mother (Rose, 1973). The puzzle of memory still remains one of the major obstacles in understanding the delicate interplay between the brain as a biochemical organ and the mind as a psychological reservoir of human experience. Even if it should be found that memories were stored in protein molecules, the question of how they are retrieved on demand would still be unanswered.

Pushing the buttons to make love or war

Stimulating the surface of the cortex reveals relatively superficial information compared with what has been discovered by probing deeper into the regions of the brain that are hidden from view. Walter Hess pioneered in developing precise technology for introducing *microelectrodes* deep into specific parts of the brain of freely moving animals. By pressing a button, Hess could send a small electrical current to the brain at the point of the electrode. Hess observed that when certain areas were stimulated, gentle cats became enraged. When other areas were stimulated, previously brave cats became fearful. Hess carefully recorded the emotional and behavioral consequences of stimulating each of forty-five hundred brain sites in nearly five hundred cats. His deep stimulation electrode technique was like a beacon that illuminated these primitive brain regions for a score of other researchers. Suddenly, at the push of a button, scientists could produce emotions and complicated behaviors in their animal subjects. The results depended on the exact placement of the wire tip. In some regions of the hypothalamus, tiny electrical currents caused well fed rats to begin immediately to eat as though starved. In other regions of the limbic system the same electrical stimulation led gentle cats to bristle with rage and hurl themselves upon a nearby object, which, in the early days, might be the startled experimenter. Sleep, sexual arousal, anxiety, or terror could now be provoked at the flick of the switch, and just as abruptly turned off. Complicated, stereotyped behavior patterns were sometimes turned on in the animals, as though the electricity were activating a prerecorded program of behavior. Cats have an unmistakable manner of stalking and capturing prey. This could be reliably produced, time after time, by stimulation through deep electrodes in the limbic system (Hess & Akert, 1955). ▲ Even pleasure can be electrified. Small currents in many regions of the brain clearly feel

▲

José Delgado is a pioneer in the brain implantation of radio-activated electrodes. His ability to find an exact spot in an animal's brain is so precise that he can trust his life to it. Here, even after the bull has started to charge, Delgado can stop it by a radio message to electrodes planted in its brain. After repeated experiences such as this, the animal becomes permanently less aggressive.

good to rats. Sometimes it arouses them sexually and even results in ejaculation, without a female rat in view. Rats and other laboratory subjects communicate the extent of their pleasure by going to great lengths to manipulate an apparatus that will deliver a jolt of that electrical current, like addicts craving drugs.

James Olds, who pioneered in this research, called these areas "pleasure centers" (Olds & Milner, 1954; Olds, 1973). Other areas of rats' brains appear to be punishing sites, and still others are both pleasurable and painful. Similar areas have been found in other species, including humans.

It is difficult to read about these experiments without being moved, for they suggest a degree of "automatic" control that we associate with machines rather than animals. While we may admit at one level that animals are in fact biological machines, the ability to control them so directly is unsettling. Recent work has shown that this control is not as total as it at first seemed to be (Valenstein, 1973). Nevertheless the conclusion remains: at least some emotions and behaviors can be "localized" in brain tissue, and can be directly and selectively manipulated by electrical stimulation.

Lesions: The cutting edge

Because the brain has no moving parts obvious to the naked eye, other more showy organs were originally thought to be the inner controls for behavior. How then did anyone first discover the true role of the brain? The simple answer is given by the third-century Greek physician Galen who refuted Aristotles' claim that the heart was the center of volition. Galen wrote:

". . . if you press so much upon a [cerebral] ventricle that you wound it, immediately the living being will be without movement and sensation. . . . this does not happen if you press the naked heart. I recall that once I permitted a certain person to grasp [the heart] with blacksmith's tongs . . . but not even thus was the animal injured in its sensation or voluntary movement, only it cried out greatly . . ." (Excerpts translated in Clarke & O'Malley, 1968)

Though gruesome and crude to us now, this was an *experiment*, a method of obtaining information that unfortunately was buried with Galen and remained lost for a thousand years. The technique he described, however, eventually became the royal road to localization of brain function. The *lesion* technique involves experimental destruction of brain areas. This is accomplished by surgically removing parts of the brain (as Lashley did in his search for the memory warehouse), by cutting connections between brain areas, or by destroying tissue by applications of intense heat, cold, electricity, or laser beams. In a variant of Galen's experiment, a region of the brain is destroyed and, after the animal recovers from the immediate effects of the operation, it is tested and any behavioral defects noted.

Experimental lesioning of the brain began in earnest in the late nineteenth century and reached its peak about twenty years ago. In that interval every distinguishable portion of the brain was, at one time or another, cut away, cauterized, frozen, or sucked out with an aspirator. The brain-damaged animals were then tested for vision, hearing, learning, motivation, sexuality, hunger, thirst, vocalization and so on in progressively more refined and quantifiable ways. Throughout this period the experimental results were repeatedly compared with the growing mass of clinical data resulting from the analysis of human behavior following brain lesions caused by disease, accidents and two world wars.

For example, the French neurologist Pierre Broca is generally credited with the discovery that the left frontal area of the brain is crucial for maintaining normal language and speech functions. During autopsies, Broca noticed that patients who had suffered from aphasia (see p. 212) turned out to have an injury in a specific area of the frontal lobe. By about 1865, Broca had observed enough cases to be able to proclaim with some degree of confidence that "we speak with the left hemisphere." Some years later, Carl Wernicke was able to identify a second region of the brain of importance for language and speech functions. This area is now commonly referred to as *Wernicke's area*. ● While Broca's area appears to be most important for generating language, Wernicke's area is primarily responsible for understanding spoken and written language. These two cortical areas are connected to each other by means of a long fiber tract known as the *arcuate fasciculus* (*arcuate* means curved). This fiber tract passes through an area of the brain called the *angular gyrus*. Centrally located between primary somatosensory, primary auditory, and primary visual areas of the brain, the angular gyrus serves important association functions. Some researchers—notably Geschwind (1970)—have suggested that the evolution of this area may be the single most important factor responsible for the advanced stage of language development seen in the human species.

●

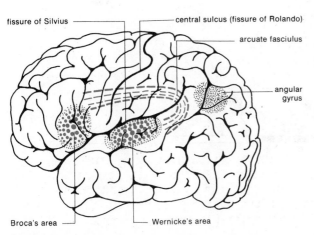

fissure of Silvius

central sulcus (fissure of Rolando)

arcuate fasciulus

angular gyrus

Broca's area

Wernicke's area

The figure is a diagrammatic representation of the left cerebral hemisphere, showing approximate location of Broca's area and Wernicke's area.

The end result of this enormous clinical and experimental research effort was a radical transformation of our concept of the brain. We could no longer regard it as an unimportant mass of tissue. Lesioning revealed it to be the highly differentiated, complex, and organized master control organ.

Lesioning is still a valuable research method, unsurpassed for quickly revealing whether a region is vitally important for a particular function. For example, it has long been known that organisms possess internal "clocks" that maintain cycles of activity with a period of about twenty-four hours. Such rhythms are important to us, and when they are out of tune with the environment we feel unwell—this is the basis of "jet lag." Such *circadian* ("about a day") *rhythms* can be clearly seen in the activity of rats, which normally are active at night. Even if rats are kept in constant darkness, this activity rhythm is maintained, showing that alternating light cycles alone do not cause it. A long search for the rat's internal clock recently paid off when it was shown that lesions in a tiny region deep in the rat's brain completely abolished the rhythm (Stephan & Zucker, 1972). ■ By itself this finding would not prove that the clock had been located, but since even very large lesions elsewhere in the brain do not disrupt circadian rhythms, the importance of this region *(suprachiasmatic nucleus)* to rhythms seems certain.

It has become fashionable to criticize the lesion technique as a crude method of analysis. It *is* crude, and it is therefore all the more remarkable that so much valuable information was gained from the ingenious and painstaking experiments that pushed the technique to its limits. Other critics have argued that lesion studies performed mostly on lower animals have little relevance to human behavior. Such criticism is blunted by observations like those in the *P&L* Close-up, The Human Relevance of Brain-Damage Research.

The lesion method has also been applied to humans in other ways, sometimes with results of dramatic significance and sometimes with quite sad consequences. Let's briefly look at two of these applications: the attempt to improve a physically diseased brain by splitting it in two, and the attempt to mend a psychologically disturbed mind by separating one part from the rest.

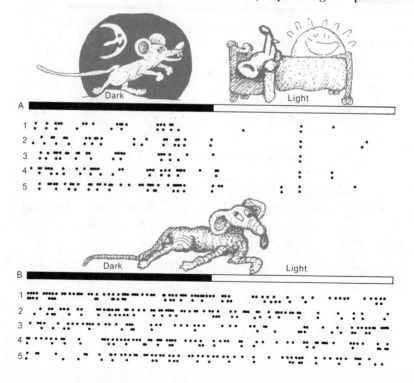

■
Rats are normally active mainly at night. The first graph shows the amount of activity and drinking during five days, each day being divided into 12 hours of dark and 12 hours of light. You can see that most activity occurs in the dark. When lesions are made in the suprachiasmatic nucleus (located within the region indicated on the rat brain), the distinction between day and night is lost, and activity continues around the clock, as shown in the second graph.

Close-up
The Human Relevance of Brain-Damage Research

Philip Teitelbaum of the University of Illinois is a physiological psychologist who has been studying the effects of brain damage on animal behavior. It is sometimes difficult to see the significance of such research for understanding human brain-behavior connections. Teitelbaum has found that brain damage simplifies complex behavior patterns, making them easier to study. Furthermore, the process of recovery from such damage shows us how behavioral components are integrated to form an effectively functioning organism. This is true because when a part of the brain is damaged, the behavior it controls may disappear completely or decompose into a simple fragmentary form. As recovery takes place, the behavioral elements are "put back into place" in much the same way they developed in the first place. Thus the study of brain damage and recovery (the brain-damaged adult goes through the sequence of reactions of a normal developing infant) gives us a view of the levels of organization involved in a particular behavior pattern.

In a series of ingenious studies, Teitelbaum and his colleagues have discovered the basis of an unusual set of reactions common to cats, monkeys, human infants, and adult patients with Parkinson's disease, or "shaking paralysis." Drugs that block certain neurotransmitter systems in the brain produce a rigidity in cats that makes them cling helplessly when placed on the back of a chair rather than climbing over it. When their eyes are bandaged, their heads fall back and they lose their grip on the chair. This "backfall reaction" is due not to loss of vision but to the pressure of the bandage on facial and cranial nerves.

The same backfall reaction is found in cats that have lateral hypothalamic damage. Because one of the brain areas affected by this damage is also involved in Parkinson's disease, Teitelbaum tested patients for this backfall reaction. He found that it does indeed occur in patients with severe Parkinsonism.

As recovery from the lateral hypothalamic damage proceeds, the backfall reaction ceases. If the recovery-development parallel holds, one should find the reaction in infants. Tests with kittens, puppies, and infant baboons indicate that it does occur. The bandage-backfall reaction is also seen in human infants under three months of age. Further research on the brain systems involved in these common reactions may shed light on normal development and lead to new forms of treatment for Parkinson patients.

Teitelbaum concludes that "Physiological psychology can be a very powerful direct approach to the analysis of animal and human behavior. Localized brain damage can simplify a behavioral system and the study of recovery can show us how it is put back together again. The abnormalities of brain damage may represent simpler levels of behavior, which are also present, though often unsuspected, in normal infant development" (1977, p. 2F).

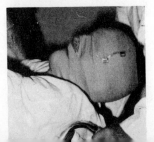

Brain splitting: Two minds in one body

Occasionally, when epileptic seizures are severe and cannot be controlled by medication, an operation is performed to sever the *corpus callosum*, which is the major connection between the two cerebral hemispheres. Following such surgery, the patient typically is freed from seizures and reports an improvement in well-being.

A by-product of the surgery is the creation of *two* brains within a single body. Each half brain acts "independently" of the other, and each seems to have its own sensations, perceptions, and memories, as well as cognitive and emotional experiences. Although the split-brain patients quickly learn ways to compensate for the loss of coordination, it has been shown experimentally by Roger Sperry and his colleagues that they are living with two separately functioning minds. ◆

There are some situations in which it appears that two brains would be better than one, as when you have to respond to two different sensory inputs. It takes you less time to react to a single stimulus than to have to press one button with your right hand when a light on your left side flashes on and to press another with your left hand when a right-side light is presented. Not so for the split-brain patient: response to the double reaction time situation is as fast as to the simple one. Each reaction is independent of the other; thus no time is lost thinking about or coordinating what is happening in each hemisphere of the brain. This is indeed a case where it is better that the right hand doesn't know what the left hand is doing (Gazzaniga, 1970).

Split-brain research has revealed that the cerebral hemispheres were designed for efficient division of labor. At first it was believed that the left hemisphere was the dominant one because it did all the talking, while the right hemisphere was the silent, observing brain. Although language control is indeed centered in the left hemisphere for about 95 percent of us, split-brain research has shown that the silence of the right hemisphere is indeed golden. Right hemisphere functioning is involved in nonverbal, intuitive thinking, in a variety of perceptual skills, in musical abilities, and in certain emotional reactions. The "warm" right hemisphere is, in a sense, the humanizing balance for the cool, verbal, analytical left side. Western societies have long prized rational intellect, while Eastern cultures and some ethnic and racial subgroups in the United States place more value on intuitive, emotional functions of mind. Current research is showing that these two views need not be in opposition. (See *P&L* Close-up, The Yin and Yang of Conscious Experience.) Our asym-

◆

Coordination between eye and hand is normal if the split-brain patients use their left hand to find and match an object that appears in the left visual field. However, when they are asked to recognize objects that they touch with their right hand, in order to match the pear seen in the left visual field, they cannot do so. Here the cup is misperceived as matching the pear. Sensory messages from the patient's right hand are going to the left cerebral hemisphere, from which there is no longer a connection to the right visual cortex.

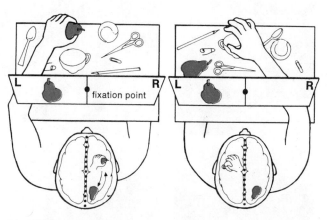

Adapted from Sperry, 1968

Close-up
The Yin and Yang of Conscious Experience

It is rather well established now that the two hemispheres of the brain are specialized to carry out different, although complementary, cognitive functions. For most people (95 percent of right-handers and about 60 percent of left-handers), the left side of the brain mediates the more verbal and analytical aspects of information processing while the right hemisphere appears to mediate the more spatial, nonanalytical, and imaginal aspects. In the remaining left-handers the situation is reversed. But which lefties are which? According to Levy and Reid (1976), it's all revealed in the way they write; those who write in a hooked hand position (hand held above the writing line) are like right-handers; their left hemisphere is specialized for language. Lefties writing with hand below the writing line (as right-handers usually do) have the opposite brain organization.

Another simple test is to observe the direction in which a person looks when asked a reflective question. Each brain hemisphere controls the motor functions of the opposite side of the body. In a right-handed person, the right hemisphere is the more spatial, nonanalytical half; thus a spatial question ("In what direction does Abraham Lincoln look on a penny?") activates the right hemisphere, causing the eyes to shift momentarily to the left. An analytical question ("What is the total of six plus three?") which activates the left hemisphere causes a shift to the right. This occurs when a person is asked such questions from behind (Kinsbourne, 1972). If the questions are asked face to face, most individuals consistently look either more to the left or to the right, regardless of the type of question (Gur, 1975). They show a systematic bias as "left-lookers" or "right-lookers." Some researchers hypothesize that the individual's preferred hemisphere is being activated. An interesting difference between these two response styles was shown by Bakan (1969) who found that left-lookers (right-hemisphere dominant) were significantly more hypnotizable than right-lookers (left-hemisphere dominant).

While these techniques give us valuable clues, their predictive accuracy remains to be verified. So far the best method for determining cerebral dominance on an individual basis is by chemically inactivating one hemisphere at a time and observing the effect on language and speech functions. If left-sided injection temporarily disrupts language and right-sided injection does not, the person may be assumed to have left hemisphere dominance for language.

Another interesting hypothesis being explored states that in normal individuals mental events in the right hemisphere can become disconnected *functionally* (through inhibition of neuronal transmission) from the left hemisphere. This may explain the phenomenon of repression and shed light on unconscious mental events. Perhaps, as with the Chinese symbol of Yin-Yang, these opposite parts must complement rather than exclude or control each other, transcending and encompassing the contradictions to form a harmonious whole that will be more than the sum of its parts. Some of the many aspects of the "Yin" and the "Yang," long a part of oriental thinking, are listed below (Ornstein, 1972).

Hemisphere specialization provides a useful framework to consider variations in cognitive style. Since research in this area is still in the early developmental stages it is controversial and exciting.

Yin	Yang
Right hemisphere	Left hemisphere
Left side of body	Right side of body
Spatial	Verbal
Intuitive	Intellectual
Gestalt	Analytic
Feeling	Thinking
Receptive	Active
Experiencing	Planning
Being	Controlling
Space	Time
Present	Past and future
Simultaneous	Sequential
Implicit	Explicit
Diffuse	Focused
Noncausal	Causal
Feminine	Masculine
Dark	Light
Night	Day
Eternity	History

metric brains may be taught to overcome cultural biases, to function more fully in the service of the ideal of being rational *and* emotionally perceptive, intuitive *and* intellectual. The hemispheres ought not to be considered dominant or subservient to each other. Rather, they should be integrated so that either faculty can be called forth to meet the challenge posed by the environment or other people. It is safe to say that few discoveries in the past decades have revolutionized our thinking about the interactions of brain, experience, and behavior as much as the split-brain research.

Psychosurgery: "All the king's horses . . ."

Science advances when clinical observations are validated through controlled experimental research. But all too often, an observation is made and a conclusion drawn that people would like to believe; then systematic scientific evidence to the contrary is ignored. Belief in "miracle drugs" or cancer cures is often based on inadequately gathered evidence, unsupported by well-conducted investigations. A more extreme example is the use of prefrontal lobotomies to stop the outbursts of rage, hallucinations, and bizarre behavior of mental patients.

In *prefrontal lobotomies* a surgeon severs the nerve fibers that connect the frontal lobes to the rest of the brain. The operation is simple, since the scalpel can be inserted underneath the eyelid and pushed into the brain, where with a few twists it can permanently disconnect the frontal lobes. The whole idea came from a report that two aggressive chimps had been permanently soothed by removal of parts of their frontal lobes. This suggested to a Portuguese psychiatrist, Egas Moniz (1937), that prefrontal lobotomies could calm his troublesome psychotic patients. Initial reports of miracle cures combined with the simplicity of the operative technique resulted in perhaps hundreds of thousands of these operations being performed throughout the world in the nineteen thirties, forties, and fifties. Over forty thousand are estimated to have been conducted in the United States alone in the decade after World War II. Many violently psychotic patients were rendered tranquil by prefrontal lobotomies. The strong emotional tone accompanying thoughts and feelings was eliminated. But so were most other feelings! Perhaps the major loss was that of the ability to plan ahead, to foresee consequences, to have a sense of the future—in effect, a loss of one's sense of self-continuity. Research has now shown that the frontal lobes are primarily involved in foresight, self-regulation, and analytical thinking (Goodman, 1978). Despite a dismal record of success and an alarming number of permanent side effects (see Chapter 20), psychosurgery is still practiced, especially in Great Britain. In the United States, prefrontal lobotomies have been largely replaced by more precise forms of psychosurgery. Some advocates of behavior control through direct intervention in the brain now want to extend psychosurgery to "help" cure criminals of their incorrigible criminal tendencies. We will have more to say about the ethics of such practices in a later chapter. (See *P&L* Close-up, The Curious Accident of Mr. Phineas Gage.)

We have seen that stimulation and lesion techniques reveal a brain in which different regions are specialized to perform highly specific functions. These techniques are, however, not suitable for providing information about *how* the brain works or what some of the principles are which underly the operation of this rather complex biological computer. For understanding of *mechanisms*, direct recording of the electrical activity of the brain is a more promising technique—particularly single-cell recordings.

Close-up
The Curious Accident of Mr. Phineas Gage

The iron bar shown here is in the collection of the Museum of Harvard Medical School, a relic of a terrible accident. In September 1848, Phineas Gage, a twenty-five-year-old railroad worker in Vermont, was tamping a charge of black powder into a hole drilled deep into rock in preparation for blasting. The powder unexpectedly exploded, blowing the tamping iron, over three feet long and weighing thirteen pounds, through Gage's head and high into the air.

Incredibly, Gage regained consciousness and was taken by wagon to his hotel, where he was able to walk upstairs. T. M. Harlow, the physician who attended him, noted that the hole in Gage's skull was 2" by 3½" wide, with shreds of brain all around it. He cleaned and dressed the wound, but two days later Gage became delirious and remained near death for the next two weeks. The wound became seriously infected, but eventually healed. In a month Gage could get out of bed without help; in two months he could walk unassisted.

Gage lived on for over twelve years. Physical impairment was remarkably slight: he lost vision in his left eye and the left side of his face was partially paralyzed, but his posture, movement, and speech were all unimpaired. Yet psychologically he was a changed man, as this summary by Harlow makes clear:

"His physical health is good, and I am inclined to say that he has recovered. Has no pain in head, but says it has a queer feeling which he is not able to describe. Applied for his situation as foreman, but is undecided whether to work or travel. His contractors, who regarded him as the most efficient and capable foreman in their employ previous to his injury, considered the change in his mind

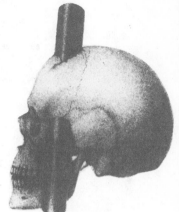

so marked that they could not give him his place again. The equilibrium or balance, so to speak, between his intellectual faculties and animal propensities, seems to have been destroyed. He is fitful, irreverent, indulging at times in the grossest profanity (which was not previously his custom), manifesting but little deference for his fellows, impatient of restraint or advice when it conflicts with his desires, at times pertinaciously obstinate, yet capricious and vacillating, devising many plans of future operation, which are no sooner arranged than they are abandoned in turn for others appearing more feasible. A child in his intellectual capacity and manifestations, he has the animal passions of a strong man. Previous to his injury, though untrained in the schools, he possessed a well-balanced mind, and was looked upon by those who knew him as a shrewd, smart business man, very energetic and persistent in executing all his plans of operation. In this regard his mind was radically changed, so decidedly that his friends and acquaintances said he was 'no longer Gage' " (Bigelow, 1850, pp. 13–22).

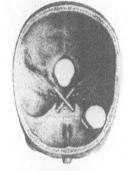

Gage's case is one of the earliest documented examples of massive damage to the frontal regions of the brain, and it illustrates the great subtlety of the psychological symptoms that accompany such lesions. Indeed, it was Gage's family and friends, rather than his doctor, who noticed the changes in him. Gage's symptoms, such as "obstinacy" or "capriciousness," are hardly so remarkable that we would attribute them to brain damage in someone whose history we didn't know. Yet it is interesting to note that they represent the very kinds of antisocial behavior that prefrontal lobotomies are supposed to *prevent*.

Neurons in concert: Recordings of the brain

Let's take a tour of the neuropsychology laboratories at Stanford University, observing several different kinds of experiments in progress. In each, researchers are recording the language of the brain. At times there is but a single voice to be heard, other times it is like a full chorus singing.

In one room a cat is on the operating table. Even though the animal is anesthetized, its brain is still active and receives messages from the sense organs. This is also true of our brains when we are "unconscious" due to either drugs or natural sleep. The cat's head is held in a special device called a *stereotaxic*, which allows a microelectrode to be accurately positioned in any region of the brain. The skull is exposed and a hole drilled in it to reach the deeper portions of the brain.

A microelectrode, a needle made of thin metal or hollow glass filled with salty water, acts somewhat like a tiny microphone. When placed near a neuron, it detects the electrical impulses, which can be greatly amplified in the same way as a singer's voice. We can then listen to the neuron's activity, and simultaneously display its signals on an oscilloscope. This is called *extracellular* (outside the cell) single-neuron recording. In this experiment the electrode is in the visual cortex, and the investigators are displaying various patterns to the cat. Almost incredibly, a given neuron prefers one specific pattern and produces a burst of impulses each time it "sees" it, but remains silent, ignoring all other stimuli of a different pattern.

Down the hall, investigators have removed the entire nervous system of a crayfish, and have placed microelectrodes *inside* several neurons. *Intracellular* recordings are about one thousand times more sensitive than extracellular ones, making it possible to record the smaller synaptic potentials that determine impulse activity. Some cells do not have impulses and so can only be studied in this way. The number of neurons in an invertebrate nervous system is small enough so that individual neurons can be identified and studied repeatedly in different animals. Studies like these will eventually establish the fundamental processes used by brains to process information.

In another laboratory, a Stanford undergraduate relaxes in an easy chair, while a researcher tapes electrodes to her scalp and forehead. The activity of the billions of neurons inside the brain generates enough electrical current to be detected even through the skull. This massed activity of the brain is called the *electroencephalogram* (EEG) or simply *brain waves*. Brain waves have characteristic forms that indicate whether the subject is relaxed, alert, or asleep, and can even discriminate various stages of consciousness (to be discussed in Chapter 15). If the subject is presented with a sudden stimulus, an *evoked potential* is recorded; its characteristics vary across the skull in complex ways. Computer analysis of these data brings out subtle features of the EEG that are not apparent from mere visual inspection of the recordings. Such analysis also permits detailed examination of the temporary electrical oscillations of the evoked potentials, making it possible to identify different profiles of brain functions. This has led to new methodologies such as *neurometrics*, developed by Roy John and his associates (1977). Through neurometric methods, John hopes to develop criteria for determining treatment strategies and assessing the effectiveness of interventions for a wide variety of diseases and malfunctions of the brain.

Each of these different recording methods has good and bad features. If we compare neurons with people, then intracellular recording is like reading someone's thoughts, extracellular recording is like eavesdropping on a conversation, and the EEG is like listening to the roar of a crowd. Only the EEG, however, can be used to study the brain activity of normal human beings.

The "liquid" brain

When you did something stupid or forgot an appointment, did your mother ever tell you "You have a brain like a sieve"? If so, her figure of speech was apt because the brain is made up mainly of salty water and organic molecules. And at times, like around final exams, do you ever suspect there is some leakage of brain material going on? Our earlier analogy between brain and computer breaks down at this point. Brains are all wet; computers must keep their electronic circuits dry. And brains can take chemicals that get them drunk and others that get them "stoned." The three classic methods of physiological psychology that we have discussed all have their chemical counterparts. We can administer chemicals that disrupt the function of certain neurons, (chemical "*lesions*"); we can use chemicals to *stimulate* neurons; or we can *record* chemical activity in the brain or blood and correlate it with behavior. All of these techniques are now widely employed.

One great advantage of using chemicals to influence the brain is that they are usually easy to administer (either by mouth or by injection) and can reach all parts of the central nervous system, yet by virture of the highly differentiated nature of neural tissue, they may have selective effects. The effects of chemical injections are longer lasting than those of electrical stimulation and, unlike the effects of physical lesions, they are reversible. But the main reason for studying the brain by means of chemical injections is that there are many areas where complex neural pathways overlap geographically and it is difficult or impossible to study these areas by lesions or electrical stimulation, both of which affect too many layers of cells.

A technique has been developed by Sebastian Grossman for stimulating or suppressing the activity of neural pathways in the deep regions of the brain by microinjections of chemicals that vary the concentration of synaptic chemical transmitter substances. Basically, the technique consists of permanently implanting a double tube (cannula) in the animal's skull. The inner cannula is removed, sterilized, filled with crystals of a given chemical, and reinserted through the outer tube into the brain area being investigated. With the same implanted tube, Grossman has been able to elicit eating by injecting one chemical and drinking by injecting another (1967).

The blood-brain barrier

Psychoactive drugs (hereafter called simply "drugs") are chemicals that change the way we feel or behave by acting directly on the brain. Obviously, drugs must be able to enter the brain in order to work. This isn't a trivial matter, because a blood-brain barrier exists to keep foreign substances out. This barrier can be traced to two structural features. First, the capillaries in the brain have walls of tightly connected cells which prevent large molecules from leaking out. Second, in some ventricles the capillaries form a structure called the *choroid plexus*. The walls of the choroid plexus are made of specialized cells which receive blood from the capillaries and secrete a colorless liquid called *cerebrospinal fluid*. Unlike the blood, this fluid contains almost no protein, and its composition of small ions is carefully regulated. The cerebrospinal fluid fills the ventricles and flows through them and over the brain, finally being absorbed into the veins. It is estimated that the whole volume of this fluid is exchanged every four hours. Neurons and glia are thus bathed in the cerebrospinal fluid, which diffuses through the narrow clefts that make up the extracellular space.

The blood-brain barrier has important consequences. For example, *morphine* is widely used as a painkiller in the U.S., but *heroin* is an illicit drug whose use is illegal even under hospital supervision. Yet the evidence is persuasive that heroin is converted to morphine by enzymes in the brain, the morphine then acting on the brain. Heroin is thus simply a convenient form of morphine, which has greater clinical efficacy because it more rapidly passes the blood-brain barrier! This rapid access to the brain is presumably responsible for the "rush," the pleasurable sensation experienced when heroin is injected intravenously.

Drugs and synapses

Once inside the brain, psychoactive drugs usually work at synapses. But since we know synapses exist in great variety, a drug that influences only one type of synapse may affect behavior in subtle ways. No one knows how many kinds of synapses exist, but at least ten compounds have been identified as possible neurotransmitters. Of these, only the distribution of three *monoamines* (norepinephrine, dopamine, and serotonin) in mammalian brains has been clearly identified. This was made possible by the spectacular discovery of *histofluorescence*. This technique involves inducing a chemical reaction between neurotransmitter molecules and formaldehyde vapors to yield a fluorescent compound so that the neurons glow brightly when irradiated with ultraviolet light. Since the reaction is specific to certain neurotransmitters that are located in discrete neuron pathways in the brain, the technique makes it possible to follow the course of these neurons through the brain. When a slice of brain tissue illuminated in this way is viewed through a microscope, it resembles the view from an airplane at night. Brightly glowing axons crisscross the field of vision like highways, and clusters of cell bodies in nuclei are reminiscent of the lights of small towns. ▪

The precise percentage of monoamine neurons in the brain was determined by simply counting the fluorescent neurons. *Acetylcholine* is the transmitter found at all skeletal neuromuscular junctions; it is also found widely throughout the brain. In recent experiments with an invertebrate organism, acetylcholine was found to be the major or exclusive neurotransmitter of perhaps 80 percent of the neurons in the nervous system (Barker, Herbert, Hildebrand, & Kravitz, 1972). Similarly, the neurotransmitter gamma aminobutyric acid (GABA) is found throughout the central nervous system, in some places associated with perhaps one third of the neuron terminal buttons.

It appears likely that a few transmitters account for the majority of neurons in the nervous system. The number of transmitters associated with the remaining neurons is unknown and may be quite large indeed.

What this all means is that a drug which selectively influences synapses

▪

In this highly magnified section of a cat's brain, some of the neurons have been stained with a special dye to make them more visible. No two-dimensional view can convey the full complexity of the three-dimensional neural network, however. In any slice of tissue, you see only a small portion of a neuron; most of its parts would be nearer or farther away. So you need to visualize a three-dimensional structure built up of the connections shown here—and many more connections.

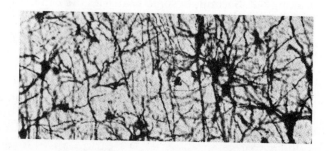

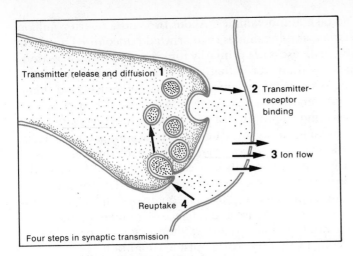

Transmitter release and diffusion **1**

2 Transmitter-
receptor
binding

3 Ion flow

Reuptake **4**

Four steps in synaptic transmission

using a given transmitter will affect the functioning of a specific portion of the brain. In the case of the monoamines, such studies have produced some very interesting results.

Monoamine neurons and amphetamine

Monoamine neurons have cell bodies almost exclusively in the brain stem. Unlike the relatively clear-cut circuits we have been studying, monoamine neurons tend to have diffuse connections. Brain researcher Seymour Kety (1967) cites evidence that a single norepinephrine-containing neuron in the brain stem sends branches to the cerebral cortex, the cerebellum, the hippocampus, and the hypothalamus, as well as other parts of the central nervous system. On an anatomical basis alone such neurons would be expected to have general effects. In fact, drugs that influence such neurons profoundly alter our alertness and our mood states.

The norepinephrine synapse shown in the reference module on p. 297 involves four basic processes: (1) release of transmitter, (2) binding of transmitter with receptor molecules, (3) brief opening of channels, (4) reuptake and oxidation of the transmitter, all four occurring each time an impulse arrives in the presynaptic terminal. Every one of these steps is vulnerable to chemical attack. ◆ Amphetamine, for example, acts in three ways. It causes release of norepinephrine, blocks its reuptake, and inhibits an enzyme that causes the breakdown of norepinephrine at the synapse. These three actions *potentiate* the norepinephrine system; that is, make it function more effectively. Many other drugs including *cocaine* also potentiate the NE system in slightly different ways. In general, any drug that enhances transmission at norepinephrine synapses (commonly called an "upper") tends to reverse depression, increase feelings of well-being and confidence, counteract fatigue, and increase alertness. The drug *ritalin*, often used with hyperactive children, may owe its effectiveness not to calming them down but to making them attend better and be appropriately alert. "Downers," drugs that depress norepinephrine synapses, have an opposite effect. Both kinds of drugs are used extensively to control mood.

Alertness and feelings of well-being are certainly desirable. In fact, the catecholamine systems that are thought to mediate such feelings are concentrated in the exact brain regions where electrical stimulation appears to be pleasurable for rats (German & Bowden, 1974). Why don't we all take amphetamines? To this question four answers can be given. The first is that a

The tranquilizer chlorpromazine

A

The neurotransmitter dopamine

B

C

great many people *do* take amphetamines. About two and a quarter million Americans take prescribed amphetamines regularly (add uncounted numbers of "street" buyers); this drug use is not primarily for legitimate medical reasons (Holden, 1976). The second answer is that some people react badly to amphetamines, becoming overexcited or anxious. Such people may find themselves drawn to tranquilizers instead. A third answer, and the most crucial one, is that drug effects diminish with use, a process known as *tolerance*. Tolerance requires that increasing doses must be taken to achieve similar effects. Hand in hand with tolerance goes *dependence*, which means that cessation of the drug causes the reappearance, usually in greatly exaggerated form, of the symptoms the drug suppressed. These effects can be tragic. The fourth, more personal answer is that reliance on drugs to pick you up or help you down often comes at the expense of self-reliance and reliance on human interaction in coping with life's problems. It also means always altering some aspect of yourself rather than attempting to alter the world outside your brain.

Chemical craziness

With very large doses and prolonged use of amphetamines, feelings of well-being give way to anxiety, fear, and delusions of persecution. These symptoms are virtually indistinguishable from the mental disturbance labeled *paranoid schizophrenia*. This has led to a great deal of research to test the hypothesis that paranoid schizophrenia and amphetamine psychosis both result from abnormalities in the brain's *catecholamine neurons*. The evidence linking these two mental disturbances to each other and to catecholamine transmission is impressive. The same kinds of tranquilizing drugs (phenothiazines, such as chlorpromazine) are effective in treating amphetamine psychosis and schizophrenia. Their relative effectiveness is also the same—that is, a powerful antipsychotic will be powerful for treating both drug and nondrug psychosis; while a weak drug will be weak for both. Furthermore, recent evidence shows that the strength with which blocking drugs bind to receptor molecules at dopamine synapses correlates with their ability to alleviate psychotic symptoms. Conversely, drugs like amphetamine will, if given to paranoid schizophrenics, make their symptoms worse. This kind of interlocking evidence is persuasive and has spurred vigorous attempts to understand the physical basis of schizophrenia (Snyder, 1974). ▲ (See *P&L* Close-up, Neurotransmitters, Rewards, Emotions, and Schizophrenia.)

In conclusion, neural processes and their mental consequences are susceptible to minor alterations in their chemical environment, but the composition of the cerebrospinal fluid which bathes the brain is buffered against changes by the blood-brain barrier. Psychoactive drugs pass through the blood-brain barrier and alter synaptic transmission. Catecholamine neurons, which can be visualized with the histofluorescence technique, have been implicated in mood, arousal, and some kinds of mental illness and drug states.

The development and evolution of the brain

We now have a picture, however imperfect, of the structure of the human brain and of the basic principles of its operation. How has this most complicated of all mechanisms come to be?

333
*The development and
evolution of the brain*

Close-up

Neurotransmitters, Rewards, Emotions, and Schizophrenia

A variety of research findings and reasoned conjecture point to an important role of neurochemicals in the prefrontal cortex of the brain. The transmitter dopamine in this region of the brain has been implicated in behaviors associated with rewards, motivational states, and emotional expression (see Wauquier & Rolls, 1976). It has also been hypothesized that an impairment to the dopamine-producing mechanism may cause a dysfunction in the systems that control goal-directed behaviors and emotions. Schizophrenic patients typically reveal such behavior problems. However, until recently there has been only indirect evidence for the role of dopamine in the prefrontal cortex.

A recent investigation now provides more *direct* evidence for the involvement of dopamine in the self-stimulation (via electrical reinforcement) of the prefrontal cortex (Mora & Myers, 1977). The research consisted of four parts: (1) First, rats were operated upon to implant a microelectrode with its tip in the prefrontal cortex. A tube was inserted close by, allowing researchers to administer radioactive chemicals and to extract cortical fluids for analysis of dopamine levels; (2) each rat was put in a self-stimulation chamber (of the kind described in Chapter 3) and trained to depress a lever in order to obtain a series of electrical im-

pulses delivered to the prefrontal cortex (the reinforcement for the lever-pressing behavior); (3) after a subject responded at a steady rate for thirty minutes (receiving the electrical stimulation), a special radioactive substance was injected into the region, enabling researchers to trace the amount of dopamine when these brain fluids were extracted and analyzed; (4) at the end of the experiment the subject was sacrificed to verify the exact position of the stimulation electrode and the injection site within the cortex.

Levels of dopamine in the region being studied increased significantly during the periods of brain stimulation. They declined rapidly in subsequent periods when stimulation ceased. On control days without any stimulation, the radioactive tests for dopamine levels in these same subjects remained normal.

This research nicely illustrates the interdisciplinary approach that is essential if we are to discover the neurochemical bases of behavior and mood states. Biochemistry, physiological psychology, and operant conditioning each contribute to piecing together the vast puzzle of how a tiny amount of a chemical in a synapse can affect our desire to work for life's rewards and to experience joy in living rather than suffer the flattened emotional life of the schizophrenic.

Development

John Locke, the British philosopher famous for founding empiricism (see p. 342) formulated the well-known concept that the mind is at birth a *tabula rasa,* a blank tablet on which all knowledge is subsequently "written" by experience. The anatomical equivalent of a *tabula rasa* would be a randomly connected brain, entirely lacking the precisely wired circuits we have been admiring. The opposing view is that at birth we already have certain forms of innate knowledge. This view (championed by Emmanuel Kant and others) is unpopular and is regarded as vaguely undemocratic. The anatomical equivalent of innate knowledge is a "prewired" brain, in which circuits develop according to genetic blueprints. The philosophical question thus reduces to a physical one that can be definitely answered: Do our brains already contain circuits at birth or do they not?

They do. The evidence for this is no longer disputable, and the embryological formation of such circuits is of great interest to physiological psychologists. We will mention only one piece of evidence in favor of inborn circuits.

The precisely arranged columns of orientation detection cells in the visual cortex, which, as we saw, depend on a staggeringly detailed network of precise connections, exist at the moment of birth (Wiesel & Hubel, 1974). ■

A great effort is now under way to show how experience modifies pre-existing circuits and establishes new ones. This work is of enormous significance for an understanding of postnatal development and learning, and is attracting some of the best researchers in science.

One of the most exciting discoveries in the field of perception in recent years is the convincing demonstration that experience can change the response properties of individual sensory neurons.

Kittens were reared in specially designed visual environments in which they saw only vertical stripes or only horizontal stripes. When they reached adulthood, measurements were made to see if there had been changes in the receptive fields of neurons in their visual systems as a result of this early experience. It was found that the adult cats had neurons sensitive only to stimuli in the orientation that they had experienced; none had neurons that responded to stimuli in the other orientation. That is, vertical-environment cats had no cells that responded to horizontally oriented stimuli and vice versa (Blakemore & Cooper, 1970).

Even more dramatic findings have emerged from a series of studies by Helmut Hirsch and his colleagues (Hirsch & Spinelli, 1970, 1971; Hirsch, 1972). Kittens were raised to the age of three months wearing masks that presented a visual field of vertical black-and-white stripes to one eye and a field of horizontal stripes to the other. Recordings of the activity of single cells in the visual cortex at ten and twelve weeks of age and again at two years showed that cortical cells connected to the eye exposed to horizontal lines could be activated only by horizontal stimuli, while cells connected to the other eye responded only to vertical stimuli.

It also seems the two eyes must learn to work together properly. Normally, many neurons in the visual cortex receive input from both eyes. However, if one eye is covered up for several days during a "critical period" of development (about twenty-three to thirty days of age in kittens), that eye loses its ability to excite cortical neurons, and becomes functionally blind (Wiesel & Hubel, 1965; Hubel & Wiesel, 1970).

A team of psychologists and physiologists at the University of California at Berkeley showed significant differences in the brains of rats reared in "enriched" and "impoverished" environments. Actually, the enriched environment provided space, toys, and other rats to interact with, and therefore ap-

■

The brain is organized without experience, as shown by the orderly arrangement of neurons in the cortex of a 17-day-old monkey whose eyes had been kept closed since birth. As the electrode was pushed through the cortex, it encountered neurons that responded to bars. The angle of the stimulus bar that most effectively stimulated the neurons changed progressively with distance, indicating a very precise neural organization.

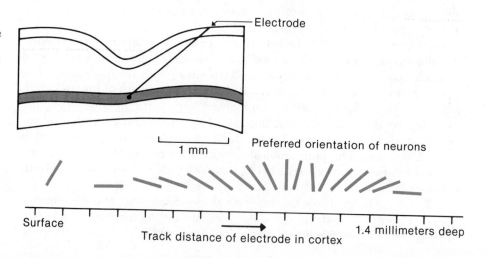

proximated a normal environment, while the "impoverished" rats were isolated in small, bare cages. The deprived rats had poorer learning test scores, and their brains had thinner cortex with fewer glial cells and less branched neurons (Rosenzweig et al., 1969). Recent studies confirm the general effect, and statistical analyses support the hypothesis that some neurons require normal sensory stimulation to develop fully (Cummins, Livesey, & Evans, 1977).

Experience can change the brain, but the newborn brain is already wired to interpret certain patterns of physical energy in predetermined ways. No one denies that humans are superbly designed for acquiring knowledge, as we saw in earlier chapters. But we begin our education with an advantage resulting from the basic structure of our brains, formed over millions of years of evolution.

Evolution

Like most scientists, psychologists take evolution for granted. This is implicit in the generalizations they make from neural processes in animals to those in humans. Although the experiments discussed were not designed to test evolutionary theory, among the clearest generalizations to emerge from modern neuroscience are: (1) the universality of many basic neural processes, (2) the orderly increase in the power of nervous systems as they grow in size and complexity, and (3) the striking similarities found in nervous systems of different species. These findings are consistent with the theory of evolution.

But the most fascinating support for evolution comes from merely observing the growth of the brain of a human fetus. Only a few days after conception, a mass of brain cells have formed into a straight tube of microscopic proportion. In less than two months, three bumps poke out from the tube. One end of the tube becomes the spinal cord, which is common to fish and all backboned creatures. Bumps near it enlarge to become the brain stem and develop other structures that control primitive reflexes. The third bump, shared by reptiles that existed one hundred million years ago, emerges as the center for basic drives and emotions. This is the old brain, or *rhinencephalon*. Most lower mammals stopped their development with this structure that has no power of specific discrimination, nor capacity for symbolization, language, or self-consciousness. Our developing fetus now shows a new structure that covers over the old brain. This neocortex, shared with higher mammals and more comparable to that of apes, vastly increases the range of intelligent learning from experience. In humans the neocortex dominates but does not totally rule the nervous and hormonal systems of the old "visceral brain." The coupling of neocortex to the rhinencephalon has been compared to "adding a jet engine to an old horse cart" (Jacob, 1977).

In the nine months of prenatal growth, the little embryonic tube will go through stages of transformations that reenact three hundred million years of evolution. This embryonic human brain makes a journey up the evolutionary ladder from fish to reptile to mammal to human being. Its individual development *(ontogeny)* in many ways reproduces *(recapitulates)* the development of the entire species *(phylogeny)*.

The twentieth-century brain

Concepts of the brain are constantly revised. It was bone marrow to the Egyptians, a radiator for cooling the blood to Aristotle, a container for vital spirits to medieval scholars. Up until the middle of this century both the telephone switchboard and the more mysterious "field potential" views of the brain were taken seriously—variations of these themes exist even today.

Whether the current fashion of viewing the brain as a computer, so useful to the study of information processing, will persist and be vindicated we cannot say. We suspect it will, but our conviction is not as strong as Aristotle's. For although we have better reasons for our view than he did for his, we also know, as he could not, just how risky it can be to theorize about the brain. But it does seem certain that the principles of neural operation established in the last quarter century are fundamentally correct. We can expect enormous elaboration of these, and new principles will be discovered—especially in the areas of very complex networks and long term changes in neuron properties—but the bedrock will remain. This is so because of the persistence and increasingly successful efforts to establish an unbroken explanatory chain from physics, to chemistry, to cellular function, to network function, to behavior.

The mechanistic, reductionistic orientation taken in these two chapters on physiological psychology has two final implications. The first is the importance of protecting our brains from environmental assault while providing enriched experiences for developing brains. Although the bony skull usually does a good protective job, many brains are still injured in auto and motorcycle accidents, sports, and even at the hands of parents. Failure to wear seat belts, helmets, or the right equipment can mean permanent damage to some of the brain's magnificent functioning. "Many slow-learning and clumsy children with IQs of 90," says pediatrician John Caffey, "might have been intelligent and normally mobile children with IQs of 120, had they not been habitually shaken and whiplashed during infancy" (1972). Overenthusiastic bouncing of a baby before its neck muscles are strong enough to support the head may result in broken vessels that retard the growth of parts of the brain. Angry slaps on the head and neck can have similar negative consequences, even for older children. Drugs that alter brain functions can affect them permanently if taken in excess. Some drugs, like the chemicals in glue, when inhaled can lead to death or a lifetime of mental retardation. Brains, especially young ones, need lots of oxygen and good nutrition. They are adversely affected by pollutants in the environment and especially when children chew on flakes of paint that contain lead. We do not yet know the long-term adverse effects of expectant mothers' cigarette and coffee addiction on the development of their babies' brains, although mothers addicted to hard drugs give birth to babies who are addicted.

The second question that arises from viewing the brain as a chemical organ is how we integrate human and spiritual values, "dignity" and "freedom," into this neuropsychological conception. Brains function on the command of nerve impulses. Some of those commands are primitive survival messages programmed into our brains by virtue of the evolutionary survival of the species. The case of Karen Ann Quinlan offers eloquent, if sad, testimony to the perseverance of the brain to keep functioning despite a coma stretching into years. Ms. Quinlan's "living death" tells us that it is possible for brains to keep up their primitive functions even after they have shut down interaction with the outside world.

However, these survival functions keep the machinery of life operating as if put on "automatic pilot." For life to have direction and meaning, the brain must be constantly stimulated by varied inputs from the environment. Much of that stimulation comes from our contacts with others, but ultimately, the human connection can only be realized through the chemical connections our exquisite brain makes possible. It is our nervous system that gives the power of action to human purpose.

In the next chapter, our attention shifts to the ways in which information about the world gets into the nervous system. How we sense physical sources of energy such as light and sound is part of the story of sensation. But beyond being sensitive recorders, we are interpreters of what we see, hear, smell, and touch. We order these inputs through perceptual processes. By understanding the principles of perception we come to appreciate how psychological reality is created out of past experience, current sensations and future expectations.

Chapter summary

The nervous system, like all matter, is structured along hierarchical lines. It is made up of vast numbers of neural circuits, or *networks*, which process information with ever increasing sophistication.

The *motor unit*, made up of a single motor neuron and all the muscle fibers it innervates, is the fundamental link between brain and behavior. Muscles involved in fine, precise movements are comprised of many more individual motor units than those with grosser gradations of force and movement.

Neural mechanisms that generate a patterned output of activity based on complex circuitry make up a *central motor program*. The two largest functional regions of the brain control the hands and vocal apparatus. The *motor cortex* initiates and integrates the voluntary action in the over six hundred muscles of the human body, working with the *cerebellum* and the *sensory cortex* to coordinate muscular activity. Information from the sensory cortex is essential in providing feedback about the progress and accuracy of motor output.

The three basic techniques researchers presently employ in studying neural activity of the brain in living humans and lower animals are *stimulation, lesions*, and the *recording* of electrical activity.

Sensory input and motor output areas can be "mapped" on the brain, largely as a result of Wilder Penfield's work with brain stimulation of conscious patients. While the *temporal lobe* has often been cited as the seat of memory, Lashley's experiments on rats indicate that memory does not have a specific location in the brain. Some investigators believe that memories may be stored in protein molecules because brain cells manufacture and use up more proteins at a higher rate than other cells in the body, and proteins may be arranged in large, complex chains suitable for coded language.

Researchers in the neurosciences have gathered revealing neurological information by introducing *microelectrodes* into specific parts of the brains of freely moving animals and sent electric currents to these locations. Stimulation at various points can induce anxiety, aggression, and a number of stereotyped behavior patterns, particularly when stimulation occurs in the *limbic system*. Pleasure and pain centers can be activated in a similar manner.

The lesion technique involves experimental destruction of the brain by cutting connections between brain areas or destroying tissue with intense heat, cold, electricity, or laser beams, and then observing the behavior of the animal after recovery from surgery. Observation of affected areas of the human brain during autopsies and therapeutic brain surgery have led scientists to assign specific functions to brain locations. For example, Broca's area in the *left* hemisphere of the brain generates language. It is connected to *Wernicke's area*, the center for understanding speech and language.

Patients with severe epileptic seizures occasionally undergo an operation in which the *corpus callosum* is severed, disconnecting the two hemispheres of the brain. The patient is usually freed of the seizures, but most must learn to cope with two separately functioning minds. *Split-brain* research has demonstrated that the left hemisphere of the brain is concerned primarily with verbal and analytical activities while the right hemisphere is involved in intuitive thinking, perceptual skills, and emotional reaction.

For many years, surgeons performed *prefrontal lobotomies* on violent psychotic patients. This severing of the nerve fibers connecting the frontal lobes to the brain induced tranquillity and eliminated strong emotional reactions in the subjects. But later findings showed that the operation also resulted in the loss of most other emotions and an inability to plan and experience a sense of continuity.

Through a method called *extracellular single-neuron recording*, scientists are able to detect electrical impulses from a single neuron and amplify them. Such recordings have demonstrated that each neuron "prefers" a specific type of sensory stimulus and remains unresponsive to other stimuli. Using invertebrates as subjects, investigators have also implanted electrodes inside neurons to make *intracellular* recordings sensitive enough to pick up synaptic potentials.

Brain waves may be detected through sensors placed lightly on the outside of a subject's skull and recorded as *electroencephalograms* (EEGs). These waves display characteristic patterns indicative of the subject's various stages of consciousness. When the subject is presented with a sudden stimulus, an *evoked potential* is recorded, and computer analyses of the resulting *brain profiles* allow for extremely subtle interpretations.

The brain is also studied by chemical means. Neural pathways in the deep regions of the brain may be stimulated or suppressed by injecting chemicals directly into the brain. The effects of these injections are longer lasting than those of electrical stimulation yet are reversible.

The composition of the *cerebrospinal fluid,* which bathes the brain, is buffered from changes in body chemistry by the *blood-brain barrier. Psychoactive* drugs bypass this barrier and may affect synaptic transmission. Studies of paranoid schizophrenia and *amphetamine psychosis* have pointed to *catecholamine neurons* as being instrumental in mood arousal, some forms of mental illness, and drug states.

The findings of neuroscience are in keeping with the theory of evolution in that many basic neural processes are universal, and there is an orderly increase in the power of nervous systems as they increase in size and sophistication. While environmental experience at critical stages of postnatal development can crucially affect the brain's efficiency and development, the brain contains at birth a number of circuits developed according to genetic blueprints.

During its nine months of embryonic development *(ontogeny),* the human central nervous system *recapitulates* the development of the human species *(phylogeny).* It develops a spinal cord, common to fish and all other vertebrates; then the *rhinencephalon,* shared by prehistoric reptiles and modern lower mammals. Finally, the human fetus develops a *neocortex,* which forms over the rhinencephalon and is common to all higher animals.

12 Perception

What do we see when we visually examine the world? Most people would say, "We see the world, of course! We see it exactly as it is!" Many psychologists would agree. People who disagree with that answer might say, "No, we see light. Light shines into our eyes and we see it." But when we go to sleep and begin to dream, we also see. That is to say, we have perceptions which we would call "seeing" when we are awake. However, while we are dreaming, the organization of our visual experience is produced by processes which originate in our brain, not in the world outside. No light is involved, yet we see.

Another instance in which sensations occur apart from their typical "waking-state" stimulus can be easily demonstrated, using a method described by Johannes Müller in the nineteenth century. Turn down the lights or shield your eyes from the light. After several minutes, close your eyes, then press *gently* with a finger against one of your eyelids. You should see a spot. If you don't, press *just a little* harder, or try a different location. Your perception of the spot is real; it is not an illusion or hallucination. Press on a different place, and the spot will move. In both of these cases, you see because of pressure, not light. Nevertheless, most people still say they "see light" when they see the spots. Old habits die hard, even if they are wrong!

Mild electric current passed across the eyeballs produces brief flashes called *visual phosphenes*. They are often described as looking like twinkling stars, sometimes white and sometimes colored. Astronauts have seen phosphenes produced by small, electrically-charged particles from space passing through their retinas (Rothwell, Filz, & McNulty, 1976). Electrical stimuli applied directly to the visual areas of the cortex also produce phosphenes. Recent efforts to develop "bionic eyes," functional artificial eyes for the blind, make use of phosphenes produced by cortical stimulation. Dobelle (1977) described the brief history of such efforts.

In 1973, two men each received temporary implants of arrays of sixty-four electrodes on the visual cortex. One was Doug, a twenty-eight-year-old social worker blinded in Viet Nam. First each electrode was stimulated individually. Because he previously had sight, Doug was able to describe the resulting sensations. The relative visual position of the phosphene produced by each electrode was determined. When the appropriate combinations of electrodes stimulated his cortex, Doug could distinguish triangles oriented in different directions. He could also identify letters and geometric patterns. As was originally planned, the electrodes were removed after three days.

In 1975, two more men received similar implants for a longer period of time. One was Craig, a 33-year-old student blind for ten years. Most of Craig's electrodes were properly positioned and functional. With no practice, when the appropriate combinations of electrodes were stimulated, he could read Braille presented as phosphene patterns. Craig could read Braille by touch at a rate of only six characters per minute; by phosphene patterns, he could read thirty characters per minute. When a television camera was connected to the electrodes, Craig could distinguish lines, orientations, and spots against a background.

Work on bionic senses focuses attention on some of the basic questions studied in perception. Do we perceive reality directly, or do we construct our perceptions of reality? Does the environment control our perceptions, or does our behavior control our perceptions? How does information from the world outside get into the nervous system and what happens once it is inside? How do culture, learning, and contexts influence perception? We will consider some of the information that research on perception has uncovered, information that begins to provide answers to such questions.

Perceiving reality

Questions about how *perceptual reality* relates to *objective reality* are at the heart of the study of perception in psychology. They also concern philosophers, physicists, dreamers, mystics, drug users, and many others.

Experiments in perception often allow us to discover how closely our perceptions of the world relate to what exists there. For example, most of us believe we can tell the difference between things that point up and down and those that are tilted, especially if we compare them to ourselves. If something *appears to be* tilted, we assume that it *is* tilted.

In a revealing set of experiments, subjects sat in an unusual chair in an unusual room. The chair and the room could be tilted, either independently or in combination. In one condition, the chair remained upright while the room was tilted. Some subjects perceived themselves as vertical and the room as tilted, while others perceived themselves as tilted and the room as vertical. The first group, called field independent, seemed to judge their body position on the basis of gravity-related cues, independently of visual cues about tilt. The second group, called field dependent, seemed to be so strongly influenced by visual cues about tilt that they did not react to gravity-related cues in their own bodies. To them, the visually tilted room meant that they were tilted themselves (Witkin, 1959).

Similar phenomena are reported outside the laboratory. Some passengers on large jets say that when the plane takes off, it appears as if the ground is receding, rather than that they are rising. Many other field dependent people, sitting firmly in a theatre seat, feel themselves powerfully pushed and pulled in the direction of the action while watching movie scenes of high-speed chases or races.

Most of the processes in perception are so automatic and "unconscious" that we normally take them for granted. Only when something goes wrong, or when an illusion occurs, do we become aware of how complex and how automatic our perceptions really are.

The processes involved in perception include *transduction*, the reception of stimulus energy by receptors and the conversion of that energy into slow potentials or generator potentials; *coding*, the patterning of activity, in groups and systems of nerve cells, which represents attributes of the original stimulus energy; *processing*, the selecting, comparing, and integrating of coded information; *subjective experience*, the sights, sounds, smells, tastes, and touch experiences which make up our personal awareness; and *behavior*, our actions which affect both the environment and our own perceptions. With so many processes involved in perception, it should be no surprise that psychologists have disagreed about whether perception of the world is direct or is constructed.

Do we perceive the world directly?

Naive observers accept the evidence of their senses uncritically. They feel that they are simply perceiving what is there. They take it for granted that they have direct contact and acquaintance with the outside world. They have a "vivid certainty" of the correctness of their perceptions and assume that other observers will perceive the situation in the same way. This position is known as *phenomenal absolutism*.

Empiricism

The question of how we come to know reality directly was of philosophical interest long before psychologists began investigating perception. In the seventeenth century, the British *associationists* (Locke, Berkeley, and Hume) proposed a general theory of knowledge and perception that is still influential. They proposed that knowledge of reality comes only through the senses. Simple sensations provide the elements of experience out of which our central nervous system builds more complex ideas by way of learned associations. Because of their emphasis on direct sensory experience as the basis for knowledge, these philosophers are also called the British *empiricists*. Their interest was not in how perception takes place, but in the role of perception in our knowledge of reality.

Early psychologists such as Wundt and Titchener accepted these assumptions. In the late 1800s they concentrated their efforts on trying to train observers to experience and report "pure sensation," uncontaminated by additives from learning. "Perception" was assumed to be a more advanced stage in which the "primary" sensory experience had been modified in various ways. They were confident that through *trained introspection* subjects could get back to the original elements of psychological experience.

More recently, the radical behaviorists tried to make psychology into a description of responses to a directly sensed "real" world. Like their founder Watson, many behaviorists admit that perception exists, but they deny that it controls behavior. B. F. Skinner describes perception as a direct response to the world as it is. Skinner flatly denies that perception involves any action by the individual upon the world, or upon any representation of the world in the nervous system (Skinner, 1974).

Differentiation theory

Eleanor Gibson (1969) regards perception as a process of progressively filtering out, or differentiating, the unessential information (noise) in sensory stimulation so that only the essential elements of a signal remain. An example would be our experience when we meet a group of new people. At first, we are unable to correctly recognize or identify each person. As our interactions with the group increase, we learn to recognize the *distinctive features* of each person; the characteristics that identify them and make them different from the others.

Gibson states that all of the information necessary to know a new situation is available from the start. All we do is focus our attention appropriately, discover the order (signal) that is there, and ignore the unessential information (noise). This process reduces our *uncertainty* about the situation (see our discussion of *entropy*, p. 130). Gibson claims that the reduction of uncertainty, accomplished by discovering invariant or unchanging features of the environment, is intrinsically reinforcing.

Do we construct our perceptions?

Many of our experiences suggest that our perception of reality is *mediated*. That is to say, perception is not always a direct reflection of the external world, but appears to be constructed out of information from the world outside. For one thing, we know that many of our everyday perceptions can be grossly incorrect, compared to the world outside. They can remain incorrect in spite of our knowledge that they are, as we will see when we examine information on illusions.

Our perceptions seem to relate fairly well to the objective world. But things are not always what they seem! If you spin in a circle until you are dizzy, then stop, you will feel yourself, and see the world, spinning in the opposite direction. You know your perception, which is real to you, is not "objectively" real. The earth looks flat, even though we know it is not. The sun seems to rise and set every day, even though we know it does not. Figures of people seem to move continuously on movie and television screens, even though we know one screen contains only a series of still pictures and the other a series of alternating lines. The perception of continuous movement while viewing discrete, individual stimuli following one another in rapid succession is called the *phi phenomenon*. It is a common feature of commercial lighting displays.

Illusions

Perceptions which relate in a seemingly unusual way to external stimuli are called *illusions*. Illusions come in many interesting forms. Look at the three photos of the author. ● Do you see me becoming twice as tall as I cross the room? If you roll a sheet of paper into a tube and look through it at the successive views, the phenomenon will be even more striking. You *know* this is impossible. What is happening?

Gestalt psychologists often used simple geometric illusions to demonstrate the principles of organization in perception. Two of those principles are the tendency to see partial outlines as being complete and the tendency to see areas that are partially bounded as being completely closed off and distinct from their background. Look at the two figures; the effects of both principles should be clear. ▲ (Did you by any chance organize your perceptions further and see the head of Darth Vader, the villain from *Star Wars*, in the dark figure?)

Illusions occur in all of the sensory systems. We will concentrate here on visual illusions, since there is not yet a good way to get sounds, smells, and tastes into a textbook. In our culture, we tend to say that perceptions of illusions are odd or deceptive. Illusions, far from being abnormal examples of runaway perception, are full of information about what is required for normal, accurate perception to take place. They do not reveal defects in our per-

●

This series of photographs was made as the author walked across the room. The room has not changed and he has not grown. How do you explain what you see?

ceptual system, but rather demonstrate the extent to which perception is independent of any one bit of stimulus information in the current environment.

How did I become a giant as I walked across the room? You saw this illusion because the room itself was distorted, with the right-hand corner actually much nearer to the camera. Because you assumed a normal room and did not have reliable distance cues, you took the larger retinal size at face value and saw the actual size of the figure as increasing. ■

Gestalt theory

Early in this century, a group of German psychologists at the University of Berlin (Köhler, Koffka, Wertheimer) attacked both the concept of *association of elements* as the basis of perception and that of *introspective analysis* as the key to primary, original experience. Rather, they emphasized innate organizing processes within the individual that produce *patterns* (Gestalts) as primary characteristics of experience.

The German word *Gestalt* has no exact English equivalent; the closest approximation is *configuration*. The configuration is seen as the basic unit of perception (and other experience). According to the Gestaltists, "the whole is different from the sum of its parts" and in many ways determines the character and behavior of the parts, instead of the other way around. A melody is

These diagrams show front and top views of the room on p. 343, which is located in the Exploratorium in San Francisco. As the author moved from point 1 to point 2 to point 3, he was actually getting closer to the camera, which was positioned at point A. Thus he appears larger in each photograph.

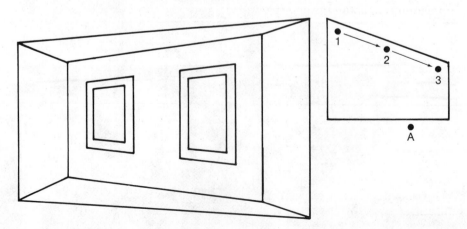

the same in one key as in another, even though the individual notes all change. Also, qualities of wholes—like the liltingness or the plaintiveness of a melody—do not reside in the individual notes. Relational properties such as these are part of the primary perception, not added later through unconscious inference. Thus, for example, no amount of introspection of the apparent movement in the phi phenomenon can make it go away.

Transactional theory

According to Ames (1951), who developed the distorted room studies (p. 343), each one of us develops—through our transactions with our own unique environment—a restricted set of perceptions to handle the infinite variety of possible retinal images that we continually receive. On the basis of our experience, we make assumptions about how reality is constructed, and it is these assumptions that determine what we will perceive. Perception becomes a learned act of constructing reality to fit our assumptions about it. His is a *transactional* theory.

How information gets in

Information from the environment outside the nervous system is detected by a variety of organs composed of specialized *receptor* cells. Generally, each type of receptor is most sensitive to one physical property of the environment— sound waves or light, for example. But the distinctions between receptors and their associated nervous systems are not absolute. In an earlier demonstration, we *saw* that the eye responds to pressure, as well as to light.

Varieties of sensory information

Our present concern will focus on vision and hearing, the senses about which most is known. In addition to these two "long-range" senses, which gather information about the environment from long distances, we also gain information about the environment through several *somatic* (body) senses that depend on direct contact. There are four somatic senses whose receptor cells are located in the skin: pressure (touch), pain, cold, and warmth. These skin senses are sometimes called the *cutaneous senses*. Each one tells the organism something different about the external world.

Two more somatic senses are located internally and intimately connected with each other. These are the *labyrinthine* sense, which helps maintain bodily balance and the *kinesthetic* sense, which informs us of the position of our arms, legs, head, and all movable parts. In addition, there are the *chemical* senses of taste and smell. The somatic and chemical senses will not be treated in further detail here.

Vision

The human eye contains major optical, muscular, and neural components. The visual nervous system performs impressive feats of information processing and analysis. The entire system seeks out and examines stimuli over a wide range of distances, from just beyond the ends of our noses to the farthest visible stars. As we saw at the beginning of this chapter, the final stage in this complex process takes place in the brain. It begins with a ray of light entering the eyeball. ◆

Structures for seeing

The human eye is made up of two visual systems combined into one. Each system has its own functions and its own distinctively shaped receptor cells; those of one system are called *cones*; those of the other, *rods*. The cones function only in intense light; they are responsible for color vision and for our sharpest visual acuity. In dim light, the cones are not stimulated and the rods function alone. The rods are extraordinarily sensitive to very dim illumination (night vision) but they do not discriminate among hues. When only our rods are operating, everything appears to be in black, white, and shades of gray.

The rods and cones are located in the back layer of the retina, which means that light must travel through several layers of nerve fibers and blood vessels before reaching them. There are more than 7 million cones in the retina, packed most closely together in the fovea and decreasing in number from the center of the retina to the periphery. Over 110 million rods are found in all parts of the retina *except* the fovea. ▲

As shown in the diagram, the receptors connect through synapses with the *bipolar cells*, which in turn synapse with the *ganglion cells*. (There are also many lateral interconnecting cells within the retina, which are not shown in the diagram.) These cells enable the retina to begin the job of processing information before transmitting it to the brain. The axons of the ganglion cells form the *optic nerve*; they synapse on cells at a relay point in the brain, the *lateral geniculate nucleus* of the thalamus. Cells in the thalamus have axons going to the *occipital cortex* at the back of the brain. At the point where the optic nerve leaves the retina, there is a *blind spot* that is not sensitive to light. (See *P&L* Close-up, Spotting Your Blind Spot.)

It has been estimated that the retina contains about 125 million receptors, a few million bipolar cells, and one million ganglion cells. There is a tremen-

◆
Cross section of the right eye viewed from above

The eyeball is composed of three layers: (1) an outer protective coat called the <u>sclera</u>, *a portion of which is the transparent* <u>cornea</u> *which acts as a refracting surface; (2) a middle layer called the* <u>choroid</u> *coat which is pigmented; and (3) a light-sensitive inner layer called the* <u>retina</u>. *When light enters the eye, it passes first through the cornea and then through the* <u>pupil</u>, *which is an opening in the pigmented* <u>iris</u>. *The pupil adjusts in size to regulate the amount of light entering the eye, which influences both the brightness and the clarity of the image. The light rays then penetrate the* <u>lens</u>, *which focuses them into the sensitive surface of the retina. Before reaching the retina, the light rays must pass through the liquid (*<u>vitreous humor</u>*) that fills the eyeball. Light from the center of the visual field (i.e., what the person is looking at) is focused on the* <u>fovea</u>, *which is at the center of the retina and is the most sensitive part of the eye in normal daylight vision. The retina contains the visual receptors that, when stimulated by light, initiate nerve impulses that travel through the* <u>optic nerve</u> *and ultimately reach the* <u>occipital lobes</u> *at the back of the brain, one in each hemisphere.*

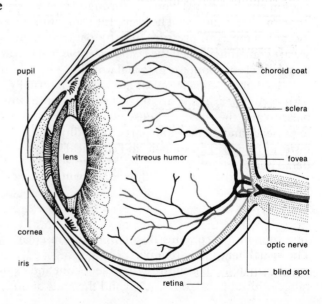

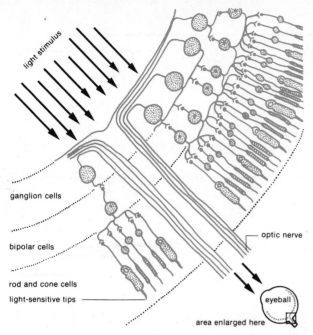

This is a stylized and greatly simplified diagram showing examples of the pathways that connect three of the layers of nerve cells in the retina. Incoming light passes through all these layers to reach the receptors, which are at the back of the eyeball and pointed away from the source of light. Through convergence, several receptor cells send impulses to each ganglion cell, while through divergence, one receptor cell may send impulses to more than one ganglion cell. Nerve impulses from the ganglion cells leave the eye via the optic nerve and travel to the next relay point.

light stimulus

ganglion cells

bipolar cells

rod and cone cells
light-sensitive tips

optic nerve

eyeball

area enlarged here

dous *convergence* of information from many receptors to one ganglion cell. However, because of the many interconnections between cells in the retina, there is also a *divergent* flow of information. Thus, one receptor connects to several bipolar cells, which in turn connect to even more ganglion cells.

But how do these receptors translate light into nerve impulses? Photopigments contained in the receptors play a major part in this transduction process. The rods have one type of photopigment, called *rhodopsin,* while each cone has one of three types of *iodopsin,* corresponding to the wavelengths of blue, green, and red light. When light hits a receptor, it is absorbed by the photopigment, causing the pigment to break down into its component parts. This process changes the polarity of the membrane of the receptor cell, producing a generator potential that activates the bipolar cells.

Millions of receptors may respond to a visual stimulus. The resulting activity is processed by the nervous system to extract information about aspects of the stimulus such as brightness, color, form, and movement. Activity from the receptor must be analyzed for several different types of information *simultaneously* at the same level. The system of anatomical divergence, mentioned earlier, provides for such multiple parallel processing of information.

How we see brightness

Receptors are activated by the absorption of light and they in turn activate chains of neurons, to produce the "perception" of light. The greater the intensity of the light, the greater will be the activity produced in the retina and transmitted to the brain, and the greater will be the sensation of brightness.

The process that prepares the eyes to see under low illumination is known as *dark adaptation.* You undoubtedly have had the experience of going into a darkened theater and being unable to find your way to an empty seat without help. Yet after a few minutes, you were able to see quite well. For most people, complete dark adaptation requires about half an hour of darkness after the last use of the eyes in bright light. (See *P&L* Close-up, The Eyes Have It.)

Close-up

Spotting Your Blind Spot

Ordinarily we are unaware of our blind spots because when we are using both eyes an image never falls on both blind spots at once, since each faces a slightly different part of the visual field. You can determine the location of your blind spots by a very simple experiment. Close your right eye, hold the book at arm's length, and fixate on the circle below. Still fixating on the circle, move the book toward you until the cross disappears.

At that point, the cross corresponds to the part of your visual field that is falling on the blind spot of your left eye. To find the location of the blind spot in your right eye, follow the same procedure, but this time close your left eye and fixate on the cross with your right eye: no circle.

How we see color

Color vision is the ability to differentiate various wavelengths of light (which we perceive as various colors) independently of their relative intensity. This is believed to be accomplished through the cones, in combination with special cells in the lateral geniculate nucleus called *opponent* cells. Each of these cells responds with excitation to impulses initiated by one wavelength and with inhibition to impulses initiated by another wavelength.

There are four basic types of opponent cells: red excitatory, green inhibitory ($+R$, $-G$); red inhibitory, green excitatory ($-R$, $+G$); yellow excitatory, blue inhibitory ($+Y$, $-B$); and yellow inhibitory, blue excitatory ($-Y$, $+B$). When light is absorbed by the cones (each of which, as you will recall, contains one of three types of photopigments), this information is passed on to the opponent cells, which subtract the output of one class of receptors from the output of another. Thus, the firing rate of a single opponent cell is dependent on the differential excitation of the two sets of receptor cells leading to it. For example, red light will excite some cones, while green light will excite others. A $+R$, $-G$ opponent cell will be excited by nerve impulses coming from red-sensitive cones and inhibited by impulses from green-sensitive cones. If only red light is present, the opponent cell will be excited above its spontaneous rate of discharge. If only green light is present, the opponent cell will be inhibited below its spontaneous rate. If equal amounts of red and green light are present, the excitatory and inhibitory

Close-up

The Eyes Have It: Dark Adaptation

Everybody with normal vision experiences dark adaptation. We know that our visual sensitivity increases the longer we are in the dark and decreases when we are in bright light. But where does the change in sensitivity occur—in the eyes or in the brain? A simple demonstration will provide most of the answer. Sit in a darkened room for several minutes—long enough to begin seeing objects in the room. Now, close one eye tightly and cover it with one hand, leaving the other eye open. Next, turn on the lights for several seconds, then turn them off. The eye that was open while the lights were on probably won't see too well. Next, close that eye and open the one that was covered in the light. Presto! You see! Where does dark adaptation occur? Clearly, the eyes have it!

effects from the cones will cancel, leaving the opponent cell at its spontaneous rate of discharge and producing a neutral response (gray). It is important to realize that "color" is always an aspect of our perceptual response; it does not exist in the world outside. Wavelength of light is out there, nerve activity and perception are in here.

How we see patterns

It was once assumed that all perceptual processing took place in the brain. That is, the input from the receptors was thought to be transmitted to the brain and mapped onto some surface there, where relationships were analyzed and interpreted and our subjective experiences of pattern vision were created. Then, in the 1950s it was discovered that particular cells at each stage in the sequence from retina to cortex were responsive only to particular features of a visual stimulus. Since then, discoveries have come thick and fast.

The *receptive field* of a particular neuron in the visual system is the area of the retina that is able to influence that neuron. (Methods of measuring the activity of a single neuron were discussed in Chapter 10.) Working with cats, Hubel and Wiesel (1959) found that the ganglion cells in the retina, each of which receives input from many receptors, have *concentric* receptive fields with either an excitatory center and an inhibitory surround or the other way around. These ganglion cells are very sensitive to *small spots* of light that just fill the center of their receptive field. In contrast to the ganglion cells, the cells in the cat's visual cortex often have elongated receptive fields, rather than concentric ones. In this case, the stimulus that produces the greatest amount of activity of the cell is a *line* of a certain width located in a particular place on the retina. Hubel and Wiesel suggest that the "line" cells in the brain are responding to the input from a group of retinal "concentric" cells whose receptive fields are in a line.

Patterns of sensory stimulation that initiate responding in particular sensory neurons are called *trigger features*. The neurons that respond selectively to them are called *feature analyzers*. The information processing that takes place as visual input is received by the retina and transmitted to the visual cortex can be inferred by studying the stimulus features that are required to trigger different neurons. It appears that the cells at higher levels become selective for increasingly complex trigger features of the stimulus. However, for a more recent, and apparently more accurate, analysis of how cortical cells detect variations in visual patterns, see the *P&L* Close-up, Seeing Bars in Place or Waves in Space?

Hearing

Our sense of hearing involves one of the most complex organs in the human body. This complicated system is able to respond to stimuli so weak that they barely have more energy than the random movement of air molecules bumping the eardrum! It also can withstand, for brief periods, extreme abuse in the form of stimuli so intense that we can feel them shaking our bodies.

How sounds get in

When an object produces sound, it creates waves of pressure differences in the surrounding air. These alternating waves of dense and thin air are the stimuli for hearing. The outer ear receives these pressure changes in the air,

Ҩ

Close-up

Seeing Bars in Place or Waves in Space?

New evidence from a brilliantly conceived series of experiments reveals that the visual cortex responds to a patterned input of light in much the same way the cochlea in the auditory system does to the variations in air pressure that make up sound waves. Cells in the visual cortex respond to spatial waveforms of light, according to research by Russel De Valois and his colleagues at the University of California, Berkeley (De Valois, Albrecht, & Thorell, 1979).

The basic units such cells are most responsive to and selective for are *not* bars and edges (as Hubel and Wiesel proposed), but rather specific frequencies of the distribution of light in space. The stimulus for detecting visual patterns is variations in sine waves of particular frequencies. In studying the responses

of cortical cells in macaque monkeys and cats to gratings and to checkerboard and plaid patterns, De Valois found that these cells are best considered as spatial-frequency filters (responding to certain two-dimensional components of patterns). Knowing how particular cells respond to the spatial frequencies of gratings allows researchers to predict precisely how those cells will respond to the other patterns (but not vice versa). Some cells are finely tuned to narrow bandwidths of spatial frequencies (like a sensitive hi-fi tuner), others to broader bandwidths. Groups of cells in the same region of a visual field are tuned to different spatial frequencies and orientations. Thus we can analyze our visual world into both fine details and complex patterns.

which are converted into vibrations in the eardrum, which are converted into lever action by the bones in the middle ear, which are converted into movement of the membrane on the *oval window*, which are converted into pressure changes in the fluid in the *cochlea*, which are converted into movements of the *basilar membrane*, which are converted into bendings of "hairs" on receptor cells, which produce generator potentials, which are converted into impulses in the auditory nerve. From there on, things start to get complicated! ▲

The ear is constructed to maximize the amount of energy that is absorbed from the sound waves hitting the eardrum. Normally, when sound waves strike a solid surface, most of their energy is reflected away. The various structures of the ear manage to conserve this energy by converting the large amplitude of the sound waves into stronger vibrations of smaller amplitude (von Békésy, 1957). The principle is like the one involved when we use a hammer to convert a large-amplitude swing of our arm into the small-amplitude, but forceful, movement of a nail into a board.

How sounds are coded

Sound is a feature of the environment, a pattern of pressure changes or vibrations in the air or in objects. *Hearing* is a perceptual experience often related to sound; it is the experience we have when certain cells in our auditory nervous systems become active in appropriate patterns.

Have you ever heard the old question, "If a tree falls in the forest and there is no one there to hear it, is there any sound?" The answer is, "Yes, but there is no hearing." A parallel question might be, "If no tree falls in the forest and a person is there, could he or she hear one fall?" The answer would be, "Yes, because hearing occurs in people, not in forests." (For example, people might hallucinate, dream, or imagine trees falling.)

Sounds have the properties of *frequency* (the number of pressure changes per second) and *amplitude* (the intensity or strength of the pressure changes). In hearing, frequency is most closely related to *pitch*, while amplitude is most closely related to *loudness*. We can count frequencies and measure amplitudes, but pitch and loudness are personal things—they are inside us and are private. However, two people with approximately normal hearing will both hear changes in pitch as we strike different keys on a piano. They will hear changes in loudness as we strike a single key repeatedly, but with varying force. How does the inner ear signal both the frequency and the amplitude of the auditory stimulus to the brain so that both pitch and loudness can be recognized?

What apparently happens is this. For sounds with frequencies above 5000 cycles per second, as the frequency of the sound changes, the place on the basilar membrane which vibrates most vigorously also changes. The places vibrating most vigorously stimulate their receptors and their nerve pathways most vigorously. The most active groups of cells in the auditory nervous system produce pitch sensations. This is the *place theory* suggested by Helmholtz before the turn of the century.

For sounds with frequencies below 5000 cycles per second, different principles work. For frequencies below 500 cycles per second, each cycle of the sound produces a distinct "burst" of nerve impulses in the auditory nerve. Many individual neurons discharge on every cycle of the sound. As the frequency of the sound varies, so does the frequency of nerve impulses; the frequency of the impulses is heard as pitch. This is the *telephone theory* suggested by the physicist Rutherford.

Since single auditory nerve fibers usually cannot produce more than 500 discharges per second, the telephone principle cannot code frequencies of sound between 500 and 5000 cycles per second. In that range, the nerve cells seem to function in groups. On *each* cycle of the sound, *some* of the cells discharge; over *several* cycles, *all* of the cells in a group will discharge at least once. This volley of discharges over a period of time codes every cycle of the sound. This is the *volley theory* suggested by Wever and Bray (1930).

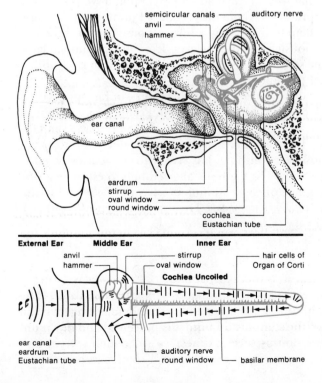

▲

Structures of the human ear

The top drawing is a cross section of the human ear. Below it is a highly simplified diagrammatic cross section of the cochlea as it would appear if it were unwound and stretched out straight.

Sound waves travel first through the outer ear and auditory canal to a thin membrane called the eardrum, which begins to vibrate. These vibrations are picked up by three small bones (ossicles) in the middle ear and are transmitted through another membrane, the oval window, to the fluid of the cochlea. One of the ossicles (the stirrup) acts like a piston, moving the fluid back and forth in the rhythm of the sound waves. The movement of the fluid makes a thin membrane within the cochlea (the basilar membrane) begin to vibrate. This, in turn, bends the hair cells of the Organ of Corti, which rests on the basilar membrane. These hair cells are the actual auditory receptors; moving them "excites" them and produces a generator potential which initiates nerve impulses in the fibers of the auditory nerve. The auditory nerve then carries the impulses to the brain.

To code increases in the intensity of a sound, the number of cells responding can increase; the rates at which certain cells discharge can increase; and, at high intensities, special cells begin to respond. When we hear a sound as complex as a human voice or a musical performance, an immensely complex and changing pattern of nerve cells, discharging at varying rates across time, is involved.

How information is organized

In the first section of this chapter, we examined the questions of whether our perceptions of the world are direct, or are constructed out of sensory information. Some theorists describe these issues in *either-or* terms: perception is determined *either* by properties of the stimulus *or* by properties of the observer; and properties of the observer are *either* innate *or* acquired. Others describe perception as the result of interactions *between* the factors. For example, Gibson emphasizes both the signal and noise properties of the environment *and* the innate search for information by the observer as determinants of perception.

In this section of the chapter, we will see how stimulus information becomes part of organized perception. In the remaining two sections, we will examine how experience and learning influence perception and how perception is directed so that it includes specific information.

Thresholds and scaling

Much of our knowledge about how information gets into perception comes from studies in physiology and anatomy. Most of the rest comes from an approach based on the idea that we can learn about perception if we put people in isolated environments, present to them only a limited number of stimuli—chosen by us—and allow them to make only a few responses—also chosen by us. Such a procedure is obviously limited. However, like similarly limited laboratory procedures in other sciences, this procedure gives us a start at understanding basic principles of perception.

The quantitative laboratory approach in perception—in fact, in psychology—began with the work of Gustav Fechner (1860). Fechner was a physicist and philosopher concerned with the problem of how the mind *(psyche)* and the physical world are related. To satisfy his own curiosity, he devised *psychophysical methods* to measure those relationships. His "ivory tower" curiosity led to the birth of modern psychology. His methods allowed him to estimate a person's sensitivity to the presence of weak stimuli *(absolute threshold)* and to differences between stimuli *(difference threshold)*. He also estimated how our sensations vary when stimuli vary *(psychophysical scaling)*.

Is anything there?

How can we measure the weakest stimulus that a person can perceive? The principle is simple, although the practice is a little more demanding. We can simply turn the intensity of the stimulus up until it is perceived and down until it is not perceived. If we do this several times, we will obtain several estimates of the intensity where our subject experiences a change in perception.

The average intensity for all of the trials is the best estimate of the *absolute threshold* for that stimulus. We have just discovered Fechner's psychophysical *method of limits*. Fechner also described several other methods and the appropriate calculations and experimental controls to be used with them.

Many researchers and theorists, including Sigmund Freud, immediately began to use Fechner's methods or his ideas of thresholds for perception. Some began to establish the "norms," or average threshold values, for various stimuli in large populations. If you ever had a vision test or a hearing test, you probably experienced Fechner's methods in an applied setting. Your individual threshold scores, when compared to standardized group norms, give the professional tester an idea of the status of your sensory systems.

Measuring how much we perceive

The methods of *psychophysical scaling* allow us to measure the magnitudes of sensations (like "heat") in the presence of different magnitudes of stimulation (like "intensity of the sun"). Such methods are necessary because the magnitude of sensation does not correspond in a direct way to the magnitude of physical stimulation. For example, if you are holding a feather and someone places a one-pound bag of sugar on your hand, you will easily notice the difference. However, if you are holding six pounds of feathers when the pound of sugar is added, the additional weight will not be so easily noticed. The discrepancies between equal amounts of change in the stimulus and the resulting nonequal changes in your perception must be a result of properties of you as an observer.

Scaling can occur at several levels of perceptual discrimination. We scale sensations whenever we identify differences between them. At the simplest level is *nominal scaling*. It occurs when we perceive things simply as being different or as belonging to general categories of things. We can then assign names or labels to them. The use of labels such as man, woman, Joe, Sue, moon, and trees requires nominal discrimination. *Ordinal scaling*, the next level in complexity, occurs when we perceive things as having different magnitudes of some property. Ordinal scaling is involved if we sort things into categories such as "small, medium, and large" or if we say, "On a scale from one to ten, that gets a seven."

The next level, *interval scaling*, occurs if we are able to estimate the equality of differences between our perceptions of things. A person who enters a nearly empty classroom and locates a seat equally distant from all of the other people in the room can estimate equal intervals. The last level of scaling, *ratio scaling*, occurs when we estimate or produce specific ratios between perceptions. Ratio scaling occurs when we adjust one stereo speaker so its loudness forms some ratio with the loudness of another. For example, we might make the first be twice as loud as the other, one fourth as loud, and so on.

Psychophysical scaling is a complex area. To explore it deeply calls for mastery of mathematical skills and procedures. However, the basic concepts of scaling are fairly direct. They are employed in all forms of psychological tests and measurements.

Getting too much of a good thing

The sense of hearing is highly sensitive, yet it is able to tolerate intense sounds for brief times. However, if a sound is too intense for too long, the auditory system may be irreversibly damaged. Irreversible damage usually means irreversible hearing loss. One study found damage to the cochlea in guinea pigs who had been exposed to eighty-eight hours of rock and roll music at 122 decibels. Guinea pigs may not normally spend much time in discotheques, but the hearing losses currently being discovered among rock musicians and disc jockeys are serious enough to make us wonder what permanent damage we may be doing by hearing too much, too long (Bohne, Ward, & Fernández, 1978).

Exposures to sounds which are less intense or of shorter duration often produce temporary threshold shift (TTS). People often experience TTS at rock concerts or in discos. While immersed in the sound, they must shout to be heard. Afterward, they must shout to hear themselves over their TTS. The condition usually disappears rather quickly. If it lasts for hours, or if the ears ring for a day or so afterwards, the risk of permanent damage from prolonged exposures to noise is fairly high. A person with such long-lasting effects probably should visit an audiologist, as a precaution.

The visual system is also influenced by high intensities of light. After exposure to bright light, we require time in the dark to recover our sensitivity. In a real example of "double jeopardy," intense strobe lights, such as those found in many light shows and discos, produce retinal degeneration, even total blindness, in experimental animals exposed to the lights for long periods (Dempsey, 1975). It is unlikely that people would be exposed to the lights for so long, but it *is* something else to consider, along with your TTS!

The structuring of perception

Measurements of threshold and of scaling give us information about how basic properties of stimuli relate to basic elements of sensory experience. Such experiences seem to be the "building blocks" out of which perception is constructed. However, Gestalt theorists argued that perception is more than a collection of building blocks; more than an assembly of basic sensations. They said that organization is a basic, innately determined, property of perception. We will briefly review some of the Gestalt principles of organization, and then examine how properties both of stimuli and of observers give rise to our perceptions of space.

Figure-ground relations

We tend to organize perception in a way which minimizes changes and differences, while maintaining unity and wholeness. Basic in this process is our seemingly automatic tendency to perceive a figure against a background, whether we are looking at the objects around us or at clouds or tea leaves (see p. 344).

Compared to the ground, the figure appears to: (a) have shape, (b) be nearer, (c) be thing-like, (d) be more vivid, (e) be more substantial in color, (f) own the common contour between them, (g) have the ground extend behind it. Some of the factors that determine what the "figure" will be are summarized in the illustration. ●

Camouflage is a familiar example of the use of these principles to change the figure seen. Whether practiced by nature to conceal prey from predators, or by armies (for the same purpose), camouflage is successful when it reduces the prominence of the figure cues, allowing the figure to be "lost" in the ground.

Not only do we create the best figure we can from the sensory information supplied us; we often tend to fill in missing parts, or see an almost circular

Why do we see the figures we do?

1. Similarity

Similar elements are seen as belonging to each other more than to other elements equally close but less similar. In this figure, do you see columns of Xs and Os or rows of alternating letters?

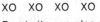

```
X  O  X  O  X  O
X  O  X  O  X  O
X  O  X  O  X  O
X  O  X  O  X  O
X  O  X  O  X  O
X  O  X  O  X  O
```

2. Proximity

Elements that are physically close are seen as belonging to each other more than to similar elements that are farther away. Below you see pairs of XOs, not OXs.

XO   XO   XO   XO

Proximity can also make things look more alike than they really are. The same figure that looks like an antelope when seen among antelopes looks like a bird in the company of other birds.

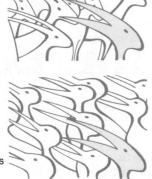

3. Closure

We tend to perceive incomplete figures as if they were complete. We see the line as a circle with a break in it and the irregular fragments as an animal.

4. Continuation

Elements are seen as belonging to each other if they appear to be a continuation of the direction of previous elements. The curving line is seen as one figure, the line with the right angles as another figure.

5. Common fate

Elements that move in the same direction are seen as belonging to each other. When alternate dancers in a ballet line step forward and make the same motion, we see them as a unit.

6. Reversible figure and ground

Occasionally a stimulus pattern is so organized that more than one figure-ground relationship may be perceived. When these conflict, they alternate in consciousness. In the example shown here, when the vase becomes "figure," the black ground seems to extend behind it; the reverse occurs when the two faces are seen as figures.

7. Good figure

The nervous system seems to prefer regular, simple forms. We see two overlapping squares here instead of a triangle and two irregular forms, equally possible from the sensory input.

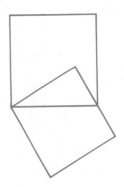

figure as more circular than it is, or in other ways make the figure more stable or regular or complete than the sensory information provides for. We tend to perceive configurations even when the elements taken individually bear no relationship at all to the composite that "emerges" from them.

Figure-ground relations exist in hearing. We can listen to one sound against a background of other sounds. One instrument or part can stand out against the rest of a group or orchestra. One voice can stand out against the sounds of a crowd.

Perceiving visual depth

Among the cues by which we perceive depth are those based on:

a. *Atmospheric perspective:* the perceptual blurring of objects farther away, because of dust, haze, or smoke in the atmosphere.

b. *Linear perspective:* the apparent decrease in size of objects farther away, and the apparent convergence of lines toward the distance.

c. *Texture gradient:* the decrease in distinctiveness of perceived texture at greater distances.

d. *Light and shadow:* the texturing of light by irregular surfaces, the distant portions tending to be darker than nearer portions.

e. *Relative position:* the concealing of far objects by near objects when both are in the same line of vision. Also, near objects usually appear at the bottom of the field of vision; far objects, at the top.

f. *Known standards:* the known size and shape of a familiar object serves as a standard for comparison of other objects.

These six cues are used by artists in attempting to create the impression of depth on a two-dimensional surface.

There are additional cues for visual depth which cannot be used on a conventional two-dimensional surface. For example, the perception of depth also involves using cues derived from changes in the lens of the eye, which bulges slightly when we look at close objects and flattens for looking at distant ones. Binocular vision greatly aids depth perception because of the extra information provided by the *convergence* of the eyes as they focus on an object near the observer. In addition, the slightly different images we get from the two eyes (called *retinal disparity*) help us perceive depth and distance. We interpret distance by automatically comparing and integrating these two images — which permits inspection "around" contours.

Perceiving auditory space

We are able to locate the positions of sources of sound, even without looking for them. An example of this ability often occurs at parties. While we talk to someone we are facing, we may hear our name in a conversation behind us. Without turning our head, we "tune in" on that conversation, while we "tune out" most of what is said by the person we face.

Most of our ability to localize sounds is a result of our having two ears located at different points in space. Sounds coming from one side of our head first reach the ear on that side. The difference in *arrival time* between the two ears can be very small, but our auditory systems are capable of detecting it.

If the frequency of a sound is higher than about 1500 cycles per second, our head can block part of the sound wave as it passes by. As a result, the ear on the side away from the sound source is in a *sound shadow*, where intensity is lower than on the side toward the source. The resulting intensity difference is an effective cue for localizing high frequency sounds.

Our heads do not block sound waves below 1500 cycles per second. However, another cue allows us to localize those sounds. Sound waves consist of alternating areas of high and low pressure, traveling through the atmosphere. All frequencies travel at the same speed—about 1087 feet per second. The result is that the distance between one high pressure wave and the next (the *wavelength*) is longer the lower the frequency of the sound. Below about 1000 cycles per second, the wavelength becomes longer than the distance across our head. Therefore, one ear can be in a high pressure part of a sound pattern while the other ear is in a low pressure portion of the pattern. This is called a difference in *phase* of stimulation and is an effective cue for localization.

Extrasensory perception

Do you believe in the existence of extrasensory perception? Do you think that people can communicate without using any of the known senses or measurable channels of communication? Recent surveys indicate that much of the public does believe so, but psychologists and scientists are divided sharply on this issue (Schmeidler, 1969). Some believe "that the available evidence for ESP is sufficient to establish its reality beyond all reasonable doubt" (McConnell, 1971); others maintain that "a great deal of experimental work has failed to provide a clear case for the existence of ESP" (Hansel, 1966).

Parapsychology

Parapsychology is the term used to label organized research concerning psychical phenomena. Researchers in parapsychology claim there are two major types of psychical phenomena: *ESP*, said to involve perception or cognition that is independent of known sensory channels, and *psychokinesis* (PK), said to involve the control of objects or events by other than known physical means. Parapsychologists usually say that ESP can be divided into the following three phenomena:

a. *Telepathy* ("mind reading"), in which one person is said to know the thoughts of another with no observable means of communication.
b. *Clairvoyance* ("second sight"), in which a person is said to obtain information about a given object, person, or event with no observable means of gaining that information.
c. *Precognition* ("divination" or "foreknowledge"), in which a person is said to have knowledge of the future thoughts of another or of future events.

Typical designs for research

In a typical telepathy experiment, an *agent*, or sender, looks at one of five symbols on a set of ESP cards and a receiver, or *percipient*, "guesses" which of the symbols is being looked at on each of two hundred trials. If the guesses were completely random, a correct guess or hit would occur in one of every five trials. In over two hundred trials then, by chance alone, the receiver would be expected to have forty hits, on the average, even if there were no ESP operating. Researchers on ESP often claim that since forty hits is the "chance level" for hits, any statistically significant deviations from forty hits provide evidence of ESP.

In a clairvoyance experiment there is no sender; the receiver guesses the identity of each card in repeatedly shuffled five-symbol sets. This becomes a precognition experiment when the receiver guesses the identity of the cards before they are shuffled and laid out. In a typical PK study, the subject tries to influence on which side of a line mechanically dropped dice will fall.

In many of these experiments, the results indicate that some subjects do score significantly above chance expectations. In addition, most of these studies utilize elaborate control procedures. So why is ESP still not regarded as "proven"?

For one thing, the terms "chance expectations" and "above chance" are frequently misunderstood and improperly used. For example, on the average, a tossed coin will fall "heads" one half of the time—that is the "chance expectation." Does that mean that for every set of four tosses you will obtain two "heads"? Certainly not, although that will be a *common* outcome. In a similar fashion, in an ESP experiment where forty hits is the average expected "chance" outcome, many more or many less hits may occur by chance in any one set of trials (Gatlin, 1977).

Demonstrations of ESP or PK by performers on the stage and on television often seem to prove that the phenomena are real. All sorts of psychic feats unfold before our very eyes. How could we doubt such evidence? Major research institutes have studied "gifted" psychics and certified their abilities. However, those same institutes have been deceived by professional magicians, who reveal their true identities only after being certified "psychic." The magicians are using standard stage tricks and gimmicks (Weil, 1974a, 1974b; Campbell, 1974). The Committee for the Scientific Investigation of Claims of the Paranormal, whose membership ranges from B. F. Skinner to "The Amazing Randi," seriously attempts to evaluate claims of psychic ability (*Science News*, 1977).

The fact that fraud or stage magic are involved in some experiments and demonstrations concerning ESP or PK *does not* disprove their existence. Many honest, capable people—scientists and nonscientists—are convinced that the phenomena cannot be easily dismissed, for there certainly is much we do not yet know about how our senses function.

Experience and contingencies in perception

We have seen that properties of stimuli and of observers influence perception. Some of the important properties of observers are apparently innately determined. We will now examine some properties of the observer which are determined by experience and by contingencies.

Experience and learning

"Of *course* perception is dependent on past experience," you say. But dependent on just what part of the vague term, "past experience," and how can we prove it? Many attempts at such a proof have studied the effects of general perceptual habits, of differential training, and of manipulated influences on psychophysical detection.

Perceptual constancy

Do our perceptions remain constant, even though stimuli change, and if so, why? Take a small box and move it slowly around, now at arm's length and then close to your face, into the sunlight and then into the shadow. It does *not* appear to change in shape, size, or brightness, although the image on the retina changes dramatically with each of these moves.

The stability of our visual world depends on this perception of *object constancy*—perception of an object as having continued existence as the same object despite changes in the size, shape, brightness, and position of the retinal image. In the competition for which source of stimulation will dominate the final perceptual judgment, the information we have about the actual object (the *distal* stimulus) must win out over that of the pattern on our retina (the *proximal* stimulus) if the perception we get is to be accurate. One of the paradoxes of perception is that this is precisely what happens: what we experience subjectively does correspond more closely with the object out there than with the pattern of the image in our retina. We perceive *size constancy,* for example, by integrating the input about retinal size with estimates of distance. Information stored in memory about usual distances and sizes of familiar objects may enter into this process.

Seen from the top of the Sears Tower in Chicago, people look like ants. When you are in a novel situation and the cues you must rely on for distance estimation are inadequate or confusing, then size constancy no longer rules and your perceptual system falls back on the information it has available—namely, the good old unreliable proximal stimulation.

The effects of training

To illustrate how even brief training can influence your perception, perform the following experiment. Carefully examine for a minute the woman's face in the drawing below. At the same time, have a friend look closely at the face on p. 361, which *you should not see.* Then both flip to p. 363 and call out, as soon as you can, what kind of face you see there. ■

When a similar experiment was first performed in the laboratory many years ago, the experimenter found that perceptual preparation with one of the first pictures was very effective in determining what the response would be to the ambiguous figure, whereas verbal preparation had no effect. He also found that when subjects saw only the ambiguous picture, twice as many of them reported seeing the young woman in it as the old one. With supposedly comparable past experience, other characteristics—perhaps in the stimulus pattern itself—tipped the balance (Leeper, 1935).

People also adapt quickly to distortions of perception. This was demonstrated in the 1890s by psychologist G. M. Stratton, who found he could adapt to wearing a set of prism lenses that both reversed the visual field and turned the world upside down. (See *P&L* Close-up, The Jim Plunkett Story.)

View I

Learning to see after being blind

Evidence for the role of experience in receiving and organizing the sensory inputs basic to perception comes from studies of adults, blind all their lives, who have suddenly received their sight.

People born with cataracts (clouding of the lens) in both eyes are totally blind. The operation to correct this defect is quite simple. However, for one reason or another, some of these people are left untreated until they are adults. Such people are completely without visual experience, but are fully as capable as any other adult with respect to most other abilities. In studying them immediately after the cataracts are removed, we have subjects who are at the earliest stage of visual development and yet able to communicate as adults about their experiences.

To demonstrate the reliance of motor performance on visual cues, I once asked Stanford Psych 1 student Jim Plunkett (later to be NFL Rookie of the Year) to serve as the subject in a test of football-throwing accuracy.

First, Plunkett threw the football with his customary pinpoint accuracy to a moving receiver at the end of a fifty-foot stage. Then he was fitted with goggles on which were glued prisms that displaced the visual field twenty degrees to the right. On his next throw, he missed the target—as the class gasped in amazement. But with only one more practice attempt he was able to correct the misinformation provided by the distorted visual feedback and hit his target perfectly—to cheers from the class, and boos for the seemingly defeated professor.

After ten more perfect trials, the goggles were removed, returning the football star to his "normal" state. "Would you please throw just once more to the receiver, just to be sure you can?" I requested. With a disdainful snicker, Plunkett raised his powerful arm and fired the football across the stage—missing the target by twenty degrees on the left side!

Did this compelling psychology lesson enhance Plunkett's ability to adapt to visual distortions on the field, thus contributing to Stanford's Rose Bowl victory over Ohio State? I'd like to think so.

Von Senden (1932) compiled data on a number of such cases. Following their operations, the patients lacked the ability to identify even the simplest objects. Each patient needed many exposures to an object in a particular setting in order to be able to name it. Even then, the patient might be unable to recognize the same object in a different setting. The patients experienced just as much difficulty in identifying the faces of friends, relatives, and other persons of great importance in their lives as they did in identifying geometric figures. One exceptionally intelligent patient could identify only four or five faces two years after the operation.

Restoring sight to adults who have learned to live in a sightless world is not always the blessing we might expect it to be. A common occurrence in many of these cases was a reluctance to rely on the newly acquired sense of sight. Gregory described the case of an Englishman, blind since the age of ten months, whose sight was restored at age fifty-two.

"We saw in dramatic form the difficulty that S. B. [the patient] had in trusting and coming to use his vision whenever he had to cross the road. Before the operations, he was undaunted by traffic. He would cross alone, holding his arm or stick stubbornly before him, when the traffic would subside as the waters before Christ. But after the operation, it took two of us on either side to force him across a road: he was terrified as never before in his life" (Gregory, 1966, p. 197).

Eventually, S. B. would not bother to turn on the lights in the evening, but would sit alone in the (comforting) darkness. In other cases, however, effective use of sensory processing has been regained by active, intelligent, well-educated patients.

Signal detection theory

Have you ever seen an unidentified flying object? If so, were you uncertain about what you saw? Did you tell anyone, or have any uncertainty about telling anyone? If you haven't seen a UFO, imagine how you might react if some day you thought you did. Project Bluebook, the U.S. Air Force study of UFO reports, involved interviews with many people who thought they made sightings; some were very reluctant to report their sightings.

In such situations, people first must decide if they saw anything, then must decide if they will say so. Because the psychophysical methods developed by Fechner to measure thresholds could not be used to describe such behavior, a new approach to measuring human sensory ability was devised (Swets, 1973). It is called signal detection theory (SDT).

What are the chances?

People are influenced by their perception of how likely they believe a stimulus to be. Pain in the left shoulder and arm may or may not be a sign of a heart attack. When a person who is always fearful of heart trouble feels such pain, it is perceived as a heart attack. However, a person who expects to live to old age free from physical infirmity probably will perceive the pain as a strained muscle. Either person might be correct or incorrect when their perception is compared to objective evidence about their heart and their muscles.

What are the consequences?

Imagine that it is 1973 and two people are having their hearing tested. One knows that if his hearing is normal, he will be inducted into the Army and sent to Viet Nam, something he would rather not do. The other knows that if hers is normal, she will be eligible to enter a flight training school, a long-term goal in her life. Will the consequences associated with the tests influence performance? Quite possibly. She might try harder, while he might hardly try.

Sensitivity and criterion

Psychophysics began by assuming that people's responses to stimuli of different types varied because of their sensitivity. If they said "yes," it meant they perceived the target stimulus; "no" meant they did not. We have seen that sensitivity is only one factor which influences such responses; consequences and the likelihood of each type of stimulus are also important. Signal detection theory provides a way to analyze the "yes" and "no" responses of a person to measure both their *sensitivity* and their *criterion*. Criterion is the willingness of the person to say "yes." One person might be very sensitive to a stimulus, but not be willing to say it is present (a "strict" criterion). Another person might be very insensitive, but be overly willing to say a stimulus is present (a "lax" criterion). There are four possible combinations of stimulus conditions and observer responses. An observer may say "yes" or "no." Either response may be correct or incorrect in a given situation, depending on whether a stimulus is or is not present. ●

The methods of signal detection theory may be used for testing sensitivity and criterion with many types of stimuli and in many settings. For example, they are useful in comparing the performance of people suffering from different clinical problems.

View II

In one study, thirty-four people who had suffered blunt head injuries were compared to thirty-four people who had not. They were tested for visual recognition memory, using SDT. Subjects viewed a series of cards containing simple designs, some of which they had seen before ("old" items) and some of which were "new." For each item, they responded "old" or "new." When "correct old" and "incorrect old" answers were analyzed, head injury patients were found to be both less sensitive to old items and more strict in their response criteria than were the control subjects; the patients had poorer memory and said "old" less often (Brooks, 1974).

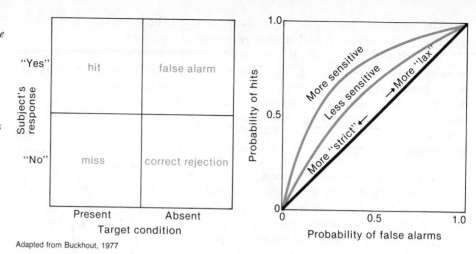

Adapted from Buckhout, 1977

How perception is directed

Perception is an active process. We do not wait passively for stimuli to force us to respond. For all of our lives, we search for and process sensory information. Sometimes the search is physically active, as when a sky diver goes through the sequence of behaviors which result in the perceptions of a free fall toward the earth. Other times, the search is private and known only to the searcher, as when a meditator goes through the practices which produce heightened perception of inner states. In all cases, the search is directed and controlled.

Attention

Many psychologists describe attention as the directive aspect of perception. As you read this page, your eyes scan the lines. At one level you perceive a sequence of words, while, at another level you perceive their meaning. At still other levels, you, as a complex system, perceive and control body posture, heart rate, blood pressure, body temperature, pupil size, and a host of other variables. You, as a describer of perceptions, usually do not seem "aware" of those other variables while you read.

Try this experiment. After reading these instructions, stop reading, sit quietly, and become aware of the sensations from your tongue. For a few minutes, perceive all you can about your tongue—without touching it. Think of nothing but your tongue. Now try it.

Now that you are reading again, did you notice anything during your experiment? Did your perceptions differ from those while you are reading? Whatever you did inside yourself to change your perceptions is called "focusing of attention." Attention focuses on one aspect of perception after another in a life-long sampling of the information available in your nervous system.

Noticing transitions

Before birth, we are sensitive to sudden changes in perception. A fetus in the womb responds when loud sounds penetrate the uterine wall. The same reflexive response to sudden intense stimuli is present after birth. It is part of a generalized *startle response* or *orienting reflex* which results in the person, infant

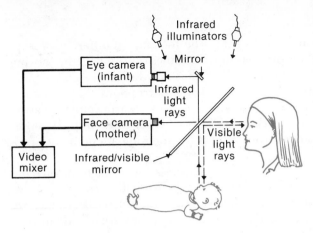

The diagram shows the apparatus used to record where infants were looking at the image of an adult face. The image of the infant's eyes is recorded along with the face of the adult. The table shows the percentage of visual fixations by infants in three age groups on each of four locations on the faces of adults.

Age groups (weeks)	Percentage of face fixations			
	Eyes	Nose	Mouth	Edges
3 to 5	29.8	7.9	4.9	57.4
7	54.8	7.2	4.2	33.8
9 to 11	48.9	12.7	5.7	32.7

Adapted from Haith, Bergman, & Moore, 1977

or adult, focusing the visual and auditory systems on the source of stimulation to maximize the intensity and clarity of perceptions of the source.

Infants and adults also share a tendency to examine less dramatic transitions, such as the edges and contours of patterns. Salapatek and Kessen (1966, 1973) demonstrated that when infants scan triangles, they concentrate most on corners, next most on edges, and least on centers. Infants also show great interest in the faces of adults.

A study compared visual fixations by infants on specific regions of the face of an adult. The figure shows a diagram of the apparatus in the study and a table of the results. Between the ages of five and seven weeks, there was a pronounced shift of fixations from edges to eyes. When the adult spoke, the infants fixated the eyes even more often. It was suggested that eye fixations by the infant facilitate the social bond between infant and adult (Haith, Bergman, & Moore, 1977). ▲

An example of sensitivity to transitions is provided by the next figure, where an edge, which is an illusion, captures our attention. Like all other visual edges, this one exists in our nervous system; unlike many others, there is no "objective" edge associated with it in the outside world. ◆

Identifying the unchanging

Gibson (1969) emphasized the importance of detecting the unchanging or *invariant* features of perception. Those invariants provide essential information about distinctive features of the environment. As we accumulate perceptual experience during our lives, we begin to identify invariants of increasing complexity. Infants cannot identify the invariants which allow us to tell dogs from cats, but a six-year-old can. Similarly, the six-year-old does not identify the invariants which identify one economy as capitalistic and another as socialistic, but some adults can.

Many unchanging aspects of perception seem to fade from awareness. In reality, they form part of the "ground" against which changing events stand out as "figure." Our response to gravity is an example. Except for brief trips by a few astronauts and cosmonauts, we live our lives in a strong gravitational field. It dominates our existence, since most of our energy goes to opposing gravity. It dominates our perception, since up, down, and horizontal are based on gravity. Try as we might, we cannot escape it unaided. Yet, this unchanging force is the basis for our nonvisual perceptions of horizontal movement, of acceleration, of falling, and of leaping.

View III

A subjective edge is visible even though the line segments run in a different direction from the curved contour and there is no brightness contrast.

Focusing

As we demonstrated earlier, attention may be focused on different perceptions by several means. You focus on different lines on the page by moving your eyes. You can focus on something which is now behind you by turning your head to look *or* by internally attending to the perceptions of sounds coming from behind you. You can focus on memories of a warm summer day by doing something which no one yet understands; by remembering. Hypnosis, meditation, and biofeedback are procedures for focusing attention and producing changes in perception.

Whatever we mean by the word "consciousness," it seems to involve the concept of attention. Perception, in the form of information coded in nerve impulses, occurs at many levels, most of which we cannot describe. In fact, we do not experience most of those levels subjectively—they are not in our consciousness. With appropriate training or feedback, we can also learn to focus attention upon them. For example, we usually are "unconscious" of the fact that we regulate our heart rate, but we can become aware of that control.

University students, selected for degree of susceptibility to hypnotic suggestion, were used in a test of the relative effectiveness of biofeedback, hypnosis, and a combination of the two. Each treatment was administered to nine subjects. Subjects were to voluntarily increase their heart rate during each of twenty one-minute trials. The biofeedback group monitored their heart rates on a meter, as did the group which used biofeedback during hypnosis, while the hypnosis group received no feedback. During the brief training period, the group combining hypnosis and biofeedback produced a statistically significant increase in heart rate. As is typical with such brief training, hypnosis or biofeedback alone produced only slight increases. The greater control demonstrated by the group receiving both treatments suggests that combining them greatly enhanced the focusing of attention on the variables controlling heart rate (Mandel, 1974).

Control system theory

At the beginning of this chapter, I suggested that you press on your closed eyelid to see a spot. Did you try it? (If you didn't, you now have a second chance!) Were you able to find your eyelid, even though your eyes were closed? Did your finger arrive gently at your eyelid, or did you poke your eye violently? Most people *can* find their eyelid and *do* touch it gently. Something controls the relationship between finger and eyelid. You might think that my suggestion controlled your actions. If that is true, then if I were to suggest that you poke your eye (which I don't), you would do it. Obviously, my suggestions influence you only if you perceive them as reasonable. You followed one suggestion in order to see a new visual perception; you ignored the other because it would produce perceptions of pain and injury. You controlled which perceptions occurred.

Doing what you want to do

After you accepted my suggestion, but before you touched your eyelid, you anticipated a perception that did not exist; your anticipation existed, but the perception did not. Powers (1973a, 1973b, 1976) calls that anticipated perception a *reference signal*. Using his concepts, you perceived your eyelid and finger in positions other than the one you anticipated; your perception of their initial positions was based on *sensory signals*, or *feedback*, from your sensory nerve endings. This feedback is simply sensory input; it is not the same as "knowledge of results." The difference between the reference signal and the sensory signals was an *error signal*. Error, in this case, simply refers to a difference condition, not to being "incorrect" or "wrong." Powers describes error signals as the nerve impulses that produce activity in muscles. Because of muscle activity, your hand moved, quickly at first, then more slowly, as the difference between the reference and sensory signals diminished to zero. Sensory feedback cancelled the error signal. Your movement then stopped and you maintained zero error by keeping your finger in one position on your eyelid. Powers' model of a perceptual control system is summarized in the *P&L* Close-up, Inside, Outside.

Close-up
Inside, Outside: Control System Units

Control theory describes in detail a way in which our perceptions relate to our behavior. The figure represents a basic control-system unit in behavior. All of the parts *above* the horizontal line (INSIDE YOU) represent events in your nervous system; while all of the parts *below* the line (OUTSIDE YOU) represent physical events outside of your nervous system. Inside, the *reference signal* is your perceptual goal or your anticipated perception; the *sensory signal*, or *feedback*, is your present perception of the existing conditions of the world and of your body; the *comparator* "subtracts" the sensory signal from the reference signal; and the *error signal* is the difference between the reference signal and the sensory signal. Outside, *disturbances* are events, other than your own behavior, which influence variables you can sense; while *stimulus energy* is the energy which comes from variables you can sense and which is able to activate your sensory receptors.

The reference signal and the feedback signal have opposite effects on the control system. For example, if the reference signal *excites* a comparator cell, and the feedback signal *inhibits* that cell, then feedback is subtracted from the reference signal. As a result, when they are unequal, error exists and the system produces behavioral output. If that output influences the environment in a way which increases the appropriate feedback signal, then the difference between feedback and the reference signal is reduced (error is reduced). The behavioral output produced by that particular error then begins to decrease. When feedback equals the reference signal, error becomes zero and the behavior which is associated with zero-error continues. Then anything which disturbs the input to the sensory feedback pathway will produce error, and behavioral output will increase, resulting in cancellation of the effect of the disturbance. Such a system works to obtain, then to maintain, a perception which is necessary or preferred.

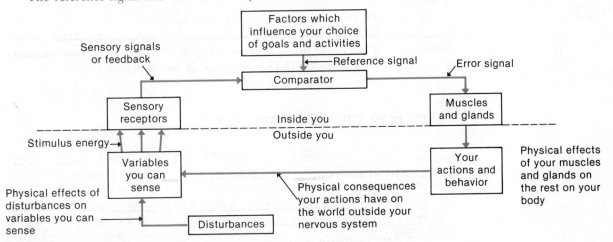

Adapted from Powers, 1973

Sensory feedback also allows a person to drive a car or ride a bicycle. The driver or rider desires to perceive the road in a specific relationship to the vehicle. The person can only move muscles, but as a result of those movements, hands and arms will move, the steering wheel or handle bars will move, the front wheels, or wheel, will turn, the vehicle will turn, and the perception of the road will change. When sensory feedback matches the desired perception, error is cancelled and efforts to steer decline. (Look, Ma, no hands!) Any disturbance of the sensory feedback creates error and produces a corrective move to exactly cancel the error. Holes in the road, blowouts, bad wheel alignment, or someone else grabbing the steering wheel will all produce disturbances. How would you correct for each one?

The chain of command

Think of the relative complexities and durations of the following organized behaviors: tensing a muscle, sitting still, daydreaming, listening to a lecture, attending a college or university, and pursuing a profession. Each of these behaviors can be described in terms of complexity and duration. For each, it is possible to identify a preferred perception, sensory signals about the present state of affairs, and error signals. It is also possible to identify a relationship between them; they could occur simultaneously. (At least, that is the impression from the front of a university or college classroom!) The most complex and long-lasting organization is made up of simpler and briefer organizations, each arranged in a hierarchy all the way down to the level of the muscle contractions that make up each of your movements or postures.

Control theory assumes that the hierarchy of organization in behavior reflects a hierarchy of perceptions and of control. Going down from the highest level of organization in the hierarchy tells us *how* a reference signal is being controlled. Pursuing a professional career *may* involve attending lectures, which *may* involve sitting still, which *may* involve daydreaming, which *may* involve tensing. The use of "may" rather than "does," is intentional. Can you think of any alternatives after each "may"? *Must* you get a degree? *Must* you daydream? (Must you!)

Going up from the lowest level of the hierarchy tells us *why* a particular action occurs, if we have all of the elements in the hierarchy. Attending the lecture occurs *because of* working toward a degree; which occurs *because of* a choice of career goals. The daydreaming tells us a person can control more than one reference signal at a time. Why might daydreaming in class occur? (See *P&L* Close-up, Does Psychology Have a Purpose?)

We will end our discussion of perception before too much daydreaming while reading begins to occur and move on in the next chapter to a further discussion of the motivations that underlie all our behavior.

Chapter summary

Perception involves a number of complex processes, including *transduction, coding, processing, subjective experience,* and *behavior.* Thus it is not surprising that psychologists are not all agreed upon the way *perceptual reality* relates to *objective reality. Phenomenal absolutism* is the belief that perceptions are direct and accurate representations of the environment. The British *associationists (empiricists)* asserted that we learn to have complex perceptions by combining simple ones.

Close-up

Does Psychology Have a Purpose?

Control-system theory is a controversial topic in psychology. The theory speaks of goals and purposes in behavior and describes perception as a controlling factor in behavior. Behaviorism (except for Tolman) has denied the usefulness of perception and the existence of purposes. As a result, many psychologists view the words "goal" and "purpose" in much the same way a bull is alleged to view a red cape!

Such reactions are probably unnecessary. The goals and purposes discussed in control theory are not always "known," in the sense that a rat could say, "I *want* to get some food now," or a person could say, "Now I *want* to raise my blood sugar level while keeping my metabolism constant." To control perceptions means to control events within the nervous system, not to be subjectively or introspectively aware of all we do and why we do it.

As an example, contingencies or schedules of reinforcement are related to behavior: if we change the number of times subjects must respond to obtain a reward, then the number of times they respond will change. Many behaviorists consider this to be a demonstration of the control of behavior by contingencies. Control theorists probably would say that schedules of reinforcement simply determine the rate at which behavior can change perceptions. If we change the number of responses needed to obtain the perception of one "reward," then subjects will change the number of responses they make in order to obtain the same total of perceptions. The subjects behave to hold constant their perceptions, not to hold constant their number of responses.

Whatever the outcome of the controversy over purpose and goals, control theory is a source of increasing interest and activity in psychology. The theory may eventually be accepted or rejected, but it certainly will cause many psychologists to reexamine their personal goals and those of psychology in general.

Other psychologists believe that our perception of reality is *mediated* by the brain rather than a direct reflection of reality. They point to the *phi phenomenon*, in which a series of stationary lights flashing on and off are perceived as moving. Such perceptions are called *illusions*; they occur in all of the sensory systems. *Gestalt* theorists hold that our perceptions are organized into *patterns*, or *configurations*, which are more than the sum of their parts.

Information from the environment is received by sensory organs composed of *receptor cells* specialized to detect stimulus energy of a particular type. Besides *vision* and *hearing*, we have a number of *somatic* (body) senses. These include the *cutaneous* (skin) senses of pressure, pain, cold, and warmth as well as the *labyrinthine sense* (balance) and *kinesthetic sense* (muscle position). The *chemical senses* are taste and smell.

The eye has two separate systems of receptors: the *cones*, specialized for daylight and color vision, and the *rods*, sensitive to very dim light but not to color. Cones are most numerous in the *fovea*, the area of sharpest vision; there are no rods in the fovea. Light passes through several layers of nerve fibers until it reaches these receptor cells, which translate it into messages carried over the *bipolar* and *ganglion* cells to the optic nerve and by it to the visual area of the brain, the *occipital cortex*. At the point where the optic nerve leaves the retina, there is a *blind spot*.

Photopigments in the rods and cones absorb light of various colors, producing the nerve potentials that activate the bipolar cells. When we move from a brightly lighted area into a darker one, a process of *dark adaptation* takes place in the retina. Four types of *opponent-process cells* in the lateral geniculate nucleus add and subtract the information reaching them, producing color vision. The perception of form, pattern, and movement depends on special-ized cells called *feature analyzers* that are activated only by certain *trigger features*—stimuli in a given spatial orientation or location.

In our perception of sound, alternating pressure differences *(sound waves)* enter the *outer ear*, are transmitted through the bones in the *middle ear* to the cochlea in the *inner ear*, and there are translated into nerve impulses. Sound waves have the properties of *frequency* and *amplitude*, which determine their pitch and loudness, respectively. The hearing of high-frequency sounds is explained by the *place theory*, and of low-frequency tones by the *telephone theory*. A *volley theory* is required to account for tones in the middle range.

Some theorists believe that perception is determined solely by the stimu-lus or solely by the observer. Others, like Gibson, see perception as the result of interactions between the individual and the environment.

Psychophysical scaling methods establish the relationship between stimulus intensity and the resulting sensations. The *absolute threshold* is determined by the average intensity required for an individual to first detect the stimulus. The four levels of scaling used in all forms of psychological tests and measure-ments are the *nominal, ordinal, interval,* and *ratio* scales.

Turning to the Gestaltist principles of organization, we find that individ-uals readily distinguish between *figure* and *ground* in both vision and hear-ing. We perceive visual depth through such cues as (a) *atmospheric perspective,* (b) *linear perspective,* (c) *texture gradient,* (d) *light and shadow,* (e) *relative position,* and (f) *known standards.* Bodily cues such as *convergence* and *retinal disparity* also help us perceive depth and distances. Differences in *arrival time, intensity,* and *phase* of sound waves assist us in locating the direction of sounds.

Parapsychology is the scientific study of psychical phenomena, such as *estrasensory perception* (ESP) and *psychokinesis.* ESP includes *telepathy* ("mind reading"), *clairvoyance* ("second sight"), and *precognition* ("foreknowledge"). Rigorously controlled research is needed to evaluate the claims of ESP.

Experience plays an important part in perception. Because of *perceptual constancy,* the perceived size of an object is in accordance with the *distal* (actual) stimulus rather than the *proximal* (retinal) stimulus. The effects of even brief training can influence perception, and most people can adapt fairly readily to perceptual distortions. The importance of experience in perception is also seen in studies of blind persons who gain sight in adulthood.

Signal detection theory provides a new approach to measuring human sensory ability. Our perceptions are influenced by our beliefs about both the *likelihood* and *consequences* of a particular stimulus occurrence. The individ-ual's *criterion* for reporting a stimulus occurrence is also important.

Perception is always an active process, directed and controlled. At-tention is the directive aspect of perception. The orienting reflex enables us to attend to changes in stimulation. It is also important that we be able to identify the unchanging aspects of the environment. With training we learn to focus on both external and internal stimuli. *Control system theory* deals with the way we control our perception. Anticipated perception provides us with a reference signal against which we can test sensory feedback and correct our responses. Control system theory assumes a hierarchy of perceptions and control that corresponds to the hierarchy of organization we observe in behavior (and in the nervous system).

Part Five

Motivation and Mind

Paul KLEE "ZWIEGESPRAECH BAUM-MENSCH"
1939, B 3 (403)
Zeichnung, Bleistift, Bambou Japon /
21 : 29, 5 / Sammlung Felix Klee, Bern,
Inv. 296

13 Motivation: The Force for Action

During questioning of Vietnamese war prisoners, some of the American in-terrogators got carried away and became physically abusive. One Green Beret sergeant described the process which led him and others to behave sadistical-ly: "First we hit them so that we could get ourselves angry. Then we hit them because they were making us angry. In the end, you strike for the sheer plea-sure of it. That was the most horrible part of it all." The experience was so personally disturbing that this American soldier refused to continue and pub-licly denounced what he and his companions were doing (*Toronto Star*, No-vember 24, 1967).

This example raises the question of *motivation*. Behind each of the actions described is a reason. In order to be perceived as threatening and tough by the enemy, the soldiers acted aggressively. Then they acted aggressively be-cause they blamed the enemy for arousing strong negative emotions in them. Next, they acted aggressively because it felt pleasurable to have power over others and to release physical energy. The sergeant eventually "blew the whis-tle" on these activities because of his concern for the suffering he saw and be-cause the actions violated his moral values. Common to each explanation is a *reason for action*. These reasons are usually stated as the *assumed causes* of a giv-en behavior. When the causes of behavior are assumed to be within the person or organism they are usually thought of as *motives*.

Some of these motives, such as hunger and thirst, stem from biological demands for the survival of the organism. Others, such as needs for social approval, develop as a consequence of social experience. Still others fall in between the biological and social, such as acting from the passion of anger or revenge, or a need to explore one's environment. Much human effort is based upon motivation to work or religious motives. In this chapter we shall first view the concept of motivation in a broad perspective, then focus on several important motives of different kinds, singling out especially hunger, achieve-ment, work, and religion.

The concept of motivation

When we ask what makes us, and other living organisms, "tick," we are proba-bly asking questions about motivation. Is human behavior driven by "animal impulse" and appetite or by love and altruism? Why does competition cause some individuals to "psych up" and succeed while others "psych out" and fail? How can children be taught to be cooperative? What can be done to increase the productivity of workers? How do TV ads make us "want" to own a particu-lar product? Is it true that people on welfare don't want to help themselves? To answer any of these questions, most of us would highlight the ways in which motivational factors influence people's lives.

If learning could explain all of behavior, we could always be sure that a given stimulus would produce a specific response. But this is not so. Food will at one time elicit the salivation response and another time be ignored. We haven't forgotten what food is—we simply are not hungry.

It is not always possible to identify the underlying motive that makes us act in particular ways on certain occasions, but it is often possible to view the motive as an *intervening variable* linking various stimulus inputs to varied re-sponse outputs. We postulate general states, such as greed or jealousy, as being responsible for behavioral consequences. Or we often see motivated behavior as stemming from some source of arousal. Motivation is characterized by the following features: (a) energy arousal; (b) direction of effort toward a particular goal; (c) selective attention to relevant stimuli (with decreased sensitivity to irrelevant ones); (d) organization of response units into an integrated pattern or sequence; and (e) persistence of this activity until the initiating conditions are changed. Thus, motivated behavior is not seen as aimless or random but as directed specifically toward (or away from) relevant stimuli. The behavior tends to be organized into general patterns. And most importantly, motivated behavior is enduring. Despite frustration, setbacks, and adversity, the motivated letter carrier gets the mail through, the spurned lover continues to send love letters to the beloved, and the rejected actor returns again and again for the next audition.

There are five different ways in which psychologists use the concept of motivation: (a) to account for behavioral variability; (b) to infer private states (from public acts); (c) to establish inner directedness; (d) to assign volition, responsibility, and blame; and (e) to link physiological processes to behavior.

Accounting for behavioral variability

The basic function of motivational analysis is explaining the observed *variability* in behavior. How can we explain the different responses to the same external situations made by different people, or even the same person at different times? When, for example, sportscaster Howard Cosell says of the winner of an athletic contest that "the man was so hungry for the win he could taste it," he is (mistakenly) using motivational rather than ability differences to explain the outcome. He is saying that A won and B lost because of a difference in level of motivation that resulted in A's putting out "more of what it takes." An obvious flaw in such an analysis is that it is retrospective, after the fact. When the verdict is in, almost any motivational explanation will do. It is quite a different matter to predict in advance the outcome on the basis of who is more "hungry for victory."

Not all variations in behavior require motivational explanations. Some behavior is a product of the way the organism is put together. One athlete performs better than another because she is physically superior. Motivational concepts are not needed to describe differences in behavior due entirely to ability or skill or intelligence or opportunity. When people are the same on these dimensions but differ in performance, motivation is used to account for the variability.

Inferring private states from public acts

'Tis e'er the wont of simple folk to prize the deed and o'erlook the motive, and of learned folk to discount the deed and lay open the soul of the doer.
John Barth
The Sot-Weed Factor

Barth's words suggest two ways of responding to someone's behavior. We might take it at face value and not look for anything more "behind" it. Or, we could see the behavior as merely the symptom of an underlying motivational state. To the greeting, "Good morning," do you respond "Good morning to you"? Or, do you wonder instead why your friend is so cheerful and what was *really* intended by that seemingly casual remark? Sigmund Freud's belief that no human behavior was accidental, coupled with his idea that sex and aggression were powerful unconscious motives, has had a profound effect on the way we think about motivated behavior. He gave us a *dynamic model* of behavior in which all action is assumed to be motivated—until proven otherwise.

"I'll run through it again. First the exhilaration of a new work completed, followed by the excitement of approaching pub date. Reviews pouring in from everywhere while the bidding for the paperback rights soars to insane figures. An appearance on Merv Griffin or Dick Cavett, sandwiched in between like Engelbert Humperdinck and Juliet Prowse. Finally, a flood of letters from people to whom your name, yesterday unknown, now has the shimmer of national renown. Hit those keys!"

Drawing by Booth; © 1972, The New Yorker Magazine, Inc..

Establishing inner direction of behavior

Radical behaviorists insist that it is reinforcement *following* behavior and not motivation *preceding* it that is significant. This approach stresses the role of the environment in controlling human behavior. It is reinforcers, not internal states, that give humans direction.

Proponents of motivational psychology claim that motivation has direct effects on behavior as well as indirect effects through making reinforcers "relevant." You do "choose" your own reinforcers. And the motivated individual does emit more responses, sooner, faster, more vigorously, and more persistently than the unmotivated one. Just as coal energizes fire, motivation energizes behavior — from within. ■

Humanists like Abraham Maslow argue that inner direction gives coherence as well as purpose to human actions. We move toward becoming "self-actualized" as our behavior falls into harmony with higher purposes in life. Satisfaction of our needs comes not from external rewards but from an inner sense of accomplishment. (We will have more to say about this point of view in Chapter 16.)

Assigning volition, responsibility, and blame

Motivation occupies an important place in law and religion. Under the law, penalties for the same crime differ if it was voluntary rather than involuntary, compelled by "overwhelming passion" or coolly planned in advance. On the other hand, motives supply reasons for crimes, but when they are too strong, they are assumed to diminish rational judgment and the ability to tell right from wrong. (See *P&L* Close-up, A Killer Is at Large.)

Many orthodox religions also require a motivated intention to do wrong for an act to be considered a sin. The person must have the maturity to know right from wrong and then forsake good to engage in evil. Motivation comes to the fore with the concept of "sin" applied to *desire* as well as to *deeds*. For example, "to *covet* thy neighbor's spouse" is no less a violation of the Ten Commandments than to *commit* adultery or kill.

We are not more ingenious in searching out bad motives for good actions when performed by others, than good motives for bad actions when performed by ourselves.

Charles Caleb Colton
Lacon

Determination of the actor's state of mind is basic to our system of justice. The same act of taking another person's life is regarded as *murder* if it is an intentional act, or as the lesser crime of *manslaughter*, if not.

We can learn much about a society's conception of human nature from its definition of those conditions under which one who takes another's life is not held responsible for that act. To see how varied such judgments can be, check below the conditions you think should "excuse" a killer and compare notes with your friends.

1. Inability to exercise reason due to:
   _____a) tender age
   _____b) mental retardation
   _____c) temporary or chronic insanity

   _____d) killer being subhuman; that is, an animal

2. Influence of controlling agents that limit exercise of free will:
   _____a) drugs and intoxicants
   _____b) sleepwalking

3. Influence of emotions that overwhelm reason:
   _____a) passions of jealousy
   _____b) uncontrollable rage

4. Situational and role-required behaviors that change intention of act or individual responsibility:
   _____a) public executioner
   _____b) police officer in line of duty
   _____c) soldier in battle
   _____d) citizen in self-defense
   _____e) parent protecting family
   _____f) doctor in mercy killing

Linking physiological processes to behavior

Early views held that a necessary condition for motivation was *deprivation* of something required for biological functioning. For example, the number of hours of food deprivation is a stimulus condition that affects hunger level which, in turn, motivates behavior to seek or work for food.

More modern views are moving away from simple deprivation concepts. Internal changes that affect dispositions to act in a given way may occur even in the absence of deprivation. The ethologists, notably Konrad Lorenz (Lorenz & Leyhausen, 1973) and Nikolaas Tinbergen (1972), have emphasized the role of genetic predispositions to engage in given behaviors at given times. These behaviors are a function of the release of hormones or responses to subtle changes in environmental stimuli, rather than of deprivation or excessive stimulation. The term *releasing mechanisms* is used in describing the process by which animals in different situations react specifically to particular aspects of their environment. In this view, behavior is elicited by internal mechanisms that selectively perceive environmental signals depending on motivation. If the animal is feeding, it may not notice a seductive display by a mate. However, if disposed to mate, it will follow ritualized patterns of responding, often synchronized to subtle cues of the other animal.

Biological drives as homeostatic mechanisms

Biologically based drives originate in the basic survival requirements of the organism. To sustain life, the individual organism must have food, water, oxygen, rest, and sleep. It also needs some means of maintaining a constant body temperature, and a signal system (pain) that will enable it to avoid bodily damage. Biological drives motivate the behavior of the organism in directions that lead to the required changes in internal environment. Yet the survival of the species entails far more than satisfying the basic physiological needs of the individual. Each species to inhabit this earth has had to face up to the alternative of sexual reproduction or extinction. Thus to insure the continuation of life from one generation to the next, sexual drives and nurturing drives (caring for the young) must come into play.

Though they vary in intensity, all biological drives, with the exception of sex, serve as regulatory mechanisms that help maintain the physiological equilibrium of the individual. An organism will go to remarkable lengths to maintain the constancy of its internal environment. This process of maintaining an internal balance, or physiologically constant level, is called *homeostasis*.

Biological drives originate in physiological conditions that have disturbed the organism's equilibrium. When an internal state is disturbed, conditions are produced that motivate activity. Such activity ceases only when the goal is attained and biological equilibrium is restored or when a stronger motive takes over. Many homeostatic activities are largely internal and automatic, such as the very complex process by which the body maintains a constant level of sugar in the bloodstream.

A recent study from a French neurobiology laboratory beautifully demonstrates the importance of homeostatic factors (also called *systemic* factors) in the regulation of ingestion and energy balance.

Adult rats were not fed by mouth but were given access to a lever that delivered nutritive fluid intravenously through an implanted tube. They quickly learned to press the bar in order to feed themselves. Because their caloric intake was low, only a third of normal, their body weight fell. Within a few weeks, however, body weight stabilized at about 70 percent of the original and was subsequently maintained at this new level, or "set point." The subjects regulated their liquid diet to balance energy expenditures at this lowered body weight. The subjects appear to have metered their caloric intake and controlled their operant lever pressing response accordingly. When they were deprived of food and their weight went below the 70 percent point, they pressed more to get more calories. When the diet of other rats was increased by doubling the number of calories they received with each lever press, they reduced their work output by half. "These [and other] results indicate that the lowered equilibrium level is defended, presumably through accurate systemic metering of energy inputs and outputs" (Nicolaidis & Rowland, 1977, p. 590).

But biological needs can never be satisfied permanently, and complex forms of activity have developed — particularly in humans — to meet the problem of recurring changes in physiology. Besides becoming able to detect very small physiological changes as cues to a change in equilibrium, many species have developed mechanisms for anticipating certain needs. Animals hoard food for winter or hibernate before snow falls. We not only have learned to eat before hunger pangs begin, but have developed elaborate systems of agriculture, food preservation, storage, and commodity exchange in order to ensure an adequate food supply at most times.

Thus homeostasis is more than the automatic maintenance of chemical conditions of the body in response to specific stimuli. It involves an active effort of the organism to establish a physical and social environment that is as constant as possible. Yet it cannot account for all types of behavior, even at the physiological level. Especially when humans are involved, even biologically based motives are affected by cognitive factors, by culturally learned ways of expressing or denying the motivational state, and by social values or personal

"tastes." Human motivation, in fact, is freed from simple mechanistic notions of behavior determined solely by energizing stimuli. This freedom has been gained by the evolution of a brain that enables *thought* to interpret stimulation and plan responding.

Manipulation and measurement

Much of our knowledge about biological drives has come from careful study of the behavior of animals under experimental conditions. Since measurement and quantification is one of the basic aims of any science, psychologists and physiologists have developed numerous ways of measuring the strength of drives. They do this by varying the intensity of drive stimulation and observing the effect produced on some facet of behavior.

To arouse drives, experimenters employ stimulus operations that disturb the organism's homeostatic balance. Deprivation of a needed substance, such as food or water, or variation in the calorie/bulk ratio of food or the salt concentration of water are most often used. As we have seen, direct stimulation of specific brain sites by electrical current or by chemical injections is being increasingly used to study biological drives. In addition, changing environmental conditions by creating an excess of heat, cold, or noxious stimulation provides another means of experimentally manipulating the antecedent variables of motivation.

The dependent consequences of the arousal of biological drives are measured by a variety of response indicators. Among them are: (a) gross motor activity; (b) autonomic nervous system activity; (c) consummatory behavior (amount, latency to begin, and patterning of eating and drinking); (d) rate or force of responding; (e) speed of learning associations that are reinforced by biologically relevant reinforcers; (f) resistance of conditioned responses to experimental extinction; (g) preference shown when given a choice between alternative activities or goal substances; (h) interference with an ongoing activity; and (i) amount of obstruction overcome or effort expended to reach an appropriate goal. (See *P&L* Close-up, We Try Harder.)

Hunger and eating

When food is available and we can consume it regularly, we tend to overlook the importance of the human activity of eating. Our attention tends to be drawn to this most basic of human functions only when someone eats to excess and becomes obese, refuses to eat and becomes malnourished, or when there is famine. In understanding the interactions between the physiology of hunger and the psychology of eating, we can learn much about motivational mechanisms of self-regulation in general.

Do you ever eat when you are not hungry? Can you easily resist the temptation of the smell of a hot pizza, the sight of a banana split, the thought of a chocolate cream pie? When a bowl of cashews or potato chips is put in front of you do you munch on only a few, or one by one do you clean the bowl? Does eating in a pleasant social environment influence the amount you eat? Such questions direct us to consider both the biological foundation of hunger and the impact of external stimuli—both physical and social—as well as conscious processes on what, where, when, and how much we eat.

Close-up
We Try Harder

To assess the relative strengths of various drives, a group of psychologists at Columbia University in the late 1920s devised an *obstruction box* that separated a motivated rat from the object of its affection by an electrified grid. The strength of a variety of drives (induced by deprivation) was pitted against a constant level of noxious stimulation that the animal had to endure in order to reach food, water, a sexually responsive mate, or its own offspring. The behavioral index of drive strength was the number of times the animal would repeatedly cross the "hot grid" in a given period of time. (It could also have been the highest level of shock intensity that would be tolerated to reach the goal.) Typical of the data obtained with this method are the patterns shown in the figure.

The motivating effects of thirst are greatest after a short period of deprivation, then decline, as does hunger, with extreme deprivation. This is called an inverted-U function. Performance at first increases with deprivation, then decreases as deprivation becomes excessive. This may be due to the debilitating effect of prolonged deprivation. In contrast, the rats kept on running at a constant rate in order to get a little sex, regardless of length of deprivation (after the first few hours). Surprisingly, mother rats overcame the greatest obstruction in order to retrieve their young. This powerful evidence for the existence of a "maternal

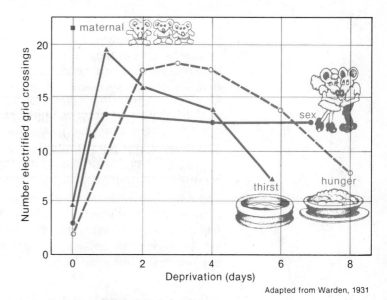

Adapted from Warden, 1931

drive" in animals went unchallenged until quite recently.

It is of interest to note another aspect of these studies. Without deprivation of any kind, the animals nevertheless crossed the grid a few times. Furthermore, even when there was nothing on the other side—except a chance to explore the novel environment—they crossed the barrier, perhaps motivated by an *exploratory drive*. This program of research is characteristic of early studies of drive, which can be criticized for focusing only on deprivation and ignoring the effects of external incentive stimuli on the motivated behavior.

What makes us hungry?

Of all the motivational states, hunger has received the most study from both psychologists and physiologists. This is because it is so easily induced in the laboratory through a simple schedule of deprivation. The number of hours without food establishes a stimulus condition that affects an organism's hunger level. The hungry organism will turn from other activities to searching the environment for food, and eating it once it is found. The *consummatory response* of eating *reduces* or temporarily eliminates the *hunger drive*. The consummatory behavior stops or becomes less probable as the animal becomes *satiated* (has had enough of the goal or activity). The *instrumental response*—the behavior of searching or working to obtain the goal—increases in strength as motivation increases in intensity and decreases with its reduction. Thus to regulate its food intake effectively, an organism must be able to detect its physiological state of hunger, initiate and organize eating behavior, meter the input and the body's energy requirements, and then stop when it has eaten enough. As we shall see, the nature of the internal conditions and regulatory mechanisms associated with hunger and eating—and cessation of eating—are quite complex.

The "feeling of hunger" is a mass of sensations seeming to come from the region of the stomach. Early research suggested that the feeling was triggered by contractions of the empty stomach (Cannon, 1934). However, more recent experiments in which the stomachs of animals were surgically removed or the neural pathways severed have resulted in only slight changes in feeding patterns. For example, in one experiment, rats whose stomachs had been removed exhibited essentially the same hunger-related behavior that normal animals (used as a control group) did. They learned mazes to obtain food just as quickly as did the controls, and they were equally active as feeding time approached. The only difference was that the rats without stomachs sought food more often than the control animals, which would be expected since they had only their intestines for food storage and hence had to eat more often (Penick, Smith, Wienske, & Hinkle, 1963). Even human patients who have had their stomachs removed experience hunger pangs (Janowitz, 1967). This would suggest that sensations originating in the stomach play, at best, a minimal role in the feeling of hunger.

Blood sugar level and hunger

The body's immediate source of the energy it needs for cellular functioning is glucose, or blood sugar. Therefore, chemical changes in blood composition should play a role in hunger. Early studies showed, for instance, that blood transfused from the body of a starving dog to that of a recently fed one can cause stomach contractions under certain conditions (Luckhardt & Carlson, 1915; Tschukitschew, 1929). It has also been found that transferring blood from a recently fed animal to a starving one stops stomach contractions in the latter (Bash, 1939). This transfusion of blood from a fed animal also brings on partial satiety in the hungry animal (Davis, Gallagher, & Ladove, 1967; Davis, Cambell, Gallagher, & Zurakov, 1971).

Hypoglycemia is a state in which glucose levels in the blood are low, below *(hypo)* normal. Injections of insulin to diabetics and to experimental subjects induce hypoglycemia. Following insulin intake, patients and subjects report increased feelings of hunger and increased pleasantness of the sweet taste of sugar. If glucose deficit induces a state of hunger, then injections of glucose should produce satiation, and they apparently do. Glucose injections inhibit eating in food-deprived animals as well as inhibiting electrical self-stimulation of brain areas presumed to be satiety centers (Balagura, 1968). How changes in glucose level in the blood are registered in the central nervous system in order to direct behavior is still uncertain, however.

A recent experiment powerfully demonstrates the significance of glucose levels within blood cells. Using advanced methodology and a fine design (utilizing multiple, independent measures of hunger), it shows that experimentally induced hunger in humans affects not only eating behavior, but metabolism, hormone release, and a variety of other correlates (Thompson & Campbell, 1977).

Five healthy, college-age male volunteers of normal weight agreed to participate in a study in which they would receive injections that might change their mood, hunger, thirst, or other reactions. Each subject was his own control (a within-subjects design), receiving in different weeks a control injection of saline (a salt solution) or the experimental drug injection. The experimental drug inhibits the use of intracellular glucose and thus should induce hunger. The drug is known as 2DG (2-deoxy-D-glucose). A special needle inserted in a vein allowed the researchers both to infuse the 2DG and to withdraw blood samples. Every thirty minutes for four hours blood samples were taken, as were pulse rate, temperature, and water intake. Subjects gave ratings of their mood, hunger, thirst, and fullness of stomach. After two hours, subjects gave estimates of the sweetness and pleasantness of a series of sugar solutions they tasted (and then spat out). They were given food by mouth 185 minutes after the injection.

Experimental hunger induced by the injection of 2DG had multiple effects. Experienced hunger increased sharply. ▲ Ratings of stomach fullness and of vigor decreased, oral temperature dropped, pulse rate went up, and sweating increased. Mood and thirst ratings were unchanged. Sucrose concentrations were judged as more pleasant after 2DG injections than after saline. Sweetness ratings were not affected. Both water intake and food intake were significantly greater in the hunger-induced condition than in the saline-control condition. Finally, there were significant elevations in concentrations of several hormones in response to the 2DG injection, including cortical and growth hormones. These data support the hypothesis that control of food intake is regulated by glucose levels in the blood. This view is called the glucostatic theory of food intake control.

The hypothalamic "feeding center"

Early evidence showed that lesions in various parts of the hypothalamus affected eating behavior as well as other consummatory responses and apparently even some motivated behaviors.

The later development of techniques for electrical stimulation of the brain generated an amazing amount of additional research focusing on the hypothalamus as the control center for hunger and the other biological drives. Stimulation of specific hypothalamic regions was thought to produce drive states that were functionally equivalent to naturally occurring drives. Even food-satiated rats could be motivated by electrical stimulation of one of these regions, the so-called "hunger center," to learn a new response for which food was the reinforcement. This and other sites were assumed to be highly specific in function, with one region of the hypothalamus controlling eating, another drinking, another aggression, and so on. Considerable evidence has accumulated lately that raises doubts whether the brain is organized in such simple function-specific sites. Many different brain regions interact to produce a given behavior. The hypothalamus may serve as the "motivation connection center" for other basic areas of the brain in the limbic region (Grossman, 1968).

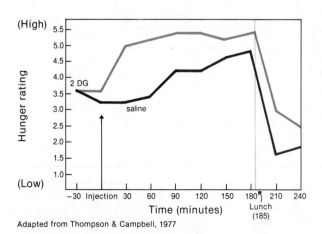

▲

Hunger ratings increase significantly within 30 minutes. Hunger is experimentally induced by injection of the glucose-inhibiting drug 2DG. Hunger shows a gradual elevation in the normal saline group as a function of food deprivation beyond 90 minutes. Eating brings immediate relief from hunger.

Adapted from Thompson & Campbell, 1977

The eating behaviors of animals electrically stimulated in the hypothalamus is often different in kind from that of animals made hungry by food deprivation. They eat whatever is presented first but don't switch to a familiar second food when the first is taken away. Nor do they eat the same food when its appearance is changed, for example by mashing it. Their consummatory behavior is very picky and highly stimulus-bound rather than being flexible in form as would be required to satisfy a general drive state.

It has been suggested that hypothalamic stimulation does not create hunger, thirst, or other drives directly. Rather, it creates the conditions that "turn on" an already established consummatory response; the act of carrying out the response may in itself be reinforcing (Valenstein, Cox, & Kakolewski, 1970).

Social and cognitive bases for eating

My mother once said, "Anyone can eat when they're hungry; it's when you eat when you're not hungry that you show your love for the cook." While the motivation to eat results largely from the body's homeostatic demands, other factors affect the appetite and eating habits of human beings. Our sensations of hunger and the starting and stopping of eating are to a large extent controlled by cognitive and social cues such as the availability of food, its tastiness, the time of day, family traditions, and so on.

Let us examine a sample of the evidence for the psychological control of eating behavior. College students ate more cashew nuts under conditions that made the nuts more prominent, such as placing the nuts under bright illumination or instructing the subjects to think about them. The effect of increasing the cue value of this food was greater for overweight subjects (Ross, 1974). Mealtime can affect eating even when the clock is rigged to give a false report of the actual time. A large wall clock was either speeded up or slowed down, leading subjects to believe that dinner time was near or distant. In both conditions, actual time passage was the same. Overweight college students who were used to eating at regular times in a dormitory snacked "according to the clock." They ate about twice as much when they thought it was dinner time than when they believed dinner was still an hour away. For normal weight subjects, the reverse occurred. They snacked less as dinner time approached because they did not want to "spoil their appetite" (Schachter & Gross, 1968).

One study found that obese patients ate more as the attractiveness of their physical and social environment was increased. They restricted their diet dramatically, however, when their meals had to be drunk through a tube projecting from a liquid dispenser (Hashim & Van Itallie, 1965). Studies suggest that overweight people are more responsive to external cues than their normal-weight peers. They may also be less sensitive to internal cues.

In the controlled laboratory research conducted by Stanley Schachter and his students, the eating of overweight college students was compared with that of a comparable normal-weight control group across a wide variety of situations. When their fear was aroused, or their stomachs were preloaded with food, normal subjects reduced their food intake, whereas these internal conditions had no effect on the eating (cracker consumption) of the obese students. On the other hand, obese subjects ate more than normals when given tasty ice cream, but less when the ice cream was bitter (Schachter, 1971).

In a related study, Schachter and Friedman (1974) found that obese subjects did *not* eat more than normals when they had to "work" for their food. Students were given either preshelled or unshelled almonds to munch on while filling out a questionnaire. The obese subjects ate more than did the controls when the almonds were already shelled, but not when they had to shell the nuts themselves. Interestingly, this effect seems to hold only in cases where the effort required is not usual for a particular food. Obese subjects ate less than normals of foil wrapped nuts—but more than normals of chocolate kisses wrapped (as usual) in the same manner (Singh & Sikes, 1974).

The suggested dichotomy between internal and external control of feeding appears now to be too simple to account for the complex interactions that comprise the control systems governing food intake. There are indeed people who are "externals." Across a great many tasks, some individuals consistently differ from others in their general sensitivity to external stimuli. Even on tasks that have nothing to do with food or eating, moderately obese people react with more external sensitivity than do any other weight group. It has been proposed by Yale University's Judith Rodin (1978) that heightened external responsiveness contributes to the development and maintenance of overeating through the crucial role it plays in short-term self-regulation. What makes some people more responsive to external cues than others is not known. However, this externality probably precedes and predisposes the person to overeat and thus become overweight in an environment of abundance. (See *P&L* Close-up, Born Fat, Not Free?)

Personal and social motives

People do not live by bread alone. They spend a lot of time and energy planning how to make a better loaf than their competitors. Often they are more concerned about who they eat with than what they eat. Indeed, for many starstruck celebrities it is vital to be seen at the "in places" with the "right" companions. Much human behavior is motivated by the desire to achieve a position of prominence, or to achieve the goal of being desirable.

We have seen that motives are inner states that energize, organize, and direct specific patterns of behavior. Biologically based motives are instigated either by conditions of deprivation or excessive stimulation at a neurophysiological level. Their satisfaction is essential for the functioning and survival of the individual and the species. In contrast stand a variety of motives that are aroused by social and cultural conditions. They are more dependent on learning than the biological drives, since they are acquired during the course of the person's transactions with people, values, and events in a given society.

Social motives, then, are acquired states of motivation that are activated by actual or imagined social stimuli. The goal response of such social motives involves eliciting particular reactions from other people. Thus for example, we need the recognition and approval of significant others in our lives. To get some, many of us comply with unreasonable demands, conforming to rules and pressures from peers to do things not always in our best interests.

There are other nonbiological motive states that may or may not involve people. Appraisal of one's own abilities and opinions requires social comparison. We often need to compare ourselves with others in order to evaluate better what we are feeling, thinking, and doing. Some personal needs may only indirectly involve others. The need to achieve one's goals, whatever they are, and motives to work are central to the psychological makeup of many of us.

Another powerful source of personal motivation which has had profound consequences not only on individual lives, but has shaped the history of

Close-up
Born Fat, Not Free?

It's no fun to be fat. More people die from medical conditions associated with excessive body weight than from any of the other addictions, including alcohol, cigarettes, and drugs (Mayer, 1968).

But the toll that obesity takes is not only physical, but psychological as well. A 1972 Gallup poll revealed that 55 percent of American women and 38 percent of American men surveyed described themselves as overweight. The fat child is taunted by playmates, while fat teenagers are likely to be ignored by peers, and fat adults retreat from the social scene or try desperately to fit the stereotyped image of the "jolly" fat person.

Richard Nisbett of the University of Michigan argues that fat people are born to be so, not made so (1972). His reasoning is based on the following ideas. How fat you are is a function of the number and size of specialized fat cells in your body. These cells, called *adipocytes*, store body fat in the form of fatty acids. Painstaking physiological research reveals that it is the greater *number* and not the larger size of these fat cells that differentiates the obese from the normal-weight individual (Björntorp, 1972). In one study the obese sample had three times as many fat cells as the average-weight group. In adults, the number of fat cells does not vary but remains stable. Dieting and starvation reduce the size of these cells but do not change their number. Overeating increases the mass of the fat cells, but not their number.

Nisbett concludes that if you have a large number of fat cells, you are programmed by nature to be fat. Two factors determine how many fat cells a person will possess in adulthood: the genetic component (fat-prone parents have fat-prone children) and an early nutritional component (being overnourished in infancy). There are critical periods in life when fat is most likely to be deposited. They are right before birth, around nine months of age, then again between six and ten years of age, and finally during late adolescence. Limiting food intake and not cleaning one's plate, especially during these fat deposition periods, can help to prevent obesity.

If you have relatively few fat cells you cannot become obese even with overeating; if you begin with a high base level of fat stores (or "*set point*" *level*), then it will be difficult in an economy of abundance for you *not* to become obese. In a sense, if you had a high set point fat level, you would be a "latent fat" even if you were skinny from dieting. This may be the reason why obesity clinics have only limited, short-term success when the latent fats return with their oversupply of underfed adipocytes to a world full of goodies.

What makes it even more difficult for a constitutionally programmed obese person to lose weight is that the "homeostatic mechanisms" in the brain are thought to adjust food intake in such a way as to maintain fat stores at that person's set point level. If this is the case, those people with a high set point level, living in our society that rewards slimness, will be hungry all the while they are maintaining the socially desired normal weight.

the human species, is religious motivation. In the next section of this chapter we shall briefly examine a selection of personal and social motives that help define key aspects of the human condition—the needs for social comparison, social approval, achievement, work, and religion.

The need for social comparison

To take effective action, it is necessary to have some sense of your strengths and weaknesses, resources and biases. How do you follow the dictum, "Know thyself"? Essentially, there are two major channels available for such information. The first involves "reality testing," in which you pit yourself against some physical attribute of the environment. Push over a large boulder, climb the highest mountain, swim the deepest ocean, throw a coin across the Potomac River, run a mile in four minutes flat, put out a fire with your bare hands. By such actions you find out what your physical capabilities are.

Whether you have succeeded in such tests of *physical reality*, however, is almost always evaluated according to tests of *social reality*: "Can other people do it too? Can they do it better? By how much?" The nonsocial motivation to know what we can do thus leads to the social motivation to use other people as yardsticks for evaluating our own accomplishments and abilities. To do so, we initiate a process of *social comparison*. Leon Festinger (1954) postulated that "there exists in the human organism a drive to evaluate his opinions and abilities." When objective criteria are not available for such evaluation, then subjective criteria are used—other people's opinions, abilities, and other characteristics. This drive for self-evaluation through social comparison has been shown to affect behavior in many ways. We observe what others say and do, and we ask questions about what they think and feel. From these tests of social reality, we come to have a picture of how strong *we* are, how bright, how emotionally responsive, how politically conservative, how attractive, and so on. From the process of social comparison we also learn "can" and "ought" relationships (Heider, 1958). We learn what we *can* do—what is possible given our mental and physical resources. On the other hand, we also learn what we *may* do—how others expect us to react in a given situation.

Not all comparison information is equally useful for forming exact and stable self-evaluations, however. The best information is derived from comparison with others whose abilities or opinions are similar to our own, or who are experiencing the same stimulus situation (Latané, 1966; Zimbardo & Formica, 1963; Bleda & Castore, 1973). You learn more about how well you write by comparing your essays with a classmate's than with the writing of J. R. R. Tolkien or Virginia Woolf. Arnold Schwartznegger or Racquel Welch are probably not the best social comparison targets for you to use if you want to check out your body development. We need to seek out people of comparable age, sex, education, experience, and background if we intend to get stable self-evaluations.

Members of a group tend to use the group standards and the performance of other members as bases for self-evaluation. Thus, an individual who is very different from others in the group makes them uncomfortable because the differences disrupt their stable base for social comparison. Typically they react by trying to force the individual to change, or, failing that, by rejecting the "deviant."

The extent to which our evaluation of our own intelligence and ability depends on comparing ourselves with others is demonstrated unhappily on every college campus each fall. Students who were "hotshot" seniors in high school (compared to their classmates) are perplexed to discover that suddenly they are only "average," at best. Half are below the average (median) compared to their new "hotshot" classmates. What has changed, of course, is not their intelligence but the basis for social comparison. An IQ of 115 is "superior" in relation to the population as a whole. But it may be "average" or even "low" in a highly selected group. First-year college students may still be big fish in the little pond back home, but on the college scene they are minnows among the sharks.

The need for social approval

At a very early age, children learn that behaving according to parental (and societal) definitions of what is right and proper results in an array of positive consequences. But such consequences, when they come from other human beings, do much more than merely increase the probability that the response will be repeated and learned. Approval from others comes to be persistently sought. Many of our highly valued activities are undertaken not for their own sake but as ways to get other people to notice, appreciate, honor, help, love, and cherish us. There are no limits to the length to which we may go to gain approval from other people, including killing someone or enduring humiliation, pain, or even death. Claude Brown relates the tale of how social approval was won (or lost) in Harlem's ghetto:

As I saw it in my childhood, most of the cats I swung with were more afraid of not fighting than they were of fighting. This was how it was supposed to be, because this was what we had come up under. The adults in the neighborhood practiced this. They lived by the concept that a man was supposed to fight. When two little boys got into a fight in the neighborhood, the men would encourage and egg them on. They'd never think about stopping the fight. . . . You had to fight, and everybody respected people for fighting. . . . A man was respected on the basis of his reputation. The people in the neighborhood whom everybody looked up to were the cats who'd killed somebody (1965, pp. 253–56).

Social approval of your actions has at least five related but distinguishable consequences:

a. approval of your behavior is a sign of recognition of *you*, and confers *visibility* and *identity*;
b. approval *legitimates* your existence, increasing your status as a person deserving to be recognized;
c. approval implies acceptance of what you have to offer, and with it the *security* of not being rejected because of inadequacy in your abilities, opinions, or feelings;
d. approval establishes a bond of contact between approver and approved, creating *liking* for the approver and perception of reciprocation by him or her;
e. approval provides one criterion of your *control* or power over the environment, by specifying how behavior on your part can generate desired consequences.

It is no wonder, then, that children's learning is strongly influenced by deprivation of social approval or by the positive social reinforcement of a nod or "Good" (Gewirtz & Baer, 1958). Consider what you would have done (or did) to get a little piece of gold paper in the shape of a star from your second-grade teacher.

The social approval of age-mates can become even more precious than

the social approval of parents and teachers, leading to "antisocial" behavior approved by the group. We can make sense of the class clown whose antics enrage the teacher, of teenagers being "recruited" into drug abuse, or of the apparently senseless violence of gang members toward an innocent victim by recognizing the power being exerted by social approval from age-mates.

People vary in how much they need the approval of others. Individual differences in need for approval are identified by scores on the Social Desirability Scale (developed by Crowne & Marlowe, 1964). Those who have a strong need to behave in socially desirable ways are likely to agree with scale statements such as:

_____ "I am always courteous to people who are disagreeable."
_____ "I always try to practice what I preach."
_____ "I have never intensely disliked anyone."

As the need for social approval becomes excessive, the individual surrenders personal values and sometimes integrity to be accepted by others. Research has shown that high scorers on the Social Desirability Scale differ from lows in their greater readiness to conform, and to suppress feelings of hostility toward others even when such feelings are justified. Sad to say, people with strong needs for social approval often tend to be social isolates, with few friends. It would appear that while being part of the social community involves actively engaging others, it cannot be bought by giving up one's identity and sacrificing one's principles.

The need for achievement

No student needs to be told that there is a strong emphasis in the United States on achievement. Business, sports, and the whole educational system all stress it. Grades are used as keys to higher levels of further competition (to admit the junior-college student to a four-year college and the college senior to graduate and professional schools). Students' characterization of the whole endeavor as one big rat race, with only a small piece of cheese in the trap, does not prevent them from joining in the race, especially if medical, law, or graduate-school admission is the prize.

The achievement motive is viewed by some investigators as a relatively general and stable characteristic of an individual, present in any situation (McClelland, 1961). It is seen as giving rise to a general *tendency to approach success*. The strength of the tendency, in a given situation, depends on three other variables: (a) expectation of success, (b) the incentive value of the particular kind of success involved, and (c) perception of personal responsibility for success (Atkinson, 1964; Feather, 1967). Two people might both have a high general-achievement orientation, but one might especially value prestige and work hardest in situations where success would mean greater prestige, whereas the other might place greater value on the satisfaction of a job well done and put forth greatest efforts in situations in which success would bring that kind of satisfaction. The concept of a motive to achieve invests individuals with an inner energy or determination to work toward goals. High achievers don't allow themselves to get distracted or easily sidetracked as they doggedly pursue their visions.

Measuring n Ach

How is this need for achievement measured? It is not enough to assume that those who work hard and meet deadlines have it, while the slouchers who get incompletes do not. Interestingly, to assess individual differences in need for achievement (labeled *n Ach*) Harvard University's David McClelland has used *fantasy* rather than the fact of work or success. He explains this approach as follows,

". . . *if you want to understand motives behind symptoms or actions, find out what's on a person's mind. If you want to find out what's on a person's mind, don't ask him, because he can't always tell you accurately. Study his fantasies and dreams. If you do this over a period of time, you will discover the themes to which his mind returns again and again. And these themes can be used to explain his actions. . . ." (1971, p. 5)*

These concerns are revealed in stories subjects tell in response to a set of pictures which portray people in ambiguous relationships or engaged in uncertain activities. This test, called the Thematic Apperception Test (TAT), was developed by Henry Murray (Murray & Morgan, 1935; Murray et al., 1938). It is a projective test that allows people to project their inner feelings, fantasies, and fears onto these ambiguous stimuli. Objective coding schemes have been developed that yield numerical scores for a person's different concerns. Differences in the strength of particular motives (needs for power, affiliation, approval, achievement) for a given individual may be identified in this way.

To be coded as a *need achievement* theme a person's story has to reveal concern to do better, to improve performance. By contrast, *need affiliation* themes reveal concern for establishing, maintaining, repairing friendly relations. And *need power* themes are filled with concern for reputation, influence, impact.

The behavioral validation of the *n Ach* measure comes from a variety of studies showing that businessmen generally score higher than professionals and that college students with high *n Ach* scores are more likely than low scorers to end up as entrepreneurs (business owners or managers). More upward mobility was found among high scorers. Sons were more likely to rise above their fathers in occupational status if they had high *n Ach* than low (Crockett, 1962).

Achievement by seeking success or avoiding failure?

The complexity of the achievement motive is partially indicated by the fact that among subjects with a high need for achievement, interesting differences have been found between those who focus on gaining success and those who focus on avoiding failure. Those who focus on attaining success tend to set more realistic goals and to choose tasks of intermediate difficulty. Those who are most concerned about avoiding failure tend to set more unrealistic goals (too low or too high in relation to their ability) and to choose tasks of low difficulty, where failure is least likely but where success, even if achieved, would be least satisfying. The importance of a feeling of responsibility for the outcome is also important in determining the level of tasks chosen. Subjects who feel highly responsible for their successes and failures tend to choose intermediate-level tasks, like the success-motivated subjects, whereas subjects who do *not* feel responsibility for their successes and failures show no preference among tasks of varying difficulty (Meyer, 1968). ■

Women and fear of success In most of the research on the need to achieve, the subjects have been men. Until recently, very little attention has been paid to achievement motives in women. Stereotyped views of the "woman's place" made it irrelevant whether she had achievement motives

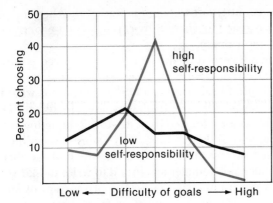

Goal setting and responsibility
Children nine to eleven years old were found to set goals of intermediate difficulty if they felt responsible for both successes and failures but to show little consistency in goal setting if they did not feel such responsibility.

Adapted from Meyer, 1968

since *n Ach* was meant largely to predict performance in work settings — traditionally the "man's place." In 1968, a dissertation by Matina Horner compared achievement themes of white college men and women. Her results uncovered a gender difference: American women appeared to fear success more than American men. Female introductory psychology students were asked to complete a story that began, "At the end of first term finals, Anne finds herself at the top of her medical school class." For male subjects, John was substituted for Anne. When the two sets of themes were analyzed for negative imagery about success, 62 percent of the women expressed conflict over Anne's success, while only 9 percent of the men expressed conflict over John's success.

Horner (1969) theorized that achievement-oriented women find themselves in a unique double-bind. On the one hand, they share with men society's general exhortation to compete and succeed; however, since successful achievement for women often brings such negative consequences as being labeled "unfeminine" or being socially rejected, women are also motivated *not* to succeed. Three main categories of fear-of-success (FOS) imagery were found by Horner:

a. Social rejection: "Anne is an acne-faced bookworm. . . . She studies twelve hours a day, and lives at home to save money. 'Well, it certainly paid off. All the Friday and Saturday nights without dates, fun — I'll be the best woman doctor alive.' And yet a twinge of sadness comes through — she wonders what she really has . . ."
b. Doubts about normality: "Unfortunately Anne no longer feels so certain that she really wants to be a doctor. She is worried about herself and wonders if perhaps she is not normal . . . Anne decides not to continue with her medical work but to take courses that have a deeper personal meaning for her."
c. Denial: "Anne is a *code* name for a nonexistent person created by a group of med students. They take turns taking exams and writing papers for Anne. . . ."

The "fear of success hypothesis" was picked up by the media as an example of a personality type created by sexist ideology — the woman who couldn't allow herself to compete successfully in a man's world. In the following decade over two hundred studies were conducted following up on various aspects of women's fear of success. However, a recent careful survey of the results of all these studies casts doubt on Horner's conclusion (Tresemer, 1976).

Fear of success is *not* a personality attribute of women. Rather, it is better conceived of as a strong avoidance reaction elicited by certain social-economic-historic conditions in *both* men and women.

When the cumulative research record of the nearly two hundred studies of fear of success (FOS) is analyzed, no gender differences appear. However, there is also a lack of standardization in scoring of FOS themes. Thus what is scored as FOS in male subjects may be different from what is evaluated as FOS in women's stories. For example, women tended to write stories depicting fear of rejection, loss of femininity, and affiliative loss. Men's stories were more cynical, hostile, violent, devalued success, and doubted the worth of sacrifices necessary to achieve success. Males and females are found to write similar stories about achieving females. Over a ten-year period the proportion of subjects showing FOS has *decreased* significantly. Finally, FOS imagery does *not* seem to be related to actual performance, especially among those high in *n Ach*. (Incidentally, the performance task typically used in FOS studies is a brief anagram test.)

Despite this lack of empirical support, fear of success may still be a useful concept. If a person is anxious about achievement but still achieves successfully, the price may be paid in ways other than poor task performance. He or she may develop health problems (migraines, ulcers, etc.), have poor social relations, become alcoholic, or pop tranquilizers. If so, that is something to be studied. In addition, the focus of research might profitably turn to situationally specific fears of success. Putting subjects in task settings where success comes at some cost may reveal both the culturally induced and neurotically centered aspects of success anxiety (Shaver, 1968). For example, in the 1960s I taught classes in which most of the women would not take part in class discussions, even though this was required for an A grade. The reason? "If we show the men we're smarter than they are, no one will want to date us"(!). In this case, the social stigma of being labeled "too bright" offset the motivation to succeed in the course.

Achievement motives in black children

Educators and psychological researchers have pointed up different patterns of achievement and achievement orientation among whites and blacks. Some have assumed that poorer academic performance by blacks reflected dispositional differences (intellectual or motivational). Others placed the blame on black parents and culture for not reinforcing the child for internalizing mechanisms of self-control. That is, they have not been taught to continue striving on tasks that have no immediate payoff. Black students were described as being "unable" to sustain effort in uninteresting tasks (Katz, 1967).

Recently Curtis Banks and his associates at Princeton University have persuasively demonstrated that the crux of the matter is not found in "deficiencies" in black (and other minority) students, but in the variable of *task interest* (Banks & McQuater, 1976). No achievement orientation differences are found between black and white adolescents on tasks that are rated of *high interest* by both groups. It is only on *low-interest* tasks that differences emerge. Blacks were found to be more concerned about the *external* consequences of these uninteresting tasks than white students (Banks, McQuater, & Hubbard, 1977). Thus black students might be expected to perform more poorly on tasks they do not value or find unattractive, especially when no external reward is present. It is only on such tasks that achievement differences are likely to emerge. A redirection of research is called for to investigate the reason certain types of tasks differ in their value or interest among different cultural groups. In trying to understand why different tasks occupy high or low positions in the value structures of whites and blacks, it may be well to examine the social-influence role of teachers and other evaluative agents on minority pupils.

Work motivation

Why do we work as hard as we do for as long as we do? If persistent effort is an index of motivation then surely work motivation is the most potent of human drives. But do we work because of what it gets us in material rewards (the payoff) or because work itself is enriching (job satisfaction)? The answer may depend on the type of job one holds, but from the employer's point of view the answer lies in "human nature." According to McGregor (1960), most organizations are structured around a set of assumptions about human nature. One such set (which he calls *Theory X*) involves the belief that people basically dislike work and will do everything possible to avoid it. Although they want security, they have little ambition and do not like to have responsibilities. In any work situation, then, people must somehow be bribed or coerced.

An alternative set of assumptions is called *Theory Y* by McGregor. Here, the belief is that people are basically creative and responsible, that the expenditure of energy in some form of work is a natural process. To the extent that work objectives fulfill personal needs (such as self-esteem, curiosity, competence), people will be intrinsically motivated to do well.

Businesses that operate on Theory X usually try to increase the quantity or quality of production by offering such standard inducements as extra pay and shorter work weeks. However, some companies have changed their organization according to Theory Y principles and have found dramatic changes in work performed. For example, instead of having assembly lines (where each person makes only a small part of the final product), some have set up small work forces where each person works on the entire product, from beginning to end. Not only do people have more pride in their work, but the chance to work in small groups allows them to develop close friendships. The workers are more satisfied, and there is less absenteeism, job turnover, and work "sabotage."

How do I motivate my workers?

The modern factory work setting has been compared to a Skinner box (see Schwartz, 1978). Workers perform specific operant behaviors with rewards (pay and fringe benefits) delivered intermittently. The reinforcement bears little or no meaningful relationship to the nature of the work. The modern worker, like the subject in an operant conditioning study, has little choice in what is to be done, or how, when, and where it is to be carried out.

In 1911, F. W. Taylor formulated a theory of "scientific management," designed for the efficient control of human labor. Time and motion studies simplified jobs and eliminated unnecessary activities. Specialization of function reduced errors and enabled work to be done automatically, often without thought. In the view of the scientific manager, motivation was simple: higher wages will result in more work (Taylor, 1911).

Frederick Herzberg disputes this simple reward notion of work motivation (1966, 1968). Poor wages will make a worker unhappy, but good wages will not make the worker want to work harder. Herzberg distinguishes "hygiene" factors from genuine motivators. Hygiene factors are aspects of the *job environment* that produce dissatisfaction if they are absent. But their presence

The "work ethic" holds that labor is good in itself; that a man or woman becomes a better person by virtue of the act of working.
Richard M. Nixon

Most of us, like the assembly line worker, have jobs that are too small for our spirit. Jobs are not big enough for people.
Studs Terkel
Working

You can't eat for eight hours a day nor drink for eight hours a day nor make love for eight hours a day—all you can do for eight hours is work. Which is the reason why man makes himself and everybody else so miserable and unhappy.
William Faulkner
Interview in *Paris Review*

does not necessarily generate satisfaction. Good wages, liberal fringe benefits, shorter work periods, human relations and sensitivity training, worker-boss communications, counseling are instances of hygienic aspects of work that reduce unhappiness, but are not real motivators. They are also instances of "positive KITA." KITA is an acronym for the direct action manager's guide to management: "a Kick In The A--." Negative KITA works even less well, though still used to punish workers physically or psychologically for not getting the job done.

Positive motivation comes only from work whose *job content* is enriching, challenging and in which the workers can assume responsibility. Where work enables a worker to achieve something of actual value, work encourages psychological growth. Growth or motivator factors that are intrinsic to the job are achievement, recognition for achievement, the nature of the work activity, responsibility, and growth or advancement. ▲ Thus it becomes a continuous function of management to discover and institute ways to enrich the jobs of their employees.

Do "enriched jobs" always have a beneficial impact upon the workers who do them? Are there *circumstances* in which enriched jobs don't have a positive effect? Outcomes in the work place are assumed to be affected by certain critical psychological states. These in turn are influenced by job characteristics, employee characteristics, and situation characteristics. Desired outcomes are high levels of internal motivation, worker satisfaction, and quality of performance. From management's point of view low absenteeism and turnover are other positive outcomes. The chart outlines the major input-mediating-output variables. ●

A study of two hundred bank employees who worked at twenty-five dif-

▲

Factors affecting job attitudes

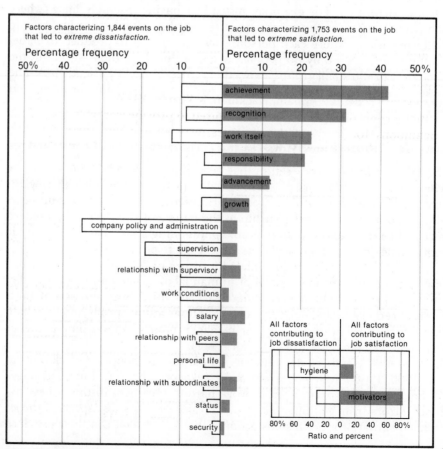

Adapted from Herzberg, 1968

Breakdown of tasks in relation to motivation

Input → Task Dimensions →	Moderating Variables → Individual and Situational Differences	Mediating Processes → Intrinsic Motivation →	Output → Task Attitudes and Behaviors
Task variety, uncertainty (difficulty)	Individual needs for: personal growth challenge learning accomplishment achievement security and structure	Challenges to skills and abilities; enjoyment of *process*	Task satisfaction
Task identity (wholeness of product) Task significance (impact on others' lives) Task-related social interaction	Individual variation in ability, technical skills, and information processing, as well as social skills for team work	Experienced meaningfulness of job; enjoyment of task within work setting	Task participation (absenteeism, turnover, volunteering for assignments)
Degree of individual responsibility for results	Instrumental orientation (money, job security-seniority) vs. "crafts" accomplishment orientation	Experienced responsibility for outcomes; enjoyment of and sense of accomplishment about *product* of labor	Task persistence (free time on task)
Knowledge of results	Work setting "climate" features: team or individual tasks peer group pressures, norms regarding rate and quality of work, employee-supervisor relations, etc.	Knowledge of job outcomes, self-efficacy, and perceived control	Quality of performance

Based on Staw, 1976; Steers & Mowday, 1977; Oldham, Hackman, & Pearce, 1975

ferent jobs revealed some of the conditions in which job enrichment has positive outcomes. Results show that employees who have strong growth needs and also are satisfied with the work context (pay, job security, co-workers and supervisors) respond positively to enriched jobs. This is in contrast to the negative reactions of others with weak needs for growth and/or dissatisfaction with the work context (Oldham, Hackman, & Pearce, 1975).

Better conceptual analysis is still required to provide workable operational definitions for many of the variables incorporated into these complex models of work definition. However, it is encouraging to see theorists and researchers using complex models to account for the obvious complexity of motivational aspects of work. One important distinction that such analyses raise is that of intrinsic versus extrinsic motivation.

Intrinsic vs. extrinsic motivation

Sometimes we work not for the reinforcing stimuli that are consequences of the work, but for the "natural reinforcement" in the activity itself. College students and professors often get pleasure from involvement in physical labor that does not involve brain power—gardening, jogging, construction work. It is the activity or the process that is reinforcing, not necessarily the product or the payoff for a good product. When reinforcers are *activities* we can think of them as *intrinsic reinforcers.* When they are *stimuli* consequent upon activities, they are *extrinsic reinforcers.* Premack (1965) has argued that reinforcers *in general* are activities and not stimuli. Operant conditioning, like most modern industrial work, relies on arbitrary, extrinsic reinforcers to control behavior rather than natural, intrinsic reinforcers (Schwartz, Schuldenfrei, & Lacey, 1977).

When work is reduced to a behavior which will only be done for the sake of a reward, the work is *extrinsically motivated*. When work is undertaken for its own sake (the task is interesting, challenging, etc.) without concern for extrinsic rewards, the work is *intrinsically motivated*. Solving crossword puzzles, keeping a diary, taking long walks in the woods, reading "optional" assignments are examples of behaviors that are probably intrinsically motivated. When you see a child work at a jigsaw puzzle, complete it, dump the pieces and start over again without concern for praise, that is intrinsic motivation at work.

What happens, however, if extrinsic rewards are imposed on intrinsic motivation? There may be a shift in attitudes away from doing the activity because it is liked, toward doing it only to get the reward. This is called the *overjustification effect*. Then, if the reward is cut off or "the price is not right," the previously enjoyed activity may become less likely.

In one demonstration with undergraduate subjects from the University of Rochester, giving them money for working on puzzles that were intrinsically interesting decreased the time they spent on the puzzles later during a free-choice period, compared with subjects who had not been paid (Deci, 1972).

The same thing can happen in the classroom as a result of the extrinsic rewards of praise, approval, and grades. Rewarding preschool children for engaging in an initially interesting, freely chosen activity lowers its value and reduces the amount of time the children later engage in the activity on their own (Lepper, Greene, & Nisbett, 1973).

The detrimental effect whereby extrinsic reward transforms intrinsically motivated children into free-enterprise entrepreneurs points up an important limitation to the laws of reinforcement. Rewards may have hidden costs. Even positive reinforcement may be counterproductive in its effect on the emission of behaviors that would have been practiced and enjoyed for their own sakes.

Religious motivation

More than two billion, five hundred million people throughout the world belong to the eleven major orthodox religions (Roman Catholic, Protestant, Jewish, Eastern Orthodox, Hindu, Moslem, Buddhist, Confucian, Shinto, Taoist, Zoroastrian—according to the *1972 Encyclopaedia Britannica Book of the Year*). Untold others are members of smaller sects. If we add individuals whose lives are guided by religious beliefs although they do not identify with any organized religion, the total number of people motivated in some way by religion swells to enormous proportions.

Throughout history, religion and beliefs in gods, spirits, or forces in the universe beyond human control have exerted a powerful—and often paradoxical—influence on the lives of individuals and nations. In the name of religion people have fought in bloody wars; others have refused to be drafted into their country's wars. Martyrs, motivated by religious dedication, have sacrificed their lives to uphold high moral principles. On the other hand, millions of innocent people have been tortured and killed in church-organized witchcraft hunts and inquisitions. Without doubt some of the world's most creative works of art, architecture, literature, and music owe their existence to powerful religious motives of the artists and their patrons. On the other hand, religious dogma has on occasion been a barrier to the acceptance of creative insights of science and to free and open inquiry. It is to the church that the sick, needy, and estranged can turn for charity. But at the same time, it is conventional (extrinsically oriented) churchgoers who tend to be intolerant and prejudiced toward minorities and deviant subgroups (Johnson, 1959).

In the United States today, we are witnessing some influential religious movements which involve and affect the lives of millions of people. Among these are the tendency for many people to turn to Eastern religions or various forms of meditation (Cox, 1977), the rise of cults such as Sun Myung Moon's Unification Church, and the dramatic rise of evangelical Christianity. Controversial news stories have emerged in this last category, including the "born-again" Christianity of President Jimmy Carter, and the reported religious conversions of Nixon "hatchet man" Charles Colson, former Black Panther Eldridge Cleaver, and Manson Family killer Charles "Tex" Watson.

The existence of these current events and historical paradoxes serves to make the psychological study of religious belief and behavior fascinating. Yet this is an area that has been largely ignored since the publication of William James' *Varieties of Religious Experience* in 1902. Today religion is rarely ever mentioned in basic textbooks in psychology. However, no account of *psychology and life* could be complete without acknowledging the power of religious beliefs to motivate human behavior. Certainly there are both personal and social *motives* for religious behavior, in addition to the personal and social *consequences* of various religious beliefs in peoples' lives. Note that when discussing the psychological aspects of religion, we must keep in mind whether we are conceptualizing the issues at the personal or at the social level of analysis. In this section, we can but touch on several basic distinctions and briefly sample from the rich complexity of ideas, theories, and data on the psychology of religious motivation.

What is religion?

Surprisingly, there is no agreed-upon definition of what constitutes "religion." One approach, at the sociological level of analysis, holds that a common factor in all conceptions of religion is "religion as seen by the general population." This is based upon affiliation with a visible church institution, and a general understanding of that institution's rules and norms. At the personal level, religion is sometimes thought of as whatever is of "ultimate concern" to the individual. Interestingly, in popular language religion is sometimes referred to as if it were a thing that some people "have" and others do not "have" (e.g., Joe Pious has "got" religion). It must be pointed out, however, that religion is not an "it" or a "thing." Rather, it is best regarded as an *area of study*, with many specific and diverse religions contained in it. Also, it is a mistake to think that the different religions are really all the same. Specific forms of religion differ greatly from each other, and peoples' motives for pursuing them are equally diverse. For example, the motives for becoming a Satanist have quite different origins and consequences than the motives for becoming a Christian.

Most social scientists prefer to view religion as both an area of study and a multidimensional variable, among the most complex of human behaviors. One conceptually clear breakdown of the religious variable into manageable dimensions was accomplished by Glock (1962). His five basic dimensions of religion include:

a. *Religious belief* (ideology): the content and type of belief, doctrine, or the values and creeds to which the individual is committed. In various religions this may be either a doctrine or an ethic.

b. *Religious practice* (ritual): the set of behaviors that are expected of a person who espouses a particular religion; the behaviors that are part of the religion itself, such as attendance at worship services, prayer, fasting, meditation, chanting, etc.

c. *Religious feeling* (experience): the inner mental and emotional states that are part of the religion. Different individuals and different religious techniques emphasize the role of feelings or experience to differing degrees.

d. *Religious knowledge* (intellectual): the information one has about the religion, about its history and origins, about data in support of or inconsistent with it.

e. *Religious effects* (consequences): the effects or consequences that one's religion has on one's "nonreligious" life. An example is an alcoholic who stops drinking after a religious conversion. The nondrinking itself is not a religious practice, but is a by-product of the person's faith.

By analyzing religion as a multidimensional variable in this way, we make ourselves better able to separate the complex facets of religious motivation. In doing so, we start to understand how these components of religion operate daily in our lives. For example, we can begin to think about how religious feelings might influence certain beliefs, or how a particular combination of knowledge of one's religion coupled with belief may result in religious effects that have an impact on the person's everyday life.

It is important to recognize that such analysis tells us nothing about the truth or falsity of any specific religious teaching or doctrine, because such questions are not within the scope of scientific inquiry. Psychological science may help us understand how various religions work, but cannot say whether any particular religion is true or false.

Intrinsic vs. extrinsic religious orientation

The intrinsic-extrinsic distinction appears in the psychology of religion, just as it does in general motivational theory. This distinction, derived from research in Protestant and Catholic churches in America, corresponds to what you might think of as mature vs. immature, true vs. false, or pure vs. perverse approaches to one's faith. The person with an extrinsic orientation tends to *use* the religion to gain some type of reinforcement, be it status, profit, an inflated ego, or a reduction of guilt feelings. This extrinsic religious motivation is incomplete, inconsistent, and utilitarian. In contrast, the intrinsic orientation connotes pure and complete, undefiled motives that can be characterized as genuine, nonhypocritical, consistent, and committed.

There is a difference in the hierarchy of motives depending on whether an individual's religion is based on intrinsic or extrinsic motives. For intrinsics, commitment to their faith becomes the master motive in life, part of the very fabric of their personality. It is superordinate to all other motives. Thus, if there is a conflict between motives (say, between the religious one and an economic or sexual one), the subordinate motives must yield to the religious one. For example, many college students refuse to engage in premarital intercourse because of their religious beliefs. For extrinsics, on the other hand, the religious motive is not superordinate and indeed is probably "used" to serve the other needs. Thus one may want to be "seen" at services to create a social impression of being honest and moral—an important illusion in business. The extrinsic orientation, therefore, leads one to compromise the religion whenever there is a conflict between the religious commitment and other motives (Allport & Ross, 1967).

The intrinsic-extrinsic distinction makes sense partly because it is consistent with the popular notion that there are both a good type and a bad type of personal religious orientation. Research data indicate, for example, that intrinsics tend to be lowest in racial prejudice and very consistent in church

attendance, whereas extrinsics tend to be higher in prejudice and only casual or "hit-and-miss" church attenders (Allport & Ross, 1967). These findings suggest that there are some negative qualities associated with "casual" religion, which are not part of the more genuine type of religious commitment.

"Church" vs. "sect"

The intrinsic-extrinsic typology at the personal level has an analog at the sociological level—the sect-church dichotomy (Dittes, 1971). This is only a rough parallel, but one worth noting. In the sociological context, "church" religion is represented by formal church and synagogue buildings, well-dressed people attending services at fixed times, professional clergy, and established organizational structure.

The "sect" form of religion is made up of people who break off from formal religious organizations and form special subgroups of their own. These sects are thought to represent a reaction against the "establishment" religious group, which they see as hypocritical and too willing to compromise their principles in order to get along well with *secular society* (the nonreligious aspects of society). According to sociological theory, sect members are motivated to *proselytize* (to seek out recruits and persuade nonbelievers to join the group). This causes the sect to increase in size and become more "church-like." Eventually, the sect becomes so big that it employs the same formalities, rules, and tendencies to compromise that were a part of the original parent organization from which it deviated in the first place. As this growth occurs, the new organization becomes a breeding ground for the development of yet new sects which will splinter off from it. There are probably both intrinsic and extrinsic individual religious orientations found in both of these sociological forms of religious groups.

The experience of conversion

"Conversion" can result in changes in one's thinking and acting that are unparalleled in their swiftness and permanence. The conversion of the Apostle Paul to Christianity (*Acts*, Ch. 9) is probably the most dramatic example of this. Examine the following statement made by a college student four years after his commitment to Christ:

*"I can honestly say that I have never been the same since! Christ has given me a new
meaning and purpose for living, a genuine joy and lasting peace within. He has freed
me from the guilt that used to plague me and replaced discouragement with hope . . .
He has given me the power to live the kind of life I have always wanted to live"
(Coleman, 1972, p. 704).*

Just what social and psychological processes motivate such profound and
enduring changes as these? And what immediate and long term experiences
and behaviors are brought about by such a complete turning point in peoples'
lives? Unfortunately there are no simple answers to these questions. The social and psychological conditions surrounding the conversion must be taken
into account, as well as the mindset of the individual convert. Most importantly, *what* the person is converting to is a crucial factor. For example, conversion
to a cult or to a type of meditation may have different motives as well as different effects from conversion to Christanity.

The process of conversion   Lofland and Stark (1965) investigated the
conditions which promote conversions to cults, stating that "for conversion a
person must:

1. Experience enduring, acutely felt tensions
2. Within a religious problem-solving perspective,
3. Which leads the person to define himself or herself as a religious seeker;
4. Encountering the [cult philosophy and its agents] at a turning point in his
or her life,
5. Wherein an affective bond is formed (or pre-exists) with one or more
converts;
6. Where extra-cult attachments are absent or neutralized;
7. And, where, if he is to become a deployable agent, he is exposed to intensive interaction." (A "deployable agent" works outside the confines of the
movement's place of business — in the community as a recruiter or fund
raiser.)

At a more theoretical level, three types of conversion—each with a corresponding psychological explanation—have been proposed by Scobie (1975),
writing with a nominally Christian context in mind. *Sudden* conversion occurs
in a very brief time period (perhaps only an hour or two) and is thought to be
emotionally based. Unconscious conflicts or frustrations are thought to be released upon conversion and "satisfied" by the various dimensions of the religion (ideology, experience, ritual). *Unconscious* conversion takes place over a
person's entire life. One's beliefs are acquired via principles of social learning
(discussed in Ch. 4). *Gradual* conversion takes place over an intermediate time
span, varying from a few days to several months or a few years. The psychological process is thought to be more rational, intellectual, and cognitive.
There may be conscious conflict coupled with a need to make "sense" out of
life and a deliberate search for meaning. The process may involve rationally
thinking through one's objections to Christianity.

Conversion and purpose in life   It becomes clear from these and other
reports (Scobie, 1973; Scroggs & Douglas, 1967) that conversions differ both
in the processes through which the newly adopted beliefs are acquired and
the nature of the belief system that is accepted by the convert. These in turn
may be related to the social motives and personal needs of people. Current
research (Paloutzian, 1976) interrelates several aspects of the conversion
experience around the "motive for meaning in life."

These empirical studies reveal that college students who claim a personal

Sample Items — Purpose-in-Life Test

1. I am usually:

   1   2   3   4   5   6   7

   completely bored   neutral   exuberant, enthusiastic

4. My personal existence is:

   1   2   3   4   5   6   7

   utterly meaningless, without purpose   neutral   very purposeful & meaningful

6. If I could choose, I would:

   1   2   3   4   5   6   7

   prefer never to have been born   neutral   like nine more lives just like this one

9. My life is:

   1   2   3   4   5   6   7

   empty, filled only with despair   neutral   running over with exciting good things

10. If I should die today, I would feel that my life has been:

    7   6   5   4   3   2   1

    very worthwhile   neutral   completely worthless

11. In thinking of my life, I:

    1   2   3   4   5   6   7

    often wonder why I exist   neutral   always see a reason for my being here

12. As I view the world in relation to my life, the world:

    1   2   3   4   5   6   7

    completely confuses me   neutral   fits meaningfully with my life

13. I am a:

    1   2   3   4   5   6   7

    very irresponsible person   neutral   very responsible person

Adapted from Crumbaugh and Maholick, 1969

relationship with Christ experience more meaning in their lives than those who do not. Within a week following their conversion, these students show a sharp increase in scores on a purpose-in-life scale (examples of which are given above). ◆ This sense of meaning tends to drop back to its preconversion level around one month after conversion; however, it then rises again to a higher level than that of non-Christians when measured six or more months later. ● Another study (Paloutzian, Jackson, & Crandall, 1978) replicates this basic finding with an older, noncollege population. Interestingly, in the adult sample, professing Christians also scored higher on a measure of social interest (concern for the welfare of others) than non-Christians.

Paloutzian also compared "born-again" Christians with people who only espoused Christian ethics. (Born agains indicate "I have received Jesus Christ into my life as my personal savior and Lord"; ethicals indicate "I respect and

● **Mean purpose-in-life scores as a function of time from conversion**

The graph shows mean purpose-in-life scores as a function of time from conversion. Students were asked if they knew themselves to be Christians within the limits of this definition: A person who has made a decision to trust Jesus Christ as savior and lord or who has received Jesus Christ into his or her life as personal savior and lord.

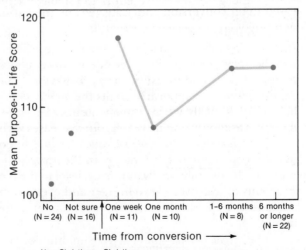

Adapted from Paloutzian, 1976

attempt to follow the moral and ethical teachings of Christ.") The two groups differed on a variety of measures designed to assess the maturity of their commitments and their ethical attitudes. Born agains scored higher on purpose in life, social interest, and intrinsic religious orientation, and lower on extrinsic religious orientation, than ethicals. Apparently, "born-again" Christians show evidence of greater internalization of Christian beliefs and ethics than do converts to ethical religious status.

Other recent research in the psychology of religion indicates that the stronger one's subjective religious experience the greater is the degree of intrinsic religious orientation (Hood, 1970, 1975). Furthermore, there is a positive correlation between intrinsic religious orientation and purpose in life (Bolt, 1975; Soderstrom & Wright, 1977; Crandall & Rasmussen, 1975).

Religious conversion sometimes involves powerful emotional experiences which become "peak experiences" that may have enduring effects over one's entire life. We turn in the next chapter to examine the nature of emotion. It is emotion that gives life its distinctive human quality, sometimes for better as in personal religious feelings, and other times for worse, as when anxiety overwhelms reason, or guilt takes the spark out of life.

Chapter summary

Motives are causes of behavior assumed to come from within the person or organism—the *intervening variables* connecting various stimuli to various responses. Motivated behavior tends toward organized patterns and endures in the face of obstacles and frustrations.

The concept of motivation is used in a variety of ways: (a) to account for variations in behavior among individuals; (b) to infer inner states from overt behavior; (c) to explain the role of inner factors in directing behavior; (d) to establish responsibility for behavior; and (e) to clarify the role of genetic and physiological factors in behavior.

Biological drives, with the exception of sex, serve as regulatory mechanisms that help the organism maintain *homeostasis* (internal balance). They originate in physiological conditions that have disturbed the equilibrium. Homeostatic mechanisms may be internal and automatic, or they may involve the organism's active effort to establish a physical and social environment that is as constant as possible.

A number of laboratory techniques have been used to measure the strength of biological drives in animal subjects. The strength of various drives may be related to specific dependent consequences of arousal such as gross motor activity and consummatory behavior. The *consummatory response* of eating *reduces* or temporarily limits the *hunger drive*. Such responding stops or becomes less likely when *satiation* occurs. The rate of an *instrumental response* increases as motivation increases, but decreases with its reduction.

The *glucostatic theory of food-intake control* hypothesizes that *glucose* levels in the blood regulate food intake. In the *hypoglycemic* state, typified by intense hunger, glucose falls below its normal level in the blood. As might be expected, injections of glucose relieve hunger and even inhibit eating in food-deprived animals as well as inhibiting self-stimulation of brain areas associated with satiety.

The *hypothalamus* plays a role in hunger and other biological drives. Yet when the hypothalamus is stimulated in laboratory animals, their consummatory behavior remains *stimulus-bound* rather than general or flexible. It appears, then, that the hypothalamus does not directly create biological drives, but probably activates already established consummatory responses.

Eating behavior is influenced by cognitive and social factors as well as purely physiological ones.

Social motives are acquired states of motivation, activated by real or imagined social stimuli. Individuals must seek out people of similar age, sex, education, and background for purposes of *social comparison* in order to evaluate their own capabilities and determine what kinds of behavior are acceptable.

The need for *social approval* is an important force in motivating people, although its strength varies from individual to individual. The potency of this need may be identified by scores on the *Social Desirability Scale*.

Similarly, the *need for achievement*, which gives rise to a general *tendency to approach success*, may vary in strength. The *Thematic Apperception Test* (TAT) is a projective test especially effective in gauging a person's need for achievement *(n Ach)*, allowing the subject to project his or her inner feelings onto ambiguous stimuli.

Research points to the fact that those who focus on success tend to set realistic goals and to prefer tasks of intermediate difficulty, while those concerned with avoiding failure tend to set unrealistic goals and to choose low-difficulty tasks. Early studies suggested that *fear of success* (FOS) was far more prevalent among American women than among American men. But more balanced assessments have shown FOS to be nonspecific to sex and unrelated to actual performance.

It has also been shown that poor academic performance on the part of black students is largely due to low *task interest* in academic situations. But black and white students perform equally well on high-interest tasks.

Employers have long assumed that workers would increase their quality and quantity of production if offered more money and an improved job environment *(hygienic inducement)*. But it is now known that positive motivation results only from work in which the *job content* is enriching, challenging, and allows the workers to assume responsibility.

Work that is undertaken for its own sake is said to be *intrinsically motivated*. *Extrinsically motivated* work is performed only for the sake of a reward which follows it. Frequently, work undertaken because of intrinsic motivation becomes extrinsically motivated when rewards are imposed on it. This can lead to the *overjustification effect*—previously enjoyed work is stopped when the reward is removed.

Religious motivation is a *multidimensional variable;* for it involves factors of belief, practice, knowledge, feeling, and effects. It may have an extrinsic orientation toward reinforcement states such as increased social standing, or an instrinsic orientation leading toward consistent, committed behavior.

Religious conversion takes many forms and can be based on widely differing motives and preconversion experiences. But recent studies have demonstrated a strong correlation between conversion and an increased sense of purpose in life. The stronger one's personal and subjective religious experience, the more intrinsic the religious orientation and the more immediate the sense of purpose and meaning.

14 Mind-Body Interactions

Emotion
  Conceptions of emotion
  Components of emotion

Pain
  Pain as a neurophysiological event
  Pain as a psychological event
  Pain as a social or cultural event

Cognitive controls on behavior
  Hope and hopelessness
  Learned helplessness
  Cognitive control of motivation
  Hypnosis as a cognitive control system

Chapter summary

Have you ever given anyone "a piece of your mind"? Did Mother ever give you one minute to "make up your mind"? Did she "pay you no mind" when you acted silly? Did Father ever get after you for "not minding your manners" or "mindlessly" endangering someone's life by your failure to realize the consequences of your actions? "Never you mind with your sassy reply, the Dean knows how to deal with your kind." Ever hear that one from a junior high school teacher? But by high-school graduation day everyone "was mindful of the solemnity of this commencement, which is not an end, but merely a beginning. . . ." "So what's on your mind?" In this chapter, mostly mind, yours and mine.

With mind so much a part of our everyday language, you might think that it must occupy an honored place at the head of psychological theorizing about human nature. In fact, mind, as a legitimate concept of scientific analysis, has only recently been invited back to the psychologist's banquet table. When behaviorism came in the front door, mind was gently ushered out the back door. Having grown used to such capricious treatment, it decided to "mind its business" until a new invitation was recently issued.

Behaviorism was not the first newcomer to unseat the mind from its privileged place. Over centuries, philosophers and other thoughtful people have wondered whether mind should be invited to the party along with body, separate from body, or not at all.

The Greeks had a word for mind; it was *nous*. *Nous* is the intelligence, reason, spiritual force that directs life and distinguishes living things from inanimate things. The mind as *nous* knows all things (like *The Shadow* of the old-time radio serial). However, mind or *nous*, being "pure thought," was assumed to have no effect upon bodily functions. "Mind is one thing, body another, and never the two shall meet." This rationalist view of human nature, which revered mind as reason, gave mind an open invitation to the banquet, but not at the same table as the body.

René Descartes turned the controversy on its head, by declaring that the mind is real but the body might not be. The only thing a thinking person could know for certain was his or her own *doubts* about what to believe. Doubts signify a consciousness that is doubting. Consciousness signifies a mind aware of its functioning. Thus thinking and mind were "real," but body could be an illusion just as the funny mirrors in the circus sideshows hold an illusion of your physical appearance. He finally accepted the existence of both, and this *dualism* consisted of erecting an absolute distinction between mental and material substance. At best, the two could peacefully coexist, side by side, as long as they did not try to interact across the table.

The separation of mind from body placed analysis of concepts such as emotion in a peculiar position.

"It is true that as the science of behavior became more complex it was felt necessary to give the psychic factors a place in the description of emotions; but even so the important writers continued a form of bookkeeping by double entry: anger, for example, might originate in the idea of a wrong afflicted but it was also a 'boiling of the blood about the heart'" (Brett, 1928, reprinted 1973, p. 391).

Emotions were from the time of Aristotle linked to bodily mechanics — but not as instances of mind acting on the body. The mind dealt only with rational considerations and the highest concerns of humanity.

Indeed, the lowly place of psychological factors in early descriptions of emotion might have kept psychologists from ever taking emotions seriously were it not for a curious invention of mid-eighteenth-century England — the novel. The hero of the novel, with the will to succeed despite adversity, set out on a sentimental journey through life, or a heroine fell hopelessly in love with her romantic ideal. Emotion was given new legitimacy through such stock characters who expressed the notion that people did not live by either bread or philosophy alone. What they felt affected their perceptions, beliefs, and actions.

Mind has been invited back into psychology, but only if it interacts on intimate terms with bodily processes. Donald Hebb, addressing the American Psychological Association in September 1973, stated firmly, "Psychology is about the mind: the central issue, the great mystery, the toughest problem of all" (1974, p. 74). Hebb went on to define "mind" in these terms: "Mind then is the capacity for thought, and thought is the integrative activity of the brain" (p. 75).

With that invitation acknowledging the rightful place of mind in psychological science has come a bold conception that mind is the active defining principle of reality. Although we live in a physical world, its meaning comes from our psychological view of it. In this chapter, then, we will look at the ways in which the mind and body interact, for better or for worse.

Emotion

We begin by considering emotion—an everyday phenomenon that falls at the intersection of mind and body. The experiences of love, hate, joy, anger, and various other *affective* states are subjective, psychological processes that also involve physiological responses (such as accelerated heart rate, trembling, or tears). Emotions can affect body functions and can influence a person's memory, thinking, and perception. Cognitive processes can in turn affect emotion or the perception of pain. An inadequate handling of emotional reactions can be a contributing factor to both mental disorders and physical illness.

Since the beginning of time, people have tried to understand these stirred-up, *affective* states. The ancient Greeks believed that there were four characteristic emotional temperaments, each based on the dominance of a particular fluid in the body: sanguinary (blood), melancholic (black bile), choleric (yellow bile), and phlegmatic (phlegm). Aristotle was the first to distinguish between the physiological and the psychological components of emotion, which he referred to as its "matter" and its "form or idea," respectively. Seventeenth- and eighteenth-century philosophers generally thought that the emotions were instinctive and nonrational and thus represented the animal side of human beings. In contrast to the emotions were the uniquely human attributes of reason and intellect, which were meant to curb people's emotions and govern their behavior in a rational way.

This rigid opposition of the emotional and the rational implied that the emotions were harmful and disruptive, and that they were an abnormal psychological process that was very different from thought and reason. Many common sense expressions still support this viewpoint, such as "I got so mad that I couldn't think straight," "I tried to do the right thing but my emotions got the better of me," or "In the heat of passion, I didn't realize what I was doing." Though extreme emotional states like panic and stage fright can interfere with ongoing behaviors, this is not true for all emotional responses. Emotions often serve the very positive function of forcing the individual to organize new adaptive responses to a changed environment. Just as human beings have achieved a far greater intellectual development than any other species, so have they achieved a greater development and constructive use of the emotions than is implied by those earlier ideas.

Conceptions of emotion

Psychologists have attempted to provide a precise definition of emotion, but find it a very difficult task. Some have defined emotions as motives while others feel that emotion is a very different process from motivation. Some define emotions as bodily changes, while others define them in terms of the subjective feelings experienced and reported by the individual. This lack of agreement is one of the factors that has hampered research in this area. However, these disagreements have also underscored the complexity of emotion and have pointed to some critical issues.

Are there good and bad emotions?

We often think of various emotions as being either positive or negative. Thus, we usually judge love and joy to be good emotions, while considering anger or fear to be bad. Although this distinction is correct in many cases, it is more useful to assess the positive or negative qualities of emotions in terms of their consequences. For example, fear can be considered a "good" emotion when it promotes survival by leading the individual to cope with anticipated danger. Similarly, the expression of joy and pleasure at someone else's suffering should probably be considered a negative emotion.

Are emotions learned or innate?

Charles Darwin (1872) postulated that emotional expressions are not functional in and of themselves, but are the evolutionary remnants of previous adaptive behaviors. For example, the facial expression of anger is derived from the snarling behavior of an animal preparing for attack. ▲ The common emotional expressions found in all infants at, or soon after, birth are one bit of evidence that supports Darwin's hypothesis. More recently, Plutchik (1962) has proposed that there are eight primary emotions, or patterned bodily reactions, each of which corresponds to an underlying adaptive biological process common to all species.

In contrast, other theorists have argued that emotions are not biologically "prewired," but are something we must *learn* to experience and express. The fact that we can modify or even inhibit our emotions (as when we smile and act calm in the midst of an upsetting situation) suggests that emotions are under learned control. Cognitions may have a primary role in determining the affective quality of a person's response. That is, the type of emotion we feel can be determined by our cognitive evaluation of the situation that elicits our arousal.

Recent analyses have moved away from an "either-or" debate and have taken the position that *both* innate and learned factors are involved in emotion. There may be genetic determinants of the basic emotions that are found universally, but differences in their expression may be due to experience, social setting, and culture.

Is emotion a state or a trait?

At times we think of emotions as short-lived phenomena that come and go as a function of the particular situation in which the person finds him- or herself.

▲

Can you see any basis for Darwin's assertion that human expressions of anger have evolved from the snarling of animals?

Something happens to make the person feel angry or frightened, but once the situation changes the emotion disappears and a different one is experienced (e.g., relief, happiness). At other times, we think of emotions as rather stable characteristics of an individual. We talk about people who are "quick-tempered" and "have a short fuse"—meaning that they are easily angered. Or we may know people who are always fearful or usually depressed.

Several theorists have pointed to this important distinction between transient forms of emotion *(states)* and the stable, individual forms *(traits)*. Emotion states are determined more by situational characteristics, while emotion traits refer to the individual's general tendency to experience a particular emotion with high frequency. State emotions last a shorter period of time than trait emotions, although they can range anywhere from a few seconds to several hours. State emotions may also be more intense than trait emotions. There is also a third category of emotion which seems to fall between state and trait. This category is known as *mood*. Moods are feelings of lower intensity and longer duration than state emotions, but are not so completely a function of individual characteristics as traits (Wessman, 1978).

Is emotion just a bodily sensation?

Whenever you have experienced a strong emotion, you have undoubtedly had a feeling of being "churned up" inside because of various bodily changes. If someone were to ask you how this stirred-up state comes about, you would probably say that your feeling of an emotion (e.g., "I am afraid") gives rise to the bodily expression of it (e.g., "therefore I am trembling"). Most people would agree with your statement—but not William James. In 1884 he proposed that the sequence of felt emotion and bodily changes was the *reverse* of the common sense one just stated; that is, "our feeling of the [bodily] changes *is* the emotion" (James, 1884). James believed that the cognitive, experienced aspects of the emotion were a *result* of physiological changes instead of the other way around. As he put it, "we feel sorry because we cry, angry because we strike, afraid because we tremble" (James, 1884). A Danish scientist named Lange presented some similar ideas at about the same time, and so this theory is known as the *James-Lange theory of emotion*. The James-Lange theory implied that in order for a person to experience different emotions, there must be discriminably different sets of physiological changes for the person to rely on as cues. Physiologist Walter Cannon disputed this notion by citing evidence that: (1) different emotions are accompanied by the *same* internal bodily state; (2) the internal organs are too insensitive for changes in them to be noticed and used as cues; and (3) internal changes are too slow to be a source of fast-changing emotional feelings (Cannon, 1929). It should be noted, however, that James had *not* limited his concept of "bodily changes" to the internal organs alone, but included such responses as crying, striking, and trembling. Thus, Cannon's criticisms do not constitute as complete an attack on the James-Lange theory as had been assumed at the time. Nevertheless, these criticisms led some theorists to postulate a nonspecific arousal (or activation) state as the physiological basis of emotion (Lindsley, 1951; Duffy, 1962).

Components of emotion

In accordance with varying definitions of emotion, psychologists have studied a wide range of responses. Some of them have been concerned with the role of such neurophysiological processes as activities of the brain, endocrine system, and autonomic nervous system. Most researchers, however, rely on verbal self-reports of emotional experiences, as well as other introspective data. Another approach has focused on overt bodily movement and facial expressions. All of these components — neurophysiological, experiential, and expressive — have to be integrated in some way by any theory that claims to be a comprehensive model of emotion. Earlier models were phrased in cause-effect terms, with theorists arguing about which component caused changes in another. There is now a growing consensus of opinion (Izard, 1978) that a better approach is to conceive of a continuous *interaction* between the various components in which each one influences, and is influenced by, the other.

The neurophysiological component

Many researchers have looked at physiological systems that could be the site of emotion. In general, there has been a particular interest in brain mechanisms. One of the most popular theories has placed the control of emotion in the limbic system (which includes parts of the cortex, thalamus, and hypothalamus). As we saw in Chapter 11, researchers have found that stimulation and lesioning of various parts of the limbic system produce changes in emotional reactions. The fact that the limbic system is made up of the primitive brain probably lent credence to the idea that the "primitive" emotions are located there. However, these supposedly phylogenetically old structures have achieved their greatest degree of evolutionary development in humans just as have the so-called "higher" cortical structures, and thus they cannot really be considered as "primitive." Moreover, stimulation and lesions of parts of the brain other than the limbic areas also produce emotional changes. As we have seen, prefrontal lobotomy has often been used to reduce strong anxieties, psychotic depression, and other types of emotional distress. These findings suggest that the emotions are controlled by many different interacting parts of the brain, rather than by any single "emotion center."

It has also been proposed that certain major developments in emotional response are linked to anatomical changes in the brain (Konner, 1977). Smiling emerges in infants of all cultures several months after birth, when the necessary nerve pathways acquire their myelin sheaths. Similarly, the fairly universal occurrence of children's fear of separation (from their parents) coincides with the development of neural tracts within the limbic system. Other research suggests that the right brain hemisphere is particularly important in regulating emotional processes (Schwartz, Davidson, & Maer, 1975).

The physiological component of emotions also involves the activity of various *endocrine glands* (see p. 304). These glands pump their *hormones* directly into the bloodstream. In sudden fear, for example, a hormone is circulated through the blood that brings about such widely diverse processes as dilation of the pupil of the eye, constriction of the blood vessels in the stomach wall, and an increase in the rapidity with which blood clots.

The adrenal glands secrete two hormones, *epinephrine* and *norepinephrine* (also called *adrenaline* and *noradrenaline*). Research has shown both increased and differential release of epinephrine and norepinephrine under different conditions of stress (Brady, 1967). Norepinephrine is also found in the brain. There is evidence to suggest that drugs that increase the accumulation of norepinephrine produce euphoria and hyperactivity, while drugs that deplete norepinephrine produce depression (Kety, 1967).

The experiential component

Does physiological activity alone determine the kind of emotion we feel? According to the James-Lange theory, the answer should be "yes." Different physiological changes should produce different emotional experiences. However, researchers have not been able to find very distinctive patterns of physiological arousal for discrete emotions. If clues from physiological activity are not the whole story, what about perceptions, expectations, interpretations, and other such cognitive processes? What role might they play in the experience of emotion? (See *P&L* Close-up, The Sound of Music.)

The two-component theory   As we saw in Chapter 12, the information provided by external stimuli is not sufficient to explain why we see things the way we do. It is only through cognitive organization and interpretation of such information after it reaches the retina that we can apprehend what is "out there." Similarly, many psychologists believe that emotion is not determined by physiological responses alone, but requires a cognitive appraisal and evaluation of the stimulus situation.

One theory argues that the physiological component of various emotions is essentially the same state of "undifferentiated arousal," and that variations in this arousal only determine the *intensity* of the emotion. The *quality* of the emotion—happiness, anger, fear, sorrow, etc.—is determined by cognitions drawn from cues in the immediate environment. Therefore, people give different emotional labels to the same experienced arousal, depending on the available situational cognitions. Thus physiological arousal is a *necessary* condition for emotion, but it is not *sufficient*. It must interact with appropriate cognitive cues to generate emotion. This interaction of physiology and cognition is called the *two-component theory of emotion*.

To test this two-component theory of emotions, male subjects in an experiment were given an injection of what was supposedly a "vitamin compound." The injection actually contained epinephrine, which usually produces a state of physiological arousal. A control group received injections of a placebo—a substance that causes no physiological reaction. Some of the experimental subjects had been told that the injection would have arousal side effects, while others had been led to expect either side effects other than arousal or no effects at all. It was assumed that these last two groups did not have an appropriate explanation of their arousal, while the others did. Each subject then spent time in a waiting room with "another subject" (actually a confederate) who began to behave emotionally. For half of the subjects, he acted in a happy and playful manner, while for the others he acted as if he were irritated and angry. The researchers reported that subjects who did not have an appropriate explanation for their arousal felt happy when the confederate acted happy, and felt angry when he acted angry. Presumably, perception of the confederate's mood provided a relevant cognition to label their own unexplained arousal. This pattern of results was not found for either the correctly informed subjects or the placebo controls (Schachter & Singer, 1962).

The theory underlying this study has been highly influential in generating new ideas about the process by which people interpret the causes of anxiety, fear, and other emotions. But, in spite of the authors' claims, the data from the experiment do *not* provide clear support for the two-component theory. Because of various methodological flaws, the experiment may not have been an adequate test of the model. A recent exact replication of this experiment, which corrected these flaws, found *no* evidence in support of the theory (Marshall & Zimbardo, 1979). Similarly, a modified replication which induced strong arousal via hypnosis instead of by drug injections also did not find the predicted pattern of results (Maslach, 1979). Instead, this research showed that subjects with unexplained arousal consistently used negative emotional terms to describe their experience, regardless of the mood expressed by the confederate. These results suggest that unexplained physiological arousal is not affectively *neutral* (as Schachter and Singer argue).

Close-up
The Sound of Music: Giving Form to Feelings

"What passion cannot music raise and quell?" asked poet John Dryden. Music has charms not only to soothe, but to excite us as well—a power which is well understood and utilized by film composers. The movie music that we hear is carefully designed to arouse certain emotions and provide insights that intensify the visual experience for us. Did you experience strong feelings of tension, suspense, and dread while watching the scenes in *Jaws* where the shark was about to attack? If so, a lot of credit for your emotional arousal should go to the jagged, rhythmic, and somewhat disturbing music that accompanied those scenes. In fact, if you were to replay those scenes in your mind, you would probably hear that music echo in your memory.

According to a psychological analysis of music by Backer and Manson (1978), here are a few examples of how the "language of emotion" works in a film:

Function of music	Example
1. Creation of mood	Raksin's *Laura*. Scene where detective roams around Laura's apartment: somber romanticism in long melodic line, often repeated but never completed throughout this long scene, helps to create mood of self-absorbed reverie that makes it more plausible that the detective is falling in love with a dead girl.
2. Evocation of time period	Goldsmith's *Planet of the Apes*. Opening scene with Heston in spacecraft: one repeated stopped note in low register of piano, and gradually increasing dynamic volume as pattern is telescoped by slide whistle, emitting unearthly glissando sigh; gives effect of putting spectator into different time and place with few bars of music.
3. Underlining unspoken thoughts of character	Arnold's *Chalk Garden*. Scene where Deborah Kerr meets judge who sentenced her for murder years before: music combines a nervous fluttering melody line with essentially slow, pulsating drumbeats, underlining Kerr's agitation about being discovered, and simultaneous silent reminders to herself that she can escape if she keeps control.
4. Revealing psychological makeup of character	Mancini's *Wait Until Dark*. Entrance of Alan Arkin to Audrey Hepburn's flat: the score reveals that Arkin is mentally disturbed with the playing of isolated notes on out-of-tune pianos.
5. Setting up audience for subsequent surprise	Herrmann's *Psycho* murder scenes: slow, underplayed phrases in the music actually loosen tension in the story, so that shock value of sudden knife murder is even greater.

Adapted from Backer & Manson, 1978

The two-component theory states that *both* physiological arousal and an emotion-relevant cognition are necessary for a person to actually experience an emotion. A subsequent modification of this theory argued that a person does not need to perceive actual arousal in order to experience an emotion, but need only *believe that he or she perceived it* (Valins, 1966). This approach suggests that cognition is of central importance in emotional experience. It sparked a series of experiments in which subjects were given *false* feedback about their physiological responses under varying circumstances and were then asked to report their emotions.

People tend to believe in the false feedback they receive from physiological equipment that allegedly measures their "inner feelings." This *bogus pipeline*, devised by Jones and Sigall (1971), leads subjects to believe in a machine's readout of their inner state even when this feedback is arbitrary and unrelated to their true subjective affect or attitude state.

The basic paradigm in these studies exposes male undergraduates to slides of female nudes while hearing sounds alleged to be of their heartbeat. This false feedback indicates that their hearts are reacting to some of the nudes but not to others. Regardless of what their true heart rate changes are, most subjects believe this externally provided information more than they do evidence straight from their own hearts. They rate those nudes paired with high false heart-rate feedback as more attractive than those paired with false information indicating no change in heart rate.

Even when some experimental subjects are debriefed — told that the feedback was false — and left alone for 10 minutes before rating the nudes, the false information about internal reactions continues to exert an effect. They like the nudes that were paired with their alleged throbbing heart more than the nudes who did not "turn on" their false heart rate (Valins, 1974).

Our reactions to stimuli with emotional value, then, are strongly determined by what we believe, as well as by what we feel.

This research approach has been critically reviewed by Harris and Katkin (1975) who argue that, in fact, real physiological responses play a more critical role in emotional experience than the cognitive theorists have been willing to admit. They propose a useful distinction between *primary emotion* (which includes physiological arousal) and *secondary emotion* (which does not require physiological excitation but can be elicited by cues in the situation). However, the occurrence of secondary emotion is dependent upon a prior learned association of these particular cues with some primary (i.e. physiologically arousing) emotional experience.

Cognitive appraisal theories   Although more investigators are becoming concerned with the role of cognitive processes in emotional and other reactions, few have tried to speculate on the dynamics of such processes. What does it mean to have a cognition that determines an emotional response? Two of the psychologists who have worked on this problem have discussed such cognitions in terms of appraisal.

Appraisal is the evaluation and judgment of the significance of a stimulus. One of the first people to use this concept in a theory of emotion was Magda Arnold (1960), who proposed a sequential model. The first step in this sequence is *perception*, in which external stimuli are received. The next step is *appraisal*, in which the stimuli are judged as good and beneficial, or bad and harmful. This appraisal then determines the emotion. The *expression* of the emotion is the pattern of physiological responses that accompanies the felt tendency. These may be organized toward approach or toward withdrawal. The final step is *action*, when actual approach or withdrawal occurs.

A more complex extension of this viewpoint postulates two basic kinds of appraisal processes: *primary appraisal*, which evaluates whether the situation is threatening or not, and *secondary appraisal*, which assesses alternative means of coping. If a situation is perceived as threatening, there are two possible *coping strategies*: (a) *direct action*, such as fight or flight, with the negative emotional states accompanying them; or (b) *benign reappraisal*, in which the person reassesses the situation as less threatening, thereby reducing the negative emotional state (Lazarus, 1968).

Both these theories argue against the notion of neutral, undifferentiated arousal proposed by the two-component model of emotion. They postulate that there *are* different patterns of physiological responses, but that such responses do *not* determine or cause the emotion. The physiological component is seen as a function of cognitive appraisal, usually following it and being incorporated into it.

The expressive component

Although we can never directly observe another person's feelings, we often make judgments about them, as when we say, "I've never seen him look this angry," or "She looks so sad today." To arrive at such classifications of emotion we often use people's *nonverbal* behavior (e.g., facial expressions and body movements) as reliable signs of what emotion they are experiencing. ■ The "look" of love communicates at least as much feeling as a verbal protestation of passion.

As we saw earlier, Darwin (1872) proposed that facial expressions are genetically determined, innate responses with biological utility in evolution. If this theory were true, then we would expect to find evidence that these expressions are universal and occur in all cultures. In fact, cross-cultural studies have shown that at least six basic emotions are universally recognized in the human face: happiness, sadness, anger, fear, surprise, and disgust (Ekman, Sorenson, & Friesen, 1969; Izard, 1971). The results suggest that innate, qualitatively distinct emotions do exist and that a particular facial expression is correlated with each one. Although some emotional expressions seem to be universal, there are cultural differences in the situations which *elicit* certain emotions. For example, a funeral may elicit sadness in one culture but be a source of happiness in another. There are also cultural differences in the rules governing *display* of emotions. Thus, males at a funeral may not display their experienced sadness because their culture considers it unseemly. Cultures have subtle "display rules" which govern emotional expression: the when, where, what kind, how strong, how long, and who, of emotional displays (Averill, 1976). This neurocultural theory of facial expression (Ekman, 1973) is perhaps best summarized by saying that: if (a) the same emotion is

Don't sigh and gaze at me,
Your sighs are so like mine;
Your eyes mustn't glow
like mine,
People will say we're in love.
Richard Rodgers
Oklahoma!

■
While a fire rages in a sixteen-story office building in New Orleans, spectators watch in disbelief and horror as four people leap to their death to escape the flames.

Can you tell from these women's facial expression what emotion they are probably experiencing?

Check your judgment on page 414.

elicited in different cultures and (b) there is no interference by display rules, then (c) the same facial expressions will occur, because the facial muscle movements are innately determined and universal. ●

This overview of psychological thinking about emotion provides a structure useful in tying down the elusive concept of emotion. But we have not touched upon the content of emotion nor the force of emotion in our lives. These topics will be our concern in subsequent chapters when we turn to consider stress and psychopathology on the one hand, and intimate relations, human sexuality, and other joys of living.

Pain

It has become clear that pain is a highly complex response that is not only a physical sensation, but a psychological and social phenomenon as well. Although at times we might wish we could be free of pain, the ability to experience pain, and its motivating properties, is actually one of nature's most valuable gifts to us. Pain should be viewed as: (a) *a signal system* that has evolved to warn us of assaults on the integrity of the body and (b) *a defensive system* triggering automatic withdrawal reflexes as well as motivated avoidance and escape behaviors. As such, it is indispensable in coping with an occasionally hostile environment and with the diseases and eventual deterioration of the living matter that is our body.

Pain as a neurophysiological event

There are two main types of pain, peripheral and central. *Peripheral pain* begins in the nerves of the extremities or body organs and is triggered by an intense or rapid change in physical energy capable of producing tissue damage (such as a cut or burn). In contrast, *central pain* starts in the spinal cord or the brain itself and is caused by such things as tumors, strokes, or spinal injuries.

Although we might think the pain we experience is determined entirely by the stimulus causing it, research findings have not supported this notion. The amount and quality of perceived pain are also affected by many psychological and social variables. Variations in pain response have led researchers to look for mechanisms in both the body and the mind that regulate pain independently of its specific source. The most influential model of pain is the *gate-control theory* which proposes that there are "gates" in the spinal cord that can open or close, thus determining the amount of nerve impulses that can reach the brain and be perceived as pain (Melzack & Wall, 1965, 1970).

There are several ways in which these hypothetical gates could be closed. ◆ One is by gentle electrical stimulation of certain large nerve fibers which transmit sensations of touch. Since these fibers transmit impulses more quickly than the pain fibers, their impulses would reach the gate earlier and close it, thus preventing pain signals from moving up to the brain. Electrical stimulation of both the spinal cord and of the skin over painful areas is now becoming a major technique for treating various types of chronic pain (such as back and paraplegic pain). Futhermore, electrical stimulation through permanently implanted brain electrodes has been effective in providing relief for patients suffering from persistent, intractable pain (Hosobuchi, Adams, & Linchitz, 1977).

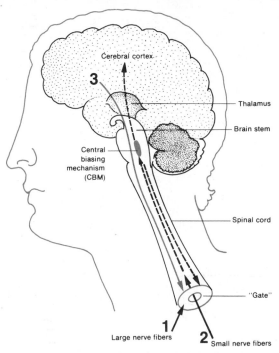

Large nerve fibers

Small nerve fibers

Cerebral cortex

Thalamus

Brain stem

Central biasing mechanism (CBM)

Spinal cord

"Gate"

Gate-control theory

Pain experts have discovered that they can use electrical stimulation, acupuncture and hypnosis to relieve chronic pain. According to the leading new theory, these techniques produce relief by closing a hypothetical "gate" in the spinal cord which blocks pain signals from reaching the brain.

1 *Gentle electrical stimulation activates large nerve fibers that close the gate in the spinal cord, blocking pain signals to the brain.*

2 *Acupuncture stimulates small nerve fibers, sending impulses through the open gate that register in the brain as an acute pain of twirling needles. When the signals reach the central biasing mechanism in the brain stem, they trigger counterimpulses that travel down the spinal cord and close the gate against the chronic pain.*

3 *Hypnosis acts directly on the cerebral cortex, sending impulses down the cord and closing the gate.*

A second way in which the gate could be closed is by activation of a "central biasing mechanism" in the brain stem, which triggers counterimpulses that travel down the spinal cord and close the gate. For example, stimulation of the small nerve fibers would send impulses to the brain that would be perceived as acute pain and would also activate the central biasing mechanism to shut the gate against chronic pain. This may be the way in which acupuncture works—the person can feel the pain of the twirling needles, but not the more severe, chronic pain. (See *P&L* Close-up, The Mystery of Acupuncture.) Thirdly, gate-control therapy postulates that the cortex (which is the brain's center for memories, expectations, anxieties, etc.) can also shut off perception of pain by sending impulses down the spinal cord and closing the gate. This may be the major way in which the mind controls pain, as well as the explanation for the effectiveness of purely cognitive processes, such as hypnosis and placebo therapies (to be discussed later in this chapter).

Although the gate-control concept has not gone unchallenged, it is by far the most influential theory about the nature of pain. It also ties in with accumulating evidence that there are opiate-like substances in the brain which appear to produce relief of pain. These substances, known as *endorphins*, are found in the area of the brain stem where gate-control theory proposes that the central biasing mechanism exists. They are considered to be the body's own "natural" form of morphine, and there is evidence that pain-reduction techniques, such as electrical stimulation, operate by releasing endorphins in the brain.

Pain as a psychological event

We tend to think of ourselves as somewhat passive participants in the pain experience—pain is something that happens *to* us, as are the common treatments for pain (such as drugs). Actually, however, we play a far more active role in our dealings with pain than we commonly believe. Our emotional state, our thoughts and memories, and our way of coping with anxiety can have an

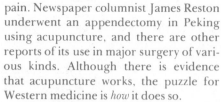

Close-up
The Mystery of Acupuncture

With the opening of China to American visitors, the news media have reported many stories about the traditional Chinese technique of pain relief called *acupuncture*. The procedure involves the insertion of long, fine needles into certain points on the person's body, and according to eyewitness acounts of American and British physicians, it really does stop pain. Newspaper columnist James Reston underwent an appendectomy in Peking using acupuncture, and there are other reports of its use in major surgery of various kinds. Although there is evidence that acupuncture works, the puzzle for Western medicine is *how* it does so.

According to gate-control theory, the answer may be that insertion of the needles produces nerve impulses that activate an inhibiting mechanism in the brain stem, which, in turn, closes the spinal cord "gate" against pain signals. However, it may be instead that acupuncture acts directly on the cortex (which then closes the gate).

Since acupuncture patients have faith in the effectiveness of the procedure and are also given explicit suggestions that they will feel no pain, their cognitive set may be very influential in reducing the pain that they feel (Melzack, 1973).

In line with the latter interpretation is research evidence that acupuncture functions not by relieving pain but by causing people to change their criterion of what constitutes severe pain (Clark & Yang, 1974).

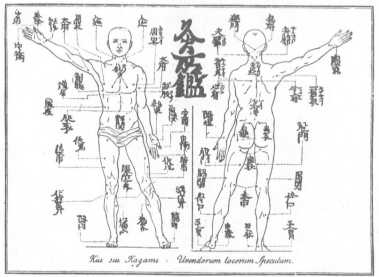

Kiu suu Kagami . Urendorum locorum Speculum.

---

enormous impact on our perception of, and response to, pain. In many instances, these psychological variables have a greater influence on pain reactions than pharmacological treatments and can even moderate their effectiveness. As one leading researcher has put it, "Thus, we can state *a new principle of drug action*: some agents are effective only in the presence of a required mental state" (Beecher, 1972, p. 178).

Placebo effects

Even when the pill or procedure administered is a placebo with no medicinal value, the individual may nevertheless be relieved of the pain and other symptoms of illness.

In a survey of 4681 patients treated with placebos for over twenty ailments or symptoms, including colds, epilepsy, and multiple sclerosis, successful results were achieved in 27 percent of the cases (Haas, Fink, & Härtfelder, 1959). According to another report, headaches were shown to be relieved by placebos in 58 percent of 4588 cases. Overall, about one third of all patients treated with placebos in fifteen test series achieved positive results (Beecher, 1959).

Even pain from incurable organic illness was lessened. In studies comparing pain relief from placebo and morphine injections for 122 patients with postoperative wound pain, 39 percent were relieved by placebos, while 67 percent were relieved by morphine. The chronic pain of cancer was temporarily relieved in 65 percent of the patients receiving a 10-mg. injection of morphine. But 10 mg. of placebo equally helped 42 percent of the cancer victims (Beecher, 1959).

Believing that a placebo will lead to pain reduction is thus sufficient to bring about major psychological (and perhaps physiological) reorganization. Recent evidence suggests that placebos somehow trigger the release of pain-killing endorphins in the brain (Levine et al., 1978).

Cognitive aspects

People's beliefs (whether rational or not) determine their *expectations* about the potential painfulness of a stimulus, and can lead them to experience more (or less) pain than is "really" there. As medical personnel can readily attest, patients are often more sensitive to pain in a medical setting than they are in their normal, everyday life. People's tolerance for pain is lower when they are sitting in a dentist's chair than in a chair in a psychology laboratory, largely because of negative expectations about going to the dentist. These expectations may not have any basis in the person's actual experience, but may be learned vicariously (as when children hear their parents bemoan their next dental appointment). Nevertheless, the influence of these expectations on a person's pain experience can be powerful.

The *meaning* a person attaches to a particular experience can also affect the reaction to pain. In a classic study, Beecher (1956) compared men who were seriously wounded in battle with men in civilian life who had received a similar "wound" in a surgical operation. Even though the extent of physical tissue damage was equivalent, only 25 percent of the soldiers wanted a narcotic for pain relief, while over 80 percent of the civilian men requested it. The difference in pain reaction was presumed to be attributable to the significance of the wound for the two groups of men. For the soldiers, the wound may have meant a ticket to safety. For the civilians, the surgical wound was more likely a disaster signal and a major disruption of the individual's life.

Fear and anxiety about pain is an important component of the pain experience. Psychological techniques that are effective in controlling pain often involve learning to relax and to alter one's cognitions. Although such techniques are now being used in specialized pain clinics and in hospital wards with a wide variety of people, their effectiveness can be demonstrated more vividly with individuals who are unusually skilled in using them (Pelletier & Peper, 1977).

Three men who were highly adept meditators were studied intensively while they voluntarily inserted steel needles into their bodies. ▲ Their physiological functioning was continuously assessed by a variety of psychophysiological measures. No pain was reported by the men, and none was observable in overt reactions. All of the men reported using a technique of "passive attention," although these differed in some ways from each other. For example, one man said:

"It's very simple. I do it by changing a single word. I don't stick a needle in my arm; [I] stick it through an arm. I move outside my body and look at the arm from a distance; with that detachment it becomes an object. It is as though I am sticking the needle into the arm of a chair. I have taught myself to move as easily outside my being as inside it" (Pelletier, 1974, p. 86).

Personality and pain

A great deal of research has been done to uncover the personality traits associated with differences in pain response. Because of some conflicting results, definitive statements can not yet be made. However, the general conclusion is that people who are most tolerant of pain "have a (probably unconscious) body

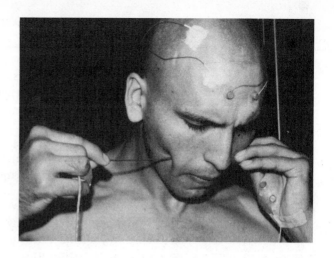

▲
This subject was able to push a sharpened bicycle spoke through his cheeks without any feeling of pain. His brain continued to show high-amplitude alpha waves throughout the process.

image with definite boundaries, are extraverted, and not neurotic and are relatively free of anxiety" (Sternbach, 1968, p. 77).

Pain is often a symptom for people with psychiatric illness, appearing most often for those with overt anxiety, other somatic symptoms, and a history of surgical operations (Spear, 1967). In a study of hospital patients, Sternbach (1974) found four types of personality patterns. The *hypochondriasis pattern* was characterized by extreme bodily preoccupation, and these patients were more likely to be "failures" in the treatment program of the pain clinic. Patients with the *reactive depression* pattern were highly depressed and willing to admit that their pain had gotten them down; they responded well to antidepressant medication. In the *somatization reaction* pattern, patients focused on bodily symptoms in order to avoid latent depression. They had adjusted to their pain and found satisfaction from their sick role. Patients with a *manipulative reaction* profile used their pain symptoms deliberately to manipulate others (a sort of "painmanship" or "pain game").

●

The woman hugging her husband has just had her name called as winner of a $1 million lottery; in the other photo the woman has just won $1,000 a month for life. Now that you know the situation, do you have any different judgments about the emotions being expressed?

Although, at some level, pain is a private, individual experience, it is shaped in important ways by the social and cultural context in which it occurs. The sensations people label as painful and the manner in which they respond to pain have been learned from other people, such as members of their family or ethnic group (Weisenberg, 1977). In fact, in some cases, patients who show exaggerated pain reactions are referred for psychiatric care when actually they are only manifesting learned behavior patterns approved in their social or subcultural group.

When surgical patients at a Bronx VA hospital were observed and interviewed (along with their families and staff), ethnic group membership generally predicted how they were handling the pain they were experiencing. The Jewish and Italian patients emotionally exaggerated the intensity of their pain, feeling free to cry out to elicit support from family or the hospital staff. By contrast, Irish and Old American patients (Anglo-Saxon Protestants from at least three generations of Americans) adopted a phlegmatic, detached, matter-of-fact orientation that inhibited any public show of emotion. When their pain became intense, they would withdraw; they would moan or cry out only when alone.

Further investigation showed that the common demonstrativeness of the Jewish and Italian patients stemmed from different concerns. The Italians focused on the immediacy of the pain experience and pain relief, whereas the Jewish patients were concerned about the meaning and future implications of the pain, and also had a distrust of pain-relief procedures.

Although both the Irish and the Old Americans were "good" patients who did not make a fuss, they too were acting from quite divergent attitudes. The Old American patients, in refusing to be seen as weak or helpless, assumed that pain was a common experience that everyone has but which threatens one's masculinity. With probing by an interviewer, however, such patients openly discussed their feelings and were optimistic about their future since "doctors are experts."

The Irish patients, on the other hand, were reluctant to speak about their pain and seemed to need to endure it alone as a unique experience. Their inability or unwillingness to share their feelings gave a superficial appearance of outward calm and lack of concern. The investigator reported that "among the four groups of patients of different ethnic backgrounds, the Irish patient presented the saddest, most depressing picture . . . not prepared to think in terms of illness and health care, he discovers in the hospital a world of human suffering of which he is a part. But he is unable to share his emotions, anxieties, and fears with a close person who would understand them and offer some comfort and support" (Zborowski, 1969, p. 235).

The basic results of this research were substantiated in a controlled laboratory study, where pain was induced (by electric shock) in housewives of various ethnic backgrounds. The Italian subjects were most sensitive to the pain, with significantly lower pain tolerance than any other group. Jewish women were able to take the greatest increase in shock level when motivated (coaxed) by the experimenter. While Yankee subjects physiologically adapted to shock more readily than any other group, the Irish housewives deliberately suppressed their suffering and concern for the implication of the pain (Sternbach & Tursky, 1965).

There were important differences, however, in the experience and interpretation of pain induced in the laboratory, as compared with pain experienced by patients in the hospital. For example, in the laboratory, where the cause of pain was obvious and controlled by the experimenter, the Jewish patients had a higher threshold for pain (as compared with the Jewish hospital patients), since the lab pain did not signal ominous future dangers.

To fully understand pain reactions, we must be careful not to overlook their function as social communications. Expressions of pain are not simply signals of physical damage, but are messages to other people about one's psychological state (Szasz, 1957). For example, a person's response to pain may be a way of saying "Don't hurt me" or "It's legitimate for me to get out of my responsibilities" or "I'm a real man—strong and tough" or "Help me, I'm vulnerable."

Cognitive controls on behavior

The psychologist attempts to formulate general laws of behavior in order to be able to explain, predict, and control such mind-body interactions as emotion and pain. For all of us attempting to cope with the demands of the environment, existence itself depends on being able to meet these goals. To discover causal relations gives meaning to events. To be able to predict the occurrence of events brings order and regularity where chaos and uncertainty would otherwise exist. To control events by means of purposeful actions leads to active mastery in place of passive dependence and submission to the environment. To be unable to exert any control over one's environment can have far-reaching pathological effects. In short, we can and do exert significant cognitive control over our noncognitive processes. Psychologists have shown that our emotions, perceptions of pain, motivations, and interpretations of immediate environmental stimuli can all be influenced by our cognition.

Hope and hopelessness

A fateful reaction of some prisoners of war has been aptly described as "give-up-itis." In this syndrome, the loss of all hope of ever being freed and consequent loss of interest in the future resulted in emotionally caused death. Bruno Bettelheim, a psychologist who himself survived imprisonment in Nazi concentration camps, characterizes one such reaction that he observed among some of his fellow prisoners in this way:

"Prisoners who came to believe the repeated statements of the guards—that there was no hope for them, that they would never leave the camp except as a corpse—who came to feel that their environment was one over which they could exercise no influence whatsoever, these prisoners were, in a literal sense, walking corpses. In the camps they were called 'moslems' (<u>Muselmanner</u>) because of what was erroneously viewed as a fatalistic surrender to the environment, as Mohammedans are supposed to blandly accept their fate.

". . . they were people who were so deprived of affect, self-esteem, and every form of stimulation, so totally exhausted, both physically and emotionally, that they had given the environment total power over them" (1960, pp. 151–52).

For the American POW of the Chinese Communists in the Korean War, there were reported to be similar feelings of abandonment by one's own people, of the day-to-day uncertainty of existence, and of the futility of resisting or escaping (Schein, 1957). Even after repatriation and return to civilian life, these men were observed to show a "zombie-like" detachment. This is also a common reaction pattern among some depressed hospitalized patients who seem to withdraw, quietly or sullenly, from all social contact. In severe cases,

". . . there is complete paralysis of the will. The patient has no desire to do anything, even those things which are essential to life. Consequently he may be relatively immobile unless prodded or pushed into activity by others. It is sometimes necessary to pull the pa-

tient out of bed, wash, dress, and feed him. In extreme cases, even communication may be blocked by the patient's inertia" (Beck, 1967, p. 28).

Although the importance of hope and hopelessness has long been recognized by clinicians, systematic research on these concepts has begun only recently. *Hope* is generally defined as an expectation of success in achieving one's goal (Stotland, 1969). This expectation that one's behavior can effect a change in the environment will motivate action toward goal attainment. Apathy and inaction are the consequences of the hopelessness that follows ineffectual responding. When an organism, human or animal, comes to believe that nothing it can do will eliminate a threat, it yields to passive resignation. (See *P&L* Close-up, The Meek Shall Inherit Ulcers.)

It well may be that the basic reinforcer that sustains broad classes of behavior over long periods of time is the confirmation of one's *competence* (White, 1959). This source of reinforcement comes from attaining mastery over one's external or internal environment, rather than from merely satisfying appetites or minimizing aversions. From the infant's elation in learning to walk to the mountain climber's pride in conquering difficult and hazardous terrain, the perception of ourselves as active, capable agents is one of our greatest joys, whereas the perception of ourselves as helpless pawns controlled by others is one of the most galling of experiences.

The acceptance of control by external factors or "fate" is not an all-or-none affair but varies with the degree to which we have had the experience of seeing that what we do makes a difference. Rotter (1966) conceives of this dimension of perceived degree of environmental control as a consistent personality trait. Some individuals ("internals") perceive that they possess considerable personal control over what reinforcements they receive. At the other end of the continuum are those people ("externals") who believe that the environment determines what happens and that nothing they could do would change the outcome. (We will have more to say about this personality variable in Chapter 17.)

Close-up
The Meek Shall Inherit Ulcers

The psychic state of loss of cognitive control over the environment has been shown to render even "normal" individuals more biologically vulnerable to a host of diseases. Medical investigators have begun to accumulate evidence suggesting that when persons respond to events in their life with hopelessness, they initiate a complex series of biological changes that foster the development of any disease potential that is present—even diabetes, heart disease, and cancer.

This link between passivity and poor health is demonstrated by some animal research. Rats that were helpless in terms of receiving uncontrollable shock were more likely to develop ulcers than rats who received controllable shock or no shock at all. The helpless rats fared worse in other ways as well, since they lost weight, drank less, and showed depletion of the transmitter norepinephrine in the central nervous system (Weiss, 1968, 1971). In another study, after animals had learned to press a bar for food, their bar pressing was suppressed when shock was given. When the shock became predictable, however, responding again occurred regularly. Six of eight subjects in an unpredictable shock condition developed ulcers after forty-five days, whereas none of eight animals given predictable shock developed ulcers (Seligman, 1968).

Although the "commonsense" belief is that the people who develop ulcers are those with greater responsibilities and more hard work, it may be that one's sense of control over the outcomes of one's work is the more critical factor.

Learned helplessness

What happens to an organism when its mastery over the environment and its sense of competence are destroyed? How would you feel if you discovered that traumatic events continue to happen to you independently of any attempts on your part to reduce or eliminate them? This general problem was first put to experimental test several decades ago.

In this study hungry rats were shocked ten seconds after they began to eat. The animals in one group were given control over the shock since it was terminated when they jumped off the shock grid. The animals in the other group had no control over the shock. It was found that the animals who could control the shock ate more often than those who had no control—even though both received the same total amount of shock. The experimenters postulated that exposure to the unavoidable shock caused the animals to eat less because they had developed a "sense of helplessness" (Mowrer & Viek, 1948).

Recently these speculations have been raised to a firm empirical level by the provocative research on learned helplessness by Seligman and his associates (Seligman, 1975; Maier & Seligman, 1978; Abramson, Seligman, & Teasdale, 1978). The term *learned helplessness* describes an organism's reaction when it is faced with important events that cannot be altered by its voluntary responses. The initial research was conducted with dogs, but has been replicated with human subjects. In Chapter 4, we discussed Seligman's research in connection with the effects of Pavlovian aversive conditioning on subsequent avoidance learning. We will review that study here as it relates to the phenomenon of learned helplessness. Dogs previously exposed to an inescapable shock could not learn to escape when placed in a novel situation. Two things had happened to these animals: they had become both unmotivated and retarded in their learning. Seligman proposes that the prior experience in the harness taught the dogs a sad lesson—their responses had no effect on their traumatic environment. Hope was extinguished and in its place there was fear and a sense of helplessness. This lesson was well learned. In the original study the effects of a prior session of helplessness seemed to wear off after forty-eight hours, but a later study showed that they could be made lasting. Repeated exposure to inescapable shock produced a failure to try to escape danger as long as a week later.

The helplessness experiments with dogs have now been replicated with college students. One experiment utilized three practice conditions: an inescapable condition in which subjects were unable to turn off a loud noise, an escape condition in which subjects could control the noise, and a no-noise control condition. After the three groups had experienced the above conditions, they were then taken to a finger shuttlebox in which a loud noise occurred when a finger was placed on one side of the box, but ceased when the finger was moved to the other side. It was found that both the escape and no-noise group subjects learned to turn the noise off by moving their hands to the other side of the shuttlebox, while the subjects who had experienced the inescapable condition did not escape the noise, but remained passive. (Hiroto, 1974).

A second experiment demonstrated cognitive deficits arising from learned helplessness. After exposure to one of the same three noise conditions (escapable, inescapable, or no noise), students were asked to solve twenty anagrams. Solution of these anagrams would be fairly easy once the person figured out that the letters were always arranged in 34251 order—e.g., ISOEN (noise), DERRO (order), and so on. However, students who had been subjected to inescapable noise had difficulty in catching on to this pattern. Furthermore, they were less able to solve each of the anagrams than were students who had received escapable noise or no noise (Hiroto & Seligman, 1975).

It has recently been demonstrated that helplessness may be learned vicariously, as well as from direct experience. Undergraduate women who merely observed another subject in an insoluble training task later showed the same performance deficits as the subjects who had actually attempted the training task (De Vellis, De Vellis, & McCauley, 1978).

Prevention and cure of helplessness

All people experience traumatic events and discover situations that are beyond their control. A number of factors have been shown to prevent, moderate, or cure helplessness that may be found in our daily lives. These include immunization, predictability, superstitious perception of control, and retroactive therapy.

"Immunization"   The most significant kind of therapy is the preventive kind in which the individual is "inoculated" against learned helplessness by prior mastery training. Mastery training in the laboratory consisted of providing sufficient prior experiences in which the dogs had a means of controlling their environment before they were exposed to inescapable trauma. When the dogs were later put into a shuttlebox where they could escape shock, they did so, unlike the helpless dogs that had not received prior mastery training.

The implications for human conditions of helplessness are obvious. The time to begin such mastery training is in childhood—and the need for parents and teachers to do so is imperative as forces in modern society increasingly make people feel anonymous, unrecognized, expendable, and powerless. (See *P&L* Close-up, Teaching Hope in the Classroom.)

Predictability   Even when aversive stimulation cannot be avoided, its disrupting effect can be reduced by making it predictable. When events are predictable, the fear and anxiety created by uncertainty about future threatening events can be reduced. Subjects prefer a shock that has a predictable warning signal over one that is unsignaled (Lockard, 1963). Rats prefer predictable shocks that are four times as long and three times as intense as unpredictable shocks (Badia, Culbertson, & Harch, 1973). Human subjects given a choice of advance information about either intensity or timing of the coming shock request information about "how soon" more often than information about "how strong" (Jones, Bentler, & Petry, 1966). Subjects also want to take inevitable shocks immediately—to "get it over with"—rather than wait for a delayed shock (Gibbon, 1967).

The following study extends these basic findings about the consequences of both behavioral and perceptual control of the environment on physiological reactions in human subjects.

Male college volunteer subjects worked for half an hour on a demanding shock-avoidance task. To keep from being shocked, they had to press a start button, quickly respond by depressing the correct lever when one of a series of lights came on, and then immediately go through the next trial. Once every forty-five seconds, on the average, they missed at some point and received a painful shock. Their arousal to this stress was recorded by elevations in systolic blood pressure (arterial pressure during a heart contraction).

At first, twelve experimental subjects were given the opportunity to call for a time-out of one minute whenever they wanted it, while twelve "yoked" controls received the same time-out periods, but only when the others requested it. Thus the only difference was in the cognition of one group that it controlled the avoidance response of calling for a time-out and of the helpless group that it did not. Over the course of the experi-

Close-up
Teaching Hope in the Classroom

Think back to your elementary school days to recall the following scene. Your teacher is questioning the class about current events that virtually everyone knows. After each question, every hand is raised in eager anticipation. "Call on me, teacher, please call on me, I know the right answer," is the refrain running through your mind and the minds of your classmates.

At last, your eyes make contact. You hear your name, stand tall, answer proudly, and the teacher smiles. As you sit back, the next question is posed to the sea of waving hands; some of the others are called on, some are not—and the period is over. What is it that you learned in this situation, and what did your friends learn who were *not* called on? Weren't there some who in fact were *never* recognized? What did they learn from this experience?

The answers are obvious. You were reinforced for raising your hand and for answering correctly, and you continued to do so, and here you are in college. The hand-raising response was simply extinguished in the others. But is that all that was being learned in that situation? Mowrer (1960) believes that specific physical responses such as hand-raising were but minor components in the total pattern of emotional responding that occurred. You were "conditioned" to feel *hope* in that situation because your responses produced gratification—they changed something in ways that were desirable to you. Your unrecognized peers were "conditioned" to feel there was no hope in this same setting because their responses were

ineffective in generating any positive consequences. Your sense of hope encourages you to take more chances, to be more active, more optimistic of success, and more competent in your mastery of the environment; you make more responses, and some of them are likely to get reinforced. In contrast, a sense of hopelessness decreases not only the question-answering response but the thinking that must precede it, as well as the intellectual curiosity and active involvement in the entire learning process. People who have learned to feel helpless in situations that are hopeless turn off, tune out, and give up. What is perhaps even worse is that they often come to blame themselves rather than the situation for their unfortunate state.

ment, systolic blood pressure was consistently higher for the helpless subjects, indicating a higher level of arousal (and, presumably, stress). ■

In a second part of the study (using different subjects), the rest period was preceded by a signal indicating that relief was on the way. The subjects again worked on the light-matching task, which was interrupted by a conditioned stimulus signaling that a time-out was thirty seconds away. The subjects had to continue working after the signal until the relief period started.

Even though they were still being shocked as often and as intensely after the safety signal as before, and had no control over its occurrence, their knowledge gave them perceptual control and their blood pressure dropped markedly as soon as the signal appeared. When, in addition, they did have control over the timing of the safety signal (both perceptual and behavioral control), the reduction in physiological stress was even greater though the number of signals and time-out periods remained unchanged (Hokanson, DeGood, Forrest, & Brittain, 1971).

Superstitious control Helplessness is often related to superstitious attempts to control the environment. Superstitions flourish when individuals do not have control over their environment and yet are faced with risky decisions. While ideas on the value and function of superstitious behavior are speculative, the widespread popularity of superstition is not. In learned helplessness we are dealing with connections between our responses, environmental outcomes, and the perception of controllability. We have seen that controllability prevents helplessness. What is surprising to consider, however, is that actual control is irrelevant. Instead it is simply the *belief* that one has control that matters.

In a study on urban stress and uncontrollability, it was demonstrated that subjects' belief that they could turn off an uncontrollable loud noise resulted in better performance on proofreading and problem-solving tasks than that of helpless subjects. Performance was also better when subjects believed that a person who could turn off the noise was accessible—even though the noise was not turned off (Glass & Singer, 1972).

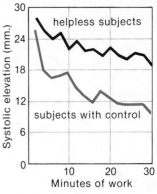

Behavioral control, helplessness, and systolic blood pressure

Adapted from Hokanson et al., 1971

This finding suggests a psychologically functional value for human superstition. Superstitions prevent learned helplessness by providing the superstitious person with an "illusion of control." (See *P&L* Close-up, Superstitions As Cultural Cognitive Control Mechanisms.) To perceive one's own knowledge, skill, and action as being effective—even if this is "merely" a superstitious belief—will not actually alter the conditions, but may prevent the negative psychological consequences of helplessness.

Treating learned helplessness

If helplessness is not prevented, it can be alleviated by treatment that comes after it has been established. Such treatment after the problem has become manifest is called *retroactive therapy*. It was found that the passive dogs in Seligman's studies could break out of the learned helplessness syndrome if they were forcibly dragged (perhaps as many as two hundred times) across from the shock compartment to the safe compartment to rediscover that responding could bring relief, and to develop self-initiated activity, as we shall see in Chapter 19.

Seligman has argued that the basic features of learned helplessness have parallels in the symptoms of depression, and that, therefore, depression may be best understood (and treated) as learned helplessness (Seligman, 1975). However, the model has been criticized for being an overly simple representation of a highly complex phenomenon, for using ambiguous concepts, and for using research designs that may not be the most appropriate ones for studying chronic depression in humans (Depue & Monroe, 1978; Buchwald, Coyne, & Cole, 1978). It may be that learned helplessness is one form of depression (rather than the basis of all depressive disorders), but more research will be needed to answer this and related issues.

Cognitive control of motivation

A hungry Fox saw some fine bunches of grapes hanging on a high trellis in a vineyard. He tried and tried to reach them by jumping as high as he could; but all his efforts were in vain, for the grapes were out of his reach. Finally, tired from his efforts, he left the

Superstitious rituals generate a sense of control. We can speculate that superstitious behavior will increase to the extent that people feel threatened, helpless, controlled, or without sufficient knowledge to make decisions that may be vital to their survival. In societies that operate on a subsistence level, depending on the vicissitudes of nature for the daily bread, fish, or game, superstitious charms and ritual behavior provide an illusion of control. There is at least something that the society can do to help tip the scales of fate, rather than passively waiting for the drought to end or the disease to abate.

In one tribe where hunting is the major source of food, someone must decide to stalk the prey during its migrating season. The herd does not always take the same route, and waiting in the wrong place may result in no food for the tribe. Such crucial decisions entail too much responsibility for any one person, and answers are typically sought by superstitious practices. Bones may be cast on the ground and the pattern "read" as a message from the gods as to where to stalk the herd. If the hunters are unsuccessful, it is assumed the gods were displeased and thus some new behaviors must be enacted to regain their favor. So even when the response has no favorable consequences, it does result in some action—which helps to prevent or forestall helplessness.

Superstitious beliefs also help to explain unusual, unnatural events and discontinuities in one's life. If a healthy child becomes sick, it is assumed in many countries of the world that an "evil eye" has been cast on the child and it must be broken. Babies in Puerto Rico, Italy, and elsewhere often wear special colors and charms (often shaped like a horn) to avert the possibility of the evil eye. Sounds strange, but did you never "knock on wood" to avert "bad luck"?

---

vineyard. With an air of unconcern he said, "I really wasn't very hungry. Besides, I thought those grapes were ripe, but I can see now they are sour" (Aesop, Fables).

Did the Fox say he wasn't hungry in an attempt to deny his heightened drive state? Or did he, in fact, effectively reduce his hunger drive by some cognitive process? When we do not get what we want (or need), have to postpone gratification or endure some unpleasant state, we can moderate the impact of biological and environmental stimuli by exercising cognitive control. Thinking can make it so, and cognitions can make it otherwise. Human beings need not react to the situation as it is given to them; they may, through their imaginative powers, *define* the situation to make it fit their needs, values, and motives.

This basic idea has been tested in experiments where subjects either believed they had free choice in their behavior or thought they had no choice at all.

One such experiment studied subjects' response to pain as a function of their perception of personal choice. In the first phase of the experiment, all subjects were given a series of electric shocks, and measures were taken of their subjective, behavioral, and physiological reactions. Then the subjects were asked to undergo a second series of shocks. In some conditions subjects agreed to go on after being given considerable justification (money, social pressure, or good reasons) for doing so. In other conditions, subjects agreed to go on after being given a <u>choice</u> to do so (or to quit) and only minimal justification. Those who committed themselves to go on under pressure and with high justification suffered the same as they had in the first phase of the study. However, those subjects who had voluntarily agreed to undergo a second set of shocks with only minimal justification for doing so, cognitively controlled the impact of this second stimulation phase of the study. The shocks did not hurt as much as they did the first time. Low-justification subjects not only said it hurt less and behaved as if it hurt less, but even at a physiological level, they *were not reacting as intensely to the painful stimulus.* ● *It is as if they persuaded themselves that it would not be so bad, and lo and behold, they were right. Motivation was brought in line with the behavioral commitment. After all, it would be "crazy" to agree to take painful shocks for no good reason when one had a choice to leave, wouldn't it? However, it would not be inconsistent if you convinced yourself that the shocks would not hurt much. Indeed, the same voltage shocks hurt these subjects less than they hurt the no-choice or high-justification controls (Zimbardo et al., 1969).*

The same pattern of findings occurred in experiments where other biological drives (hunger, thirst) or strong social motives (achievement, approval, frustration, aggression) were substituted for pain. People who chose to subject themselves to additional aversive stimulation for minimal justification were <u>less</u> *affected by that stimulation at all levels of functioning, subjective, behavioral and physiological (Zimbardo, 1969).*

These results empirically support the hypothesis that cognitive control processes can change the usual relationship between a physical stimulus and the body's reaction to it (see *P&L* Close-up, Cognitionless Comprehension). But just how far can we push this notion of choice as a potent cognitive control variable? According to some recent studies of elderly individuals in homes for the aged, the perception of choice may have an important relationship to people's life expectancy. In the first of these studies, it was found that women who had died within a month of making application to an old-age home usually had not chosen to apply; their families had made the application for them. Based on prior interview responses, these women were divided into those who perceived they had no choice but to go to the home, and those who perceived that they did have other alternatives even though they were going to the home. Within ten weeks of being admitted to the home all but one woman in the no-choice group had died. In sharp contrast, all but one of the choice group were still living! Examination of the medical records revealed there were no medical health differences between the women in these two groups upon admission to the institution (Ferrare, 1962).

If it is the exercise of choice that is the independent variable accelerating or retarding death, then by providing a perception of choice, it should be possible to prolong life. Even for those who have no "real" choice about entering the home, a series of minimal choices might be presented, such as which day to enter, which floor to be housed on, which of several activities to engage in,

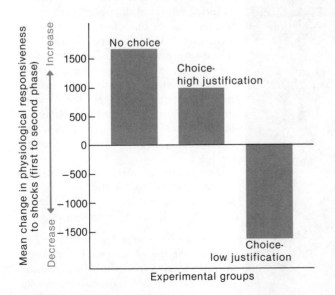

● **Responsiveness
to shocks**

Adapted from Zimbardo et al., 1969

and so on. If perceived helplessness results in death, then manipulating the environment to create an "illusion of choice" and mastery through decision making should delay death or promote life.

Such a study has just been done — with remarkable results.

The sample consisted of ninety-one residents, ages sixty-five to ninety, all well enough to be walking about. Half of the participants in the study were randomly assigned to a condition in which they received instructions that emphasized the need for them to take more responsibility for caring for themselves and for improving the quality of life in the home. They were then asked to choose a plant from among a box of them as a present — but they had to care for it. In contrast, a second group of patients was given instructions that stressed the responsibility of the staff to provide good services for the residents. They were handed a plant as a present and informed that the nurses would water it for them.

The results of the enhanced sense of personal responsibility were dramatic. On questionnaire ratings and behavioral measures, the experimental group ("I'll do it myself") showed significant improvement over the comparison group ("let George do it for you")

Close-up
Cognitionless Comprehension

There have been several claims that the subjective state of consciousness produced by Zen meditation can profoundly alter the relation of people to their inner and outer realms of reality. Just what is Zen, and what is the evidence for its power as a cognitive control?

The original meaning of *Zen* was "quiet meditation," but over time the term came to include "wisdom," and now its objective is "enlightenment." The essence of Zen Buddhism is to acquire a fresh, new viewpoint on life and things generally. The state of mind sought through Zen meditation is one of alert emptiness, in which the mind is like a mirror, simply reflecting what impinges upon it from the outside. The means by which a practitioner realizes enlightenment, or "nonconceptual comprehension" *(satori)* are three:

a) Zazen — exercises to regulate posture and the body, exercises to regulate breathing, and exercises to regulate the mind;

b) Kōan — intellectual exercises of meditating on riddles and questions that logic can never resolve, such as, "What is the sound of one hand clapping?" "How does one look before one's father and mother have met?" To comprehend the Kōan, one must discard rational cognitive processes, since the Kōan can be grasped but never explained. Concentration on the meaning of the Kōan frees the mind of other concerns until only the Kōan remains. Later, the Kōan, too, vanishes, leaving only the mind as a "blurless mirror";

c) Sanshi-Mompō — the practice of "going to a master to ask the way." It consists of disciplined study by a disciple with a Zen master for a long period of time.

As we have seen (p. 303), the Zen master's mind can become so perfect a mirror that even the fundamental physiological process of habituation to repeated stimuli does not take place.

Interaction, choice, and responsibility can increase alertness, participation, and sense of well-being as well as length of life.

on alertness, active participation, and general sense of well-being (Langer & Rodin, 1976).

Eighteen months later, these positive results still persisted, as indicated by nurses' higher ratings of the happiness, sociability, and vigor of the personally responsible group. But most startling of all, inducing the residents to be responsible for themselves and their plants made them live longer! The overall death rate for the entire nursing home during an eighteen-month period prior to the experiment was 25 percent. Following the experiment, only 15 percent of the personally responsible residents died, compared to twice as many for the no-responsibility group (Rodin & Langer, 1977). ■

Thus, psychological interventions of this kind not only improve mood and attitudes, they can affect the very process of life and death itself. The existentialist philosopher Jean-Paul Sartre (1957) has said that "man makes himself" and "through his choice he involves all mankind, and he cannot avoid making a choice." If the helpless, hopeless person can be provided with more meaningful alternatives, his or her final choice may be life, rather than death. And if society provides its citizens with more meaningful options, the quality of social life will be improved and enriched. We do not yet know the extent of cognitive control that people possess over both external stimuli and their internal environment, but it may approach the vision seen by the Roman poet, Marcus Manilius, many centuries ago:

"No barriers, no masses of matter however enormous, can withstand the powers of the mind; the remotest corners yield to them; all things succumb; the very Heaven itself is laid open" (Astronomica I, c. 40 B.C.*).*

Hypnosis as a cognitive control system

Imagine that in front of you on the lecture stage sit two students from your class engaged in a contest of endurance. On your left is Steve, a big, burly, 235-pound varsity letterman from the football team, eager to show his stuff. On the right side demurely sits Cynthia, her compact 5'3", 120-pound frame also preparing for the "one-on-one" competition. They roll up their sleeves, and on the count of three plunge the right arm deep into an ice chest. When the ice is up to their biceps, the contest of strength is on. It is strength of imagination (or will power) that is being contested. The contestant who keeps the arm submerged in the ice pack longest is the winner.

They call out subjective reports of the pain they are experiencing—pain mounts rapidly in response to the intense cold. Initially both reports are at the "0," "1," "2" levels. After a few minutes Steve moves to "3," "5," then up to "7." "It's freezing in here, man!" Cynthia smiles, nods to her opponent, and repeats her "2" report. Steve is now struggling in his seat, no way he's going to let this little girl beat him. "Eight," "it's 8," "no, 9," says he, and listens with disbelief as his frail opponent says, "Yes, it is getting colder, I'd say 3."

"Ten," shouts Steve ripping his blue arm up through the ice. "I can't take any more, I give up."

Cynthia does not gloat over her victory, in fact, she seems coolly detached from the competition. When the instructor requests, she lifts her blue arm out of the ice chest and with a faint smile says, "Maybe it's 4."

"It's rigged, the fix has got to be on somehow," declares Steve who is positive that he can endure a lot more pain than most people. He's right, of course, the contest was rigged. Cynthia had been hypnotized. She was given an hypnotic suggestion for <u>analgesia</u>, to the effect that <u>she</u> would feel little pain even though <u>her arm</u> might get cold. Somehow these words got translated into a code that her body responded to accordingly.

"I've seen it, but I still don't believe," muttered Steve as he rejoined the audience in my introductory psychology course.

Over the years, hypnosis has been valued largely for the stage effects it can produce. Today, psychologists are beginning to consider it a topic for serious study. Much of what appears to be due to hypnosis can be reproduced merely by heightened motivation in unhypnotized people.

Steve is like many others who take an *incredulous* or skeptical view of hypnosis. They doubt the testimony of hypnotic subjects, and believe hypnotic phenomena are all pretense. The *credulous* view accepts the hypnotized subject's testimony as an adequate representation of reality. In between is the scientific view that "doubts with an open mind." Before accepting even the apparent evidence of our senses, data must be collected according to the scientific method (Chapter 2). That methodology helps impose the precision and control essential to minimize possible sources of error in drawing inferences from evidence. But the true scientist allows for all conceivable possibilities, especially those that do not fit current theories. Belief is suspended until all the available reliable data are evaluated.

Many claims are made for hypnosis which are not substantiated under rigorous testing conditions. ▲ However, there is a reliable body of evidence bolstered by expert opinion that strongly suggests hypnosis can exert a powerful influence over a variety of psychological and bodily functions. (See *P&L* Close-up, Mesmer's Magnetism and the God of Sleep.)

Hypnosis is not easy to define because different theorists and researchers emphasize different aspects of the phenomenon. Our conceptual definition views *hypnosis* as a cognitive process induced by a variety of techniques that are characterized generally by deep relaxation, increased susceptibility to hypnotic suggestions, and alterations in self-control and motivational level.

Hypnotic susceptibility

These effects are most pronounced in (or in some cases limited to) individuals who are hypnotizable. *Hypnotizability* is the degree to which an individual is or is not responsive to standardized hypnotic suggestions, administered following a routine induction of suggested relaxation and eye closure or arm levitation. This objective measure of hypnotizability has been found to be a good predictor of responsiveness to a variety of hypnotic phenomena. However, few personality or social factors have been found to relate to hypnotizability. The percentage of subjects who are at various levels of hypnotizability the first time they are given the induction-test procedure is shown in the graph. ◆

Hypnotic susceptibility is a trait that appears to remain relatively stable over a period of years (Morgan, Johnson, & Hilgard, 1974). It may have a

Mesmer's Magnetism and the God of Sleep

In the eighteenth century Anton Mesmer, a Viennese physician, startled the world when he began to cure afflicted persons by application of *animal magnetism*. He believed that a universal fluid influenced the planets and all living things. A diseased body could be restored to its harmony with the universe by magnets placed on it to induce a flow of healing magnetic fluid.

Mesmer's brand of therapy involved principles of old-fashioned faith healing dressed up in scientific terminology, with a little medieval mysticism and ancient astrology thrown in for good measure. The power of *mesmerism* achieved such fame that as hundreds of patients experienced relief from pain, thousands more came. To handle the demand, Mesmer "magnetized" virtually everything in sight and proclaimed that contact with these objects (e.g., trees) would be curative.

Animal magnetism was eventually discredited as having no physical basis by a commission of the French Academy of Science, led by Benjamin Franklin. Their verdict was, "Nothing proves the existence of magnetic animal fluid; imagination without magnetism may produce conversions; magnetism without imagination produces nothing." That is an interesting conclusion for its time because it proclaimed imagination and suggestability (the mind) as influences on the body.

Hypnosis replaced animal magnetism through the efforts of James Braid, who discovered in 1843 that the nervous system could be induced artificially into a state of "nervous sleep." He eventually called this state "hypnosis," after the Greek god of sleep. It was demonstrated that this special state of sleep could be produced merely by concentrated attention or "fixity of gaze." The person in this state was found to be very responsive to verbal suggestions given by the hypnotist.

From 1845 to 1853, a Scottish surgeon working in India, James Esdaile, performed nearly 300 painless major operations including amputations and cataract removals, with mesmerism as the only anesthetic. The subsequent discovery of ether, however, led surgeons to prefer that physical drug treatment to the psychic one of hypnosis, although the latter was shown to be equally effective and to lead to fewer side effects and a lower mortality rate for many types of operations.

Hypnosis was revived in France through the demonstrations of hypnosis by Jean Charcot, with whom Freud and Breuer studied. They were later to use hypnosis as a technique to study the unconscious processes in hysteria.

It was not until the 1930s, however, that the current era of psychological experimentation in hypnosis began, with the work of Clark Hull, known to psychologists for his major contributions to learning theory. During World War II and the Korean War, American psychiatrists and clinical psychologists discovered the advantages of hypnotherapy for treating a variety of pathological problems created by combat stress. Medical practitioners became more attracted to the potential of hypnosis for relief of pain.

In recent years the scientific standard-bearers for hypnosis have been Ernest Hilgard of Stanford University, and Martin Orne of the University of Pennsylvania. Through the productivity of their research laboratories and the rigor and ingenuity with which they and their students have studied the process, correlates, and consequences of hypnosis, the mystery is being replaced with sound fact and testable theory (Hilgard, 1973; Orne, 1970).

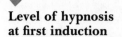

**Level of hypnosis
at first induction**
*The graph shows results for
533 subjects hypnotized for
the first time. Hypnotizability
was measured on the
Stanford Hypnotic
Susceptibility Scale, which
consists of 12 items.*

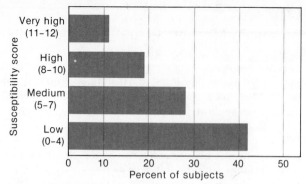

Based on Hilgard, 1965

genetic component, since identical twins have been found to have greater similarity in hypnotizability than do fraternal twins (Morgan, 1973). It has been suggested that hypnotic susceptibility is not so much a trait as a special state. Researchers like Charles Tart (1975a) argue that hypnosis, for some subjects, is a unique state of consciousness (the topic of our next chapter).

Other investigators have argued that all hypnotic phenomena represent nothing more than strong states of motivation. Theodore Barber (1970) has shown that many behaviors attributed to the "state of hypnosis" can be reproduced even in unhypnotized subjects simply given a set of motivating instructions in the waking state.

Although some of the effect of hypnosis is attributable to the same motivation that operates in faith healing (Frank, 1963), there is an effect over and above the placebo effect that is unique to hypnosis.

Hypnosis in the relief of pain

Hypnosis is a potent technique for relieving the psychological experience of pain. In controlled laboratory tests, hypnotizable subjects given appropriate suggestions are able to reduce their sensitivity to usually painful stimuli much more than when they are in a waking state or than unhypnotized subjects.

Hypnosis appears to be even more effective in clinical settings than it is in controlled laboratory investigations. This is probably due to the patient's heightened motivation to relieve his or her chronic pain or to block the anticipated pain of medical and surgical procedures. For experimental subjects the meaning of limited "safely administered pain" is quite different and less compelling.

Hypnosis has been found to be effective in the treatment of migraine and vascular headaches which do not respond to traditional medical treatment. The power of hypnosis to increase a person's potential control over the impact of a threatening environment is demonstrated by the finding that even in terminal cancer, intense pain can be brought under patients' cognitive control so that they no longer need to depend on morphine during the last phase of their lives (Sacerdote, 1966).

The use of hypnosis in childbirth has much to recommend it. In addition to reducing or actually eliminating the intense pains of labor and delivery hypnotic instructions can reduce later back pain and facilitate more rapid recovery. One obstetrician successfully used hypnosis as the sole form of anesthesia in 814 out of 1000 deliveries—some of them caesarian (Hilgard & Hilgard, 1974).

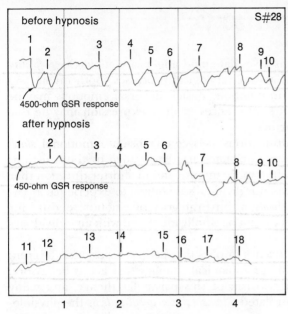

before hypnosis

S#28

1
2
3
4
5 6
7
8
9
10

4500-ohm GSR response

after hypnosis

1
2
3
4
5 6
7
8
9 10

450-ohm GSR response

11 12
13
14
15
16
17
18

Minutes

1
2
3
4

Adapted from Zimbardo, Rapaport, & Baron, 1969

Volunteer subjects were given a series of constant-intensity, painful electric shocks, both before and after receiving a hypnotic suggestion for analgesia. As compared to a control group, these hypnotic subjects reported feeling much less pain and showed less physiological responsivity to the shocks. One subject's reactions to the shocks are shown in the graph.

Hypnotic altering of control systems

A subject "who spoke only German at age six and who was age regressed to that time answered ["Nein"] when asked whether he [understood] English. . . . When this question was rephrased to him 10 times in English, he indicated each time in German that he was unable to comprehend English, explaining in childlike German such details as that his parents speak English in order that he not understand. While professing his inability to comprehend English, he continued responding appropriately in German to the hypnotist's complex English questions" (Orne, 1972, p. 427).

This subject shows "trance logic"; he can tolerate paradoxes without insisting on ordinary logical reasoning to make sense of his experiences. Trance logic involves registration of information at one level of processing, but denial of it at other levels. This phenomenon should remind you of the "hidden observer" we encountered in Chapter 1. Under hypnosis there appears to be a dissociation of different levels of such processing. Hilgard (1976, 1977) postulates that hypnotic phenomena are best understood within the framework of an information processing model (of the kind we detailed in Chapter 5). The multiple controls over our programs for thinking, feeling, and acting can be directly affected by hypnotic suggestions. Parallel processing is facilitated, with more than one cognitive event occurring simultaneously. Furthermore, the information being processed by one channel may be denied access to conscious awareness by an executive processor.

This use of an information processing model and dissociation concepts offers exciting possibilities. It may, if justified by empirical research, help provide a solid foundation that links hypnosis to basic psychological phenomena on one hand, as well as to less clearly understood phenomena that link mental and bodily processes. In the next chapter, we shall examine the nature of consciousness that hypnosis seems to alter, as well as other means of changing our states of consciousness.

Chapter summary

Emotional experiences such as love, hate, and anger, are subjective, *affective* states involving psychological and physiological processes. Both innate and learned factors are involved in emotion. Basic, universal emotions may be genetically determined, but the differences in their expression may be due to cultural and experiential factors.

Theorists often make distinctions between transient emotional *states* and stable, individual *traits*. Emotion states are determined by the situations in which they occur and are often more intense and of shorter duration than emotion traits, which describe an individual's tendency to experience a particular emotion frequently. *Moods,* a third category of emotion, endure for longer periods than states, yet cannot be wholly identified with an individual's characteristic traits.

The *James-Lange theory of emotion* implies that people experience different emotions as a result of specific physiological changes that act as behavioral cues. There has been much criticism of this particular theory, and many psychologists have instead postulated a *nonspecific arousal state* as the physiological basis of emotion.

The most successful psychological models of emotion view the neurophysiological, experiential, and expressive components of emotional experience as interacting closely with each other. The physiological component involves both the brain and the endocrine glands. Researchers have found that stimulation of areas in the *limbic system* produces changes in emotional reactions, as does stimulation or surgery in other brain regions such as the frontal lobes. Anatomical changes in the brain may be involved in the development of emotional response in infancy.

The *endocrine glands,* which pump *hormones* directly into the bloodstream, are known to be associated with emotional reaction. The regulatory center for the endocrine system lies in the *hypothalamus.* The *pituitary,* attached to the underside of the hypothalamus, secretes a number of hormones, some of which act directly on endocrine glands such as the *adrenals.* When stimulated, the adrenal glands secrete *epinephrine* and *norepinephrine,* both associated with conditions of stress. Research has also linked these hormones to states of euphoria and depression.

The *two-component theory* of emotion stresses the interaction between physiology and cognition. It suggests that the physiological component of various emotions is really one *undifferentiated* state of arousal that determines the intensity of emotion—the quality of emotion being determined by cognitions drawn from environmental cues. Thus, physiological arousal would be a necessary condition for emotion but not a sufficient one. Recent research, however, points up the fact that the physiological component is not necessarily neutral and that cognition may have more subtle and complex impact on the perception of emotion than the theory assigns it.

Cognitive appraisal theories are concerned with the impact of an individual's evaluation and judgment of the significance of a stimulus on his or her emotional response. While the theories differ somewhat in the complexity of their approach, they all maintain that emotion involves distinct patterns of physiological response acting as functions of cognitive appraisal.

Studies of the expressive component of emotion, which is often of a nonverbal nature, have pointed out that certain innate responses that have had biological utility in evolution are found universally in humans. This has been convincingly demonstrated with comparisons of emotionally based facial expressions. There are, however, important cultural differences in which strikingly dissimilar emotional reactions are elicited by identical situations.

Pain is both a *signal system* that has evolved to warn us of assaults on the body and a *defensive system* initiating automatic withdrawal reflexes, motivated avoidance, and escape behaviors. *Peripheral* pain is triggered in the nerves of the body's organs or extremities, while *cerebral* pain begins in the brain or spinal cord. Pain actually experienced is not wholly determined by the stimulus causing it; it is interpreted according to the context in which it occurs.

The *gate-control theory* of pain suggests that there is a "gate" in the spinal cord that can open and close, determining the amount of nerve impulses that reach the brain and are eventually perceived as pain.

Psychological variables may have a tremendous influence on people's perception and reaction to pain. Studies have shown that subjects administered *placebos* they were told would reduce pain, experienced such a reduction. The personality traits of a subject and the significance he or she attributes to pain may also affect its perceived intensity.

Pain may be shaped by the social and cultural context in which it appears. Responses to it may be learned from familial or societal examples, and they may also be used as a means of communicating a psychological state, such as vulnerability or anxiety, to others.

Cognition, then, can exert control over noncognitive processes. Hope, for example, leads to motivated action toward goal attainment and changing one's environment, whereas hopelessness leads to ineffectual responding and can result in physical deterioration and death.

The confirmation of one's competence seems to be a basic reinforcer that sustains broad classes of behavior over long periods of time. An individual's perception of the degree of control that he or she exerts over the environment is considered a consistent personality trait by some psychologists.

Learned helplessness describes an organism's reaction when it is faced with important events that cannot be altered by its voluntary responses. In such a reaction, hope is extinguished and is replaced by fear and a sense of helplessness.

The perception of choice provides another example of cognitive control over physical stimuli and the body's response to them. Individuals who can exercise some measure of choice do not experience the degree of helplessness of those denied the opportunity to make choices. Elderly people who perceive themselves as having the power of choice tend to live longer than those who do not.

An as yet little understood form of cognitive control takes place under *hypnosis*. Hypnosis is usually induced by deep-relaxation techniques and results in increased susceptibility to hypnotic suggestion and changes in levels of self-control and motivation.

The *hypnotizability* of an individual may vary in degree and remains fairly stable over a period of years. Hypnosis can be a powerful tool for relieving the psychological experience of pain and is especially effective in the treatment of migraine and vascular headaches which do not respond to traditional medical treatment.

A particularly unusual aspect of the hypnotic state is that hypnotized subjects often display *trance logic*. They accept paradoxical facts that would seem illogical in a nontrance state, suggesting that hypnosis may involve a dissociation of the various levels of information processing.

States of Consciousness

Helen is undergoing exploratory surgery. She has been given a deep general anesthesia because her surgery involves painful probing of the mouth region.

"Good gracious. . . . It may not be a cyst at all," exclaims the physician. "It may be cancer!" Fortunately, the biopsy proves the cyst to be benign and the physician's reaction merely a false alarm. No need for Helen to worry now.

But Helen *is* depressed. The next day she cries uncontrollably for no apparent reason. Attempts to relax her and restore her usual good spirits are unsuccessful. Under hypnosis, a therapist asks Helen to lift her hand if something is disturbing her. Helen's hand rises suddenly.

"Good gracious," she exclaims. "The cyst may be cancerous!" After being able to express her fear openly and being reassured, Helen's depression lifts. Was it possible that in her unconscious anesthetized state, some part of Helen's mind was still conscious of its surroundings? Could she still be registering information though seemingly unconscious?

To investigate this possibility, a formal study was conducted to see if anesthetized patients were responsive to information presented during an operation. Ten patients were anesthetized and their EEG brain waves monitored. At the point when each patient's brain-wave pattern indicated he was profoundly anesthetized, the anesthetist said in an urgent tone:

"Just a moment. I don't like the patient's colour. The lips are too blue, very blue. More oxygen please (pause). . . . Good, everything is fine now."

None of the patients recalled anything about the operation. However, when they were hypnotized and a suggestion given to reexperience the operation, four of the ten "were able to repeat practically verbatim the traumatic words used by the anesthetist. A further four patients displayed a severe degree of anxiety while reliving the operation. At a crucial moment they woke from the hypnosis and refused to participate further. The remaining two patients, though seemingly capable of reliving the operation under hypnosis, denied hearing anything" (Levinson, 1967, p. 202).

In other studies recorded suggestions for quick recovery, given during general anesthesia, had positive effects. Postoperative pain-killing medication was needed less (Hutchins, 1961), and patients could be released from the hospital two and a half days sooner than control-group patients who heard either music or silence during their anesthesia (Pearson, 1961).

These studies force us to recognize a new dimension of complexity in human functioning. Even when deeply anesthetized by powerful drugs, we may still remain conscious of significant events taking place in our environment. Furthermore, even when we have no memory of those events in our normal waking state, they may continue to influence our moods, behavior, and physiological reactions.

In these instances, the usual operation of conscious awareness was altered — first by drugs and then by hypnotic procedures. But consciousness can be changed in other less dramatic ways. You practice mind alteration every time you daydream or indulge in fantasy. At night you enter another realm of consciousness when you fall asleep and change reality by dreaming. In this chapter the spotlight is on normal and alternate states of consciousness.

What is consciousness?

Consciousness in its normal state is typically assumed to reflect what we are aware of, attending to, thinking about. In some views, consciousness is an intellectual, rational, logical ego state. It is a state in which the ego processes information about both the external environment and internal functioning. It does so with the goal of understanding reality in order to adapt to it. Simply put, ordinary *consciousness is awareness of one's own thought processes and of external events*. It is not an entity, an all-or-none condition, but rather a process and a continuum of experience.

Consciousness, one might say, is what occurs when the mind looks in on the brain's activity. We can experience an awareness that is distinct from the particular *content* of that awareness at a given time. In addition, there is sometimes an awareness of our being aware—a self-awareness. At other times, we become so absorbed in mental activity that we lose our self-awareness totally.

A useful orientation is provided for us by Charles Tart, one of the pioneers in the study of states of consciousness. He writes:

"For any given individual, his normal state of consciousness is the one in which he spends the major part of his waking hours. That your normal state of consciousness and mine are quite similar and are similar to that of all normal men is an almost universal assumption, albeit one of questionable validity. An altered state of consciousness for a given individual is one in which he clearly feels a <u>qualitative</u> shift in his pattern of mental functioning; that is, he feels not just a <u>quantitative</u> shift (more or less alert, more or less visual imagery, sharper or duller, etc.) but also that some quality or qualities of his mental processes are <u>different</u>. Mental functions operate that do not operate at all ordinarily, perceptual qualities appear that have no normal counterparts, and so forth. There are numerous borderline cases in which the individual cannot clearly distinguish just how his state of consciousness is different from normal, where quantitative changes in mental functioning are very marked, etc., but the existence of borderline states and difficult-to-describe effects does not negate the existence of feelings of clear, qualitative changes in mental functioning that are the criterion of altered states of consciousness" (Tart, 1969, pp. 1 – 2).

The use of the term *altered* has been criticized because it implies that there is one standard, desirable state of consciousness. Most researchers today prefer to speak of *alternate* or *extended* states of consciousness, since these words carry no implication of abnormality.

Ordinary waking consciousness is the most familiar state of consciousness. Daydreaming, fantasy, and sleep dreaming are the alternate states with which we are most familiar. Consuming large quantities of alcohol or other drugs leads to other alternate states that many people are acquainted with. ◆ Changes in consciousness are also brought about through meditation, prayer, and spiritual or mystical experiences. In one survey, two out of every five Americans questioned reported having had some sort of "mystical" experience (Greeley & McCready, 1975). Less familiar to most of us are the alternate states of consciousness associated with trance, biofeedback (to be discussed in Chapter 18), and psychotic hallucinations.

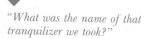

◆
"What was the name of that tranquilizer we took?"

Drawing by Alan Dunn; © 1957, The New Yorker Magazine, Inc.

Psychology and the study of consciousness

In the early days of psychology, consciousness was the "mental stuff" to be analyzed scientifically. It was different from the material substance that biologists and physicists dealt with, but at the same time had more substance than the vague concepts philosophers talked about. Psychology was defined in those nineteenth-century days as "the science of consciousness." Its data were the contents of subjects' awareness. Its analytical method was introspection (see p. 25). In America, William James gave the study of consciousness legitimacy by his attempt to analyze the "stream of consciousness." This everchanging flow of awareness seemed to be an important and central aspect of mental life. Freud went further in postulating an *unconscious* stream of sensations and perceptions. In Freudian theory unconscious mental activity is the *primary process* through which we experience reality directly. When that experience is filtered through intellectual, rational thought patterns to make it more socially acceptable, it becomes *secondary process*.

As we saw in Chapter 3, John Watson and the early behaviorists would have nothing to do with consciousness, be it the ordinary kind or the unconscious variety. The pragmatic force of behaviorism held sway in the United States for more than the next fifty years.

In the last decade, consciousness has quietly slipped back into psychology. Concern with issues of consciousness and a fresh approach to their investigation has come from a variety of areas within psychology. Neuroscientists are discovering that we have two minds in one head. Sperry and Gazzaniga have shown that each of the cerebral hemispheres carries out quite different, although complementary, functions (see Wittrock et al., 1977). Sleep researchers have perfected a technology for objectively measuring the depth of sleep. Hypnosis research and the notion of dissociated consciousness (see Chapters 1 and 14) have gained new respectability through the rigorous research of Ernest Hilgard (1977). Meanwhile, humanistic psychology has emphasized the study of the whole human organism — the thinking, feeling part as well as the acting, behaving part. In addition, the openness of the humanistic approach led to a new tolerance for and interest in "esoteric psychologies." These are psychologies not in the western analytical tradition, but rather in the oriental traditions of Zen, Yoga, mind control, and those based on nonordinary reality (Tart, 1975b).

Two other movements also paved the way for a reemergence of consciousness in psychological study. The drug cultures of the sixties offered considerable firsthand evidence of the profound impact of psychedelic agents on transforming normal levels of awareness. At a more academic level, many psychologists realized that the "rat psychology" which grew out of behaviorism's attempt to get rid of human subjectivism, had run its course into a dead end. Once psychologists discovered the value of an information-processing approach, they had to admit there might be "deep cognitive structures" and "internal representations." (See *P&L* Close-up, Worldwide Consciousness Alteration.)

Describing consciousness

It is important to recognize that the concept of consciousness is itself a construction of our minds. There is no validation by others for your experience of consciousness, normal or otherwise. The events that change your consciousness might have no effect on someone else, or be a very different qualitative experience for each of you. To study consciousness scientifically involves the use of multiple operations, which taken together yield a coherent picture. Among the operations employed are subjects' self-reports, performance measures under different conditions, behavioral observations, and physiological recordings.

While we make a great point about our conscious, monitoring self, we are usually not conscious of all those things in our daily experience which are most *habitual*. We are not aware or our clothes, gravity, the room temperature, or our breathing because we have habituated to them, put them out of consciousness because they are constant, recurring, and "uneventful." Jaynes

Close-up
Worldwide Consciousness Alteration

Anthropologists have observed that most societies have distinct conceptions of "the secular, or profane" and "the holy, or sacred." The secular involves all attempts to adapt to the environment as perceived realistically through the senses. Work, technology, education, ego control, career are aspects of the secular world. In contrast stands the sacred world which is more highly charged emotionally since it originates in the attempt to adapt to basic anxieties. Sacred knowledge derives from revelations given to ancestors, dreams of prophets, or visions of culture heroes believed to have a "direct line" to the mystical world of the supernatural.

Sacred rituals usually occur in a special holy place, removed from the profane reality of everyday life. Critical reality testing, and logical reasoning may be dulled by repetitive prayers, music, dance, paradoxes, and confusion. This leads to a willing opening of self to mystical union with supernatural forces. Often this possession by spirits is facilitated by states of intoxication with alcohol or hallucinogenic substances. The society may encourage dreaming, trances, or drug taking to make contact with and gain control over supernatural forces (La Barre, 1975).

Among the Jivaro Indians of the Ecuadorian Amazon, "normal waking life is simply a 'lie,' or illusion, while the true forces that determine daily events are supernatural and can only be manipulated with the aid of hallucinogenic drugs" (Harner, 1973, p. 16). While this is an extreme reversal of our (secular) view about what is reality, many societies practice techniques to alter reality-based consciousness. In a survey of 488 societies covering every region of the world, 90 percent were found to engage in one or more institutionalized, culturally patterned forms of altering consciousness. The highest incidence of culturally institutionalized altered states (97%) is found among societies of aboriginal North America and the lowest (80%) among those around the Mediterranean. These institutionalized altered states are classified by anthropologist Erika Bourguignon (1973) into two broad categories: (1) states interpreted by the societies in which they occur as due to possession by spirits (termed "possession trance"), and (2) states not so interpreted (termed "trance"). *Possession trance* generally "involves the impersonation of spirits—the acting out of their speech or behavior. It does not involve hallucinations, and it is typically followed by amnesia." Possession trances tend to be public, enacted in rituals and psychologically "contagious." *Trance* "may involve the repetition of messages of spirits to an audience, the imitation of the actions of spirits, or the narration of the subject's spirit journey; or it may involve a private, isolated hallucinatory experience of the individual, as in the vision quest of North American Indians" (p. 12). Trances usually include hallucinations, but no amnesia for the experience (see also Bourguignon, 1976).

(1976) has pointed out six things consciousness is not. It is *not*: (1) necessary for learning, (2) necessary for thinking, (3) necessary for concepts, (4) necessary for reason, (5) localized in a particular place, and (6) it is not even a carbon copy of experience. To demonstrate the last point, perform a bit of introspection: visualize the last time you went swimming. If you are like most people, you *imagined seeing yourself swimming*. But in your direct experience you did not observe yourself from an outsider's perspective. Your experience was what you saw in front of you and felt as your arms lifted out of the water, and so forth.

How do you describe the sensations, impressions, and ideas of your consciousness? Even though consciousness is a unique subjective experience, nevertheless we can communicate to one another some of its basic similarities. A framework for analyzing states of consciousness developed by Caryl Marsh (1977) combines four features:

a. *Focus* is the directing of one's attention either to external objects, people and events, or inwardly to our own process of thought and feeling. It is a continuum like that of the focus adjustment on your camera or TV set.

b. *Structure* of consciousness is divided into *background, foreground,* and *aerial view.* In the *background* are the more constant, general aspects of reality, such as knowledge of time, place, space, identity, and bodily functioning. In the *foreground* are the momentary, fleeting impressions, desires, and reactions that capture our attention. The *aerial* dimension of structure is provided by an overview of one's awareness of oneself observing this framework of consciousness. Each of these structural properties may shift with changes in states of consciousness.

c. *Attributes* of consciousness are those qualities that describe the image, the action, and the setting of conscious experience. Images of one's self and of others may be: passive/active; controlled/controlling; distorted/realistic; blurred/clear; and so forth. Attributes of the scenario of consciousness may also be: familiar/unfamiliar; organized/jumbled; significant/meaningless; continuous/disjointed; etc.

d. *Flow* is the movement of conscious awareness. It is the constantly shifting change of focus, the stream that carries along our associations, wishes, memories, and sense impressions. Novelists James Joyce and Virginia Woolf developed a "stream-of-consciousness" literary style. In it they explored different levels of awareness, especially the preverbal level we rarely express.

> ". . . *Sticks too like a summer cold, sore on the mouth. Cut with grass or paper worst. Friction of the position. Like to be the rock she sat on. O sweet little, you don't know how nice you looked. I begin to like them at that age. Green apples. Grab at all they offer*" (Joyce, <u>Ulysses</u>, 1934, p. 370).

Though ever changing, the states of consciousness somehow seem to hang together with an identifiable constancy—identified, of course, by the individual who is monitoring his or her own consciousness. Are there common characteristics among the many varieties of altered states of consciousness? Surprisingly, many similar qualities have been described despite the differences in the settings giving rise to the experiences. (See *P&L* Close-up, What Are Alternate States of Consciousness Really Like?)

It should be apparent to you by now that consciousness is a "fuzzy concept" and its alternate states even fuzzier. Perhaps you can better appreciate why the behaviorists wanted to build a science of psychology upon a firmer foundation. But then again, maybe the metaphor is wrong. It may be better not to think of consciousness as the foundation in the basement, but the skylight at the top of the human edifice.

Daydreaming

After reading the following instructions, close your eyes, and determine how clearly you can visualize each one of the following: (a) a full moon coming over the horizon; (b) inheriting a million dollars; (c) your happiest birthday; (d) what you should have said to the teacher you disliked most in elementary or high school; (e) your next vacation.

These "pictures in the mind's eye," when arranged in some scenario of

Close-up
What Are Alternate States of Consciousness Really Like?

The following seven characteristics have often been found in reports of alternate or extended states of consciousness.

1. *Distortions of perceptual processes, time sense, and body image.* A common characteristic is distortion of many familiar perceptions, including those of the visual and auditory senses, as well as those of time and space. A sense of being separate from one's body, or of having portions of the body feel and/or look very different from usual, is often reported.

2. *Feelings of objectivity and ego-transcendence.* This is the sense that one is viewing the world with greater objectivity, more able to perceive phenomena as if they were independent of oneself and even of all human beings. One seems to be able to divorce oneself from personal needs and desires and see things as they "really" are, in some ultimate, impersonal sense. Sometimes this sense of objectivity is experienced as a loss of control, a feeling of being outside oneself. This may be either positive or negative.

3. *Self-validating sense of truth.* The experience may be seen as more "real" or "true" than the perceptions of ordinary consciousness. Knowledge itself is experienced at an "intuitive" level and one "sees" beyond appearances into essential qualities.

4. *Positive emotional quality.* Joy, ecstasy, reverence, peace, and overwhelming love are frequently reported when transcendent experiences are interpreted within a religious or philosophical framework. In the reports of Eastern mystics, the experience is less one of ecstasy than of a deep and profoundly restful peace in which the individual seems in harmony with all things.

5. *Paradoxicality.* Descriptions of alternate states of consciousness tend to seem contradictory and illogical when analyzed on logical, rational grounds. The polarities of life seem to be experienced simultaneously, to reach some resolution, and yet to remain separate.

6. *Ineffability.* Individuals frequently claim an inability to communicate the experience. The qualities seem so unique that no words seem appropriate. Often, too, the experience seems to contain so many paradoxical qualities that it makes no sense to describe it.

7. *Unity and fusion.* Distinctions and discontinuities may disappear between self and others, between past, present, and future, between animate and inanimate, between inner and outer reality, and between actual and potential. The separateness of self vanishes, the boundaries dissolve, and there is a fusion of self with what previously was nonself. Other characteristics sometimes mentioned in various reports are feelings of rejuvenation, sudden, intense emotionality, extreme suggestibility, loss of control, and ideas that assume new significance and meaning (Ludwig, 1966; Nideffer, 1976).

wish fulfillment, playful imagining, planning or obsessional rehearsal, are the stuff of daydreams. Jerome Singer (1966, 1976) has systematically examined the nature of daydreaming. His pioneering research has done much to reveal the psychological significance of daydreams.

Daydreaming means a shift of attention away from an ongoing physical or mental task, or away from a perceptual response to external stimulation toward a covert response to some internal stimulus. The *operational definition of daydreaming* is: "the report of thoughts that involve a shift of attention away from an immediately demanding task" (Singer, 1975, p. 730). Do you daydream, according to such definitions? You're in good company if you do. Almost all people surveyed report that they daydream. In one sample of 240 respondents ages eighteen to fifty, with some college education, 96 percent reported daydreaming daily. Most daydreaming was reported by young adults (ages eighteen to twenty-nine), with a significant decline with age (Singer & McCraven, 1961).

Novelist James Thurber has given us the marvelous character Walter Mitty (1942), whose mundane life is spiced by heroic, wish-fulfilling daydreams. But daydreaming is less likely to involve wild speculations of a wishful nature than fairly practical, immediate concerns, especially future interpersonal behavior. Next in frequency come daydreams dealing with sexual satisfaction, altruistic concerns, unusual good fortune (inheriting money), and likely future events (vacations).

In general, research shows that daydreaming is a common human activity when people are alone and in restful motor states. Most daydreaming is reported to occur in bed shortly before sleep. Daydreaming is least frequent upon awakening in the morning, and during meals or sexual activity. Most people report that they enjoy daydreaming and deny that it embarrasses them because they feel it is a normal function. In fact, it well may be that daydreaming, in part, is a form of visual imagery that allows the individual to explore possible options and to take trial actions toward the constructive solution of present and future problems. Wishes and reality-testing activities form the basic core of our daydreams. ■

The characteristics of daydreams can be distinguished using the framework for describing consciousness. In daydreams *focus* of attention is turned inward; *structure* has both foreground and background, but no overview; *attributes* of the contents of the daydream include imagined, improbable, meaningful, familiar actions that are clear and organized, but "blurred around the edges"; *flow* is slow, as sense of time is abandoned or purposely slowed down.

Why is it that our daydreams seem pale in comparison to the vividness of night dreams? During the night external stimulation is reduced to a minimum, overt movements stopped, and competing activities brought to a halt. A direct consequence of shutting out the noises of living is opening ourselves to the inner sounds of imagining. All of our mental energies can be directed inwardly to the dream show. By contrast, during waking hours, daydreams are imposed upon ongoing mental and behavioral functioning. We have to keep open and engage the same sensory processing channels for daydreaming as for daytime coping. Indeed when dreams in the day seem as vivid as those in sleep, you are probably close to having a more profound alteration of consciousness—a hallucination.

■

Daydreaming is natural for people of all ages. It provides a means of transcending time and space. We can try out new roles, have our wishes fulfilled, travel to exciting places—all in a matter of moments. Only when such activity becomes more "real" and important than the world around us should we begin to worry.

Hallucinations

Hallucinations are vivid perceptions in the absence of objective stimulation. The images and sensations experienced are the products of the hallucinator's mind and not the consequence of external inputs. But who is to say your vision is unreal, or the voices I hear are not really there? Because hallucinatory activity poses a threat to our conception of reality based on consensual validation, it is often considered a sign of mental illness. Under some circumstances, however, hallucinations are not dismissed as the fantasies of madness, but honored as the insights of visionaries.

Hallucinations can occur "naturally" during states of high fever, epilepsy, migraine headaches, sensory deprivation, and nervous disorders. They have also been associated with heightened arousal states and religious ecstasies. Drug-induced hallucinations come from ingestion of LSD, hashish, peyote, and other psychedelics, as well as from withdrawal of alcohol in alcoholics (delerium tremens or the "DTs"). There are, in fact, a surprisingly large number of situations which give rise to hallucinatory experiences.

Analysis of four properties of visual hallucinations will help us categorize the situations in which hallucinations occur (Horowitz, 1975).

a. There is a shift from verbal representations to images.
b. Internal sources of information take precedence over the external.
c. The images are appraised incorrectly as if they reflected the immediate outer realm of information.
d. The hallucinatory episode intrudes upon all other functioning without intention, and often without awareness of its intrusiveness.

From this analysis, it follows that hallucinatory activity can become more prominent under the following circumstances:

a. Increased visual imagery relative to verbal thought.
b. Failure to label and appraise images accurately.
c. Reduced external sensory stimulation (sensory deprivation).
d. Heightened arousal and states of intense needs, strong drives, high stress (overload).
e. Lowered self-awareness as a critical thinker.
f. Inability to suppress threatening, unconscious thoughts.
g. Isolation from normal sources of reality appraisal, such as critical feedback from trusted others in a familiar setting.

Instead of asking what turns hallucinations on, some psychologists wonder "why do we not hallucinate all the time?" Their answer is that the ability to hallucinate is always present in each of us, but inhibited. It is prevented from manifesting itself under certain conditions (the ones opposite to those outlined above). To suppress hallucinations, according to this view, requires adequate sensory input, reality testing, and interaction feedback from the environment.

Sensory deprivation and overload

The distortions of experience that occur under conditions of sensory deprivation were perhaps the first altered states of consciousness to be studied seriously by psychologists. It was found that any situation that involves unusual or prolonged reduction in the normal level of stimulus input or in the individual's motor functioning can give rise to such experiences. Prolonged solitary confinement, sensory and social deprivation (as occurs in the Arctic or at sea), and even prolonged immobilization in a body cast or an iron lung have been shown to result in hallucinations and other changes in cognitive functioning.

It seems clear from present experimental findings that meaningful sensory experiences are necessary for the normal functioning of the brain. The complex, continually active brain, which never even allows itself forty winks, apparently demands that the environment, too, stay awake and provide stimulating conversation. Sensory isolation may be thought of as a means of "destructuring the environment." The subject, made uncertain and anxious by the lack of an orientation in space and time, has a tendency to try to structure the environment and restore meaning to the situation. In this attempt, the fantasies, hallucinations, and perceptual distortions that appear are in accordance with the subject's personality and past environment, as well as with the experimental setting.

Reduced or impaired sensory input is responsible for hallucinations among people suffering progressive hearing losses and those with progressive blindness from cataracts. They are similar to the phantom limb syndrome in which an amputated limb is hallucinated as still giving rise to sensations. In the absence of familiar peripheral stimuli the brain may compensate by providing stored memories of the activities of these senses and motor systems. (See *P&L* Close-up, I Am My Brother's Keeper.)

In sensory isolation experiments sense information is artificially reduced or depatterned. (You can achieve such an effect by taping half a Ping-Pong ball over each eye and sitting quietly for an hour, with your eyes open.)

In one study of sixteen subjects who underwent a week or more of sensory isolation in a chamber where auditory and visual stimulation were virtually eliminated, eleven experienced hallucinations. They were mostly flashes of light, flickering lights, dim glowing lights, and so on, that lacked shape and usually appeared in the peripheral field of vision. The hallucinations were usually of very short duration, about five to ten seconds, although some were reported to last for as long as fifteen minutes.

In addition to visual hallucinations, several auditory hallucinations were reported. These were usually very realistic, such as howling dogs, a ringing alarm clock, and the sound of a typewriter. Two tactual-kinesthetic hallucinations were also reported. One consisted of cold steel pressing on the subject's forehead and checks; the other was a sensation of someone pulling the mattress from under the subject. In most instances, the auditory and tactual hallucinations were reported during the last two days of isolation (Zubeck, Pushkar, Sansom, & Gowing, 1961).

Other studies demonstrated that a low level of diffuse visual and auditory stimulation had even more profound effects than an absence of stimulation. The following changes were reported in one such study.

Visual hallucinations were generally quite simple at the beginning, but later became more vivid and complex. At first there was a general lighting of the visual field, then dots or lines of light, then geometric figures and patterns. Finally full scenes appeared. One man thought he saw things coming at him and withdrew his head accordingly when this occurred; one was convinced that pictures were being projected on his goggles; another felt that someone was with him in the cubicle. These hallucinations were more vivid than normal imagery and appeared to be projected as on a movie screen in front of the subject, rather than in the "mind's-eye" as is normally the case with imagery. Such experiences could be endured for only a few days, even though the subjects were being paid $20 a day (Heron, 1961).

The need to be alert and vigilant for a long time can also result in hallucinations or changed perceptions. Such experiences frequently arise from prolonged vigilance during sentry duty, fervent prayer, intense mental absorption in some all-consuming task, or concentrated attention on an external object or internal sensation.

Many similar instances are reported following such "overstimulating" experiences as mob riots, religious revival meetings, prolonged dancing (such as is done by "whirling" dervishes), extreme fright or panic, trance states during primitive ceremonies of numerous kinds, or moments of extreme emotion (whether the emotion be ecstatic love or unbearable grief).

Common patterns of hallucination

Hallucinations are private events, but they have much in common from person to person within a given kind of experience. While schizophrenic hallucinations tend to be auditory (hearing voices), visual ones are more likely in drug intoxication. Experiments by Ronald Siegel and Murray Jarvik (1975) show that, in a wide variety of hallucinatory conditions, there are common types of hallucination which develop systematically over time and with intensity of the experienced state. For instance, there are two stages in drug-induced imagery. In the first stage simple, constant form patterns appear.

In the process of doing the background research for this chapter I discovered the explanation for a most extraordinary hallucination I had about fifteen years ago. It was my first day back to work after recovering from a traumatic automobile accident. I was lucky to be alive with only torn ligaments in my leg and a concussion; the driver had been killed by the impact of the head-on collision. As I hobbled up the three flights of stairs supported by a crutch, my initial joy of returning to school was suddenly suspended. With each step I took a strange sensation occurred: I could "feel" myself *becoming* my younger brother, George. Not *imagine* "as if" I were George, but being transformed physically to be him.

I perceived my face changing to be his face and my body doing likewise. My limp became more pronounced, and it took great strength to climb the last flight. In a panic, I shut myself in my office, not wanting anyone to witness this strange transformation. I avoided looking at my reflection in the window for fear I would see his face and not mine. Had I really become my brother or was I *merely* hallucinating?

Time passed during which I tried frantically to relax, "to pull myself together," and make sense of my distorted sense impressions. After all, I was a normal, serious scientist type not given to such flights of fancy. I lived by the reality principle.

My secretary and colleagues knocked and came into the office before I could say I was busy. They were worried by my abrupt disappearing act. They were relieved to see I was "my old self again," and I was relieved to see them responding to me as if I were Phil and not George. A glance at my reflection confirmed my hope. I had changed back, "or was no longer George, . . . or George was no longer manifesting himself in me." Whatever? Weird, no? But why?

The source of explanation is to be found in an article on the determinants of hallucinatory experiences (Horowitz, 1975). I learned from it that memories of early motor response systems and reflex responses can be retained and reactivated later in similar sensory situations. Such motor response memories are called *enactive thought.* "The memory of information capable of transformation into enactive representations would grow from two sources: the memory of motor actions by the self which have a successful effect, and the *retention of mimicry [imitation] responses to the motor activity of someone else*" (p. 168).

When we were children, George had infantile paralysis and for a time had to wear leg braces and walk with crutches. I would accompany him to therapy sessions and observe his frustration, embarrassment, and anger at not being able to function normally. Since we were only eighteen months apart in age, I could readily empathize with his feelings. I may have also felt guilty at being glad I too was not crippled. Once I recall volunteering to exchange places with him in the swimming pool exercises, but the nurse chided me, "being crippled is not fun and games, young man." I was about four at the time.

As I hobbled up the stairs to my office some twenty-five years later, the pattern of feedback sensory stimulation reactivated this prerecorded motor action plan. Memories of George's posture and movement were being enacted. I had retained mimicry responses of his motor activity that I had observed so intensely. Now I was changing places with him, but not consciously and not volitionally. The suddenness and vividness of the hallucination was frightening because it was so real, yet at the same time contradicted my knowledge of reality.

The four primary forms are: lattices, cobwebs, tunnels, and spirals. They can occur separately or together and may be brightly colored and moving. There are similar form constants that can sometimes accompany severe migraine attacks. In the second stage more complex forms appear which may incorporate the simpler constant forms. The hallucinating person "sees" landscapes,

These paintings were made by Huichol Indians using yarn and beeswax on wood. They depict hallucinations induced by use of the drug peyote. The first is an eyes-open hallucination of a tree; the second depicts deer's heads rotating around the brightness of the fire god.

faces, people, familiar places and objects. The specific forms experienced tend to be of images activated from those stored in memory.

In a review of more than five hundred hallucinations induced by LSD, about two thirds of the subjects experienced the simple geometric form constants, while nearly 80 percent reported similar complex images. Friendly small animals and humans in caricatures or cartoons were the most commonly hallucinated images (Siegel, 1977). Curiously, similar stages are found in psychedelic experiences in the modern industrialized world and in peyote states of Huichol Indians, as shown in their weaving and art. ●

Subjects were trained to recognize and rapidly report three categories of visual imagery. Then trained and untrained subjects were tested in weekly sessions where they received either a hallucinogen, a stimulant, a depressant, or a placebo. The results were startling. Black-and-white random forms moving about aimlessly were the images that accompanied placebos, amphetamines, and phenobarbitol. Hallucinogens (LSD, psilocybin, and mescaline) brought an explosion of pattern, color, and movement into the hallucinations. Initially black-and-white hues turned blue, then over time shifted to red, orange, and yellow. The forms were organized in geometric patterns that increased in complexity. The movement was pulsating but organized. Complex imagery began 90 to 120 minutes into the drug experience. These images tended to be childhood memories and emotionally charged events that were embellished into fantastic scenes.

At the peak of the hallucinatory experience, the subjects reported merging with the visualized scene. They were part of their hallucination, not outside looking in on it. The feeling of bodily dissociation was frequently reported. Scenes changed rapidly, as many as ten images changed per second. Trained subjects were better able to describe the complexity of their rapidly shifting images (Siegel, 1977).

Religious visions might represent states of hysteria, psychoses, ecstasies, intoxication, epilepsy, or migraines. A unique example is the visions of the nun and mystic Hildegard of Bingen (1098–1180), which have been interpreted as "indisputably migrainous" (Sacks, 1973). The visions she recorded can be accounted for by consistent patterns of visual imagery produced by migraines. ▲

▲ *This drawing by the mystic Hildegard of Bingen depicts a vision of a shower of brilliant stars, extinguished after its passage. It is typical of a migraine-induced hallucination.*

Sleeping and dreaming

We slip daily between states of consciousness as we move from waking to sleeping and then to dreaming. And in that drowsy interval between being awake and sleeping is the hypnagogic state, which itself is a uniquely altered state of consciousness. Few areas of human behavior have been the subject of such intensive recent research as that of sleep. Hundreds of studies have been conducted in the past decade that reveal an incredible amount of mental and physiological activity taking place when we are asleep and apparently "out of it."

If sleep is a mysterious part of life, then how much more so is dreaming? Our dreams violate the usual principles of rationality, logic, perception, time, and space as well as many of our habits and moral standards; yet while they are taking place, they seem quite normal and real. There is no certain knowledge about why we dream or what dreams mean or even if they *have* a meaning. Nevertheless, each of us knows that something strange, wonderful, or frightening occurs in our heads when we abandon the ordinary consciousness that guides our everyday journeys.

The behavior we call "sleep"

In studying sleep, psychologists are concerned primarily with *internal* behavior—that is, processes that are presumed to take place inside each person. However, as we have seen, before we can study such behavior, we must find a way to make it external so it can be observed and measured.

The lack of early research on sleep was due primarily to the lack of appropriate methodology. The methodological breakthrough for the study of sleep came with the development of the *electroencephalograph* (EEG) that allowed investigators to "listen" to the brain (see Chapter 11). In 1937, Loomis and his associates made the important discovery that brain waves change in form with the onset of sleep and show further systematic changes during the entire sleep period.

The next significant advance in sleep research occurred when it was found that bursts of rapid eye movements appeared at periodic intervals (Aserinsky & Kleitman, 1953). When these rapid eye movements during sleep were linked to dreams (Dement & Kleitman, 1957) many investigators were excited by this new path into the previously hidden side of human activity.

States and stages of sleep

There are two distinct sleep states: non-rapid eye movement sleep (NREM, pronounced non-Rem) and rapid eye movement sleep (REM, pronounced Rem). NREM sleep is also called *orthodox sleep,* while REM sleep has been termed *paradoxical sleep.* Within NREM sleep, three distinct stages have been identified. The basis for objectively determining which kind of sleep and what stage a sleeper is experiencing comes from distinctive EEG patterns of electrical activity of the brain.

Most EEG patterns can be described by two features: their *amplitude* (how high each wave is when its voltage level is translated into movement of a recording pen across a chart), and their *frequency* (the number of cycles of ups and downs occurring each second). Together, amplitude or voltage, and frequency or speed define the *form* of a wave pattern. There are other features of these electrical tracings that the trained observer (and now computers) can recognize. The wave patterns typical of the various stages of sleep are shown in the diagram. ■ In addition to EEG pattern changes, researchers also record electrical changes in muscle action (EMG) and in eyeball movement (EOG, electroculargram).

Let's review what is known about the seemingly simple process of going to sleep. As the normal sleeper relaxes, closes his or her eyes, and becomes

■

EEG patterns of human sleep stages

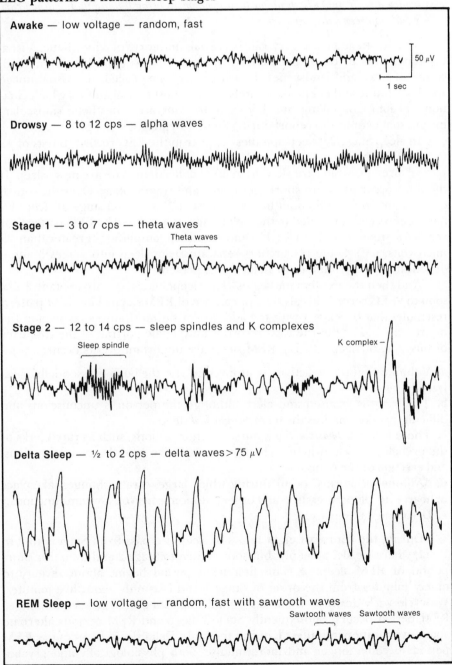

Adapted from Hauri, 1977

drowsy, the EEG pattern shifts from low voltage, and random, fast frequency to an *alpha wave* pattern characterized by waves of 8 to 12 cycles per second (CPS).

Stage 1 is the transition stage between being awake and sleeping. It is usually a short period, lasting less than ten minutes, in which *theta* waves (3 to 7 CPS) occur. Stage 1 sleep has features of both sleep and awake states, so is better considered as the *hypnagogic state*. In the hypnagogic state reactivity to outside stimuli is reduced, thoughts drift, the anchor of reality is cast off, and hallucinations arise. In the *Leviathan* (1651), Thomas Hobbes provided an early account of the hypnagogic experience:

A man shall in the dark, though awake, have the images of lines and angles before his eyes; which kind of fancy hath no particular name, as being a thing that doth not commonly fall into men's discourse (p. 6).

The hypnagogic imagery can be visual, auditory, or kinesthetic. Visual imagery tends to be of geometric forms and unrecognized, though vivid, scenes of faces and landscapes. Hearing your name called, the visual image speak, or music and chimelike sounds are the most typical auditory hallucinations. Feelings of falling and bodily distortions are kinesthetic (muscular) images that people also report during Stage 1 hypnagogic sleep.

In sleep Stage 2, "sleep spindles" appear in the EEG record (bursts of 12 to 14 CPS that last a half second to two seconds). There are also "K complexes" present, which are slow, large EEG deflections. You are now asleep. If thoughts occur, they are short, mundane, and fragmentary. Over the course of the night you spend about half your time in this second stage of sleep. Finally, deep sleep is reached in the Delta stage. It is defined by EEG patterns of very slow frequency (½ to 2 CPS) and very large amplitude (greater than 75 microvolts, μV). Some researchers separate Delta sleep into Stages 3 and 4 depending on the number of delta waves present.

And then the excitement begins! The sleeper goes back up to Stage 2 and soon the EEG record reveals the appearance of REM sleep. The REM pattern resembles that of Stage 1 with the addition of sawtooth waves (as seen in the figure on p. 445). But the EEG record is only a pale portrait of the character of this state of sleep. During REM sleep five important events occur:

a. Voluntary muscular activity is suppressed and the body is essentially paralyzed.
b. The brain is aroused and alert, although the person is unconscious and difficult to wake up; thus the term *paradoxical* sleep.
c. There is much *phasic activity*, bursts of short actions, such as rapid jerks of the eyeballs, muscle twitches, changes in pupil size, middle ear contractions, and erection of the penis.
d. "Autonomic storms" occur during which large, erratic changes take place in heart rate, blood pressure, and other autonomic nervous system functions.
e. Dreaming takes place.

During the course of eight hours of sleep, we pass from Stage 1 to 2 to Delta, where we sleep deeply, but soon return to Stage 2 and then to a short period of REM sleep. ▲ This first REM period begins about seventy to ninety minutes from the onset of Stage 1 and lasts only about five minutes. We cycle back down to Delta sleep and Stage 2 before the second, longer REM period occurs. Subsequently Stage 2 sleep and REM periods alternate about every ninety minutes. Later in the night Delta sleep drops out as REM periods become longer and more intense, both physiologically and psychologically. Even in people who sleep well, sleep is interrupted by body move-

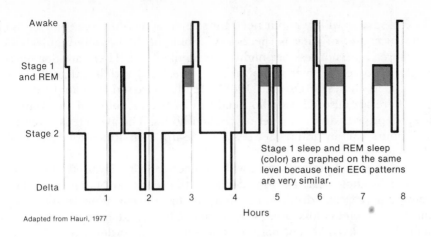

Stage 1 sleep and REM sleep (color) are graphed on the same level because their EEG patterns are very similar.

Adapted from Hauri, 1977

ments and a series of brief awakenings. It appears that too many body movements are as detrimental to sound sleep as are too few; the optimal number is about one every fifteen minutes.

This progression varies somewhat from person to person according to individual circumstances, but it is relatively constant for healthy young adults. No sex differences have been found in the cycles of sleep, but age does make an important difference. Infants and children up to about age four spend substantially more of their total sleep time in the REM and Stage 4 periods. In elderly people the REM period is slightly shorter and the Stage 4 period is much shorter than when they were younger. Apparently older people get less sleep and less deep sleep. ●

Things that go wrong in the night

How much sleep do we need? What happens when we don't get enough? Can we get by with less? What are sleep disorders?

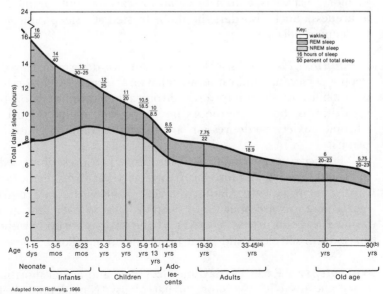

Adapted from Roffwarg, 1966

● **Patterns of human sleep over a lifetime**

The graph shows changes with age in total amounts of daily sleep, both REM and NREM, and percentage of REM sleep. Note that the amount of REM sleep decreases considerably over the years, while NREM sleep diminishes less sharply.

We vary so widely in our need for sleep that it seems to be entirely an individual matter of what is "necessary." Some healthy adults regularly sleep only three hours or less per night with no ill effects. There are documented cases of people who manage to function effectively with less than one hour's daily sleep (Jones & Oswald, 1968; Meddis, Pearson, & Langford, 1973). But there are also adults who need ten to twelve hours of sleep and feel sleep deprived when they get only seven hours. The average is seven and a half hours for an adult. (See *P&L* Close-up, Ten Rules for Better Sleep Hygiene.)

An extended period of time without sleep can alter a variety of physiological and psychological reactions. Some of the results are fatigue, headaches, tremor, perceptual distortions, difficulty in concentration, disorientation, immediate memory loss, brain-wave abnormalities, and, in some people, paranoid ideas and vivid hallucinations. The effects of sleep deprivation, however, are not merely a simple function of how long the person has gone without sleep; environmental, personality, motivational, and age variables also determine its impact on behavior.

But one good night's sleep is enough to restore ordinary functioning. In a group of four healthy adult males who were closely studied as they underwent 205 hours of sleep deprivation, their psychopathological reactions did not extend beyond the actual period of sleep deprivation itself (Kollar et al., 1969).

We can't live without sleep or function well with prolonged periods of sleep deprivation, but we can sleep less than we do. A recent study trained people to reduce the amount of time spent sleeping (Mullaney, Johnson, Naitoh, Friedman, & Globus, 1976). Couples gradually reduced their total sleep time by thirty minutes every two weeks until they were sleeping only six hours. Thereafter they continued to reduce their sleep time by thirty minutes over every three-year period. Participation was terminated at different total sleep times. One year after completion of the study, the majority of participants still slept one to two-and-a-half hours less than they had before the experiment began. There were no visible signs of distress.

Pathological sleep problems that result in excessive sleepiness over long periods of time can dramatically alter consciousness in about 95 percent of the patient population. Among the most common consequences are lapses of memory, blackouts, automatic behavior (carrying out routine actions without awareness). Such disorders should be treated at a sleep clinic, *not* by resorting to sleeping pills.

Insomnia *Insomnia* is a sleep disorder not determined by the amount of sleep a person has, but rather in behavioral terms: "A person has insomnia if his inability to sleep interferes chronically with efficient daytime function, regardless of how many hours he sleeps each night" (Hauri, 1977, p. 17). Chronic anxiety or depression are the most common causes of such complaints.

Physicians traditionally treat insomniacs by prescribing sedatives. Nothing could be worse because this treatment transforms temporary psychological distress into a longer lasting medical problem, that of drug-related insomnia. Tolerances are built up to sleeping pills, so over time greater amounts become less effective as sedatives. If the drug is abruptly withdrawn, nightmare-disturbed sleep and heart problems often follow.

Narcolepsy Excessive daytime sleepiness and actual short naps are a primary and disabling symptom of narcolepsy. Narcoleptics go limp and fall asleep at the most inopportune times—while working, making love, or throw-

Not poppy nor mandragora
Nor all the drowsy syrups
of the world,
Shall ever medicine thee to
that sweet sleep
Which thou owed'st
yesterday.
Shakespeare
Othello

Close-up
Ten Rules for Better Sleep Hygiene

"1. Sleep as much as needed to feel refreshed and healthy during the following day, but not more. Curtailing time in bed a bit seems to solidify sleep; excessively long times in bed seem related to fragmented and shallow sleep.

2. A regular arousal time in the morning seems to strengthen circadian cycling and to finally lead to regular times of sleep onset.

3. A steady daily amount of exercise probably deepens sleep over the long run, but occasional one-shot exercise does not directly influence sleep during the following night.

4. Occasional loud noises (e.g., aircraft flyovers) disturb sleep even in people who do not awaken because of the noises and cannot remember them in the morning. Sound attenuating the bedroom might be advisable for people who have to sleep close to excessive noise.

5. Although an excessively warm room disturbs sleep, there is no evidence that an excessively cold room solidifies sleep, as has been claimed.

6. Hunger may disturb sleep. A light bedtime snack (especially warm milk or similar drink) seems to help many individuals sleep.

7. An occasional sleeping pill may be of some benefit, but the chronic use of hypnotics is ineffective at most and detrimental in some insomniacs.

8. Caffeine in the evening disturbs sleep, even in persons who do not feel it does.

9. Alcohol helps tense people to fall asleep fast, but the ensuing sleep is then fragmented.

10. Rather than trying harder and harder to fall asleep during a poor night, switching on the light and doing something else may help the individual who feels angry, frustrated, or tense about being unable to sleep."

Reprinted from Hauri, 1977, p. 26.

ing a ball. Unlike normal sleepers, narcoleptics go immediately into **REM** sleep. A typical narcoleptic can suffer fifteen to twenty of these sudden "sleep attacks" a day, each lasting fifteen minutes or less. Narcolepsy may be the result of an inherited brain abnormality. It is readily diagnosed at a sleep clinic and stimulant drugs can reduce its impact. Sadly, many people assume it is a psychological problem, waste money on psychotherapy, and often end up feeling worthless and not in control of their lives. Proper diagnosis is often a great relief to the victim and his or her family.

Air-starved snorers About one of every twenty patients who go to a sleep clinic with complaints of excessive daytime drowsiness suffer from a stoppage of their breathing while sleeping. This disorder is called *sleep apnea*. The usually reliable autonomic control of breathing somehow gets disrupted in these individuals as they fall asleep. Respiratory movements stop, and the reduced oxygen intake upsets the delicate balance of blood chemistry. The patient awakes slightly, struggles for a gulp of air (emitting a loud snore in the process), gets the needed air, and falls asleep again. As soon as sleep begins, the cycle is repeated throughout the night. One sleep apnea sufferer was recorded as having stopped breathing 534 times in one night. He also let out at least 534 snores. Such people find themselves tired and often irritable throughout the day—and irritating at night to anyone within earshot of their snoring (Guilleminault, Billiard, Montplaisir, & Dement, 1975).

To sleep, perchance to dream

When a sleeper is awakened during a REM period, chances are he or she will report having a dream. Subjects aroused during REM sleep recall ongoing

Dreaming during REM and NREM sleep

Definition of Dreaming Used in Study	Percent Recalling REM Dreams	Percent Recalling NREM Dreams
• "any item of specific content"	87	74
• "visual, auditory, or kinesthetic imagery"	82	54
• "a dream recalled in some detail"	69	34
• self-definition by each subject	85	24
• "specific content of mental experience"	86	23
• "detailed dream description"	74	7
• "coherent, fairly detailed description"	79	7
• "any sensory imagery with . . . progression of the mental activity"	81	7
• self-definition by each subject	60	3
• self-definition by each subject	88	0

Adapted from F. R. Freemon, SLEEP RESEARCH: A CRITICAL REVIEW, 1972. Courtesy of Charles C Thomas, Publisher, Springfield, Illinois

visual images that form a coherent drama, are vivid, and may be in color with sound. Despite bizarre or fantasy qualities of the plot, the unreal situation is accepted by the sleeper as "natural." Some dreaming also takes place during NREM periods, but it is of a different quality. Dreaming associated with NREM states is usually devoid of dramatic story content. It is full of specific thoughts but has minimal sensory imagery. The percentage of dreaming reported from REM and NREM awakenings in ten studies and the definitions they used are summarized in the table. ■

The meaning of dreams

Dreams offer a royal road to the mind when it is in a state governed by rules and principles quite different from those that apply during waking.
Hobson & McCarley, 1977

One physiological explanation recently advanced proposes that dreams are the brain's attempt to make a coherent interpretation out of essentially incoherent bursts of ongoing cortical activity during REM sleep. The cortex retrieves memories that could be associated with the signals it is receiving from deep within the brain stem. Finding no logical connections, it makes illogical remote associations or fills the gaps with recent memories (Hobson & McCarley, 1977).

But according to Freud, dreams are much more than the brain in search of a good story to account for its electrical discharges. Dreams are thought to be symbolic expressions of unconscious wishes that have been carefully disguised by an internal "censor." In Freudian terms, what you remember and report of your dreams is the *manifest content*. The real meaning of a dream, however, is in its *latent* (hidden) content—ideas that represent unconscious impulses and wishes that have been denied overt gratification and appear in dreams in disguised form. The manifest content is the acceptable version of the story; the latent content represents the socially or personally unacceptable version—but nevertheless the "true, uncut one." In sleep, the usually vigilant censor is relaxed, and by a variety of psychological processes, unacceptable unconscious material is transformed into an acceptable manifest story line and so slips by. Through *displacement,* for example, emphasis is shifted from the central "naughty" theme to the unimportant but "nice" element.

It is evident from Freud's writing in his classic *Interpretation of Dreams* (1900) that *his* mind was on sex. Thus dream symbols were largely sex symbols in varying states of undress.

" —All elongated objects, such as sticks, tree trunks and umbrellas (the opening of these last being comparable to an erection) may stand for the male organ—as well as all long, sharp weapons, such as knives, daggers and pikes. . . . —Boxes, cases, chests, cupboards and ovens represent the uterus, and also hollow objects, ships, and vessels of all kinds.— Rooms in dreams are usually women; if the various ways in and out of them are represented, this interpretation is scarcely open to doubt. . . . A dream of going through a suite of rooms is a brothel or harem dream. . . . —It is highly probable that all complicated machinery and apparatus occurring in dreams stand for the genitals (and as a rule male ones). . . . Nor is there any doubt that all weapons and tools are used as symbols for the male organ: e.g., ploughs, hammers, rifles, revolvers, daggers, sabres, etc.— In the same way many landscapes in dreams, especially any containing bridges or wooded hills, may clearly be recognized as descriptions of the genitals. . . ." (pp. 354–56)

According to Freud, the two main functions of dreams are to guard sleep and to serve as sources of wish fulfillment. They allow uninterrupted sleep by draining off psychic tensions created during the day, and they allow us to achieve the unconscious fulfillment of our wishes in hallucinated form.

Dreams are real while they last. Can we say more of Life?
Havelock Ellis

Nightmares

When my son, Adam, was four years old he let out a scream of terror in the middle of the night. I tried in vain to comfort him.

"There's a bear chasing me! He's going to hurt me."
"There's no bear; you were sleeping and were only having a nightmare."
"But I'm afraid! It's a real bear."
"Go back to sleep now; the bear will be gone. You'll see it was only a nightmare."
"But how do I know that I'm awake now and not dreaming, and that you're not part of that nightmare thing and that the bear won't come back as soon as I do what you say?"

How indeed? Can we really be so sure that we know what is real and what is imaginary and which form of our consciousness is normal? When was the last time you had a nightmare? Nightmares are surprisingly widespread; 86 percent of a college sample reported at least one in the past year, and 5 percent indicated they had them at least once a week (Feldman & Hersen, 1967).

Nightmare themes often center around catastrophes that the dreamer is helpless to do anything about. Danger, dread, debilitation, and death are common core themes of nightmares. Falling, being chased, and being immobilized when action is necessary are also very frequent. Animals are among the most prominent nightmare characters retrospectively reported by the dreamer.

In laboratory studies of nightmares, where the dreamer is awakened and immediately reports on the nature of the nightmare, some thematic differences occur between REM sleep and Delta sleep. While REM nightmares contain anxiety and threatening material, those occurring in Delta sleep tend to include more internally directed aggression—falling, being crushed, choked, etc., accompanied by screams, vocalization, and more fright than REM dreams. REM nightmares often are continuations of nonnightmare REM dreams (Fisher et al., 1970).

Night terrors, sleepwalking, sleep talking, and nocturnal enuresis (bed wetting) occur in Delta sleep, are most prevalent in young children, and are accompanied by large physiological changes. While there are many intriguing questions one might pose regarding the causes, correlates, and consequences of these terrors of the night, few sound answers are available at the present time.

These two children are enacting dreams which are variations on the common theme of immobilization. The girl had recurrent dreams of being alone in a deserted house, unable to move; the boy of being trapped in a cage within a cage.

Changing consciousness with chemicals

Saturday, April 10, 1965
"I had been experiencing brief flashes of disassociations, or shallow states of nonordinary reality. . . . In going over the images I recalled from my hallucinogenic experience, I had come to the unavoidable conclusion that I had seen the world in a way that was structurally different from ordinary vision. In other states of nonordinary reality I had undergone, the forms and the patterns I had visualized were always within the confines of my visual conception of the world. But the sensation of seeing under the influence of the hallucinogenic smoke mixture was not the same. Everything I saw was in front of me in the direct line of vision; nothing was above or below that line of vision.

"Every image had an irritating flatness, and yet, disconcertingly, a profound depth. Perhaps it would be more accurate to say that the images were a conglomerate of unbelievably sharp details set inside fields of different light; the light in the fields moved, creating an effect of rotation.

"After probing and exerting myself to remember, I was forced to make a series of analogies or similes in order to 'understand' what I had 'seen'" (Castañeda, 1968, pp. 181–182).

This entry from the journal of anthropologist Carlos Castañeda is part of a fascinating record of a five-year apprenticeship to a Mexican Indian "sorcerer," Don Juan, who trained him to achieve awareness and mastery of a world of "nonordinary reality" through the use of peyote, jimson weed, and other plants that produce hallucinatory experiences (1968, 1971, 1972).

This drug-induced alteration in the functioning of mind and in the nature of consciousness was popularized in the 1954 publication of *The Doors of Perception* by Aldous Huxley. Huxley took mescaline as a personal experiment to test the validity of poet William Blake's assertion in *The Marriage of Heaven and Hell*:

"If the doors of perception were cleansed every thing would appear to man as it is, infinite.
"For man has closed himself up, till he sees all thro' narrow chinks of his concern."

Experimenting with other realities

Watch children stand on their heads or spin around in order to make themselves dizzy, and ask them why. "So everything looks funny." "It feels weird." "To see things tumble around in my head." These are the kinds of answers you might get. They underscore the assumption that "human beings are born with a drive to experience modes of awareness other than the normal waking one; from very young ages, children experiment with techniques to change consciousness" (Weil, 1977, p. 37).

Since ancient times, people everywhere have experimented on themselves by ingesting drugs that assisted in altering their perception of reality.

"Every culture throughout history has made use of chemicals to alter consciousness — except the Eskimos, who had to wait for the white man to bring them alcohol, since they could not grow anything" (Weil, quoted in Brecher, 1972, p. 195).

There is archeological evidence for the uninterrupted use of *sophora* seed (called mescal bean) for over ten thousand years in southwestern United States and Mexico. From the ninth millennium B.C. to the nineteenth century, New World peoples smoked sophora to bring on ecstatic hallucinatory visions. Sophora was replaced by the more benign peyote cactus, which is still held as sacred in the rituals of many Indians.

European explorers and missionaries to the New World in the fifteenth and sixteenth centuries helped carry part of this drug culture "back to civilization." They imported coffee and tea (caffeine), tobacco (nicotine), coca leaves (cocaine), marijuana, opium, and other native plants. Despite scientific and governmental opposition to such drugs, once tried in a country they are rarely given up by the people.

It is likely that people learned to seek out mind-altering chemicals in natural plants by observing their reactions on other animals. Field observations and laboratory experiments show that some infrahuman species search out hallucinogens and also hallucinate with them. African elephants have a "passion" for alcohol-filled fruit from the umganu-tree and after eating them become quite tipsy and playful (Carrington, 1959). Like the native Chukchki people in Asia, their reindeer eat hallucinogenic *Amanita muscaria* mushrooms and have been reported to be "intoxicated" (Wasson, 1968).

In modern-day use, drugs are less associated with "sacred" communal rituals to reach new plateaus of mystical awareness. Instead, they tend to be used by individuals to feel mellow, to cope with stress, or to tune out the unpleasantness of current realities.

Drugs that affect mental processes are called *psychoactive* drugs. Among these, the ones that can produce sensory hallucinations are termed *hallucinogenic* and those that can produce abnormal patterns of thought and arousal that mimic psychotic patterns are called *psychotomimetic*. Humphry Osmond, an early researcher in this area, used the term "psychedelic" to indicate the psychological consequences of drugs like LSD. *Psychedelic* means "mind manifesting" and was originally intended to be a scientifically neutral term to characterize drugs that led to altered states of consciousness. It is now generally used to refer to hallucinogenic drugs.

Chemistry in our daily lives

The use of tobacco is growing greatly and conquers men with a certain secret pleasure, so that those who have once become accustomed thereto can later hardly be restrained therefrom.
Sir Francis Bacon

In this section we will briefly review some of the main characteristics and psychologically interesting features of drugs that affect consciousness. ▲

a. *Nicotine*   The nicotine in tobacco can act as a stimulant, depressant, or tranquilizer. In higher concentrations than exist in cigarette tobacco, nicotine was the active ingredient used to attain mystical states or trances by certain native Indian shamans. Unlike modern users, the Indians knew nicotine was an addictive substance and chose when to be under its influence.

b. *Caffeine*   One to two cups of coffee or tea administer enough caffeine to stimulate the central nervous system. Caffeine is taken to allay drowsiness and fatigue, sustain attention, reduce reaction time, and produce more rapid and clearer flow of thoughts. In large doses caffeine can have a profound effect on heart, blood, and circulatory function. Cola drinks, hot chocolate, and cocoa all contain significant quantities of caffeine.

The effects of caffeine, like those of many drugs, depend as much on psychological aspects of the drug-taking situation and the drug taker's personality as they do on the chemical action of the drug. This effect was shown in a study that compared the reactions of habitual coffee drinkers and nondrinkers to drinking a cup of instant coffee.

Housewives volunteered to report their mood states before and after drinking a cup of instant coffee. The coffee contained either no caffeine, 150 mg., or 300 mg. caffeine (equivalent to two or three cups of coffee). Before they had their morning caffeine, the thirty-eight regular drinkers felt less alert, active, and content, and also more sleepy and irritable. Caffeine-free coffee did not change these feelings. The stronger the caffeine in their coffee cup the fewer headaches reported and more pleasant feelings. Among the eighteen nonusers the effects were reversed. On caffeine mornings they reported an increase in unpleasant stimulant effects; they were jittery, nervous, and had gastrointestinal complaints (Goldstein, Kaizer, & Whitby, 1969).

▲
A wide variety of drugs is in daily use in our society. Cultural groups may differ as to which drugs and what uses of them are acceptable, but the fact remains that we are a drug-using culture and the line between use and abuse is not always an easy one to draw.

c. *Alcohol*   Under the influence of alcohol, our social inhibitions are lifted and we feel freer to act out our impulses. Thus alcohol makes for livelier parties—and auto accidents and murders. Alcohol intoxication seriously impairs reality testing, affects mood, slows reaction times, disrupts coordination, and diminishes many cognitive functions. Its emotional effects are varied. Some people become silly, boisterous, friendly, and talkative. Others get abusive and violent. Still others are made quietly depressed by alcohol.

Dependency of the alcoholic upon alcohol leads to serious malnutrition and neurological damage. Withdrawal from such dependency often results in one of the most undesirable involuntary alterations of consciousness, delirium tremens, the shaking fits of DTs in which the alcoholic suffers delirious hallucinations.

It is commentary worth noting that in our society alcohol is not treated as a "drug." There are over forty thousand liquor stores, hundreds of thousands of bars, taverns, lounges, restaurants dealing it daily and more than $250 million spent every year to advertise its desirability.

The drugstore

The World Health Organization Expert Committee on Drugs (1965) declared that the term "addiction" had become an unusable omnibus word. They proposed that the term "dependence" be used, and that a clear distinction be made between psychological dependence on the effects of the drug and physical dependence, or actual bodily need of it.

Tolerance, the homeostatic process by which a drug's effect is reduced because it has been used before, develops quickly, and a high physiological and psychological dependence occurs. Use may continue in the absence of any pleasurable effects merely to avoid the traumatic withdrawal symptoms. No chronic tissue damage is caused, but death from overdose during initial uses is a real danger.

A given drug may have multiple effects on an organism, and tolerance for all the effects may not occur uniformly. For example, results of the use of narcotics include drowsiness, reduced ability to concentrate, euphoria, a sense of detachment, reduction of hunger, thirst, and sex drives, feelings of heaviness of the limbs, itchiness, constipation, nausea, and pupillary constriction. Tolerance may develop to most of these effects to the extent that doses far exceeding the formerly lethal dose may be administered with virtually no effects, pleasurable or adverse, except for constipation and pupillary constriction, which may continue about as before.

The phenomenon of tolerance is what leads addicts to have to keep increasing the dosage or frequency with which they "shoot up." It is as if the demand is always greater than the supply, and—what makes the situation intolerable—when the need is supplied, it is not enough to produce the effect it used to. This results not only in escalation of drug abuse but frustration, anxiety, and experimentation with any and all drugs that might produce the desired high (or low).

Marijuana

The initial effects of marijuana are comparable to those of alcohol: mild euphoria, stimulation of the central nervous system, and subjective feelings of "mellowness" and "conviviality."

It is a preparation from the *cannabis* plant, a more potent derivative being *hashish*. Cannabis has been used for thousands of years in India both as an intoxicant and an aid to meditation. It was brought to the western world by the crusaders after their religious wars with the Moslems (1096–1279 A.D.). Laborers and peasants in North Africa, India, the Middle East, and elsewhere use it to create a state of well-being that helps transcend the boredom and strain of their work.

Before the 1960s marijuana use in the U.S. was centered in the ghettos and in selected circles of users, such as artists. From there it entered the "hippie" countercultures, then the mainstream of American life. The initial reasons for trying marijuana were tied to values of humanism, desire for genuineness, spontaneity, hedonism, and experimentation with other systems of reality (Keniston, 1968). Boredom, curiosity, and conformity induced others to smoke. Once begun, marijuana use is maintained because it relieves tension, induces euphoria, and facilitates social interaction.

In the United States, marijuana use is a social phenomenon; people smoke it in groups of friends and at parties to intensify fellowship and promote group cohesion (Goode, 1969). Among underprivileged youths, use of marijuana and other drugs is not an "escape from reality." Quite the contrary. Since it is valued by their subculture, drugs are taken as a positive effort to get *into* the mainstream of their reality. (See *P&L* Close-up, A Friend in Weed Is a Friend Indeed.)

Marijuana has only a moderate potential for psychological dependence, and no physical dependence results from its use. Preliminary research reveals no indication of chronic pathology, and a lethal dose is virtually unattainable. Some users report enhancement of their powers of concentration, some impairment. Some find it sexually stimulating, some the opposite. Behavior under marijuana use depends more than other drugs on social and personal factors. In larger quantities, the drug effect may be more like those of the psychedelic drugs, with distorted time sense and new dimensions in perception. The altered state is more controllable, and generally less intense, although high doses may cause panic states and failure of judgment and coordination.

While marijuana decreases verbal analytical reasoning, it has been shown to enhance performance on certain nonanalytical tests of a holistic-visuospatial nature (Harshman, Crawford, & Hecht, 1976). This finding is in line with earlier experiential ones that report marijuana enhancement of nonverbal perception, visual depth sensation, and the perception of meaning in forms that would ordinarily be seen as meaningless lines or shapes (Tart, 1971).

Amphetamines

Stimulants like "speed" initially reduce sensitivity to the feelings of others and promote feelings of ability, invulnerability, and power. But greater doses produce irritability, anxiety, paranoid fears, and auditory hallucinations. A high degree of tolerance develops quickly, and there is a high potential for psychological dependence. Soon high doses must be taken intravenously to maintain the desirable effects. But these desirable effects cannot be maintained long. Use rapidly becomes abuse (Goodman & Gilman, 1970).

"It is the desire to re-experience the flash and the desire to remain euphoric, and to avoid the fatigue and the depression of the 'coming down,' which drives the users to persist and necessarily to increase their dose and frequency of injection. And it is this persistence of use and these large doses which bring on all the other effects of these drugs. It takes ever more drug to recreate this chemical nirvana" (Kramer, 1969, p. 4).

This run-crash cycle may be repeated for several months. "Speed freaks" cannot readily function in the "straight" world. The temporal patterns, ag-

A Friend in Weed Is a Friend In Deed

Among the factors responsible for adolescent students using drugs, one of the most potent is social conformity pressures. A large-scale 1971 survey of over 8000 secondary school students in New York State reveals that adolescents are much more likely to use marijuana if their friends do than if their friends do not (Kandel, 1973).

In this sample, 29 percent reported having used marijuana, with the freshman low of 16 percent escalating to the senior high of 41 percent. Of the users, a third were heavy users, having used it forty times or more. The vast majority of these heavy users (90 percent) also "were into" a variety of other drugs.

To some extent, initiation into the drug scene is a function of modeling parental drug use; students who perceived their mothers to be users of tranquilizers were more likely to become marijuana users than those who perceived their mothers to be nonusers. But the most striking finding was the crucial role that peers played. Association with other drug-using adolescents was the most important correlate of adolescent marijuana use. ". . . Only 7 percent of adolescents who perceive none of their friends use marijuana use marijuana themselves, in contrast to 92 percent who perceive all their friends to be users" (p. 1068).

As can be seen in the figure, the influence of best friends overwhelms that of parents. Marijuana use is related in a small way to parental drug use, but it does not make much of a difference if your parents do not use drugs if your best friend does—chances are then that you will too. And, on the other hand, if your best friend does not use drugs, it does not make much of a difference if your parents do—chances are you will *not*.

It seems reasonable to conclude, then, that drug use is encouraged by social peer pressures and, in turn, forms a basis for association among friends. That is why I say only half facetiously that "a friend in weed is a friend in deed."

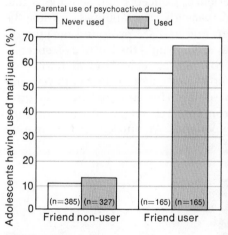

Parental use of psychoactive drug
☐ Never used ☐ Used

(y-axis) Adolescents having used marijuana (%)

Friend non-user: (n=385) (n=327)
Friend user: (n=165) (n=165)

Adapted from Kandel, 1973

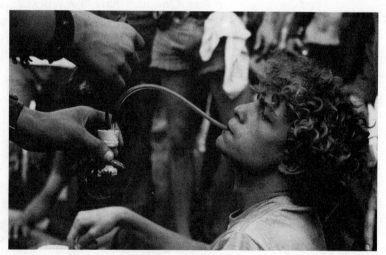

gressiveness, paranoia, and irritability make it very difficult for a speed freak to hold a job or even to keep any "straight" friends.

Hallucinogens

The hallucinogens, or psychedelics, include LSD-25, psilocybin (the "magic mushroom"), mescaline, and DOM (STP). The chemistry of their action is not fully understood, but they act primarily on the central nervous system and perhaps interfere with the filtering mechanisms of the brain (Shulgin, 1969).

Drugs of this type closely resemble certain natural chemicals essential at various stages of the transmission of nerve impulses. Hallucinogens may block the action of these chemicals or act as a substitute for them (Seiden, 1971).

The hallucinogens uniquely and profoundly alter perception, resulting in greater sensitivity to all forms of stimulation (visual, auditory, tactile, etc.) and greater emotional sensitivity. They also create a sense of timelessness. On rare occasions they can cause psychotic reactions. These drugs build up complete tolerance after four to five days, which is lost just as rapidly, and physiological dependence does not develop. There is a slight potential for psychological dependence. There is no substantive evidence to suggest that these drugs cause any tissue or brain damage (Irwin, 1971; Harvey, 1971).

The hallucinogens, or psychedelic drugs, are the most powerful of the mind-altering drugs. The label "hallucinogen" is not entirely accurate, since there is a physiological basis for the perceptions that occur. Actual hallucinations are not common with the use of the psychedelics. There are more likely to be acute changes in perception and interpretation and pseudohallucinations, in which an individual distorts perceptions and projects other meanings and images into them but is still aware of their realistic basis. For instance, the walls may "melt" or brown foam may creep out of drains, but the walls and drains are there and the user usually realizes that a distortion is occurring. ●

"Psychoactive" is indeed a good adjective to describe the effects of LSD and other psychedelic drugs. The variety of effects is staggering. Existence seems more interesting. A sense of timelessness may result, whereby a minute seems like an hour, and the past, present, and future seem like one. Stimuli of every sort may seem overwhelming; stimuli of one sort may be perceived in other forms, for example, music may be seen as waves of astonishingly vivid colors. One may have a mystical experience. Concepts and sensations that normally seem paradoxical may seem amazingly compatible—black may be white, life and death may exist together, one may see profound meaning in what normally seems trivial, a flower may seem to hold the key to existence.

The integration of drugs such as LSD, mescaline, and peyote into a religious experience, as occurs in American Indian tribes in the Southwest and Mexico, is hardly likely in a laboratory setting. However, psychedelic "transcendental" reactions may be elicited from research subjects if the drug variable is made part of a total "religious" experience. An unusual and fascinating study did just that (Pahnke, 1963, 1967).

● **LSD-induced visual imagery**

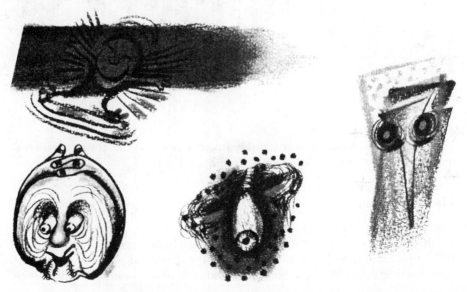

Forty theological students were prepared for the drug experience first by attending "indoctrination" meetings about religious potentials. Then half of them received thirty thousand micrograms of psilocybin prior to attending a lengthy Good Friday service. The service included prayers, songs, music, and personal meditation. Other subjects were randomly assigned to an active placebo condition in which they received nicotinic acid, which produces sensations of warmth and tingling. Thus set, setting, and prior history of the drug user all combined to maximize the religious interpretation of any psychedelic reactions.

On a detailed questionnaire given immediately after the experience, those who were in the psilocybin condition reported significantly more mystical, transcendental experiences than did the placebo controls. These differences persisted on a follow-up interview six months later.

In reviewing the results of research relating subject expectations, LSD dose, and drug effects, Theodore Barber concluded: ". . . at least one third of the variance in response to a relatively small dose of LSD (25 – 100 micrograms) is independent of the drug *per se* and is related to factors which determine response to a placebo, such as subjects' expectancies as to what effects are likely to occur" (1970, p. 17).

As with other relationships between physical-biological variables and psychological ones, the psychological variables exert relatively less influence on behavior as the physical ones become stronger, bigger, more intense. When powerful drugs are administered in large doses or are taken without awareness of their intended effects, they will affect perception, thinking, time sense, and emotional stability regardless of the psychological and social situation.

Drug discrimination and state-dependent learning

One feature of the use of drugs that warrants mention here is their function as discriminative stimuli and their role in state-dependent discrimination learning (see Ho, Richards, & Chute, 1978).

A drug is an unconditioned stimulus that consistently elicits a physiological and behavioral unconditioned response. However, this response produces stimulation within the individual which can become a discriminative stimulus if the drug has distinctive, consistent effects (see p. 81). Drug effects can serve as sensory signals that are associated with conditioned discriminative responses. A drug in moderately high dosage that affects the central nervous system can become a signal for different motor responses (perhaps also cognitive and emotional responses). Appetitive (food) and aversive (shock) unconditioned stimuli are associated with the drug condition through principles of classical conditioning. The motor responses that lead to obtaining a positive reward or avoiding a negative one are associated with the stimuli produced by the drug through principles of operant or instrumental learning. Thus, for example, when a particular drug is associated with a food reward that can be obtained by making a given response, that drug will become a discriminative stimulus eliciting that response.

The discriminative response learned with one drug generalizes to other drugs that have similar effects. But humans and animal subjects can discriminate between different dosages of drugs and different categories of drugs (Barry & Krimner, 1978). When learning takes place during a particular drug-induced state, there is a loss of information or performance efficiency when the individual is tested in a different or nondrug state. This change in performance with changes in state gives rise to the concept of *state-dependent learning*. When learning is state dependent, it is specific to the given state and does not generalize to dissimilar states.

The discriminable cues associated with the particular state during which learning occurred are necessary for the person to retrieve the information stored in memory. That information is not lost, but merely inaccessible when the individual is tested in a different state. If subjects are provided with powerful retrieval cues, the stored events will reappear regardless of the state in which testing is done.

State-dependent learning and the phenomenon of drug discrimination have given impetus to the development of the new field of behavioral psychopharmacology. Drug discrimination enables investigators to study the ways in which internal stimuli can elicit or guide the selection of an organism's responses. State dependency describes the effects that one's physiological state has upon the coding and retrievability of stored information (Overton, 1974).

Throughout recorded history, human beings have not been content with "reality" as given or consciousness as ordinarily experienced. We have sought means to enter new realms of awareness, to go beyond merely perceiving appearances to "seeing" essences. Of the many ways in which the limits of consciousness have been expanded, one has been by the eating and smoking of plants provided by nature.

Whether such desires to transcend the empirical reality of the here-and-now by means of drugs is "right," "good," and "proper" is debatable on moral and social-philosophic levels and is established in legal terms. On a psychological level, we can say that each day millions of Americans use a variety of drugs, some of which sometimes alter their view of the world. The drug experience may be a trivial social exercise in adolescent rebelliousness to society (and conformity to the gang), a unique mystical revelation, a trapdoor to madness, or a ticket to prison. It cannot be denied, however, that through such experiences human beings have altered their consciousness, leading psychologists to a renewed concern with the nature of human consciousness.

Chapter summary

Consciousness may be defined as an awareness of one's own thought processes and of external events. Ordinary waking consciousness is the most familiar state of consciousness. *Alternate* or *extended* states of consciousness signify a qualitative change in the pattern of mental functioning.

A workable framework for analyzing states of consciousness examines features of focus, structure, attributes, and flow. *Focus* refers to the directing of attention; *structure* to divisions of consciousness into *background*, *foreground*, and *aerial view*; *attributes* to qualities ascribed to image, action, and setting of conscious experience; and *flow* to the movement of conscious awareness.

Daydreaming has been defined as the shift of attention away from an immediately demanding task. Wishes and reality-testing activities form the basic core of most daydreams. Night dreams are usually more vivid than daydreams because external stimulation and overt movements are at a minimum at that time.

Hallucinations are perceptions in the absence of objective stimulation

They may occur during states of high fever, epilepsy, migraine headaches, sensory deprivation, and nervous disorders. They may also be drug-induced or result from alcohol withdrawal. In hallucinations there is a shifting from verbal representation to visual imagery; internal sources of information take precedence over external ones; images are experienced as if they reflected the immediate outer environment; the hallucinations intrude upon all other functions.

Prolonged sensory and social deprivation may result in hallucination and other changes in cognition. Intense concentration or sensory overload may have similar effects. Schizophrenics tend to have auditory hallucinations, while individuals on drugs usually experience visual ones.

There are two distinct sleep states: *non-rapid eye movement* sleep (NREM) and *rapid eye movement* sleep (REM). The first is called *orthodox* sleep, the second is *paradoxical* sleep. The first stage of sleep, the *hypnagogic* stage, is really a transition state between waking and sleeping—thoughts drift and hallucinations arise. Sleep Stage 2, with characteristic brain-wave patterns, follows. Finally, deep sleep, or the *Delta* stage, is reached. The sleeper then goes back to Stage 2 and into REM sleep. During this stage, the body is essentially paralyzed, the brain is aroused and alert though the subject is unconscious. *Phasic* activity, *"autonomic storms,"* and dreaming take place. During the course of eight hours of sleep, a person passes in cycles from stage to stage.

While the amount of sleep required to maintain health varies with the individual, an extended period of time without sleep can result in fatigue, headaches, tremor, disorientation, and in some cases, hallucinations. However, one good night's sleep usually restores ordinary functioning.

Insomnia is a sleep disorder in which a person's inability to sleep interferes with efficient daytime functioning. This condition is usually caused by chronic anxiety or depression. Sedation may worsen the insomnia by prolonging it and making it drug-related. Those suffering from *narcolepsy,* on the other hand, display excessive daytime sleepiness and can fall asleep in the middle of activity, often several times a day. *Sleep apnea* is a syndrome in which those affected repeatedly experience stoppage of breathing while sleeping, resulting in loud snores and a restless night.

Subjects aroused during REM sleep have usually been dreaming and can recall vivid visual images from the coherent drama of their dreams. (Dreams that occur during NREM sleep usually have no story content, but are composed of separate thoughts.) One physiological explanation for dreaming is that it is the brain's attempt to interpret unrelated bursts of ongoing cortical activity during REM sleep. But Freudian theory proposes that dreams express unconscious wishes disguised by an internal censor. In this context, what individuals remember of their dreams is the *manifest content,* the real meaning of the dreams being their *latent content.*

Drugs that affect mental processes are called *psychoactive* drugs. Among these, the ones that can produce sensory hallucinations are termed *hallucinogenic* or *psychedelic,* and those producing patterns of thought and arousal mimicking psychotic patterns are called *psychotomimetic. Tolerance* is the homeostatic process by which a drug's effect is reduced by previous use. It is important to distinguish physiological dependence from psychological dependence. *Nicotine* may act as a stimulant, depressant, or tranquilizer, while *caffeine* also has diverse effects, including increased alertness and reduced reaction times. *Alcohol* intoxication leads to the lifting of social inhibitions and encourages impulsive action. It disrupts coordination and cognitive functioning, and affects emotion. If alcohol dependence results, lead to *delirium tremens.*

Initial effects of *marijuana* are usually mild euphoria, stimulation of the central nervous system, and subjective feelings of conviviality. This drug has a moderate potential for psychological dependence and does not cause physical dependence. Behavior under marijuana depends to a large extent on social and personal factors.

Amphetamines such as "speed" reduce sensitivity to the feelings of others and promote feelings of ability, invulnerability, and power. But in greater doses, they produce anxiety, paranoid fears, and auditory hallucinations. Tolerance develops quickly and there is a high potential for psychological dependence.

Hallucinogens, or *psychedelics,* include LSD-25, psilocybin, mescaline, and DOM (STP). While the chemistry of their action is not fully understood, it is apparent that they act primarily on the nervous system, perhaps blocking the action of chemicals active at various stages of nerve impulse transmission. These substances profoundly alter perception, on rare occasions causing psychotic reactions. The drugs build up complete tolerance in four or five days but this tolerance is lost just as quickly, and physiological dependence does not develop. There is a slight potential for psychological dependence. Subjective mystical and transcendental experiences may occur under their influence.

While a drug is an *unconditioned stimulus* that consistently elicits a physiological and behavioral *unconditioned response,* the drug can become a *discriminative* stimulus if it has distinctive, consistent effects. When learning takes place during a particular drug-induced state, there is a loss of information or performance efficiency when the individual is tested in a different or nondrug state, resulting in *state-dependent* learning.

Part Six
Personality and Clinical Psychology

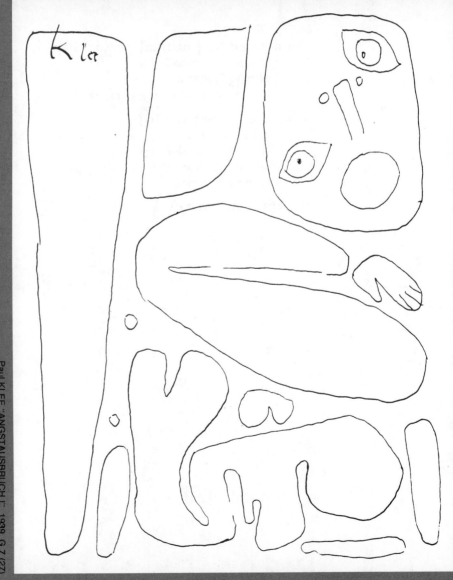

16 Personality: Issues and Theories

Imagine that you are at the reunion of your high school graduating class. It has been years since you last saw most of your old friends and classmates! You wonder, somewhat anxiously, whether they will remember you and if they will think you have changed. If so, hopefully for the better. And what about them? What will you look for as clues to whether they have changed or remained pretty much the same as when you were all in your teens?

Of course, your attention is first drawn to appearances. Are the "beautiful people" still the best looking? Has time given some faces a more interesting character, while those marked earlier by "cuteness" did not age quite so well? You notice the flabbiness of the class athlete who didn't make the college varsity. There's the new slim line of formerly "Fat Freddie." It's a puzzle what that beautiful woman saw in plain old Charlie, or why your handsome lab partner was attracted to a wife of such modest looks.

But there is more to you and your friends than meets the eye. We expect age to take a toll on our looks, but not to change our "real selves." You look beneath surface appearances to seek out those personal qualities that distinguished particular classmates. Is George still gregarious? What about Steven, the silent, shy guy—did he even come tonight? Will Jeanette still be the same gentle, caring person with whom you could share your feelings? And will domineering Don be as pushy as ever, or stingy Sarah as uptight about money?

Will the others notice your greater maturity? After all, college did more than just fill your head with information. You've developed what you think of as "your style" in relating to people. You are not as impulsive as you once were, you plan things out, reflect, and analyze the consequences. You've learned how to listen to the problems of other people and be compassionate even when you can't give the counsel they seek. But maybe, they see you as "straight" or "square." Have career and security become too important for you? Whatever happened to your concern for social justice and . . . .

In this scenario you are both an observer and an actor. You are observing how other people behave in the situation in order to determine characteristic patterns of reaction of different individuals. But *you* are also part of the total situation to which the others react. Perhaps your presence encourages or inhibits certain reactions in other people. If you are a talker, most people will be less talkative around you than if you are a more silent type. If you are solemn, others will probably not tell jokes to you, and if religious, certainly not dirty jokes. This means that you are always an actor in life's drama, even when you are not consciously aware of playing a part. But in addition, it means that what we think of as general "characteristics" of other people may, in fact, be specific reactions that only are elicited by us. Put differently, the "you" your parents know may not correspond well to the "you" your closest friends know—or think they know. If not, why? Has your personality changed or do different situations bring out different aspects of your personality? But just what is "personality," and how do psychologists attempt to understand your personality and mine? That will be our concern in this chapter.

The worst part of a person who becomes an important person is, they call him a celebrity. It's not the person who changes, but the persons who surround him. My parents have become so conditioned to reacting for the benefit of local newsmen and television cameras that they smile when the light goes on in the refrigerator at home.

Guillermo Vilas (Argentine tennis star)

Understanding normal personality

In popular usage, "personality" is like "attractiveness," "charm," or "charisma." "She may not be pretty, but she has a nice personality." "Be careful, he has a very forceful personality." It is also used in everyday language as a quality movie stars and those politicians we like have a lot of, while the rest of us must make do with less. Even as a child, you had probably developed and put to use your own system of appraising your own personality and that of others. It was of vital importance to be able to distinguish between friends and foes, to judge the moods of your parents, to size up and "psych out" competitors, and to determine your own strengths and weaknesses. Your judgments were, in fact, primitive personality assessments. These naive judgments are based largely on intuition and limited observations that are open to many sources of error. We will see later that in the *formal* assessment of personality by psychologists much effort is directed toward minimizing these errors and biases.

Some nonpsychologists make their living by being "naive personality theorists." Among them are the fortune-tellers, the pool hustlers, and the "confidence artists" (we applauded some in the movie *The Sting*). These people are skilled pseudoprofessionals who operate on the basis of a naive personality theory built upon keen observational skills, a knowledge of human nature, and considerable *chutzpah* (nerve). The basic tools of the trade include an ability to classify people quickly on the basis of age, appearance, marital status, and so on. They also have a shrewd knowledge of what kind of problems a given type of individual is most likely to have. Implicit in such techniques are the fortune-teller's profound faith in the stereotypes of the culture and an enormous dependence on characteristics inferred from the outward appearance of clients.

When we casually observe human beings and their behavior, we are struck by their remarkable similarities and continuities. But the closer we look, the more we become aware of their differences and discontinuities. It is exactly like putting your two hands side-by-side, palms up, and noting how identical each finger on your left hand is to its corresponding right-hand member. But now look closely at your fingers and see how different the fingerprints are on each. There are no recorded cases of two identical fingerprints. So too, there are no two people, not even "identical" twins, who are not different in many respects.

There are four basic questions that are central to our discussion of the psychological study of personality:

a) What makes different people behave alike in the same situation?
b) What makes different individuals in the same situation behave differently?
c) What makes the same person behave similarly in different situations?
d) What makes every person uniquely different from all others?

The first question is at the core of our general science of psychology. It seeks to account for the apparent diversity of human behavior by discovering environmental stimuli that control behavior according to patterns of lawful regularity. The goal of the behaviorist, for example, is to understand, predict, and control behavior of any and all individuals in a given environment. Behavior is assumed to be a function of environmental stimuli. Adequate knowledge of the stimulus is assumed to be the necessary and sufficient condition for valid predictions of behavior. Differences between individuals are ignored, considered irrelevant, or assumed to be variations due to *error* rather than to the operation of psychological laws.

However, there are few situations in everyday life in which everyone behaves the same. There is usually a range of reactions to be seen in almost any setting. Think of the last party you attended. Would you say that all (or even most) people there were behaving identically in the same stimulus situation? Even in a common environment, people often react quite differently. At a party, some dance, others are wallflowers; some sing, others are listeners;

There never were, since the creation of the world, two cases exactly parallel.
Lord Chesterfield
Letters to His Son

some drink, others are teetotalers; some try to "make out" with one partner, others watch them.

Thus our second question directs attention to the observed differences in the behavior of different individuals in response to apparently the same situation. The variability in behavior that is *not* accounted for by the stimulus situation is attributed to *individual differences*. The study of personality is in large part the study of individual differences in reaction to a given stimulus, person, or environmental setting. What does one person bring to a behavior setting that leads to a different interpretation of it and reaction to it than that of another individual? Behavior is a function of the stimulus situation *and* the person, in this view.

At a personal level, we rarely stop to inquire why we have acted the way we have when everyone else acts as we do. It is only when we behave differently from others, or when someone else deviates from the rest, that we pause to wonder why. It is in this pause that the study of individual differences originated. Thus the personality theorist has a special interest in trying to understand why people's behavior still differs after all of the known environmental factors have been specified. It has been the function of personality tests (psychological assessment) to quantify these individual differences in functioning.

The third question we posed focuses upon the *consistency* of personality. Just as there are perceptual constancies (see p. 358), there seem to be some personal qualities that do not change much from one situation to another. The physical appearance and intellectual ability of a friend do not change as he or she goes from one to another situation. Similarly, expressive behaviors, such as use of hand and facial gestures, and other forms of "body language" tend to be characteristics of an individual that are seen in different situations. But what about "generosity," "honesty," "friendliness," "shyness," and other aspects of personality? Is there consistency in an individual's behavior in different situations that can be attributed to personality traits? "Yes," is the answer given by traditional personality approaches that emphasize traits and types of personality. ● (We will see later that there is much controversy over the issue of whether personality traits show cross-situational consistency.)

Finally, the last question confronted by the psychological study of personality centers on discovery of *unique characteristics* that distinguish individuals from one another. Although we are alike in many ways, aren't there some characteristics you possess that you feel are special to you, aspects of your personality that identify you as *you?* As we get to know someone better, we usually discover distinguishing characteristics not obvious on casual contact. "Oh, that's just like Adam, he always does things like that." When we relate to the unique aspects of other people we probably are responding more to unique *response styles* that form behavioral patterns than to specific personality traits.

●
"All right, I'm labeling you. Did it ever occur to you I wouldn't label you if you weren't such a type?"

Defining "personality"

Although psychologists give a variety of definitions for "personality," common to all of them are concepts of uniqueness, characteristic responses, and situational consistency. *Personality is the sum of the unique psychological qualities of an individual that influence a variety of characteristic behavior patterns (both overt and covert) in relatively consistent ways across different situations and over time.*

We expect also that there will be some stability to personality from one time to the next as well as *consistency* from one situation to another. That is why at our high-school reunion we assume that the passage of time will not have altered the unique characteristics of people we know well. Only to the extent that such stability and consistency exist, does individual behavior become predictable. Without such consistency we can predict only the probable average response of a sample of people to specific stimuli. Opponents of traditional personality psychology argue in favor of this latter position.

Just as radical behaviorists reject unobservable concepts such as consciousness and even motivation, they and others believe "personality" to be an explanatory fiction. It is only used, they assert, when someone is ignorant or unaware of the true causal determinants of a given behavior. For them the study of individual differences is the refuge of those who are unable to discover the true situational determinants of behavior. In reply, personality theorists ask their brethren to come out of their sterile laboratories and observe the variety and profusion of personality types, as well as the uniqueness of individuals in the real world.

Defining "normal"

A common misconception perpetuated by newspaper advice columnists is that normal human beings function pretty much alike. Moreover, to be normal, one *ought* to be functioning like others who are in some way comparable (of similar age, sex, or education, for example). Parents worried that their baby has not yet begun to walk are told the age at which the "normal" baby does, while adolescents are told when it is "normal" to begin dating according to surveys of when the "average" teenager does. Problems arise when *descriptions* of what most people do (a statistical normality) become *prescriptions* for what everyone should do (culturally or socially imposed normative standard).

The myth of the normal, average, human function was dispelled in a thorough analysis by Williams (1956) showing the enormous range of variation in the location, size, and operation of internal human organs. Nearly every organ is several times larger in some "normal" individuals than in other individuals equally "normal." Similar differences are reported in neural structure, chemical composition and activity, and reactions to drugs and various stimuli.

When such an array of physiological differences is added to the infinite variety of life experiences individuals have, it is no wonder that there is such diversity of human behavior, even among people in the same situation. These differences among individuals are problems to researchers looking for general laws. They are usually either overcome by studying powerful stimuli in simple situations or averaged out by combining the varied responses of a large number of subjects.

Most personality theorists, however, take a quite different view of this "problem." What makes people behave as individuals is looked on not as a problem to get rid of, but as *the* problem to be studied. This does not mean that psychologists working in personality are not interested in finding general laws. As in other areas of psychology, many personality theorists believe that eventually psychologists will discover principles that can be applied to all human beings. But in personality theory the principles must also be able to account for differences among people. Not all personality theories emphasize individual differences, but all must be able to account for them. They must be able to say what makes one person different from another, what makes one person behave consistently in different situations, and what makes people either remain the same or change over a period of time.

The *statistical* aspect of normality describes the extent to which individuals deviate from the average reaction of a comparison population. Normal is equated with the numerical "average," the representative case, the central tendency. Abnormal is the atypical case, those individuals at the extremes of the distribution on various tests and measures of psychological functioning. Geniuses and the mentally retarded are by this definition both "abnormal."

But we usually mean something more by the normal-abnormal distinction. Abnormal has a negative connotation; it is "bad," while normal is "good." Geniuses are statistically exceptional, but we don't think of them as "really abnormal." The study of normal personality implies exclusion of the "abnormal." Personality researchers generally study individuals who, within a broad range, would be considered normal, average, typical. The study of abnormal personalities is reserved for psychiatrists, clinical psychologists, and those interested in psychopathology. In our text, it is reserved for Chapter 19.

The easiest way to study normal personality is to select subjects who are functioning in a *setting* that is viewed as normal, and avoid those in settings that are not normal. Thus students in college are studied rather than patients in mental hospitals. (But sometimes, as we both know, the setting may conceal people who do not really belong there—both "students" and "patients.")

Another definition of normality is whether the person's behavior is *situationally appropriate*. Do you do the right thing at the right time in a particular situation? If you laugh at the accidental death of a friend, talk to God in the movies, and express anger loudly in church, you are behaving inappropriately. Chances are you will be judged "abnormal" compared to the person who laughs in the movies, talks to God in church, and expresses anger over the accidental death of a friend. Beyond the particular standards of "correct" behavior in a given situation, *cultural values* also determine normality. ▲

Finally, there is a criterion of *effective adjustment*. Using this criterion, normality can be defined as the state of psychological functioning that enables an individual: (a) to adjust effectively to situational demands, (b) to perform adequately in line with his or her abilities and capacities, and (c) to have a balanced mental attitude and emotional temperament that responds appropriately to social reality.

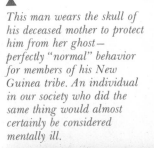

▲ *This man wears the skull of his deceased mother to protect him from her ghost—perfectly "normal" behavior for members of his New Guinea tribe. An individual in our society who did the same thing would almost certainly be considered mentally ill.*

Approaches to studying personality

Should psychology study *variables* or *people*? Is it possible to construct a science of psychology based upon the intensive study of the unique features of individual personality? These questions have been hotly debated for many years, without yet being resolved. Psychologists who propose that the study of individual differences must center around variables and general traits follow the nomothetic approach (see p. 53). In contrast, those who agree that people and their unique traits represent the proper study of personality carry the idiographic banner.

The nomothetic approach

The experimental research tradition adopts what is called the *nomothetic* approach. It tries to establish general functional relationships between behavior and causal determinants assumed to be shared by all individuals (or identifiable subgroups of people).

Applied to the study of individual differences, the nomothetic approach assumes that there is an underlying basic structure to personality, or universal trait dimensions common to everyone. In this view, individuals differ only in the degree to which they possess those traits identified by the researcher. The research paradigm dictated by the nomothetic study of personality first measures a set of traits (such as "honesty," "helpfulness," "persistence") in a large group of individuals. The numerical scores of each person on each trait are then correlated with other criterion performance scores derived from behavioral observation or tests. The resulting correlation coefficient represents the degree of relationship between the predictor trait variable and the criterion variable *averaged* across the group studied. When the correlation is very high, knowledge of a person's score on the trait dimension is predictive of his or her behavioral response in the criterion test situation. But the correlation is a single score which, in lumping all individuals together, forfeits the unique contribution of any particular person. When the correlations among traits or between traits and behaviors are *low*, then neither average tendencies nor individual characteristics can be validly predicted. *Low correlations between traits and trait-related behaviors in different situations are the rule.* It does not appear possible then to predict the behavior of even most of the people most of the time, using personality traits as predictors.

Three investigations illustrate the predictive failure of the nomothetic trait-based approach to personality. Hartshorne and May in their classic *Studies in the Nature of Character* (1928, 1929) found little consistency among different measures of moral character. It was not possible, for example, to predict whether a child who cheated in one situation would lie in another. "Honesty" was therefore declared to be composed of situation-specific habits rather than a constellation of general traits.

"Punctuality" seems a good candidate for general trait status. Getting to class on time, keeping appointments promptly, not being late for the start of movies or church services ought to be components of a general personality trait of punctuality. Not so, found Dudycha (1936) in his study of over three hundred college students. More than fifteen thousand observations were made of their time of arrival to various college-related events. The average correlation in punctual behavior across situations was a mere +.19. Hardly robust enough to set your watch by.

When Walter Mischel (1968) surveyed a large body of literature on trait consistency across situations, he was forced to conclude its presence was modest at best. The highest correlation found in these studies is about +.30. Mischel is one of the strongest critics of general personality traits as links unifying stimulus events and responses across diverse situations. *Behavioral specificity,* rather than trait generality, is found when cross-situational consistency is sought in psychological research. He maintains that what seem to be "inconsistent" reactions to subtle changes in environmental stimuli are, in fact, due to the fine discriminative ability of human beings (Mischel, 1976). However, his position on the situational consistency question should not be taken to mean that personality doesn't exist. "No one seriously doubts that lives have coherence and that we perceive ourselves and others as relatively stable individuals who have substantial identity and continuity over time" (Mischel & Mischel, 1977, p. 335).

But we might inquire if even that perception of consistency in ourselves and others is "really there" or exists primarily in the eye of the beholder. This tendency to perceive consistency in other people seems to be an extension of a more general tendency to perceive consistency in all events. As we found in our study of perception in Chapter 12, the attempt to impose stability and constancy on variability is the hallmark of human perception. Thus perceiving consistency in personality is part of a general process of organizing our world in such a way as to make it coherent, orderly, and more readily predictable. (See *P&L* Close-up, The Search for Consistency.)

To investigate whether personality traits show stability over time, psychologists rely on the longitudinal method (see p. 224). Such studies of individual lives through time are difficult to carry out; thus relatively few have been conducted. However, two notable studies deserve mention.

At the Institute of Human Development of the University of California at Berkeley, researchers began collecting data over forty years ago on two samples of children: 248 infants and 212 fifth graders. Today, this study is continuing to gather data on about one third of the subjects still available from the original sample. Some of the results of this longitudinal program of research have been summarized by Jack Block (1971). Although the complex patterns of relationship among the dozens of variables studied cannot be fully summarized here, a general finding of the research was that, with some exceptions, people show little consistency of specific personality characteristics from adolescence to adulthood. For example, while achievement and IQ seemed moderately stable over time, expressions of sexual interests, hostility, impulsiveness, power orientation, morals, fantasizing, and competitiveness show no stability over an extended time period.

Shortly after World War I, Lewis Terman at Stanford University began his longitudinal study of gifted children, those with very high IQ's (Terman & Oden, 1947, 1959). Many items of data were collected on each of 857 boys and 671 girls who constituted the original sample. By the time of the most recent evaluation in 1972 literally thousands of items of data were available for every one of the remaining 75 percent of the original sample. In this recent report of the results using early life variables to predict later life behaviors, Robert Sears (1977) presents the following conclusions: (a) the direct predictive value of a variable *diminishes* with time (it may have a continuing indirect value, but its degree of influence then is difficult to assess); (b) correlations between earlier measured personality variables and later-life variables (such as satisfaction with family life, work) tend to be low; and (c) self-descriptive qualities seem to have high consistency over the three decades from age thirty to sixty. Adulthood may be a time of stability and little change in character. But it may also be that one's *feelings* about one's *self,* rather than one's actions, constitute the stable dimension of personality.

The idiographic approach

Does the failure of the nomothetic approach to find general traits that predict behavior across situations and over time mean there is no consistency in per-

Close-up
The Search for Consistency

It certainly seems to be the better part of common sense that people can be characterized according to some dominant traits that they exhibit across different situations. We all know "gregarious" people, "shy" ones, "honest" ones, "impulsive males," "dependent females," and so forth. Despite our confidence in these intuitions, there is considerable research evidence that suggests our intuitions are wrong.

Here we have an intriguing paradox. On the one hand our naive view is in accord with the basic assumption of most theories of personality—namely, there *is* consistency in personality from one situation to another. On the other hand, systematic research that tries to predict behavior of the person in a given situation from personality-trait scores or from his or her behavior in different situations shows rather poor predictability. A resolution of these discrepant views may come from analyzing the reasons why we (and some personality theorists) might perceive consistency to exist *within* individuals to a greater extent than it actually does.

There are at least ten good sources of bias that give us *an illusion of consistency* of personality:

a. We each carry around an "implicit personality theory" by which we link observed behavior to inferred traits and then predict to other unobserved behaviors. Such theories encourage us to fill in missing observations of what *is* with what *ought to be*—according to our theory of personality. In addition, we overgeneralize from available evidence of areas where there is some consistency (such as in intellectual ability or cognitive style) to areas of the person where consistency is not really present.

b. We rely too heavily on a language of traits to describe human behavior, having over 18,000 trait names in our vocabulary. We tend to *think* in terms of the language we have at our disposal—in terms of traits rather than situations.

c. Perhaps the reason we have such an overabundance of individual trait terms is the emphasis both in psychology and in our society on the individual. We tend to locate "problems" in people rather than in situations. This results in a tendency to label people according to their "problem," and the label often sticks.

d. We underestimate subtle situational forces that may produce different reactions in different people. We especially ignore the situational impact when it affects others but not us.

e. We usually see certain people only in a limited number of situations (sometimes only one, as with teachers and students in school) and generalize our observations to other unobserved situations.

f. Often others will behave the way they think we want them to, thus exaggerating how consistent they appear to us (but sometimes they act quite differently for another observer).

g. Most of us are free to choose the situations we enter, and we enter those we predict that we will feel comfortable in and can handle. Those situations tend to be familiar ones, where the opportunities for new stimulation, conflict, or challenge are limited. It is no wonder that we act consistently in situations we have chosen for the sake of their constancy.

h. Our judgments of others often come not from what we observe them doing but from what they tell us they do. Such self-reports are often biased.

i. Our first impressions bias us strongly, and subsequent evaluations are reinterpreted so as to fit in with the original "true" view. Once established, a belief needs little evidence to support it, but much to refute it.

j. We tend to see consistency where it is not because we have come to equate consistency with goodness, reliability, stability, and so on. As Mark Twain put it: "There are those who would misteach us that to stick in a rut is consistency—and a virtue, and that to climb out of the rut is inconsistency—and a vice" ("Consistency," 1923).

sonality? Gordon Allport refused to accept such a negative conclusion. Allport was the champion of the idiographic approach to personality. For him, the study of personality meant discovering those traits that both characterize and are relevant to an individual — from the person's own perspective (1937). Each trait, he held, is unique in the way it functions within a person's total makeup. Traits cannot be averaged across people to get composite scores or correlations without destroying their uniqueness. For Allport, then, the method by which to uncover the uniqueness of personality was the *idiographic* approach: an intensive, long-term analysis of individual cases that relied on the person's own phenomenological view.

When low correlations are found between traits and behavior, as in the studies of honesty, Allport believed it proved only that "children are not consistent *in the same way,* not that they are inconsistent with *themselves*" (1937, p. 250). They may not behave consistently according to the researcher's arbitrarily imposed general trait dimension, because it is not relevant for them. For example, you may tell a lie to avoid hurting a friend's feelings, or cheat by giving test answers to someone in danger of flunking out. Are you then a *dishonest* person, in your own eyes? Or was Daniel Ellsberg *immoral* for stealing the Pentagon Papers and releasing them for publication in order to expose the immorality of his government? However, might we have predicted from his behavior in this situation other actions he would take to protest the U.S. involvement in the Vietnam War? Is there consistency within *one person* over situations? Allport believed so. The major inconsistencies uncovered by nomothetic research are thus seen as occurring between different concepts of personality held by the *researchers* and those of the *individuals studied* — rather than in real inconsistencies within the individual.

A resolution: Predicting some personalities sometimes

We can have a nomothetic science of personality and an idiographic approach to individual assessment if two conditions are accepted (Bem & Allen, 1974). First, idiographic assessment permits the prediction of only certain behaviors across certain situations for certain people — and no more than that. Secondly, the determination of which behaviors are relevant in which situations must be made by the individual(s) studied.

George Kelly's (1955) psychology of personal constructs is a prime example of an effective idiographic approach. The individual is asked to generate trait descriptions (or constructs) that characterize both his or her self and the social world. In addition, the individual determines which behaviors express a given construct in particular settings. Thus, I may think of myself as "generous" because I give money to the needy, advice to relatives, and my limited time to social causes. This personal construct is not challenged by the apparent "lack of generosity" shown by my refusal to loan someone my toothbrush or my spouse. It is not that such acts exceed the limits of my generosity, for I do not perceive them as reflections of generosity, but rather of hygiene and personal morality. Thus an important point in the controversy over personality consistency is *whose* view of consistency is being studied.

Daryl Bem proposes a different resolution to the controversy: use idiographic assessment methods within a nomothetic research paradigm (Bem & Allen, 1974). Use only people who define themselves as cross-situationally consistent on the general trait dimension, then study their behaviors that are assumed to be characterized by the investigator's personality construct.

College student subjects were classified initially according to their self-reports on two questions: (a) how friendly they were (on a seven-point scale), and (b) how much they varied in friendliness from one situation to another. Subjects were designated as being high or low in variability if they were above or below the median (respectively) of the distribution of same-sex subjects at the same point on the degree of friendliness trait scale. Independent assessments of friendliness were obtained by reports from each subject's father, mother, and a friend, as well as behavioral observations in a group discussion and with a solitary stranger.

Using self-rated friendliness as the only predictor variable was of little value in predicting how others evaluated the subject's friendliness or how friendly the subject behaved in the test situations. However, the subjects' self-reported variability did relate highly to their degree of cross-situational consistency in friendliness. Those who perceived themselves as low in variability (generally friendly or generally not) showed consistency in the friendliness variable across the different ratings and test situations. For the high variability people the correlations between their self-reported friendliness and the ratings of others and with their overt behavior were low. In fact, a high variability subject's evaluation of his or her own friendliness had no relationship (r = −.06) to their spontaneous friendly behavior during a waiting period with a stranger. For subjects not variable in how friendly they were from one situation to another, the correlation between self-reported friendliness and their actual overt friendly behavior was sizable, r = +.61. A similar set of results was found for a second trait of "conscientiousness" studied by these investigators.

Theories of personality

The many theoretical approaches to understanding personality may be conveniently reduced to four major ones: trait theories, psychodynamic theories, humanistic theories, and learning theories.

Trait theories

Just as the young child seems to be always asking for labels by which to classify things in its environment, we also label and classify people by their psychological characteristics. Classification helps to organize diversity and minimize the number of separate entities to which we have to attend. It is the first step in imposing order on our experiences. The many are reduced to a few. Concrete and variable instances are replaced by general, abstract uniformities. Once the classification is established, and people are assigned to it, we then search for all the ways in which members of a given category are similar. We proceed to predict the likelihood that any person who is assigned to a particular category will share in these personality and behavioral characteristics. Do you ever use any of the following classifications to order people in your psychological environment? College class, sex, race, nationality, religion, body build, fraternity or sorority affiliation, academic major? These categorizations sort people into distinctive categories or *types*. Types are all-or-none classifications in which a person is assigned to one of a small number of possible categories that do not overlap with any others.

Personality typologies attempt to simplify the relationship between an individual's behavior and a simple, highly visible characteristic of the person, or assumed characteristic of the categorical class. If fat, then jolly; if an engineering major, then conservative; if female, then emotional; and so it goes. Such typologies have traditionally had much popular appeal because they give an illusion of simplicity to the complicated business of understanding and predicting human nature.

The Italian criminologist Cesare Lombroso developed a typology of facial types by which one could allegedly predict a person's criminal predispositions.

"In striking contrast to the narrow forehead and low vault of the skull, the face of the criminal, like those of most animals, is of disproportionate size, a phenomenon intimately connected with the greater development of the senses as compared with that of the nervous centres. . . . Asymmetry is a common characteristic of the criminal physiognomy. The eyes and ears are frequently situated at different levels and are of unequal size, the nose slants towards one side, etc. This asymmetry, . . . is connected with marked irregularities in the senses and functions" (Ferrero, 1911, pp. 12, 13). ◆

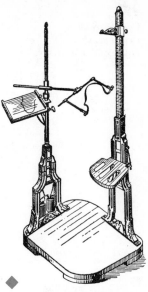

◆

Using instruments like the "craniograph" shown here, Cesare Lombroso measured the skulls of criminals and developed a classification of criminal types.

But the most well developed type theory of personality was that advanced by an American physician, William Sheldon (1942). Sheldon sought to relate physique to temperament. He rated body builds *(somatotypes)* on seven-point scales according to whether they fit into the categories of: *endomorphic* (fat, soft, round), *mesomorphic* (muscular, rectangular, strong) or *ectomorphic* (thin, long, fragile). A person with a rating of 1:3:7 would be an ectomorph with some muscles and no fat, perhaps a long-distance runner. A 7:5:1 on the other hand, might characterize a Japanese sumo wrestler. ■ But the point of the typology was to associate physique (or constitutional differences) to personality. Sheldon's personality theory created obvious associations between body size and type with activities and preferences. Endomorphs are relaxed, love to eat, sociable, gut-oriented. Mesomorphs are physical people filled with energy, courage, and assertive tendencies. The ectomorphs are brainy, artistic, introverted temperaments who think about life rather than consuming it or acting upon it. Sheldon's typology has proven to be of little value in predicting an individual's behavior from somatotypes—once stereotypes that bias raters' judgments are eliminated (Tyler, 1956).

■
Sheldon's somatotype theory was an attempt to equate body build with personality characteristics. It has not, however, proved useful in predicting the behavior of individuals.

Traits are to types as dashes are to dots. While types assume discrete, discontinuous categories, traits assume there is an underlying continuous dimension. A *trait* is a psychological construct or personality dimension on which individuals may be placed according to how much of the characteristic they possess. J. P. Guilford has said, "A trait is any distinguishable, relatively enduring way in which one individual varies from another" (1959, p. 6).

Allport's trait theory

Gordon Allport (1937, 1961, 1966) was the most influential of the trait theorists. In his view, traits are the building blocks of personality, the guideposts for action, the source of uniqueness of the individual. *Traits are defined as inferred predispositions that direct the behavior of an individual in consistent and characteristic ways.* Furthermore, traits produce consistencies in behavior because they are *enduring* attributes and they are *general* or broad in their scope. That is, they stand between and unify a variety of specific stimuli and responses. ●

Traits may act as intervening variables, relating groups of stimuli and responses that might seem at first glance to have little to do with each other.

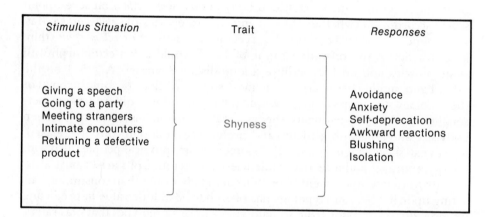

Stimulus Situation	Trait	Responses
Giving a speech Going to a party Meeting strangers Intimate encounters Returning a defective product	Shyness	Avoidance Anxiety Self-deprecation Awkward reactions Blushing Isolation

Allport identified three types of traits. *Cardinal traits* are highly generalized dispositions around which a person organizes his or her whole life. For some it may be power or achievement, while others of us are disposed toward self-sacrifice for the good of others. Less dominant or in less total control of behavior are *central traits*. They are, however, still broad and general in their influence. The specific traits that guide our actions in more limited channels are called *secondary traits*.

Traits form the structure of personality which, in turn, determines an individual's behavior. Allport saw personality structure rather than environmental conditions as the critical determiner of psychological reality. "The same fire that melts the butter hardens the egg," he said as a way of showing that stimuli had different effects on different individuals. Although he recognized *common* traits that were shared by individuals in a given culture, Allport was most interested in discovering the *unique traits* that made each person a singular entity. In a later paper (1966), he made it clear that the core concept of "trait" was a basic, general term covering all "the permanent possibilities for action." These include long-range sets, attitudes, "perceptual response dispositions," and "cognitive styles." As the "most acceptable unit for investigation in the psychology of personality" (1937), Allport saw traits as "biophysical facts" — the personal realities whereby neural and mental energies affect how we think, feel, and act.

Three other notable trait theorists are Raymond Cattell (1965), J. P. Guilford (1959, 1967), and British psychologist Hans Eysenck (1967, 1973). (See *P&L* Close-up, Extraverts Fade While Introverts Flourish.) Despite some differences in their approaches, they share in common the following beliefs:

a. Traits are the basic unit of personality organization.
b. Traits are inferred from behavioral indicators (usually paper-and-pencil personality tests).
c. By integrating behavior and stimulus events, traits give personality continuity and consistency.
d. Traits may be either *surface traits* (clusters of overt responses that are interrelated) or *source traits* (underlying processes that determine the surface manifestations).
e. The task of personality assessment is to distinguish superficial from basic traits and to identify the smallest number of these basic units of personality that will explain the greatest amount of the variability in human behavior.

Close-up
Extraverts Fade While Introverts Flourish

Eysenck has developed a personality inventory that can identify people who vary along the trait dimension of extraversion-introversion. Extraverts are sociable, outgoing, active, impulsive, "tough-minded" people. Introverts are their psychological opposites; they are "tender-minded" individuals, noted for being withdrawn, inner directed, passive, cautious, and reflective (Eysenck & Eysenck, 1967).

Introverts are assumed to be born with a more sensitive, easily arousable autonomic nervous system than extraverts. Introverts have been shown to have lower thresholds than extraverts for pain, and to condition faster with weak unconditioned stimuli or partial reinforcement training. Other research has shown that associations learned in the presence of low-arousal stimuli are better recalled immediately than those learned in the presence of high arousal. The theory developed to explain this finding argued that high arousal results in greater consolidation of the information being learned. High consolidation was considered to interfere with immediate recall but to be more permanent and to facilitate retention over long time intervals. Eysenck combined these ideas to predict memory differences between extraverts and introverts.

British students who were extreme extraverts or introverts were tested for their recall on a paired associate learning task (see p. 173) over five time intervals.

It was predicted that introverts would perform poorly initially because their high arousal would interfere with short-term recall. Good initial performance was expected for extraverts. However, over time both of these effects should reverse. The greater consolidation by the introverts should facilitate later performance, while the weaker consolidation of the extraverts, although interfering less at the shorter time intervals, should be less permanent and therefore not enhance long-term retention. The data shown in the figure clearly reveal the predicted effects. While they flourish initially, the lower-arousal extraverts fade over time (Howarth & Eysenck, 1968).

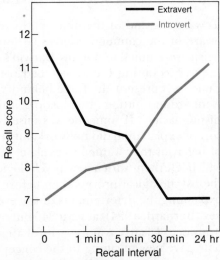

Adapted from Eysenck, 1973

f. The development of a sophisticated test methodology is used to quantify individual differences on underlying trait dimensions. Using the psychometric method (the psychological measurement of individual differences), trait theorists collect personality test responses from large samples of subjects under standardized test situations. By using powerful statistical techniques (such as factor analysis), the patterns of association between traits across all the individuals are reduced to the minimal number that presumably form the core of personality.

Criticism of trait theories

Trait theories have been criticized as not being real theories in that they do not *explain* how behavior is *causally* determined, but merely identify trait labels that are *correlated* with behavior. Furthermore, trait theories offer no conception of the development of personality. Emphasis is on the structure of personality and its elements with no corresponding concern for its origins or the dynamic interrelation of the traits that together are assumed to form personalities. We have seen that nomothetic trait approaches have failed to demonstrate empirically that traits have any substantial cross-situational or temporal consistency. Allport's ideal idiographic approach based on the intensive study of unique cases is rarely followed. To the contrary, modern trait theorists sacrifice individual uniqueness in personality in the effort to discover basic common source traits that explain differences between individuals in their reaction to the same situation.

A positive value of the trait theory approach, however, has been in the recognition that predictions of behavior are usually improved by taking account of *both* situational variables and dispositional variables. Psychological reality is rarely found in simple, main effects where one stimulus variable predicts behavior. More often, the rule is *interaction* of variables. The effect of a given variable on the behavior being studied is not direct; it usually *depends* on one or more other variables. Thus, in the study of extraversion and memory (above), to predict a person's recall we need to know both the extraversion-introversion category and the recall interval. The personality trait *interacts* with the stimulus event to determine performance on the task.

Psychodynamic theories

Toward the end of the nineteenth century, Charles Darwin made the world aware of the common bonds that link human beings and animals. Psychologists were quick to borrow Darwin's concept of "instinct." From its original use in accounting for stereotyped patterns of animal behavior, this concept came to represent the force behind virtually all human actions. If a person went around hitting other people, it might be because of an inborn "instinct of pugnacity." If someone was miserly, it was a "hoarding instinct." Yet, this sort of explanation did not work out very well. If psychologists had a new kind of behavior they wanted to explain, they had only to postulate a new instinct, which left them with a new psychological term but no more understanding of the psychological process than before. Naming something is not the same as explaining the determinants of the event. By the 1920s, according to one survey (Bernard, 1924), at least 849 different classes of human instincts had been proposed. Clearly a more fruitful approach was needed. Sigmund Freud not only gave new meaning to the concept of human instincts, he revolutionized the very conception of human personality.

Freud's ideas about the origins, development, and expression of both normal and abnormal personality are complex, numerous, and subtle. You should supplement the bare structure to be sketched here with your own reading of Freud's *Psychopathology of Everyday Life* (1904), *Introductory Lectures on Psycho-analysis* (1923), and also Munroe's *Schools of Psychoanalytic Thought* (1955).

Fundamental concepts

A number of basic concepts characterize Freud's approach to understanding personality. Despite some differences in emphasis between Freud and certain of his followers (such as Jung, Adler, and Sullivan), five basic ideas form the core of the psychodynamic approach. They are: (a) an extreme psychological determinism; (b) a genetic approach; (c) biosocial instincts; (d) unconscious processes; and (e) goal-directed motivational dynamics.

Determinism   In the late 1800s *hysteria* was a common European illness without an adequate explanation. Patients had impairments in bodily functioning with no apparent physical basis. Paralysis and blindness, for example, occurred in people (mostly women) with intact nervous systems and no organic damage. Freud, a physician, studied and attempted to treat the bizarre symptoms of this mental disorder. Along with his colleague Breuer, Freud discovered that a particular physical symptom usually *made sense* in terms of a prior forgotten event in the patient's life. Under hypnosis a blind patient might recall, for instance, witnessing in childhood her parents having intercourse. As an adult, anticipation of her first sexual encounter aroused powerful feelings associated with this earlier, disturbing and psychologically injurious episode. Her blindness represented the patient's attempt to undo not only seeing the original event, but perhaps also to deny sexual feelings in herself. Her symptom also had a secondary function *(secondary gain)*. It made her helpless and dependent, and this brought her attention, comfort, and sympathy from others.

Freud's analysis revealed that symptoms were not arbitrary nor accidental, but were related in a meaningful way to significant life events. By careful, intensive analysis of each patient's life history, Freud believed it was possible to reconstruct the origins of bizarre mental disorders as well as of the irrational behavior that even normal individuals engage in from time to time.

His extreme *determinism* can be summed up in the phrase "no behavior is accidental." The determinants of behavior might not be obvious, but *psychoanalysis could uncover the causal determinants of any and all human action.* Thus empirical investigation and rational analysis became tools that could unlock the secrets of both pathological and normal personality.

Genetic origins   Significant aspects of adult personality functioning are seen as the product of the person's adaptive experiences in coping with demands placed upon him or her. There is assumed to be a *continuity* of personality development from "womb to tomb." But it is in infancy and early childhood where experience has its most profound impact on personality formation. Freudian theory made the scientific study of infant and child behavior respectable and fashionable. Interestingly, Freud based his theories on adult patients' descriptions of their childhood experiences and *not* on direct observations of children.

Instincts   Freud searched for a way to relate the mental abnormalities he observed in his patients to a common, normal biological foundation. Because

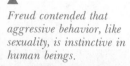

Freud contended that
aggressive behavior, like
sexuality, is instinctive in
human beings.

of his training as a physician, he sought that foundation in psychobiology. Because of the ideas of his times, he found the mechanism in human instincts. He believed that behavior receives its force from instincts which, in turn, are derived from the bodily processes of the individual. Recurring states of excitation of the body provide the energy for our various instincts. Instincts are inborn tension systems created by the organs of the body. The goal of instinctive behavior is to reduce the tension experienced. Tension reduction is experienced as pleasure. There are many ways (behaviors) to satisfy a given instinct. It thus becomes the task of psychoanalysis to discover the underlying instinctual basis of observed actions (or symptoms).

Two major categories of instinct are: ego instincts and sexual instincts. Ego instincts are part of the system of self-preservation. Sexual instincts involve the need for survival of the species. But Freud greatly expanded the notion of human sexuality with his view of the sexual or life instinct, also called *eros.*

The urge for sexual union was only one expression of eros. It involved all attempts to seek pleasure, to make physical contact, and even to strive for creative synthesis. The force that drives it is called the *libido.* As we have seen (p. 240), the sexual instinct does not arise in puberty but is already operating in early childhood. Infantile sexuality was a radical concept in Victorian times. For Freud it meant the infant's pleasure from physical stimulation of genitals and other sensitive areas of the body. These other "erogenous" areas include the mouth and anus. The sexual instinct was seen as a primitive, uncompromising force that demanded satisfaction—seeking pleasure and avoiding pain (called the *pleasure principle*). At times, the satisfaction of eros is indirect and disguised in wishes, fantasies, dreams, or actions that do not seem to make sense.

Clinical observation of patients who had suffered from traumatic experiences associated with World War I led Freud to go beyond the pleasure principle. *Thanatos,* or the death instinct, is a tension that drives people toward aggressive and destructive behaviors. It is part of the tendency for all living things to return to an inorganic state, to entropy.

What is important for us to remember is that sexuality and aggression are proposed here as central aspects of the *normal* personality. The pleasure of destroying someone's sand castle with one swift kick, or defacing a building with graffiti, or smashing an automobile is indeed readily observable in normal children and adults. ▲

Unconscious processes Though reaction was strong against the loss of innocence in the notion of infantile sexuality, it was stronger in opposition to another of Freud's novel ideas—the unconscious. Other writers had pointed to such a process but Freud put the concept of the unconscious determinants of human thought, feeling, and action on a very special pedestal. The unconscious is a *process,* not an entity, or part of the mind. Behavior can be motivated by drives of which we are not conscious. We may act without knowing why, or without direct access to the true cause of our actions. There is a *manifest* content to our behavior—what we say, do, perceive. But there may also be a *latent* content that is concealed from us by unconscious processes. The *meaning* of neurotic symptoms, as well as dreams, slips of the pen and tongue, and other psychopathological aspects of normal behavior are to be found at the unconscious level of thinking and information processing. ●

What evidence is there that such conflicts actually take place? Freud's answer has passed into the popular culture as the "Freudian slip." According to Freud, these unacceptable impulses within us, even though inhibited, sup-

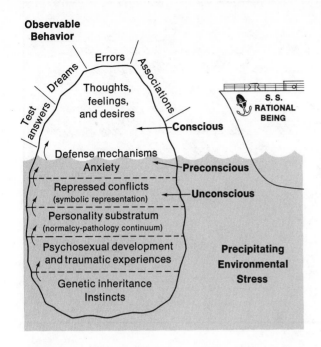

Observable Behavior

Before Freud, it had been assumed that people's actions were influenced largely by conscious thought and rational choice applied to present situations. Freud believed that the thoughts and behavior of which a person was aware constituted only a small portion of his or her ongoing experience and that the major influences on both conscious thoughts and observable behavior were irrational, unconscious, and historical, each layer influencing those above it.

pressed, or repressed, still strive for expression. Our desire to confess our imagined transgressions against society "oozes from our pores" and takes on many forms. For example, "forgetting" an important appointment with the dentist or being consistently late for dates with a particular person may not be accidental but may be an instance of this tendency to express the way we *really* feel. Telling unwanted guests on their arrival, "I'm so sorry—oh, I mean glad you could come," may reveal the true intention of the host or hostess. When a faculty member at Oxford University asked the invited guests to raise their glasses in a toast to their "dear queen," was there another intention being expressed when it came out as "Let us toast our queer dean"?

According to Freud, such slips are meaningful, the meaning being in the unconscious intention. Such "errors" can be explained in terms of the final result produced, even though some other meaning was expected by the hearer or apparently intended by the speaker; such slips indicate the true intention. ■

Dynamic motivation The term *psychodynamic* refers to a human motivational system that is goal-directed. For Freud, all behavior has a purpose of its own. There are good reasons why people forget certain unpleasant events and why they may risk their lives or even act foolishly in public. As the wish is parent to the deed, so our actions emerge from what we desire. Prominent among our desires are sexual and aggressive wishes which drive unconsciously motivated actions toward or away from specific goals. Thus Freudian theory holds that in adjusting to life's demands, individual behavior is continually driven by both conscious and unconscious processes.

The structure of personality

Freud accounted for individual differences in personality by suggesting that different people deal with their fundamental drives (eros and thanatos) in different ways. To explain these differences, he pictured a continuing battle

As an exercise in detecting Freudian slips, read this letter quickly once. Now reread it more carefully. What message is Mama unconsciously telegraphing to her son, who has just broken the news of his engagement to a woman from Richmond, Virginia? See if your friends find all the slips.

My dear Son,

The news of your engagment came as a delightful surprise. Naturally we are very peased at the resluts of your efforts. When must we meet the fair lady again? She seemed just to divine when we saw her at your new year's petty. Richmond is such a long way—I hope you won't be going to Vaginia so often that you have no time left for studies.

We look forward to the future knowing that I have not lost a sun but a daugter.

Conratulations,

Mother

between two parts of the personality, the id and the superego, moderated by a third aspect of the self, the ego.

The *id* is conceived as the primitive, unconscious part of the personality, the storehouse of the fundamental drives. It operates irrationally; impulses push for expression and gratification "no matter what," without considering whether what is desired is realistically possible or morally acceptable.

The *superego* is the storehouse of an individual's values, including moral attitudes implanted by society. The superego corresponds roughly to the *conscience*; it develops when a child *internalizes* the prohibitions of parents and other adults against certain kinds of actions. The superego also includes the *ego ideal*, which develops as a child internalizes the views of others as to the kind of person he or she should strive to become. Thus the superego, society's representative in the individual, is often in conflict with the id, survival's representative. The id wants to do what feels good, while the superego insists on doing what is "right."

The *ego* plays the part of arbitrator in this conflict. The ego represents the individual's picture of physical and social reality, of what will lead to what and which things are possible in the world as it is actually perceived. Part of the ego's job is to choose kinds of action that will gratify id impulses without having undesirable consequences. Thus the ego would probably block an impulse to fly by leaping from a cliff, and might substitute sky diving or a trip on a roller coaster. When the id and the superego are in conflict, the ego generally tries to find a compromise that will at least partially satisfy both.

Ego defense mechanisms

Sometimes the compromise involves putting a lid on the id. The desires of the id are *repressed*. They are put out of conscious awareness and their overt expression curtailed. When, for example, a child has strong feelings of hatred toward a parent which, if acted out, would be dangerous, repression takes over. The hostile impulse is no longer consciously pressing for satisfaction. However, though not seen or heard, repressed urges are not gone. They continue to play a role in personality functioning. Repression is the most basic mental strategy the ego uses to defend itself from the conflicts experienced in the normal course of human development. *Repression* separates our cognitions about an urge or instinct from its motivational force.

When we are in a situation where the repressed conflict is about to be reexperienced, we feel *anxious*. For Freud, anxiety is a danger signal that a repressed conflict is about to emerge into consciousness. A second line of defense is then called into action in the form of one or more other ego defense mechanisms. ◆ For example, by using reaction formation, the person transforms the unacceptable impulse to its opposite: "I don't hate my child, I love my child. See how I smother the dear little thing with love?"

Ego defense mechanisms are thus vital to the psychological adaptation of the individual. "From a psychoanalytic point of view, ego mechanisms of defense are mental processes that attempt to resolve conflicts among drive states, attacks, and external reality . . . they moderate levels of emotion produced by stress, they help keep awareness of certain drives at a minimal level, they provide time to help an individual deal with life traumas, and they help deal with unresolvable loss" (Plutchik, Kellerman, & Conte, 1978).

According to Freudian theory, we all have some urges that are unacceptable in our society and thus all use these defense mechanisms to some extent. Overuse of them, however, constitutes *neurosis*. People who are neurotic spend so much of their energy deflecting, disguising, and rechanneling unacceptable urges that they have little energy left over for productive living or satisfying relationships.

◆

Summary chart of ego defense mechanisms

Compensation	Covering up weakness by emphasizing desirable trait or making up for frustration in one area by overgratification in another
Denial of Reality	Protecting self from unpleasant reality by refusal to perceive it
Displacement	Discharging pent-up feelings, usually of hostility, on objects less dangerous than those which initially aroused the emotion
Emotional Insulation	Withdrawing into passivity to protect self from being emotionally hurt
Fantasy	Gratifying frustrated desires in imaginary achievements ("daydreaming" is a common form)
Identification	Increasing feelings of worth by identifying self with person or institution of illustrious standing
Introjection	Incorporating external values and standards into ego structure so individual is not at the mercy of them as external threats
Isolation	Cutting off emotional charge from hurtful situations or separating incompatible attitudes by logic-tight compartments (holding conflicting attitudes which are never thought of simultaneously or in relation to each other); also called *compartmentalization*
Projection	Placing blame for one's difficulties upon others, or attributing one's own "forbidden" desires to others
Rationalization	Attempting to prove that one's behavior is "rational" and justifiable and thus worthy of the approval of self and others
Reaction Formation	Preventing dangerous desires from being expressed by endorsing opposing attitudes and types of behavior and using them as "barriers"
Regression	Retreating to earlier developmental level involving more childish responses and usually a lower level of aspiration
Repression	Preventing painful or dangerous thoughts from entering consciousness, keeping them unconscious; this is considered to be *the most basic of the defense mechanisms*
Sublimation	Gratifying or working off frustrated sexual desires in substitutive nonsexual activities socially accepted by one's culture
Undoing	Atoning for, and thus counteracting, immoral desires or acts

Freud's conception of a healthy or well-adjusted person is one who can successfully engage in both "love and work." He was rather pessimistic about the chances for escaping neurosis. Perhaps because he grew up in the Victorian era, he believed that any society must teach its children that most expression of their basic drives is bad. Hence nearly everyone will have to be defending against such impulses nearly all the time.

Criticisms of Freudian theory

Critics of Freudian theory and its application to both normal personality and the treatment of neurosis through psychoanalysis raise a number of objections.

a. Many concepts are vague and not operationally defined. Thus much of the theory is difficult to evaluate by means of empirical tests and testable predictions. Because it cannot be disproved even in principle, its theoretical status remains questionable.

b. The theory explains everything *after the fact,* but predicts much less in advance of the facts. It is applied retrospectively, as a historical reconstruction of events and motives that could have determined a behavior in question.

c. Its overemphasis on historical origins of current behavior may misdirect attention away from current situational stimuli that induce and maintain the behavior. ●

d. It has developed from speculation based on clinical experience with people suffering from neuroses and other problems of adjustment, people in whom something has gone wrong. Thus it has little to say about life-styles that are not primarily defensive or defective.

e. Finally, the entire basis of the theory offers a pessimistic view of human nature as developing out of conflicts and traumas, fixations and anxieties. As such, it does not fully acknowledge the positive side of our existence nor offer a view of the healthy personality striving for happiness and realization of its fullest potential.

Even Freud's severest critics, however, recognize his contributions to modern psychological thinking about personality. Among them, we should remember his emphasis on the unconscious determinants of behavior and the understandable origins of the most irrational and bizarre behaviors. Furthermore, the significance he attributed to early life origins of adult behavior gave impetus to the psychological study of child development. In addition, the psychoanalytic perspective paved the way for the scientific study of human sexuality and revealed its importance as a source of conflict and adjustment problems. Finally, his method of treatment of neurosis through psychoanalysis has added to our understanding of how normal personality can "go wrong" as well as helping some patients get back on the right track toward effective personal functioning.

Neo-Freudian theories

Many of those who came after Freud kept his basic picture of personality as a battleground in which unconscious primal urges fight it out with social values. Most, however, made a few changes. Some, like Alfred Adler and Carl Jung, offered different candidates for the most important "primal urges" to replace Freud's broadly defined sex drive.

Adler (1929) accepted the notion that the whole of personality is determined by unrecognized wishes: "Man knows more than he understands." But

●
"All right, deep down it's a cry for psychiatric help — but at one level it's a stick-up."

he rejected the significance of the pleasure principle in favor of what he saw as a more powerful wish: *the desire to be superior*. For Adler this is the central goal of the human personality and it motivates all of human action. Personality is structured around this underlying striving for superiority. Because as helpless, dependent small children, we all experience feelings of inferiority, our lives become dominated by the search for paths to superiority. Life-styles are often developed around compensations for feelings of inferiority. Personality conflict arises when external environmental pressures are incompatible with the person's internal striving for superiority or perfection—and not from competing urges within the person.

Carl Jung (1953) greatly expanded the conception of the unconscious. For him, it was not confined to the individual's unique life experiences but was filled with fundamental psychological truths shared by the whole of the human race. This *collective unconscious* is evidenced in our intuitive understanding of primitive myths, art forms, and symbols—which are the universal archetypes of existence. Libido was also much more than sexual force for Jung. It was the energy of life, the vital force that is indestructible and everlasting and binds individuals to the cycle of nature.

Other neo-Freudians upgraded the role of ego as equal in significance to id and superego and not merely the go-between that arbitrates their conflicts. Still others, like Karen Horney (1950) and Erich Fromm (1947), have believed that Freud overemphasized the biological influences on personality at the expense of the social influences. They have attempted in their writings to redress the balance. In Chapter 8 we outlined the developmental theories of two other neo-Freudians, Erik Erikson and Harry Stack Sullivan.

Humanistic theories

Humanistic approaches to understanding personality are characterized by their: (a) reliance upon a field-theory orientation, (b) insistence on a holistic view of personality, (c) concern for the integrity of the individual's personal, private experience (the phenomenal field), (d) emphasis on growth motivation, and (e) stress on the importance of self-actualization.

Humanistic personality theorists such as Carl Rogers and Abraham Maslow have stressed a basic drive toward self-actualization as the organizer of all the diverse forces whose interplay continually creates what a person is. In the process they have developed theories that seem more "human" than many that preceded them. These theories emphasize the importance of how people perceive their world and of processes of health and growth. In their view, psychological events always take place within fields of force that are in dynamic and constantly shifting equilibrium. Such mental events represent a balance and interaction of many forces, and a change anywhere in the system is seen as affecting the whole system. Thus behavior is seen as shaped not by individual chains of cause and effect, but by the combination of forces that make up the entire field.

Carl Rogers

For Carl Rogers (1947, 1951, 1977), therapy is "client-centered" and personality theory is "person-centered." It is the private world of the individual—his or her *phenomenal field*—which must be understood. His advice is to listen to what people say about themselves. Attend to their concepts and to the significance they attach to their experiences. Such an approach is in part a reaction against the imposition of a priori theoretical conceptions as in Freudian theory, and the reliance by behaviorists on the objective, external situation.

Rogers believes the most basic drive of the human organism is toward *self-actualization*—the constant striving to realize our inherent potential. Unfortunately, this drive at times comes into conflict with the need for approval or *positive regard* from both the self and others. If other important people in a child's environment express dismay at some of the things the child does without making it clear that this "conditional regard" applies to the *behavior* rather than to the *child* as a person, he or she may begin to do and think only things that are "acceptable" (recall our Chapter 4 distinction between punishing a response and punishing a person). In that case, *incongruence* will develop between the child's "real" feelings and fulfilling activities, on the one hand, and the "acceptable" things that are allowed, on the other. Mental illness comes when one does not dare to be oneself or to acknowledge one's real experiencing self as legitimate. (See *P&L* Close-up, Self-concepts.)

Close-up
Self-concepts: Public Roles or Private Places?

For humanistic psychologists the self is the irreducible unit out of which the coherence and stability of personality emerge. The notion of a self-concept is hardly new. "Know thyself" is an inscription carved on the shrine of the Delphic oracle in ancient Greece. Sociologist Charles Cooley proposed a "looking-glass self" that reflected the appraisals we imagine others hold of us (1902). G. H. Mead extended this idea; he believed that identity develops from incorporating the orientations other people have toward us (1934). Self, in such a view, is the direct product of real or symbolic interactions in one's social environment. Within psychology, the concern for analysis of the self found its strongest advocate in William James (1890). James identified three components of self-experience: the *material me* (bodily self, along with physical objects one is surrounded by); the *social me* (one's awareness of his or her reputation in the eyes of others) and the *spiritual me* (the self that monitors private experiences of thinking and feeling).

There are two definitions of self in current use in psychology. One definition considers the self as an *object* of a person's self-conception. Research utilizing this definition has focused on the importance of self-esteem for the way we feel and behave. The second type of definition focuses on the self as a *process* of perceiving, thinking, evaluating, and so on. Undoubtedly, people utilize both of these types of conceptions of self, but it may be that some people more often focus on themselves as objects, while others more frequently experience self as process. Or it may be that most people use both of these conceptions, but at different periods in their lives.

The concept of self may develop out of our relations with and appraisals by others, but once formed, it also exerts a *biasing* influence on how we process information. For example, once we think highly of ourselves and have positive self-esteem, negative feedback is explained away or treated as an exception to the rule. On the other hand, once we have developed low self-esteem, positive feedback does little to change it because *it* is seen as the exception, whereas any failure or bad experience is readily accommodated as "expected" evidence.

Our self-conceptions influence not only our relations with others but the goals we aspire to, and—perhaps most important—the quality of our private emotional life.

Once the alternatives are clearly perceived and adequately symbolized, however, Rogers believes that the individual chooses the path of growth. Thus in therapy it is the patient's own inner urge toward growth and wholeness that makes recovery possible. The therapist's task, as we shall see in Chapter 20, is to provide a safe and encouraging climate that promotes such growth.

Abraham Maslow

Another theorist who found self-actualization a fruitful concept was Abraham Maslow (1968, 1971). Feeling that psychology had concentrated too much on human weaknesses, while neglecting strengths, Maslow sought to round out the picture by studying emotionally healthy individuals. He regarded human nature as basically good, but saw the innate tendency toward growth and self-actualization as rather weak and fragile, easily overcome by social pressures. Maslow distinguished between *deficiency motivation*, in which individuals seek to restore their physical or psychological equilibrium, and *growth motivation*, in which individuals seek to go beyond what they have done and been in the past. People may welcome uncertainty, an increase in tension, and even pain if they see it as a route toward greater fulfillment of their human potential.

According to Maslow, a person's inborn needs are arranged in a *hierarchy* of priority. As those on one level are satisfied, those on the next level take precedence. Thus when the physiological needs such as hunger and thirst are satisfied, the needs on the next level—safety needs—press for satisfaction. After these come, in order, needs for belongingness and love, needs for esteem, and needs for self-actualization. At the top of the needs hierarchy is the sixth stage of "transcendence." Maslow added this highest level to represent the ultimate human need which goes beyond self-actualization, the quest for identity, even beyond individual humanness. ▲

The psychological investigation of transcendent experiences is part of the newly emerging field of "transpersonal psychology." *Transpersonal psychology* has become a distinct field of inquiry into higher states of consciousness and the spiritual search as basic aspects of human life (Roberts, 1974).

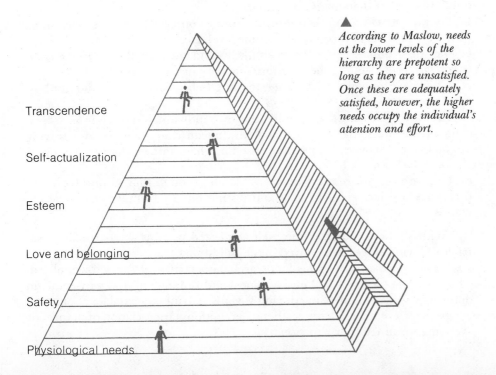

▲

According to Maslow, needs at the lower levels of the hierarchy are prepotent so long as they are unsatisfied. Once these are adequately satisfied, however, the higher needs occupy the individual's attention and effort.

Transcendence

Self-actualization

Esteem

Love and belonging

Safety

Physiological needs

Although for most people self-actualization is only a hope or a goal, something wished for and striven toward, a few appear to achieve it to a large degree. Maslow studied a group of such persons, although he never made it very clear just how he chose his sample and carried out his investigations. He did include both historical personages, such as Beethoven and Lincoln, and persons alive at the time of the study, including Einstein and Eleanor Roosevelt. On the basis of his findings, Maslow formulated a list of fifteen characteristics of self-actualized persons. Would you consider yourself "actualized" according to the following standards?

a. Self-actualized persons perceive reality more effectively than most people do and have more comfortable relations with it. That is, they *live close to reality* and to nature, can judge others accurately, and can tolerate ambiguity or uncertainty more easily than most people can.

b. They can *accept themselves* and their various characteristics with little feeling of guilt or anxiety and, at the same time, can readily *accept others*.

c. They show a great deal of *spontaneity* in both thought and behavior, although they seldom show extreme unconventionality.

d. They are *problem-centered*, not ego-centered, often devoting themselves to broad social problems as a mission in life.

e. They have a *need for privacy* and solitude at times and are capable of looking at life from a detached, objective point of view.

f. They are relatively *independent of their culture and environment* but do not flaunt convention just for the sake of being different.

g. They are capable of *deep appreciation* of the basic experiences of life, even of things they have done or seen many times before.

h. Many of them have had *mystic experiences* such as having felt a deep sense of ecstasy, having felt limitless horizons opening to them, or having felt very powerful and at the same time very helpless but ending with a conviction that something significant had happened.

i. They have a *deep social interest* and identify in a sympathetic way with people in general.

j. They are capable of very *deep, satisfying interpersonal relations*, usually with only a few rather than many individuals.

k. They are *democratic* in their attitudes toward others, showing respect for all people, regardless of race, creed, income level, etc.

l. They discriminate clearly between means and ends but often *enjoy the means toward their ends* ("getting there") more than impatient persons do.

m. They have a good *sense of humor*, tending to be philosophical and nonhostile in their jokes.

n. They are highly *creative*, each in their own individual way. They have "primary creativeness that comes out of the unconscious" and produces truly original, new discoveries. This shows itself in whatever field the self-actualized person has chosen.

o. They are *resistant to enculturation*. That is, although they fit into their culture, they are independent of it and do not blindly comply with all its demands.

With all these characteristics, self-actualized persons are particularly capable of loving and of being loved in the fullest way.

Peak experiences of various kinds are characteristic of the self-actualized. These are "moments of highest happiness and fulfillment" and may come, in differing degrees of intensity, during various activities—sexual love, parental experiences, creative activity, aesthetic perceptions, appreciation of nature, or even intense athletic participation.

Criticism of humanistic theories

It is difficult to criticize theories that are on the side of the angels. Who could possibly object to the importance of self-concepts, to self-actualization, to fulfilling one's human potential, or to motives for growth? Behaviorists do. They criticize humanistic concepts as being fuzzy, without clear definitions. Is self-actualization an inborn tendency or socially defined? Humanistic theories have difficulty in accounting for the *specific* kinds of consistency that characterize particular individuals, except in a very general way. It is as if they were theories of human nature rather than of humans beings. Objective behaviorists also claim that the general level at which such theories are formulated minimizes their research value. (Roberts, however, has developed an extensive bibliography that suggests otherwise [1973].) They go on to note that overemphasis on the self as a unitary source of experience and action neglects the important environmental variables that behaviorists have shown to control behavior.

Learning theories

In the heyday of football at the United States Military Academy at West Point, "Doc" Blanchard made yardage running straight ahead inside the opposing line, while Glenn Davis did so running around end, on the outside. Their nicknames of "Mr. Inside and Mr. Outside" also seem to be apt characterizations of two of psychology's leading ball carriers, Carl Rogers and B. F. Skinner. We have seen that Rogers focuses his attention on what is going on inside the person. Skinner is the "Mr. Outside" of psychology.

B. F. Skinner

Skinner's approach ignores what is "in" the person and outright denies that the inside approach has any psychological validity. For him and other behaviorists, behavior and personality are shaped by the outside environment. Personality, in such a view, is the sum total of covert and overt response systems that are reliably elicited as a consequence of particular reinforcement histories. The sources of individual differences are to be found in variations between people in their personal histories of reinforcement—and also in our ignorance of the true external causes of behavior. According to Skinner, "Science insists that action is initiated by forces impinging upon the individual, and that caprice is only another name for behavior for which we have not yet found a cause" (1955, p. 53).

Clearly then, such an empirically based view would argue that the observed consistencies in behavior which give rise to a search for personality are not to be found in trait dispositions, primal instincts, or free-floating self-concepts. For the behaviorist, the search begins with a *functional analysis* of the ways behavior varies as environmental conditions change. It ends by specifying the external variables that can be shown to alter responding. No mental states, no inferred dispositions are allowed in explanations of behavior. You will recall from our discussions in earlier learning chapters that the crux of the Skinnerian approach was the discovery of environmental contingencies (reinforcing circumstances) that control behavior.

John Dollard and Neal Miller

John Dollard and Neal Miller worked together at Yale University (1950) to reconcile the behaviorist approach with the Freudian. They combined a concern for the sorts of problems discussed by Freud with an appreciation for the methodological rigor of Hull's learning theory. So they set about trying to find a way to put the two together. At first sight, Freud's rich theory seems very different from the sort of statements usually generated by studies of rats running around in mazes. In fact, however, there are some strong points of similarity. First, Freud's conceptualization, like Hullian learning theory, was a *tension-reduction* theory: both conceived of the organism as acting in order to reduce "tension" produced by unsatisfied drives. Second, both kinds of theory stress the importance of *early learning* in determining what an organism does later in life. Although the two theoretical systems use very different words to describe their conclusions, they thus come out with models of the human organism that have important parallels.

An interesting example of Dollard and Miller's translation of Freudian concepts into experimental learning terms is their handling of the personal characteristic of "indecisiveness." Consider, they suggested, the case of a lover contemplating marriage. The perfect mate has been found, and the appropriate arrangements have been made. But as the day of the wedding approaches, the lover's doubts increase. Finally, to the consternation of all concerned, the whole thing is called off at the last minute. A week later, the lover decides to go through with it after all. But again, when the day approaches, the wedding is canceled. How are we to account for this wishy-washy, vacillating behavior? And how are we to account for the scores of lovers who, in spite of increasing doubts at the last minute, go ahead and get married anyway?

Miller (1944) listed four principles derived from animal research that seem to help us understand this sort of conflict situation:

a. The tendency to approach a desired goal gets stronger the nearer the subject is to it *(approach gradient)*.
b. The tendency to go away from a feared place or object also gets stronger the nearer the subject is to it *(avoidance gradient)*.
c. The strength of the second (avoidance) tendency increases more rapidly than that of the first (approach). In other words, it may be said that the avoidance gradient is steeper than the approach gradient.
d. The strength of both tendencies varies with the strength of the drive on which the tendencies are based. A high level of drive may thus be said to raise the height of the entire gradient.

The two graphs show how these principles help us understand our different lovers. ■ Such an example is an intriguing illustration of Dollard and Miller's approach, but it has more to do with how people behave in relatively

■
In the first figure, the avoidance gradient has outstripped the approach gradient, causing the wedding to be canceled. Now, however, the wedding is further away, so the approach tendency is the stronger—and the process is repeated. In the second figure, the approach tendency is so strong the avoidance tendency never exceeds it— and the wedding takes place on schedule.

From Neal E. Miller—"Experimental Studies of Conflict" in *Personality and the Behavior Disorders,* edited by J. McV. Hunt, Copyright 1944, renewed © 1972. The Ronald Press Company New York.

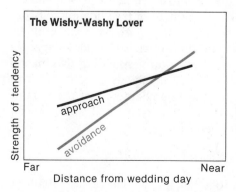

The Wishy-Washy Lover

Strength of tendency

approach

avoidance

Far · Near
Distance from wedding day

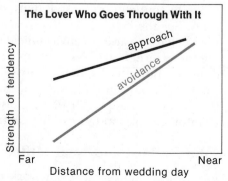

The Lover Who Goes Through With It

Strength of tendency

approach

avoidance

Far · Near
Distance from wedding day

transient situations than with the kinds of consistency over time and place with which personality theorists are usually concerned.

Albert Bandura and Walter Mischel

The systematic development of an approach to personality that recognizes the importance of behavioral learning processes that occur in social settings and influence both cognitions and actions is found in the work of Albert Bandura and Walter Mischel of Stanford University. Through their theoretical writing and extensive programs of empirical research with children and adults, Bandura (1977) and Mischel (1973) are eloquent champions of the new social-learning approach to understanding personality.

Social learning theory does not view human beings as being driven by inner forces or as being the helpless pawns of environmental influences. Rather, it proposes that "psychological functioning is best understood in terms of a continuous reciprocal interaction between behavior and its controlling conditions" (Bandura, 1971). Any individual's unique characteristics are determined by such factors as social stimuli, social and personal reinforcements, past learning history, and so on.

In contrast to other theories of learning, the social-learning approach stresses the uniquely human cognitive processes that are involved in acquiring and maintaining patterns of behavior. The theory points out that people can learn things *vicariously* through observation of other people, in addition to learning by direct experience. Furthermore, people can use *symbols* to represent external events cognitively, thus allowing them to foresee the possible consequences of their actions without having to actually experience them. Also, people are capable of *self-regulatory processes*, whereby they evaluate their own behavior (according to personal standards) and provide their own reinforcements (e.g., self-approval or self-reproach). This self-regulating capacity allows people to control their own actions, rather than being controlled by external forces.

Much of what we do, the things we believe in and value are not best thought of as emerging properties of the self. Instead, as we saw in Chapter 4, actions, thoughts, feelings, and values can be developed, maintained, or changed by observing influential models. We learn general rules and principles through such observational learning, as well as specific stimulus-response pairings.

Mischel's analysis (1973) highlights the interaction of selected personal variables with specific situational variables. Individual differences in response to a specific environmental input may be due to any or all of the following variables (or processes):

a. *Competencies.* What you know, what you can do, and your ability to generate certain cognitive and behavioral outcomes.

b. *Encoding strategies.* The way you process incoming information, selectively attending, categorizing, and making associations to it.

c. *Expectancies.* Your anticipation of likely outcomes for given actions in particular situations.

d. *Personal values.* The importance you attach to stimuli, events, people, and activities.

e. *Self-regulatory systems and plans.* The rules you have developed to guide your performance, to set goals, and evaluate your effectiveness.

Each of these variables is assumed to have been learned through reinforced transactions with people in one's social-cultural environment and with inanimate aspects of the physical environment.

Criticisms of learning theories

Some critics hold that behaviorist approaches to personality have thrown out the baby and kept the bath water. In placing such emphasis on environment, they have lost contact with the person. Is it variables or people that personality is all about, they ask? If one insists that personality is built upon the learned repetition of reinforced responding, where is the origin of creative achievements, innovative ideas, inventions, and works of art? Other criticisms focus on the narrowness of situationally bound views of behavior that deny choice and the freedom that can be used even to reject one's past history of reinforcement. In addition, much of the learning observed by behaviorists is performance that is reinforced because the organism is in a state of deficiency motivation (hungry, thirsty, etc.). The full realization of human potential comes not from acting out of appetitive motives in common with brute beasts, but from those motives that make people aspire to joy, immortality, altruism, and love—that do put us on the side of angels.

Some of the earlier criticisms leveled against the radical behaviorism of Skinner lose their force when confronted by the broader and more flexible theoretical perspectives of the cognitive social-learning theorists. Moreover, other related theoretical ventures, like Arthur Staats' social behaviorism (1975), are currently being developed to provide a rapprochement between basic principles of behaviorism and traditional personality approaches.

A unified theory of personality that the majority of psychologists can agree with remains a promise for future theorists. A summary of the areas of differences between the major theories discussed is outlined in the chart. ●

It might help to think of the comparison between these conceptions of personality that we've reviewed using the following analogy of the human vehicle. Trait theories provide a catalogue which describes the parts and structures of the vehicle. Psychodynamic theories add an engine and the fuel to get the vehicle moving. Learning theories supply the steering wheel, directional signals, mirror, and other regulation equipment. Humanistic theories put a person in the driver's seat—a man or woman who wants to travel to a unique place and to enjoy the trip as much as arriving at the destination. In the next chapter, we will see how psychologists give that person a "psychological driver's test" by objectively measuring personality.

● **Importance of selected variables and processes in major theories of personality**

Variables and Processes	Theory			
	Trait	Psychodynamic	Humanistic	Social-Learning
Heredity	M to H	H	L	L
Biological Foundations	H	H	L	M
Learning Process	L	L	M	H
Early Experience	L	H	L	H
Unconscious Processes	L	H	M	L
Personality Structure	H	H	L	L
Self-concept	H	M	H	L
Uniqueness	H	M	M	L

Key: H = High (emphasized); M = Moderate; L = Low (not emphasized)

Adapted from Hall & Lindzey, 1957

Chapter summary

Personality is the sum of the unique psychological qualities of an individual that influence characteristic behavior patterns (both overt and covert) in relatively consistent ways across situations and over time.

Personality researchers generally study individuals who, within a broad range, would be considered normal, average, or typical. Subjects are usually studied in a setting which is viewed as normal. Investigators also determine normality by ascertaining whether or not a person's behavior is *situationally appropriate*.

The *nomothetic* approach in personality assumes that there is a basic structure to personality. Its adherents measure a set of traits in a large group of individuals, then correlate the scores of each person on each trait with other *criterion performance scores* derived from behavioral observation or tests. Repeated studies show that low correlations between these behaviors are the rule, however.

To investigate the stability of personality traits over a period of time, psychologists have employed the *longitudinal* method of observing or testing a sampling of individuals at an early stage in their lives and then reevaluating them at regular intervals. One such study of gifted children, begun by Lewis Terman, has extended over nearly sixty years and has shown that while direct predictive variables diminished with time, self-descriptive qualities had a high consistency from age 30 to 60. This suggests that it may be one's feelings about oneself that constitute stability in personality.

Gordon Allport believed that personality consistency could be demonstrated through the *idiographic* approach. He held that consistency existed within one person over many situations, and that traits that characterize and are relevant to an individual should be studied in terms of that individual's own phenomenological view.

There are four major theoretical approaches to understanding personality: *trait theories*, *psychodynamic theories*, *humanistic theories*, and *learning theories*.

Personality *typologies* attempt to relate an individual's behavior to simple, highly visible characteristics of the individual. Such typologies in general appear to have little validity. While *types* assume discrete, discontinuous categories, *traits* refer to distinguishable, relatively enduring ways in which individuals vary from each other. Allport, the most influential of the trait theorists, defined traits as inferred predispositions directing the behavior of an individual in consistent and characteristic ways. He distinguished *cardinal traits*, highly generalized dispositions around which a person organized his or her whole life; *central traits*, the less dominant but still broad influences; and *secondary traits*, the more specific traits, limited in scope.

Freud's *psychodynamic* approach embraced concepts of *psychological determinism, genetic origins, biosocial instincts, unconscious processes,* and *goal-directed motivational dynamics.* He held that no behavior was accidental and that the origins of mental disorder and irrational behavior could be uncovered through rational analysis of the patient's life history. Freud's emphasis on *genetic origins* suggested that a person's adaptive experiences, especially in childhood, had profound influences on many aspects of adult personality. He also viewed sexuality and aggression as instincts centrally important to the normal personality. Freud insisted that in addition to the *manifest* content of our behavior there is a *latent* content, concealed from us by *unconscious processes*. Further, all behavior, conscious or unconscious, was seen as *psychodynamic*—having a purpose of its own. *Neo-Freudian* theories, for the most part, kept to Freud's basic picture of personality; they have differed in the emphasis placed upon the various inner drives and have expanded upon concepts such as the *libido*.

Humanistic approaches to personality rely upon *field-theory orientation,* a *holistic* view of personality, and emphasize personal experience, growth motivation, and *self-actualization*. Humanistic psychologists like Carl Rogers see self-actualization, the realization of inherent potentials, as the most basic drive among humans. Within Rogers' framework, the *phenomenal field* of the individual takes precedence, so his therapy is *client-centered,* and his personality theory is *person-centered*. He has pointed out that people tend to behave according to internalized pictures of themselves, rejecting or distorting information which conflicts with this picture. Mental illness, then, results when an individual does not acknowledge his or her real experiencing self as legitimate.

Abraham Maslow, too, placed self-actualization in a central position in his theory, emphasizing *growth motivation,* in which individuals seek to fulfill their human potential. He believed that the individual's inborn needs were arranged in a hierarchy of priority. As those on one level were satisfied, those on the next level would take precedence. *Transcendence* was placed at the top of the hierarchy, following self-actualization as the highest aspiration of human beings.

B. F. Skinner and other behaviorists have developed an approach to personality that ignored internal psychological events and attempted to explain personality and behavior solely from environmental factors. They began with a *functional analysis* of the ways in which behavior varies as environmental conditions change and concluded by demonstrating external variables that alter responding.

John Dollard and Neal Miller reconciled Freudian theory and the behaviorist approach by stressing aspects both have in common — *tension reduction* and *early learning*. Albert Bandura and Walter Mischel have taken a *social learning* approach to understanding personality. This approach proposes that the unique characteristics of an individual are determined by social stimuli, social and personal reinforcements, and past learning history, suggesting that much of human behavior results from imitating influential models.

Chapter

17

Personality Assessment and Individual Differences

What type of person are you, anyway? Tell me something about yourself. In this chapter our interest will be on the ways in which personality is measured and some personality types that such assessment reveals. You will get a better feel for this measurement approach if you first complete the following simple personality test: In the margins are numbers from 1 to 20. In each space write a statement beginning with the words 'I am." When you have completed your list, analyze your responses according to the four categories given below (Kuhn & McPartland, 1954).

a. Put an A next to descriptions that refer to physical characteristics such as size, sex, race, and address. These should be statements that can be easily validated using a mirror, yardstick, scale, or other nonsocial measure.

b. Next to references to your social status, such as mother, student, carpenter, put a B. This category contains descriptions which must be socially defined and validated. Implied in these descriptions are relationships to others.

c. A third category of descriptors are those describing abstract characteristics that transcend situations, such as "I am friendly" and "I am a rock music fan." Next to these types of descriptions, place a C. These will be comments that leave you free to vary your behavior across situations, but characterize you in terms of your personal style.

d. Finally, place a D next to statements that are very vague and global, such as "I am a person" or "I am at one with the universe."

Now add up the number of A's, B's, C's and D's used to describe yourself. Which category do you use most often? Which next, and least, to describe yourself? Give the test to others and see how your self-portrait compares to theirs.

In the 1950s, when people were asked to describe themselves as you did above, the majority of people gave responses in the *B mode*. That is, they responded by describing their group memberships and their roles within society. However, a recent series of studies by Louis Zurcher (1977) has found that people today tend to use the C mode most frequently. He believes this is because the world is changing so rapidly that people no longer feel comfortable defining themselves in terms of their place in the social structure.

Zurcher set out to determine whether differences in people's self-description were related to other characteristics. Comparing B, C, and D mode respondents, he found that B-moders had the greatest sense of social belonging and social purpose. D-moders felt the most distant and detached from society and also had a greater sense of autonomy and self-esteem. C-moders were characterized as having high levels of anxiety and experiencing life stress more intensely than the others.

Zurcher theorizes that we all experience all four modes at different stages of development. The A mode is predominant as children develop the sense of a physical self separate from others. The B mode comes as they learn and internalize social roles. But with adolescence comes a period of role confusion (see p. 262). As adults, we choose among a large array of roles and we may be forced into some roles unwillingly. It is almost inevitable that we begin to question who we really are. To cope with these times of questioning and change, a C-mode self-concept emerges, defining the self as stable across roles. But as we settle into a comfortable set of roles again, we realize that different roles require different types of behavior. Unless we shift back to a B mode at this point, the result can be anxiety and maladjustment.

This analysis of self suggests that shifts from B mode to C mode and back to B mode should be considered a routine part of daily living. This view of self is different from other views of personality in that it emphasizes the *changing* self rather than the stable self. Indeed, Zurcher argues that an adaptive trans-

_____ 1. I am

_____ 2. I am

_____ 3. I am

_____ 4. I am

_____ 5. I am

_____ 6. I am

_____ 7. I am

_____ 8. I am

_____ 9. I am

_____ 10. I am

formation would be for us to come to define stability in terms of change. Thus, the healthy self would be one that is capable of sliding between modes as required by the changing society we live in. Fixation at any particular mode would be maladaptive since it would inevitably lead to stress. This changing conception of self is called *the mutable self*. Our society tends to emphasize the importance of stability of self. We have been trained through years of education to value and strive for consistency in our lives. This analysis implies that it may be necessary to retrain people to evolve mutable selves so they can adequately cope with a changing society. Such training would help the person understand transitions from one mode to another. It would also emphasize that the person can choose which mode to utilize, and further, that it is acceptable, indeed desirable to move from one mode to another.

Assessment of individual differences

Assessing differences between individuals in their abilities, intelligence, personality, and creativity is a relatively new enterprise in psychology. We will see that it grew out of practical concerns created by the needs for mass education, and mass induction of draftees into the Army during World Wars I and II.

But long before Western psychology began devising *tests* to see how people "measured up," assessment techniques were commonplace in ancient China. Actually, China employed a sophisticated program of civil service testing over four thousand years ago, when officials were required to demonstrate their competence every third year at an oral examination. Two thousand years later, during the Han Dynasty, batteries of written civil service tests were used to assess competence in the areas of law, the military, agriculture, and geography. Finally, after another thousand years, civil service testing grew to be a nationwide practice in China. During the Ming Dynasty (1368–1644 A.D.) public officials were chosen on the basis of their performance at three stages of an objective selection procedure. Examinations were first given at a local level. The 4 percent who passed these tests had to endure nine days and nights of essay examinations on the classics. The 5 percent who passed the essay exams were allowed to complete a final set of tests conducted at the nation's capital.

China's selection procedures were transmitted to Western culture by British diplomats and missionaries who visited China in the early 1800s. Modified versions of China's system were soon adopted by the British, and finally by the Americans, for selection of civil service personnel (Wiggins, 1973).

Assessment has been described as "the scientific art of arriving at sufficient conclusions from insufficient data" (OSS Staff, 1948, p. 8). In our everyday life we often try to make prophecies about how someone we know will function in a setting sometime in the future. Your parents probably wondered if you "had it in you" to "make it in college." If they predicted incorrectly it would be financially and emotionally costly. The *error* in such predictions, of course, can go in either of two directions: it is possible to predict failure (and withhold a college education) when the student would have been effective, or to estimate success (and support a college education) when the student is actually ineffective and flunks out. Similarly, of course, there are two kinds of accurate predictions: those in which success is predicted and achieved, and those in which failure is predicted and observed.

_____ 11. *I am*

_____ 12. *I am*

_____ 13. *I am*

_____ 14. *I am*

_____ 15. *I am*

_____ 16. *I am*

_____ 17. *I am*

_____ 18. *I am*

_____ 19. *I am*

_____ 20. *I am*

In many areas of our lives we also want to predict the future behavior of someone under circumstances that are largely unknown or uncertain. Your choice of a person to live with you as roommate or later as spouse and perhaps as parent of your children involves an important assessment prediction. So does choosing a career for yourself. While you are acting as assessor, you are also being assessed by others—potential dates, mates, employers, judges, superior officers, and others who are sizing up your qualifications. Scientific psychology attempts to formalize the procedures by which such predictions about individual behavior can be made with a minimum of error and a maximum of accuracy.

Formally, *assessment is the use of specified testing procedures to evaluate or differentiate individuals on the basis of certain characteristics* (see Kelly, 1967). Such assessment begins with the measurement of a limited number of individual personality attributes and samples of behavior. From this narrow body of information about the person in the testing situation(s), predictions are made about his or her likely reactions at some future time in some other situation (not identical to the test situation).

Psychologists use assessment techniques to make sense of the incredible range of individual differences. They want to understand how different traits go together to form a unique personality. They are curious to discover ways of describing the diversity of individual behavior. By testing, classifying, and categorizing individuals who share similar traits, psychologists can correlate behavioral differences with personality types. Part of such research is designed to test the predictive value of different theories of personality looked at in the previous chapter.

Another aspect of the scientific concern for assessment has to do with learning about how people develop. At what ages do children develop which skills, attitudes, and ways of dealing with the world? How important are sex, race, intelligence and other human characteristics in predicting specific behavioral outcomes? The personality psychologist is interested in general answers to these and similar questions about relationships between the average behavioral tendency of people with certain characteristics. While the clinical psychologist's goal is to make predictions about the individual client, the research psychologist's goal is to discover consistencies and regularities in personality that predict to behavior in general. In all such testing, the goal is to find out more information that will further the development of psychology as a theoretical and applied science.

Basic features of assessment

Three methodological requirements must be met before assessment procedures can yield information that will be useful in classification and selection of individuals. In developing instruments for the measurement of personality, the psychologist is concerned with the concepts of reliability, validity, and standardization.

A test is *reliable* if it measures something *consistently* and *precisely*. If your bathroom scale gives you a different reading each time you step on it within a short time period (when you have not eaten or changed your clothing) it is not giving you a reliable estimate of your weight. Or, if you took the same test twice and got very different scores (without more learning in between), that test would be an unreliable measure of your knowledge of the subject.

In addition to being consistent, reliable test instruments must be accurate. Reliability is the precision with which an instrument makes its measurements. A sundial is not as reliable as a clock, which in turn, is an imprecise instrument if you are measuring fractions of a second. Depending on our purposes, we are willing to accept a certain degree of unreliability in the form of less precise estimates of the true underlying value. Precision is always more expensive than approximation. A sundial is reliable enough if you want to know only whether it is morning or afternoon. Thus we try to increase the reliability of an instrument without unduly increasing its cost to construct and administer. There are three ways of estimating the reliability of a test.

Test-retest reliability is a measure of the correlation between the scores of the same people on the same test given on two different occasions. A perfectly reliable test would have a correlation of +1.00, while a totally unreliable test would result in a .00 reliability coefficient. Reliability coefficients between .70 and .90 are found in the best psychological tests. By comparison, achievement tests constructed by classroom teachers generally range in reliability from lows of .30 to only moderate levels of .60 (Kelly, 1967). These correlations are for objective, true-false, and multiple-choice tests; you already know about the unreliability of essay-test scores.

Two other ways of assessing reliability include administering alternate, *equivalent forms* of the test to the same persons, or measuring the *internal consistency* of scores on a single test. For example, a reliable test should yield approximately the same scores if we compare responses to equivalent forms of the same test, or if we compare scores on the odd-numbered and even-numbered items of a single test. In either case, a mathematical correlation can be obtained, showing the relative stability (reliability) of scores. Sources of unreliability are introduced by variables that change over time and *temporarily* affect the thing we are measuring. Fatigue, attention, emotional arousal, mood, and motivation are among the factors that can operate to make your measured performance deviate from what your true performance should be.

Validity tells us if the test is doing the job for which it was designed. The *validity* of a test refers to whether it is measuring what is intended to be measured. Simply put, do scores on the test relate to something that we really want to know about? Our primary interest is in that "something"; the test is merely a means to estimate whether the person has that something or has enough of certain attributes to be effective at that something. Validity must always be determined for specific purposes. The validity of test scores is assessed by the extent to which they correlate with (predict to) some explicit measurable *criterion*. The criterion is the thing of interest, the outcome you are really concerned about, such as success in college. Often problems of validity arise not simply because the test itself is defective, but because the criterion is not adequately conceptualized. These criteria of appraisal are the yardstick against which the effectiveness of the assessment is determined. They are the target of prediction and should be well formulated even before the assessment procedure is instituted.

To be most useful, a measuring device should be *standardized*—administered under standard conditions to a large group of persons representative of the group for which it is intended. This procedure yields *norms*, or standards, so that an individual's score can be compared with those of others in a defined group. The test must, of course, also be administered to all subjects in the same way and under the same conditions, or comparisons will be meaningless.

Ways to measure personality

The systematic effort to study and measure personality traits in a quantitative fashion (using tests) is called the *psychometric trait approach*. *Psychometrics* is the general term for the branch of psychology that deals with assessment.

In their effort to measure personality by tests, psychometricians have developed instruments to assess traits, aptitudes, skills, achievement, temperament, needs, values, attitudes, interests, conflicts, and more. In subsequent sections we will devote considerable attention to intelligence testing and measures of creativity. Here we will outline five general approaches to measuring other aspects of personality functioning: human judges, situational-behavior sampling, self-inventories, projective tests, and personality scales.

Use of human judges

For some kinds of evaluation people who know the individual well may be used to assess his or her various attributes. Psychologists, parents, friends, teachers, counselors, co-workers and others can be asked to make these judgments.

Rating scales Rating scales are used to record systematic judgments in a standardized format. For example, I invite you to be a judge of the interest level and informational value of each chapter of *Psychology and Life* that you have read (see evaluation form at end of the book). You might indicate which chapter you like best and rank it *1*, next best, *2*, and so on until you have given your *relative rating* of each of the chapters you have read so far.

Absolute rating scales ask the judge to assign a score to each individual item (chapters of this text, movies you've seen, your teachers) on each trait being rated. The thing being judged is evaluated according to some standard that is independent of other things being considered. Using 5-point absolute-rating scales, indicate your judgment of the two chapters noted (1 and 11) on the two dimensions indicated. It is hoped by the author that you would (at least) rate Chapter 1 high in interest value and Chapter 11 high in information value. Depending on your background, physiological psychology may also be interesting to you or deadly dull. By comparing the ratings of judges with certain characteristics (type of major, college class, sex) it is possible to find out whether the evaluation is shared by most people or differs according to specifiable characteristics of the judges.

Relative Ratings		Absolute Ratings	
		Information value	**Interest value**
———— Rank	Chp. 1	1 2 3 4 5 High Average Low	1 2 3 4 5 High Average Low
———— Rank	Chp. 11	1 2 3 4 5 High Average Low	1 2 3 4 5 High Average Low

Other types of rating scales are: (a) *adjective checklists* (select from a large list of adjectives those that best describe a particular person), and (b) *forced-choice scales* (of three or four adjectives that would describe a person, select the most and least descriptive ones).

Q-sort technique A rating scale of considerable value, that has not been used as extensively as it might, is the Q-sort method of personality description (Block, 1961). The rater is given a large set of items (say, one hundred) each of which is a descriptive personality characteristic. For example:

a. is critical, skeptical, not easily impressed
b. tends to be self-defensive

c. is productive, gets things done
d. is personally charming
e. does not vary roles; relates to everyone in the same way.

Each of the items (printed on separate cards) is sorted into one of nine categories, with those in category one being most representative and those in category nine least representative of the person. A specified number of items must be assigned to each of the nine categories to form a symmetrical distribution of ratings: category 1, 5 items; 2, 8; 3, 12; 4, 16; 5, 18; 6, 16; 7, 12; 8, 8; 9, 5. The hundred descriptive phrases are forced into a standard distribution (see p. 515). This method ensures that different judges use a common vocabulary to describe and rate the personality of the person being judged.

The interview   The interview has long been the central technique used by clinical psychologists and psychiatrists in their attempts to study and treat personality disorders. It has also been used extensively by employers in selecting new workers. In one form, the interview may be fairly loose and open-ended. In this form, however, it has proved to be a rather undependable device for yielding impressions that predict future behavior, at least in a job setting. This undependability probably results in part from its vulnerability to errors in judgment or bias on the part of the interviewer.

Many difficulties can be circumvented by using a *standardized interview schedule*, whereby predetermined questions are asked in a prearranged order. Such an approach yields data that are less subject to interviewer bias and that can be scored and evaluated objectively.

Judgmental bias   Human judgments are subject to two very important unconscious errors of judgment: halo and stereotype. The *halo effect* is the tendency to judge a likable or intelligent person as "good" in other respects as well. (See *P&L* Close-up, The Halo Effect.) *Stereotypes* are preconceived notions as to what we expect a given kind of person (Russian, politician) to be like. Both errors can be minimized by having the judge rate all the individuals on only one trait at a time, so that the earlier ratings of a given person will be less likely to influence the later ones.

Because the rating scale and the interview inevitably depend so much on the subjective judgments of the raters, however, they are usually regarded as inferior to the more objective psychological tests to be described below. Certainly the value of the ratings will depend both on a judge's ability to evaluate others and on his or her definition of the traits being assessed. To some extent these factors can be appraised by a check on how well two sets of judges agree on their ratings of the same individuals and on how reliable the same judges are on their ratings of the same individuals on successive occasions.

Behavior sampling

Personality variables are also inferred from observations of people in particular situations. The situations may vary in how structured they are, how natural or contrived they are, and how comparable they are to the criterion situation. Sometimes the person is aware of being observed; other times the behavior samples are collected covertly (by informers, hidden cameras or microphones, etc.) Scores from this technique have most validity when the person perceives the test and the criterion situation as psychologically comparable and his or her behavior is under similar contingencies in both settings.

The most ambitious use of behavior-situation assessment tests was that

Close-up
The Halo Effect

One of my relatives has the infuriating habit of losing a contact lens in her shag carpet, usually when the family is late for an outing. "Infuriating" to all who have to help find it—except to her new, loving husband. In his eyes, it's just part of her charm, a kind of a scatterbrained eccentricity.

There you have the halo effect in action! Our overall impression of another person colors our judgment of his or her specific traits and behaviors. If I like you, you can do no wrong; if you don't like me, I can do no right. Of special psychological interest is the unconscious nature of this process. It goes on without our awareness; indeed, we are likely to deny the influence that our judgments of person and performance are not objective and independent.

The clearest demonstration of this phenomenon of bias in human judgments comes from a recent experiment by Richard Nisbett and Timothy Wilson (1977a). College students were randomly assigned to view one of two videotaped lectures by a professor. In one, he acted cold and was seen as unlikable, while in the other presentation he projected a warm manner that made him seem likable. Students then rated several specific aspects of his physical appearance, his expressive style, and his strong French ac-

cent. Those who were exposed to the cold professor did not like him overall, nor in the particular. The opposite was true of those who saw the warm lecturer. He was generally liked and also positively evaluated on the specific dimensions.

To examine the link between general liking and evaluation of personal characteristics, the researchers posed the question in two different ways. Half the subjects were asked if their specific evaluations affected their overall judgment. The other half of the subjects were asked whether their overall liking had any influence on their ratings of individual attributes.

The pattern of results indicates that: (a) people believe they develop overall impressions from evaluations of individual traits and (b) they deny that their rating of individual traits is influenced by their overall impressions. Not only have they "gotten matters precisely backward," they cannot be persuaded they are guilty of a halo effect bias, because it operates at an unconscious level.

I wonder if my new cousin would have been so willing to stoop for the missing lenses had love not conquered the objectivity of his judgments. But then again, what better adversary to lose your rationality to, than the cosmic halo effect called love?

developed in the Army's Office of Strategic Services (1948). The reactions of over 5000 recruits were intensively observed as they were put through a large variety of test situations. Some of these involved overcoming obstacles, problem solving, handling stress, taking charge, handling different assignments, etc. Teams of observers assessed and numerically rated each person on each test. Over a thousand of these recruits were then rated by superior officers and associates when they went overseas on "cloak and dagger" wartime missions for the OSS. The results of this assessment program and related follow-ups lead to four conclusions:

a. there is good interjudge reliability of personality trait evaluations from miniature life situations,

b. judges' ratings are moderately well correlated with other measures of the same traits,

c. ratings based on single situations or brief behavior samples have low validity (in part because some variables take time to manifest themselves, such as loyalty, patience, tolerance, capacity for leadership, etc.),

d. the assessment program was not efficient since it proved very expensive in terms of money and professional personnel required (Kelly & Fisk, 1951).

Self-inventories

Standard self-inventories require subjects to give information about *themselves*. They may be asked to tell what they like or dislike, what emotional reactions they tend to have in certain situations, whether they admire or condemn various figures in public life, and so on. The self-inventory is valuable in that it goes below the surface appearance to tap the individual's own personal experience and feelings. It is also convenient to give because it does not require the services of skilled raters or interviewers. Its chief disadvantage is that the individuals tested do not altogether understand themselves and therefore cannot always give an accurate report. Or, if they wish, they can easily lie about themselves in an attempt to make the results look more favorable.

The first self-inventories were developed for the purpose of classifying individuals in terms of either occupational interest or psychopathology. There are several interest inventories of this type in general use. Because of its high validity, the most widely used test is the Strong Vocational Interest Blank. The basic principle underlying its scoring system is that a person who marks a great majority of the items in the same way as, for example, doctors would be likely to be happy as a doctor.

There is substantial evidence that young people who choose occupations that are consistent with their interest scores find greater satisfaction in their work than those who do not choose occupations consistent with their scores.

Projective tests

Undoubtedly you have sometimes "seen" a face or the shape of an animal in a cloud. But if you mentioned this to friends, you may have discovered that they saw a tree or a castle or something else quite different. Psychologists rely on a similar phenomenon in their use of *projective* techniques of personality measurement. The subject is presented with a standardized set of ambiguous or neutral stimuli—inkblots or pictures that have no definite meaning but can be interpreted in various ways—and is encouraged to interpret freely what is "seen" in them. Thus the subject can "project" onto each neutral stimulus some special, private meaning—much as you projected the face or animal onto the cloud. Psychologists have suggested that such projections reflect the differing needs and emotional adjustments of individuals and thus help reveal their underlying personality patterns.

Projective tests are difficult to fake because there are no obviously right or wrong answers; they have the further advantage of tapping deeper levels of needs and fears than other measurement methods. They are not, however, entirely satisfactory. One major limitation is that the psychologists must rely to a large extent on their own subjective judgment in scoring the subject's responses. Although objective standards have been set up for evaluating various types of responses, skillful interpretation on the part of the examiner is still required. This means that the judgment of the examiner influences the final "score" to a greater extent than it does with objective tests. In addition, considerable training is necessary for using projective tests as a diagnostic tool.

The Rorschach test The *Rorschach* technique, one of the oldest projective methods, makes use of a series of inkblots. Some are black and white, some colored, and they vary in form, shading, and complexity. Subjects observe the cards in a prescribed order and describe what they "see" in each one. This often gives information about their personality structure that is not brought out by clinical interviews. For example, the way subjects react to the color in the blots may throw light on their emotional responses to their environment. ■

■
An inkblot similar to those used in the Rorschach test. What do you see in it? Ask one or two of your friends what they see.

In addition to analyzing the content of the subject's descriptions, the Rorschach expert detects clues to personality functioning from stylistic aspects of the response. Does the person respond to the whole stimulus or only to parts? Do form and structure predominate over movement and action in the subject's attempt to organize the ambiguity in the test materials? Such analyses help the clinician identify the individual's style of perceiving the world, areas of conflict, and the extent of pathology. (See *P&L* Close-up, Looking into the Minds of Nazi War Criminals.)

The Thematic Apperception Test (TAT)   Another projective technique is the Thematic Apperception Test (see p. 386). This test is composed of three series of ten pictures, each picture representing a different situation. The subject is asked to make up a story about each picture, describing the situation, the events that led up to it, how the characters felt, and what the outcome will be. By evaluating both the structure and the content of these stories, as well as the subject's behavior in telling them, the examiner tries to discover the personality characteristics of the subject. For example, the examiner might evaluate the subject as being "conscientious" if the subject told TAT stories about "people who lived up to their obligations" and told them in a very serious, orderly way. ▲

The interpretation of the TAT stories (as well as the Rorschach) is very much a subjective judgment of the clinician, in which inferences are made about the subject's motives, values, attitudes, defenses, and more. Basically, the clinician puts together a theory about the subject that accounts for as much as possible of that person's history and responses. In practice, the TAT is used in conjunction with several other types of assessment techniques, which form a balanced set, or *battery*, of tests.

Close-up

Looking into the Minds of Nazi War Criminals

During the period of the Nuremberg trial (1945–46), Rorschach tests were administered to many of the major Nazi leaders accused of war crimes. These tests were conducted by Gustave Gilbert, the prison psychologist assigned to the trial. The projective responses of sixteen of these notorious Nazis (among them were Speer, Goering, and Hess) were independently analyzed recently by Florence Miale (Miale & Selzer, 1975).

Were these men ordinary people blindly obeying authority and mindlessly following orders—as Hannah Arendt and Stanley Milgram's analyses suggest (see p. 11)—or were they possessed of perverted, sadistic personalities? Maile and Selzer argue for the position that "the Nazis were not psychologically normal or healthy individuals" (p. 287). This diagnosis is based upon their interpretation of Rorschach response patterns that are full of depression, violence, concern for status, rejection of responsibility, death, grotesqueness, distorted qualities,

rejection of feeling. "In general, these appear to be individuals who are undeveloped, manipulative, and hostile in their relationships with others" (p. 278). The verdict of those two Rorschach experts is: guilty of possessing a psychopathic personality. (Psychopaths are people who engage in antisocial behavior without any apparent feelings of guilt or remorse.)

Before one could concur with that verdict it would be necessary to repeat the procedure using other Rorschach experts who were unaware of the histories of the people behind the inkblots. We might also insist that "control" test protocols be mixed with those of the war criminals. Some of these would be from normal citizens, and others psychiatric patients. Psychologist Molly Harrower (1976) has done exactly that. Her "blind" panel of fifteen Rorschach experts found no consistent personality differences between the responses of the Nazis and those of comparison subjects.

Selected personality types and variables

If "birds of a feather flock together," then we can predict something about the likely flocking behavior of certain birds from knowledge of the characteristics of their feathers. In a similar fashion, personality researchers are able to predict some behavioral possibilities of people by identifying traits they share with others of the same "feather."

Sometimes the effect of a stimulus condition on behavior differs depending on the type of person and his or her habitual way of responding to such inputs. Let's look at four different examples of personality types and personality variables. They will provide a wide range of reaction patterns that I think you may find interesting: The internal or external personality, the Machiavellian mentality, the shy individual, and the androgynous person.

Internal vs. external locus of control

To what extent do you believe that what happens to you is determined by forces that are *external* to you—fate, chance, powerful others, unpredictable world events? To what extent do you feel the controlling influence is *internal*, that is, comes from within you? People differ in the extent to which they tend to perceive that the controlling influences on their behavior come *from within* themselves or are imposed on them *from without*. Knowledge of these individual differences improves our prediction of how a person will interpret the role of his or her efforts in achieving a particular goal. Are you likely to get what you want if you work hard enough for it, or is it "impossible to beat the system"? The internal-external metaphor is popular in many approaches to personality (see Collins et al., 1973). In part, that interest has been due to the underlying

God grant me the serenity to accept the things I cannot change, courage to change the things I can, and wisdom to know the difference.
Reinhold Niebuhr

dynamic conception of the individual (internal) in combat with the forces of society (external). As social problems become more complex and social pressures more intense, people everywhere begin to feel more overwhelmed and powerless. Do people control their social order, or are they mere puppets in society's drama?

We have seen that humanists such as Abraham Maslow have contended that the ideal character is that of the *self-actualized* person who is free of both peer-group external constraints and internal constraints imposed by the socialization process. This self-actualization results in greater autonomy and creativity.

The dimension of *introversion-extraversion* found in the Eysenck Personality Inventory (see p. 477) uncovers individual differences in the degree to which people need others as sources of reward and cues to appropriate behavior. The outgoing, impulsive extravert needs people to interact with, while the reserved, cautious introvert relies less on other people for stimulation and more on books or nonsocial sources. These personality types present other contrasts as well. Introverts are more unchangeable, passive, careful, pessimistic, peaceful, controlled, reliable, and anxious. Extraverts tend toward being changeable, active, impulsive, optimistic, aggressive, excitable, and carefree. Eysenck (1976) has related measured differences in introversion-extraversion to a host of social, intellectual, and learning behaviors.

In the United States the internal-external personality metaphor has been developed in the social learning theory approach of Julian Rotter and associates (1954; Rotter, Chance, & Phares, 1972; Lefcourt, 1972; Phares, 1976).

The internal-external personality types are extremes on the continuum of beliefs about *locus of control*; that is, about whether sources of reinforcement are primarily internal or external. "Internal" people perceive that reward is contingent on their own behavior and/or their personal attributes. "Externals" perceive that rewards occur independently of their actions and are controlled by external forces.

While other approaches to internal-external personality types have emphasized the *origins* of an individual's goals, values, and motives, Julian Rotter's internal-external control dimension focuses on *strategies* for attaining goals regardless of the origins of these goals. The measurement of locus of control in individuals has been primarily accomplished by a forced-choice questionnaire (the I-E Scale). For one who has a belief in the internal locus of control, the world should be seen as a predictable place where one's actions have consequences. For an "external" person, on the other hand, the world is unpredictable and one's behavior does not necessarily gain rewards or help avoid pain.

The I-E Scale asks you to choose one of two alternatives from a large set of items such as:

1a. In the case of the well-prepared student there is rarely if ever such a thing as an unfair test.
1b. Many times exam questions tend to be so unrelated to course work that studying is really useless.
2a. The average citizen can have an influence in government decisions.
2b. This world is run by the few people in power, and there is not much the little guy can do about it.
3a. Most people don't realize the extent to which their lives are controlled by accidental happenings.
3b. There is no such thing as "luck."

4a. What happens to me is my own doing.
4b. Sometimes I feel that I don't have enough control over the direction my life is taking (Rotter, 1971).[1]

There is evidence that internals are more resistant to social influence, less conforming, and more independent than are externals. Successful management of one's behavior requires planning of means-ends relationships and the ability to "steer around obstacles toward desired goals." Thus, internals should be more likely to utilize available information in the situation that is relevant to their decisions and goals. This prediction has been verified in several ways. Among tuberculosis patients (matched for hospital experience and socioeconomic class), internals more often than externals made efforts to find out about their disease, and tried to do something about it (Seeman & Evans, 1962).

Many poor people and minorities have learned that, in fact, they exercise little control over their lives. They are controlled by a complex set of external conditions within their political-economic-social situation. They have available many fewer options than others in their society as to where they will live, work, and play. Poverty makes education a luxury, but without education and the skills and "certification" it brings, poor people are the last to be hired, first to be fired, even on menial jobs.

"In all of the reported ethnic studies, groups whose social position is one of minimal power either by class or race tend to score higher in the external-control direction. Within the racial groupings, class interacts so that the double handicap of lower-class and 'lower-caste' seems to produce persons with the highest expectancy of external control. Perhaps the apathy and what is often described as lower-class lack of motivation to achieve may be explained as a result of the disbelief that effort pays off" (Lefcourt, 1966, p. 212). ●

---

[1]Internals tend to choose 1a, 2a, 3b, 4a; externals are more likely to select the other alternative.

●

People with internal locus of control see themselves as being in command of their circumstances. Hence they are more likely to work actively at improving their surroundings than are externals, who believe that things "just happen" to them.

A recent review of this literature (Phares, 1976) indicates that perceived locus of control is a relatively stable characteristic that people carry from situation to situation as a generalized belief about their power and control. In addition, it can be viewed as a relatively narrow expectancy determined by the specific environmental situations the person is functioning in. Only the most extreme internals may be able to remain optimistic and active when the situation appears hopeless.

The Machiavellian mentality

Imagine yourself in the following situation with two other people. Ten one-dollar bills are put down on the table to be distributed among you in any way; the game is over as soon as any *two* of you agree to how it will be split. Obviously, the fair allotment would be $3.33 each—if all three had to decide how to share it. However, a selfish pair could cut the third party out and each have $5.00. One person suggests this alternative to you. Before you can agree or refuse, the left-out third party offers to give you $5.50, taking $4.50 as his or her share and cutting out the other person. What do you do? Do you manipulate the others to maximize your "take" before agreeing either to cut out one of the two, or to have them share what is left over after your portion? Or, is it likely that you will even be bargaining to get a small piece of the prize and not be cut out by the other two?

When this situation is actually staged in an experiment, over many trials, the typical pattern is for one person to come out with about $5.57, one to get $3.14, and one to get only $1.29. Which of the three would *you* be?

Niccolò Machiavelli has provided in his writings (notably *The Prince*, 1532, and *The Discourses*, 1531) the origins of a social-personality theory that helps answer that question. He was concerned with how people can be manipulated, and with what orientations and tactics differentiate those who wield influence from those who are influenced.

Traits of Machiavellians

From anecdotal descriptions of power tactics and the nature of influential people. Richard Christie constructed a questionnaire scale to measure "Machiavellianism." The questions were organized around a cluster of beliefs about tactics, people, and morality. Examples of each are (Christie & Geis, 1970):

Tactics
High Mach: "A white lie is often a good thing."
Low Mach: "If [something is] morally right, compromise is out of the question."
View of People
High Mach: "Most people don't really know what's best for them."
Low Mach: "Barnum was wrong when he said a sucker is born every minute."
Morality
High Mach: "Deceit in conduct of war is praiseworthy and honorable."
Low Mach: "It is better to be humble and honest than important and dishonest."

The "Mach" scales differentiate between High and Low Machiavellians on the basis of the extent to which they endorse Machiavelli's rules of conduct in human relations. The scales place at one end of the continuum people who have *relative* standards of behavior ("Never tell anyone the real reason you did something, unless it's useful to do so"). At the other extreme are those with *absolute* standards ("Honesty is always the best policy"). Between the extremes of the High Machs and the Low Machs fall the middle group, who endorse some part of the Machiavellian philosophy. Essentially, this philosophy is one of pragmatism: "if it works, use it."

In the game described above, the people who get the lion's share consistently are those who score high on these scales. They are included in every *winning* coalition, whereas the Low Mach scorers are lucky to be included in any coalitions and have to be content with the leftovers. The Moderate Mach scorers get only slightly less than would be expected by a fair one-third split.

In other experimental situations, High Machs have been shown not to cheat more, but to cheat *better*. When they lie, they can look their accusers in the eye and convince them that they did not cheat. When competing against other students, they are more effective at "psyching out" their competitors (they work harder at it and devise more creative disturbances). When they have behaved irrationally or in a manner inconsistent with their private attitudes, they can tolerate this cognitive dissonance without changing their attitudes to fit the behavior. In psychology experiments, they manipulate not only other subjects, but often the experimenter as well!

What makes a High Mach high?

The essence of the High Mach is "to keep one's cool when others are blowing theirs." Machiavellians maintain emotional distance, do not get involved in others' behavior, or even in their own. Their behavior is guided by what they know rationally, not by what they feel emotionally.

High Machs flourish where three general situational features exist:

a. Interaction is face-to-face (rather than impersonal or indirect);
b. Rules and guidelines are minimal and there is considerable latitude for them to improvise and structure the ambiguity;
c. Emotional arousal is high (thus interfering with task performance) for the Low Machs, but not for them.

The silent prisoner of shyness

Shyness may mean something different to the President and his wife, Rosalynn, than it does to you. How, indeed, can they say they are shy, yet choose to be in the public eye? Don't shy people avoid social situations and public performances? Not all shy people and not all such situations. Some of our notable celebrities are people who label themselves as shy—except when they are in their "power domain," performing in settings in which their role is structured and rehearsed. Comedians such as Carol Burnett and Phyllis Diller, TV interviewer Barbara Walters, singers Johnny Mathis and Liza Minnelli, actors Robert Young, Henry Fonda, and Lynn Redgrave, athletes Fred Lynn of the Boston Red Sox and Terry Bradshaw of the Pittsburgh Steelers are just some of the shy set. They are *privately shy,* that is, their shyness is felt psychologically even though it may not interfere with their overt behavior. The more common variety of shyness that we tend to notice is that of the *publicly shy*. When the inner experience of shyness spills over to disturb or inhibit public actions then the publicly shy person suffers even more.

Shyness is a multi-dimensional concept, and as it is commonly used, it can include a variety of social anxieties: performance difficulties in large group settings, public-speaking anxieties, lack of assertiveness, and anxieties about informal social contacts with members of both the same and opposite sexes.

Rosey and I are both naturally shy. She's one of the most naturally shy people I've ever known. I don't know how to explain it, how we can be shy and campaign the way we do. It doesn't come easy.
President Jimmy Carter
Quoted by S. Quinn,
Washington Post, April 1, 1976

Here we shall define shyness as *a tendency to avoid social situations, to fail to participate appropriately in social encounters, and to feel anxious, distressed, and burdened during interpersonal interactions.* Shyness therefore includes cognitive, affective, physiological, and behavioral components that are elicited by certain types of people and social situations. Some of the most common shyness reactions among colleges students are given in the table. ◆

Shyness, to the extent that it encourages social isolation and personal withdrawal, has at least three negative consequences. First, it drastically reduces the rewards available from one of the most potent reinforcers in the environment—other people. By avoiding the anxiety associated with social encounters, shy people also eliminate the potential rewards that such encounters can provide. A lack of adequate social reinforcement may play a critical role in the development of subsequent difficulties such as depression (cf. Lewinsohn, 1974). Second, shyness limits the general availability of the social support provided by significant others. As a result, shy people may be more vulnerable to life stresses ordinarily moderated by the advice and encouragement of relatives, friends, and acquaintances. Third, shyness, by limiting interaction, deprives isolated people of valuable social comparison information. Excessively harsh self-evaluations (and other cognitive aspects of anxiety states) arise in part from ignorance about the commonness of such social anxiety, and also a lack of realistic standards against which to judge one's social behavior. Paradoxically, it is only because the shy are so concerned about others that many organize their lives around avoiding their evaluation, while also shunning desired intimate association with other people. ■

The Stanford Shyness Survey

In Chapter 1 we discussed the development of the Stanford Shyness Survey (see pp. 16–18). As we noted, over 80 percent of the individuals surveyed labeled themselves as "shy" or "formerly shy." Men reported themselves to be shy as often as women did, dispelling the myth that shyness is a female trait. Nor is shyness just a stage children pass through; about a quarter of the shy adults said they had been shy all their lives. About the same proportion had overcome their shyness once they got past the struggles of adolescence. Most people view shyness in primarily negative terms. Of the presently shy, 79 percent do not like being shy and nearly two thirds say shyness poses a personal problem for them (Zimbardo, 1977).

Among the negative consequences of shyness reported by the majority of those surveyed were:

◆

Inventory of shyness reactions

	% Shy Students		% Shy Students		% Shy Students
Physiological Reactions		**Thoughts and Sensations**		**Overt Behaviors**	
Increased pulse	54%	Self-consciousness	85%	Silence	80%
Blushing	53%	Concern about impression		No eye contact	51%
Perspiration	49%	management	67%	Avoidance of others	44%
Butterflies in stomach	48%	Concern for social evaluation	63%	Avoidance of action	42%
Heart pounding	48%	Negative self-evaluation	59%	Low speaking voice	40%
		Unpleasantness of situation	56%		

Adapted from Zimbardo, Pilkonis, & Norwood, 1974

By withdrawing from social
contact, the shy individual
misses out on the pleasures—
as well as the pains—of
interacting with other people.

a. creates social problems; makes it difficult to meet new people, make new friends, enjoy potentially good experiences;

b. has negative emotional consequences; creates feelings of loneliness, isolation, depression;

c. prevents positive evaluations by others (e.g., one's personal assets never become apparent because of one's shyness);

d. makes it difficult to be appropriately assertive, to express opinions, to take advantage of opportunities;

e. allows incorrect negative evaluations by others (e.g., one may unjustly be seen as unfriendly or snobbish or weak);

f. creates cognitive and expressive difficulties and inhibits the capacity to think clearly while with others and to communicate effectively with them;

g. encourages excessive self-consciousness, preoccupation with oneself.

Other perspectives on shyness

Research has shown that individuals who labeled themselves "shy persons" were less extraverted, less capable of monitoring their social behavior, and more socially anxious than their not-shy peers. As shyness increases so does poor personal adjustment, as reflected in high neuroticism scale scores (Pilkonis, 1977a, 1977b). In other research, those who labeled themselves shy have been found to differ from nonshys in the same setting in a number of ways. When their self-awareness is heightened shys suffer memory deficits and are more easily persuaded. Shys have less sexual experience of all kinds and tend to enjoy less the sexual contacts they do make. Among naval personnel and business people, shys report more job dissatisfaction, generally associated with feelings of 'being passed over" and not being recognized.

Although shyness is a personal reaction, it is created and maintained by basic social values and cultural programming. The prevalence of shyness is higher in ego-oriented cultures than in group- or community-centered cultures. Where cultural norms overvalue competition and achievement and control behavior through shame and social expectation, shyness thrives.

However, where group goals are of primary importance, as on an Israeli *kibbutz* or in mainland China, shyness is less common. Cross-cultural perspectives also reveal that the label of shyness and its interpretation may differ from our own. Among a sample of Tokyo University students who were generally quite shy, a minority did view shyness in positive terms since it creates a modest, appealing impression, does not intimidate others, prevents one from being aggressive, and enables one to be a good listener (G. Hatano, 1975).

The androgynous person

Please stop and check the appropriate box at left.

Sex

☐ *male*

☐ *female*

Sexual identity

☐ *masculine*

☐ *feminine*

☐ *other*

In our society, males are supposed to be masculine and females to be feminine. We are born with a certain sexual gender, but we are trained (perhaps socially programmed) to develop a sexual identity that fits the inherited gender. *Masculine:* he, tough, brave, fearless, dominant, rational, assertive, aggressive. *Feminine:* she, tender, sensitive, timid, submissive, emotional, passive, gentle. Right? Wrong!

The training for sexual identity begins before birth with anticipation and planning for the kind of clothes, furniture, toys, and color scheme for the newborn. Blue for a boy and pink for a girl. Names drawn from the right sex list help distinguish boy from girl. But so do the different patterns of play and responsiveness most parents unwittingly show to the different sex offspring. Rough with boys, gentle with girls, and so on.

When behavior is not in step with the traditional sex role, one's very self-concept is questioned. If you like ballet, romantic novels, playing with babies, and cooking, it's fine—unless you also happen to be male. If you stand up and assert your rights, have a mind of your own, like to be financially independent, and have a beer while you watch Monday night football, people will wonder where you went wrong if you are a woman.

Masculinity and femininity are viewed as polar opposites in our society. Standard psychological tests to measure these traits also reflect this orientation. A person is allowed to be high or low on one *or* the other dimension. You can't be both.

Or can you? The concept of *androgyny* refers to a blending of the behaviors and personality traits traditionally associated with one or the other sexual identity. The androgynous person (from the Greek *andro*, male, and *gyne*, female) is *both* masculine and feminine, and is able to respond to situational demands with the type of behavior most appropriate and effective in each situation faced. The androgynous male can be tender and gentle and emotionally responsive when relating to others in intimate encounters. He can as readily be competitive when competition is necessary to achieve some goal. Similarly, the androgynous female is not locked into a narrow self-concept. She can drive trucks, be a marathon runner, enjoy mathematics, and be nurturant—and be or do whatever she has interests in and talents for. In the truly androgynous person masculinity and femininity are totally integrated to make a more fully human, well rounded, and adaptable personality.

Sandra Bem (1974, 1978) has pioneered the thinking and research on the androgynous personality. Her strategy involved: (a) developing a new sex-role inventory, (b) classifying people by their masculinity-femininity scores, and (c) comparing reactions of masculine, feminine, and androgynous college subjects in various situations where traditional sex roles restrict behavioral options.

The Bem Sex Role Inventory (BSRI) consists of a series of sixty adjectives (twenty "masculine," e.g., ambitious, self-reliant; twenty "feminine," e.g., affectionate, gentle; and twenty "neutral" characteristics, e.g., happy, truthful). You answer by indicating how well each characteristic accurately describes you (on a seven-point scale where one equals "never or almost never true" and seven equals "always or almost always true"). The average number of points assigned by the person to the feminine items is the Femininity Score, while the average number of points assigned to the masculine characteristics constitutes the Masculinity Score. Androgyny is operationally defined as having high scores on both masculinity and femininity dimensions.

Studies of androgynous individuals reveal that an expanded range of possibilities is open to them in comparison to the straitjacket imposed by sex-typed identity. In her research, Bem has found such individuals to be both more independent and more nurturant and supportive. She also found that feminine subjects of both sexes were more dependent, while masculine subjects were low in nurturance. Spence and Helmreich (1978) found that men and women had greater self-esteem, social competence, and achievement orientation when they were high in *both* masculine and feminine characteristics. They suggest that our traditional view of masculine and feminine as "bipolar opposites" may be incorrect. Successful people may need to display androgynous behaviors. ●

Greater intellectual development has also been shown to correlate consistently with cross-sex typing, masculine girls and feminine boys showing the most advanced general intellectual functioning. To find those who are lowest in overall intelligence, spatial ability, and creativity we have only to look to masculine males and feminine females. To better appreciate the role of intelligence and creativity in human behavior and personality, we turn to our final sections.

●

Androgynous individuals, whose interests and competencies span a broad range of what have traditionally been considered "masculine" or "feminine" areas, appear to lead the fullest and best-adjusted lives.

Intelligence and IQ tests

Intelligence is the capacity to profit from experience and to go beyond the given to the possible. It is in our intellectual development that we humans have been able to transcend our physical frailty and gain dominance over more powerful or numerous animals. No wonder, then, that intelligence is our most highly prized possession. But what is intelligence? What are its origins? How can it be assessed? What are its advantages?

Intelligence tests were originally designed as a democratic means of ensuring that qualified children would be given the opportunity provided by free, mass public education. If it were possible to determine how intelligent a child was, the admission into the public education system would not have to rely on the subjective biases of teachers and administrators. Thus all children who had the capacity to profit from the educational experience would be entitled to it. In addition, by identifying those who performed poorly on intelligence tests, special education programs could be developed for them. In this way the search for individual differences in intelligence was guided by pragmatic educational philosophy.

Binet's first test

The year 1905 marked the first published account of a workable intelligence test. Alfred Binet had responded to the call of the French Minister of Public Instruction to study the problem of how best to teach mentally retarded children in the public schools. Binet and his colleague, Theophile Simon, believed that before a program of instruction could be planned, it was necessary to develop a way of measuring the intelligence of the children they were studying.

Their approach was *empirical*, trying out different tasks on groups of children of various ages in standard schools and institutions for the retarded. They began by preparing a test of intelligence containing problem situations that could be scored objectively, were varied in nature, were little influenced by differences in environment, and called for judgment and reasoning rather than mere rote memory (Binet & Simon, 1911).

The results of these tests were expressed in terms of the age at which normal children could make a particular score. This was called the mental age of the child. For example, when a child's score on the test was equal to the mean (average) of the scores of a comparison group of five-year-olds, the child had an MA of five, regardless of his or her actual (chronological) age. As we have seen (p. 234), the relationship between mental age (MA) and chronological age (CA), known as the intelligence quotient (IQ), is computed as follows:

$$IQ = \frac{MA}{CA} \times 100.$$

Thus a child who performs at a mental age equivalent to his or her chronological age has an IQ of 100. Most scores cluster around this mean, and there is no break between the dull, the average, and the bright. (See *P&L* Close-up, The "Normal" Curve.)

IQ testing in America

Lewis Terman of Stanford University realized the significance of Binet's method for assessing intelligence. He adapted the questions for American

The "Normal" Curve

The figure shows the distribution of scores that would be expected if 1000 randomly selected persons were measured on weight, IQ, or other continuous traits. Each dot represents an individual's score. The baseline, or *horizontal axis*, shows the amounts of whatever is being measured; the *vertical axis* shows how many individuals have each amount of the trait, as represented by their scores. Usually only the resulting curve at the top is shown, since this indicates the frequency with which each measure has occurred. Actual curves only approximate this hypothetical one, but come remarkably close to it with very large samples.

This curve is very useful to psychologists because they know that in a large, randomly selected group, a consistent percentage of the cases will fall in a given segment of the distribution. For example, if the trait is one that is distributed normally, 68 percent will fall in the middle third of the range of scores.

The standard deviation, as you saw in Chapter 2, is a measure of the variability of the scores. It indicates the typical amount by which the scores differ from the mean. The more widely the scores are spread out, the larger will be the standard deviation. Most of the scores in a distribution fall within three standard deviations above the mean and three standard deviations below it (but usually a few scores in an actual distribution will be lower and a few higher).

The distance of the standard deviation from the mean can be indicated along the baseline of the curve, as is done below. Since the standard deviations are equally spaced along the range of the scores, they are convenient dividing points for classification. For further explanation of the standard deviation and of the uses of both it and the normal curve, see the Appendix.

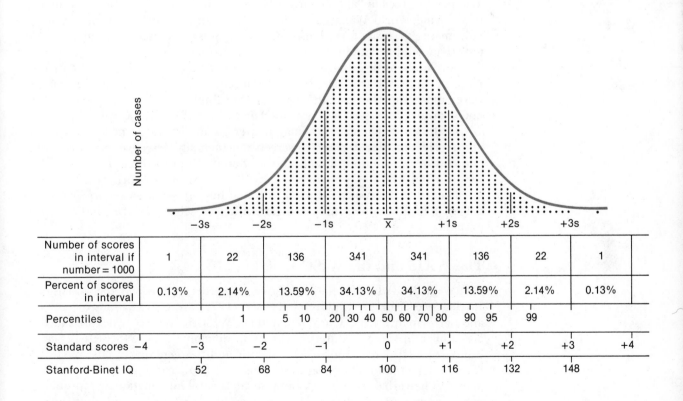

	−3s	−2s	−1s	X̄	+1s	+2s	+3s	
Number of scores in interval if number = 1000	1	22	136	341	341	136	22	1	
Percent of scores in interval	0.13%	2.14%	13.59%	34.13%	34.13%	13.59%	2.14%	0.13%	
Percentiles		1	5 10	20 30 40 50 60 70 80	90 95	99		
Standard scores	−4	−3	−2	−1	0	+1	+2	+3	+4
Stanford-Binet IQ		52	68	84	100	116	132	148	

schoolchildren, standardized administration of the test, and developed age-level norms by giving the test to thousands of children. In 1916 he published the Stanford Revision of the Binet Tests, commonly referred to as the *Stanford-Binet*, which soon became a standard instrument in clinical psychology, psychiatry, and educational counseling (Terman, 1916).

In subsequent revisions of the test (Terman & Merrill, 1937), the upper limits of the scale were extended to differentiate among adults of superior intelligence, with scores determined on a statistical basis rather than an age ratio. It was also extended downward in age, making it possible to assess the intelligence of children as young as two years. Parallel forms (of high reliability) were designed to allow for retesting without worry about practice effects. The last revision of the Stanford-Binet intelligence test was made in the early 1970s (Terman & Merrill, 1973) to take account of vocabulary changes over time. More than a million Americans a year take the Stanford-Binet or one of the other standard intelligence tests. Psychologist Julian Stanley has stated:

Though "IQ tests" are much maligned, especially because results from them can be misused greatly, the Stanford-Binet Intelligence Scale remains a psychometric marvel. No other instrument spans so well almost the entire range of mental ability from slow-learning preschoolers to brilliant adults. No other one mental test can provide the well-trained school or clinical psychologist with as valid a single IQ. Because it must be administered by the examiner to examinees individually and must be scored carefully, use of the Stanford-Binet is slower and more expensive than group testing, but for many persons it is well worth the cost (1976, p. 668).

Mass testing of intelligence

The need to recruit "able-bodied and able-brained" personnel into the military during World War I gave additional impetus to the intelligence testing movement. Necessity forced individually administered tests to be replaced by tests that could be administered in large group settings. Another change was the development of *performance tests* that could be used in addition to, or in place of, the standard tests that were largely verbal. Because many recruits were immigrants who had little command of English, their intelligence could not be properly assessed by a test based on the use of English words.

General intelligence examinations were administered to nearly two million recruits in World War I to screen out mentally defective individuals at one end of the continuum and also to identify those at the upper end with superior IQs who could be trained for special services. In World War II, mass intelligence testing was conducted with another nine million service personnel. Such tests became routine for generations of school children and job applicants.

The WAIS and the WISC-R

The Wechsler Adult Intelligence Scale (Wechsler, 1955) and the Wechsler Intelligence Scale for Children—Revised (1974) are combinations of verbal and performance tests. The WAIS and the WISC-R, as these scales are called, are similar in content, differing chiefly in difficulty. The WISC-R has been standardized for children of ages six through sixteen years. The WAIS is for age sixteen and over. Both tests consist of two parts—verbal and performance. The verbal section includes tests of general information, comprehension, vocabulary, similarities between words, arithmetic, and digit span (repeating a series of digits after the examiner).

The performance section also has several parts. In the block design test, the subject tries to reproduce a series of designs shown on cards by fitting together blocks with colored sides. In the picture arrangement test, the task is to arrange a series of pictures in the correct sequence so that a meaningful story is depicted. Some of the other performance tests include mazes (in the WISC only), picture completion, and object assembly.

Sources of variability in IQ scores

If two people have differing IQ scores, can we infer the one with the higher score is the more intelligent? Not necessarily. To see why that is so, let us first distinguish two types of IQ, then consider an analogy with strength. The IQ score obtained on a given test is the *phenotypic IQ*; it reflects *intellectual performance*. Such a score may or may not accurately reflect intellectual capacity or *genotypic intelligence*. The phenotypic IQ may not adequately express the person's genotypic intelligence for many reasons. Some of these reasons for the discrepancy between intellectual performance and underlying ability are more evident in a familiar test of physical strength.

"Step right up and ring the gong by driving the lever up with a swing of the hammer!" This carnival measure of phenotypic strength can give a false picture of your genotypic strength because of factors unrelated to strength and certain aspects of the test situation. For example, you might be strong but poorly coordinated or not have experience swinging a hammer. Or your arms might be fatigued, or you might be anxious about performing in public. The carnival barker might intimidate you or psych you up. Similarly, phenotypic IQ can be a *biased* measure of intellectual capacity when test scores vary as a function of characteristics of the test, background factors, or motivational and experiential variables.

IQ tests do not measure "pure" intelligence. In addition to the intelligence of the test taker, they reflect values, attitudes, and information from the culture of the test designer and the normative population. For example, one IQ test asks what you would do if you found a stamped, addressed envelope. "Mail it" is scored as the only correct answer. If you were poor and said, "Check it out for money before mailing it," that would be scored wrong. Intellectually wrong or morally wrong? An IQ test item asking who was the first President of the United States is easy—if you know American history. The heavy emphasis on vocabulary penalizes those whose native language is not standard English. In short, if IQ tests are not culture-free, then phenotypic IQ scores are "contaminated" by differences between test takers who vary along cultural, ethnic, and social class lines. (See *P&L* Close-up, What Color Is an IQ?)

A large-scale, longitudinal study of 26,760 children identified a variety of factors in the first years of life that related to Stanford-Binet IQ scores at age four. The investigators studied 169 independent variables as possible predictors of IQ (including prenatal, neonatal, infant variables as well as family and parental background factors). Of these the two that were the best predictors were the family's socioeconomic index and the level of the mother's education. In this study as in others, females had higher IQs than males, white children scored higher than black children (Broman, Nichols, & Kennedy, 1975).

The adverse effects of poverty can affect intellectual functioning in many ways: through poor prenatal health of the mother, poor nutrition of the child, a lack of books and other materials for verbal stimulation, a "survival orientation" that leaves little time or energy for parents to play with and intellectually stimulate children. Racial differences in IQ scores have been found in a num-

Critics of intelligence tests claim that one reason that blacks and other minorities score lower is that the tests are written in a "foreign" language. The test instructions and questions, written in "standard" (white) English and testing "standard" concepts, may not make sense to children who use a different (but not inferior) language to deal with "nonstandard" concepts (see also p. 199).

To illustrate the gap between standard and "black" English, sociologist Adrian Dove developed the Dove Counterbalance General Intelligence Test (1968), a set of thirty multiple-choice questions. This test, also known as the "Chitling test," uses "black English" to test knowledge of black cultural concepts. For example, could you answer the following questions?

What is a "blood"?[1]
"Bird or yardbird was the jacket jazz lovers from coast to coast hung on _____."[2]
Do you know the difference between a "gray" and a "spook"?[3]

Psychologist Robert L. Williams feels that the differences in language can be much more subtle than the black English used on test items on the Chitling test. He and L. Wendell Rivers designed a study to measure the actual effect of this language gap on IQ scores (1972). They enlisted the aid of black teachers and graduate students to translate the instructions of an IQ test into nonstandard English. The test they used was the Boehm Test of Basic Concepts (BTBC), an IQ test that asks children to mark the picture that matches a concept of time, space, or quantity. Their subjects were 890 black children attending either kindergarten, first, or second grade. The children were divided into two groups, and the psychologists controlled for the variables of the scores received on other IQ tests, age,

sex, and grade level. One half was given the standard version of the Boehm and one half was given the nonstandard version. The results? The children who took the nonstandard version scored significantly higher than those who took the test with the standard instructions. What is surprising is that the nonstandard instructions seem to differ little from the standard version. For example, the instructions on the standard version read "*behind* the *sofa*," while the nonstandard version asked the child to mark a picture of something that was "*in back of* the *couch*."

The Black Intelligence Test of Cultural Homogeneity (the BITCH test) was Williams' next experiment in designing a culture-specific test for blacks. Williams administered 100 vocabulary items, selected from a slang dictionary and his personal experiences, to a group of 200 sixteen- to eighteen-year-old subjects. Half were black and half were white. On this IQ test, the whites got the lower scores — an average score of 51, compared to an average of 87 for the blacks.

As Williams demonstrated, psychologists can develop a test that favors a particular group rather easily. However, the problem that has confronted the designers of tests is how to design a test that will apply to all groups fairly. And, after the test is designed, how do we best use the data they provide? Williams (1974) stresses that we must remember that an IQ is *only* a score on a test that measures fairly specific skills. An IQ should not be used to label children (as it often is). In addition, illiteracy (or just a different type of literacy) should not be confused with intellectual ability. Nor can an IQ score be used to measure an individual's ability to adapt to and function effectively in society.

Should IQ tests have color and culture? Is separate but equal the best alternative when it comes to IQ tests? Or should we just be more careful in using IQ scores? What do you think?

---

[1] A Negro.
[2] Charlie Parker, who spent time in prison ("on the yard").
[3] Grays are pale-faced Caucasians; spooks are Negroes.

ber of studies (see Loehlin, Lindzey, & Spuhler, 1975). These phenotypic IQ differences have created a controversy over whether they stem from underlying differences in genotypic intelligence. The controversy reflects the "nature-nurture" conflict we examined in Chapter 8.

It has been suggested that poverty can lower IQ in yet another way. Robert Zajonc (1976) has found that birth order and family size are significant determinants of a child's IQ. IQ scores are lower in children from large families, particularly those who are later born and close in age to their siblings. Zajonc believes that the intellectual environment of such children is less stimulating than that of peers who are the eldest in small families, with a wide age gap between siblings. To the extent that poor people and minority groups are more likely to have many children close in age, their IQ level as a group will be lower than the standardized norms.

Intelligence, mental abilities, and talent

Remember our discussion of validity (p. 499). If we ask what is the criterion validity of intelligence test scores, the answer is they correlate highly with academic grades. Intelligence can then be operationally defined as "what IQ tests measure," and IQ test scores appear to be a valid predictor of academic success (Tyler, 1965; Wing & Wallach, 1971).

Intelligence tests, then, do nothing more than sample a small portion of an individual's current *performance* in order to predict his or her *potentialities* for various future tasks. A basic assumption has always been that intellectual performance reflects intellectual *capacity*. This capacity is assumed to derive from physiological factors in the brain and nervous system (Thorndike, 1926). Such a view taken by many psychometricians leads to the conception of intelligence as a trait (largely inherited) that sets the limits on the levels of a person's intellectual functioning. There is, however, no available evidence to suggest that intelligence is related to the number of associative connections in the brain or other physiological factors (Estes, 1970).

Although childhood IQ is a good predictor of adult IQ (Honzik, 1973), it is much less satisfactory in predicting adult educational and occupational success (Jencks et al., 1972). In a recent longitudinal study that related early IQ with later adult success, about 75 percent of the variability in adult attainment was *not* reflected in childhood IQs. The best predictor of a child's likelihood of educational and occupational status was the father's educational level (McCall, 1977).

Although there are situations in which it is helpful to know the general overall level of a person's intelligence, as indicated by an IQ score, research has shown that "general intelligence" is actually a composite of a number of "special intelligences" or *primary abilities* that are relatively independent of each other. Two people who obtain the same IQ may have a very different pattern of specific abilities and deficiencies: one may do best on the verbal and abstract reasoning questions, the other on the memory and motor skill items. Thus psychologists have developed tests of primary mental abilities that distinguish between such intellectual abilities as verbal, numerical, perceptual, spatial, and reasoning.

Most countries outside the United States use examinations that test specific areas of *achievement,* instead of IQ tests, to diagnose and predict academic and vocational success. Even in France, IQ tests have been used only as Binet intended them, to screen for subnormal children who need remedial education. In the Soviet Union pure achievement tests are used to identify children with talent for particular occupational needs of the country, such as teachers, architects, nuclear physicists, etc. The rejection of IQ tests in favor of this assessment of more specialized talent is justified by one Soviet psychologist in these terms:

"we hold that a correct investigation of abilities is possible only if the child's activities are performed under his ordinary conditions of life, and when his abilities are not investigated statistically, but in their development and change, in connection with the whole personality of the child, his instructions and education, his entire life" (Smirnov, 1974, p. 74).

In the United States many psychologists are calling for a modification of our traditional reliance on IQ tests. William Estes (1974) proposes that the tests be used only to reveal performance deficits. Then through analysis of the learning processes involved in the test behavior (such as encoding strategies, retrieval processes, and others), educational measures can be developed to improve intellectual performance. Michael Wallach (1976) also proposes that traditional ability tests be used only for screening out those who score below an established cut-off level. For those scoring above that performance threshold, IQ scores, G.P.A., S.A.T. scores would be ignored. Instead, *talent* would be recognized from displays of excellence in a person's accomplishments. If you want to major in English, you provide evidence of the worth of your written work; in art, of your creative products; in science, of research accomplished or proposed. Potential for success would thus be assessed not by performance on tests of abstract mental abilities but by products of one's particular talents.

Creativity

Of those attributes that help define our humanity—language, tender emotions, a time sense, abstract reasoning—none is more mysterious or desired than the creative urge. We see the earliest signs of creativity in the artistic expression of prehistoric cave dwellers. ▲ Throughout history every religion has offered some explanation of the *creation* of the universe. Our passion to create, "to bring into being, to cause to exist," is revealed in the fantasies of our children's doll play, in our imaginative involvement with nonordinary reality.

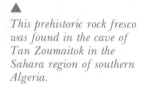

▲
This prehistoric rock fresco was found in the cave of Tan Zoumaitok in the Sahara region of southern Algeria.

When we think of the creative person, great artists, inventors, scientists, and poets spring to mind—Michelangelo, Ludwig van Beethoven, William Shakespeare, Marie Curie, Emily Dickinson. But ordinary, average people can be creative, even without public acclaim for their accomplishments. For example, let's look at the responses that a ten-year-old ghetto boy of average IQ gave to the question, "How many uses can you think of for a newspaper?"

"You can read it, write on it, lay it down and paint a picture on it. If you didn't have covers, you could put it around you. You can burn it, put it in the garage and drive the car over it when you wash the car, lay it down and put your baby on it, put it on a busted window, put it in your door for decoration, put it in the garbage can, put it on a chair if the chair is messy. If you have a puppy, you put newspaper in its box or put it in your back yard for the dog to play with. When you build something and you don't want anyone to see it, put newspaper around it. Put newspaper on the floor if you have no mattress, use it to pick up something hot, use it to stop bleeding, or to catch the drips from drying clothes. You can use newspaper for curtains, put it in your shoe to cover what is hurting your foot, make a kite out of it, shade a light that is too bright. You can wrap fish in it, wipe windows, or wrap money in it and tape it [so it doesn't make noise]. You put washed shoes on newspaper, wipe eyeglasses with it, put it under a dripping sink, put a plant on it, make a paper bowl out of it, use it for a hat if it is raining, tie it on your feet for slippers. You can put it on the sand if you had no towel, use it for bases in baseball, make paper airplanes with it, use it as a dustpan when you sweep, ball it up for the cat to play with, wrap your hands in it if it is cold" (Ward, Kogan, & Pankove, 1972).

In evaluating this boy's answers, you might say that he is very creative because he gave many unusual responses that you would never have thought of. In fact, if you were to compare his answers to those of other ten-year-old children of average IQ, his performance might be even more impressive. But where does such an ability come from? Is it a general characteristic that he was born with, or is it something that he learned? If we look at this boy's answers again, we might say that *experience* is an important factor. Clearly, the more often a person has had to use something in different ways, the more likely he or she is to think of other uses for it. Perhaps this child's responses would be considered less creative by other people of his own socioeconomic background. If so, this would imply that creativity is a relative quality that exists only when someone thinks it does. Many psychologists dispute such a viewpoint, however, and maintain that creativity *is* a personal characteristic that can be reliably measured and assessed.

What is creative?

The most widely used definition of creativity is that it is the occurrence of *uncommon or unusual, but appropriate responses*. This assumption underlies most of the tests that have been developed to measure creativity. ■

Although originality is usually taken for granted as a major factor in creativity, the importance of appropriateness is not always recognized. However, it is the criterion that distinguishes between creative and nonsensical acts. Solutions to a problem that are unique but totally worthless or irrelevant cannot be considered as creative responses.

There are different facets to creativity and the creative enterprise. First, there is the perceptual element involved in one's *heightened sensitivity* to features of the world that other people do not usually notice. Then there is the generation of nonverbal images or *internal representations* of a spatial or visual

Common Responses
1. Smudges
2. Dark clouds

Uncommon Responses
1. Magnetized iron filings
2. A small boy and his mother hurrying along on a dark windy day, trying to get home before it rains

Common Responses
1. An ape
2. Modern painting of a gorilla

Uncommon Responses
1. A baboon looking at itself in a hand mirror
2. Rodin's "The Thinker" shouting "Eureka!"

Common Responses
1. An African voodoo dancer
2. A cactus plant

Uncommon Responses
1. Mexican in sombrero running up a long hill to escape from rain clouds
2. A word written in Chinese

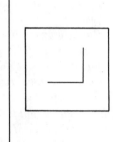

Two projective tests used to distinguish between creative and uncreative individuals are shown here. In the inkblot test, the individual must attribute order and meaning to vague configurations. The average individual is apt to concentrate on their simple, obvious features. The creative person is more likely to impose an elegant new order on the figure. In the drawing completion test, the average individual is satisfied with a simple figure that "makes sense" (above), while the creative individual produces a more complex and meaningful drawing (below).

character. The creative product is the tangible "externalization" of these private images, in terms of theories, inventions, or works of art (Shepard, 1978). Creativity also involves *synthesis*, the ability to make connections that relate one's observations or ideas in meaningful ways.

In scientific creativity the stage of *obtaining* good ideas can be distinguished from the stage of *criticizing* those ideas to determine which are worthwhile, which worthless. At a conference on creativity attended by outstanding scientists, it was generally agreed that "getting the idea" cannot be taught in universities. Only the critical side of creativity could be learned in an apprentice relationship—one where the master models how to ask and answer the right kind of questions (see Maugh, 1974).

Finally, there must be some element of will, some *self-assertion* and courage to translate one's private experience into a public product. Of central importance in the creative process is this "push from within." The intrinsic, self-imposed motivation to discover, to see anew, to recast old forms in new molds suffers when external constraints are imposed. In *The Act of Creation* (1964), Arthur Koestler speculates that the highest forms of creativity emerge under conditions when we are free from control, when our minds can regress to unconscious, preverbal, playful levels of thought.

Using a rigorous experimental paradigm, Teresa Amabile (1977) demonstrated that the introduction of an external constraint for performance of an activity leads to lower creativity. Collages produced by college women were scored lower on creativity when subjects knew they were to be evaluated by experts. The products of other subjects not expecting to be evaluated were scored higher on creativity.

Creativity, then, seems to depend upon the cognitive freedom that accompanies the state of intrinsic motivation.

Who is creative?

How can creative people be identified? What characteristics distinguish them from less creative people? How did they get to be the way they are? (Could you get there too?) The search for answers to these questions has been undertaken by many psychologists.

In general, studies have shown that creative persons are distinguished more by their interests, attitudes, and drives than by their intellectual abilities (Dellas & Gaier, 1970). The lack of a strong correlation between creativity and intelligence may seem surprising, but research conducted so far has supported this conclusion (Wallach & Kogan, 1965). For example, not one of a large sample of people with superior intelligence studied by Lewis Terman over a forty-year period produced any outstanding creative works (Terman & Oden, 1959).

Other cognitive variables do seem characteristic of creative people, however. One of the most distinctive of these is a cognitive preference for *complexity*, as opposed to simplicity. This is revealed in a preference for figures that are asymmetrical, dynamic, and even chaotic, rather than those that are regular, neat, and simple.

Much creativity research has been concerned with the personality characteristics of creative individuals. The results have pointed to a group of characteristics that includes impulsivity, independence, introversion, intuitiveness, and self-acceptance. Creative architects (MacKinnon, 1961) and creative research scientists (Gough, 1961) were remarkably similar in these personality traits, despite the differences in the content of their professional work. Crea-

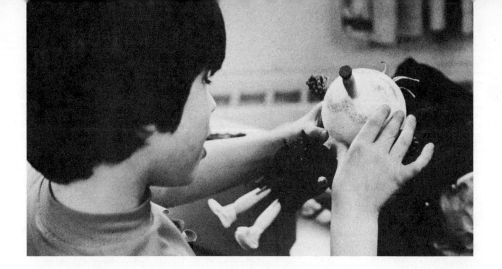

tive writers displayed a similar complex of traits, although they showed greater originality and an emphasis on fantasy (Barron, 1963).

Independence, in both attitudes and behavior, is perhaps the most striking characteristic of the creative personality. Practically all studies have found that creative individuals are not very concerned with other people's opinion of them. As the Gershwins said,

*"They all laughed at Christopher Columbus when he said the world was round;
They all laughed when Edison recorded sound;
They all laughed at Wilbur and his brother when they said that man could fly.
They told Marconi wireless was a phony; it's the same old cry."*
Gershwin & Gershwin, "They All Laughed"

Another personality variable that distinguishes creative individuals is a pattern of androgyny. Creative men are able to accept the feminine aspects of their personality without experiencing any sexual conflict, thus leading them to a greater openness to emotions and feelings, and to a greater aesthetic sensitivity (Hammer, 1964). According to the research of Ravenna Helson (1967) on creative women mathematicians, these women differ from the less creative in that they retain their femininity despite admission of some masculine traits. Overall, they are often *less* "masculine," than uncreative women. Perhaps certain characteristics traditionally identified as "masculine" inhibit creativity rather than promote it. Only much more research can shed light on the extent to which there is a real sex difference in the creative process—if indeed there is any difference.

One popular view of exceptionally creative people is that while they are geniuses, they are also crazy. The madness of such artists as Van Gogh or Nijinsky is often cited as a "typical example." What psychological evidence is there for a relationship between creativity and psychopathology? The answer is that there is almost none. Instead, creative people appear to have superior ego strength and a constructive way of handling problems (Cross, Cattell, & Butcher, 1967). It may be that such characteristics as independence and originality, which lead creative individuals to think in ways that are taboo or considered "strange," cause the rest of the world to think of them (erroneously) as mentally unbalanced.

Despite our differences, your uniqueness and mine, we are often subject to the same challenges and environmental "insults." Although we may react to them each in our own way, such stressors put a heavy burden on us. In the next chapter we shall concern ourselves with the ways we adapt to life's stresses—and what happens when we fail to do so.

Chapter summary

Assessment is the use of specified testing procedures to evaluate or differentiate individuals on the basis of certain characteristics. In developing instruments for the measurement of personality, psychologists are concerned with *reliability, validity,* and *standardization.* A test is reliable if it measures something consistently and precisely from one occasion to the next. The *validity* of a test refers to whether or not it is actually measuring that which it is intended to measure. In order to produce *norms* or standards so that individual scores may be compared, a measuring device must be *standardized*—administered under standard conditions to a large group of persons representative of the group for which it is intended.

Investigators use the *psychometric trait approach* to measure personality traits quantitatively. In some cases, people who know the individual well are asked to assess his or her various attributes. *Rating* may be *relative* or it may employ *absolute* rating scales in which the thing being judged is rated according to a standard independent of the other items being rated. In the *Q-sort* technique, the rater is given a large set of items, each of which is a descriptive personality characteristic. Each of the items is to be sorted into one of nine categories according to which are most representative of the person being described.

Interviewing as a technique tends to be open-ended, but it can be made more dependable by using a standardized interview schedule with predetermined questions in prearranged order.

Human judgments may introduce unconscious errors such as the *halo effect* and the *stereotype.* These can be minimized by having the judge rate all the individuals on only one trait at a time, so earlier ratings of a given person will be less likely to influence later ones.

Behavior sampling is a means by which personality variables are inferred from observations of people in particular situations. Sometimes the person is aware of being observed; in other cases the behavior samples are collected covertly. Scores from this type of assessment are most valid when the person views the test and the criterion situation for which he or she is being tested as psychologically comparable.

Standard self-inventories require subjects to give information about themselves directly, while *projective tests* allow subjects to project private meaning onto standardized sets of ambiguous neutral stimuli. Psychologists assume that such tests as the *Rorschach* and the *Thematic Apperception Test* bring out projections that reflect the differing needs and emotional adjustments of individuals, revealing their underlying personality patterns.

The dimensions of *introversion-extraversion* found in the *Eysenck Personality Inventory* demonstrate individual differences in the degree to which people need others as sources of reward and cues to appropriate behavior. The *extravert* is found to be more impulsive and dependent upon interaction with others, while the *introvert* is more controlled, relying less on others.

Julian Rotter and his colleagues have used the *internal-external* personality dichotomy to place individuals on a continuum of *locus of control. Externals* perceive that rewards occur independently of their behavior, while *internals* perceive that rewards are contingent on their own behavior. The *I-E Scale,* a *forced-choice* questionnaire, has been designed to assess individuals according to where they fall on this continuum.

Richard Christie has constructed a questionnaire scale that measures *Machiavellianism*—the degree to which individuals are manipulative and pragmatic. At one end of the continuum are *High Machs,* people with relative standards of behavior, and at the other end, those who are *Low Machs* and have absolute standards. Machiavellians are characterized by emotional distance and are guided by what they know rationally, rather than emotionally.

Shyness is a tendency to avoid social situations, to fail to participate appropriately in social encounters, and to feel anxious, distressed, and burdened during interpersonal interactions. Shy individuals are less extraverted, less capable of monitoring their social behavior, and more socially anxious than their "not-shy" peers. A high degree of shyness is frequently reflected in poor personal adjustment.

The concept of *androgyny* refers to a blending of the behaviors and personality traits traditionally associated with one sex or the other. Androgyny is associated with high scores on both masculinity and femininity dimensions of such tests as the Bem Sex Role Inventory. The androgynous person integrates masculinity and femininity into a well-rounded and adaptable personality.

Alfred Binet and Theophile Simon pioneered the first empirical intelligence test in France at the beginning of this century. The results of the tests were scored in terms of the mental age (MA) of the children who took them. The relationship of mental age to chronological age (CA) was known as the *intelligence quotient* (IQ). Lewis Terman developed the Stanford-Binet test, a revision of Binet's original assessment tool, standardizing it and developing norms for American schoolchildren.

During World Wars I and II, the armed forces administered performance and general intelligence examinations, geared to measure mental fitness and intelligence, to millions of recruits. The *Wechsler Intelligence Scale for Children* (WISC) and the *Wechsler Adult Intelligence Scale* (WAIS) also assess intelligence by testing verbal and performance abilities.

IQ tests do not measure "pure" or *genotypic* intelligence. Rather they measure *phenotypic* IQ or *intellectual performance.* Because such tests draw upon values, attitudes, and information from the culture of the test designer and the normative population, variability in IQ may be due to the socioeconomic and cultural background of the test-takers. In addition, research has shown that general intelligence is actually a composite of relatively independent primary abilities, and new tests have been developed to distinguish between them.

Creativity is usually defined as the occurrence of uncommon or unusual but appropriate responses. Different facets of creativity include heightened sensitivity, internal representation, ability to synthesize, and the cognitive freedom that accompanies the state of *intrinsic motivation.* Creative individuals tend to show a great deal of independence in both attitudes and behavior.

18

Understanding and Managing Stress

It started out as most school days do—only bleaker. I was late because I over-slept, having set the radio-clock alarm to 7:00 P.M. instead of 7:00 A.M. (a Freudian wishful fantasy, no doubt). But I was still tired, hadn't slept well, worrying all night about my promotion decision which was to be handed down today by the senior faculty. If anyone ever deserved to be promoted I did just on sheer effort, devotion, and energy above and beyond the call of duty. But they might not see it that way.

Gulped down my coffee and bagel, checked to see if my socks were the same color, fly zipped, lecture notes all together, and raced down the four flights of stairs to head off "Machine-gun" Rattner. Police Officer Rattner had earned his reputation by being the fastest and most prolific ticket writer on the force. He had already tagged me for over $200 worth of them, and I was determined not to get stung again. But with alternate street parking from 8:00 A.M. and overcongested traffic, it was a Mission Impossible situation.

7:58 and counting down. But where was my car? I forgot where I parked it last night, because every night it was parked on a different street. I gambled on 71st—and lost. Running down 68th Street, I saw Rattner getting my car in his sights. Too late; in an instant the ticket was issued and I owed the city another $15.00.

My outrage slowly turned to anger as I drove away. Nearly ran a pedestrian down at the corner (he deserved to be frightened for walking so slowly). We exchanged obscenities. In no time I was *there*—stuck in the morning rush traffic jam, in the tunnel. Horns honking, exhaust fumes building up, tempers boiling.

Eleven minutes late to Psych 1, beg departing students to return, most do so resentfully. Lecture goes badly; I can't concentrate my attention or get my emotions under sufficient control. Feel guilty for having forced the class to stay. Promise myself to give a dynamite lecture tomorrow to make up for to-day's disaster.

During office hours, my research assistant tells me she has to leave school to work full time because her father died and she has to support her family. She cries over the loss of her father and her education. I'm distressed over the loss of the only reliable, normal graduate assistant I have. I take some aspirin for my headache which gets progressively worse during endless student counseling hours.

The afternoon mail is a mixed bag. First letter tells me my research article was accepted for publication in a prestigious journal. Joy! Second letter informs me I'm overdrawn at the bank and it's ten days before the next payday. Begin thinking about what I could sell or whom I could borrow from—but not my kid brother again. Too humiliating. Begin to feel overwhelmed with money problems. No way out. Depressed.

Chairman invites me into his office. "We all respect the kind of work you've been doing" . . . *But . . . But . . . But* . . . No promotion. "Some people feel you need more time to mellow . . . too brash, and . . ." Sad: they're right, I'm not any good. Angry: they're all wrong. Result: feeling more depressed.

Forget to keep my appointment for a medical checkup on the headaches and chest pain I've been having lately. Lose my temper with the secretary for not finishing the typing I gave her yesterday. She cries. I apologize. Decide to call it a day. Take a few stiff drinks before heading home.

Stuck in evening rush-hour traffic, as usual. But finally home. Or, almost so. Ride up 69th, down 70th, up 71st, down 72nd—in search of the elusive 10 × 4 feet of unoccupied asphalt in which to bury my car.

And so today ended as most work days do—only somewhat more stressful.

Stress and adaptation

This modern-day college professor seems far removed from the isolated ivory towers of learning inhabited by academics of earlier times. He is suffering from the "disease of civilization"—the stresses induced by intense environmental stimulation. He reacts at four interrelated levels to these environmental demands. There are the *emotional* responses: sadness, anger, irritation, frustration, rage, and even elation. There are the *behavioral* reactions which show up in changes in performance: poor concentration, forgetting, lessened productivity, or inability to get along with other people. In addition, stress may induce a third type of response, changes in *physiological* functioning. At this level, the bodily tensions that stress creates may lead to headaches, backaches, high blood pressure, and ultimately to diseases that kill. Finally, at a *cognitive* level, the person may begin to think of him- or herself in certain ways that lower self-esteem and lead to feelings of helplessness and hopelessness. At that point, serious forms of depression take over which can necessitate hospitalization, or even end in suicide.

Research on the psychological aspects of health, sickness, and medical treatment has recently been integrated as a special area of science called *behavioral medicine*. This new, interdisciplinary field brings the methods and concepts of the behavioral sciences to aid in the maintenance of health, the prevention of disease, and more effective treatment of illness. Topics of concern include the management of stress, cognitive strategies that influence susceptibility to disease states, and behavior patterns of patients and physicians that affect the outcome of medical practices. Behavioral medicine adopts a *holistic* view of the person—one in which mind and body, thoughts and emotions, beliefs and behavior are not separated but function as interdependent systems. The range of issues being studied is already great and promises to become even broader: How can a physician get a patient to follow the prescribed course of treatment? How are cultural beliefs about illness related to the types of illness that actually occur? Why don't certain populations in a society utilize available health resources even when they are free? Does society's emphasis upon competition and achievement encourage habits destructive to health? Such questions call for research by investigators in many different fields—social psychologists, behavior modifiers, cognitive psychologists, personality psychologists as well as sociologists, anthropologists, and medical researchers.

In this chapter, we will take a close look at how we face up to the demands for adaptation to our environment and what happens when we fail to adapt to the stresses of everyday living. Finally, we will examine what *you* can do to cope more effectively with stress and better adjust to the diseases of civilization that intrude on your life space.

Human adaptability

Human beings are organisms of incredible adaptability. They don't just "make do" with what they have to work with; they adapt to what is available sometimes by altering the environment to make it more livable. The capacity to imagine an environment better suited to our needs and the ability to create it are hallmarks of the human species. The survival of our species has been challenged by the most traumatic natural catastrophes: famines, floods, droughts, earthquakes, volcanic eruptions, and more. Still greater threats to survival have come from hostile forces within the species—those who would commit violent crimes, start wars, practice genocide.

But the greatest threat to our adaptive ability is much newer. In the process of modifying our environment to make it serve the goals of comfort and luxury, we have created an industrial technology that has potentially lethal side effects. We are beginning to witness the impact on our lives, as individuals and as a society, of air, water, and noise pollution, escalating energy consumption, pressures toward excessive work, an increased tempo of life, and a dizzyingly rapid rate of change of almost everything (Toffler, 1970). Even to these environmental "insults" we adapt. But, as we shall see, sometimes we pay a high price for this adaptability.

What accounts for human adaptability? We know from our earlier study that the answer lies in our highly evolved nervous system. It allows us to share in common with lower species primitive types of adaptation through the signal learning of classical conditioning and the consequent learning of operant conditioning. But it is the refined development of our cerebral cortex that enables us to think, plan, and solve problems through manipulation of abstract symbols. Through cognition and the use of language we can profit from our past mistakes to transform the present into a more desirable future. Adaptability is given a big boost by our ability to learn much from merely observing the effects that follow upon the actions of others. And through our cultural heritage such knowledge is passed on over generations by oral tradition or through the printed word. Because animals of the wild must adapt biologically to their environment, the mechanisms are coded in their genes and limited by the slow timetable of evolutionary processes. Human beings adapt not only biologically, but psychologically.

The key to human adaptation goes beyond survival at any cost. It is found in the delicate balance of our internal environment—minds and physical functioning—with the demands imposed by the external environment. This equilibrium is challenged when the demands are intense or chronic, and we are not psychologically prepared or biologically fit to respond optimally to the challenge. Disease results when we fail to respond adaptively. Health is signaled by our ability to respond effectively in a total way—by our thoughts, feelings, and actions—to the environmental demands faced. René Dubos, professor emeritus of environmental biochemistry at Rockefeller University, instructs us that: "Human health transcends purely biological health because it depends primarily on those conscious and deliberate choices by which we select our mode of life and adapt, creatively, to its experiences. Many have affirmed that human ability to create our own selves and shape our own lives" (1978, p. 80).

The professor in our opening example made choices (to eat a poor diet, not to have adequate rest and relaxation, to live in an overcrowded, noisy city, to own an automobile, to work at a competitive job, to spend more than he earned) that had a variety of negative consequences. In addition, he allowed himself to get emotionally upset by these and other events he experienced. His sadness at the report of someone's death as well as the joy and elation at receiving good news were also strong internal adjustments to external inputs. Over and over again in this one day's slice of life we witness the operation of stress.

Stress is the nonspecific response of the body to any demand made on it (Selye, 1973). Although the causes of stress are many and varied, and can be either pleasant (such as a passionate kiss) or unpleasant (such as the loss of one's job), they all demand readjustment or adaptation. The biological stress response to this demand (regardless of the source) is always essentially the same. As we shall see, this response involves the activities of various hormones, and it occurs in several phases. Contrary to popular opinion, stress is not some terrible

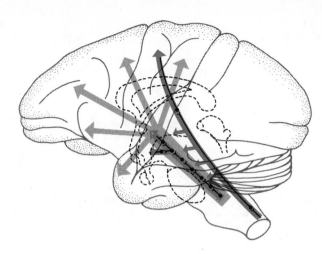

Lateral view of a monkey's brain, showing the ascending reticular system in the brain stem receiving input from sensory pathways and projecting primarily to the association areas of the hemisphere.

circumstance to be avoided; rather, it is a process that is continually evoked throughout one's life. No matter what you do, there will always be demands to perform necessary tasks or adapt to changing influences. Instead of avoiding stress, we need to learn how to deal with it in the best way possible.

Arousal and stress pathways

Emotional arousal is one of the most frequent causes of stress. But all arousal is not stressful. Imagine being gently wakened from a sound sleep with a tender kiss, and a whisper "It's time." You move from a state of inactivity toward one of action—but gradually. Surely you "wake up" more slowly than if someone had screamed, "Fire, run for your life!"

It is the brain's *reticular activating system (RAS)* that has the job of "waking up the cortex." It makes the organism vigilant and aware of what is happening in the environment and to it. The RAS is a bundle of nerve fibers running from the spinal cord through the medulla into the cortical regions of the brain. These fibers receive inputs from all the senses, thus helping put the total organism in better contact with its environment. ▲ They then make the organism alert, aroused, and sensitive to changes in environmental stimuli. This generalized arousal, coupled with appropriate information about bodily needs and environmental demands, plays an important role in determining the ultimate expression of behavior.

Our activity level may vary from the low level of sleep to the high level of alert excitement. As arousal increases, there is a generalized increase in the strength of instrumental responses, whether or not they are actually useful in satisfying the motivational requirement. The capacity of sensory stimulation to guide behavior is poor when arousal is very low or very high. With very low arousal, the sensory message does not get through; with very high arousal, too many messages get through and prevent the individual from responding selectively to the correct stimulus message. Thus an intermediate level of arousal produces optimal performance, because more useful information can be extracted from the relevant cue stimuli to guide the behavior. Such an intermediate level has been shown to be most effective for both rats in mazes and students in a test-taking situation. This relationship between arousal and effectiveness of performance is called an inverted-U function. ◆

Several variables must be considered to predict an individual's performance from this general inverted-U function. The arousal continuum differs according to an individual's tolerance for, and definition of, "high arousal." For some people, a double-loop roller-coaster ride is not really extreme arous-

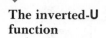

**The inverted-U
function**

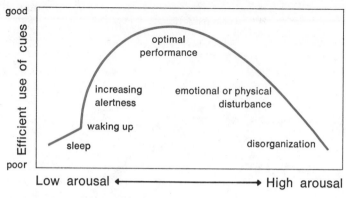

Adapted from Hebb, 1958

al. Others faint at the sight of blood or the touch of a hypodermic needle. Thus the arousal dimension is in part subjectively determined. Furthermore, the same degree of arousal may facilitate performance of simple, well-practiced tasks, but disrupt complex, unfamiliar ones. Arousal may have cumulative effects when a person is faced with continual or chronic episodes of arousal, as a front-line surgeon in wartime or a volunteer on a suicide "hot line." Performance may deteriorate more quickly or more completely over time as the same level of repeated emotional arousal takes its toll and wears one down. (Some students report a comparable reaction on the last day of a week of final exams.)

Relaxation and arousal are not the poles of a simple continuum; they involve an intricate balance of nervous system and hormonal factors. Contact with a stressor stimulates a complex system of the hypothalamus, the cerebral cortex, the reticular formation, the limbic system, the autonomic nervous system, and the endocrine system. This complex physiological response marshals the body's full energy resources almost instantly. It does so without conscious preparation—which would waste precious time when action and not reflection is in order.

The general adaptation syndrome

Stress is a psychobiological state manifested by a *syndrome*, that is, a set of symptoms. Hans Selye has spent over forty years studying the syndrome of "just being sick" (1956, 1976). According to Selye's theory, the body's reaction under stress, which he calls the *general adaptation syndrome*, occurs in three major phases: the *alarm reaction*, the *stage of resistance*, and the *stage of exhaustion*.

The *alarm reaction*, sometimes called the *emergency reaction*, consists of the physiological changes that are the organism's first response to a stress-provoking agent, or *stressor*. *A stressor is anything injurious to the organism*, whether physical (such as inadequate food, loss of sleep, disease, bodily injury) or psychological (such as loss of love or personal security). The alarm reaction consists of various complicated bodily and biochemical changes that usually have the *same* general characteristics regardless of the exact nature of the stressor. This accounts for the similarity in general symptoms of people suffering from diverse illnesses. All seem to complain of such symptoms as headache, fever, fatigue, aching muscles and joints, loss of appetite, and a general feeling of being "run down."

If exposure to the stress-producing situation continues, the alarm reaction is followed by the *stage of resistance*. This is the second phase of the general adaptation syndrome. Here the organism seems to develop a resistance to the particular stressor that provoked the alarm reaction. The symptoms that occurred during the first stage of stress disappear, even though the disturbing stimulation continues, and the physiological processes that had been disturbed during the alarm reaction appear to resume normal functioning. Resistance to the stressor seems to be accomplished in large part through increased level of secretions of the anterior pituitary and the adrenal cortex (ACTH and *cortin*, respectively).

If exposure to the injurious stressor continues too long, a point is reached where the organism can no longer maintain its resistance. It then enters the final phase of changes related to stress, the *stage of exhaustion*. The anterior pituitary and adrenal cortex are unable to continue secreting their hormones at the increased rate. This means the organism cannot continue to adapt to the chronic stress. Many of the symptoms of the alarm reaction begin to reappear. If the stressor continues to act upon the organism after this time, death may occur. It is rare, however, for stress not to be relieved before the stage of total exhaustion is reached. ●

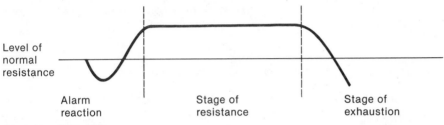

Level of normal resistance

| Alarm reaction | Stage of resistance | Stage of exhaustion |

The general adaptation syndrome

Adapted from Selye, 1956

The body shows the changes characteristic of the first exposure to a stressor. At the same time, its resistance is diminished and, if the stressor is sufficiently strong (severe burns, extremes of temperature), death may result.

The second stage ensues if continued exposure to the stressor is compatible with adaptation. The bodily signs characteristic of the alarm reaction have virtually disappeared and resistance rises above normal.

Following long continued exposure to the same stressor, to which the body has become adjusted, eventually adaptation energy is exhausted. The signs of the alarm reaction reappear, but now they are irreversible, and the individual dies.

The concept of the general adaptation syndrome has been exceptionally valuable in explaining disorders that had baffled physicians. Within this framework, many disorders can be viewed as the results of stress or of the physiological processes involved in adaptation to stress. The value of administering additional ACTH and cortisone in treating some of these diseases can also be understood. In effect, such treatment may be regarded as a way of helping the anterior pituitary and the adrenal cortex maintain the body's resistance to some stressor.

Consequences of stress

In the fourth century B.C., Plato boldly asserted that "all diseases of the body proceed from the mind or soul." It is now believed by those who specialize in the study and treatment of psychologically induced physical illness that stress is a contributing factor in 50 to 80 percent of all disease (Pelletier, 1977). It is estimated that about thirty million Americans suffer from sleep-onset insomnia. Stress contributes to insomnia, as you may know personally from

■

Would you believe that only six months separate the two Nixons? The first photo was taken in January 1974, the second in June of the same year, shortly before the Watergate scandal forced his resignation.

those sleepless nights before a big event. Nearly as many Americans are afflicted with *hypertension* (high blood pressure). Hypertension can lead to complications that are lethal.

Living under the flight paths leading to and from major airports may induce stressful reactions of serious proportion. At Los Angeles International Airport, for example, more than three hundred jets a day fly over densely populated neighborhoods. Their noise sometimes exceeds one hundred decibels. Its other stressful aspects include suddenness, unpredictability, and unpleasantness. For some people the noise also arouses fears of a plane crash.

Many residents report sleep disturbances. More serious is the greater likelihood of mental hospital admissions for those living in the maximum noise area compared to adjacent areas. The chances of developing a psychological disorder requiring hospitalization were 29 percent greater for those living under the jetways. A similar figure of 31 percent more "nervous breakdowns" was found among Britishers living near London's Heathrow Airport (Meecham & Smith, 1977, p. 50).

Aging itself is a stress-related disease, but its deteriorating effects can be exaggerated by excessive stress. A comparison of two photographs of former President Richard Nixon graphically depicts the visible effects of stress. ■ How much older is the troubled Nixon in the second photo than the happier Nixon above?

Emotions and physical illness

In the face of repeated stressful arousal, the physiological defenses of the body may be maladaptive and injurious. Deterioration in bodily functioning that is *psychogenic* (has a psychological-emotional source) is called, appropriately, a *psychosomatic disorder* (*psyche* = "mind," *soma* = "body"). This term is used to refer to the symptoms involved in a persistent stress reaction, such as rapid pulse and high blood pressure, and to actual tissue damage that may result, such as a gastric ulcer. Emotional factors have been clearly demonstrated in the development of some cases of ulcers, high blood pressure, colitis, migraine, low back pain, dermatitis, obesity, asthma, and many other ailments.

Is it really bad for your health to "bottle up" your emotions? Yes, according to research evidence; certainly as far as feelings of frustration and pent-up aggression are concerned.

In separate studies employing over 160 college-age subjects of both sexes, frustration was experimentally aroused by the blocking of goal activity, or by ego threats. Some of the subjects were allowed to aggress physically, verbally, or in their fantasy against the frustration, while others were given no such opportunity.

The results clearly indicated that both heart rate and systolic blood pressure rose significantly following the frustrating experience. Opportunity to aggress physically or verbally lowered these levels, whereas when subjects were not allowed to express their strong feelings overtly, the physiological changes persisted (Hokanson & Burgess, 1962).

The stress of having to deal with a stranger in an interview situation can affect your blood pressure. This was shown in an experiment where subjects were interviewed under conditions that varied the interview content, the novelty of the setting, and the amount of social intervention. The data suggest that the process of social interaction (and presumably the emotions it arouses) has a powerful effect upon raising diastolic blood pressure. It did so more than novelty or content of the interview (Williams, Kimball, & Williard, 1972).

Although prolonged stress can lead to a wide range of serious disorders, psychosomatic reactions cannot be predicted solely on the basis of exposure to behavioral stress. Constitutional factors and specific kinds of past experience appear to play a role not only in whether stress will result in a psychosomatic reaction, but in the kind of reaction as well. In the study cited above, students who had learned to express their anger outwardly toward the source of the stress displayed different physiological responses than those who had developed a characteristic reaction of fear or self-blame (Funkenstein, King, & Drolette, 1957). Convincing evidence that physical and psychological factors may combine to cause disease also comes from a study using mice as subjects.

Mice were stressed for three days by being given cues for anticipating shock plus the shock itself, then inoculated with Coxsackie B virus and stressed for four additional days. Neither stress alone (for some control groups) nor virus alone (for others) was sufficient to cause disease. Only a combination of the two—environmental stress plus the viral agent—resulted in disease (Friedman, Ader, & Glasgow, 1965).

In another recent study mice were exposed to a daily auditory stressor for varying lengths of time. This stress induced a change in their immune response to infection. The depression of the body's immune function was associated with an increase in circulating levels of adrenal corticosteroids. However, environmental stressors were also shown to en-hance as well as depress the immune reaction. Research is in progress to establish the conditions under which stress may enable the body to resist disease or make it less vulnerable (Monjan & Collector, 1977).

After reviewing the available evidence on factors related to acquiring or resisting infectious disease, a team of physicians concluded that "relatively subtle psychological and environmental factors appear to influence susceptibility to a wide range of infectious and parasitic agents" (Friedman & Glasgow, 1966, p. 323). Emotional factors have also been implicated in the onset of cancer. (See *P&L* Close-up, Emotions and Breast Cancer.) Most physicians have long realized that even when symptoms are due primarily to physical causes, emotional strain can work against successful treatment.

At the other end of the spectrum are the many cases on record of patients determined to get well who have done so despite a physician's opinion that they were beyond recovery. It has been reported that old people are more likely to die after a holiday or birthday than before, as though they were determined to live until a certain target date. Emotional factors are particularly important in such organic disorders as tuberculosis, heart disease, diabetes, and epilepsy. In treating tuberculosis, for example, care must be taken to avoid emotional disturbances, since the patient is not allowed to engage in vigorous physical exercise and is thus denied an important natural means of working off emotional tensions. Unless efforts are made to help the patient maintain a cheerful mood, a disease that is essentially organic may be intensified by emotional factors.

It is likely that at least as many patients are cured by a doctor's reassuring "bedside" manner as by any of the medicines prescribed. Physicians are now being cautioned to be more responsive not only to the whole patient but to the social-emotional network in which the patient lives. Although the significance of the "mind" in physical illness is receiving greater attention in medical circles, it may be that the general trend away from family doctors and general practitioners to clinics and specialists means that the patient's emotional needs will receive less attention than the family doctor would give. ▲

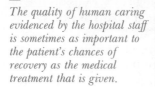

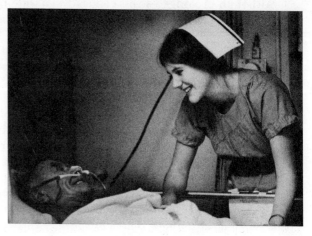

The quality of human caring evidenced by the hospital staff is sometimes as important to the patient's chances of recovery as the medical treatment that is given.

The holistic approach

As economic conditions have improved and medical science has specialized in the problems of infectious diseases and serious injuries, disease patterns in Western countries have changed. Advances in surgery, nutrition, hygiene, and epidemic control have made these problems less prevalent. At the same time, there has been an increase in the relative prevalence of heart disease, high blood pressure, ulcers, anxiety disorders, colitis, and arthritis. These stress-related and degenerative diseases are collectively known as "diseases of adaptation" or "afflictions of civilization" (Dubos, 1965).

Traditional medical approaches are ineffectual when confronted with the nonspecific syndrome of stress-related illness. Medicine has had its best success in dealing with specific agents (such as germs) that cause a particular disease. The alternate approach holds that a person's habitual life-style (diet, exercise, smoking habits) and habitual reaction to perceived stress can lead to any of a variety of disorders. It is both a new and an ancient doctrine. The conception that the way we live is intimately associated with our vulnerability to disease has been "clearly expressed in Taoism and in traditional Chinese medicine, and in the Hippocratic teachings which dominated Western medicine until the nineteenth century" (Stoyva, 1976).

The new version of these ancient doctrines is found in *holistic medicine*. Holistic medicine combats illness by treating the whole person, not just the physical organs. The holistic approach concentrates on helping individuals reorient their life-styles, if necessary, to prevent stress-induced health problems. This may involve changing jobs or moving away from areas that are highly stressful. It may mean altering daily patterns of living that are not healthful. The focus is on health maintenance and growth rather than cure of existing illness.

If intense demands are put on the body to perform adaptive functions and stress is the body's nonspecific response to such demands, then it is not possible to establish simple, direct cause-effect relationships. (See *P&L* Close-up, Executive Pressure or Emotional Personality?) Experimental medicine faces problems in trying to pin down the physiological consequences of pollution, diet, lack of exercise, noise, excessive work output, hostility in the home, and other such general stress agents. Similarly, on the output side, a number of diseases appear to be stress-related — respiratory disease, arthritis, migraine, hypertension, arteriosclerosis, cancer, and others. But which agents are re-

Women with diagnosed breast cancer may have developed the illness in part because of emotional traumas they had experienced. Rose Kushner, of the Breast Cancer Advisory Center, Washington, D.C., states that in her experience with over four thousand women with breast cancer an "overwhelming" number had suffered from an earlier major loss in their lives. This observation is supported in a West German study of eight thousand patients with various types of cancer. The disease usually shows up during periods of severe stress involving "loss and separation." Breast cancer could be linked to repression of emotions such as anger and despair, according to Dr. S. Greer of King's College, London. Emotional stressors may create both depression and hormonal imbalances which, in turn, interfere with immunological defenses against cancer.

Little research is being directed toward this problem area because of the difficulty in establishing a clear link between depression, hormones, and cancer. Cancer itself causes hormone changes, so it is difficult to determine if hormone imbalance causes or follows the malignancy. Also, cancer develops slowly over long time periods, so it is difficult to isolate specific stress factors.

However, it is possible to include emotion histories as well as disease histories in patient intake interviews. This would help establish the correlation on a firmer data base. More research could be directed at understanding the psychology of women under stress. If breast cancer potential increases following certain stress reactions, then women could be cautioned to make more careful inspection of their breasts for lumps following periods of emotional arousal.

Even though cause-effect conclusions are hardly at hand as yet regarding the link between emotions and breast cancer, the precautions involved are simple enough to warrant a practical implication: check your body for malignancy for some time after exposure to emotional stress, and report any suspicions of lumps to a physician (*Behavior Today*, October 11, 1976).

sponsible and how they work are still unanswered questions. If diseases of adaptation are thought of as psychosomatic disorders, then both mind and body must be treated. Furthermore, the model employed must be flexible enough to search for consistent patterns of correlation between environmental inputs and bodily reactions, and not demand causal proof before taking action. Such thinking underlies the methodological approach of holistic medicine.

Sources of stress

Many things that happen to us are stressful in some degree. Most of these are not serious and we readily adjust to them. It is when we must cope with too many pressures at one time or with continuing pressure over an extended period that stress becomes a serious problem. In this section we shall examine some of the types of changes in our lives that can build up to damaging levels of stress. Continuing job pressures, whether they stem from too much or too little change, can be a chronic source of harmful stress and we will look at these as well.

Life crises and health

Even with diseases such as cancer or leukemia, emotional experiences early in life may contribute to the development of the disease. More surprising is the evidence that such events may not show their effects until many years later.

In a study investigating the history of early psychic traumas in cancer patients, a psychic trauma was defined as an experience in which "emotional relationships brought pain and desertion." Of 450 cancer patients, 72 percent (as compared to only 10 percent of a noncancerous control group) were found to have suffered such an experience early in life. It was theorized that the cancer patients had, as children, responded to these crises with feelings of guilt and self-blame. During adolescence and early adulthood, these feelings were submerged as desires and energies were concentrated on school, job, and meaningful relationships with others, particularly the spouse. However, often after as long as forty years, when the pattern was changed, perhaps by retirement from work or by the death of the spouse, and the individuals could find no substitute source of satisfaction and meaning in their life, their feelings of guilt and inadequacy returned. Usually the first symptoms of cancer appeared from six months to eight years after this second life crisis (LeShan, 1966).

Close-up
Executive Pressure or Emotional Personality?

"Executive monkeys develop ulcers" was the conclusion of a famous study done back in 1958 that has been widely quoted both in the popular press and in psychology textbooks (Brady, Porter, Conrad, & Mason, 1958). The investigators placed pairs of monkeys in an environment where they both received electric shocks following a cue light, unless one of them operated a switch that prevented the onset of the series of shocks. The monkey in charge of the switch was, of course, labeled the *executive monkey* because it had all the responsibility. The other monkey could do nothing to control the situation. In this study the executive monkeys developed ulcers and died; the passive control monkeys remained healthy.

The obvious conclusion is that "pressure to perform" produced the ulcers—a conclusion that, if true, would have obvious implications for human executives. It has recently been suggested, however, that the conclusion is probably a false one, and probably resulted from a bias in the way the monkeys were assigned to the two conditions. Instead of assigning the monkeys at random to the "executive" or "passive" condition, the researchers chose the monkeys that had shown the most initiative in lever-pressing to avoid shock—the ones that were the fastest starters—to be the executives. The "slowpokes" were the controls. It has since been found that monkeys that respond most quickly when shocked are those that are most "emotional" to begin with (perhaps with a low threshold for pain and anxiety). Thus an interaction effect exists: *emotional* executives are more likely to get ulcers than are *unemotional* observers.

When researcher Joy Weiss at Rockefeller University (1968, 1971) randomly assigned rats to the executive and passive treatments, the helpless animals fared worse, losing more weight, drinking less, defecating more, and getting more severe ulcers than did the executives. Perhaps, then, executives develop ulcers not so much because of their greater responsibility or even hard work, but from biting off more than they can control.

Events	Scale of Impact	Events	Scale of Impact
Death of spouse	100	Son or daughter leaving home	29
Divorce	73	Trouble with in-laws	29
Marital separation	65	Outstanding personal achievement	28
Jail term	63	Spouse begins or stops work	26
Death of close family member	63	Begin or end school	26
Personal injury or illness	53	Change in living conditions	25
Marriage	50	Revision of personal habits	24
Fired at work	47	Trouble with boss	23
Marital reconciliation	45	Change in work hours or conditions	20
Retirement	45	Change in residence	20
Change in health of family member	44	Change in schools	20
Pregnancy	40	Change in recreation	19
Sex difficulties	39	Change in church activities	19
Gain in new family member	39	Change in social activities	18
Business readjustment	39	Mortgage or loan less than $10,000	17
Change in financial state	38	Change in sleeping habits	16
Death of close friend	37	Change in number of family get-togethers	15
Change to different line of work	36	Change in eating habits	15
Change in number of arguments with spouse	35	Vacation	13
Mortgage over $10,000	31	Christmas	12
Foreclosure of mortgage or loan	30	Minor violations of the law	11
Change in responsibilities at work	29		

But how does one measure a "life crisis"? Psychiatrists at the University of Washington School of Medicine developed a scale for rating the degree of adjustment required by forty-three different life changes, both pleasant and unpleasant (Holmes & Holmes, 1970). Their scale of stress values is measured in *life change units* (LCU).

In a group of almost four hundred subjects, a consistent relationship was found between the number of life change units, according to the scale, and major health changes during the same ten-year period. Of those with moderate crisis scale scores, 37 percent had had a major health change; of those with substantial life crisis scale scores, 70 percent had showed a major health change. In addition, those who usually remained well during flu epidemics were more likely to have flu after a major life change (Rahe & Holmes, 1966).

Holmes and his colleagues predict that people run the risk of developing a major illness in the next two years if they total more than 300 LCU points. It might be well to calculate your personal LCU rating.

My LCU = _____

A recent improvement in the methodology of relating life changes to illness is the development of the Life Experiences Survey (Sarason & Johnson, 1976). This instrument extends the usefulness of LCU ratings. (See *P&L* Close-up, A Critical Look at LCU and Illness.) The Life Experiences Survey asks the respondent to indicate the type and extent of impact that each of a series of life event changes had at the time the event occurred (from "extremely negative" through "no impact" to "extremely positive"). Such a procedure distinguishes between positive and negative changes and allows individualized ratings of both events and degree of impact. Thus for example, death of a spouse who was disliked, abusive, and left a big inheritance represents a positive LCU that has less impact on subsequent stress than death of a dearly loved spouse.

The breakdown of social networks

Underlying most critical life events is a separation from other people. Someone dies, you move away, you get another job, you're promoted, graduated, or demoted, but in all cases you are distanced from your former associates.

Close-up
A Critical Look at LCU and Illness

The extensive research by investigators Holmes and Rahe has directed attention to an important relationship between psychosocial factors and somatic illness (Holmes & Masuda, 1974; Rahe, 1974). Because of the theoretical and practical implications of their work, we must be cautious in accepting the evidence and sufficiently critical in our appraisal of what has been found. Some points of contention are:

Methodological
(a) Many of the studies correlate retrospective accounts of life changes with other retrospective accounts of illness. In some studies subjects reported on life changes and illness simultaneously — making the purpose of the study all too clear and possibly biasing subjects' responses. (b) When predictive follow-up of illness is the dependent variable, prior LCU of 6 months predicts illness rather than LCU of two years as in earlier studies. (c) The correlations are generally quite small but are statistically significant with larger samples. (d) Some of the LCU life events may be presymptomatic indicators of the illness and not independent of the predictor variable (such as changes in eating or sleeping). (e) Independent and dependent variables are often not clearly defined. (f) The use of a unidimensional scale to represent an obviously complex domain of symptoms may lead to limited and erroneous conclusions.

Theoretical
(a) No specific biological mechanisms for the relationship are given. (b) The LCU measure may be a better predictor of "treatment-seeking behavior" than of actual illness. (c) "No change" may be stressful, when change is expected, as in loss of an expected promotion or refusal of a marriage proposal. (d) There is no provision for the broader context in which the changes take place, social contacts, capacity to deal with stress, established ways of handling such changes. (e) The differences between positive and negative changes in the person's interpretation and subsequent illness reaction need to be established. (f) Perhaps both LCU and illness involve losses of close social contacts which is the important mediating process (Cohen, 1975; Rabkin & Struening, 1976).

Even a positive event such as marriage often involves a separation from an established network of friends and family. We may reasonably ask then whether there is an association between social disconnection or isolation and disease processes. Two studies in progress point convincingly to the importance of social relationships to physical and psychological health:

Nearly seven thousand adults were surveyed in 1965 to determine health and health-related behaviors, as well as other background factors and the extent of their social relationships. Mortality (death rate) data were collected for a nine-year period on 96 percent of this original sample. A <u>social network index</u> was computed for each person consisting of the number and relative importance of social contacts. This index of social disconnection was significantly correlated with overall mortality rates as well as each specific cause of death. For every age group and both sexes, more people with minimal social contacts died than people with many social contacts. This effect was independent of health status at the time of the initial survey or of socioeconomic status. Furthermore, people who were socially isolated were more likely to engage in poor health behaviors (smoking, drinking, overeating, irregular eating, inadequate sleep, etc.). But the extent of one's social contacts still predicts mortality over and above the effects of any or all of these poor health practices. Thus likelihood of death can be predicted better by knowing how isolated or connected a person is than by knowledge of the person's smoking history, even though smoking clearly increases mortality. The data warrant the researcher's conclusion that "social and community ties may be powerful determinants of consequent health status" (Berkman, 1977, p. 7).

In the other large-scale study, psychological distress was related to the social nature of life change events over a two-year period. Thoits (1978) distinguished life change, iso- lating events (deaths, separation, divorce, child leaves home, unemployment, institution- alization, etc.) from integrating events (marriage, reconciliation, birth, child returns home, employment or schooling begins, etc.). She also examined life events that increased or decreased one's prestige. Distress was assessed by a scale of self-reported psychophysio- logical symptoms (nervousness, weight loss, exhaustion, insomnia, etc.).

Events that are isolating and those that decrease one's prestige raise the distress level in all groups studied. Among married males, integrating events, even though they have high LCU values, reduce distress. However, they have no effect on distress level for married females. Also, the impact of each isolating event on distress level is greater for males already isolated than for those who are part of a social network. But the impact of integrating effects on reducing distress is also greater for isolates than connected males. Thus life change events have less effect on males who are socially connected than those who are isolated. (The effects for females are more complicated and less consistent.)

The "romantic notion" that people need the warmth of human contact to survive (which we discussed in Chapter 1) is being given a solid empirical foundation by research such as this.

Occupational stress

Many of us spend more time each day working than in any other activity. If some kinds of work can be identified as stress-inducing, then the demands of adapting to one's job could be costly, and perhaps even death-dealing. But what makes a job a stress agent? What features of an occupation mark it out as hazardous to one's health? And what is the evidence that certain occupations are really stressful?

Occupational stress may be defined as "the condition in which some factor, or combination of factors, at work interact with the worker to disrupt his [or her] psychological or physiological homeostasis" (Margolis & Kroes, 1974, p. 15). Stress on the job is most likely to occur when there is a poor fit between person and environment. This can happen when the job makes demands be- yond the worker's abilities *(overload)*, or when the worker's needs are frustrat- ed by an unstimulating job *(stimulus underload)*. Overload can be created by jobs in which there is excessive and often conflicting information about one's expected role. "We play it cool here, don't be pushy—but you'd better be pro- ductive and exceed the quota." Uncertainty about performance criteria, what is expected of you, ambiguity about the best way to do the job or how one ought to relate to co-workers and superiors all contribute to the stress factor of a job.

Executives in certain departments of a large company were placed in a new organiza- tional system of decision making, which proved to be a very inefficient one. Their frustra- tion with the structure of their job was not only reflected in lowered sales and increased staff infighting, but in a high frequency of psychosomatic complaints (Ruma, 1973).

In another study of the effects of switching workers from a fixed monthly salary to the more demanding schedule of a piecework rate, the result was also a negative psycho- logical reaction and a corresponding change in bodily state. Although the women work- ers were earning more money as their average production rate rose by 113 percent, they reported more strain and fatigue and there was a sharp increase in secretion of stress hormones (Levi, 1972).

Work overload has been shown in a number of studies to produce at least nine different kinds of psychological and physiological strain in the worker

(French & Caplan, 1971). Work overload is related to job dissatisfaction, increased levels of cholesterol, elevated heart rate, and excessive smoking—all risk factors in heart disease. Overloaded workers were also found not to be utilizing their knowledge or their intellectual, administrative, and leadership skills. At conscious or unconscious levels such workers perceive their job as a threat to their mental and physical well-being.

Even highly glamorous occupations like that of career diplomats on foreign assignments can be stress factors. A physician assigned to the American Embassy in Moscow reported that the Moscow assignment was associated with unusually high levels of psychic stress. For many diplomats it is their most important assignment, but one that is under much restriction and surveillance. In addition, most are separated from families for long periods. The consequences: a high proportion develop ulcers, insomnia, colitis, anxiety problems, sexual failure, or "nervous breakdowns" (Osnos, 1977).

Sexual impotence may also be a stress-related consequence of the tensions associated with police work. "I've seen great numbers of men who, after they've been in law enforcement about five years, become impotent," says a psychologist who counsels law officers. He believes the responsible stress agents are abnormal work hours, and the violence and squalor in their work (*San Francisco Examiner* & *Chronicle,* October 17, 1976). (For other effects of high-stress jobs see *P&L* Close-up, Tensions in the Tower.)

Close-up
Tensions in the Tower

Air-traffic controllers at Chicago's O'Hare Airport are responsible for more than thirty-seven million passengers a year. About 666,560 takeoffs and landings occur, one every twenty seconds. Any letup from constant vigilance, a slight error in instructions, or a switch missed can result in a fatal air crash. This intense stress is comparable to battle fatigue and has been labeled "collisionitis."

By their own estimates, there are two or three near-misses every day. These near-misses might be avoided if the controllers followed the FAA regulations which specify the minimum distance between landing aircraft—five miles apart for big jets, three miles apart for standard size planes. That is the theory—in practice, the controllers cannot "go by the book" because the volume of traffic is too great. The standards become the maximum, not the minimum. When peak traffic reached 220 takeoffs and landings in one hour, the controllers were commended by their superiors. Commended in part for violating the safety standards! Role confusion added to the stress of vigilance overload.

When the medical records of four thousand flight controllers were compared with those of eight thousand second-class airmen the results were startling. High blood pressure was four times as common and developed at an earlier age among the controllers. Twice as many controllers also suffered from peptic ulcers as did the airmen. These psychosomatic illnesses as well as anxiety, insomnia, loss of appetite, irritability, and depression were found to be greatest among controllers at the busiest airports. And O'Hare is the busiest one of all (Martindale, 1976).

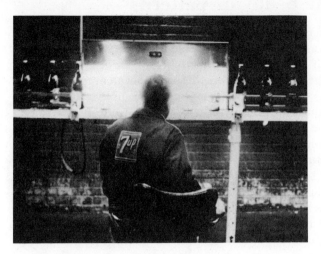

Boredom rating

Assembler (work paced by machine)	207
Forklift-truck driver	170
Assembler (working at own pace)	160
Monitor of continuous flow goods	122
Accountant	107
Engineer	100
Computer programmer	96
Electronic technician	87
White-collar supervisor	72
Scientist	66
Administrator	66
Policeman	63
Air-traffic controller (large airport)	59
Professor	49
Physician	48

On the other hand, if overload doesn't get you, underload might. People are not ever bored to death by their jobs, but there is good evidence that they can be "bored to sickness." Researchers at the Institute for Social Research of the University of Michigan found that boring jobs are hardest on health (Caplan et al., 1975).

In this study of over two thousand males in twenty-three different occupations, the researchers found that general working conditions (hours worked, quantitative work load) had less effect on job dissatisfaction than personal factors such as opportunities to use one's skills and to participate in decision making. As job dissatisfaction increases so do anxiety, depression, irritation, and psychosomatic illnesses. Assembly-line workers have boring jobs, but ones that do not involve long hours, unwanted overtime, much concentration, or responsibility. They report the most dissatisfaction with their job and show the greatest stress-related disorders. By contrast, family physicians who work the most hours per week (an average of 55), with much demand for their free time, mental concentration, and personal responsibility are most satisfied with their jobs. They also have fewest somatic complaints or other stress effects of any occupation studied. The ratings of the boredom levels of fifteen of these occupations are given in the table. ●

●
Through interviews, 2010 workers rated the boredom of their jobs. The higher the rating, the more boring the job. A rating of 100 was considered to be "average boredom."

But perhaps not having a job when you want one is worse than having a stress-producing one. When health statistics are related to economic cycles over a 127-year period in the U.S., it can be shown that increased deaths follow periods of economic depression two to four years later (Brenner, 1973). This research points up the importance of the political, economic, and social context of behavior.

Dysfunctional coping patterns

Human life is shaped by the genetic code, by modes of adaptation to the environment, and by the ability to perceive alternatives and choose among them. It is through the exercise of our choice of action possibilities that we can most radically alter—for good or for ill—the way we adapt to environmental demands. In this section we shall consider two forms of ineffective coping behavior.

Coronary-prone behavior patterns

One style of coping behavior has been shown to increase the likelihood of heart disease. Physicians are currently recognizing the fact that high-pressure, "go-getting" businessmen are especially prone to heart conditions. According to one report, coronary heart disease strikes these men seven times as often as it does individuals in the general population. Several cognitive factors have been discovered to be characteristic of these coronary-prone men. Among them are: feelings of time urgency, a sense of unrelenting external demands, intense striving for achievement, competitiveness, easily provoked impatience, abruptness of gesture and speech, excess drive and hostility, and behavioral patterns of compulsive activity designed to ward off impending harm (Jenkins, Rosenman, & Friedman, 1967; Friedman & Rosenman, 1974; Jenkins, 1976). This has been labeled Type A, coronary-prone behavior. It should be emphasized that this pattern is not "stress," but a characteristic attempt to cope with stressful situations.

One study used a reaction-time task to compare a group of Type A individuals with Type B people, who do not exhibit these coronary-prone behaviors. The task instructions emphasized the need for rapid and accurate performance. The Type A subjects showed more increases in heart rate and systolic blood pressure, suggesting that in the daily course of the pressure of events they face, they react with greater sympathetic arousal than do the Type B's (Dembroski, MacDougall, & Shields, 1977).

When college students are placed under stress in an experiment, their preferences for being alone or with others are related to their coronary-prone behavior pattern (Dembroski & MacDougall, 1978). Type A subjects preferred to affiliate with others while *waiting* for the anticipated stress much more than did Type B subjects. However, this preference changes dramatically when it comes to the working period. Type A's choose to work *alone* under high threat significantly more than do their noncoronary-prone peers. In other correlational studies, coronary patients reported a greater preference for working alone under pressure than did matched controls. While there are many possible reasons why Type A's prefer to work under pressure alone, by isolating themselves they forsake the values of social exchange. Perhaps it is possible to retrain them to work in collaboration rather than in competition with colleagues in supportive social settings. The dysfunctional coping style of Type A individuals is learned and can be modified through reeducation. For many "go-getters," learning new behavior patterns may mean additional years to "go," although at a more relaxed pace (see Glass, 1977).

The coronary-prone behavior pattern is more prevalent among men than among women. "Competitive," "aggressive," "impatient" might almost seem to be sex-linked descriptors of males in the United States. Actually, they describe only Type A males. Research tells us that these Type A behaviors are found in some women as well. Although fewer employed women than employed men are among Type A, more employed women than housewives are Type A.

Is it the personalities of these Type A men and women that direct them toward competitive social and work environments, or does functioning in such settings promote the coronary-prone behavior pattern? The available evidence puts the blame on cultural and socioeconomic pressures. For example, the Type A behavior pattern is much rarer in nonindustrial societies. One survey of this evidence concludes that it is these social pressures "related to the roles of men in our society [that] push them to develop the Coronary Prone Behavior Pattern, and that this makes a major contribution to men's

Close-up
Why Do Women Live Longer Than Men?

Women live longer than men. A woman in the United States today can expect to live to age seventy-five. In 1920 her life expectancy would have been only fifty-six. But while the male child of the 1920s could expect to live only two years less than his sister, now he dies eight years sooner. Statistical projections indicate that this mortality gap will continue to increase in the future.

What is killing off men at a greater rate than women? Much of the 60 percent higher male mortality rate is accounted for by arteriosclerotic heart disease. Heart disease risk is greater among men because they smoke cigarettes more and are more likely to develop the competitive coronary prone behavior pattern. Men commit suicide in greater numbers than do women. They are involved in more fatal motor vehicle accidents, and all types of other accidents as well. They die more often from cirrhosis of the liver, respiratory cancers, and emphysema. Of the major causes of death in the U.S., women lead men in only four categories, breast cancer, genital cancer, diabetes, and strokes. In 1975, the male death rate (per 100,000 population) was 1013; the female was only 770 (U.S. Bureau of the Census, 1977).

Analysis of the causes of death that contribute most to the sex differential in mortality indicates that the responsible agent is *behavior*, and not genetic factors. An analysis by biologist Ingrid Waldron (1976) leads to the conclusion that "each of these causes of death is linked to behaviors which are encouraged or accepted more in males than in females: using guns, drinking alcohol, smoking, working at hazardous jobs, and seeming to be fearless. Thus, the behaviors of males in our society make a major contribution to their elevated mortality" (p. 2).

higher risk of coronary heart disease" (Waldron, 1976, p. 8). (See *P&L* Close-up, Why Do Women Live Longer Than Men?)

Among Type A individuals, more than twice as many men under the age of fifty have coronary heart disease as premenopausal women. The prevalence of such disease among Type B's is equally low for both sexes. This suggests that men who adopt a less competitive, less intense life-style are able to avoid coronary heart disease to the same extent as Type B women; they are even three times less likely to develop it than are Type A women. Thus, dysfunctional coping styles are not inevitably determined by one's sex. The choice to live a high-pressured life creates behavioral consequences that have adverse effects upon the quality of one's life and health.

Suicidal behavior

When stress is chronic, when we have lost a loved one or suffered a blow to our self-esteem, and when we believe the future won't be any better, then for some suicide becomes an alternative strategy for adaptation. Surely all of us experience times in our lives when we simply cannot face another day; when life just doesn't seem worth the agony and pain it forces us to endure. Perhaps we've just lost a parent or an intimate friend; a lover has disappointed us; we've just failed a course or been fired from a job we liked. Yet however "appropriate" and strong these feelings of utter hopelessness and the fleeting impulse to end it all, most of us do not give in to the impulse. As Nietzsche once said, "The thought of suicide is a great consolation. By means of it one gets successfully through many a bad night."

Tragically, for some thousand people each day, self-destruction is a great deal more than a fleeting impulse; it is the final reality of life. According to the World Health Organization, almost half a million persons a year commit suicide, a statistic that becomes even more sobering when we realize that as many more try unsuccessfully to end their lives as succeed. As a cause of death, suicide now ranks seventh in the U.S. and among the first ten in the industrialized world. What are the reasons for and the kinds of people who contribute to these statistics? What do we know of the human element in this life-and-death equation? (See *P&L* Close-up, Suicide Among College Students.)

Suicide is most succinctly defined in terms of two basic characteristics: *intention* and *outcome*. "True" suicides involve people who intend to kill themselves and who actually do so. Although outcomes are obvious—the individual either survives or dies—intentions are not so easily recorded. Some cases quite clearly indicate lethal intention: a jump from the roof of a high building or

Close-up
Suicide Among College Students

Ten thousand students in the United States attempt suicide each year, and over a thousand succeed. The greatest incidence of suicidal behavior occurs at the beginning and the end of the school quarter or semester. Approximately three times more female than male students attempt suicide, but as with the general population, males are more successful at killing themselves.

When a college student attempts suicide, it is assumed that he or she was doing poorly in school. However, suicidal students are, as a group, superior students. While they tend to expect a great deal of themselves in terms of academic achievement and to exhibit scholastic anxieties, the significant precipitating stresses are *not* usually grades, academic competition, or pressure over examinations. Moreover, when academic failure does appear to trigger suicidal behavior—in a minority of cases—the actual cause of the behavior is generally considered to be loss of self-esteem and failure to live up to parental expectations, rather than the academic failure itself. For most

suicidal students, the major precipitating stress appears to be either the failure to establish, or the loss of, a close interpersonal relationship. Loneliness kills.

A change in mood and behavior is a most significant warning in students who may be planning suicide. Characteristically, students become depressed and withdrawn, undergo a marked decline in self-esteem, and show deterioration in habits of personal hygiene. This is accompanied by a profound loss of interest in studies. Often they stop attending classes and remain in their rooms most of the day. Usually they communicate their distress to at least one other person, often in the form of a veiled suicide warning. Many leave suicide notes.

Although most colleges and universities have mental health facilities to assist distressed students, few suicidal students seek professional help. Thus, it is of importance for those around to notice the warning signs and to try to obtain assistance for fellow students (Coleman, 1976).

the firing of a bullet through the brain. Others, such as the taking of a few extra sleeping pills immediately followed by a telephone call to friends informing them of the action, or a superficial cutting of the wrists just as the spouse's car is pulling into the garage, seem to suggest less than lethal intent.

Direct psychological research on suicide can involve only historical reconstruction of cases where the outcome of the attempt was successful. Therefore, investigation of the antecedents and psychosocial dynamics of suicide obviously focuses on those people who fail, whether intentionally or unintentionally. Indeed, we can learn much that may help us understand this flight from living by studying those people who tried but did not succeed.

When is life not worth living?

Suicidal individuals are often plagued by the crushing combination of hopelessness and helplessness, the feeling of despair that nothing can be done and no one can do it. Without question, the single most outstanding characteristic of those who attempt suicide is depression.

A study of 384 suicide attempters clearly indicates that hopelessness is the catalytic agent in suicidal behavior. Suicide attempters were seen twice for psychiatric interviews within forty-eight hours of admission to the hospital. These interviews offer support for the role of hopelessness in leading to negative expectations about the success of any attempts to obtain major personal goals. When the resulting depression becomes pervasive, then suicide seems to be the only alternative (Beck, Kovacs, & Weissman, 1975). Therapy, then, should focus on reducing hopelessness through building renewed competence. Research on the syndrome of learned helplessness, discussed in Chapter 14, is providing some new leads to the causes and, hopefully, effective treatment strategy for those so depressed that they find life not worth living.

Beverly Howze of the University of Michigan has found "an alarming pattern of alienation and self-destructiveness" among black youth, leading to a disproportionate increase in suicides. On the basis of her study of 341 Detroit teenagers, she attributes this to an extraordinarily high degree of estrangement from the community, school, and peers among these lower-class black youth (*Behavior Today,* July 10, 1978, p. 5).

Any sudden and radical change that removes an individual's basic sources of security and predictability can make that person more susceptible to suicide. Rapid social and economic change, the unexpected loss of a loved one, or strong feelings of life's injustice coupled with a sense of powerlessness to exert any control can become a precondition for suicide.

Another study compared the life histories of white males who had committed suicide with those of murderers and nonviolent mental patients. The experience of some personal loss was found to be a key factor. These three samples were analyzed in terms of the number and kind of losses they had suffered during their lives: death of parents, wife, or children, dropped out of school, been demoted or lost a job. The suicide victims had lost the most, the homicide groups ranked second, the mental patients third.

Perhaps even more important than the extent of their loss was the way the loss was experienced. The homicidal subjects experienced losses early in life, which they interpreted as obstacles to be overcome. The losses were thus perceived to be external barriers that frustrated goal-seeking activity. Aggression against others is seen as one way to reduce such frustration. In contrast, most of the suicidal men seem to have had an ideal childhood and earlier life, with indulgent parents, happy school days, a good marriage, and a nice family. Then the roof fell in. It may be the abrupt reversal, the dramatic dis-

ruption of the status quo, that leaves the person without adequate coping devices. Then suicide is considered as a rational alternative to a life that has become "cursed" (Humphrey, 1977).

Suicide prevention

Surprisingly, we have only just begun to take suicide seriously as a human problem deserving scientific and humanitarian interest. The first Suicide Prevention Center was founded in Los Angeles by Edwin Shneidman as recently as 1958. Fortunately, such centers are being founded in increasing numbers. Hospitals are instituting new programs of therapy for those who have attempted suicide, and many cities have suicide-alert phone numbers that potential suicides are urged to call. But it is obvious that for any program to work, the suicidal people must either take the initiative and identify themselves or be unsuccessful in an attempted suicide. Suicide prevention efforts obviously fail when potential suicides decide to kill themselves without giving the so-called cry for help.

It would seem that attempts at prevention need to start earlier. Instead of trying to spot a person already so desperate that he or she is prepared to die, we need to find ways of identifying children and young adults who are potential suicides.

Meanwhile, many people do overtly threaten to commit suicide before they actually do so. In fact, it is unusual for a person to commit suicide without giving some prior indication of intent. Therefore, the most important response to any suicide threat is to take it seriously—as if somebody's life depended on *your* being concerned.

Effective stress management

Stress is a part of life, but too much stress is a partner of death. We can avoid excessive levels of stress by consciously choosing occupations, dwelling places, and general life-styles that are conducive to health maintenance. For example, recent national mortality statistics reveal that your life expectancy is greater if you live in the "hang-loose" atmosphere of Hawaii than in the physically and psychologically more stressful environments of Alaska or our nation's urban centers. In addition to making more rational life-style choices, we may learn to adjust better to the stress of our environment by controlling our bodily stress reactions, by utilizing effective cognitive coping strategies, and by participation in experiential groups. After examining these, we will look at some strategies you might want to use to enhance your personal effectiveness in adjusting to your own life demands.

Relaxation and physiological control

Just as stress is the nonspecific response of the body to any demand that is made upon it, there is growing evidence that there is an anti-stress response, a "relaxation response" (Benson, 1975). Benson finds that in this response muscle tension *decreases*, cortical activity decreases, heart rate and blood pressure decrease, and breathing slows. The stimuli necessary to produce this response, according to Benson, include: (a) a quiet environment, (b) closed eyes, (c) a comfortable position, (d) a repetitive mental device. The first three factors lower afferent input to the nervous system, while the fourth lowers the internal stimulation of the nervous system. This allows the nervous system and body to reach a low level of arousal and recuperate from stress. Benson finds that these four requirements of the relaxation response are met by most traditional and religious techniques of meditation and prayer, and suggests that in addition to whatever spiritual function they may serve, such techniques are directly promoting recuperation from stress.

Progressive relaxation is a technique that has been widely used in American psychotherapy. Designed by Edmund Jacobson (1970), the approach teaches people to alternately tense and relax their muscles. In this way they learn the experience of relaxation, and how to extend it to each specific muscle. After several months of daily practice with progressive relaxation people are able to achieve deep levels of relaxation.

A system of relaxation called *autogenic training* has been used extensively in Europe, Japan, and the U.S.S.R. as a therapy for psychosomatic disorders. It consists of paying attention to different body parts while concentrating on mental images of heaviness and warmth in the body (Luthe, 1969).

Meditation

A form of meditation that is attracting many disciples is called *Transcendental Meditation*, or TM. Its originator, Maharishi Mahesh Yogi, defines it as "turning the attention inwards towards the subtler levels of thought until the mind transcends the experience of the subtlest state of thought and arrives at the source of the thought." TM gained much notoriety when the Beatles journeyed to India and the Mahesh Yogi in search of new spiritual values and personal contentment.

The basic procedure utilized by TM is remarkably simple, but the effects claimed for it are extensive. One simply sits comfortably, closes the eyes, and engages in an effortless mental repetition of a special sound for short periods of time (usually twenty minutes twice daily). The practice of TM involves neither religious beliefs nor changes in life-style.

The special sounds or syllables that are silently repeated are called *mantras*. Mantras are not written down but are recorded in an oral tradition and individually given out from teacher to student. Each meditator's mantra is a specially chosen sound which will help him or her experience deep relaxation.

TM is considered to be a form of *Mantram Yoga*. In some ways it is similar to practices common in Christian and Hebrew services. They too have rituals for focusing attention away from the external material world to the inner spiritual reality, such as repetition of prayers, singing or chanting of hymns, concentration on symbolic forms, and restricted body movements. However, over the generations, such religious exercises have too frequently become automatic rituals that do not lead the practitioner to the kinds of altered consciousness reported by earlier religious figures. It may be that TM's popularity represents a rediscovery for Westerners of what was once a vital element in the mystical aspect of Western religious traditions.

What does TM do? After a review of the physiological, psychological, and social consequences of the TM experience, one is more likely to ask, "Is there anything TM does *not* do?" The following are some of the physiological changes attributed to TM by researchers Robert Wallace and Herbert Benson (1972): increased blood flow, decreased oxygen consumption and carbon dioxide production, increased skin resistance, alert "watchfulness" brain-wave patterns, and a generalized "quiescence of the sympathetic nervous system" (usually overstimulated by the stresses of modern life). ■

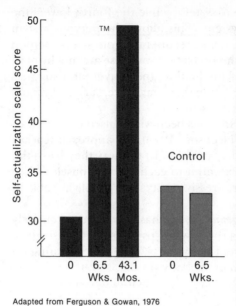

Increased self-actualization, as indicated by a higher score on the Northridge Self-Actualization Scale, was shown by both short- and long-term meditators as compared to nonmeditating controls. Measures were taken before and after the short-term group began TM.

Adapted from Ferguson & Gowan, 1976

In a variety of other studies, the benefits of TM were revealed in improved learning performance and lessened anxiety, hostility, and aggression. It has also been used effectively to improve therapeutic progress among mental patients, prisoners, and drug abusers (see Kanellakos & Ferguson, 1973; Schwartz, 1974).

Biofeedback

Individuals can be taught to control a variety of internal body processes by a technique known as *biological feedback*, or *biofeedback*. In biofeedback, small changes occurring in the body or brain are detected, amplified, and displayed to the person and/or researcher. Sophisticated recording and computer technology make it possible for a person to attend to subtle changes in heart rate, blood pressure, temperature, and brain-wave patterns that would normally be unobservable. ◆

These ongoing biological processes are thus made available as continuous feedback to the individual. A "goal" is established, such as altering the brain-wave pattern in a particular direction. The individual continuously monitors his or her progress toward that goal. The physiological response becomes an operant response to be modified in a specific direction (e.g., lowered blood pressure). The reinforcement for altering this response is the person's perceived satisfaction in achieving a noticeable change in the desired direction. The ability to gain control over one's bodily processes also leads to an increased sense of mastery — a potent reinforcer.

Subjects have been able to use this technology to change skin temperature by up to 9° F.; reduce blood pressure 15 percent; increase or decrease heart rate; relax tense muscles; alter alpha, beta, and theta EEG frequencies on command; and change still other activities once thought to be beyond human voluntary control. For example, blood pressure can be raised while heart rate is lowered. This is contrary to the normal pattern in which both responses go up or down together (Schwartz, 1972).

The most effective use of biofeedback, however, has been for its general (rather than specific) effects of training tense people to relax. It accomplishes this end more quickly than most other relaxation techniques, although it is not any more effective (Stoyva, 1976). Because the apparatus used with biofeedback amplifies biological signals and provides immediate feedback, control can be more precise than it is with other relaxation techniques. For example, the person may obtain objective information about the functioning of a set of tense muscles. Through a trial-and-error process using mental relaxation and visual imagery, the person discovers what responses change the system being monitored. In this way, biofeedback utilizes the principles of operant conditioning to achieve a therapeutic effect. Biofeedback is being combined in the clinical treatment of stress with other general relaxation approaches to create a holistic treatment approach.

Neal Miller, a pioneer in establishing the scientific legitimacy of biofeedback, calls for more basic research using double-blind procedures to control for placebo effects. He also points up problems of maintaining the degree of control obtained in laboratory and hospital settings when the person practices (or fails to practice) biofeedback at home. Issues of patient motivation, distractions, and the psychological meaning of various bodily symptoms all add complexity to what initially appeared to be a simple technological solution to stress control.

Students interested in the inexpensive do-it-yourself biofeedback devices being marketed should exercise caution and skepticism. It is unlikely that the average person could alter alpha-wave production to any substantial degree using a cheap device and without proper training by an expert. In addition, it is dangerous to rely on biofeedback technology to put your brain and body back into normal working condition rather than altering your habits and lifestyle to achieve that goal. We have all become too intolerant of pain and anxiety and too eager to reach for the quick and easy solution—even though we know intellectually that happiness is not going to come commercially prepackaged.

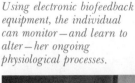

Using electronic biofeedback equipment, the individual can monitor—and learn to alter—her ongoing physiological processes.

Cognitive coping strategies

A soldier about to go into battle, a premed student being given a medical school "stress" interview, or a novice parachutist readying for a leap into open space, all face stress directly. If they cannot master their fear, their performance will suffer, with obviously disastrous personal consequences.

Appraisal of threat

Obviously, stressful situations do not always lead to psychosomatic illness or behavioral dysfunctioning. Under what conditions do they *not* do so? The research that is being done on this question has consistently pointed to the importance of psychological factors in coping with stress. How the person perceives the situation and what emotion he or she feels can drastically affect the outcome of the event. The cognitive appraisal one makes of the stressor can increase or limit its autonomic impact. A research project in which subjects were exposed to films with high stress content studied the effects of different types of cognitive appraisal on stress reactions.

In one study, subjects watched a film that showed some very crude genital operations carried out as part of male initiation rites in a primitive Australian tribe. The sound track that accompanied the film either emphasized the dangers of the operation, denied such dangers, or discussed them in an intellectualized, detached way. The investigators hypothesized that these sound tracks would alter the subjects' cognitive appraisal of (and thus their emotional response to) the threatening film. They found that, as compared with arousal by the film alone, levels of physiological arousal were higher with the "danger" sound track and lower with the "denial" and "intellectualization" tracks (Speisman, et al., 1964; see also Lazarus, 1968).

In another experiment, subjects who watched a film about unexpected, dramatic accidents in a woodshop (such as an accident in which a man was impaled by a plank of wood while operating a circular saw) showed less physiological arousal, as measured by skin conductance (galvanic skin response) and heart rate, if they had cognitively rehearsed, or imagined, the threatening scenes prior to seeing the film. ■ *Relaxation training also helped reduce stress, but the opportunity for advance cognitive appraisal was clearly more effective (Folkins, Lawson, Opton, & Lazarus, 1968).*

Adequate preparation for stressful events then is an important principle in stress management. However, research—as well as your own observation—makes it clear that warnings of danger are not always accepted and acted on. Even when they are believed, as in the case of VD, drug abuse, and cancer related to smoking, they sometimes only increase the individual's emotional arousal without also increasing the likelihood of one's initiating preventive behavior.

In a series of studies focused on the problem of how a person can be made to act to promote his or her own health, one researcher set up information booths at the New York World's Fair, several state fairs, and also in conjunction with college health centers. He found that many of the people most in need of the preventive action refuse it in an attempt to maintain their illusion of personal invulnerability. Among a group of smokers encouraged to have chest X rays, 53 percent of those with moderate levels of fear were willing to do so, as compared with only 6 percent of those with high fear, demonstrating that those with the greatest fear were not the ones most likely to take action to safeguard their health (Leventhal, 1970).

In the same way, people who are afraid they might have VD or cancer often put off seeing a doctor.

For fear warnings to serve an effective function, they must: (a) establish a reasonable (not excessive) level of fear; (b) not only arouse fear but also

■

Stress induced by highly arousing films can be lowered to some extent by relaxation training. "Emotional inoculation" through cognitive rehearsal of the stressful scenes lowers the stress response even more.

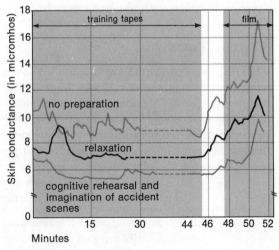

Adapted from Folkins et al., 1968

Preparation
I can develop a plan to deal with it.
Just think about what I can do about it. That's better than getting anxious.
No negative self-statements, just think rationally.

Confrontation
One step at a time; I can handle the situation.
This anxiety is what the doctor said I would feel. It's a reminder to use my coping
    exercises.
Relax; I'm in control. Take a slow deep breath. Ah, good.

Coping
When fear comes just pause.
Keep focus on the present; what is it I have to do?
Don't try to eliminate fear totally; just keep it manageable.
It's not the worst thing that can happen.
Just think about something else.

Self-reinforcement
It worked; I was able to do it.
It wasn't as bad as I expected.
I'm really pleased with the progress I'm making.

Adapted from Meichenbaum, 1975

change general attitudes toward doing something about the feared activity or event; and especially (c) provide clear guidelines for coping action in *concrete terms of what the person must do, how,* and *where.* Finally, recommendations for action are more likely to be followed if the person is induced to make a public commitment to act in the prescribed way. So when you give your fear warnings to friends and family, don't just cry "wolf"; follow the ABC's outlined above for best results.

Verbal self-instruction

Stress management can also be approached as a problem in altering the verbal instructions a person gives to him- or herself when stress looms ahead. You can train yourself to deal with stress situations through a four-stage approach: preparation, confrontation, coping with feelings of being overwhelmed, and self-reinforcement. Some examples of coping self-statements during each of these stages are outlined in the table. ▲ The value of this self-instructional package for inoculating yourself against stress has been demonstrated in research and therapy by Donald Meichenbaum (1975), the cognitive behavior modifier we met back in Chapter 4. He describes five such values of stress-coping statements. Clients are encouraged to:

a. assess the reality of the stress situation,
b. control negative, self-defeating, anxiety-arousing thoughts and images,
c. acknowledge the anxiety felt and possibly relabel it,
d. "psych themselves up" to perform well,
e. cope with possibly intense fear, and
f. reinforce themselves for having coped.

Encounter groups, or personal growth groups, provide an opportunity to practice emotional expressiveness and to experiment with different modes of behaving and perceiving.

The group experience

Many people find resources for coping with the stresses of life in group inter-action and sharing. During the 1960s there occurred a virtual explosion in the number of groups offered in this country for psychological purposes. The evolution of what have variously been called "experiential groups," "growth groups," or, more generally, "encounter groups" is having a profound and perhaps lasting effect on our society.

The basic goal of encounter groups is to provide an intensive interper-sonal experience in a small group, focusing on the interactions and feelings that emerge within the group setting itself in an atmosphere encouraging openness, honesty, emotional sensitivity, and expression. A major aspect is thus prompt and honest feedback. A member usually receives a good deal of encouragement and affection for qualities seen as good by the other group members and unequivocal criticism for qualities seen as bad. The leader may be either directive or nondirective.

When we consider how much we conceal ourselves, the many masks we wear, and the general tendency to hide our true reactions, it is clear that hon-est group probing in a climate of openness can be an important learning expe-rience. Group members can become more open-minded, more aware of their own needs and feelings, and more sensitive to the needs and feelings of others. They can also begin to understand better the sources of their re-sponses to others and the reason for other people's reactions to them and can begin to build more honest and open relationships.

Many students find that even in brief encounter group sessions, the ex-perience and self-knowledge they derive can be a source of joy to them. Just to be able to reach out and touch another person and in return to share ten-derness is for many students a new experience. It *ought* to be part of our everyday life, but until we can change our society to make that happen, ex-periential groups help form a bridge from isolation to independence to inter-dependence. ●

The stated goal of most encounter groups is not to treat emotional problems but to enrich life for normal men and women. There is little doubt, however, that such groups do attract people with emotional problems and inef-fective coping skills. To complicate matters even further there is the problem of amateur leaders whose only "training" has been their own participation in such a group. Unlike professional psychotherapists, encounter group leaders need not be licensed or certified, and many lack the necessary skills for dealing with severe emotional problems.

Findings from one extremely well-designed and executed study evaluating the effectiveness of encounter groups indicate both the value and possible dangers of this "therapeutic" experience. Some important findings were:

a. Seventy-five percent of those in groups reported a positive change in themselves, most of them feeling the change was a lasting one.

b. Wide variations in outcome were found with different leaders and in different groups. In some groups, the experience had virtually no effect on the participants; in others, almost every participant reported being affected by the experience. In some of these groups, as many were affected negatively as positively. Some groups had no dropouts; others had 40 percent quitting.

c. Group leaders varied considerably in the amount and style of stimulation and "leadership" they provided, which had an impact on the norms of appropriate group behavior that developed within their groups.

d. What students felt they got out of the encounter groups also varied—acceptance for some, understanding or involvement for others, advice or intellectual stimulation for yet others.

e. Sixteen students were adversely enough affected by the experience to warrant psychiatric follow-up treatment.

Groups with high risk in terms of casualties resulting from the group experience were characterized by highly aggressive stimulation and relatively high charisma on the part of their leader. In addition, there was no evidence to support the widely held notion that high risk is necessary in order to achieve a high level of growth. Quite the contrary, it was those leaders who were rated as high on *caring* dimensions and as supplying a cognitive framework on how to change who produced the highest positive outcomes and had the fewest casualties. Although it is evident that clear-cut positive results can and do occur for some participants of encounter groups, it is equally clear that a serious danger exists in terms of psychological casualties from such groups. Whether any single group has more of one kind of result than the other seems to depend considerably on the social-psychological attributes of the leader.

The researchers conclude: "It thus appears that the generic title 'encounter groups' covers a wide range of operations by leaders that lead to many kinds of group experiences, and perhaps to many types of learning" (Lieberman, Yalom, & Miles, 1973).

Preserving your mental health

As limitless as are the pathways to the fulfillment of human potential, so too are the roads to the perversion of that potential of mind and spirit. We can, if we so choose, become our own worst enemy, able to destroy ourselves more totally than any adversary could with the most advanced weapons of modern technology.

In the next chapters we catalogue the extreme forms of madness that can afflict us, and go on to describe how professional therapists treat neurotic and psychotic problems. But you do not have to be "crazy" to be depressed, nor is it "abnormal" to question the value of your life or to act strange at times. Not enough people who could benefit from therapy, seek it out. And not enough people who could help themselves or others through temporary periods of extreme stress and distress, do so effectively. Your concern (and that of psychologists and psychiatrists) should be directed toward ensuring mental health rather than acting only to cure mental illness. Health maintenance, prevention of sickness, and improving the quality of life are primary goals to be actively sought by us all.

Although this textbook is meant to be an academic survey of the current state of psychological research and knowledge and *not* a personal adjustment manual, I believe that the following principles may be of value in the quest for sanity and mental health. They are presented only as guidelines to encourage you to think more rationally and to act more effectively about matters that relate to your mental health.

1. Look for the causes of your behavior in the current situation or in its relation to past situations, and *not* just for some defect in yourself.

2. Compare your reactions, thoughts, and feelings with those of other comparable individuals in your current life environment to assess their appropriateness and relevance.

3. Have several close friends with whom you can share your feelings, joys, and worries.

4. Don't be afraid to show others you want to be their friend or even to give and accept love. Rejection should not deter you from trying again—after "cleaning up your act."

5. Never say bad things about yourself; especially never attribute to yourself irreversible, chronic, negative traits—such as "stupid," "ugly," "uncreative," "incorrigible," "a failure." Find the sources of unhappiness in elements that can be modified. Make criticism constructive.

6. Always take full credit for your successes and happiness (and share the positive feeling with others).

7. Keep an inventory of all the things that make you special and unique, those qualities you have to offer to others. For example, a shy person can offer a talkative person the gift of being a good listener. Know your sources of personal strength.

8. When you feel intense physiological reactions, which you typically interpret as "anxiety": (a) analyze the components of this physiological reaction objectively (count your pulse, note as many bodily changes as possible); (b) consider whether there is some explanation for your physiological reaction other than psychological "anxiety"—perhaps it was something you ate; perhaps the room is too hot, etc.

9. When you feel you are losing control over your emotions (hyperexcited or depressed), distance yourself from the situation you are in by: (a) physically leaving it; (b) role playing the position of some other person in the situation or conflict; (c) projecting your imagination into the future to gain temporal perspective on what seems like an overwhelming problem here and now; (d) talk to someone who is sympathetic.

10. Don't dwell on past misfortunes or sources of guilt, shame, failure. The past is gone and only thinking about it keeps it alive in memory. Nothing you have said or done is new under the sun.

11. Remember that failure and disappointment are sometimes blessings in disguise, telling you that your goals were not right for you or saving you from bigger letdowns later on. Learn from every failure experience.

12. Don't judge your behavior and that of others as "normal" or "crazy," but rather as situationally and culturally appropriate or inappropriate, and try to discover ways of modifying undesirable *behavior* rather than undesirable people (including yourself). Understand the context of your behavior.

13. If you see someone you think is acting strangely, intervene in a concerned, gentle way to find out if anything is wrong and how you can help. Often listening to someone's troubles is all the therapy needed if it comes soon enough. Don't isolate the "stranger."

14. If you discover you cannot help yourself or the other person in distress, seek the counsel of a trained specialist in your student health department. In some cases the problem may seem to be a psychological one but is really physical, as with thyroid glandular conditions.

15. If it is not a medical problem, then consult a psychiatrist or clinical psychologist recommended by your family doctor, the student health department, or your local hospital. Learn what mental health resources are available in your school and your town — before you need them.

16. Assume that everyone would be better off if they had the opportunity to discuss their problems openly with a mental health specialist; therefore, if you do go to one there is no need to feel stigmatized.

17. Develop long-range goals in life — what you want to be doing five, ten, twenty years from now — and think about alternative ways of getting there.

18. Take time to relax, to meditate, to enjoy hobbies and activities that you can do alone and by means of which you can get in touch with yourself. Even if you do so only fifteen minutes a day, do so.

19. Think of yourself not as a passive object to which bad things just happen, but as an active agent who at any time can change the direction of your entire life. You are what you choose to be and you are seen by others in terms of what you choose to show them.

20. As long as there's life, there's hope for a better life, and as long as we care for one another, our life will get better. (See also p. 619.)

Chapter summary

Stress, often called the "disease of civilization," is the nonspecific response of the body to any demand made on it. It brings about important reactions on an emotional, behavioral, physiological, and cognitive level.

The *reticular activating system* (RAS), a bundle of nerve fibers running from the spinal cord to the brain, is an integral part of the physiology of stress response. It receives input from all the senses and is responsible for keeping an organism aroused, alert, and sensitive to environmental changes. An intermediate level of arousal produces optimal performance. Such a relationship is called an *inverted-U function.*

According to Hans Selye, the body's reaction under stress occurs in three major phases: the *alarm reaction,* the *stage of resistance,* and the *stage of exhaustion.* Together, they make up the *general adaptation syndrome.* Should continued exposure to an injurious stressor result in the stage of exhaustion (in which the interior pituitary and adrenal cortex are unable to continue secretion of the stress-reducing hormones *ACTH* and *cortin*), the symptoms that appeared in the alarm reaction will reappear, and death may occur with total exhaustion.

Many specialists believe stress to be a contributing factor in 50 to 80 percent of all disease. It is known to contribute to the syndromes of *insomnia* and *hypertension.* Aging is also a stress-related disease.

Deterioration in bodily functioning that is *psychogenic* (has a psychological-emotional source) is called a *psychosomatic* disorder. This term is used to refer to symptoms involved in persistent stress reactions, such as rapid pulse and high blood pressure. Constitutional factors and past experiences, as well as behavioral stress, are important in determining whether or not there will be a psychosomatic reaction and what type it will be.

Holistic medicine combats illness by treating the whole person, not just the physical organs. Its focus is on health maintenance, so its practitioners are concerned with helping individuals arrange their life-styles in order to prevent stress-induced health problems.

Studies correlating stress to life changes have found that people do experience a higher degree of stress during major changes in their lives, especially when these changes are isolating or decrease their prestige. It was also demonstrated that people with no social ties have higher mortality rates than those socially connected.

Occupational stress is the condition in which some factor or combination of factors at work interact to disrupt the worker's psychological or physiological homeostasis. Chief among these are *work overload* and *stimulus underload*.

Some individuals cope with stress in ways that can be physically harmful. For example, *coronary-prone men,* also labeled *Type A,* display characteristic attempts to cope with stress such as excessive drive, hostility, competitiveness, impatience, and a host of other maladaptive behaviors.

Stress resulting in feelings of hopelessness and depression is the single most outstanding characteristic of those who attempt *suicide.* Therapists aim at reducing these feelings by helping depression victims to build renewed competence. Often suicide victims have experienced social and economic changes or the sudden loss of a loved one.

The *relaxation response* is an anti-stress response that decreases muscle tension, cortical activity, heart rate, and blood pressure and breathing rates. The stimuli required for this sort of relaxation are identical with those employed in meditation practices.

Progressive relaxation and *Transcendental Meditation* (TM) both enable the practitioner to undergo deep relaxation. TM in particular, which utilizes the repetition of a *mantra* as part of its meditation technique, causes physiological changes in the nervous, circulatory, and respiratory systems.

Individuals may be taught control of internal body processes by *biofeedback* techniques which allow the individual to observe, via sophisticated electronic apparatus, subtle changes in heart rate, blood pressure, temperature, and brain-wave patterns. But the most effective use of biofeedback has been for its general effects in training people to relax. Patients using biofeedback are able to learn relaxation more quickly than those attempting meditation, but the results of biofeedback do not exceed those of meditation.

It has also been demonstrated that the *cognitive appraisal* one makes of the stressor can increase or limit its autonomic impact. Adequate preparation for stressful events is an important principle in *stress management.* For fear warnings to be effective, they must establish a reasonable (not excessive) level of fear, change attitudes toward doing something about the feared activity or event, and provide clear guidelines for coping action. Stress management may also be approached through *verbal self-instruction* during stages of preparation, confrontation, coping with feelings of being overwhelmed, and self-reinforcement.

The basic goal of *encounter groups* is to provide an intensive interpersonal experience in a small setting. A member usually receives encouragement and affection for qualities seen as good by other members and unequivocal criticism for qualities seen as bad. Although clear-cut positive results can and do occur for some participants of encounter groups, some danger exists in terms of casualties from such groups. Much depends on the leader's personality.

19

Deviance, Pathology, and Madness

☥

Nine-year-old Joey was a "mechanical boy." He functioned as if he were a remotely controlled robot. When he entered the dining room he would plug himself into an imaginary electric outlet in order to get energy to eat. When the inner machinery was working, Joey could be animated and the center of attention. But when the machinery was idle, Joey would be so quiet and motionless as to disappear from notice.

Joey was not a "sometimes robot." His fantasy world totally engulfed him so that every action was part of his mechanical character. He needed an imaginary carburetor to breathe, motors to run him during the day, exhaust pipes through which he exhaled, and assorted apparatus to "live him" through each night. Many times a day he would noisily shift gears to higher levels of functioning until he exploded with screams of "crash, crash." Interestingly, children and adults responded to his pantomime with respect for its reality in Joey's mechanical brain. They carefully stepped over Joey's "wires" so as not to interrupt his apparent life force.

On one level, Joey seemed like a highly complex piece of machinery, a surprisingly advanced programmed humanoid with a superiority complex. But at a more basic level, little Joey was a fragile, barely developed infant. Why had Joey become a nine-year-old automaton?

Psychologist Bruno Bettelheim, who treated Joey and reported his case (1959), traces the origins of Joey's delusional system to a totally impersonal, indifferent rearing by parents who completely ignored him. Joey's mother, insecure, detached, and self-preoccupied, reported: "I never knew I was pregnant," his birth "did not make any difference," "I did not want to see or nurse him. I had no feeling of actual dislike—I simply didn't want to take care of him." When his father was on leave from the Army his only response to the child was to discharge his own frustrations by punishing Joey when he cried at night.

Robust and responsive at birth, by eighteen months Joey was frail, irritable, quite remote, and growing more inaccessible. He was like one of the children we discussed in Chapter 1 whose development was stunted by emotional deprivation. Early in life he began to withdraw into himself, to talk only to some inner listener of his imaginary tales. He also became obsessed with the workings of machines, like an old electric fan which he took apart and put together again and again.

*An early self-portrait by
Joey, the "mechanical boy."*

In time, machines replaced people as his role models. He believed they were better, stronger, harder, and besides, they didn't break. So why not become one? To do so, Joey substituted mechanical parts for his vital organs and machinery for his thought processes and feelings. A "criticizer" machine prevented him from "saying words which have unpleasant feelings." His "tubes" bled when they hurt, and when a potential playmate rebuffed one of his rare advances, Joey cried, "He *broke* my feelings."

Joey was a schizophrenic child who was imprisoned in a fantasy. He had created a delusional system in order to survive in a world that did not allow him to be human. Human emotions were transformed into inhuman energy sources which could not suffer any more pain. Joey's survival strategy "worked"; it made him too *remote* to be controlled and abused by any uncaring people.

After three years of intensive treatment, Joey was able to exchange the machinery for his humanity. When he was twelve, Joey made this slogan for a parade flag—"Feelings are more important than anything under the sun." Bettelheim draws this lesson for us: "Feelings, Joey had learned, are what makes for humanity; their absence for a mechanical existence. With this knowledge Joey entered the human condition" (p. 9).

Not all little Joeys reenter society once they have been abandoned or have lost contact with the reality principle that guides most other people's everyday lives. The study of psychopathology is an inquiry into the nature of madness. It is an investigation of the forms of deviant behavior, distorted thinking, and impoverished feelings of the "mentally ill." We shall in this chapter be concerned with the range of human reactions that set some of our brothers and sisters apart as "unusual," "weird," "deviant," "strange," "disturbed," "neurotic," or "psychotic." In the following chapter we will learn how clinical psychologists and psychiatrists treat people suffering from the many different kinds of psychopathological conditions.

The problem of mental illness

The unknown, the unusual, the unexplained, the mysterious have always held a peculiar fascination for human beings. They stimulate our curiosity to explore, to investigate, to understand. The driving force of ignorance has been institutionalized in our quest to undo it or contain it through education, science, and creative works of art. But things which do not make sense, which we are not able to comprehend, also evoke strong fears. From such primitive emotions emerge pagan religious practices, witchcraft, magic, and belief in the occult. What is not understood is not controlled, or if evil, can come to control us. At different times, in different cultures, the person whose actions were different, whose demeanor was alien, was set apart as divinely inspired or demoniacally possessed. Such people who were "beyond normal" have emerged as leaders, priests, shamans, soothsayers, and eccentric critics of society. However, they have more often been branded "mad."

It is likely that abnormal psychology is one of the areas of psychology in which you are most interested. If so, ask yourself why. For the layperson the whole of psychology is equated with the study of abnormal behavior. You now know that it is just one small part of the scientific study of mind and behavior — but a most fascinating part filled with curious problems and with suffering people who need our intellectual understanding as well as our compassion.

The scope of the problem

The scope of this nation's "mental health problem" is vast. We are faced with a bewildering array of situations that have a debilitating effect on our emotional and psychological well-being. Mental disorders due to inherited defects, organic causes, or inability to cope with life's traumas and the stresses of everyday living are numerous and increasing. Beyond the traditionally defined forms of "psychiatric disorders," the neuroses and psychoses, are legions of psychological disorders in which the will rebels, the emotions recoil, and the intellect surrenders. Violence against people, property, and one's self, prejudice, abuse of addictive substances, alienation, learning disabilities, mental retardation, and indifference to the needs of others — these, too, are all part of the pervasive web of psychological and social malfunctioning.

It is difficult to document with any precision the number of people who currently have a mental health problem. It is even less possible to estimate accurately what those statistics will be for the next generation. The best estimates are based upon identified populations, such as mental hospital patients, other institutionalized populations, clients in therapy, and the dollar costs of various mental health treatment programs. Such statistics underestimate the scope of the problem by not accounting for the number of people who do not come forth to be counted. Many disturbed people are cared for at home, others have learned to conceal their anxieties and frustrations and not to "act crazy" in public, and still others discover socially acceptable ways to act out their unacceptable impulses. The President's 1977 Commission on Mental Health offers a dismal perspective of the current mental health picture in the United States. ■

These statistics are the surface of the mental illness iceberg; not figured in are the millions of neurotics and psychopaths, the people who have attempted suicide, those imprisoned for serious criminal offenses, the senile, the lonely people cut off from society, and the untold number who are more often unhappy, sad, and angry than filled with joy, peace, and love. And it must not be forgotten that psychological malfunctioning contributes to many physical illnesses (as we saw in Chapter 18).

Response to the problem

Specific strategies for treating some of these disorders will be discussed in detail in the next chapter. In this chapter we will analyze the major categories of abnormal reaction patterns. Before we can treat or solve a problem, it is necessary to define what the problem is and ideally to understand its origins, symptoms, and consequences. However, analysis of such disorders of affect and action depend in turn upon the general "model of madness" one adopts. Thus the response of any society to its "mental health problem" first depends on the way the problem is conceptualized.

Models of mental illness

Before the modern conception of "mental illness" existed, such behavior was attributed to possession of the mind and body by demons, the invisible powers that were assumed to cause the evil, pain, and suffering that were everywhere in evidence. The only hope lay in preventing such spirits from entering one's body, for once they gained entry, the process of driving them out was as likely

---

■

Seventeen billion dollars per year is the current direct cost of providing mental-health care for Americans.

20 to 30 million Americans need some kind of mental-health care at any one time
10 million people have a significant alcohol-related problem
8 million children need help for psychological disorders
6 million people are mentally retarded
2 million youth have specific learning disabilities
2 million people suffer profound depression
2 million Americans are or have been schizophrenic
1 million Americans have organic psychosis (toxic, neurological origin, or other brain diseases)
500,000 are addicted to heroin
200,000 child-abuse cases are reported annually
1 of every 3000 children is autistic

The word _lunatic_ reflects the belief that the mentally ill were affected by the moon. This seventeenth-century French engraving shows a group of "moonstruck" women dancing in a town square.

to result in death as in a return to normalcy. People wore charms and amulets (usually fashioned from parts of sacred animals) to ward off evil. To be "different" in the Middle Ages was interpreted as a sign of Satan's handiwork, for which imprisonment, torture, and death were the only remedies. ▲

The Renaissance brought widespread social and intellectual changes, supplanting superstition with reason and scientific investigation. The developing science of neurology separated body from spirit, and mental disturbance was attributed to disease rather than to demons. The emergence of this _medical model_ focused attention on the description and classification of "mental disease" and the search for its causes. Such a model applies the general schema for physical disease to the understanding of mental problems. Aberrant behavior is seen as a symptom of underlying disease. The ultimate cause of that disease is typically sought in genetic, biochemical, or organic malfunctioning, rather than in external events. Treatment involves medical intervention and often hospitalization to cure the sick individual.

Sigmund Freud rejected what had been essentially a static model of the suffering individual as a passive victim of demons or disease. Freud transformed these views into more dynamic ones by implicating the individual as an active (though unknowing) agent in his or her mental anguish.

The dynamic forces that accounted for much that was "abnormal" were unconscious motivation and the repression of unacceptable impulses. Freud developed psychoanalytic theory to the point where it made rational much that was thought to be irrational and senseless in neurotic behavior. His ideas profoundly changed our basic conception of human nature, for he believed that neurosis was simply an extension of "normal processes" of psychic conflict and ego defense.

Freudian theory is an extension of the disease model. It postulates an inner core of mental disturbance from which spring the manifest symptoms that are observed. But Freud's vision also provided a foundation for a new psychological approach in which learning, thought processes, and social relationships play key roles.

Freudian theory was quickly accepted by American clinical psychologists and psychiatrists; we have seen that Dollard and Miller (1950) recast some of the basic Freudian notions into the language of learning theory prevalent in the early 1950s to give psychoanalytic thought more respectability and utility among research-oriented psychologists. The learning model, however, differs from all previous approaches in its emphasis on the conditions in the present environment that elicit and maintain undesirable behavior patterns. Behavior is seen as the problem to be treated, not as a symptom of some inferred disease. The learning model thus is more concerned with consequences than with causes, and with seeking relevant reinforcers rather than with unconscious motivators.

A learning approach to understanding maladaptive behaviors examines the inadequate coping strategies people use or the possibly effective ones they fail to use in solving the problems and stresses that confront them. Often behavior is inhibited or ineffective not because the person does not know intellectually what to do, but because high levels of anxiety interfere with translating those plans into meaningful actions. High anxiety often results in dominant behaviors becoming rigid and inappropriate to the changing demands of the current situation. This is assumed to occur because the *cognitive structures* that guide responding become inflexible when anxiety mounts too high.

Labeling abnormal behavior

Models of demons, disease, and dysfunctional habit patterns are all similar in that they locate the source of psychopathology *in* the person. There is something wrong with the person; he or she must be changed in some way in order to function normally again.

But is psychopathology within or without? With physical illness there are objective criteria of disease (blood cell counts, X rays, blood pressure, etc.); in mental illness the criteria are more subjective. A person is mentally ill, is neurotic, psychotic, or insane (the legal term) only when another human being in a position of authority judges him or her to be so. In our society today we generally consider individuals mentally ill on the basis of some combination of the following evidence:

a. They are under psychiatric care.
b. Respectable, influential members of the community (teachers, judges, parents, spouses, priests) agree that the behavior represents a given degree of maladjustment.
c. A psychiatrist or clinical psychologist diagnoses mental disturbance.
d. Their test scores on psychological self-report inventories deviate by a specified extent from standards of a group designated as normal.
e. They declare themselves to be "mentally sick" either directly by applying this term to themselves or indirectly by expressing feelings such as unhappiness, anxiety, and inadequacy that are associated with emotional disturbance.
f. They behave publicly in such ways as to call attention to their behavior as deviating from standards accepted by the majority of others in the society.

The decision to declare someone to be insane or mentally ill is always a judgment about *behavior*. We have seen throughout our study of psychology that the *meaning* of behavior is jointly determined by its *content* and the *context* in which it occurs. The same act in a different setting conveys very different

Close-up
On Being Sane in Insane Places

Could a normal, "sane" person who has never suffered from serious psychiatric symptoms be admitted to an insane asylum and not detected as sane once inside?

This is a fear I harbored as a graduate student visiting a local mental hospital. What would happen if by accident I were locked in, how could I convince the staff I did not belong there? A fascinating study by David Rosenhan (1973) offers the disturbing answer that maybe we could *not* persuade the authorities that we were sane. His study demonstrates that diagnosis and treatment of mental illness is relative to the context in which the individual is observed. If a person is in a locked mental hospital ward and is not staff, then . . .

Rosenhan and seven other people had themselves committed to twelve different mental hospitals in five different states on the East and West Coasts. Each of these pseudopatients presented the same complaint: "I hear voices, unclean voices. I think they say 'empty,' 'hollow,' 'thud.'" Except for this falsehood and altering their name, vocation, and employment, everything else they said was truthful and represented their nonpathological current or past histories. In almost every case they were diagnosed "schizophrenic"; the exception being at the only private hospital in the sample, where "manic depressive" was the diagnosis. (This diagnosis has more favorable chances of recovery or cure.) Once on the psychiatric ward, the pseudopatients immediately ceased simulating any symptoms. Each pseudopatient behaved as "normally" as possible in every way.

How quickly were they detected? "Despite their public 'show' of sanity," Rosenhan reports, "the pseudopatients were never detected. Admitted in the main with a diagnosis of schizophrenia, each was discharged with a diagnosis of schizophrenia 'in remission'" (still present but with no symptoms in evidence). Length of hospitalization ranged from seven to fifty-two days, with an average commitment of nineteen days. Release was typically accomplished with the intervention of spouses or colleagues, but not by any staff member realizing that an admissions "error" had been made or that a sane person was in an insane place.

To demonstrate further the subjectivity of judgment and the unreliability of psychiatric diagnosis of mental illness, Rosenhan (1973) performed a simple companion study at a hospital whose staff learned of the above study and refused to believe such errors could occur in *their* hospital. He told them that sometime in the next three months one or more pseudopatients would seek admission to their hospital. Staff members were thus set to detect imposters, and systematically rated their confidence in their belief that each of 193 patients admitted to the hospital during this time period was either a sane pseudopatient or an insane real patient. Forty-one of the patients admitted were confidently judged to be pseudopatients by at least one staff member, and 19 of these patients were judged to be sane pseudopatients by *both* a psychiatrist and a staff member. How many pseudopatients had Rosenhan sent over to the hospital? You probably guessed it already. *None.*

The results of Rosenhan's study have been used as ammunition in the battle against mental hospital institutionalization. Fascinating as it is, the methodology and evaluation of the research has been subject to criticism by psychiatrists and clinical psychologists (see Fleischman, 1973, Lieberman, 1973).

meanings. A man kisses another man: brotherly affection, homosexual advance, ritual greeting (in France), Mafia "kiss of death" (in Sicily) are but a few of the meanings this behavior could have depending on its context. (See *P&L* Close-up, On Being Sane in Insane Places.)

The stigma of mental illness   The diagnosis of "mentally ill" carries with it the dual consequences of public degradation and self-devaluation. The social stigma associated with "mental illness" is more potent and enduring than virtually any other form of stigmatism. Fear of such stigmatism may lead people to deny the need for psychological counsel and treatment when it is called for in themselves and others. Becoming a "mental patient" in itself contributes to the anxiety of the individual so labeled, lowering self-esteem and perhaps working as a self-fulfilling prophecy.

Rather than conceive of themselves as ordinary individuals who have been unable to solve certain ongoing problems posed by their society and environment, mental patients learn that they are persons to be feared, pitied, disliked, degraded, and isolated. Often they are viewed as malingerers, weak-willed and unassertive in overcoming their personal problems (Fletcher, 1967). First Lady Rosalynn Carter has focused national attention on the mental health problems of the United States and the plight of being stigmatized as mentally ill.

"So stigma is a problem in getting people into treatment in the first place; it's a problem during treatment; and it's a problem in trying to get the patient re-involved in the community. . . . Mental illness is simply not an acceptable condition people want to talk about or deal with. We must work harder to replace each myth about mental illness with a reassuring truth" (1977, p. 4).

Mental illness as deviance

From a sociological point of view, the mentally ill are classified as "deviant." Deviance can be defined in a purely statistical sense (see p. 515). To what extent is a given behavior different from that of the majority or from typical behavior of similar people in the same situation? Deviance in this usage is simply an expression of the degree of "deviation" from the population average.

However, "deviance" and "abnormality" are rarely used in a value-free statistical sense when people judge other people's behavior. In effect, the status of "deviant" connotes moral inferiority, social rejection, and biased labeling by those who either have power or want some. In addition, the term *deviant* implies that an individual "is different in kind from ordinary people and that there are no areas of his personality that are not afflicted by his 'problem'" (Scott, 1972, p. 14).

It has been proposed (Erikson, 1966) that each society defines itself negatively by pointing out what is *not*, rather than what *is*, appropriate. Society thus sets boundaries on social acceptability. Deviants, since they clarify these boundaries, may be a necessary part of society; they serve to make the rest of the society feel more normal, healthy, sane, good, moral, and law abiding.

Another sociological issue is that of conformity to a possibly "unhealthy" societal norm. Societies differ both in what the norm is and in how much variability they will tolerate before the behavior differences are seen as significant deviations. But there is always a tendency to protect the social status quo by punishing nonconformers or treating them in a variety of ways designed to bring them back to the norm or eliminate them, in order not to permit the average response ("what most people do") to shift in their direction. (See *P&L* Close-up, "Let the Punishment Fit the Crime.")

Mental health professionals function as agents of the society. The view that what is good for the average person is what is *healthy* can make deviants of critics and maniacs of nonconformers. It becomes obvious that the "normality" of any group's norm must in turn be judged by some other criteria. Was the anti-Semitic norm in Nazi Germany "normal"? If everyone in your

Close-up
"Let the Punishment Fit the Crime"

This figure illustrates a continuum of behaviors that are deemed increasingly unacceptable and are responded to with increasing severity. Basically, all these reactions are punishments for deviance; thus behavior toward those who behave neurotically or psychotically can be seen to resemble that toward criminals and other antisocial deviants. This occurs even though we acknowledge that the mentally ill should not be held legally or personally responsible.

Like antisocial deviants, those showing psychopathology may be seen as threatening people's lives and property. They behave in unpredictable ways, thus weakening the social control function. And, more basically, they appear unable to control their behavior toward goals defined as desirable. They bring into question fundamental assumptions about the dignity and integrity of human nature. However, it should be noted that for some people mental hospital commitment is sought as a refuge or asylum from society, and some staff have a genuine desire to help, not punish, the suffering patient.

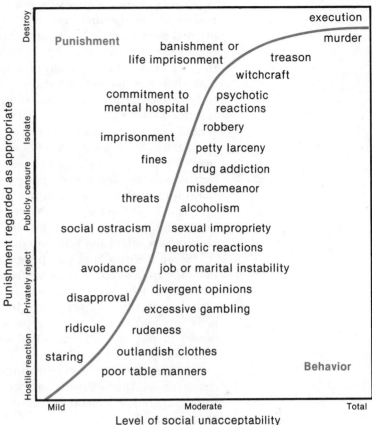

Adapted from Haas, 1965

college decided to take heroin, would it be "normal" to conform? Would it have been abnormal to be a slave owner before the Civil War? Is it a sign of insanity to be a political dissident in the Soviet Union today?

The notion of situational or cultural relativity of psychiatric labels argues that there is nothing about the patient that is abnormal per se. But this argument is not without its limitations. There are some symptoms of mental illness which appear to be universal manifestations of affliction that are not relative to particular cultural settings. Similar kinds of disturbed behavior are, in fact, labeled abnormal in such distinctly contrasting groups as the Eskimos of northwest Alaska and the Yorubas of rural tropical Nigeria. The labels of insanity refer to a pattern of related behaviors, and the label is not applied until three or four of the signs are manifest. The labels refer to beliefs, feelings, and actions that are thought to come from the person's mind, over which he or she has lost control. The particular pattern of afflictions resembles what is diagnosed as schizophrenia in the United States (Murphy, 1976).

It is reasonable to conclude that there are both universal aspects of mental illness and culturally specific aspects. There are also culture-bound and situationally relevant dimensions of mental illness within a given culture. Such a view leads to the conclusion that there is a reality to the phenomenon of mental illness; in fact, there are many.

Personality disorders

A person's character structure is a product of habitual attitudes, values, and reactions toward human relationships. The foundation for this structure is often laid down early in life and extends over a long period of time. When these characteristic ways of behaving become exaggerated to a degree that they are inappropriate, it may be a sign of a personality disorder. A personality or character disorder is a chronic or long-term behavior pattern that is disturbing to other people because of its inappropriateness or offensiveness, but is rarely a source of anxiety or distress to the individual with the disorder and is not judged to be neurotic or psychotic.

Personality disorders are not easy to classify. In general what we see are people with a peculiar, stereotyped style of relating to other people. Since personality disorders involve patterns of reaction with a long history, they are difficult to treat with conventional therapy. The person often does not perceive that he or she has a "problem," has little motivation to change, and does not get immediate feedback for any change attempts (because the changes required are broad and reactions to them are diffuse).

Some theories hold that personality disorders are inborn. Others maintain they grow out of inadequate parent-child relationships with deficient role models or inconsistent childrearing practices. A related view specifies that such disorders are the result of a history of reinforcement for inappropriate behaviors and lack of training (in school and community as well as in the home) in internalizing the social norms and values that regulate human relationships.

Among the more commonly found types of disorders of personality and character are the following: inadequate personality, explosive personality, passive-aggressive personality, obsessive-compulsive personality, and antisocial personality.

1. *Inadequate personality.* In this category are largely ineffective people with an inability to sustain interest in study, work, or social relationships. They tend to have a poorly developed sense of responsibility and not to ever mature psychologically or emotionally. They have been described as society's "drifters," "floaters" who contribute little to other people.

2. *Explosive personality.* Under most circumstances, this person would appear to be pleasant and well adjusted. However, minor frustrations or setbacks, and the slightest hint of rejection could ignite the fuse that results in a rage reaction. The hostility may initially be verbally assaultive (critical, argumentative, and intimidating), but can end in physical violence. The sense of potentially explosive rage being tentatively suppressed so long as all goes well creates much fear, appeasement, and deference among the families and acquaintances toward those with this personality disorder—to prevent "all hell from breaking loose."

3. *Passive-aggressive personality.* Passivity can be a reaction against one's intense feelings of anger and hostility. Fearing retaliation for directly expressing such feelings, the individual assumes a passive role. But interpersonal hostility is still expressed in subtle, devious ways. Through acting helpless and becoming dependent, the passive-aggressive personality limits the freedom of others by becoming a burden for which they are responsible. Another passive type achieves the indirect hostility effect by resisting everything. By acting negatively, being stubborn, sullen, and obstructive, this personality type may prevent others from fulfilling their needs or carrying out their plans.

4. *Obsessive-compulsive personality.* This person reveals an exaggerated sense of

control over every element in his or her life. Control takes the form of ordering physical elements (neatly arranged desk, closets, drawers), activities (by means of schedules and "to do" lists), or human relationships (through insisting others do it their way). The need for order results in a rigid, formal, inhibited, and perfectionistic behavior pattern. Principles of duty, respect for authority, cleanliness, and obedience mark the obsessive-compulsive personality. It is difficult for others to feel comfortable around such people because they are never spontaneous and open and insist others follow their standards. Freudians believe that this character disorder stems from repressed hostility toward parents, usually over their harsh toilet-training practices. The child fears this hostility will emerge and lead to loss of love or rejection. Denial of all strong emotions—which are by their nature impulsive and uncontrollable—is supported by establishing control over all other aspects of one's life. When faced with a situation in which they can not exercise their usual control over the external environment, such people may react with violence, with obsessive repetition of thoughts and formulas, and with rigidly stereotyped behavior.

5. *The antisocial personality*. The antisocial personality has also been called the sociopathic or psychopathic personality. The psychiatric diagnostic manual (DSM-II) defines antisocial personalities as:

> . . . *individuals who are basically unsocialized and whose behavior pattern brings them repeatedly into conflicts with society. They are incapable of significant loyalty to individuals, groups, or social values. They are grossly selfish, callous, irresponsible, impulsive, and unable to feel guilt or to learn from experience and punishment. Frustration tolerance is low. They tend to blame others or offer plausible rationalizations for their behavior (p. 43).*

Such people create trouble for other people and for society. They start early in life disrupting class, getting into fights, running away from home, having promiscuous sexual experiences, never keeping their jobs. Many end up breaking the law, and wind up in jail. Others, with a superficially charming manner and easygoing style, coupled with a high degree of intelligence, may become highly "successful" confidence men. (See *P&L* Close-up, The Case of Terrible Tommy.)

Neurosis

When an individual feels chronically threatened by life's hazards and inadequate to the task of coping with them, the ordinary ego defenses we all use are not enough. Gradually such a person may come to rely excessively on one or more neurotic defense patterns. These patterns have in common: *the search for relief from anxiety*. Thus they are characterized by an absence of joy in living and by actions aimed at lessening pain rather than at positive accomplishment or the constructive solution of objectively real problems. They provide enough temporary relief from anxiety that many individuals cling to them desperately despite the fact they do not solve their basic problems and may even worsen them. Thus they are self-defeating in the long run. The tragedy of neurotics is that often their evaluations of the world as threatening and of themselves as ineffectual are faulty. With more realistic perceptions there would be no need for this loss of joy or a tortured preoccupation with worries and threats.

One of the most extreme cases I know of antisocial personality is that of a graduate student in psychology, "Terrible Tommy." Brilliant, energetic, and productive, Tom was admired by the faculty because he got things done, and often with a flair. As a first year student, when his peers were trying to survive without making waves, Tom would be sure to ask the first question after a speech by famous visiting guest lecturers. His one-liners might go like this: "There must have been something more interesting in your research than what you've told us today, otherwise an obviously intelligent person like you would not have spent five years doing it. What might that be?"

Tom "got things done" because he had informed a naive new student that he had been assigned to work as Tom's assistant (as part of an experimental "big peer" apprenticeship program). He had this hapless student running errands for him, soliciting research subjects at midnight in local all-night diners, and more.

The student flunked out at the end of the year because he had not been keeping up with his studies or assisting faculty—there wasn't time left after Tom had used him.

Tom's girlfriend gave him a birthday party one year and invited all the other graduate students. Tom arrived late with a beautiful girl on his arm and proceeded to distress everyone by necking with her most of the evening—totally ignoring his girlfriend's hurt and embarrassment. At the end of the party he told his by now outraged former girlfriend he was surprised at her thoughtlessness in not buying him a present!

The exploits of Terrible Tommy were legendary. Years later, old friends would meet and soon be exchanging Tom anecdotes. "Did I ever tell you the one when Tom . . ." That says something unpleasant about our fascination with the power wielded by emotionless manipulators. (Were *you* angered or amused by Tom's escapades?)

In general, the normal person functions as an organized whole and deals with frustrations more or less effectively. But "normality," for the psychologist, includes a wide range of behavior rather than a single fixed point on a scale. Thus there is no clear dividing line between the normal and the neurotic: the difference is one of degree. The neurotic's defenses are regarded as abnormal because they represent seriously and chronically ineffective ways of coping with life's demands. However, they are rarely severe enough to require hospitalization.

If there is a continuum from normal to neurotic, at what point can we identify a person as being disturbed enough to justify assigning the label of "neurotic"? What are the behavioral signs used to identify the neurotic individual? Six fairly distinct neurotic patterns that have been identified will be described here: anxiety neurosis, phobias, "obsessive-compulsive" neurosis, hysterical neurosis, hypochondria, and existential neurosis.

Anxiety neurosis

"The patient feels very sick. He is tired and apprehensive, his heart pounds and his breathing is labored. From time to time he is overcome by fright and the conviction that he is seriously ill or even about to die" (Pitts, 1969, p. 69).

This patient is suffering from anxiety neurosis.

Because anxiety is the chief characteristic in *all* neurotic disorders, it may seem strange for a subcategory to be named "anxiety neurosis." The diagnosis of this neurotic syndrome is made when anxiety attacks and symptoms occur in the *absence* of other recognizable symptoms.

Characterized by an almost continual anxiousness for which there is no apparent cause, the feeling has been called "free floating" anxiety. The person simply does not know why he or she feels this way, and this in itself generates even more anxiety.

Periodically, the sufferer may experience an *acute anxiety attack*. Such attacks, which typically last a few minutes, are periods where anxiety symptoms become particularly severe. Suddenly the heart may begin to flutter and the head to pound; dizziness and terror set in. Often the onset is abrupt and patients will frequently report, "I feel like I'm going to die." Anxiety neurotics who consult a physician (or two or three) are all too often met with the same old responses: "There's nothing wrong with you," "It's just nerves, relax!" Yet this is the most common of all neuroses.

Freudian theory explains anxiety attacks as the signal to the neurotic that repressed conflicts are threatening to emerge. The psychic energy used in keeping these conflicts out of conscious awareness is thought to cause the general anxiety. The anxiety neurotic, then, is a person who is habitually at the mercy of anxiety attacks, their anticipation, or their aftereffects. It is also possible that anxiety reactions can be learned by being reinforced with attention from significant others. If an individual is anxious, whatever the reason, and "tea and sympathy" follow, anxiety can become a conditioned response.

Neurotic anxiety can be differentiated from objective anxiety or fear. Fear is a rational reaction to an objective, identified external danger and may involve flight or attack in self-defense. In neurotic anxiety the emotional arousal is just as strong, but the danger is internal: neither identifiable nor shared as a common threat by others in the situation (see Sarnoff & Zimbardo, 1961).

The failure to explain the "unexplained arousal" itself constitutes a threat to one's feelings of self-control. One of the main functions of psychotherapy is to identify the original source of anxiety in order to convert it to a tangible, manageable fear. "Put a name on it and you can do something about it" (Grimmett, 1970).

Phobias

Phobic neurosis is easily distinguished from anxiety neurosis; in the phobia, anxiety becomes attached to a definite object in the external environment. Typically the object is not a source of physical harm or biological danger. Thus, neurotics often realize that their acute reaction is irrational—but that recognition only makes their anxiety more unbearable.

Many of our fears have a basis in reality: some snakes are poisonous, some insect bites cause painful irritations, people do drown in oceans, and planes occasionally drop out of the sky. ● However, a phobia is based more on the symbolic meaning of an activity or situation than on its actual danger. Small garter snakes or ordinary flies may create strong anxiety, even though the person recognizes their harmlessness. The phobic reaction is an avoidance reaction, and neurotics may go to great lengths to alter their life-style in order to avoid the object of their fear.

Virtually any stimulus that can be perceived can come to be a conditioned stimulus for a phobic avoidance reaction. ◆ Phobias are much more common among women than among men. The most prevalent type, agoraphobia, occurs three times as often in females, and 95 percent of all zoophobics are thought to be women (Davison & Neale, 1974).

The psychoanalytic view of phobia is that these neurotics handle their

"It's not the <u>dark</u> I'm afraid of . . . it's the stuff in it I can't <u>see!</u>"

inner conflicts by externalizing them onto some object. For example, a boy intensely afraid of the ocean, swimming pools, or even bathtubs might actually be repressing persistent thoughts of drowning his mother. As long as the substitute objects can be avoided, these people can avoid confronting the real terror within themselves. Some behaviorists contend that phobias can result from a traumatic event being paired with a certain object (recall the case of little Albert in Chapter 8). These fears are extremely resistant to extinction because each time the feared object is successfully avoided, so is the anxiety associated with it. This avoidance response is, therefore, reinforced because of the relief it brings in terms of anxiety reduction. Avoidance also prevents the person from confronting the cause of the irrational fear and thus coping with it directly (Eysenck, 1963; Rachman & Costello, 1961).

Obsessive-compulsive neurosis

Obsessions and compulsions are separate types of reactions that may occur quite independently of each other, but they occur together so often that they are generally considered as two separate aspects of a single behavior pattern.

Obsessions

An obsession is a persistent and irrational thought that comes into consciousness inappropriately and cannot be banished voluntarily. Almost everyone has some sort of mild obsessional experience occasionally, such as the intrusion of petty worries, "Did I really lock the door?" or "Did I turn off the oven?" or the persistence of a haunting melody we simply cannot shake from our consciousness. Most of us have at times felt a bit better after a ritual crossing of fingers or knocking on wood.

Although mild obsessions such as persistent tunes can be irritating, true neurotic obsessions are much more insistent and so disturbing that they come to interfere with all facets of the individual's daily life. Often they center around morbid thoughts of death or suicide or continual fantasies of committing murder in some brutal fashion. Extreme obsessional reactions can be almost completely disabling—patients may be so overwhelmed by uncontrollable obsessive thoughts that they find it almost impossible to concentrate on anything else.

Compulsions

Compulsive behavior consists of repetitive ritualistic actions which the person feels must be carried out. Compulsions are the "action" of obsessional thought. Even though such rituals are highly charged emotionally for neurotic people, they may remain unaware of their meaning. By becoming preoccupied with carrying out these minor everyday tasks repeatedly, however, the compulsive neurotic has no time or energy left to carry out the impulsive action that is unconsciously being guarded against. In some cases, guilt feelings for real or imagined sins may find expression in compulsive rituals designed to undo them; an example is excessive hand washing—a kind of Lady Macbeth reaction. Mild obsessive behaviors may be seen as annoying little personality quirks, but they sometimes grow so out of proportion as to virtually enslave a person.

Consider the case of a forty-three-year-old woman who accidentally smashed a dish one night while serving the family dinner. Seized with a sudden fear that the fragments of glass might get into her husband's food and kill him, she insisted on resetting the table completely before the meal could proceed. Her anxiety continued, and she began to fear that she and the children might eat contaminated food.

Soon the compulsions became more and more elaborate. Each piece of household glassware had to be examined for chips before use. If even the slightest chip was discovered, she would take the piece outside and throw it away. After completing this task she would carefully search the house for the missing chip. Later still she began to worry about infections spreading from the bathrooms into the kitchen and about outdoor pesticide contamination.

Psychotherapy revealed that sometime before breaking the dish she had become aware of her husband's extramarital affair. Concealing (or denying) this discovery, she was bottling up both her anger and her shame. At the time of the dish breaking incident, she was aware of a wish that her husband eat the glass and die (Cameron, 1963).

One explanation of obsessions and compulsions is that they serve to impose order on impulses and desires that are perceived (at some level) as being unacceptable. The obsessive-compulsive rituals act as barriers that stop forbidden thoughts from turning into forbidden actions.

Learning theory accounts of this disorder are somewhat related to this analytical conception. A person who has what he or she considers highly immoral thoughts can avoid them by substituting some activity that puts the mind to work on something else. The removal of such thoughts is rewarding; therefore the activity is reinforced. Whenever the thoughts return, the person will repeat the action (however ridiculous) that had previously removed them.

Hysterical neurosis

It is not uncommon for students to forget appointments with the dentist or get sick on the day of a final exam, for singers to get laryngitis before an audition, or for track athletes to develop "charley horses" that prevent them from competing in a meet. These represent some of the "normal" forms of avoiding an unpleasant, feared situation. These escapes are not consciously sought. In fact, the individuals using them vigorously deny that they are "escapes": they just "happen" in situations of anticipated stress. But losing one's memory or becoming physically incapacitated does remove the person from a situation that is threatening psychological well-being or self-esteem and does so in such a way that the individual cannot be blamed for not facing it.

When such a mechanism is carried to the extreme that the person becomes physically paralyzed or has a total loss of memory—without any organic defect—then the condition is abnormal and is labeled *hysterical neurosis*. Included under this general heading are related disorders: *conversion reactions, hysteria,* and *dissociated states.*

Conversion reactions and hysteria

Though conversion and hysteria are disorders that often occur together, a distinction between them should be made. A *conversion reaction* is a loss of sensory or motor function for which there is no organic cause. A working part of the body may suddenly be "converted" into nonfunctionality. Individuals may wake up to find they cannot hear or see or speak or may find their legs or arms paralyzed. It is important to remember that in a conversion reaction no actual biological change is involved. This is clearly demonstrated by the fact that when the individual is asleep or under hypnosis the symptoms generally disappear. For instance, patients who suffer from paralysis may be entirely incapable of moving their legs, but under hypnosis they may be made to get up and walk across the room. Moreover, these symptoms may come and go or even appear at different times in different areas of the body; occasionally a patient who is "blind" in the right eye on one day may unconsciously shift the ailment to the left eye the next day.

Whereas *conversions* are specific organ or limb "disabilities," the term *hysteria* refers to persons consistently reporting a large range of physical difficulties. Something seems to be wrong with almost every organ in their bodies, with some form of pain being the most characteristic symptom. Sexual problems, including menstrual pain and frigidity, are frequent among female hysterics (Woodruff, Goodwin, & Guze, 1974). As we noted earlier, many hysterics also have conversion reactions. ▲

In the case of a person who is blind in the right eye on Tuesday and in the left eye on Wednesday, the difficulty is obviously psychological. It is often difficult, however, for a physician to determine whether a patient is suffering from an organic ailment or a hysterical one. Interestingly, conversion reactions are less common in areas having better educational and medical facilities than in areas where the educational level is low. The disorder serves little purpose when symptoms violate generally available medical knowledge.

Dissociated states

We have noted throughout this text how important it is for people to see themselves as basically in control of their behavior—including their emotions, cognitions, and actions. Essential to this perception of self-control is the sense of selfhood—the consistency and continuity of our personality. It is thought that in dissociated states, individuals escape from their conflicts by giving up this precious consistency and continuity and, in a sense, disowning part of themselves. One way is through *somnambulism* (sleepwalking), in which the individual may walk about while sleeping and perform some action of symbolic significance of which there is no recollection when awake.

The loss of memory for what one did during states of somnambulism

▲

The most frequent symptoms of hysteria and the percentage of hysterics reporting them are shown in the table.

Symptom	%	Symptom	%
Nervous	92	Abdominal pain	80
Back pain	88	Headache	80
Dizziness	84	Nausea	80
Extremity pain	84	Chest pain	72
Joint pain	84	Difficulty in breathing	72
Fatigue	84	Trouble doing anything	
Weakness	84	because of feeling bad	72

Adapted from Perley & Guze, 1962

can assume a more extreme form by occurring during waking. In cases of *amnesia*, people perform their usual waking actions—eating, speaking, reading, driving, and so on, but have no memory of their own identity. By obliterating the past through amnesia, the person in one deft stroke cuts off the present from these ties to an unhappy past and is able to start all over again, constructing the present on its own terms. In many cases, amnesics are people whose life history and habitual patterns of psychological reaction have made them exceptionally good at escaping from situations with which they simply cannot cope.

Often an amnesic person who has given up an old identity may actually travel to some other place, either a completely new one or a familiar place that was emotionally supportive at some earlier time. This is called a *fugue* episode, from the Latin word meaning "to flee." Mrs. R. J., whom we met in Chapter 6, had experienced such an episode. Once in a new place, the person may assume a new identity and create a new life-style, dissociated psychologically, temporally, and geographically from a prior unacceptable life-style. Cases have been reported where such persons were rediscovered several years after their disappearance. Of course, we do not know how many remain undiscovered and lead the rest of their lives as their "recycled" selves.

The most extreme form of dissociation is the multiple personality. This disorder is thought to be extremely rare; only ninety case reports have been documented. Ralph Allison, a therapist with extensive experience in treating this disorder, feels that the actual incidence rate is much higher, with many cases going undiagnosed (1977). This would not be surprising, since hypnosis is often required to confirm its presence, and only about 10 percent of American therapists use hypnosis.

Multiple personality is frequently confused with schizophrenia, which literally means "split personality." Multiple personality is actually a severe form of neurosis; whichever personality is "in command" at any given moment remains in contact with reality. Schizophrenia, as we shall see, is a *psychotic* disorder in which the individual's functioning is "split off" from external reality.

In the multiple personality reaction, the individual develops two or more distinct personalities that alternate in consciousness, each taking over conscious control of the person for varying periods of time. Usually, though not always, each personality is completely unaware of the other. In some cases one personality may be aware of the other but not vice versa.

This dramatic form of reaction is illustrated by the widely publicized case of Eve White. Eve, twenty-five years old and separated from her husband, had sought therapy because of severe, blinding headaches, frequently followed by "blackouts." During one of her early therapy sessions Eve was greatly agitated; she reported that she had recently been hearing voices. Suddenly she put both hands to her temples, then looked up at the doctor with a provocative smile and introduced herself as "Eve Black."

It was obvious from the voice, gestures, and mannerisms of this second Eve that she was a separate personality. She was fully aware of Eve White's doings, but Eve White was unaware of Eve Black's existence. Eve White's "blackouts" were actually the periods when Eve Black was in control, and the "voices" marked unsuccessful attempts of Eve Black to "come out." With extended therapy, it became evident that Eve Black had existed since Eve White's early childhood, when she occasionally took over and indulged in forbidden pleasures, leaving the other Eve to face the consequences. This habit had persisted, and Eve White frequently suffered Eve Black's hangovers. After about eight months of therapy, a third personality appeared. This one, Jane, was more mature, capable, and forceful than the retiring Eve White; she gradually came to be in control most of the time.

As the therapist probed the memories of the two Eves, he felt sure that some shocking event must have precipitated the actual development of distinct personalities in the disturbed child. In a dramatic moment, the climax of therapy, the missing incident came to light. Jane suddenly stiffened, and in a terrified voice began to scream, "Mother . . . Don't make me! . . . I can't do it! I can't!" When the screams subsided, a new personality took over. She was able to recall the shocking event that lay at the bottom of the personality dissociation. At the age of six Eve White had been led by her mother to her grandmother's coffin and been forced to place a good-bye kiss on the dead face (Thigpen & Cleckley, 1954, 1957; Thigpen, 1961).

"Eve" has recently revealed herself to be Chris Sizemore, a Fairfax, Virginia, housewife. She has manifested twenty-one different personalities over the past two decades. Each time they came in sets of three very different personalities, but her last split selves "died" in 1974, leaving Chris now ready to make it on her own (Sizemore & Pitillo, 1977).

The appearance of additional personalities after the "cure" of reexperiencing the event that supposedly precipitated the neurosis calls into question the claim of a cure. Some clinicians believe that all cases of multiple personality reflect the efforts of highly suggestible patients to please their therapists. To develop a multiple personality requires imaginative involvements with fantasy. Such imagination is a good predictor of hypnotic suggestibility. These patients then are invariably responsive to hypnotherapy, but they also may be so suggestible as to reconstruct their scripts to fit what they believe the therapist would like to hear (J. Hilgard, 1970).

Hypochondria

Even a hypochondriac gets ill sometimes..

Neurotic individuals frequently show an extreme concern about their health and physical condition, dwelling morbidly on every minor bodily sensation as a possible sign of some serious organic disorder. When such a preoccupation is the main feature of the neurosis, it is called *hypochondria*. One explanation of hypochondria is that the individual feels separated from his or her body and is attempting to know it, but by analyzing and describing it rather than by being and experiencing it. It may also be that in the process of trying to explain vague feelings of anxiety, tension, and mysterious emotional arousal, some people find it more reasonable and less threatening to the ego to have an organic problem than to have a psychological one. For such people, the choice may be between "crazy" and being "ill."

In any case, hypochondriacs are often said to "enjoy poor health," for their greatest satisfaction seems to be in finding bodily symptoms that confirm their dire predictions. These supposed ailments not only prevent active engagement in life—with its risk of failure—but also may bring secondary gains in attention, sympathy, and service from others. On the other hand, these demands for extra consideration and enormous medical consultation fees and useless surgery bills sometimes lead the patient's exasperated family to forget that the discomfort, however irrational, is subjectively real.

Existential neurosis

Steve is twenty-five and lives at home with his parents, having flunked out of college at twenty-two. That's really all there is to say, since Steve doesn't do anything anymore. He finds life totally meaningless. The little he does do has no value, import, or use to him. He is always bored and possesses no emotion. Three years ago he used to have bouts of depression, but no more; it's too much trouble. His life is geared toward minimal action and minimal decision making. He vegetates.

From time to time, most people wonder "Is life really worth all the effort?" When a person's doubts about the significance of life and the meaninglessness of existence become chronic and result in anxiety or extended bouts of depression the condition is called *existential neurosis*. It has been described as a "settled state of meaninglessness, apathy, and aimlessness such that contradictory states of commitment, enthusiasm, and activeness are the exception rather than the rule" (Maddi, 1967, p. 313).

Individuals most prone to this state tend to think of themselves as being mere players of social roles, enacting other people's scripts. Once life has no purpose, suicide becomes an alternative, as does living from day to day, for the pleasures of the moment. Such an individual becomes an existential neurotic as a result of stress. Maddi (1967) describes three main sources of this stress.

a. The knowledge that you are going to die, as experienced by the terminal cancer patient.
b. Gross disruption of social order. An example might be the fall from "riches to rags." This reversal of previous life-style is thought to disintegrate the social roles so necessary to these people's lives.
c. The third type is harder to define. This stress is gradual, accumulating over time, and seems to come from the realization that the person lacks certain capabilities for deep and meaningful experiences that others have. They are aware something is missing in their lives, having been confronted by others who point out the person's existential failures. This is a frequent theme in movies by Italian director Michelangelo Antonioni.

Existential neurosis is not recognized as being a separate disorder, but these symptoms have been reported and in some ways do differ from other neuroses. If you can, stop here for a second and try to imagine having absolutely *no* emotions and *no* passions for *anything*. It might feel like not being human at all.

Neurosis as loss of control

Each of these types of neurosis seems to be an expression of loss of personal effectiveness and an inability to control the anxiety within or human relationships without. Neurotic coping strategies are ways in which neurotics prove to themselves and the world that they are impotent, unable to deal with their problems through no fault of their own. The phobic says, "I am terrified by this; I must avoid it." The obsessive-compulsive says, "I *have* to think or do this." The hysteric says, "I cannot move from where I am; I cannot face the part of me I don't like." The hypochondriac says, "If I weren't so sick, I could deal with other problems." The existential neurotic says nothing.

What all these neurotic patterns have in common is a mechanism for limiting anxiety by avoiding any direct confrontation with its source, and an inability to contemplate any other way to handle the problem. Neurotic individuals see "no exit" from their problems and no choices among alternative ways of being. As theologian Paul Tillich once said, "Neurosis is the way of avoiding nonbeing by avoiding being" (1952, p. 66).

When therapy is successful with such people, it changes their self-concept

"The symptoms of the neurosis all point to a rather comprehensive psychological death, where there is no longer even anguish or anger to remind the person that he [or she] is a person . . ."
Salvatore Maddi
"The Existential Neurosis"

by getting them to accept the fact that they can exert control. By rediscovering the power of decision making and action, or simply by having a visible effect on the environment and recognizing it as their doing, neurotic patients learn that they not only can cope with their particular present problems but also can begin to shape their life along new dimensions that can bring pleasure, satisfaction, and feelings of accomplishment. Many of the therapeutic procedures to be described in the next chapter are directed at the neurotic reaction patterns described above. Although varying in approach, the different therapies share the basic goals of making the neurotic person less helpless and hopeless by helping increase self-acceptance and self-efficacy.

Psychotic reactions

Psychosis is the general term for the most severe form of psychopathology. It is marked by a loss of contact with reality and extreme disturbances in perceptual, affective, and cognitive functioning. To be a psychotic is, in lay terms, to be "crazy," "mad," or "insane." It is the most feared and unacceptable "mental disease." Psychosis has been characterized as "a mind loosed from its moorings," a rebellion of the will against conventional thoughts, expected feelings, and standard actions. Some type of psychotic reaction exists in virtually every known society.

Insanity is not a psychiatric or psychological term but a legal concept. It is applied to any mental condition that renders the individual incapable of knowing right from wrong and therefore of being legally responsible for actions committed. An alternative legal definition involves an irresistible compulsion or urge to behave in ways judged dangerous to society. For example, a person who threatens the life of the President of the United States, even in a letter, is likely to be arrested and required to undergo psychiatric evaluation. Thus the term *insanity* can include not only psychotic disorders but also extreme, severely incapacitating neurotic reactions.

While there is an underlying continuum between normal and neurotic reactions, psychosis represents a qualitatively different experience from neurosis. The psychotic person does not necessarily pass through a neurotic stage, nor do very disturbed neurotics eventually become psychotic. There are, however, some cases where the symptoms of the two disorders may be mixed. The psychotic individual is one who refuses to accept both the empirically based definition of what is real and the socially agreed-upon definition of reality.

Thus psychotics often lump together "what is" and "what ought to be." Or they may dissociate effects from their causes, actions from thoughts, feelings from actions, conclusions from premises, or truth from evidence. In one sense, what appears as the psychotic's bizarre, inappropriate, and irrational behavior follows from the creation of a closed system that is self-validating and internally consistent. It has been suggested that whereas most of us evaluate the reality of our inner world against criteria established in the external world, psychotics *reverse* the usual reality-testing procedure. Inner experience is the criterion against which they test the validity of outer experiences (Meyer & Ekstein, 1970). Theirs is a world in which thinking makes it so.

Causes of psychosis

What causes psychosis? Unfortunately, despite years of research by psychologists, psychiatrists, and a host of medical investigators, there is no satisfactory answer to this critical question. There are still heated debates about what factors constitute psychotic reactions, or whether there can be objective criteria of mental health (Moore, 1975). Some radical psychiatrists like Ronald Laing (1976) and Thomas Szasz (1961) have even rejected the view that psychosis is abnormal. They prefer to conceptualize the psychotic state as a radical revolt against questionable societal assumptions about the purpose of life, means-ends relationships, and a too-limited view of human thought and subjective reality.

Medically oriented researchers argue for an inherited, genetic basis for some types of psychosis or point to metabolic deficiencies and malfunctioning. Biologically oriented psychiatry holds that abnormal behavioral and emotional states represent deviations from the basic neurobiological processes that underlie all human functioning. Research in this area, therefore, looks for problems with body and brain mechanisms.

Psychologists and analytically oriented psychiatrists emphasize instead a constellation of psychosocial factors in the development of psychopathology. The two approaches are reflected in a basic distinction between organic and functional psychoses.

Some psychotic reactions and other mental disorders are obviously *organic* — that is, associated with brain damage due to physical causes such as diseases of the nervous system, brain tumors, brain injuries, overdoses of gases, drugs, alcohol, or metallic oxides, and disturbances in arterial circulation occurring in old age.

More prevalent are the *functional* psychoses that stem from no *known* physical defect in brain tissue, but rather from deficits in functioning. They fall into three major classifications, as shown in the chart. ■ It is these psychoses whose origin is the subject of so much debate. We will examine them in detail after outlining alternative views on the causes of psychosis.

As we have seen, it is most difficult to specify with confidence what events are both *necessary* and *sufficient* causes of a given behavior. Most causes of behavior are insufficient in themselves to bring about a given reaction; the *interaction* of other variables is required. Thus we saw in Chapter 18 that physiological stress reactions arise from a combination of biological, psychological, and social factors. An increasing number of experts believe that virtually all disease states are influenced by the interaction of genetic and metabolic factors with life experiences and psychological processes. Despite this multi-factor orientation, most researchers are trained in only a single speciality. They look for causes where they believe they will be found and

■

Classification of the functional psychoses

Schizophrenic Reaction
Major Symptoms: Retreat from reality, with emotional blunting, inappropriate emotional reactions, and marked disturbance in thought processes; delusions, hallucinations, and stereotyped mannerisms common.
Major Subgroups: Childhood; Simple; Paranoid; Catatonic; Hebephrenic; Undifferentiated.

Paranoid Reaction
Major Symptoms: Logical, often highly systematized and intricate delusions with personality otherwise relatively intact.
Major Subgroups: Paranoia; Paranoid state.

Affective Reaction
Major Symptoms: Extreme fluctuations of mood or intense, prolonged depression or euphoria, with related disturbances in thought and behavior.
Major Subgroups: Manic reaction; Psychotic depression; Involutional melancholia.

where their training qualifies them to look. Some seek the key to the mysteries of madness in human nature, others in patterns of human nurture. We shall briefly review the contributions of these two major approaches as they bear on one type of psychotic reaction, schizophrenia.

Is nature the cause?

The two primary sources of evidence that emerge from a biological perspective on schizophrenia are genetic transmission and biochemical mechanisms.

Genetic transmission   It is known that schizophrenia tends to run in families (Kallman, 1946; Paul, 1977). Less certain is the genetic contribution to that effect. Social psychological factors in a family where one or both parents have schizophrenia are obviously different from families with nonaffected parents. One method for separating the hereditary from the experience component is by studying children of schizophrenic parents adopted and reared by normal parents. The subsequent incidence of pathology is then compared with the rate for adopted or foster-care children of normal parents. Such data support the notion of a major role played by the genetic factor in schizophrenia (Rosenthal et al., 1975; Heston, 1970). A summary of a large body of empirical research suggests that genetic transmission of schizophrenia potential is substantial (Gottesman & Shields, 1976). The incidence of schizophrenia in any given culture is about 1 percent of the total population. Where one member of a pair of identical twins is schizophrenic the chances of the other being also affected is four to five times greater than among pairs of nonidentical twins. When both parents are schizophrenic the schizophrenia risk of their offspring ranges from 35 to 50 percent. The risk for the offspring drops sharply where either parent is normal. It is greatest in families with many affected relatives and where their schizophrenic reactions are severe (see Hanson, Gottesman, & Meehl, 1977). ● It appears that schizophrenia definitely runs in families, but for unknown reasons as many children are "invulnerable" to the affliction as are vulnerable to the high risk it creates.

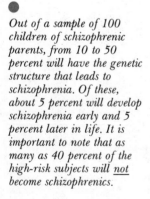

Out of a sample of 100 children of schizophrenic parents, from 10 to 50 percent will have the genetic structure that leads to schizophrenia. Of these, about 5 percent will develop schizophrenia early and 5 percent later in life. It is important to note that as many as 40 percent of the high-risk subjects will <u>not</u> become schizophrenics.

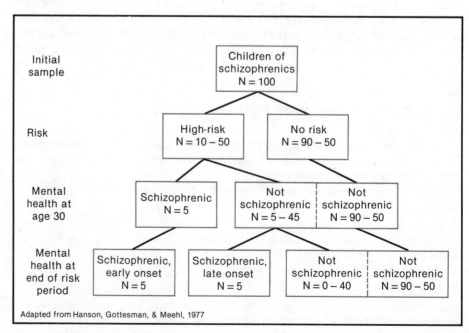

Adapted from Hanson, Gottesman, & Meehl, 1977

A consequence of the genetic approach to schizophrenia is the development of research on "children at risk" (Garmezy, 1974; Garmezy & Streitman, 1974). The hope in studying high-risk offspring is the early detection of the schizophrenic process. By identifying children genetically vulnerable to schizophrenia, researchers will be able to better study the factors that contribute to the development of the disease. In addition, strategies of prevention and early therapeutic intervention can be designed and utilized.

Biochemical transmitters A genetic predisposition for schizophrenia would be triggered by natural gene products such as neurotransmitters in the CNS (see Chapters 11 & 12). Research has shown that certain drugs which reduce movement abnormalities in Parkinson's disease produce schizophrenic-like symptoms. Other drugs designed to reduce schizophrenic symptoms have the side effect of increasing abnormal motor behaviors. Discovery of these "side effects" have led to a theory that a common neurochemical mechanism is responsible for the control of both movement and madness. *Dopamine* is the neurotransmitter substance most likely to exert that dual control. The *dopamine hypothesis* holds that schizophrenia is associated with a relative excess of dopamine at specific CNS receptor sites (Snyder, 1972; Meltzer & Stahl, 1976). Researchers are studying the relationships between drugs that alter dopamine availability or its reception and changes in patterns of movement and madness. It is unlikely that the complexity of madness can be distilled in a test tube, but this research is providing important clues about the biochemistry of schizophrenia.

Is nurture the cause?

One of the most obvious differences between the biologically and psychologically proposed causes of schizophrenia lies in their degree of specificity: genes versus the social and political structure of families, neurotransmitters versus environmental stressors. It becomes as difficult to prove a highly specific biological factor is sufficient to cause the disease as it is that a vague general psychological one is a necessary condition. At best, what we can expect to discover is the relative contributions of each of a complex of variables that together produce a schizophrenic reaction pattern. Just as genetic factors can make an individual biologically vulnerable, so environmental factors like parental rejection or overprotection, excessive or inconsistent discipline, or extreme insecurity can predispose some individuals psychologically to mental disorder. Studies of the family structure of schizophrenics, as well as of other features of their social life, reveal the extent to which functional psychosis may represent learned ways of attempting to cope with chronic stress and unresolvable conflicts.

One of the most reliable prognostic indicators of future schizophrenic development is an early pattern of *social isolation* in which the adolescent withdraws from interacting with others. This may be a consequence of feeling different or "abnormal" in some way, or of not having learned how to relate to other people in a positive, meaningful way, or both. Many studies clearly show that one of the most abnormal things about schizophrenic children is the relationship between their parents and the parents' use of the child to work out their own feelings of frustration and hostility. The child may be cast in the role of "buffer" or mediator and made to feel responsible for the continuation or failure of the marriage.

Family interaction studies show less responsiveness and interpersonal sensitivity in the speech of families with a schizophrenic member than in normal families. In families with the most disturbed offspring, the members do not listen to each other or spend as much time in information exchange as normal families (Ferriera & Winter, 1964). Those in families with withdrawn adolescents are less able to predict each other's responses in a test situation.

Within our own society, people from lower socioeconomic classes are more likely to become schizophrenic and those most affluent to become neurotic (Hollingshead & Redlich, 1958). It may be that the higher rate among lower-class families can be traced to their patterns of childrearing (Lane & Singer, 1959). It may also be that many of the environmental consequences of being poor—powerlessness, frustrated ambitions, rootlessness, a losing battle for survival—provide fertile soil for psychotic pathology.

The apparent differences in who develops which disorder may also reflect bias in how patients are diagnosed and treated. For example, poorer disturbed patients, unable to pay for therapy, may be committed to state hospitals as "out-of-contact psychotics," while those with similar symptoms who can afford psychotherapy are perceived and labeled as "neurotics in need of treatment to work through their conflicts."

Schizophrenic reactions

There exists no greater puzzle and challenge to medical and behavioral science than the understanding and control of schizophrenia. Between two and three million living Americans at one time or another have suffered from this most mysterious and tragic mental disorder. Half of the beds in this nation's mental institutions are currently occupied by schizophrenic patients. The estimate that 2 percent of the population will have an episode of schizophrenia during their lives rises in certain social settings—the urban ghetto for example—to a frightening 6 percent, or more than one in twenty persons.

Schizophrenia is a chronic disorder characterized by: (a) delusions and hallucinations, (b) disorganized thinking, (c) emotions that are blunted, shallow, or situationally inappropriate, (d) odd or occasionally bizarre motor behavior, and (e) disintegration of personality. Although early reports indicated unreliability in diagnosing schizophrenia, high reliability can be achieved when those who make the diagnosis are competent, motivated, and work from accurate detailed sources of information (Meehl, 1972).

The problem of diagnosis and labeling is a persistent one, however, and one of the big obstacles to a better understanding of schizophrenic behavior is a disagreement among clinicians on the best criteria for classifying it. While there is some consensus about a number of the prominent symptoms associated with schizophrenia, no one patient shows them all, and any single patient may exhibit a variety of them over time. For convenience, clinicians distinguish several types of schizophrenia, each with a characteristic cluster of behaviors. Six such types are summarized in the table. ◆ The most common of these subclasses of schizophrenia is the paranoid.

Analysis of changes in schizophrenia diagnosis over a fifteen-year period (for patients admitted to psychiatric facilities in Monroe County, New York) reveals a sharp decline in the paranoid category, an increase in undifferentiated schizophrenia, and a lower, more stable percentage of other subtypes (Romano, 1977).

Early views of schizophrenia were pessimistic about the likelihood of recovery. It is now recognized that schizophrenics often show spontaneous remission of the disease symptoms; that is, they recover in time without any treatment. The prognosis varies depending upon a number of factors. ■

◆
Types of schizophrenia

Childhood Schizophrenia
Inability to relate to other people and to environmental stimulation in the ordinary way, including: impairment of emotional relationships; serious retardation in most skills; self-directed aggression; pathological attachment to particular objects; resistance to environmental change; abnormal perceptual experiences; acute and illogical anxiety; underdeveloped speech; and distorted patterns of movement (Davison & Neale, 1974). A second category of childhood psychosis is *early infantile autism*. Autistic infants are psychologically detached from the moment of birth and remain isolated from human relationships.

Simple Schizophrenia
Reduction of external interests and attachments, apathy, withdrawal, inconspicuous delusions or hallucinations, some disintegration of thought processes, often aggressive behavior, hypochondriacal experiences, and sex and/or alcohol indulgence.

Paranoid Schizophrenia
Poorly systematized delusions; often hostile, suspicious, aggressive. Delusions are often of omnipotence, remarkable talents, and high social status. Delusions are combined with personality disorganization.

Catatonia
More sudden onset than other types with vivid hallucinations and grandiose delusions. Alternation between stupor and excitement; in stupor, there is a sudden loss of animation, and a stereotyped position may be maintained for some time, during which patient will not eat, drink, or take care of other bodily functions. Catatonic schizophrenics are the most likely to recover.

Hebephrenia
Most severe disorganization: silliness; inappropriateness of affect; incoherence of thought, speech, action; unusual mannerisms; auditory and visual hallucinations; fantastic delusions; obscene behavior; lack of modesty; hypochondriasis; emotional indifference; regression to childish behavior.

Undifferentiated
Acute or chronic reactions with a hodgepodge of symptoms.

There are several intriguing characteristics of the schizophrenic reaction that are being discovered through controlled psychological research. Schizophrenics exhibit a greater sensitivity to perceptual stimuli. This results in more distractability and a "flooding" by external stimulation. Such hypersensitivity makes it difficult for them to find constancy in their sensory environment. Disturbed thought patterns may be the consequence of an inability to give sustained attention to events or processes taking place in the environment. The perceived vividness of stimuli might make the stimuli more potent. In order to think, the schizophrenic may attempt to shut out external stimulation. The attempt is not completely successful because the immediate stimulus situation keeps intruding. Not being able to filter out and ignore irrelevant stimuli results in a confusion of "signals" and "noise." Studies on thought disorders in schizophrenics reveal a loss of abstract thinking in favor of concrete. More research is called for that investigates schizophrenic thinking and memory within the kinds of information processing framework we outlined in Chapter 5.

The schizophrenic's speech seems to be under the control of immediate stimuli. Distracted from completely expressing a simple train of thought by constantly changing sensory input and vivid inner reality, the schizophrenic

Prognosis for recovery from schizophrenia

Diagnostic criteria	Good prognosis	Poor prognosis
Mode of Onset	Acute	Insidious, gradual
Precipitating Events	Frequently reported	Usually not reported
Pre-psychotic History	Good	Poor; frequent history of "schizoid" traits (aloofness, social isolation)
Confusion	Often present	Usually absent
Affective Symptoms	Often present and prominent	Usually absent or minimal; affective responses usually "blunted" or "flat"
Marital Status	Usually married	Often single, especially males
Family History of Affective Disorder	Often present	May be present but less likely
Family History of Schizophrenia	Absent or rare	Likely

does not make sense to a listener. The incomprehensibility of schizophrenic speech is due, in part, to bizarre intrusions. These intrusions are thoughts irrelevant to the verbalized statement being uttered which are *not* suppressed. Long interconnected strings of words cannot be maintained. Speaking requires remembering what was said (past), monitoring where one is (present), and directing the spoken sentence toward some final goal (future). Brendan Maher (1968) argues that bizarre schizophrenic speech is a particular brand of nonsense. It deviates from normal whenever a vulnerable word is uttered that has multiple meanings. Then the incorrect, or personally relevant but semantically inappropriate, word is used. A patient says "Doctor, I have pains in my chest and hope and wonder if my box is broken and heart is beaten." Chest is a vulnerable word; it can mean respiratory cage or container like a *hope* chest. Wonder could mean *Wonder Bread,* kept in a bread box. Similarly hearts *beat* and are *broken.* The oversensitivity to stimuli also leads the schizophrenic to overrespond to the sound of his speech which leads to association by sound rather than by meaning (called *clang* associations). By carefully listening to the schizophrenic's speech it is often possible to decode the sense that appears to be just nonsense (Forrest, 1976).

Paranoid reactions

Unlike the other psychotic reaction patterns, which may be quite varied, paranoid reactions are marked by one major pathological symptom — persistent delusions. A *delusion* is a firmly held belief that is maintained by the individual in the face of objective evidence to the contrary and despite lack of social support. In the *paranoid state,* the delusions are transient and not well organized into a coherent story. Patients may exhibit hallucinations, but their personalities are otherwise intact. As the pathology progresses, the delusions become more systematized, coherent, and internally logical, while hallucinatory activity disappears. This condition is termed *paranoia.*

There are three types of delusions that occur in paranoid disorders and sometimes in the other psychotic states:

a. *Delusions of grandeur.* Individuals believe they are some exalted being, such as the Virgin Mary, a millionaire, a great inventor, or even God.

b. *Delusions of reference.* Individuals misconstrue chance happenings as being

directly aimed at them. If two people are seen in earnest conversation, para-
noiacs immediately conclude that they are talking about them.

c. *Delusions of persecution.* Individuals feel that they are constantly being spied
on and plotted against and are in mortal danger of attack. Delusions of persecution may accompany delusions of grandeur — the patient is a great person,
but is continually being opposed by evil forces.

The intellectual and economic level of the paranoid is usually higher than
that of other psychologically disturbed patients. These individuals can usually
function for some time without anyone realizing the need for treatment and
hospitalization. Among the psychological factors frequently found to be important in the dynamics of paranoid disorders are guilt over immoral or
unethical behavior, repressed homosexuality, inferiority feelings, and unreal-
istically high ambitions. There is sometimes a "grain of truth" in paranoid
delusions, an initially valid element that gets distorted or exaggerated out of
all proportion. Thus fears of being caught masturbating might be the kernel
around which an elaborate spy scenario is developed.

It may also be that when the individual first begins to develop these paranoid ideas, they go unchallenged by sympathetic friends and relatives. As time
goes by the delusions become more systematized, that is, more logical and
apparently rational. Thus we have the curious paradox that the more serious
the condition becomes, the more logical the person's reasoning appears. Such
people resist therapy because it is easier to assume that the therapist is part of
an enemy plot than to accept the fact that one's thought processes are illogical.

Affective reactions

In one group of psychotic disorders, the major characteristic is extreme distortion of mood. Here the usual symptom is a deep depression, accompanied
by a generalized slowing down of mental and physical activity, with gloom,
morbid thoughts of disease or death, and feelings of worthlessness. During
such *depressive* episodes, patients may attempt to commit suicide and must be
carefully watched. The speech of psychotically depressed patients is slow and
without emotion. When they do speak, it is generally to express their suffering
and suicidal desires.

In sharp contrast to psychotic depression is the *manic* reaction, which is
characterized by high excitement, elation, and restless activity. Manic patients
indulge in frequent boisterous laughter and eloquent, loud speeches. They
walk about wildly and gesture dramatically, banging upon the walls and furniture.

Most patients show only a manic pattern or only a depressive one, but
some patients alternate between manic and depressive periods, often in a cycle of great regularity. Sometimes there are long periods of apparent normality between episodes. With or without treatment, the episode typically runs its
course (perhaps a few weeks or months) and then subsides.

Depression has been called the "common cold of psychopathology." Of
all the forms of pathology described in this chapter, it is the one most students
are likely to have already experienced. We have all at one time or another
been depressed at the loss of or separation from a loved one, the failure to
achieve a desired goal, or from chronic frustration and stress. This normal,
"garden-variety" depression is transitory and situationally specific.

In neurotic depression the symptoms are more intense, prolonged, recurrent, and disabling. The boundary between neurotic and psychotic depres-

▲
Characteristics of depression

Emotional

Dejected mood	Self-dislike
Loss of gratification	Loss of attachments
Crying spells	Loss of mirth response

Cognitive-Motivational

Negative expectations	Loss of motivation
Suicidal wishes	Low self-evaluation
Distorted self-image	Self-blame, self-criticism
Indecisiveness	

Vegetative-Physical

Loss of appetite	Loss of sexual interest
Sleep disturbance	Constipation
Fatigability	

Delusional

Worthless	Sinner

Appearance

Sad faced	Speech slow, reduced, not
Stooped posture	spontaneous

Adapted from Beck, 1967

sion is not clearly drawn, since the general concept of "depression" denotes a cluster of symptoms rather than a single defining characteristic. ▲ The psychotic forms of depression would not only be characterized by their severity and chronicity but also by associated loss of contact with present reality. The depressed psychotic requires hospitalization and intensive care.

In any given year, it is estimated that 15 percent of adults between eighteen and seventy-five years may have serious depressive symptoms. However, this common illness is greatly overlooked in the United States today, with only a small percentage of the estimated twenty million depressives receiving treatment (Bielski & Friedel, 1977).

Depressive behavior is difficult to categorize, however. It is felt by many that there are actually two types of depression: endogenous and reactive. This distinction is based on the presence or absence of precipitating external factors (such as stress, conflict, or loss).

Endogenous depression is assumed to be caused by internal (biochemical or genetic) factors. The symptoms of this form of depression include: retardation, severe depression, lack of reactivity to the environment, loss of interest in life, insomnia, weight loss, guilt, suicidal tendencies (Mendels, 1970). In contrast, *reactive depression* is less severe but is marked by self-pity, inadequate personality features, and the presence of precipitating stressors. It is possible, however, that such stressors are in fact present in endogenous depression but the patients are not aware of them. Martin Seligman (1974) has proposed parallels between depression in humans and the model of learned helplessness. (See *P&L* Close-up, Learning to Be Depressed.)

One form of extreme depression in middle life or later (after the age of forty or so), which occurs more frequently among women than among men, is called *involutional melancholia*. The psychological features of this reaction are apprehension, agitation, and hopelessness, as well as feelings of guilt and failure. It has been suggested that this disorder is related to physiological

Close-up
Learning to Be Depressed

Learned helplessness in a variety of lower animals is shown to occur when responding and reinforcement are not contingently related. In research with college students, Seligman and his associates have found that both depressed students and students who were not depressed but were made helpless show the same sort of performance deficits. Seligman has extended this conception to reactive depression, theorizing that the common core is the development of a belief in the futility of active responding. The depressed person becomes passive only with repeated lack of positive reinforcement for responding. Some depressed persons make many responses that lack "social awareness," that is, behaviors that others seldom reinforce. Reinforcement then comes primarily through the attention that is given to the person's depressive reactions (a "secondary gain" of the pathology).

This learned helplessness model of depression has generated research that has had mixed results. Critics point out that the analogy does not hold up well because people think in ways lower animals do not. We think not only about the present failure of our actions to effect desired outcomes, but also about our past track record. We compare our situation with performance-outcome relations of other people in similar circumstances. Sometimes when we fail we don't get depressed because we know we weren't properly prepared, the competition was out of our league, or the outcome was more a matter of luck than our ability or effort. Such ideas constitute attributions that interrelate tasks, outcomes, social comparisons, and perceived self-efficacy. To what extent is the experienced helplessness personal or universal ("I am a failure" vs. "no one else succeeded")? What does the person foresee as possible outcomes? What degree of control does he or she perceive can be exerted over those outcomes? How significant is the particular outcome to the person; what meaning is attributed to one's failure to get it? These are but some of the questions that a human model of clinical depression must answer.

Finally we should recognize that depressed people often control other people through their passivity and other dependent symptoms even when they do not achieve impersonal control (over tasks, work, etc.). Secondly, failure can convey positive messages: "to clean up your act," reevaluate your goals, develop new tactics or strategies or move on to greener pastures that are more personally controllable. A theory is needed that can predict when particular attributions will be made and when they will lead to depression and passivity on the one hand or reappraisal and activation on the other (see Abramson, Seligman, & Teasdale, 1978; Wortman & Dintzer, 1978; Buchwald, Coyne, & Cole, 1978).

© *1977, United Feature Syndicate, Inc.*

"change of life" involving reproductive functions. It has recently been shown, however, that there is no greater risk of an affective disorder during menopause than at other times in a woman's life (Winokur, 1973). It may be that when some people take stock of themselves at significant stages or "passages" in their adult life cycle, they become depressed over not having realized their ambitions. Others, having achieved their life's goal of "getting to the top" (gaining material wealth or status), begin to question its value relative to all they had to give up along the way.

Our understanding of madness does more than enable society to reclaim its "familiar strangers." In making sense of madness, we are forced to come to grips with basic conceptions of normality, reality, and social values. A mind loosed from its moorings does not just go on its solitary way; it bumps into others, sometimes challenging their stability. Treatment and prevention of mental illness is a major goal of many psychologists, as we shall see in the next chapter.

Chapter summary

Mental disorders have always been widespread in our society. They include inherited or organic defects, neuroses, psychoses, and a whole range of psychological and social malfunctioning. Before modern times, mental disturbance was attributed to demonic possession, but the Renaissance brought with it a scientific, investigative approach which attributed such disorders to disease. Eventually, the *medical model* emerged, classifying abnormal behavior as the symptoms of genetic, biochemical, or organic malfunction. Medical intervention, including hospitalization, was the prescribed treatment.

Freudian psychoanalytic theory changed this view of the patient as the victim of disease, ascribing to the individual an active, though unknowing part in his or her mental anguish. The dynamic forces of unconscious motivation and repression of unacceptable impulses accounted for abnormality from this viewpoint. Neurosis was seen as an extension of normal processes, but the Freudian approach was still akin to the disease model, assuming a core of mental disturbance from which overt symptoms originated.

The *learning model* places far less emphasis on historical origins of psychological disturbance, concentrating instead on the present environment eliciting the undesirable behavior patterns. Psychologists who use this model concentrate on the inadequate coping strategies people use or the effective ones they neglect to use.

Insanity is a legal term. An individual is usually considered to be mentally ill on the basis of a judgment, made by someone in authority, as to how appropriate that individual's behavior has been in terms of content and context. From a *sociological* point of view, a mentally ill person is a *deviant*—displaying a degree of deviation from the population average. Although the view that what is good for the average person is necessarily what is healthy for all is erroneous, certain symptoms of mental illness are *universal* and do not appear to be culturally or situationally relative.

A *personality* or *character disorder* is a chronic, long-term behavior pattern disturbing to others because of its inappropriateness or offensiveness. It is rarely, however, a source of anxiety to the individual manifesting it. Common types of personality disorders include the *inadequate personality*, the *explosive personality*, the *passive-aggressive personality*, and the *antisocial personality*.

Neurosis is essentially a search for relief from anxiety. It is a state in which the individual feels chronically threatened by life events and inadequate to the task of coping with them. While there is no clear dividing line between the "normal" individual and the neurotic one, there are certain patterns of behavior recognized and labeled as neurotic. These include: *anxiety neurosis*, *phobias*, *obsessive-compulsive neurosis*, *hysterical neurosis*, *hypochondria*, and *existential neurosis*.

Psychosis is the general term used for the most severe form of psychopathology. It involves loss of contact with reality and extreme disturbance in perceptual, affective, and cognitive functioning. Inner experience is the criterion against which psychotics test the validity of outer experience.

There is disagreement over what causes psychosis. While some psychotic reactions are obviously *organic* in nature, *functional psychoses* stem from no known physical defect in the brain. A few theorists have suggested that psychosis is not abnormal but is a radical revolt on the part of the individual against prevailing societal norms and notions of reality. Most, however, consider it to be pathological behavior. Whether its causes are genetic and biochemical, or social and experiential, is a question over which there has been much debate.

Schizophrenia, for example, is known to run in families. Thus the tendency to develop this affliction is to some degree heritable. The *dopamine hypothesis* holds schizophrenia to be associated with an excess of dopamine at specific receptor sites in the central nervous system. On the other hand, an early pattern of social isolation is one of the most reliable prognostic indicators of schizophrenic development. Schizophrenic children tend to come from lower-class families in which they have been cast in the role of "buffer" between their parents.

Schizophrenic reactions are characterized by delusions and hallucinations, disorganized thinking, blunted or inappropriate emotions, odd or occasionally bizzare motor behavior, and disintegration of the personality. Schizophrenics exhibit a greater sensitivity than most people to perceptual stimuli, making it difficult for them to find constancy in the sensory environment. Schizophrenics' speech seems to be under the control of immediate stimuli. It has also been suggested that the bizarre speech of schizophrenics is due to the intrusion into verbal utterances of internal thoughts that have not been suppressed. It is interesting to note that many schizophrenics show spontaneous remission of disease symptoms with no treatment.

Paranoid reactions, another form of psychosis, are characterized by persistent delusions—usually delusions of *grandeur, reference,* or *persecution.* The disorder generally begins with the *paranoid state,* progressing to the more severe stage of *paranoia.*

Affective psychotic reactions are episodes of extreme mood distortion. These may include *manic* or *depressive* episodes and, in the case of a small number of patients, *manic-depressive cycles.*

Depressions may be *endogenous* (biochemically or genetically based) or *reactive* (less severe and usually accompanied by inadequate personality features and precipitating stressors). *Involutional melancholia* is a severe form of depression occurring most frequently in middle-aged and older women.

20

Therapeutic Modification of Behavior

Biomedical therapy
Psychosurgery
Shock therapy
Chemotherapy
The medical model

Psychodynamic therapy
Freudian psychoanalysis
Neo-Freudian approaches

Behavioristic therapy
Contingency management
Extinction and counterconditioning

Existential-humanistic therapy
Existential psychotherapy
Humanistic psychotherapy

Comparisons, evaluation, and alternatives
Making the madness fit the therapy
Does psychotherapy work?
Alternatives to traditional treatment

Chapter summary

Suppose you were to become mad, mentally ill, insane, emotionally disturbed—in a word, "crazy." What kind of treatment might you expect to receive? It depends. The treatment for madness has varied in different times and in different countries depending on prevailing views of mental health, illness, and the origins of deviant behavior. One of the best ways to discover the perspective on human nature taken by a society is by examining how it treats its mentally ill.

In ancient Roman law, mental illness was evidence only for mental *incompetence*. Thus, the legally insane person had to be protected from making contracts (wills, marriage, business deals, etc.) the implications of which they could not comprehend. Moreover, the insane were exempted from penalty for crime, while family members who neglected to care for their own insane relatives were legally penalized.

At the start of the Middle Ages, the insane were generally treated well in Europe. The way they were treated was much affected by the influential writing of the Catholic friar Bartholomew, whose book *The Properties of Things* was in continuous use for several hundred years. Bartholomew listed the causes of insanity as: overwork, too deep thought, passion, sorrow, and fear. The treatment for such ills consisted of a change of environment to remove the sufferer from the source of his or her agitation. Music and planned occupational and recreational therapy were also proposed (Graham, 1967).

Hundreds of years later during the Jacksonian era in the United States, a similar view of the "stress-induced" nature of mental illness gave rise to the creation of mental hospitals. They were literally "asylums" erected in the countryside away from the turmoil of the cities which were assumed to contribute to mental disturbance (Rothman, 1971).

But during the intervening centuries several events occurred that dramatically changed the treatment of mental illness—for the worse. Population increases coupled with migration to big cities created unemployment, poverty, and alienation. Special institutions arose to warehouse the poor, the criminals, and the insane. In 1403, St. Mary of Bethlehem, a London hospital for the poor, admitted its first insane patient—and Bedlam broke loose. *Bedlam* (a corruption of Bethlehem) came to stand for chaotic confusion and the most dehumanized treatment of people the world had seen. For the next three hundred years patients were chained, tortured, and exhibited like animals in zoos for the amusement of the public who paid admission to see the mad beasts perform their antics. ▲

Canst thou not minister to a mind diseas'd;
Pluck from the memory a rooted sorrow,
Raze out the written troubles of the brain;
And with some sweet oblivious antidote
Cleanse the stuff'd bosom of that perilous matter
Which weighs upon the heart?
William Shakespeare
Macbeth

▲
In this famous engraving, artist William Hogarth depicted the conditions that existed in the London mental institution known as Bedlam in the 1730s. Two society women are viewing the inmates.

Meanwhile, an even more sinister plot was unfolding in fifteenth-century Germany. The Inquisition saw psychosis as witchcraft; the mad were assumed to be possessed by the devil and evil spirits. The printing of the book, *Malleus Maleficarum (Hammer of Witches)* in 1487 provided the religious rationale needed for the torture and execution of those people suspected of being deprived of their reason by the forces of Satan. This "operational manual of psychopathology" was the clinical textbook used for diagnosis and therapy of madness in any form that threatened the security of the established order.

The dignity of mentally ill people was reaffirmed with the nineteenth-century view that they were just *sick* people. During this age of enlightenment and revolution, Phillipe Pinel expressed a new conception of mental illness. "The mentally ill," wrote Pinel in 1801, "far from being guilty people deserving of punishment are sick people whose miserable state deserves all the consideration that is due to suffering humanity. One should try with the most simple methods to restore their reason" (quoted by Zilboorg & Henry, 1941, 323–24). ■

■
In the early nineteenth century, French physician Philippe Pinel literally struck the chains from the mentally ill and instituted more humane forms of treatment. He is shown here removing the shackles from inmates at Salpêtrière Hospital.

Not only did Pinel's conception of mental illness as *disease* help cast off the shackles of institutionalized patients, his view made it scientifically legitimate and thus medically acceptable to study and treat mental disease. Such malfunctioning was assumed to reflect diseases of the nervous system. We will see that current therapy based upon a *biomedical* model still tries to change disturbed brain and nervous system function by surgery, shock treatment, and drugs.

In contrast, *psychological* approaches to mental disorder have focused upon psychological factors assumed to cause dysfunctional reaction patterns. Three major treatment categories have evolved from the assumption that aberrant behavior is a function of psychological rather than biological variables.

In Freud's *psychodynamic* view, mental illness was to be studied and treated in terms of traumatic life experiences that create conflicts and neurotic suffering. *Psychoanalysis* treats mental illness with words, insights, and a sympathetic ear for the sufferer's interpretation of critical life conflicts. All other psychological approaches to the understanding and treatment of psychopathology "argue their positions with reference to psychoanalysis" (Korchin, 1976, p. 88).

Therapy by *behaviorists* and those of a social-learning persuasion seeks to change reinforcement contingencies that maintain deviant or pathological reactions. They reject the notion of an inner-disease state that gives rise to symptoms. Instead, they treat the symptoms directly as the disturbed behavior that must be modified. In addition, appropriate skills for social living are taught as part of a social-learning approach to therapy.

The fourth major category of treatment we will consider in some detail in this chapter is the *existential-humanistic* approach. Therapies that have emerged from this tradition emphasize the relationship between the *values* of the patient and those of the society. As you might expect from our discussion of this approach to personality functioning (Chapter 16), existential-humanistic therapies are more directed toward self-actualization, psychological growth, restoring meaningful interpersonal relationships, and enhancing freedom of choice.

In this chapter we shall examine the assumptions, procedures, and strategies utilized by these four therapeutic approaches. (See *P&L* Close-up, Psychotherapy Overview.) They represent the most common types of formal therapy in contemporary Western societies. Then we will be in a better position to evaluate the basic goals, purposes, and effectiveness of psychotherapy in general, as well as in specific types of therapy.

Biomedical therapy

The relationship of human functioning to its biological underpinnings is unquestionably important. We are, after all, an animal species subject to many of the same limitations as other species in nature. Our internal ecology is held in a delicate balance that may be upset by nutritional deficiencies, under- or over-secretion of hormones, the failure of certain enzymes to perform their required function, and many other biological mishaps.

In this view, mental ailments have their basis in physical-biological disorders. Physiological psychologists search for the origins of mental illness in the biological substrata of human functioning. Therapists who assume that disturbances of the nervous system have an *organic* basis turn to *physical* methods of treatment. Their goal is to change the patient's abnormal patterns of reaction as *directly* (and quickly) as possible.

If mental disease stems from malfunctioning of the central nervous system, metabolism, or endocrine system, then the faulty mechanism is the target for intervention. The "hardware" of the defective human computer is changed and not merely its programming instructions. That may mean disconnecting parts of the brain through psychosurgery, scrambling nerve circuits through electroconvulsive shock therapy, or altering neuronal and hormonal functioning by the administration of drugs *(chemotherapy)*. Other medical measures (which we will not discuss here) include special diets, megavitamin therapy, induced prolonged sleep (popular in the Soviet Union), and hydrotherapy designed to relax "agitated nerves" in hot baths. It should be emphasized that such "physical psychiatry" is not always intended to cure the individual's emotional disorder but may be used in an attempt to prevent some extreme act such as homicide or suicide or to make the disturbed patient receptive to psychotherapy.

Psychotherapy Overview: Problems, Purposes, Participants, Principles, Practices, and Places

"Psychotherapy describes any intentional application of psychological techniques by a clinician to the end of effecting sought-after personality or behavioral change" (Korchin, 1976, p. 281). People who have problems in the areas of thought, emotion, or behavior are treated by specially trained professionals who intervene with the goal of changing the troubled person in some particular way.

People become patients in therapy when their everyday functioning violates societal criteria of normality and/or their own sense of personal adjustment. A person with a problem may seek therapy on his or her own initiative or may do so on the advice of others or by coercion.

The purpose of all therapeutic intervention is to reduce suffering, increase the patient's sense of well-being, and assist the person to develop effective means of coping with everyday demands and stresses. The ultimate goals of therapy involve replacing mental illness or inadequate personality and behavioral functioning with improved mental health and effective coping and character styles.

These general goals are translated into therapeutic *principles* that differ widely according to the theory of normal personality and psychopathology the therapist holds. In part, this belief system of the therapist is a product of his or her cultural values and training in a particular mental-health speciality. The actual practices or tactics of therapists from different schools, however, often share more in common than do their abstract theories. Most therapists fit their approach to the needs of the patient and "borrow" effective techniques from other approaches. This flexibility and eclecticism blur theoretical distinctions but function in the best interests of the patient.

Therapy can take place in a variety of settings with many different types of therapists. Usually, the more severe the disturbance, the more intensive and isolated from society is the treatment. Psychotic patients and those with severe neurotic problems are treated in hospitals. In clinics and private practice we find neurotic patients and those with character disorders that are not incapacitating. Psychological problems of a more limited kind are treated in nonclinical settings—in schools and work places by counselors, in the home by psychiatric social workers, in churches and synagogues by pastoral counselors. Psychiatrists, psychoanalysts, and clinical psychologists are the primary mental-health professionals (see p. 19).

If you had a personal psychological problem, which of these therapists would you be more likely to consult? Probably none of them—at least not initially. Most people turn to parents, friends, teachers, bartenders, cabdrivers, and their beauticians for advice, support, love, and a chance to "talk it out." These informal therapists carry the bulk of the daily burden of relieving human suffering. Only when the problems become severe and persist is formal therapy called into action.

Psychosurgery

Among the most dramatic, most widely publicized, and most disappointing innovations in psychiatry has been the brain surgery used in the treatment of severe emotional disorders, as we saw in Chapter 11. The best-known form of psychosurgery is the *prefrontal lobotomy*, an operation that severs the nerve fibers connecting the prefrontal lobes of the brain with the lower-brain centers, especially the hypothalamus.

Clinical experience has shown that lobotomy does often diminish the emotional tone accompanying the individual's thoughts and memories. Psychosurgery is not thought to remove the *sources* of the patient's disturbance; its goal is to eliminate the emotional torment of disturbing ideas or hallucinations.

These benefits must be set against the following list of negative side effects: (a) a loss of interest in body and in the relation of the self to the environment, (b) an inability to foresee the consequences of a planned series of personally relevant acts, (c) an indifference to the opinions of others, (d) an increase in some forms of impulsive behavior, since remorse, guilt, and fear are banished, (e) a reduced capacity to form a unified self-image and project it into the future (Robinson & Freeman, 1955). Psychosurgery, once performed, cannot be undone or reversed. Because its results are uncertain, it has been considered a method of last resort and is less widely used today than it has been in the past.

Originally psychosurgery was recommended as a cure for schizophrenia, depression, criminal behavior, addictive disorders, and even homosexuality and childhood behavior disorders. Today, patients whose behavior is labeled as showing a *dyscontrol syndrome* (assaults, impulsive sexual behavior, pathological intoxication, and traffic violations and accidents) are assumed to be the best targets for psychosurgery (Mark & Ervin, 1970). The evidence of the success of this newest attempt at brain control of violence is questionable. Even more so are the assumptions that violence proneness can be located in regions of the brain rather than in the patient's interactions with other people and social forces (Valenstein, 1973).

Until recently, there has been no protection against psychosurgery being performed against the will of involuntarily committed hospital patients. A Michigan court has now ruled that "involuntarily confined mental patients" cannot give valid informed consent to undergo psychosurgery for two reasons. First, because true consent is not possible for those who live in a coercive environment and second, because the effects of the treatment are permanent and not reversible (*Kaimovitz* v. *Michigan Department of Health,* 1973). This decision has broad implications for creating needed safeguards against this violation of individual rights.

Shock therapy

Severely disturbed patients who would once have been considered hopeless have responded favorably in some cases to artificially induced seizures or convulsions. Such treatment, known as *shock therapy,* became routine in most mental hospitals after World War II, but it has been less frequently used since the discovery of new techniques of chemotherapy. Although a number of different techniques have been used in shock therapy, they all induce a state of coma lasting for several minutes to several hours after the shock. It is not entirely clear whether the coma itself is the therapeutic factor or whether the value of shock is due to some other factor—such as physiological changes in nervous system circuits, or the creation of a violent psychological reaction.

The most recently developed and by far the most widely used form of convulsive therapy is electroconvulsive shock. The patient is secured to a bed, and electricity ranging from 70 to 130 volts is applied for a fraction of a second through electrodes fastened to the temples. Twenty or more such treatments may be given over a period of weeks or months. Electroconvulsive shock has proved particularly effective in cases of severe depression.

Conflicting findings have been obtained, however, in regard to its benefits. Many psychiatrists believe that this drastic form of treatment will be used less and less in the future; it is already being supplanted by drugs and new techniques of psychotherapy. There is some evidence that electroconvulsive shock has adverse effects on learning and retention (Leukel, 1957; Stone &

*Electroconvulsive shock
therapy induces brief
unconsciousness. It has
proved effective in the
treatment of severe
depression. Unfortunately,
it can also be misused to
"keep patients in line."*

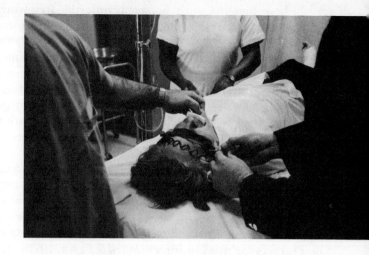

Bakhtiari, 1956) and may also cause brain damage (as reported by Maher, 1966). Certainly it disrupts the integrated functioning of the organism.

In large state institutions that are understaffed, shock therapy has been used rather indiscriminately and sometimes as a threat or punishment. One of my most disturbing memories is of the first time I witnessed such a procedure in a local mental hospital. One after another, nearly two dozen sobbing women patients were strapped to a wheeled cot, begging the nurses "not to turn on the juice" again. The staff ignored the patients' reactions—probably in their own emotional self-defense. Once the current was applied to a patient's temples, she began jerking spastically, foamed at the mouth, and lost consciousness. Upon recovery the women were disorganized and frightened. This experience made me aware that the patient's view of the treatment must always be considered. As Ken Kesey reminds us in his novel, *One Flew Over the Cuckoo's Nest* (1962), we must be wary of any form of "therapy" that may be just a disguise for suppressing dissent and making patients easier to manage.

Chemotherapy

The most dramatic change in hospitalized mental patients over the past twenty years is that they now rarely "run around like lunatics," exhibiting themselves, shouting obscenities, threatening, screaming, or showing extreme emotional displays. The reason is *chemotherapy*, the use of drugs in the treatment of mental and emotional disorders.

Tranquilizers

In 1955 there were about 560,000 patients in U.S. mental hospitals, most of whom required long-term custodial care. It was projected that in the next fifteen years this population would increase to over 750,000. The prediction was wrong. Less than half the projected number occupied state mental hospitals by 1971. Moreover, the average patient remained on the hospital ward about two months.

Bizarre schizophrenic symptoms seemed to vanish. "Incurable" patients were suddenly more receptive to psychotherapy. The diagnosis of schizophrenia was no longer seen as a "death sentence." This "revolution" in the treatment of hospitalized schizophrenics was brought about by two antischizophrenic drugs, *reserpine* and *chlorpromazine* (CPZ).

These drugs, though chemically different, have similar effects on particular aspects of brain functioning. Patients become calm and tranquil, but remain alert. Thus, psychotherapy becomes possible for the first time with many such patients.

Reserpine is the trade name for the drug *Rauwolfia*, extracted from the Indian snakeroot plant. Chlorpromazine is the name of the drug derived from the parent compound *phenothiazine*. Because reserpine has more undesirable side effects, such as lowering blood pressure, chlorpromazine is generally preferred. According to one of the foremost researchers on the effects of drugs on the brain, Seymour Kety of Massachusetts General Hospital, there is "general agreement that the introduction of the phenothiazine group of drugs in the treatment of schizophrenia has been the outstanding single contribution to psychiatry over the last twenty years" (in Swazey, 1974, p. xii). Curiously, the discovery of chlorpromazine did not come out of a master plan of research on the treatment of mental illness. Rather, it emerged from a strange accumulation of basic research findings in unrelated areas. (See *P&L* Close-up, CPZ.)

Antidepressant drugs

Depressed patients are frequently helped by *psychic energizers* such as *imipramine* and by a group of substances known as *monoamine oxidase inhibitors*. Two other drugs prescribed as antidepressants are *lithium* and *amphetamines*. Lithium therapy exerts a protective effect against recurring psychotic mood variations in manic-depressive disorders. One virtue of this drug is that it does not dull the senses as do many tranquilizers; therefore it does not interfere as much with creative work. Unlike all other psychoactive drugs lithium is not metabolized, it does not break down or bind to any blood or tissue proteins. This enables physicians to monitor the amount of this active agent in the brain by simple blood analyses. Thus, a patient's dosage may be systematically adjusted to achieve a particular therapeutic effect instead of using rigid fixed dosages. A review of research on its clinical effectiveness indicates seven or eight of every ten manic patients treated with lithium have a good chance of recovery—even where other treatments have failed (N.I.M.H., 1977).

Amphetamines have been prescribed in cases of mild neurotic depression because of their ability to induce euphoria, alertness, and increased muscular energy. Amphetamines, or "speed," have long been a key ingredient in diet pills due to their capacity to suppress hunger. Amphetamine abuse is a special problem because neurotically depressed people are the kind most likely to get "hooked" on the drug. Its psychiatric use in cases of depression is now questionable.

Curiously, one type of amphetamine, with the brand name of *Ritalin*, is used with children who are diagnosed as "hyperactive." Hyperactivity describes a syndrome of behaviors in children of normal intelligence, characterized as being easily distractable, unable to focus attention or to sit still in class or at home. The same drug that has an energizing effect in depressed adults appears to have the opposite effect in children (Kolata, 1978). Actually it does not calm them down, but rather decreases their distractability. By enabling them to concentrate better and prolonging their attention span, this amphetamine enables some hyperkinetic children to function more effectively. However, many critics question the use of drugs to modify the behavior of essentially normal children (see Rapoport et al., 1978). They point to the vague definition of the "disease," the learned dependence on drugs as the

CPZ: The Therapeutic Miracle of Drug Research

The development of chlorpromazine in the treatment of mental illness has followed a fascinating path. Students interested in how scientific ideas evolve, or in discovering the intellectual history of a major innovation in therapy, are encouraged to read Judith Swazey's account in *Chlorpromazine in Psychiatry* (MIT Press, 1974).

We also learn from the story of CPZ an important message of appreciation for the unforeseen practical effects of basic research. "None of the crucial findings or pathways that led, over the course of a century, to the ultimate discovery of chlorpromazine would at first have been called relevant to the treatment of mental illness even by the most sophisticated judge" (p. xii).

The synthesis of CPZ in 1950 from phenothiazine by French chemist Paul Charpentier marked the beginning of the modern era of psychopharmacology. But it also was the endpoint of a long series of investigations that had nothing at all to do with mental illness. The French chemist and his staff were searching for a drug that would act on the central nervous system to reduce the amount of anesthesia necessary in surgery. They were aware of the work of the French surgeon Henri Laborit who had discovered that the antihistamine promethiazine given before an operation reduces surgical shock. His patients seemed to be calm, relaxed, and rested. "Even after major operations," he reported, "they are never excited, not complaining and appear to really suffer less." Laborit had used antihistamines because of their anticipated effect of preventing the drop in blood pressure

that is a major symptom of surgical shock. However, that wasn't the effect. The drug was a tranquilizer. It is still used as an adjunct to surgical anesthesia.

The identification and synthesis of phenothiazine by a German chemist in 1883 was the result of an attempt to manufacture a new blue dye in the laboratory for industrial applications in the German dye industry. On the basis of decades of intervening research, an Italian pharmacologist discovered antihistamines in 1937. Histamines are released from body cells in allergic reactions and this new wonder drug was very effective in treating asthma and other allergic reactions. The basic formula of an antihistamine incorporated the phenothiazine structure. The rush by drug companies to develop more effective antihistamines led in 1945 to the introduction in the United States of promethiazine as the first major antihistamine derived from phenothiazine. At that point we rejoin Laborit and Charpentier's discoveries.

Once CPZ was seen to have psychiatric value in calming manic patients (in its first use in 1952), psychiatrists were ready to exploit its psychotropic effects. It fit into their medical model of an organic or biologic basis for mental illness which must be treated by physiologic or physiochemical means. Thus as Pasteur said "chance favors the prepared mind." The serendipitous (unexpected) discovery of CPZ as chemotherapy for mental illness involved many scientific disciplines in research labs in many countries over decades. But once its tranquilizing effect was noted, a new era of pharmacology emerged in a moment's time.

means to handle personal and social problems, and the failure of responsible adults to adjust the school and home environment to meet the needs of these hyperactive children. Ritalin therapy, they argue, only adjusts the child's brain to the established system making him (most are male) easier to manage (Bruck, 1976; Vonder Haar, 1975).

Some second thoughts about chemotherapy

The use of tranquilizing and energizing drugs has certainly played an important role in reducing the length of hospitalization of mental patients. Such drugs have decreased the incidence of the more extreme forms of maladaptive, bizarre behaviors previously associated with psychotic reactions. They have also made it possible for some types of patients previously "unreachable" to become amenable to psychotherapy. But there is no evidence of permanent "cure" via drugs; instead drug therapy has lubricated the "revolving door" phenomenon in mental hospitals. The higher discharge rate in mental hospitals is now being compensated for by an even higher return rate of formally "cured" patients.

These drugs do not "cure" in the usual sense of that term; they merely decrease the frequency of occurrence of certain behaviors that are undesirable and apparently unexplainable. Hospitalized mental patients are kept on *daily* medication for prolonged periods of years. When discharged, such patients must continue outpatient drug medication indefinitely, or risk a return of psychotic symptoms. Even when drug use is continued regularly after discharge from the hospital, the majority of psychotic outpatients seldom make more than a marginally successful adjustment to the community (Rickles, 1968).

Among the hazards of long-term chemotherapy are: (a) an overreliance on drug therapy in place of psychosocial and "human contact" therapies; (b) various physical side effects, including some visual impairments, spastic motor behavior, and facial tics; and (c) most serious of all, the development of a psychological dependence on drugs as a way to avoid developing adequate behavior patterns for coping with life's problems (Davison & Valins, 1969).

The medical model

Any physical therapy for psychopathology assumes a medical model of mental disorder (see pp. 561–562). One of the problems of using a medical model in describing and treating behavior disorders is that the "symptoms" of the "disease" are behavioral rather than physical; thus the changes, too, must be in behavioral terms. But descriptions of behavior are subject to bias by the observer. Many psychologists believe that the terms derived from the disease model *(sickness, cure, relapse,* even *patient)* are not really suitable terms for describing or understanding what they believe is primarily a behavioral-psychological process. As we have seen, some investigators totally reject the "myth of mental illness" (Szasz, 1961, 1965) as having brought more disadvantages with it than beneficial consequences. ◆ Meanwhile, others continue the search for more objective physical indicators both of psychopathology and of "cure" in consistent patterns of brain waves or chemical composition of the blood.

Clearly, drugs can change behavior and mental processes, both directly

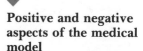

◆
Positive and negative aspects of the medical model

Positive Aspects	Negative Aspects
Development of physiological therapies	Stigma of "disease" label
	Deviance as "sickness"
More humane treatment of patients	Concept of "incurable"
	Treatment costly, limited availability
Money, facilities, legislative lobbies, and respectability, due to medical involvement	Lessened community involvement
	Psychiatry a medical discipline, nonbehavioral
	Long-term hospitalization, isolation from community
	Vested professional interests and status hierarchies
Intradisciplinary medical research	Emphasis on curing individual pathology, disregard of social pathology

and indirectly. To the extent that normal functioning depends on an intact brain and nervous system functioning smoothly, physical agents to restore or maintain such functioning will provide physical readiness for healthy adjustment. But to the extent that effective behavior depends on learning in a social setting, one can expect that relearning and social interaction will need to be part of therapy in order for new behavioral repertoires to be acquired. And to the extent that effective adjustment depends on a perception of one's own control over oneself and one's destiny, therapy must increase that perception; dependence on pills or other external physical agents is likely to work in the other direction.

The notion that mental illness is an entity, a form of neurological disease, does injustice to the subtle interplay of the underlying cognitive, social, and experiential processes.

Psychodynamic therapy

The psychodynamic view of psychopathology, like the biomedical one, locates the core of the disturbance inside the disturbed person. It accepts a general model of a disease core that shows up in symptoms. However, it emphasizes ongoing, intense psychological processes rather than physical imbalances. As we saw in previous discussions of Freudian theory, neurosis is viewed as the inability to resolve adequately the inner conflicts between the unconscious, irrational impulses of the *id* and the internalized social constraints imposed by the *superego*. According to this view, biology determines the sexual stages an individual progresses through from infancy to adulthood. It is the particular psychological experiences at each stage that determine whether there will be a fixation at an immature stage and a failure to progress to a more mature, healthy level of development. The goal of psychoanalysis is the establishment of intrapsychic harmony that expands one's awareness of the forces of the id, reduces overcompliance with superego demands, and strengthens the role of the ego.

Freudian psychoanalysis

Psychoanalytic therapy, as developed by Sigmund Freud, is an intensive and prolonged technique for exploring the patient's unconscious motivation. Special importance is attached to conflict and repression stemming from problems in the early stages of psychosexual development. Patients recover, according to the psychoanalytic view, when they are *released from repression* established in early childhood (Munroe, 1955). The aim of psychoanalysis then is to help the patient bring repressed memories into consciousness and to enable the patient to express strong repressed feelings. The technical word for this expression of affect during therapy is *abreaction*.

Psychoanalytic therapy is based upon Freudian views of the early life origins of pathology. The process by which such repressed conflicts are uncovered and resolved is typically slow and long, sometimes daily sessions continue for many years. The medium of therapy is the intellectual exchange of words and the release of feelings. Ultimately, the therapist's goal is to remove the presenting symptoms that brought the suffering neurotic into treatment by changing the individual's basic personality structure. Psychoanalysts use

Sigmund Freud's ideas were not always taken seriously by his contemporaries. This caricature shows Freud psychoanalyzing a figure of himself that is spouting Freudian imagery.

several techniques for bringing repressed conflicts to consciousness and helping the patient resolve them. These include free association, dream analysis, analysis of resistances, and analysis of transference. ●

Analysis of free associations

The principal procedure used in psychoanalysis to probe the unconscious and release repressed material is *free association*. The patient sits comfortably in a chair or lies in a relaxed position on a couch. His or her mind wanders freely, giving a running account of thoughts, wishes, physical sensations, and mental images as they occur. The patient is encouraged to reveal every thought or feeling, regardless of how personal, painful, or seemingly unimportant.

Freud maintained that free associations are not random but predetermined. The task of the analyst is to track the associations to their source and to identify what is beneath the surface in the psychoanalytic "iceberg" (see p. 481).

Analysis of resistances

During the process of free association, the patient may show *resistances*—that is, inability or unwillingness to discuss certain ideas, desires, or experiences. Resistances prevent the return to consciousness of repressed material that is painful to recall. This material is often connected with the individual's sexual life or with hostile, resentful feelings toward parents. Sometimes a resistance is shown by the patient's coming late to therapy or "forgetting" it altogether. When such material is finally brought into the open, the patient generally claims that it is either too unimportant, too absurd, too irrelevant, or too unpleasant to be discussed.

The psychoanalyst of the Freudian school attaches particular importance to subjects that the patient does *not* wish to discuss. Such resistances are conceived of as *barriers* between the unconscious and the conscious. The aim of psychoanalysis is to break down resistances and bring the patient to face these painful ideas, desires, and experiences. Breaking down resistances is a long and difficult process but is considered essential in order to bring the whole problem into consciousness where it can be solved.

Analysis of dreams

Psychoanalysts believe that dreams are an important source of information about the patient's unconscious motivation. When a person is asleep, the ego is presumably less on guard against the unacceptable impulses originating in the id, so that a motive that cannot be expressed in waking life may find expression in a dream.

Some motives are so unacceptable to the conscious self, that they cannot be revealed openly even in dreams but must be expressed in disguised or symbolic form. Thus, as we saw in Chapter 15, a dream has two kinds of content. The *manifest* (openly visible) content of the dream is that which we remember and report upon awakening. Beneath the manifest content is the *latent* (hidden) content—the actual motives that are seeking expression but that are so painful or unacceptable to us that we do not want to recognize their existence. The therapist attempts to uncover these hidden motives by studying the symbols that appear in the manifest content of the dream. For example, a male student who is filled with anxiety about failing an examination and being expelled from school may dream that he is pushing his way through a heavy snowstorm, pursued by wild animals.

Analysis of transference

During the course of psychoanalytic treatment, the patient usually develops an emotional reaction toward the therapist. The therapist may be identified with a person who has been at the center of an emotional conflict in the past. This emotional association between patient and therapist is called *transference*. In most cases, the analyst is identified with a parent or a lover. The transference is called *positive transference* when the feelings attached to the therapist are those of love or admiration. *Negative transference* occurs when these feelings consist of hostility or envy. Often the patient's attitude is *ambivalent*, including a mixture of positive and negative feelings.

The analyst's task in handling the transference is a difficult and dangerous one because of the patient's emotional vulnerability. However, it is a crucial part of treatment. The therapist helps the patient to interpret the present transferred feelings by understanding their original source in earlier experiences and attitudes.

However, it must be remembered that the therapist is not a perfectly programmed, objective analyzer of patient input. Despite attempts to maintain an emotional detachment, he or she may still react to the patient's problems in a personal way. In the intense relationship that develops over the prolonged personal therapeutic contact, it is difficult for the analyst to avoid personal reactions. Thus, *countertransference* may also develop during the period of analysis. In countertransference the therapist comes to like or dislike the patient at a personal level because of perceived similarity of the patient to significant others in the therapist's life. In working through this countertransference therapists may discover some unconscious dynamics of their own. Failure to recognize the operation of countertransference interferes with the effectiveness of therapy.

Neo-Freudian approaches

The differences between orthodox psychoanalysts and neo-Freudians is more a difference in emphasis than in basic ideology. In therapeutic practice the differences are even less striking, since, as was noted earlier, most therapists have pragmatic goals of helping particular patients rather than proving particular theories. In general, neo-Freudians place *more* emphasis than Freud did on: (a) the patient's *current* social environment (less on the past); (b) the continuing influence of life experiences in later development (not just infancy and childhood); (c) the role of interpersonal interaction (less on biological demands); (d) the significance of ego functioning and self-concept (less on id-superego conflicts).

Neo-Freudian therapists place *less* emphasis on unconscious processes and the place of sex and aggression as determinants of pathology. But their therapeutic practice still relies on intensive "talking therapy" designed to uncover personality dynamics that shape the neurotic behavior patterns of the patient.

Behavioristic therapy

To change behavior, change its consequences. This basic conception is at the core of behavior therapy. Pathology is not treated by behaviorists as a disease of the nervous system nor the manifestation of repressed conflicts. Functional mental illness is nothing more in this view than self-defeating habits, self-destructive behavior patterns, and learned life-styles that are nonproductive and undesirable. These forms of *behavior pathology* are changed by discovering and then modifying existing stimulus conditions that maintain (reinforce) such behavior.

We saw in earlier chapters that behaviorism represents a view that is pragmatic, empirical, and grounded in research. Inferred concepts such as the unconscious are rejected because they are not amenable to empirical verification. The central task of all living organisms is seen as *learning* how to adapt to their current environment. When organisms have not learned how to cope effectively with the demands of their social and physical environment, their maladaptive reactions, it is believed, can be overcome by therapy based on principles of learning (or relearning). The unique aspect of this treatment is thus that it is directed toward a modification of *behavior*, rather than of something within the individual.

Behavior modification is defined as "*the attempt to apply learning and other experimentally derived psychological principles to problem behavior*" (Bootzin, 1975). The terms *behavior therapy* and *behavior modification* are often used interchangeably. Both refer to the systematic use of principles of learning to increase the frequency of desirable behaviors and/or decrease that of problem behaviors. The range of deviant behaviors and personal problems that are treated by behavior therapy is extensive, including various types of mental illness, fears, compulsions, addictions, aggression, and delinquent behaviors. Watson showed us that phobias could be learned through the process of emotional conditioning. Recall also that Mary Cover Jones (1924) showed how the same fears in a child could be unlearned by using principles of counterconditioning (see pp. 243–244). Behavior therapy uses learning principles to build effective skills and response patterns while breaking down ineffective, problematic ones.

Before we examine the therapeutic tactics of "behavior mod," an important question must be resolved. If a problem behavior—a symptom—is cured won't the underlying conflict remain to produce a new symptom? This threat of "*symptom substitution*" made by traditional therapists assumes that problem behaviors flow from a deep-seated disease process. The available evidence consistently shows that there is *no* support for the symptom substitution hypothesis. "On the contrary, patients whose target symptoms improved often reported improvement in other, less important symptoms as well" (Sloane et al., 1975, p. 219; see also Montgomery & Crowder, 1972).

In examining strategies of behavior modification, we will make use of the distinction between operant conditioning and classical conditioning. In operant conditioning response patterns are changed by their learned association with reinforcing consequences. What changes in classical conditioning is the stimulus value of a particular (neutral) stimulus. The production of desirable behaviors and skills usually follows operant conditioning principles of contingency management. Changing neurotic fears and undesired emotional reactions follows classical conditioning principles of counterconditioning and extinction.

Contingency management

Find the contingency that will maintain a desired response, apply it, evaluate its effectiveness. This is the basic approach of changing behavior by controlling its consequences. The application of positive reinforcement of desired responses according to systematic schedules has been successfully applied in the classroom, in penal and mental institutions, and in many other settings. Even patients who have been totally mute for many years but are physically capable of speech have been trained to speak by the use of operant techniques (Sherman, 1963).

Dramatic success has also been obtained in the application of operant conditioning procedures to the behavior problems of children with psychiatric disorders. The following is one such case.

The patient was a three-year-old boy who was hospitalized with a diagnosis of childhood schizophrenia. He lacked normal social and verbal behavior and was given to ungovernable tantrums and self-destructive behavior. He had had a cataract operation, but refused to wear the glasses that were essential for the development of normal vision.

To counteract this problem, the psychologists decided to use the technique of shaping. First the child was trained to expect a bit of candy or fruit at the clicking sound of a toy noisemaker. The sound soon became a conditioned reinforcer. Then training began with empty eyeglass frames. The child was reinforced first for picking them up, then for holding them, then for carrying them around. Slowly and by successive approximation, he was reinforced for bringing the frames closer to his eyes. After a few weeks, he was putting the empty frames on his head at odd angles, and finally he was wearing them in the proper manner. With further training the child learned to wear his glasses up to twelve hours a day (Wolf, Risley, & Mees, 1964).

Imitation of models

Positive reinforcement alone can be quite satisfactory for strengthening behavior that already occurs some of the time, but it can be a long and tedious technique when new behaviors are to be learned. New responses, especially complex ones, can be acquired more easily if the person can observe and imitate a model. Imitation is often used in combination with positive reinforcement.

In one program, schizophrenic children were first treated for muteness by a variety of techniques, including reinforcement for imitation. First, the children were rewarded simply for making sounds. Later they were rewarded for vocalization only when the sound was similar to a "model" sound made by the therapist. When the children had

The first photo shows an early imitation session with Billy, who at seven could not talk at all and was subject to violent tantrums and self-destructive behavior. In the second photo, Billy and another boy receive immediate food reinforcement of social interaction.

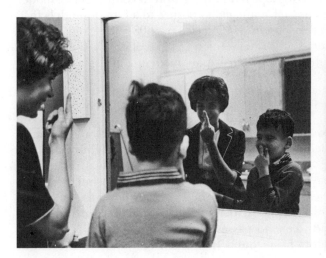

learned to imitate sounds, rewards were given for duplicating words spoken by the therapist. By building on the children's growing repertoire of vocal behaviors, and their growing readiness to imitate, more intricate communicative and social behaviors were eventually established (Lovaas, 1968). ■

Such a therapeutic approach requires considerable patience and diligence on the part of the therapist. One of the autistic children with whom Ivar Lovaas worked required 90,000 trials before he could reliably label two objects.

In the treatment of phobias (such as the fear of snakes) the therapist will first demonstrate fearless approach behavior at a relatively minor level, such as approaching the snake's cage or touching the snake. The client is then aided, through demonstration and supportive encouragement, to model the therapist's behavior. Gradually the approach behaviors are shaped to the point where the client can pick the snake up and let it crawl freely over him or her. ● At no time is the client forced to perform any behavior, and, if a re-

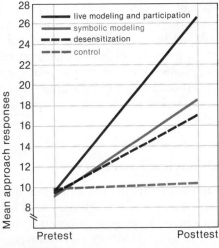

Adapted from Bandura, 1970

● *The subject shown in the photo first watched a model make a graduated series of snake-approach responses, then repeated them herself. She eventually was able to pick up the snake and let it crawl about on her. The graph shows a variety of approach responses in participant modeling and in other conditions.*

quest is met with overt resistance, the therapist returns to the previously successful approach behavior and starts over again. The remarkable power of this form of participant modeling can be seen in the research of Albert Bandura and his colleagues (1970) depicted in the graph. It compares live modeling with symbolic modeling (self-managed exposure to a film of models fearlessly handling a large snake), desensitization (see pp. 608–609), and a control (without any form of therapeutic intervention). Snake phobia was eliminated in eleven of the twelve subjects in the participant modeling group.

Token economies

When desirable behaviors are followed with immediate, tangible rewards, they become more frequent. In a *token economy*, patients are tangibly rewarded for socially constructive activities such as maintaining personal cleanliness, arriving on time for meals, and performing assigned tasks. Payment consists of tokens (such as poker chips) that may be used later to "purchase" such luxuries as more elegant dining facilities, increased television time, private sleeping accommodations, and weekend passes.

Hospital administrators have found that token economies can often be quite effective in eliciting desired behaviors, even on the part of rather severely disturbed patients. It usually is necessary to start gradually, however. Thus patients may initially be rewarded for merely approaching nurses or other patients. Then, through a process of shaping, it may be possible to coax them to strike up conversations. Finally, they can be rewarded for more complex forms of interpersonal interaction as well as for other activities.

From the learner's point of view, token economies have the value of: (a) providing an unambiguous indication of approval, (b) introducing consistency and predictability into the situation by making clear exactly what must be done to achieve what effect, (c) not being dependent on the mood or personal values of the contingency manager, (d) allowing the learner to have complete freedom in determining what he or she is willing to work for (among the options available), and (e) guaranteeing that even minimally appropriate responses will be observed, acknowledged, and reinforced.

Critics, however, shudder at the thought of a system based on the profit motive in therapeutic, rehabilitative, and educational settings. They argue that this extrinsic reinforcement changes behavior but perhaps at the cost of the person's intrinsic motivation to want to continue to engage in the task for its own sake. More serious criticism is that token economies rely on a prior state of *deprivation* in order to exert their positive reinforcing effect. It works only when people have no independent means of obtaining what the token will purchase. As used in prisons, token economies and behavior modification often have the objectionable feature of starting prisoners at the maximum deprivation level. They must work and exhibit desirable (from the staff's viewpoint) behaviors in order to get tokens exchangeable for such "privileges" as showers, hot meals, a decent bed, or the opportunity to exercise (see Holden, 1978).

Behavioral contracts

One way to involve the individual more directly in his or her own contingency management is through the use of behavioral contracts. A *behavioral contract* is an explicit agreement (often in writing) that states what consequences will follow what behaviors. Such contracts are often required by behavior therapists working with patients on obesity or smoking problems. The contract may specify what the patient is expected to do (patient's obligations) and what in turn the patient can expect from the therapist (therapist's obligations). Patients may be asked to put down a sum of money as a deposit, which is returned in part for each therapy session attended or therapeutic goal reached. Therapists may indicate in advance the expected duration of treatment and specific criteria for terminating treatment—as "success" or "other."

The elements of a good behavioral contract are:

a. explicitness as to benefits and privileges to be gained through specific performances,
b. specified consequences for failure to meet terms of contract,
c. bonuses for compliance with contract terms,
d. monitoring of contracted activities,
e. record-keeping of benefits earned,
f. voluntary participation of both parties in specifying contract terms,
g. right to third-party arbitration in instances of alleged contract violation (see Stuart, 1971).

Generalization techniques

Are behaviors modified by token reinforcements or other forms of contingency management still practiced when the person leaves the therapeutic setting? This question of the generalizability of treatment effectiveness from therapy to real life is important for all therapeutic approaches. The "cure" must go beyond the couch, the hospital, or the laboratory to where the person lives.

Most research indicates that unless the responses are also reinforced in the new setting, the therapeutically modified behavior will deteriorate. To counteract this effect, generalization techniques must be part of the treatment program (see Kazdin & Bootzin, 1972). Such techniques all have in common attempts to *increase the similarity* of target behaviors, reinforcers, and stimulus demands between the therapeutic and real-life setting. Thus behaviors are taught which are likely to be reinforced naturally in the person's environment (e.g., politeness or acting with consideration for others). Dependence on token reinforcement is *faded out* gradually, while social approval and other more naturally occurring consequences are introduced. Opportunities are also provided to practice new behaviors under the guidance of a staff member on "field trips" away from the institution. Halfway houses also help transfer programs from hospital and prison settings to the community setting (Fairweather, Sanders, Maynard, & Cressler, 1969).

Extinction and counterconditioning

Elimination of an unwanted behavior occurs if it can be put on an extinction schedule by removing its reinforcing consequences. To weaken the association between a patient's responses of anxiety to particular environmental cues, counterconditioning strategies are used.

Extinction strategies

Why do people continue to do something that causes pain and distress when they are capable of doing otherwise? Many forms of behavior (or symptoms) have multiple consequences—some negative, some positive. Often subtle positive reinforcements keep the behavior going despite its obvious negative consequences. This is often found in cases of stuttering, where the inordinate tension, embarrassment, and inconvenience generated by stuttering are counterbalanced, in part, by the attention, sympathy, and ready excuses for failure or rejection that stuttering provides.

Unintentional reinforcement has been found to maintain and encourage psychotic behavior. It is standard procedure in many mental hospitals for the staff to ask patients frequently how they are feeling. This may suggest to the patients that the "appropriate" behavior is to be thinking and talking about one's feelings, unusual symptoms, hallucinations, and so on. In fact, the more bizarre the symptoms and verbalizations, the more attention may be shown by the staff in their efforts to understand the "dynamics" of the case (Ayllon & Michael, 1959). When I asked a hospitalized patient if there was "anything else that was bothering him," he responded, "You mean *halicinations* or *sublimitions*?" He had learned how to talk about those experiences to which the staff paid attention. Dramatic decreases in psychotic behavior have been observed when the staff was simply instructed to ignore the psychotic behavior and to attend to the patients only when they were behaving normally (Ayllon & Michael, 1959).

In addition to simply withholding reinforcement for undesirable behaviors, it is sometimes necessary to force the patient to face the anxiety-arousing stimulus. If neurotic behavior is the conditioned avoidance of anxiety-arousing stimuli, neither the anxiety nor the behavior will ever extinguish if the person is allowed to deny, avoid, or escape it (Stampfl & Levis, 1967).

In order to extinguish an irrational fear most effectively, it may be necessary for the client to experience a full-blown anxiety reaction without suffering any harm. The therapeutic situation is arranged so that the frightening stimulus occurs in circumstances where the client cannot run away. The therapist describes an extremely frightening situation relating to the client's fear and urges the client to imagine being in it, experiencing it through all the senses as intensely as possible. In this way the client is *flooded* with rapid exposure to anxiety-eliciting sensations.

Such imagining is assumed to cause an explosion of panic. Since this explosion is an inner one, it is called an *implosion*; hence the term *implosive therapy*. As this happens again and again and no harm is forthcoming, the stimulus loses its power to elicit anxiety. When anxiety no longer occurs, the neurotic behavior employed to avoid it disappears. In other words, extinction occurs.

Systematic desensitization

It is difficult to be both happy and sad, or relaxed and anxious, at the same time. This principle is applied in therapy in the *reciprocal inhibition* technique developed primarily by Joseph Wolpe (1958, 1973). One type of reciprocal inhibition is *systematic desensitization*. Since anxiety is assumed to be a major cause of inability to approach positive goals and of fixation on negative ones, the client is taught to prevent anxiety arousal by relaxing.

Desensitization therapy involves three major steps. It begins by identifying the stimuli that provoke anxiety in the client and arranging them in a *hierarchy* ranked from weakest to strongest. For example, a student suffering from severe test anxiety constructed the following hierarchy. Note that she rated immediate anticipation of the examination as more stressful than taking the exam itself. ▲ Next, the client is trained in a system of progressive deep-muscle relaxation. Relaxation training requires several sessions; hypnosis or

Hierarchy of anxiety-producing stimuli

1. On the way to the university on the day of an examination.
2. In the process of answering an examination paper.
3. Before the unopened doors of the examination room.
4. Awaiting the distribution of examination papers.
5. The examination paper lies face down before her.
6. The night before an examination.
7. One day before an examination.
8. Two days before an examination.
9. Three days before an examination.
10. Four days before an examination.
11. Five days before an examination.
12. A week before an examination.
13. Two weeks before an examination.
14. A month before an examination.

Adapted from Wolpe, 1973

drugs may be used to help tense clients learn to achieve complete relaxation (pp. 548–549). Finally, the actual process of desensitization begins. The client, in a relaxed state, is told to imagine as vividly as possible the *weakest* anxiety stimulus on the list (opposite to the implosion strategy). If anxiety reactions occur, the client stops and concentrates on relaxation again. When the weakest stimulus can be visualized without discomfort, the client goes on to the next stronger one. After a number of sessions, the most distressing situations on the list can be imagined without anxiety—even the one that could not be faced originally. Great care is taken not to arouse anxiety during this process of gradually approaching the "unthinkable" stimulus. If anxiety is evoked, the therapist terminates the imagery production and relaxes the client, and they begin again with a weaker stimulus.

As in other conditioning, once anxiety is extinguished to a particular scene due to the pairing of that stimulus with relaxation, there is a *generalization* of this inhibition to related stimuli, including those next stronger in the hierarchy. Thus desensitization works both directly, by reducing anxiety to a particular stimulus through relaxation, and indirectly, through generalization of anxiety reduction to similar stimuli. Desensitization is ideally suited for treatment of specific phobic reactions that are maintained by the relief experienced when the anxiety-producing stimuli are avoided or escaped. It has been successfully applied to a diversity of human problems, including such generalized fears as test anxiety, stage fright, impotence, frigidity, and a variety of phobias (Paul, 1969).

Aversive learning

Some behaviors are followed by positive immediate pleasure, but long-term negative consequences. Most addictive reactions fit this description. In order to modify the "temptation value" of stimuli that elicit deviant desires and behaviors, counterconditioning procedures are employed. Stimuli that have come to arouse unwanted responses (such as alcoholic drinks) are paired with noxious stimuli such as electric shocks or nausea-producing drugs.

One problem with the clinical use of aversive therapy is getting the person to submit to it willingly (and even to pay to be tormented). Aversive therapy is not designed to encourage a person to endure it freely or come back for more. Especially if the positive, immediate gains of the "bad habit" are strong, the motivation to receive aversive stimulation will not be strong unless the person is impressed with long-term negative consequences of engaging in the undesirable behavior. Such "impression" involves education, indoctrination, and sometimes mass propaganda. It is also counteracted by those segments of society that depend for economic survival on the "bad habit" — liquor, tobacco, gambling industries, among others.

Rehearsal: Cognitive and behavioral

In addition to counterconditioning of fears and problem behaviors by desensitization and aversive learning, it is possible to do so more directly and less painfully. One way is through the use of models (often the therapist) who verbalize reassuring statements to themselves while engaging in an activity the client fears or a habit the client wants to break. We have seen in earlier chapters that Meichenbaum (1977) advocates a strategy of teaching clients how to make self-statements (see p. 553). Cognitive rehearsal of the setting in which self-defeating statements are usually made coupled with practice in making successful coping statements is effective in building cognitive and behavioral skills.

Building *expectations of being effective* increases the likelihood of behaving effectively. Setting attainable goals with realistic strategies for attaining them and monitoring feedback from performance is the way people develop a sense of mastery and *self-efficacy* (Bandura, 1977b).

Social learning therapists advocate behavior rehearsal to build new social skills as well as to overcome problem behaviors. Indeed, one of the major therapeutic innovations in this decade is *social-skills training* (Hersen & Bellock, 1976). Many problems arise for the psychotic, the neurotic, and even the troubled normal person simply because they are socially inhibited, inept, or unassertive. *Behavior rehearsal* is a procedure for establishing and strengthening basic skills (personal hygiene, work habits, social skills) through modeling, explicit instruction, behavioral contracting, and repeated practice. Social skills training has been used to modify abusive verbal outbursts in psychiatric patients (Foy, Eisler, Pinkston, 1975; Frederiksen, Jenkins, Foy, & Eisler, 1976). Patients were taught to handle interpersonal disagreements not by their usual strategies of avoidance, intimidation, or violence, but by learning to make appropriately assertive responses in those situations.

Common to much social-skills learning is the production of more effectively *assertive* behavior. Andrew Salter (1949) pioneered procedures for assertiveness training in normals (as well as patient populations). Rules for assertion involve: clearly describing verbally what the disagreement or problem is as you see it; expressing how you feel about it in emotional terms (but not getting overemotional); specifying desirable behavioral alternatives and options for yourself and the other party; and proposing positive consequences for agreement with a satisfactory alternative (see Bower & Bower, 1976).

Existential-humanistic therapy

Among the primary presenting symptoms that bring students for therapy in college student health centers across the country are general dissatisfaction, feelings of alienation, and failure to achieve one's ego ideals. Problems in everyday living, the lack of meaningful human relationships, and the absence of significant goals to strive for have become part of the "existential crises" of our times. Humanism and existentialism have emerged as new orientations toward a therapy that addresses itself to such contemporary needs.

The term *existentialism* comes from the Latin *existere* — "to merge or stand out" — which fully describes the focus on the *existing* human being as he or she is emerging or becoming. Existentialism is an attempt to understand our unique position in the universe: feelings of love, hate, anguish; self-awareness; and the knowledge of one's own imminent death. We have seen in the previous chapter and earlier (in Chapter 1) that the humanistic movement grew out of a reaction to the pessimistic view of human nature afforded by psychoanalytic determinism and the mechanistic view taken by early radical behaviorists.

One important factor that unites humanism and existentialism is the insistence that all human knowledge is based on experience. Both stress the importance of an openness and readiness to accept the data of experience as they merge. The observer attempts to put aside all preconceived notions concerning a person or event and all judgments of value.

At the core of both humanistic and existential therapies is the concept of the whole person in the continual process of changing and of becoming. Although environment and heredity place certain restrictions on the process of becoming, we remain always free to choose what we will become by creating our own values and committing ourselves to them through our decisions. However, along with this freedom to choose comes the burden of responsibility. Since we are never fully aware of all the implications of our actions, we experience anxiety and despair. We also suffer from guilt over lost opportunities to achieve our full potential.

The humanistic and existential approaches to therapy are alike in many respects. Both view human beings as the source of values and focus in their potential for self-actualization. Both stress the concepts of responsibility, freedom, and commitment. There are several points of disagreement, however. In accordance with the flavor of the American outlook, humanistic psychology is much more optimistic and positive than European existentialism. We are seen as not only responsible for actualizing our potential, but as having a positive drive and need to do so. The humanistic view also places heavy emphasis on the value, dignity, and worth of the individual with a correlated focus on positive aspects of human behavior such as love, joy, creativity, friendship, play, fun, ecstasy, and so forth. ◆

◆
Humanistic and existential therapies stress the uniqueness of the individual and his or her potential for growth. Therapists in this tradition seek to help their clients accept responsibility for their own behavior and recognize the choices they make.

As we turn to the therapeutic application of existentialism and humanism, we find considerable diversification in method and style. Existentialism is not a technique, theory, or systematic explanation of human behavior, but rather an attitude one maintains toward oneself and others. Thus we may find therapists trained in psychoanalysis calling themselves existential psychotherapists because they share that basic attitude and value orientation.

Existential psychotherapy

The existential movement in psychiatry was formed by a number of Europeans who were dissatisfied with orthodox psychoanalysis. Realizing that the most common problem of a modern individual was a feeling of alienation from the world, a loss of the sense of identity or belonging, these psychiatrists and psychologists felt that psychoanalysis often tended to increase the problem by fragmenting the individual still further. For them, the basic reality was the individual's current experience.

One school of existential analysis, called *logotherapy*, focuses on the need to see meaning in one's own life. The "will-to-meaning" is regarded as the most human phenomenon of all. This school emphasizes Nietzche's statement, "He who knows a Why of living surmounts almost every How." The human being finds the "Why" through self-realization, which involves both freedom to choose a course of action and responsibility to choose in such a way as to further spiritual values. Thus logotherapy lays particular stress on the development of spiritual and ethical values (Weisskopf-Joelson, 1955).

Logotherapy is the only school of existential psychiatry to have evolved specific psychotherapeutic techniques. One such technique, called *paradoxical intention*, is found useful in the short-term treatment of obsessive-compulsive and phobic patients. Viktor Frankl, originator of logotherapy, speaks of the vicious circle in which the phobic person is caught. It is not so much the feared object or occurrence that concerns the patient, but the *fear of fear itself* and the potential effects of such fear, such as fainting or heart attack. Frankl (1959) calls such phobic reactions a "flight from fear" and sees the patient as reacting to "the fearful expectation of the recurrence of the event." This expectation, however, triggers off exactly what the patient fears will happen: a phobic reaction. Paradoxical intention is a technique for dealing with this anticipatory anxiety by encouraging the patient "to do, or wish to happen, the very thing he fears." There is an obvious similarity between this technique and implosive therapy discussed previously. Here, however, we find the chief responsibility for applying the technique rests with the patient rather than the therapist. Furthermore, paradoxical intention is deliberately formulated in as humorous a manner as possible, since humor involves self-detachment.

It is not felt that paradoxical intention or even logotherapy itself is applicable to all individuals seeking therapy, nor is it believed that any such techniques will have long-lasting effects unless the individual also establishes a commitment to purposeful goals.

Humanistic psychotherapy

One of the clearest and earliest examples of a humanistic approach to treatment is *client-centered therapy*, developed originally by Carl Rogers in the 1940s. This nondirective therapy is based on the premise that individuals who are sufficiently motivated can work through their own problem if they can become free enough from self-deception and fear to recognize their problem for what it is. Accordingly, the therapist neither praises nor blames but accepts whatever is said, perhaps rephrasing it or helping clients to clarify their own reactions, paying specific attention to both the overt feelings expressed and the covert ones being experienced.

Therapy is regarded as a "growth process" in which clients utilize their own potentialities to achieve a more mature level of emotional adjustment. From the beginning, they are responsible for their own behavior and decisions, as well as for the course of therapy. The idea that "the doctor knows best" is unheard of in this form of therapy. Superficially the role of the therapist is that of "reflecting" the feelings the client has expressed. Actually, however, the therapist's attitude of acceptance and concern is probably of greatest significance, for it helps the client develop the self-confidence and strength to handle difficult problems of adjustment.

An important aspect of client-centered therapy has been the willingness to submit its techniques to investigation and to modify the approach in light of such experience. In fact, Rogers was the first clinician to tape-record his sessions, which led to the first meaningful analysis of the process of therapy (Meader & Rogers, 1973).

The general perspective behind the existential-humanistic approach to therapy has produced the human potential movement. Therapy for growth, personal enrichment, increased interpersonal sensitivity, for greater joy in sex, love, and living is the offspring of the union of existential and humanistic views of human nature. Many of the new breed of therapies, Gestalt therapy, family and couples therapy, est, and others, find their intellectual origin in those views. Of special significance for treatment is the effect of the humanistic-existential orientation on the development of personal growth groups, which we discussed in Chapter 18.

Comparisons, evaluation, and alternatives

You now should have a general familiarity with the four major approaches to the treatment of mental illness, behavioral pathology, and removal of barriers to the fuller realization of the human potential. There are a great many other therapies which do not fit neatly into one of these categories but straddle them or present yet other approaches, notably Albert Ellis' rational-emotive therapy (1962), Victor Raimy's cognitive misconception therapy (1975), and Arnold Lazarus' multimodal behavior therapy (1976). You can discover more about them on your own or through advanced courses in personality theory or abnormal behavior.

In this final section, we will be able to only briefly address ourselves to three broad issues in treatment. First we will make some comparisons across the different therapeutic approaches. Next we have to face the fundamental question of evaluation: does therapy work? Finally, let's consider major alternatives to the therapeutic approaches we've examined: institutional care and community care, as well as non-European, or Anglo-American therapies.

One of the best summaries of the positions taken by psychoanalytic, behavioral, and existential-humanistic psychologists on the key premises, issues, and therapeutic strategies is provided by Sheldon Korchin (1976). ∎

Comparison of psychoanalytic, behavioral, and humanistic-existential approaches to psychotherapy

Issue	Psychoanalysis	Behavior Therapy	Humanistic-Existential Therapy
Basic Human Nature	Biological instincts, primarily sexual and aggressive, press for immediate release, bringing people into conflict with social reality.	Like other animals, people are born only with the capacity for learning, which develops in terms of the same principles in all species.	People have free will, choice, and purpose; the capacity for self-determination and self-actualization.
Normal Human Development	Growth occurs through resolution of conflicts during successive stages. Through identification and internalization, mature ego controls and character structures emerge.	Adaptive behaviors are learned through reinforcement and imitation.	A unique self-system develops from birth on. The individual develops personally characteristic modes of perceiving, feeling, etc.
Nature of Psychopathology	Pathology reflects inadequate conflict resolutions and fixations in earlier development, which leave overly strong impulses and/or weak controls. Symptoms are defensive responses to anxiety.	Symptomatic behavior derives from faulty learning of maladaptive behaviors. The symptom *is* the problem, there is no "underlying disease."	Incongruence exists between the depreciated self and the potential, desired self. The person is overly dependent on others for gratification and self-esteem. There is a sense of purposelessness and meaninglessness.
Goal of Therapy	Attainment of psychosexual maturity, strengthened ego functions, reduced control by unconscious and repressed impulses.	Relieving symptomatic behavior by suppressing or replacing maladaptive behaviors.	Fostering self-determination. authenticity, and integration by releasing human potential and expanding awareness.
Psychological Realm Emphasized	Motives and feelings, fantasies and cognitions.	Behavior and observable feelings and actions.	Perceptions, meanings, values.
Time Orientation	Oriented to discovering and interpreting past conflicts and repressed feelings, to examine them in light of the present.	Little or no concern with early history or etiology. Present behavior is examined and treated.	Focus on present phenomenal experience; the here-and-now.
Role of Unconscious Material	Primary in classical psychoanalysis, somewhat less emphasized by neo-Freudians.	No concern with unconscious processes or with subjective experience even in conscious realm.	Though recognized by some, emphasis is on conscious experience.
Role of Insight	Central; emerges in "corrective emotional experiences."	Irrelevant and/or unnecessary.	More emphasis on "how" and "what" rather than "why."
Role of Therapist	A *detective*, searching out root conflicts and resistances; detached, neutral, and nondirective, to facilitate transference reactions.	A *trainer*, helping patient unlearn old behaviors and/or learn new ones. Control of reinforcement is important; interpersonal relation is minor.	An *authentic person* in true encounter with patient, sharing experience. Facilitates patient's growth potential. Transference discounted or minimized.

Adapted from Korchin, 1976

Making the madness fit the therapy

The therapist's theoretical perspective influences his or her basic perception of the "problem" — "mental illness," "emotional conflict," "inappropriate reinforcement contingencies," or "self-alienation." Each therapist is thus *set* to interpret a given behavioral event in terms that are consistent or harmonious with the guiding assumptions of a particular theoretical framework — while ignoring the alternatives. Thus, different therapists treat the *same* manifest problem according to their different *perceptions* of its origins.

Patients, then, must make a tacit contract with the particular therapist of their choice to be "sick" in a way the therapist can treat. It is not unreasonable to suggest that the first task of the patient is learning to play the correct role in the therapist's scenario. This requires learning to use the special language of the therapist to describe symptoms and past events. It may also involve a kind of conversion to the therapist's belief system, enabling the patient to notice and label as "significant" and "relevant" the same events and variables the therapist does.

The psychoanalyst's patient thereby becomes a "historian," discovering historical precedents, and the historical continuity that links present ills to their past origins. The behaviorist's client becomes sensitized to the future environmental consequences of current behavioral responses and to attaching an S to every R and an R to every S. The self-actualized patient emerges from existential-humanistic therapy focusing on the present, on the here and now of existing, being, and becoming, while talking about "sharing, meaning, choice, and freedom." Finally, the person treated by the biomedically oriented therapist comes away from "successful" treatment with the attitude that "doctor knows best," and with little feeling of responsibility for the "problem" or its alleviation.

Does psychotherapy work?

Now that you have some idea of what goes into different forms of psychotherapy, it is reasonable to inquire about what comes out. Does psychotherapy work? Are some therapies more effective than others? Since psychotherapy is the *application* of ideas about mental illness and the determinants of behavior disorders, our concern now is a practical one. It does not matter which theory of therapy is more intellectually stimulating. What matters is the utility of a given set of therapeutic procedures to accomplish certain specific goals.

This concern reduces to: (a) specifying those goals and subgoals; (b) determining the extent to which the goals have been realized; (c) accounting for the time and real costs required to achieve those results; (d) estimating the extent to which even the most effective therapeutic resources are actually utilized by the general population of people "in need" or "at risk."

Therapeutic goals

Interventions by different therapists are based on the expectation of accomplishing one or more of the following goals or purposes (Sundberg & Tyler, 1962):

a. strengthening the patient's motivation to do the right thing,
b. reducing emotional pressure by facilitating the expression of feeling,
c. changing habits,
d. releasing the potential for growth,

e. modifying the person's cognitive structure,

f. gaining self-knowledge,

g. facilitating interpersonal relations and communication.

But each of these goals covers a lot of ground and must be translated into more concrete subgoals. For example, a therapeutic subgoal might be to change the specific habit of making obscene phone calls. One advantage of behavioral approaches is an emphasis on accountability for attainment of limited goals agreed upon in advance by therapist and client. The broader and more vaguely stated the goal of therapy, the more difficult it becomes to collect the kind of evidence necessary for assessing therapeutic effectiveness. By establishing in a therapeutic contract explicit, specific goals, that can be evaluated within a given time period, therapists and clients can determine the value of their therapeutic experience.

Therapeutic effectiveness

British psychologist Hans Eysenck created a furor some years ago (1952) by reporting that persons receiving no therapy still had a higher cure rate than did those receiving either psychoanalysis or other forms of insight therapy. A later study (not open to some of the criticisms leveled at Eysenck's research) shows that conclusion to be a bit too extreme—but not far from the truth. It was found that untreated subjects improved almost as much as those who received psychotherapy (Bergin, 1971). Across seven studies that compared changes in untreated subjects with those given psychotherapy, the *average* amount of change was the same. However, the *variability* in outcome was greater among those who had received treatment: some got much better, while others got worse or did not change. Those people who improved considerably with therapy might not have done so without it, so for them psychotherapy deserves credit for their "cure." For others, the mere passage of time was sufficient to "heal all wounds."

Richard Stuart (1970) concluded from his review of twenty-one studies that "it can be said that persons who enter psychotherapy do so with a modest chance of marked improvement, a much greater chance of experiencing little or no change, and a modest chance of experiencing a deterioration in their functioning" (p. 50). However, it is still also the case that some individuals with certain types of problems can be helped best by a particular type of therapy and therapist and would get worse without any therapy.

For unknown reasons, some percentage of mental patients improve without any professional intervention. This *spontaneous recovery* effect—estimated to be around 30 percent for neurosis (Bergin, 1971)—is the baseline against which to assess the "cure rate" of other therapies. Simply put, doing something must be shown to lead to a significantly greater percentage of improved cases than occurs when nothing is done, or time simply passes.

Placebo therapy must also be distinguished from substantive therapeutic approaches to determine whether client improvement depends on specific clinical procedures. Some psychologists believe that the patient's *belief* that therapy will help and the therapist's social influence in conveying this suggestion are the key ingredients in the success of therapy (Fish, 1973). When about one hundred therapy outcome studies of "reasonable" quality were evaluated, positive therapeutic effects were reported in 80 percent of them (Meltzoff & Kornreich, 1970). People are helped more often than not by their therapeutic experience.

An even more positive conclusion emerges from the best controlled recent evaluation study of whether therapy works (Sloane et al., 1975). Behavior therapy and analytical psychotherapy were compared to each other and to a minimal treatment control group. Among the noteworthy features of its research design are:

a. *random assignment* of all patients to the control group and the two treatment groups, from a population of patients seeking help at a university psychiatric outpatient clinic;

b. therapists experienced in each form of treatment;

c. standardized testing procedures to assess kind and extent of pathology and its effect on outcome;

d. monitoring of in-therapy procedures;

e. independent assessment by judges of all data; and

f. multiple measures of therapeutic outcome collected at several times after termination of therapy.

The results indicate that all three groups improved significantly. But both therapy groups improved more than the control group of "wait-listed" patients. The initial improvement was maintained by most patients without further treatment over the two-year follow-up. Behavior therapy was the most effective in improving patients' social adjustment and work adequacy. The investigators conclude optimistically that: "therapy in general 'works,' that the improvement of patients in therapy is not entirely due either to 'spontaneous recovery,' or to the placebo effect of the nonspecific aspects of therapy, such as arousal of hope, expectation of help, and an initial cathartic interview" (p. 224).

Cost accountability

In this study the single most important part of both treatments according to the ratings of successful patients was the personal interaction with the therapist. In psychotherapy, but not behavior therapy, the patients who were liked by their therapists showed the most improvement. The patient most likely to succeed in psychotherapy is young, intelligent, verbal, well educated, affluent, not too seriously disturbed, with an introverted type of neurosis. Among hospitalized mental patients, there is a patient status hierarchy based on sociability. Compared to likable patients, those patients the staff likes least are more avoided and are recommended for more drug medication and transfers to other wards, or for discharge (despite the fact they are judged as more mentally ill). Well-liked patients are judged to be improving and see themselves as mentally healthy (Katz & Zimbardo, 1977).

This finding raises fundamental questions about the "cost accountability" of therapies that take a long time to do their thing, are expensive, and only work for a highly select subgroup of patients. Conventional psychotherapies are unavailable or ineffective for many segments of the population: the poor, the uneducated, the unintelligent, minorities, the nonverbal, the addicted, the psychopathic, and the psychotic.

Finally, some critics have suggested that psychotherapy is an expensive way for people to purchase temporary friendships. That the friendship aspect may be a crucial part of successful therapy for many patients is suggested by a study illustrating "student-friend power." Psychotic patients who were "treated" for five months by untrained, inexperienced college students showed greater gains than comparable patients given no treatment or given group treatment by a psychiatrist or a psychiatric social worker (Posner, 1966).

Such criticisms and new developments have had a positive effect in directing a greater interest toward: group therapy; more practical, short-term therapy; utilization of educational TV for self-help therapy and programs; and a reexamination of the assumptions, values, and goals of psychotherapy.

Notwithstanding these negative views, individual psychotherapy may still be the best treatment for certain people with certain problems when practiced by a perceptive and sensitive therapist. (See *P&L* Close-up, A Practical Guide to Therapy.)

Alternatives to traditional treatment

Traditional treatment of mental illness in Western industrialized societies takes place in isolation from the rest of the community. Clients are treated by professionals in private offices and clinics, while patients are treated in mental hospitals. This isolation factor speaks to our conception of the "disease" nature of mental illness, and to the stigma attached to this alien entity. It also creates additional problems for the disturbed person who experiences the stigma attached to being "sent away." It raises for such people the problems of adjusting to a lonely, faraway, impersonal institution and the equally difficult problem of coming back to the community after a long absence and trying to find a viable place in it again.

When we learn that a majority of hospitalized patients suffer relapses after being discharged, is that evidence for the severity and "depth" of their illness or the disturbance in the environment into which they are discharged? It is curious that the high recidivism rate of mental patients is comparable to that of psychiatrically normal prisoners who have also been institutionalized for long periods of time. "Dumping" a person back into a setting that was unsupportive to begin with (and may have deteriorated in the interim) is likely to provide the stimulus for deviant responses. It is also critical to realize the difficulty in readjusting to one's family and friends after any prolonged absence. Returning American POWs from Vietnam were given "reentry" training, but in a fair number of cases were not able to adjust to a family that had gotten along without them for a number of years and a "community" that really never noticed they were gone. If this is true of those given a hero's welcome, what are the reentry problems of the ex-schizophrenic or ex-convict? We must recognize that sometimes the source of the "problem" is not in the troubled person but in his or her environment. As this fable nicely illustrates, sometimes we need a radical therapy to attack the source of social pathology and not simply to help suffering people adapt better to their sick society:

"Two friends were walking on a riverbank when a child swept by downstream in the current, screaming and drowning. One of the pair jumped in and rescued the kid. They had just resumed their stroll when another child appeared in the water, also struggling for air. The rescuer jumped in again and pulled the victim to safety. Soon a third drowning child came by. The still-dry friend began to trot up the riverbank. The rescuer yelled, 'Hey, where are you going? Here's another one.' The dry one replied, 'I'm going to get the bastard that's throwing them in'" (Wolman, 1975, p. 3).

Community mental health care

An exciting alternative to institutional care of the mentally ill is the concept of community-based mental health care. Community mental health is an exciting and necessary approach to treatment, where innovation should be the rule rather than the exception. Clearly, if the psychological needs of large numbers of people are to be met, clinicians must leave the confines of the institution and search out the needs of the people instead of waiting for people in need to come to them. But even more important is the concept of treatment and *prevention* for the entire community akin to public health programs to immunize the community against sources of disease such as smallpox. Sources

Close-up
A Practical Guide to Therapy

Many of us have developed (or been taught) the feeling that we ought to be able to work out our own problems and not burden others with our troubles. It somehow seems a sign of weakness to admit that we might need help. There is little doubt, however, that almost everyone sometimes experiences feelings of depression or loneliness, or the inability to cope. Numerous life experiences have the potential of inducing such personal crises. It is important to realize that everyone faces such crises at one time or another and that there is nothing wrong or unusual about reacting to them emotionally. Seeking help at such times may not be easy, but it seems preferable to muddling through alone.

When our usual emotional supports, such as parents or close friends, are absent or unavailable, we should not hesitate to seek help from other sources. The duration of crisis is usually short for most people (from 4 to 6 weeks) and contains both the danger of increased psychological vulnerability and the opportunity for personal growth. The outcome seems to depend to a large degree on the availability of appropriate help and one's own attitude and definition of the "problem."

In terms of prevention, however, it would make better sense to seek out sources of help *before* they are needed. An interesting and worthwhile project would be to identify various sources of psychological support available to you now. First of all, you should list the available sources of help outside the mental health profession, such as family, friends, teachers, clergy, "rap centers," etc. Perhaps a visit to a local church or drop-in center would be instructive in terms of whether or not you think these places could be of help to you. You can simply explain that you are trying to identify sources of emotional support in the community (as a class project).

Most problems are in fact minor ones that will go away in time, that diminish in intensity as we look back on them. But the process of working them through helps us get in touch with ourselves and perhaps reduces the stressfulness of such problems in the future. However, there are also cases of real distress where perhaps you or a friend might become severely depressed, seriously contemplate suicide, or else begin to develop paranoid feelings of persecution, hallucinations, or other signs of major psychological stress. For such problems you should go at once to an accredited professional therapist for help. Go early, before the symptoms themselves become problems (causing poor grades, etc.).

It is not unreasonable to talk ahead of time about the "therapeutic contract"—what you get for what you give. If you think it appropriate, you might want to explore the therapist's view of human nature and the causes of emotional and behavioral disturbance. Of course, feeling comfortable with the therapist and being able to develop feelings of trust are more important than knowing his or her philosophy. This can best be accomplished through sharing your problems and concerns and gauging the helpfulness of the response you get. Remember, though, most therapists refrain from giving advice, but seek to help the client achieve his or her own resolution to the problem. You may judge for yourself whether or not this is what you need.

Therapy is an intimate social exchange in which you pay for a service. If you feel the service is not benefiting you, discuss this openly with the therapist, expose the possibility that failure of therapy represents the *therapist's failure* as well as your own. Discuss criteria for successful termination of therapy—when will the two of you know you are "really" better? Also discuss the issue of terminating therapy if you are unsatisfied with it. This may itself be a positive step toward self-assertion. Professionals understand that no therapist relates well with everyone, and a good one will sometimes suggest that a client might do better with another therapist.

of environmental or organizational stress can be identified, and plans can be formulated to alleviate or circumvent them as well as to increase people's resistance to specific sources of stress.

While some of our emotional problems undoubtedly stem from early-life unresolved conflicts and inappropriate learning, nevertheless, the major sources of stress we face come from the conditions under which we live our daily lives—violence, prejudice, forms of ecological deterioration, social isolation, crime, unemployment, poverty, wars between governments, and the powerlessness felt in trying to change the global systems that control and manipulate us. This concept, given impetus by the Community Mental Health Centers Act (1963), was designed to transfer responsibility for care and treatment of the mentally ill away from large "dehumanizing" state institutions to small centers in the patients' own communities. It was hailed as a revolution in psychiatric treatment.

Fifteen years later the resident population of large mental hospitals has been reduced by two thirds. Part of the initial hopes have been realized. Unfortunately, many of these patients are being sent out "to a lonely existence in hostile communities without adequate care" (Bassuk & Gerson, 1978, p. 46). A Ralph Nader study group offers a similar dismal conclusion on the failure of the community mental health program in the United States (Chu & Trotter, 1974). The usual unresponsiveness of federal bureaucracy, poor planning, inadequate funding, and other reasons have been given for this failure of a dream. Nader's analysis suggests "this grievous failure reflects in turn the failure to involve the concerned portions of the community and generate citizen participation and accountability" (p. xiv). The community must care; the well must want to help the unwell to get better before the concept of community mental health can have any real meaning.

Community mental health in other cultures

Among the Navaho and African cultures, healing is a matter that always takes place in a social context and involves the sick person's beliefs, family, work, and life environment. Recently the African use of group support in therapy is being expanded into a procedure called "network therapy." The patient's entire network of relatives, co-workers, and friends become involved in the treatment (Lambo, 1978).

The contrast with our society is obvious. The European world view emphasizes: individuality, uniqueness, competition, independence, survival of the fittest, a mastery over nature, and personal responsibility for success and failure. In the African world view we see instead: groupness, sameness, commonality, cooperation, interdependence, tribal survival, unity with nature, and collective responsibility (Nobles, 1976). Such fundamental differences in philosophies and basic belief systems may underlie the ways in which people become mentally ill and the paths they find available back to mental health.

When therapy for mental illness must follow an isolated path it is neither as swift nor as sure a journey as when the path is populated with people. The ultimate therapy may consist in having someone care enough about you to help you reestablish the powerful bonds of the human connection. In that network of mutual concern we are united in our common journey through life and strengthened against the fears, frustrations, and failures that sometimes await us. No man or woman should ever have to be an island separate unto themselves. In isolation there is madness, in community there is might. We turn next in our last section of *Psychology and Life* to social psychology, the study of behavior in a social context—where people confer meaning on one another's existence.

Chapter summary

The treatment of the mentally ill has historically reflected the attitudes of the cultures in which such treatment has been practiced. Present-day approaches to therapy are based on the *biomedical model,* in which the thrust is toward changing the brain and nervous system through surgery, shock, or drugs, and the *psychological* approach, which encompasses the *psychodynamic, behaviorist,* and *existential-humanistic* views.

Biomedical therapy assumes mental ailments to be *organic. Psychosurgery* is a process in which parts of the brain are disconnected. The *prefrontal lobotomy,* once widely used, severs nerve fibers connecting the prefrontal lobes with lower brain centers, diminishing the emotional tone that accompanies thoughts and memories and eliminating emotional anguish and hallucination. The numerous side effects associated with this procedure have presently limited its use primarily to those exhibiting a *dyscontrol syndrome.*

Shock therapy, also widely used after World War II, has diminished in recent years. Such treatment induces a state of coma for several minutes or hours after a shock. *Electroconvulsive shock* treatments have been particularly effective in treating depressed patients.

It is *chemotherapy* that has had the largest impact on mental health care in the last twenty years. Hospitalization has been dramatically reduced with the use of *tranquilizers* such as *reserpine* and *chlorpromazine* for schizophrenics and *antidepressant psychic energizers* such as *imipramine* and *monoamine oxidase inhibitors* for depressed patients. In addition, *lithium* has proved highly successful in treating *manic-depression* and various *amphetamines* have been used for those suffering from mild depression. *Ritalin* in particular has been prescribed for *hyperactive* children.

Critics of drug therapy point out that drugs merely decrease the frequency of undesirable behaviors but do not actually "cure" the problems, and patients may develop an overreliance on drug therapy to the exclusion of human contact therapy. Lastly, biomedical approaches do not sufficiently account for the interplay between cognitive, social, and experiential processes.

Psychodynamic therapy, particularly *Freudian psychoanalysis,* is an intensive, long-term technique for exploring the patient's unconscious motivation, with special importance attached to conflict and repression stemming from problems in the early stages of *psychosexual development.* It attempts to bring about *abreaction,* a process by which the patient brings repressed memories into consciousness and expresses strongly repressed feelings. Psychoanalysts use techniques of *free association, analysis of resistances, dream analysis,* and *analysis of transference* to accomplish this.

Neo-Freudians place more emphasis on the patient's current social environment, emphasizing the role of interpersonal interaction and the significance of ego functioning and self-concept. Less stressed are sex and aggression as determinants of pathology. In general, the neo-Freudian outlook is less pessimistic and in some ways, more *existentially* oriented than the traditional Freudian one.

Behavioristic therapy approaches functional mental illness as a set of self-defeating habit patterns and so bases *behavior modification* on principles of *learning theory. Contingency management* employs operant conditioning principles to produce desirable behavior and skills and classical conditioning principles to change neurotic fear and undesired reactions. Among the best-known contingency management therapies are: *modeling,* useful for aiding clients to learn new responses or overcome phobias, *token economies,* in which patients are tangibly rewarded for socially constructive activities, and *be-*

havioral contracts, explicit agreements that state what patients are expected to do and what they may expect from the therapist.

In order to ensure that modified behavior patterns persist after the patient has left the hospital or discontinued therapy, *generalization techniques* are employed. These increase the similarity between therapeutic target behaviors, reinforcers, and stimulus demands and those encountered in real-life settings.

Extinction strategies such as *implosive therapy* diminish unwanted behavior by gradually removing its reinforcing consequences. *Counterconditioning* strategies such as *systematic desensitization* weaken the association between patients' responses of anxiety to particular environmental clues. *Aversive learning,* on the other hand, pairs noxious stimuli with stimuli that have come to arouse unwanted responses, in order to change these responses. Finally, *cognitive* and *behavioral rehearsal* allow patients to build new skills through learning effective coping statements and coping behavior in the midst of settings that usually evoke unwanted behavior. *Social skills training* employs most of the behavior modification techniques for the acquisition of basic social skills, especially that of becoming appropriately assertive.

Existential-humanistic therapies stress the importance of openness and the readiness to accept the data of experience. *Responsibility, freedom,* and *commitment* are the cornerstones of this approach. The existential approaches recognize feelings of alienation and loss of identity as central human problems. *Logotherapy,* in particular, encourages patients to find meaning through self-realization and spiritual and ethical values. *Paradoxical intention* is a form of existential therapy geared toward treating phobic and obsessive-compulsive ailments—overcoming the fear of fear itself. The patient is encouraged to do or wish to have happen the very thing feared. *Humanistic* psychotherapy, especially as practiced by Carl Rogers, is *nondirective* and encourages clients to use their own potentialities to achieve more mature levels of emotional adjustment. This perspective has contributed to the growth of the *human potential movement.*

Because different therapists treat the same manifest problem according to their different perceptions of its origin, some critics have suggested that eventually patients come to act "sick" in the way their therapists implicitly suggest. Indeed, a number of studies have shown that untreated subjects improved as much as those who received psychotherapy, although the *variability* in outcome was greater among those who had received treatment. The *spontaneous recovery effect* is the baseline against which the cure rate of other therapies must be assessed. A recent comparative study showed behavior therapy to be the most effective in improving patients' social adjustment and work adequacy. Much of the success in other therapies may be due to the "friendship" factor between therapist and client.

An alternative to traditional treatment is that of *community-based* mental health care. New programs involve formulating plans to avoid and alleviate environmental and organizational stress and to increase people's resistance to certain forms of stress. The community approach has been a successful and integral part of mental health care in other cultures, especially in Navaho and African cultures.

Part Seven

Social Psychology

Paul KLEE "BRUDERSCHAFT", 1939, ZZ 12 (952)
Zeichnung, Bleistift, Briefpapier /
20, 8 : 29, 6 /
Sammlung Paul Klee-Stiftung,
Bern, Inv. Z 1923.

21 The Social Bases of Behavior

The dynamics of groups
Norms
Leadership
Intergroup conflict

Prejudice
Prejudice as the denial of legitimacy
Racism: High-powered color blindness
The unconscious ideology of sexism

Persuasion and attitude change
The many faces of persuasion
What produces—and changes—attitudes?
Your vulnerability to influence

Chapter summary

The Sunday-morning quiet in Palo Alto, California, was shattered by a screeching siren as police swept through the city picking up college students in a surprise mass arrest. Each suspect was charged with a felony, warned of his constitutional rights, spread-eagled against the police car, searched, handcuffed, and carted off to the police station for booking. After fingerprinting and paperwork were completed, each prisoner was blindfolded and transported to the "Stanford County Prison." Here he was stripped naked, skin-searched, deloused, and issued a uniform, bedding, soap, and towel.

The prisoner's uniform was a loosely fitting smock with an identification number on front and back. A chain was bolted around one ankle, and he had to wear a nylon stocking cap to cover his hair. Orders were shouted at him, and he was pushed around by the guards if he didn't comply quickly enough. The guards wore khaki uniforms which gave them "group identity." No names were used, and their silver reflector sunglasses made eye contact with them impossible. Their symbols of power were billy clubs, whistles, handcuffs, and the keys to the cells and the main gate. Most of the nine youthful prisoners sat on the cots in their barren cells, dazed and shocked by the unexpected events that had transformed their lives so suddenly. Just what kind of prison was this?

It was, in fact, an experimental "mock prison" — created by social psychologists specifically for the purpose of investigating the psychological effects of imprisonment (Zimbardo, 1975; Haney & Zimbardo, 1977). Both the guards and the prisoners had been recruited through newspaper ads calling for student volunteers for a two-week study of prison life at fifteen dollars a day. Participants were chosen because they were judged to be emotionally stable, physically healthy, "normal-average" on the basis of extensive personality tests, and law-abiding. Their assignment to the condition of "guard" or "prisoner" was *randomly determined* by the flip of a coin.

At the start of the study, then, there were no measurable differences between the "guards" and the "prisoners." The "correctional officers" received no special training. They were told merely to "maintain law and order" in the prison and not to take any nonsense from the prisoners. Physical violence was forbidden.

The "prison" was in the basement of the Stanford psychology building, which was deserted after the summer session. Three small laboratory rooms were made into cells with barred doors and three cots each. A small, dark storage closet opposite the cells served as solitary confinement. Data collection consisted of videotaping the interactions of guards and prisoners, direct observations by the research team, and interviews with the subjects, as well as their reactions on a battery of self-report questionnaires, in diaries, letters, daily reports, and a two-year-long follow-up.

This mock prison represented an attempt to simulate *functionally* some of the significant features of the psychological state of imprisonment. The intention was not to make a *literal* copy of a real prison setting, but to achieve some equivalent *psychological* effects despite differences in the physical details.

In a remarkably short time, a perverted relationship developed between the prisoners and the guards. After an initial rebellion was crushed, the prisoners reacted passively as the guards daily escalated their aggression. In less than thirty-six hours, the first prisoner had to be released because of uncontrolled crying, fits of rage, disorganized thinking, and severe depression. Three more prisoners developed similar symptoms and also had to be released on successive days. A fifth prisoner was released from the study when he developed a psychosomatic rash over his entire body, triggered by rejection of his parole appeal by the mock Parole Board.

Social power became the major dimension on which everyone and everything was defined. Although there were no initial differences between those assigned to play the roles of prisoner and guard, enacting those roles in a social situation that validated the power differences created extreme behavioral and emotional differences between the two groups.

Every guard at some time engaged in abusive, authoritarian behaviors. Many appeared to enjoy the elevated status that accompanied putting on the guard uniforms, which transformed their routine, everyday existence into one where they had virtually total control over other people. As these differences in behavior, mood, and perception became more evident, the need for the now "righteously" powerful guards to rule the obviously inferior (and powerless) inmates became sufficient justification to support almost any indignity of man against man.

The power of this simulated prison situation had transformed college students into people that they themselves would not have recognized one short week before.

When normal college students, within a few days, come to treat each other not as peers but as dehumanized enemies, we might well ask what goes on in groups that can transform everyday patterns of behavior so dramatically. *Social psychology* is the study of group processes and structures, and of the impact of people on each other.

Through the dynamics of group interaction, people develop and maintain a powerful *social reality*. It is a reality that, through processes of persuasion and interpersonal influence, serves to stabilize and also to change group members' attitudes and beliefs about themselves and other people. One such attitude is prejudice — stereotyped perceptions of people on the basis of group membership and identification. It is to these important topics — group dynamics, prejudice, persuasion, and attitude change — that social psychologists devote much of their research efforts. By studying these interpersonal processes, psychologists hope to understand the social bases of human behavior in the great variety of situations in which it occurs: the prison, the classroom, the home, at work, at play, in making love or making war.

In studying the social nature of the human animal, social psychological investigations focus sometimes on the dependent variable of social *behavior*, and sometimes on the independent variable of social *stimuli*. In this chapter both social stimuli and social responses will be considered, as well as the concepts that unite them in meaningful psychological relationships. Our level of analysis will typically be a molar one, and the variables will be more complex than in the research described in earlier chapters.

The dynamics of groups

The Stanford prison study demonstrates the power that people, acting together in groups, have to induce situationally specific behavior from individuals in the group. This experiment is by no means typical of the kind of research carried out by social psychologists. Nevertheless, it highlights a number of concepts that are important in understanding group dynamics: norms, roles, and power.

Norms

Given an infinite variety of possible ways to react in different situations, we are guided by the *expectations* held by fellow group members. Expectations are attitudes people have about social reality—for example, about the appropriate conduct for members of their group. Social norms are expectations *shared* by the members of a group. Norms are the potential "pressure" in situations that: (a) helps to define the nature of social reality, (b) forms the foundation upon which people base their interaction, and (c) provides a common referent for members' self-evaluation. Through these mechanisms norms increase feelings of personal and group identity.

The pressure of social norms has two major sources: agreement (*consensus*) and the strength of people's expectations. For example, in some college circles, students expect each other to drink at particular times and in specific amounts. At Leisure College, students are in strong agreement that frequent drinking is appropriate. In contrast, students at Grind University care much less about whether people drink, and they approve of relatively infrequent to moderate consumption patterns.

The difference in drinking norms at these two schools helps to explain why alcoholism is less of a problem at Grind University and why there are three times as many liquor stores within walking distance of Leisure College. The norm at Leisure College encourages fairly frequent drinking, while at Grind University the relatively weak norm tends to keep drinking behavior from becoming excessive.

Norms shape behavior by providing limits within which people can receive social approval for their behavior. In our example, the range of tolerable behavior is different for the two schools. Grind University's norm constrains behavior to a smaller range of drinking than Leisure College's norm. Outside these ranges, students at each school will encounter negative expectations for their drinking. Thus, as members of college groups, students have a basis for estimating how far they may go before experiencing the normative power of ridicule, rejection, and loss of status among their friends and acquaintances. If you visited these two schools, at which one do you think you would find the most partying? At which would you feel most comfortable?

The function of social norms

Although group norms backed by powerful punishments for violations can restrict behavioral freedom and promote excessive uniformity, they nevertheless serve three indispensable functions. First, norms contain the collective power to create and regulate social reality. Awareness of the norms operating in a group situation enables each participant to anticipate how others will enter the situation (for example, what they will wear) and what they are likely to say and do, as well as what behavior on one's own part will be expected and approved. For example, participants in a given class share expectations regulating the meeting place and time. Running the class overtime or changing the day it is to meet is likely to evoke negative student response. An instructor's status and prestige among students depend upon his or her conformity to countless norms governing student-faculty interaction (Santee & VanDerPol, 1976). Similarly, faculty response to students will be affected by their conformity to the faculty's norms.

Second, norms help to interlock the *roles* that people perform in social situations. *Roles are the socially programmed behaviors available for self-expression in group situations:* sister-brother, coach-athlete, minister-parishioner. Knowing what is expected from each role performance—one's own role and others' roles—oils the machinery of social interaction. Sometimes it does so only too well, as we saw in the Stanford prison study, where students performing the prisoner and guard roles quickly fell to displaying all the behaviors that have come to be associated in our society with those roles.

628

For three days, twenty-nine staff members at Elgin State Hospital in Illinois were confined to a ward of their own—a mental ward on which they performed the role of "patient." Trained observers and video cameras recorded what transpired throughout. "It was really fantastic the things that happened in there," reported Norma Jean Orlando (1973), director of the research. In a short time the mock patients began acting in ways indistinguishable from real patients: six tried to escape, two withdrew into themselves, two wept uncontrollably, one came close to having a nervous breakdown. Most experienced a general increase in tension, anxiety, frustration, and despair. They reacted most strongly to the total invasion of their privacy, to being treated as incompetent children, ignored, and obliged to conform to the often arbitrary rules of the staff.

One staff-member-turned-patient who suffered during his weekend ordeal gained the insight to declare: "I used to look at the patients as if they were a bunch of animals; I never knew what they were going through before."

The positive outcome of this study was the formation of an organization of staff members dedicated to raising the consciousness of the rest of the hospital personnel about the way patients were being mistreated, as well as to working at personally improving their own relationship to patients.

The Stanford study illustrates the *power of norms* to control and regulate behavior by interlocking role performances into a microcosmic social reality of crime and punishment. The subjects became so locked into their role interdependency that after six days the researchers had to stop the planned two-week simulation. Pathological reactions were being elicited in subjects who were chosen precisely for their normality, sanity, and emotional stability. Since the subjects were randomly assigned to guard and prisoner roles, showed no prior personality pathology, and received no training for their roles, how can we account for the ease and rapidity with which they assumed these roles? Presumably, they, like the rest of us, had learned stereotyped conceptions of guard and prisoner roles from the mass media as well as from social models of power and powerlessness (for example, parent and child). (See *P&L* Close-up, When Role Playing Becomes Reality.) The "role-driven script" (see p. 150) of prisoner and guard overwhelmed the "person-driven scripts" of the volunteers. In less than a week, a lifetime of values, ethics, and personality were overcome by the new, alien roles (but only within the setting of the mock prison).

A third function of social norms is the distribution of behavioral content across roles. Not everyone is expected to perform their roles in the same way. In a given group, a very important type of behavior that is differentially distributed across roles is decision making, the rights and obligations of choosing among alternatives that have consequences for the group and its members. The shape of this distribution is the *authority structure* of a group. If important decisions are concentrated in the hands of a very few role performers, we say authority is *centralized*. Total institutions, such as prisons and mental hospitals (and maybe residential colleges), where the "client" spends 24 hours a day, are group settings where decision making is controlled entirely by one group of role performers to the exclusion of another. In the Stanford prison study, as in real prisons, authority was vested in the guards.

Situations create roles that people fill. When in those roles they may exercise certain prerogatives and enjoy advantages purely as a function of the role. For example, the MC of a TV quiz show asks questions of contestants but does not have to answer their questions. When asked to judge the general knowledge of the game show host and the guests, most people judge the host to be smarter. In doing so, they fail to correct adequately for the self-presentation advantage that the role confers on the actor. When college students were *arbitrarily* assigned to play questioner, contestant, or observer their judgments of how smart each of the participants was depended on which role they had been assigned *by chance.* They all agreed the questioner was smartest (Ross, Amabile, & Steinmetz, 1977).

Development of norms

Twin Oaks began in the late 1960s as a thriving commune in Virginia patterned after B. F. Skinner's utopian community described in *Walden Two* (1948). How did normative control develop at Twin Oaks during the first years? Norms emerge in a group through two processes: *diffusion* and *crystallization* of expectations. When new members arrived at the commune, they brought with them their own expectations that they had acquired through previous group memberships and the mass media. These expectations diffused into the commune as the new members communicated with other group members who were persuaded to accept the expectations as their own.

But another interesting thing happened. As the members talked with each other, their expectations began to converge or crystallize into a shared perspective on appropriate solutions to group problems and the proper performance of roles. Their social reality emerged out of this communication process, which finally resulted in an attempt to formalize their norms in a code of rules: "We don't publicly complain"; "We don't boast of individual accomplishments"; "We clean up after ourselves." Initially, sexual relations were socially controlled through a norm of monogamy—one mate at a time. However, when a large number of new members joined the commune all at once, the diffusion into the group of new expectations was pronounced, and a new norm crystallized that discouraged exclusive possession and encouraged sexual freedom.

A classic study in social psychology was designed by Muzafer Sherif (1935) to experimentally demonstrate norm crystallization through the convergence of expectations and perceptions. Sherif brought his subjects into a dark room in which there was a stationary spot of light. Without any frame of reference, such a light appears to move about erratically. This illusion is called the *autokinetic effect.*

Male subjects were asked to judge the movement of the light individually at first. Their judgments varied widely: some saw movement of a few inches, while others reported that the spot moved many yards. Each subject soon established a range within which most of his reports would fall. But then, when he was put into a group with two or three others, his estimates and theirs would converge on a new range on which they would all agree. After this happened, his judgment would continue to fall in this new range even when he was in the room by himself.

For a fascinating demonstration of how norms can develop and take a frightening stranglehold on reality, see the *P&L* Close-up, Creating Nazis in a High-School History Class.

Norms and conformity

Once norms are established in a group, they tend to perpetuate themselves. When new members arrive, they not only begin to compare themselves to others along normative dimensions but they find themselves subject to active

Close-up
Creating Nazis in a High-School History Class

The development of norms and power of roles to transform reality has never been better demonstrated than by a California high-school history teacher. Ron Jones was leading a sophomore history class discussion on Nazi Germany when he decided he had to modify his medium in order to make the message meaningful. Like many of us, Ron's students could not comprehend how such a social-political movement could thrive, and how the average citizen could be ignorant or indifferent to the suffering it imposed on so many people. The teacher told the class they would simulate some aspects of the German experience. Despite this fore-warning, the role-playing "experiment" that took place over the next five days was a serious matter for the students and a shock for the teacher. Simulation and reality merged as these high-school students created a totalitarian system of beliefs and coercive control that was all too much like that fashioned by Hitler (Jones, 1978).

First there were new classroom rules. All answers must be limited to three words or less. When no one challenged this and other arbitrary rules, the classroom atmosphere began to change. The more verbal students lost their positions of prominence as the less verbal took over. The next day the classroom movement was entitled "The Third Wave" and a cupped-hand salute was introduced. Slogans were shouted out in unison, "Strength through discipline," "Strength through community." Actions followed the slogans — making banners that were hung about the school, enlisting new members, teaching other students mandatory sitting postures, and so forth.

The original core of twenty soon swelled to 100 eager Third Wavers. Membership cards were issued. Some of the brightest students were ordered out of class. The in-group was delighted and abused their "former" classmates as they were taken away.

Jones then confided to his followers that they were part of a nationwide movement to discover students who were willing to fight for political change. They were "a *select* group of young people *chosen* to help in this cause," he told them. A rally was scheduled for the next day at which a national presidential candidate was supposed to announce on TV the formation of a Third Wave Youth program. Over 200 students filled the auditorium at Cubberley High School in eager anticipation of this announcement. Banners were hung by exhilarated Third Wave members wearing white-shirted uniforms with homemade armbands. While muscular students stood guard at the door, friends of the teacher posing as reporters and photographers circulated among the mass of true believers. The TV was turned on and everyone waited — and waited — for the announcement. Instead, Ron Jones projected a film of a Nuremberg rally; the history of the Third Reich appeared in ghostly images. "Everyone must accept the blame — no one can claim that they didn't in some way take part." That was the final frame of the film and of the simulation.

Well, almost. The teacher explained the reason for the simulation and what he had learned from it, concluding his summation with a prediction that, "you won't admit to participating in this madness . . . of being manipulated . . . a follower . . . you will keep this day and this rally a secret." As far as anyone can tell, never was heard a discouraging word.

That's how the follies of earlier generations get repeated, because they cover up their mistakes and embarrassments rather than learning from them and communicating the message to the innocents in the next generation. For example, it is only recently that German textbooks have broken silence and begun to analyze the Hitler era of four decades ago.

attempts to obtain their conformity to group norms — a process called *socialization*. ▲ People become socialized into the culture of a particular group when they behave in accordance with its dominant normative values. Often the process is so gradual and subtle that you don't perceive the external forces acting on you to change, to become their kind of person. It is the rare cucumber who can emerge from the vinegar vat as anything but a pickle. The more one relies on the social reward structure of the group for his or her sense of self-worth and legitimacy, the greater the pressures toward conformity the group can bring to bear on the individual.

Faced with agreement among group members about the nature of reality, the lone individual may find dissent in public quite difficult. Solomon Asch decided to find out just how independent people could be when confronted with a social reality that conflicted with their perceptions of the world.

Groups of seven to nine male college students were shown cards with three lines of differing lengths and asked to indicate which of the three was the same length as the line on a standard card. Ordinarily, mistakes on this task would be made less than 1 percent of the time. All but one of the members of each group, however, were confederates of the researcher who gave incorrect answers unanimously on twelve of the eighteen trials. Under this group pressure, the minority subjects, overall, accepted the majority's wrong judgments in 37 percent of the trials. But this figure is misleading, for individual differences were marked. Of the 123 minority subjects, about 30 percent nearly always yielded, while another 25 percent remained entirely independent. All who yielded underestimated the frequency of their conformity.

Next, the design of the experiment was changed slightly to investigate the effects of the size of the opposing majority. Pitted against just one person giving an incorrect judgment, the subject exhibited some uneasiness. When a majority of three opposed him, errors rose to 31.8 percent. When the subject was given an agreeing partner, the effects of the majority were greatly diminished—errors decreased to one fourth of what they had been with no partner, and the effects lasted even after the partner left (Asch, 1955). ■

"Yes, it does make you look stupid, but all the with-it people are looking stupid this year."

The pressures to conform to group norms are present not simply in social psychology experiments but in all social settings, including college campuses. What impact does membership in a college community have on the attitudes and values of its students? This question is of obvious concern to every student caught between twin pressures to become part of the group and to maintain his or her independence and individuality. A study begun back in 1935 in a small New England college for women offers some insights.

■

The concern of the dissenting subject is evident as he leans forward to check his judgment. In general, subjects found this a very disturbing situation. The graph compares the average errors under normal circumstances with those made under social pressure both with and without a supporting partner.

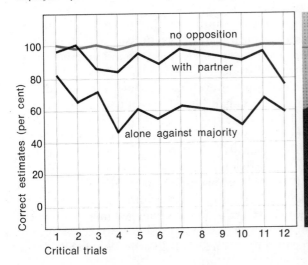

The prevailing norm at Bennington College was one of political and economic liberalism. On the other hand, most of the women had come from conservative homes and brought conservative attitudes with them. The question studied, then, was what impact this "liberal atmosphere" would have on the attitudes of individual students.

The conservatism of the freshman class steadily declined with each passing year. By their senior year most students had been "converted" to a clearly liberal position. This seemed to be due both to faculty and upper-class social approval for expression of liberal views and to the greater availability of politically oriented information in the college community.

The students who had resisted this pervasive norm and retained their conservatism fell into two classes. Some, part of a small, close-knit group, simply had been unaware of the conflict between their conservatism and the prevailing campus attitudes. Others had maintained strong ties with their conservative families and continued to conform to their standards (Newcomb, 1958).

Twenty years later, the marks of the Bennington experience were still evident. Most women who had left as liberals were liberals, and those who had resisted remained conservatives. For the most part, they had married men with comparable values, thus creating a supportive home environment. Of those who left college as liberals but married conservative men, a high proportion returned to their freshman-year conservatism (Newcomb, 1963).

Group norms, then, have the power to produce fundamental changes in people, since deviance brings some degree of social ostracism and conformity results in approval and acceptance. *Sanctions* — rewards and punishments contingent on conformity — serve to reinforce the controlling effect of norms. But norms and sanctions are intrinsically neither good nor bad. The effects they have on our behavior, our attitudes, and our basic identity must be evaluated on the merits of the individual case.

As we saw in the Asch experiment, even a single partner can bolster an individual's resistance to group pressure. The pressure of the group on a dissenter is often evident in jury deliberations. "You can't hold off an army by yourself." With these words, the last of twelve jurors explained her vote for the conviction of Wendy Yoshimura (accomplice of Patty Hearst) for illegal possession of explosives. The last holdout for Yoshimura's innocence—a sixty-one-year-old retired hospital housekeeper—found herself under intense group pressure to make the vote for conviction unanimous. "I got tired. . . . I couldn't hold out no more. If someone held out with me I could [have held out too] but when everyone went against me, well . . . You can't hold off an army by yourself" (Rubenstein & Snyder, 1977).

But can a small minority turn the majority around to create new norms using only the same basic psychological principles that usually help to establish the majority view? A group of French psychologists found that if two confederates in groups of six female students consistently called a blue light green, almost a third of the naive subjects eventually followed their lead, and some continued to call it green when again tested individually (Faucheux & Moscovici, 1967; Moscovici, Lage, & Naffrechoux, 1969). If a minority can win adherents to this extent even when it is wrong, there is abundant hope for a minority with a valid cause. Serge Moscovici (1976) argues convincingly that conflict between a group and the individual is not a destructive force on the person's integrity. Rather, it is an essential precondition of the innovation that leads to positive social change. It is always the few with ideas, courage, and conviction that sway the majority. The individual is engaged in a two-way exchange with society, adapting to its norms, roles, and status prescriptions, but also acting upon it to reshape its image. The minority who would change the group's reality must: (a) present a consistent unvarying position, (b) be seen as strongly invested or personally committed to the issue at stake, and (c) give the appearance of autonomy, of each having come to the expressed point of view independently. In this way, the rule of the many may be undercut by the conviction of the few.

Leadership

When an individual is elevated to a position of leadership, the power of the group is invested in him or her. But what determines who will emerge from the body of the faceless group to become its head, guide its direction, and often give it a unique identity? For centuries political and social analysts have puzzled over the ingredients that go into the recipe for leadership. ◆

Are great leaders born with special traits that give them a *charisma*, a special emotional appeal and attraction? Or do great leaders emerge because momentous situational demands happen to occur at a given point in history and "put them on the spot"? Questions such as these focus our attention on two approaches to studying leadership: the *trait approach* and the *situational approach*.

◆

Are great leaders born or made? Social psychological research has shown that the answer lies somewhere in between.

Do leaders "have what it takes"?

In one early analysis of the "essence of political leadership" several interesting hypotheses were presented:

"In ordinary politics it must be admitted that the gift of public speaking is of more decisive value than anything else. Experience has shown that no exceptional degree of any other capacity is necessary to make a successful leader. . . . The successful shepherd thinks like his sheep, and can lead his flock only if he keeps no more than the shortest distance in advance. He must remain, in fact, recognizable as one of the flock, magnified no doubt, louder, coarser, above all with more urgent wants and ways of expression than the common sheep, but in essence to their feeling of the same flesh with them. In the human herd the necessity of the leader having unmistakable marks of identification is equally essential" (Trotter, 1916).

Recent research has confirmed that leaders tend to be the most verbally active members of their groups. In fact, in an experimental group of strangers, any member with an artificially induced high verbal output comes to be perceived as the leader (Bavelas, Hastorf, Gross, & Kite, 1965).

It also appears that to maintain their effectiveness, leaders must empha-size their community with the rank-and-file. The downfall of leaders is often traced to their losing contact with their roots and identifiability with those who have given them leadership.

The attempt to find a standard set of traits to characterize leaders in gen-eral has been fruitless, and it is little wonder. Could we possibly expect consis-tent traits for leaders of, say, the Daughters of the American Revolution, a Sunday-school choir, a suburban wife-swapping group, and a labor union? It seems obvious that an effective leader must possess whatever resources are needed by the individual members of the group and by the group as a unit in order to reach its goals—and that these needed resources will be somewhat different for every situation.

There is evidence that in many situations more than one leader is needed. Bales (1970) has distinguished between two general types of leaders: (a) *task leaders*, whose orientation is to get the job done as efficiently as possible, and (b) *social-emotional leaders*, whose perspective favors creating and maintaining a good psychological climate within the group, responsive to the personal needs, problems, and uniqueness of individual members. Evidently, effective leadership depends on neither personality characteristics nor situational fac-tors alone but on an optimal combination of leader personality and situational demands.

Do different leadership "styles" have different effects?

Putting aside the problems of uncovering personality traits that "make" lead-ers, a team of social psychologists wondered whether particular styles that leaders use in relating to their groups make any difference in how a group behaves. In 1939, at the time the study was initiated, the example of Hitler's autocratic domination in Germany was frightening people who believed that democratic leadership was not only more desirable, but more effective. Some were even proposing that the best leaders were those who were nondirective, who led by providing resources only when requested to do so, and let things go as they might—a *laissez-faire* style. This complex problem was studied in a classic experiment by Kurt Lewin, one of the leading figures in the develop-ment of social psychology.

The subjects were four five-member groups of ten-year-old boys who met after school to engage in hobby activities. Four men were trained in each of three leadership styles. An <u>autocratic</u> leader was to make all decisions and work assignments but not participate in group activity. A <u>democratic</u> leader was to encourage and assist group decision-making and planning. Finally, a <u>laissez-faire</u> leader was to allow complete freedom for the group with a minimum of leader participation. At the end of each six-week period, each leader was transferred to a different group, at which time he also changed his leadership style. Thus, all groups experienced each style under a different person. ●
The following generalizations emerged from this experiment (Lewin, Lippitt, & White, 1939).

a) The laissez-faire atmosphere is not identical to the democratic atmosphere. Less work—and poorer work—was done by the laissez-faire groups.
b) Democracy can be efficient. Although the quantity of work done in autocratic groups was somewhat higher, work motivation and interest were stronger in the democratic groups. Originality was greater under democracy.
c) Autocracy can create much hostility and aggression. The autocratic groups showed as much as thirty times more hostility, more demands for attention, more destruction of their own property, and more scapegoating behavior.
d) Autocracy can create discontent that may not appear on the surface. Four boys

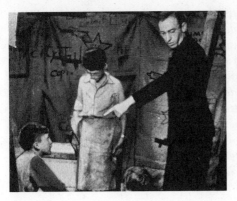

These photos from Lewin's classic study of group dynamics show the three leadership styles in action. The autocratic leader directs the work, the democratic leader works with the boys, and the laissez-faire leader remains aloof.

dropped out during autocratic periods. Nineteen of the twenty boys preferred their democratic leader, and more discontent was expressed in autocracy than in democracy.

e) Autocracy encourages dependence and less individuality. There was more submissive or dependent behavior in autocratic groups, and conversation was less varied, more confined to the immediate situation.

f) Democracy promotes more group-mindedness and friendliness. In democratic groups mutual praise, friendly remarks, and overall playfulness were more frequent, and there was more readiness to share group property.

This was the pioneering study in "group dynamics." It demonstrated that group interaction and group-related variables could be studied experimentally in a controlled setting to yield conclusions of a causal nature. It showed that the same person, no matter what his own "traits," had a markedly different impact when he employed one leadership "style" as opposed to another.

Intergroup conflict

Group dynamics operate not only within groups but between them. Within a group, social norms serve as a basis for generating change in basic attitudes, values, and self-identification. They also discourage change and promote stability once the individual is in conformity. Further, to the extent that the individual's goals and expectations are in agreement with group norms, the individual develops a sense of identification with the group, a feeling of loyalty, and a desire to cooperate with other group members. But what happens when the members of one such group are confronted with those of another such group, as frequently occurs in everyday life? To study the process by which *in-groups* develop cohesive friendships and a shared sense of social reality that includes the labeling of others as members of *out-groups* and hence as enemies, a special summer camp was created.

In this camp, friction was generated between two groups of boys and was later overcome as the groups worked toward common goals. In the beginning, the experimenters put the groups in different bunkhouses and kept them separate for daily group activities. By the end of this part of the experiment, the two groups had acquired definite group structures, including leaders, names for themselves (Rattlers and Eagles), nicknames, private signals, cooperative patterns within the group, flags, and other identification symbols.

Next, rivalry between the groups was stimulated by a series of competitive events. As predicted, this both increased in-group solidarity and produced unfavorable stereotypes of the out-group and its members. After losing a tug-of-war, the Eagles burned the Rattlers' flag. The Rattlers retaliated, and a series of bunkhouse raids ensued, accompanied by name calling, fist fights, and other expressions of hostility. During the conflict, a physically daring leader emerged to replace the less aggressive boy who had led the "peacetime" Eagles. In this way relations with other groups will cause changes within a group.

An attempt was then made to break down the hostility and induce the two groups to cooperate with each other. First, the rival groups were brought into close contact in pleasant activities — such as eating and shooting off firecrackers. The groups refused to intermingle, however, and the activities merely provided them with further opportunities for expressions of hostility, indicating that intergroup contact does not in itself decrease tension.

Situations were then contrived to bring about interaction of the groups to achieve superordinate goals — that is, important goals that required the combined efforts of both groups. The most striking episode in this period was one in which the tug-of-war rope, formerly the central object in a most antagonistic situation, served as a tool. On an overnight trip, a truck that was to bring their food "stalled," and the boys hit upon the idea of using the rope to pull the vehicle. After looping the rope through the bumper, the two groups pulled on different ends, but the next day, when the truck "stalled" again, members of the two groups intermingled on the two lines, obliterating group divisions. ◆

Further evidence of the change in the boys' attitudes was obtained from friendship choices made at the end of the period of intense competition and again at the close of the experiment. Rattlers' choices of Eagles as friends went up from 6 to 36 percent of their total friendship choice. Eagles' choices of Rattlers went up from 8 to 23 percent. The boys were also asked to rate each other on six characteristics designed to reveal the presence of stereotyped images. During the period of antagonism, Eagles received few favorable ratings from Rattlers, and Rattlers few from Eagles; but at the close of the experiment there was no significant difference in the ratings of in-group and out-group members (Sherif & Sherif, 1956).

Clearly this study has many implications for the overcoming of bitterness between national groups and between antagonistic groups within our own society.

◆

In the first stage of the study a cooperative atmosphere developed within each group; here the Rattlers work together carrying canoes to the lake. During the second stage, intergroup rivalry became intense, with raids and counterraids and a tug-of-war that ended in a complete impasse. In the third stage of the experiment, intergroup cooperation was fostered as the groups worked together to repair the camp's water supply system.

Prejudice

Prejudice between people is often one consequence of normative processes occurring within groups. Many groups exhibit an "ethnocentric" attitude which postulates: "my group, right or wrong; your group, rarely right and probably wrong until proven otherwise." We have seen that group membership gives us security, status, a basis for reality testing, and much more that we need for both survival and the full flowering of the human spirit. But being identified as a member of a certain group can also bring us insecurity, loss of self-esteem, and a precarious existence—if others with power choose to label our group as inferior. The consequences of prejudice take many forms, but common to all of them is a less human reaction to other people and a diversion of psychological energy from creative to destructive directions.

Prejudice may be defined as a cluster of learned beliefs, attitudes, and values held by one person about others that: (a) is formed on the basis of incomplete information, (b) is relatively immune to contrary informational input, (c) makes a categorical assignment of individuals to certain classes or groups that are (typically) negatively valued. *Prejudice,* then, is the internal state or psychological set to react in a biased way toward members of certain groups. *Discrimination* is the behavior(s) that prejudice may give rise to.

Prejudice as the denial of legitimacy

Our self-image and esteem depend upon many variables, as we saw in Chapter 16. Perhaps these inputs can be summarized as coming from two sources: (a) the individual's appraisal of personal worth derived from social and physical feedback of his or her *competence,* and (b) cultural feedback of the *legitimacy* of the person's primary reference groups (Clark & Khatib, 1978).

Competence knowledge comes from observing the consequences of your actions, what you achieve, how your abilities, skills, and talents are realized. *Legitimacy knowledge* comes from a variety of cultural sources by which your important group memberships—religious, racial, ethnic, sexual, age group, and others—are recognized as acceptable and worthwhile. Denial of the legitimacy of one's significant group identification can isolate the individual from those who control desired social and material reinforcers within a culture. In addition, the reasons given to justify rejection of the group and the personal feelings of helplessness that result from arbitrary discrimination can have a negative impact on performance, lowering even competence-based esteem. To the extent one accepts the values of, and is dependent on, the reward structure of a cultural group that denies the legitimacy of one's own subgroup, one's self-esteem is likely to suffer. Legitimacy is often denied not through hostile, obvious acts of discrimination, but in subtle patterns of prejudice that simply ignore one's existence.

Categorical rejection of the individual because of perceived membership in some nonaccepted group is a general phenomenon of prejudice. When you were a child, did friends of your parents or even relatives ignore your presence after they said the usual, "My, how you've grown"? Have you ever done likewise to aged people; that is, ignored them as persons because they are members of an out-group? Have you ever treated a person who was performing a service for you as if he or she were nothing more than a machine?

One of the most effective demonstrations of how easily prejudiced attitudes may be formed and how arbitrary and illogical they can be comes from a third-grade class in Riceville, Iowa. The teacher, Jane Elliott, wanted to provide her students from this all-white, rural community with the experience of prejudice and discrimination in order to draw from it the implications of its seductive appeal and devastating consequences. She devised a remarkable experiment, more compelling than many done by professional psychologists.

One day, blue-eyed Mrs. Elliott announced to her class of nine-year-olds that brown-eyed people were more intelligent and better people than those with blue eyes. The blue-eyed children, although the majority, were simply told that they were inferior and that the brown-eyed children should therefore be the "ruling class." Guidelines were laid down so the inferior group would "keep their place" in the new social order. They were to sit at the back of the room, stay at the end of the line, use paper cups (instead of the drinking fountain), and so on. The "superior" students received extra privileges, such as extra recess time for work well done.

Within minutes the blue-eyed children began to do more poorly on their lessons and became depressed, sullen, and angry. They described themselves as "sad," "bad," "stupid," "dull," "awful," "hard," "mean." One boy said he felt like a "vegetable." Of the brown-eyed superiors, the teacher reported, "What had been marvelously cooperative, thoughtful children became nasty, vicious, discriminating little third-graders . . . it was ghastly."

To show how arbitrary and irrational prejudice and its rationalizations really are, the teacher told the class on the next school day that she had erred, that it was really the blue-eyed children who were superior and the brown-eyed ones who were inferior. The brown-eyes now switched from their previously "happy," "good," "sweet," "nice" self-labels to derogatory ones similar to those used the day before by the blue-eyes. Their academic performance deteriorated, while that of the new ruling class improved. Old friendship patterns between children dissolved and were replaced with hostility.

The children reacted with relief and delight at the end, when they were "debriefed" and learned that none of them were "inferior" to others. Hopefully they had learned to empathize with those they might see being made targets of prejudice in the future (Elliott, 1977). ●

Besides the observable changes in the children's overt behavior toward each other and in their schoolwork under the two conditions of the experiment, Jane Elliott obtained measures of their feelings under each condition by having them draw pictures of how they felt. One pair of these drawings is reproduced here. When the children were "on top," they felt competent and capable and exulted in their feeling of power and superiority. When they were "on the bottom," they felt small, glum, and pushed down, evidently accepting the discriminators' image of them as inferior and unworthy.

The reality of the emotional strain the children had undergone during the brief two-day experiment is also reflected in the exuberance with which they crowded around the teacher at the end as one united, happy group, in which everyone could accept and be accepted by everyone else.

This experiment has been repeated with other classes and even adult groups with the same results. In each case the assumption of power by one group over another based on supposed superiority has led to discriminatory behavior, disruption in the social structure, loss of self-esteem, changes in performance by the "inferior" members in accord with their ascribed status, and justification by the superiors for the pattern of discrimination sanctioned by the "system."

Once you adopt the derogatory stereotype as a valid indicator of *your* lack of worth, then you may want to dissociate yourself from the despised group—to "pass" on your own via a name change, nose job, hair straightening, and other alterations of your appearance as well as by changing your friends and maybe even rejecting your family. Such a prejudice-induced reaction is one of the most insidious effects of prejudice since it turns the individual not only against his or her own group but against self as well.

Racism: High-powered color blindness

The difference between *prejudice* and *racism* (broadly defined) is a difference between individuals and systems. While prejudice is carried in the minds and actions of individuals, racism is perpetuated across generations by laws and treaties, group norms and customs. It is carried by newspapers, textbooks, and other communications media.

A prevailing racist ideology in a culture constantly provides the "informational" support and social endorsement for discrimination despite personal evidence of its invalidity and injustice. Such ideas become unquestioned assumptions that are seen not as biased opinions or distorted values, but as self-evident truths. They are a major contributor to racial differences in the quality of employment, housing, schooling, health care, and nutrition. They also contribute to crime and violence, and in other cultures and other times have led to "holy wars."

Overt racism

Under the banner of the "white man's burden," it was possible for colonialists to exploit the resources of black Africa. Native Americans could be deprived of their land, liberty, and ecological niche in the United States by newly arrived European immigrants whose desires for wealth, homesteads, and new frontiers were in conflict with the "menace of the red savages." ▲

The "yellow peril" was another journalistic fiction to set people's thinking against Americans of oriental ancestry. After their usefulness was over as laborers on the railroads, mines, and other manual jobs, the press and labor groups mounted campaigns to deport the Chinese, to deprive both them and Japanese immigrants of the rights and privileges of American citizenship. Over 100,000 Japanese Americans were put into concentration camps in the Western states at the start of World War II. Their property was sold at small return, and millions of dollars of their money held by the government and used by American bankers for thirty years (without any interest). Nothing comparable was done to those of German or Italian ancestry—America's other two enemies during that same war.

When a group becomes the target of prejudice and discrimination, it is socially segregated, preventing normal interchange and destroying or blocking channels of communication. This isolation, in turn, allows rumors and stereotypes to go unchecked, fantasies to surface and grow, and the "strange-

In the end, as any successful teacher will tell you, you can only teach the things that you are. If we practice racism, then it is racism that we teach.
Max Lerner
Actions and Passions

▲

In some countries, like South Africa, segregation is still a way of life and the lines are strictly enforced.

ness" of the group, real and fancied, to increase over time. The isolation of American Indians on reservations and the segregated housing patterns in our cities increase the alienation between groups and prevent either reality checks or casual interaction.

Covert racism

The public opinion poll is one way of assessing the extent of racism in a society. If you can believe what people say, there is a decreasing amount of negative stereotyping and adverse attitudes of whites toward blacks in the United States. (In Great Britain the opposite trend can be seen.) Americans seem to be changing their attitudes about racial integration (Gallup, 1975). White parents in the North and South were asked if they had any objection to sending their children to schools with different racial balances. As the table shows, serious objections seem to be diminishing. ◆

Americans of all races, while almost wholly opposed to busing to achieve integration, would favor changing school boundaries to achieve a more heterogeneous racial mix (31%) or the creation of housing for low-income people in middle-class neighborhoods (18%). However, nearly one in five of those surveyed did not endorse any plan for desegregation. As we will see later in this chapter, attitudes often are not readily translated into behavior.

Are overt expressions of prejudice diminishing or merely being suppressed? Measures of covert racial prejudice use content analysis of public media to discern if the same old attitudes are still there, but under wraps. One recent study deserves to be highlighted for the subtle form of covert racism it reveals—so subtle that you have probably been exposed to it and never realized its impact on your thinking.

A blind psychology professor, Raymond Rainville, found that while listening to live broadcasts of professional football games he was able to identify the race of the players even though it was never mentioned. Rainville reasoned that the white announcers were communicating messages about basic racial differences, perhaps at an unconscious level.

Transcripts of the televised commentaries of sixteen NFL games were analyzed according to a variety of content categories. The researchers compared descriptions of a black and a white player of the same position who had comparable performance statistics, such as running backs O. J. Simpson and Larry Csonka. Players were designated as "Smith" or "Jones," and names of teams, teammates, and cities were disguised. Three independent raters were able to identify each player correctly as black or white on eleven of twenty-five rating categories.

◆

Attitudes toward school integration

Parents not wanting to send their children to school with:	1963	South 1970	1975	1963	North 1970	1975
A few blacks	61%	16%	15%	10%	6%	3%
Half blacks	78	43	38	23	24	24
More than half blacks	86	69	61	53	51	47

Adapted from Gallup, 1975

All differences found were favorable to whites and unfavorable to blacks. Whites were significantly more often: (a) recipients of sympathy, positive focus, and play related praise, (b) described as executors of aggression, and (c) credited with positive cognitive and physical attributes. Blacks were more often described as: (a) being the recipients of aggression and (b) having a negative nonprofessional record (problems in college, with the police, etc.) (Rainville & McCormick, 1977).

All of these players are exceptional athletes to begin with. Yet the white players were described as active causal agents on the field and the black players as passive objects moved by external forces.

Overcoming prejudice and racism

Once established, prejudice and racism are relatively resistant to extinction because of the several needs they may serve for the individuals and the group and the many conditions that may encourage and maintain existing attitudes. We have a few clues but have been woefully inadequate so far in overcoming this serious social problem.

1. *Change actions.* Research has shown that *contact* between antagonistic groups can promote better intergroup relations and lessen existing hostilities if—but *only* if—many other factors are favorable; mere exposure does not help and is more likely to intensify existing attitudes. Changes as a result of contact are most likely to occur when the contact is rewarding rather than thwarting, when a mutual interest or goal is served, when status is equal, and when the participants perceive that the contact was the result of their own choice.

2. *Change the rules and the reinforcements.* Although "righteousness cannot be legislated," a new law or regulation provides a new system of rewards and punishments and can thereby create a new social norm, which then becomes a powerful influence on individuals to conform to the new pattern. The same results may be achieved by more informal agreements to change "ground rules."

3. *Change the self-image of victims of prejudice.* Young people who are targets of prejudice may be "inoculated" against the crippling psychological effects of it—and thus be helped to develop and demonstrate their real potentials—if they can establish a sense of pride in their origins, history, and group identity. The "Black is beautiful" movement represents an effective instance of this approach, as do "Gray Power" and "Gay Power."

4. *Change competitive encounters to cooperative ones.* Environments that foster interpersonal competition are often breeding grounds for envy, jealousy, hostility, and self-derogation. By creating conditions in which students must depend on one another for learning required material, teachers can help overcome some interracial conflicts that exist in traditional classrooms. Elliot Aronson (1978) has developed a "jig-saw" technique for promoting group cooperation. Each student is given part of the total material to master and then share with other group members. Performance is evaluated on the basis of the overall group presentation. Thus every member's contribution is equally valuable. Students are made to feel like partners not competitors, and those in desegregated settings discover the advantages of sharing knowledge (and friendship) with "equal and interdependent" peers—regardless of race, creed, or sex. ■

Prejudice and racism are
learned behaviors. There is
no need to teach them to our
children.

The unconscious ideology of sexism

*Nature intended women to
be our slaves . . . they are
our property; we are not
theirs. . . . What a mad
idea to demand equality
for women! . . . Women
are nothing but machines
for producing children.*
Napoleon Bonaparte

Which sex do *you* believe is the more emotional, sensitive, affectionate, squeamish, protective, intuitive, jealous, catty, and talkative? Which do you think is more rational, creative, assertive, cool, mechanically and mathematically inclined, and tough? Which would not make a good President or Little League outfielder? Which looks foolish changing an infant's diapers or puttering around the kitchen? A Martian visitor might answer "Golly, I don't know, but maybe it has something to do with whether an infant started life on Earth under a pink or a blue baby blanket."

While boys are playing with guns and mechanical erector sets, girls get dolls and are encouraged to "play house" in preparation for the role of obedient, dedicated wives and self-sacrificing mothers. They are more likely than male students of equal ability to be counseled to go to commercial high schools or "finishing schools." Unless they are exceptional, they are less likely to receive encouragement to continue with higher education. ●

If they are exceptional and do the original work required for a Ph.D. degree, the chances of getting a good job that will be personally and financially rewarding are low. Of the thirty-five million women in the work force, nearly two thirds work as domestics or as clerical, service, or sales workers. In 1974, a woman with four years of college training earned an average of $6477 a year—the same as a man with only an eighth-grade education—and much less than her male classmates, who averaged $14,401 (U.S. Bureau of the Census, 1974). The ideology, often unconscious, that leads to such discrimination is called *sexism*. The two major factors responsible for perpetuating sexist thinking and practices are biological barriers and sex-role socialization training.

Biological barriers

Because women have wombs and bear children, and because artificial control of the reproductive function has always been imperfect, woman has always been defined primarily as *childbearer*. Any supplementary activities that might alter the power of social control over her reproductive capacities have been seen as threatening to the very foundation of society itself and "contrary to

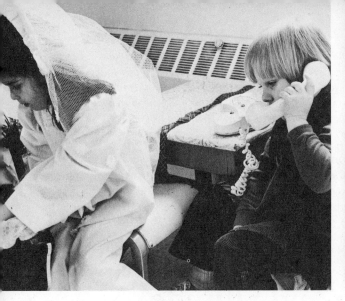

nature." Thus the basic dichotomy in humanity—different reproductive roles—has been used to rationalize all the other supposed differences between men and women and to justify the discriminatory treatment of women. Without the ability to limit her own reproductiveness, a woman's other "freedoms" were illusions that could not really be exercised (Cisler, 1970).

The improved technology of birth control, along with social changes in awareness of the need for reduced population growth, egalitarian male-female relationships, alternative life-styles (single mothers, communal families, etc.), and more day-care facilities are combining to permit more varied self-fulfillment for women.

Sex-role socialization

If discrimination begins early enough and is consistently applied in many spheres of the person's life, then that is the only social reality available on which to base one's self-identity and from which to derive a sense of self-worth. Many studies have documented the general acceptance by women of the stereotype of inferiority.

In one study six articles, on subjects ranging from education to law, were read by college women. Nothing was said about the authorship of the articles, but for each subject half the articles were supposedly by a male author and half by a female author. The same articles were consistently rated as more authoritative and more interestingly written when attributed to male authors than when attributed to female authors (Goldberg, 1968).

Stereotyped thinking about what girls and women can or cannot do—as well as what they should do—develops through bias in both *commission* and *omission*. Take TV, for example, which gets more of many children's time than school. What they see on TV, according to an extensive study of prime-time Canadian TV viewing, are women who are poor models for achievement (Manes & Melynk, 1974). Frequent themes are financially independent female characters portrayed as having unsuccessful marital relations or having happy marriages destroyed by a decision to take a responsible job. A thorough analysis of elementary-school texts published in the 1960s revealed clear sex-role stereotypes.

Female characters (a) occurred less frequently than males, (b) followed orders rather than gave them, (c) were more likely to be engaged in fantasy than in problem solving,

(d) were more conforming and verbal, and (e) were more often found indoors. In addition, whereas positive outcomes were attributed to male actions, happy outcomes after female action were attributed to the situation or to the goodwill of others. With increased grade level, there was an increase in sex differentiation on these dimensions and a more divergent presentation of the "appropriate" characterizations of males and females (Saario, Jacklin, & Tittle, 1973).

Even in many commonly used college psychology texts, sexism is manifest in a variety of ways, most significantly by omission: women rarely appear except as "mothers." The excessive use of the masculine pronoun and the generic term *man* also help to convey the picture of psychology as the study of the "he-man" and not as the study of people's behavior (APA Task Force Report, 1974).

Persuasion and attitude change

In June 1973 Kathy Crampton, age nineteen, was abducted from a commune belonging to the fundamentalist Church of Armageddon in Seattle by a woman and two men. When a state trooper stopped the car, Kathy told him she had been taken against her will. She also told him that her name was Corinth Love Israel, she was eighty-five years old, and her mother was the "spiritual vision of peace." The officer allowed her abductors to drive her off to San Diego. The woman Kathy accused of kidnaping her was her mother; the men were her sister's fiancé and Ted Patrick, an expert on "deprogramming."

This photo of Patricia Hearst was released by the Symbionese Liberation Army fifty-eight days after her kidnaping. The taped message accompanying the photo revealed that Patty had chosen to join the cause of the SLA.

Kathy claimed that she had freely given her life to the founder of the Church of Armageddon to become a child of God. After 102 hours of coercive reindoctrination, including religious services, intensive questioning, emotional attacks, and physical challenges, the deprogramming apparently succeeded. But the next day Kathy escaped and returned to Seattle and the Church of Armageddon, where she was renamed *Dedication* Israel (CBS Evening News Special, August 13, 14, 15, 1973. See also *Los Angeles Times*, December 4, 1972).

In February 1974 Patricia Hearst, age nineteen, was abducted from her apartment in Berkeley, California, by a woman and two men belonging to the Symbionese Liberation Army. After demands for millions of dollars of ransom in the form of food for the poor were met by her father, Randolph Hearst, Patty was scheduled to be released. Then, about sixty days after her kidnaping, the Hearst family and much of the nation were stunned by the tape-recorded announcement that Patty Hearst—renamed Tania—had chosen to stay with the SLA. ■

During the nineteen months that she eluded "recapture" by the FBI, Tania was involved in at least one bank robbery and other illegal activities. Her sensational trial in San Francisco centered around the nature of free will versus the power of social forces of persuasion and indoctrination. Defense lawyer F. Lee Bailey based his case on a form of "brainwashing." He contended that she was under a state of such duress that it conditioned her to unthinking obedience to her captors' wishes. Thus her behavior was not rational, but influenced and forced through fear and primitive needs for survival. The jury did not accept that view, finding her guilty of participating in a bank robbery.

It seems reasonable to conclude that Patty made an ideological conversion to the romantic political belief system of the SLA—in many ways similar to Kathy Crampton's religious conversion. The physical fear she initially experienced was likely to make her grateful to her captors when she was released from close confinement and allowed to eat, sleep, and interact with other young people. Their ideals and rhetoric of justice, equitable distribution of wealth, and racial equality when part of a Robin Hood life-style must have been very appealing to a young person of no firm political, religious, or social ideology.

Both Kathy and Patty experienced the tremendous power of groups of people acting together to achieve a specific goal: in this case, to dramatically and swiftly change a person's way of life. Both women were initially converted, and both were subsequently separated from their new friends. The difference in the two cases is that Kathy did not become resocialized into conformity with family expectations, while Patty, after the deaths of most of her SLA companions, had nowhere to turn but back to her former affiliations.

These cases underscore the role of group pressure in stabilizing or changing attitudes and behavior, but they also raise two basic issues for the social psychologist. What are the face-to-face conditions occurring during interaction that cause individuals to change their attitudes, their beliefs, and their behavior? And how can it be determined whether such a conversion is "genuine" or only overt compliance? That is, how do we know whether any act—by ourselves or others—is freely chosen or is the consequence of coercive pressures? (See *P&L* Close-up, Converts, Brainwashed, Programmed?)

The many faces of persuasion

Virtually every day we are bombarded by systematic attempts to influence the way we think, feel, and act. Our senses are assaulted through the mass media by advertisers who want us to buy various products and services whether or not we want them, need them, or can afford them. Politicians try to influence our votes; teachers try to influence our thinking; religious leaders try to influence our moral behavior and spiritual values. Our friends influence our style of dress, vocabulary, "taste" in music, and ideas of what constitutes an acceptable date, while our parents press on us the importance of eating spinach, cleaning our room, personal hygiene, certain sexual attitudes, and much more.

We have come to accept such attempts as facts of life. Examples of persuasion like those cited above, however, still distress us. One-sided social influence is considered unacceptable when: (a) the "victim" is unable to resist because of "tender age," "weak intellect," or dependence on the influencer; (b) the influencer employs coercive power and has control of most of the relevant resources; (c) the "victim" gains nothing while the influencer gains something; and, most important, (d) there is a high probability that the influence attempt will be successful—no one cares about social influence that does not work.

Education vs. propaganda

A person can choose freely only to the extent that he or she is aware of all the options and of the possible consequences and contingencies. Many educators believe that their primary task is to teach students *how* to think and not *what* to think—to encourage students to seek out alternatives and learn how to evaluate them rather than accept someone else's definition of the problem or choice of solution.

Close-up
Converts, Brainwashed, Programmed?

"I am a thinker. I am your brain. What I wish must be your wish" (Reverend Sun Myung Moon).

The issue of individual freedom versus coercive social control has gained recent prominence in the growing debate over a new religion. Religious converts to the Family of the Unification Church—"Moonies"—allegedly have lost their power to think, replacing it with slavish devotion to Moon's *Divine Principles*.

Has the Church in fact deprived these young people of their individual freedom to make choices? Are they "brainwashed"? What is the nature of the Church's social control? The answers to these questions require an understanding of both the religious sect's techniques of conversion and individual susceptibility to influence.

Unlike the approach of the SLA or of prisoner-of-war interrogators, the Family uses "friendly persuasion." Potential recruits are given dinners at Unification centers with introductory lectures as the dessert. The emphasis is on forming strong friendship bonds with the recruit, coupled with the weaning away from existing ties to parents and friends.

From there, decisions indicating increased commitment are requested. Weekend workshops are followed by week-long and month-long training periods. Potential converts are increasingly isolated and insulated from competing group pressure, their time monopolized and structured into long eighteen-hour days of ceaseless, programmed activity.

Within the Family, strong group pressures are generated through a com-

bination of warmth, supportiveness, and cohesion; repetitive communication of stock phrases as answers to all questions ("You've got to 'shine up' your soul"), resulting in a highly crystallized and shared social reality; and the exclusive power to control positive and negative sanctions. The satisfaction of basic needs—for food, sleep, sex, and self-esteem—is contingent on "proper" behavior and exclusively controlled by the Family members. As a result of this extremely powerful group pressure, individuals often make basic changes in self-identification (perhaps taking a new name), in attitude, and in behavior.

Who might be particularly susceptible to Unification pressures for conversion? The alienated in society who have no deep commitments to existing institutional structures—the young, for example—are particularly ripe for a way of life that offers a meaningful answer to gnawing problems and despair. Perhaps they have reached a "turning point"—the loss of a loved one, a career, a friend—just as the Church appears on their horizon, and with few alternative commitments, they find themselves swept away (see Solomon, 1979).

Is the mushrooming "cult" phenomenon in the United States—typified by the "Moonies," the People's Temple, and Synanon—a symptom of our need for the security of regimented communal life or of alienation from a society grown too complex and impersonal to care for its individual members? Or is it simply a vivid manifestation of normal processes of social behavior?

Propaganda, in contrast, is defined as the systematic, widespread promotion of particular ideas, doctrines, or practices to further one's own cause or to discredit that of one's opposition. Effective propaganda usually involves concealing both the intention to persuade and also the true source of the propaganda.

But if propaganda works best when it is subtle and not obvious because it fits into an available social context, then it is sometimes indistinguishable from what passes as education. In teaching students how to think, textbooks and teachers must use content. In the content they select or fail to use, we may discover the operation of a bias that qualifies some education as propaganda, according to the standard dictionary definition. To cite just one example, by their absence from our history books, minority peoples have been systematically overlooked as contributors to the development of the United States.

When is persuasion coercive?

More carefully calculated are the efforts of lawyers, police interrogators, and leaders of the state to gain our "freely given" consent or assent. Louis Nizer (1961), a famous trial lawyer, describes the subtle psychology of the jury, which, he feels, must be played upon since "the opportunity to condition the jury is as limitless as the attorney's art" (p. 42).

The manuals for training police in the art of interrogation may take some of the credit for the fact that 80 percent of all arraigned suspects confess following a period of interrogation (see Inbau & Reid, 1967). In these manuals the physical excesses of the old "third degree" have been replaced by the "sophistication" of applied psychology used in ethically questionable ways. (See *P&L* Close-up, Confess, My Child.)

Normally, we would assume that the tests for coercion might include the following criteria: (a) sudden, dramatic conversion of beliefs and values rather than gradual evolution of a new position; (b) inaccessibility to one's usual sources of information, approval, and social comparison; (c) being detained in a situation where informational inputs, as well as sources of social reinforcement, are controlled; (d) intensive contact with persuasive agents; (e) promise that the present situation is only temporary and that return to one's former situation is possible.

"Brainwashing" fits these criteria. It is not a scientific term but a word coined by a reporter to account for the conversions apparently produced by the Chinese Communists in some American POWs during the Korean War. (see Schein, 1961; Hinkle & Wolff, 1956).

What produces — and changes — attitudes?

An *attitude* is a relatively stable, emotionalized predisposition to respond in some consistent way toward some person or group of people or situations. The question of how attitudes are learned — and changed — is of concern to us all. Not only are we targets of the kinds of persuasion outlined above, but it is the rare person who has never tried to influence someone else, to change someone's mind by a "line," "reason," example, appeal, threat, or bribe in disguised form.

Attitudes have three components: (a) *beliefs*, or propositions about the way things are or ought to be; (b) *affect*, or emotion associated with these beliefs, measurable in terms of physiological reactions or intensity and style of response; and (c) an action-intention component, with a given probability of responding in specific ways.

We form attitudes about many things in our lives, some of which we know about only indirectly, through information provided by others. Thus one source of attitude formation is *information*, be it through direct observation, information from others, or inferred information. Other sources, already discussed in earlier chapters, include *observation of models* and of the consequences of their actions, and *rewards and punishments* (usually social) meted out by our peers or family for holding or not holding a given attitude. The attitudes we form may also be by-products of repressed conflicts or displaced forms of them. This *ego-defensive* function of attitudes is assumed to play a potent role in the development of some of our most strongly held and "irrational" attitudes, as in racial and religious prejudices (Sarnoff, 1960).

If attitudes are formed in these several ways, then we can expect that changing them will take place through exposure to new information, observation of new models or old models with new reinforcement contingencies,

⚲ *Close-up*
Confess, My Child, and You Shall Be Saved—in Prison

Interrogation manuals claim that they do not "coerce" confessions, but rather elicit them as voluntary statements from suspects actually guilty of committing crimes. After giving a sixty-one-page typewritten murder confession, suspect George Whitmore, Jr., said he felt closer to his interrogating officer than to his own father. It was subsequently proven that Whitmore's confession was false, and had been subtly coerced by means of an old standard technique known as the *Mutt and Jeff approach.* Two detectives work as a pair: Mutt, the "heavy" who leans on the suspect, is abusive and menacing. Jeff, who is kindly and gentle, pretends to be distressed by Mutt's degrading attacks on the suspect, whom he tries to protect. Jeff is the only source of friendship in the barren, hopeless situation. A confession to him will help straighten things out, will enable Jeff to put Mutt in his place, and give him a chance to help out his new-found friend-in-distress. In such a situation, Whitmore obliged with an incredibly detailed description of two murders he had never committed.

Variations on this theme include the "bluff on a split pair," in which two suspects are separated, and Suspect 1 is taken into a back room while Suspect 2 waits in the front office. After hearing screaming and loud noise from the back room, Suspect 2 hears the secretary called in over the intercom. Later, the secretary returns to the front office and begins typing, occasionally stopping to ask Suspect 2 for some vital information that gets typed into the report. Eventually, the detective in charge appears and says there is no need to interview Suspect 2 because the case is closed: the partner has "spilled the beans," turned state's evidence, and put the finger on Suspect 2. In many cases, the unsuspecting Suspect 2 then pleads innocence while describing the crime in detail and accusing the partner of it. After this "voluntary" confession, Suspect 1, who up to this point has said nothing, gets a chance to read the confession and take the full rap—or further implicate the deceived accomplice.

In a "reverse lineup," a suspect in a minor crime may be identified by several reputable-looking witnesses (police confederates) as a child molester, kidnaper, armed robber, or whatever. Against the possibility of a twenty-years-to-life sentence, pleading guilty to the lesser crime with a one-to-five-year sentence seems the better part of wisdom for many naive suspects.

Besides describing tactics such as these, interrogation manuals tell detective candidates how to dress, talk, and size up the suspect, as well as how the room should be arranged for maximum persuasive impact.

changed rewards and punishments for our own attitudes, and resolution of our psychodynamic conflicts. Social psychological research has concentrated on attitude change through exposure to persuasive communications (see Eagly & Himmelfarb, 1978; Bakker, 1975).

Who says what to whom with what effects?

Aristotle, in his *Rhetoric,* attributed the persuasive impact of a communication to three distinguishable factors: *ethos, logos,* and *pathos.* These correspond to communicator characteristics, message features, and the emotional nature of the audience. The scientific study of communication effectiveness has followed Aristotle's lead in its investigation of "*who* says *what* to *whom*—and with what effect" (Hovland, Janis, & Kelley, 1953).

Even though the research has concentrated on only the three variables—source, message, and audience—complex interactions have typically been found rather than simple main effects. The reason becomes apparent when we consider only a few of the dimensions on which source, message, and audience may vary:

1. *Source* — expertise, trustworthiness, status, coercive and reward power, age, sex, race, ethnic group, physical appearance, attractiveness, voice qualities, identification with audience's initial attitude, and so on.
2. *Message* — use of rational or emotional appeals, type of emotional appeals (fear, guilt, shame, etc.), organizational features (builds to climax or starts out as hard-hitting), language style (formal, colloquial, slang, profanity, slogans), presents both sides of the issue or only one side, presents positive or negative points first, and so on.
3. *Audience* — sex, intelligence, educational level, and personality traits (self-esteem, dependency, dogmatism, extraversion); also their involvement and informational level on the issue, the extremity of their initial attitude, and so on.

Do people do what they say?

Social psychologists have studied the process of changing attitudes because they have assumed that attitudes are "predispositions to act." Thus, knowledge of the conditions that control the formation and change of attitudes has been expected to provide an efficient means of predicting and controlling behavior change. How valid are these assumptions and explanations?

Unfortunately, many studies have found a very weak correlation between measured attitudes and other behavior. For example, attitudes of prejudice toward ethnic groups bear little relationship to how one behaves toward minorities; one's attitude toward cheating fails to predict how much one will cheat. It appears that what people say and what they do are not as closely intertwined as common sense might suggest.

This low correlation between attitude and behavior is not surprising since the conditions under which verbal statements on attitude scales are elicited differ from the conditions under which the overt target behavior is elicited. Each type of behavior is also partly under the control of its own reinforcement contingencies. Thus a written questionnaire on which an individual expected approval for expressing tolerance might show no prejudice, whereas the same individual might reveal quite different attitudes in the company of prejudiced friends.

Various intervening factors bring a person's actions into line with his or her sentiments and attitudes. Would you help someone who is being mugged? Of course! But have you? Probably not, because you must have the *opportunity* to act on your attitudes. But given the chance to act, you then must have *knowledge* of what courses of action lie open to you in order to prevent the violence — call the police, assume a karate stance. You must also have the *competence* to perform the action deftly and effectively; for example, without knocking out the victim instead of the mugger. Therefore, the connection between the behavior and the attitude is often weak because of the nature of the situation and the difficulties involved in performing the appropriate role in the situation.

Under what conditions do people's attitudes predict how they will behave? First, an attitude predicts behavior when they are of equal generality. A person's attitude about the importance of environmental conservation does not accurately predict participation in a community bottle recycling project. His or her attitude toward taking part in community recycling projects more accurately predicts such behavior.

Second, an attitude is not tied to any particular behavior, but predicts one's overall *pattern* of behavior toward the attitude object. While a Methodist's attitude toward the church may not predict attendance on any given Sunday, it is related to church behaviors taken as a whole, including attendance, tithing, church socials, etc. The more positive one's attitude, the more positive behaviors one is likely to engage in.

Third, the *salience* of the attitude affects the extent of its impact on behavior toward the attitudinal object. Students' attitude toward affirmative action affected their verdict of liability in a mock court case dealing with sex discrimination when they thought about affirmative action prior to their judgments (Snyder & Swann, in press). Furthermore, people's attitudes are salient, well-defined, and strong—and hence more likely to determine behavior—when they are formed through *direct experience* rather than indirectly through media communication or word-of-mouth (Regan & Fazio, 1977; Zanna & Fazio, 1977). Attitudes and behavior are linked if people have cognitive schemas (see p. 149) for thinking about the attitude object (Tesser & Leone, 1977). Together, these findings suggest that attitudes do affect behavior, and that one may change behavior by first changing attitudes, provided that the variables of generality, behavioral patterning, and attitudinal salience are taken into account.

Do people say what they do?

Investigators have begun a new approach to understanding attitudes and attitude change, based on the wisdom shown in Aristotle's statement that "men acquire a particular quality by constantly acting in a particular way." In fact, there is considerable evidence now to support the view that attitude change is best accomplished *after* exposure to a situation in which behavior is first changed directly. If behavior is changed, a change in attitude will usually follow. ▲

One way of changing behavior, as we saw in our study of group dynamics, is to place people in positions where group norms constrain and direct them to perform new roles. Seymour Lieberman (1956) investigated whether new attitudes would follow from the change to roles that demanded new behavior.

Early one year, over two thousand employees of the Rockwell Corporation reported their attitudes toward plant management and toward the union that organized plant workers. By December of the next year, twenty-three workers had been promoted to foreman and thirty-five workers elected to union steward positions. When their attitudes were reassessed, it was found that, in comparison to workers who had not changed roles but who were similar in other respects, the new foremen had become more pro-management and the new stewards more pro-union.

Individuals can be induced to perform roles that are contrary to their relevant attitudes. Incentives for such attitude-discrepant role performance are numerous: for personal gain (getting an "A"), to avoid punishment or ridicule, to further some transcendent cause (to advance science), to develop skills (as a member of the debate team), to help a friend or neighbor, and so on. Will attitudes change regardless of the reason the person enacts the role? No, the amount of change will depend on variables described in the theory of cognitive dissonance.

▲

Which comes first, the attitude or the behavior? A positive attitude toward environmental conservation is likely to grow out of participation in a specific recycling project. On the other hand, the behavior will not necessarily follow from a vaguely positive general attitude.

Cognitive dissonance

Simply performing a counterattitudinal activity is not enough to produce attitude change. To the extent that they can attribute their compliant act to *external* forces (such as reward or coercion), people can maintain their original attitude even though their behavior contradicts it. However, stimulus conditions that can get people to perform a discrepant act and see it as of their own choosing create a state of *cognitive dissonance*. Leon Festinger's (1957) cognitive dissonance theory assumes that people cannot tolerate inconsistency and will work to eliminate or reduce it whenever it exists. According to the theory, a state of *dissonance* will be aroused whenever a person simultaneously has two cognitions (bits of knowledge, beliefs, opinions) that are psychologically inconsistent. Since this state is an unpleasant one, the individual will be motivated to reduce the dissonance in some way and achieve greater *consonance* (consistency). This reduction of dissonance between an act and an attitude can take place in a number of ways: (a) change the attitude to fit the behavior; (b) change the behavior to fit the attitude; (c) reevaluate the importance of the attitude or behavior; and (d) bolster or support with new cognitions either one's belief about one's behavior or one's attitude.

For example, suppose the two dissonant cognitions are a piece of knowledge about oneself ("I smoke") and a belief about smoking ("Smoking causes lung cancer"). To reduce the dissonance involved here, one could: (a) change one's belief ("The evidence for lung cancer is not very convincing"); (b) change one's behavior (stop smoking); (c) reevaluate the behavior ("I don't smoke very much"); (d) add new cognitions ("I smoke low-tar cigarettes") that make the inconsistency less serious.

The more *important* the cognitions are for the individual, the greater the dissonance will be. For example, if our smoker didn't care about getting lung cancer (was ninety years old and had already lived a full life), then there would be little dissonance between "I smoke" and "Smoking causes lung cancer." For a younger person very frightened of becoming ill or dying, however, the dissonance would be much greater.

The amount of dissonance is also a function of the *ratio* of dissonant to consonant cognitions. According to the theory, the amount of dissonance that is produced is very important to an understanding of the individual's later behavior, since the greater the dissonance, the harder the person will try to reduce it.

In a later modification of the original theory, Brehm and Cohen (1962) postulated that dissonance is more likely to occur in a given situation if one *commits* oneself to an inconsistent course of action publicly while believing that one has a genuine *choice* to do otherwise. For example, you might feel considerable dissonance if you publicly supported a politician for whom you had contempt. But if you saw no other choice (you would lose your job otherwise), then you could disown the support as not personally caused and feel no dissonance.

Brehm and Cohen's hypothesis allows us to make predictions as to how dissonance will be reduced. Since public actions are observed by others, while private ideas and beliefs are not, any public behavior will be more "fixed" in reality and less susceptible to change than private thoughts. For example, suppose you are experiencing dissonance between an overt behavior ("I chose to do this job") and a covert belief ("This job is boring"). Since you have already made the behavioral commitment, it would be very hard for you to change that cognition ("I did not choose to do this job"). Your private belief, however, is less anchored in external reality and thus is more amenable to change ("Actually, this job is interesting—I'm learning a lot").

A number of studies have been conducted to test such dissonance-reduction hypotheses.

In one experiment, subjects participated in a very dull task and were then asked (as a favor to the experimenter) to lie to another subject by saying that the task had been fun and interesting. Half the subjects were paid twenty dollars to tell the lie, while the others were paid only one dollar. The former group saw the money as sufficient external justification for lying. The one-dollar payment was seen as an inadequate reason for telling the lie, so members of the second group were left with two dissonant cognitions: "The task was dull" and "I chose to tell someone it was fun and interesting." To reduce their dissonance, these subjects changed their evaluation of the task and later expressed the belief that "It really was fun and interesting—I might like to do it again." In comparison, the subjects who lied for twenty dollars did not change their evaluation of the dull task (Festinger & Carlsmith, 1959).

In sum, when induced by incentives to perform a public role that demands counterattitudinal behavior, people will *not* change their private attitudes if they can deny personal responsibility by attributing the action to external forces and constraints. Maximum dissonance and subsequent attempts to reduce it through attitude change are found when your discrepant commitment is refused by several other group members whom you perceive as similar to yourself, especially when they give personal reasons for not going along with the counterattitudinal act (Haney, 1978). In this case, the irrationality of the dissonant action (behavior without sufficient cause) is compounded by the sense that one has deviated from the group. The individual resolves this conflict by saying, "I did it because I like it; in fact, I've always liked it—sort of." This attitude change is then internalized as a rational, normal process.

Thus we arrive at an answer to the initial questions we posed in regard to

Kathy Crampton and Patty Hearst. They are likely to have seen their own belief conversion as free and uncoerced to the extent that they were unaware of or insensitive to situational forces sufficient to cause their actions. If powerful physical forces, threats, rewards, and other types of extrinsic justification were used to elicit their public compliance, it is unlikely that their private beliefs would have been similarly affected. Once the extrinsic pressures were off, their private beliefs would have reemerged. But we have seen that when public compliance is induced with minimal apparent extrinsic justification, then the accompanying private changes in beliefs and values are not only seen by the individual as "genuine" and "inner-directed" but are likely to endure.

Your vulnerability to influence

Whether or not we succumb to social influence attempts is often a matter of what we tell ourselves rather than how persuasive the orator or con artist is. We saw in Chapter 5 that causal schemas organize information about the determinants of behavior. They establish what we consider to be effective, reliable causal agents and what we believe are weak and insignificant ones. In addition, our schemas about change processes include conceptions about our own changeability or susceptibility to persuasion and group pressures. Are your attitudes easily changed? Are your opinions shaped by the media? Are you a sucker for a well-wrought ad? How many people do you suppose would also answer "No"? Probably most of us. But then who is left that is being socialized, persuaded, educated, sold, changed?

Our vulnerability to social influence is proportional to the degree to which we *underestimate* the power of social forces and *overestimate* our personal power to resist them and totally control our actions. We attribute more power to *dispositional* factors (personality, character, morals, personal values, family upbringing) than is warranted. At the same time, we do not acknowledge the true potency of *situational* forces (norms, roles, status, protocol, etiquette, group pressures). This egocentric power orientation is called the *attribution error* (Ross, Bierbrauer, & Polly, 1974).

This error of overestimating the importance of an actor's *dispositions* and underestimating the importance of *situational* forces occurs across a wide range of everyday situations. It is seen in our belief that *we* would not have acted the way so-and-so did in a given situation.

It is inconceivable to most people that they could have acted as Lt. Calley or the other members of Charlie Company did in the My Lai massacre, or as the National Guard did—shooting defenseless Kent State students, or as Nixon and his Watergate circle of advisors did.

But it was also inconceivable to the psychiatrists—and perhaps to you—that the majority of subjects in Milgram's obedience studies would go all the way in giving electric shocks to an innocent victim. Similarly, in the Stanford prison study, all subjects who were later prisoners asserted that they were absolutely certain they would last the full two weeks—whereas half of them did not last even five days. And the guards did not believe they would ever act in the brutal manner they did. Said one before the study began, "As I am a pacifist, I cannot imagine ever being aggressive toward another person." Yet he became one of the most cruel, abusive guards.

A major conclusion from all the research on attribution is that while people are remarkably susceptible to situational pressures, they are even more remarkably insensitive to and unaware of the extent to which these pressures are determining their behavior (see Nisbett & Wilson, 1977b).

The laws of behavior that most *experimental* research generates are empirical statements relating situational variables to certain outcomes. Such laws explain the variability of comparable subjects' behavior in different situations; differences between people are ignored. The generalizations of *personality* research, on the other hand, attempt to explain the variability of different people's behavior in the same situation. There is also a third class of explanations: those involving *interactions* between situational and dispositional variables—the situation has a different but predictable impact on different types of people. Taken together, these three types of explanation account for all the possible variation (other than random) in the behavior of people across situations.

In the next chapter we will concentrate on the way people behave in one-to-one social situations—situations of potentially intimate human contact.

Chapter summary

Social psychology is the study of group processes and structures and the impact of people on each other. *Social norms* are the expectations shared by the members of a group. They define the nature of social reality, the forms and foundations upon which people base their interaction, and the common referent for members' self-evaluations. Social norms distribute the *roles* of group members according to an *authority structure*.

Norms emerge in a group through the *diffusion* and *crystallization* of expectations. The expectations of incoming group members eventually crystallize around perspectives shared with other group members. People become *socialized* into the culture of a group when they behave in accordance with its dominant normative values. The more an individual relies on the group for a sense of self-worth and *legitimacy,* the greater the pressure toward conformity the group can bring to bear on him or her. *Sanctions* are the rewards and punishments contingent on conformity. Norms can be changed by a minority when it is able to present a consistent position, strong commitment, and an appearance of autonomy.

While there is little evidence that group leaders all share the same personality traits, they do tend to be the most verbally active members of groups, and they emphasize their community with the rank and file. Bales has distinguished two types of leaders—the *task-oriented* and the *social-emotional*. But good leadership is usually a matter of an optimal combination of leadership personality and situational demands. A pioneering study by Kurt Lewin demonstrated that the same leader, regardless of his own traits, had a markedly different impact on a group when he employed one *leadership* style as opposed to another. The range of styles employed were: *laissez-faire, democratic,* and *autocratic.*

Intergroup conflict arises because the cohesive friendships and shared sense of reality in an *in-group* often includes the labeling of others as members of *out-groups. Prejudice* is an internal state or psychological set to react in a biased way toward members of certain groups. *Discrimination* is behavior that prejudice may give rise to. Victims of discrimination may experience a *denial of legitimacy* and *isolation* from the power structure of a culture. This may eventually lower *competence-based self-esteem.* Numerous experiments have shown that the assumption of power by one group over another based on supposed superiority leads to discriminatory behavior, disruption in social structure, loss of self-esteem by the "inferior" group, and justification by the "superiors" for their behavior in terms of *sanctions* in the "system."

Racism differs from prejudice in that rather than merely being carried in the minds and actions of individuals, it is perpetuated across generations by group norms and customs. It may occur in obvious *overt* forms and in more subtle *covert* forms. Overcoming racism and prejudice involves increasing the positive contacts between antagonistic groups, changing social rules and reinforcements, changing the self-image of victims of prejudice, and changing competitive encounters to cooperative ones.

The two major factors responsible for perpetuating *sexist* thinking and practice are *biological barriers* and *sex-role socialization training*. The basic dichotomy in humanity—different reproductive roles—has been used to rationalize all other supposed differences between men and women and to justify discriminatory treatment of women. Further, *stereotyped* thinking about girls and women as presented in the media, general language usage, and early child-rearing practices perpetuates sexist attitudes in society at large and in the self-images formed by the women themselves.

Systematic, widespread promotion of particular ideas, doctrines, or practices to further one's cause or to discredit that of one's opposition may be termed *propaganda*. But *propaganda* and *persuasion* are only *coercive* when certain conditions are met. For example, studies have shown that jurors and subjects of police interrogations may be psychologically *coerced* by lawyers and police investigators.

Attitudes are relatively stable, emotionalized predispositions to respond in some consistent way toward a person or group. Attitude components are *beliefs, affect,* and *action*. They are formed on the basis of *information, observation of models,* and *rewards and punishments*. Attitudes in themselves may serve as important ego-defense mechanisms. Surprisingly, there is a low correlation between attitudes and actual behavior. The nature of a situation and the difficulty involved in performing an appropriate role in the situation discourage people from acting upon their attitudes. Only when they are formed by *direct experience,* are *salient,* and are of *equal generality,* are attitudes effective in predicting behavior. But if behavior is changed, a change in attitude is likely to follow.

According to the theory of *cognitive dissonance,* people will change their attitudes or behavior, or add new cognitions when they are in a state of *dissonance*—when they are confronted simultaneously with two cognitions that are psychologically inconsistent. They will be motivated to achieve greater *consonance* with these changes. A maximum state of dissonance occurs, for example, when an individual holds a commitment that is refused by several other group members perceived as similar to the individual.

Individuals are susceptible to social influence attempts to the extent that they underestimate the powers of social forces and overestimate their personal powers to resist them. We tend to attribute more power to *dispositional* factors than is warranted, not acknowledging the full impact of *situational* forces. This egocentric power orientation is called the *attribution error*.

22 Liking, Loving, and Sexual Relationships

Liking, loving, and sexual relationships forge the bonds of the human connection. This person-to-person connection expands the boundaries of our individual functioning by liberating the self from its solitary confinement.

The "chemistry" that occurs between two people in love cannot be fully understood from even the most intensive analysis of the individual elements involved. The relationship is the secret ingredient—the "we" that transforms the "you" and the "me." Interaction is the special process—the mutual sharing that emerges from individuals giving and taking. The sound of one hand clapping is silence and not half-hearted applause. So too, for example, is the sound of one person trying to tickle him or herself. It is not partial laughter, but silence. You will never know whether you are ticklish by judging how you respond to tickling yourself. Try it and discover that even such an apparently physical response requires the presence of another person. It is not clear why this should be, but it is evident that it takes two to tickle.

The primary relationship between people is that which links a parent and a child. As part of an affectionate, stable family unit, the growing child develops a sense of personal integrity and security, while also learning to trust others, to share with them, and to enjoy their companionship. Self-respect and a sense of identity are developed in this crucible of positive regard and recognition by others. In less ideal social environments, we see other patterns forming: envy, jealousy, mistrust, exploitation, submission, and fear of authority.

The child or adult who cannot reach out for the hand of another, or whose extended hand is not grasped in turn by another person, is cut adrift from the moorings of society. In many ways we have seen in our study of *Psychology and Life* that the isolated individual is vulnerable to the pathologies of a self-centered existence: loneliness, depression, paranoia, suicide, and antisocial reactions.

We need to like and be liked in return. *Liking relationships* are characterized by positive attitudes of each person toward the other, backed up by tendencies to approach and interact. Liking can turn casual, impersonal encounters with strangers into friendships. When we are young, we want many friendships because they index our popularity. As we mature we become selective, narrowing down the range of our friendships by substituting quality for quantity. We want to be with people around whom we can feel comfort-

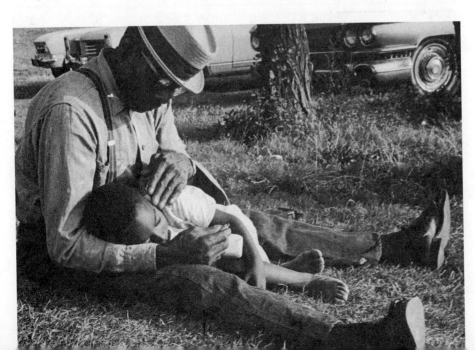

able, "let down our hair," and "be our real selves." Close friends get to let down their defenses, take off their masks of sociability, and just be people. Once formed, such relationships can endure for a lifetime even when friends live far apart and only rarely have direct contact. Friendship may survive on a diet of good thoughts warmed in the glow of pleasant feelings.

Intense liking and the desire for more exclusive and permanent contact between two people shapes itself into a *loving* relationship. But love is not just a lot of liking, it is one of the most complicated of all human experiences. It can ennoble or demean. It can be the source of creation or the reason for destruction. Love may be many things to different people, but it is a powerful force psychologists have just begun to reckon with in their attempt to understand human nature.

Curiously, some loving relationships may develop with little or no liking. They may be based upon strong arousal, often sexual in nature, that is labeled as "love." Sometimes such love is more like an addiction than a preference for companionship. The physiological changes going on within the sexually maturing young adult give new meanings to interpersonal relationships. Other people become sources of erotic thoughts and romantic feelings as well as the means of gratifying sexual impulses. The power of sexual urges to bring young people into closer union has been a matter of concern to the elders of most societies everywhere. By a variety of tactics, strategies, and social programming, the two sexes have been put into adversary positions—to encourage making war and not love (before marriage). Little wonder then that most people have difficulty accepting the humanness of their own sexuality and, even more so, comfortably relating to anyone else on a sexual level.

In this chapter, then, we will study some close encounters of a special kind, not through rendezvous with alien creatures, but by studying those qualities of life that seek their own affirmation. What are the determinants and consequences of our attempts to contact another mind, to embrace a kindred spirit, to touch, be touched in return, and breathe existence into another generation in our own image?

Falling in like

Does "absence make the heart grow fonder," or is it "out of sight, out of mind"? Do "birds of a feather flock together," or does "familiarity breed contempt"? Or which wisdom shall we follow from Shakespeare: "They do not love that do not show their love," or "Love looks not with the eyes, but with the mind"?

When it comes to friendship, liking, and love, every human society has a vast accumulation of knowledge collected over the ages to guide the social psychologist's inquiry. But as the quotations above nicely indicate, common sense and literary wisdom have enjoyed a long life by the simple expedient of being all things to all people. There are clichés, quotations, folk wisdom, and down-home good sense to handle all outcomes—so long as you select the one that suits the occasion and conveniently ignore its contradiction.

Despite the obvious importance of attraction between people in creating the foundations of social life, it is only recently that energetic young researchers have begun to recast the flowery verse of the poets and the essence of common sense into testable hypotheses. From this emerging enterprise we may soon learn some valuable lessons to help us love each other both wisely and well (see Huston & Levinger, 1978).

The ABC's of liking

Why do we like some people more than others? Basically, research has shown that we are attracted to people who bring us maximum rewards or gratifications at a minimum expense. For example, we are more attracted to people who are nearby than to those who are farther away. We like people who are already attracted to us, and who demonstrate their attraction by doing us favors and saying nice things about us. We like people who satisfy our needs and who have needs that we can satisfy.

Proximity

All other things being equal, we tend to like people who live close to us more than those who live far away. People who are nearby are more easily accessible to us, and our contact with them is likely to be more frequent. Early evidence of this proximity-liking effect is seen in a study of marriage license applications in Philadelphia in 1931. It was found that one of every four couples had lived within two city blocks of each other (Bossard, 1940). A similar study in Columbus, Ohio, showed that in 50 percent of the cases where both partners were residents of that city, they lived within fourteen standard blocks of each other (Koller, 1953).

"Oh, I just adore the boy next door . . ."
Martin & Blane
"The Boy Next Door"

The most famous study of proximity and friendship choice was conducted in a housing development for married students called Westgate West. Residents of seventeen structurally similar apartment buildings were asked to name their closest friends and the people they saw most often socially. Researchers found that residents most often chose other residents who lived on the same floor and in the same building as they did. The functional distance among residents also produced proximity effects. Functional distance is determined by the design or structure of the buildings and residential area that allows more or less contact among different residents. ●

● **Schematic diagram of a Westgate West building**

Adapted from Festinger, Schachter, & Back, 1950

People living in apartments 1 and 5 near the stairs, for example, chose residents from the upper floor more often than people in other apartments on the first floor. People in apartment 5, near the mail boxes, tended especially to choose more upper-level friends, particularly residents of apartments 9 and 10. Furthermore, people who lived in apartments that faced onto the central court area had twice as many friends in the building than did people whose apartments faced out onto the street (Festinger, Schachter, & Back, 1950).

Why should nearness to people promote liking for them? Presumably, it is because we have more frequent exposure to people who are close by, and "if the frequency of interaction between two or more people increases, their degree of liking for one another will increase" (Homans, 1950).

If proximity is a powerful force for mutual liking, then what predictions can we make about interpersonal attraction? Although we all assume that students who like each other will sit next to each other in class, the proximity principle leads to the reverse prediction as well: students who sit close to each other in classrooms will like each other more than students who sit at opposite sides of the room. Likewise, friends who are separated for extended periods of time should gradually become less attached or attracted to each other. This prediction is often borne out when a student who returns home after a semester away from old friends expects to find relationships unchanged. Most of us have experienced the distress of having "nothing to say" to old friends from whom we have been physically separated.

There is a limit, however, to the proximity-liking effect. If we are annoyed or disturbed by certain things that people do, then we will dislike the people who do them near to us more than those who do them farther away. For example, the student who continually drums on the arm of a chair or whispers to a neighbor during lectures will be more disturbing the closer he or she is to you. Research has found that if you dislike such people (presumably because they "spoil" your environment in some way), proximity to them will *decrease* your attraction rather than increase it (Ebbesen, Kjos, & Konecni, 1976).

Physical attractiveness

*Beauty is a greater
recommendation than any
letter of introduction.*
Aristotle

Generally speaking, we like beautiful people more than we like plain or ugly ones. This finding may contradict our beliefs in equality and in the irrelevance of external appearance to personal relationships, but it has been demonstrated in a number of experiments. For example, in one study college students attended a dance in which they thought their dates had been assigned to them on the basis of a computer analysis (actually, the dates were randomly assigned). Interview data indicated that the *physical attractiveness* of the date was the only factor significantly related to liking and anticipation of future dates. Neither personality nor intelligence proved to be influential factors in determining interpersonal attraction (Walster, Aronson, Abrahams, & Rottman, 1966). In another experiment, male subjects were paired with either an attractive or unattractive female partner for a laboratory task. Subjects liked the attractive partner more, spent more time thinking about her long after the experiment was over, and remembered more details about her appearance (Kleck & Rubinstein, 1975).

The "prejudice" in favor of physically attractive individuals appears to be fairly well established early in life. Boys and girls (ages five to six) who are physically attractive are better liked by others of their age group than are children who are judged physically less attractive (Dion, Berscheid, & Walster, 1972). Furthermore, adults assign different personality and behavioral characteristics to children according to the child's physical attractiveness.

In one study, subjects were shown pictures of children who had supposedly misbehaved. Some children were highly attractive; others were not. Respondents tended to rationalize the misbehavior of the beautiful children and to describe such children as basically well-mannered, unselfish, and sociable. Less attractive children who had committed the same misdeed were described as bratty, potentially antisocial, maladjusted, and were perceived as likely to cause problems (Dion, 1972).

It would appear that our society has internalized the premise that "what is beautiful is good." Thus we perceive beautiful people as more intelligent, more successful, more pleasant, and happier than other people, even if there is no objective basis for these judgments.

So far, the research on physical attractiveness has been done in situations where people did not know each other or were only beginning to get acquainted. It may be that physical attractiveness plays a more important role in these initial, "getting to know you" stages than later on in a relationship.

Competency

In general, we like people who are able and competent, rather than those who have difficulties in doing things well (Stotland & Hillmer, 1962). Presumably, this is because competent people can make life easier for everyone as a result of their knowledge and efficiency.

We don't love qualities, we love persons; sometimes by reason of their defects as well as of their qualities.
Jacques Maritain
Reflections on America

However, it is possible to be too competent for one's own good. Highly competent people may be better liked if they show some human weaknesses or blunder occasionally than if they are too perfect. ◆

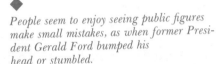

◆
People seem to enjoy seeing public figures make small mistakes, as when former President Gerald Ford bumped his head or stumbled.

In one study subjects listened to one of four tape recordings of a "candidate for the College Quiz Bowl." The same voice was used on each tape, but on two of the tapes the candidate was presented as highly intelligent and as having done well both academically and in extracurricular activities. On the other two tapes, the candidate was presented as average in intelligence and as having done only moderately well in school. On two of the tapes (one involving the superior person, one involving the average person), the candidate committed an embarrassing blunder by clumsily spilling a cup of coffee all over himself.

After listening to each tape, subjects were interviewed about their impressions of the candidate, how much they liked the candidate, and so on. "The results were clear-cut: The most attractive stimulus person was the superior person who committed a blunder, while the least attractive stimulus person was the person of average ability who also committed a blunder. . . . there was nothing charming about the blunder itself; it had the effect of increasing the attractiveness of the superior person and decreasing the attractiveness of the average person" (Aronson, 1969, p. 149).

These results may be interpreted in a number of ways. Some suggest that the superior "bunglers" seem more attractive because they become more "human" and hence more like us. Or perhaps we rationalize the mistake in terms of outside circumstances rather than in terms of personal attributes. The superior person's mistake will probably be seen as an "exception"—not a rule. When an average person makes a mistake, however, it may be attributed to already perceived ineptitude or interpreted as further evidence of incompetence. Although it may not seem fair, average people are not given as much latitude as superior people.

Reciprocal liking

*To make people like you
. . . become genuinely interested in other people.
. . . Be a good listener.
Encourage others to talk
about themselves.*

Dale Carnegie
*How to Win Friends and Influence
People*

As Dale Carnegie taught, we like people who express liking for us and who show a "genuine interest" in us. Evidence for this reciprocal liking effect was found by Backman and Secord (1959), who told members of discussion groups that certain other group members liked them very much. Later, when two-person teams were formed, subjects chose more often to be paired with those people who expressed liking for them than with other group members.

Although we tend to like people who like us, it would be a mistake to equate liking behavior with flattery or insincere, manipulative actions. If someone else's expression of praise or affection toward us is viewed as ingratiating, rather than sincere, we will like them less (Jones, 1964). How do we evaluate a person's sincerity? If we think that the other person is trying to get something from us, we will see his or her behavior as manipulative. Also, we are prone to dismiss praise that seems excessive and deviates greatly from our own estimate of ourselves.

For example, if you think of yourself as an "ugly duckling," being called "beautiful" or "handsome" will probably be taken as insincere flattery, whether or not it is intended as such. To be effective, positive statements or compliments should not be obviously inconsistent with the recipient's self-perception. While giving compliments is an important part of liking, learning to *receive* compliments is equally important. (See *P&L* Close-up, When in Doubt, Say "Thanks!")

Similarity and complementarity

One of the most consistent findings in research on attraction is that people like others who are similar to themselves. This principle that "like attracts like" holds true for physical appearance, since there is a tendency for people to like, date, and ultimately marry individuals who are physically similar to themselves (Murstein, 1972). More importantly, there is much evidence to suggest that persons who share similar attitudes, values, and beliefs are more likely to be attracted to each other. For example, when a group of previously unacquainted male subjects spent a great deal of time together under very adverse conditions (ten days in a small, hot fallout shelter), they tended to like those of their comrades who held attitudes similar to their own (Griffitt & Veitch, 1974).

In another field study, college students completed an attitude questionnaire and then were later paired up into male-female couples for a supposed experiment on computer dating. Half of the couples were matched for maximum similarity of attitudes, while the others were matched for maximum attitude dissimilarity. Each couple spent thirty minutes together on a "Coke date" at the student union. After they returned to the experimenter's office, their attraction to each other was measured by how closely they stood next to each other and by their responses on a questionnaire. Couples with similar attitudes

liked each other more (both immediately after the date and several weeks later) and indi-cated a greater desire to date each other (Byrne, Ervin, & Lamberth, 1970).

Why should a similar person be so attractive? One possible reason is that similarity is *reinforcing*. We are less likely to argue or have unpleasant encounters with someone who generally agrees with us, and are more likely to feel confident in the correctness of our attitudes. Furthermore, we may believe that similar people will more likely become attracted to us. Similarity may also lead to attraction because it allows us to maintain *consistent*, balanced relationships with our friends. Thus we like those who like what we like. Another explanation is that we are attracted to people with similar attitudes for reasons of *social comparison*. As we saw earlier, we usually look to other people to give us information about our own abilities, feelings, and beliefs. In other words, we may be attracted to people who are reflections of ourselves or of what we would like to be.

Not *all* similarity breeds such liking, however. There is some evidence that attraction is the result of having *complementary* needs or personality styles. For example, the person who is very domineering may like someone who is quiet and submissive, rather than another domineering individual. Women who hold traditional views of husband and wife roles may prefer men with traditionally masculine traits to complement their own feminine characteristics (Seyfried & Hendrick, 1973).

It may be that at different times, different factors are important to the development of a couple's relationship. For example, similarity of values may be most critical at the early stages, when the two people are beginning to get to know each other. Once they have established that they share certain values and attitudes, and have decided to consider a more long-term relationship, then the complementarity of their needs may take on more significance.

A study of college couples who were seriously considering marriage found that the importance of value similarity and need complementarity was related to the length of time the couple's relationship had existed. For short-term relationships (less than eighteen months), couples who were more similar in values reported more progress towards a permanent commitment. Need complementarity did not play a significant role at this point. However, for long-term relationships (more than eighteen months), greater need complementarity predicted a greater movement toward marriage while similar values did not (Kerckhoff & Davis, 1962).

We must resemble each other a little in order to understand each other, but we must be a little different to love each other.
Paul Géraldy
L'homme et l'amour

Do you enjoy receiving compliments? Do you make the person who gives one feel good or do you disown the compliment or maybe pretend you didn't hear it? How often do you give compliments and nice strokes to others? How are they received? A remarkable number of people can't accept a compliment.

"You like *this* dress? It's just a cheap thing I picked up at a sale. I don't know why I bought it. It's not my color and it's not made very well . . ."

"Naw, it's no big deal. I just put my mitt out and the ball plunked in. Any lamebrain could have done the same thing."

"Really, my A in psychology is nothing to brag about. I studied hard for the test but it was so simple an idiot could have racked up a perfect score. . . . You got a C? Oh, well, hmm."

"Thanks" is the one-word way to acknowledge a compliment. When you disavow the compliment, you make its giver look stupid, unsophisticated, or insensitive. You might extinguish not only compliments toward you, but also the giver's tendency to give compliments to

other people who would like to get them. An aversion to compliments may stem from a sense of modesty that makes you want to neutralize a compliment in order to avoid appearing conceited. A negative response may also arise from your awareness of being evaluated. Even if someone is evaluating you positively, they are still in the superior position of judging you—and they might be more critical in the future. However, if we perceive compliments as an attempt to single us out for special regard, we should reinforce the compliment givers for their efforts.

We can even use compliments to start a conversation—and a relationship.

"Thank you for the compliment. I wasn't sure it was my color when I bought it on sale, so I'm glad to hear you say it looks good."

"I'm glad you think so. I've been practicing that Willie Mays special for a long time, so it's nice to have it work for me."

"It's good of you to say so. Psychology is my major and I put a lot of desk hours into it. I'm thinking of taking more courses. What about you?"

Why do we like the people we like?

As more research is done on the antecedents of attraction, attempts have been made to pull them all together into a comprehensive theory. The most typical approach has been to explain attractions in terms of reinforcement principles. However, more recent theories have gone beyond the notion of reinforcement to develop more complex models of interpersonal attraction.

Reinforcement theory

According to reinforcement models, our attraction to people is based on the feelings we have associated with them. People who reward us in some way arouse positive feelings in us, and thus we like them. Conversely, people who punish us arouse negative feelings and dislike. Not only do we like people who reward us directly, but we also like those people who are present when we receive rewards, even though they are not the source of them. In reinforcement terms, such people have become associated with rewards and function as conditioned reinforcers. Similarly, we dislike people who are simply associated with our being punished, even when they are not the cause of it (Byrne & Clore, 1970; Lott & Lott, 1974).

Reinforcement principles can be used to explain the effects on attraction of the characteristics we have discussed so far. For example, a physically attractive person may provide direct aesthetic rewards or may vicariously reward his or her companion by drawing favorable attention to both of them when they are together. People who are close by can provide rewards more quickly and more often than can acquaintances who live farther away. Competent people may be rewarding because they can put others at ease and can take care of various problems. Similarity is rewarding because it validates our view of reality and because it becomes easier for us to predict how the other person will behave. Both similarity and social approval (reciprocal liking) have been demonstrated to be effective reinforcers across a wide range of situations.

Exchange theory

According to several theorists (Homans, 1961; Thibaut & Kelley, 1959), whenever we interact with others we go through a process of analyzing both the rewards and costs of the interaction. Unless both participants feel the rewards of interacting are greater than the costs, and they are making a psychological "profit" from the exchange, the interaction will not continue. This theory approaches human interaction, or exchange, from the perspective of economics. In the "interpersonal marketplace" you attempt to "give the other man behavior that is more valuable to him than it is costly to you and to get from him behavior that is more valuable to you than it is costly to him" (Homans, 1961, p. 62).

One of the advantages of exchange theory over a pure reinforcement model is that it explicitly recognizes that there are *many* rewards and punishments (costs) present in most interactions. For example, you may be receiving affection from someone, but expending a great deal of time and effort for it. Also, it points out that it is the relationship between these rewards and costs, their sum total, that will determine whether attraction will occur. However, both reinforcement and exchange theories have some limitations. First of all, neither of them can adequately explain behaviors that seem to occur in the absence of rewards, such as altruism or unrequited love. Secondly, neither of them deals with the wide range of individual differences in what constitutes a reward or a cost—to update an old proverb, "what is one person's meat is another person's poison."

© 1977, United Feature Syndicate, Inc.

Equity theory

In an attempt to handle these shortcomings of simple reinforcement principles, equity theory has developed some additional propositions about the role of rewards in a social context. Basically, it assumes that a group of people can maximize their collective reward by working out a system for "equitably" dividing the rewards and costs among the group members. *Equity* is defined in terms of relative outcomes, such that people's outcomes are proportional to their inputs (the more you put into a relationship, the more you should get from it). The group will reward people for adhering to this system of equity and punish them for behaving inequitably. Consequently, when a person is participating in an inequitable relationship, he or she will feel distressed and will try to restore equity to the relationship. The greater the inequity that exists, the more distress he or she will feel, and the harder he or she will try to restore equity. Restoration of equity can take two forms: actual and psychological. People can make direct changes in their inputs or outcomes (as by reducing the number of gifts they give to someone who is providing little

A proposal of marriage in our society tends to be a way in which a man sums up his social attributes and suggests to a woman that hers are not so much better as to preclude a merger or partnership in these matters.
Erving Goffman
On Cooling the Mark Out

affection). Or, they can distort reality and convince themselves that they really *are* getting just what they deserve (as by reinterpreting criticism as an expression of true love). In addition to attraction, equity theory has been applied to the analysis of altruism and exploitative relationships (Walster, Walster, & Berscheid, 1978).

Equity theory has led to the proposal of a "matching hypothesis": romantic relationships that are equitable will be most successful, and thus people will try to get partners who "match" them in terms of their level of social worth. This matching could involve a similar characteristic (for example, highly attractive people will choose highly attractive partners) or could be based on a more complex weighting of different characteristics (for example, someone who is beautiful and dull might "match" someone who is plain and intelligent).

In one experiment, male college students were given feedback on an "intelligence test" they were taking. Some were led to believe they were doing extremely well, while others were told they were doing poorly. During a coffee break, each subject was casually introduced by the experimenter to a woman (actually a confederate). Half of the time, this woman had a highly attractive appearance, while for the other half she appeared to be very unattractive. The experimenter left, and the woman and the subject talked for a while. The subject's behavior was scored for its "romantic" level (e.g., asking the woman for a date, offering to buy her a snack or coffee). Subjects who had been told they had done well on the intelligence test behaved more romantically toward the attractive confederate than the unattractive one. However, subjects who had been told they had performed poorly showed the opposite pattern—they behaved more romantically towards the unattractive confederate, presumably because she "matched" more closely their level of desirability (Kiesler & Baral, 1970).

Overall, the evidence for this "matching" hypothesis is somewhat mixed. Although individuals do tend to choose partners of approximately the same social worth, they still persistently try to attract partners who are far more socially desirable than they. In other words, we strive for the ideal, but our choices tend to be based on the reality of what we have to offer someone else.

Gain-loss theory

Liking is not determined entirely by the other person's characteristics and the extent to which they "match" our own. In situations where attraction is involved, the individual's own ego is at stake, and liking may depend as much or more on one's feelings about oneself as on the characteristics of the other person. One's self-esteem is often based on the feedback one gets from other individuals, and the response that occurs is not always in line with reinforcement predictions.

Aronson (1969) has developed a model called the *gain-loss theory of attraction* to deal with this area of feedback and liking. According to this theory, *changes* in another person's evaluation of us will have more impact on our liking for him or her than if the evaluation were constant. Thus we will like a person whose esteem for us increases over time (a "gain" situation) better than someone who has always liked us. Similarly, we will dislike a person whose evaluation of us becomes more negative over time (a "loss" situation) more than someone who has always disliked us.

Why should this be so? One reason is that we are more likely to attribute a change in the person's attitude to something that *we* did ("She's changing her mind because she's gotten to know me better"), while attributing an unchanging attitude to the person's disposition ("He always says that—it's just the way he is and has nothing to do with me"). Thus we take the change in opinion more personally. Another possible reason involves the arousal and reduction of anxiety. People arouse anxiety in us by saying negative things; when they later say positive things ("gain"), these evaluations not only are rewarding in and of themselves, but also reduce the previous anxiety and are thus doubly rewarding. Just the opposite would be the case for the "loss" part of the theory.

To test this model, a study was conducted in which female subjects interacted in two-person groups over a series of brief meetings. After each meeting, it was possible for one subject to eavesdrop on a conversation between the experimenter and the "partner" (actually a confederate) in which the partner evaluated the subject. There were four major experimental conditions: (1) positive—the evaluations were consistently favorable; (2) negative—the evaluations were consistently unfavorable; (3) gain—the evaluations began as unfavorable, but gradually became as positive as those in the positive condition; (4) loss—the evaluations began as favorable, but gradually became as negative as those in the negative condition.

If liking depended on the number of rewards received by each subject, then there should have been most liking in the positive condition, least in the negative condition, and an intermediate amount in the gain and loss conditions. This did not occur. Rather, it was the pattern or sequence of reinforcements that was the major determinant of liking. Subjects liked the confederate in the "gain" condition better than the confederate whose evaluations were all positive. Similarly, the confederate in the "loss" condition tended to be disliked more than the confederate who gave negative evaluations every time (Aronson & Linder, 1965).

Hatred which is entirely conquered by love passes into love, and love on that account is greater than if it had not been preceded by hatred.
Benedict Spinoza
Ethics

Loving you, loving me

Given the importance of love in promoting happiness and making the world go 'round, it may seem surprising that psychologists have only recently begun systematic research on this topic. Partly this was due to a widespread taboo about even discussing the subject (Bloom, 1967). Partly it was because of the popular belief that love is so mysterious and mystical that it defies rational explanation. To try to study it scientifically would only lead to stripping it of its romance, and so scientists should leave well enough alone. Even today there are still those who espouse this "don't tell us about love" attitude. For example, when Senator William Proxmire criticized the National Science Foundation in 1975 for funding social psychological research on romantic attraction with taxpayers money, he stated his opinion that,

"I believe that 200 million other Americans want to leave some things in life a mystery, and right at the top of things we don't want to know is why a man falls in love with a woman and vice versa. . . . Here, if anywhere, Alexander Pope was right when he observed, 'if ignorance is bliss, 'tis folly to be wise.' "

However, general support for this viewpoint has dwindled considerably in the last decade. Both social scientists and the lay public have come to realize the importance of increasing our knowledge about the whys and wherefores of love. As Abraham Maslow expressed it, "We must understand love; we must be able to teach it, to create it, to predict it, or else the world is lost to hostility and to suspicion" (1954).

What is love, anyway?

Another reason for the relative scarcity of research on love is the difficulty in defining it. Philosophers and social scientists have often differed on what are the components of love and on what forms love takes. The ancient Greeks distinguished between three types of love: *eros,* or romantic love; *philia,* or friendship; and *agape,* which originally meant the love of God for humankind but now usually refers to humanitarian concern for people in general. In his classic book, *The Art of Loving* (1956), Erich Fromm proposed five different kinds of love: brotherly love (love of all humanity), parental love (love of parents for their child), erotic love (craving for union with one other person), self-love (love of one's own being), and love of God (religious love). Bloom (1967) proposed a developmental model of seventeen life stages, each of which has a corresponding form of love. For example, the stage of marriage and progeny involves contractual or married love, the development of the grandparent or patron role involves romantic-immortality love, and so forth.

Another approach has been to define love in terms of its different components. For example, Prescott has described four aspects of love:

1. *Love involves more or less* <u>empathy</u> *with the loved one. A person who loves actually enters into the feelings of and shares intimately the experiences of the loved one and the effects of these experiences upon the loved one.*
2. *One who loves is deeply* <u>concerned for the welfare,</u> *happiness, and development* <u>of the beloved.</u> *This concern is so deep as to become one of the major organizing values in the personality or self-structure of the loving person. . . .*
3. *One who loves finds* <u>pleasure in making his resources available</u> *to the loved one, to be used by the other to enhance his welfare, happiness, and development. Strength, time, money, thought, indeed all resources are proffered happily to the loved one for his use. A loving person is not merely concerned about the beloved's welfare and development, he does something about it.*
4. *Of course the loving person seeks a maximum of participation in the activities that contribute to the welfare, happiness, and development of the beloved. But he also* <u>accepts fully the uniqueness and individuality of the beloved and . . . accords [him] full freedom to experience, to act, and to become what he desires to become.</u> *A loving person has a nonpossessive respect for the selfhood of the loved one (reprinted from Prescott, 1957, p. 358).*

In recent years, social psychologists have begun to develop very systematic measures of love based on their own assessments of the nature of love. One of the important questions has centered on the distinction between love and liking. Is the difference a *quantitative* one, such that love is simply an intense form of liking? Or is there a *qualitative* difference between liking and love? Although there is not yet much evidence to resolve this question, Berscheid and Walster (1978) argue that love and liking appear to differ in three important ways:

1. Fantasy plays a far more important role in love, while liking is more reality-bound;
2. Love relationships can involve both positive and negative feelings (e.g., loving and hating the same person), while liking relationships involve just one type of affect;
3. Liking becomes more durable over time, while romantic love tends to weaken.

Would you agree with these proposed differences? Can you think of any other ways in which love and liking may be distinguished from each other?

On the scale of love

One attempt to study both love and liking involved the development of scales to measure these two concepts (Rubin, 1973). The "Love Scale" included three major components: (a) affiliative and dependent needs, (b) predisposition to help, and (c) exclusiveness and absorption. The "Liking Scale" had items assessing variables such as perceived similarity, maturity, adjustment, and intelligence.

Rubin administered the two scales to 182 dating couples at the University of Michigan. Each member of a couple was instructed to respond to both scales twice, first with their date in mind and second with a close friend of the same sex in mind. Each partner filled out the questionnaires independently of the other. Results indicated that dating partners both liked and loved each other more than they liked or loved their friends. Women tended to express a greater liking for their dates than did men and were also more loving and liking toward friends of the same sex.

According to Rubin, "while women do not typically have more same-sex friends than men, women's friendships tend to be more intimate, involving more spontaneous joint activities and more exchanging of confidences" (1973, p. 221). Rubin believes that women's friendships are more intense because established cultural norms permit them greater freedom in expressing affection and affiliation.

The researcher was also curious to know if a couple's scores on the Love Scale were related to their actual behavior toward one another. Operating on the notion that romantic love includes a tendency to be completely absorbed with each other, he unobtrusively watched couples who were sitting alone waiting for the experiment to begin. He found that couples who had high scores on the Love Scale were more likely to gaze into each other's eyes than couples with low love scores.

Six months later, Rubin asked the couples to fill out a questionnaire about their relationship at that time. As predicted, their initial love scores were positively related to their reports on whether or not their relationships had made progress toward permanence.

Some psychologists have criticized the fact that Rubin's scale uses only one score to measure a concept that is so complex as love. Thus, a new "Love

Scale" has been developed which is composed of five subscales that assess different components of love (Pam, Plutchik, & Conte, 1975). The five subscales are: respect, congeniality, altruism, physical attraction, and attachment. This Love Scale has been completed by three groups of subjects: people who were in love with someone, people who were dating someone but were not in love with him or her, and people who had a friendship with someone but were not dating. The results showed that love relationships had significantly higher scores than dating or friendship relationships on all of the subscales except congeniality. The most important aspects of each of these relationships (as judged by the highest mean scores for each subscale) were as follows: for love relationships, the most important aspects were physical attraction and attachment; for dating relationships, congeniality and physical attraction; and for friendship relationships, congeniality and respect.

Falling in love

Poets, songwriters, and lovers the world over have long celebrated the intoxicating and ecstatic experience of falling in love. This is the "many splendored thing," the peak experience in which the love-struck person is ruled more by the heart than by the head. The term "falling" conveys the abrupt and often precarious nature of the experience. Suddenly, one's life changes dramatically as the result of a chance encounter with another person. "Falling" in love is also somewhat brief and impermanent (after one falls in love, one either shifts to "being in love" or else "falls out" of love). The complete absorption of the lover with his or her beloved and the intense physical raptures of this "magnificent obsession" suggest that love may have an addictive quality.

Falling in love seems to be reserved exclusively for romantic passion, as opposed to other forms of love (for example, one does not "fall in love" with one's child or friend). This may be due to the presence of physiological arousal and sexual excitement in passionate love. Walster and Walster (1978) define *passionate (or romantic) love* as a state of intense absorption in another, accompanied by a state of intense physiological arousal. Sometimes "lovers" are those who long for their partners' love and for complete fulfillment. Sometimes "lovers" are those who are ecstatic at finally having attained their partners' love and, momentarily, complete fulfillment. Although little research has been done on passionate love, several theories have been proposed to account for its development.

The pleasure and the pain of passion

As you will recall from Chapter 14, the two-component theory of emotion proposes that people's emotional experience is a function of the cognitive labels they attach to their feelings of physiological arousal (Schachter & Singer, 1962). The same state of arousal could be interpreted as "joy" (if one meets a good friend), as "fear" (if one meets an enemy), or as some other emotion, depending on the label given it. Although the empirical support for this theory is weak (see p. 406), it has been used by Walster and Berscheid (1974) to explain the logical and sometimes illogical aspects of passionate love. Basically, they argue that any sort of physiological arousal can be interpreted as passionate love, given the presence of an appropriate cognition. For example, a person caught up in the excitement of a college football game might interpret his or her arousal as romantic passion if an attractive date is close by. However, a person not accompanied by a date will probably interpret the arousal in other terms. ●

According to one theory, the physiological arousal we feel on a thrilling amusement park ride or similar setting may be attributed to the presence of a pleasant and attractive companion.

The physiological arousal which we label as romantic love can be produced by intensely joyful and happy experiences. Sexual arousal would be another facilitating source of passion, as would any thrilling and exciting event. Such positive bases of arousal are probably the cause of romantic love for most people. However, it is also possible that even negative sources of arousal could, under the right conditions, facilitate romantic passion.

To test the theory that emotional arousal (of whatever kind) can promote feelings of passionate love, Dutton and Aron (1974) placed subjects in a fear-provoking situation. They wanted to know if a physiologically aroused male would attribute his state to the presence of an attractive female (rather than to fear). Male subjects in this study were requested to cross a narrow wooden bridge that wobbled above rocks 230 feet below. A second group of male subjects crossed a strong bridge that transversed a stream 10 feet below. As they crossed the bridge, subjects in both groups were interviewed by a female who requested that they respond to a brief questionnaire and make up a story in response to a Thematic Apperception Test (TAT) stimulus picture. Following each interaction, the female interviewer gave the subject her name and phone number in case he later wanted more information about the experiment.

The two groups differed significantly in terms of responses to the TAT. The "fear-aroused" group used more sexual imagery in their stories than did the no-fear group. Also, more members of the fear-aroused group telephoned the female interviewer at a later time (an indication of sexual attraction).

If fear, frustration, or anger could actually *heighten* one's feelings of love, this might explain some puzzling paradoxes of passion, such as the presence of conflicting emotions (i.e., both love and hate) or the instances where the pain and suffering caused by jealousy lead people to conclude that they must truly be in love. It may also provide an insight into why some people fall in love with those who are unattainable, or who spurn and reject them, or who play "hard to get." It should be noted, however, that recent research does *not* support the popular belief that the challenge posed by the person playing "hard to get" makes him or her more desirable. In a series of experiments, researchers found that men liked hard-to-get and easy-to-get women equally well. However, if the woman was *selectively* hard-to-get (was eager to date the particular man, but was reluctant to date any others), then the man's liking for her increased significantly (Walster, Berscheid, & Walster, 1973).

Another source of negative arousal in a love relationship, which could then (according to this two-factor theory) be interpreted as romantic passion, involves parental interference. Parents who openly oppose the romantic choice of their offspring may unwittingly defeat their own purpose. If opposition is perceived by couples as an infringement upon their personal freedom and a source of frustration, parental attempts to terminate such romantic involvements may backfire. This is popularly referred to as the *Romeo and Juliet* effect.

A team of researchers asked 140 couples to respond to a love scale similar to Rubin's. Their hypothesis was that feelings of romantic love between individuals would intensify if there was a threat to one's freedom of choice—in this case, parents who objected to the match. To test this, the 91 married couples and 49 pairs of dating couples were asked to complete, in addition to the love-scale questionnaire they had already filled out, a questionnaire concerning the degree of parental interference that had been experienced or perceived. Results showed a positive correlation between feelings of romantic love and degree of parental interference experienced by the couples. That is, the greater the parental interference, the greater the feelings of romantic love shared by couples.

The passage of time did not change this situation. Some months later, responding to questionnaires again, the couples reported no lessening of romantic love when parental objections persisted; if the interference had increased during the interim, feelings of romantic love intensified. Similarly, if the parents had reduced their interference, the couple's romantic feelings diminished (Driscoll, Davis, & Lipetz, 1972).

Reducing fear increases love

Although research has shown that romantic attraction does increase under adverse circumstances, it is still not clear why this should be so. At first glance, these results would appear to be contradictory to reinforcement principles, and better understood as a "mislabeling" of negative arousal (as proposed by the two-factor theory of passion). However, Kenrick and Cialdini (1977) have proposed the opposite interpretation: that there are problems with the "mislabeling" model and that the findings can be best explained in terms of reinforcement. More specifically, they argue that increased romantic attraction under aversive conditions is due to conditioning and the effects of *negative reinforcement* (the termination or reduction of aversive stimuli). In other words, we love those people who *reduce* our negative arousal by allaying our fears, calming our anger, and providing sexual release. So the notion that having a "lover's spat" is not so bad, because the making up is so much fun, would fit in nicely with this *fear-reduction* model of love.

According to this alternative argument, the "mislabeling" process could only work when the person was unaware of the true source of his or her physiological arousal. A person who knew what was actually causing the arousal would be very unlikely to mistake that arousal for romantic love. Instead, his or her increased attraction toward a particular person would reflect the fact that that person had reduced the fear or anxiety in some way. According to Kenrick and Cialdini, none of the studies cited as support for the two-factor model attempted to disguise the true source of the subject's arousal; thus subjects were probably not in any doubt about the emotion they were experiencing. For example, in the Dutton and Aron experiment described above, subjects who were crossing the high bridge may have been well aware that their arousal was due to fear. When they met the female experimenter who asked them to fill out the questionnaires, her relaxed and comfortable presence on the bridge may have reduced their fears about it or distracted them from the view below. Thus, they may have been more attracted to her because she reduced their fearfulness and *not* because they "mislabeled" their fear as romantic passion.

Long-term relationships

According to fairy tales, after the prince and princess fall in love, they live "happily ever after." Such a successful long-term relationship is something that is often sought but less often found. If the rising divorce rate in the United States is any indication, an increasing number of people are finding it difficult to keep a commitment to another person "until death do us part." What are the factors that maintain a relationship over time? Are they different, perhaps, than those which start the relationship in the first place? According to the theories to be presented in this section, the answer is "yes." As relationships grow and mature, their dynamics change and new elements take on special significance. As opposed to the intense and often short-term nature of passionate love, the love that is involved in a long-lasting commitment has been termed *compassionate love*. It is defined as the affection we feel for those with whom our lives are deeply intertwined.

How does this "intertwining" develop? Each of the following theoretical models describes a process of sequential stages, in which two people move from superficial relationships to more intimate ones. At each stage, both people evaluate the relationship and, if it is satisfactory for each of them (that is, the rewards outweigh the costs), the relationship will continue to the next stage.

Love is a symbol of eternity. It wipes out all sense of time, destroying all memory of a beginning and all fear of an end.
Madame de Staël
Corinne

Establishing trust

One of the key elements in a long-term relationship is the development of a sense of trust between the two partners. This confident belief in the integrity and reliability of the other person is often achieved through a process of reciprocal self-disclosure of personal information. (See *P&L* Close-up, Try a Little Trust.)

At the beginning of any relationship, there is very little self-revelation and thus no basis for trust. The theory of *social penetration* proposes that trust begins when one person initiates self-disclosure. If the other person responds in kind, it means that the trust has been accepted and that the basis for a closer relationship has been established. The two partners continue to trade self-disclosures and gradually move through deeper levels of intimacy, as long as each level is mutually satisfying. The final level of intimacy that is achieved will depend on the needs and interpersonal skills of the two people involved. In some cases, the relationship will stop at a more superficial level, while in others, it will continue to grow and deepen (Altman & Taylor, 1973).

Intimacy is achieved not only by verbal statements of self-disclosure, but by various nonverbal behaviors such as touch, eye contact, forward leaning, and reduced interpersonal distances (Argyle & Dean, 1965; Mehrabian, 1969). According to one model, sufficient changes in one person's nonverbal intimacy behaviors will produce a noticeable change in arousal in the other person (Patterson, 1976). Depending upon the type of relationship, the setting, and other factors, the person will label his or her arousal state as either a posi-

674

Try a Little Trust

Trust is perhaps the most important dimension in human relationships. It washes away the fears of rejection, ridicule, and betrayal that haunt many people's existence. It paves the way to friendship and intimacy. It is at the core of love for another person and acceptance of oneself.

You can create a climate of trust in your home or work environment by doing the following things:

1) Make it acceptable for other people to talk openly about themselves;
2) reciprocate with your own openness;

3) express support and unconditional acceptance of your loved ones, even though you disapprove of some of their specific *behaviors* (make them aware of this difference);
4) be consistent (but not rigid) in your standards, values, and behavior;
5) be available to listen, express warmth, and empathize, even when you do not have an answer or a solution;
6) do not make promises you do not intend to keep, or cannot deliver (Zimbardo, 1977).

tive emotion (liking, love) or a negative emotion (embarrassment, anxiety). If it is labeled positively, the person will reciprocate with intimacy behaviors (and these, in turn, will encourage further intimate responses from the other). If it is labeled negatively, the person will back off and engage in *less* intimate responses (which will signal the other that his or her behaviors were inappropriate).

The notion that there is an optimal level of self-disclosure and intimacy in any two-person relationship is paralleled by Jourard's (1964) theory that there is an optimal level of self-disclosure for any healthy, well-adjusted individual. A person who never discloses will not be able to have close, meaningful relationships with other individuals. On the other hand, a person who overdoes it by disclosing everything to anyone who will listen is viewed as maladjusted and excessively self-centered. Ideally, according to Jourard, one should disclose a moderate amount of personal information to most acquaintances, and only reveal a lot about oneself to a very few close friends.

Establishing mutuality

One consequence of reciprocal self-disclosure is that the two people acquire a great amount of shared knowledge which can, in turn, facilitate the development of shared viewpoints, goals, and decisions. This emerging "we-ness" or mutuality is another important aspect of long-term relationships. A theoretical model of the development of "relatedness" has been proposed by Levinger and Snoek (1972).

This model conceptualizes relationships in terms of different levels of "relatedness," as shown in the diagram. ◆ At first, there is complete unrelatedness between any pair of people (P and O) who have not yet met and are unaware of each other. This level of relationship is known as Zero Contact (Level 0). Subsequently, three levels of relationship may develop between the two people, as they come into increasing contact. At the stage of Awareness (Level 1), one person (P) is aware of the other (O) and has formed some impressions or attitudes about O, but has not actually interacted with him or her. In the next stage of Surface Contact (Level 2), the two people have met, formed some evaluations of each other, and have interacted to some extent. However, this interaction is limited to the stereotyped "surface" roles that

Levels of Relationship

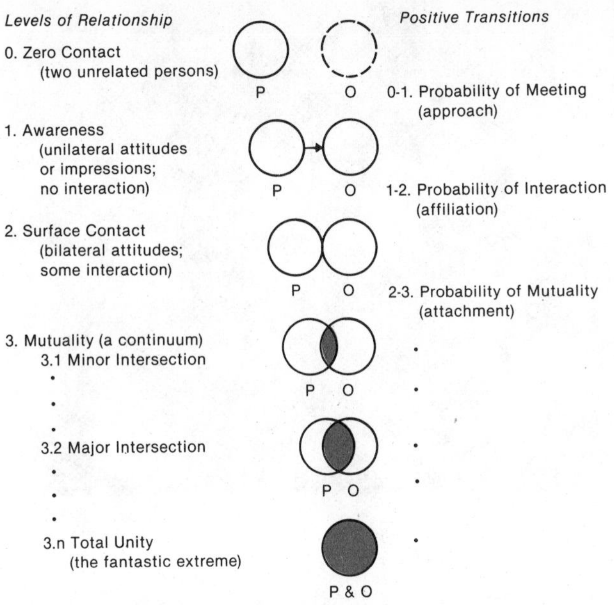

Positive Transitions

0. Zero Contact
(two unrelated persons)

P   O

0-1. Probability of Meeting
(approach)

1. Awareness
(unilateral attitudes
or impressions;
no interaction)

P   O

1-2. Probability of Interaction
(affiliation)

2. Surface Contact
(bilateral attitudes;
some interaction)

P   O

2-3. Probability of Mutuality
(attachment)

3. Mutuality (a continuum)
3.1 Minor Intersection

P   O

3.2 Major Intersection

P O

3.n Total Unity
(the fantastic extreme)

P & O

Adapted from G. Levinger and J. D. Snoek, Attraction in relationship: A new look at
interpersonal attraction, 1972. Copyright to the authors, 1978.

people adopt in their public self-presentations, and does not involve any self-disclosure.

The next stage of Mutuality (Level 3) is actually a continuum of states in which the two people become increasingly interdependent. Each person's actions and attitudes are strongly influenced by those of the other, and the development of joint attitudes, joint behavior, and joint possessions constitutes an "intersection" in the lives of the two people. (This is represented by the shaded overlapping sections of the two circles in the diagram.) Self-disclosure is an important part of this stage, and there is a great deal of shared information about both partners. Each person assumes some responsibility for ensuring that the other receives positive outcomes from the relationship. Furthermore, the two partners develop their own personal rules for regulating their interaction, rather than letting it be governed by external cultural norms. With increasing mutuality and interdependence, the intersection between the partners' lives becomes greater.

Several transition processes that could move a couple from one stage to another are shown in the diagram. The transition from Zero Contact to Awareness is called "approach" and involves the probability that any particular two people are likely to meet each other. This probability is increased by such variables as close proximity and similar social status. The move from Awareness to Surface Contact is called "affiliation" and concerns the probability that one person will initiate interaction with the other. Important variables in this process include the other's physical attractiveness, similarity to the person, and readiness to reciprocate contact. (Parenthetically, it is this transition stage that has received the most research attention from social psychologists.) Finally, the transition from Surface Contact to Mutuality, in which mutuality is gradually increased, is called "attachment." The factors that promote attachment include reciprocal liking, satisfaction with the joint outcomes of the relationship, extension of the partners' interaction beyond the usual role requirements, the formation of norms specific to the partners, and a compatibility of attitudes, values, and needs. (Developmental psychologists have studied attachment behavior, but primarily between mother and child.)

Choosing a marriage partner

Deep, meaningful long-term relationships can occur between many different pairs of people. The Levinger and Snoek model is as applicable to parent-child relationships and those between old friends or colleagues as it is to the commitment between husband and wife. However, other theories are concerned exclusively with the marriage relationship and with the factors that determine whom one selects for a mate. One of the earliest of those models was Winch's (1958) theory of *complementary needs*. Winch proposed that our choice of a spouse will be a person whose needs are complementary to our own and who can provide us with maximum need-gratification. This view is similar to equity theory's "matching principle" (see p. 666) which suggests that we choose a mate who has the same level of social worth as ourselves.

Another model for marital choice is Murstein's (1976) *stimulus-value-role theory*. At first, in the "stimulus" stage, most of what we know about the other person is based on a minimal interaction with him or her. The stimulus impact of this other will depend on such surface characteristics as physical attractiveness, social skills, and reputation. In the second, "value" stage, the two people discuss their attitudes and values, and if these turn out to be similar, then attraction is strengthened and the couple's relationship is likely to continue into the third and final "role" stage. At this point, both of the individuals are concerned about their ability to function as a unit, or as a "we." If the various roles they each play fit together and complement each other, then the relationship will be a satisfying one and the couple is likely to go on to marriage.

The prevailing belief in American society is that people get married because they have fallen in love. However, there is also an economic basis for mate selection, particularly for women since their choice of a husband has traditionally been a choice of a standard of living. Thus women are often cautioned to be selective in their romantic attachments and not fall in love with the wrong person. This notion that women may actually be more practical than sentimental in their affairs of the heart is supported by recent evidence that goes against some standard stereotypes. Women do not fall in love as readily as men, and they fall *out* of love more quickly and easily than men do (Hill, Rubin, & Peplau, 1976). Furthermore, women are more likely to perceive problems in premarital relationships and are somewhat more likely to precipitate a breakup of such a relationship when problems exist. It may be that women's criteria for falling in love and choosing a mate are higher than men's, and that they are more sensitive to the possible positive and negative outcomes of a long-term marriage relationship.

One area where trust, intimacy, and mutuality blend is in the sexual union of two people in love. While sexual intercourse may be engaged in for self-centered reasons, it takes on new meaning when it is an integral part of a loving relationship. But precisely because the sexual experience can be so fulfilling, when it is not, the long-term relationship is often in peril. And conversely, when such relationships are beginning to sour, the symptoms show up in unsatisfactory sexual relations between the partners. In the final section of this chapter, our focus will be on human sexuality.

Human sexuality

"Dear Dr. Reuben: Don't you think there's entirely too much attention paid to sex these days? I'm a physical education major and I think that it's much better for people to devote themselves to good clean pursuits like sports and exercise rather than occupying so much of their time and energy with something like sex. Don't you agree?" (Reuben, 1973)

Well, do *you?* or don't you?

The implications of the above letter are that sexual thoughts (and worse, sexual actions) are the opposite of "good clean pursuits." This attitude that sex degrades the purity of human conduct and the nobility of human spirit is somewhat less prevalent than it was in the days of your parents and grandparents.

It was not too long ago that marriage manuals described sexual behavior as "a dangerous evil which, unfortunately, is necessary for the perpetuation of the race." Since open discussion of sexual behavior was taboo for males and unthought of for those of the "gentle, more tender persuasion," these marriage manuals carried the burden of sexual education of the literate masses. Typically such manuals, though written by physicians, were designed to instill fear, guilt, shame, and the urgency of endless vigilance on the part of parents who hoped to nip "the vicious habit" in the bud! It is difficult for us to imagine the psychological impact of this indoctrination on the minds of untold numbers of parents, except to realize that without that era of sexual repression, it would not have been necessary for us to have to be "liberated" now. (See *P&L* Close-up, S–X.)

It is only in the last thirty years or so that human sexuality has begun to be a legitimate area of scientific inquiry in the United States. The investigation into normal sexual behavior in humans was given the first important impetus by the work of Alfred Kinsey and his colleagues (1948, 1953). They interviewed some seventeen thousand Americans about their sexual behavior and revealed—to a generally shocked American public—the extent to which certain behaviors, previously considered rare and even "abnormal," were actually quite widespread and, in fact, statistical norms. But it was really William Masters and Virginia Johnson (1966, 1970) who broke down the traditional taboo and legitimized the study of human sexuality by directly observing and recording under laboratory conditions the physiological patterns involved in human sexual response. ●

Close-up
S – X: *The Vicious Habit*

From an informative pseudomedical pocket guide published in 1902 (*The Ladies Guide in Health and Disease,* by J. H. Kellogg, M.D.), which is chock full of helpful hints to parents regarding sex and how to prevent its outbreak in their children, we quote without comment from a section dealing with one of the greatest of all human vices: "self-abuse" (masturbation).

"*Vicious Habits.*—Many mothers are wholly ignorant of the almost universal prevalence of secret vice, or self-abuse, among the young. It is exceedingly common among girls as well as boys. The nature of this vice is such that it may be acquired and continued months and even years, possibly during the greater part of a lifetime, without its existence being suspected by those who are not skilled in its detection. We have met scores of such cases in which it was impossible to convince the doting mother that her daughter could be guilty of such an offense, although the marks of vice were too plain to be mistaken. A careful study of this too prevalent vice and a wide opportunity for observation have convinced us that this is one of the great causes of the large increase of nervous diseases and diseases peculiar to the sex, which has been so marked among women during the last half century. A pungent writer who has devoted himself almost exclusively to the treatment of the diseases of females, asks pertinently: 'Why hesitate to say firmly and without quibble that personal abuse lies at the root of much of the feebleness, paleness, nervousness, and good-for-nothingness of the entire community?' . . .

"Much of the nervousness, hysteria, neuralgia, and general worthlessness of the girls of the rising generation originates in this cause alone. The pale cheeks, hollow eyes, expressionless countenances, and languid air of many school-girls, which are likely to be attributed to over-study, are due to this one cause. . . .

"The habit of self-pollution is one which when thoroughly established, is by no means easily broken. The victim of this most terrible vice is held in the most abject slavery, the iron fetters of habit daily closing the prisoner more and more tightly in their grasp. . . .

"The mother should first carefully set before the child the exceeding sinfulness of the habit, its loathsomeness and vileness, and the horrible consequences which follow in its wake. . . .

"Reform is not impossible, however, for anyone who really desires to reform; but the work of reformation must begin with the mind. The impure thoughts and images which have been harbored must be banished. The mind must be cleansed from every taint of evil. This is a task which requires no little patience, and in many cases more than human strength" (1902, pp. 144–65).

Physiology of sexual arousal

What Masters and Johnson began to study in the mid-1950s was, as they defined it, "what happens to the human male and female as they respond to effective sexual stimulation." Their subjects—619 females and 654 males—were observed in about ten thousand sexual response cycles, including both intercourse and masturbation. Masters and Johnson concluded that physiologically male and female sexual responses are very similar, no matter what the source of arousal or who is involved.

Physiologically, in both males and females sex with a partner (either of the same or opposite sex) or sex without a partner is characterized by a pooling or collecting of blood *(vasocongestion),* particularly in the genitals, and increased muscle tension *(myotonia).* But though sexual reactions are generally very similar, there are great variations from person to person and from occasion to occasion.

For convenience in analysis, Masters and Johnson divided the sexual re-

William Masters and
Virginia Johnson, shown
here interviewing patients
in their clinic in St. Louis,
Missouri, have studied human
sexuality under laboratory
conditions since the mid-
1950s.

sponse cycle into four phases: *excitement, plateau, orgasm,* and *resolution.* During the excitement phase, individual sexual arousal begins. This phase, which may last for a few minutes to several hours, is characterized by elevation and enlargement of the genital areas—in males, erection of the penis and thickening or flattening of other genital areas; in females, vaginal lubrication and engorgement of the clitoris (the female analogue of the penis in terms of sexual response) and other genital areas. During the plateau phase, sexual arousal is greatly heightened and is reflected in both males and females by increased heartbeat and blood pressure, increased glandular secretions, and both voluntary and involuntary muscle tension throughout the body. "Sex flush," a coloring of the body, may also be experienced, particularly by females. During orgasm, both sexes experience a very intense, very pleasurable sense of release from the sexual tension that has been building up. Orgasm is characterized by rhythmic contractions that occur every eight-tenths of a second in the genital areas in both sexes, and in males by ejaculation, a sudden release of semen. Blood pressure reaches very high levels in both males and females and heart rate may double. During the resolution phase, there is a gradual return of the body to its normal, preexcitement state with both blood pressure and heartbeat slowing down in both sexes.

According to Masters and Johnson's research, females and males do differ in one major respect: females are potentially capable of multiple orgasms—several orgasmic reactions in fairly rapid succession. But males generally are not. After one orgasm, most males enter a *refractory* period, lasting anywhere from a few minutes to several hours (or even days), during which no further orgasm is possible. ▲

A number of myths that have troubled many generations were dispelled by the landmark Masters and Johnson studies. One of the most prevalent was that women—at least "nice" women—were not as erotically inclined as men. This disparaging view of female sexuality was not simply folklore but enshrined as "scientific" fact. Even as recently as 1957 a medical textbook on women claimed that they, unlike men, were neither interested in nor capable of orgasm. The evidence that women could be multiorgasmic shattered these stereotyped views and suggested that in terms of sexual response, women were not the "weaker" but rather the "stronger" sex (Hall, 1969).

The degree to which human sexuality is basically a *psychological* process was perhaps the most important discovery of Masters and Johnson's research on the physiology of sex. A key aspect of their work was a conclusive demonstration that problems in sexual response, particularly *lack* of sexual response

*If a woman hasn't got a
tiny streak of a harlot in
her, she's a dry stick as a
rule.*
D. H. Lawrence
Pornography and Obscenity

The orgasmic cycle in human sexual intercourse

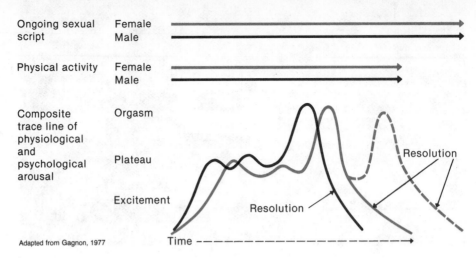

Ongoing sexual script	Female
	Male
Physical activity	Female
	Male
Composite trace line of physiological and psychological arousal	Orgasm
	Plateau
	Excitement

Resolution

Resolution

Adapted from Gagnon, 1977

Time

(what we commonly call *impotence* in males and *frigidity* in females), can be effectively treated. These conditions are largely the result of psychological rather than physiological problems.

Although poor nutrition and excessive use of alcohol or drugs can diminish sexual drive and performance, most often it is a preoccupation with personal problems, fear of the consequences, or anxiety about the partner's evaluation of one's performance that lie at the basis of a person's sexual dysfunction. *Human beings engage in sexual activities with their bodies in order to satisfy their minds.* Whether it is a "positive" or "negative" experience depends almost entirely on the psychological programming they bring to their sexual ventures. For example, shy college students not only report less sexual activity of all kinds than do their nonshy classmates (in an anonymous survey), but those that have had sexual experiences describe them as more negative (Zimbardo, 1977).

Varieties of sexual experience

Sex, like hunger and thirst, is a biological drive. But unlike hunger and thirst, it is a drive that need not be satisfied. It is not a critical necessity for the survival of the individual, only for the survival of the species. Lifelong *celibacy*—abstention from sexual relations—however, is not considered desirable in our society except in certain religious groups where it is valued as a virtue of self-restraint. Of course, celibacy may be practiced at some times out of necessity and at other times out of choice, "to get sex off the mind."

There are three main varieties of sexual experience in our culture: *autosexuality* (sex without a partner), *homosexuality* (sex with a partner of the same sex), and *heterosexuality* (sex with a partner of the opposite sex). Of these, only heterosexuality—and specifically heterosexuality within the framework of marriage—has long been recognized as the "appropriate" and "socially acceptable" mode of sexual activity.

Heterosexuality

Many of our social conventions and institutions are based on the premise that heterosexuality is the only right and proper way for individuals to relate sexually. This attitude has its historical origins in the Judeo-Christian doctrine that any sexual activity not directly aimed at reproduction was sinful. Thus very strong sexual taboos have existed in our culture, not only against such forms of sexual activity as masturbation and homosexuality, but against premarital, extramarital, and postmarital intercourse.

Prohibitions against sexual activity have not always applied equally to both sexes. For example, in the case of premarital sex, the predominant social norm has traditionally been the "double standard," whereby young males were encouraged and young females discouraged from engaging in sexual intercourse.

These societal standards, however, were not entirely upheld. Kinsey's surveys revealed that about 54 percent of college-educated males (1948) and 33 percent of college-educated females (1953) had engaged in premarital intercourse. In the years since then, the percentages have grown even higher. One recent survey reported that 73 percent of the college-age males and females surveyed had engaged in premarital sex (Bauman & Wilson, 1974). Another reported even higher percentages: 82 percent for males, and 85 percent for females (Jessor & Jessor, 1975). Though these recent surveys do not reflect samples as large as those of the Kinsey researchers, there is no doubt that a major shift has occurred in American attitudes toward the acceptability of premarital intercourse. With the widespread availability of contraceptives, the feminist movement, and the more permissive attitudes engendered by the "sexual revolution" of the late 1960s, the double standard has faded among many groups of young Americans. Young women now feel freer to engage in sexual activities before marriage, and numerous surveys have indicated that, at least among the college-educated, women are quickly catching up to men in every aspect of sexual experience.

Still, there remain sex differences in behavior, and the traditional sex roles have not entirely disappeared. Among 231 college-age couples in one survey, men still tended to be the aggressive initiators and women the passive resisters in sexual activity. Moreover, intercourse, if not linked to marriage, was still linked to love. The majority of couples surveyed felt intercourse was permissible for couples who were in love (Peplau, Rubin, & Hill, 1977). This sexual standard has been labeled "permissiveness with affection" (Reiss, 1967). Only 20 percent of the students and significantly fewer women than men approved of "casual sex"—no emotional intimacy between the participants.

Autosexuality

Despite the fact that heterosexuality is the norm for most people in our culture, autosexuality is by far the most common sexual experience. Besides masturbation, other widespread forms that autosexuality may take are sex fantasies and sex dreams. Almost all males and nearly 75 percent of females dream about sex at some point in their lives, most females and males occasionally engage in sexual fantasy during waking hours, and more than 90 percent of all males and 85 percent of all females masturbate (Kinsey et al., 1948, 1953). These activities may or may not result in orgasm. In a study of daydreaming during a rather ordinary introductory psychology lecture, about 20 percent of the students were very likely to be having thoughts of a sexual nature at any given time (Cameron et al., 1968).

Despite their prevalence, such sexual activities are often undertaken in secret and accompanied by great guilt and anxiety. The prohibitions relating to masturbation have been particularly strong not only from the religious point of view, which has looked on it as sinful, but from a medical point of view, which has regarded it as unhealthy.

We now know that masturbation is not physically harmful. Some researchers would even argue that it has beneficial effects, permitting sexual release when no other means are available (Sarnoff & Sarnoff, 1979). Probably the greatest danger in masturbation is coming to enjoy the sense of control it provides more than the pleasure of sex with a partner where control must be shared. Another problem arises when the sexual fantasies associated with masturbation become necessary conditioned stimuli for arousal when having sex with a real person. But for most people, masturbation and other autosexual activities rank as a poor second, a pallid substitute to be tolerated until "the real thing" comes along. Most prefer sex with another person.

Homosexuality

Whereas autosexual activities are widely practiced, exclusive homosexuality is not. It has been estimated that up to 7 percent of American males and females are exclusively homosexual. The percentage of those who have had some limited homosexual experiences is higher, perhaps as high as 50 percent.

Like masturbation, homosexuality has been regarded in the past as immoral and in many cases illegal. Until recently, most states in the union condemned private acts of homosexuality between consenting adults as criminal. In 1977 such acts were still punishable in seven states by life imprisonment and in thirty-five others the maximum penalty was at least ten years. However, with the advent of the "gay liberation" movement and the growing acceptance by "straight" society of the right to alternate life-styles, the trend in the last decade has been to liberalize such punitive laws and to end repressive penalties against homosexuals.

Until fairly recently psychiatry, too, regarded the homosexual as a sick person. Though various theories had been proposed about the origins of homosexuality—that it was caused by genetic, hormonal, or environmental abnormalities—none had found full acceptance. The psychiatric approach to homosexuals was to treat them with prolonged therapy until they rejected this inappropriate attachment in favor of heterosexuality. (Some overzealous behavior modifiers chose simply to attach electrodes and shock the homosexual every time a sexual response was made to a same-sex visual stimulus, then reprogram the individual to get "turned on" by the opposite sex.)

But is homosexuality a mental disorder? On December 14, 1973, homosexuals were considered mentally ill sexual deviants. On December 15, 1973, homosexuals were no longer considered psychiatric deviants. This turnabout was not achieved by mass therapy, but by a vote of the trustees of the American Psychiatric Association. They declared homosexuality to be a "sexual orientation disturbance" not requiring treatment unless an individual desires it. The emphasis now in psychiatric treatment is generally to help a homosexual who is troubled toward a more positive self-concept and self-acceptance.

Bisexuality

Some individuals claim an affinity for both homosexual and heterosexual relations; that is, *bisexuality*. Indeed, in recent years, bisexuality has taken on a certain chic in our society, with a number of people in the entertainment and literary world publicly proclaiming such a sexual orientation.

Kinsey's data revealed that many people have a certain fluidity in their sexual preferences. At one point in their lives, they may be homosexual; at other times, heterosexual. Kinsey himself suggested that the rigid categories "homosexual" and "heterosexual" be abandoned in favor of a continuum ranging from exclusive heterosexuality to exclusive homosexuality. Determination of an individual's place on the continuum would be made in terms of the percentage of homosexual and heterosexual acts he or she engaged in.

We have considered here only the main sexual patterns in our culture. Theoretically, the varieties of sexual experience are endless.

The sexual script

What determines the form our sexual drive will take? Most sex researchers have concluded that biology gives us the means, but our experience and our culture define the pattern the sexual drive will take. Ford and Beach, in a study of sexual behavior across species and cultures, have written:

"Human sexuality is affected by experience in two ways: First, the kinds of stimulation and the types of situations that become capable of evoking sexual excitement are determined in a large measure by learning. Second, the overt behavior through which this excitement is expressed depends largely upon the individual's previous experience" (1951, p. 262).

In other words, we cannot separate the physical act of sex from the psychological context in which it takes place. Sex is not just a biological experience but a social and psychological experience as well. For many individuals the most important element is not what happens during sex, but the attitudes, motives, expectations, anxieties, and cultural values each partner brings to bed—their social programming about sexual matters. Sociologist John Gagnon has referred to this social programming as a *sexual script.* How do we acquire our sexual scripts? Gagnon believes we learn them as we learn everything else.

"In any given society, at any given moment in its history, people become sexual in the same way they become everything else. Without much reflection, they pick up directions from their social environment. They acquire and assemble meanings, skills, and values from the people around them. Their critical choices are often made by going along and drifting. People learn when they are quite young a few of the things that they are expected to be, and continue slowly to accumulate a belief in who they are and ought to be throughout the rest of childhood, adolescence, and adulthood. Sexual conduct is learned in the same ways and through the same processes; it is acquired and assembled in human interaction, judged and performed in specific cultural and historical worlds" (1977, p. 2).

Sexual scripts are like other scripts we discussed in Chapter 5. They are higher-order knowledge packages that combine social norms, individual expectations, and preferred sequences of behavior. They include not only scenarios of what you think is appropriate on your part, but also guidelines for a sexual partner. Different scripts can come into conflict and create problems of adjustment when they are not discussed, but acted upon and imposed on the other person.

Of course, the most noteworthy aspect of sexual scripts is that they are continually changing. What were once regarded as unthinkable activities are now commonplace; what was once disapproved is now approved or at least accepted. We seem to be searching in our culture, both at the individual level and at the collective level, for a less judgmental, more tolerant view of human sexuality than that based on the traditional, rather rigid framework of the scripts of yesteryear.

Beyond the pleasure principle

Not so long ago sex was regarded as a sinful activity, necessary only for reproduction; fortunately we now regard it in a more positive sense. Rather than inducing emotions of fear, guilt, and shame—attitudes that dominated much of our thinking in the past—we now tend to view sex as a source of joy and pleasure. But beyond that, there is in the healthy sexual experience a source of self-renewal and self-fulfillment, a vital part of the life force that affirms and expresses our basic humanity.

Sex researchers have played a large part in changing these attitudes. Sigmund Freud made us aware of the pervasive and significant role played by our sexual urges in so many aspects of our lives. Kinsey showed us what was normative, what were the "standard" sexual behaviors in our society. Ford and Beach revealed that variety is the principle in sexual behavior in different animal species and human societies. Masters and Johnson demonstrated that sex is primarily psychological, a learned set of social-emotional and behavioral skills. Thus, we can remedy our shortcomings in this as we can in other areas of learned behavior. Sex researchers are now less concerned with what is normative or therapeutic and more concerned with the place of sex in the life of the average person. The focal point of current sex research is the interactional aspects of sexuality, the individual's sexual experiences, the social context in which they take place, the meaning the individual and society as a whole ascribe to these experiences.

How does this approach apply to our own lives? To promote a positive development of our own sexuality, we need to remember that sex is more than just a set of learned techniques, a performance of bodies in space, a giving or receiving of pleasurable physiological sensations. We need, as a very first step, to accept our own body and the responsibility for someone else's. We must want to give and be open to receive. We need to be willing to learn over time how best to give our gift and to accept the gift of another. But it is not enough to know what to do physically. For many, the most satisfactory sex takes place within a loving, caring relationship between two people. If we want sex to reach its potential as a fulfilling human experience, we need to develop attitudes of trust and sharing. Sex strips us literally and figuratively of our protective garments. It lays bare our vulnerability. That is why sex can at the same time be so frightening if misused with hostility and so glorious if filled with assurances of love and respect.

Sex contains all, bodies, souls,
Meaning, proofs, purities, delicacies, results, promulgations,
All hopes, benefactions, bestowals, all the passions, loves, beauties, delights of the earth,
All the governments, judges, gods.
Walt Whitman
A Woman Waits for Me

Within your own ethical and moral standards, sexual experiences should allow you to feel an elevation of spirit, a sense of unique closeness with another human being. For as with liking and loving relationships, a sexual relationship is good if it is communicative, if it helps us to bridge the currents that separate us as people.

Chapter summary

Liking and loving have not until recently been considered legitimate topics of psychological research. But investigators are finding predictable patterns in this area of human relationships. It has been demonstrated, for example, that we are generally attracted to those in close proximity to us, who are physically attractive and competent, who reciprocate our liking for them, and who are similar to us in attitudes, values, and beliefs.

A number of theories have been developed to explain these statistical findings. *Reinforcement theory* suggests that people who reward us in some way arouse positive feelings in us and consequently cause us to like them. Conversely, those who punish us in some way will arouse negative feelings and dislike. It is also suggested that through the process of simple conditioning, we come to like people who are present when we receive rewards, and come to dislike those present when we are punished. Such elements of attraction as reciprocal liking and shared attitudes easily fit into this reinforcement paradigm.

Exchange theory has an economic perspective in that it proposes that unless both participants in a relationship feel the rewards of interacting are greater than the costs, and they are making psychological "profit" from the exchange, the interaction will not continue.

Equity, as the concept is used in *equity theory,* is defined in terms of *relative outcomes* — people's outcomes are proportional to their inputs. Thus, inequity in a relationship will lead to attempts at *restoration,* either *actual* or *psychological.* *Matching theory,* a corollary of equity theory, suggests that successful romantic relationships are equitable ones because the people involved try to acquire partners who "match" them in social worth.

According to the *gain-loss theory of attraction,* changes in another person's evaluation of us will have more impact on our liking for him or her than if evaluation were constant. Therefore, we tend to especially like a person who originally had a bad impression of us but revised this to a good impression.

Psychological theorists have approached a definition for love from many vantage points. Erich Fromm postulated five different types of love: brotherly, parental, erotic, self-love, and religious love. Other attempts at defining love have involved breaking it into components and comparing it with behaviors such as liking.

Rubin designed a "Love Scale" and "Liking Scale" on which he scored dating couples' responses to questionnaires and their overt behavior toward each other. His research showed that the most important components in love relationships are physical attraction and attachment; in liking relationships, congeniality and respect.

The term "falling in love" is used exclusively for romantic passion. This experience may be due in part to the presence of physiological arousal and sexual excitement. Indeed, the *two-component theory of emotion* holds that any sort of physiological arousal can be interpreted as passionate love, given the presence of an appropriate cognition — an attractive person.

The *fear-reduction* model of love suggests that we love those who *reduce* our negative arousal by allaying fears, calming anger, and providing sexual release. Thus, falling in love may be a result of *negative reinforcement.*

As relationships grow and mature, and become long-term, their dynamics change. *Passionate* love becomes *compassionate* love, and trust comes to occupy a key place in the relationship. The theory of *social penetration* sees trust beginning with a simple self-disclosure which is reciprocated. Continued trading of self-disclosures gradually moves to deeper levels of intimacy. It appears that every relationship has an optimal level of self-disclosure and intimacy. *Mutuality* or *relatedness* is also important in long-term relationships. The people involved gradually progress from initial contact to an increasing interdependency.

Similar models have been constructed to explain how marriage partners are chosen. The *complementary needs* approach sees the process as the seeking of an individual whose needs are complementary to ours and who can gratify our needs. The *stimulus-value-role* theory proposes a sequence of an initial *stimulus* or attraction stage, a *value* stage in which values and attitudes are found to be similar, and a *role* stage in which each individual finds his or her role in the relationship satisfying.

The study of human sexuality has become an important area of research in recent years, pointing up previously little-known facts about this aspect of human life. Masters and Johnson have found that male and female sexual responses are very similar physiologically, characterized by *excitement, plateau, orgasm,* and *resolution.* They have further demonstrated that problems in sexual response, particularly *impotence* and *frigidity,* are largely the result of psychological problems and can be effectively treated.

The three main varieties of sex in our culture include: *autosexuality, homosexuality, heterosexuality. Autosexuality* is the most common sexual experience and may involve masturbation, sex fantasies, and sex dreams. While masturbation is essentially harmless, most individuals find it less rewarding than experiencing sex with another person.

Homosexuality occurs in about 7 percent of the American population. While it has been regarded in the past as immoral and in many cases illegal, the trend has been to liberalize laws and end repressive penalties against homosexuals. In recent years, it has been termed a "sexual orientation disturbance," not requiring treatment unless the individual desires it.

Heterosexuality is the most socially conventional and thus sanctioned form of sexuality. In the past, the Judeo-Christian ethic, which prohibits masturbation, premarital, extramarital, and postmarital sex, has prevailed in society. But these norms were often accepted in terms of a *double standard,* with young males being encouraged to experience sex and young females discouraged from doing so. Kinsey shocked the American public in the late 1940s and early 1950s when he presented studies showing that, in actuality, a large percentage of young adults engaged in premarital sex. Because of changing attitudes and the availability of contraceptives, the double standard has faded and premarital sex has become widespread. Some of the traditional roles remain, however. Men still tend to be the aggressive initiators in sex, and permissiveness with affection is preferred to casual sex.

Individuals who engage in sexual relations with members of both sexes are called *bisexuals.*

Humans acquire a *sexual script* from their culture. Their sexual drives are linked to a higher-order knowledge that combines social norms, individual expectations, and preferred sequences of behavior. Scripts can change—what was once regarded as immoral may eventually become commonplace.

Social Pathology

[*The historical account of humans is a*] *heap of conspiracies, rebellions, murders, massacres, revolutions, banishments, the very worst effects that avarice, faction, hypocrisy, perfidiousness, cruelty, rage, madness, hatred, envy, lust, malice, and ambition could produce.*
. . . I cannot but conclude the bulk of your natives to be the most pernicious race of little odious vermin that nature ever suffered to crawl upon the surface of the earth.
Jonathan Swift
Gulliver's Travels

Although Swift's total condemnation has been dismissed as the work of a cynical hater of the human condition, many others concerned about "human nature" over the centuries have echoed similar sentiments. A basic theme in Western literature is that Man has suffered a great fall from his original state of perfection.

According to biblical scholars, the Fall originated with Adam's one defect—his pride—which led to his disobedience to God and banishment from Paradise. In other schemes, the corrupting force is not within the person but from without—as exemplified by the social influence of Eve, who, tempted by Satan in snake's clothing, persuaded Adam to disobey God's command not to eat the fruit of the tree of knowledge.

This theme of the corrupting influence of social forces was developed by Rousseau. He envisioned human beings as noble, primitive savages diminished by contact with society. To recapture and preserve their essential goodness, individuals must escape from civilization. For Americans, Thoreau's isolated cabin at Walden Pond, Massachusetts, has become a symbol of breaking the bonds of dependence on social convention. More recently, many young people have responded to this same primitive appeal by forming and joining small communes in rural areas.

Standing in opposition to this general view of human beings as the innocent victims of an all-powerful, malignant society is the view that people are basically evil. According to this view, people are driven by desires, appetites, and impulses unless they are transformed into rational, reasonable, compassionate human beings by education, or controlled by firm authorities.

Where do *you* stand in this argument? Are we born good and corrupted by an evil society, or born evil and redeemed by a good society? Before casting your ballot, consider an alternative perspective. Maybe each of us has the capacity to be a saint or a sinner, altruistic or selfish, gentle or cruel, dominant or submissive, sane or mad. Maybe it is the social circumstances we experience and how we learn to cope with them that determine which potential we develop. In fact, maybe the potential for perversion is inherent in the very processes that make us able to do all the superbly wonderful things we can do.

The preceding chapters have documented the complex development and supreme specialization that have resulted from untold millions of years of evolution, growth, adaptation, and coping. We have become the rulers of this planet, controlling the other animals and the physical matter of the earth for our survival, comfort, and happiness. This reign is currently being extended to life beneath the oceans as well as to outer space. We have reached this position because of our capacity for learning new relationships, for remembering old ones, for reasoning, inventing, and planning action strategies. We have developed both natural and computer languages to manipulate symbols and transmit our thoughts and information to others. Our perceptual, cognitive, and motor skills allow us to see, reflect, and act in countless intricate ways to avoid pain, gain pleasure, and change our surroundings to suit ourselves.

But each of these unique attributes can also become cancerous. Implanted in the very potential for perfectibility are the seeds of perversion and breakdown. A partial catalog of human traits and attributes and their possible positive and negative consequences is given in the table. ■

In this chapter our attention will be directed toward some of the psychological processes that are occurring when people "go wrong." Only with a knowledge of what can go wrong and how, can we reformulate our modes of relating to one another and design social institutions more appropriate for the fulfillment of each of our individual lives.

Attribute	Positive Enables Us to	Negative But Can Also Lead Us to
Memory	Profit from past mistakes Develop and use complex concepts Relate present to past Distinguish novel events from previously experienced ones	Carry grudges, suffer from former conflicts and past traumatic events Lose spontaneity of behavior because of commitments and obligations Feel excessive remorse or sense of loss
Time sense	Develop a history and sense of continuous self Relate present behavior to the future Distinguish between transience and permanence	Fear change, live in the past, feel guilt Dread an unknown future, become anxious Experience disappointments from unfulfilled expectations Concentrate on past or future, ignoring the present
Ability to associate elements and infer unseen events	Create, imagine events not experienced Generalize from partial data Construct theories, hypotheses	Form negative, crippling associations Misperceive self or others, develop stereotypic and delusional thinking
Perception of choice	Not be stimulus bound, be independent See ourselves as responsible agents Hope, build for future	Experience conflicts, indecision Suffer from inability to act when action is necessary
Responsibility, self-evaluation	Take pride in accomplishments Delay gratification, undertake difficult or unpopular tasks Be concerned about effects of our actions on others	Feel inadequate Feel guilt for not living up to standards or for letting someone down Feel constrained by obligations
Competence motivation	Do work well, set high standards Gain benefits of hard work Advance technologically, use resources to meet our needs	Fear failure, suffer feelings of inadequacy Be anxious about tests of our ability Work for self-aggrandizement, to be "number one," to beat others down
Ability to use language and other symbols	Communicate with others, present and absent, for information, comfort, pleasure, planning, social control	Circulate and be prey to rumors and falsehoods; conceal true feelings Mistake the symbol for the reality
Susceptibility to social influence	Follow group standards Learn and transmit values Cooperate; establish community	Overconform, sacrifice integrity Reject innovation and stifle creativity in ourselves and others
Love	Experience tender emotions Nurture growth and independence of others Support, encourage, comfort others Feel wanted and special	Become jealous, vengeful Possessively limit another person's freedom Become depressed and suicidal from loss of love

Aggression and violence

The world we live in is often a violent one. The daily news accounts of murders, muggings, riots, suicides, and wars are ample evidence of the extent to which people can inflict injury on others and on themselves. How can "abnormal" social behavior be understood? Can it be controlled?

Psychologists concerned with these questions have focused on the study of *aggression*, which can be defined as *physical or verbal behavior with the intent to injure or destroy*. Research evidence on aggression has been drawn from a wide variety of sources, including physiological studies, clinical observations, and studies of aggressive interactions in both the laboratory and the "real world." In addition, aggression in animals has received a great deal of attention in the hope that it will clarify our understanding of aggression in humans. In this section we will review several of the theories that have been proposed to account for aggressiveness.

Aggression as inborn

In his famous essay "Leviathan," Hobbes argued that people are naturally selfish, brutal, and cruel toward other people. He expressed this concept by the phrase *Homo homini lupus* — "Man is [like] a wolf to [his fellow] man." Although the wolf is unjustly maligned by this phrase (wolves are actually quite peaceful and gentle with others of their own species), it expresses a common belief that human beings are instinctively aggressive animals.

Freud's death instinct and the concept of catharsis

One of the first psychologists to elaborate on this belief and develop it into a theory was Sigmund Freud. As we saw in Chapter 16, he believed that from the moment of birth a person possesses two opposing instincts: a life instinct (eros), which causes the person to grow and survive, and a death instinct (thanatos), which works toward the individual's self-destruction. He believed that the death instinct is often redirected outward against the external world in the form of aggression toward others.

According to Freud, energy for the death instinct is constantly being generated within the body. If this energy cannot be released in small amounts and in socially acceptable ways, it will accumulate and eventually be released in an extreme and socially unacceptable form. Thus a highly aggressive or violent person can be assumed to be someone who: (a) generates a great deal of aggressive energy and (b) is unable to discharge that energy appropriately.

Freud visualized this energy as being like water accumulating in a reservoir until finally it spilled over in some aggressive act. It could be drained off in various "safe" ways, however. One such way was *catharsis* (a Greek word meaning purification or cleansing), in which the emotions were expressed in their full intensity through crying or words or other symbolic means. Aristotle first used the concept of catharsis to explain the way in which good drama first built up and then purged feelings of intense emotion in the audience.

Some experimental support for the catharsis hypothesis of aggression is found in a study by Robert Sears (1961). Male children high in aggressiveness at age five were also high at age twelve. Some were still overtly and antisocially aggressive. However, the others, though low in *antisocial* aggression, showed high *prosocial* aggression (aggression for socially acceptable purposes, such as law enforcement or punishment for rule-breaking) and more *self-aggression* than did boys who were still highly antisocial aggressors. ▲ Furthermore, the prosocial aggressors were more anxious and fearful of antisocial aggression than the antisocial aggressors.

In spite of some supporting evidence, however, Freud's theory has been criticized by psychologists for failing to specify any factors that could be used to predict the occurrence of aggression or the direction or form it will take. It

Home they brought her warrior dead, She nor swooned nor uttered cry. All her maidens, watching said, "She must weep or she will die."
Alfred, Lord Tennyson
The Princess

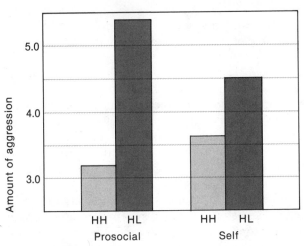

▲

Two groups of boys were both high in antisocial aggression at age five. The boys who became low in antisocial aggression by age twelve (HL) showed more prosocial and self-aggression than did the boys whose antisocial aggression remained high (HH).

Adapted from Sears, 1961

has a lovely literary, after-the-fact, descriptive quality but little scientific utility. Indeed, in his later writings Freud himself abandoned reliance on this death instinct, although others have continued to incorporate it into their conception of human nature.

The "aggressive instinct"

Another theory stressing the innateness of aggression is that of the well-known ethologist Konrad Lorenz (1966). On the basis of studies of animals, he argues that aggression is a spontaneous, innate readiness to fight, which is critical for an organism's survival. In other species, however, aggressiveness between members of the same species rarely involves actual injury or death because one animal will eventually "signal" appeasement or submission. According to Lorenz, human beings have somehow lost this means of inhibiting aggression while retaining the instinct to aggress, and thus have become killers. Lorenz argues that aggression results from *territoriality*, which is an innate drive to gain and defend property. Animals of some species will mark off their living area by urination or some other means. Other members of the species respond to these markers by withdrawing from the territory or else risk aggressive confrontation with the owner.

However, the evidence for Lorenz' theory is not all that clear-cut. Many instances of within-species killing among animals have been observed (Wilson, 1973). Humans often act in response to memories and ideas as well as to the immediate situation. Because of their tool-making capacities and ability to plan ahead, they can carry out virtually unlimited injury on a totally impersonal basis, with "no hard feelings." Animals' responses to "appeasement gestures" are in fact quite variable, much as with humans (Barnett, 1967). Sometimes displays of weakness and submission elicit sympathy and "fair play." But at other times they simply elicit even more intense violence on the part of the aggressive individual or group. Furthermore, not all species of animals display territorial behavior (Crook, 1973). Thus, Ardrey's (1966) popular argument that a territorial instinct is the basis for human aggression is not well supported by the evidence. While territorial issues may well be the reason for some human conflicts (for example, the Israeli-Arab border disputes), there is no need to assume that they derive from an innate drive rather than learned needs for power and security.

Physiological bases of aggression

The relationships between aggression and biology are complex and unclear. We will mention here only the role of the brain and of genetic and hormonal factors.

The *hypothalamus* and the *amygdala* (and probably other regions of the brain) seem to be involved in some aggressive behavior (see p. 320). There appears to be a complex chemical and anatomical specificity of the brain mechanisms controlling aggression. For example, one drug injected into the lateral hypothalamus of rats made usually spontaneous mouse-killers stop such killing, whereas a different drug injected into exactly the same brain site of normally peaceful rats induced them to kill mice (Smith, King, & Hoebel, 1970).

Some types of aggressive behavior in humans are often related to brain disorders. For example, brain disease of the limbic system or temporal lobe has sometimes been found in persons exhibiting a *dyscontrol syndrome*, characterized by senseless brutality, pathological intoxication, sexual assault, or repeated serious automobile accidents. Tumors in the brain may influence aggressive behavior, as suggested by the case of mass murderer Charles Whitman. In the summer of 1966, Whitman killed his wife and mother, and then climbed to the top of a tower at the University of Texas. Armed with a high-powered hunting rifle equipped with a telescopic sight, he shot thirty-eight people, killing fourteen, before he himself was gunned down. A postmortem examination of Whitman's brain revealed a highly malignant tumor the size of a walnut in the area of the amygdala (Sweet, Ervin, & Mark, 1969).

What part do specific genes play in aggressive behavior? Although animals such as bulls and cocks can be selectively bred for their fighting and killing abilities (Scott, 1958), the evidence is less clear that this holds true for human beings.

In both humans and animals, males are characteristically more aggressive than females—a fact apparently due in part to the early influence of sex hormones on the brain. Female animals that have been injected with male sex hormones often display increased aggressive behavior (Edwards, 1971). On the other hand, there are different physiological patterns in different kinds of aggression. In fact, Moyer (1976) distinguished between *seven* different neural and hormonal patterns, depending on whether the aggressive behavior was: (1) predatory (attack behavior directed against natural prey); (2) intermale (ritualized fights between males); (3) fear-induced (attacks against threatening agent preceded by attempts to escape); (4) territorial (defense of territory against intruder); (5) maternal (protection of young); (6) instrumental (aggression followed by positive reinforcement); or (7) irritable (attack without attempts to escape—includes uncontrollable rage, annoyance, threat, halfhearted attack). Clearly, there is not a simple one-to-one correspondence between physiological factors and aggression. The relationship is far more complex, largely because of the importance of learned and situational factors as well.

Aggression as an acquired drive

Almost twenty years after Freud proposed the existence of a death instinct, a group of academic psychologists at Yale University formally presented an alternative view of aggression called the *frustration-aggression hypothesis* (Dollard, Doob, Miller, Mowrer, & Sears, 1939). Aggression, they said, was a drive acquired in response to frustration. *Frustration* was defined as the condition that exists when a goal response is blocked. Its intensity is a function of three factors: (a) the strength of the motivation toward the goal response; (b) the degree of interference with it; and (c) the number of prior goal-response sequences interfered with. The greater the amount of frustration, the stronger the resulting aggressive response.

It soon became obvious, however, that not every act of aggression is preceded by frustration and that not every frustration results in aggression. The original frustration-aggression hypothesis was revised to state that every frustration produces an *instigation* to aggression, but that this instigation may be too weak to elicit actual aggressive behavior (N. Miller, 1941). These theorists agreed with Freud that the aggressive drive would increase if not expressed (if frustration continued). However, they saw the origin of aggressive behavior in *external* factors (accumulated frustrating experiences), rather than in *internal* factors (aggressive "instinct").

When frustration occurs, the first and strongest aggressive impulse is toward the source of the frustration. Thus, if a child sees a piece of candy, but is not allowed it, the child is most strongly motivated to be aggressive toward the parent. However, such aggression may be inhibited because of the threat of punishment. According to the frustration-aggression theory, the child will then *displace* the aggression onto some target other than the original source of frustration, perhaps mistreating a younger sibling or the family pet. According to the theory, the less similar the target is to the source of frustration, the weaker is the displaced aggression and the less complete the cathartic effect. However, recent research has suggested that displaced aggression is as strong as aggression directed at the source of frustration, and that it can be as effective in reducing subsequent tendencies toward aggressive behavior (Konecni & Doob, 1972). ◆

The frustration-aggression theory applied to prejudice predicts that when a powerful frustrator is feared or impossible to retaliate against, aggression may be displaced onto a *scapegoat*. Presumably, minorities and members of out-groups are favorite targets of displaced aggression. They are identifiably different from members of the in-group (against whom aggression must not be vented), and they are already in vulnerable positions and thus are not likely to retaliate.

Recently, the frustration-aggression hypothesis has been revised to stress the importance of both inner and outer factors. According to Berkowitz

If the Tiber overflows into the city,
If the Nile does not flow into the countryside,
If the heavens remain unmoved,
If the earth quakes,
If there is famine and pestilence,
At once the cry goes up:
"To the lions with the Christians."
Tertullian
Roman historian

◆
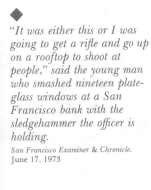
"It was either this or I was going to get a rifle and go up on a rooftop to shoot at people," said the young man who smashed nineteen plateglass windows at a San Francisco bank with the sledgehammer the officer is holding.
San Francisco Examiner & Chronicle,
June 17, 1973

(1969), the probability that people will aggress depends on both their *internal readiness to aggress* and *external cues* that elicit their aggression and provide a target. A habitually aggressive person has a strong "readiness" and needs only mild outside provocation. However, even a mild-mannered individual may become aggressive if he or she is subjected to strong, repeated frustration and potent provocation (Berkowitz & LePage, 1967).

Aggression as socially learned

Another answer to the "why" of aggression is that it is learned just like many other kinds of behavior. It is not due to some instinct or drive but is the result of the norms, rewards, punishments, and models that the individual has experienced (Bandura, 1973). According to this *social learning approach*, aggression can be the result of (a) aversive experiences and/or (b) anticipated benefits or incentives. Any kind of aversive experience (not only frustration) produces a general state of emotional arousal. This arousal can then lead to a number of different behaviors, depending on the individual's prior learning history. For example, aggression can generalize across situations. Boys who have been reinforced for aggressive responses in one situation tend to respond aggressively in other situations even when no rewards are provided (Horton, 1970). Thus, when they are upset, some people become aggressive, some withdraw, some turn to others for help, some engage in constructive problem solving, and so on. Aggression, like other responses, can also occur in the absence of emotional arousal if the individual feels that it will lead to some desired outcome (as when a child hits a younger one in order to get a toy).

Models for aggression

As we saw in Chapter 4, one of the basic ways in which people learn new behaviors is by watching other people perform them. Bandura and his associates pioneered in studies showing the power of aggressive models to produce aggressive behavior in children.

Nursery-school children were exposed to one of several conditions: a real-life aggressive model, a film of a model acting aggressively, an aggressive cartoon character, or no model at all. Soon after this experience, all the children were mildly frustrated. The frustrated children who had observed the aggressive models exhibited many imitative aggressive responses, while the frustrated children who had not observed a model were barely aggressive at all. Furthermore, the children who saw the filmed model were just as aggressive as those who saw the real-life model (Bandura, Ross, & Ross, 1963). ▲

Suppose the children saw a model being punished for aggressive behavior; would they then be less likely to imitate aggression?

Children were shown a film in which a model demonstrated four novel aggressive responses. One group saw a version in which the aggressive behavior was rewarded; another saw a version in which the model was punished; for a third group there were no consequences for the model. After viewing the film, children who had seen the model punished displayed fewer imitative aggressive acts (Bandura, 1965).

But did the observation affect their *learning* of aggression or only the *performance* of aggressive behavior?

After the experiment proper was supposedly over, the experimenter offered each child a prize for doing just what the model had done. Given this positive incentive all children readily performed the aggressive responses in imitation of the model. Evidently the ag-

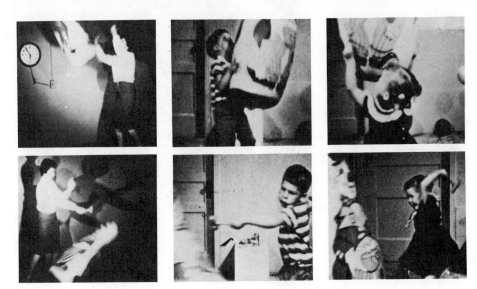

▲ *The model's attacks on an inflated doll were faithfully imitated by these two young subjects.*

gressive act had been learned plus the knowledge that such acts were inappropriate in that situation. When the payoff was changed, the act was performed (Bandura, 1965).

More recent research has shown that children who are emotionally aroused (as when they are participating in competitive games) are more likely to imitate a model's behavior whether the model is displaying aggressive or nonaggressive behavior (Christy, Gelfand, & Hartmann, 1971).

Do as I say, not as I do

A number of experiments have shown that some models are more effective than others in producing imitation. The most effective models are nurturant, high-status adults who have control over the rewarding resources. The people most affected by models are those who are dependent and moderately aroused and who have been previously rewarded for displaying imitative responses (Bandura, 1969). All in all, it would be hard to program an environment more conducive to the learning of aggression than that provided in the home of Mr. and Mrs. Average Punishing Parent.

Obviously, if a parent always punishes a child for behaving aggressively when the aggression is discovered, the child will soon learn to inhibit aggression in the presence of the parent. However, from Bandura's research we would expect that the imitative aggressive response would be powerfully learned, but would be withheld in the presence of the parent and performed in other situations—and it is. Mothers who punished aggression in the home were found to have children who behaved more aggressively in nursery school (Sears, Maccoby, & Levin, 1957). A study of overly aggressive adolescent boys showed that their fathers severely punished aggression in the home and that, consequently, few of the boys exhibited aggressive behavior there. In fact, many of the parents were surprised to learn that their "good boys" were highly aggressive in school (Bandura & Walters, 1959). Paradoxically, then, parents who physically punish a child for aggression are modeling and fostering the very behavior they are trying to eliminate.

Parents can also teach aggression in other ways. By telling their son to "be a man," always fight back, and use his fists, parents are explicitly training and encouraging him to be aggressive toward other people. Such parents not only condone aggressive behavior; they demand and reward it.

This little girl in war-torn Beirut has learned to handle an automatic weapon by imitating her older companions.

The broader cultural environment too can encourage violent behavior. By providing many aggressive models and by giving approval and prestige for violent acts, the community can put much pressure on individuals — especially young ones — to conform to the aggressive norm. ■

Expression of aggression: Catharsis or goad?

Because social learning theory does not postulate any aggressive drive or instinct, it rejects the concept of catharsis — that the expression of aggressive feelings will lessen aggressive actions. In fact, it predicts just the opposite result: that expressing aggressive impulses or watching aggressiveness in others will *increase* the probability of future aggression. This hypothesis is supported by studies such as the ones cited earlier, which show that aggression increases after exposure to aggressive models. In addition, studies have demonstrated that the expression of aggressive behavior in a permissive setting maintains the behavior at its original level, instead of reducing it.

Subjects were exposed to an anger-arousing antagonist; then half of them were allowed to express their anger and hostility to a sympathetic interviewer. The other subjects did not have such an interview but merely sat for a while. Later, subjects who had experienced the cathartic interview disliked the antagonist more (rather than less) and remained more physiologically aroused than the control subjects (Kahn, 1966).

These results suggest that therapeutic procedures that encourage the person to act out aggressive feelings may have an effect opposite to that intended.

Such findings contradict instinct and drive theories of aggression. They also seem to run counter to the common-sense notion that it is good to "let off steam" and "get it all off one's chest." It may help us to understand this contradiction if we make a distinction between *expressing emotional feelings* and *acting aggressively.* Giving vent to your feelings (as in crying, laughing, or talking to others) may make you feel better or relieve your anxiety. However, displaying aggression against your enemy, either verbally or in overt action, is *not* going to reduce the likelihood that you will do so again.

Violence and the mass media

Anyone who watches television is very likely to see both drama and comedy episodes in which people are killed or injured in a wide variety of ways, cartoons with lovable but sadistic characters, and news programs with on-the-spot coverage of wars, assassinations, riots, and "crime in the streets." Given the high rate of television viewing by most people in this country (between twenty and forty-five hours per week), the potential psychological impact of all of this televised violence is enormous. Some members of the television industry have argued that they are simply giving the public what it wants to see and that violent programs are the most popular. However, violent programs usually contain lots of action and suspense as well, and it may be these other factors that account for the high ratings of some violent shows.

This notion is supported by recent research in which viewers evaluated an adventure program which either portrayed violence or did not. Subjects viewed an episode of "Police Woman" which dealt with a gang of extortionists enforcing the payment of huge interest rates on loans the gang had made. Half of the subjects saw the original, uncut version which contained such violent scenes as forcing a man's hand into boiling water, releasing a car jack so that the car drops onto a mechanic underneath, beating criminals in order to get information, and so forth. The comparison subjects saw an edited version of the episode in which these violent scenes had been deleted. Although the uncut version was clearly rated more violent than the edited one, the subjects did not show greater liking for it. Thus violence per se does not appear to be a necessary condition for high ratings of particular TV shows. Good acting, action, and plot may be all that is necessary (Diener & DeFour, 1978).

Recently, much public attention and debate has focused on the possible effects of televised violence on the viewer. Does he or she become *more* aggressive as a result of watching television? According to proponents of both instinct and drive theories of aggression, the viewing of violence is cathartic and thus serves a positive social function by decreasing aggressive energy. The opposite point of view is taken by social learning theorists, who argue that television programming (as well as other media) provides models and sanctions for violent actions and is thus a major factor in the promotion of antisocial behavior.

So far, the research evidence generally supports the social learning viewpoint. As mentioned earlier, the modeling of aggression has been shown to influence the level of children's aggressive behavior. Not only do they learn

the aggressive responses immediately, but they can reproduce many of them several months later (Hicks, 1968).

It is difficult to prove conclusively that people's aggressive actions have been directly caused by televised violence. However, there have been several instances in which the link between television and subsequent crime appears to be quite strong. In a film called *Fuzz,* there was a scene showing teenagers setting derelicts on fire for "kicks." A few days after this film was aired on TV, real-life incidents of derelicts being set on fire and killed by teenagers occurred in Boston and Miami. *Born Innocent,* a controversial TV special, had a scene in which a young girl was brutally assaulted by a gang of girls in a reform school. Several days later in San Francisco, a girl was actually raped in the same manner by three girls who had seen the show and had admitted being influenced by it. ●

Although there have been some studies claiming that media violence is cathartic and decreases aggressive tendencies, major methodological flaws have reduced the credibility of these studies. More well-controlled research has supported the opposite conclusion: boys who view movie violence become *more* aggressive than those who see nonviolent films (Parke, Berkowitz, Leyens, West, & Sebastian, 1977). Also, boys who see a great deal of television violence during their childhood are far more aggressive in their behavior ten years later than boys who see very little violence (Eron, Huesmann, Lefkowitz, & Walder, 1972). Not only are children more prone to act aggressively after viewing violence, but they become more tolerant of aggressive behavior in others. They are less likely to take responsible action and intervene, for example, in a fight between two younger children (Drabman & Thomas, 1974). Similar effects have been found in studies of television viewing among adults (Gorney, 1976).

What are people learning from their repeated exposure to media violence? In addition to finding out *how* to act in various aggressive ways, viewers come to believe that aggression is an appropriate and normal reaction to any sort of conflict or frustration (Thomas & Drabman, 1978). Furthermore, people who watch a lot of TV tend to exaggerate the danger of violence in their own lives. They come to expect that they are potential victims of criminal actions, which makes them more generally fearful (Gerbner & Gross, 1976). Not only does television give a misleading impression of the *amount* of crime in our society, but it presents a false picture of the *kinds* of crimes that are committed and the individuals who commit them. For example, TV criminals are frequently depicted as mentally abnormal or pathologically greedy; real criminals are typically sane and poor (Haney & Manzolati, 1978).

●

Fifteen-year-old Ronny Zamora was convicted of robbery and murder in October 1977. His defense attorney had argued that Ronny was not guilty because he was intoxicated by television violence when he shot an elderly woman.

Violent encounters

Up to this point, we have been focusing on aggressive tendencies *within* the individual. However, aggression typically occurs in a social context, involving other people and a social structure.

Violence in the home

One of the most basic and critical social relationships is that existing between parent and child. This relationship is not always a normal, healthy one, since some parents neglect their children, provide inadequate care, and do not express feelings of love for them. And it has become very clear in recent years that some parents physically abuse their children, even to the point of death.

Accurate statistics are hard to come by, since many people are unwilling to admit that they abuse their own children. However, the most recent study of violence within the family concludes that each year well over 1.5 million children experience an attack by their parents that could cause severe bodily harm or death (Gelles, Straus, & Steinmetz, 1978). Child abuse occurs in both single-parent and intact families, in rich homes as well as in poor ones.

Why does such abuse occur? Are battering parents unusually sadistic people? Research on these questions has shown that there is a distinct pattern in abusive families, but that the adults can rarely be viewed as pathological "deviants."

Battered children are more likely to emerge from families in which there is marital stress (as well as other emotional problems) and a strong reliance on physical means of discipline. (See *P&L* Close-up, There's Only One Way to Teach the Little Brats . . .) Abuse is often directed at one particular child, rather than all of them, and it appears that anything that causes the child to be seen as strange, different, damaged, or abnormal increases the probability of abuse of that child (Friedrich & Boriskin, 1976). Such "differentness" might arise from an unwanted pregnancy, prematurity and low birth weight, mental retardation, or a physical handicap. Abusive mothers are often very lonely people who have little contact with other people outside the home. They usu-

Close-up
"There's Only One Way to Teach the Little Brats . . ."

Physical force is well accepted as a form of punishment in the United States, with about 80 percent of parents of young children (age three to nine) using some form of corporal punishment to discipline their children. (Interestingly, the acts that parents carry out on their children in the name of acceptable punishment could, if done to strangers or adults, be considered chargeable assault). In some cases, punishment of children is carried to extremes, such that children are seriously abused—physically and psychologically damaged. What distinguishes the discipline practices of abusing parents? In an attempt to answer this question, interviews were conducted with the mothers of "abused" children and those in a comparison group whose children were not abused. *Abused* in this study was defined as "multiple bone fractures traceable to physical assault by parents" (Elmer, 1971).

In families where child abuse was present, discipline was achieved by a variety of physical means of control, including whipping, scolding, shaming, shaking, and deprivation. Reasoning or avoidance of conflicts were rare. Many of these mothers believed that even very young, immature children of six to nine months had "tempers," acted out of spite, knew right from wrong, and deliberately did the wrong thing. They were more likely to interpret crying, soiling of diapers, or breaking a toy as deliberate attempts to misbehave and cause trouble. When asked how they would respond if their baby (of six months of age or older) struck or spat at them, the overwhelming majority replied that they would retaliate physically "to show him that he is *not* to do that kind of thing."

Many of the parents of nonabused children also punished their babies physically—the difference being in the severity and frequency of the punishment. Eighty-seven percent of *all* the mothers studied were slapping the hands or buttocks of their children by the time they were twenty-four months of age. Interesting social class differences were found. According to the mothers' reports, upper-class mothers tended to punish more for aggressive acts, middle-class mothers for excessive, irritating, or dangerous activities, and lower-class mothers for "misconduct," such as excessive demands, disobedience, or crying.

Speak roughly to your little boy,
And beat him when he sneezes;
He only does it to annoy,
Because he knows it teases.
Lewis Carroll
Alice's Adventures in Wonderland

ally have basic misconceptions about child development, perceiving their children as far more capable and potentially responsible than they really are. Such people have little basis for social comparison (which could help to correct their misconceptions) and also lack the support of friends or relatives in times of personal stress. Mothers are more likely than fathers to abuse their children physically, at least in terms of slapping, spanking, or throwing something at the child (Gelles, Straus, & Steinmetz, 1978). This is one of the few situations where women openly display as much aggression as (if not more than) men.

The attention of social service, medical, and government agencies has been most clearly focused on the incidence of violence by parents against the child. But the reverse can happen as well. According to recent Congressional testimony, elderly people are suffering more and more beatings at the hands of their adult children in order to "make them mind" or to change their mind about wills, financial management, or the signing of other papers. The abused old person shares a number of traits with the abused child—both are dependent on others, both are supposed to be under the love and care of a family, and both cause emotional, physical, and financial strain (*San Francisco Chronicle*, February 16, 1978).

Domestic violence can also take the form of violence between spouses and the last few years have witnessed a growing concern about the plight of battered wives. Statistics on the incidence of wife beating are extremely difficult to come by, since it is believed that wife beating is the most underreported crime in the country—even more so than rape, which is estimated to occur at least ten times for every case reported. Even when wife beating is reported to the police, they are unlikely to intervene. However, as more and more evidence accumulates, it is clear that many "commonsense" notions about wife beating are myths. For example, it has often been assumed that marital violence only occurs in low income or minority groups. However, battered wives come from all social classes, ethnic groups, and religions. Wife beating among poor people may be more visible because they have no other options but to call the police, while people with more money can seek out some form of escape or private therapy (Martin, 1976).

A recent study of battered wives found that they tended to be reserved, easily upset, timid, and low in self-esteem. They had grown up in conservative and restrictive home environments in which they had been taught traditional male and female sex-roles. They tended to be passive, dependent, inhibited, and acquiescent in their behavior—a pattern which enhanced their victimization by a dominating and aggressive spouse (Star, 1977). Battering husbands often grew up in homes where physical abuse was frequent; they are insecure, suffer from job-related frustrations, and often resent their wife's (and children's) dependence on them. They also have difficulty in expressing emotions, and their violence may represent an extreme form of the traditional male role of toughness and aggression which has been inculcated in them by society (Martin, 1976).

While some recent evidence suggests that wives are almost as likely to strike out at their husbands during fights as vice versa (Gelles et al., 1978), it is clear that the men, with their greater strength and physical prowess, are more likely to inflict serious damage. Nevertheless, it is estimated that nearly 5 percent of all married men in any given year (approximately 2 million) are the victims of serious assaults by their wives (Straus, 1978).

In many cases, women continue to live with their abusive husbands, even though they are battered repeatedly. Because of this, the erroneous belief has arisen that they are masochistic, want to be beaten, and even bring the beatings upon themselves by deliberately displeasing their husbands. In fact, the main reason women remain in violent marriages is because they have no place else to go. They often do not have access to much money, and they may not have the practical skills to get a job to support themselves and their children. They are made to feel that it is highly important to keep the family together and are sometimes counseled (by their relatives and friends) to be dutiful wives and "suffer a little" to prevent the family breakup. Finally, they are often afraid that their husband's retaliation for their leaving will be more violent than the beatings, and so they do learn to suffer in silence (Martin, 1976).

In recent years, some shelters have been established to provide battered women and their children with an alternative place to live, to receive needed counseling, legal assistance, and other services. This is obviously an important step in the right direction. However, efforts must be made to help abusing men as well if our society hopes to reduce the incidence of marital violence and the toll it takes in destroying our romantic conception of living "happily ever after."

It takes two to fight

Interpersonal aggression is rarely a case of one person being completely at fault and the other being totally innocent. More typically, both people are involved in escalating violence to the point where an assault occurs. This pattern is shown in interactions between police officers and individuals being arrested.

One analysis of 344 arrest reports found that in the cases where violent incidents occurred, both parties were reacting to what they perceived as threats against their own integrity and self-esteem. Often the encounter began with an officer's request for information or identification or an order to "move on," "break it up." In 60 percent of the episodes studied, the civilian reacted negatively to the officer's approach and failed to cooperate. The officer viewed this uncooperativeness as "irrational," disrespectful, and perhaps concealing criminal activity, whereas the individual had perceived the original request as unwarranted or discourteous or as an expression of personal hostility. A chain of events was then set off in which both parties contributed to the spiraling potential for violence (Toch, 1969).

Toch's analysis of these encounters is that violence generally follows a standard, two-step pattern. The first step is some action by either person that is seen by the other as a *provocation*. In many of the incidents involving police, the officer's initial verbal approach was such an action. To the officer, the approach was just part of the job, but to the civilian, it was a threat to personal dignity and autonomy. This is a common theme in most violent encounters— neither participant takes the other's point of view into account.

Following the initial provocation, the second step of a violent interaction is *escalation and confrontation*. Each person reacts not only to what the other one does but also to his or her perception of the *intention* behind the act, thereby gradually increasing the level of aggressiveness. This escalation ends in a final violent confrontation, unless one or the other breaks off the sequence. In interactions between police officers and resisting civilians, the officer's requests eventually become orders, and then escalate to threats or arrests. The civilian, on the other hand, will often move from resistance to verbal abuse, either to an attempt to flee, or to an assault against the officer. As these mutual provocations and escalations occur with increasing intensity, we can begin to understand some of the causes of "police riots." ◆

◆

*It is never easy to evaluate
charges of "police violence,"
for confrontations between
police officers and civilians
generally involve both
provocation and escalation.*

Deindividuation

In many instances of violence, people behave in ways that appear to involve a loss of control. They "get carried away," "lose their heads," and do things that normally they would never do. For example, "good citizens" have been known to loot, set fires, disrupt traffic, and assault other people when social controls were disrupted, as when New York City suffered a blackout in 1977 or the Montreal police went on strike in 1969. Since we know that human beings are capable of reason and responsible action, how can we understand these occasional instances of seemingly impulsive and irrational behavior?

A model that can explain these two sides of human nature has been proposed by Zimbardo (1970). *Deindividuation* is a complex process in which a series of social conditions lead to changes in perception of self and of other people. The individual does not monitor his or her own behavior and is less concerned about evaluation by others. Consequently, there is a weakening of the controls on behavior based upon guilt, shame, fear, and commitment. As a result, behavior that is normally restrained and inhibited is "released" in violation of established norms of appropriateness. Some behaviors are antisocial ones which can be characterized as selfish, greedy, power-seeking, hostile, lustful, and destructive. However, deindividuation can also lead to positive behaviors which are not normally expressed overtly, such as intense feelings of happiness, crying in public, and openly expressing love for others.

What conditions produce this reduction of self-monitoring and a loss of concern for social evaluation? One major contributor to deindividuation is the psychological state of *anonymity*. Anonymity may result when a person is "lost in the crowd," disguised, masked, part of a uniformed group, or hidden by darkness. When a person is anonymous, he or she cannot be identified by other people, and thus cannot be evaluated, criticized, judged, or punished by them. Emotions or impulses that would otherwise be held in check by conformity to social norms and fear of social disapproval may be released under the mask of anonymity. "You don't know who I am and I don't care who you are."

In one laboratory experiment, anonymity was created by having groups of female students wear baggy lab coats and hoods that covered their faces. In addition, they sat in a darkened room and were never referred to by name. Other women wore name tags, were frequently called by name, and saw the faces of the others in their group.

The subjects were told that the experimenter was studying empathy. Electric shocks were to be given to two young women (who were supposedly undergoing a conditioning experiment anyway). Two subjects would give the shock while the other two would only observe; then all would make empathy judgments. To determine who would do the shocking, they drew lots (which were rigged so that each subject believed that she and one other would deliver shocks). Subjects were led to believe that the same amount of shock was delivered whether one or more buttons were pressed and that the experimenter would not know which subjects were doing the shocking.

The subjects listened to a taped interview with each victim before watching her twist, squirm, and jump in reaction to each "shock" they gave her (actually she was a confederate who received no shock). In one condition the victim was portrayed as obnoxious, prejudiced, "bitchy"; in the other, as sweet, warm, loving, and altruistic.

As predicted, the anonymous subjects shocked the victims more than did the identifiable subjects. ■ *Furthermore, the aggression by the anonymous subjects did* not *vary as a function of the characteristics of the victim. They shocked the victim more and more over time, regardless of whether she was nice or obnoxious. In contrast, the identifiable subjects* did *respond to the victim's stimulus characteristics, shocking her less over a period of time if she was nice and more if she was obnoxious (Zimbardo, 1970).*

Simply creating a psychological state of anonymity was sufficient to increase

■

The anonymous subjects delivered more shock and gradually increased the amount of shock they gave both victims. Identifiable subjects gave only about half as much shock and decreased the amount they were giving the "nice" victim in the course of the experiment.

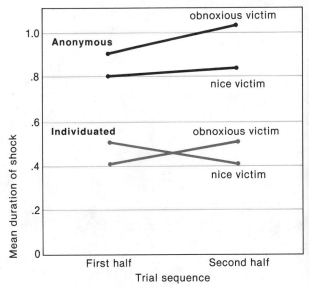

Adapted from Zimbardo, 1970

aggression toward a stranger, without any pressures by the experimenter to obey the authority.

A body of subsequent research supports the basic conclusion of this study—under conditions fostering anonymity, people are more likely to act aggressively or to behave in other antisocial ways. College student subjects were more likely to cheat or steal from the researcher's office when they were treated as anonymous "guinea pigs" than when they were treated humanely as individuals (Kiernan & Kaplan, 1971). Similarly, Halloween trick-or-treaters were more likely to steal extra candies and money when their identities were concealed by costumes than when they had previously been asked to reveal their identity to the adult host (Diener, Fraser, Beaman, & Kelem, 1976).

In an earlier study, anonymity was shown to increase aggression even when the aggressor had to pay a high price to be aggressive. Eight children were invited to an experimental Halloween party where they were allowed to play at aggressive or nonaggressive games in which they could win tokens. These tokens could be exchanged for attractive toys at an auction held at the end of the party. Playing the aggressive games involved physical competition (pushing and shoving) and took more time, thus earning fewer tokens and not being instrumental to the goal of getting the best toys later. The aggressive and nonaggressive games were similar in content. For example, competing with another child to retrieve a bean bag from a tunnel, or being timed while retrieving it alone.

At first, the children played these games in their normal street clothes (condition A); then they were dressed in Halloween costumes that made them appear anonymous (condition B); finally, they were unmasked and wore their regular clothing again (condition A). The A-B-A research design makes it possible to compare the behavior of the same person in the experimental and control conditions (Fraser, 1974). ▲

But maybe aggression is its own reward. Social conditions other than anonymity can foster deindividuated behavior. People may be more willing to engage in antisocial acts if they do not feel personally responsible for the consequences. This sense of *diffused responsibility* can result from sharing it with

▲

Aggression vs. rewards
The effects of simply being made anonymous are dramatic. Aggression was much higher in the anonymous condition despite the fact that its consequences were not in the children's best interests; they earned far fewer tokens during this period.

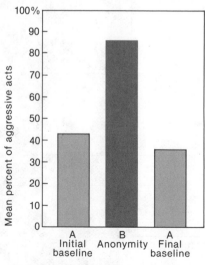

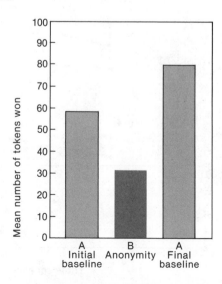

Based on Fraser, 1974

others, turning it over to some higher authority, or being unable to see the relationship between an action and its consequences. The presence of a *group* not only promotes anonymity and diffused responsibility, but can provide models for actions and serve as a catalyst by triggering behavior in a given direction or toward a given object.

A state of *arousal* increases the likelihood that intense, emotional behaviors will be released and that situational cues that would normally inhibit responding will not be noticed. Situational cues are also less powerful when the person is in a *novel or unstructured situation.* Finally, the cognitive and intellectual controls on behavior can be weakened by *sensory overload, altered states of consciousness,* and a reliance upon *noncognitive feedback* (such as physical absorption in the act).

Although much of the research on deindividuation has focused on its role in promoting antisocial behavior, such as aggression, some studies have looked at how it can enhance more positive behaviors. For example, people who were in an anonymous and unstructured situation (a dark room with several other strangers) were more likely to touch and hug each other and to enjoy the situation than people who were in a lighted room and did not feel anonymous (Gergen, Gergen, & Barton, 1973).

Recently, it has been proposed that deindividuation leads to an increase in behaviors not typical of an individual because it stimulates his or her *search for a unique identity,* rather than releasing restraints (Dipboye, 1977). Alternatively, deindividuation may have both benefits and drawbacks for the individual, since it allows behavioral freedom on the one hand but reduces one's sense of uniqueness and distinctiveness. Thus, it is possible that people will seek out deindividuation in some circumstances but avoid it in others. In support of this idea, Maslach (1974) found that subjects will try to become anonymous in a threatening environment, where there is the possibility of negative consequences. However, in a supportive environment, they will try to individuate themselves, making themselves stand out from the crowd in order to enhance their chances of receiving available positive rewards.

Social support for evil

Auschwitz. My Lai. Kent State. Attica. Jackson State. Cambodia and . . . . For many people these names have come to symbolize modern versions of evil. *Evil* is a term applied to "situations when force, violence, and other forms of coercion exceed institutional or moral limits" (Smelser, 1971). The three classes of situations that qualify as "evil" by this definition are those in which individuals or groups: (1) exercise coercive power over others when they are not legitimately empowered to do so; (2) exceed the limits of their legitimate authority to exercise coercion; or (3) exercise coercive or destructive control over others that violates a higher standard of humanity or morality even though it may be within politically sanctioned authority.

Those who engage in evil deeds rarely, if ever, see them as such. For the evil-doer, there is always sufficient justification to make the deed appear not only reasonable but absolutely necessary. Here again is the paradox of human perfection—the same mind that can comprehend the most profound philosophical and metaphysical truths can distort reality so that "evil" becomes "good."

People who violate basic laws of humanity typically rationalize their behavior according to some principle acceptable to others in their society. In addition, they often have some degree of social or political support or institutionalized structure that helps make it possible to redefine the act in other than its human terms. Consider Hitler:

"Thus, if we review all the causes of the German collapse, the final and decisive one is seen to be the failure to realize the racial problem and, more especially, the Jewish menace. . . . Thus do I now believe that I must act in the sense of the Almighty Creator: by fighting against the Jews I am doing the Lord's work" (1933, p. 25).

Lieutenant William Calley was found guilty of the massacre of more than four hundred civilians by Charlie Company in My Lai, Vietnam, on March 16, 1968. But an analysis of the conditions that led to this act of atrocity reveals it to be "only a minor step beyond the standard, official, routine United States policy in Vietnam" (Opton, 1971).

It might be argued that Calley and the other soldiers were responding to intense situational pressures that overdetermined their behavior. But now, in a cool analysis that distance and time from that atrocity provide, does the average citizen judge this action as evil? Is it likely to happen again, or was it a once-in-a-wartime event? A survey of a representative sample of nearly a thousand respondents across the United States found that under certain circumstances "large segments of the population . . . would consider such an action at least justifiable, probably acceptable, perhaps even desirable" (Kelman & Lawrence, 1972, p. 212).

As historian Hannah Arendt (1965) has pointed out, although evil behavior is often dramatic in its consequences, the circumstances in which evil occurs is the contrary—often banal and commonplace. Evil occurs frequently without raging emotions or confrontations between id and superego—it is often just a job to be done, an unpleasant interlude in one's life.

While some of these violent actions have been expressions of feelings of hate and anger, much collective violence is coolly instrumental—a means to an end. It can be used either to maintain power and preserve the status quo, or to change the existing society and achieve power.

Over the years, collective and institutionalized violence have taken many different forms. Governments have continually exhorted their citizens to take up arms against foreign invaders or to go forth to conquer new lands. In countries like the United States, where the threat of outside attacks has been small, violence has been directed toward the "enemies" within—the American Indians, for example, whose ranks were brutally cut from 850,000 to less than 400,000 in a series of "skirmishes." When governments have become oppressive, people have often joined together to fight their rule and overthrow them. Many massacres have been committed in the name of religious principles.

Blind obedience to authority

When you think of the long and gloomy history of man, you will find more hideous crimes have been committed in the name of obedience than have been committed in the name of rebellion.

C. P. Snow
"Either-Or"

We began your introduction to psychology with an analysis of Milgram's research on obedience. In a series of studies, Milgram found that the majority of subjects obeyed the experimenter's orders to deliver painful and dangerous electric shocks to another person. Even when subjects protested that they should not be doing it, they eventually went on to administer shocks when ordered to do so. This distinction between *dissent* and *disobedience* is dramatically underscored by the results of a more recent experiment in which college students were asked to train a puppy on a discrimination task by punishing it with increasing levels of shock whenever it made an error. The male and female students could actually see the puppy react to the shocks (which were low enough not to be harmful), and they not only dissented, but they expressed personal distress and, in some cases, even wept. Nevertheless, three-fourths of the students continued to obey the experimenter's demands, delivering the maximum intensity shock to the helpless puppy whose pain they could witness directly (Sheridan & King, 1972).

The argument that is proposed by both the obedience research and the mock prison study (in Chapter 21) is that evil deeds are not simply the actions of evil people but rather reflect the impact of evil situations on good, well-meaning individuals. In analyzing the obedience situation, three conditions can be distinguished that lead to a "blind obedience to authority" in violation of one's self-image and moral values.

1. Obedience is fostered by the presence of a *legitimate authority* who is trusted, who is seen as a valid representative of society, and who controls significant reinforcers. An authority who is not face-to-face with the subject loses some of this power.
2. Obedience is enhanced when a *role relationship* is established and accepted in which the individual is subordinated to another person. In this role, people perceive that they are not personally responsible for their behavior since they are not spontaneously initiating action but merely carrying out orders. However, when subjects see two other people refuse to accept the experimentally imposed role, 90 percent of them will defy authority commands themselves.
3. Obedience is nurtured by the presence of *social norms* that are seen as relating oneself to others in the situation and providing proscriptions as to protocol, etiquette, and socially approved and acceptable behaviors. These norms come to govern and constrain what is perceived as possible and appropriate. One subject in the original Milgram study said to the experimenter, "*I don't mean to be rude, sir,* but shouldn't we look in on him? He has a heart condition and may be dying."

Thus individuals often perceive social forces as so binding that they are locked into behaviors and interactions that they must carry out regardless of what they feel is right or believe is just. The values prescribed by the situation replace their individual values; "duty" and "loyalty" to the group and its norms supersede the dictates of conscience. (See *P&L* Close-up, Comparing Notes on Obedience to Authority.) Not long ago, over 900 U.S. citizens in a small religious settlement in South America stunned the world with mass suicide and murder in obedience to their leader, the Reverend Jim Jones. ■

Have you learned something from the principles presented here and in Chapter 21 that might help you "make sense" out of the senseless horrors that took place at the People's Temple in Jonestown, Guyana, in November 1978?
© *The Washington Post 1978, Frank Johnston/WOODFIN CAMP.*

The dynamics of groupthink

In many organizations and institutions, important decisions or policies are made by *groups* of people, rather than by any single individual. The advantage of such a group process is that there will be several different perspectives on the problem, so that the decision does not depend solely on one person's biases or errors in judgment. Even with a variety of inputs, however, group decisions can sometimes turn out to be extremely bad ones—the kind that later lead smart people to ask, "How could we have been so stupid?"

In an attempt to understand how the group process can go wrong, Irving Janis (1972) made an intensive analysis of several major policy decisions that turned out to be fiascoes, such as the Bay of Pigs Cuban invasion in 1961 and

Comparing Notes on Obedience to Authority: Dean and Milgram

Presidential counsel John Dean eventually broke away from obedience to authority and blew the whistle on his Watergate teammates.

In October, 1977, a symposium on "Obedience to Authority" was conducted in New York. An interesting discussion occurred between psychologist Stanley Milgram, who had conducted the laboratory experiments on obedience, and John Dean, the former presidential counsel whose own obedience to authority had enmeshed him in the Watergate scandal:

Milgram: I began my work on obedience to authority in 1961, before Vietnam and before Watergate, but we had certain historical episodes to inform us about what happens when a person is locked into a structure of authority, and I concluded my book, *Obedience to Authority: an Experimental Inquiry* (1973), with a few generalizations as to how people perform when they are locked into an authority situation. I'd like to read a few brief comments and ask you if it corresponds to the experience as you know it. . . . .

There's a frequent modification of language so that the acts at a verbal level do not come into any direct conflict with the verbal moral concepts that are part of everyone's upbringing. Euphemisms come to dominate language not frivolously, but as a means of guarding the person against the full moral implication of his acts.

Dean: Very true, and I'll give you some specifics on that. The money that I talked about. We never talked about the money, we talked about "the bites out of the apple." . . .

Milgram: The actions are almost always justified in terms of a set of constructive purposes, and come to be seen as noble in the light of some high ideological goal.

Dean: Well I'll tell you from my own experience what would document that, and still does in the minds of some of those who were involved: . . . this would never have been done had it not been done to protect a president. And for a long time I had trouble separating the man from the office. . . .

Milgram: There is always some element of bad form in objecting to the destructive course of events or, indeed, in making it a topic of conversation. Thus in Nazi Germany, even among those most closely identified with the "Final Solution," it was considered an act of discourtesy to talk about the killing. Subjects in the experiments described in the book most frequently experienced their objections as embarrasssing.

Dean: Well, there was some of that. For example, when I first went in to start dealing with the President I talked about the cover-up and the problems in terms of generalities. It wasn't until later that I started raising these problems flat out and in as graphic and as brutal a way as I could. But it took a long time for me to get there.

Milgram: When the relationship between subject and authority remains intact, psychological adjustments come into play to ease the strain of carrying out immoral orders. What kind of adjustments did you feel yourself making as you were under pressure to carry out these acts? . . .

Dean: Well, I suppose the adjustment I made, the rationalizations I made, were that it wasn't me that was actually doing the dirty work, I was just the man in the middle. I think the point that you made about a person in that position feeling that he has become an agent is so true. It even appears on the tapes where I'm explaining my behavior as being that of a mere agent of others. And when my lawyer analyzed it from a legal standpoint he said, "John, you're nothing but a mere agent." So there's a parallel between the law and where my head was.

Milgram: Yes. . . . We've talked about obedience to authority in this symposium, and some people may feel that that has to do with someone issuing a command, a finger pointing out at another person cowering in the face of that demand. But I think obedience does not take the form, necessarily, of a dramatic confrontation of opposed wills or philosophies; but is typically imbedded in a larger atmosphere where social relationships, career aspirations and technical routine set the dominant tone. Typically, we do not find a heroic figure struggling with conscience, nor a pathologically aggressive man ruthlessly exploiting a position of power, but a functionary who's been given a job to do and who strives to create an impression of competence in his work.

APA Monitor, January 1978, p. 5

the invasion of North Korea. After analyzing thousands of pages of historical documents, Janis found that these blunders were the result of what he calls *groupthink* — a mode of thinking that persons in highly cohesive groups engage in when they become so preoccupied with seeking and maintaining unanimity of thought that their critical thinking is rendered ineffective. Instead of carefully weighing the pros and cons of a decision, considering alternatives, raising moral issues, etc., the group has an overriding concern with *consensus*, which makes them vulnerable to committing serious blunders.

Groupthink has eight major characteristics:

1. An illusion of invulnerability, which creates excessive optimism and encourages taking extreme risks;

2. Collective rationalizations of the group's actions, which allow the group to discount any evidence that is contrary to the decision;

3. An unquestioned belief in the group's inherent morality, which leads the group to ignore the ethical or moral consequences of the decision;

4. Stereotyped views of the enemy as weak, evil, and/or stupid;

5. A strong internal pressure on group members to conform to the group norm and not to dissent;

6. Individual self-censorship of thoughts and ideas that deviate from the group consensus;

7. An illusion of unanimity on the decision, which is partly the result of the conformity pressures mentioned above;

8. The emergence of self-appointed *mind guards* — group members who suppress inconsistent information and reproach anyone who deviates from the group consensus.

Groupthink is not a trait of certain kinds of people. Rather, it is a process that can take place in all types of groups, even those composed of the best and the brightest. The important question, then, is "When is groupthink most likely to occur?" Janis has suggested three conditions that encourage groupthink: (a) high cohesiveness of the decision-making group; (b) insulation of the group from other, more balanced, outside information and authorities; and (c) endorsement of the policy by the group leader. These conditions work together to produce a group that is likely to arrive at an early consensus and, once the consensus has been reached, to force the members to support it for better or for worse. Such factors appear to have been at work behind the scenes in the Watergate scandal. This scandal exposed a plot by the President's closest aides and the Committee to Re-elect the President in the 1972 election to bug and to burglarize the Democratic headquarters in the Watergate building in Washington, D.C. When discovered, those involved tried to cover up their crimes. As condemning evidence mounted, it became apparent that the leaders of our government had perverted their good offices in the name of "national security."

How could so many decent, respectable government officials abdicate their sense of morality so totally? The most significant factors were those that encouraged the "groupthink" atmosphere among the aides and associates of the President. The parallels here to the general conditions outlined by Janis are surprisingly close. Prominent among them were: (a) the emphasis on *secrecy;* (b) the collective *paranoia* against hippies, antiwar radicals, and other critics of the administration; (c) the insulated belief that in using the resources of the government against *their* enemies, they were safeguarding the "national security"; (d) the emphasis on being a good "team player."

Given the disastrous consequences that can result from groupthink, what can be done to prevent it from happening? Janis makes several proposals, all

Master, go on, and I will follow thee,
To the last gasp, with truth and loyalty.
William Shakespeare
As You Like It

of which change the process of group decision making so that independent thinking is encouraged. For example, he recommends using procedures that force group members to evaluate critically both their own and others' ideas. There must also be channels of information, feedback, and criticism from *outside* experts or groups. He also recommends that the group be required to both analyze and role play the opposition's reactions and strategies. No research has been done to test the validity of these recommendations. However, it should be pointed out, as a historical note, that some of these techniques were intuitively adopted by President Kennedy after the Bay of Pigs fiasco. In the following year, basically the same group of men were faced with the Cuban missile crisis, and by using these different group techniques, they were able to arrive at a more effective group decision.

There is much research evidence accumulating to make us believe that decision making by crowds, mobs, large groups, or even powerful small groups is dangerous (Buys, 1978). Anthropologist Weston La Barre (1972) concludes that: "If anything, group membership blunts ethical perception and fetters moral imagination, because we then uncritically and passively let others think for us. The function of the group ethic, of course, is simply to maintain the group" (p. 14).

Dehumanized relationships

Would you ever deliberately humiliate, embarrass, or degrade another person? Can you imagine turning down a poor family's request for some food or clothing if you were in a position to authorize it just by signing your name? Is it conceivable that you would ever decide that certain groups were unfit and order their extermination? What would it take to make *you* kill another person?

These and other antisocial behaviors become possible for normal, morally upright, and idealistic people to perform under conditions in which people stop perceiving others as having the same feelings, impulses, thoughts, and purposes in life that they do. Such a psychological erasure of human qualities is called *dehumanization*. The result is that the people are seen and treated as objects, rather than as human beings.

When you are not responding to the human qualities of other persons, it becomes more possible to act inhumanely toward them. The golden rule then becomes "Do unto others as you would." It is easier to be callous or rude toward dehumanized "objects," to ignore their demands and pleas, to use them for your own purposes, and even to destroy them if they are irritating. The attempted genocide of Jews and gypsies by the Nazis could be carried out with the same efficiency as occurs daily at the animal slaughterhouses in Omaha by the simple expedient of perceiving these fellow human beings as inferior forms of animal life.

In a laboratory experiment, subjects were led to believe that they were studying the effects of punishment on decision making. They supervised the work of a group of male students and had the option of punishing them with electric shock whenever inadequate decisions were made. Some of the subjects overheard the experimenter characterize the students as being perceptive and understanding people. Other subjects overheard a dehumanized characterization of the students as an animalistic, rotten bunch. Control subjects did not receive any description of the potential victims. Subjects who thought of their "victims" in dehumanized terms chose much higher levels of shock as punishment and felt

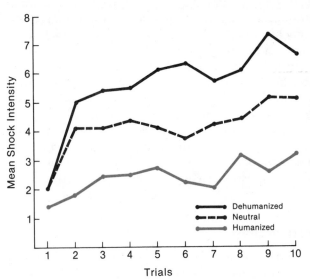

"Overheard" cues that humanized or dehumanized performers affected the intensity of shocks that subjects administered to them. Shock victims who were described in humanized terms were shocked less than the neutral control group, while the dehumanized subjects categorized as "animals" were shocked the most—and increasingly so over the ten trials.

Adapted from Bandura, Underwood & Fromson, 1975

less personal responsibility for the consequences of their punitive actions. Subjects given a humanized description of the victims showed less aggression against them than did the controls (Bandura, Underwood, & Fromson, 1975). ◆

The functions of dehumanization

The conditions that encourage people to treat others as objects are related to the functions that dehumanization can serve—the apparent benefits it can bring to the one doing the dehumanizing. Dehumanization may be: (a) socially imposed, (b) imposed in self-defense, (c) imposed deliberately for self-gratification, or (d) rationalized as the necessary means toward some noble end.

Socially imposed dehumanization

Dehumanization can occur in various work situations as a result of the way in which the job is defined by society. Such definitions fall into two major categories: (a) the job requires that the individual dehumanize other people in order to deal with them; and (b) the job itself dehumanizes the worker because it permits no opportunity for expression of either personal feelings or uniquely human abilities.

Examples of the first category include situations in which a large number of people have to be processed efficiently—such as college students during registration, subway commuters during rush hour, prisoners or mental patients during the institutional mealtime. In order to do this, administrators of institutions often become concerned with "managing the flow," monitoring time schedules, and minimizing disrupting influences. Once the number of individuals requiring a given service becomes too great, they stop being seen or treated as "individuals." Moving mental patients in and out of the cafeteria and the showers may take precedence over therapeutic concerns. Being shoved around by the employees hired as subway "packers" in the Tokyo Transit System can be as dehumanizing as being given an administrative runaround or being told that there can be no (human) exceptions to "the rules."

You can't take pride any-
more. It's hard to take
pride in a bridge you're
never gonna cross, in a
door you're never gonna
open. You're mass-
producing things and you
never see the end result
of it.

Steelworker quoted in
Working by Studs Terkel

The second category of socially imposed dehumanization in a work situation is perhaps best illustrated by that marvel of American technology, the assembly line. On an automobile assembly line, cars may pass by each work station at the rate of over fifty an hour. Each person has less than a minute to perform a task, and must repeat it hour after hour. ■

Work on such assembly lines is so depressing and exhausting that workers no longer feel meaningfully related to the product of their labors. The result has been high rates of absenteeism, high turnover, poor quality of work, alcoholism and drug abuse on the job, massive worker dissatisfaction, increasing mental health problems, lower productivity, and unsafe autos that have to be recalled—all measures of how prevalent dehumanization is in the contemporary work scene (Congressional Hearings on Worker Alienation, 1972).

Dehumanization in self-defense

Individuals in many health and service professions must function in situations that ordinarily arouse very intense emotional feelings, elicit painful empathy, and/or involve "taboo" behaviors, such as invasion of privacy or violation of the human body. In order to perform efficiently in such situations, the individual may develop defenses against these disruptive emotions through techniques of dehumanization. By treating one's clients or patients in an objective, detached way, it becomes easier to perform necessary interviews, tests, or operations without experiencing strong psychological discomfort. To some extent, this form of dehumanization is positive.

For example, surgeons have reported that before they could perform their role effectively, they had to learn not to perceive a whole person under their scalpel but only an organ, tissue, or bone. Within the profession itself, this process is called "detached concern," a term that better conveys the difficult (and almost paradoxical) position of having to dehumanize people in order to help or cure them (see Lief & Fox, 1963).

However, it is possible for this "detachment" to go to an extreme. If the psychological stress and strain of the job become too severe (as when a social worker is faced with trying to help several hundred poor and suffering families), the person may "burn out" emotionally and lose all human feeling for the people being served. (See *P&L* Close-up, The Loss of Human Caring.)

■
Dehumanization can result
from being treated as an
object rather than an
individual, as in the Tokyo
subway during rush hours, or
from holding a job that offers
no opportunity for expression
of either personal feelings or
uniquely human abilities.

The Loss of Human Caring

Intense involvement with people occurs on a large scale, continuous basis for individuals in various health and social service professions. Hour after hour, day after day, these professionals must *care* about many clients or patients. However, in all too many cases, they are unable to cope with this continual emotional stress, and eventually "burn-out" occurs. Burn-out is a syndrome of emotional exhaustion, in which the professionals lose all concern or emotional feeling for the people they work with, and come to treat them in detached and even dehumanized ways.

Recent research on this syndrome (Maslach, 1976) has identified several social and situational factors that can affect the level of burn-out:

1) *Ratio.* The quality of the professional interaction is greatly affected by the number of people for whom the professional is providing care. As this number increases, the general result is greater cognitive, sensory, and emotional overload for the professional.

2) *Amount of direct contact.* Longer work hours are correlated with more stress and negative staff attitudes *only* when they involve continuous direct contact with patients or clients. This is especially true when the nature of the contact is very difficult and upsetting (patients who are dying, clients who are physically or verbally abusive). The emotional strain of such prolonged contact can be eased by varying the professional's work so that he or she is not constantly in such high-stress situations and by providing temporary withdrawals when needed.

3) *Time-outs vs. escapes.* Opportunities for withdrawing from a stressful situation are critically important for these professions. The most positive form of withdrawal are "time-outs." These are opportunities for the professional to voluntarily choose to do some less emotionally stressful work while other staff take over his or her responsibilities with clients and patients.

Most other types of withdrawals represent a negative form of "escape." Here, the professional's decision to take a break from work always comes at the expense of clients or patients. In such situations, the professionals are more likely to feel trapped by their total responsibility for these people, and can not temporarily withdraw without feeling some guilt.

4) *Social-professional support system.* The availability of formal or informal programs in which professionals can get together to discuss problems, and get advice and support, is a way of helping them to cope with job stress more successfully. Such a support system provides opportunities for analysis of both the problems they face and their personal feelings about them, for humor, for comfort, and for social comparison.

5) *Analysis of personal feelings.* Since the arousal of strong emotional reactions is a common feature of health and social service occupations, efforts must be made to deal constructively with them and prevent them from being entirely extinguished. Burn-out rates are lower for those professionals who actively express, analyze, and share their personal feelings with their colleagues either informally, or through social-professional support groups, special staff meetings, or workshop group sessions.

6) *Training in interpersonal skills.* Health and social service professionals need to have special training and preparation for working closely with other people. While they are well trained in certain healing and technical service skills, they are often not well equipped to handle repeated, intense, emotional interactions with people.

The conclusion to be drawn from Maslach's analysis is that burn-out is not a function of "bad" people who are unfeeling and brutal. Rather, it is a function of "bad" situations in which originally idealistic people must operate. Hopefully, implementation of some of the ideas she proposes can be a start towards changing these health and welfare situations such that they promote human values rather than destroy them.

Dehumanization for self-gratification

Sometimes others are used solely for one's own gain, pleasure, or entertainment, with no concern given to their feelings or thoughts. An example of this process is prostitution, in which a person openly buys the privilege of dehumanizing another individual. Parenthetically, the prostitute reciprocates in kind, viewing the purchaser as just another "trick" to be turned. Men for whom sexual intercourse is only a self-gratifying experience—with a woman simply the means—show this dehumanization when they call a woman "a piece," "a real dog," "a cow," etc.

The depths to which this insensitivity to other human beings can go are revealed in news accounts of people being entertained by suicide attempts and taking advantage of robbery victims.

In Miami, Florida, an eighty-seven-year-old man, depressed from years of loneliness, threatened to commit suicide by jumping off a bridge. Instead of trying to prevent his death, a group at the scene taunted him: "Come on, jump! Jump! Jump!" He took their advice and jumped. One young man hurried to his aid, dragged him from the river, and tried in vain to revive him—as the apathetic crowd watched without offering any assistance (Knight Newspapers Service, August 17, 1973).

In Chicago, a gas station was robbed and the two attendants were tied up by the burglars. When a customer arrived shortly afterwards, the attendants called out for help. Instead, the customer helped himself to a free tank of gas and two cartons of cigarettes and drove off. This scene was repeated in one form or another by nearly one hundred drivers in the next two hours, before someone finally called the police (United Press International, December 13, 1975).

Dehumanization as a means to an end

There have been many times in history when people have viewed a particular group of others as obstacles to the achievement of their goals. By perceiving such people in a dehumanized manner as "the enemy," "the masses," "a threat to national security," "inferior," etc., it becomes less of a problem to take action against them in the name of some great cause, such as peace, victory, liberty, the revolution. Their suffering, injury, or destruction is then justified as a means toward a "noble" end. Many examples of such dehumanization come to mind, including the dropping of the atomic bomb on the residents of Hiroshima in order to "bring peace," the mass killing of Jews by the Nazis because "they are unfit," and the denial of medical treatment to black men afflicted with syphilis (the control group in a controversial study at Tuskegee, Alabama) in order to "study the course of the disease."

To demonstrate the ease with which people can adopt this dehumanized view of others, a psychologist studied the reactions of 570 students at the University of Hawaii to an alleged threat to their security. The students were assembled to hear a brief speech by a professor who asked them to assist in the application of scientific procedures to eliminate the mentally and emotionally unfit. The problem was convincingly presented as a high-minded scientific project, endorsed by scientists, planned for the benefit of humanity, and actually even a kindness to those who would be eliminated. It was further "justified" by an analogy to capital punishment, and those whose opinions were being solicited were flattered as being intelligent and educated, with high ethical values. In case there might be any lingering misgivings, assurances were made that much careful research would be carried out before action of any kind would be taken with human beings. A questionnaire was then administered to the students (Mansson, 1972). The startling results of this study are all too apparent in the table. ● *In a later replication of this study, a surprising 29 percent even supported the final solution when applied to their own families! (Carlson & Wood, 1974).*

This study of the "final solution" should give you pause, for it shows how little effort might be necessary to translate these "artificial" experimental findings into the same nightmare of reality that occurred in Germany in World War II—and in other places and other times before that.

The techniques of dehumanization

What are the methods or strategies that people use to achieve dehumanization and emotional detachment? Surprisingly, very little research has been done on this question. In fact, there is only one relevant experimental study showing that people can indeed control their emotional reactions to upsetting stimuli (Koriat, Melkman, Averill, & Lazarus, 1972). Subjects were asked to watch a very disturbing film of industrial accidents, and were told to try to *detach* themselves from it psychologically. Apparently, these verbal instructions were sufficient to make subjects feel less emotionally aroused by the film (even though their physiological responses were still high). In contrast, subjects who were told to become *involved* in the film showed significantly more physiological arousal and also reported that they felt more emotionally upset.

How did these subjects actually suppress or enhance their emotional response? At the moment, we have to rely on some supportive evidence and

●
Student opinions concerning the "final solution"

1. Do you agree that there will always be people who are more fit in terms of survival than others?	*Agree*	90%
	Disagree	10%
2. If such killing is judged necessary, should the person or persons who make the decisions also carry out the act of killing?	*Yes*	57%
	No	43%
3. Would it work better if one person were responsible for the killing and another person carried out the act?	*Yes*	79%
	No	21%
4. Would it be better if several people pressed the button but only one button would be causing death? This way anonymity would be preserved and no one would know who actually did the killing.	*Yes*	64%
	No	36%
5. What would you judge to be the best and most efficient method of inducing death?	*Electrocution*	1%
	Painless poison	9%
	Painless drugs	89%
6. If you were required by law to assist, would you prefer to:		
(a) *be the one who assists in the decisions?*		85%
(b) *be the one who assists with the killing?*		8%
(c) *assist with both the decision and the killing?*		1%
No answer		6%
7. Most people agree that in matters of life and death extreme caution is required. Most people also agree that under extreme circumstances, it is entirely just to eliminate those judged dangerous to the general welfare. Do you agree?	*Yes*	91%
	No	5%
	Undecided	4%

Adapted from Mansson, 1972

speculation for our answer. There appear to be several techniques by which humans become able to dehumanize other humans. In different ways, all of them help the individual to: (a) perceive the other person(s) as less human; (b) perceive the relationship with the other person(s) in objective, analytical terms; and/or (c) reduce the amount of experienced emotion and physiological arousal.

a. *Relabeling.* The use of certain kinds of language is perhaps one of the most visible techniques of dehumanization. A change in the labels or terms used to describe people is one way of making them appear more objectlike and less human. Some of these dehumanizing terms are derogatory ones, such as "gook," "queer," "half-breed," "hippie." Others are more abstract labels that refer to large, undifferentiated units—like "aliens" or "the masses."

Another form of dehumanizing language describes people in terms of the functional relationship the individual has with them. For example, social-welfare workers often speak of "my caseload" when referring to the people they deal with, while poverty lawyers talk about "my docket." Substituting verbs with less emotional meaning can have the same effect—e.g., "to waste" a person instead of "to kill." Similarly, it becomes easier to steal from the college bookstore if it is relabeled as "ripping off the establishment."

b. *Intellectualization.* A related technique of dehumanization is one in which the individual recasts the situation in more intellectual and less personal terms. By dealing with the abstract qualities of other people (rather than the more human ones), the individual can "objectify" the situation and can react in a less emotional way. For example, physicians may view their patients in terms of their illness ("I admitted two coronaries yesterday").

c. *Compartmentalization.* To the extent that a particular situation or type of activity can be separated from the rest of an individual's life, it becomes easier to detach it from one's personal values and feelings. An example is the belief that "Thou shalt not kill"—except in wartime for the good of your country.

d. *Withdrawal.* Another technique for reducing emotional arousal is to minimize one's involvement in an interaction with others that might be stressful. This can be done in a number of ways, such as by spending less time with the other person, physically distancing oneself (standing farther away from the person or not making eye contact), communicating with the other person in impersonal ways (e.g., superficial generalities, form letters), and so forth.

e. *Diffusion of responsibility, social support, humor.* In attempting to deal with strong emotional feelings, an individual will often turn to others for help and support. If such actions reduce psychological stress and discomfort, they can be used to promote dehumanization. Having other people say, "It's not so bad" or "Why don't you look at it *this* way," helps the person achieve detachment. A perceived diffusion of responsibility can also aid in dehumanization. If the individual knows that other people feel the same way or are doing the same thing, he or she may have fewer qualms about engaging in a particular behavior.

Being able to joke and laugh about a stressful event is another way of reducing the tension and anxiety that one may feel. It can also make the situation seem less serious, less frightening, and less overwhelming. Observers have noted the "sick" humor of medical students who are dissecting a cadaver for an anatomy class, and have suggested that it serves these purposes.

The cataloging and analysis of social pathology is depressing to write about and to read about because it should not be done with scientific detachment, but with a sense of personal concern and urgency. One feels helpless to know where to begin to suggest remedies. The perversion of our human potential flows not merely from the distortion of psychological processes. Economic, political, historical, and cultural levels of influence interact with the psychological to determine both human nature—and our inhumane reactions.

Perhaps in some future edition of *Psychology and Life* there will be no need for a chapter on social pathology. Rooting out such pathology involves our concerted action directed toward improving the quality of our lives—one of the goals of psychology outlined in Chapter 2. Psychologists are becoming increasingly concerned about studying psychological phenomena at a level appropriate to its everyday complexity. In addition, many of us want to contribute our research talents, wisdom, and insights to help create and broaden the positive conception of humanity. In the final chapter of our journey we shall examine one such endeavor, the ecological approach to psychological experience.

Chapter summary

Aggression is physical or verbal behavior with the intent to injure or destroy. Freud approached aggression as an *inborn* component of human behavior. He postulated two opposing instincts—*eros,* the life instinct that promotes survival and growth, and *thanatos,* the death instinct that generates aggressive, self-destructive energy. Aggressive energy could be drained off in safe ways, through *catharsis.* But a highly aggressive or violent person who generated a great deal of aggressive energy would be unable to discharge it appropriately in small amounts.

Some ethologists have theorized that human aggressiveness, like the aggressive behavior of other animals, is *instinctive.* According to this theory most animals do not kill their own kind because one animal will eventually signal appeasement or submission to the other. Humans have somehow lost this inhibitory instinct, while retaining the instinct to aggress. Aggression is thought to arise from an innate sense of *territoriality.* This theory has been criticized because it does not take into account the cognitive factors that divorce human aggression from the immediate situation. Other research suggests that inhibitory behavior in animals is not innate.

A third approach to aggression emphasizes its physiological basis. The *hypothalamus* and *amygdala,* in particular, have been associated with aggressive behavior. Brain disease of the limbic system is sometimes found in those exhibiting a *dyscontrol syndrome.* There does not, however, appear to be a one-to-one correspondence between physiological factors and aggression.

The *frustration-aggression hypothesis* holds that aggression is a drive acquired in response to frustration. The greater the amount of frustration, the stronger the resulting aggressive response. This theory was later revised to state that every frustration produces an *instigation* to aggression. When frustration occurs, the frustrated individual is often unable to vent aggression on his or her primary target and so *displaces* it onto some other persons or objects (*scapegoats*). A further development of this hypothesis suggests that the probability of aggression is dependent upon the individual's *internal readiness to aggress,* as well as the *releasers,* or external cues associated with violence, that are present.

The *social learning* approach states that aggression can be the result of aversive experiences and/or anticipated benefits. *Aggressive models,* particularly parents and the media, are extremely powerful in producing aggressive behavior in children. Thus, social learning theory rejects the idea of catharsis, insisting rather that experiencing aggressive feelings or watching others do so increases rather than lessens the probability of future aggression. Because research supports this view, great concern has arisen over the impact of violence in the media, especially television.

It is now known that the degree of aggression and abuse within the home does not correlate with socioeconomic level. Instead, other patterns have come to light. Families with *battered children* tend to have marital stress and other emotional problems and to abuse a child who is "different" in some way—physically or mentally. Abusive mothers are generally lonely, have had little contact outside the home, and harbor misconceptions about child development.

Elderly people, too, suffer abuse at the hands of their adult children, usually because of the physical and financial strain their dependency brings. Battered wives have been found in all social and ethnic groups. They tend to be reserved, timid, low in self-esteem, and the products of conservative, restrictive homes. Battering husbands, on the other hand, tend to suffer from job-related frustrations and have usually grown up in homes where physical abuse was frequent.

Violence between two people generally begins with an action by one person seen by the other as *provocation*. This is followed by *escalation* and violent confrontation.

Deindividuation is an important factor in violence and aggression because it causes an individual to stop monitoring his or her own behavior and become less concerned about the evaluation of others. *Anonymity, diffused responsibility, states of arousal* in *nonstructured situations, sensory overload, altered states of consciousness,* and reliance on *noncognitive feedback* all contribute to this state.

"Evil" situations may be defined as those in which individuals or groups exercise coercive power over others when they are not legitimately empowered to do so, exceed the limits of their legitimate authority to coerce, and coerce or destructively control others, violating a higher standard of humanity or morality, even if their actions are socially and legally sanctioned.

People with "good" intentions often perform "evil" acts through *blind obedience to authority,* or through *groupthink,* in which persons in highly cohesive groups become so preoccupied with seeking and maintaining unanimity of thought that their critical thinking is rendered ineffective.

When people are perceived and treated as objects rather than as human beings, they are *dehumanized.* Professionals such as doctors and social workers often practice dehumanization on patients and clients in *self-defense,* thus preventing constant emotional turmoil and preserving their effectiveness. Others may dehumanize purely for *self-gratification,* or as a means to an end. People may employ many means to dehumanize others. Among them are *relabeling, intellectualization, compartmentalization, withdrawal, diffusion of responsibility, social support,* and *humor.*

24 Ecological Psychology

In southern Illinois it has been discovered that the nitrates in fertilizers used on the surrounding farms have seeped into the water supply of the nearby city. Using these fertilizers greatly increases the yield. But when they get into the water supply, the nitrates are converted into *nitrites*, which are highly toxic and can lead to a serious children's disease. Meanwhile, however, the farms have come to depend on the extra yield they are getting by using the fertilizers. Otherwise, their farming would not be economically feasible. The whole city, in turn, is economically dependent on the success of its farming community. The farmers cannot just give up using nitrates because it would upset the whole system and ruin them financially. Yet while they continue, they are endangering the health of their own children.

A similar case has been reported in Idaho. In a mining community, dangerous levels of lead have been discovered in the blood of young children in the area, levels sufficient to cause irreversible brain damage. The nearby mining company responded to the news by assurances that it would cooperate with health officials. It played down the danger, however, pointing out that it was not the only possible source of the lead. Residents, too, tended to discount the reports of danger as distorted. Only those outside the situation of economic dependence on the mine were alarmed: both the governor and the state health department authorities regarded it as extremely serious (*San Francisco Chronicle*, September 25, 1974, p. 25).

Just as we have come to realize that we are part of a biological ecosystem in which all parts are interdependent, so we are discovering that we are interdependent parts of social systems too. Much of our social behavior has its roots in this psychosocial interdependence rather than in either our character traits or the particular stimuli of the moment.

Social systems do not become apparent when we study the behavior of single individuals. Conclusions based on laboratory research alone are often limited because all influences other than a few independent variables have been carefully excluded. It is no wonder, then, that such conclusions sometimes do not predict what happens outside. They do not predict that individuals who have always been kind and decent will kill helpless villagers in a war, or that a crowd will taunt a frightened boy who is threatening suicide, or that a seminary student hurrying to deliver a sermon about the Good Samaritan will fail to *be* one when he meets a person who needs help. Nor do they explain why competing fishermen overfish even though they know they are depleting the stocks of fish they all need for their livelihood or why nations that already have enough weapons to kill their enemies many times over keep devising more terrible ways of killing human beings while reducing funds that are badly needed for social and health services for their citizens.

To understand behaviors like these, we have to develop new tools. We have to learn how to take into account the whole context in which behavior occurs. This new approach is called *ecological psychology*.

Systematic study of the effects of the larger environment on behavior began in the 1950's with studies of behavior in psychiatric wards, where different physical designs seemed to produce different behavior on the part of the patients. Such studies have led to the new field of *environmental psychology*. Environmental psychologists study the relationships between psychological processes and physical environments, both natural and humanmade environments. For example, how do people use space and architectural design to express their feelings and meet their needs?

Ecological psychology overlaps environmental psychology but goes beyond it in studying both physical and social environments. It also emphasizes the systems in which behavior is enmeshed. For example, an ecological psy-

The formula for survival is not power; it is symbiosis.
Lord E. Ashby
Encounter

The reciprocal interplay between humankind and the earth can result in a true symbiosis, the word being used here in its strong biological sense to mean a relationship of mutualism so intimate that the two components of the system undergo modifications beneficial to both.
René Dubos
Symbiosis between the Earth and Humankind

chologist would point out that the continued use of nitrates by the Illinois farmers makes sense only when you recognize the social and economic systems of which they are a part.

Most psychology focuses on how the environment influences our behavior. Ecological psychology is as much interested in how our actions affect our environment. Thus in the long term, it is interested in quality of life, in how human beings can make their interdependence with each other and with their environment mutually nourishing. The Greek word *oikos*, from which *ecology* is derived, means "house" or "household." In the broadest sense, ecological psychology is concerned with what the human species will have to do to put its house in order.

In this final chapter we will first look more closely at the contrasts between traditional and ecological psychology and then see how ecological concepts can help us to understand the social structures in crowded urban centers that lead to social pathology. We will then return to the possibility of designing a nourishing environment for ourselves to live in.

The ecological approach

The ecological psychologist differs from the traditional one in focusing on (1) molar, ongoing behavior in its physical and social context, (2) the systems in which behavior occurs, and (3) the two-way influence of person and environment—how they affect each other.

Molar, ongoing behavior in a context

A *reductionist* approach is one that tries to understand behavior by describing processes on the level below the behavior itself. For example, thinking is described in terms of the activity of neurons in the brain. Or psychologists trying to understand short- and long-term memory look for different kinds of electrochemical changes in the brain. This is also a *molecular* approach, an attempt to understand a process by understanding its parts.

The ecological psychologist argues that a behavior can never be completely described by processes at a lower level of organization. At each level, new properties emerge that are not predictable from the parts that went into it. The sadness or sprightliness of a tune cannot be seen in the individual notes. Similarly, the content of our feelings and thoughts would never be predicted from the behavior of neurons. Hopes and fears occur in persons but not, so far as we know, in neurons or glands. They are of course made possible by physiological processes, but they in turn influence the working of those processes. Just compare the reactions of a hopeful individual with those of a panic-stricken one. Respiration, heart rate, adrenal secretion, ability to remember, coordination—all are different. But to look only at the body processes would miss the importance of the psychological context in which they occur, the meaning of the situation for the conscious individual. So the ecological psychologist studies *molar* behavior—the overt behavior as it looks to another person—and tries to explain it on the level where it occurs rather than on the level below.

An ecological approach also looks at the next level up. Human beings not only *have* subsystems but *are* subsystems of larger systems, as we have seen. On these higher levels of organization, too, new properties emerge that exert influence over the functioning of their parts. Much of the meaning of what happens on one level can best be understood by looking at the level above it. Understanding the ecology of behavior requires a look at all the levels where processes are taking place that influence it.

The need for this newer approach has been well put by ecologist Eugene Odum (1977):

"It is self-evident that science should not only be reductionist in the sense of seeking to understand phenomena by detailed study of smaller and smaller components, but also synthetic and holistic in the sense of seeking to understand large components as functional wholes. A human being, for example, is not only a hierarchical system composed of organs, cells, enzyme systems, and genes as subsystems, but is also a component of supraindividual hierarchical systems such as populations, cultural systems, and ecosystems. Science and technology during the past half century have been so preoccupied with reductionism that supraindividual systems have suffered benign neglect. We are abysmally ignorant of the ecosystems of which we are dependent parts. As a result, today we have only half a science of man" (p. 1289).

Studying behavior in context means devising new research methods for studying larger units of behavior than single stimulus-response chains. It also means studying more naturally occurring behavior. We need to start with the broadest possible net to be able to catch and identify all the factors that are important influences on everyday behavior.

Finally, studying behavior in context means studying ongoing behavior in its time context. Looking at isolated segments of stimulus and response, with no past and no future, we miss the continuity that helps give behavior its direction and meaning. To understand a person's behavior we need to understand his or her picture of the past, present, and future; that is, a person's or group's sense of temporal perspective.

Systems as settings for behavior

When you study the influences of the context, you are not looking at just a collection of independently acting influences but at systems. The decision of the Illinois farmers to keep using their fertilizers or of the Idaho residents to keep the mine going is influenced by a whole network of factors that interact with each other and keep each other going. There are multiple, interdependent causes, multiple effects, and dynamic interrelationships among the parts.

Networks of causes

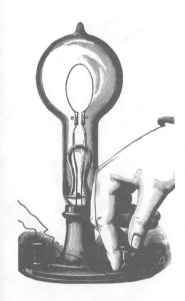

In a system there is not a simple causal chain with one event causing another. Our traditional experimental paradigm of manipulating a single independent variable and looking for changes in particular dependent variables is too simple.

Flicking a light switch turns on a light only if there is an intact circuit, a good bulb, an energy source of the right voltage to tap into, the nation's energy resources, and so on. All these other elements are part of the cause of the light's going on, not just the flicking of the switch. Isolating one "independent" variable for study often leads us to forget the continuing influence of all the variables that we did *not* manipulate.

If you use similar subjects and try different reinforcement schedules, holding everything else constant, it is easy to conclude that reinforcement schedules are the key factor in determining behavior. Likewise, if you hold reinforcement and other environmental factors constant, and study the responses of subjects differing in motivation, it is easy to conclude that the motivations were what determined the reactions you saw. This helps explain why behaviorists regard the environment as the key determinant of behavior while personality psychologists see "traits" and other internal conditions as the important variables. Each type of psychologist is holding a different set of variables constant as they conduct their own observations of behavior.

The ecological psychologist points out that the variable you manipulate is no more causal than the ones you hold constant. They are still operating too. If they were absent or even just held constant at a different level, the behavior might be very different. A change anywhere in the system of causes could change the behavior.

Another complicating factor is that the same causal factor can have different effects in different networks. The whole explains the parts rather than the other way around. Take the potent force of peer pressure, for example. In a delinquent gang, it can lead to auto thefts; in a Boy Scout troop, to obedience and cooperation with society's rules; in a drug culture, to use of drugs. The behavior that peer pressure leads to depends on the norms of the group in which it occurs.

Sometimes a variable that we have been holding constant or ignoring turns out to be so important that it breaks through the constraints of a research design. That is, the variables the experimenter expected to be important may not be, while some variable that was very nearly ignored turns out to have a major effect. An example is found in an exhaustive study of factors related to academic achievement of black children. To everyone's surprise, objective factors in the school situation such as class size, teacher-pupil ratio, physical plant, and money spent per pupil turned out to have little or no consistent relationship to achievement. Family factors had more, but the thing that was most highly correlated with doing good schoolwork was discovered almost by accident. It was a *sense of personal control*, a belief that one's actions could make a difference in shaping one's life. Little attempt had been made to assess this factor, but it was such an important one that it broke through the research design in the students' self-reports. The investigators had to revise their hypotheses about the causes of academic achievement (Coleman, 1969).

It is the nature of science to seek lawful consistency within complex phenomena. Only occasionally, however, can a single, central cause be found that accounts for most of the variability in reactions. Most important events have many causes that are multiply determined. Furthermore, they are operating not just independently and additively but as a network, interactively. So they have to be studied as a network, as interdependent, interacting variables. Studying them separately, as "independent variables," may give us an inaccurate picture as well as an incomplete one.

Multiple effects

Our recent awareness of the fragility of our ecosystem has given us a helpful analogy for trying to understand social, political, and economic systems. In dealing with the natural world, it is clear that what happens anywhere in it affects the whole system. With the best intentions you can introduce a new chemical that kills a bothersome weed only to find later that you have put a poison into the food chain that is killing people.

◆ *The Pruitt-Igoe public housing project in St. Louis was abandoned and partially demolished when it became obvious that the design of the buildings not only rendered them inefficient but encouraged crime and delinquency.*

The public housing built in several large cities in the 1950s seemed to meet the requirement of better living space for many poor families but had other effects that were quite unexpected. The buildings were so massive that tenants had no feeling of belonging. More important, they replaced social neighborhoods with anthills of strangers—thousands to the block. There were no natural, comfortable places to meet where one could feel in control. Public areas were so unsafe that tenants would walk up seven flights to avoid being caught in the elevator. So many new sources of insecurity were created that people would not live there. Many of the buildings have since been torn down or burned out; others stand half empty. ◆

When we put children into grade school for eight years, they may or may not learn what they are "taught" by teachers and textbooks, but they will learn many lessons. They may learn to love or hate school, to feel self-esteem or lack of confidence. They may also perform well at the time, as measured by grades, but develop ulcers later on from pressure and strain. They may learn to be obedient and docile or questioning and skeptical.

The ecological psychologist is concerned with *all* the effects of a given intervention, including remote effects in other parts of the system and delayed effects that do not show up right away. The Aswan dam in Egypt provides a good example of short-term success in achievement of an objective, with unanticipated problems in other parts of the system. The dam has done what it was designed to do—control flooding on the Nile River and bring irrigation and electrical power to the area. But downstream it has had other effects. It destroyed the complex life cycle in which flooding brought rich nutrients from phytoplankton to zooplankton to sardines to humans. Fisheries at the Nile delta that used to produce eighteen hundred tons of sardines a year dropped to a production of five hundred tons. Whole fishing villages lost their livelihood. Even upstream, there is concern that minerals left on the land by the irrigation water may ruin the land. In addition, since the dam was built, there has been a disturbing increase of *schistosomiasis*, a waterborne intestinal disease.

As our technology grows more powerful, so does our power for long-term damage from interventions that bring benefit in the short term. Citizens of a democratic society are plagued by the fact that political leaders, to be re-elected, must show results during their term of office. Yet the measure that would be best in the long run may be one that will not show any results for several years—or one that is more expensive or painful at the beginning. It takes a courageous politician and an enlightened electorate to judge measures by their long-term promise instead of their short-term advantages—and in fact, the long-term consequences cannot always be foreseen. (See *P&L* Close-up, Doing Time.)

Social traps

Any system provides certain choices and not others to people within it. So the choices open to you depend in part on the systems you are part of. Sometimes systems become traps because all the choices they give you are unacceptable but you see no escape. They require you to do things that you realize are self-defeating, but you do not know how to extricate yourself.

One type of social trap occurs when an act has positive consequences for the individual but harmful effects for the group of which that individual is a member. The situation of the Illinois farmers is such a trap. If they continue to use the nitrates, they poison their children; if not, they face ruin. Likewise, in the Idaho mining community, residents see a choice between their jobs and their children's health. As a society, we are in a trap because of our dependence on foreign oil. If it were cut off, our whole economy would be disrupted, yet our growing trade deficit, due largely to our oil imports, is undermining our economy just as surely.

Another type of social trap consists of situations in which the immediate consequences of an activity are positive but the long-term consequences are negative. Familiar examples of such social traps are world overfishing and the arms race. Overfishing has been so extensive that the great whales are almost gone, and some other species that were once common have been nearly depleted. All the fishermen know that their livelihood depends on there

Close-up
Doing Time: When Less Leads to More

Indeterminate sentencing of convicted prisoners was introduced a number of years ago. It was thought that if there could be greater flexibility in deciding how long the prison term should be, the punishment could be fitted to the criminal instead of to the crime. Prisoners who were rehabilitated more quickly could be released sooner than those who were not. It was thought that this would be a fairer procedure and would result in shorter average sentences.

The actual results, however, have been largely the opposite. Indeterminate sentencing has put prisoners at the mercy of the parole board's annual evaluation of their case. In a study of one hundred such parole hearings, the average time given a prisoner to plead his case was only

fifteen minutes. The deliberations by the two hearing officers (during which they decided to keep him in prison for another year or to free him) averaged only slightly more than one minute (Garber & Maslach, 1978).

Indeterminate sentencing makes life less predictable for the prisoners. Instead of having a clear-cut requirement to fulfill for release, they have to satisfy the personal judgment of a particular hearing officer. Prisoners never know exactly what behaviors or what length of time served will bring release. Average time served has turned out to be longer rather than shorter. So indeterminate sentencing, begun to overcome one abuse, has created others.

being enough fish in the future, but their immediate need is to make a living this year, and they all keep taking what they have to in order to do that.

In the arms race too, everyone knows that a big buildup of armaments makes war more likely, and today's armaments are more horrible and more expensive than ever. Yet over $350 billion of the world's treasure is going into armaments each year without buying security for anyone, while funds for schools and other social purposes are cut back. Irrational as it is, no one knows how to stop it.

What can you do when you find yourself in such a situation? Is there any solution? Laboratory studies are not encouraging.

In one ingenious study where the overfishing situation was simulated, the researcher explained carefully just what the "sustainable yield" was — how fast the available pool of reinforcers would be replenished. In addition, subjects were permitted to discuss the situation as they "fished." Yet in every case they took from the supply too fast and it ran out (Brechner, Boyce, Cass, & Schroeder, 1975).

As a victim in a trap, it would appear that your only hope is either in removing yourself from it or in working to restructure it to change the choices it offers. Sometimes you *can* remove yourself by moving away or changing to a new job. Some fisherman can change to a new field. Many individuals are trying to lessen their own dependence on oil and other nonrenewable resources by adopting a simpler life style. But the society as a whole has found no such escape.

John Platt (1973), studying the social trap phenomenon and possible solutions to it, offered three suggestions of ways that restructuring could come about:

1. In situations like overfishing, where people are dependent on limited resources, they can sometimes agree to be bound by quotas and set up mechanisms for enforcing the decisions they make together. Binding decisions and enforceability are needed if the choice of taking too much is actually to be cut off. Reaching such an agreement becomes more difficult as total available resources fall below the total really needed.

2. In traps like the arms race, it may take a third party or a superordinate power to change the ground rules and set up a new system that offers the security nations are seeking but not achieving through armaments. As long as nation states have no better means of defense, they are unlikely to agree voluntarily to give up their armies or their freedom to arm.

3. Some restructuring also occurs in the normal course of events. Systems try to maintain their equilibrium and resist change, but are always vulnerable to change resulting from shifts either in their component parts or their own environments. The discovery of new chemicals or new farming methods or a shift in economic relationships could give the farmers new choices.

Two-way influence

Traditional psychology has studied the effects of the environment on the individual—rarely the reverse. Independent variables have been environmental stimuli, if possible manipulated by the experimenter, who was also part of the environment. Dependent variables have been responses of the organism. The influence has been seen as one-way, with control of behavior thus resting in the environment.

In recent years, feedback loops have been postulated to describe the way in which, over time, the organism tests and corrects hypotheses about environ-

The urban environment often fosters anonymity and the loss of a sense of personal identity among its residents. Here, youngsters have responded by asserting that they "are who they are" and leaving their mark on a part of their environment.

mental conditions and makes its responses more adaptive. But the role of the organism in creating its environment and initiating interactions with it — especially at the human level — has hardly been touched.

Chess and her colleagues (1965) have recognized that even very young babies help to establish the relationships that develop between mother and child. That is, inborn differences in infant temperament influence the mother's responses from the very beginning. Clinical theories, such as Adlerian psychology, have always postulated an active organism, initiating action and using environmental resources for its own needs and purposes. But laboratory psychology has preferred the reactive model.

The ecological approach emphasizes the reciprocity and mutual influence in the organism-environment relationship. Organism and environment influence each other, and both keep changing as a result. The organism reacts to stimuli but also makes a continuing attempt to meet its own needs out of what the environment offers and also to meet the demands of the environment without losing its own integrity. So we see a circular pattern; humans change the natural environment and create physical and social structures. These, in turn, confine, direct, and change us, encouraging certain behaviors, while discouraging or preventing others, often in ways we did not anticipate. ▲

In any case, ecological psychology is oriented not toward past determinants so much as toward the future that is being created. This means, in turn, that it has to be concerned with values. Some environments are more nourishing for us than others, and some uses of the environment, as we have discovered, are destructive. Ecological psychology is concerned with identifying what makes environments nourishing and what human behaviors will create those environments — while not trespassing on the health of the ecosystem that makes life possible in the first place. (See *P&L* Close-up, A Safe and (Un)Happy Home.)

Urban design: Can we make cities livable?

People have traditionally been attracted to cities because of the economic opportunities they provide and also for their cultural and social functions. The urban centers are "where the action is."

Close-up
A Safe and (Un)Happy Home

Before adding a small, rare bird called the "Bearded Tit" to the birdhouse of a European zoo, the curator spent considerable time, effort, and patience investigating the bird's natural habitat and way of life. He designed a zoo environment that was ecologically correct for this species, and the male and female birds appeared to be very happy in it. The birds liked their new environment so much that they not only ate and drank and groomed and flew freely about; they sang, mated, made a nest, laid eggs, and hatched their young.

The delighted zookeeper was horrified a few days later to discover that all the babies were lying dead on the ground. The parents were still as active and "cheerful" as ever, so he concluded that it must have been an accident. But when the mating cycle recurred and a new brood was hatched, they, too, were soon all dead.

Careful observation revealed that the parents were the killers — pushing the babies out of the nest onto the ground, where they died! This cycle of mating, hatching the young, and pushing them out of the nest to die was repeated several times. But why? Why would these apparently happy, "normal" parents behave in this "abnormal" way in their carefully designed environment?

The curator returned to the natural habitat to observe whether there was something he had overlooked in his design. He discovered that the infant birds there spent many hours crying for food while the parents spent much time searching for food (which was scarce) and feeding their demanding young. In addition, the parents kept the nest clean by shoving out any inanimate object, such as a leaf, eggshell, or feather.

The solution! In their "perfectly designed" environment, food was in abundance so that the needs of the babies could be quickly satisfied. After being fed, the babies fell asleep — during daylight hours while the parents were still awake. The babies then became "inanimate objects" and were shoved out of the nest by the parents. When food was made scarce and harder to find in the designed environment, the infants stayed awake crying for it, the parents were kept busy working for it, and they all lived happily ever after (Willems, 1973).

But today, for many people, the action is too much, too fast, and too unpredictable and uncontrollable. The tempo and pace seem nonstop; there is too much competition for limited and often deteriorating resources (such as taxis, seats in subways, nursery schools); and there are too many people willing to "con" you, too much incivility, and too little neighborly concern. The advantages of urban-style living are increasingly counterbalanced by the adaptations an individual must make to the sensory-cognitive overload and stress created by such a life. While cities represent our greatest technological control over nature, they have begun to limit the power of the individuals within them to regulate the quality of their own lives.

In the summer of 1970, a temperature inversion trapped hot air and air pollutants over New York City, causing temperatures to soar and creating respiratory problems. The technological solution was simple: air conditioners and dehumidifiers were turned on everywhere. But the demand overtaxed the electrical supply, leading to reduced electrical power not only for the air conditioners but for the subways as well. This increased the frustration of stranded and late passengers, many of whom then turned to their cars for transportation. Naturally, the greater use of cars in an already overcrowded city not only created maddening traffic jams, but also added to the air pollution. And so did the greater effort by the utility companies to generate more electricity. As so often happens in a complex system, solving parts of the problem kept making other parts worse.

In the aftermath of New York's 1977 blackout, a police officer guards what little remains in stores gutted by looters and the bits and pieces of their contents left strewn across the sidewalk.

A more serious crisis hit New York in 1977. The utility companies, after the 1965 blackout of much of the Northeast and part of Canada, had taken measures that they thought would prevent another large blackout. But then one stifling July night four strikes of lightning in quick succession at strategic points upset their calculations. New York went black and remained so for a night and a day and well into the next night. This time, unlike the earlier occasion, there was widespread looting and burning by people of all ages, often in a festival atmosphere. Over 3700 people were arrested, over 400 policemen hurt, and the hospital emergency rooms, lit by candlelight, were crowded with the wounded. Two things stood out: the utter dependence of all these millions of people on a human-made environment that wasn't working and the peer support for "grabbing what you can get away with." ■

Is pathology inevitable in a big city? With people all over the world flocking to the urban areas, we need to learn how to design cities that will serve us instead of entrapping us. (See *P&L* Close-up, The Commuter Blues.)

Physical structures within social ones

People live in physical structures that all can see. These physical structures, in turn, are imbedded in social structures that are not so visible but may be much more important.

There is ample evidence of the influence of physical design on psychological activities and processes. Different physical arrangements have been studied in hospital settings, work places, homes, and whole cities; different moods, self-images, and overt behaviors have been consistently found to be related to these physical differences.

For example, when mental hospital wards were designed to bring patients constantly into contact with each other, the patients developed strategies for ignoring each other. Paradoxically, the introduction of chances for privacy led to more sociability, which the researchers attributed to the patients' increased opportunity for choice and control over their interactions (Ittleson, Proshansky, & Rivlin, 1970).

Close-up
The Commuter Blues

In the large urban areas that have good public transportation, many people avoid traffic congestion and parking problems by becoming commuters on trains or buses or the underground. But at what psychological cost?

A psychiatrist distributed one hundred questionnaires to the faithful waiting for the 7:12 A.M. "bullet" train from Long Island into Manhattan. From the forty-nine completed questionnaires returned, it was determined that these average commuters had just gulped down their breakfast in less than eleven minutes, if at all; were prepared to spend three hours each day in transit; and had already logged ten years of rail time—about 7500 hours, assuming two-week vacations and no time off for illness. Two thirds of the commuters believed their family relations were impaired by their commuting, 59 percent experienced fatigue, 47 percent were filled with conscious anger, 28 percent were anxious, and others reported headaches, muscle pains, indigestion, and other symptoms of the long-term consequences of beating the rat race in the city by living in the country (Charatan, 1973).

The way space is partitioned can help bring people together or isolate them. The type of windows in an apartment house can encourage residents to look out at activities on their streets and "keep an eye on the neighborhood" or, if they are small, high casement windows, can cut off such "people watching." An architect can design space to appeal to snobbery, or to invite informality, or to induce confusion and frustration. The judge's bench uses space to awe.

You wouldn't think that a simple thing like length of corridor in a dormitory would have any appreciable influence on college students' approach to life problems, but a recent study found changes after only a few months.

Subjects from long-hall or short-hall dormitories came singly for "an experiment on impression formation." They were asked to wait a few minutes with another person (a confederate of the experimenter). After a few minutes, they filled out questionnaires and were interviewed by the experimenter, who asked them to choose between two vaguely described experimental conditions.

Long-corridor subjects sat farther away and interacted less with the confederate than did short-corridor subjects. They indicated more discomfort at waiting and asked fewer questions about the vaguely described conditions. They also expressed more negative feelings about the quality of residential interaction and expressed greater helplessness when questioned about possible improvements in their dormitories. This confirmed the hypothesis that residents of the less regulated long-corridor dormitories would give up more readily and be less likely to make choices or try to control their environment. The avoidance of social contact may have been adaptive in the dormitory, but it could lead to unadaptive behavior in other settings.

In a second test, when long- and short-hall subjects were given a task permitting more opportunity for social interaction and either cooperative or competitive behavior, the long-hall subjects initiated less social interaction and showed more competitive and less cooperative behavior than the short-hall subjects (Baum & Valins, 1977). Other research has shown that competitive responding may occur in the early stages of the learning of helplessness (Wortman & Brehm, 1975).

Social structures can also counteract negative effects of a physical environment.

For example, studies of several slum neighborhoods where urban renewal had not taken place found that residents reported many sources of satisfaction. They saw the area as "home" and reported positive feelings toward both the local places and the people. Most had relatives and close friends in the neighborhood and did not want to leave it. One said, "This is my home. It's all I know; everyone I know is here; I won't leave" (Fried & Gleicher, 1976, p. 553).

Clearly, there is no one-to-one relationship between the physical attributes of a setting and the satisfactions that people in it experience. The finest physical setting is unsatisfactory if the social structure is wrong; a setting full of physical problems can be enjoyable if the social setting is right.

Does crowding cause pathology?

Overcrowding has been linked to both physical and social pathology. Higher rates for death and disease, higher rates of mental illness, and more antisocial behavior are found among both young people and adults in the more crowded area of our cities. In a study of five Chicago communities, one of the best predictors of social pathology was the average number of persons per room in a given area (Galle, Grove, & McPherson, 1972).

Does this mean that the high population density is responsible for the pathology? How do we separate the effects of crowding from the effects of poverty, high mobility, alienation, and other conditions that are also typical in crowded urban areas? To what extent was the simple physical fact of too many people crowded together a cause of the looting and violence in the slum areas of New York during the blackout?

Crowding among animals

The most thorough investigation of the relationship between population density and social-emotional pathology in animals has been conducted by John Calhoun at the National Institute of Mental Health over the past two decades (Calhoun, 1962, 1976). Colonies of wild or tame rats or mice have been reared in artificial habitats where the effects of increasing population could be observed over several generations.

In one series of experiments, a kind of "housing project" was created in which there were four interconnected units reached by a winding staircase. To reach the end units, the animals had to pass through the center ones, which soon became the focal point for social activity. When the population grew to about 80 rats—48 would have been optimal— life-destroying behaviors began to emerge.

Despite the presence of ample physical resources, such as food and nest-building materials, there were frequent vicious fights between the males as well as unprovoked attacks on females and infants. Some males were extremely aggressive, while others withdrew and became passive. Hypersexuality, homosexuality, and bisexuality increased tremendously. Social order broke down completely to the point that such normal activities as nest building and infant care were ignored by the females, cannibalism

● *Rats in this "high rise apartment complex" survived happily until the "neighborhood" became overcrowded, destroying the family structure and leaving the young to roam the area in aimless packs.*

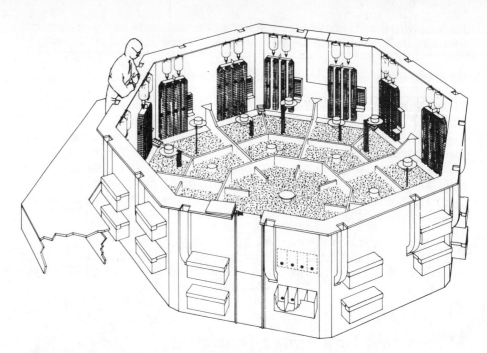

occurred, and no infant reached maturity. Deviations in endocrine functioning were common, especially among the animals at the bottom of the social hierarchy.

In another version, living quarters were arranged as "high-rise apartments" around an open area, again with ample food and nesting materials and freedom from germs, predators, and bad weather. ● *Breakdown began when all the desirable physical spaces and social roles were filled. Dominant males started to break down, worn out from defending their territories. Females chased their young out of the nest early and became more aggressive and dominating. Young adults stopped struggling for territory of their own. With neither territory nor a useful role in the community life, they never had a chance to develop the interactive social behaviors needed for the survival of the group. Instead they took to a pathological life "on the streets" in the large open central area. Even breeding ceased in the community. The last mouse died less than five years after the start of the study.*

Calhoun is now conducting a study in which young rats will be able to get water only if they cooperate in a lever-pressing sequence. They will also be put into "neighborhood groups" within the larger community. Each residential area will have an equal number of males and females, some members of all the surviving generations to date. Calhoun predicts that these measures will increase the capacity for coping and will prevent the pathologies that have occurred with the eightfold increase in density in the earlier studies.

But can these findings from animal studies be carried over to the human situation? Calhoun thinks so. He thinks that the pathological behaviors seen in his studies can be expected in human societies too, once the optimum population has been passed, unless measures are taken to see that young people have a chance to learn the complex behaviors on which our survival depends. As the worldwide unemployment of youth increases, we will see more young people fall into what Calhoun calls the "behavioral sink."

Crowding among humans in the laboratory

At the opposite extreme from these conclusions are those of J. L. Freedman. Not only has he studied crowding with human subjects, but he has concluded that crowding does not cause pathology. In fact, Freedman argues that crowding may even be beneficial because it is associated with the high level of intellectual and cultural stimulation that cities provide.

Freedman (1975) points out the need to distinguish between *high density* and *crowding*. High density of population is the physical situation, so many people per so much space. Crowding is the psychological phenomenon, the *perception* of too many people too close. Although they tend to co-vary, there is not a one-to-one relationship because whether you feel crowded depends on what you are trying to do, your cultural background, and other factors in addition to the actual density. In fact, Ittleson and his colleagues (1974) have concluded that the key element in feeling crowded is not mere numbers or density but the feeling that the achievement of some purpose is being interfered with by the presence of others.

Freedman has studied the effects of both *spatial* density (the same number of people in large or small rooms) and *social* density (the same size room with different numbers of people in it. His subjects have been given tasks of varying complexity to perform under these different conditions.

Some interesting sex differences have been demonstrated. For example, whereas men sometimes react to high density with aggression and competitive behavior, women sometimes seem to enjoy it and are more likely to develop cooperative strategies. And in a study where subjects listened to recorded court cases, the men gave more severe judgments in the small, crowded room than in a large, less crowded one, whereas the women showed no difference in severity under the two conditions. This study is especially interesting because when they did their judging in a mixed-sex group, the men gave *less* severe judgments than when in an all-male group (Freedman, 1975). The presence of women reduced the competitiveness and aggressiveness of the men. Here is another example of the "same" factor having different effects when operating in different causal networks.

But overall, Freedman has concluded that the effect of high density is mainly to amplify whatever is already going on: whatever the individual's reaction to the other aspects of the situation, it will be intensified by feelings of being crowded.

In Freedman's analysis, high population density is not necessarily even a stressor. He cites as evidence the fact that his subjects' performance on complex tasks did not suffer under high density conditions, as would have been predicted if the high density were a stressor (Freedman, Klevansky, & Ehrlich, 1971). He also points out that there are many life situations where we choose and enjoy high density, as in a packed stadium at a football game. Some people find the crowds of a big city exhilarating. Crowds add to the excitement and fun of a festival like the Mardi Gras. ▲

To what extent are Freedman's "high-density" lab rooms like high-density conditions in the city? His subjects were not too crowded to have their own private space to work in. Even his most dense conditions were not really very uncomfortable or inconvenient, and they were temporary. They did not seriously interfere with the subjects' vital needs or long-term goals. The subjects did not have to compete for scarce resources or struggle with threatening problems of life-and-death importance to them. One person's success did not mean another's failure. Perhaps most important, there was no larger social setting to give a meaning to the density: it was not a signal for fun, as at a football game, or for feelings of inadequacy, as in a crowded tenement. It had no social significance. What subjects did in these rooms would have no effect on their lives tomorrow. So we do not know how far Freedman's findings can be meaningfully applied to city crowding.

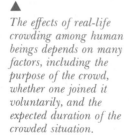

The effects of real-life crowding among human beings depends on many factors, including the purpose of the crowd, whether one joined it voluntarily, and the expected duration of the crowded situation.

Crowding in the real world

What about studies of the effects of high density in natural settings, in dense human settlements? Here the problem is complicated by all the confounding variables (poverty, low education, high mobility, etc.) that typically are present along with the high density. It is enormously difficult to find situations that differ only in density, with everything else comparable—or to control the other variables statistically. In addition, different investigators have used different indications and measures of "density," "poverty," "pathology," and so on. So putting the various findings together is difficult and we sometimes get apparent contradictions.

For example, in a study of residential sections of Honolulu that differed in population per acre, no correlation was found between density of living conditions and several measures of pathology when people per acre were held constant. This was true even when income and education were controlled (Schmitt, 1966). In a Chicago study, Winsborough (1955) actually found *less* disease and need for welfare associated with high density, except under living conditions of seven persons per room. Social pathology rates are lower where there is home ownership and higher in high, multiple dwelling units. In the latter, it increases with the number of floors above ground level (Factor & Waldron, 1973; Mitchell, 1971).

Evidently the relationship between population density and social pathology in humans is never simple and direct. The effect of the density is confounded not only directly, by factors like poverty, poor housing, and high mobility, but also more indirectly by social, political, and economic factors that involve segregation of poor and minorities, greater surveillance of them by police, less tolerance by courts, poorer schools and recreational facilities—all of which increase the chances of antisocial behavior, arrest, and confinement (Sengel, 1978).

It appears that density does not have any constant effect in and of itself. The presence or absence of all those other variables helps determine what effect the density itself will have. Again it is the whole network of causes that need to be studied together. In our poor urban areas, the cluster of conditions that includes crowding typically includes several distinct kinds of stress:

1. psychic overload, too many sensory inputs, too many signals to be interpreted and evaluated, too many decisions to be made — all with too few resources to draw on;

2. loss of privacy, infringement on one's psychological "breathing space";

3. too many strangers, too many hurried, impersonal contacts with people performing fragmentary functions instead of meaningful interactions with whole persons;

4. being treated as a number, a nonentity; having no environmental supports for one's sense of worth, no feeling of having a useful role in a caring community;

5. continuing frustration from the unsuccessful competition for limited resources and from the expectation that it will always be like this.

Such stresses set the stage for various defensive maneuvers, including the learning of helplessness.

Rodin (1976), hypothesized that children in crowded living quarters would come to see themselves as less able to control their environment and regulate their social interactions than comparable children from less crowded homes. First, children were taught to obtain candy from an apparatus. Then they were given the choice of selecting the candy themselves or having the experimenter choose it. Children from more crowded homes opted to choose their own candy less often than did the children from less crowded apartments in the same housing development.

In a second part of the experiment, both groups were given an unsolvable problem followed by a solvable one. The children from the more crowded homes did more poorly on the solvable problems. Rodin concluded that both these findings supported her hypothesis. These children, less than nine years old, were evidently learning not to expect to have an effect on their environment or to be able to meet its demands.

Stokols (1978) defines a stressor as an environmental condition that taxes or exceeds the individual's ability to cope adequately with it. Asking whether crowding is a stressor is too simple a question. It depends on the individual and the context. Crowding is a stressor for an individual when it occurs in a physical and social situation that taxes or exceeds that person's ability to build a satisfying life.

Crowding in a controllable environment

Tokyo has a population density of twenty thousand people per square mile — far higher than that of New York. But it does not have the serious social pathology that we see in New York. Why?

The answer seems to be that the high density in Tokyo occurs in a wholly different social network. Tokyo is not a city of strangers or migrants from somewhere else. There is low unemployment and low mobility. But most important, there is a strong sense of connectedness, with a close and controlling family life. Even young adult children stay at home or close by. Tokyo is also made up of closely knit neighborhoods, in which there is a high degree of participation in community decisions. And child rearing in Japan encourages conformity to the needs of the group rather than individual self-expression (Douglas, 1978).

The Japanese have also developed successful strategies for combatting the potential stress of high density and living graciously in limited space. Japanese houses are small and scantily furnished, with rooms serving multiple purposes. People sit and sleep on mats on the floor so do not need chairs or beds. Tables are small and simple, easily moved; even walls are movable. Miniaturization, too, has long been a means of making maximum use of limited space; open spaces are kept and beauty is created and prized. Some writers see Japanese politeness and ritual formality as a strategy developed to lessen the stress of so many people in a small space.

Vandalism: the destructive power of anonymity

Living among strangers with whom one has only superficial, impersonal, and often unpleasant contacts can lead to apathy, alienation, and cynicism. Partly this is a means of coping with the stress by psychologically distancing oneself. Partly it is a self-defense against getting "taken." The extent to which city dwellers develop a lack of trust of each other was demonstrated in an interesting field experiment.

In middle-income apartments in Manhattan and in apartments in small towns in surrounding counties, student investigators, working singly, rang doorbells and asked to use the telephone, explaining that they had misplaced the address of a friend who lived nearby. The researchers wanted to see whether there would be a difference between the city and town dwellers in their willingness to help a stranger with such a request.

The differences were striking. Male students were allowed to enter half of the homes in the small towns but only 14 percent of the homes in the city. The females were admitted more often, but the difference between town and city held for them too. They were admitted to 94 percent of the town homes but to only 60 percent of the city ones (Altman, Levine, & Nadien, 1970).

Big-city living not only robs people of many of the potential benefits of social living but often nibbles away at one of their most precious possessions — a sense of personal identity and uniqueness, being recognized and appreciated by those around them. Though surrounded by people, the individual becomes anonymous. It is easy to get the feeling, "No one knows or cares who I am — so why should I care about anyone else?" Jane Jacobs (1961) describes what it means to be an anonymous child:

"On the old-city side, which was full of public places and the sidewalk loitering so deplored by Utopian minders of other people's leisure, the children were being kept well in hand. On the project side of the street across the way, the children, who had a fire hydrant open beside their play area, were behaving destructively, drenching the open windows of houses with water, squirting it on adults who ignorantly walked on the project side of the street, throwing it into the windows of cars as they went by. Nobody dared to stop them. These were anonymous children, and the identities behind them were an unknown. What if you scolded or stopped them? Who would back you up over there in the blind-eyed Turf? Would you get, instead, revenge? Better to keep out of it. Impersonal city streets make anonymous people. . . ." (p. 57).

Being anonymous decreases the chances of being either approved for socially beneficial behavior or punished for antisocial behavior. Emotions or impulses that would otherwise be held in check by fear of disapproval may be released under the mask of anonymity.

In the previous chapter we have seen how inducing feelings of anonymity in college students led to antisocial reactions. This deindividuated behavior may also take the form of destruction of property. The enormous release of such destructive energy in the form of vandalism has become an ecological problem of major proportions in our nation. Often it seems wanton and utter-

◆
An abandoned building is an invitation to vandalism in an area that permits little opportunity for constructive play and discourages supervision by caring adults.

ly senseless. Rare trees in a park garden are cut up, wrecked, and demolished; animals in a sanctuary are tortured and killed, birds defeathered; churches are desecrated, synagogues sacked; schools are burned, windows broken; comfort stations are set afire; public telephones are ripped from their booths; parked cars are stripped and battered; gravestones are overturned. ◆

Such is only a partial listing of the daily activities not of a conquering enemy army but of a curious breed of citizens called *vandals*, so-called after the barbarians who invaded Western Europe in 455 A.D. Vandalism is the destruction of property and life without any apparent goal beyond the act of destruction itself. Such behavior seems to be motiveless and irrational since the perpetrators put a lot of effort into an activity that seems to have no instrumental value to them.

When is destruction vandalism?

To a large extent, vandalism is what someone has *called* vandalism. Derailing a train by putting obstacles on the track is "mischief" if done by children, "vandalism" if the perpetrators have attained the age of reason, or "sabotage" if the cargo of the train is related to the national defense. Even killing animals becomes a sport if the killer has a license to hunt. While polluting the environment by littering is a criminal act that draws a fine if done by an individual, pollution of the air, water, and earth by factories did not even draw public censure until the recent ecology movement identified these acts as vandalism against the property of the human race.

A number of important consequences follow from calling a given destructive act vandalism. The first is to deny that it could result from legitimate motives. The second is to identify certain people as "deviants" whose irrationality is a danger to everyone. The third is to absolve the society: people blame the supposedly disturbed mind of the vandal instead of looking for possible causes in the individual's transactions with society.

Finding sense in the "senselessness."

If vandalism were indeed "senseless" we could never hope to control it, because an effect without a cause does not fit into any systematic plan that could limit it. Fortunately, it *is* possible to make sense of even apparently senseless, malicious vandalism. History can give us some clues, as can talking to gang members, observing the behavior of college students engaged in acts of physical destruction, and various kinds of field experiments. In the eighteenth century, when a group of workers called *Luddites* began destroying factory machines, they were stereotyped as "frenzied" and "mad," and their actions as "pointless." But they were part of an earnest movement aimed at the betterment of their society. They were protesting against the evils of the industrial system. Similarly, the property destruction that occurred during the racial disturbances in Watts, Newark, and other American cities in the late 1960s appeared "mindless" until it was noted that the targets chosen were not arbitrary but appeared to be deliberate attacks on white-owned businesses believed to be unfair or disrespectful toward members of the community.

Analysis of the behavior of gangs reveals several interrelated causal factors in their violent acts. Gang members, like many individuals in lower socio-economic groups, typically lead lives with little hope of change or significant improvement, without feelings of ownership or relatedness to society. Social conditions have limited their accessibility to the traditional means of "making it," of gaining status, prestige, and social power. They have reacted by becoming outsiders, forming a counterculture with its own norms. But they still need to *use* the traditional culture in order to "make it" in their own subculture. One gang member said,

"If I would of got the knife, I would have stabbed him. That would have gave me more of a build-up. People would have respected me for what I've done and things like that. They would say, 'There goes a cold killer.' It makes you feel like a big shot" (Yablonsky, 1968, pp. 230–31).

For such a youth, vandalism against property and violence against people may be a way of transforming boredom into excitement. On the basis of our prior analysis, we would also predict that vandalism would be used as a means of gaining a measure of self-recognition. Indeed, a recent vogue among big-city vandals has been *"identification graffiti."* The vandal leaves his or her calling card sprayed on walls of everything in sight: houses, churches, public buildings, mass transit vehicles, toilets, and more (Ley & Cybriwsky, 1974).

At a deeper level, vandalism may be an affirmation that powerless people can at times rebel and be the controllers. Malicious vandalism can be seen as an acceptance of society's rejection and an active attempt to establish oneself as an outsider—one to be feared. Apparently, in fact, an act that appears senseless receives *more reinforcement* than one that is understandable and predictable. People make their mark, gain a reputation, are more remembered or feared for behavior that is out of the ordinary, unaccountable, and unlikely to be performed by others in the same situation.

Who becomes a vandal?

Is violent destructiveness something that only people with warped personalities from bad neighborhoods would engage in? Evidently not: one need only provide an old car, a sledgehammer, and permission to smash the car, and an astonishing degree of violence is unleashed in even the most timid of middle-class college students.

●
These college students so thoroughly demolished the car that the tow-truck operator who removed it said that the last car he had seen in that condition had been hit by an express train.

One freshman dormitory group I invited to a "smash-in" not only demolished the car in a short time, but set it ablaze, tried to prevent firemen from extinguishing it, and eventually had to be restrained at gunpoint by police order from attacking it again. Graduate students who were invited to try their hand at "just denting an old car a bit" were reluctant at first, but got carried away with the exhilarating feeling of physically destroying it. At one point, one student was stomping on the roof, two others were trying to pull the doors off, and another was energetically trying to break all the glass. ●

In a more systematic effort to observe who the people are that actually vandalize automobiles on the street and what conditions are associated with such vandalism, a simple field demonstration was performed in New York City and Palo Alto, California.

Two used automobiles in good condition were abandoned on the streets with their license plates removed and their hoods raised. One was placed a block from the New York University campus in the Bronx, the other a block from the Stanford University campus. Hidden observers watched, photographed, and took notes on all those who came into contact with the "bait." The researchers expected to find that the greater anonymity in New York City would lead to a greater incidence of vandalism to the New York car and that most of the vandals would be adolescents and young children.

The first prediction was confirmed; the second was certainly not. Only ten minutes after the New York car was staked out, the first auto strippers appeared — a mother, father, and young son. The mother acted as lookout while father and son emptied the trunk and glove compartment, then hacksawed out the radiator and pulled out the battery. Soon after they drove off, another passing car stopped and its adult driver jacked up the abandoned car and removed the best of its tires. By the end of the day, a steady stream of <u>*adult vandals had removed every conceivable removable part of the car.*</u> ■

Then random destruction began, as other passersby stopped to examine the car and then cut up a tire, urinated on the door, broke all windows, and dented in the hood, fenders, door, and roof.

"In less than three days what remained was a battered, useless hulk of metal, the result of twenty-three incidents of destructive contact. The vandalism was almost always observed by one or more other passersby, who occasionally stopped to chat with the looters. Most of the destruction was done in the daylight hours, not at night (as had been anticipated), and the adults' stealing clearly preceded the window-breaking, tire-slashing fun of the youngsters. The adults were all well dressed, clean-cut whites

■

A "respectable" middle-class family were the first to begin stripping the car. Adult vandals systematically removed the rest of the usable parts, eventually leaving the battered remains to be picked over and further abused by youngsters.

who would, under other circumstances, have been mistaken for mature, responsible citizens demanding more law and order."

That anonymity provides a release of inhibitions against engaging in such anti-social behavior is inferred from the startling contrast between what occurred in the two different locations. In the town of Palo Alto, not a single item was stolen, nor was any part of the car vandalized during the full week it was left abandoned. Instead, as a sign of the greater prevailing sense of social consciousness in this community, one man passing by in the rain protectively lowered the hood, preventing the motor from getting wet! (Zimbardo, 1973)

Motives for vandalism

It would appear that "vandalism" includes many kinds of behavior, by many kinds of people, in a variety of settings. Far from being senseless, acts of vandalism can be sorted into at least six categories according to the significance that the destructive behavior seems to have for the person:

1. *Acquisitive vandalism* — Property damage done to acquire money or goods, such as breaking open vending machines or telephone coin boxes, stripping parts from cars or fittings from housing project heating systems.
2. *Tactical vandalism* — Property damage as a means to draw attention to a grievance or to force a reaction. Such a tactical approach is exemplified by prisoners who destroy their cells or the mess hall to protest inadequate facilities or a man who breaks a store window to get arrested so that he will be institutionalized.
3. *Ideological vandalism* — Similar to tactical vandalism, but carried out to further an ideological cause. Examples are painting antigovernment slogans on embassy buildings, pouring blood on draft files, burning down R.O.T.C. headquarters, and "trashing" on college campuses as a tactic to make the administration call the police onto campus, in hopes that their expected over-reaction will then radicalize apathetic students and faculty. At some point ideological vandalism gets labeled "sabotage" or "treason."
4. *Vindictive vandalism* — Damage done to a selected target for revenge. Sometimes a group of students demolish a classroom because they feel the teacher has been unjust.
5. *Play vandalism* — Damage to property in the context of a game: who can break windows on the highest level, shoot out the most street lamps, jam telephone receivers most ingeniously.

6. *Malicious vandalism*—Damage done to property as part of a general expression of rage or frustration. This vandalism may be indiscriminate but often is directed at symbols of the middle class, public institutions, and anonymity-promoting systems, such as subways, schools, and automobiles (Cohen, 1973).

Help! Who will help me?

In a big city one is surrounded by literally hundreds of thousands of people, hears them on radio, sees them on television, eats with them in restaurants, sits next to them in movies, waits in line with them, gets pushed around in subways with them, touches them—but remains unconnected, as if they did not exist.

For a woman in Queens, they did not exist, when she most needed them.

"For more than half an hour, thirty-eight respectable, law-abiding citizens in Queens [New York] watched a killer stalk and stab a woman in three separate attacks in Kew Gardens.

"Twice the sound of their voices and the sudden glow of their bedroom lights interrupted him and frightened him off. Each time he returned, sought her out and stabbed her again. Not one person telephoned the police during the assault; one witness called the police after the woman was dead" (The New York Times, March 13, 1964).

This newspaper account of the murder of Kitty Genovese shocked a nation that could not accept the idea of such apathy on the part of its responsible citizenry. Yet only a few months later there was an even more vivid and chilling depiction of how alienated and out of contact one can be in the midst of people. An eighteen-year-old secretary had been beaten, choked, stripped, and raped in her office and then finally broke away from her assailant. Naked and bleeding, she ran down the stairs of the building to the doorway screaming, "Help me! Help me! He raped me!" A crowd of forty persons gathered on the busy street and watched passively as the rapist dragged her back upstairs. Only the chance arrival of passing police prevented her further abuse and possible murder (*The New York Times*, May 6, 1964).

Would *you* have called the police if you had lived in Kew Gardens? Would you have intervened to help the woman being raped? Will you (when your chance comes) do anything other than "your own thing"?

When will bystanders intervene?

Since the murder of Kitty Genovese our city streets have become increasingly unsafe by night and sometimes even by day. The failure of bystanders to intervene to help is certainly not the cause of the crimes that occur. But a higher likelihood that observers would help might deter an attacker and in any case could improve the victim's chances of survival.

Why don't bystanders intervene in cases like these? And what would make them more likely to do so? A classic study of the bystander intervention problem was carried out soon after the Kitty Genovese murder.

Two social psychologists ingeniously created in the laboratory an experimental analog of the bystander-intervention situation. A college student, placed in a room by himself, was led to believe that he was communicating with other students via an intercom. During the course of a discussion about personal problems, he heard what sounded like one of the other students having an epileptic seizure and gasping for help.

During the "fit" it was impossible for the subject to talk to the other students or to find out what, if anything, they were doing about the emergency. The dependent variable

The Eyewitness

I was the man on the spot.
  I was the first at the crime.
I got a story in hot;
  I wasn't wasting no time.

I got my name in the news.
  I got my face on TV.
I had the stuff they could use;
  I got a nice little fee.

I saw the van hit the cab;
  I saw the man with the gun;
I saw the smash and the grab;
  I saw the driver get done.

I saw the gang get away;
  They passed me as close as could be,
I could have—What's that you say?
  Why didn't I stop them? Who, me?

Peter Suffolk

was the speed with which he reported the emergency to the experimenter. The major independent variable was the number of people he thought were in the discussion group with him.

It turned out that the likelihood of intervention depended on the number of bystanders he thought were present. The more there were, the slower he was in reporting the fit, if he did so at all. As you can see by the graph, everyone in a two-person situation intervened within 160 seconds, but nearly 40 percent of those in the larger group never bothered to inform the experimenter that another student was seriously ill. ● Personality tests showed no significant relationship between particular personality characteristics and speed or likelihood of intervening (Darley & Latané, 1968).

Related studies have since shown that if you are a victim in an emergency, your chances of being helped are better if the bystanders:

a. are black rather than white,
b. are men rather than women,
c. have witnessed a model similar to themselves helping someone else (but not if they have witnessed people like themselves *not* helping),
d. see the situation as a clear emergency,
e. see that you are trying to help yourself,
f. do not perceive the situation to be a formal, structured one.

More hope in the real world

When similar investigations are carried out in field situations, the victim's chances of getting help are quite a bit better. For example, compare the following field experiment with those of Darley and Latané.

A man on a moving New York subway train suddenly collapses and falls to the floor. This event is witnessed by a number of bystanders. The experimenters manipulate the situation by varying the characteristics of the "victim" — an invalid with a cane, or a drunk smelling of liquor, or, in a companion study, the invalid seemingly bleeding (or not bleeding) from the mouth. They then unobtrusively record the bystander responses to these emergency situations.

●
**Bystander
intervention in
an emergency**

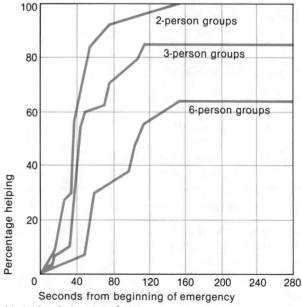

Adapted from Darley & Latané, 1968

Despite the newspaper stories of the "callous" city folk, one or more persons responded directly to almost every emergency (81 out of 103) and did so with little hesitation. Help was slower when the apparent cost of intervening was higher (that is, slower for a bloody victim than for a simple collapse), but still it came, even if it was indirect, such as by a question: "Is there a doctor in the subway?" (Piliavan, Rodin, & Piliavan, 1969; Piliavan & Piliavin, 1972).

Why the difference? Helping may be inhibited in the laboratory setting for the following reasons: (a) the college student subjects have already adopted the *passive* role of "the subject"; (b) they assume that the experimenter in charge is ultimately responsible for everything that occurs during the experimental session, which itself is an artificial situation; (c) they often do not actually see the victim-in-distress; and (d) their physical locomotion is severely restricted by obedience to an unstated rule of the laboratory setting—"You stay in your seat; you stay put and follow instructions until told otherwise." In unstructured, informal settings none of these conditions hold, the decision to intervene is probably based more on the observer's weighing of the personal costs of intervening or of not intervening.

Despite the higher rate of helping in field studies, however, the fact remains that many people do *not* help and that some settings render helping less likely than others. For example, when the man on crutches put on his act in an airport, the percent of those who helped was much lower than in the subway —41 percent as compared with 83 percent. The important factor seemed to be familiarity with the environment: the subway riders felt more at home on the subway platform, dirty and noisy as it was, and thus were more likely to deal with the trouble that arose (Latané and Darley, 1970).

No time to say "Hello"

One of the most perplexing characteristics of our modern way of life is that everything seems to be moving and changing faster than we can psychologically cope with. Especially in big cities, anything that stands still is ticketed, towed away, vandalized, or buried.

The ultimate test of the degree to which being in a hurry can destroy the foundation of social life was created in a remarkable experiment with seminary students at Princeton University.

Forty students studying for the ministry at Princeton Theological Seminary volunteered for an alleged study on religious education and vocations. After being briefed about the study in one building, each student was supposed to report to another building in order to give a speech. Some of them expected to give a speech on jobs for which seminary students would be effective: the others were prepared to deliver a sermon on the parable of the Good Samaritan (from the Gospel of Luke, Chapter 10).

Before each seminary student left to deliver his speech, the experimenters systematically manipulated his perception of how much time he had to get to the other building. A third were told they were early but might as well start over there; a third were told that it was just time, so they should go right over; the final third were told that they were already late so should hurry.

As the subject passed down an alley to the other building, guess what he found? Sure enough, slumped over in a doorway was a man coughing, groaning, head down, eyes closed. Here was the opportunity to be a Good Samaritan, to stop and help this poor victim. The "victim," who did not know which experimental condition any subject was in, noted whether or not each subject helped and also the kind of help offered. The seminary students eventually made their speeches and then filled out a questionnaire that contained questions about helping people in need and specifically about when they had last seen such a needy person and whether they had helped. Then they were debriefed and the purpose of the study was explained fully.

The results are startling and depressing: overall, 60 percent of the subjects did not stop to help the victim. The fact that they were on their way to give a sermon on the Good Samaritan parable had no effect on increasing the likelihood that they would act like one. Most significantly, the best predictor of who would stop to help was the situational variable of the degree to which a subject was in a hurry. Of those not in a hurry, 63 percent helped; of those somewhat in a hurry, 45 percent helped. Only 10 percent of the seminary student subjects who were late, in a big hurry to deliver the Good Samaritan sermon, stopped to help a fellow man in need of their help (Darley & Batson, 1973).

When the experiment was replicated later with the same task, the same dismal results were obtained. But when an unimportant task was substituted, 70 percent of those most in a hurry stopped to help. Failure to help in the earlier case was evidently not due to callousness but to a conflict of task demands on the would-be Good Samaritan (Batson et al., 1978).

Creating good environments for people

Our ability to influence our environment as well as be influenced by it gives us the possibility of creating optimum conditions for ourselves. We do not have to just adapt to what exists but can change our environment to make it provide what we need. We do not have to wait until we are overwhelmed by stress and then get therapy: we can change the stressors in our environment. In an age of dependence on experts and prepackaged solutions, we can decide to take responsibility for our own health and well-being and can change the lifestyles that now make us so vulnerable to many illnesses. And as a society, we can work to change systems that give people only unacceptable choices and trap them in self-defeating behavior. We can try to build a nourishing environment that maximizes people's ability to achieve the life they want.

Is it possible to plan cities that will support the many complex activities that must take place in them and still provide challenge and enrichment for those who live in them? Saegert (1976) has suggested that the stressfulness of cities can be reduced and the challenge and enrichment of their inhabitants increased by (a) keeping the human scale in mind in the design, (b) providing alternative kinds of environments and flexible access to them, and (c) keeping environments understandable so that the options they offer will be recognized and used and people will feel comfortable with them. Others have pointed out the possibility of making environments restorative by providing opportunities for quiet and meditation and for the enjoyment of beauty. And finally, it is important for planners to get the ideas of those who will live in the community if it is to fit them and their needs. (See *P&L* Close-up, Designing Environments for Living.)

It is customary now for legislative bodies to insist on an environmental impact report before approving a new development. But such reports cover only the expected effects on the physical environment: what the program will do to water, land, air, and other physical resources. Yet many of the programs now being undertaken will have profound effects on our satisfactions and choices. Some will change our way of life in basic ways.

As architects, developers, politicians, psychologists, physicians, lawyers, and others combine to plan what is good for us, the time has come to insist that a psychological impact report be included too and thoroughly checked out before any intervention is undertaken. What will the program do to people's life-styles? to feelings of crowdedness? to esthetic satisfactions? How will it affect the ways people relate to each other? Will they have more control over their lives or less?

Close-up
Designing Environments for Living

The interplay of behavioral science and architectural design is also leading to new developments in "humanizing the city environment." In the forefront of this movement is Lawrence Halprin, who designs fountains, recreation areas, and other urban mini-environments that are for people. As one reviewer of his approach to people-architecture put it: "His point—the fundamental one—is that working toward predetermined goals is a bad approach to design or to anything, because en route to the preordained solution, the real problems and opportunities are often overlooked. A lot of beautiful buildings, whole new towns, have failed because they've been aesthetic band-aids applied to trouble spots in the environment, creating new problems rather than eradicating existing ones because they were made to fulfill limited 'ideal' life-styles, not the needs of real live people."

Halprin's nongoal-oriented approach evolved (in the way of most innovative techniques or philosophies) from his isolation of a phenomenon that was so enmeshed in the social fabric that it had eluded social awareness. Halprin simply recognized that people are going to *move* and *live* in the spaces he designs—not merely look at finished structures and scenery. And he believes that people who will be participants in the final product *must be in on the process of making it* (Schoen, 1972, pp. 14, 15).

It is not enough to consider only efficiency and economic practicality in planning new programs that will affect people. Without an anticipation of the long-term psychological effects before an intervention is begun, it may be discovered too late that the new environment, despite its apparent physical efficiency, is less hospitable and supportive than the present one. Psychological impact statements would have warned against the urban renewal projects of the 1950s that broke up existing social networks in old neighborhoods. To be supportive, it is not enough for an environment to consider only people's physical needs. A good environment must enhance the power of those who live in it to achieve their goals and carry out the activities *they* regard as important.

The ecological principle here is a sound one; people should not be fitted into marginally livable environments, nor should someone else's conception of what constitutes a good environment be imposed upon us. Rather, we *are* the environment; people, not inanimate objects, are the important features of human environments. It is our purposes that should guide the architect's designs. Our values and expectations should be the planner's yardstick. But human desires must be tempered by knowledge of past failures, short-sighted visions, greed, and the many social and ecological traps to which we are vulnerable. People must enter a new creative partnership with their environment. As ecologist René Dubos has said.

"The earth is to be seen neither as an ecosystem to be preserved unchanged nor as a quarry to be exploited for selfish and short-range economic reasons, but as a garden to be cultivated for the development of its own potentialities of the human adventure. The goal of this relationship is not the maintenance of the status quo, but the emergence of new phenomena and new values. Millennia of experience show that by entering into a symbiotic relationship with nature, humankind can invent and generate futures not predictable from the deterministic order of things, and thus can engage in a continuous process of creation"(1976, p. 462).

Psychology for a better life

When we added to the traditional goals of psychology the notion of "improving the quality of life," we stepped beyond the purely scientific, academic pursuit of knowledge for its own sake into the realm of social action where knowledge is an instrument for change. The apparent simplicity of the phrase "improving the quality of life" leads virtually everyone to nod in agreement, "Sounds fine with me," "Sure, why not?" "I'll buy some in pastel shades." All would-be reformers, leaders of religious or political groups, or even garden-club members would espouse that high-sounding principle. But didn't Hitler believe that was what he was doing, and so too the Watergate "plumbers," and even Mafia hit men? "Whose life will be improved at whose cost and at whose gain?" is the question we must pose.

In this now optimistic era of psychology where there is much talk of "giving psychology away," "psychology for the people," and "for the 'human enterprise,'" some more conservative scientists shudder at the grandiosity of such plans and at the dangers involved in becoming a problem-solving discipline. To the layperson—or to the scientist as a citizen—there is also a sinister ring to the notion of *control* of human behavior.

But it can be argued that any joint enterprise involving two or more people requires control over behavior. Our major problems derive from things that people *do* or *don't do*. Pollution, resource-depletion, discrimination, individual and group violence—all are the result of human action or inaction. Thus why they happen and how they can be changed are, at least in part, psychological problems. While we are aware that effective behavior-control methods are subject to abuse, we also believe that efforts to solve human problems without dependable knowledge about human behavior can lead to great waste of effort, disastrous failure, and quite likely the creation of new and greater problems.

Psychologists are being called upon more and more to add their knowledge and orientation to the decision-making processes that occur in various legal, social, and political settings. Awareness of behavioral dynamics, of subtle sources of motivation, of the impact of situational forces on behavior, of the sources of subjective bias are but some of the contributions a psychologist may bring to such deliberations (see Brodsky, 1973).

There are a host of other examples we might cite of psychology for the good of people and society—going all the way from new approaches to controlling hypertension to antilitter research projects and citizen training in crime prevention through re-creating a sense of community values. Some psychologists are at work trying to elevate the level of moral functioning of prison guards and inmates, while others are studying the elements that will contribute to a sense of perceived control among otherwise hopeless institutionalized people. Some are trying to discover means of overcoming feelings of shyness and loneliness, while their colleagues strive to uncover the basis for lasting commitments and affectional bonds. This is a psychology quite different from that envisioned by Wilhelm Wundt in his little brass-instrument laboratory in Leipzig a hundred years ago. But we are witnessing a curious merger of the scientific search for knowledge, regularity, and order and the humanistic quest for understanding, acceptance, and personal fulfillment. There is no reason why modern psychology cannot do both.

However, before rushing out to put a Band-Aid on the world, it is well for psychologists and psychology students to heed the wisdom of Judge David Bazelon (1972). He asked a group of correctional psychologists:

"Why should we even consider fundamental social changes or massive income redistribution if the entire problem can be solved by having scientists teach the criminal class—like a group of laboratory rats—to march successfully through the maze of our society? In short, before you respond with enthusiasm to our pleas for help, you must ask yourselves whether your help is really needed, or whether you are merely engaged as magicians to perform an intriguing sideshow so that the spectators will not notice the crisis in the center ring. In considering our motives for offering you a role, I think you would do well to consider how much less expensive it is to hire a thousand psychologists than to make even a minuscule change in the social and economic structure" (p. 6).

And so we conclude your introduction to psychology. I hope you will see it as a challenge to start out on new intellectual and practical journeys, and that *Psychology and Life* has helped prepare you for the exciting places to which those journeys lead you. Thanks for letting me be your guide this far.

Every exit is an entry somewhere else.
Tom Stoppard
Rosencrantz and Guildenstern Are Dead

Chapter summary

Ecological psychologists focus on molar, ongoing behavior in its physical and social context, on the systems in which behavior occurs, and on the *two-way influence* of person and environment. The ecological approach deals with both molar behavior and the behavior of the larger systems in which humans interact, taking into consideration peoples' *temporal perspective,* or sense of continuity, and the *natural settings* in which behavior occurs.

Unlike behaviorists and trait psychologists, ecological psychologists do not see behavior as a simple causal chain with one event causing another. Instead, they approach it as a *network* of causes — a change anywhere in the system of causes having impact on other parts of the network. Psychological and ecological variables are placed in an *interactive* model. In addition to the immediate changes resulting from an action, investigators must take into account unforeseen, long-term *multiple effects.*

Social traps are defined as systems that present individuals with choices that are unacceptable but unavoidable. In social-trap situations, the action taken may bring about positive consequences for an individual and harmful ones for the group, or may have positive immediate consequences but negative long-term effects. Escape from the trap might involve self-enforced regulatory activity of those involved, the construction of a new system by an authoritative third party, or restructuring that occurs normally in the course of events.

Ecological psychologists recognize a *two-way influence* in which reciprocity and mutual influence exist between the organism and the environment, with both continually changing as a result. They attempt to identify what human behaviors will create the most nourishing environments.

There is much evidence for the influence of physical design of cities and buildings on psychological activities and processes. But while moods, self-images, and overt behaviors are related to physical environments, social structures can reinforce or counteract these effects.

Studies with laboratory animals have shown that overcrowding leads to antisocial, pathological behavior. But laboratory research with human beings suggests that a qualitative difference exists between an individual's perceptions of *high-density* conditions and *crowding.* Crowding is seen to have definitely negative effects, but high density may tend to amplify whatever feelings individuals had toward other aspects of the environment. Field studies in urban areas have turned up no direct evidence correlating crowding to pathology because so many other variables are involved. Slum areas, for example, combine crowding with loss of privacy, anonymity, and the frustration arising from unsuccessful competition.

There is little pathological behavior in some crowded cities, such as Tokyo, because such environments are seen as *controllable* and potentially nourishing. Individuals retain control of their lives, achieve their goals, and enjoy attractive surroundings and the support of a caring community.

In other cities, however, conditions are quite different, and there is a high rate of *vandalism.* Vandalism seems to be related to factors of boredom, the need for self-recognition, and the desire of otherwise powerless people to take control. Types of vandalism include: *acquisitive, tactical, ideological, vindictive, play,* and *malicious.*

A number of grisly incidents in large cities have demonstrated that victims of assault often go unaided by bystanders. Studies of this phenomenon indicate that bystanders are most likely to help if they have previously seen someone in a similar situation giving aid, see the situation as a clear emergency, believe that the victim is trying to help him- or herself, are in an unstructured situation, and are familiar with the surroundings. Individuals who are "in a hurry" are less likely to come to the aid of a stranger.

Investigators have learned much about the design and organization of planned communities. They have found that stress can be reduced and enrichment increased by keeping human scale in mind in design, providing alternative kinds of environment and flexible access to them, and keeping these environments understandable, so the options they offer will be recognized and people will feel comfortable with them. Environmental psychologists suggest that city planners and building designers take into account *psychological impact reports* before proceeding with their projects. These would examine how best to meet the values and expectations of the people who would be using the facilities. Modern psychology is becoming ever more concerned with using the scientifically developed knowledge gained from basic research to help improve the quality of life for all people.

Appendix

Research Methods and Data Analysis:
The Challenge of Knowing How to Do What About Why
Prepared by Teresa M. Amabile and William DeJong

Prior to Valentine's Day, 1977, Fred Cowan of New Rochelle, New York, was described by relatives and acquaintances as a "nice quiet man," a "gentle man who loved children," and a "real pussycat." But on that day, Cowan strolled into work toting a semiautomatic rifle and shot four co-workers, a policeman, and, finally, himself. In subsequent interviews, people who had known Cowan expressed shock and amazement at what he had done. One neighbor said that Cowan belonged to "the best family on the block." The principal of his Catholic elementary school reported that Cowan had received grades of "A" in courtesy, cooperation, and religion. And yet, this quiet, courteous young man who, according to a co-worker, "never talked to anybody and was someone you could push around," opened and ended the only truly violent day in his life with six senseless murders.

News items such as this lead us—laypeople and research psychologists alike—to wonder about the meaning and causes of human behavior. How could a seemingly gentle man like Fred Cowan so lose control of himself that he could go on such a violent rampage? How can it be that the first aggressive crime he ever committed was mass murder? What kind of person can become a "sudden murderer"? A group of researchers at Stanford University asked themselves these same questions, and then conducted a psychological study to help shed some light on this phenomenon. Their basic idea was this: Perhaps there is a constellation of personality traits that distinguishes "sudden murderers" from killers who committed other violent crimes before their first murder. Quite simply, they had a hunch that sudden murderers would have a personality quite different from that of other murderers and that this difference might point the way to better understanding the psychology of men like Fred Cowan.

These researchers (Lee, Zimbardo, & Bertholf, 1977) argued that sudden murderers are typically shy, quiet people who keep passions and impulses in check. For most of their lives, they silently suffer many injuries, seldom, if ever, expressing anger—no matter how angry they really feel. On the outside they appear cool and unbothered, but on the inside they might be fighting to control a furious rage. Then, something explodes; at the slightest provocation, and sometimes with no obvious provocation at all, they release the stifled violence that has been building up for so long.

To test this idea about sudden murderers, the researchers obtained permission to administer psychological questionnaires to a group of prison inmates who were serving time for murder. Those nineteen inmates (all male) who were willing to participate in the study filled out three different questionnaires. The first was the Stanford Shyness Survey (see p. 16). The most important item on this questionnaire asks the person if he considers himself to be a shy person; the answer is a simple "yes" or "no." The second questionnaire was the Bem Sex Role Inventory (BSRI), which presents a list of sixty trait adjectives, such as "ambitious" and "gentle," and then asks subjects to indicate how well each adjective describes them (on a scale from 1 to 7). One-third of the items on the BSRI are characteristically "masculine," one-third are "feminine," and one-third are neutral. The final questionnaire given to the inmates was the Minnesota Multiphasic Personality Inventory (MMPI), which is designed to measure many different types of personality traits. The part of the MMPI which is most relevant to the purposes of this study is the "Ego-Overcontrol" section, which measures the degree to which a person acts out or controls impulses. It was predicted that, compared to murderers with a long history of violent crime, the sudden murderers would more often describe themselves as shy, would show up as more feminine than masculine on the BSRI, and would be higher in ego-overcontrol as measured by the MMPI.

Each of these predicted results was found. A startling 80 percent of the sudden murderers described themselves as shy, while only 11 percent of the habitually violent murderers did so. Among a group of inmates convicted for crimes other than murder, 25 percent labeled themselves as shy, and among the general American population, 40 percent say they are shy. On the BSRI, 70 percent of the sudden murderers showed up as more feminine than masculine, while most of the habitual criminals (78 percent) indicated that the masculine adjectives more accurately described them than did the feminine adjectives. Finally, as expected, the sudden murderers were higher in overcontrol of impulses than were the habitually violent murderers.

But what do these results really mean? Can we

now say that all persons with a "clean" criminal record who suddenly commit a murder are probably shy, feminine, and overcontrolled? If we know a man who seems somewhat feminine, shy, and nonimpulsive, can we predict with any certainty that he will some day go on a killing spree? Can we even draw meaningful conclusions about the particular subjects in this one study? Can we say that their shyness and overcontrol *caused* them to become sudden murderers? Perhaps their act of murder caused them to become shy afterwards. These important questions, and dozens like them, are typical of the questions that can be asked about almost any psychological study. How shall we answer them?

This Appendix is intended as a general introduction to the methods of research and data analysis commonly used by psychological investigators. We will begin with a discussion of the plans and purposes of psychological research and from there we move on to a more detailed explanation of results of the Sudden Murderers study. Finally, we outline a laboratory experiment that could be carried out to further investigate the ideas suggested by the results. In so doing, we hope to give you a simple, yet complete overview of the enterprise of psychological science.

If you have looked ahead through the next few pages, and if you are like most students, you were "turned off" by the sight of numbers and equations. We understand your apprehension; in fact, many psychological researchers began their careers as dyed-in-the-wool math-haters. So try to keep this one thought in mind: You do not need to be "good in math" to be able to understand the concepts we will be discussing. Actually, all you need is an understanding of what an equation means, plus the courage to see mathematical symbols for what they are: a shorthand way of representing simple ideas and arithmetic operations. Moreover, we will present only the most basic concepts of methodology and statistics. The mathematical equations and calculations have, for the most part, been relegated to special sections which you may read or ignore as your needs, your abilities, your interests (and your professor) dictate.

Stay with us. The "mystery" of scientific experimentation is really no mystery at all, and it actually can be downright exciting.

The methods of psychological science

For hundreds of years, human beings have been involved in the business of observing other people and drawing conclusions from those observations. This process became more systematized and logical (and trustworthy) with the advent of what is called the *scientific method*. The scientific method is a collection of general rules that scientists follow in gathering and analyzing their observations. It involves seven basic steps: (1) getting ideas on what to study; (2) formulating these ideas into simple, testable *hypotheses*; (3) devising a plan or *design* for the study; (4) selecting a sample of *subjects* (people or animals) to study; (5) conducting the experiment, which involves setting up proper conditions for observation and then making those observations; (6) looking for meaningful patterns in the results (analyzing the *data*); and (7) reporting the results and the conclusions that can be drawn from them. Each of these steps must be carried out with care if researchers are to have the scientific community—and the rest of the world—pay attention to their work and trust their results.

Getting the idea

The basic idea is, of course, the heart of any psychological study. Good experimental methodology can help make sense out of confusing or complex events, but even the best methodology is without value if it is used to test uninteresting or ill-formed ideas. In one sense, then, getting a good idea is the most difficult part of research. But human behavior presents all sorts of interesting puzzles that are almost begging to be studied. Ideas are everywhere. They can come from informal observation or personal experience, or they might emerge after careful thought about special, puzzling occurrences such as the Cowan murders. They can come from surprising or contradictory experimental results, or from a theory that needs to be tested. Obviously, this phase is the least controlled part of the scientific method. In getting ideas, anything goes.

Formulating a hypothesis

Most people do not come up with ideas in a form that can readily be tested. For example, informal personal observation might suggest to you that women cry more easily than men. Can this idea be tested as it is presently stated? Not satisfactorily. How exactly do we define "crying"? Do we think this is generally true of men and women, or does it depend on the situation? What exactly do we mean by "more easily"? A hypothesis needs to be formulated; the idea needs to be translated into more concrete terms. One possible hypothesis might be stated as follows: "Women will cry more tears while reading a Gothic romance novel than will men." Another might be: "Women will start crying sooner than men while watching *Love Story*." In either case, there is something specific that we can measure—the number of tears, or the number of seconds before crying begins, and our measurements are made under a well-defined, if limited, set of conditions.

Choosing a research method

In formulating an experimental design or plan for a study, the experimenter has many different types of designs to choose from. Some are easier to implement than others; some are more likely to give clear-cut results. And, in many cases, there is one research design that is best suited to testing a particular hypothesis. Although there are many different kinds of experimental designs, we will discuss only the three simplest and most widely used ones.

One type of study is the *field observation*, which was used in the Sudden Murderers study. The investigator simply makes systematic observations of events occurring out in the world (in the "field" as opposed to the laboratory). If the idea to be tested is that people who own inexpensive cars drive more recklessly than the owners of luxury cars, a researcher might begin by formulating this hypothesis: "A higher percentage of Volkswagen sedan drivers than Lincoln Continental drivers run stop signs." To test this hypothesis, the researcher could send questionnaires to a small sample of licensed drivers who own one of those two automobiles. But while questionnaires are easy to administer, people can lie, fill them out carelessly, or simply be unable to give accurate answers. The method of field observation, in which our experimenter would make careful, systematic observations of drivers' stopping behavior at street corners, is best suited to answering this particular question.

A second method often employed by psychological researchers is the *field experiment*. As with field observation, the experimenters work in the "real" world. But instead of merely observing people as they go about their daily business, the experimenters actually *do* something to their subjects and then observe how they react. For example, Freedman and Fraser (1966) wanted to know whether the so-called "foot-in-the-door" technique—that time-honored ploy of the door-to-door salesman—actually does work. If you can induce people to comply to some small, unimportant request, will they then be more likely to comply to a larger request made at a later time? The field experiment is the best method to use here, for if we want to learn something about sales tactics, we should put ourselves in the position of a door-to-door solicitor in making our observations. That is exactly what

Freedman and Fraser did. They went to a number of homes in Palo Alto, California, and asked housewives if they would be willing to sign a petition asking for legislation designed to "keep California beautiful" (the small request). Another interviewer approached the women a few days later and asked them if they would allow a huge, ugly billboard about driving safety to be placed in their front yards (the large request). Another group of women was not approached with the first request, but only with the second, much larger request. In analyzing their data, Freedman and Fraser looked at the percentage of women in each group who agreed to have the billboard installed. They found a rather sizable foot-in-the-door effect. The women who had been approached with the questionnaire were much more likely to agree to the second request than were those who had not been contacted previously.

The third type of experimental method—the one people usually think of when they envision a "psychology study"—is the *laboratory experiment*. With this method, the experimenter exerts more control over what is going on, making it much easier to determine what factor *caused* a particular pattern of results to occur. This method is most useful when the researcher wishes to investigate a behavior or process that could possibly be affected by many different variables. Indeed, this is true of most things which psychologists are interested in studying. For example, social psychologists have long been interested in the process of attitude change. What makes people change their minds or make up their minds about some issue? How can people most effectively be persuaded?

Since there are so many variables which could affect attitude change in the real world, many researchers have chosen to study this process using the method of the laboratory experiment. This allows them to control or *hold constant* those variables they are not especially interested in at the time (for example, the communicator's physical attractiveness or the room temperature), and they can systematically vary or *manipulate* only that one variable whose effects they wish to examine (for example, the communicator's trustworthiness). Researchers might have two groups listen to the same communicator make the same speech about a certain household product. One group of subjects, told that the woman they will listen to is an average homemaker, might be expected to see her as a trustworthy communicator. Subjects in a second group might be told that the woman is an advertising executive who has something to gain personally by successfully promoting the product. Because all subjects listen to the same woman, many variables which could otherwise influence their attitudes have been

"I think they've spotted the hide, Neville."

held constant. Only one—the trustworthiness of the communicator—has been manipulated. If the experimenter has correctly followed the other rules of a well-run experiment, any differences found between the two groups could be attributed to that variable.

Each of these three methods has its advantages and its disadvantages. Field observation and the field experiment are often more trouble to conduct than the laboratory experiment. But because people may behave more naturally in the "field" than they do in a psychology laboratory, we might be inclined to see the results of field studies as more meaningful. On the other hand, there are so many factors that could influence a person's behavior in the real world that we will feel more confident of the results with a laboratory study. No single method is perfect, however. In some cases, the best choice might be to formulate several related hypotheses and test them experimentally in *both* field and laboratory settings.

Independent and dependent variables

Typically, psychologists want to look at the effect of one particular variable upon one particular behavior. They hypothesize that a given stimulus causes a particular response. The stimulus becomes the *independent variable*. The response behavior is called the *dependent variable*. It depends upon or is affected by the independent variable in some way. In the attitude-change experiment, trustworthiness was the independent variable, and attitude toward the product was the dependent variable.

You may have noticed in the examples of experiments we have given that we have gone from rather broad, general concepts like "shyness," "trustworthiness," and "crying" to rather specific things that can be measured, such as "saying yes or no on the shyness questionnaire" or "describing the communicator as a housewife or an advertising executive." These concrete, measurable things are *operational definitions* of the more abstract concepts. We need operational definitions to reduce the ambiguity that is present in any descriptive term. For example, "shyness" can mean different things to different people, or the same behavior might be seen as "shy" in one situation, but not in another. One study asked mothers whether or not their sons were shy, intending to use that answer as a measure of the boys' shyness. As it turned out, no mother of a boy over the age of fourteen described her son as shy! Perhaps they viewed shyness as a feminine trait, not acceptable in their teenage sons. When boys this age report on their own shyness, more than half label themselves as shy.

Of course, both the independent and dependent variables must be operationally defined before an experiment can be conducted. But even after the experimenters have carefully defined their dependent measure, they must still be concerned about both the measure's *validity* and its *reliability*. A measurement is considered to be *valid* if it really measures what the experimenter designed it to measure. This is often quite difficult to determine. For example, how does the experimenter know that the inmates' answers to the items on the MMPI questionnaire actually reveal their degree of "impulse control"? Does saying "yes" or "no" on the shyness survey really tell us if that person is shy? In order to satisfy ourselves that the latter is a valid measure, we might want to compare responses on the shyness questionnaire with measures of blushing or other criterion behaviors thought to be indicative of shyness.

A measurement is considered *reliable* if subjects end up with about the same score each time the measurement is made. Thus, we might ask whether or not those inmates rated as "feminine" on the basis of the BSRI would be so rated if they filled out the questionnaire a second or third time. It is important to realize that score might vary slightly from measurement to measurement, even if the subject has not changed drastically during the intervening time. For example, an inmate might overlook one of the sixty adjectives, or might be in a better mood the second time. Maybe he just sees himself differently on different days. Any of these things could influence the reliability of the BSRI questionnaire. Obviously, if a measure is too unreliable, it simply cannot be trusted. If you weigh in one day at one hundred sixty pounds, and the next day at two hundred or more, it's time to buy a new, more reliable scale.

Control groups

In the examples we have looked at, you may have noticed that not all subjects in a study were treated in the same way. In the attitude change experiment, some subjects would be told that the woman was a housewife, others that she was an advertising executive. In the foot-in-the-door experiment, some of the subjects were asked to comply with an initial small request, others were not. Why is it necessary to have more than one group of subjects? The reason is simple. We learn almost nothing unless we can make some kind of comparison between two different groups that were not treated the same way. Suppose that every subject who was told that the communicator was trustworthy ended up being persuaded to her point of view. This would not prove that trustworthy communicators are more persuasive, *unless* those subjects could be compared to another group that had been told she was not trustworthy. In the Sudden Murderers study, 80 percent of the sudden murderers described themselves as shy. This fact, by itself, means little in terms of the hypothesis being tested. It is informative only when it is *compared* to the results for another group—in this case, criminals who have a long history of violent crime.

It would be fair to say, then, that *the key to good research is making appropriate comparisons between groups.* Often, a laboratory or field experiment will be set up so that a group which has received some kind of manipulation (the *experimental group*) is compared to a group to which nothing has been done (the *control group*). An example of this kind of research design was the foot-in-the-door study. The experimental group was approached with an initial request, but the control group was not. As we described it, the attitude-change experiment did not use a control group. Rather, it utilized two variations of an experimental treatment—high and low trustworthiness. But a control group for that study could easily be included as part of the design. Subjects in such a group could simply not be told anything at all about the communicator. Why would we want to run such a group? If we did not, and we found that more subjects in one experimental group than the other had been persuaded by the communicator's arguments, we would not know what the nature of that difference was. Did believing that the communicator was an advertising executive decrease her persuasiveness, or did believing that she was a housewife increase it? Without a "base-line" control group, we cannot say. But suppose the subjects in a control group found the communicator just as persuasive as did those who thought she was a housewife. We could then conclude that being perceived as untrustworthy lowers a communicator's persuasiveness.

Why else might a control group be necessary? Imagine an experiment in which subjects are given a test of mathematical ability, after which they are put through a special one-week crash course designed to develop skills in that area. Afterwards, the subjects are given a different test to see how much they have learned during the past week. If those subjects scored better on the second test, would this prove the utility of the special course? It would not. Perhaps the subjects became more familiar with the format of the examinations, and thus did better the second time. Perhaps the second test was easier. Perhaps the students learned something in their regular class that helped them do better. But if we had a control group that took both tests at the same times as the experimental group, with no special instruction in between, these problems would vanish. If our experimental group showed greater improvement than this control group, then we would know that the new course had been useful. If other factors had an impact on how well students did the second time, we would expect them to influence the subjects in our two groups about equally.

In some experiments it is simply not possible to include a suitable control group as part of the research design. In the crying experiment, for example, we wanted to compare the reactions of men and women to the movie *Love Story*. A control group is not possible, since the independent variable of gender has only two possible *values*, male and female. In the Sudden Murderers study, the researchers compared two groups of murderers with a group that had been convicted of nonviolent crimes. We have three different groups, but is any of them a real *control* group? Probably not. In such experiments, it can only be said that we have two or more *comparison groups*.

Experimental bias

Researchers must also be concerned about possible sources of *bias* which could contaminate the results. There are two types of bias.

Experimenter bias may result from the way the experimenter behaves during the course of the experiment. In the foot-in-the-door experiment, it was extremely important that the researcher making the second request not know whether a particular subject had experienced the first request. Someone who knew might have some kind of expectations about how the subject would respond to the large request. Such an experimenter might inadvertently suggest to the subjects in the control group that they were not really expected to comply. Through tone of voice or a hesitant manner, he or she might communicate a belief that the billboard request was absurd. It is not always easy, but the experimenter should always make an effort to avoid this type of experimental bias by remaining "blind" to the particular experimental condition to which each subject has been assigned.

Subject bias may come from the subjects' attempts to second-guess the experimenter. It is a rare subject who is not curious about what the experimenter is up to. Subjects who know (or think they know) the purpose of the experiment might not behave naturally. They might even try to "help" the experimenter by producing the desired results. To guard against this kind of bias, experimenters often go to great lengths to provide subjects with a *cover story* — a false or incomplete description of the experiment's purpose. (Obviously, an experimenter investigating the relative effectiveness of trustworthy and untrustworthy communicators would not want to announce that purpose to the subjects before the speaker came to the podium. Instead, subjects in both conditions might be told that the experimenter was interested in their evaluation of the woman's speaking style.)

Defining the sample

After deciding on a research method, the experimenter must define the *population* or group of people to be studied and must then choose a *sample* from that population to observe. It is usually impossible to observe an entire population of subjects in a given situation. Moreover, observing or testing an entire population is really unnecessary. If a sample is chosen correctly, and if the experiment is designed and run properly, not much more information would be gained by observing the whole population than by observing this representative sample. For example, public opinion polls are able to predict national voting trends quite accurately using samples of a few thousand voters when, in fact, tens of millions are registered.

A sample should be selected so that each member of the population has an equal chance of being chosen; a sample picked in this way is called a *random sample*. If we were sampling from the population of undergraduates at a particular college we could achieve a fairly good random sample by drawing names out of a bin containing slips of paper with the name of an undergraduate on each. Our sample would *not* be random if we chose all our subjects from the beginning of the alphabet, or from one particular dormitory, or from those students who happened to be in the student union at a particular time of day.

Choosing a random sample assures us that the sample is *representative* of the population. Researchers who think they are using random sampling methods sometimes end up with quite nonrepresentative samples. For example, in the 1936 election, pollsters randomly selected names from telephone directories and asked those people whom they preferred in the presidential race. Their prediction: Landon, the Republi-

can, would win. Unfortunately, the pollsters overlooked the fact that many more Republicans than Democrats had telephones; their sample was not wisely selected. Roosevelt won by a landslide.

How large should the sample be? That depends a great deal on what results the experimenter expects to find. Consider again the problem of predicting the outcome of an election. If one candidate does, in fact, win by a landslide, a relatively small sample would have allowed the pollster to predict the results with confidence. But in a close race, the pollster will need a much larger sample to make any kind of reasonable prediction. At the extreme, an election might simply be too close to call, no matter how large the sample (short of polling the entire population). The same principle applies when a researcher is doing a field or laboratory experiment. An experimenter who believes that the effect he or she wishes to demonstrate is weak will need a large sample to detect it. If the effect is expected to be quite powerful, a smaller sample will do.

Data analysis

After all of the subjects in the experiment have been tested, researchers examine the results *(data)* for all of the dependent measures and look for differences between the groups. Data analysis can involve many different procedures, some of them surprisingly simple and straightforward. For most experimenters in psychology, this is an exciting step. They can now find out if their results will contribute to a better understanding of a particular aspect of behavior, or if they have to go back to the beginning and redesign their research. In the next section we will lead you through a step-by-step analysis of the data from the Sudden Murderers study.

The methods of data analysis

The measures obtained from the nineteen inmates in the study by Melvin Lee and his colleagues are listed in the table. ■ As you can see, there were ten inmates in the Sudden Murderers group, and nine in the Habitual Criminal Murderers group. When first glancing at these data, any researcher would feel much the same thing that you feel: confusion. What do all these scores mean? Do the two groups of murderers differ from one another on these various personality measures? It's difficult to say. Some way of

Raw data from the Sudden Murderers study

Inmate #	Shyness[a]	BSRI Femininity	— Masculinity	= Difference[b]	MMPI Ego-overcontrol[c]
Group 1 — Sudden Murderers					
1	yes	97	92	+5	17
2	no	99	100	−1	17
3	yes	78	74	+4	13
4	yes	103	42	+61	17
5	yes	99	80	+19	13
6	yes	101	60	+41	19
7	no	78	107	−29	14
8	yes	84	61	+23	9
9	yes	109	122	−13	11
10	yes	101	96	+5	14
Group 2 — Habitual Criminal Murderers					
11	no	100	112	−12	15
12	no	104	118	−14	11
13	yes	74	107	−33	14
14	no	101	109	−8	10
15	no	98	105	−7	16
16	no	99	96	+3	11
17	no	66	83	−17	6
18	no	85	79	+6	9
19	no	91	101	−10	12

Lee et al., 1977

[a]Each subject's response to the question, "Do you consider yourself to be a shy person?" is listed.

[b]Each subject was asked to indicate how much each "feminine" adjective was true of himself by using a seven-point scale (1 = "never or almost never true"; 7 = "always or almost always true"). The femininity score is the sum of those ratings for all twenty feminine adjectives. The masculinity score is similarly calculated. The difference score is calculated by subtracting the masculinity score from the femininity score.

[c]The "ego-overcontrol" subscale of the MMPI is scored so that the higher a subject's score, the more ego-overcontrol the subject exhibits.

summarizing these scores must be found so that we can get an overall picture.

Measurement scales

Before we can begin to clarify these data, however, we must determine what kinds of *scales* were used. There are four different types of measurement scales, two of which were used in this study. The first is the *nominal* scale, on which scores are simply grouped into categories. The shyness ratings were made on a nominal scale: answers fall into one of two categories, "yes" or "no." Other nominal scales might be male–female; Black–Caucasian–Oriental; or fall–winter–spring–summer. The nominal scale tells us nothing about quantity or magnitude; it is merely a way of classifying things or giving them a name. The *ordinal* scale does tell us something about magnitude, because measurements on this type of scale are *rank ordered*. For example, placements in a

race are made on an ordinal scale. The person who came in first ran faster than the person who came in second who, in turn, ran faster than the person who came in third. Measurements on this scale say nothing about how much faster number one was than number two, but say only what their relative ranking was.

The *interval* scale not only indicates relative positions, it also tells us something about *quantity*. There is equal spacing between points on an interval scale of measurement; thus the difference between points one and two is the same as the difference between points 14 and 15, or between points 71 and 72. Finally, the *ratio* scale has all the properties of the interval scale and, in addition, a "real zero point." For example, the Fahrenheit temperature scale is an interval scale; the difference between 10° and 11° means the same as the difference between 58° and 59°. But this scale does not have a real zero point; 0° F does *not* mean that there is a total absence of heat. In contrast, the Kelvin temperature scale is a ratio scale; 0° K really does mean the complete absence of all heat.

Distribution

The shyness data are easy to summarize. Out of 19 scores, there are 9 yes's and 10 no's. Let's look next at the BSRI *difference* scores; of the 19 scores, 9 are positive and 10 are negative. This means that 9 of the murderers described themselves (by checking the various adjectives) as more feminine than masculine, and 10 described themselves as more masculine than feminine. These scores vary from +61 down to −33; their *range* is 94 points. The range of the MMPI overcontrol scores is 13 points (from 6 to 19).

To get an even clearer picture of how the scores are distributed, we can draw up *frequency distributions* for the BSRI and the MMPI data. The first step in doing this is to *rank order* the scores from lowest to highest (or vice versa). For the BSRI difference scores, this rank ordering would be:

Highest	+61	
	+41	−7
	+23	−8
	+19	−10
	+6	−12
	+5	−13
	+5	−14
	+4	−17
	+3	−29
	−1	−33 **Lowest**

The second step is to place these rank-ordered scores into a small number of categories, called intervals. There is no hard-and-fast rule for deciding on the number of categories to use. In general, we should not have so many categories that we end up with only one or two scores in each, but, at the same time, we should not have so few categories that the highest and lowest scores are not really separated from one another. In this example, in which we have only 19 scores, a total of 10 categories will probably be about right, but this decision is fairly arbitrary. Researchers may use more or fewer categories, depending on how finely they wish to break their data down.

If we divide the range of the BSRI scores, which equals 94, into 10 equal-size parts, each category will cover 94/10 or 9.4 points. Categories of 10 points would be easier to handle, so we will use that. It will also be more convenient for us if our categories are constructed so that each *lower bound* is a multiple of ten. (Thus, the score of +61 will fall within the category, +60 to +69.) The third step is to construct the *frequency distribution* table, listing intervals from highest to lowest and noting the *frequency* (number of scores) within each interval:

Category	Frequency
+60 to +69	1
+50 to +59	0
+40 to +49	1
+30 to +39	0
+20 to +29	1
+10 to +19	1
0 to +9	5
−10 to −1	4
−20 to −11	4
−30 to −21	1
−40 to −31	1

Our frequency distribution shows us that most of the scores are clustered between −20 and +9; this means that, for the most part, the inmates' difference scores did not deviate too far from zero. (Try making several distributions with fewer categories of larger intervals.)

Methods of graphing can also help us obtain a clear picture of the results. In order to look at differences between the two groups of murderers, we can draw a *bar graph.* ◆

◆

Shyness bar graph for two groups of murderers

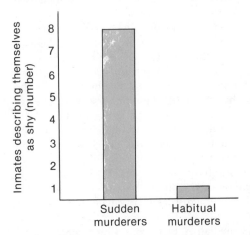

For interval or ratio-scaled data, such as the BSRI and MMPI scores, we can construct a *histogram.* (The histogram is similar to the bar graph, except that the bars are directly adjacent to one another, and the intervals of a frequency distribution are used on the horizontal axis.) A histogram of the BSRI scores makes the frequency distribution data even clearer. ▲ Most of the scores cluster between −20 and +9, and there are only a few extremely positive scores.

▲

Histogram of BSRI scores

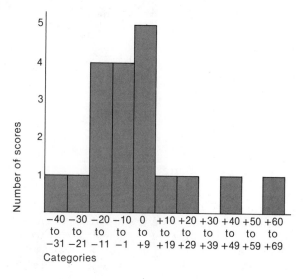

Categories

Average

What we have done so far has served to give us a general picture of how the scores are distributed, and it has certainly increased our understanding of the experimental results. But it would also be useful to know what the *average* or typical score is. Actually, there are three different averages which can be used: the *mode*, the *median*, and the *mean*.

The mode is that score which occurs more often than any other. For the measure of shyness, the modal response by the inmates was "no"; a majority of the murderers (ten out of nineteen) said they were not shy. Refer back to the original data on page 756. You will see that the BSRI femininity scores have two modes; they are *bimodal*. The scores of 99 and 101 each appear three times. The masculinity data also have two modes: 96 and 107. The BSRI difference scores have a single mode, +5, and the MMPI overcontrol scores have three modes, 11, 14, and 17. The mode can be used with any measurement scale. It is the easiest average score to calculate, but it is often the least useful.

The median is that score which separates the upper half of the scores in a distribution from the lower half. Fifty percent of the scores are larger than the median, and fifty percent are smaller. For the BSRI difference scores, the median score is −1. If you will look back at the rank ordering of those 19 scores, (p. 757), you will see that nine scores are higher than −1, and nine scores are lower. In order to calculate a median, it must be possible to rank order the scores; thus, this average can be found only

for ordinal-, interval-, or ratio-scaled data. It should be noted that the median is "insensitive" to extreme scores. For example, if the highest BSRI difference score had been +140, the median value would still have been −1. That score would still separate the upper half of the data from the lower half.

The mean is what most people think of when they hear the word *average*. It is also the statistic most typically used to describe a set of data that is interval- or ratio-scaled. To calculate the mean, we simply add up all of the scores, and then divide that sum by the total number of scores. This operation is summarized by the following formula:

$$\bar{X} = \frac{\Sigma X}{N}$$

In this formula, X stands for each individual score, and the symbol, Σ (sigma), means "sum all." N represents the total number of scores, and $\bar{X}$ (X-bar) stands for the mean. The means of the BSRI femininity and masculinity scores would be calculated as follows:

Masculinity: $\bar{X} = \frac{\Sigma X}{N} = \frac{1767}{19} = 93.0$

Femininity: $\bar{X} = \frac{1744}{19} = 91.79$

The mean describes a distribution of scores in terms of a "most typical" representative value, but in order to describe the distribution more completely, we need a statistic which will tell us how closely the scores are clustered, or vary, around that average value.

Variability

A statistic that can tell us how spread out the scores are is the *variance*. To calculate the variance, we need to know only the individual scores and their mean. The variance (S^2) is calculated in the following way:

$$S^2 = \frac{\Sigma(X - \bar{X})^2}{N}$$

As before, X is a symbol for the individual scores, and $\bar{X}$ represents their mean. The total number of scores is represented by N, and Σ is the summation sign. To obtain the variance of the BSRI difference scores, for example, we would first take each individual score and subtract the mean from it $(X-\bar{X})$, giving us a set of numbers known as *deviation scores*. Next, we would square each deviation score and add all 19 squared values. Finally, we would divide that sum by 19, giving us the value of the variance, S^2.

Why do we need to square the deviation scores before adding them? Couldn't we simply average them? The answer is quite simple. Scores above the mean will give us positive deviation scores, and scores falling below the mean will give us negative deviation scores. These positive and negative scores will always "cancel" one another, giving us a sum of zero, and therefore an average of zero.

We get around this problem by squaring each deviation score before we take the sum. But this leaves us with another problem: the variance is stated in square units. For example, if our dependent variable happened to be measured in terms of number of feet, the variance of those scores would be measured in square feet. This is a bit cumbersome, so we typically take the square root of the variance to return us to our original units of measurement. This new statistic is called the *standard deviation (S)*, and it is the most commonly used measure of variability for interval- or ratio-scaled data. Sample calculations of variances and standard deviations on the data from the Sudden Murderers study are presented in the table. ●

The standard deviation tells us exactly how variable a set of scores is. The larger the standard deviation, the more spread out the scores are. For example, the standard deviation of the BSRI difference scores for the Sudden Murderers is 25.92, but only 11.38 for the Habitual Criminals. This means that there was much less variability in the scores in the Habitual Criminals group. In other words, those scores clustered much more closely about their mean than did those of the Sudden Murderers.

Standard scores (z)

The standard deviation serves a second important function. With it, a score can be computed for each subject which indicates where that subject falls in the overall distribution of scores for the group. This measure, which tells us how many standard deviations away from the mean a particular score lies, is called the *standard score*. To obtain a standard score for any subject, we subtract the mean from that subject's score, and then divide that difference by the standard deviation. For example, consider Inmate 1, whose femininity score is 97. The standard deviation for the set of all 19 femininity scores is 11.92, and their mean is 93.0. This inmate's standard score is calculated as follows:

$$z = \frac{X - \bar{X}}{S} = \frac{97 - 93}{11.92} = +.34$$

Since the standard score is symbolized by z, it is often referred to as the *z-score*. As you can see by examining the formula, if a person's "raw score" (X) is equal to the mean $(\bar{X})$, the z-score for that person will be 0. If the raw score is greater than the mean, the z-score

●

Calculating the variance and standard deviation

If we are interested only in the variance of a particular sample, we can use the variance formula below:

$$S^2 = \frac{\Sigma(X - \bar{X})^2}{N}$$

To calculate the variance of the femininity scores, we subtract their mean from each score, square each difference, sum the squares, and divide that sum by 19:

$$S^2 = \frac{(97 - 93)^2 + (99 - 93)^2 + \ldots + (85 - 93)^2 + (91 - 93)^2}{19} = 2556/19 = 134.53$$

To calculate the standard deviation, researchers usually make a slight correction in the variance formula. Rather than divide by N, they divide by $N - 1$. This change is statistically appropriate when dealing with samples and not with entire populations. This "unbiased" variance is symbolized with a lower-case letter:

$$s^2 = \frac{\Sigma(X - \bar{X})^2}{N - 1}$$

The "unbiased" variance of the femininity scores is:

$$s^2 = \frac{(97 - 93)^2 + (99 - 93)^2 + \ldots + (85 - 93)^2 + (91 - 93)^2}{18} = 2556/18 = 142.00$$

The unbiased standard deviation of the femininity scores, then, is:

$$s = \sqrt{s^2} = \sqrt{142} = 11.92$$

will be positive, and if the raw score is less than the mean, the z-score will be negative. Thus, we can tell by looking at the sign of the z-score whether the person's score was higher or lower than average, and the size of the z-score tells us how *far* from average the person's score was. The larger the z-score (either positive or negative), the farther the raw score deviated from the average.

The z-score for Inmate 1 tells us that his raw score fell above the mean, since it is positive, and that it fell about one-third of a standard deviation above the mean. Inmate 9, whose raw score is 122, has a much more extreme femininity score. His z-score is +2.43, almost two and a half standard deviations above the mean.

The normal curve

Several types of measurements—such as IQ scores, college students' height and weight, and the wingspans of monarch butterflies—are known to follow what is called the *normal curve*, also called a *bell curve*. 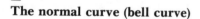 Along the horizontal axis are standard scores (z-scores), and the height of the curve above the axis indicates the frequency of scores. Given enough subjects, a pattern of scores distributed like the bell curve will emerge.

Several facts about this curve should be noted: (1) The center of the curve represents the mean score. (2) Most scores fall at or near the mean. A score far from the mean is less common than one close to the mean.

If we gathered femininity scores for a large number of inmates (certainly more than the nineteen we have in the Sudden Murderers study), the greatest number of scores would fall right at the mean, and the number receiving each z-score value would gradually become smaller and smaller as the scores became more and more extreme, both above and below the mean. But we actually know more about these scores than that. Standard scores in a normal distribution can be converted to *percentile scores*. A z-score of 0 (the mean) is always at the 50th percentile (that is, 50 percent of all scores fall at or below that point). A z-score of +1.00 is at the 84th percentile; a z-score of −1.00 is at the 16th percentile. A z-score of 1.64 means that 95 percent of the scores were equal to or lower than that score. There are tables that can tell us what percent of the scores fall below each of the possible z-score values. By referring to such a table, we can figure out exactly how extreme a particular score is. Inmate 1 had a z-score on the femininity measure of +.34. Were we to administer the BSRI scale to a very large number of inmates, we would ex-

The normal curve (bell curve)

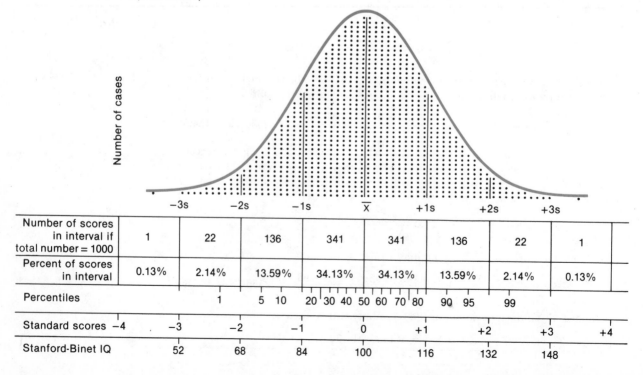

Number of scores in interval if total number = 1000	1	22	136	341	341	136	22	1
Percent of scores in interval	0.13%	2.14%	13.59%	34.13%	34.13%	13.59%	2.14%	0.13%

pect this inmate's score to be greater than the scores of 63 percent of his fellow prisoners. Inmate 9 had a more extreme score ($z = 2.43$); we would expect his score of 122 to be higher than the scores of 99 percent of all inmates.

Correlation

Another useful statistic is the *correlation coefficient*, which indicates the degree of relationship that exists between two variables (such as BSRI score and MMPI score). It tells us if, in general, scores on one measure predict scores on another measure. If high scores on one variable tend to be matched with high scores on the other variable, the correlation coefficient will be *positive*. If, however, high scores on one variable tend to go with low scores on the other, the correlation will be *negative*. If there is really *no* consistent relationship between the scores on the two variables, the correlation will be close to zero.

As it is calculated, the correlation coefficient can range from -1.00 to $+1.00$. For example, we might expect that IQ scores would be highly correlated with math scores on the Scholastic Aptitude Test (SAT). In general, we would expect a person with a high IQ score to do well on the SAT, and we would expect a person with a low IQ to do poorly. Of course, some individuals would be exceptions, but overall, we would expect this pattern to hold true. If we actually had these scores for a group of subjects and computed the correlation coefficient, we might get a correlation of $+.85$. This would be a very high positive correlation, and it would mean that there is a very close correspondence between those two scores.

Let's consider the variables at hand. We might think, intuitively, that a person's sex-role score on the BSRI would be correlated positively with his MMPI overcontrol score; that is, we might expect that a person who scored higher on femininity than masculinity would also score relatively high on ego-overcontrol. Actually obtaining a correlation coefficient would help to tell us how the two variables are related and whether our prediction is a good one. ◆

Our prediction was supported by the data. But this correlation also tells us that there were a number of exceptions to that pattern. A correlation of $+1.00$ would have told us that the correspondence between the two variables was exactly as we had predicted.

The correlation coefficient can be useful in several ways. First, it gives us a general idea of which variables tend to be related to one another. If we construct two questionnaires and expect them to measure the same thing, and the scores on them have a correlation of almost zero, then we know that our thinking was misguided. Second, the correlation coefficient serves the important function of helping us make predictions. If there is known to be a substantial correlation between two variables, and we know a person's score on one of those variables, we can be more confident in predicting that person's score on the other measure, based on that information. (There are mathematical formulas dictating just how such a prediction is to be made.)

This ability to make predictions often leads people to think that the existence of a correlation between two variables means that one caused the other. For example, some have assumed that a correlation between the amount of time children spend watching

---

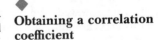

Obtaining a correlation coefficient

In order to calculate the actual correlation between sex-role scores and overcontrol measures, we need to know: (1) the total number of subjects, (2) each subject's BSRI difference score, and (3) each subject's MMPI overcontrol score.

These are the symbols used in the correlation formula:

X_i is a particular subject's BSRI difference score
Y_i is that subject's MMPI overcontrol score
N is the number of subjects

The formula for the correlation coefficient (r) is:

$$r = \frac{N(\Sigma X_i Y_i) - (\Sigma X_i)(\Sigma Y_i)}{\sqrt{[N(\Sigma X_i^2) - (\Sigma X_i)^2][N(\Sigma Y_i^2) - (\Sigma Y_i)^2]}}$$

If we plug the appropriate BSRI and MMPI scores into this formula and carry out the calculations, we obtain a correlation coefficient of $r = +.35$. This means that the sex-role score and the overcontrol score are positively correlated to a moderate degree: in general, when one is high the other will tend to be high, and when one is low the other will tend to be low.

television and their "aggressiveness" during play *proves* that television fosters violence. But the fact is that correlation tells us nothing about causation. Just because there is a high correlation between the number of water puddles on the street and the number of people carrying umbrellas, we obviously cannot say that the water on the street caused people to carry umbrellas, or vice versa. Clearly, this is a case where *both* variables were caused by a third related occurrence; namely, the rain. Of course, there are times when something might be caused by another factor which is well correlated with it. But the point is that, on just the basis of the correlation coefficient, we cannot say whether or not this is the case.

The procedures we have outlined so far — calculating ranges, averages, standard deviations and standard scores, forming frequency distributions, and drawing graphs — are examples of what are commonly known as *descriptive statistics*. These statistics help us describe the overall results and tell us where a particular score stands in relation to other scores. They give us a good grasp of what the numbers are, but they do not tell us what conclusions we are permitted to draw.

The methods of inferential statistics

At this point, we have used a number of descriptive statistics to describe the data from the Sudden Murderers study, and this information has been useful in giving us an idea of the overall pattern of results in this study. But some basic questions of interest remain unanswered. Can we say for sure that Sudden Murderers are more shy than those murderers with a long history of violent crime? Are they more feminine? More ego-controlled or nonimpulsive? The statistics we have computed so far tell us that these statements *seem* to be true. While 80 percent of the Sudden Murderers described themselves as shy, only 11 percent of the Habitual Criminals did so. The mean BSRI difference score was +11.50 for that first group, and it was −10.22 for the second. The mean MMPI overcontrol score was 14.40 for the Sudden Murderers and only 11.56 for the others. But are these differences large enough to be meaningful? Should we believe them? Do they accurately reflect the true state of the world? Are they reliable? If we did this study again with another group of sudden murderers and habitual criminals, could we expect the general pattern of results to be the same? *Inferential statistics* are used to answer these kinds of ques-

tions; they help us decide what conclusions can be legitimately drawn from our data.

Chi-square

Since the shyness data are so straightforward ("yes" or "no"), we can use a simple *statistical test* to look at the difference between the two groups. This is the *Chi-Square* test (pronounced "kī-square"); the chi-square statistic that we compute is symbolized by χ^2. This test contrasts the total number of "yes" and "no" answers in the two groups by comparing them with the hypothetical totals that would be expected if there were absolutely *no* difference between the two groups. Statisticians have derived simple formulas for computing these hypothetical or "expected" values. Once the expected values are determined, we can use the χ^2 test to determine the significance of the difference between expected and obtained values. A large χ^2 indicates that the two groups are quite different from one another; a χ^2 close to zero shows that the two groups are nearly identical. ■

t-tests

With both the BSRI and MMPI scores we have interval-scaled measurements. The appropriate test for this type of data, when we have just two groups being compared, is the *t-test*. In a general sense, this test looks at the difference between the two group means on a particular variable (like the BSRI), takes into consideration the variability of the scores and the number of subjects in each group, and computes a statistic ("t") which helps us decide whether or not that difference is reliable. A large value of t tells us that the groups are quite different from one another; if we repeated the experiment with two new samples of subjects, we would expect to find the same kind of difference between them. ●

Statistical significance

For the shyness data we obtain a χ^2 of 9.02, for the BSRI difference scores we get a t of 2.32, and for the MMPI overcontrol scores we obtain a t of 1.99. Are these statistics large enough to make us conclude there really are differences between the two groups? If there really are *no* differences between them, what are the chances that we would have just happened to get a χ^2 (or a t) this large by luck? It may actually be the case that the whole population of Sudden Murderers is *not* more shy, more feminine, and more ego-controlled than the population of Habitual Criminal Murderers. But for some reason we may

For this test, we need to: (1) compute the total number of "yes" answers and "no" answers obtained in each group, (2) calculate the hypothetical "expected," "yes," and "no" totals for each group, and (3) plug these values into the χ^2 formula.

We begin by putting the frequencies of "yes" and "no" responses from each group into a table:

Chi-square test for the shyness data

Observed Frequencies

	"Yes"	"No"	Total
Group 1	8	2	10
Group 2	1	8	9
Total	9	10	19

We need to compare these frequencies with what we would have expected by chance. But how do we know the "expected" values? We calculate them on the basis of the row totals and the column totals in the "observed" table.

$$\text{Expected frequency} = \frac{(\text{row total}) (\text{column total})}{\text{overall total}}$$

So, for the first cell (Group 1, "Yes"), the expected frequency would be

$$\frac{(10) (9)}{19} = \frac{90}{19} = 4.74$$

Expected Frequencies

	"Yes"	"No"
Group 1	4.74	5.26
Group 2	4.26	4.74

Here are the symbols used in the χ^2 formula:

O_i stands for the observed value of a particular cell
E_i stands for the expected value of a particular cell

The χ^2 formula is:

$$\chi^2 = \Sigma \frac{(O_i - E_i)^2}{E_i}$$

So, for the shyness data, the χ^2 calculation would be:

$$\chi^2 = \frac{(8 - 4.74)^2}{4.74} + \frac{(2 - 5.26)^2}{5.26} + \frac{(1 - 4.26)^2}{4.26} + \frac{(8 - 4.74)^2}{4.74} = 9.02$$

have just happened by chance to test a sample of Sudden Murderers that is particularly shy, feminine, and controlled. By consulting the appropriate statistical tables, we can tell how likely it is that this could be the case—that there really is no difference between these two types of murderers, but that we just happened to get such a large difference by luck.

If the table for a particular statistic indicates that there is less than a 5 percent chance of obtaining such a large statistic just by luck, researchers usually will feel comfortable in saying the obtained difference is real. By consulting a χ^2 table and looking under the appropriate heading (two groups, one *degree of free-*

dom; that is, only two possible answers), we discover that there is only a 1 percent chance of obtaining a χ^2 of 9.02 just by luck. We can conclude that, in general, Sudden Murderers really do feel more shy than Habitual Criminal Murderers; there is a 1 percent chance that we are wrong in making that assertion, but that is an acceptable level of risk. For the BSRI and MMPI statistics, we need to consult a table for the *t*-statistic. By checking under the appropriate heading (ten subjects in one group, nine in the other), we discover that there was less than a 5 percent chance of obtaining a *t* as large as 2.32 just by luck, but there was *more* than a 5 percent chance of ob-

t-tests for the BSRI and the MMPI data

Although the formula for obtaining *t* looks complicated, all we need in order to carry out the computation are: (1) each individual score on the measure of interest, (2) the number of subjects in each group, and (3) the mean for each group.

Here are the symbols used in the formula:

X_i stands for the individual scores in Group 1
Y_i stands for the individual scores in Group 2
$\bar{X}$ is the mean for Group 1
$\bar{Y}$ is the mean for Group 2
N_1 is the number of subjects in Group 1
N_2 is the number of subjects in Group 2

The formula for *t* is:

$$ t = \frac{\bar{X} - \bar{Y} - 0}{\sqrt{\left(\frac{1}{N_1} + \frac{1}{N_2}\right)\left(\frac{\Sigma X_i^2 - N_1\bar{X}^2 + \Sigma Y_i^2 - N_2\bar{Y}^2}{N_1 + N_2 - 2}\right)}} $$

The zero in the numerator means that we want to see if the difference between the two means is really greater than zero.

If we carry out the *t*-tests on the BSRI difference scores, the starting formula will be:

$$ t = \frac{11.50 - (-10.22) - 0}{\sqrt{\left(\frac{1}{10} + \frac{1}{9}\right)\left(\frac{\Sigma X_i^2 - 10(11.50)^2 + \Sigma Y_i^2 - 9(-10.22)^2}{10 + 9 - 2}\right)}} $$

After squaring and summing all the separate X_i and Y_i as required, and carrying out all the final calculations, we end up with $t = 2.32$ for the BSRI data.

If we plug the MMPI data into the formula, we get a $t = 1.99$.

taining a *t* of 1.99. Thus, the BSRI data does show a *statistically significant* difference. A researcher would symbolize the level of significance as $p < .05$, which means that the probability of obtaining the result by chance was less than 5 percent. But the MMPI over-control data does *not* show a statistically significant difference ($p > .05$). However, since the results on the MMPI overcontrol scale *are* in the direction we expected (Group 1 more controlled than Group 2) and the difference is fairly pronounced, we might try to investigate this idea further using a different sample of murderers, or increasing the size of the present sample by testing additional inmates. (The statistical test used when more than two groups are being studied is called the *F-test,* or *analysis of variance.*)

Since we obtained statistically significant differences between our groups on two of the major dependent measures and a strong trend on the third, we can tentatively conclude that there are some important personality differences between men who commit murders after leading a seemingly "model" life and men who commit murders as just another in a series of violent crimes. The Sudden Murderers

are clearly more shy and perceive themselves as more feminine than the other group, and they may also be more ego-overcontrolled. But these results are by no means definitive. First, this pattern of findings may only be true for male criminals. Remember that only men were tested. Second, we cannot even say that their shyness and femininity led these Sudden Murderers to suddenly lose control and kill someone. Since we tested them *after* the murders had been committed, it is theoretically possible that having committed the sudden murder made them ashamed, which in turn led them to feel more shy and less stereotypically masculine. Third, even if it is true that Sudden Murderers overcontrol their impulses, but then suddenly lash out in violence, we still do not know precisely what factors might lead to the kind of "blowup" that we have been describing. In this kind of situation, when we have some interesting, but inconclusive observations or results from a field experiment, we need to investigate our hypotheses further in the more controlled setting of the laboratory. Here, unlike the field situation, we can hope to determine the causes of the effects we see.

A proposed laboratory experiment

The Sudden Murderers study was actually carried out and the data we presented earlier are real. Here we will propose one possible laboratory experiment that might be carried out to answer some of the questions raised by the results of that study. By doing so we hope to give you a firsthand look at the problems a researcher faces and the procedures that must be followed in devising a carefully controlled experiment.

Design of the experiment

There are many intriguing questions raised by the Sudden Murderers study—questions about shy people, about murderers, about sex roles, about aggression, and about ego-overcontrol. But before we can plan any particular experiment we need to narrow our focus, directing it to only one specific idea. (The other ideas can be tested in other, separate experiments.) For example, it might be worthwhile to study differences between shy and nonshy people in their reactions to verbal provocation. From this idea, we need to formulate a specific hypothesis which can be tested experimentally: "Shy people will take longer than nonshy people to respond to verbal provocation, but once they do, their initial reaction will be stronger than the initial reaction of nonshy people." In this study, then, the independent variable (whose effects we are studying) would be the subject's shyness or nonshyness. The two dependent variables (the behaviors which are assumed to be affected) are the subject's latency in responding to provocation, and the strength of the subject's initial response.

Now that we have identified the independent and dependent variables, we need operational definitions for the general concepts that appear in our statement of the hypothesis. For example, we need a way of operationally defining "verbal provocation," "shy," and "response to provocation." We might measure shyness by the same means used in the Sudden Murderers study: the answer given to the self-description question on the Stanford Shyness Survey. To operationalize "verbal provocation," we could hire an actor to make various anger-provoking or insulting remarks to each subject, having him start out mildly and get progressively more abusive. Finally, "response to provocation" might be defined as the first thing the subject says after the verbal abuse begins. The latency would be measured by the length of time it takes the subject to first respond to the insults, and the "strength" of response would be the hostility of

the subject's first remark, as rated by some independent judges who later listen to tapes of the interactions.

We now have the basic skeleton for the study: an idea, a hypothesis, independent and dependent variables, and a set of operational definitions. Next, the researcher would flesh out this skeleton with: (1) a plan for administering the Shyness Survey to a large group of people before subjects need to be chosen for the experiment itself; (2) a detailed procedure, including a standardized "script" for what the experimenter would say to each subject to introduce the study; (3) a step-by-step outline so that the procedure followed will be identical for all subjects; (4) a plan for reducing both experimenter and subject bias; and (5) a "pretest" in which a few subjects are actually tested so that the procedure can be "debugged" before the experiment itself is started.

Research ethics

One consideration should be particularly important for researchers who are planning to use human subjects: the ethics of the research. This means, quite simply, that the researcher should show a concern for the subjects' physical and psychological well-being. Many psychological experiments—especially those on perception and learning and memory, in which the subject is merely asked to perform some routine tasks—carry little risk to the subject. But experiments which study subjects' emotional reactions, self-images, and attitudes could potentially be upsetting or somehow psychologically disturbing to the subjects. In these experiments, it is crucial that the researcher make the experience as pleasant and non-threatening as possible for the subject, within the constraints of sound experimental design. Subjects should be assured in advance that they may leave the experiment at any time they wish, and they should be carefully "debriefed" at the end of the experiment. That is, the experimenter should take the time to explain the hypotheses and purposes of the experiment in detail, and should make sure that the subject does not leave the experiment feeling upset or embarrassed. In addition, care should be taken that all responses to questionnaires and personality profiles, as well as records of subjects' behaviors during the experiment, be kept strictly confidential. Because of growing concern about the ethics of experimentation, most universities and research institutes now have a committee which reviews all proposals for research involving human subjects before allowing that work to begin. Generally, if the review committee feels that an experiment involves some potential risk to subjects, the proposal will only be approved if the experiment will result in benefits to the subjects or to scientific knowledge which outweigh those risks.

The experiment that we are proposing here raises questions about the ethics of deception, since it would be necessary to deceive subjects about the experiment's true purpose. Obviously, it will be important that subjects not know we chose them on the basis of their shyness or nonshyness, or that we are interested in their reactions to verbal provocation. For this reason, we will need to devise some plausible cover story to give our subjects as a rationale for the study. But, in keeping with the ethical principles of research, we will need to find a careful, sensitive, and tactful way to debrief subjects at the end of the experiment, explaining our deception and its purpose.

Procedure and data collection

Consider, then, this experimental procedure which could be used to test our hypothesis: We will have two groups of subjects, each representing a different "level" of the independent variable (shy or nonshy), and we will have both males and females in each group. We will administer the Shyness Survey to some large population (say, the introductory psychology class at a large university) and, from that population, randomly choose a sample of shy subjects and a sample of nonshy subjects. Then, we will test each subject in the experiment individually. Since the independent variable is something that exists in the subjects already and is not something we are manipulating, the procedure should be identical for all subjects, no matter which group they are in. This feature of the design is especially nice, since it will be possible to keep the experimenter completely ignorant of each subject's experimental condition; this should eliminate the possibility of experimenter bias. We will try to reduce subject bias as much as possible by making the cover story as plausible as we can.

When each subject arrives, the experimenter will explain that the purpose of the experiment is to investigate the "getting acquainted" process. Another person will be present. The subject will think that this person is just another subject, the person with whom he or she will get acquainted, but, in fact, this person will be an actor—a "confederate" of the experimenter. The experimenter will say that the confederate was "randomly chosen" to talk first in the getting-acquainted conversation, and she will then leave the two people alone to talk. As she departs, she will tell them that, after the conversation, they will answer a questionnaire about their first impression of the other person. The confederate will go first, saying exactly the same thing to each subject. At first he will

merely be belligerent and sarcastic, but then he will become rude and insulting to the subject. As soon as the subject has made his or her first response, the experimenter will reenter the room, ask the confederate to leave, and debrief the subject. A permanent record of each session will be made by tape-recording.

This is just a rough sketch of one procedure that might be used in the laboratory to answer some of the questions raised earlier; such a study has not yet been conducted. (Perhaps you can think of others.) The data collected would be: (1) the number of seconds from the time the confederate started talking to the subject's first response, and (2) the strength of the subject's response, as assessed by a group of judges who did not know whether a given subject was shy or not.

Analyzing and communicating the results

The results could be analyzed by using the descriptive statistics discussed earlier and by statistical tests similar to the *t*-tests that were used on the Sudden Murderers data. We could look not only for differences between shy and nonshy persons, but also for differences between men and women. By examining the descriptive statistics and consulting the appropriate tables for our inferential statistics, we could then draw tentative conclusions about the experimental hypothesis and the idea with which we started. If the shy subjects respond as we would predict, we can probably reject the notion that Sudden Murderers become shy *after* committing their crime.

Once the data from a study have been analyzed, the researchers must decide whether the results are sufficiently important that they should be publicized to the scientific community—and, perhaps, the general public. Usually, only results which show a statistically significant difference between groups are considered worthy of publication, but occasionally studies are designed so that even "negative" (nonsignificant) results can be instructive. Once researchers have made the decision to publish a study, they must decide on the best way to introduce their idea and to discuss the results they found. In addition, the final report should include a detailed description of the experimental procedure and the data analysis. This is particularly important because scientific research is published with two major goals in mind. First, to add to the existing body of knowledge on a given problem, and second, to give others the opportunity to *replicate* or reproduce the study in their own laboratories. It is crucial to the scientific process that a result—even a statistically significant one—be obtained more than once with a given procedure.

We began this chapter by raising several questions about two seemingly different types of murderers. We tried to show that, no matter what our intuitions tell us about people, we need to rely upon careful psychological research to be able to answer such questions definitively. You have seen that there are several different methodologies that might be used in psychological studies, there are many fine points of experimental procedure which must be considered, and there is a vast array of descriptive and inferential statistics which can be used in examining experimental results. From start to finish, the enterprise of psychological research is fascinating and complex. But if you understand how it works, you can understand and even evaluate the answers that psychologists give to the basic questions about human behavior. And, perhaps, you can begin to tackle some of the unanswered questions yourself.

Glossary

Abnormal behavior. Behavior considered to be maladaptive or deviant by the individual or the social group of which the person is a member. (564)

Abreaction. The expression of affect (often strong repressed feelings) during therapy. (600)

Absolute rating scale. See *Rating scale.*

Absolute refractory period. Period of a few milliseconds after an axon has fired during which the membrane is temporarily unexcitable, and during which the axon cannot be fired again regardless of the stimulus energy level. (295)

Absolute threshold. The lowest level of stimulus intensity necessary for that stimulus to be detected. (353)

Accommodation. Process postulated by Piaget by which previously developed cognitive structures are modified on the basis of new experiences. (239)

Acetylcholine. Chemical transmitter substance that probably facilitates the passage of a nerve impulse from one neuron to another across the synapse. (330)

Achievement need. *(n ach)* A learned motivational state which gives rise to a general tendency to approach success. (385)

ACTH. A hormone secreted by the anterior pituitary, which interacts with the secretions of the adrenal cortex—an important factor in physiological reactions to prolonged stress. (533)

Action potential. The sudden electrical charge in a neuron resulting from a change in the permeability of the cell membrane which allows ions to pass through it. (291)

Activation. Arousal or energy mobilization, which enables an organism to pursue its goals. (531)

Adipocytes. Specialized cells that store body fat in the form of fatty acids; obese individuals have a greater number of these cells than do normal individuals. (382)

Adolescence. In humans, a transitional stage between puberty and maturity; an arbitrary classification. (262)

Adrenal cortex. Outer part of the adrenal glands, which secretes cortin, a hormone important in physiological reactions to prolonged stress. (304)

Adrenal glands. A pair of endocrine glands located at the upper end of the kidneys; consist of inner adrenal medulla, which secretes the hormones adrenaline and noradrenaline (also called *epinephrene* and *norepinephrine*) during strong emotion, and outer adrenal cortex, which secretes hormones that influence maturation. (304)

Adrenaline. See *Epinephrine.*

Affective reactions. Category of psychotic disorders characterized by severe fluctuations of mood or feeling. (585)

Affective states. Emotional states or experiences whether the emotions involved are mild or intense, pleasant or unpleasant. (402)

Afferent neuron. See *Sensory neuron.*

Affiliation. Tendency or desire to be with other people; a basic social need or motive of gregariousness basic for common life. (675)

Age regression. A special case of memory distortion in which hypnotized subjects are induced to reexperience events that occurred at some earlier period of their lives. (483)

Aggression. A response that destroys objects, causes harm to others or to oneself (or the explicit intention to do so); assumes many forms. (689)

Alarm reaction. See *General adaptation syndrome.*

Alcohol. A type of psychoactive drug that acts to depress the central nervous system; it has a high potential for psychological and physiological dependence and leads to irreversible tissue damage. (455)

Alcoholism. A dependence on or addiction to alcohol; perhaps best described as a disease process wherein physical damage becomes progressively greater with the increased consumption of alcohol over time. (455)

All-or-none principle. Principle stating that if a nerve fiber responds at all, it responds at its full strength. That is, as long as the stimulus strength is above the stimulus threshold, the nerve impulse fired by a particular neuron is always the same magnitude. (291)

Alpha waves. The electrical rhythm or EEG frequency typical of the brain during a relaxed state. (550)

Alternate states of consciousness. States of consciousness in which an individual feels that there has been a qualitative shift in his or her pattern of mental functioning away from the "normal" waking state of experiencing consciousness. (438)

Amnesia. Loss of memory, especially of past personal experiences; may be a type of dissociative state. (575)

Amphetamine psychosis. A psychotic reaction induced by excessive doses of amphetamine. (332)

Amphetamines. Drugs that stimulate the central nervous system, usually administered to lift depressive mood states and control appetite. In street usage called "speed." (456)

Amplitude. A measure of the extent or amount of a response. (351)

Amygdala. Structure in the limbic area of the brain associated with flight and defense responses, primitive emotion, and sexual behavior. (312)

Anal stage. In psychoanalytic theory, the second stage of psychosexual development during which bowel control is achieved and the focus of pleasure is the eliminative processes. (240)

Androgynous. Exhibiting both "masculine" and "feminine" characteristics. (512)

Anonymity. State of being unknown; not imparting a sense of clearly marked individuality. (The anonymity of urban living robs individuals of their sense of identity.) (702)

Antidepressant drugs. Drugs that elevate mood and relieve depression; used in chemotherapy. (597)

Antisocial aggression. Aggression expressed in socially unacceptable ways. For example, rape. (690)

Antisocial personality. A type of personality disorder in which the individual is poorly socialized to live with others. Such people are immature, selfish, impulsive, and guilt-free. (569)

Anxiety. The experience of apprehension, tension, and dread without an appropriate causal determinant. (569)

Anxiety neurosis. Type of neurosis characterized by chronic "free-floating" anxiety and apprehension. In Freudian theory, neurotic anxiety stems from the imminent emergence of repressed conflicts. (570)

Aphasia. Impairment of ability to use or understand language, even though hearing and speech mechanisms are unimpaired; due to disease or damage to certain association areas of the brain. (211)

Appetitive conditioning. A form of respondent conditioning in which the conditioned response is a kind of "seeking," appetitive behavior, such as salivation. (67)

Appraisal. The evaluation and judgment of the significance of a stimulus; it may result in moving the organism to action. Primary appraisal establishes threat potential, secondary appraisal assesses coping strategies to use on perceived threat. (408)

Approach gradient. Strengthening of the tendency to approach a desired goal as the subject draws nearer to it. Important in the understanding of certain conflict situations. (490)

Archetypes. In Jung's personality theory, universal symbols and predispositions inherited in the "collective unconscious"; may appear in dreams. (485)

Arousal. General energizing component of attention and motivation; involves organs controlled by both central and autonomic nervous systems. (531)

Assertiveness training. Training in expressive social skills that enable a person to be more direct and effective in resolving interpersonal conflicts. (610)

Assimilation. Process whereby new cognitive elements are altered to make them more similar to familiar, already experienced ones, and to fit more easily into existing cognitive structures. (239)

Atmospheric perspective. A cue in depth perception based on the learned difference in clarity between near and far objects. (356)

Attachment. A set of behaviors that elicit and maintain nearness between two people, especially between parent and infant. Also, the social-emotional bond that develops from such intimate contact. (253)

Attention. The directive aspect of the perceptual process, involving orientation to a particular set of events. Attention requires postural and physiological adjustments, cognitive focusing on stimuli with particular characteristics, and motivation to sustain the information processing. (362)

Attitude. A learned tendency to respond to people, concepts, and events in an evaluative way. Attitudes are composed of beliefs, feelings, and action tendencies. (647)

Attribution. Process of attributing to individuals or their behavior inferred underlying conditions and causes. (150)

Attribution error. Tendency, in explaining or understanding a given action, for an individual to overestimate the importance of the actor's disposition while underestimating the importance of situational factors. (653)

Attribution theory. Theory that we give both meaning and predictability to the events of our lives by developing both a reality orientation and a control orientation to the world through finding causal attributions for actions and events we perceive. (150)

Audience. Those to whom a message is directed; a variable in the study of attitude change. (649)

Auditory nerve. Nerve that carries impulses from the auditory receptors in the inner ear to the brain. (350)

Autism. Extreme form of childhood mental disturbance in which the child does not communicate or relate well to others or to the environment, or form an adequate self-concept. (583)

Autistic thinking. Thinking as an end in itself and not a means to an end; determined primarily by the individual's needs or desires, as in daydreaming. (139)

Autonomic nervous system (ANS). The part of the peripheral nervous system that regulates bodily activities not ordinarily subject to voluntary control, including the visceral changes that occur during emotion; composed of the *sympathetic* and *parasympathetic* divisions. (65)

Autosexuality. Sexual arousal or excitement arising through oneself, without the participation or stimulation of another individual. (681)

Aversive control. A form of conditioning in which the conditioned response is an attempt to avoid or escape from an aversive stimulus or punishment. (101)

Avoidance conditioning. A form of operant conditioning in which an organism can prevent (avoid) an aversive stimulus by making an appropriate response. (101)

Avoidance gradient. Strengthening of the tendency to go away from a feared place or object as the subject draws nearer to it; it is steeper in slope than approach gradient; important in the understanding of certain types of conflict situations. (490)

Axon. Long fiber leading away from the cell body of the neuron; transmits nerve impulses to other neurons or to a muscle or gland. (292)

Axonal conduction. Nerve impulse transmission in which the depolarization of the nerve membrane triggers an all-or-none impulse which rapidly moves down the length of the axon. (291)

Basilar membrane. Membrane of the ear within the cochlea; movements of this membrane stimulate the hair cells of the organ of Corti, producing the neural effects of auditory stimulation. (350)

Battered children. Children who are seriously beaten, tortured, and injured by their parents, siblings, or other relatives. (699)

Behavioral contract. An explicit agreement (often in writing) stating the consequences for both parties to the contract that will follow upon certain desired behaviors. Used by behavior therapists especially with clients being treated for addictions. (606–607)

Behavioral medicine. A new interdisciplinary field in which physicians, psychologists, psychiatrists, and other health specialists are working to develop illness prevention strategies, health maintenance programs, and means of delivering health care knowledge and practice more effectively. (529)

Behavioral variability. The observed phenomenon that different individuals respond differently to the same external situation; motivational analysis is an attempt to explain this occurrence. (372)

Behaviorism. An approach that views measurable behavior as the only acceptable content for the science of psychology. It emphasizes the functional relationship of behavior to its stimulus determinants. (24)

Behavioristic therapy. Type of psychotherapy that focuses on observable behavior, using learning principles (such as the use of reinforcement) to discover the stimulus conditions that maintain behavior pathology and to change them so as to modify such behavior. (603)

Behaviorists. Psychologists whose work can be described as the scientific study of the overt behavior of organisms. They are concerned only with observable, objectively measurable behavior and the discovery of predictable and specific stimulus-response relationships. (24)

Behavior modification. Behavioristic therapy that involves the use of operant conditioning procedures, emphasizing observation of behavior, its controlling variables, and contingent reinforcement. (603)

Behavior sampling. Personality measurement technique in which the examiner observes the subject's behavior in a specified situation. (501)

Beliefs. A component of attitudes, they are propositions about the way things are or ought to be. (617)

Bell-shaped curve. See *Normal curve.*

Beta waves. The EEG frequency associated with problem solving and tension. (550)

Biofeedback. Technique by which organisms are taught to change and control internal body processes formerly thought to be involuntary (e.g., blood pressure and brain waves); it involves giving the subject immediate feedback or knowledge of the bodily changes as they occur. (550)

Biological drives. Unlearned motivational states induced by deprivation conditions (e.g., hunger, thirst) or excessive physical stimulation (e.g., pain). (374)

Bipolar cells. First neurons in the visual pathway; conduct messages from the rods and cones to ganglion cells. (346)

Bisexual. Individual whose sexual preferences involve members of both the same and the opposite sex. (682)

Bit. The amount of information needed to distinguish between two equally likely alternatives; used in information theory and artificial intelligence. (131)

Blind obedience to authority. Compliance with the wishes or orders of another even in violation of one's self-image and moral values; may be fostered or enhanced by the presence of a legitimate authority, social norms, or a superior-subordinate role relation. (706)

Blind spot. Region of the retina where the optic nerve leaves the eye; thus it contains no receptor cells. (346)

Blood-brain barrier. A structural-chemical barrier that keeps foreign substances in the bloodstream from flowing into the brain. (329)

Body image distortion. A perceptual distortion that is often characteristic of altered states of consciousness; a condition in which awareness of the body or its parts may be considerably altered. For example, there may be a sense of being separated from one's body or a feeling that certain portions of the body are enlarged or weightless. (438)

Brain mapping. The process of identifying the functions controlled by specific regions of the brain. (316)

Brain stem. A collection of structures lying between the new brain and the spinal cord; includes the thalamus, the hypothalamus, and the reticular formation. (312)

Brainwashing. Intensive form of propaganda conducted under stressful conditions designed to induce major changes in thinking; a journalistic term derived from Korean war experiences. (644)

British empiricists (associationists). Seventeenth-century philosophers who stated that knowledge of reality could only come from information processed through the sensory apparatus; complex thoughts were seen as being built by association between simple sensory elements. (342)

Cannula. A double tube (a tube within a tube) inserted into a body cavity, duct, or blood vessel and used for various purposes such as drainage of fluids or the administration of chemical substances into selected brain sites or other body parts. (329)

Catatonia. Type of schizophrenia characterized by motionless, unresponsive stupor; vegetative existence, but responds well to therapy. (583)

Catecholamines. Special neurotransmitters that act on the central nervous system to alter mood and arousal. (331)

Catharsis. The process and beneficial effect of expressing one's strongly felt, but usually inhibited feelings; getting "things off one's chest." (690)

Causal determinants. Variables that have been specified by theory or shown by research to have a systematic influence on changing a particular behavior. Frustration may be a causal determinant of aggression in some situations. (35)

Causation. Relationship between behavior and stimulus condition whereby the occurrence of the stimulus invariably results in the simultaneous or subsequent occurrence of the behavior and is a necessary condition for it. (39)

Cell body. Part of a cell that contains the nucleus and from which, in neurons, the axon and several dendrites project. (288)

Central motor program. The neural mechanisms that generate patterned output (also called *motor score*). (315)

Central nervous system (CNS). The brain and spinal cord, as distinct from the peripheral nervous system. (285)

Cerebellum. The part of the brain that controls the coordination of movements necessary to maintain balance, posture, and other regulatory mechanisms least involved in psychological functions. (312)

Cerebral hemispheres. The two halves of the human brain. (312)

Cerebral specialization. The two cerebral hemispheres have a specialization of functions. The dominant hemisphere controls speech, writing, and mathematical calculations, while the nondominant hemisphere controls perceptive tasks; also referred to as *lateralization of function*. (324)

Cerebrospinal fluid. A liquid that fills the ventricles, flows over the brain, and is absorbed into the veins in a complete exchange every four hours. Neurons and glia are bathed in this fluid. (329)

Chaining. Type of operant conditioning in which the subject learns to perform a *series* of responses in order to obtain reinforcement. (99)

Charisma. An extraordinary personal quality of leadership, actual or perceived, marked by a special emotional appeal and attraction on the part of the leader to a group of followers. (633)

Chemical senses. The senses of taste and smell. (345)

Chemotherapy. A form of biological or somatic therapy using drugs in the treatment of mental and emotional disorders; heavily used in institutional settings for patient management as well as rehabilitation. (596)

Chi-square (χ^2) test. Test of statistical inference; a test for comparing the obtained frequencies of various possible events with the frequencies that would be predicted by chance alone. (762)

Chlorpromazine. Tranquilizing drug widely used in treatment of schizophrenia; it facilitates the production of serotonin. (303)

Chromosomes. Large molecules consisting of DNA and proteins, which contain the genes responsible for hereditary traits. Every human cell contains 46 chromosomes except the sex cells, or *gametes*, which have 23.

Chronological age (CA). An individual's age in years. (514)

Chunking. Organization of material to be learned or remembered into smaller units that are familiar; increases recall ability. (180)

Circadian rhythms. The rhythmic biological cycle of sleep and activity peculiar to each species. It reflects the energy requirements of the individual and the ecological character of its habitat. (302)

Clairvoyance. Form of extrasensory perception in which a person supposedly becomes aware of an external object without the use of the sense organs. (357)

Classical conditioning. A form of learning in which behavior (conditioned response) is elicited by a stimulus (conditioned stimulus) that acquired its power through association with a biologically significant stimulus (unconditioned stimulus). Also called *Pavlovian* or *respondent* conditioning. (65)

Client-centered therapy. A nondirective technique of humanistic psychotherapy based on the theory that many individuals can work through their own problems by "talking them out" in a permissive and supportive atmosphere. (612)

Clinical psychologist. A psychologist with a Ph.D. whose training involves hospital and/or clinical experience; involved in the practice of psychotherapy using verbal-behavioral treatment; trained in diagnosis using methods of testing, interviewing, and research. (19)

Cochlea. Part of the inner ear containing fluid that is set in motion by vibrations of the oval window and which in turn stimulates the basilar membrane. (350)

Cognition. The act, process, or product of knowing and perceiving. Cognitions are bits of information individuals maintain about themselves, the environment, and their interrelationship. (108)

Cognitive appraisal. A theory of emotion that emphasizes the person's evaluation of the significance of a stimulus, resulting in a felt tendency to approach it or withdraw. (408)

Cognitive control. Control of motivational, emotional, perceptual, and behavioral responses through engagement of cognitive processes, such as cognitive dissonance, choice, beliefs in placebos or in taboos. (416)

Cognitive dissonance theory. Principle that dissonant (discrepant or incongruous) cognitions motivate the individual to reduce the perceived inconsistency, to achieve greater consonance. This can happen if one of the cognitions is changed, or if new ones are added; theory developed by Festinger. (651)

Cognitive maps. Learning of stimulus (S – S) relationships in the environment which help structure and give purpose to one's behavior; used by Tolman to account for expectancies and learning without overt responding. (108)

Cognitive processes. Those processes by which individuals think, know, and gain an awareness of objects and events; includes learning, reasoning, remembering, decision-making, creating, etc. (126)

Cognitive rehearsal. A behavior modification strategy in which the client makes positive self-statements and attempts to stop making negative ones. (553, 610)

Cohort. A group of individuals similar in some way. For example, birth cohorts are individuals born at the same time. (224)

Collective unconscious. In Jungian theory, that part of an individual's unconscious which is inherited, evolutionarily developed, and common to all members of the species; a sort of storehouse of racial memories deeper than the personal unconscious. (485)

Communication. Process by which individuals give and receive information. (144)

Community mental health. Approach to mental health that emphasizes the prevention of mental illness and the need for broader and more effective mental health services based within the community; stresses local needs and resources. (618)

Compartmentalization. A defense mechanism or technique of dehumanization by which a particular activity or situation can be separated from an individual's life, values, and feelings; also called *isolation*. (483)

Complementarity. Possession of traits that complement (go well with) those of another individual; a property that makes one person attractive to another. (662)

Compulsion. Bizarre, irrational, repetitive action which the individual does not understand but nevertheless feels impelled to perform; usually symbolic in nature. (572)

Concrete operations. Third of Piaget's stages of cognitive development (from 7 – 11 years); characterized by logical-mathematical thinking and conservation. (259)

Conditioned reinforcement. See *Secondary reinforcement.*

Conditioned response (CR). The learned or acquired response to a conditioned stimulus. (67)

Conditioned stimulus (CS). An originally neutral stimulus that, through repeated pairings with an unconditioned stimulus, acquires the ability to elicit the response originally elicited only by the unconditioned stimulus. (68)

Cones. Retinal receptor cells responsible for color vision and high visual acuity. (346)

Conflict. The simultaneous presence of opposing or mutually exclusive impulses, desires, or incompatible responses (i.e., to approach and to avoid). (490)

Conformity. Adherence of attitudes, values, and/or behavior to social norms. (629 – 630)

Confrontation. The culminating act in a sequence of violent interaction; a result of escalation. (701)

Conscience. Internal functioning of socially learned standards of right and wrong by which an individual judges his or her own behavior; corresponds to the superego. (482)

Conscious. In Freudian theory, the thoughts, ideas, feelings, and desires that an individual is aware of at any given moment. (481)

Consciousness. State of awareness of internal events (such as thought processes) and of the external environment; normal waking state. (433 – 434)

Consummatory response. Action that represents the completion of goal-seeking activity. For example, eating. (377)

Contiguity. Relationship between a conditioned stimulus and a response in the environment which appear close together in space and time. According to current psychological theories it is a necessary, but not sufficient, condition to account for learning associations. (107)

Contingency, behavioral. A specified relationship between a given response and the timing or frequency of reinforcement. (90)

Continuity hypothesis. Theory that problem solving is essentially a gradual learning procedure based on trial-and-error behavior. (142)

Continuous reinforcement. Reinforcement given regularly after each correct response. (87)

Control, conceptually guided. Control exercised over the processing of information at a high level of intellectual function, involving systems evaluation and conceptual guidance. (128)

Control, data driven. Control over information processing determined by new inputs, by current data which interrupt ongoing programs. (128)

Control group. Group of subjects that shares all of the characteristics and procedures of the experimental group except exposure to the independent variable the effect of which is being studied. A control group establishes a no-treatment baseline against which to compare the treatment effects on the experimental group. (48)

Control orientation. A view of the world that recognizes our need to be able to predict and influence events important in our lives; assumed by attribution theory. (151, 653)

Control system theory. A theory that accounts for the way sensory feedback is maintained and utilized to control perceptions and motor activities. (364)

Convergence. Distributing process in the nervous system whereby impulses from many neurons or receptor cells reach the same neuron or effector. (346 – 347)

Conversion reaction. Neurotic reaction to stress or anxiety in which psychological distress is converted into bodily symptoms. (574)

Coping strategies. The possible means of dealing with a situation that an organism perceives as threatening; various coping strategies possible in a given situation are assessed in the process of secondary appraisal. (408)

Coronary-prone behavior pattern. A coping style found to increase the risk of heart disease. The stress response typical of Type A coronary-prone individuals (often males) involves compulsive activity, competitiveness, time urgency, and hostility. (544)

Corpus callosum. Heavy bundle of nerve fibers connecting the two cerebral hemispheres. When this is severed, separate functions of each hemisphere are not integrated, leading to "two minds in one brain." (312)

Correlation. Measure of the degree to which two variables are related; generally a prediction relating one behavior to another rather than relating behavior to a stimulus condition. A precise quantitative measure of the degree of correlation is given by the coefficient of correlation. (39 – 40, 761)

Cortex. A thin, grayish rind of tissue covering the cerebrum and consisting of neurons and their connectors; active in conscious experience and higher mental processes; also called *gray matter*. (312)

Cortin. A hormone secreted by the adrenal cortex, which interacts with ACTH, a pituitary hormone, and is an important factor in the physiological reaction to prolonged stress. (533)

Counterconditioning. The replacement of a particular response to a stimulus by the establishment of another, often quite different, response; often used in behavior therapy to eliminate unwanted behavior and replace it with a more desirable response. (74, 609)

Countertransference. Process in which the analyst develops personal feelings about the patient because of perceived similarity of the patient to significant others in the therapist's life; reversal of the usual process of transference. (602)

Covert. Not directly observable; rather hidden or concealed from public scrutiny, as are one's thoughts.

Creativity. The uninhibited, imaginative thought processes involved in the act of creating, of "bringing into being, causing to exist." (521)

Criterion validity. The validity of test scores is assessed by the extent to which they correlate with (predict to) something of interest, some outcome of particular significance. (499)

Cross-sectional design. A research approach that selects and compares individuals of different ages at one time of testing. (222)

Crowding. The perception of too many people in too little space, which may affect behavior adversely if other variables are operating. (731)

Crystallized abilities. Abilities largely determined by learning experiences in a particular culture (such as vocabulary or mechanical knowledge). (271)

Cue-producing responses. Responses that mediate between an initial external stimulus and the next observable response in a behavior sequence—as in counting, where "2" is a response that serves as the cue for "3." (111)

Cumulative record. Measure of response rate; a graph plotting the responses as they occur and recording a cumulative total for a given time interval. (86)

Cybernetics. The study of feedback control and communications in both machines and living organisms. (128)

Cutaneous senses. Senses of pressure, pain, warmth, and cold, receptors for which are located primarily in the skin. (345)

Cytoplasm. Substance of a cell (excluding the nucleus), in which most of the biochemical reactions of the cell take place. (287)

Dark adaptation. Process by which the eyes become more sensitive so that they can see under low illumination. (347)

Data. Reports or measurements of observed events. (32)

Daydreaming. The report of thoughts that involve a temporary shift of attention away from an ongoing task. (438)

Decay theory. Theory of forgetting that states that learned material leaves a trace in the brain, which fades away if unused. (170)

Deductive reasoning. The mode of reasoning that starts with propositions and derives inescapable conclusions from them. (140)

Deep structure. The basic, underlying meaning of a sentence; the same deep structure can be used to generate several different surface structures by the use of transformational rules. (201)

Defense mechanism. An unconscious mode of coping with situations that arouse anxiety or threaten self-esteem; examples include displacement, projection, rationalization, regression, and sublimation. (482)

Deficiency motivation. Motivation in which the individual seeks to restore his or her physical or psychological equilibrium rather than move toward personal growth. (487)

Dehumanization. Psychological erasure or cancellation of human qualities and values of other people; leads to the treatment and perception of people as objects or subhuman animals. (710)

Deindividuation. Subjective state of the loss of one's identity as an accountable, responsible self. It results in weakening of the usual controls that restrain impulsive and antisocial behavior; may be fostered by such conditions as anonymity or altered states of consciousness. (702)

Delayed effect. An effect resulting from a given intervention, which does not appear immediately, but rather occurs after some time has elapsed. (724–725)

Delay of reinforcement. Principle which states that responses occurring close in time or space to the delivery of the reinforcement are learned more quickly than responses remote from reinforcement. (89)

Delerium tremens. Violent physical and perceptual reactions (hallucinatory experiences) occurring as a result of chronic, excessive alcoholic indulgence. (455)

Delta sleep. Deep sleep stage defined by EEG patterns of slow frequency and large amplitude. (446)

Delusion. A strong belief opposed to reality and maintained in spite of logical persuasion and evidence to the contrary; symptom of paranoid states. Three main types: *delusion of grandeur* (belief that one is an exalted personage), *delusion of persecution* (belief that one is being plotted against), and *delusion of reference* (egocentric belief that chance happenings and conversations concern oneself). (584–585)

Demonic possession. Archaic conception of mental illness, based on the belief that physical sickness and mental aberrations were caused by the "possession" of the patient's body by evil spirits. (592)

Dendrites. Highly branched fibers that extend from the cell body at the receiving end of a neuron; usually quite short. (288)

Denial. A defense mechanism by means of which an individual protects self from external threat by refusing to perceive or think about it; however, this unrealistic fear level may have negative results. (483)

Dependence. Physiological or psychological need for any of a number of psychoactive drugs. (455)

Dependent variable. A particular behavior that is observed and measured in psychological research. It is the response predicted to vary depending upon variations in antecedent stimuli or with concurrent responses. (46)

Depression. Emotional state of dejection, feelings of worthlessness, and usually apprehension; it is the most prevalent psychiatric disorder in the United States and bears a marked similarity to the symptoms of learned helplessness. (585)

Depressive episodes or reactions. Psychotic reactions characterized by periods of extreme depression; may alternate with manic episodes. (585)

Depressive neurosis. A type of neurosis characterized by exaggerated sadness and depression in response to a loss or threatened loss; a reactive expression of helplessness and feelings of failure. (414)

Deprivation. Lack of, or withholding of, need-satisfying stimulation or of something necessary for biological or psychological functioning.

Deprivation dwarfism. A condition of defective physical growth and maturation in children as a consequence of emotional deprivation. (7)

Deprogramming. Systematic attempt to force individuals to renounce their beliefs, usually newly acquired beliefs assumed to have been coercively programmed in. (644)

Descriptive statistic. A single number that represents or describes a series of measurements on a group or individual, such as central tendency, variability, coefficient of correlation. (755)

Desensitization. Behavioral therapy process of reconditioning in which stimuli lose their power to elicit anxiety through the individual's graded exposure to them from mild forms to more severe ones. (608)

Determinism. The theory that all events are determined by preceding causes. The theory assumes that this relationship is invariant and, therefore, that an event is predictable when the relevant causes are known. (51, 479)

Determinism, reciprocal. A conception of the mutual controlling influence of person, behavior, and environment. This interdependency proposed by Bandura is central in developing programs for self-regulation of behavior. (119)

Developmental psychology. The area of psychology concerned with the systematic study of changes in individual functioning due to age. (218)

Deviance. Behavior that is viewed by society as being markedly different from the group average or norm expected in a given situation under given conditions. (566)

Differentiation theory. Theory that perception is a process of reduction of sensory input, filtering out essential signal elements from the abundance of stimulus "noise." (342)

Discontinuity hypothesis. Theory that problem solving is primarily a matter of insight and perceptual reorganization, and that solutions are discovered or realized all at once, rather than in a gradual fashion, (143)

Discrimination. The ability to detect differences between two stimuli; in conditioning, the ability to pick out and respond to relevant stimuli and to inhibit responses to irrelevant stimuli. (70) Prejudicial response or behavior, as in racial discrimination. (637)

Discriminative stimulus (S^D). In operant conditioning, a stimulus that signals that reinforcement is or is not available following the operant behavior. (81)

Disobedience. Refusal or negligence to obey, to carry out a rule or command. (9–10, 707)

Displaced aggression. Transfer of hostility from the object or person actually causing frustration to some other object or person or to the self. (693)

Displacement. A dream process by which material is disguised so that something important in real life is unimportant in a dream or vice versa. (450) A defense mechanism by which feelings of hostility, etc., are discharged against a substitute object. (483)

Dispositional attribution. Attribution of causes of an action or event to relatively stable, internal, nonmodifiable characteristics within the individual; that is, his or her personality traits, character, and inner dispositions to act. It allows for the categorization of "problem people" rather than analysis of problem situations. (653)

Dissent. Objection, a withholding of assent based on a difference of opinion; does not necessarily imply contrary action. (9–10, 707)

Dissociated states. Neurotic reactions to extreme stress in which entire episodes of life are repressed from consciousness; mental processes may be split off from the main personality or lose their normal thought-affect relationships, as in *amnesia, fugue,* and *multiple personality.* (574)

Distal stimulus. The actual object providing stimulation of the retina. (359)

Divergence. Distributing process in the nervous system whereby impulses from a single neuron or receptor cell reach many neurons or muscles. (347)

DNA. Deoxyribonucleic acid; the principal component of genes, consisting of long chains of pairs of nucleotide bases arranged like a twisted ladder or spiral staircase.

Double-bind. Situation that involves two or more inconsistent messages that require incompatible responses. (387)

Double-blind test. A methodological control used to conceal the treatment from the subject as well as from the person (researcher) who administers the treatment. A safeguard against expectation or set effects; especially used in drug evaluation research. (34)

Dream analysis. Psychoanalytic technique involving the interpretation of dreams in order to gain insight into the patient's unconscious motivation; based on the belief of Freud and others that dreams are symbolic representations of unconscious impulses, conflicts, and desires. (450, 480)

Drive. Motive; internal conditions directing an organism toward a specific goal, usually involving biological processes. (374–375)

Drive reduction. Theory of learning stating that a motivated sequence of behavior is best explained as moving from an aversive state of tension (drive) to a goal state in which the drive is reduced. (79)

Drug abuse. Use of a drug to the point where it interferes with the individual's health or with economic or social adjustment. (455)

Dualism. Descartes' view of the human organism as comprising two independent elements: the mechanistic body and brain, and the spiritualistic soul and ephemeral mind. (284)

Dynamism. In Sullivan's personality theory, a prolonged, recurrent behavior pattern; a habit. (242)

Dyscontrol syndrome. Pattern of senseless brutality or other repeated offenses assumed to be brought about by disease of the limbic system or the temporal lobe of the brain. (595)

Eardrum. Thin membrane at the end of the auditory canal between the outer and middle ear. (350)

Eclectic approach. Approach to the study of psychology that stresses a wide variety of theories, assumptions, kinds of research, and levels of analysis rather than advocating any one as superior to others. (56)

Ecological psychology. A new approach to psychology concerned with understanding the psychosocial interdependence between the individuals in a community and their physical and biological environment. (720)

Ecology. The mutual relations between organisms and their physical environment. (720)

Ecosystem. A total ecological community considered together with the nonliving elements of its environment as a unit.

Effector neurons. Neurons that excite or inhibit the activity of glands. (290)

Effectors. The organs (muscles or glands) that perform the actual response functions upon receiving nerve impulses from motor neurons. (285)

Efferent nerve fiber. Carries messages from the central nervous system to an organ of response such as a muscle or gland; also known as a *motor nerve fiber.* (285)

Efficacy. Sense of personal competence, effectiveness, mastery, or self-worth. (120)

Ego. In Freud's psychoanalytic theory, the rational aspect of the personality; regulates the impulses of the id in order to meet the demands of reality and maintain social approval and self-esteem. More generally, the individual's concept of self. (482)

Ego-defense mechanism. See *Defense mechanism.*

Ego ideal. The individual's view of the kind of person he or she should try to become; part of the *superego.* (482)

Ego transcendence. Condition often characteristic of altered states of consciousness; an experience of separation from self and personal needs, enabling one to view reality more objectively from a detached vantage point. (438)

Eidetic imagery. Ability to retain an image (usually visual) with great clarity and accuracy for a fairly long period of time. (183)

Einstellung. A mental set to perceive and/or solve a problem in a particular way. Previously learned problem-solving strategies are frequently applied to new problems even though they may be indirect or ineffective. (144)

Electroconvulsive shock treatment. A form of biomedical therapy using shock treatments in which electric current is passed briefly through the patient's head, producing temporary coma and convulsions with the intention of alleviating depression or other severe symptoms. (595)

Electroencephalogram (EEG). Recording of the minute electrical oscillations in the cerebral cortex known as brain waves; used to detect sleep stages and disturbances or pathology in brain functioning. (135)

Electromyogram (EMG). Recording of electrical activity associated with muscular responses. (135)

Elicited behavior. In conditioning, a response already in the organism's repertoire which is initiated or drawn out by some recognizable, external, physical stimulus. (97, 108)

Embryo. An organism in the early stages of prenatal development; in humans, during the first eight weeks of pregnancy. (335)

Emergency reaction. See *General adaptation syndrome.*

Emitted behavior. Behavior caused by internal conditions, which appears without the use of an external stimulus to initiate it; can be modified by operant conditioning. (108)

Emotion. A complex, subjective, cognitive process, which may be induced by environmental stimuli and mediated by physiological variables; it may have the power to motivate an organism to action. It is a felt tendency toward stimuli appraised as good, and away from those appraised as bad. (402, 405)

Emotional inoculation. Preparatory process to enable individuals to moderate anxiety and plan future reactions to an impending threatening event. (552)

Empiricism. The scientific method of relying on verifiable, factual information such as observation, sensory experience, or experimentation rather than on untestable or unobservable concepts and speculations. (342)

Encounter groups. Small therapy or personal growth groups designed to provide an intensive interpersonal experience, focusing on the current interactions and feelings that emerge within the group in an atmosphere of honesty and emotional sensitivity. (554)

Endocrine system. System composed of glands that secrete hormones which act to regulate metabolism, coordinate various body processes, and may influence emotion. (405)

Endogenous depression. Type of depressive behavior assumed to be caused by internal biochemical or genetic factors; symptoms may include retardation, insomnia, suicidal tendencies, and severe depression. (586)

Endorphins. Morphinelike substances occurring naturally in the brain and pituitary gland which mimic the effects of opiates in the body; may be neurotransmitters. (411)

Energizer. Drug with a stimulating effect, used in chemotherapy to enable a patient to feel more energetic; *imipramine* is an example of such a drug. (597)

Entropy. The amount of uncertainty in an informational system (as opposed to *redundancy*). (130)

Environmentalists. Psychologists who stress environmental rather than hereditary factors in the development of human nature, placing an emphasis on "nurture" as the determining factor. They see human nature as modifiable. (52)

Epinephrine. Hormone secreted by the adrenal medulla, the inner part of the adrenal glands, in strong emotion; associated with fear and anger reactions; also called *adrenaline*. (405)

Epileptic seizures. A nervous system disorder marked by sudden violent convulsions ending in loss of consciousness.

Epistemology. The philosophical study of the origin, nature, methods, and limits of human knowledge. (148)

Equity theory. Theory that applies to human relationships, stating that people will try to maximize their outcomes by achieving the greatest possible rewards at the minimum costs. (665)

Erogenous zones. Local body areas which upon tactile stimulation trigger sexual arousal or excitement. (239)

Eros. According to Freudian theory, the "sex instinct" or "life instinct"; encompasses all striving for creative synthesis, thus being much broader than sex drive alone. (480)

Escalation (of aggression). Second step of a violent interaction in which the individuals involved react to previous responses, the initial provocation, and the inferred perception of the intention behind the act. (701)

Escape conditioning. A form of operant conditioning in which a negative, aversive stimulus can be terminated if the organism makes the appropriate response. (101)

Ethics. A set of principles or values dealing with what is good and bad or right and wrong or with moral duty and obligation. (42)

Ethnocentrism. Tendency to hold prejudiced attitudes toward all groups different from one's own, which is assumed to be the best. (637)

Ethologist. Researcher who studies the behavior of animals in their natural habitat. (374)

Etiology. Causation; the systematic study of the causes of disorders. (32)

Euphoria. A feeling of extreme well-being or elation.

Evaluative reasoning. Critical thinking that involves judging the soundness, appropriateness, condition, or significance of an idea or product. (141)

Evil. A modern definition applies this term to situations in which force, violence, and other forms of coercion exceed institutional or morally justifiable limits. (705)

Exchange theory. Theory that human interactions can best be understood from an economic perspective, by analyzing the rewards and costs to each participant. (665)

Existential-humanistic therapy. Type of therapy which emphasizes the here-and-now of an individual who must be treated, understood, and attended to; sees individual experience rather than physical events as the basic reality; focuses on the whole organism as a complex system and not just its biology, behavior, or unconscious; also encourages a more concerned, caring orientation of therapist toward patient. (611)

Existential neurosis. Persistent anxiety about the meaninglessness of human existence that is sufficiently intense to interfere with the person's daily functioning. (576)

Existentialism. An introspective philosophy which emphasizes that individuals are responsible for their own lives and realize their existence fully through the art of choice. (611)

Experiential groups. Groups like encounter groups that provide intensive interpersonal experience. (554)

Experimental group. Group of subjects for whom the experimenter alters the independent variable or treatment variables, the influence of which is being investigated. See *Control group.*

Experimental method. Highly formalized version of the scientific method which attempts to establish a causal relationship between the independent and dependent variable. A hypothesis is tested under precisely specified conditions controlled to eliminate the effects of all extraneous variables. (45)

Experimental neurosis. Neurotic reactions produced in animals when a conditioning process involves prolonged stress and inescapable conflicts. (74)

Explosive personality. A type of personality disorder in which violent outbursts of temper may erupt into a dangerous rage reaction if the person is frustrated or rejected. (567)

Extinction. Gradual disappearance of a conditioned response when the conditioned stimulus repeatedly occurs without being followed either by reinforcement or by the unconditioned stimulus. (71) May be used as a form of behavior-modifying psychotherapy to reduce or eliminate undesirable responses. (607)

Extrasensory perception (ESP). Perception or experience not mediated by any known source of stimulation of, or activity in, the sense organs. (357)

Extrinsic motivation. Instigation for undertaking or maintaining an activity perceived as arising from external circumstances; doing something only for the sake of an anticipated reward. (392)

Facial display. A form of nonverbal expression that concerns facial movements, positions, or expressions; e.g., a smile. (409)

Factor analysis. Statistical technique used in identifying and measuring the relative importance of the underlying variables, or factors, which contribute to a complex ability, trait, or form of behavior. (478)

Fear. A rational reaction to an objective, identifiable, external danger; distinguished from free-floating, neurotic anxiety; social consequences usually depend on its situational appropriateness.

Feature analyzers. Neurons that respond selectively to trigger features. (350)

Feedback. Process by which information about the correctness of previous responses under one's control returns to the individual's "control center" so that corrections and regulations can be made where necessary to guide subsequent responding; knowledge of results. (128, 130)

Fetus. The developing mammal in the womb; from the third month after conception until birth in humans. (250)

Field. Natural environment or habitat as opposed to the laboratory; much social psychological research takes place in the field. (752)

Figure-ground relations. The tendency to perceive things as objects or events (figures) against a background, even when the stimuli are ambiguous and the foreground-background relationships are reversible. (354)

Fissures. Deep clefts or grooves separating the lobes of the cortex; major ones are named *Rolando*, vertical groove separating frontal and parietal lobes, and *Sylvius*, horizontal groove separating temporal from parietal and frontal lobes. (312)

Fixation. In Freudian theory, arrested development through failure to pass beyond one of the psychosexual stages as a result of an excess of frustration or gratification at this stage. (240)

Fixed interval schedule (FI). Intermittent schedule by which reinforcement is given regularly at the end of a certain period of time, such as every two minutes. (88)

Fixed ratio schedule (FR). Intermittent schedule by which reinforcement is given regularly after a certain number of correct responses. (87)

Flattened affect. Characteristic of some schizophrenic states in which emotions are blunted, subdued, or not expressed. (582)

Fluid abilities. Abilities determined largely by maturation or physiological factors. For example, memory span and inductive reasoning. (271)

Formal operations. The fourth of Piaget's stages of cognitive development (from 11 years on); characterized by abstract thinking and conceptualization. (193)

Forward conduction, law of. Sequence of neural activity; information is transmitted in only one direction along neurons and synapses, from dendrites to cell body to axon to synaptic knobs across synapse to next dendrites. (296)

Fovea. Area at the back of the retina which forms the point of sharpest vision. (346)

Free association. Principal psychoanalytic procedure used to probe the unconscious; patient lets his or her mind wander freely, giving a running account of every thought and feeling. (23, 601)

Free-floating anxiety. Anxiety not referable to any specific cause or situation; type of anxiety that is experienced in anxiety neurosis. (570)

Frequency. Measure of how often a response occurs; the frequency of a response per unit of time is its *rate*. (351)

Frequency distribution. An array of individual scores arranged in order from highest to lowest; the frequency with which each score is represented in a given distribution. (757)

Frequency of response. A measure of the strength of response based on the rate of making a given response.

Frigidity. A disorder in sexual functioning in females (often psychological) characterized by indifference or nonreceptivity to appropriate sexual advances and sexual stimuli. Also, the inability to experience orgasm during intercourse despite appropriate stimulation. (680)

Frustration. Denial or thwarting of motives by obstacles that lie between organism and goal. Physiological changes, as in heart rate and systolic blood pressure, may occur and persist if no opportunity for aggression against the frustration presents itself. (692)

Frustration-aggression hypothesis. A theory which holds that aggression is a drive acquired as a direct response to frustration; the greater the amount of frustration, the stronger the resulting aggressive response. (692)

F-test. Test of statistical inference used for comparing between-group variability with within-group variability for two or more groups. (764)

Fugue. Neurotic dissociative state; entails loss of memory accompanied by actual physical flight from one's present life situation to a new environment or less threatening former one. (575)

Functional analysis. The analysis of responding in terms of variations in stimulus conditions; behavior is viewed as a function of environmental contingencies.

Functional fixedness. An inhibition in perceiving a new use for an object previously associated with some other purpose, adversely affecting problem solving and creativity. (145)

Functional invariants. A concept in Piaget's theory of cognitive development; primary shapers of intellectual growth that are basic modes of interacting with the environment to make behavior appropriate to what has previously been experienced, as well as to modify behavior to fit new intellectual challenges. *Assimilation* and *accommodation* are the most important functional invariants. (237)

Functional psychosis. Severe mental disorder precipitated primarily by psychological stress, and not attributable to organic, physical causes. (579)

Gain-loss theory of attraction. Model of interpersonal attraction stating that changes in positive or negative evaluation have more impact on interpersonal attraction than does constant, unvarying evaluation; a theory developed by Aronson. (666)

Galvanic skin response (GSR). Minute changes in electrical conductivity of, or activity in, the skin, detected by a sensitive galvanometer. The reactions are commonly used as an indicator of emotional reactivity.

Ganglion. A collection of nerve cell bodies located outside the central nervous system. (312)

Ganglion cells. Neurons that connect the bipolar cells to relay areas in the brain. (346)

Gate-control theory of pain. Melzack's theory of a control system that continuously interacts to modulate pain; involves the control of afferent input by efferent processes. (410)

General adaptation syndrome. Theoretical approach developed by Selye to explain the body's reaction under continued stress, consisting of the *alarm reaction*, during which the body makes a number of complicated physiological changes in response to a stressor; the *stage of resis-*

tance, during which the organism, with the aid of increased secretions of the adrenal glands, is able to withstand the stressor for a time without showing symptoms; and the *stage of exhaustion*, in which the organism can no longer resist the stressor and may die if stress does not cease. (532)

Generalization. An important principle of learning in which stimuli perceived to be similar to those in the original learning situation come to elicit the learned response. As discrimination becomes finer, generalization becomes weaker. (69)

Generalization decrement. Process whereby responses to stimuli not directly subject to extinction will also extinguish in proportion to the similarity of the stimuli to the conditioned stimulus. (71)

Generalization techniques. Procedures introduced during and following therapy to increase the likelihood that positive changes in therapy will generalize (carry over) to the client's everyday environment.

Genes. Ultramicroscopic areas of DNA within the chromosomes; the basic unit of hereditary transmission. (227)

Genital stage. In Freudian theory, last stage of psychosexual development, starting at puberty with turning away from autoeroticism to normal interest in genitalia of others. (240)

Genotype. The genetic constitution of an organism or class of individuals; the underlying, inherited characteristics which may not be directly observable in the appearance of the phenotype. (517)

Geropsychology. The area of developmental psychology that deals with the study of old age. (219)

Gestalt psychology. A school of psychology which teaches that psychology should study the whole pattern of behavior instead of analyzing it into elements, since the whole is more than the sum of its parts. (344–345)

Give-up-itis. Syndrome afflicting some prisoners of war characterized by the loss of all hope of ever being freed and consequent loss of interest in the future; the result is emotionally caused death. (416)

Glucostatic theory. Hypothesis that food intake is regulated by feedback to the brain regarding glucose (sugar) levels in the blood. (378)

Goal-directed behavior. According to Tolman, behavior is given meaning by being purposive rather than merely mechanistic; it is directed toward particular goals and states of satisfaction. (107)

Grammar, case. Analysis of syntax in terms of the way meaningful parts of the sentence are related. (202)

Grammar, phrase structure. Analysis of the underlying structure of language according to phrase units rather than words. (200)

Grammar, transformational. Analysis of syntax in terms of the productive aspects of language and the ways in which the structure of a sentence can be altered to determine its semantic interpretation. (201)

Group dynamics. Psychological study of the dynamic properties of social interaction within groups. (626)

Group therapy. Any form of psychotherapy practiced on a group basis; more than one person treated at same time in same setting; usually nondirective in form and under the guidance of a therapist. (620)

Groupthink. Mode of decision making engaged in by people in highly cohesive groups in which a preoccupation with unanimity limits critical thinking and realistic appraisal of options. (709)

Growth motivation. Motivation in which the individual seeks to go beyond level attained in the past; to develop potentials. (487)

Habit strength. In Hull's theory of learning, a learned connection between stimulus and response; the unit of learning and a mediating variable. (79)

Habituation. Diminished physiological and psychological responsiveness to stimulus input; cessation of the orienting reaction, when the stimulus has become familiar, is constantly repeated, or is expected, thus lowering its informational value to the individual. (303)

Hallucination. Sensory impression of external objects in the absence of appropriate stimulus energy in the environment; origin of the perception is internal and not external. (439)

Hallucinogenic. Able to produce sensory hallucinations. (453)

Hallucinogens. A group of hallucinogenic, psychoactive drugs, also called the psychedelics; they include LSD-25, psilocybin, and mescaline among others, and can cause profound perceptual alteration. (453)

Halo effect. An error of judgment to which rating scales are subject; it is the tendency, when interviewing or rating an individual on a particular trait, to be influenced by one's opinion of some other trait or by one's overall impression of the individual. (502)

Hebephrenic schizophrenia. Form of schizophrenia in which the most severe disorganization appears; characterized by inappropriate affect, and silly, childlike behavior, frequent hallucinations, and other grossly inappropriate thoughts, affect, and behavior. (583)

Hedonism. Doctrine that asserts that personal pleasure or happiness is the sole good and chief goal in life. (52)

Heterosexuality. Primary sexual interest in members of the opposite sex. (680–681)

Heuristics. The informal cognitive strategies, or "rules of thumb" used in making judgments or solving problems. (151)

Hidden observer. That part of the self which maintains an intellectual awareness and contact with reality even under hypnosis. (14)

Hierarchy of needs. According to Maslow's theory of personality, the arrangement of a person's inborn needs according to certain priorities; needs at a low level in the hierarchy must be satisfied before those on higher levels take precedence. (487)

Higher-order conditioning. Process by which, once a conditioned response has been established, the conditioned stimulus may in turn function as an unconditioned stimulus in setting up a conditioned response to a third (or higher-order) neutral stimulus. (70)

Higher-order knowledge structures. The organization of information into coherent molar units that allow for the efficient transformation and integration of new information on the basis of our accumulated wisdom. (149)

Hippocampus. A subcortical structure of the brain that is crucial for recent memory and important in mating. (312)

Holistic approach. A psychological approach to the study of behavior stating that the proper perspective for the analysis of behavior must be in terms of the whole organism, not merely in terms of its functioning parts. (284)

Holistic medicine. An approach to health care that attempts to reorient a person's whole life-style rather than to treat only diseased organs. (536–537)

Homeostasis. The complex process of maintaining stability between the internal and external environment so that the body's chemical balance can be maintained and social and biological needs can be satisfied; homeostasis on the physiological level is largely automatic. (375)

Homosexuality. Primary sexual interest in members of one's own sex. (682)

Homunculus. Miniature human figure, thought by some early scientists to exist in the sperm cells, needing only nourishment and time to unfold and develop into an adult. (218)

Hope. Cognitive concept concerning the expectation of the instrumental value of one's behavior for effecting a change in the environment. (417)

Hopelessness. A state of being without hope, which results in apathy, inaction, and passive resignation. (416)

Hormone. Any of various internally secreted compounds, formed in the endocrine glands, that affect the functions of specifically receptive organs or tissues when transported to them by body fluids. (282)

Humanism. An approach to psychology in which the emphasis is on studying human experience, both private and public behavior, and the uniqueness and wholeness of individuals. (27)

Hygienic inducement. In the field of work motivation, those motivational factors that are aspects of the job environment necessary to avoid dissatisfaction, but insufficient to create satisfaction. (389)

Hyperactive child. A child of normal intelligence exhibiting a syndrome of behaviors characterized as being highly distractable, unable to focus attention or sit still in class. (597)

Hypertension. A symptom of stress-related disease in which the diastolic blood pressure registers above the medically acceptable level of 90. (534)

Hypnagogic imagery. Visual or other sensory experiences without adequate external sensory stimuli that occur during stage 1 sleep, the transition phase between being awake and sleeping. (446)

Hypnosis. An alternate state of awareness induced by a variety of techniques and characterized by deep relaxation, increased susceptibility to hypnotic suggestions, changes in sense of self-control and in level of motivation. (426)

Hypnotic analgesia. Upon suggestion, the insensitivity to pain of a hypnotized subject. (428)

Hypnotizability. The level of susceptibility to hypnosis of an individual; the ease with which one comes to be hypnotized as measured by a hypnotic susceptibility scale. (426)

Hypochondria. Neurotic preoccupation with the body's activities and the state of one's health. (576)

Hypoglycemia. Lowered blood-sugar level, as following an injection of insulin. (378)

Hypothalamus. A key structure of the subcortex, important in the regulation of metabolism, temperature, hunger, thirst, and emotional behavior; control center for much of the endocrine system through connections with the pituitary gland. (313)

Hypothesis. A tentative explanation or statement of the relation between two (or more) events or variables, often based on the results of previous observations, that is tested in an experiment. Experimental results may reject or support it although it can never be conclusively proven. (38)

Hysterical neurosis. Type of neurosis characterized by involuntary psychogenic loss of motor or sensory function. For example, physical paralysis or loss of memory. (573)

Iconic representation. Representation of stimuli that are conceptually stored according to their perceptual, sensory image. (160)

Id. In Freud's three-part division of the personality, the primitive part of the unconscious, composed of instinctive organic cravings and characterized by unrestrained pleasure-seeking impulses. (482)

Identification. A cognitive process whereby one person adopts the point of view (perspective) of another person or a character in a story. During child development the desire to be like some powerful authority figure creates pressures toward social conformity. (19)

Idiographic approach. Psychological approach to understanding human nature which focuses on the special circumstances and unique aspects of each individual's personality in order to understand him or her. (53, 472)

Illusion. A misinterpretation of the relationships among presented stimuli, so that the percept does not correspond to the physical reality that gives rise to it. (343)

Images. Mental pictures of actual sensory experience in the absence of any external stimulus. (138)

Implosive therapy. Form of behavior therapy developed by Stampfl; extinction occurs as frightening stimuli are imagined without harmful result; called *implosive* because the frightening stimuli produce an inner explosion—an *implosion*—of panic. (608)

Impotence. A disorder of sexual functioning in the male (often psychological), involving the inability to get or maintain an erection or achieve orgasm. (680)

Inadequate personality. A type of personality disorder in which social skills, work motivation, and sense of responsibility are not adequately developed. (568)

Independent variable. Factor whose effects (on the dependent variable) are being studied, and which is systematically manipulated while the other variables are held constant; in psychological experiments it is often a stimulus condition (S) whose effect on a response (R) is being studied. The independent variable is also the *predictor* variable used to predict outcomes or behaviors. (46)

Index variable. A variable that is itself not causal but is a manifest sign of an underlying causal variable. Age is an index variable in developmental psychology. (221)

Inductive reasoning. Method of reasoning by which, on the basis of specific observations and instances, an inference is drawn about a general state or abstract concept which organizes and makes meaningful those separate elements. (141)

Ineffability. Often characteristic of an alternate state of consciousness; individuals often profess an inability to put into words, to communicate, a description of their experiences. (438)

Inference. A conclusion or decision reached by reasoning from known facts or evidence. The inference often goes beyond observations, is broader, more general than the evidence on which it is based. (762)

Inference strategies. Cognitive strategies used in the process of making predictions, explanations, and decisions. (152)

Information processing. Approach to the study of cognitive processes that uses computer programs as a precise, rigorous model for thought. (127)

Information store. The memory subsystem where facts are stored as data within an information processing system. (127)

Inhibition. Suppression or restraint of behavior or an event; term has many specific meanings at all levels of analysis. (70)

Innate. Inborn or inherited; not learned. (480)

Inner-directed person. An individual who is controlled by early implanted values and goal orientations; such individuals perceive themselves as having a greater amount of control over their environment than do "externals." (391, 394)

Insanity. A legal concept applied to any mental condition that renders the individual incapable of ethical and moral judgment and legally not responsible for his or her actions. (578)

Insomnia. A sleep disorder in which inability to sleep interferes with efficient daytime functioning. (448)

Instinct. Innate behavior pattern that is unaffected by practice; invariant sequence of complex behaviors that is observed in all members of a species and released by specific stimuli in the apparent absence of learning. (479)

Instrumental conditioning. A type of behavioral conditioning in which the subject learns to make a response that leads to a reward or prevents a punishment; in contrast to respondent conditioning, no eliciting stimulus is presented. (62)

Instrumental response. The reinforcement-seeking response; in a motivational state, an organism's behavior of searching or working to obtain a goal or reward. (377)

Insulin. Hormone secreted by the pancreas which helps the body to metabolize sugar and keep the blood sugar level steady. (378)

Intellectualization. Process or defense mechanism that reduces anxiety in a threatening situation by turning it into an abstract problem or by explaining it in such a way as to reduce the threat. (716)

Intelligence. The global capacity to profit from experience; it is a complex mental ability that includes such primary abilities as verbal comprehension, space visualization, reasoning ability, numerical ability; operationally defined, intelligence is what intelligence tests measure. (514)

Intelligence quotient (IQ). Measure of intelligence obtained by dividing the individual's mental age (MA), as determined by performance on standardized test items, by chronological age (CA) and then multiplying by 100. An IQ of 100 is considered to be average. (514)

Interference theory. Theory that forgetting is caused by new information interfering with what has already been learned. (171)

Internal representations. Nonverbal mental images of a spatial or visual character that play an important role in the creative process. (139)

Interneurons. Nerve cells with many short dendrites and a short axon, the latter often giving off branches called collaterals; interconnect sensory input pathways and motor output pathways within the central nervous system; also called *associative neurons* or *internuncial neurons.* (290)

Interval scale. Scale of measurement possessing all of the properties of the nominal and ordinal scales in addition to the property of equal units; i.e., that equal differences in scores represent equal differences in what is being measured. (756)

Intervening variables. Inferred processes that link stimuli and responses. They are assumed to be affected by experience with (measurable) stimulus events and in turn, to influence specific responding. (108)

Intrinsic motivation. Perceived source of energy for responding in a given context coming from within the person; doing something for its "own sake." (392)

Introspective analysis. Careful self-observation of mental content; technique for retrieving original elements of psychological experience, without the distortion of meaning and interpretation. (342)

Introversion—extraversion. A personality dimension that describes people by the degree in which they need other people as sources of reward and cues to appropriate behaviors. Extraverts are more socially responsive than introverts, who rely more on nonsocial stimulation. (477, 506)

Invertebrates. Creatures without a backbone.

Inverted-U function. Relation between arousal and effectiveness of performance—increased arousal increases efficiency only up to a point and beyond that has negative effects. (531)

Involuntary response. An unlearned, automatic response of an organism to an eliciting stimulus (65)

Involutional melancholia. Psychotic reaction characterized by abnormal anxiety, agitation, delusions, and depression; occurs in later years without previous history of psychosis; may be characterized chiefly by depression or can center around paranoid ideas, more frequently diagnosed in women. (586)

Iodopsin. Photopigment found in the cones of the eye; three types of iodopsin correspond to the wave lengths of blue, green, and red light. (347)

James-Lange theory. Theory that emotion consists of the bodily changes that occur in response to an exciting event, holding that we feel sad because we cry rather than vice versa; it was the first to challenge the idea that mental processes control bodily reactions. (404)

Kinesthetic sense. Somatic sense of active movement. (345)

Labyrinthine sense. Somatic sense of passive movement and body position. (345)

Laissez-faire style of leadership. Nondirective, nonparticipatory style of leadership in which the leader provides resources only when requested to do so. (634)

Language. An arbitrary system of signs, symbols, or sounds agreed upon by two or more language users that enables communication between them through encoding and decoding thoughts and experiences. (188)

Latency of response. A measure of the strength of conditioning based on the length of time elapsing between the onset of the conditioned stimulus and the response. (71)

Latent. Condition of existing in a hidden, dormant, or repressed form, but capable of being evoked or elicited at a later time.

Latent content. In Freudian dream analysis, the hidden content of a dream, which indicates the individual's true wishes; changed to the symbolic but more acceptable manifest content. (450)

Latent fat. Condition in which individuals with an abundance of adipocytes have a potential to become obese because of their high base level of fat stores, even if they are currently skinny as a result of dieting. (382)

Latent learning. Associations learned from experience and observation that are not performed until the organism is appropriately motivated. (109)

Latent stage. In Freudian theory, fourth stage of psychosexual development, during which less conscious sexual interest is thought to be present. (240)

Lateral geniculate nucleus. Relay point in the thalamus, through which impulses pass going from the eye to the occipital cortex. (346)

Lateral specialization. "Two sidedness" of brain function unique to humans, such that the two hemispheres of the brain are specialized to carry out different functions. (324)

Law of effect. A theory formulated by Thorndike that S-R connections are strengthened by satisfying events and weakened by unsatisfying or unsuccessful ones. (79)

Leadership. Capacity possessed by individuals who exert more influence than other members on a group; the traits possessed by an effective leader include intelligence, achievement, responsibility, participation, and status. (633)

Learned helplessness. A sense of helplessness when an organism learns as a result of prior experience that its responses have no effect on a noxious, aversive, traumatic environment; has negative effects on motivation, learning, and performance; analogous to depression in humans. (418)

Learning model. An orientation to the study of human nature that emphasizes the environmental conditions which elicit and maintain behaviors (both desirable and undesirable ones).

Legitimacy knowledge. The learned awareness that the significant group(s) one identifies with are recognized as acceptable and worthwhile—or not. (637)

Legitimate authority. One seen as a valid representative of society, authorized to demand compliance, and who controls significant reinforcers; presence may foster blind obedience to authority. (707)

Lens. Transparent structure of the eye which focuses light rays onto the sensitive retina. (346)

Lesion. Destruction of a portion of the brain (or other tissue) by accident, by disease, or through an operation of either an experimental or medical nature. (320)

Libido. Broadly conceived sexual forces; the energy of Freud's creative drive, *Eros.* (480)

Life change rating. A scale developed to measure the degree of adjustment required by various kinds of life changes, both positive and negative. (539)

Limbic system. Region around the upper end of the brain stem that is active in functions of attention, emotion, motivation, and memory. (313)

Linear perspective. Perceptual phenomenon of objects appearing both smaller and closer together as they become more distant. (356)

Lithium. Psychoactive drug used in therapy to prevent recurring psychotic mood swings in manic-depressive disorders. (597)

Locus of control. Generalized beliefs (expectancies) about whether one's behavior and desired outcomes are contingent on one's own behavior (internal), or on external forces. (506)

Logotherapy. School of existential analysis originated by Frankl which focuses on the individual's need to see meaning in his or her life; emphasizes spiritual and ethical values; concepts beyond the material ones in a given life environment. (612)

Longitudinal design. Research approach in which individuals from the same birth cohort are tested repeatedly at different ages. (224)

Long-term memory. Relatively permanent memory system with a theoretically unlimited capacity; however, information is not always readily accessible. (164)

Lysergic acid diethylamide (LSD). Hallucinogenic drug capable of producing vivid imagery, hallucinations, disorganization of thought processes, and symptoms of mental disorder; has also been used in psychotherapy and in cases of terminal illness. (457)

Machiavellians. Individuals who share in common with Machiavelli a set of beliefs about manipulative tactics and relative standards of morality; those who score high on the Christie Mach scale. (508)

Mach scale. A scale of measurement that differentiates the degree to which individuals endorse Machiavelli's rules of conduct; Low Machs are those with absolute standards of behavior, while High Machs are those who have relative standards of manipulative behavior. (508)

Manic reactions or episodes. Psychotic reactions characterized by periods of extreme elation, unbounded euphoria usually without sufficient reason; may alternate with depressive episodes. (585)

Manifest content. In Freudian dream analysis, the surface content of a dream that we remember; masks the unacceptable, emotionally painful latent content. (450)

Mantra. A sound pattern that can be meditated on; in transcendental mediation, syllables drawn from the Hindu holy books that are silently chanted by meditators, who exclude all other thoughts from their minds. (549)

Marijuana. Psychoactive drug derived from the cannabis plant; behavioral effects depend to a great extent upon personal and social factors, but there is no potential for physical addiction. (455)

Masochism. A deviant use of pain motivation, it is a desire to inflict pain on oneself, or to suffer pain at the hands of others; a form of pain as pleasure. (701)

Mean. Measure of central tendency, more familiarly known as the average; obtained by adding a group of measurements together and dividing the sum by the number of measurements; also called the *arithmetic mean.* (49, 758)

Means-ends-readiness. An action tendency that an organism brings to a learning situation (due to its heredity and prior experience). Tolman proposed that it caused the selective responsiveness of organisms to particular environmental stimuli. (108)

Mechanistic approach. An approach to the study of physiological processes put forth by Descartes which holds that perception and other bodily processes are mechanistically determined, that is, completely explainable according to the scientific laws of physics and chemistry. (283)

Median. A measure of central tendency of scores or measures in a distribution; the median is the middle measure when the scores have been ordered in order of magnitude, that is, the same number of scores will be higher or lower than the median. (49, 758)

Mediating variable. Unseen, inner process inferred to be intervening between observed stimuli and observed response, also called *intervening variable* or *hypothetical construct.* (108)

Medical model. Model of psychopathology in which psychological and psychiatric behavior problems are viewed as symptoms of a disease state. (563, 599)

Meditation. Conscious concentration of attention and awareness on a single unvarying source of stimulation for an extended period of time; often practiced in the hope that it will facilitate alternate states of consciousness in which one can perceive the spontaneous flow of experience. (549)

Memory. The mental capacity for, or the product of, storing and retrieving previous experiences. (157)

Menopause. The period of time in which mature women undergo abrupt physiological and psychological changes as a result of the end of menstruation and the menstrual cycle. (266)

Mental age (MA). Degree of mental development as measured by standardized intelligence tests; based on age at which a representative group of children make a given score; used in determining IQ. (514)

Mental illness. Term from medical model of psychological disturbance referring to a variety of abnormal behavior patterns severe enough to interfere with the ordinary conduct of life; includes motivational, emotional, and social maladjustments. (561)

Mental retardation. Below-normal intelligence (IQ below approximately 68), due to chronic defects in cognitive capacity such that mental age lags far behind chronological age.

Mescaline. A hallucinogenic drug derived from the peyote cactus, the action of which is similar to that of epinephrine; investigation has found that it can induce a state comparable to schizophrenia; has been used for therapeutic and religious purposes. (457)

Mesmerism. Hypnotic induction by Mesmer's method; believed to involve animal magnetism, an alleged spiritlike force from the planets which could be contained and transmitted to others for therapeutic purposes. (427)

Message. The content and ideas that are communicated; a variable in the study of attitude change. (648)

Metabolism. Chemical processes that take place in all living tissue involving the breakdown of nutrients, by which energy is provided to carry on the life processes. (304)

Metaphor. Figure of speech in which a word that usually denotes one thing is used to describe something else that it does not literally denote, as in the metaphor of the brain as computer. (147)

Method of loci. A mnemonic device for improving memory by associating people or items to be recalled with particular locations (such as clock positions, seats around a table, etc.) (182)

Microelectrode. Fine wire inserted into brain regions through which minute electrical current may be passed to stimulate cortical activity, or from which such activity can be recorded. (319)

Microscopic level. Level of psychological analysis wherein interest centers on the smallest discernible parts, events, and subunits of the organism (e.g., study of biochemical reactions within a brain cell). (55)

Mind. The capacity for thought, where thought is the integrative activity of the brain. (401)

Mnemonic strategies. Techniques for encoding material to be learned for more efficient remembering. (181)

Mode. A measure of central tendency; the most frequently occurring measure in a distribution. (49)

Model. Theoretical framework or structure developed in one field, but applied to another in order to lend a clearer, more familiar perspective for understanding, although the model itself is not the explanation. (21)

Molar level. Level of psychological analysis concerned with the functioning of the whole organism or of whole systems within the organism. For example, the study of emotional disorders or vandalism. (55)

Molecular level. Intermediate level of psychological analysis; concerned with processes larger than those at a microscopic level, yet still small, quantifiable units. For example, study of a specific brain-wave pattern of arousal or reaction times to stimulus events. (55)

Mood. A distinctive emotional quality subjectively experienced by the person. (404)

Motivation. The source of energy within an organism assumed to affect its tendency toward action. Motivation that arises from states of deprivation makes reinforcers effective, but motivation may also arise from one's values and beliefs, as in esthetic or religious activities. (96)

Motivational theory of forgetting. Theory that forgetting may be intentional; that individuals will forget or remember items of information according to their value and importance to the individual. (177)

Motive. A condition, usually social or psychological, which serves to direct the individual toward a certain goal. (371)

Motor cortex. The part of the brain which is responsible for initiating and integrating the voluntary action of the muscles of the body. (315)

Motoric reproduction processes. Factor influencing observational learning whereby the performance of learned behavior depends upon an individual's ability or skill to carry out the modeled activity. (117)

Motor nerve fiber. See *efferent nerve fiber.*

Motor neurons. Neurons that excite the muscles to respond. (290)

Multidimensional. General term for events that are characterized as having more than one dimension; in measurement, the analysis of behavior in terms of its many different dimensions. (393)

Multiple personality. Extreme neurotic dissociative state in which the individual develops two or more distinct personalities that alternate in consciousness, each personality being based on sets of motives which are in conflict with those of the others; though dramatic, multiple personality is a rare occurrence. (575)

Mutt-and-Jeff approach. A tactic used in police interrogations in which an investigator who seems pleasant is switched with a cruel or relentless investigator in order to increase belief in and willingness to confess to the friendly investigator. (648)

Myelin sheath. Fatty white covering that surrounds axons and nerve branches of large diameter. Nerve impulses travel faster and with less energy expenditure along these myelinated paths. (292)

Naive realism. The belief that what one perceives is the only reality. This early developmental stage is altered with the emergence of logical and abstract reasoning. (236)

Narcolepsy. A serious sleep disorder in which an individual falls suddenly into REM sleep during the daytime. These brief "sleep attacks" are probably due to brain abnormalities. (448)

Nativists. Psychologists who hold that human nature is determined by innate, hereditary factors. They believe that the environment merely develops a nature that is already genetically determined. (52)

Nature-nurture controversy. In determining the relative contributions to a particular characteristic, such as intelligence or personality, psychologists differ in the importance they attach to heredity (nature) vs. environmental experiences, such as learning (nurture). (234)

Need. Biological or psychological motive condition that serves to direct an individual toward a certain goal. (487)

Negative discriminative stimulus. A stimulus in whose presence responding is not reinforced, and is thus inhibited. (82)

Negative reinforcer. A reinforcer whose termination increases the probability that the response it follows will occur again under similar circumstances. (101)

Negative transference. Instance of transference in which the feelings attached to the analyst are those of hostility, envy, or some other negative emotion. (602)

Neocortex. Cortex of the brain, which has become more complex during the upward development of more complex species of animals; most highly developed in humans. (335)

Neo-Freudian theories. A group of personality theories held by modern psychoanalysts who have modified Freud's basic theory in various ways; includes Jung's and Adler's theories. (484)

Nerve impulse. Electrochemical excitation propagated along a neuron or chain of neurons; the means of receiving and transmitting information in the nervous system. (291)

Neural network. A large assembly of neurons organized to process information of particular kinds for specified functions, as in visual networks. (311)

Neuroglia. Network of cells in which the entire complex of neurons is embedded and that nourish and protect the neurons; also called *glial cells.* (288)

Neurology. Psychiatric, medical study of the brain and nervous system and the diseases thereof.

Neuron. Individual nerve cell; the basic unit of the nervous system. (287)

Neuroscience. The interdisciplinary scientific study of nervous system functioning (by neurologists, physiological psychologists, biochemists, and others).

Neurosis. Emotional disorder characterized by loss of joy in living and excessive anxiety, the true cause of which is not recognized, and overuse of defense mechanisms against anxiety. (569)

Neurotransmitter. Chemical substance released into the synapse at the presynaptic terminal allowing information transmission from one neuron to others. (331)

Nodes of Ranvier. Regularly occurring points of constriction along the myelin sheath; they serve to improve the reliability and velocity of nervous signal transmission by allowing the impulse to skip from node to node along the axons. (292)

Nominal scale. Scale of measurement in which numbers are used solely to differentiate one individual or class from another; the numbers involved do not represent an amount; a qualitative classification, naming. (353)

Nomothetic approach. Psychological approach to understanding human nature which tries to establish general relationships between behavior and causal conditions presumed to be shared by all individuals. (53, 470)

Non-rapid eye movement (NREM) sleep. Sleep in which the rapid eye movements characteristic of REM sleep do not occur; consists of four stages varying in sleep depth and brain wave patterns. Also called *orthodox sleep*. (444)

Nonsense syllable. Syllable consisting of a vowel between two consonants, which is meaningless; invented by Ebbinghaus for use in the study of memory. (169)

Nonverbal expression. Any transmission of information or communication without words or word symbols. (409)

Noradrenaline. See *Norepinephrine*.

Norepinephrine. Hormone secreted by the inner part of the adrenal glands, the adrenal medulla, during strong emotion; associated with anger reactions; brings about a number of bodily changes, including constriction of the blood vessels near the body's surface; also called *noradrenaline*. (405)

Norm. Standard based on measurement of a large group of people; used for comparing the standardized score of an individual with those of others within a defined group. See also *Social norm*. (499)

Normal. Conforming to the usual or the norm of expected reactions or values; also used to mean healthy, adequate adjustment. (468)

Normal curve. Graph of the normal distribution in the ideal case, where mean, median, and mode are identical and distribution is symmetrical around this central value. (515, 760)

Normal distribution. Tendency for most members of a large population to cluster around a central point or average with respect to a given trait, with the rest spreading out to the two extremes in a symmetrical bell-shaped curve. (515)

Nucleus. Specialized protoplasm in each cell that directs activities in the cytoplasm. It contains the chromosomes, and is necessary for cell reproduction; also, a group of nerve cell bodies located within the CNS. (287)

Null hypothesis. Hypothesis that the variable being manipulated has *no* effect on the behavior being measured; that following experimental treatment, there will be no difference between the experimental and control groups. Statistical inference tests are designed so as to reject or fail to reject the null hypotheses (H°). (46)

Obesity. Excessive body weight; food addiction; a social disease common in an affluent society like our own, it has serious psychological and physiological effects. (380)

Objective anxiety. See *Fear*.

Objective reality. The independently measurable and verifiable physical world. (341)

Observational learning. Learning by observing and identifying with a model; important in childhood learning; influenced by attentional, retention, motoric reproduction, and reinforcement and motivational processes. Concept important in social learning theories. (115)

Obsession. Persistent and irrational idea, usually unpleasant, that comes into consciousness and cannot be banished voluntarily. (568–569)

Obsessive-compulsive neurosis. A neurotic pattern characterized by the presence of anxiety, with persisting unwanted thoughts and/or the compulsion to repeat ritualistic acts over and over. (568–569)

Occipital lobe. Portion of the cortex located at the back of the brain that receives nerve impulses from the eye. (312)

Ontogeny. The course of development of an individual organism. (335)

Operant behavior. Voluntarily emitted response already within an organism's behavioral repertoire that serves to operate on (i.e., have an effect on) its environment. (67)

Operant conditioning. A form of learning in which the rate of occurrence of an emitted response varies as a function of its stimulus consequences. Behavior is studied as it is contingently related to schedules of reinforcement. Also called *Skinnerian conditioning*. (79)

Operationism. A means of defining an abstract concept like hunger, or an internal event such as a dream, by framing the definition in terms of the operations used to measure or observe it. Hunger might be defined operationally as "x number of hours without food." Such definitions are important in reducing ambiguity from scientific concepts for experimental replication. (33)

Opponent cells. Cells in the lateral geniculate nucleus that make color vision possible by subtracting the output of one type of cone from the output of another. (348)

Oral stage. In Freudian theory, the first stage of psychosexual development, in which the mouth is the primary source of pleasure. (240)

Ordinal scale. An ordered scale of measurement that serves to distinguish one individual or score from another, and also to indicate whether one individual has more or less of the trait being measured. (353)

Organic psychosis. Mental disorder resulting from injury to the nervous system or from such conditions as glandular deficiency or poisons. (579)

Organ of Corti. The receptor for hearing, which is located in the cochlea and contains the hair cells where the fibers of the auditory nerve originate. (350)

Orgasm. The physical (and emotional) sensation experienced at the culmination of a sexual act; typically followed by ejaculation of semen in the male and vaginal discharge in the female. (679)

Orienting reflex. A set of behavioral and physiological adjustments induced by the perception of a novel, significant, or threatening stimulus. (362)

Orthogenetic principle. In developmental psychology, the principle that growth and responsiveness proceed from general and diffuse to specific and focused. (231)

Oscilloscope. Instrument used for the study of the brain's activity in which the sudden voltage change that occurs with the firing of neurons appears as a visible wave pattern upon a fluorescent screen. (294)

Ossicles. The three small bones (the hammer, anvil, and stirrup) located in the middle ear. (350)

Outer membrane. Cell structure that contains the cell contents and separates the cellular material from the external environment. (287)

Oval window. Membrane situated between the middle and inner ear. (350)

Overjustification effect. The change in the quality and the quantity of a product of work when external rewards are imposed upon the original intrinsic motivation for engaging in the activity. (392)

Overlearning. Technique for improving memory that involves additional practice after achieving mastery. (179)

Overt. Open to view; not concealed; public and directly observable.

Paired-associate learning. Learning in which the subject is first presented with paired items and must then respond with one word or syllable when given the other word or syllable with which it had been paired. (173)

Paradigm. An example or pattern; in research it is a basic procedure or design which represents the essential features of a process being investigated. (67)

Paradoxical intention. A technique of logotherapy useful in the short-term treatment of obsessive-compulsive and phobic patients, which deals with their anticipatory anxiety by encouraging them to do or think about the very thing they fear; similar to implosive therapy. (612)

Paranoia. Psychosis characterized by systematized, intricate delusions. (584)

Paranoid reactions. A psychotic pattern of reaction marked by the pathological symptom of persistent delusions. (584)

Paranoid schizophrenia. Type of schizophrenia characterized by poorly systematized, often hostile, suspicious, aggressive delusions, and delusions of grandeur; also personality disorganization. (583)

Parapsychology. The scientific study of psychical phenomena. (357)

Partial reinforcement. Intermittent reinforcement of a response; responses acquired under these conditions are more resistant to extinction than those developed under schedules of continuous reinforcement. (87)

Passive-aggressive personality. A type of personality disorder in which hostility is expressed indirectly in passive ways through dependence and resistance. (568)

Pathology. Diseased or abnormal physical, mental, emotional, or social state.

Pattern recognition. Identification of a stimulus according to its form or features that allow it to be assigned to particular categories. (160)

Pavlovian conditioning. See *Classical conditioning.*

Peak experiences. According to Maslow's theory of personality, moments of highest happiness and fulfillment; experienced by self-actualized individuals. (488)

Perceived reality. An individual's experience of objective reality. (341)

Perception. The process through which organisms understand their environment by means of their senses. (341)

Perceptual constancy. The perceptual-cognitive process through which a stimulus object is recognized as unchanged despite apparent changes perceived by the retina of its varied size, shape, or brightness. (358)

Performance test. Test in which muscular responses rather than verbal ones are required; may be used for intelligence testing. (516)

Peripheral nervous system. A system of fibers connecting the receptors to the central nervous system or connecting the central nervous system to muscles and glands (effectors). (285)

Personality. What characterizes an individual; the sum total of the ways in which an individual characteristically reacts to and interacts with others. (467)

Personality assessment. Describing and analyzing differences between individuals in their abilities, intelligence, creativity, and personality by means of objective measurements. (498)

Personality disorder. A form of psychopathology characterized by chronic behavior patterns that disturb others but rarely the person; also called character disorder. (568)

Personification. In Sullivan's theory, an image a person has of someone else; largely determines how he will react to that individual. (242)

Persuasion. Systematic attempts to influence another person's thoughts, feelings, and actions by means of communicated arguments. (645)

Phallic stage. In psychoanalytic theory, the third stage of psychosexual development (between third and fifth year) when genital manipulation and exploration occurs and there is a strong attraction for the parent of the opposite sex, with jealousy toward the same-sexed parent. (240)

Phenomenal absolutism. Uncritical certainty of the naive observer that he or she is perceiving in a direct, unmediated way the attributes of various objects. (341)

Phenomenal field. In Carl Rogers' personality theory, private world of individual experience, that makes up a person's unique frame of reference. (485)

Phenomenologists. Psychologists who approach the study of human nature by seeking to understand consciousness. In contrast to the behaviorists they are interested in making use of subjective individual experience, introspective reports, and mental processes to derive their understanding of the world from the subject's point of view. (26)

Phenotype. The observable appearance or constitution of an organism that results from the interaction of the genotype and the environment. (517)

Pheromone. Odor cues that arouse sexual desire in animals. (303)

Phi phenomenon. Perception of a moving light when, in reality, the stimulus is two stationary lights going on and off in succession. (343)

Phobic reaction. A neurotic defense pattern, it is a process of displacing free-floating anxiety onto some external environmental object which there is no objective reason to fear; leads to avoidance of that specific object or situation. (571)

Phonemes. Basic, distinctive units of sound that make up a particular language. (195)

Phonological level. Level of linguistic analysis concerned with the units of sound (phonemes) that make up speech. (194)

Phrenology. The false belief that the personality consists of various distinct "faculties," each located in a specific area of the brain and evidenced through "bumps" on the skull. (317)

Phylogeny. The evolutionary development of a species. (335)

Physiological dependence. Property of certain addictive drugs such that prolonged drug use makes the body physically dependent on the chemical for continued normal functioning. (294, 474)

Physiological psychology. Branch of psychology which studies the relationship between the biological and physiological functioning of an organism and its experience and behavior. (283)

Pituitary gland. Endocrine gland associated directly with growth. It releases pituitary growth hormone when activated by the hypothalamus. It is in turn responsible for activating many of the other endocrine glands. (304)

Placebo. A chemically inactive substance administered in such a way that patients or research subjects believe they are receiving an active drug. In some cases reactions to the placebo are comparable to those of the active drug. (412)

Place theory. A theory of hearing developed by Helmholtz, who maintained that the basilar membrane consisted of a series of resonating fibers each tuned to a different frequency. (351)

Plateau. The portion of a performance curve in which response strength temporarily stops changing (levels off) with further reinforced practice. If the leveling off is permanent then the response is said to be at asymptote. (679)

Pleasure centers. Certain sites in the brain, electrical stimulation of which is positively reinforcing to the organism. (319)

Polarized state. The steady or resting state of a neuron in which it is not transmitting any information. The electrical condition of the cell is such that inside the membrane is negatively charged while outside is positively charged. (290)

Population. The total group from which samples are selected for study; also called *universe.* (48)

Positive regard. Approval of an individual obtained both from self and others; need for positive regard may conflict with an individual's drive toward self-actualization in terms of overreliance on acceptance of others. (486)

Positive reinforcer. A reinforcer whose presentation increases the probability that the response it follows will occur again under similar circumstances. (95)

Positive transference. Instance of transference in which the feelings attached to the analyst are those of love, admiration, or some other positive emotion. (602)

Posthypnotic suggestion. A suggestion given a hypnotized subject to carry out at a time after the termination of the hypnotic experience in response to a given cue. (428)

Precognition. Form of extrasensory perception involving knowledge of future events. (357)

Preconscious. In Freudian theory, the ideas, thoughts, and images which a person is not aware of at a given moment, but which can be brought into awareness, made conscious, with little or no difficulty; includes anxiety and defense mechanisms. (481)

Predictability. Foreknowledge of the likelihood of events, it prevents against learned helplessness by reducing uncertainty; it serves to increase a subject's perceptual control of the environment. (419)

Predisposition. Likelihood that an individual will develop certain symptoms (for example, schizophrenic reactions) under certain stressful conditions because of prior factors, such as hereditary ones and early life experiences. (581)

Prefrontal lobotomy. Form of psychosurgery in which the nerve fibers connecting the hypothalamus with the prefrontal lobes of the brain are severed, the purpose being to cut intellectual processes off from the emotional processes which normally accompany them; not currently as widely used as in earlier years. (326)

Prejudice. A cluster of learned beliefs, attitudes, and values (usually negative) that bias an individual toward the members of a particular group and give rise to behavioral discrimination; usually based on incomplete information and relative immunity to contrary informational input. (637)

Prelinguistic period. Period of language development preceding the appearance of the beginnings of "true" speech; covers approximately the first year of life. (205–206)

Preoperational thought. Second of Piaget's stages of cognitive development (from 2–7 years); characterized by transductive reasoning, egocentrism, and development of the capacity to represent the external world symbolically. (258–259)

Primary mental abilities. The relatively independent abilities, identified through factor analysis, which make up "general intelligence." Among them are verbal, spatial, numerical, and reasoning abilities. (236)

Primary motor area. The portion of the neocortex concerned with motor functions; located immediately in front of the fissure of Rolando. (318)

Primary reinforcer. A stimulus whose power to alter the strength of responding derives from its biological significance to the organism, such as food or water to hungry or thirsty people. (89)

Proactive inhibition. The interference produced by earlier learning on subsequent memory or performance with newly learned materials. (172)

Proactive interference. Difficulty in remembering certain material because of the interference of material or associations learned prior to it. (171)

Problem solving. Mode of response that will achieve a goal through the elimination of obstacles. (141–142)

Processors. Those aspects of an information processing system that carry out the system's operations. They retrieve stored information and programs, search for additional information and direct attention to new inputs. (128)

Productive memory. Theory of memory as a process of active reconstruction, rather than simple retrieval. (175)

Projective techniques. Methods of measuring personality traits in which the subject is presented with a standardized set of ambiguous or neutral stimuli and is encouraged to interpret freely what he sees in them. (503)

Propaganda. Systematic, widespread promotion of particular ideas, doctrines, or practices to further one's cause or to discredit that of the opposition; often the real purpose or source of this form of persuasion is hidden from the intended target; usually directed toward changing political beliefs. (646)

Prosocial aggression. Aggression directed toward socially acceptable purposes, for example, punishment for rule-breaking or defending a child against a bully. (690)

Protocol. Systematic record of the thought processes involved in problem solving; used in developing computer programs for the study of artificial intelligence. (133)

Provocation. Inciting to action, the first step of a violent interaction; interpersonal aggression is often initiated by mutual provocation, often intentional. (701)

Proximal stimulus. The retinal pattern of an object (as opposed to the object itself). (359)

Pseudoconditioning. Phenomenon in which behavior similar to conditioned behavior is obtained without the typical pairing of stimuli, which is the essence of true conditioning. (73)

Psychedelic. Term meaning "mind manifesting," originally a neutral term used to connote any psychoactive drug; now refers to hallucinogens. (453–454)

Psychiatrist. Medical doctor specializing in the treatment of mental, emotional, and neurological illness; may utilize physical-medical forms of therapy such as psychosurgery, shock, drugs, etc., in addition to verbal-behavioral therapies. (19)

Psychiatry. Field of medicine concerned with understanding, assessing, treating, and preventing mental and neurological disorders. (19)

Psychic determinism. Theory of behavior, both normal and abnormal, postulated by Freud, which holds that mental events are never random, but can be meaningfully or causally related if explored deeply enough. (479)

Psychic trauma. Stressful experience of a severely traumatic or disturbing nature; psychic traumas occurring early in life may not show their effects until many years later. (538)

Psychoactive drug. A drug that affects mental processes. (453)

Psychoanalyst. A psychotherapist who has received advanced training in the Freudian approach to understanding and treating neuroses and other psychological problems. (19, 480)

Psychoanalytic movement. School of psychology, originated by Freud, which emphasizes the study of unconscious mental processes; also a theory of personality and a method of psychotherapy that seeks to bring unconscious desires into consciousness and make it possible to resolve conflicts that usually date back to early childhood experiences. (23)

Psychoanalytic theory. Systematic personality theory put forth by Freud emphasizes childhood experiences, sexuality, and unconscious processes as they affect personality development and its distortions. (479)

Psychodynamics. The systematic study of personality and behavior that emphasizes motivational forces and past experiences. Freudian theory is a psychodynamic model of human behavior. (22)

Psychodynamic therapy. View of psychotherapy emphasizing causes within the individual, but stressing ongoing intense psychological processes rather than physical deficits, excesses, or imbalances as set forth in the biological or somatic view. (600)

Psychogenic. Caused by psychological-emotional factors rather than organic or physiological factors. (534)

Psychokinesis (PK). A form of extrasensory perception in which objects and events are supposedly controlled by an act of thought or will. (357)

Psycholinguistics. The psychological study of language and how it is learned. (187)

Psychological dependence. A strong emotional need for pleasure or the relief of discomfort, stress, or anxiety; often develops in connection with an addiction substance such as a drug. (455)

Psychology. The scientific study of the behavior and experiences of organisms; the study of the interactions of biological organisms and their perceived social and physical environments. (3)

Psychometrics. The measurement of aspects of psychological functioning by standardized tests to establish a quantifiable basis for individual differences. (220)

Psychophysical scaling. Techniques for measuring psychological response to physical stimuli. (352)

Psychosis. A severe form of mental or emotional disorder usually requiring major intervention in the person's life, often through hospitalization and drug therapy. (578)

Psychosocial stages. Stages of ego development as formulated by Erikson, incorporating both sexual and social aspects. (240)

Psychosomatic illness. Physical symptoms, often including actual tissue damage, that are attributable to emotional stress or other psychological causes. (534)

Psychosurgery. A form of biological or somatic psychotherapy that involves brain surgery used in the treatment of severe emotional disorders by severing nerve fibers connecting various brain areas, by removing cortical matter, and by lesioning specific brain sites. Recent use in control of violence is in dispute. (326, 593)

Psychotherapy. The general term for all psychological treatment of mental disorders and abnormalities in thought, emotion, or behavior. (594)

Psychotomimetic. A drug whose effect on the body (and mind) is similar to (mimics) the effect of a naturally occurring chemical substance in the body. (453)

Puberty. The period of adolescent development marked by the appearance of mature sexual characteristics. (261)

Punishment. An aversive stimulus that follows an undesired response, thus producing a decrease in the rate of that response. (101)

Purposiveness. An important principle of Tolman's theory of behavior stating that learning is rationally directed and involves hypotheses, expectations, explicit goals, etc. (107)

Q-sort technique. A specialized method of personality evaluation in which one or more raters describe the subject as he or she appears to them (on a series of standard items) at the time of observation. (500)

Racism. Form of prejudice in which negative evaluations and discrimination are directed at individuals because of their race. (639)

Random sampling. Method of drawing a sample so that each member of the population has an equal chance of being selected, and so that the probability of each member being selected is independent of whether or not any other member is selected; also chance sampling. A necessary feature of assigning subjects to experimental groups. (46, 755)

Range. Simplest measure of variability; the difference between the highest and lowest measurements. (49)

Rapid eye movement sleep (REM). A state of sleep during which rapid eye movements occur; it is characterized by a suppression of voluntary muscle action, major changes in the autonomic nervous system, phasic activity, and an aroused, alert brainwave pattern; dreaming is more probable during this time. (444)

Rating scale. Device for recording the rater's judgment of himself or others on defined traits. On relative rating scales, the rater ranks the subjects in order from highest to lowest in the group on the trait in question. On absolute rating scales, the judge assigns an absolute value or score to the individual on each trait being rated. (500)

Ratio scale. Scale of measurement that possesses all of the properties of nominal, ordinal, and interval scales with the additional property of an absolute zero as its point of origin; common physical measurements of weight and length are examples of such scales. (353)

Reaction formation. Defense mechanism in which the individual's conscious attitudes and overt behavior patterns are the opposite of his or her unconscious wishes, which have been repressed; prevents dangerous desires from being expressed by endorsing opposing attitudes and behavior as a barrier. (483)

Reaction time. The interval of time elapsing between stimulus presentation and a designated response to that stimulus. (137)

Reactive depression. Type of depressive behavior induced by external, situational stressors, not inner "disease" causality. (586)

Realistic thinking. Thinking closely tied to reality; concerned with the features, requirements, and demands of the objective, external situation. (139)

Reality orientation. A way of viewing the world that recognizes our need to develop an understanding of predictable relations in order to lend stability and meaning to our lives; assumed by attribution theory. (151)

Reasoning. Realistic thinking directed toward problem solving. (140)

Recall. Method of measuring retention; with a bare minimum of cues, subject must reproduce a response learned earlier. (170)

Receptive field. That specific area of the retina from which a given neuron receives its impulses. (349)

Receptor cells. Structures in the nervous system that are sensitive to specific stimulus qualities (light, sound, pressure, etc.) and that set up nerve impulses in the sensory nerve fibers. (285)

Recidivism. A shift back to one's original attitude, behavior, or condition after a period of therapy or rehabilitation treatment; a measure of the failure of the intervention. (76)

Reciprocal inhibition. Technique of desensitization developed by Wolpe and used in behavior therapy in which responses antagonistic to anxiety, like relaxation, are paired with anxiety-eliciting stimuli. (608)

Recognition. A measure of forgetting that involves the ability to identify whether a currently presented stimulus was previously experienced. (170)

Reconstruction. A form of recall in which only part of an informational item is stored and recalled; the rest is reconstructed from the clues provided by the stored information. (170)

Reductionism. An approach for understanding complex processes and phenomena through the study of their simpler units and component terms. Often used by physiological psychologists in understanding human behavior and the functioning of the brain as they study the many discrete neurological and biochemical events and substances of the brain. (56)

Redundancy. Repetition within a signal or message. (130)

Reflex. Specific, automatic response involving only a part of the body, such as salivation or the grasping reflex of an infant; unlearned reactions elicited by stimuli and important for survival of the organism. (65)

Reflex arc. A physiological sequence of sensory input to the central nervous system and then to behavioral output. (289)

Rehearsal. Active repetition of information in order to enhance subsequent access to it. (162)

Reinforcement. Stimulation that serves to strengthen a response. In classical conditioning, the process of following the conditioned stimulus with the unconditioned stimulus; in instrumental conditioning, the reward of the learner for appropriate responses. (79, 81)

Reinforcement scheduling. The pattern of administration of reinforcement, whether regular or haphazard. (85)

Reinforcing stimulus. A stimulus that maintains a response or increases its strength, when presented in a proper temporal relationship to that response. (78)

Relative rating scale. See *Rating scale*.

Relative refractory period. Short period during which a stronger than normal stimulus is required to cause the firing of another nerve impulse. It follows the absolute refractory period, and immediately precedes the membrane's return of responsiveness to its usual stimulus level. (295)

Releaser stimuli. External signal stimuli or cues, such as disliked objects or objects already associated with aggression, which interact with internal conditions to elicit aggression and provide a target for its expression. (693–694)

Reliability. The degree to which individuals earn the same relative scores each time they are measured according to a certain measuring instrument. (498)

Remission. Term used in the medical model of psychopathology to refer to the improvement or disappearance of the *symptoms* of a mental illness, with implication that the core of disease is still present in latent form.

Remote effects. Effects resulting from an intervention that appears in some part of the system apart from that being specifically studied. (724)

Replication. Repetition of an experiment under the same conditions to see if the same results can be obtained a second time—usually by an independent investigator. (45)

Repression. Defense mechanism in which painful or guilt-producing thoughts, feelings, or memories are excluded from conscious awareness; such repressed material may remain active at an unconscious level, resulting in bizarre behavior. (483)

Reproductive memory. Theory of memory as a reproductive process consisting of the retrieval of previously learned material stored in the brain. (175)

Reserpine. Tranquilizing drug widely used in the treatment of mental patients. (596)

Resistances. In psychoanalysis, inability or unwillingness to discuss certain ideas, desires, or experiences, particularly during free association; conceived to be psychological barriers preventing the return to consciousness of painful, repressed material and conflicts. (601)

Resistance to extinction. A measure of the strength of conditioning based on the persistence of a conditioned response during extinction trials or the number of trials necessary to cause extinction. (71)

Respondent behavior. Behavior that is an unlearned, involuntary response to an eliciting stimulus. Essentially a reflex action, it acts to change the organism in order to better adapt it to the environment, rather than changing the environment itself. (67)

Respondent conditioning. See *Classical conditioning*.

Retention processes. Factor influencing observational learning whereby a model's influence depends on the individual's ability to remember its actions. (116)

Reticular activating system (RAS). The fibers going from the spinal cord to the higher centers, acting as a general arousal system and mobilizing the organism for action. (313)

Retina. Inner layer of the eye, containing the light-sensitive rods and cones. (346)

Retinal disparity. The slight difference in the retinal image which the two eyes get from the same object; helps make depth perception possible. (356)

Retroactive inhibition. The interference produced by learning something new on the memory or performance of earlier learned material. (172)

Retroactive therapy. Treatment to alleviate a condition (e.g., learned helplessness) after it has already occurred or been established. (421)

Reward conditioning. A form of operant conditioning in which a positive reinforcing stimulus occurs if the organism makes the appropriate responses. (85)

Rhinencephalon. Primitive area in the brain containing both olfactory and emotional centers; the "nose brain." (335)

Rhodopsin. Photopigment found in the rods of the eye. (347)

Ritalin. Brand name for one type of amphetamine prescribed for hyperactive children because it apparently enhances their concentration and attention. (597)

Rods. Retinal receptor cells extremely sensitive to low intensities of light and capable of producing sensations of black, white, and gray (but not color). (346)

Rorschach test. A projective test making use of a series of symmetrical inkblots. (503)

Rote recall. Recall for material leaned verbatim, without regard for meaning. (170)

R−R relationship. Relationship between responses, used in correlational analysis. Causality cannot be assumed from such a relationship. (64)

R→S relationship. Relationship that expresses the effect of a response on stimulus events (the physical and social environment); characterizes consequence learning. (64)

Sample. A specific group upon which measurements are taken; should be representative of some population or universe about which an inference is to be made. (501)

Satiation. Condition wherein an organism is satisfied or has had enough of a particular goal or activity. (377)

Scalloping. Typical response pattern of FI schedules; the organism ceases relevant responding after reinforcement, and then sharply increases its response in the period immediately before reinforcement is due to occur. (88)

Scapegoat. A target other than the original source of frustration onto which aggression is displaced; minorities and unpopular, powerless groups are favorite targets of displaced aggression as applied to prejudice. (693)

Schema. A higher-order knowledge structure which organizes information (and gives it meaning) according to learned conceptions, general rules, or context features. (150)

Scheme. As used by Piaget, a cognitive structure that relates means to ends (manipulating objects to receive desired stimulation). (237)

Schizophrenia. Psychosis characterized by the breakdown of integrated personality functioning, withdrawal from reality, emotional blunting and distortion, and disturbed thought processes. (582)

Scripts. Learned knowledge structures about the organization of a concrete sequence of interrelated events. Scripts may influence our interpretation and memory of events and direct behavior. (150)

Secondary gain. Reinforcement an individual receives from others for manifesting certain abnormal symptoms; positive side effects of negative reactions, such as attention for tantrums. (479)

Secondary reinforcement. Reinforcement provided by a stimulus that has gained reward value by being previously associated with a primary reinforcing stimulus, although it does not directly satisfy a need. (89)

Selective attention. A characteristic of motivation wherein an organism is attentive to stimuli relevant or central to its goal-directed behavior, but shows decreased sensitivity to stimuli irrelevant or peripheral to this purpose. (112)

Selective permeability. Property of the cell membrane of a neuron that allows certain ions to pass through it more easily than other ions, thereby changing the polarization of the neuron and permitting the transmission of nerve impulses. (290–291)

Self-actualization. Constant striving to realize one's full inherent potentials, regarded by Goldstein, Rogers, Maslow, and others as the most fundamental goal of the human personality. (486)

Self-concept. The individual's awareness of his or her continuing identity as a person; develops gradually from an infant's discovery of the parts of his or her own body and comes to include all of the individual's thoughts, feelings, attitudes, values, and aspirations; a differentiated portion of one's phenomenal field. (486)

Self-efficacy. A general sense of competence and the belief in one's abilities and personal resourcefulness to successfully achieve desired outcomes. (120)

Self-inventory. Instrument for measuring personality traits by having the individual give information about himself or herself, validity limited by subject's lack of self-understanding and by desire to put best self forward. (503)

Self-managed reinforcement. Control of the contingencies of reinforcement by the individual whose behavior is to be changed. (90)

Self-regulatory process. Capacity allowing individuals to control their own actions whereby they evaluate their own behavior according to personal standards and provide their own reinforcements; concept stressed in social learning theories. (119)

Self-system. A dynamism, according to Sullivan, which develops as the individual learns to avoid threats to his security; tends to interfere with ability to deal effectively with others because it becomes isolated from the rest of the personality. (242)

Semantic processing. The search for meaningful relationships (comprehension) between information units stored in long-term memory. (165)

Semantics. The study of meaning. (202)

Sensation. Awareness of the stimulation of a sensory receptor; first stage in perception.

Sensory cortex. The part of the brain which integrates incoming information and provides feedback about the organism's motor output and its consequences. (314)

Sensory deprivation. Sensory stimulation well below the normal level of sensory input, achieved by eliminating as much visual/auditory/tactual stimulation as possible; may lead to hallucinations and delusions. Deprivation may also be in terms of lack of the *variety* of sensory input required by our complex brain. (440)

Sensory information store. A memory system that retains sensory information for a very brief period of time, usually less than a half of a second. (160)

Sensory-motor arc. Functional unit or basic pattern of the nervous system; a chain composed of sensory input at a receptor neuron, one or more interneurons in the spinal cord or brain, and an effector neuron that initiates behavioral output. (289)

Sensory-motor period. First of Piaget's stages of cognitive development (from about 0–2 years); characterized by development in self-identification, efficacy, and causality. (256)

Sensory neuron. Carries messages toward the central nervous system from a sensory receptor cell, for instance in the eye or ear; also known as an *afferent* neuron. (289)

Sensory overload. Increased sensory input caused by excessive motor activity and/or intense emotional arousal, which may precipitate altered states of consciousness. (441)

Sequential design. Research approach in which several different birth cohorts are tested repeatedly for a span of years. (224)

Serendipity. Chance discovery of something not sought for, often while looking for something else.

Serial learning. Learning and remembering stimulus materials in the exact sequence in which they were presented. (174)

Serial position effect. In memory, the tendency for the earlier and later items in a series to be easier to recall than the middle ones. (174)

Serotonin. A neurotransmitter substance produced in the brain; important in inducing nightly sleep and implicated in schizophrenic behavior. Research with cats has shown that when its production is blocked, brain-wave patterns similar to those characteristic of animals deprived of REM sleep are produced. (330)

Set. Readiness to respond in a particular way to some stimulus situation. (112)

Set point level. The base level or initial stable level used as a point of reference. (382)

Sex drive. The motive that leads to the satisfaction of the individual (through tension reduction) and the perpetuation of the species through successful reproduction—enhancing sexual receptivity and increasing approach to a variety of sex-related goals. (680)

Sexism. Prejudice and discrimination solely on the basis of sex of the individual. (642)

Sex-role socialization. Socially accepted stereotypes presented by society that prescribe what is right, proper, and appropriate behavior, values, and appearance for its male and female members. (227, 643)

Sexual script. A socially learned set of expectations about the roles, actions, and consequences of sexual encounters. (683)

Shaping. Form of operant conditioning used in training in which all responses that come close to the desired one are rewarded at first, then only the closest approximations, until the desired response is attained. (99)

Shock therapy. A form of biological or somatic psychotherapy, it is a method of treating severe mental disturbances by inducing convulsions, which are followed by a state of coma; usually induced by electricity or insulin. (595)

Short-term memory. A limited capacity memory system in which information is stored for only a short length of time and is easily accessible. (161)

Shyness. An awareness of one's inability to take social action when one both wants to and knows how to; a subjective state influenced by the label one attaches to a given set of reactions. (510)

Sigma (Σ). Greek letter used to stand for the phrase "the sum of . . ." (758)

Signal detection theory. A theory combining sensory and decision-making processes in perceptual judgments. The observer's sensitivity is analyzed independently of the criterion the observer uses to make the decision. (361)

Signal learning. An acquired, learned expectation that one stimulus (the signal) will be followed by a certain other stimulus. (63)

Sign-gestalt-expectation. A learned expectancy that in a particular context certain stimuli will be related to (predict to) other stimuli. Tolman proposed this concept to account for a broader type of learning than just experienced S→R associations. (108)

Significant difference. A research convention which sets in advance the formulation of a probability estimate that can be regarded as a statistically trustworthy measure of an effect, that is, real change, not merely that which might be due to chance; usually that difference is: $p < .05$, probability less than 5 times in 100 by chance. (48)

Simple schizophrenia. Type of schizophrenia characterized by reduction in interpersonal relationships, apathy, withdrawal, disintegration of thought processes, and inconspicuous delusions or hallucinations. (579)

Simulation. A means of explaining behavior by the artificial representation of the essential elements of a system; often involves a computer which processes information as specified by a model (its program designed by psychologists in an attempt to simulate actual human behavioral processes. (132)

Situational attribution. Attributing actions or events to causes and properties in the environment, situation, or personal interaction, rather than to the individual. (653)

Size constancy. Tendency to perceive the actual size of a familiar object, regardless of its distance from the observer. (359)

Skinner box. Simplified apparatus used in experiments on operant conditioning; a box that contains a bar or other device that the experimental organism must manipulate (operant response) in order to trigger the delivery of food or stop an aversive stimulus. (86)

Sleep apnea. A sleep disorder in which excessive day-time drowsiness is caused by breathing problems while asleep. (449)

Sleep deprivation. A prolonged period of time without sleep, which can alter various physiological and psychological reactions, and may result in fatigue, disorientation, brain-wave abnormalities, paranoid ideas, perceptual distortions, and other behavioral abnormalities depending on a variety of factors. (448)

Social approval. A process and a postulated need, of acting in ways designed to elicit the acceptance and social reinforcement provided by certain other people. (384)

Social behavior. Social response; an individual behavior involving or taken with respect to others; response to social stimuli. (626)

Social comparison. A process, and a postulated need, in which individuals seek out and make subjective comparisons with certain other people in order to assess their own ability, opinions, and emotions. (382)

Social context. The part of a total environment that includes other people, whether actual, imagined, or represented symbolically.

Social-emotional leaders. Leaders who stress creating and maintaining good psychological conditions within the group rather than task efficiency; concerned with process more than product. (634)

Socialization. The process of social learning by which an individual (usually a child) comes to recognize, practice, and identify with the values, attitudes, and basic belief structure of the dominant institutions and representatives of his or her society. (241)

Social learning theory. Theory stating that current psychological functioning is best understood in terms of a continuous reciprocal interaction between behavior and its controlling conditions, i.e., the environmental influences which include social stimuli, social and personal reinforcement, and past learning history. (115)

Social motives. Motivational states induced by social and cultural conditions, acquired during one's transactions with people, values, and events in one's society. (381)

Social norms. Group-defined standards concerning what behaviors are acceptable or objectionable in given situations. (626)

Social pathology. Abnormal social conditions in institutions, environments, or systems that create, facilitate, or sustain reactions that are pathological in individuals living under those conditions. (688)

Social penetration. Concept that proposes the development of trust between two persons when one person initiates self-disclosure. (673)

Social psychology. Field of psychology that studies the effect of social variables on individual behavior, attitudes, motives, and perceptions; the study of the effect of others and social environments on an individual's responses. (626)

Social trap. Situation that occurs within a social system in which individuals discover themselves behaving in a manner that they perceive will be harmful in the long run, but that they do not know how to stop or control at present. For example, the nuclear arms race. (725)

Somatosensory areas. Areas of cerebral cortex concerned with kinesthesis and the cutaneous senses; primary area lies just back of the fissure of Rolando and body surface is projected onto it. (318)

Somnambulism. Sleepwalking; may be a kind of dissociative state. (574)

Sound localization cues. Cues that enable organisms to locate the position of sound sources in terms of distance and direction, including the difference in phase, time, and intensity of sound waves as they stimulate the two ears. (356)

Sound spectrograms. Visual representations of spoken sounds, with time shown along the horizontal axis, frequency along the vertical axis, and intensity indicated by the varying shades of darkness of the pattern. (196)

Source. The communicator of the message; that from which the message comes; it is a variable in the persuasive impact of a communication. (649)

Species-specific characteristics. Characteristics found only in a given species. (209)

Spinal cord. Part of the central nervous system, it is a longitudinal cord of nervous tissue connecting the brain and the peripheral nervous system. (313)

Split-brain research. Research in which the corpus callosum is severed in intact organisms, thus creating two independently functioning cortical hemispheres. (324)

Spontaneous recovery. The return of a conditioned response following extinction, after an interval of no stimulation. (71) Also, the remission of all signs of mental disturbance without therapeutic intervention. This self-generated "cure" with the passage of time must be taken into account in evaluating the effectiveness of therapy. (616)

S→R approach. A psychological approach that is concerned with the stimulus-response connection as a unit for studying an organism's overt behavior. It is assumed that reinforced practice establishes and stresses the S→R connection. (24, 64) See *Behaviorists*.

S−S relationship. Relationship between two stimulus events in the environment. (64)

Stage. Concept used by developmental psychologists to signify qualitatively different behaviors that occur in fixed sequences at certain times in the life of the organism. (221)

Stage of exhaustion. Final phase of the body's reaction to prolonged stress in which adaptation anxiety is exhausted, alarm reaction reappears, and death becomes imminent. See also *General adaptation syndrome*. (533)

Stage of resistance. See *General adaptation syndrome*.

Standard deviation. A measure of the average variation of scores from the group mean; equal to the square root of the variance. (49)

Standardized interview schedule. Interview in which predetermined questions are asked in a set order; a method of making the interview a more objective behavior sampling technique. (501)

Standardized measuring device. Property of a useful measuring device by which it is administered to a large group of subjects representative of the group for which it is intended; then it is administered to all subjects in the same way under the same conditions in order that comparison can be made. (47)

Standard score. Score expressed in terms of standard deviations from the mean. (759)

Stanford-Binet test. A version of the Binet intelligence test, it is an individual test using age level subtests; most widely used children's intelligence test. (516)

State-dependent learning. Learning of a response in a particular environmental context or emotional or physiological state, such that the optimal performance of that response depends upon the presence of those specific state-related cues. (459)

Statistical inference. Procedure of drawing general conclusions of a probabilistic nature by studying samples of behavior. (762)

Stereotype. According to Sullivan, a personification held in common by a group of people. (242) A preconceived, often biased, notion as to how people of a given race, nationality, or occupation will appear or behave. (501)

Stigmatize. To mark or label as deviating from a norm; to single out for discrimination because individual or group is assumed to possess an undesirable trait or history, as ex-convicts or former mental patients, for example. (565–566)

Stimulants. Psychoactive drugs that stimulate the central nervous system, such as amphetamines, methamphetamine (speed), cocaine, and caffeine (found in coffee, tea, and colas). (456)

Stimulation threshold. The transitional point at which the energy level of an incoming stimulus is sufficient to activate a sensory neuron, causing it to fire. (290)

Stimulus control. Control of the occurrence of a response by means of a dependable signal (S^D) that a reinforcer is available; the responses will thus occur consistently in the presence of the stimulus, but not in its absence. (81)

Stimulus generalization. Tendency for a conditioned response to be evoked by a range of stimuli similar (but not identical) to the conditioned stimulus. (69–70)

Story chain. A mnemonic strategy for improving memory of unrelated items by linking them together in a story. (182)

Stress. Nonspecific physiological and psychological response of an individual to any environmental demand or challenge to the integrity of the individual. (530)

Stressor. Anything potentially injurious to the organism, either physically or psychologically, that taxes the adaptive capacity of the organism. (532)

Sublimation. A defense mechanism by means of which socially acceptable forms of activity are substituted for unacceptable motives or instinctual drives. (483)

Successive reproduction. Technique used in the study of productive memory in which meaningful material is recalled several times by subjects, and any transformation of the original material is noted. (172)

Suicide. The act of taking one's own life. (546)

Superego. According to Freudian psychoanalytic theory, that part of the personality controlling the internalized moral values learned by the individual as a child; consists of two components, the conscience and the ego ideal. (482)

Superstitious behavior. Behavior based on a coincidental relationship between a response and a reinforcing stimulus event; individual perceives causality when in fact there is none. (84)

Superstitious control. Belief that one has control of one's environment, although this belief is mere superstition and false, which serves to prevent the development of learned helplessness. (421)

Surface structure. The component parts of a sentence and their relations; the superficial structure. (201)

Syllogism. A deductive analysis of a formal problem that consists of two premises and a conclusion. (140)

Symbol. Most sophisticated means of mental representation, which involves the use of an image or word to represent something else. (138)

Symbolic learning. Learning general rules, principles, relationships of the form "if→then." Context, timing, and response strategies are learned by using abstract symbols to represent concrete events. (118)

Symptom. Evidence or manifestation of a disease.

Synapse. Functional region between neurons where nerve impulses are transmitted from one neuron to another. (297)

Synaptic transmission. Nerve impulse transmission between neurons in which a chemical transmitter substance crosses the synaptic gap between an active neuron and adjacent ones; excitation or inhibition of postsynaptic neurons is critical in processing information. (290)

Syntax. A branch of linguistic analysis concerned with the order of and relation between words and phrases used to form sentences; (198) also called *grammar*.

Systematic desensitization. A form of behavior therapy in which specific fears are weakened through counterconditioning. (608)

Task leaders. Leaders oriented to complete a task or job as efficiently as possible; concerned chiefly with product. (634)

Telepathy. Form of extrasensory perception in which perceptions are supposedly based on thought transference from one person to another. (357)

Telephone theory. A frequency theory of hearing, according to which the basilar membrane plays the role of a telephone transmitter, relaying impulses of various frequencies to the brain. (351)

Temporal lobe. Portion of the new brain separated from the frontal and parietal lobes by the fissure of Sylvius; lies just beneath the temples; location of the auditory projection areas. (313)

Terminal buttons. Structures at the end of an axon that synapse with another cell. (292)

Terminal drop. The notable decline in any one of a variety of cognitive performances in the elderly which predict imminent death (less than five years). (271)

Territoriality. The perceived spatial area in which an organism feels "at home," safe from intruders. In animals it is the mating and offspring rearing place which is defended against intrusion. (691)

Thalamus. Brain structure that is a part of the brain stem and a relay station for incoming sensory messages from all parts of the body; important in sensations of pain. (313)

Thanatos. According to Freudian theory, the "aggressive instinct" or "death instinct," one of two drives present at birth; includes all striving toward self-destruction or breaking down of order. (480)

Thematic Apperception Test (TAT). A projective technique making use of pictures about each of which the subject is asked to make up a story, the themes of which are then analyzed for the existence of various sources of motivation. (504)

Theory. A systematic statement of the organization and relationships of assumptions, principles of behavior, and various observed facts and deductions. Theories account for what is known, integrate phenomena, and help predict the unknown. (36)

Theta waves. An EEG frequency; a possible sign of inhibitory activity. (446)

Thinking. Behavior carried on in terms of ideas, which involves symbolic, representational, and transformational processes. (135)

Time distortion. A perceptual distortion, characteristic of some alternate states of consciousness; distortion can make an hour seem like a second, or a second seem like an hour, or distortion may be changes in past, present, or future orientation. (438)

Token economy. Technique of positive reinforcement often employed by mental hospitals and other custodial institutions in which patients are rewarded for socially constructive behavior by tokens, which may later be exchanged for privileges. Major virtues are clear goals and explicit behavioral criteria. (606)

Tolerance. Physiological process by which the effect of a particular drug is reduced by virtue of its having been taken before; thus increased amounts of a drug must be taken in order to achieve the same effects previously produced by a smaller dose. (455)

TOTE. An acronym for a planned hierarchy of operations (cognitive processes) that are guided by feedback: Test-Operate-Test(again)-Exit. (129)

Trace decay theory. A theory of forgetting which holds that learned events leave traces or impressions in the brain. These traces weaken and disappear over time. (170)

Trait. A relatively stable characteristic of individuals that personality psychologists assume can be observed in behavior or measured. (404)

Trait theory. An approach to the study of personality that analyzes the differences between people according to measurable traits that are assumed to be relatively stable characteristics of a person. (476)

Trance logic. Tolerating paradoxes under hypnosis rather than relying on ordinary logical reasoning to make sense of strange experiences. (429)

Tranquilizers. Drugs used in chemotherapy for antipsychotic purposes; they serve to reduce anxiety and tension. (596)

Transactional approach to perception. Theory stating that perception is the result of our learned transactions with objects and events in our environment; reality is thus constructed from our assumptions and hypotheses about how things, people, and actions are related on the basis of prior transactions with them. (345)

Transcendental meditation (TM). A form of meditation that involves repeated chanting of and the focusing of attention on a mantra, away from the external material world. (549)

Transduction. Process by which an organism obtains information about the intensity of a stimulus. (341)

Transference. Process by which a patient in psychoanalytic therapy attaches to the therapist feelings formerly held toward some person who figured in a past emotional conflict, often a parent or a lover; may be negative, positive, or ambivalent feelings. (601)

Transformational rules. Rules applied to a kernel sentence to achieve different meanings and kinds of expression; used in converting the deep structure of meaning into the surface structure of spoken sentences, according to Chomsky's theory of language. (201)

Traumatic events. A physical or psychological event that is injurious, stressful, or shocking; such occurrences early in life are thought by psychoanalytic theorists to be the source of adult fears or neurosis.

Trial and error. Attempts to solve a problem by trying out alternative possibilities and discarding those that prove to be unsatisfactory. (98)

Trigger features. Patterns of sensory stimulation that initiate responding in particular sensory neurons. (350)

t-test. Test of statistical inference; used to determine whether the probability that the means of two sets of scores come from the same population or can be assumed to be different. (762)

Two-component theory of emotion. View of emotion as the interaction of cognitive cues and physiological arousal where the general arousal state is given its affective quality by available social cognitions. (406)

Typology. A characterization of psychological differences between people in terms of visible characteristics that form a limited number of categories (such as Sheldon's somatotypes). (474)

Unconditioned response (UCR). Response made to an unconditioned stimulus; often an inborn reflex, as in the case of salivation in response to food in the mouth. (67)

Unconditioned stimulus (UCS). Stimulus that elicits a response in the absence of conditioning. (67)

Unconscious. Lack of conscious, rational awareness; in Freudian theory, that portion of the psyche that is a repository for repressed conflicts and desires not directly accessible to consciousness. (480)

Unity and fusion. Often characteristic of an alternate state of consciousness; the notion of the separateness of self seems to vanish and be replaced by the experience of a collective identity. (438)

Validity. The extent to which an instrument actually measures what it is intended to measure; the "goodness" of the concept, idea, measuring instrument. Validity may be assessed by external criteria or by internal consistency. (499)

Vandalism. Seemingly senseless acts of destruction of property; however, it may serve a specific purpose: acquisitive, tactical, ideological, vindictive, malicious, or playful. (737)

Variable. Any quantity or property subject to change. (46)

Variable interval schedule (VI). Intermittent schedule by which reinforcement is given after differing lengths of time, regardless of the number of correct responses made in between. (88)

Variable ratio schedule (VR). Intermittent schedule by which reinforcement is given after a variable number of responses. (87)

Variance. A measure of variability that is computed by adding the square of the difference between each measurement and the mean, and dividing by the number of measurements; square of the standard deviation. (758)

Vertebrates. Animals with a brain enclosed in a skull and a segmented spinal column, such as mammals, birds, reptiles, amphibians, and fishes.

Vicarious learning. Learning based entirely upon observation of the behavior of others and its consequences, without personally performing the response or experiencing its effects. Bandura's social learning theory emphasizes this process. (115)

Viscera. The internal organs in the cavities of the body, such as the intestines and stomach.

Volley theory. Auditory theory that nerve fibers operate in groups and that various fibers discharge their volleys of impulses at different times, making it possible for a bundle of fibers to reproduce high frequencies. (351)

Wechsler Adult Intelligence Scale (WAIS). Intelligence test battery for adults which includes both performance and verbal subtests; used also to diagnose cognitive defects through variability in a pattern of subtest scores. Children's version (WISC) also available. (516)

Whorfian hypothesis. Theory that the language patterns of a cultural group shape the thought patterns and the perceptions of the individuals in that culture. (210)

Yoga. A system of beliefs and practices the goal of which is to attain a union of self with Supreme Reality; popularly, it is meditation based on physical posturing and breathing. (549)

Zeigarnik effect. Tendency to have greater recall of tasks interrupted before completion than of completed ones. (177)

Zen. A Japanese school of Buddhism that teaches self-discipline, deep meditation, and the attainment of enlightenment. (424)

References

Abramson, L. Y., Seligman, M. E. P., & Teasdale, J. D. Learned helplessness in humans: Critique and reformulation. *Journal of Abnormal Psychology*, 1978, *87*, 49–74.

Adams, J. *Conceptual blockbusting.* Portable Stanford Series. Stanford, Calif.: Stanford University Press, 1976.

Adler, A. *The practice and theory of individual psychology.* New York: Harcourt, Brace & World, 1929.

Ahammer, I. M. Social-learning theory as a framework for the study of adult personality development. In P. B. Baltes & K. W. Schaie (Eds.), *Life-span developmental psychology: Personality and socialization.* New York: Academic Press, 1973.

Ainsworth, M. D. S., & Bell, S. M. Attachment, exploration, and separation: Illustrated by the behavior of one-year-olds in a strange situation. *Child Development*, 1970, *41*, 49–67.

Albright, G. L., & Gift, H. C. Adult socialization: Ambiguity and adult life crises. In N. Datan & L. H. Ginsberg (Eds.), *Life-span developmental psychology: Normative life crises.* New York: Academic Press, 1975.

Allison, R. B. Diagnosis and treatment of multiple personality. Paper presented at Annual Meeting of American Psychiatric Association, Toronto, Canada, May 1977.

Allport, G. W. *Personality: A psychological interpretation.* New York: Holt, Rinehart & Winston, 1937.

Allport, G. W. *Pattern and growth in personality.* New York: Holt, Rinehart & Winston, 1961.

Allport, G. W. Traits revisited. *American Psychologist*, 1966, *21*, 1–10.

Allport, G. W., & Ross, J. M. Personal religious orientation and prejudice. *Journal of Personality and Social Psychology.* 1967, *5*, 432–442.

Altman, D., Levine, M., & Nadien, J. Unpublished research cited in S. Milgram, The experience of living in cities. *Science*, 1970, *167*, 1461–68.

Altman, I., & Taylor, D. A. *Social penetration: The development of interpersonal relationships.* New York: Holt, Rinehart, & Winston, 1973.

Amabile, T. Effects of extrinsic constraint on artistic creativity. Unpublished Ph.D. dissertation, Stanford University, 1977.

American Psychological Association. Ethical principles in the conduct of research with human participants. *American Psychologist*, 1973, *28*, 79–80.

American Psychological Association Task Force Report. On issues of sexual bias in graduate education (Jan Birk, Chairperson), 1974.

Ames, A. Visual perception and the rotating trapezoidal window. *Psychological Monographs*, 1951, *65* (7, Whole No. 234).

Appleton, T., Clifton, R., & Goldberg, S. The development of behavioral competence in infancy. In F. D. Horowitz (Ed.), *Review of child development research* (Vol. 4). Chicago: University of Chicago Press, 1975.

Ardrey, R. *The territorial imperative.* New York: Atheneum, 1966.

Arendt, H. *Eichmann in Jerusalem: A report on the banality of evil.* New York: Viking, 1965.

Argyle, M., & Dean, J. Eye-contact, distance, and affiliation. *Sociometry*, 1965, *28*, 289–304.

Arnold, M. B. *Emotion and personality.* New York: Columbia University Press, 1960, 2 vols.

Aronson, E. Some antecedents of interpersonal attraction. In W. J. Arnold & D. Levine (Eds.), *Nebraska symposium on motivation.* Lincoln: University of Nebraska Press, 1969.

Aronson, E. *The jigsaw classroom.* Beverly Hills, Cal.: Sage, 1978.

Aronson, E., & Linder, D. Gain and loss of esteem as determinants of interpersonal attractiveness. *Journal of Experimental and Social Psychology*, 1965, *1*, 156–71.

Asch, S. E. Opinions and social pressure. *Scientific American*, 1955, *193*(5), 31–35. Copyright © 1955 by Scientific American, Inc. All rights reserved. Reprinted by permission.

Aserinsky, E., & Kleitman, N. Regularly occurring periods of eye mobility and concomitant phenomena during sleep. *Science*, 1953, *118*, 273–274.

Atkinson, J. W. *An introduction to motivation.* Princeton: Van Nostrand, 1964.

Attneave, F. *Applications of information theory to psychology: A summary of basic concepts, methods and results.* New York: Holt, Rinehart & Winston, 1959.

Averill, J. R. Emotion and anxiety: Sociocultural, biological, and psychological determinants. In M. Zuckerman and C. D. Spielberger (Eds.), *Emotion and anxiety: New concepts, methods and applications.* Hillsdale, N.J.: L. Erlbaum Associates, 1976, 87–130.

Ayllon, T., & Michael, J. The psychiatric nurse as a behavioral engineer. *Journal of the Experimental Analysis of Behavior*, 1959, *2*, 323–334.

Azrin, N. H., & Foxx, R. M. *Toilet training in less than a day.* New York: Pocket Books, 1976.

Azrin, N. H., & Holz, W. C. Punishment. In W. K. Honig (Ed.), *Operant behavior.* New York: Appleton-Century-Crofts, 1966.

Backer, T. E., & Manson, E. L. In the key of feeling. *Human Behavior*, February 1978, *7*, 63–67. Copyright © 1978 by *Human Behavior* Magazine. Reprinted by permission.

Backman, C. W., & Secord, P. F. The effect of perceived liking on interpersonal attraction. *Human Relations*, 1959, *12*, 379–384.

Baddeley, A. D. *The psychology of memory.* New York: Basic Books, 1976.

Badia, P., Culbertson, S., & Harch, J. Choice of longer or stronger signalled shock over shorter or weaker unsignalled shock. *Journal of the Experimental Analysis of Behavior*, 1973, *19*(1), 25–32.

Baer, D. M. An age-irrelevant concept of development. *Merrill-Palmer Quarterly of Behavior and Development*, 1970, *16*, 238–246.

Bailey, R. H. *The role of the brain.* New York: Time-Life Books, 1975.

Bakan, P. Hypnotizability, laterality of eye movement and functional brain asymmetry. *Perceptual and Motor Skills*, 1969, *28*, 927–938.

Bakker, C. Why people don't change. *Psychotherapy: Theory, research and practice*, 1975, *12*, 164–172.

Balagura, S. Influence of osmotic and caloric loads upon lateral hypothalamic self-stimulation. *Journal of Comparative and Physiological Psychology*, 1968, *66*, 325–328.

Bales, R. F. *Personality and interpersonal behavior.* New York: Holt, Rinehart & Winston, 1970.

Baltes, P. B., Reese, H. W. & Nesselroade, J. R. *Lifespan developmental psychology: Introduction to research methods.* Monterey, Calif: Brooks/Cole, 1977.

Ban, P. K. The use of generalized gradients for the study of mediational processes. Unpublished Master's thesis. University of Hawaii, 1975.

Ban, P. K., & Minke, K. A. *Verbal pretraining effects upon the central tendency shift.* Paper presented at the meeting of the Western Psychological Association, San Diego, April 1979.

Bandura, A. Influence of models' reinforcement contingencies on the acquisition of imitative responses. *Journal of Personality and Social Psychology*, 1965, *1*, 589–595.

Bandura, A. *Principles of behavior modification.* New York: Holt, Rinehart & Winston, 1969.

Bandura, A. Modeling therapy. In W. S. Sahakian (Ed.), *Psychopathology today: Experimentation, theory, and research.* Itasca, Ill.: Peacock, 1970.

Bandura, A. *Social learning theory.* (Module) Morristown, N.J.: General Learning Press, 1971.

Bandura, A. *Aggression: A social learning analysis.* Englewood Cliffs, N.J.: Prentice-Hall, 1973.

Bandura, A. *Social learning theory.* Englewood Cliffs, New Jersey: Prentice-Hall, 1977(a).

Bandura, A. Self-efficacy. *Psychological Review*, 1977, *84*, 191–215 (b).

Bandura, A., Ross, D., & Ross, S. A. Imitation of film-mediated aggressive models. *Journal of Abnormal and Social Psychology*, 1963, *66*, 3–11.

Bandura, A., Underwood, B., & Fromson, M. E. Disinhibition of aggression through diffusion of responsibility and dehumanization of victims. *Journal of Research in Personality*, 1975, *9*, 253–269.

Bandura, A., & Walter, R. H. *Adolescent aggression.* New York: Ronald, 1959.

Banks, W. C., & McQuater, G. V. Achievement motivation and black children. *IRCD Bulletin, 11,* 1976, 1–8.

Banks, W. C., McQuater, G. V., & Hubbard, J. L. Task-liking and intrinsic-extrinsic achievement orientations in Black adolescents. *Journal of Black Psychology,* 1977, *3*(2), 61–71.

Barber, T. X. *LSD, marihuana, yoga and hypnosis.* Chicago: Aldine, 1970.

Barbizet, J. *Human Memory and Its Pathology.* (Trans. D. K. Jardine) San Francisco: W. H. Freeman, 1970.

Barker, D. L., Herbert, E., Hildebrand, J. G., & Kravitz, E. A. Acetycholine and lobster sensory neurones. *Journal of Physiology,* 1972, *226,* 205–229.

Barnes, J. M. & Underwood, B. J. "Fate" of first-list associations in transfer theory. *Journal of Experimental Psychology,* 1959, *58,* 97–105.

Barnett, S. A. Attack and defense in animal societies. In C. D. Clemente & D. B. Lindsley (Eds.), *Aggression and defense.* Los Angeles: University of California Press, 1967.

Barron, F. X. *Creativity and psychological health: Origins of personal vitality and creative freedom.* Princeton, N.J.: Van Nostrand, 1963.

Barry, H., & Krimner, E. C. Pharmacology of discriminative drug stimuli. In B. T. Ho, D. W. Richards, & D. L. Chute (Eds.), *Drug discrimination and state dependent learning.* New York: Academic Press, 1978, 3–45.

Bartlett, F. C. *Remembering: A study in experimental and social psychology.* New York: Macmillan, 1932.

Bash, K. W. Contribution to a theory of the hunger drive. *Journal of Comparative Psychology,* 1939, *28,* 137–60.

Bassuk, E. L., & Gerson, S. Deinstitutionalization and mental health services. *Scientific American,* 1978, *238,* 46–53.

Batson, C. D., Cochran, P. J., Biederman, M. F., Blosser, J. L., Ryan, M. J., & Vogt, B. Failure to help when in a hurry: Callousness or conflict? *Personality and Social Psychology Bulletin,* 1978, *4,* 97–101.

Baum, A. & Valins, S. *Architecture and social behavior: Psychological studies of social density.* Hillsdale, N.J.: L. Erlbaum Associates, 1977.

Bauman, K. E., & Wilson, R. R. Sexual behavior of unmarried university students in 1968 and 1972. *Journal of Sex Research,* 1974, *10,* 327–333.

Bavelas, A., Hastorf, A. H., Gross, A. E. & Kite, W. R. Experiments on the alteration of group structure. *Journal of Experimental and Social Psychology,* 1965, *1,* 55–70.

Bayley, N. On the growth of intelligence. *American Psychologist,* 1955, *10,* 805–818.

Bazelon, D. L. Appendix A: Psychologists in corrections—are they doing good for the offender or well for themselves? In S. L. Brodsky, *Psychologists in the criminal justice system.* Champaign: University of Illinois, 1972.

Beatty, J., & Wagoner, B. L. Pupillometric signs of brain activity vary with level of cognitive processing. *Science,* 1978, *199,* 1216–1218.

Beck, A. T. *Depression,* New York: Harper & Row, 1967.

Beck, A. T., Kovacs, M., & Weissman, A. Hopelessness and suicidal behavior. *Journal of the American Medical Association,* 1975, *234,* 1146–1149.

Beecher, H. K. Relationship of significance of wound to the pain experienced. *Journal of the American Medical Association,* 1956, *161,* 1609–1613.

Beecher, H. K. Generalization from pain of various types and diverse origins. *Science,* 1959, *130,* 267–268.

Beecher, H. K. The placebo effect as a non-specific force surrounding disease and the treatment of disease. In R. Janzen, W. D. Keidel, H. Herz, C. Steichele, J. P. Payne, & R. A. P. Burt (Eds.), *Pain: Basic principles, pharmacology, therapy.* Stuttgart: West Germany: Georg Thieme, 1972.

Bem, D. J., & Allen, A. On predicting some of the people some of the time: The search for cross-situational consistencies in behavior. *Psychological Review,* 1974, *81*(6), 506–520.

Bem, S. L. The measurement of psychological androgyny. *Journal of Consulting and Clinical Psychology,* 1974, *42,* 155–162.

Bem, S. L. Beyond androgyny: Some presumptuous prescriptions for a liberated sexual identity. In J. Sherman & F. Denmark (Eds.). *The future of women: Issues in psychology.* New York: Psychological Dimensions, 1978.

Bengtson, V. L., & Haber, D. A. Sociological approaches to aging. In D. S. Woodruff & J. E. Birren (Eds.), *Aging: Scientific perspectives and social issues.* New York: Van Nostrand, 1975.

Benson, H. *The relaxation response.* New York: Morrow, 1975.

Bergin, A. E. The evaluation of therapeutic outcomes. In A. E. Bergin, & S. L. Carfield (Eds.), *Handbook of psychotherapy and behavior change: An empirical analysis.* New York: Wiley, 1971.

Berkman, L. F. Psychosocial resources, health behavior, and mortality: A nine-year follow-up study. Paper presented at the American Public Health Association Annual Meeting, Washington, D.C. October 1977.

Berkowitz, L. The frustration-aggression hypothesis revisited. In L. Berkowitz (Ed.), *Roots of aggresssion: A re-examination of the frustration-aggression hypothesis.* New York: Atherton, 1969.

Berkowitz, L., & LePage, A. Weapons as aggression-eliciting stimuli. *Journal of Personality and Social Psychology,* 1967, *7,* 202–207.

Bernard, J. & Sontag, L. W. Fetal reactivity to tonal stimulation: A preliminary report. *Journal of Genetic Psychology,* 1947, *70,* 205–210.

Bernard, L. L. *Instinct.* New York: Holt, Rinehart & Winston, 1924.

Bernstein, I. S. Alternatives to violence. *Mental Health Program Reports, No. 4.* Publication No. 5026. Chevy Chase, Md.: National Institute of Mental Health, 1970.

Berscheid, E., & Walster, E. H. *Interpersonal attraction.* Second edition. Reading, Mass.: Addison-Wesley, 1978.

Bettelheim, B. Joey: A "mechanical boy." *Scientific American* reprint, March 1959. San Francisco: Freeman, 1959.

Bettelheim, B. *The informed heart.* New York: The Free Press, 1960.

Bielski, R. J., & Friedel, R. O. Subtypes of depression, diagnosis and medical management. *The Western Journal of Medicine,* 1977, *126,* 347–352.

Bigelow, H. J. Dr. Harlow's case of recovery from the passage of an iron bar through the head. *American Journal of Medical Science,* 1850, *20,* 13–22.

Billow, R. M. Metaphor: A review of the psychological literature. *Psychological Bulletin,* 1977, *84,* 81–92.

Binet, A., & Simon, T. La mésure du développement de l'intelligence chez les jeunes enfants. *Bulletin de la Société Libre pour L'Étude Psychologique de L'Enfant,* 1911, *11,* 187–284.

Birren, J. E., & Woodruff, D. S. Human development over the life span through education. In P. B. Baltes & K. W. Schaie (Eds.), *Life-span developmental psychology: Personality and socialization.* New York: Academic Press, 1973.

Björntorp, P. Disturbances in the regulation of food intake. *Advances in Psychosomatic Medicine,* 1972, *7,* 116–127.

Blakemore, C., & Cooper, G. F. Development of the brain depends on the visual environment. *Nature,* 1970, *228,* 477–478.

Bleda, P. R., & Castore, C. Social comparison, attraction, and choice of a comparison other. *Memory and Cognition,* 1973, *1,* 420–424.

Block, J. *The Q-sort method in personality assessment and psychiatric research,* Springfield, Ill.: C. C. Thomas, 1961.

Block, J. *Lives through time.* Berkeley, Calif.: Bancroft Press, 1971.

Bloom, M. Toward a developmental concept of love. *Journal of Human Relations,* 1967, *15,* 246–263.

Boakes, R. A., & Halliday, M. S. (Eds.), *Inhibition and learning.* New York: Academic Press, 1972.

Bohne, B. A., Ward, P. H., & Fernandez, C. Irreversible inner ear damage from rock music. *Audiology and Hearing Education,* 1978, *4,* 8, 10–13.

Bolt, M. Purpose in life and religious orientation. *Journal of Psychology and Theology,* 1975, *3,* 116–118.

Bongiovanni, A. *A review of research on the effects of punishment in the schools.* Paper presented at the conference on child abuse. Children's Hospital National Medical Center, Washington, D.C. 1977.

Bootzin, R. R. *Behavior modification and therapy: An introduction.* Cambridge, Mass.: Winthrop, 1975.

Bornstein, M. H. Chromatic vision in infancy. In H. W. Reese & L. P. Lipsitt (Eds.), *Advances in child development and behavior* (Vol. 12). New York: Academic Press, 1978.

Bossard, J. H. S. *Marriage and family.* Philadelphia: University of Pennsylvania Press, 1940.

Bourguignon, E. Introduction: A framework for the comparative study of altered states of consciousness. In E. Bourguignon (Ed.), *Religion, altered states of consciousness, and social change.* Columbus: Ohio State University Press, 1973.

Bourguignon, E. *Possession.* San Francisco, Calif.: Chandler & Sharp, 1976.

Bower, G. H. Improving memory. *Human Nature,* 1978, *1*(2), 64–73.

Bower, G. H. & Clark, M. C. Narrative stories as mediators for serial learning. *Psychonomic Science,* 1969, *14,* 181–182.

Bower, S. A., & Bower, G. H. *Asserting yourself.* Reading, Mass.: Addison-Wesley, 1976.

Bower, T. G. R. Object perception in infants. *Perception,* 1972, *1,* 15–30.

Bowes, W. A., Jr., Brackbill, Y., Conway, E., & Steinschneider, A. The effects of obstetrical medication on fetus and infant. *Monographs of the Society for Research in Child Development,* 1970, *35* (4, Serial No. 137).

Bowlby, J. *Attachment and loss.* Vol. 1. *Attachment.* London: Hogarth (New York: Basic Books), 1969.

Brady, J. V. Emotion and the sensitivity of psychoendocrine systems. In D. C. Glass (Ed.), *Neurophysiology and emotion.* New York: Rockefeller University Press, 1967.

Brady, J. V., Porter, R. W., Conrad, D. G., & Mason, J. W. Avoidance behavior and the development of gastroduodenal ulcers. *Journal of the Experimental Analysis of Behavior,* 1958, *1,* 69–73.

Bransford, J. D. & Franks, J. J. The abstraction of linguistic ideas. *Cognitive Psychology,* 1971, *2,* 331–350.

Brazelton, T. B. *Neonatal Behavioral Assessment Scale.* Philadelphia: Lippincott, 1973.

Brecher, E. M. *Licit and illicit drugs.* New York: Consumers Union, 1972.

Brechner, K. C., Boyce, J., Cass, R. A. & Schroeder, D. A. Social traps. Paper presented at American Psychological Association, September, 1975.

Brehm, J. W., & Cohen, A. R. *Explorations in cognitive dissonance.* New York: Wiley, 1962.

Brenner, M. H. *Mental illness and the economy.* Cambridge, Mass.: Harvard University Press, 1973.

Brett, G. S. Historical development of a theory of emotions. In M. L. Reymert (Ed.), *Feelings and emotions: The Wittenberg Symposium, 1928.* New York: Arno Press, 1973, pp. 388–397.

Brodsky, S. L. *Psychologists in the criminal justice system.* Urbana, Ill.: University of Illinois Press, 1973.

Broman, S. H., Nichols, P. I., & Kennedy, W. A. *Preschool IQ: Prenatal and early developmental correlates.* Copyright © 1975 by Lawrence Erlbaum Associates, Inc., Publishers. Reprinted by permission.

Brooks, D. N. Recognition memory after head injury: A signal detection analysis. *Cortex,* 1974, *10,* 224–230.

Brown, C. *Manchild in the promised land.* New York: MacMillan, 1965. Copyright © Claude Brown 1965. Excerpt reprinted by permission of Macmillan Publishing Co., Inc. and Jonathan Cape Ltd.

Brown, J. W. *Aphasia, apraxia, and agnosia,* Published 1972 by Charles C. Thomas, Publisher. Courtesy of Charles C. Thomas, Publisher, Springfield, Illinois.

Brown, R. W. Language and categories. In J. S. Bruner, J. J. Goodnow, and G. A. Austin (Eds.) *A study of thinking.* New York: Wiley, 1956.

Brown, R. W., Cazden, C. B., & Bellugi-Klima, U. The child's grammar from I to III. In J. P. Hill (Ed.) *Minnesota symposia on child psychology, vol. 2.* Minneapolis: University of Minnesota Press, 1969.

Brown, R. W. & McNeil, D. The "tip-of-the-tongue" phenomenon. *Journal of Verbal Learning and Verbal Behavior,* 1966, *5,* 325–337.

Bruck, C. Battle lines in the Ritalin war. *Human Behavior,* August, 1976.

Bruner, J. S. The course of cognitive growth. *American Psychologist,* 1964, *19,* 1–15.

Bruner, J. S. *Toward a theory of instruction.* Cambridge: Belknap Press, 1966.

Bruner, J. S. *Beyond the information given.* New York: Norton, 1973.

Brush, S. G. Should the history of science be rated X? *Science,* 1974, *183,* 1164–1172.

Buchwald, A. M., Coyne, J. C., & Cole, C. S. A critical evaluation of the learned helplessness model of depression. *Journal of Abnormal Psychology,* 1978, *87,* 180–193.

Buckhout, R. Psychology of the eyewitness. In P. G. Zimbardo, *Psychology and life* (9th ed., Diamond Printing). Glenview, Ill.: Scott, Foresman, 1977.

Buhler, C. Genetic aspects of the self. *Annals of the New York Academy of Sciences,* 1962, *96,* 730–764. (Cited in Havighurst, 1973).

Bullock, T. H., Orkand, R., & Grinnell, A. *Introduction to the nervous system.* San Francisco: W. H. Freeman, 1977.

Buxton, C. E. Latent learning and the goal gradient hypothesis. *Contributions to Psychological Theory,* 1940 *2*(6), 1–75.

Buys, C. Humans would do better without groups. *Personality and Social Psychology Bulletin,* 1978, *4,* 123–125.

Bykov, K. M. *The cerebral cortex and the internal organs.* New York: Chemical Publishing Co., 1957.

Byrne, D., & Clore, G. L. A reinforcement model of evaluative responses. *Personality: An International Journal,* 1970, *1,* 103–128.

Byrne, D., Ervin, C., & Lamberth, J. Continuity between the experimental study of attraction and real-life computer dating. *Journal of Personality and Social Psychology,* 1970, *16,* 157–165.

Caffey, J. On the theory and practice of shaping infants. *American Journal of Diseases of Children,* 1972, *124,* 10.

Caldwell, D. K. & Caldwell, M. C. Dolphins communicate—but they don't talk. *Naval Reviews,* June–July 1972, 23–27.

Calhoun, J. B. A "behavioral sink." In E. L. Bliss (Ed.), *Roots of behavior.* New York: Harper & Row, 1962.

Calhoun, J. B. Scientific quest for a path to the future. *Populi, Special Section,* 1976, vol. 3 no. 1.

Cameron, N. *Personality development and psychopathology: A dynamic approach.* Boston: Houghton Mifflin, 1963. Copyright © 1963 by Norman Cameron. Used by permission of Houghton Mifflin Company.

Cameron, P., Frank, R., Lifter, M., & Morrissey, P. Cognitive functionings of college students in a general psychology class. Paper presented at the meeting of the American Psychological Association, San Francisco, September 1968.

Campbell, C. Uri and the fisheye. *Psychology Today,* 1974, *8,* 76–77.

Cannon, W. B. *Bodily changes in pain, hunger, fear and rage.* (2nd ed.) New York: Appleton-Century-Crofts, 1929.

Cannon, W. B. Hunger and thirst. In C. Murchison (Ed.), *A handbook of general experimental psychology.* Worcester, Mass.: Clark University Press, 1934.

Caplan, G. A psychiatrist's casebook. *McCall's,* November 1969, p. 65.

Caplan, R. D., Cobb, S., French, J. R. P., Van Harrison, R., & Pinneau, R. *Job demands and worker health: Main effects and occupational differences.* Washington, D.C.: National Institutes for Occupational Safety and Health, 1975. Used by permission.

Carey, S., & Diamond, R. From piecemeal to configurational representation of faces. *Science,* 1977, *195,* 312–313.

Carlson, J. G., & Wood, R. D. Need the final solution be justified? Unpublished manuscript. University of Hawaii, 1974.

Carmichael, L. Ontogenetic development. In S. S. Stevens (Eds.), *Handbook of experimental psychology.* New York: Wiley, 1951.

Carmichael, L. The onset and early development of behavior. In P. H. Mussen (Ed.), *Carmichael's manual of child psychology* (Vol. 1, 3rd ed.). New York: Wiley, 1970.

Carrington, R. *Elephants.* New York: Basic Books, 1959.

Carter, R. Remarks for World Federation for Mental Health. Vancouver, British Columbia, August 25, 1977. Excerpt reprinted by permission.

Castaneda, C. *The teachings of Don Juan: A Yaqui way of knowledge.* New York: Ballantine Books, 1968. Copyright © 1968 by the Regents of the University of California. Excerpt reprinted by permission of The Regents of the University of California.

Castaneda, C. *A separate reality: Further conversations with Don Juan.* New York: Simon & Schuster, 1971.

Castaneda, C. *Journey to Ixtlan.* New York: Simon & Schuster, 1972.

Cattell, R. B. *The scientific analysis of personality.* Baltimore: Penguin, 1965.

Charatan, F. Personal communication to the author, Spring 1973.

Chess, S., Thomas, A., & Birch, H. G. *Your child is a person.* New York: Viking, 1965.

Chomsky, C. S. *The acquisition of syntax in children from 5 to 10.* Cambridge, Mass.: MIT Press, 1970.

Chomsky, N. *Aspects of a theory of syntax.* Cambridge, Mass.: MIT Press, 1965.

Christie, R., & Geis, F. L. (Eds.). *Studies in Machiavellianism.* New York: Academic Press, 1970.

Christy, P. R., Gelfand, D. M., & Hartmann, D. P. Effects of competition-induced frustration on two classes of modeled behavior. *Developmental Psychology*, 1971, *5*, 104–11.

Chu, F. D., & Trotter, S. *The madness establishment.* New York: Grossman Publishing, 1974.

Cisler, L. Unfinished business: Birth control and women's liberation. In R. Morgan (Ed.), *Sisterhood is powerful.* New York: Random House, 1970.

Clarizio, H. Some myths regarding the use of corporal punishment in schools. Paper presented at the Annual Meeting of the American Educational Research Association, April 2, 1975.

Clark, C. X., & Khatib, S. M. *Social change and the communication of legitimacy.* Oakland, Cal.: Society for the Study of African Sciences, 1978.

Clark, E. V. On the acquisition of the meaning of *before* and *after. Journal of Verbal Learning and Verbal Behavior*, 1971, *10*, 266–75.

Clark, W. C., & Yang, J. C. Acupunctural analgesia? Evaluation by signal detection theory. *Science*, 1974, *184*, 1096–1098.

Clarke, E., & O'Malley, C. D. *The human brain and spinal cord.* Berkeley: University of California Press, 1968.

Cohen, F. Psychological factors in the etiology of somatic illness. Unpublished report. Stanford University, 1975.

Cohen, S. Property destruction: Motives and meanings. In C. Ward (Ed.), *Vandalism.* London: Architectural Press, 1973.

Coleman, J. *Abnormal psychology and modern life* (4th edition). Copyright © 1972, 1964 by Scott, Foresman and Company.

Coleman, J. C. *Abnormal psychology and modern life* (5th ed.). Glenview, Ill.: Scott, Foresman, 1976.

Coleman, J. S. A brief summary of the Coleman report. In Equal educational opportunity: Symposium. *Harvard Educational Review*, 1969, *39*, 164–167.

Collins, A. M., & Quillian, M. R. Retrieval time from semantic memory. *Journal of Verbal Learning and Verbal Behavior*, 1969, *8*, 240–247.

Collins, B. E., Martin, J. C., Ashmore, R. D., & Rose, L. Some dimensions of the internal-external metaphor in theories of personality. *Journal of personality*, 1973, *41*, 471–92.

Condon, W. S. & Sander, L. W. Neonate movement is synchronized with adult speech: interactional participation and language acquisition. *Science*, 1974, *183*, 99–101.

Conger, J. J. *Current issues in adolescent development.* Master lectures on developmental psychology. Washington, D.C.: American Psychological Association, 1976.

Congressional Hearings on Worker Alienation. Hearings before the Subcommittee on Employment, Manpower, and Poverty. Washington, D.C.: U.S. Government Printing Office, 1972.

Conrad, R. Acoustic confusions and immediate memory. *British Journal of Psychology*, 1964, *55*, 77–84.

Cooley, C. H. *Human nature and the social order.* New York: Scribner, 1902.

Cooper, L. A., & Shepard, R. N. The time required to prepare for a rotated stimulus. *Memory and Cognition*, 1973, *1*, 246–250.

Cox, H. Eastern cults and Western culture: Why young Americans are buying oriental religions. *Psychology Today*, July 1977, 36–42.

Craik, F. I. M. & Lockhart, R. S. Levels of processing: A framework for memory research. *Journal of Verbal Learning and Verbal Behavior*, 1972, *11*, 671–84.

Crandall, J. E., & Rasmussen, R. D. Purpose in life as related to specific values. *Journal of Clinical Psychology*, 1975, *31*, 483–485.

Crockett, H. J. The achievement motive and differential occupational mobility in the U.S. *American Sociological Review*, 1962, *27*, 191–204.

Crook, J. H. The nature and function of territorial aggression. In M. F. A. Montagu (Ed.), *Man and aggression* (2nd ed.). New York: Oxford University Press, 1973.

Cross, P. G., Cattell, R. B., & Butcher, H. J. The personality patterns of creative artists. *British Journal of Educational Psychology*, 1967, *37*, 292–299.

Crowne, D. P., & Marlowe, D. *The approval motive.* New York: Wiley, 1964.

Crumbaugh, J. C., & Maholick, L. T. *The purpose-in-life test.* Copyright © 1969 Psychometric Affiliates. Reprinted by permission.

Cummins, R. A., Livesey, P. J., & Evans, J. G. M. A developmental theory of environmental enrichment. *Science*, 1977, *197*, 692–694.

Curran, J. P. Skills training as an approach to the treatment of heterosexual-social anxiety: A review. *Psychological Bulletin*, 1977, *84*, 140–157.

Darley, F. L. Treatment of acquired aphasia. In W. J. Friedlander, *Advances in neurology 7.* New York: Raven Press, 1975.

Darley, J. M., & Batson, C. O. From Jerusalem to Jericho: A study of situational variables in helping behavior. *Journal of Personality and Social Psychology*, 1973, *27*, 100–108.

Darley, J. M., & Latané, B. Bystander intervention in emergencies: Diffusion of responsibility. *Journal of Personality and Social Psychology*, 1968, *8*(4), 377–83.

Darwin, C. *The expression of the emotions in man and animals,* London: Murray, 1872.

Datan, N., Antonovsky, A., & Maoz, B. *A time to reap: The middle age of women in five Israeli sub-cultures.* Baltimore: Johns Hopkins University Press, 1978 (in press).

Davis, J. D., Cambell, C. S., Gallagher, R. J., & Zurakov, M. A. Disappearance of a humoral satiety factor during food deprivation. *Journal of Comparative and Physiological Psychology*, 1971, *75*, 476–482.

Davis, J. D., Gallagher, R. J., & Ladove, R. Food intake controlled by a blood factor. *Science*, 1967, *156*, 1247–1248.

Davison, G. C., & Neale, J. M. *Abnormal psychology: An experimental clinical approach.* New York: Wiley, 1974.

Davison, G. C., & Valins, S. Maintenance of self-attributed and drug-attributed behavior change. *Journal of Personality and Social Psychology*, 1969, *11*, 25–33.

Deci, E. L. Intrinsic motivation, extrinsic reinforcement, and inequity. *Journal of Personality and Social Psychology*, 1972, *22*, 113–120.

Deese, J., & Hulse, S. H. *The psychology of learning.* 3rd edition. New York: McGraw-Hill, 1967.

Dellas, M., & Gaier, E. L. Identification of creativity: The individual. *Psychological Bulletin*, 1970, *73*, 55–73.

Dembroski, T. M., & MacDougall, J. M. Stress effects on affiliation preferences among subjects possessing the Type A coronary-prone behavior pattern. *Journal of Personality and Social Psychology*, 1978, *36*, 23–33.

Dembroski, T. M., MacDougall, J. M., & Shields, J. L., Physiological reactions to social challenge in persons evidencing the Type A coronary-prone behavior pattern. *Journal of Human Stress*, 1977, *3*, 2–9.

Dement, W. C., & Kleitman, N. Cyclic variations in EEG during sleep and their relations to eye movement, body mobility and dreaming. *Electroencephalography and Clinical Neurophysiology*, 1957, *9*, 673–690.

Dempsey, D. Eye openers. July 20, 1975, *The New York Times Magazine*, pp. 10 ff.

Depue, R. A., & Monroe, S. M. Learned helplessness in the perspective of the depressive disorders: Conceptual and definitional issues. *Journal of Abnormal Psychology*, 1978, *87*, 3–20.

De Robertis, E. Submicroscopic morphology of the synapse. *International Review of Cytology*, 1959, *9*, 61–69.

De Valois, R. L., Albrecht, D. G., & Thorell, L. G. Cortical cells: Bar and edge detectors, or spatial frequency filters? In S. Cool (Ed.), *Frontiers of visual science.* New York: Springer-Verlag, 1979 (in press).

DeVellis, R. F., DeVellis, B. McE., & McCauley, C. Vicarious acquisition of learned helplessness. *Journal of Personality and Social Psychology*, 1978, *36*, 894–899.

Developmental Psychology Today (2nd ed.). New York: CRM (Random House), 1975.

Diener, E., & DeFour, D. Does television violence enhance program popularity? *Journal of Personality and Social Psychology*, 1978, in press.

Diener, E., Fraser, S. C., Beaman, A. L., & Kelem, R. T. Effects of deindividuation variables on stealing among Halloween trick-or-treaters. *Journal of Personality and Social Psychology*, 1976, *33*, 178–183.

Dillard, J. L. Negro children's dialect in the inner city. *The Florida FL Reporter*, Fall 1967.

Dillard, J. L. Non-standard Negro dialects—convergence or divergence? *The Florida FL Reporter*, Fall 1968.

Dillard, J. L. *Black English.* New York: Random House, 1972.

Dion, K. L., Berscheid, E., & Walster, E. What is beautiful is good. *Journal of Personality and Social Psychology*, 1972, *24*, 285–290.

Dipboye, R. L. Alternative approaches to deindividuation. *Psychological Bulletin*, 1977, *84*, 1057–1075.

Dittes, J. E. Typing the typologies: Some parallels in the career of church-sect and extrinsic-intrinsic. *Journal for the Scientific Study of Religion*, 1971, *10*, 375–383.

Dobelle, W. H. Current status of research on providing sight to the blind by electrical stimulation of the brain. *The Journal of Visual Impairment and Blindness*, 1977, *71*, 290–297.

Dodwell, P. E., Muir, D., & DiFranco, D. Responses of infants to visually presented objects. *Science*, 1976, *194*, 209–211.

Dolinsky, R. Remembering jokes and non-jokes. Colloquium presentation, 1978.

Dollard, J., Doob, L. W., Miller, N., Mower, O. H., & Sears, R. R. *Frustration and aggression.* New Haven: Yale University Press, 1939.

Dollard, J., & Miller, N. E. *Personality and psychotherapy.* New York: McGraw-Hill, 1950.

Donchin, E. On evoked potentials, cognition, and memory. *Science*, 1975, *190*, 1004–1005.

Dooling, D. J. & Lachman, R. Effects of comprehension on retention of prose. *Journal of Experimental Psychology*, 1971, *88*, 216–222.

Douglas, J. Letter from Tokyo:(4) Pioneering a non-western psychology. *Science News*, 1978, *113*(10), 154–158.

Dove, A. Taking the chitling test. *Newsweek*, July 15, 1968, 51–52.

Drabman, R. S., & Thomas, M. H. Does media violence increase children's tolerance of real-life aggression? *Developmental Psychology*, 1974, *10*, 418–421.

Driscoll, R., Davis, K. E., & Lipetz, M. E. Parental interference and romantic love: The Romeo and Juliet effect. *Journal of Personality and Social Psychology*, 1972, *24*, 1–10.

(DSM-II) *Diagnostic and Statistical Manual of Mental Disorders.* Washington, D.C.: American Psychiatric Association, 1968.

Dubos, R. *Man adapting.* New Haven: Yale University Press, 1965.

Dubos, R. Symbiosis between the earth and humankind. *Science*, 1976, *193*, 459–462. Copyright © 1976 by the American Association for the Advancement of Science. Reprinted by permission of the association and the author.

Dubos, R. Health and creative adaptation. *Human Nature*, January 1978, *1*, 74–82.

Dudycha, G. J. An objective study of punctuality in relation to personality and achievement. *Archives of Psychology*, 1936, (204), 1–53.

Duffy, E. *Activation and behavior.* New York: John Wiley, 1962.

Duncker, K. On problem solving. *Psychological Monographs*, 1945, *58*(5), Whole No. 270.

Dutton, D., & Aron, A. Some evidence for heightened sexual attraction under conditions of high anxiety. *Journal of Personality and Social Psychology*, 1974, *30*, 510–517.

Dwornicka, B., Jasienska, A., Smolarz, W. & Wawryk, R. Attempt of determining the fetal reaction to acoustic stimulation. *Acta Oto-Laryngologica*, Stockholm, 1964, *57*, 571–574.

Dyer, W. *Your erroneous zones.* New York: Funk & Wagnalls, 1976.

Eagly, A. H., & Himmelfarb, S. Attitudes and opinions. In M. Rosenzweig & L. W. Porter (Eds.), *Annual Review of Psychology*, 1978. Palo Alto, Ca.: Annual Reviews Press.

Ebbesen, E. B., Kjos, G. L., & Konecni, V. J. Spatial ecology: Its effects on the choice of friends and enemies. *Journal of Experimental Social Psychology*, 1976, *12*(6), 505–518.

Ebbinghaus, H. *Memory.* Teachers College, Columbia University, 1913, (Originally published: Liepzig: Altenberg, 1885).

Edwards, A. E., & Acker, L. E. A demonstration of the long-term retention of a conditioned galvanic skin response. *Psychosomatic Medicine*, 1962, *24*, 459–463.

Edwards, D. A. Neonatal administration of androstenedione, testosterone, or testosterone propionate: Effects on ovulation, sexual receptivity, and aggressive behavior in female mice. *Physiological Behavior*, 1971, *6*, 223–228.

Eich, J. E., Weingarten, H., Stillman, R. C., & Gillin, J. C. State-dependent accessibility of retrieval cues in the retention of a categorized list. *Journal of Verbal Learning and Verbal Behavior*, 1975, *14*, 408–17.

Eimas, P. D., Siqueland, E. R., Jusczyk, P. & Vigorito, J. Speech perception in infants. *Science*, 1971, *171*, 303–6.

Ekman, P. Cross-cultural studies of facial expression. In P. Ekman (Ed.), *Darwin and facial expressions: A century of research in review.* New York: Academic Press, 1973.

Ekman, P., Sorenson, E. R., & Friesen, W. V. Pancultural elements in facial displays in emotion. *Science*, 1969, *164*, 86–88.

Elliott, J. The power and pathology of prejudice. In P. G. Zimbardo & F. L. Ruch, *Psychology and life*, 9th Ed., Diamond Printing. Glenview, Ill.: Scott, Foresman, 1977.

Ellis, A. *Reason and emotion in psychotherapy.* New York: Lyle Stuart, 1962.

Elmer, E. Studies of child abuse and infant accidents. *Mental Health Program Reports, No. 5.* (DHEW) Publication No. (HSM) 72-9042. Chevy Chase, Md.: National Institute of Mental Health, 1971.

Encyclopedia Brittanica, 1974 *Vol. 2* Macropaedia, p. 506.

Engen, T., Lipsitt, L. P., & Kaye, H. Olfactory responses and adaptation in the human neonate. *Journal of Comparative and Physiological Psychology*, 1963, *56*, 73–77.

Erickson, J. R., & Jones, M. R. Thinking. In M. R. Rosenzweig & L. W. Porter (Eds.), *Annual Review of Psychology*, 1978, Vol. 29. Palo Alto, Calif.: Annual Reviews Press, 1978, 61–90.

Erikson, E. H. *Childhood and society* (2nd ed.). New York: Norton, 1963.

Erikson, K. T. *Wayward puritans: A study in the sociology of deviance.* New York: Wiley, 1966.

Eron, L. D., Huesmann, L. R., Lefkowitz, M. M., & Walder, L. O. Does television violence cause aggression? *American Psychologist*, 1972, *27*, 253–263.

Estes, W. K. *Learning theory and mental development.* New York: Academic Press, 1970.

Estes, W. K. Learning theory and intelligence. *American Psychologist*, 1974, *29*, 740–749.

Evans, R. I. (Discussions with A. Bandura) In *The making of psychology.* New York: Knopf, 1976.

Eysenck, H. J. The effects of psychotherapy: An evaluation. *Journal of Consulting Psychology*, 1952, *16*, 319–24.

Eysenck, H. J. Behavior therapy, symptom remission and transference in neurotics. *American Journal of Psychiatry*, 1963, *119*, 867–871.

Eysenck, H. J. *The biological basis of personality.* Springfield, Ill.: C. C. Thomas, 1967.

Eysenck, H. J. *Eysenck on extraversion.* New York: Wiley, 1973.

Eysenck, H. J., & Eysenck, S. B. G. *Personality structure and measurement.* London: Routledge & Kegan Paul, 1967.

Eysenck, H. J. & Eysenck, S. B. G. *Eysenck personality inventory.* San Diego: Educational and Industrial Testing Service, 1968.

Eysenck, M. W. Extraversion, verbal learning and memory. *Psychological Bulletin*, 1976, *88*, 75–90.

Factor, R. M., & Waldron, I. Contemporary population densities and human health. *Nature*, 1973, *243*, 381–384.

Fairweather, G. W., Sanders, D. H., Maynard, R. F., & Cressler, D. L. *Community life for the mentally ill: Alternative to institutional care.* Chicago: Aldine, 1969.

Fantz, R. L. Pattern vision in newborn infants. *Science*, 1963, *140*, 296–97.

Faucheux, C. & Moscovici, S. Le style de compôtement d'une minorité et son influence sur les résponses d'une majorité. *Bulletin du Centre d'Etudes et Recherches Psychologiques*, 1967, *16*, 337–360.

Feather, N. Valence of outcome and expectation of success in relation to task difficulty and perceived locus of control. *Journal of Personality and Social Psychology*, 1967, *7*, 372–386.

Fechner, G. T. *Elements of psychophysics.* H. E. Adler (Trans.) D. H. Howes & E. G. Boring (Eds.) New York: Holt, Rinehart, & Winston, 1966. (First German edition, 1860.)

Feldman, M. J., & Hersen, M. Attitudes toward death in nightmare subjects. *Journal of Abnormal Psychology,* 1967, *72,* 421–425.

Ferguson, G. A. On learning and human ability. *Canadian Journal of Psychology,* 1954, *8,* 95–112.

Ferguson, G. A. On transfer and the abilities of man. *Canadian Journal of Psychology,* 1956, *10,* 121–131.

Ferguson, P. C., & Gowan, J. C. TM: Some Preliminary Findings. *Journal of Humanistic Psychology,* 1976, *16*(3).

Ferrare, N. A. Institutionalization and attitude change in an aged population. Unpublished doctoral dissertation. Western Reserve University, 1962.

Ferrero, G. L. *Criminal man according to the classification of Cesare Lombroso.* New York: Putnam's, 1911.

Ferriera, A. J., & Winter, W. W. Information exchange and silence in normal and abnormal families. In W. W. Winter & A. J. Ferriera (Eds.), *Research in family interaction.* Palo Alto, Calif.: Science & Behavior Books, 1964.

Festinger, L. A theory of social comparison processes. *Human Relations.* 1954, *7,* 117–140.

Festinger, L. *A theory of cognitive dissonance.* Stanford, Calif.: Stanford University Press, 1957.

Festinger, L., & Carlsmith, J. M. Cognitive consequences of forced compliance. *Journal of Abnormal and Social Psychology,* 1959, *58,* 203–211.

Festinger, L., Schachter, S., & Back, K. *Social pressures in informal groups: A study of human factors in housing.* New York: Harper & Row, 1950.

Fillmore, C. J. The case for case. In E. Bach & R. T. Harms, (Eds.) *Universals in linguistic theory.* New York: Holt, Rinehart & Winston, 1968, pp. 1–88.

Fillmore, C. J. Pragmatics and the description of discourse. In C. Fillmore, G. Lakoff, & R. Lakoff (Eds.). *Berkeley studies in syntax and semantics.* Berkeley: University of California Press, 1974.

Fischetti, M., Curran, J. P., & Wessberg, H. W. Sense of timing: A skill deficit in heterosexual-socially anxious males. *Behavior Modification,* April 1977, *1*(2), 179–194.

Fish, J. M. *Placebo therapy.* San Francisco: Jossey-Bass, 1973.

Fisher, C., Byrne, J. V., Edwards, A., & Kahn, E. REM and NREM nightmares. In E. Hartman (Ed.), *Sleep and Dreaming,* Boston: Little, Brown, 1970.

Flavell, J. H. *Cognitive development.* Englewood Cliffs, N.J.: Prentice-Hall, 1977.

Fleischman, P. R. Letter to *Science* concerning "On being sane in insane places." *Science,* April 27, 1973.

Fletcher, C. R. Attributing responsibility to the deviant: A factor in psychiatric referrals by the general public. *Journal of Health and Social Behavior,* 1967, *8,* 185–96.

Folkins, D. H., Lawson, K. D., Opton, E. M., Jr., & Lazarus, R. S. Desensitization and the experimental reduction of threat. *Journal of Abnormal Psychology,* 1968, *73,* 100–113.

Ford, C., & Beach, F. *Patterns of sexual behavior.* New York: Paul Hoeber, 1951.

Forrest, D. V. Nonsense and sense in schizophrenic language. *Schizophrenia Bulletin,* 1976, *2,* 286–381.

Fouts, R. S. Personal communication, July, 1977.

Foxx, R. M., & Azrin, N. H. Dry pants: A rapid method of toilet training children. *Behaviour Research and Therapy,* 1973, *11,* 435–442.

Foy, D. W., Eisler, R. M., & Pinkston, S. Modeled assertion in a case of explosive rages. *Journal of Behavioral Therapy and Experimental Psychiatry,* 1975, *6,* 135–137.

Frank, J. D. *Persuasion and healing.* New York: Schocken Books, 1963.

Frankl, V. E. *Man's search for meaning.* Boston: Beacon Press, 1963. (Originally published, 1959).

Fraser, S. C. Deindividuation: Effects of anonymity on aggression in children. Unpublished mimeograph report. University of Southern California, 1974.

Frederiksen, L. W., Jenkins, J. O., Foy, D. W., & Eisler, R. M. Social-skills training to modify abusive verbal outbursts in adults. *Journal of Applied Behavior Analysis,* 1976, *9,* 117–125.

Freedman, J. L. *Crowding and behavior.* San Francisco: Freeman, 1975.

Freedman, J. L., & Fraser, S. C. Compliance without pressure: The foot-in-the-door technique. *Journal of Personality and Social Psychology,* 1966, *4,* 195–202.

Freedman, J. L., Klevansky, S., & Ehrlich, P. R. The effect of crowding on human task performance. *Journal of Applied Social Psychology,* 1971, *1,* 7–25.

Freemon, F. R. *Sleep research: A critical review.* Springfield, Ill.: Charles C. Thomas, 1972. Reprinted by permission.

French, J. R., & Caplan, R. D. Occupational stress and individual strain. Unpublished paper. University of Michigan Institute for Social Research, 1971.

Freud, S. *The interpretation of dreams, Vol. 5. The standard edition of the complete psychological works of Sigmund Freud.* London: Hogarth Press, 1900.

Freud, S. Psychopathology of everyday life. In J. Strachey (Ed.), *The standard edition of the complete psychological works of Sigmund Freud.* London: Hogarth Press, 1960. (First English edition, 1904).

Freud, S. *Introductory lectures on psycho-analysis.* J. Riviera (Tr.). London: Allen & Unwin, 1923.

Fried, M. & Gleicher, P. Some sources of resident satisfaction in an urban slum. In H. M. Proshansky et al., *Environmental Psychology,* 2nd ed., New York: Holt, Rinehart & Winston, 1976.

Friedman, M., & Rosenman, R. F. *Type A behavior and your heart.* New York: Knopf, 1974.

Friedman, S. B., Ader, R., & Glasgow, L. A. Effects of psychological stress in adult mice inoculated with coxsackie B viruses. *Psychosomatic Medicine,* 1965, *27,* 361–368.

Friedman, S. B., & Glasgow, L. A. Psychologic factors and resistance to infectious disease. *Pediatric Clinics of North America,* 1966, *13,* 315–335.

Friedrich, W., & Boriskin, J. The role of the child in abuse: A review of the literature. *American Journal of Orthopsychiatry,* October 1976.

Fromm, E. *Man for himself.* New York: Holt Rinehart & Winston, 1947.

Fromm, E. *The art of loving.* New York: Harper & Row, 1956.

Fry, D. *Homo loquens: Man as a talking animal.* Cambridge, England: Cambridge University Press, 1977.

Funkenstein, D. H., King, S. H., & Drolette, M. E. *Mastery of stress.* Cambridge, Mass.: Harvard University Press, 1957.

Gagné, R., & Briggs, L. *Principles of instructional design.* New York: Holt, Rinehart & Winston, 1974.

Gagnon, J. H. *Human sexualities.* Glenview, Ill.: Scott, Foresman, 1977.

Galle, O. R., Grove, W. R., & McPherson, J. M. Population density and pathology. *Science,* 1972, *176,* 23–30.

Gallup, G. The growing acceptance of racial integration. *San Francisco Chronicle,* October 13, 1975.

Gantt, W. H. Reflexology, schizokinesis, and autokinesis. *Conditional reflex,* 1966, *1,* 57–68.

Garber, R. M., & Maslach, C. The parole hearing: Decision or justification? *Law and Human Behavior,* 1977, *1,* 261–281.

Gardner, L. Deprivation dwarfism. *Scientific American,* 1972, *227,* 76–82.

Gardner, R. & Gardner, B. T. Teaching sign language to the chimpanzee. *Science,* 1969, *165,* 664–672.

Garmezy, N. Children at risk: The search for the antecedents of schizophrenia, Part II. *Schizophrenia Bulletin,* 1974, *1*(9), 55–125.

Garmezy, N., & Streitman, S. Children at risk: The search for the antecedents of schizophrenia, Part I. *Schizophrenia Bulletin,* 1974, *1*(8), 13–90.

Gatlin, L. L. *Information theory and the living system.* New York: Columbia University Press, 1972. Copyright © 1972 Columbia University Press. Excerpt reprinted by permission.

Gatlin, L. L. Meaningful information creation: An alternative interpretation of the psi phenomenon. *The Journal of the American Society for Psychical Research,* 1977, *71,* 1–18.

Gazzaniga, M. S. *The bisected brain.* New York: Appleton-Century-Crofts, 1970.

Gelles, R. J., Straus, M. A., & Steinmetz, S. K. *Violence in the American family,* 1978, in press.

Gerbner, G. & Gross, L. The scary world of TV's heavy viewer. *Psychology Today,* April 1976, *9*(11), 41 ff.

Gergen, K. J., Gergen, M. M., & Barton, W. H. Deviance in the dark. *Psychology Today,* October 1973, pp. 129–130.

German, D. C., & Bowden, D. M. Catecholamine systems as the neural substrate for intracranial self-stimulation: A hypothesis. *Brain Research*, 1974, *73*, 381–419.

Geschwind, N. The organization of language and the brain. *Science*, 1970, *170*, 940–944.

Gewirtz, J. L., & Baer, D. M. Deprivation and satiation of social reinforcers as drive conditions. *Journal of Abnormal and Social Psychology*, 1958, *57*, 165–172.

Gibbon, J. Discriminated punishment: Avoidable and unavoidable shock. *Journal of the Experimental Analysis of Behavior*, 1967, *10*, 451–60.

Gibson, E. *Principles of perceptual learning and development.* New York: Appleton-Century-Crofts, 1969.

Gibson, E. J. & Walk, R. D. The "visual cliff." *Scientific American*, 1960, *202*(4), 67–71.

Glanzer, M. & Cunitz, A. R. Two storage mechanisms in free recall. *Journal of Verbal Learning and Verbal Behavior*, 1966, *5*, 351–60.

Glass, D. C. *Behavior patterns, stress and coronary disease.* Hillsdale, New Jersey: L. Erlbaum Associates, 1977.

Glass, D. C., & Singer, J. E. *Urban stress: Experiments on noise and social stressors.* New York: Academic Press, 1972.

Glock, C. On the study of religious commitment. *Religious Education*, 1962, *57*.

Glucksberg, S. & Danks, J. H. *Experimental psycholinguistics.* Hillsdale, N. J.: L. Erlbaum Associates, 1975.

Goldberg, P. Are women prejudiced against women? *Transaction*, 1968, *5*(5), 28–30.

Goldstein, A., Kaizer, S., & Whitby, O. Psychotropic effects of caffeine in man. IV. Quantitative and qualitative differences associated with habituation to coffee. *Clinical Pharmacology and Therapeutics*, 1969, *10*, 489–497.

Goode, E. Multiple drug use among marijuana smokers. *Social Problems*, 1969, *17*, 48–64.

Goodman, D. A. Learning from lobotomy. *Human Behavior*, 1978, *7*(1), 44–49.

Goodman, L. S. & Gilman, A. *The pharmacological basis of therapeutics.* (4th ed.) New York: Macmillan, 1970.

Goodwin, D. W., Powell, B., Brener, D., Hoine, H. & Stone, J. Alcohol and recall: state-dependent effects in man. *Science*, 1969, *163*, 1358–1360.

Gorney, R. Paper presented at annual meeting of the American Psychiatric Association, 1976.

Gottesman, I. I., & Shields, J. A critical review of recent adoption, twin, and family studies of schizophrenia: Behavioral genetics perspective. *Schizophrenia Bulletin*, 1976, *2*, 360–401.

Gough, H. G. Techniques for identifying the creative research scientist. In *Conference on the creative person.* Berkeley: University of California, Institute of Personality Assessment and Research, 1961.

Graham, T. F. *Medieval minds.* London: Allen & Unwin, 1967.

Greeley, A. M., & McCready, W. C. Are we a nation of mystics? *New York Times Magazine*, Jan. 26, 1975, 12–25.

Gregory, R. L. *Eye and brain: The psychology of seeing.* New York: McGraw-Hill, 1966. Copyright © 1966 McGraw-Hill. Excerpt used with permission of McGraw-Hill Book Company.

Griffitt, W., & Veitch, R. Preacquaintance attitude similarity and attraction revisited: Ten days in a fall-out shelter. *Sociometry*, 1974, *37*, 163–173.

Grimmett, H. Personal communication to the author, October 1970.

Gross, C. G., Rocha-Miranda, C. E., & Bender, D. B. Visual properties of neurons in inferotemporal cortex of the macaque. *Journal of Neurophysiology*, 1972, *35*, 96–111.

Grossman, S. P. Neuropharmacology of central mechanisms contributing to control of food and water intake. In C. Code (Ed.), *Handbook of physiology.* Baltimore: Williams & Wilkins, 1967.

Grossman, S. P. Physiological basis of specific and nonspecific motivational processes. In W. J. Arnold (Ed.), *Nebraska symposium on motivation.* Lincoln: University of Nebraska Press, 1968.

Guilford, J. P. *Personality.* New York: McGraw-Hill, 1959.

Guilford, J. P. *The nature of human intelligence.* New York: McGraw-Hill, 1967.

Guilleminault, C., Billiard, M., Montplaisir, J., & Dement, W. C. Altered states of consciousness in disorders of daytime sleepiness. *Journal of the Neurological Sciences*, 1975, *26*, 377–393.

Gur, R. E. Conjugate lateral eye movements as an index of hemispheric activation. *Journal of Personality and Social Psychology*, 1973, *31*, 751–757.

Guthrie, R. V. *Even the rat was white: A historical view of psychology.* New York: Harper & Row, 1976.

Haas, H., Fink, H., & Hartfelder, G. Das placeboproblem. *Fortschoritte der Arzneimittleforschung*, 1959, *1*, 279–454. Translated in *Psychopharmacology Service Center Bulletin*, 1959, *2*(8), 1–65. U. S. Department of Health, Education and Welfare, Public Health Service.

Haas, K. *Understanding ourselves and others.* Englewood Cliffs, N.J.: Prentice-Hall, 1965.

Hadanard, J. *The psychology of invention in the mathematical field.* Princeton, N.J.: Princeton University Press, 1945.

Haith, M. M., Bergman, T., & Moore, M. J. Eye contact and face scanning in early infancy. *Science*, 1977, *198*, 853–854.

Hall, G. S., & Lindzey, G. *Theories of personality.* New York: Wiley, 1957. Reprinted by permission.

Hall, M. H. A conversation with Masters and Johnson *Psychology Today*, 1969, *3*(2), 50–58.

Halverson, H. M. An experimental study of prehension in infants by means of systematic cinema records. *Genetic Psychology Monographs*, 1931, *10*, Nos. 2–3, 107–286.

Hamill, R., Wilson, T. D., & Nisbett, R. E. Ignoring sample bias: Inferences about populations from atypical cases. Unpublished manuscript, University of Michigan, 1978.

Hammer E. F. Creativity and feminine ingredients in young male artists. *Perceptual and Motor Skills*, 1964, *19*, 414.

Haney, C. Consensus information and attitude change. Unpublished Ph.D. dissertation, Stanford University, 1978.

Haney, C., & Manzolati, J. Television criminology: Network illusions of criminal justice realities. Unpublished manuscript, Stanford University, 1977.

Haney, C., & Zimbardo, P. G. The socialization into criminality: On becoming a prisoner and a guard. In J. L. Tapp & F. L. Levine (Eds.), *Law, justice and the individual in society: Psychological and legal issues.* New York: Holt, Rinehart & Winston, 1977, 198–223.

Hansel, C. E. M. *ESP: A scientific evaluation*, New York: Scribner's, 1966.

Hanson, D., Gottesman, I. & Meehl, P. Genetic theories and the validation of psychiatric diagnosis: Implications for the study of children of schizophrenics. *Journal of Abnormal Psychology*, 1977, *86*, 575–588.

Harlow, H. F. The formation of learning sets. *Psychological Review*, 1949, *56*, 51–65.

Harlow, H. F. Learning set and error factor theory. In S. Koch (Ed.), *Psychology: A study of a science.* Vol II, New York: McGraw-Hill, 1959.

Harlow, H. F., & Suomi, S. J. Induced depression in monkeys. *Behavioral Biology*, 1974, *12*, 273–296.

Harner, M. J. The sound of rushing water. In M. J. Harner (Ed.), *Hallucinogens and shamanism.* Oxford: Oxford University Press, 1973, pp. 15–27.

Harris, V. A., & Katkin, E. S. Primary and secondary emotional behavior: An analysis of the role of autonomic feedback on affect, arousal, and attribution. *Psychological Bulletin*, 1975, *82*, 904–916.

Harrower, M. Were Hitler's henchmen mad? *Psychology Today*, July 1976, 76–80.

Harshman, R. A., Crawford, H. J., & Hecht, E. Marijuana, cognitive style, and lateralized hemispheric functions. In S. Cohen & R. C. Stillman (Eds.), *The therapeutic potential of marijuana.* New York: Plenum, 1976, 205–254.

Hart, J. T. Memory and the memory-monitoring process. *Journal of Verbal Learning and Verbal Behavior*, 1967, *6*, 685–91.

Hartshorne, H., & May, M. A. *Studies in the nature of character.* Vol. 1. *Studies in deceit.* New York: Macmillan, 1928.

Hartshorne, H., & May, M. A. *Studies in the nature of character.* Vol. 2. *Studies in service and self-control.* New York: Macmillan, 1929.

Harvey, J. A. Behavioral tolerance. In J. A. Harvey (Ed.), *Behavioral analysis of drug action.* Glenview, Ill.: Scott, Foresman, 1971.

Hashim, S. A., & Van Itallie, T. B. Studies on normal and obese subjects with a monitored food dispensing device. *Annals of the New York Academy of Sciences*, 1965, *131*, 654–61.

Hatano, G. Personal communication to the author, August, 1975.

Hauri, P. *The sleep disorders.* The Upjohn Company, copyright ©, 1977. Reprinted with permission from Scope® Publications and the author.

Havighurst, R. J. History of developmental psychology: Socialization and personality development through the life span. In P. B. Baltes & K. W. Schaie (Eds.), *Life-span developmental psychology: Personality and socialization.* New York: Academic Press, 1973.

Haviland, S. E., & Clark, H. H. What's new? Acquiring new information as a process in comprehension. *Journal of Verbal Learning and Verbal Behavior,* 1974, *13,* 512–521.

Hawkins, G. *Stonehenge decoded.* Garden City, N.Y.: Doubleday, 1965.

Hayes, J. R. Memory, goals, and problem solving. In B. Kleinmuntz (Ed.), *Problem solving: Research, method, and theory.* New York: Wiley, 1966.

Hayes, K. J. & Hayes, C. Imitation in a home raised chimpanzee. *Journal of Comparative and Physiological Psychology,* 1952, *45,* 450–9.

Hazlitt, W. On taste. In *Sketches and essays.* London: John Templeman, 1839.

Hebb, D. O. *Organization of behavior.* New York: Wiley, 1949.

Hebb, D. O. *A textbook of psychology.* Philadelphia: Saunders, 1958.

Hebb, D. O. What psychology is about. *American Psychologist,* 1974, *29,* 71–79.

Heider, F. *The psychology of interpersonal relations.* New York: Wiley, 1958.

Helson, R. Sex differences in creative style. *Journal of Personality,* 1967, *35,* 214–33.

Heron, W. Cognitive and physiological effects of perceptual isolation. In P. Solomon et al. (Eds.), *Sensory deprivation.* Cambridge, Mass.: Harvard University Press, 1961.

Herrera, G. Effects of nutritional supplementation and early education on physical and cognitive development. Paper presented at the West Virginia University Conference on Life-Span Developmental Psychology: Intervention, Morgantown, W. Va., June 1978.

Hersen, M., & Bellock, A. J. Assessment of social skills. In A. R. Ciminero, K. R. Calhoun, & H. E. Adams (Eds.), *Handbook of Behavioral Assessment.* New York: Wiley, 1976.

Hershenson, M., Munsinger, H. & Kessen, W. Preference for shapes of intermediate variability in the newborn human. *Science,* 1965, *147,* 630–631.

Herzberg, F. *Work and the nature of man.* Cleveland: World Publishing Company, 1966.

Herzberg, F. One more time: How do you motivate employees? *Harvard Business Review,* January–February, 1968.

Hess, W., & Akert, K. Experimental data on the role of hypothalamus in the mechanism of emotional behavior. *Archives of Neurological Psychiatry,* 1955, *73,* 127–129.

Heston, L. L. The genetics of schizophrenia and schizoid disease. *Science,* 1970, *112,* 249–256.

Hicks, D. J. Effects of co-observer's sanctions and adult presence on imitative aggression. *Child Development,* 1968, *39,* 303–9.

Higbee, K. L. *Your memory: How it works and how to improve it.* Englewood Cliffs, N. J.: Prentice Hall, 1977.

Hilgard, E. R. *Hypnotic susceptibility.* New York: Harcourt Brace Jovanovich, 1965.

Hilgard, E. R. The domain of hypnosis. With some comments on alternative paradigms. *American Psychologist,* 1973, *28,* 972–82.

Hilgard, E. R. Neodissociation theory of multiple cognitive control systems. In G. E. Schwartz & D. Shapiro (Eds.), *Consciousness and self-regulation,* Vol. 1. New York: Plenum, 1976, pp. 137–171.

Hilgard, E. R. *Divided consciousness: Multiple controls in human thought and action.* New York: Wiley, 1977.

Hilgard, E. R., & Hilgard, J. R. Hypnosis in the control of pain. *The Stanford Magazine,* Spring-Summer 1974, 58–62.

Hilgard, E. R., & Hilgard, J. R. *Hypnosis in the relief of pain.* Los Altos, Calif.: W. Kaufman, 1975.

Hilgard, J. R. *Personality and hypnosis.* Chicago: University of Chicago Press, 1970.

Hill, C. T., Rubin, Z., & Peplau, L. A. Breakups before marriage: The end of 103 affairs. *Journal of Social Issues,* 1976, *32,* 147–168.

Hinkle, L. E., & Wolff, H. C. Communist interrogation and indoctrination of "Enemies of the state." *Archives of Neurology and Psychiatry,* 1956, *76,* 115–174.

Hiroto, D. S. Locus of control and learned helplessness. *Journal of Experimental Psychology,* 1974, *102*(2), 187–93.

Hiroto, D. S., & Seligman, M. E. P. Generality of learned helplessness in man. *Journal of Personality and Social Psychology,* 1975, *31,* 311–32.

Hirsch, H. V. B. Visual perception in cats after environmental surgery. *Experimental Brain Research,* 1972, *15,* 405–423.

Hirsch, H. V. B., & Spinelli, D. N. Visual experience modifies distribution of horizontally and vertically oriented receptive fields of cats. *Science,* 1970, *168,* 869–871.

Hirsch, H. V. B., & Spinelli, D. N. Modification of the distribution of receptive field orientation in cats by selective visual exposure during development. *Experimental Brain Research,* 1971, *13,* 509–527.

Hitler, A. *My Battle.* E. T. S. Dugdale (Trans.). New York: Houghton Mifflin, 1933.

Hitt, W. D. Two models of man. *American Psychologist,* 1969, *24,* 651–658.

Ho, B. T., Richards, D. W., & Chute, D. L. *Drug discrimination and state dependent learning.* New York: Academic Press, 1978.

Hobbes, T. *Leviathan.* London: A Crooke, 1651.

Hobson, J. A., & McCarley, R. W. The brain as a dream state generator: An activation-synthesis hypothesis of the dream process. *American Journal of Psychiatry,* 1977, *134,* 1335–1348.

Hockett, C. D. The origin of speech. *Scientific American,* 1960, *203,* 88–96.

Hokanson, J. E. & Burgess, M. The effects of three types of aggression on vascular processes. *Journal of Abnormal and Social Psychology,* 1962, *64,* 446–49.

Hokanson, J. E., DeGood, D. E., Forrest, M. S., & Brittain, T. M. Availability of avoidance behaviors in modulating vascular-stress responses *Journal of Personality and Social Psychology,* 1971, *19*(1), 60–68.

Holden, C. Amphetamines: Tighter controls on the horizon. *Science,* 1976, *194,* 1027–1028.

Holden, C. Patuxent: Controversial prison clings to belief in rehabilitation. *Science,* 1978, *199,* 665–668.

Holliman, N. B. Some principles as applied to human learning. Mimeo paper, Midwestern State University, 1976.

Hollingshead, A. B., & Redlich, F. C. *Social class and mental illness: A community study.* New York: Wiley, 1958.

Holmes, T. H., & Masuda, M. Life change and illness susceptibility. In B. S. Dohrenwend & B. P. Dohrenwend (Eds.), *Stressful life events: Their nature and effects.* New York: Wiley, 1974.

Holmes, T. S., & Holmes, T. H. Short-term intrusions into the life-style routine. *Journal of Psychosomatic Research,* 1970, *14,* 121–32.

Homans, G. C. *The human group.* New York: Harcourt, Brace & World, 1950.

Homans, G. C. *Social behavior: Its elementary forms.* New York: Harcourt, Brace & World, 1961.

Homans, G. C., Interview with B. F. Skinner. *Harvard Magazine,* July–August 1977, 53–58.

Honzik, M. P. The development of intelligence. In B. B. Wolman (ed.). *Handbook of general psychology.* Englewood Cliffs, N.J.: Prentice-Hall, 1973.

Hood, R. W., Jr. Religious orientation and the report of religious experience. *Journal for the Scientific Study of Religion,* 1970, *9,* 285–292.

Hood, R. W., Jr. The construction and preliminary validation of a measure of reported mystical experience. *Journal for the Scientific Study of Religion,* 1975, *14,* 29–41.

Horn, J. L. Organization of data on life-span development of human abilities. In L. R. Goulet & P. B. Baltes (Eds.), *Life-span developmental psychology: Research and theory.* New York: Academic Press, 1970.

Horner, M. S. Fail: Bright women. *Psychology Today,* November 1969, *3,* 36–38. Copyright © 1969 Ziff-Davis Publishing Company. Excerpt reprinted by permission.

Horney, K. *Neurosis and human growth.* N.Y. Norton, 1950.

Horowitz, M. Hallucinations: An information-processing approach. In R. K. Siegel & L. J. West (Eds.), *Hallucinations: Behavior, experience, and theory.* New York: Wiley, 1975, 163–196.

Horton, L. E. Generalization of aggressive behavior in adolescent delinquent boys. *Journal of Applied Behavior Analysis,* 1970, *3,* 205–211.

Hosobuchi, Y., Adams, J. E., & Linchitz, R. Pain relief by electrical stimulation of the central gray matter in humans and its reversal by naloxone. *Science,* 1977, *197,* 183–186.

Hovland, C. I., Janis, I. L., & Kelley, H. H. *Communication and persuasion.* New Haven: Yale University Press, 1953.

Howarth, E., & Eysenck, H. J. Extraversion, arousal, and paired associate recall. *Journal of Experimental Research in Personality,* 1968, *3,* 114–116.

Howes, E. R. Twin speech: a language of their own. *New York Times,* Sept. 11, 1977. Copyright © 1977 by the New York Times Company. Excerpts reprinted by permission.

Hubel, D. H., & Wiesel, T. N. Receptive fields of single neurones in the cat's striate cortex. *Journal of Physiology* (London), 1959, *148,* 574–591.

Hubel, D. H., & Wiesel, T. N. The period of susceptibility to the physiological effects of unilateral eye closure in kittens. *Journal of Physiology,* 1970, *206,* 419–436.

Hudgins, C. V. Conditioning and the voluntary control of the pupillary light reflex. *Journal of General Psychology,* 1933, *8,* 3–51.

Hull, C. L. *Principles of behavior: An introduction to behavior theory.* New York: Appleton-Century-Crofts, 1943.

Hull, C. L. *A behavior system: An introduction to behavior theory concerning the individual organism.* New Haven: Yale University Press, 1952.

Hultsch, D. F. Adult age differences in retrieval: Trace dependent and cue dependent forgetting. *Developmental Psychology,* 1975, *11,* 197–201.

Humphrey, J. A. Social loss: A comparison of suicide victims, homicide offenders and non-violent individuals. *Diseases of the Nervous System,* 1977, *38,* 157.

Humphrey, T. The development of human fetal activity and its relation to postnatal behavior. In H. W. Reese & L. P. Lipsitt (Eds.), *Advances in child development and behavior* (vol. 5.) New York: Academic Press, 1970.

Huston, T. L., & Levinger, G. Interpersonal attraction and relationships. *Annual Review of Psychology,* 1978, *29,* 115–56.

Hutchins, D. The value of suggestion given under anesthesia. *American Journal of Clinical Hypnosis,* 1961, *4,* 26–29.

Huxley, A. *The doors of perception.* New York: Harper & Row, 1954.

Hyman, I. A. McDowell, E., & Raines, B. Corporal punishment and alternatives in the schools: An overview of theoretical and practical issues. In J. H. Wise (Ed.), *Proceedings; Conference on corporal punishment in the schools.* Washington, D.C.: National Institute of Education, 1977, 1–18.

Inbau, F., & Reid, J. E. *Criminal interrogations and confessions.* (2nd ed.). Baltimore: Williams & Wilkins, 1967.

Irwin, O. C. Effect of systematic reading of stories. *Journal of Speech and Hearing Research,* 1960, *3,* 187–190.

Irwin, S. Drugs of abuse: An introduction to their actions and potential hazards. *Journal of Psychedelic Drugs,* 1971, *2,* 1–16.

Itard, J. M. G. *The Wild Boy of Aveyron.* G. & M. Humphrey (Trans.) New York: Appleton-Century-Crofts, 1962.

Ittleson, W. H., Proshansky, H. M., & Rivlin, L. G. The environmental psychology of the psychiatric ward. In H. M. Proshansky, W. H. Ittleson, & L. G. Rivlin (Eds.), *Environmental psychology: Man and his physical setting.* New York: Holt, Rinehart & Winston, 1970.

Ittleson, W. H., Proshansky, H. M., Rivlin, L. G., & Winkel, G. H. *An introduction to environmental psychology,* New York: Holt, Rinehart & Winston, 1974.

Izard, C. E. *The face of emotion.* New York: Appleton-Century-Crofts, 1971.

Izard, C. E. (Ed.). *Emotions, conflict, and defense.* New York: Plenum Press, 1978.

Jacob, F. Evolution and tinkering. *Science,* 1977, *196,* 161–166.

Jacobs, J. *Death and life of great American cities.* New York: Vintage Books, 1961. Copyright © 1961 by Jane Jacobs. Excerpt reprinted by permission of Random House, Inc.

Jacobson, E. *Modern treatment of tense patients.* Springfield, Ill.: C. C. Thomas, 1970.

Jacoby, L. L. Encoding processes, rehearsal and recall requirements. *Journal of Verbal Learning and Verbal Behavior,* 1973, *12,* 302–310.

James, W. What is an emotion? *Mind,* 1884, *9,* 188–205.

James, W. *The principles of psychology* (2 vols.). New York: Holt, 1890.

Janis, I. L. *Victims of groupthink: A psychological study of foreign-policy decisions and fiascoes.* Boston: Houghton Mifflin, 1972.

Janis, I. L., & Frick, F. The relationship between attitudes toward conclusions and errors in judging logical validity of syllogisms. *Journal of Experimental Psychology,* 1943, *33,* 73–77.

Janowitz, H. D. Role of gastrointestinal tract in the regulation of food intake. In C. F. Code (Ed.). *Handbook of Physiology: Alimentary Canal I.* Washington, D.C.: American Physiological Society, 1967, 219–224.

Jaspers, K., *General psychopathology.* Manchester, England: Manchester University Press, 1963.

Jaynes, J. *The origin of consciousness in the breakdown of the bicameral mind.* Boston: Houghton Mifflin, 1976.

Jencks, C., Smith, M., Acland, H., Bane, M. J., Cohen, D., Gintis, H., Heyns, B., & Michelson, S. *Inequality.* New York: Basic Books, 1972.

Jenkins, C. D. Recent evidence supporting psychologic and social risk factors for coronary disease. *New England Journal of Medicine,* April 29 and May 6, 1976, *294,* 987–994 and 1033–1038.

Jenkins, C. D., Rosenman, R. H., & Friedman, M. Development of an objective psychological test for the determination of the coronary-prone behavior pattern in employed men. *Journal of Chronic Diseases,* 1967, *20,* 371–379.

Jenkins, J. G., & Dallenbach, K. M. Obliviscence during sleep and waking. *The American Journal of Psychology,* 1924, *35,* 605–612.

Jenni, D. A., & Jenni, M. A. Carrying behavior in humans: Analysis of sex differences. *Science,* 1976, *194,* 859–860.

Jensen, A. R. Verbal mediation and educational potential. *Psychology in the Schools,* 1966, *3*(2), 99–109.

Jensen, A. R. Cumulative deficit in IQ of blacks in the rural south. *Developmental Psychology,* 1977, *13,* 184–191.

Jessor, S., & Jessor, R. Transition from virginity to nonvirginity among youth: A social-psychological study over time. *Developmental Psychology,* 1975, *11,* 473–484.

John, E. R., et al. Neurometrics. *Science,* 1977, *196,* 1393–1410.

Johnson, D. M. *A systematic introduction to the psychology of thinking.* New York: Harper & Row, 1972.

Johnson, N. F. The psychological reality of phrase-structure rules. *Journal of Verbal Learning and Verbal Behavior,* 1965, *4,* 469–75.

Johnson, P. E. *The psychology of religion.* (Rev. ed.). New York: Abingdon, 1959.

Jones, A., Bentler, P. M., & Petry, G. The reduction of uncertainty concerning future pain. *Journal of Abnormal Psychology,* 1966, *71,* 87–89.

Jones, E. E. *Ingratiation: A social psychological analysis.* New York: Appleton-Century-Crofts, 1964.

Jones, E. E., & Nisbett, R. E. The actor and the observer: Divergent perceptions on the causes of behavior. In E. E. Jones et al. (Eds.). *Attribution: Perceiving the Causes of behavior.* Morristown, N.J.: General Learning Press, 1972.

Jones, E. E., & Sigall, H. The bogus pipeline: A new paradigm for measuring affect and attitude. *Psychological Bulletin,* 1971, *76,* 349–364.

Jones, H. S., & Oswald, I. Two cases of healthy insomnia. *Electroencephalography and Clinical Neurophysiology,* 1968, *24,* 378–380.

Jones, M. C. A laboratory study of fear: The case of Peter. *Pedagogical Seminary and Journal of Genetic Psychology,* 1924, *31,* 308–315.

Jones, R. The third wave. In A. Pines & C. Maslach (Eds.), *Experiencing social psychology.* New York: Knopf, 1978.

Jourard, S. M. *The transparent self.* Princeton, N.J.: Van Nostrand, 1964.

Judson, A. I., & Cofer, C. N. Reasoning as an associative process: I. "Direction" in a simple verbal problem. *Psychological Reports,* 1956, *2,* 469–476.

Jung, C. *Collected works.* H. Read, M. Fordham & G. Adler, Eds. New York: Bollinger Series, Pantheon Books, 1953.

Kagan, J. The baby's elastic mind. *Human Nature,* 1978, *1* (1), 66–73.

Kahn, M. The physiology of catharsis. *Journal of Personality and Social Psychology,* 1966, *3,* 278–286.

Kahneman, D., & Tversky, A. On the psychology of prediction. *Psychological Reviews,* 1973, *80,* 237–251.

Kalish, R. A. *Late adulthood: Perspectives on human development.* Monterey, Calif.: Brooks/Cole, 1975.

Kallman, F. J. The genetic theory of schizophrenia: An analysis of 691 schizophrenic index families. *American Journal of Psychiatry,* 1946, *103,* 309–322.

Kandel, D. Adolescent marijuana use: Role of parents and peers. *Science,* 1973, *181;* 1067–1070. Copyright © 1973 by the American Association for the Advancement of Science. Figure and excerpt reprinted by permission of the association and the author.

Kandel, E. R. *Cellular basis of behavior.* San Francisco: W. H. Freeman, 1976.

Kanellakos, D. P., & Ferguson, P. *The psychobiology of transcendental meditation.* Los Angeles: Maharishi International University, Spring 1973.

Kaplan, E. L. & Kaplan, G. A. Is there such a thing as a prelinguistic child? In J. Eliot (Ed.) *Human development and cognitive processes.* New York: Holt, Rinehart & Winston, 1970.

Kaplan, J. Let's go, big beige machine! *Sports Illustrated,* 1977, *47* (8), 42.

Kasamatsu, A., & Hirai, T. An EEG study on the Zen meditation. *Folia Psychiatria Neurologica Japonica,* 1966, *20,* 315–336.

Kastenbaum, R. Is death a life crisis? On the confrontation with death in theory and practice. In N. Datan & L. H. Ginsberg (Eds.), *Life-span developmental psychology: Normative life crises.* New York: Academic Press, 1975. Copyright © 1975 by Academic Press. Excerpt reprinted by permission of Academic Press and the author.

Katchadourian, H. *The biology of adolescence.* San Francisco: W. H. Freeman, 1977.

Katz, I. The socialization of academic motivation in minority group children. In D. Levine (Ed.). *Nebraska symposium on motivation.* Lincoln: University of Nebraska Press, 1967.

Katz, J. J. & Fodor, J. A. The structure of a semantic theory. *Language,* 1963, *39,* 170–210.

Katz, M., & Zimbardo, P. G. Making it as a mental patient. *Psychology Today,* April 1977, *10*(11), 122–126.

Kaye, H. Infant sucking behavior and its modification. In L. P. Lipsitt & C. C. Spiker (Eds.), *Advances in child development and behavior* (vol. 3). New York: Academic Press, 1967.

Kazdin, A. E., & Bootzin, R. R. The token economy: An evaluative review. *Journal of Applied Behavior Analysis,* 1972, *5,* 343–372.

Kelley, H. H. Attribution theory in social psychology. In D. Levine (Ed.), *Nebraska symposium on motivation.* Vol. 15. Lincoln: University of Nebraska Press, 1967.

Kellogg, J. H. *The ladies' guide in health and disease.* Chicago: Modern Medicine Publishing Co., 1902.

Kelly, E. L. *Assessment of human characteristics.* Belmont, Calif.: Brooks/Cole, 1967.

Kelly, E. L., & Fisk, D. W. *The prediction of performance in clinical psychology.* Ann Arbor: University of Michigan Press, 1951.

Kelly, G. A. *The psychology of personal constructs.* (2 vols.) New York: Norton 1955.

Kelman, H. C., & Lawrence, L. H. Assignment of responsibility in the case of Lt. Calley: Preliminary report on a national survey. *Journal of Social Issues,* 1972, *28,* 177–212.

Keniston, J. Heads and seekers: Drugs on campus, countercultures and American society. *American Scholar,* 1968, *38,* 97–112.

Kenrick, D. T., & Cialdini, R. B. Romantic attraction: Misattributions versus reinforcement explanations. *Journal of Personality and Social Psychology,* 1977, *35,* 381–391.

Kerckhoff, A. C., & Davis, K. E. Value consensus and need complementarity in mate selection. *American Sociological Review,* 1962, *27,* 295–303.

Kesey, K. *One flew over the cuckoo's nest.* New York: Viking Press, 1962.

Kessen, W., Haith, M. M., & Salapatek, P. H. Infancy. In P. H. Mussen (Eds.), *Carmichael's manual of child psychology.* New York: Wiley, 1970.

Kety, S. S. Psychoendocrine systems and emotions: Biological aspects. In D. C. Glass (Eds.), *Neurophysiology and emotion.* New York: Rockefeller University Press, 1967.

Kiernan, R. J., & Kaplan, R. M. Deindividuation, anonymity, and pilfering. Paper presented at the Western Psychological Association meeting, San Francisco, April 1971.

Kiesler, S., & Baral, R. The search for a romantic partner: The effects of self-esteem and physical attractiveness on romantic behavior. In K. Gergen & D. Marlowe (Eds.), *Personality and social behavior.* Reading, Mass.: Addison-Wesley, 1970.

Kinsbourne, M. Eye and head turning indicates cerebral lateralization. *Science,* 1972, *176,* 539–541.

Kinsey, A. C., Martin, C. E., & Pomeroy, W. B. *Sexual behavior in the human male.* Philadelphia: Saunders, 1948.

Kinsey, A. C., Pomeroy, W. B., Martin, C. E., & Gebhard, R. H. *Sexual behavior in the human female.* Philadelphia: Saunders, 1953.

Klaus, M. H., & Kennell, J. H. Mothers separated from their newborn infants. *Pediatric Clinics of North America,* 1970, *17,* 1015–1037.

Kleck, R. E., & Rubenstein, C. Physical attractiveness, perceived attitude similarity, and interpersonal attraction in an opposite-sex encounter. *Journal of Personality and Social Psychology,* 1975, *31,* 107–114.

Koestler, A. *The act of creation.* New York: Dell, 1964.

Kohlberg, L. Development of moral character and moral ideology. In M. L. Hoffman & L. W. Hoffman (Eds.), *Review of child development research* (Vol. 1). New York: Russell Sage Foundation, 1964.

Kohlberg, L. Moral and religious education and the public schools: A developmental view. In T. Sizer (Ed.), *Religion and public education.* Boston: Houghton Mifflin, 1967.

Kohlberg, L. Continuities in childhood and adult moral development revisited. In P. B. Baltes & K. W. Schaie (Eds.), *Life-span developmental psychology: Personality and socialization.* New York: Academic Press, 1973.

Kohler, W. *The mentality of apes.* New York: Harcourt Brace Jovanovich, 1926.

Kolata, G. B. Hormone receptors: How are they regulated? *Science,* 1977, *196,* 747 ff.

Kolata, G. B. Childhood hyperactivity: A new look at treatments and causes. *Science,* 1978, *199,* 515–517.

Kolers, P. A. & Palef, S. R. Knowing not. *Memory and Cognition.* 1976. *4.* 553–558.

Kollar, E. J., et al. Psychological, psychophysiological, and biochemical correlates of prolonged sleep deprivation. *American Journal of Psychiatry,* 1969, *126,* 488–97.

Koller, M. R. Residential and occupational propinquity. In R. F. Winch & R. McGinnis (Eds.), *Marriage and the family.* New York: Holt, Rinehart & Winston, 1953.

Konecni, V. J. & Doob, A. N. Catharsis through displacement of aggression. *Journal of Personality and Social Psychology,* 1972, *23,* 379–387.

Konner, M. J. Research reported in Greenberg, J. The brain and emotions. *Science News,* 1977, *112,* 74–75.

Korchin, S. J. *Modern clinical psychology.* New York: Basic Books, 1976.

Koriat, A., Melkman, R., Averill, J. R., & Lazarus, R. S. The self-control of emotional reactions to a stressful film. *Journal of Personality,* 1972, *40,* 601–619.

Kramer, J. C. Introduction to amphetamine abuse. *Journal of Psychedelic Drugs,* 1969, *2,* 1–16. Reprinted with permission of STASH, Inc.

Krueger, W. C. F. The effect of overlearning on retention. *Journal of Experimental Psychology,* 1929, *12,* 71–78.

Kubler-Ross, E. *On death and dying.* Toronto: Macmillan, 1969.

Kuffler, S. W., & Nicholls, J. G. *From neuron to brain.* Sunderland, Mass.: Sinauer Associates, 1976.

Kuhn, C. M., Butler, S. R., & Schanberg, S. M. Selective depression of serum growth hormone during maternal deprivation in rat pups. *Science,* 1978, *201,* 1034–1036.

Kuhn, M. H. & McPartland, T. S. An empirical investigation of self attitudes. *American Sociological Review,* 1954, *19,* 68–76.

Kupalov, P. S. Some normal and pathological properties of nervous processes in the brain. In N. S. Kline (Ed.), *Pavlovian conference on higher nervous activity. Annals of the New York Academy of Sciences*, 1961, *92*, 1046–1053.

LaBarre, W. *The ghost dance,* New York: Delta, 1972.

LaBarre, W. Anthropological perspectives on hallucination and hallucinogens. In R. K. Siegal & L. J. West (Eds.), *Hallucinations: Behavior, experience, and theory.* New York: Wiley, 1975, pp. 9–52.

Labov, W. The logic of non-standard English. *The Florida FL Reporter,* Spring/Summer, 1969, 60–169.

Labov, W. *The study of non-standard English.* Urbana, Ill.: National Council of Teachers of English, 1970.

Labov, W., Cohen, P., Robins, C., & Lewis, J. *A study of the non-standard English of Negro and Puerto Rican speakers in New York City.* Vols. 1 & 2. Columbia University, Cooperative Research Project No. 3288, U.S. Office of Education, 1968.

Laing, R. *The facts of Life: An essay in feelings, facts, and fantasy.* New York: Pantheon Books, 1976.

Lambo, T. A. Psychotherapy in Africa. *Human Nature,* 1978, *1* (3), 32–39.

Lane, H. *The wild boy of Aveyron.* Cambridge: Harvard University Press, 1976.

Lane, R. C., & Singer, J. L. Familial attitudes in paranoid schizophrenics and normals from two socioeconomic classes. *Journal of Abnormal and Social Psychology,* 1959, *59,* 328–339.

Langer, E. J., & Rodin, J. The effects of choice and enhanced personal responsibility for the aged: A field experiment in an institutional setting. *Journal of Personality and Social Psychology,* 1976, *34,* 191–8.

Lashley, K. S. *Brain mechanisms and intelligence.* Chicago: University of Chicago Press, 1929.

Latané, B. (Ed.). Studies in social comparison: Introduction and overview. *Journal of Experimental Social Psychology,* 1966, *2,* Supplement No. 1.

Latané, B., & Darley, J. M. *The unresponsive bystander: Why doesn't he help?* New York: Appleton-Century-Crofts, 1970.

Lawrence, D. H. Acquired distinctiveness of cues. I. Transfer between discriminations on the basis of familiarity with the stimulus. *Journal of Experimental Psychology,* 1949, *39,* 770–784.

Lazarus, A. A. *Multimodal behavior therapy.* New York: Springer, 1976.

Lazarus, R. S. Emotions and adaptation: Conceptual and empirical relations. In W. J. Arnold (Ed.), *Nebraska symposium on motivation.* Lincoln: University of Nebraska Press, 1968.

Lee, M., Zimbardo, P., & Bertholf, M. Shy murderers. *Psychology Today* November 1977, *11*(6), 68–70; 76; 148.

Leeper, R. W. A study of a neglected portion of the field of learning: The development of sensory organization. *Journal of Genetic Psychology,* 1935, *46,* 41–75.

Lefcourt, H. M. The internal versus external control of reinforcement: A review. *Psychological Bulletin,* 1966, *65,* 206–220.

Lefcourt, H. M. Recent development in the study of locus of control. In B. A. Maher (Ed.). *Progress in experimental personality research. Vol. 6.* New York: Academic Press, 1972.

Lefford, A. The influence of emotional subject matter on logical reasoning. *Journal of General Psychology,* 1946, *34,* 127–151.

Leiberman, S. The effects of changes in roles on the attitudes of role occupants. *Human Relations,* 1956, *9,* 385–402.

Lenneberg, E. H. On explaining language. *Science,* 1969, *164,* 635–643. Copyright © 1969 by the American Association for the Advancement of Science. Excerpt reprinted by permission.

Lepper, M. R., Greene, D., & Nisbett, R. E. Undermining children's intrinsic interest with extrinsic reward: A test of the over-justification hypothesis. *Journal of Personality and Social Psychology,* 1973, *28*(1), 129–137.

LeShan, L. An emotional life-history pattern associated with neoplastic disease. *Annals of the New York Academy of Sciences,* 1966, *125,* 780–793. Used by permission of The New York Academy of Sciences and the author.

Leukel, F. A comparison of the effects of ECS and anesthesia on acquisition of the maze habit. *Journal of Comparative and Physiological Psychology,* 1957, *50,* 300–306.

Leventhal, H. Findings and theory in the study of fear communications. In L. Berkowitz, (Ed.), *Advances in Experimental Social Psychology,* Vol. 5. New York: Academic Press, 1970. Used by permission of Academic Press and the author.

Levi, L. Occupational stress: A psychophysiological overview. *Occupational Mental Health,* 1972, *2,* 6–9.

Levine, J. D., et al. Paper presented at the World Congress on Pain, Montreal, August, 1978.

Levinger, G., & Snoek, J. D. *Attraction in relationship: A new look at interpersonal attraction.* Morristown, N.J.: General Learning Press, 1972.

Levinson, B. W. States of awareness during general anesthesia. In J. Lassner (Ed.), *Hypnosis and psychosomatic medicine.* New York: Springer-Verlag, 1967, pp. 200–207.

Levy, J., & Reid, M. Variations in writing posture and cerebral organization. *Science,* 1976, *194,* 337–339.

Lewin, K., Lippitt, R., & White, R. K. Patterns of aggressive behavior in experimentally created social climates. *Journal of Social Psychology,* 1939, *10,* 271–299.

Lewinsohn, P. M. A behavioral approach to depression. In R. M. Friedman & M. M. Katz (Eds.). *The psychology of depression: Contemporary theory and research.* New York: Wiley, 1974.

Ley, D. & Cybriwsky, R. Urban Graffiti as territorial markers. *Annals of the Association of American Geographers,* 1974, *64,* 491–505.

Liddell, H. S. *Emotional hazards in animals and man.* Springfield, Ill.: C. C. Thomas, 1956.

Lieberman, L. R. Letter to *Science* concerning "On being sane in insane places." *Science,* April 27, 1973.

Lieberman, M. A., Yalom, I. D., & Miles, M. D. *Encounter groups: First facts.* New York: Basic Books, 1973.

Lieberman, P., & Crelin, E. S. On the speech of Neanderthal man. *Linguistic Inquiry,* 1971, *2,* 203–222.

Lief, H. I., & Fox, R. C. Training for "detached concern" in medical students. In H. I. Lief, V. F. Lief, & N. R. Lief (Eds.). *The psychological basis of medical practice.* New York: Harper & Row, 1963.

Lilly, J. C. *Programming and metaprogramming in the human biocomputer.* New York: Bantam, 1974.

Lindsay, P. H., & Norman, D. A. *Human information processing.* 2nd edition. New York: Academic Press, 1977. Copyright © 1977 Academic Press. Excerpt reprinted by permission.

Lindsley, D. B. Emotion. In S. S. Stevens (Ed.), *Handbook of experimental psychology.* New York: Wiley, 1951.

Lipsitt, L. P. Learning in the first year of life. In L. P. Lipsitt & C. C. Spiker (Eds.), *Advances in child development and behavior* (vol. 1). New York: Academic Press, 1963.

Lipsitt, L. P. *Developmental psychobiology: The significance of infancy.* Hillsdale, N. J.: L. Erlbaum Associates, 1976.

Lipsitt, L. P. The study of sensory and learning processes of the newborn. *Clinics of Perinatology,* 1977, *4,* 163–186.

Lipsitt, L. P., & Reese, H. W. *Child development.* Glenview, Ill.: Scott Foresman, 1979.

Lipsitt, L. P., Reilly, B., Butcher, M. J., & Greenwood, M. M. The stability and interrelationships of newborn sucking and heart rate. *Developmental Psychobiology,* 1976, *9,* 305–310.

Lockard, J. S. Choice of a warning signal or no warning signal in an unavoidable shock situation. *Journal of Comparative and Physiological Psychology,* 1963, *56,* 526–530.

Loehlin, J. C., Lindzey, G., & Spuhler, J. N. *Race differences in intelligence.* San Francisco: W. H. Freeman, 1975.

Lofland, J., & Stark, R. Becoming a world-saver: A theory of conversion to a deviant perspective. *American Sociological Review,* December 30, 1965, 862–875.

Loftus, E. F. & Palmer, J. C. Reconstruction of automobile destruction: an example of the interaction between language and memory. *Journal of Verbal Learning and Verbal Behavior,* 1974, *13,* 585–589.

Loftus, G. R., & Loftus, E. F. *Human memory: The processing of information.* Hillsdale, N.J.: L. Erlbaum Associates, 1976. Copyright © 1976 by Lawrence Erlbaum Associates, Inc. Excerpt reprinted by permission.

Logan, F. A. *Incentive.* New Haven, Conn.: Yale University Press, 1960.

Logan, F. A. Experimental psychology of animal learning and now. *American Psychologist,* 1972, *27*(11), 1055–1062.

Longstreth, L. E. *Psychological development of the child* (2nd ed.). New York: Ronald, 1974, p. 504. Reprinted by permission.

Lopata, H. Z. Widowhood: Societal factors in life-span disruptions and alternatives. In N. Datan & L. H. Ginsberg (Eds.), *Life-span developmental psychology: Normative life crises.* New York: Academic Press, 1975.

Lorenz, K. *On aggression.* New York: Harcourt Brace Jovanovich, 1966.

Lorenz, K., & Leyhausen, P. *Motivation of human and animal behavior: An ethological view.* (Translated by B. A. Tonkin). New York: Van Nostrand Reinhold, 1973.

Lott, A. J., & Lott, B. E. The role of reward in the formation of positive interpersonal attitudes. In T. L. Huston (Ed.), *Foundations of interpersonal attraction.* New York: Academic Press, 1974.

Lovaas, O. I. Learning theory approach to the treatment of childhood schizophrenia. In California Mental Health Research Symposium, No. 2. *Behavior theory and therapy.* Sacramento, California: Department of Mental Hygiene, 1968.

Lovitt, T. C., & Curtiss, K. A. Academic response rate as a function of teacher and self-imposed contingencies. *Journal of Applied Behavior Analysis,* 1969, *2,* 45–53.

Luchins, A. S., & Luchins, E. H. New experimental attempts at preventing mechanization in problem solving. *Journal of General Psychology,* 1950, *42,* 279–297.

Luckhardt, A. B., & Carlson, A. J. Contributions to the physiology of the stomach. XVII. On the chemical control of the gastric hunger contractions. *American Journal of Physiology,* 1915, *36,* 37–46.

Ludwig, A. M. Altered states of consciousness. *Archives of General Psychiatry,* 1966, *15,* 225–234.

Lummis, R. C. Speaker verification: A step toward the "checkless" society. *Bell Laboratories Record,* September, 1972, 254–259.

Luria, A. R. *The mind of a mnemonist: A little book about a vast memory,* translated from the Russian by Lynn Solotaroff. Copyright © 1968 by Basic Books, Inc., Publishers, New York. Excerpt from pp. 17–18 reprinted by permission of Basic Books, Inc., Publishers and Jonathan Cape Ltd.

Luthe, W. (Ed.) *Autogenic therapy.* (Vols. I-VI). New York: Grune & Stratton, 1969.

Lynch, J. *The broken heart.* New York, Basic Books, 1977.

MacKinnon, D. W. The study of creativity and creativity in architects. In *Conference on the creative person.* Berkeley: University of California, Institute of Personality Assessment and Research, 1961.

Maddi, S. R. The existential neurosis. *Journal of Abnormal Psychology,* 1967, *72,* 311–325.

Maher, B. A. *Principles of psychopathology: An experimental approach.* New York: McGraw-Hill, 1966.

Maher, B. A. The shattered language of schizophrenia. *Psychology Today,* November 1968, pp. 30ff.

Mahoney, M. J. & Thoresen, C. E. *Self-control: Power to the person.* Monterey, Calif.: Brooks/Cole, 1974.

Maier, S. F., & Seligman, M. E. P. Learned helplessness: Theory and evidence. *Journal of Experimental Psychology: General,* 1978, *105,* 3–46.

Mandel, A. R. *Biofeedback, hypnosis, and heart-rate control.* Unpublished master's thesis. Stephen F. Austin State University, Nacogdoches, Texas, 1974. Also presented to Division 31 (clinical hypnosis) of the American Psychological Association, Chicago, Illinois, 1975.

Mandler, J. M. & Johnson, N. S. Rememberance of things parsed: story structure and recall. *Cognitive Psychology,* 1977, *9,* 111–151.

Manes, A. L., & Melynk, P. Televised models of female achievement. *Journal of Applied Social Psychology,* 1974, *4,* 365–374.

Mansson, H. H. Justifying the final solution. *Omega,* 1972, *3* (2), 79–87.

Margolis, B. K., & Kroes, W. H. Occupational stress and strain. In A. McLean, (Ed.), *Occupational stress.* Springfield, Ill. C. C. Thomas, 1974, 15–20.

Mark, V., & Ervin, F. R. *Violence and the brain.* New York: Harper & Row, 1970.

Marks, L. E. & Miller, G. A. The role of semantic and syntactic constraints in the memorization of English sentences. *Journal of Verbal Learning and Verbal Behavior,* 1964, *3,* 1–5.

Marsh, C. A framework for describing states of consciousness. In N. E. Zinberg (Ed.), *Alternate states of consciousness.* New York: Macmillan, 1977, pp. 121–144.

Marshall, G., & Zimbardo, P. G. The affective consequences of inadequately explained physiological arousal. *Journal of Personality and Social Psychology,* 1979, in press.

Martin, D. *Battered wives.* San Francisco: Glide Publications, 1976.

Martindale, D. Torment in the tower. *Chicago,* April 1976, 96–101.

Maslach, C. Social and personal bases of individuation. *Journal of Personality and Social Psychology,* 1974, *29,* 411–425.

Maslach, C. Burned-out. *Human Behavior,* 1976, *5,* 16–22.

Maslach, C. Burn-out: A social-psychological analysis. Paper presented at annual meeting of American Psychological Association, San Francisco, August 1977.

Maslach, C. Negative emotional biasing of unexplained arousal. *Journal of Personality and Social Psychology,* 1979, in press.

Maslach, C. & Pines, A. The burn-out syndrome in the day care setting. *Child Care Quarterly,* 1977, *6,* 100–113.

Maslow, A. H. *Toward a psychology of being.* (2nd edition). New York: Van Nostrand, 1968.

Maslow, A. H. *Motivation and personality.* New York: Harper & Row, 1954.

Maslow, A. H. *The farther reaches of human nature.* New York: Viking, 1971.

Masters, W. H., & Johnson, V. E. *Human sexual response.* Boston: Little, Brown, 1966.

Masters, W. H. & Johnson, V. E. *Human sexual inadequacy.* Boston: Little, Brown, 1970.

Matson, F. W. Humanistic theory. *The Humanist,* March/April 1971, 7–11.

Maugh, T. H. Creativity: Can it be dissected? Can it be taught? *Science,* 1974, *184,* 1273.

May, R. Values, myths, and symbols. *American Journal of Psychiatry,* 1975, *132,* 703–706.

Mayer, J. *Overweight: Causes, cost and control.* Englewood Cliffs, N.J.: Prentice-Hall, 1968.

Mayer, R. E. *Thinking and problem solving.* Glenview, Ill.: Scott, Foresman, 1977.

McArthur, L., & Post, D. Figural emphasis and person perception. *Journal of Experimental Social Psychology,* 1978, In press.

McCall, R. B. Childhood IQ's as predictors of adult education and occupational status. *Science,* 1977, *197,* 483–483.

McCandless, B. R. Socialization. In H. W. Reese & L. P. Lipsitt (Eds.), *Experimental child psychology.* New York: Academic Press, 1970.

McClelland, D. C. *The achieving society.* Princeton: Van Nostrand, 1961.

McClelland, D. C. *Motivational trends in society.* Morristown, N.J.: General Learning Press, 1971.

McConnell, R. A. *ESP curriculum guide.* New York: Simon & Schuster, 1971.

McGregor, D. *The human side of enterprise.* New York: McGraw-Hill, 1960.

McGuigan, F. J. Imagery and thinking: Covert functioning of the motor system. In G. E. Schwartz & D. Shapiro (Eds.), *Consciousness and self-regulation: Advances in research.* Vol 2. New York: Plenum, 1978.

McGuigan, F. J., Keller, B., & Stanton, E. Covert language responses during silent reading. *Journal of Educational Psychology,* 1964, *55,* 339–343.

McGuigan, F. J., & Tanner, R. G. Covert oral behavior during conversational and visual dreams. *Psychonomic Science,* 1971, *23,* 263–264.

McMahon, D. Chemical messengers in development: A hypothesis. *Science,* 1974, *185,* 1012–1020.

McNeil, D. *The acquisition of language: the study of developmental psycholinguistics.* New York: Harper & Row, 1970.

Mead, G. H. *Mind, self and society: From the standpoint of a social behaviorist.* Chicago: University of Chicago Press 1934.

Meader, B. D., & Rogers, C. R. Client-centered therapy. In R. Corsini (Ed.), *Current psychotherapies.* Itasca, Ill.: Peacock, 1973.

Meddis, R., Pearson, A., & Langford, G. An extreme case of healthy insomnia. *Electroencephalography and Clinical Neurophysiology*, 1973, *35*, 213–214.

Meecham, W. C., & Smith, H. G. Decibels and nervous breakdowns. Reported in *Human Behavior*, November 1977, p. 50. Copyright © 1977 *Human Behavior*. Used by permission.

Meehl, P. E. A critical afterword. In I. I. Gottesman & J. Shields, *Schizophrenia and genetics: A twin study vantage point*. New York: Academic Press, 1972.

Mehrabian, A. Significance of posture and position in the communication of attitude and status relationships. *Psychological Bulletin*, 1969,*71*, 359–372.

Meichenbaum, D. A self-instructional approach to stress management: A proposal for stress innoculating training. In D. C. Spielberger and I. G. Sarason, (Eds.), *Stress and anxiety*, Vol. I. New York: Wiley, 1975, 237–263. Copyright © 1975 by Hemisphere Publishing Corporation. Table reprinted by permission.

Meichenbaum, D. *Cognitive-behavior modification: An integrative approach*. New York: Plenum, 1977.

Melton, A. W. & Irwin, J. M. The influence of degree of interpolated learning on retroactive inhibition and the overt transfer of specific responses. *American Journal of Psychology*, 1940, *53*, 173–203.

Meltzer, H. Y., & Stahl, S. The dopamine hypothesis of schizophrenia. *Schizophrenia Bulletin*, 1976, *2*, 19–76.

Meltzoff, J., & Kornreich, M. *Research in psychotherapy*. New York: Atherton, 1970.

Melzack, R. How acupuncture works: A sophisticated Western theory takes the mystery out. *Psychology Today*, 1973, *7* (6), 28–37.

Melzack, R., & Wall, P. D. Pain mechanisms: A new theory. *Science*, 1965, *150*, 971–979.

Melzack, R., & Wall, P. D. Psychophysiology of pain. *International Anesthesiology Clinics*, 1970, *8*, 3–34.

Mendels, J. *Concepts of depression*. New York: Wiley, 1970.

Meyer, D. E., & Schvaneveldt, R. W. Meaning, memory structure, and mental processes. *Science*, 1976, *192*, 27–33.

Meyer, M. M. & Ekstein, R. The psychotic pursuit of reality. *Journal of Contemporary Psychotherapy*, 1970, *3*, 3–12.

Meyer, W.-U. In H. Heckhausen, Achievement Motive Research, from W. J. Arnold (Ed.), *Nebraska symposium on motivation 1968*. Lincoln: University of Nebraska Press, 1968.

Miale, F. R. & Selzer, M. *The Nuremberg mind: The psychology of the Nazi leaders*. New York: New York Times Book Co., 1975.

Miernyk, W. H. The changing life cycle of work. In N. Datan and L. H. Ginsberg (Eds.), *Life-span developmental psychology: Normative life crises*. New York: Academic Press, 1975.

Milgram, S. Some conditions of obedience and disobedience to authority. *Human Relations*, 1965, *18*(1), 57–76.

Milgram, S. *Obedience to authority*. New York: Harper & Row, 1974.

Miller, G. A. Speech and language. In S. S. Stevens (Ed.) *Handbook of Experimental Psychology*. New York: Wiley, 1951, p.p. 789–810.

Miller, G. A. The magic number seven plus or minus two: some limits on our capacity for processing information. *Psychological Review*, 1956, *63*, 81–97.

Miller, G. A. *The psychology of communication: seven essays*. New York: Basic Books, 1967.

Miller, G. A. Psychology as a means of promoting human welfare. *American Psychologist*, 1969, *24*(12), 1063–1075.

Miller, G. A., Galanter, E., & Pribram, H. K. *Plans and the structure of behavior*. New York: Holt, Rinehart & Winston, 1960.

Miller, G. A. & Isard, S. Some perceptual consequences of linguistic rules. *Journal of Verbal Learning and Verbal Behavior*, 1963, *2*, 217–28. Excerpt reprinted by permission of Academic Press and G. A. Miller.

Miller, N. E. The frustration-aggression hypothesis. *Psychological Review*, 1941, *48*, 337–342.

Miller, N. E. Experimental studies of conflict. In J. McV. Hunt (Ed.), *Personality and the behavior disorders*. Vol. 1. New York: Ronald Press, 1944.

Miller, N. E. Liberalization of basic S-R concepts: Extensions to conflict behavior, motivation, and social learning. In S. Koch (Ed.), *Psychology: A study of a science*. Vol. II. New York: McGraw-Hill, 1959, 196–292.

Miller, N. E. Learning of visceral and glandular responses. *Science*, 1969, *163*, 434–445.

Miller, N. E. Fact and fancy about biofeedback and its clinical implications. *Journal supplement abstract service, Catalogue of Selected Documents in Psychology*, 1976, *6*, 92.

Miller, N. E., & Dollard, J. *Social learning and imitation*. New Haven, Conn.: Yale University Press, 1941.

Milner, B. & Penfield, W. The effect of hippocampal lesion on recent memory. *Transactions of the American Neurological Association*, 1955, *80*, 42–48.

Minami, H. & Dallenbach, K. M. The effect of activity on learning and retention in the cockroach. *American Journal of Psychology*, 1946, *59*, 1–58.

Minke, K. A., & Carlson, J. G. *Psychology and Life Unit Mastery System* (Rev. ed). Glenview, Ill.: Scott, Foresman, 1975.

Mischel, W. *Personality and assessment*, New York: Wiley, 1968.

Mischel, W. Toward a cognitive social learning reconceptualization of personality. *Psychological Review*, 1973, *80*, 252–283.

Mischel, W. *Introduction to personality*. (2nd edition). N.Y.: Holt, Rinehart & Winston, 1976.

Mischel, W., & Mischel, H. N. *Essentials of Psychology*. New York: Random House, 1977.

Mitchell, G., & Schroers, L. Birth order and parental experience in monkeys and man. In H. W. Reese (Ed.), *Advances in child development and behavior* (Vol. 8). New York: Academic Press, 1973.

Mitchell, R. E. Some social implications of high density housing. *American Sociological Review*, 1971, *36*, 18–29.

Moniz, E. Prefrontal leucotomy in the treatment of mental disorders. *American Journal of Psychiatry*, 1937, *93*, 1379–1385.

Monjan, A. A., & Collector, M. I. Stress-induced modulation of the immune response. *Science*, 1977, *196*, 307–308. Copyright © 1977 by the American Association for the Advancement of Science. Used by permission of the association and the author.

Montgomery, G. T., & Crowder, J. E. The symptom substitution hypothesis and the evidence. *Psychotherapy*, 1972, *9*, 98–102.

Moore, M. S. Some myths about mental illness. *Archives of General Psychiatry*, 1975, *32*, 1483–1497.

Moore, R. B. The role of directed Pavlovian reactions in simple instrumental learning in the pigeon. In R. A. Hinde & J. Stevensen-Hinde (Eds.), *Constraints on learning*. New York: Academic Press, 1973.

Mora, A., & Myers, R. D. Brain self-stimulation: Direct evidence for the involvement of Dopamine in the prefrontal cortex. *Science*. 1977, *197*, 1387–1389.

Morgan, A. H. The heritability of hypnotic susceptibility in twins. *Journal of Abnormal Psychology*, 1973, *82*, 55–61.

Morgan, A. H., Johnson, D. L., & Hilgard, E. R. The stability of hypnotic susceptibility: A longitudinal study. *International Journal of Clinical and Experimental Hypnosis*, 1974, *22*, 249–257.

Morgan, C. T. & Deese, J. *How to study*, (2nd Ed.) New York: McGraw-Hill, 1969.

Moscovici, S. *Social influence and social change*. London: Academic Press, 1976.

Moscovici, S., Lage, E., & Naffrechoux, M. Influence of a consistent minority on the responses of a majority in a color perception task. *Sociometry*, 1969, *32*, 365–80.

Mowrer, O. H. *Learning theory and behavior*. New York: Wiley, 1960.

Mowrer, O. H., & Viek, P. An experimental analogue of fear from a sense of helplessness. *Journal of Abnormal and Social Psychology*, 1948, *43*, 193–200.

Moyer, K. E. *The psychobiology of aggression*. New York: Harper & Row, 1976.

Mullaney, D. J., Johnson, L. C., Naitoh, P., Friedman, J. K., & Globus, G. G. Sleep before and after gradual sleep reduction. In M. H. Chase, M. M. Mitler, & P. L. Walter (Eds.), *Sleep research*. Los Angeles, Brain Information Service/Brain Research Institute, UCLA, 1976, *5*, 193.

Munroe, R. L. *Schools of Psychoanalytic thought*. New York: Dryden, 1955.

Munroe, R. L., & Munroe, R. H. *Cross-cultural human development*. Monterey, Cal.: Brooks/Cole, 1975.

Munsterberg, H. *On the witness stand: Essays on psychology and crime*. New York: Clark Boardman, 1927. (Originally published: New York: Doubleday, 1908.)

Murphy, J. M. Psychiatric labelling in cross cultural perspective. *Science,* 1976, *191,* 1019–1028.

Murray, H. A., et al., *Explorations in personality.* New York: Oxford, 1938.

Murray, H. A., & Morgan, C. D. A method of investigation of fantasies. *Archives of Neurological Psychiatry,* 1935, *34,* 289–306.

Murstein, B. I. Physical attractiveness and marital choice. *Journal of Personality and Social Psychology,* 1972, *22*(1), 8–12.

Murstein, B. I. *Who will marry whom? Theories and research in marital choice.* New York: Springer, 1976.

Muuss, R. E. *Theories of adolescence.* New York: Random House, 1962.

National Institute of Mental Health. *Lithium in the treatment of mood disorders.* DHEW Publication No. (ADM) 77–73. Washington, D.C.: U. S. Government Printing Office. Reprinted 1977.

Neisser, U. *Cognitive psychology.* New York: Appleton-Century-Crofts, 1967.

Nesselroade, J. R., & Baltes, P. B. Adolescent personality development and historical change: 1970–1972. *Monographs of the Society for Research in Child Development,* 1974, *39* (1, Whole No. 154).

Neugarten, B. L. *The psychology of aging: An overview.* Master Lectures on developmental psychology. Washington, D.C.: American Psychological Association, 1976.

Newcomb, T. M. Attitude development as a function of reference groups. In E. E. Maccoby, T. M. Newcomb, & E. L. Hartley (Eds.), *Readings in social psychology.* New York: Holt, Rinehart & Winston, 1958.

Newcomb, T. M. Persistence and regression of changed attitudes: Long-range studies. *Journal of Social Issues,* 1963, *19,* 3–4.

Newell, A., Shaw, J. C., & Simon, H. A. Elements of a theory of human problem solving. *Psychological Review,* 1958, *65,* 151–166.

Nicolaidis, S., & Rowland, N. Intravenous self-feeding: Long-term regulation of energy balance in rats. *Science,* 1977, *195,* 589–591.

Nideffer, R. M. Altered states of consciousness. In T. X. Barber *Advances in altered states of consciousness and human potentialities,* Vol. 1. New York: Psychological Dimensions, Inc. 1976, p. 3–35.

Nisbett, R. E. Hunger, obesity and the ventromedial hypothalamus, *Psychological Review,* 1972, *79,* 433–453.

Nisbett, R. E., & Ross, L. *Human inference: Strategies and shortcomings in social judgment.* Prentice-Hall, 1979, in press.

Nisbett, R. E., & Wilson, T. D. The halo effect: Evidence for unconscious alteration of judgments. *Journal of Personality and Social Psychology,* 1977, *36,* 250–256. (a)

Nisbett, R. E., & Wilson, T. D. Telling more than we can know: Verbal reports on mental processes. *Psychological Review,* 1977, *84,* 231–259. (b)

Nizer, L. *My life in court.* New York: Pyramid, 1961.

Nobles, W. W. African psychology: Foundations for black psychology. In R. L. Jones (Ed.), *Black psychology.* New York: Harper & Row, 1972.

Nobles, W. W. Black people in white insanity: An issue for black community mental health. *Journal of Afro-American Issues,* 1976, *4,* 21–27.

O'Brien, C. P. Experimental analysis of conditioning factors in human narcotic addiction. *Pharmacological Review,* 1975, *27*(4), 533–543.

O'Brien, C. P., Testa, T., O'Brien, T. J., Brady, J. P. & Wells, B. Conditioned narcotic withdrawal in humans. *Science,* 1977, *195,* 1000–1002.

Odum, E. P. The emergence of ecology as a new integrative discipline. *Science,* 1977, *195,* 1289–1293.

Office of Strategic Services Staff. *Assessment of men selection of personnel for the Office of Strategic Services.* New York: Holt, Rinehart & Winston, 1948.

Oldham, G. R., Hackman, J. R., & Pearce, J. L. *Conditions under which employees respond positively to enriched work.* Technical Report No. 4. Yale University Department of Administrative Sciences. September, 1975.

Olds, J. Commentary on positive reinforcement produced by electrical stimulation of septal areas and other regions of rat brain. In E. S. Valenstein (Ed.), *Brain stimulation and motiva-*

tion: Research and commentary. Glenview, Ill.: Scott, Foresman, 1973.

Olds, J., & Milner, P. Positive reinforcement produced by electrical stimulation of septal area and other regions of the rat brain. *Journal of Comparative and Physiological Psychology,* 1954, *47,* 419–427.

O'Leary, K. D., Kaufman, K. F., Kass, R. E. & Drabran, R. S. The effects of loud and soft reprimands on the behavior of disruptive students. *Exceptional Children,* 1970, *37,* 145–155.

Oppenheimer, R. Analogy in science. *American Psychologist,* 1956, *11,* 127–135.

Opton, N. Lessons of My Lai. In R. Buckhout (Ed.), *Toward social change.* New York: Harper & Row, 1971.

Orlando, N. J. The mock ward: A study in simulation. In O. Milton & R. G. Wahler (Eds.), *Behavior disorders: Perspectives and trends.* Philadelphia: Lippincott, 1973.

Orne, M. T. Hypnosis, motivation and the ecological validity of the psychological experiment. In W. J. Arnold & M. M. Page (Eds.), *Nebraska symposium on motivation.* Lincoln: University of Nebraska Press, 1970.

Orne, M. T. On the simulating subject as a quasi-control group in hypnosis research: What, why, and how? In E. Fromm & R. E. Shor (Eds.), *Hypnosis: Research developments and perspectives.* Chicago: Aldine, 1972.

Ornstein, R. E. *The psychology of consciousness.* San Francisco: Freeman, 1972.

Osgood, C. E. Exploration in semantic space: a personal diary. *Journal of Social Issues,* 1971, *27*(4), 5–64. Excerpt reprinted by permission.

Osgood, C. E., Suci, G. J. & Tannenbaum, P. H. *The measurement of meaning.* Urbana, Ill.: University of Illinois Press, 1957.

Osnos, P. American doctor: Moscow imposes psychic stress. *Washington Post,* Jan. 23, 1977.

Osofsky, J. D. Neonatal characteristics and mother-infant interaction in two observational situations. *Child Development,* 1976, *47,* 1138–1147.

Overmier, J. B., & Seligman, M. E. P. Effects of inescapable shock upon subsequent escape and avoidance responding. *Journal of Comparative and Physiological Psychology,* 1967, *63* (1), 28–33.

Overton, D. A. Experimental methods for the study of state-dependent learning. *Federation Proceedings,* 1974, *33,* 1800–1813.

Owens, J., Dafoe, J., Bower, G. H. Taking a point of view: Character identification and attributional processes in story comprehension and memory. Paper presented at the meeting of the American Psychological Association, San Francisco, August 1977.

Pahnke, W. N. Drugs and mysticism: An analysis of the relationship between psychedelic drugs and mystical consciousness. Unpublished doctoral dissertation, Harvard University, 1963.

Pahnke, W. N. LSD and religious experience. In R. C. DeBold & R. C. Leaf (Eds.), *LSD, man and society.* Middletown, Conn.: Wesleyan University Press, 1967.

Paloutzian, R. F. Purpose-in-life and value changes following conversion. Paper presented at the meeting of the American Psychological Association, Washington, D.C., September, 1976.

Paloutzian, R. F., Jackson, S. L., & Crandall, J. E. Conversion experience, belief system, and personal and ethical attitudes. *Journal of Psychology and Theology, 6,* 1978 (in press).

Pam, A., Plutchik, R., & Conte, H. R. Love: A psychometric approach. *Psychological Reports,* 1975, *37,* 83–88.

Parke, R. D., Berkowitz, L., Leyens, J. P., West, S. G., & Sebastian, R. J. Some effects of violent and nonviolent movies on the behavior of juvenile delinquents. In L. Berkowitz (Ed.), *Advances in Experimental Social Psychology,* Vol. 10. New York: Academic Press, 1977.

Parke, R. D., & Walters, R. H. Some factors influencing the efficacy of punishment training for inducing response inhibition. *Monographs of the Society for Research in Child Development,* 1967, *32* (1, Whole No. 109).

Patterson, F. G. Linguistic abilities of a young lowland gorilla. Paper presented at American Association for the Advancement of Science symposium: An account of the visual mode: man versus ape, Denver, 1977.

Patterson, M. L. An arousal model of interpersonal intimacy. *Psychological Review*, 1976, *83*, 235–245.

Paul, G. L. Outcome of systematic desensitization. II. Controlled investigations of individual treatment technique variations, and current status. In C. M. Franks (Ed.), *Behavior therapy: Appraisal and status*. New York: McGraw-Hill, 1969.

Paul, S. M. Movement and madness: Towards a biological model of schizophrenia. In J. D. Masei & M. E. P. Seligman (Eds.), *Psychopathology: Experimental models*. San Francisco: Freeman, 1977, 350–386.

Pearson, R. E. Response to suggestions given under general anesthesia. *American Journal of Clinical Hypnosis*, 1961, *4*, 106–114.

Pelletier, K. R. Neurological psychophysiological, and clinical differentiation of the alpha and theta altered states of consciousness. Unpublished doctoral dissertation. University of California, Berkeley, 1974. Reprinted by permission.

Pelletier, K. R. *Mind as healer, mind as slayer: A holistic approach to preventing stress disorders*. New York: Delta, 1977.

Pelletier, K. R., & Peper, E. Developing a biofeedback model: Alpha EEG feedback as a means for main control. *The International Journal of Clinical and Experimental Hypnosis*, 1977, *25*, 361–371.

Penfield, W. *The excitable cortex in conscious man*. Liverpool: Liverpool University Press, 1958.

Penfield, W., & Baldwin, M. Temporal lobe seizures and the technique of subtotal temporal lobectomy. *Annals of Surgery*, 1952, *136*, 625–634.

Penick, S., Smith, G., Wienske, K., & Hinkle, L. An experimental evaluation of the relationship between hunger and gastric motility. *American Journal of Physiology*, 1963, *205*, 421–426.

Peplau, L. A., Rubin, Z., & Hill, C. T. Sexual intimacy in dating relationships. *Journal of Social Issues*, 1977, *33*(2), 86–109.

Perley, M., & Guze, S. B. Hysteria: The stability and usefullness of clinical criteria. *New England Journal of Medicine*, 1962, *266*, 421–26. Table reprinted by permission.

Peterson, L. R. & Peterson, M. J. Short-term retention of individual verbal items. *Journal of Experimental Psychology*, 1959, *58*, 193–198.

Phares, E. J. *Locus of control in personality*. Morristown, N.J.: General Learning Press, 1976.

Piaget, J. Piaget's theory. In P. H. Mussen (Ed.), *Carmichael's manual of child psychology* (Vol. 1, 3rd ed.). New York: Wiley, 1970.

Pierrel, R., & Sherman, J. G. Train your pet the Barnabus way. *Brown Alumni Monthly*, February 1963, 8–14.

Piliavin, I. M., Rodin, J., & Piliavan, J. A. Good Samaritanism: An underground phenomenon? *Journal of Personality and Social Psychology*, 1969, *13*, 289–300.

Piliavin, J. A., & Piliavin, I. M. Effect of blood on reactions to a victim. *Journal of Personality and Social Psychology*, 1972, *23*, 353–361.

Pilkonis, P. A. Shyness, public and private, and its relationship to other measures of social behavior. *Journal of Personality*, 1977, *45*, 585–595. (a)

Pilkonis, P. A. The behavioral consequences of shyness. *Journal of Personality*, 1977, *45*, 596–611. (b)

Pinel, J., Treit, D., & Rovner, L. Temporal lobe aggression in rats. *Science*, 1977, *197*, 1088–1089.

Pitts, F. N. The biochemistry of anxiety. *Scientific American*, 1969, *220*, 69–75.

Platt, J. Social traps. *American Psychologist*, 1973, *28*, 641–651.

Plutchik, R. *The emotions: Facts, theories, and a new model*. New York: Random House, 1962.

Plutchik, R., Kellerman, H., & Conte, H. Q. A structural theory of ego defenses and emotions. In C. Izard, (Ed.), *Emotions and psychopathology*. N.Y.: Plenum, 1978, in press.

Polya, G. *How to solve it*. Garden City, N.Y.: Doubleday Anchor, 1957.

Posner, E. G. The effect of therapists' training on group therapeutic outcome. *Journal of Consulting Psychology*, 1966, *30*, 283–289.

Postman, L. & Rau, L. Retention as a function of the method of measurement. *University of California Publications in Psychology*, 1957, *8*(3).

Powers, W. T. Feedback: Beyond behaviorism. *Science*, 1973, *179*, 351–356. (a)

Powers, W. T. *Behavior: The control of perception*. Chicago: Aldine, 1973. (b)

Powers, W. T. Control-system theory and performance objectives. *Journal of Psycholinguistic Research*, 1976, *5*, 285–297.

Premack, D. Reinforcement theory. In D. Levine (Ed.). *Nebraska symposium on motivation*. Lincoln: University of Nebraska Press, 1965.

Premack, D. The functional analysis of language. Paper presented at the meeting of the American Psychological Association, Washington, D.C., 1969.

Premack, D. The education of Sarah. *Psychology Today*, 1970, *4* (4), 54–8..

Prescott, D. A. *The child in the educative process*. New York: McGraw-Hill, 1957. Copyright © 1957 McGraw-Hill Book Company. Used with permission of McGraw-Hill Book Company.

President's Commission on Mental Health. Preliminary report to the President, September 1, 1977.

Proxmire, W. Quote on the National Science Foundation, 1975. Reprinted by permission.

Rabkin, J. G., & Struening, E. Life events, stress, and illness. *Science*, 1976, *194*, 1013–1020.

Rachlin, H. *Introduction to modern behaviorism* (2nd ed.), San Francisco: W. H. Freeman, 1976.

Rachman, S., & Costello, C. G. The etiology and treatment of children's phobias: A review. *American Journal of Psychiatry*, 1961, *118*, 97–105.

Rahe, R. H. The pathway between subjects' recent life changes and their near-future illness reports: Representative results and methodological issues. In B. S. Dohrenwend & B. P. Dohrenwend (Eds.), *Stressful life events: Their nature and effects*. New York: Wiley, 1974.

Rahe, R. H., & Holmes, T. H. Life crisis and major health change. *Psychosomatic Medicine*, 1966, *28*, 744.

Raimy, V. *Misunderstandings of the self*. San Francisco: Jossey-Bass, 1975.

Rainville, R., & McCormick, E. Extent of covert racial prejudice in pro football announcer's speech. *Journalism Quarterly*, 1977, *54*, 20–26. Used by permission.

Rapoport, J. L., Buchsbaum, M. S., Zahn, T. P., Weingartner, H., Ludlow, C., & Mikkelsen, E. J. Dextro amphetamine: Cognitive and behavioral effects in normal prepubertal boys. *Science*, 1978, *199*, 560–563.

Razran, G. The observable unconscious and the inferable conscious in current Soviet psychophysiology. *Psychological Review*, 1961, *68*, 81–147.

Reardon, F. J., & Reynold, R. N. *Corporal punishment in Pennsylvania*. Harrisburg, Pa.: Penn. State Department of Education, 1975.

Reese, H. W. Attitudes toward the opposite sex in late childhood. *Merrill-Palmer Quarterly of Behavior and Development*, 1966, *12*, 157–163.

Regan, D. T., & Fazio, R. H. On the consistency between attitudes and behavior: Look to the method of attitude formation. *Journal of Experimental Social Psychology*, 1977, *13*, 28–45.

Reiss, I. *The social context of premarital sexual permissiveness*. New York: Holt, Rinehart and Winston, 1967.

Rescorla, R. A. Pavlovian conditioned inhibition. *Psychological Bulletin*, 1969, *72*, 77–94.

Restle, F., & Davis, J. H. Success and speed of problem solving by individuals and groups. *Psychological Review*, 1962, *69*, 520–36.

Restle, F., & Greeno, J. G. *Introduction to mathematical psychology*. Reading Mass.: Addison-Wesley, 1970.

Reuben, D. Letter to Dr. David Reuben. *San Francisco Examiner/Chronicle*, Dec. 16, 1973. Copyright © 1973 by Dr. David Reuben, M.D. Excerpt reprinted by permission of Harold Matson Co., Inc.

Ribble, M. A. *The rights of infants*. New York: Columbia University Press, 1943.

Rickles, K. Non-specific factors in drug therapy of neurotic patients. In K. Rickles (Ed.), *Non-specific factors in drug therapy*. Springfield, Ill.: C. C. Thomas, 1968.

Riegel, K. F. Dialectical operations: The final period of cognitive development. *Human Development*, 1973, *16*, 346–370.

Riegel, K. F., & Reigel, R. M. Development, drop, and death. *Developmental Psychology*, 1972, *6*, 306–319.

Roberts, T. B. Maslow's human motivation needs hierarchy: A bibliography. *Research in Education*. ERIC document ED-069-591, 1973.

Roberts, T. B. Transpersonal: The new educational psychology. *Phi Delta Kappan*, Nov. 1974, 191–193.

Robinson, M. R., & Freeman, W. J. *Psychosurgery and the self*. New York: Grune & Stratton, 1955.

Rodin, J. Density, perceived choice, and response to controllable and uncontrollable outcomes. *Journal of Experimental Social Psychology*, 1976, *12*, 564–578.

Rodin, J. Stimulus-bound behavior and biological self-regulation: Feeding, obesity, and external control. In G. Schwartz & D. Shapiro (Eds.). *Consciousness and self-regulation* (Vol. II). New York: Plenum Press, 1978.

Rodin, J., & Langer, E. J. Long-term effects of a control-relevant intervention with the institutionalized aged. *Journal of Personality and Social Psychology*, 1977, *35*, 897–902.

Roffwarg, H. P., Muzio, J. N., & Dement, W. C. Ontogenetic development of the human sleep-dream cycle. *Science*, April 1966, *152*(29).

Rogers, C. R. Some observations on the organization of personality. *American Psychologist*, 1947, *2*, 358–368.

Rogers, C. R. *Client-centered therapy: Its current practice, implications and theory*. Boston: Houghton-Mifflin, 1951.

Rogers, C. R. *On becoming a person*. Boston: Houghton-Mifflin, 1961.

Rogers, C. R. *On personal power: Inner strength and its revolutionary impact*. New York: Delacorte, 1977.

Romano, J. On the nature of schizophrenia: Changes in the observer as well as the observed (1932–77). *Schizophrenia Bulletin*, 1977, *4*, 532–559.

Rose, S. *The conscious brain*. New York: Knopf, 1973.

Rosenhan, D. L. On being sane in insane places. *Science*, 1973, *179*, 250–58.

Rosenhan, D. L. Personal communication to the author. August, 1974.

Rosenthal, D., Wender, P. H., Kety, S. S., Schulsinger, F., Welner, J., & Rieder, R. Parent-child relationships and psychopathological disorder in the child. *Archives of General Psychiatry*, 1975, *32*, 466–476.

Rosenzweig, M. R., Bennett, E. L., Diamond, M. C., Wu, Su-Yu, Slagle, R. W. & Saffran, E. Influences of environmental complexity and visual stimulation on development of occipital cortex in rats. *Brain Research*, 1969, *14*, 427–45.

Ross, L. Effects of manipulating the salience of food upon consumption by obese and normal eaters. In S. Schachter & J. Rodin (Eds.), *Obese humans and rats*. Hillsdale, N.J.: Erlbaum/Halsted, 1974.

Ross, L. Some afterthoughts on the intuitive psychologist. In L. Berkowitz (Ed.), *Cognitive theories in social psychology*. New York: Academic Press, 1979 (in press).

Ross, L., Amabile, T., & Steinmetz, J. Social roles, social control and biases in the social perception process. *Journal of Personality and Social Psychology*, 1977, *37*, 485–494.

Ross, L., Bierbrauer, G., & Polly, S. Attribution of educational outcomes by professional and nonprofessional instructors. *Journal of Personality and Social Psychology*, 1974, *29*, 609–618.

Roth, S. M. Attitudes toward death across the lifespan (Doctoral dissertation, West Virginia University, 1977). *Dissertation Abstracts International*, 1978, *38*, 3858B. (University Microfilms No. 7732097)

Rothman, D. J. *The discovery of the asylum: Social order and disorder in the new republic*. Boston: Little, Brown, 1971.

Rothwell, P. L., Filz, R. C., & McNulty, P. J. Light flashes observed on Skylab 4: The role of nuclear stars. *Science*, 1976, *193*, 1002–1003.

Rotter, J. B. *Social learning and clinical psychology*. New York: Prentice-Hall, 1954.

Rotter, J. B. Generalized expectancies for internal versus external controls of reinforcement. *Psychological Monographs*, 1966, *80*(1, Whole No. 609).

Rotter, J. B. External control and internal control. *Psychology Today*. 1971, *5* 37–42, 58–59.

Rotter, J. B., Chance, J., & Phares, E. J. (Eds.) *Applications of a social learning theory of personality*. New York: Holt, Rinehart & Winston, 1972.

Rubenstein, S., & Snyder, G. Last one to vote guilty. The *San Francisco Chronicle*, Friday, January 21, 1977.

Rubin, Z. *Liking and loving*. New York: Holt, Rinehart & Winston, 1973.

Ruma, S. J. Easier said than done: Theory and practice in applying social psychology. In M. Deutsch & H. A. Hornstein, *Applying social psychology: Implications for research, practice, and training*. Hillsdale, N.J.: L. Erlbaum Associates, 1975, pp. 193–210.

Rumbaugh, D. M. & Gill, T. V. The mastery of language-type skills by the chimpanzee (Pan). In S. R. Harnad, H. D. Steklis, and J. Lancaster (Eds.) Origins and evolution of language and speech. *Annals of the New York Academy of Sciences*, 1976, *280*, pages 562–78.

Rumbaugh, D. M., Gill, T. V., & von Glasersfeld, E. C. Reading and sentence completion by a chimpanzee. *Science*, 1973, *182*, 731–3.

Rumelhart, D. E., & Norman, D. A. *Accretion, tuning, and restructuring: Three modes of learning. Technical Report No. 63*. Center for Human Information Processing. University of California, San Diego, August, 1976.

Saario, T. N., Jacklin, C. N., & Tittle, C. K. Sex role stereotyping in the public schools. *Harvard Educational Review*, 1973, *43*, 386–416.

Sacerdote, P. Hypnosis in cancer patients. *American Journal of Clinical Hypnosis*, 1966, *9*, 100–108.

Sachs, J. S. Recognition memory for syntactic and semantic aspects of connected discourse. *Perception and Psychophysics*, 1967, *2*(9), 441.

Sacks, O. *Migraine: Evolution of a common disorder*. Berkeley: University of California Press, 1973.

Saegert, S. Stress-inducing and reducing qualities of environments. In H. M. Proshansky et al, *Environmental Psychology*, 2nd ed. New York: Holt, Rinehart & Winston, 1976.

Salapatek, P., & Kessen, W. Visual scanning of triangles by the human newborn. *Journal of Experimental Child Psychology*, 1966, *3*(2), 155–167.

Salapatek, P., & Kessen, W. Prolonged investigation of a plane geometric triangle by the human newborn. *Journal of Experimental Child Psychology*, 1973, *15*, 22–29.

Salmon, W. Confirmation. *Scientific American*, 1973, *228*(12), 75–83.

Salter, A. *Conditioned reflex therapy*. New York: Capricorn Books, 1949

Santee, R. T., & VanDerPol, T. L. Actor's status and conformity to norms: A study of students' evaluations of instructors. *The Sociological Quarterly*, 1976, *17*, 378–388.

Sarason, I. G., & Johnson, J. H. The life experiences survey: Preliminary findings. *Office of Naval Research Technical Report*, May, 1976.

Sarnoff, I. Psychoanalytic theory and social attitudes. *Public Opinion Quarterly*, 1960, *24*, 251–79.

Sarnoff, I., & Zimbardo, P. G. Anxiety, fear, and social affiliation. *Journal of Abnormal and Social Psychology*, 1961, *62*, 356–363.

Sarnoff, S., & Sarnoff, I. *Sexual excitement/sexual peace: The place of masturbation in adult relationships*. New York: M. Evans, 1979 (in press).

Savage-Rumbaugh, E. E., Rumbaugh, D. M., & Boysen, S. Symbolic communication between two chimpanzees (Pan troglodytes). *Science*, 1978, *201*, 641–44.

Scammon, R. E. The measurement of the body in childhood. In J. A. Harris, C. M. Jackson, D. G. Patterson, & R. E. Scammon, *The measurement of man*. Minneapolis, University of Minnesota Press, 1930.

Schachter, S. *Emotion, obesity and crime*. New York: Academic Press, 1971.

Schachter, S., & Friedman, L. The effects of work and cue prominence on eating behavior. In S. Schachter, & J. Rodin (Eds.), *Obese humans and rats*. Hillsdale, N.J.: L. Erlbaum Associates, 1974.

Schachter, S., & Gross, L. Manipulated time and eating behavior. *Journal of Personality and Social Psychology*, 1968, *10*, 98–106.

Schachter, S., & Singer, J. Cognitive, social and physiological determinants of emotional state. *Psychological Review*, 1962, *69*, 379–99.

Schank, R. C., & Abelson, R. P. *Scripts, plans, goals and understanding*. Hillsdale, N.J.: L. Erlbaum Associates, 1977.

Schein, E. H. Reaction patterns to severe, chronic stress in American Army prisoners of war of the Chinese. *Journal of Social Issues*, 1957, *13*(3), 21–30.

Schein, E. H., with **Schneier, I.,** & **Barker, C. H.** *Coercive persuasion: A sociopsychological analysis of the "brainwashing" of American civilian prisoners by the Chinese Communists.* New York: Norton, 1961.

Schmeidler, G. *Extrasensory perception.* New York: Atherton Press, 1969.

Schmitt, R. C. Density, health, and social disorganization. *Journal of American Institute of Planners,* 1966, *32,* 38–40.

Schoen, E. Lawrence Halprin: Humanizing the city environment. *The American Way,* Nov. 1972, 13–23.

Schwartz, B. *Psychology of learning and behavior.* New York: Norton, 1978.

Schwartz, B., Schuldenfrei, R., & **Lacey, H.** Operant psychology as factory psychology. Paper presented at Midwestern Association for Behavior Analysis, 1977. Submitted for publication.

Schwartz, G. E. Voluntary control of human cardiovascular integration and differentiation through feedback and reward. *Science,* 1972, *175,* 90–93.

Schwartz, G. E. The facts on transcendental meditation: Part II. TM relaxes some people and makes them feel good. *Psychology Today,* April 1974, 7 39–44.

Schwartz, G. E., Davidson, R. J., & **Maer, F.** Right hemisphere lateralization for emotion in the human brain: Interactions with cognition. *Science,* 1975, *190,* 286–288.

Science News, 1977, *112*(8), 118.

Scobie, G. E. W. Types of Christian conversion. *Journal of Behavioral Science,* 1973, *1,* 265–271.

Scobie, G. E. W. *Psychology of religion,* New York: Halsted Press, 1975.

Scott, R. A. A proposed framework for analyzing deviance as a property of social order. In R. A. Scott & J. D. Douglas (Eds.), *Theoretical perspectives on deviance.* New York: Basic Books, 1972.

Scott, W. A. Research definitions of mental health and mental illness. *Psychological Bulletin,* 1958, *55,* 29–45.

Scroggs, J. R., & **Douglas, W. G. T.** Issues in the psychology of religious conversion. *Journal of Religion and Health,* 1967, *6,* 204–216.

Sears, R. R. Relation of early socialization experiences to aggression in middle childhood. *Journal of Abnormal and Social Psychology,* 1961, *63,* 466–92.

Sears, R. R. Sources of life satisfaction of the Terman gifted men. *American Psychologist,* 1977, *32,* 119–128.

Sears, R. R., Maccoby, E. E., & **Levin H.** *Patterns of child rearing.* New York: Harper & Row, 1957.

Seeman, M., & **Evans, J. W.** Alienation and learning in a hospital setting. *American Sociological Review,* 1962, *27,* 772–783.

Seiden, L. S. Neurochemical basis of drug action: Introduction. In J. A. Harvey (Ed.), *Behavioral analysis of drug action.* Glenview, Ill.: Scott, Foresman, 1970.

Selfridge, O. G. Pandemonium: A paradigm for learning. In *The mechanisation of thought processes.* London: Her Majesty's Stationery Office, 1959. As cited in Klatzky, R. L. *Human memory.* San Francisco: Freeman, 1975.

Seligman, M. E. P. Chronic fear produced by unpredictable electric shock. *Journal of Comparative and Physiological Psychology,* 1968, *66,* 402–11.

Seligman, M. E. P. Depression and learned helplessness. In R. J. Friedman & M. M. Katz (Eds.), *The psychology of depression: Contemporary theory and research.* Washington, D.C.: V. H. Winston & Sons, 1974.

Seligman, M. E. P. *Helplessness: On depression, development and death.* San Francisco: W. H. Freeman, 1975.

Seligman, M. E. P., & **Maier, S. F.** Failure to escape traumatic shock, *Journal of Experimental Psychology,* 1967, *74*(1), 1–9.

Selye, H. *The stress of life.* New York: McGraw-Hill, 1956.

Selye, H. The evolution of the stress concept. *American Scientist,* 1973, *61,* 692–99.

Selye, H. *Stress in health and disease.* Woburn, Mass.: Butterworth, 1976.

Sengel, R. A. A graph analysis of the relationship between population density and social pathology. *Behavioral Science,* 1978, *23,* 213–224.

Seyfried, B. A., & **Hendrick, C.** When do opposites attract? When they are opposite in sex and sex-role attitudes. *Journal of Personality and Social Psychology,* 1973, *25,* 15–20.

Shannon, C. & **Weaver, W.** *The mathematical theory of communication.* Urbana, Illinois: University of Illinois Press, 1949.

Shaver, P. Questions concerning fear of success and its conceptual relatives. *Sex Roles,* 1976, *2,* 305–320.

Sheldon, W. *The varieties of temperament: A psychology of constitutional differences,* New York: Harper, 1942.

Shepard, R. N. Externalization of mental images and the act of creation. In B. S. Randhawa & W. E. Coffman (Eds.), *Visual learning, thinking, and communicating.* New York: Academic Press, 1978 (in press).

Shepard, R. N., & **Feng, C.** A chronometric study of mental paper folding. *Cognitive Psychology,* 1972, *3,* 228–43.

Shepard, R. N., & **Metzler, J.** Mental rotation of three-dimensional objects. *Science,* 1971, *171,* 701–3.

Shepard, R. N., & **Metzler, J.** Transformational studies of the internal representation of three-dimensional objects. In R. Solso (Ed.), *Theories in cognitive psychology: The Loyola Symposium.* Hillsdale, N.J.: L. Erlbaum Associates, 1974.

Shepard, W. O. Intelligence: Development and correlates. In H. W. Reese & L. P. Lipsitt (Eds.), *Experimental child psychology.* New York: Academic Press, 1970.

Sheridan, C. L., & **King, R. G.** Obedience to authority with an authentic victim. *Proceedings of the 80th Annual Convention, American Psychological Association, Part 1,* 1972, *7,* 165–66.

Sherif, M. A study of some social factors in perception. *Archives of Psychology,* 1935, 27(187).

Sherif, M., & **Sherif, C. W.** *An outline of social psychology.* (2nd ed.). New York: Harper & Row, 1956. Used by permission of Harper & Row, Publishers, Inc.

Sherman, J. A. Reinstatement of verbal behavior in a psychotic by reinforcement methods. *Journal of Speech and Hearing Disorders,* 1963, *28,* 398–401.

Sherrod, K., Vietze, P., & **Friedman, S.** *Infancy.* Monterey, Calif.: Brooks/Cole, 1978.

Shirley, M. M. *The first two years: A study of twenty-five babies.* Vol. II. *Intellectual development.* Institute of Child Welfare Monograph Series No. 7. Minneapolis: University of Minnesota Press, 1933.

Shulgin, A. Psychotomimetic agents related to the catecholamines. *Journal of Psychedelic Drugs,* Fall 1969, *2,* 27–29.

Shuman, E. Computer crazy. *Human Behavior.* August 1976, 56–59.

Siegel, R. K. Hallucinations. *American Scientist,* Oct, 1977, 132–140.

Siegel, R. K., & **Jarvik, M. E.** Drug-induced hallucinations in animals and man. In R. K. Siegel & J. L. West (Eds.), *Hallucinations: Behavior, experience, and theory.* New York: Wiley, 1975, 81–161.

Singer, J. L. *Daydreaming: An introduction to the experimental study of inner experience.* New York: Random House, 1966.

Singer, J. L. Navigating the stream of consciousness: Research in daydreaming and related inner experience. *American Psychologist,* 1975, *30,* 727–738.

Singer, J. L. Fantasy: The foundation of serenity. *Psychology Today,* 1976, *10,* 32 ff.

Singer, J. L. & **McCraven, V. J.** Some characteristics of adult daydreaming. *Journal of Psychology,* 1961, *51,* 151–164.

Singh, D., & **Sikes, S.** Role of past experience on food-motivated behavior of obese humans. *Journal of Comparative and Physiological Psychology,* 1974, *86*(3) 503–508.

Sizemore, C. C., & **Pitillo, E. S.** *I'm Eve.* New York: Doubleday, 1977.

Skeels, H. M. Adult status of children with contrasting early life experiences. *Monographs of the Society for Research in Child Development,* 1966, *31*(3).

Skinner, B. F. *The behavior of organisms.* New York: Appleton-Century-Crofts, 1938.

Skinner, B. F. *Walden II.* New York: Macmillan, 1948.

Skinner, B. F. *Science and human behavior.* New York: Macmillan, 1953.

Skinner, B. F. Freedom and the control of men. *The American Scholar,* 1955–56, *25,* 47–65.

Skinner, B. F. *Verbal Behavior.* New York: Appleton-Century-Crofts, 1957.

Skinner, B. F. *Beyond freedom and dignity.* New York: Knopf, 1971.

Skinner, B. F. *About behaviorism.* New York: Knopf, 1974.

Slamecka, N. J. Retroactive inhibition of connected discourse as a function of practice level. *Journal of Experimental Psychology,* 1960, *59,* 104–8.

Sloane, R. B., Staples, F. R., Cristol, A. H., Yorkston, N. J., & **Whipple, K.** *Psychotherapy versus behavior therapy.* Cambridge, Mass.: Harvard University Press, 1975.

Smelser, N. J. Some determinants of destructive behavior. In N. Sanford & C. Comstock (Eds.). *Sanctions for evil.* San Francisco: Jossey-Bass, 1971.

Smirnov, A. cited in Good, P. *The individual.* New York: Time-Life books, 1974.

Smith, D. E., King, M. B., & Hoebel, B. C. Lateral hypothalamic control of killing: Evidence for a cholinoceptive mechanism. *Science,* 1970, *167,* 900–901.

Smith, K. U. *Delayed sensory feedback and behavior.* Philadelphia: Saunders. 1962.

Snyder, M., & Swann, W. B., Jr. When actions reflect attitudes: The politics of impression management. *Journal of Personality and Social Psychology,* in press.

Snyder, S. H. Catecholamines in the brain as mediators of amphetamine psychoses. *Archives of General Psychiatry,* 1972, *27,* 169–179.

Snyder, S. H. Catecholamines as mediators of drug effects in schizophrenia. In F. O. Schmitt & F. G. Worden (Eds.), *The neurosciences: Third study program.* Cambridge, Mass.: MIT Press, 1974, pp. 721–732.

Soderstrom, D., & Wright, E. W. Religious orientation and meaning in life. *Journal of Clinical Psychology,* 1977, *33,* 65–68.

Solomon, R. L., Kamin, L., & Wynne, L. C. Traumatic avoidance learning: The outcome of several extinction procedures with dogs. *Journal of Abnormal and Social Psychology,* 1953, *48,* 291–302.

Solomon, T. Integrating the "Moonie" experience: A survey of ex-members of the Unification Church. *Journal of Social Issues,* 1979, in press.

Spear, F. G. Pain in psychiatric patients. *Journal of Psychosomatic Research,* 1967, *11,* 187–193.

Speisman, J. C., Lazarus, R. S., Mordkoff, A. M., & Davison, L. A. The experimental reduction of stress based on ego-defense theory. *Journal of Abnormal and Social Psychology,* 1964, *68,* 367–80.

Spelke, E., Hirst, W. & Neisser, U. Skills of divided attention. *Cognition,* 1976, *4,* 215–30.

Spence, J. T., & Helmreich, R. L. *Masculinity and femininity: Their psychological dimensions, correlates, and antecedents.* Austin, Texas: University of Texas Press, 1978.

Spence, K. W. *Behavior theory and conditioning.* New Haven: Yale University Press, 1956.

Sperling, G. The information available in brief visual presentations. *Psychological Monographs,* 1960, *74* (whole no. 498).

Sperry, R. Neurology and the mind-brain problem. *American Scientist,* 1952, *40,* 291–312.

Sperry, R. W. Mental unity following surgical disconnection of the cerebral hemispheres. *The Harvey Lectures,* Series 62. New York: Academic Press, 1968.

Spitz, R. A. Hospitalism: An inquiry into the genesis of psychiatric conditions in early childhood. In O. Fenichel et al. (Eds.), *Psychoanalytic study of the child* (vol. 1). New York: International Universities Press, 1945.

Staats, A. W. *Social behaviorism.* Homewood, Ill.: Dorsey Press, 1975.

Stampfl, T. G., & Levis, D. J. Essentials of implosive therapy: A learning theory-based psychodynamic behavioral therapy. *Journal of Abnormal Psychology,* 1967, *72,* 496–503

Standing, L., Conezio, J., & Haber, R. N. Perception and memory for pictures: Single trial learning of 2560 visual stimuli. *Psychonomic Science,* 1970, *19,* 73–4.

Stanley, J. The study of the very bright. *Science,* 1976, *192,* 668–669.

Star, B. *Haven House research report.* Presented at Conference on "Battered Women: Defining the issues," Stanford University, May, 1977.

Staw, B. M. *Intrinsic and extrinsic motivation.* Morristown, N.J.: General Learning Press, 1976.

Steers, R. M., & Mowday, R. T. The motivational properties of tasks. *Academy of Management Review,* 1977, *2,* 645–58.

Steiner, J. E. Human facial expressions in response to taste and smell stimulation. In H. W. Reese & L. P. Lipsitt (Eds.), *Advances in child development and behavior* (Vol. 13). New York: Academic Press, 1978.

Stephan, F. K., & Zucker, I. Circadian rhythms in drinking behavior and locomotor activity of rats are eliminated by hypothalamic lesions. *Proceedings of the National Academy of Sciences, U.S.A.,* 1972, *69:*1583–1586.

Stern, D. N., Jaffe, J., Beebe, B., & Bennett, S. L. Vocalizing in unison and in alternation: two modes of communication within the mother-infant dyad. In D. Aaronson and R. W. Rieber (Eds.) Developmental psycholinguistics and communication disorders. *Annals of the New York Academy of Sciences,* 1975, *263,* 89–100.

Sternbach, R. A. *Pain: A psychophysiological analysis.* New York: Academic Press, 1968.

Sternbach, R. A. *Pain patients: Traits and treatment.* New York: Academic Press, 1974.

Sternbach, R. A., & Tursky, B. Ethnic differences among housewives in psychophysical and skin potential reponses to electric shock. *Psychophysiology,* 1965, *1,* 241–46.

Sternberg, S. High speed scanning in human memory. *Science,* 1966, *153,* 652–4.

Stokols, D. Environmental psychology. *Annual Review of Psychology,* 1978, *29,* 253–295.

Stone, C. P., & Bakhtiari, A. B. Effects of electroconvulsive shock on maze relearning by albino rats. *Journal of Comparative and Physiological Psychology,* 1956, *49,* 318–20.

Stotland, E. *The psychology of hope.* San Francisco: Jossey-Bass, 1969.

Stotland, E., & Hillmer, M. L., Jr. Identification, authoritarian defensiveness, and self-esteem. *Journal of Abnormal and Social Psychology,* 1962, *64,* 334–342.

Stoyva, J. Self-regulation and the stress-related disorders: A perspective on biofeedback. In D. Mostofsky (Ed.). *Behavior control and modification of physiological activity.* Englewood Cliffs, N.J.: Prentice-Hall, 1976.

Straus, M. Quoted in Twenty percent of American husbands abused by their wives? *Behavior Today,* February 13, 1978, *9* (5), 2–3.

Stuart, R. B. *Trick or treatment: How and why psychotherapy fails.* Champaign, Ill.: Research Press, 1970.

Stuart, R. B. Behavioral contracting with families of delinquents. *Journal of Behavior Therapy and Experimental Psychiatry,* 1971, *2,* 1–11.

Stunkard, A. New therapies for the eating disorders: Behavior modification of obesity and anorexia nervosa. *Archives of General Psychology,* May 1972, *26*(5) 391–98.

Suffolk, P. The Eyewitness. From A Big Bowl of Punch, 1964 Simon & Schuster. © Punch, London. Poem reprinted by permission of Rothco Cartoons, Inc.

Sullivan, H. S. *The interpersonal theory of psychiatry.* New York: Norton, 1953.

Sullivan, W. The Einstein papers: Childhood showed a gift for the abstract. *The New York Times,* March 27, 1972, p. 1.

Sundberg, N. J., & Tyler, L. E. *Clinical psychology.* New York: Appleton-Century-Crofts, 1962.

Swazey, J. P. *Chlorpromazine in psychiatry: A study of therapeutic innovation,* Cambridge, Mass.: MIT Press, 1974.

Sweet, W. H., Ervin, F., & Mark, V. H. The relationship of violent behavior to focal cerebral disease. In S. Garattini & E. Sigg (Eds.), *Aggressive behavior.* New York: Wiley, 1969.

Swets, J. A. The relative operating characteristic in psychology. *Science,* 1973, *182,* 900–1000.

Szasz, T. *Pain and pleasure.* New York: Basic Books, 1957.

Szasz, T. S. *The myth of mental illness.* New York: Harper & Row, 1961.

Szasz, T. S. *Psychiatric justice.* New York: Macmillan, 1965.

Tanner, J. M. Physical growth. In P. H. Mussen (Ed.), *Carmichael's manual of child psychology* (Vol. 1, 3rd ed.). New York: Wiley, 1970.

Tart, C. T. *Altered states of consciousness.* New York: John Wiley & Sons, Inc. Copyright © 1969 by John Wiley & Sons, Inc. Reprinted by permission.

Tart, C. T. *On being stoned: A psychological investigation of marijuana intoxication.* Palo Alto, Calif.: Science and Behavior Books, 1971.

Tart, C. T. *States of consciousness.* New York: Dutton, 1975(a).

Tart, C. T. (Ed.). *Transpersonal psychologies.* New York: Harper & Row, 1975(b).

Tavris, C., & Offir, C. *The longest war: Sex differences in perspective.* New York: Harcourt Brace Jovanovich, 1977.

Taylor, F. W. *Principles of scientific management.* New York: Norton, 1967. (Originally published in 1911.)

Taylor, S. E., & Fiske, S. T. Salience, attention and attribution: Top of the head phenomena. In L. Berkowitz (Ed.), *Advances in experimental social psychology.* Vol. 11. New York: Academic Press, 1978.

Teitelbaum, P., The physiological analysis of motivated behavior. In P. Zimbardo & F. L. Ruch, *Psychology and Life*, 9th ed., Diamond Printing. Glenview, Ill.: Scott, Foresman, 1977. Copyright © 1977 Philip Teitelbaum. Excerpt reprinted by permission.

Terman, L. M. *The Measurement of intelligence.* Boston: Houghton Mifflin, 1916.

Terman, L. M. & Merrill, M. A. *Measuring intelligence.* Boston: Houghton Mifflin, 1937.

Terman, L. M. & Merrill, M. A. *The Stanford-Binet intelligence scale* – Third revision. Boston: Houghton Mifflin, 1973.

Terman, L. M., & Oden, M. H. *Genetic studies of genius. Vol. IV. The gifted child grows up.* Stanford, Calif.: Stanford University Press, 1947.

Terman, L. M., & Oden, M. H. *Genetic studies of genius. Vol. V. The gifted group at mid-life.* Stanford, Calif.: Stanford University Press, 1959.

Tesser, A., & Leone, C. Cognitive schemas and thought as determinants of attitude change. *Journal of Experimental Social Psychology*, 1977, *13*, 340–356.

Thibaut, J. W., & Kelley, H. H. *The social psychology of groups.* New York: John Wiley, 1959.

Thigpen, C. H. Personal communication to the author. August 1961.

Thigpen, C. H., & Cleckley, H. A. A case of multiple personality. *Journal of Abnormal and Social Psychology*, 1954, *49* (1), 135–44.

Thigpen, C. H., & Cleckley, H. A. *The three faces of Eve.* New York: McGraw-Hill, 1957.

Thoits, P. Life events, social isolation and psychological distress. Unpublished doctoral dissertation. Stanford University, 1978

Thomas, J. C., Jr. An analysis of behavior in the hobbits-orcs problem. *Cognitive Psychology*, 1974, *6*, 257–69.

Thomas, M. H., & Drabman, R. S. Effects of television violence on expectations of other's aggression. *Personality and Social Psychology Bulletin*, 1978, *4*, 73–76.

Thompson, D. A., & Campbell, R. G. Hunger in humans induced by 2-Deoxy-D-Glucose: Glucoprivic control of taste preference and food intake. *Science,* 1977, *198*, 1065–1068.

Thorndike, E. L. Animal intelligence. *Psychological Review Monograph Supplement*, 1898, *2* (4, Whole No. 8).

Thorndike, E. L. *The elements of psychology.* New York: Seiler, 1905.

Thorndike, E. L. *Measurement of intelligence.* New York: Teacher's College, Columbia University, 1926.

Thurber, J. The secret life of Walter Mitty. In *My world and welcome to it.* New York: Harcourt Brace Jovanovich, 1942.

Tillich, P. *The courage to be.* New Haven: Conn.: Yale University Press, 1952.

Timberlake, W., & Grant, D. L. Auto-shaping in rats to the presentation of another rat predicting food. *Science*, 1975, *190*, 690–692.

Tinbergen, N. *The animal and its world: Forty years of exploratory behavior by an ethologist.* London: Allen & Unwin, 1972.

Toch, H. *Violent men.* Chicago: Aldine, 1969.

Toffler, A. *Future Shock,* New York: Random House, 1970.

Tolman, E. C. *Purposive behavior in animals and men.* Berkeley: University of California Press, 1949. (Originally published, 1932.)

Tolman, E. C., Ritchie, B. F., & Kalish, D. Studies in spatial learning. I. Orientation and the short cut. *Journal of Experimental Psychology*, 1946, *36*, 13–24.

Trabasso, T. R., & Bower, G. H. *Attention in learning.* New York: Wiley, 1968.

Treas, J. Aging and the family. In D. S. Woodruff & J. E. Birren (Eds.), *Aging: Scientific perspectives and social issues.* New York: Van Nostrand, 1975.

Tresemer, D. (Ed.). Current trends in research on "Fear of success." *Sex Roles*, 1976, *2*, Whole issue.

Troll, L. E. *Early and middle adulthood: The best is yet to be—maybe,* Monterey, Calif.: Brooks/Cole, 1975.

Trotter, W. *Instincts of the herd in peace and war.* London: T. Fisher Unwin, 1916.

Tschukitschew. *Contributions of the Timiriazer Institute,* 1929, 36. Cited in R. D. Templeton & J. P. Quigley. The action of insulin on the motility of the gastrointestinal tract. *American Journal of Physiology*, 1930, *91*, 467–74.

Tulving, E. Episodic and semantic memory. In E. Tulving and W. Donaldson (Eds.) *Organization and memory.* New York: Academic Press, 1972.

Tversky, A. Features of similarity. *Psychological Review*, 1977, *84*, 327–352.

Tversky, A., & Kahneman, D. Causal schemata in judgments under uncertainty. In M. Fishbein (Ed.), *Progress in social psychology*. Hillsdale, N.J.: L. Erlbaum Associates, 1978 (in press).

Twain, M. (S. L. Clemens) *Mark Twain's speeches.* New York: Harper & Row, 1923. Reprinted by permission of Harper & Row, Publishers, Inc.

Tyler, L. E. *The psychology of human differences.* 3rd ed. New York: Appleton-Century-Crofts, 1965.

U'Ren, M. B. The image of women in textbooks. In *Woman in sexist society: Studies in power and powerlessness.* V. Gornick and B. K. Moran, (Eds.). New York: New American Library, 1971, 318–346.

U.S. Bureau of the Census, *Statistical Abstract of the United States: 1977.* (98th edition.) Washington, D.C., 1977.

U.S. Department of Commerce Bureau Census Reports, 1974. (Series P60-101). Washington, D.C., U.S. Government Printing Office.

Valenstein, E. S. *Brain control: A critical examination of brain stimulation and psychosurgery.* New York: Wiley, 1973.

Valenstein, E., Cox, V., & Kakolewski, J. Reexamination of the role of the hypothalamus in motivation. *Psychological Review*, 1970, *77*, 16–31.

Valins, S. Cognitive effects of false heart-rate feedback. *Journal of Personality and Social Psychology*, 1966, *4*, 400–408.

Valins, S. Persistent effects of information about internal reactions: Ineffectiveness of debriefing. In H. London & R. E. Nisbett (eds.), *Thought and feeling: Cognitive alteration of feeling states.* Chicago: Aldine, 1974, 116–124.

Van Riper, C. Historical approaches. In J. G. Sheehan (Ed.), *Stuttering: Research and therapy.* New York: Harper & Row, 1970.

Vaughan, E. Misconceptions about psychology among introductory psychology students. *Teaching of Psychology*, 1977, *4*, 138–141. Copyright © 1977 by Division Two of the American Psychological Association. Excerpt reprinted by permission.

von Békésy, G. The ear. *Scientific American*, 1957, *197*(2), 66–78.

Vonder Haar, T. A. Chaining children with chemicals. *The Progressive*, March 1975.

von Senden, M. *Raum-und Gestaltauffassung bei operierten Blindgeborenen vor und nach der Operation.* Leipzig: Barth, 1932. Cited in D. O. Hebb, *The organization of behavior,* New York: Wiley, 1949.

Waldron, I. Why do women live longer than men? *Journal of Human Stress*, March, 1976, 2–13.

Wallace, R. K., & Benson, H. The physiology of meditation. *Scientific American*, 1972, *226*, 84–90.

Wallach, M. A. Tests tell us little about talent. *American Scientist*, 1976, *64*, 57–63.

Wallach, M. A., & Kogan, N. *Modes of thinking in young children: A study of the creativity-intelligence distinction.* New York: Holt, Rinehart & Winston, 1965.

Wallas, G. *The art of thought.* New York: Harcourt Brace Jovanovich, 1926.

Wallechensky, D., Wallace, I., & Wallace, A. *The people's almanac presents the book of lists.* New York: Morrow, 1977.

Walsh, D. A. Aging differences in learning and memory. In D. S. Woodruff & J. E. Birren (Eds.), *Aging: Scientific perspectives and social issues.* New York: Van Nostrand, 1975.

Walster, E., Aronson, V., Abrahams, D., & Rottman, L. The importance of physical attractiveness in dating behavior. *Journal of Personality and Social Psychology*, 1966, *4*, 508–516.

Walster, E., & Berscheid, E. A little bit about love: A minor essay on a major topic. In T. L. Huston (Ed.), *Foundations of interpersonal attraction.* New York: Academic Press, 1974.

Walster, E., Berscheid, E., & Walster, G. W. New directions in equity research. *Journal of Personality and Social Psychology*, 1973, *25*, 151–176.

Walster, E., & Walster, G. W. *A new look at love.* Reading, Mass.: Addison-Wesley, 1978.

Walster, E., Walster, G. W., & Berscheid, E. *Equity: Theory and research.* Boston: Allyn and Bacon, 1978.

Walther, R. J. Economics and the older population. In D. S. Woodruff & J. E. Birren (Eds.), *Aging: Scientific perspectives and social issues.* New York: Van Nostrand, 1975.

Ward, W. C., Kogan, N., & Pankove, E. Incentive effects in children's creativity. *Child Development,* June 1972, *43* (2), 669–676.

Warden, C. J. *Animal motivation: Experimental studies on the albino rat.* New York: Columbia University Press, 1931.

Warner, R. The relationship between language and disease concepts. *The International Journal of Psychiatry in Medicine,* 1976–77, *7,* 57–68.

Wason, P. C. Problem solving and reasoning. *British Medical Bulletin,* 1971, *27*(3), 206–10. Excerpt reproduced by permission of the Medical Department, The British Council.

Wasserman, E. A. Pavlovian conditioning with heat reinforcement produces stimulus-directed pecking in chicks. *Science,* 1973, *181,* 875–877.

Wasson, R. G. *Soma, divine mushroom of immortality.* New York: Harcourt Brace Jovanovich, 1968.

Watson, J. B. Psychology as the behaviorist views it. *Psychological Review,* 1913, *20,* 158–77.

Watson, J. B. *Behaviorism.* New York: Norton, 1925.

Watson, J. B., & Rayner, R. Conditioned emotional reactions. *Journal of Experimental Psychology,* 1920, *3,* 1–14.

Wauquier, R., & Rolls, E. T. (Eds.), *Brain stimulation reward.* Amsterdam, North-Holland, 1976.

Wechsler, D. *Wechsler adult intelligence scale.* New York: Psychological Corp., 1955.

Wechsler, D. *Wechsler intelligence scale for children—Revised.* New York: Psychological Corp., 1974.

Weg, R. B. Changing physiology of aging: Normal and pathological. In D. S. Woodruff & J. E. Birren (Eds.), *Aging: Scientific perspectives and social issues.* New York: Van Nostrand, 1975.

Weil, A. Parapsychology: Andrew Weil's search for the true Uri Geller. *Psychology Today,* 1974, *8,* 45–50.(a)

Weil, A. Parapsychology: Andrew Weil's search for the true Geller—Part II: The Letdown. *Psychology Today,* 1974, 8, 74–78, 82.(b)

Weil, A. T. The marriage of the sun and the moon. In N. E. Zinberg (Ed.), *Alternate states of consciousness.* New York: Free Press, 1977, 37–52.

Weiner, H. R., & Dubanoski, R. A. Resistance to extinction as a function of self- or externally-determined schedules of reinforcement. *Journal of Personality and Social Psychology,* 1975, *31,* 905–910.

Weiner, N. *Cybernetics.* New York: Wiley, 1948.

Weiner, N. *The human use of human beings.* Boston: Houghton Mifflin, 1954.

Weisenberg, M. Cultural and racial reactions to pain. In M. Weisenberg (Ed.), *The control of pain.* New York: Psychological Dimensions, 1977.

Weiss, J. M. Effects of coping responses on stress. *Journal of Comparative and Physiological Psychology.* 1968, *65,* 251–60.

Weiss, J. M. Effects of coping behavior in different warning signal conditions on stress pathology in rats. *Journal of Comparative and Physiological Psychology,* 1971, 77, 1–13.

Weisskopf-Joelson, E. Some comments on a Viennese school of psychiatry. *Journal of Abnormal and Social Psychology,* 1955, *51,* 701–3.

Wessman, A. E. Moods: Their personal dynamics and significance. In C. E. Izard (ed.), *Emotions, conflict, and defense.* New York: Plenum Press, 1978.

Wever, E. G., & Bray, C. W. Present possibilities for auditory theory. *Psychological Review,* 1930, *37,* 365–80.

Wheeler, L. R. A comparative study of the intelligence of East Tennessee mountain children. *Journal of Educational Psychology,* 1942, *33,* 321–334.

Whelan, E. *Boy or girl?* New York, Pocket Books, 1978.

Whitaker, H. A., & Ojemann, G. A. Graded localisation of naming from electrical stimulation mapping of left cerebral cortex. *Nature,* 1977, *270,* 50–51.

White, R. W. Motivation reconsidered: The concept of competence. *Psychological Review,* 1959, *66,* 297–33.

Whorf, B. L. *Language, thought, and reality.* J. B. Carroll (Ed.). New York: Wiley, 1956.

Wickens, D. D. Encoding categories of words: an empirical approach to meaning. *Psychological Review,* 1970, *77,* 1–15.

Wiesel, T. N., & Hubel, D. H. Comparison of the effects of unilateral and bilateral eye closure on cortical unit responses in kittens. *Journal of Neurophysiology,* 1965, *28,* 1029–1040.

Wiesel, T. N., & Hubel, D. H. Ordered arrangement of orientation columns in monkeys lacking visual experience. *Journal of Comparative Neurology,* 1974, *158,* 307–318.

Wiggins, J. S. *Personality and prediction: Principles of personality assessment.* Reading Mass.: Addison-Wesley 1973.

Willems, E. P. Go ye into all the world and modify behavior: An ecologist's view. *Representative Research in Social Psychology,* 1973, *4,* 93–105.

Williams, R. B., Kimball, C. P., & Williard, H. N. The influence of interpersonal interaction on diastolic blood pressure. *Psychosomatic Medicine,* 1972, *34,* 194–198.

Williams, R. J. *Biochemical individuality.* New York: Wiley, 1956.

Williams, R. L. The silent mugging of the black community. *Psychology Today,* 1974, *7*(12), 32–41; 101.

Williams, R. L., & Rivers, L. W. The use of standard and nonstandard English in testing black children. Paper presented at the meeting of the American Psychological Association, Honolulu, September 1972.

Wilson, E. O. The natural history of lions. *Science,* 1973, *179,* 466–467.

Winch, R. F. *Mate selection: A study of complementary needs.* New York: Harper & Row, 1958.

Wineman, D., & James, A. *Policy statement: Corporal punishment in the public schools.* Detroit: Metropolitan Detroit Branch of the ACLU of Michigan, 1967.

Wing, C. W., & Wallach, M. A. *College admissions and the psychology of talent.* New York: Holt, Rinehart & Winston, 1971.

Winokur, G. The types of affective disorders. *Journal of Nervous and Mental Diseases.* 1973 *156*(2), 82–96.

Winsborough, A. H., 1955. Cited in Ittleson et al., 1974.

Witkin, H. A. The perception of the upright. *Scientific American,* 1959, *200,* 50–56.

Wittrock, M. C., Beatty, J., Bogen, J. E., Gazzaniga, M. S., Jerison, H. J., Krashen, S. D., Nebes, R. D., & Teyler, T. J. *The human brain.* Englewood Cliffs, N.J.: Prentice-Hall, 1977.

Wolf, M., Risley, T., & Mees, H. Application of operant conditioning procedures to the behavior problems of an autistic child. *Behavior Research and Therapy,* 1964, *1,* 305–12.

Wolman, C. Therapy and capitalism. *Issues in Radical Therapy,* Winter 1975, *3* (1). Reprinted by permission.

Wolpe, J. *Psychotherapy by reciprocal inhibition.* Stanford: Stanford University Press, 1958.

Wolpe, J. *The practice of behavior therapy,* 2d ed. New York: Pergamon, 1973.

Wong, P. T. P. Durable partial reinforcement effects and social learning in the rat. *Learning and Motivation,* 1977, *8,* 275–283.

Woodruff, R. A., Goodwin, D. W., & Guze, S. B. *Psychiatric diagnosis.* New York: Oxford University Press, 1974.

World Health Organization Expert Committee on Drugs. Drug dependence: its significance and characteristics. *Bulletin of the World Health Organization,* 1965, *32,* 721–733.

Wortman, C. B., & Brehm, J. Responses to uncontrollable outcomes. In L. Berkowitz (Ed.), *Advances in Experimental Social Psychology,* 1975, *8,* 278–336.

Wortman, C. B., & Dintzer, L. Is an attributional analysis of the learned helplessness phenomenon viable?: A critique of the Abramson-Seligman-Teasdale reformulation. *Journal of Abnormal Psychology,* 1978, *87,* 75–90.

Yablonsky, L. The violent gang. In S. Endleman (Ed.), *Violence in the streets.* Chicago: Quadrangle Books, 1968.

Yakovlev, P. I. & Lecours, A. R. The myelogenetic cycles of regional maturation in the brain. In A. Minkowski (Ed.), *Regional development of the brain in early life.* Oxford: Blackwell, 1967.

Yates, A. J. Delayed auditory feedback. *Psychological Bulletin,* 1963, *60,* 213–32.

Yates, B. T., & Zimbardo, P. G. Self-monitoring, academic performance, and retention of content in a self-paced course. *Journal of Personalized Instruction* 2(2), June 1977.

Zajonc, R. B. Family configuration and intelligence. *Science*, 1976, *192*, 227–236.

Zanna, M. P., & Fazio, R. H. Direct experience and attitude-behavior consistency. Paper presented at the Annual Meeting of the American Psychological Association, San Francisco, August 1977.

Zborowski, M. *People in pain.* San Francisco: Jossey-Bass, 1969.

Zeaman, D., & Smith, R. W. Review and analysis of some recent findings in human cardiac conditioning. In W. F. Prokasky (Ed.), *Classical conditioning.* New York: Appleton-Century-Crofts, 1965.

Zeigarnik, B. Uber das Behalten von erledigten und unerledigten Handlungen. *Psychologische Forschung*, 1927, *9*, 1–85.

Zeilberger, J., Sampen, S. E., & Sloane, H. N. Jr. Modification of a child's problem behaviors in the home with the mother as therapist. *Journal of Applied Behavior Analysis*, 1968, *1*, 47–53.

Zilboorg, G., & Henry, G. W. *A history of medical psychology.* New York: Norton, 1941.

Zimbardo, P. G. *The cognitive control of motivation.* Glenview, Ill.: Scott, Foresman, 1969.

Zimbardo, P. G. The human choice: Individuation, reason, and order versus deindividuation, impulse, and chaos. In W. J. Arnold & D. Levine (Eds.), *Nebraska Symposium on Motivation, 1969.* Lincoln: University of Nebraska Press, 1970.

Zimbardo, P. G. A field experiment in auto-shaping. In C. Ward (Ed.), *Vandalism.* London: Architectural Press, 1973.

Zimbardo, P. G. On transforming experimental research into advocacy for social change. In M. Deutsch & H. Hornstein (Eds.), *Applying social psychology: Implications for research, practice, and training.* Hillsdale, N.J.: L. Erlbaum Associates, 1975.

Zimbardo, P. G. *Shyness: What it is, what to do about it.* Reading, Mass.: Addison-Wesley, 1977.

Zimbardo, P. G., Cohen, A., Weisenberg, M., Dworkin, L., & Firestone, I. The control of experimental pain. In P. G. Zimbardo (Ed.), *The cognitive control of motivation.* Glenview, Ill.: Scott, Foresman, 1969.

Zimbardo, P. G., & Formica, R. Emotional comparison and self-esteem as determinants of affiliation. *Journal of Personality*, 1963, *31*, 141–162.

Zimbardo, P. G., Pilkonis, P. A., & Norwood, R. M. The silent prison of shyness. Office of Naval Research Technical Report Z-17. Stanford, Calif.: Stanford University, November, 1974.

Zubeck, J. P., Pushkar, D., Sansom, W., & Gowing, J. Perceptual changes after prolonged sensory isolation (darkness and silence). *Canadian Journal of Psychology*, 1961, *15*, 83–100.

Zurcher, L. A. *The mutable self: A self-concept for social change.* Beverly Hills, Calif.: Sage Publications, 1977.

Acknowledgments

Credits for illustrations and photographs not given on page where they appear are listed below. Credits for quoted material will be found in the References. To all, the authors and publisher wish to express their appreciation.

7 Photograph by Ken Heyman.

9 Courtesy of Philip G. Zimbardo, Inc.

10 Courtesy of Philip G. Zimbardo, Inc.

12 Brown Brothers.

15 Reproduced with permission from *Hypnosis in the Relief of Pain,* by E. R. Hilgard and J. R. Hilgard. Copyright © 1975 by William Kaufmann, Inc., Los Altos, CA 94022. All rights reserved.

18 Copyright, 1977, Universal Press Syndicate.

21 Owens, J., DaFoe, J., and Bower, G. "Taking a Point of View: Character Identification and Attributional Processes in Story and Comprehension and Memory." Reprinted by permission.

23 Brown Brothers.

25 Photograph by Ken Heyman

28 The Bettmann Archive.

35 © 1979 Sidney Harris.

38 Aerofilms Limited.

42 Mary Ellen Mark/Magnum Photos.

43 © 1979, Sidney Harris.

44 Courtesy, Jester of Columbia University (left); Wide World (center); courtesy of Dr. Philip G. Zimbardo (right).

52 Woodcut by M. C. Escher, *Heaven and Hell,* from the collection of C. V. S. Roosevelt, Washington, D.C.

62 From "Solution for a Burning Issue," copyright © 1971 The Associated Press. Reprinted by permission.

66 Culver Pictures (top); The Bettmann Archive (bottom).

69 Photoworld/FPG.

72 From Hudgins, Clarence V. "Conditioning and the Voluntary Control of the Pupillary Light Reflex." *The Journal of General Psychology,* January 1933, 8(1), 30. Copyright by the Journal Press, Provincetown, Mass. Reprinted by permission.

78 Charles Biasiny-Rivera/En Foco Inc.

86 Courtesy of Grason-Stadler Company.

87 Courtesy of Dr. Warren R. Street, Central Washington State College/Reprinted by permission of APA Monitor.

90 Weiner, Howard R. and Dubanoski, Richard A. "Resistance to Extinction as a Function of Self- or Externally Determined Schedules of Reinforcement." *Journal of Personality and Social Psychology,* 1975, 31(5), 905-910. Copyright 1975 by the American Psychological Association. Reprinted by permission.

98 © 1979, Sidney Harris.

99 Michael Johnson.

105 Culver Pictures.

106 Washington Star Syndicate, Inc. (top); graphs from O'Leary, "The Effects of Loud and Soft Reprimands on the Behavior of Disruptive Students." *Exceptional Children,* 1970, 37, 145-155. Copyright 1970 by The Council for Exceptional Children. Reproduced by permission (bottom).

109 Tolman, E. C., Ritchie, B. F., and Kalish, D. "Studies in Spatial Learning. I. Orientation and the Short-Cut." *Journal of Experimental Psychology,* February 1946, 36(1). Copyright 1946 by the American Psychological Association. Reprinted by permission.

110 From Frank A. Logan, *Incentive,* Ch. 3, p. 52. Copyright 1960 by Yale University Press. Reprinted by permission (top); UPI (bottom).

113 From Harlow, Harry F. "The Formation of Learning Sets." *Psychological Review,* 1949, 56(1), 53.

117 Thomas Brand (left); Wendy Rosen Malecki (right); © 1977 Erika Stone/Photo Researchers, Inc. (bottom).

119 From Bandura, A. "Self-reinforcement: The Power of Positive Personal Control." *Psychology and Life* (9th ed., Diamond Printing). Copyright by Scott, Foresman and Company, 1978.

121 Courtesy of Philip G. Zimbardo, Inc.

126 © 1979, Sidney Harris.

129 Adapted from *Plans and the Structure of Behavior* by George A. Miller, Eugene Galanter and Karl H. Pribram. Copyright © 1960 by Holt, Rinehart and Winston, Inc. Reprinted by permission of Holt, Rinehart and Winston.

130 Adapted with permission from *Encyclopaedia Britannica* (15th ed.), 1974, 2, p. 506.

131 From Attneave, Fred, *Applications of Information Theory to Psychology: A Summary of Basic Concepts, Methods, and Results.* Copyright © 1959 by Henry Holt and Company, Inc. Reprinted by permission of Holt, Rinehart and Winston.

132 Washington Star Syndicate, Inc.

133 Loftus, Geoffrey R., and Loftus, Elizabeth F. *Human Memory: The Processing of Information.* Copyright © 1976 by Lawrence Erlbaum Associates, Inc. Reprinted by permission.

139 "Mental Rotation of Three-Dimensional Objects," Shepard, R. N., and Metzler, J., *Science,* February 19, 1971, Vol. 171, pp. 701-703. Reprinted by permission.

141 Mayer, Richard E., *Thinking and Problem Solving: An Introduction to Human Cognition and Learning.* Copyright © 1977 Scott, Foresman and Company.

143 Photo by Baron Hugo Van Lawick.

150 Wide World.

163 "High Speed Scanning in Human Memory," Sternberg, S., *Science,* Vol. 153, pp. 652-654, Fig. 1, August 5, 1966. Reprinted by permission.

165 Adapted from D. E. Meyer and R. W. Schvaneveldt, "Meaning, Memory Structure, and Mental Processes," *Science,* April 2, 1976, Vol. 192, pp. 27-33. Diagram reprinted by permission. (Originally from A. M. Collins and M. R. Quillian, "Retrieval Time from Semantic Memory," *Journal of Verbal Learning and Verbal Behavior,* 1969, 8, 240-247. Reprinted by permission of Academic Press and the author.)

166 Sachs, Jacqueline S. "Recognition Memory for Syntactic and Semantic Aspects of Connected Discourse." *Perception and Psychophysics,* 1967, 2. Reprinted by permission.

169 From Ebbinghaus, H., *Memory,* 1885.

172 From an article by Jenkins and Dallenbach in *American Journal of Psychology,* 1924, 35, 605-612. Champaign, Ill.: University of Illinois Press. Reprinted by permission.

174 From A. W. Melton & J. M. Irwin, "The Influence of Degree of Interpolated Learning on Retroactive Inhibition and the Overt Transfer of Specific Responses." *American Journal of Psychology,* 1940, 53, 173-203. Champaign: University of Illinois Press. Reprinted by permission.

175 From Postman, L. and Rau, L. *Retention as a Function of the Method of Measurement.* University of California Publications in Psychology, 1957, 8(3). Reprinted by permission.

176 From J. M. Mandler and N. S. Johnson, "Remembrance of Things Parsed: Structure and Recall." *Cognitive Psychology,* 1977, 9, 111-151, Academic Press, New York. Reprinted by permission.

192–193 From Patterson, F. G., "Linguistic Abilities of a Young Lowland Gorilla," a paper presented to the American Association for the Advancement of Science, 1977. Reprinted by the permission of the author.

194 Dr. David Premack (top left); Yerkes Regional Primate Center of Emory University (top right); Dr. Ronald Cohn, The Gorilla Foundation (bottom).

196, 197 From Cutting, J. E. and Day, R. "Perceptual Competition between Speech and Nonspeech." Eighteenth annual meeting of the Acoustical Society of America, Houston, 1970. New York: Acoustical Society of America. Reprinted by permission.

199 Copyright, 1973, G. B. Trudeau, distributed by Universal Press Syndicate.

201 From Johnson, N. F. "The Psychological Reality of Phrase-Structure Rules." *Journal of Verbal Learning and Verbal Behavior*, 1965, *4*, 469–475. Reprinted by permission of Academic Press and the author.

204 From Katz, J. J. and Fodor, J. A. "The Structure of a Semantic Theory." *Language*, 1963, *39*(2), 186. Reprinted by permission of Linguistic Society of America.

206 Courtesy of Children's Television Workshop (bottom).

218 Drawing by Niklaas Hartsoeker, from *Early Theories of Sexual Generation* by the late Professor F. J. Cole (top); photo by A. G. Schering, Berlin, as published in *Nature*, courtesy of *Science News* (bottom).

219 Bayley, N. "On the Growth of Intelligence." *American Psychologist*, 1955, *10*, 805–818, Fig. 16–3. Copyright © 1955 by the American Psychological Association. Reprinted by permission.

225 From Nesselroade, J. R. and Baltes, P. B. "Adolescent Personality Development and Historical Change: 1970–1972." *Monographs of the Society for Research in Child Development*, Vol. 39 (1, Serial No. 154), 1974. © The Society for Research in Child Development, Inc.

226 Scammon, R. E., "The Measurement of the Body in Children." In Harris et al., *The Measurement of Man*, Fig. 67, p. 184. Minneapolis: University of Minnesota Press, 1930. Reprinted by permission.

228 From *The First Two Years* by Mary M. Shirley, by permission of University of Minnesota Press.

229 From *Genetic Psychology Monographs* by Hsiao Hung Hsiao, by permission of Clark University Press.

231 Photos by William Vandivert, courtesy of *Scientific American*.

233 Photos, Susan Carey and Rhea Diamond, Massachusetts Institute of Technology; graph from S. Carey and R. Diamond, "Piecemeal to Configurational Representation of Faces," *Science*, January 21, 1977, *195*, 312–313, fig. 2. Reprinted by permission.

235 From Wheeler, L. R. "A Comparative Study of the Intelligence of East Tennessee Mountain Children." *Journal of Educational Psychology*, 1942, *33*, 321–334.

238 Wide World.

243 Photos by Dr. J. E. Steiner, from *Advances in child development and behavior*, Vol. 13, by H. W. Reese and L. P. Lipsitt, by permission of Dr. J. E. Steiner and Academic Press Inc.

250 Stern/Black Star.

253 Photograph by Ken Heyman.

254 Suzanne Szasz/Photo Researchers, Inc.

259 Lynn McLaren/Photo Researchers, Inc. (bottom).

261 Rohn Engh/Van Cleve Photography.

263 "Carrying Behavior in Humans: Analysis of Sex Differences," Jenni, D. A. and Jenni, M. A., *Science*, November 19, 1976, Vol. 194, pp. 859–860, Fig. 1 and 2. Reprinted by permission.

264 Jean-Claude Lejeune/Stock, Boston.

265 Adaptation of tables 7–1 and 7–2 from *Marriage and Family Development* (5th ed.), by Evelyn Mills Duvall. Copyright © 1957, 1962, 1967, 1971, 1977 by J. B. Lippincott Company. Reprinted by permission of Harper & Row Publishers, Inc.

268 George Bellerose/Stock, Boston.

269 Nat Farbman, *Life Magazine*, © 1947 Time Inc. (left); Christa Armstrong/Photo Researchers, Inc. (right).

272 Geoffrey Gove/Photo Researchers, Inc.

275 From *Demographic Yearbook 1972*, Table 3.2, p. 34. Copyright, United Nations 1972. Reproduced by permission.

277 John Launois/Black Star (left and right).

288 Reprinted by permission of the publishers from *The Postnatal Development of the Human Cerebral Cortex*, Volumes 1 and 6, by Jesse LeRoy Conel, Cambridge, Mass.: Harvard University Press, Copyright © 1939, (renewed 1967), 1959 by the President and Fellows of Harvard College."

294 Tektronix, Incorporated.

297 From De Robertis, E. "Submicroscopic Morphology of the Synapse," *International Review of Cytology*, 1959, *9*, 61–96. New York: Academic Press, Inc. Reprinted by permission.

300 From Kuffler and Nicholls, in *From Neuron to Brain*, 1976. Reprinted by permission of author.

310 From Penfield, W. "The Excitable Cortex in Conscious Man." Liverpool, Liverpool University Press, 1958.

316 From *Perception and Motion: An Analysis of Space-Structured Behavior* (Fig. 4-1, p. 59 and Fig. 5-16, p. 83), by Karl U. Smith & W. M. Smith, W. B. Saunders, Publishers, 1962.

320 Dr. José M. Delgado.

323 Courtesy of Dr. Philip Teitelbaum, University of Illinois at Urbana-Champaign.

324 From R. W. Sperry from The Harvey Lectures, Series 62, 1968. New York: Academic Press, Inc. Reprinted by permission.

325 Ornstein, Robert E. Adapted from THE PSYCHOLOGY OF CONSCIOUSNESS. Copyright © 1972 W. H. Freeman and Company. Reprinted by permission.

327 From *American Journal of the Medical Sciences*, Vol. 20, 1850.

330 University College, London.

332 From S. H. Snyder, "Catecholamines as Mediators of Drug Effects in Schizophrenia." In F. O. Schmitt & F. G. Worden (Eds.), *The Neurosciences: Third Study Program*. Cambridge, Mass.: MIT Press, 1974. Reprinted by permission.

334 Wiesel, T. N. and Hubel, D. H. "Ordered Arrangement of Orientation Columns in Monkeys Lacking Visual Experience," *Journal of Comparative Neurology*, 1974, *158*, 307–318. Reprinted by permission.

343 Photos by Alan Ross.

344 Courtesy of the Institute for International Social Research (bottom).

355 From *Patterns of Discovery* by Dr. Norwood R. Hanson, 1958, by permission of Cambridge University Press.

362 Graph by Robert Buckhout found in *Psychology of the Eyewitness*. Reprinted by permission of the author.

363 "Eye Contact and Face Scanning in Early Infancy," Haith, M. M., Bergman, T., & Moore, M. J., *Science*, November 25, 1977, Vol. 198, pp. 853–855, Fig. 1. Reprinted by permission.

365 "Feedback: Beyond Behaviorism," Powers, W. T., *Science*, January 26, 1973, Vol. 179, pp. 351–356, Fig. 1. Reprinted by permission.

371 From *Toronto Star*, November 24, 1967.

377 From Warden, C. J. *Animal Motivation: Experimental Studies on the Albino Rat*, 1931. Reprinted by permission of Columbia University Press.

379 "Hunger in Humans Induced by 2-Deoxy-D-Glucose: Glucoprivic Control of Taste Preference and Food Intake," Thompson, D. A. and Campbell, R. G., *Science*, December 9, 1977, Vol. 198, pp. 1065-1067, Fig. 2. Reprinted by permission.

382 Harvey Stein.

385 Patricia Hollander Gross/Stock, Boston.

387 From W.-U. Meyer, page 127 in H. Heckhausen, "Achievement Motive Research," from *Nebraska Symposium on Motivation 1968,* W. J. Arnold (Ed.). Copyright © 1968 by University of Nebraska Press. Reprinted by permission of University of Nebraska Press.

389 Cowley, M. "Interview with William Faulkner," *Writers at Work: The Paris Review Interviews* Vol. 1. Copyright © The Paris Review, Inc., 1957, 1958. Reprinted by permission of Viking Penguin, Inc.

392 Cary Wolinsky/Stock, Boston.

393 The Cleveland Museum of Art, Purchase from the J. H. Wade Fund.

394 Courtesy of the Wurttembergisches Landesmuseum, Stuttgart.

395 Peter L. Gould/FPG.

396 From Lofland, J., and Stark, R. "Becoming a World Saver: A Theory of Conversion to a Deviant Perspective," *American Sociological Review,* December 30, 1965. Copyright © 1965 American Sociological Association. Reprinted by permission.

397 From a paper presented by Dr. Raymond Paloutzian at the American Psychological Association in Washington, D.C., September 1976.

403 From *The Expression of the Emotions in Man and Animals* by Charles Darwin, Preface by Konrad Lorenz, by permission of The University of Chicago, publisher (top); Wide World (bottom).

409 Wide World.

410 Wide World (both photos).

411 Diagram on Gate-Control Theory by Harry Carter, in *Newsweek,* April 25, 1977, p. 50.

412 The Bettmann Archive.

414 Gay Luce © 1971 by The New York Times Company, reprinted by permission (top); Wide World (bottom left and right).

421 Hokanson, J. E., Degood, D. E., Forrest, M. S., Brittain, T. M. "Availability of Avoidance Behaviors in Modulating Vascular-Stress Responses." *Journal of Personality and Social Psychology,* 1971, *19,* 60–68. Copyright © 1971 by the American Psychological Association. Reprinted by permission.

423 "Mean Change in GSR" Figure 3 from Zimbardo, Cohen, Weisenberg, Dworkin, and Firestone. In P. G. Zimbardo, *The Cognitive Control of Motivation.* Copyright © 1969 by Scott, Foresman and Company.

424 Rene Burri/Magnum Photos.

425 Ann Hagen Griffiths/DPI.

426 The Bettmann Archive.

427 The Bettmann Archive.

428 Based on Ernest R. Hilgard, *Hypnotic Susceptibility.* Copyright © 1965 by Harcourt Brace Jovanovich, Inc. Reprinted by permission of the publisher.

429 "Pain Reduction Under Hypnosis," Figure 4 from Zimbardo, Rapaport, and Baron in *The Cognitive Control of Motivation.* Copyright © 1969 by Scott, Foresman and Company.

439 Lerner, A. J., and Loewe, F. *On the Street Where You Live.* Copyright © 1956 by Alan Jay Lerner and Frederick Loewe. Chappell and Company, Inc., owner of publication and allied rights. International Copyright secured. All rights reserved. Used by permission.

439 Photograph by Ken Heyman.

443 From *Hallucinations* by R. K. Siegel and L. J. West (left); from *Hallucinations* by R. K. Siegel and L. J. West, painting by Martin de la Cruz (top right); from *Migraine: The Evolution of a Common Disorder* by Oliver Sacks with a forward by William Gooddy, by permission of University of California Press.

447 "Ontogenetic Development of the Human Sleep-Dream Cycle", Roffwarg, H., et al, *Science,* Vol. 152, pp. 604–619, Graph, 29 April 1966 (bottom).

452 Arthur Tress (both).

453 Elizabeth Hamlin/Stock, Boston.

454 Leonard Freed/Magnum Photos (left); David A. Krathwohl/Stock, Boston (right).

457 Leonard Freed/Magnum Photos.

457 Kandel, D. "Adolescent Marijuana Use: Role of Parents and Peers," *Science,* Vol. 181, pp. 1067–1070, Fig. 1, September 14, 1973. Copyright © 1973 by the American Association for the Advancement of Science. Reprinted by permission of the association and the author.

458 From *Hallucinations* by R. K. Siegel and L. J. West, by permission of Oscar Janiger.

467 © William Hamilton.

468 *Miss Peach* by Mell Lazarus. Courtesy of Mell Lazarus and Field Newspaper Syndicate.

469 John Scotfield, © 1962 National Geographic Society.

472 Twain, Mark. "Consistency" from *Mark Twain's Speeches,* 1923. Reprinted by permission of Harper & Row, Publishers, Inc.

475 From G. L. Ferrero: *Criminal Man According to Classification of Cesare Lombroso,* 1911 (top); Michael I. Valeri/FPG (bottom left); Photograph by Ken Heyman (bottom right).

477 Figure 1 of mean recall scores from Eysenck, H. J. *Eysenck on Extraversion,* 1973, p. 173. England: Granada Publishing Limited. Reprinted by permission.

480 Wayne Miller/Magnum Photos.

483 Plutchik, R., Kellerman, H., and Conte, H. A Structural Theory of Ego Defenses and Emotions, in *Emotions and Psychopathology,* C. Izard (Ed.). New York: Plenum Publishing Corporation, 1978.

484 © Punch, London.

486 Leo M. Johnson/Image Inc.

490 From Miller, Neal E. "Experimental Studies of Conflict" found in *Personality and the Behavior Disorders,* 1944, p. 440. New York: The Ronald Press Company.

492 Hall, C. S., and Lindzey, G. "Dimensional Comparison of Theories of Personality," from *Theories of Personality.* Copyright © 1957 by John Wiley & Sons, Inc. Reprinted by permission.

503 Scott, Foresman staff.

505 Van Bucher/Photo Researchers, Inc.

507 Charles Gatewood/Magnum Photos.

510 From Zimbardo, P. G., Pilkonis, P. A., and Norwood, R. M. "The Silent Prison of Shyness." The Office of Naval Research Technical Report Z-17, November 1974. Stanford, Cal.: Stanford University Press. Reprinted by permission.

511 © Bob Combs '74/Photo Researchers, Inc.

513 Vannucci Photo Services/FPG (left); © Alice Kandell/Rapho-Photo Researchers, Inc. (right).

517 © Bob Krueger '76/Photo Researchers, Inc.

520 © George Holton '72/Photo Researchers, Inc.

521 From an interview for a study by W. C. Ward, N. Kogan, and E. Pankove, "Incentive Effects in Children's Creativity," from *Child Development,* June 1972, pp. 669–676. Reprinted by permission.

522 Courtesy of Dr. Frank Barron.

523 James C. Hershey-Photoworld/FPG (left); Scott, Foresman staff (right).

524 Gershwin, G., and Gershwin, I. *They All Laughed.* Copyright © 1936 by George Gershwin. Copyright renewed, assigned to Chappell and Company, Inc. International Copyright Secured. All rights reserved. Used by permission.

524 Photograph by Ken Heyman.

531 From Magoun, H. W. *Brain Mechanisms and Consciousness,* Delafresnay, J. F. (Ed.), 1954. Copyright by Blackwell Scientific Publications Limited. Reprinted by permission (top); Orville Andrews/FPG (bottom).

532 From Hebb, D. O. *A Textbook of Psychology,* p. 235, 1966. Reprinted by permission of W. B. Saunders Company, Philadelphia, Pa.

533 From Hans Selye, *Stress in Health and Disease.* Woburn, Mass.: Butterworth (Publishers) Inc., 1976. Reprinted with the permission of the publisher.

534 Ken Regan/Camera 5 (top); Frank Fisher/GAMMA/LIAISON (bottom).

536 Sherry Suris/Photo Researchers, Inc.

538 U.S. Army photo, courtesy of Walter Reed Army Institute of Research.

539 From "Short Term Intrusions into the Life-style Routine" by T. S. Holmes and T. H. Holmes. *Journal of Psychosomatic Research,* Vol. 14, pp. 121–132, June 1970. Reprinted by permission of Pergamon Press, Ltd. and T. H. Holmes.

542 Nicholas Sapieha/Stock, Boston.

543 Courtesy of Philip G. Zimbardo, Inc.

545 Arthur Grace/Stock, Boston.

550 From Ferguson, P. C., Gowan, J. C. "TM: Some Preliminary Findings." *Journal of Humanistic Psychology,* 1976, 16. Copyright by the Association for Humanistic Psychology. Reprinted by permission (left); Barbara Alper/Stock, Boston (right).

551 © Ray Ellis '77/Photo Researchers, Inc.

552 Folkins, Lawson, Opton, and Lazarus. "Desensitization and the Experimental Reduction of Threat." *Journal of Abnormal Psychology,* 1968, 73, 100–113. Copyright 1968 by the American Psychological Association. Reprinted by permission.

554 Photograph by Ken Heyman.

555 Washington Star Syndicate, Inc.

560 Courtesy of Dr. Bruno Bettelheim.

562 From *Preliminary Report to the President from the President's Commission on Mental Health.* Thomas E. Bryant, Chairperson. Washington, D.C.: September 1, 1977.

563 The Bettmann Archive.

567 From Haas, K. "Let the Punishment Fit the Crime." *Understanding Ourselves and Others,* 1965. Reprinted by permission of Prentice-Hall, Inc., Englewood Cliffs, New Jersey.

571 *Dennis the Menace* ® used by permission of Hank Ketcham and © Field Enterprises, Inc.

572 Photograph by Ken Heyman.

576 © Mel Calman, 1978. Reprinted through the courtesy of Field Newspaper Syndicate.

580 Hanson, Gottesman, Meehl. "Genetic Theories and the Validation of Psychiatric Diagnosis: Implications for the Study of Children of Schizophrenics." *Journal of Abnormal Psychology,* 1977, 86, 575–588. Copyright 1977 by the American Psychological Association. Reprinted by permission.

586 From Beck, A. T., *Depression,* p. 28. Harper & Row Publishers, Inc., 1967. Reprinted by permission of the author.

586 Photograph by Ken Heyman.

591 Culver Pictures.

592 The Bettmann Archive.

596 Paul Fusco/Magnum Photos.

601 The Bettmann Archive.

605 © 1965 by Allan Grant (both top); Courtesy of Philip G. Zimbardo, Inc. (bottom).

609 From J. Wolpe, *The Practice of Behavior Therapy* (2nd ed.). United Kingdom (and New York): Pergamon Press, 1973.

611 Marc J. Pokempner.

614 Table 14–2 from *Modern Clinical Psychology: Principles of Intervention in the Clinic and Community,* by Sheldon J. Korchin, © 1976, Basic Books, Inc., Publishers, New York.

625 Courtesy of Philip G. Zimbardo, Inc.

626 Courtesy of Philip G. Zimbardo, Inc.

627 Jean-Claude Lejeune/Stock, Boston.

631 Reprinted by permission of the Chicago Tribune-New York News Syndicate, Inc. (top); photo by William Vandivert, reprinted by permission of *Scientific American* (bottom right).

633 © The Times (left); Press Information Bureau, Government of India (center); UPI (right).

635 Courtesy of Dr. Ronald Lippitt.

636 Sherif, M., and Sherif, C. W. *An Outline of Social Psychology* (2nd Ed.). Adapted from pp. 301–331. Copyright 1948, © 1956 by Harper & Row, Publishers, Inc. Reprinted by permission of Harper & Row, Publishers, Inc.

638 Courtesy of Mrs. Jane Elliott and ABC Television; photos by Charlotte Button.

639 Hughes Vassal/LIAISON.

640 Chicago Sun-Times, by George Gallup. Reprinted with permission from The Chicago Sun-Times.

642 Photograph by Ken Heyman.

643 Alice Kandell/Rapho-Photo Researchers, Inc. (left); Abigail Heyman/Magnum Photos (right).

644 UPI.

646 Owen Franken/Stock, Boston.

651 Daniel S. Brody/Stock, Boston.

657 George Gardner.

659 Quote from *The Boy Next Door,* words/music by Hugh Martin and Ralph Blane. Copyright 1944, renewed 1972 Leo Feist, Inc., New York, New York. Used by permission; drawing adapted from *Social Pressures in Informal Groups* by Leon Festinger, Stanley Schachter, and Kurt Back, with the permission of the publishers, Stanford University Press. Copyright © 1950 by the Board of Trustees of the Leland Stanford Junior University.

661 UPI.

663 Photograph by Ken Heyman.

666 *Miss Peach* by Mell Lazarus. Courtesy of Mell Lazarus and Field Newspaper Syndicate.

671 Peter Menzel/Stock, Boston.

673 Chester Higgins, Jr./Photo Researchers, Inc.

676 Rick Smolan/Stock, Boston.

679 Ben Martin.

680 Gagnon, John H., *Human Sexualities,* p. 207, 1977. Copyright © 1977 by Scott, Foresman and Company.

682 Peter Southwick/Stock, Boston.

684 J. Berndt/Stock, Boston.

690 © Mel Calman, 1977. Reprinted through the courtesy of Field Newspaper Syndicate.

691 From R. R. Sears, "Relation of Early Socialization Experiences to Aggression in Middle Childhood," *Journal of Abnormal and Social Psychology,* 1961, 63, 446–492.

693 San Francisco Examiner.

695 Courtesy of Dr. Albert Bandura.

696 Sarah Webb Barrell/The New York Times.

697 Jean-Claude Lejeune/Stock, Boston.

698 UPI.

702 Peter Southwick/Stock, Boston.

703 Graph adapted from P. G. Zimbardo, "The Human Choice: Individuation, Reason, and Order Versus Deindividuation, Impulse, and Chaos." In W. J. Arnold & D. Levine (Eds.), *Nebraska Symposium on Motivation 1969* (left); photo courtesy of Philip G. Zimbardo, Inc. (right).

704 Photograph by Ken Heyman.

708 UPI photo; symposium dialogue from Milgram, S., "Comparing Notes on Obedience to Authority: Dean and Milgram," in *APA Monitor,* January 1978. Copyright © 1978 by the American Psychological Association. Reprinted by permission.

712 Martha Cooper Guthrie (left).

715 Table, Mansson, H. H. From "Justifying the Final Solution," *Omega,* 1972, 3(2), 79–87. Copyright © 1972, Baywood Publishing Company, Inc.

724 UPI.

725 Wide World.

727 Julie O'Neil/Stock, Boston.
729 UPI.
734 Chicago Tribune Photo.
737 Photograph by Ken Heyman.
739 Courtesy of Philip G. Zimbardo, Inc.
740 Courtesy of Philip G. Zimbardo, Inc. and Dr. Scott C. Fraser.
741 From *The New York Times,* March 13, 1964. Copyright © 1964 by The New York Times Company. Reprinted by permission.

742 Darley and Latané "Bystander Intervention in Emergencies: Diffusion of Responsibilities." *Journal of Personality and Social Psychology,* 1968, *8*(4), 377–384. Copyright 1968 by the American Psychological Association. Reprinted by permission.
743 Michael Vollan.
745 Paul Ryan.

Physiological drawings by Cecilia Duray-Bito. Charts and graphs by ANCO/Boston and Slug Signorino.

Name index

Subject index

Feedback, please!

I need your reactions and ideas if *Psychology and Life* is to serve students better. What did you like best and least? What would you like to have more or less of? How could it have been handled better? Please jot down your suggestions, cut out this page, fold and tape or staple it, and mail it to me. No postage is needed.

Many thanks!
Phil Zimbardo

For every chapter that you read, please make a check mark on each line to indicate your evaluation of it. It is ideal if you can do this as soon as you finish reading each chapter.

Chapter	Informational Value			Interest		
	high	average	low	high	average	low
1 Psychology and Life						
2 Unraveling mysteries						
3 Conditioning and learning						
4 Changing patterns of human behavior						
5 Thinking and reasoning						
6 Memory						
7 Language						
8 Developmental theory						
9 Developmental stages						
10 Nervous system						
11 Brain						
12 Perception						
13 Motivation						
14 Mind and body						
15 Consciousness						
16 Personality theory						
17 Personality assessment						
18 Stress						
19 Pathology						
20 Therapy						
21 Social behavior						
22 Intimacy						
23 Social pathology						
24 Ecological psychology						
Appendix Research methods						

What did you like best about *Psychology and Life?*

How could *Psychology and Life* be improved?

Your name and address (if you wish)

_____

_____   Size of your psychology class _____

Male _____ Female _____ Age _____   Were you in a discussion section? _____

Your course grade _____   Besides the text, did you use:

Will you take more psychology? _____   *Mastering Psychology and Life* _____

Your probable major _____   *Psychology for Our Times* _____

School _____   Other supplementary material _____

fold here

Overall evaluation of *Psychology and Life* 10th

All things considered, how does *Psychology and Life* compare to introductory
texts you have used in other courses?

| much better | better | about average | worse | much worse |

Would you recommend its continued use at your school?

_____ Definitely yes
_____ Yes
_____ Uncertain
_____ No
_____ Definitely no

fold here

cut page out

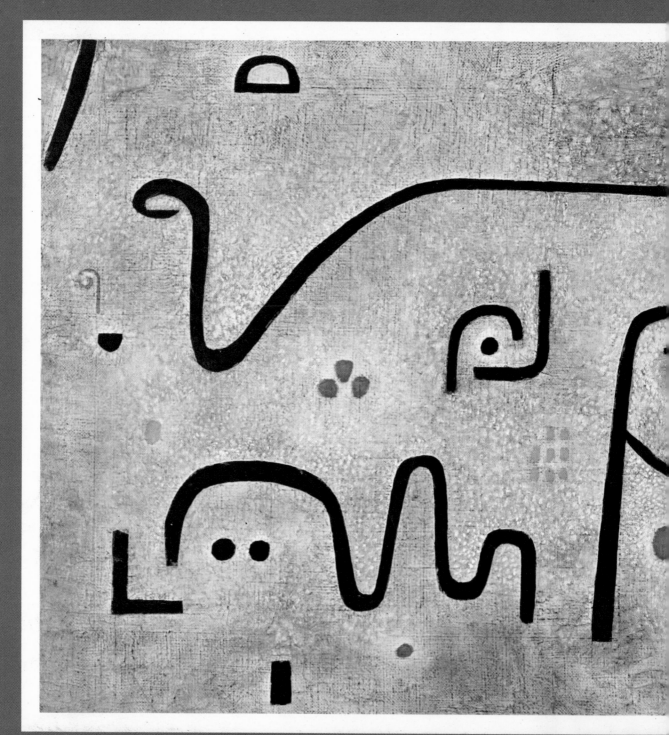